Part I: Mainline perspectives on consumer behavior

- The seven keys — Chapter 1
- Marketers' and consumers' views — Chapter 2
- The consumer marketplace — Chapter 3
- Market segmentation — Chapter 4

Part V: Special topics

- Public policy perspectives — Chapter 21
- Organizational buyer behavior — Chapter 22

Part II: The consumer as an individual

- Consumer motivation (I) — Chapter 5
- Consumer motivation (II) — Chapter 6
- Consumer information processing — Chapter 7
- Consumer perception (I) — Chapter 8
- Consumer perception (II) — Chapter 9
- Consumer learning — Chapter 10
- Consumer attitudes — Chapter 11

Part III: External influences

- Culture, cultural change, and cross-cultural influences — Chapter 12
- Social and situational influences — Chapter 13
- Household and family — Chapter 14
- Salespersons' influences — Chapter 15
- Advertising's influences — Chapter 16

Part IV: The consumer decision process

- Prepurchase processes — Chapter 17
- Purchase processes — Chapter 18
- Postpurchase processes — Chapter 19

◼ WE WANT TO HEAR FROM YOU!! ◼

By sharing your opinions about this book, you will help us ensure that you are getting the most value for your textbook dollars. After you've used the book for awhile, please fill out this form fold, tape and drop it in the mail.

Course Title:_____ Text Title & Author: _____

1. Are you a major in this subject? ❑ yes ❑ no ❑ undecided
   Were you required to purchase this text? ❑ yes ❑ no

2. Did you purchase this book: ❑ for yourself? ❑ for yourself and at least one other student?
   Was a copy available when you needed one? ❑ yes ❑ no

3. Was a study guide available for purchase? ❑ yes ❑ no ❑ don't know
   If yes, did you purchase it? ❑ yes ❑ no
   Might you purchase it in the future? ❑ yes ❑ no

Fold Here

4. Were any other supplements to the text available (for example, software, a workbook, etc.)?
   ❑ yes ❑ no   If yes, what? _____
   Did you purchase any other supplement? ❑ yes ❑ no

5. How far along in the course are you? ❑ only starting ❑ less than midway
   ❑ more than midway ❑ completed

6. How much have you used this text? ❑ only skimmed it ❑ read/studied a few chapters
   ❑ read/studied most chapters ❑ read/studied entire text

7. Have you read the introductory material (such as the preface)? ❑ yes ❑ no
   Do you feel you know how to effectively use this book? ❑ yes ❑ no

8. Even if you've only skimmed the text, please rate your perception of it in terms of the following:

   a) Value as a reference   ❑ highly valuable   ❑ somewhat valuable   ❑ not valuable
   b) Readability   ❑ consistently clear   ❑ sometimes clear   ❑ generally unclear
   c) Illustrations/photos   ❑ very effective   ❑ somewhat effective ❑ ineffective
   d) Design/use of color   ❑ very effective   ❑ somewhat effective ❑ ineffective
   e) Study help in the text   ❑ very effective   ❑ somewhat effective ❑ ineffective
   f) Level   ❑ too difficult   ❑ appropriate   ❑ too easy/not challenging
   g) Problems   ❑ too difficult   ❑ appropriate   ❑ too easy/not challenging
   h) OVERALL PERCEPTION: ❑ better than average ❑ average   ❑ less than average

Fold Here

9. Do you find the examples in the text relevant to you? ❑ yes ❑ no
   Note any that you find particularly relevant_____

10. By looking at the text, do you think it treats the subject as interestingly as possible?
    ❑ yes ❑ no ❑ hard to tell

11. What do you like most about this book?_____
    What *don't* you like about this book? _____

12. At the end of the semester, what do you intend to do with this text?
    ❑ keep for future reference ❑ sell back to bookstore or other students ❑ unsure

◼ **THANK YOU FOR YOUR HELP!** ◼

WILEY

Name _____   School _____

May we quote you?   ☐ Yes   ☐ No

Student Comments

CONSUMER BEHAVIOR

THIRD EDITION

CONSUMER BEHAVIOR

WILLIAM L. WILKIE

University of Notre Dame

JOHN WILEY & SONS, INC.

New York   Chichester   Brisbane

Toronto   Singapore

ACQUISITIONS EDITOR Timothy J. Kent
ASSISTANT EDITOR Ellen Ford
MARKETING MANAGER Debra Riegert
PRODUCTION Publication Services and Deborah Herbert
DESIGNER Dawn L. Stanley
MANUFACTURING MANAGER Andrea Price
PHOTO RESEARCHER Lisa Passmore, Joan Meisel, Linda Sykes, and Sarah Katzka
ILLUSTRATION Jaime Perea

This book was set in 10.5/12 Palatino by Publication Services and printed and bound by Von Hoffman Press. The cover was printed by Phoenix Color Corp.

Library of Congress Cataloging in Publication Data:
Wilkie, William L.
    Consumer Behavior/William L. Wilkie.–3rd ed.
        p.   cm.
    Includes bibliographical references and indexes.
    ISBN 0-471-54517-1
    1. Consumer behavior.   I. Title.
    HF5415.3.W536   1994
    658.8′342–dc20   93-37613
                                                                                            CIP

Printed in the United States of America

10 9 8 7 6 5 4 3 2 1

Throughout the long days devoted to developing, then twice revising, this text, my family provided me with encouragement and much assistance in this effort. In so doing, they made room in their lives for me to work and gave up much of the time I might have shared with them.

With much love and great appreciation I dedicate this book to Barbara, and to Will, Alexandria, and James.

ABOUT THE AUTHOR

William L. Wilkie is the Aloysius and Eleanor Nathe Professor of Marketing Strategy at the University of Notre Dame, where he teaches popular undergraduate and graduate courses in consumer behavior and consults for business and government agencies on consumer behavior topics. Dr. Wilkie has served as president of the Association for Consumer Research, an international professional group with members in 30 nations around the world. He has also served as a member of the editorial boards of the *Journal of Consumer Research, Journal of Marketing, Journal of Marketing Research, Journal of Public Policy and Marketing,* and *Journal of International Consumer Marketing.* Dr. Wilkie's research in marketing and consumer behavior has received a number of awards and recognitions. He is listed in *Who's Who in America.* He has been recognized as one of the most-cited authors in the field of marketing; one of his articles has been named a "Citation Classic in the Social Sciences" by the Institute for Scientific Information. He has also served as a member of the American Marketing Association's Task Force on the Development of Marketing Thought and as a member of the Academic Advisory Council of the Marketing Science Institute.

Dr. Wilkie holds a B.B.A. degree from the University of Notre Dame, where he majored in marketing and minored in management science. He holds M.B.A. and Ph.D. degrees from Stanford University, where he was also a fellow in the year-long Stanford-Sloan Executive Development Program. Prior to joining the University of Notre Dame, he served as in-house consultant to the Federal Trade Commission in Washington, D.C., as research professor at the Marketing Science Institute in Cambridge, Massachusetts, and as a faculty member at Purdue University, Harvard University, and the University of Florida. He now lives in South Bend with his wife, Barbara; three children, Will, Allie, and Jim; and his dog, Blaze.

PREFACE

This book reflects my belief that consumer behavior is a fascinating topic. It is about people and the way we live. It is about consumers buying and marketers selling. It is about many forms of influence, from the subtle shaping of our culture, through the social forces from our family, friends, and peers, to the persuasive attempts by advertising and salespersons. It is about the benefits we seek through our purchase decisions and the satisfactions we obtain through consuming products and services.

For all these reasons, consumer behavior is important. It plays a significant role in our lives, from literally sustaining life itself (foods, medicines, . . .), to providing comfort and convenience (electricity, clothing, cars, . . .), to enriching our leisure and social lives (perfumes, education, entertainment, . . .). Moreover, because it is an activity in which we all engage, consumer behavior has *huge* economic impacts in our society. When consumer purchasing is high, jobs are created and profits encourage more business investments. For any particular firm, customer patronage is the key determinant of success or failure.

In addition to being important, consumer behavior also poses some really interesting questions. Why are people attracted to some products but not to others? Why do some consumers spend frugally while others run up large debts? What role does the marketing system play in all of this behavior? Is influencing consumer behavior an easy task for a marketer, or is it actually quite difficult? What are some of the guidelines that marketers use when interacting with consumers? How does advertising really work? These questions can go on and on, of course, but they represent only a few dimensions of what is truly a fascinating field.

My Goals for the Book

As a student, I came to appreciate those occasions when a book would capture my interest and stimulate me to think more about a particular idea or theory. I especially appreciated those books that were able to provide me with useful frameworks to help guide my further thinking—frameworks that would reveal how the basic elements related to one another, and what implications these basic relations might have. When I decided to write this textbook, my goal was to produce this type of book for others to read and enjoy. As a professor, however, I also wanted the book to contain the best and latest concepts, findings, and applications. And, to the extent possible, I wished to see the book make a useful contribution to knowledge in the field as well as to the knowledge of its individual readers.

In this book, therefore, you will find a number of interesting and useful *frameworks*. These frameworks tie concepts together and bring them to the level of the real world that we experience in our lives as marketers and consumers. In some chapters I was able to use frameworks that are already widely accepted, whereas in other chapters I needed to develop new frameworks especially for this text.

Another basic element of this text is its reliance on the importance of *perspective,* or the view we choose to take of a particular topic. Just as a person looks different from the back than from the front, and different still if viewed from the side, so too will a topic appear different depending on the perspective we use in analyzing it. Recognizing this, I have included several chapters that directly discuss key perspectives on consumer behavior.

The Style of This Book

In accordance with my goals, the style of this book attempts to capture the innate excitement of consumer behavior while also delivering the best of theory and applications. It seeks to stimulate a personal interest in reading the material and thinking more about it, simply because the topics are interesting. It provides many examples of the real world of marketing and consumer behavior; in addition to adding interest, these examples indicate the differing ways in which concepts relate to reality. Occasionally it asks the reader to hazard a prediction of how a study turned out or to suggest another way to resolve a realistic marketing problem.

Also in accord with my goals, great attention was paid to effectively communicating the material to the reader. As the first edition was being written, 50 focus groups of student readers were conducted to provide feedback and suggestions on individual chapters; following each session, the chapter was revised to clarify and to streamline the discussion. The second, and now the third, editions have been further refined based on professors' and students' suggestions in actual coursework as well. At this point I am able to report that almost all of the consumer behavior students who have read this text are enthusiastic about it; they report that they find the book to be stimulating, to provide clear explanations, and to be a pleasure to read.

This text, in striving to present the best of theory and concepts, adopts the approach of stressing the basic issues in each area. Students and professors who wish to go beyond these basics in any given area will find that a strong foundation has been laid for this effort and that extensive reference notes have been provided at the back of the book. Thus students and professors who wish to move on to the next topic will find that they can do so without being diverted. In a sense, then, this book has been written for several levels of reader involvement and to support different forms of teaching orientations. The text is thus suitable for both undergraduate and graduate courses. Sufficient background on research approaches is provided that advanced readings can be assigned to extend text discussion. Sufficient marketing-decision orientation is included that cases can be assigned to extend the application of concepts to the reality of a marketing manager's role. Given the interesting nature of the topics, moreover, a class discussion format is easily supported, as are lectures to explain and to extend topic coverage.

By far the majority of consumer behavior courses are presently taught within marketing departments of business schools. This book maintains this general orientation and has been designed to be successful in this setting. There is no reason, however, that students with other majors should not be able to enjoy and use it effectively as well. (Students without a basic background in marketing should pay careful attention to Chapter 2, however, to learn the rudiments of this significant perspective.)

Improvements in This Edition

Readers familiar with the earlier editions will notice several positive additions in the present book. The topical coverage has been somewhat reorganized to more closely reflect the order in which many professors prefer to teach this course. The book has been shortened slightly with the deletion of one chapter and the relocation of its key discussions to adjacent chapters. Additional photos and advertisements have been added (some in color) to lend tone to the coverage. Many recent marketing applications and "state-of-the-art" consumer behavior topics have also been added to this edition. And, to better serve the interests of both those readers who will not consult the references and those who wish to spend much time with them, an expanded and up-to-date Notes section has again been compiled at the back of the book rather than at the end of each chapter. In addition, a short list of managerially oriented Suggested Readings has been added at the end of each chapter. Finally, to enhance both the teaching and learning associated with this text, an extensive glossary has been added at the back of the book and a "running glossary" of brief key term definitions has been added in page margins throughout the text.

Acknowledgments

This project and each of its revisions has taken a long time to complete, and over the years many people have helped in its development and refinement. For the first edition, graduate students at the University of Florida, especially Henry Morehead, Melanie Albert, Alain D'Astous, Carolyn Simmons, Amardeep Assar, William Baker, Kunal Basu, Amitava Chattopadhyay, Alan Dick, Douglas Hausknecht, Howard Marmorstein, Darrell Miller, Prakash Nedungadi, Elizabeth Moore-Shay, and Jane Petty, offered useful insights at various stages. Many daily work activities at the University of Florida were much assisted by the pleasant personalities of Jody Imperi, Carrie Patterson, Astrid Barranco, Yvette Ellison, Connie Kaminski-Krueger, and Jackie Liszak-May. At the University of Notre Dame, the two revisions have depended on the help of my student assistants: Megan Duffy, Brian Vogel, Kathy Fitzgerald, Edward Balog, Marilou Thielen, Brian Dineen, and Shannon Windsor. Donna Smith, Dee Sequin, Chris Breisch, and Jennifer Huggins have done fine work on much of this revision, and have earned my respect and gratitude.

At John Wiley, Tim Kent has been a fine and stimulating editor, continually pushing this author to practice the marketing concept, and being interested in discussing ways to make this the best book possible. I have also enjoyed my (numerous) telephone interactions with the talented members of the acquisition, editorial, design, photo, and production teams associated with Wiley, including Ellen Ford, Sally Ann Bailey, Jaime Perea, Kristina Williamson, Doris Cadd, Shelley Clubb, Debra Riegert, Dawn Stanley, Joan Micelli, and Lisa Passmore.

The insightful reviews and suggestions I have received from numerous faculty members have clearly helped to shape each of the editions of this book. For the first edition inputs I wish to again thank:

David Aaker (*California, Berkeley*)	William O. Bearden (*South Carolina*)
Tim Hartman (*Ohio U.*)	Harold Kassarjian (*UCLA*)
Richard J. Lutz (*Florida*)	George Prough (*Akron*)
Mary Lou Roberts (*Massachusetts*)	Carol Scott (*UCLA*)

For the second revision, I wish to again acknowledge the insightful reviews and suggestions by:

Raymond Burke (*Harvard*)	Peter Dacin (*Wisconsin*)
Richard Durand (*Maryland*)	Jack Faricy (*Florida*)
Ron Goldsmith (*Florida State*)	Jeff Kasmer (*Calif. State, Long Beach*)
Debbie MacInnis (*Arizona*)	Naresh Malhotra (*Georgia Tech*)
Lee Meadow (*Salisbury State*)	Jim Muncy (*Clemson*)
Ivan Ross (*Minnesota*)	Debra Stephens (*Villanova*)
Jeff Stoltman (*Wayne State*)	Judy Vilmain (*Kent State*)

and to offer special thanks to Dr. Darrel Miller (Queens College), who contributed the organizational buying chapters to this book.

This third edition has been significantly enhanced by both detailed suggestions and broader reactions offered by a talented group of reviewers. My thanks and appreciation to:

Jacqueline Brave (*Loyola U., Chicago*)	Gary Gaeth (*Iowa*)
Arthur Heimbach (*San Francisco State*)	Ronald Hill (*Villanova*)
Raj Javalgi (*Cleveland State*)	Steve Lysonski (*Marquette*)
William Rice (*California State, Fresno*)	Debra Stephens (*Villanova*)
Jeff Stoltman (*Wayne State*)	Russel Wahlers (*Ball State*)
Joseph Zinnes (*Temple*)	

For their special contributions to the original and the revised editions, I wish to express my warmest appreciation to my friends and colleagues, Joel Cohen and John Lynch (University of Florida) and Rich George (Saint Joseph's University). They have offered me encouragement from the very start, while also providing useful critiques, feedback from course testing, and ideas for specific sections. Rich also worked many hours to produce our fine original instructor's manual. For this third edition, I wish to thank Doug Hausknecht and George Prough (U. of Akron), who have developed the supplementary materials to enhance teaching and learning. Finally, I wish to express my deepest thanks to my wife, Barbara, for her support, encouragement, and insightful critiques of virtually every draft on every topic.

WILLIAM L. WILKIE
South Bend, Indiana
January 1994

CONTENTS IN BRIEF

xiii

CONTENTS

4 MARKET SEGMENTATION, *84*

7 CONSUMER INFORMATION PROCESSING, *175*

8 CONSUMER PERCEPTION (I) : Attention to Marketing Cues, 205

9 CONSUMER PERCEPTION (II) : Interpreting Marketing Cues, 231

Where do you suppose they keep the Range Rover?

A Range Rover is quite at home in weather that would keep other luxury cars, well, at home.
After all, with its permanent 4-wheel drive and powerful V-8 engine, you can plow through unplowed roads.
Tool along slushy streets.
Make it up sleet-covered hills.
And easily cope with conditions that would discourage a sled dog.

In fact, the Range Rover County even comes with an anti-lock braking system considered by many to be the most sophisticated one on four wheels.

RANGE ROVER

Which not only means you can drive with a reassuring amount of control.
You can stop with it too.
So why not call 1-800-FINE-4WD for the name of a dealer near you?
Granted, with Range Rovers starting at just under $39,000, it's not the sort of thing one should take lightly.
But then, neither is a ton of snow.

3 customers for Campbell's coming up

Pretty soon now, they'll be good and ready for something good and hot. Make it Campbell's Soup. Campbell's Tomato Soup, or Chicken Noodle, or Vegetable. Nothing else takes the chill out of children quite so fast. Nothing quite so warming tastes so good. And it heats in just 4 minutes.

Soup this good just has to be *Campbell's*

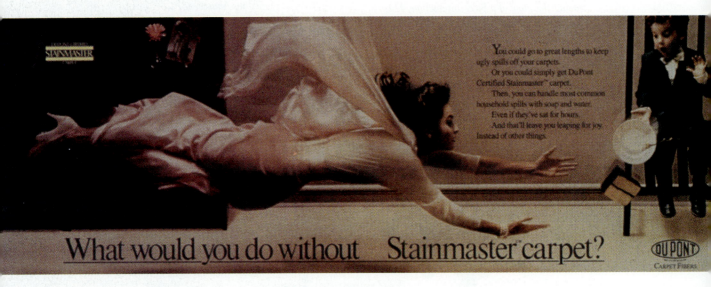

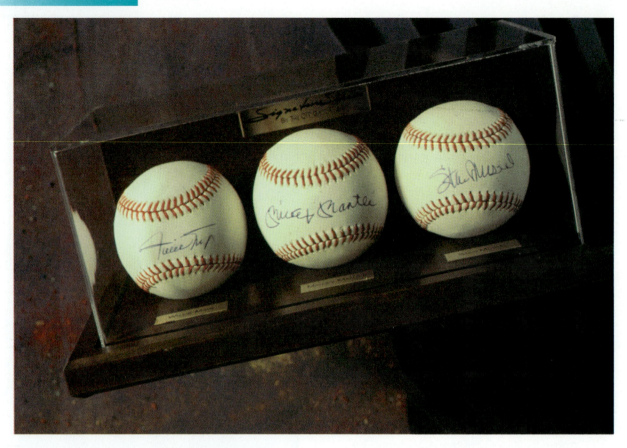

CONSUMER BEHAVIOR

Part I

INTRODUCTION TO CONSUMER BEHAVIOR

IN THIS part of the book—Chapters 1–4—we examine the major viewpoints used to understand the fascinating field of consumer behavior. In Chapter 1, we look at the academic aspects of the field: what is included in this area and how we study it. In Chapter 2, we consider the two major "players" in this field, reflecting on how marketers view consumer behavior and how consumers view their own behavior. In Chapter 3, we look at the huge and dynamic consumer market, examining both the size and the emerging trends. Finally, in Chapter 4, Market Segmentation, we consider how the larger market can be usefully divided into key target segments of consumers.

As you'll see, there is much fascinating material in the pages ahead, so let's get started!

THE FASCINATING FIELD OF CONSUMER BEHAVIOR

WHAT ARE THEY *REALLY* SAYING?

Consumer behavior is both an important and an interesting subject. As a marketer, you will want to understand as much as possible about it. For example, consider these quotes (taken from the chapter) from two consumers:

> I was so happy for Amanda when she married Jonathan! She's my best friend, and I know they'll be happy together...The trip, hotel, and my outfit were expensive, and so was my gift—a vase from Gump's. But money was no object...I like the "finer things in life" for my friends and myself.
>
> JENNIFER ANDERSON, ATTORNEY

> I had a very hard time deciding on a college....I thought about location, costs, activities, academics, and a lot of other things. I sent for some catalogs and visited a couple of places. I also talked with my folks and relatives about it, and the school counselor, too. My older sister Kim was a big help—she's a junior at State. I didn't talk about it as much with my friends as I thought I would...we're starting to go different ways, and it was a little awkward. Mark came here, though, and I'm glad I knew somebody from home....(pause) I don't know, sometimes I think I made a bad decision, but most of the time it's okay.
>
> MICHAEL TAYLOR, STUDENT

In this chapter, we'll learn a few powerful concepts that will help us to understand more about what's going on in these cases (and in millions of others).

Welcome to the fascinating field of consumer behavior!

Consumer behavior is an exciting and challenging subject! It's about people—what we purchase and why we purchase the way we do. It's about marketing—how products and services are designed for, and sold to, consumers in the marketplace. And it's about the consumer marketplace itself, in which *billions* of individual purchases occur each year, in *millions* of marketing outlets.

The chapter is organized in three major sections. The first describes some of the basic characteristics of consumer behavior as it exists today, and how it has evolved to its present status. The second provides an overview of the major academic concepts in this field. The closing section summarizes "where we are going" in the remainder of the book and shows how the many interesting aspects of consumer behavior are related.

■ CHARACTERISTICS OF MODERN CONSUMER BEHAVIOR

CONSUMER BEHAVIOR IS...

Subtle and Interesting

In many ways consumer behavior is a subtle phenomenon: it is not just "common sense." The reasons for our behavior are not always clear. Our actions as consumers are sometimes difficult to predict, and sometimes even hard to explain. As we examine this field, we'll be asking such interesting questions as

- Why do different consumers purchase different products?
- What is the best way for a consumer to go about buying a particular product?
- How does advertising work to influence consumer preferences?

In addressing many questions such as these, we will encounter some of the subtle complexities of this field of study.

Relevant Personally and Professionally

Each of us has spent a goodly portion of our lives observing others' consumer behavior, as well as participating in our own consumer decisions. This experience base can provide us with a strong "feel" for the subject matter—we can easily recognize the key issues and see why they are important.

However, we'll also see that, despite all this experience, most consumers do not possess a great deal of insight regarding their own behaviors. As consumers, most of us are not highly aware of the external influences that guide us toward purchases nor of our own internal processes at work to bring the decisions to fruition. Increased understanding of consumer behavior can thus improve our personal consumer behaviors in our daily lives.

On a professional level, most readers of this text are involved in marketing, advertising, and related fields of endeavor. As we'll see, an understanding of consumer behavior is increasingly recognized as a key factor in success in these fields. The careful study of the material in this text can lead to a competitive advantage for those who are able to use it well in their careers.

All Around Us

We are all consumers: each of us undertakes many forms of consumer behavior every day of our lives. If we could step back and view this in the aggregate, we'd see a massive amount of consumer and marketing activity at work across the country and around the world. For example, the U.S. market alone consists of some 260 million persons, each consuming food, housing, transportation, and thousands of other products and services, day after day after day. The consumption system operates continuously and is ingrained in our daily styles of living.

A Major Contributor to Society

Although we might have never thought about it this way, we can see that this staggering level of consumer activity plays an important role in the economic and social fabric of our society. Consumer spending in the United States alone accounts for about two-thirds of the nation's gross national product (GNP) each year. As we enter the mid-1990s the U.S. GNP is over $6 trillion, and *U.S. consumers are spending about $4 trillion per year!*[1]

Of course, $4 trillion is hard to imagine in the abstract. Exhibit 1-1, however, offers a graphic representation of how far $4 trillion would extend if the actual dollar bills were stretched end to end. The dollars spent by consumers in the United States each

XHIBIT 1-1 _____

How Far Does the Consumer's Dollar Stretch?

As of the mid-1990's, U.S. consumers are spending enough dollar bills each year to stretch for two round trips from the Earth to the sun!

year would stretch all the way from the Earth to the sun, around the sun (assuming no scorching factor!), back to and around the Earth, *back* to the sun again, and then again back to the Earth! Examined another way, $4 trillion is such a huge number that, if we were to try to count to it, at one dollar per second, it would take us over 100,000 years, or much longer than the history of civilization!

Consumers' purchases form the backbone of our economic system. Consumers' purchases provide profits for marketers who deliver valued goods and services and jobs and incomes for employees of these firms. *Changes* in consumer spending have important effects on the overall health of the economy, affecting a business's chance of success, a worker's chance of being unemployed, prospects for economic recession, the prices we pay, the interest rates we are charged, and so on.

Socially, consumer purchases help to mold society. Consider, for example, how such consumer products as food, travel, and clothing all help us to live our daily lives. Even more broadly, telephones, television, and magazines not only serve as sources of entertainment, but also serve important communication functions for us. These are, of course, supported with consumer dollars through both advertising revenues and direct purchases.

Further, consumer behavior involves more than physical goods. Consumers' use of *services*, such as medical care, auto repair, or hair styling, accounts for about one-half of all consumer spending, equal to product purchases. In addition, we engage in other types of consumer "purchases" as well—as voters, students, patients, worshippers, and so on. All these acts are also studied in the field of consumer behavior. In total, then, consumer behavior constitutes a broad and important set of activities in our society.

WHO STUDIES CONSUMER BEHAVIOR?

The field of consumer behavior comprises a broad set of people who are interested in describing, understanding, predicting, or influencing behavior by consumers. Compared to most academic fields, it is very young. The first major textbook did not appear until 1968. Most colleges did not even offer this course until the 1970s!

In recent years, however, the field has grown rapidly. For example, a small professional group—the Association for Consumer Research (ACR)—was formed in 1970. By the 1990s, ACR has grown to some 1,500 members, in 30 nations of the world. Many companies have hired persons with consumer behavior training in marketing, advertising, and consumer affairs positions. Government agencies, consulting firms, and not-for-profit organizations (e.g., universities, hospitals, religious groups) have also begun to hire persons with consumer behavior knowledge.

Historical Forces

Although the formal field is young, consumer behavior itself has been of interest for a long time. Since early peoples began to barter and trade, they have had to decide what they wanted and what they were willing to give up to get it. As money economies began to develop, consumers faced new questions of saving versus spending—and how to allocate their money across purchase categories.

The impact of technology and the Industrial Revolution led to significant changes in consumer behavior and our marketing systems. For example, during the early years of the twentieth century, the telephone, radio, and moving pictures provided new ways of informing consumers about the products available to them. Automobiles opened new vistas for recreation and fueled the growth of a mass consumer market. The success of the auto industry provided jobs for hundreds of thousands of workers in auto plants and in support businesses (raw materials, components, dealerships, road construction, gas stations, repair shops, etc.). The new income available for these workers was, in turn, used for consumer purchases that provided jobs in the manufacturing and selling of consumer products. As the industrial wheel turned faster, the beginnings of a mass consumer market emerged during the Roaring Twenties. Much of this momentum was halted by the Great Depression in the 1930s, however.

Then, during World War II, millions of people were earning money in the military and in civilian jobs, but couldn't spend it freely. Manufacturing capacity was redirected toward military uses: civilian production (houses, cars, clothing, etc.) was restricted in support of the war effort. When the war ended, consumers had both the money and the desire to purchase the items they had been denied during the years of sacrifice. This burst of consumer demand coincided with the "baby boom" of the late 1940s through the early 1960s. Demand for new homes, big enough for growing families, pushed out from city neighborhoods, and the suburbs were born.

Large chain stores, which had begun during the Great Depression of the 1930s, pushed to expand to the suburbs to meet the huge demand. The shopping center appeared in the 1950s and became a popular suburban gathering spot. A new U.S. interstate highway system added to the momentum, helping marketers to distribute mass-produced goods efficiently by truck from centralized warehouses. Finally, a key element took hold in the 1950s—television. Every night, in every corner of the land, millions of families watched, listened, and learned from the same network program. From the marketing viewpoint, a single commercial offered instantaneous communication with millions. The era of the mass consumer market had been born.

Recent Forces

The availability of a mass market meant huge profit opportunities for marketers who could successfully develop products that would satisfy consumers' desires. The **marketing concept** was introduced shortly after World War II by the General Electric Company. It was explicit recognition of the potentials in mass markets:

> Rather than making what you've always made, and then trying to sell it, find out what will sell, and then try to make it.

Descriptive consumer research: Research that describes the actual state of the consumer marketplace.

Inferential consumer research: Research that helps the marketer discover why consumers behave the way they do or how they will likely react to new types of products or services.

"Finding out what will sell" meant that marketers needed to solve two problems. First, they had to discover *what* was selling, what was not selling, *who* was buying, and who was not. This required **descriptive consumer research** to describe the actual state of the consumer marketplace. Second, the marketer had to discover *why* consumers were behaving as they were, and *how* they would likely react to new types of products or services. This required **inferential consumer research** (as we'll discuss, consumers are typically unable to provide complete answers to these questions, so consumer researchers need to *infer* what the true answers are). Thus the growth of the mass market required a growth of consumer research during the 1950s.

In earlier years some economists had been studying how consumer spending patterns were influenced by economic factors. During the 1950s these economists were joined by a number of researchers in marketing, who were interested in how marketing factors worked to influence consumer behavior. Unfortunately, there was still no efficient way to handle the data that were obtained; arduous manual calculation was the order of the day for the commercial analysts who studied consumer markets.

Then came the *computer* and tremendous advances in analytical methods. The quantitative approach to research in marketing and advertising began to blossom during the 1960s. In 1964, for example, the *Journal of Marketing Research* was founded, four years after the *Journal of Advertising Research*. Researchers were now able to gather information from large samples of consumers about their purchases, attitudes, and backgrounds. The computer's flexibility in data analysis allowed researchers to test various approaches. For example, the capability of trying out different ways of segmenting consumer markets served to advance dramatically the use of market segmentation within marketing.

By the late 1960s many researchers in marketing had decided that they should focus on consumer behavior as a subject in its own right. During the 1970s they were joined by persons from home economics (who had been studying how to help consumers to buy more wisely for many years) and some psychologists, sociologists, and anthropologists (who saw the consumer setting as an important context in which human behavior could be studied). People in business and government organizations also played key roles in identifying problems and supporting research efforts. Another new publication, the *Journal of Consumer Research*, was started in 1974, joining the *Journal of Consumer Affairs*, which had begun in 1967. The Association for Consumer Research began to publish the proceedings of its annual conference under the title *Advances in Consumer Research*, while the American Marketing Association continued to give consumer behavior a great deal of attention in its conferences and publications. Thus, by the mid-1970s, the field of consumer behavior research had clearly arrived as a significant area for study, and this course had been started at colleges across the United States. Now, in the 1990s, the field continues to flourish. Persons who have studied consumer behavior have gained authoritative positions in businesses of all types as well as in universities, marketing research firms, and advertising agencies. Numerous journals and trade publications are now available, including such recent entries as the *Journal of Consumer Psychology* and the *Journal of Consumer Marketing*. Further, marketers are continuously conducting consumer research to help make better marketing decisions. As just one example of how important the study has become, Kraft Foods recently reported that over a 10-year period, it had run more than 5,000 consumer research studies at a total cost of over $100 million![2]

■ KEY CONCEPTS IN THE STUDY OF CONSUMER BEHAVIOR

FROM QUOTES TO CONCEPTS

How can we best begin our study of consumer behavior? One interesting approach is to participate in trying to observe what actual consumers do and say, and then try to understand and explain what is really going on. To begin this approach, please now turn to Exhibit 1-2 and read carefully the consumer quotes there (we'll be referring to these in our discussions that follow).

While the vignettes are not a representative sample of all consumer behavior, they do portray the wide range of the consumer experience that exists. Notice also how easily we can relate to them: how familiar or normal they seem to be. This indicates that we already possess implicit or hidden theories about this field. For example, in reading the quotes most of us implicitly accept that there is an underlying system at work, that the behavior is not simply random. If we take any individual quote, we can usually pick out one or more consumer characteristics—sex, age, marital status, and so on—that we would expect to have a fairly reliable relationship to the consumer behavior being reported. Scott Campbell's quote isn't too surprising coming from him, for example, but what if Martha Lindsey were making this statement? In each instance we see as typical, we are reflecting our beliefs about an underlying system for consumer behavior.

$\mathcal{E}$XHIBIT 1-2

Quotes from Consumers

I was a little down, and I called home to my mother. She tried to cheer me up; she suggested I buy something nice as a sort of reward for doing well in my classes. So I...just leisurely looked at clothes. Finally I saw just what I wanted. It was a beige satin blouse with puffed sleeves and pearl buttons. It made me look soft and curvy. The only problem was the price—it was almost $120! The saleslady showed me how it was well made and told me how nice it looked on me. I gulped and bought it!

JILL PRADO, *student*

*My car decision was real easy... I knew just what I wanted. The Camaro was for me...
long, low, powerful, dark and handsome. Alriggght!*

SCOTT CAMPBELL, *student*

*I was so happy for Amanda when she married Jonathan! She's my best friend, and I know
they'll be happy together.... The trip, hotel, and my outfit were expensive, and so was
my gift—a vase from Gump's. But money was no object... I like the "finer things in life"
for my friends and myself.*

JENNIFER ANDERSON, *attorney*

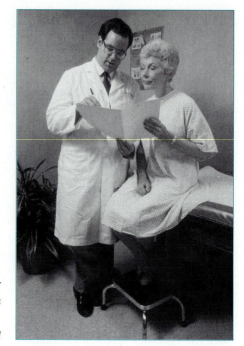

I've started to take a new "miracle drug" for my arthritis, and I'm feeling a lot better now. I thank Dr. Reed for prescribing it for me. The cost? It's expensive, I bet, but my medical plans cover most of it.

MARTHA LINDSEY, *retired*

Dad, no offense, but you really don't get it about shoes . . . we have to wear the new Nikes 'cause they really are the best. Besides, the kids at school do notice what someone wears, you know!

WILL, ALLIE, and JIM WILKIE, *ages 14, 12, and 10*

I just saw an ad for used tools at a garage sale, so I'll be there early in the morning. Deb and I are adding a room, and I don't have all the tools I need. Since my wallet's thin, I'm hoping to get them cheap.

ANTHONY GRANT, *production manager*

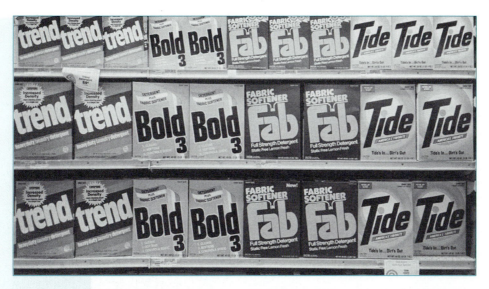

I'd never use [detergent brand]! My daughter plays with a neighbor's child whose clothes have a yellowish tinge, which doesn't say much for her mother. She uses it. I'll only use Tide; it's the best one. I think it's one of the leading sellers, too.

JANET RODGERS, *housewife*

I had a very hard time deciding on a college. . . . I thought about location, costs, activities, academics, and a lot of other things. I sent for some catalogs and visited a couple of places. I also talked with my folks and relatives about it, and the school counselor, too. My older sister Kim was a big help—she's a junior at State. I didn't talk about it as much with my friends as I thought I would . . . we're starting to go different ways, and it was a little awkward. Mark came here, though, and I'm glad I knew somebody from home . . . (pause) I don't know, sometimes I think I made a bad decision, but most of the time it's okay.

MICHAEL TAYLOR, *student*

However, while there is an underlying system at work within consumer behavior, it is also true that most of the relationships we'll examine are far from being perfect or straightforward. Throughout the remainder of this text we will be striving to (1) *deepen* our understanding of the causes of consumer behavior and (2) *broaden* our appreciation of how consumer behavior knowledge can be applied to solve problems.

DEFINITION OF CONSUMER BEHAVIOR

Consumer behavior: The mental, emotional, and physical activities that people engage in when selecting, purchasing, using, and disposing of products and services so as to satisfy needs and desires.

A formal definition of terms helps us to focus attention on key points and concepts. **Consumer behavior** is here defined as

> The mental, emotional, and physical activities that people engage in when selecting, purchasing, using, and disposing of products and services so as to satisfy needs and desires.

While this definition is short, it is rich in basic implications about the topic. Understanding these implications is the key to knowing this field, as indicated in our following discussion of the "Seven Keys" to consumer behavior.

THE "SEVEN KEYS" TO CONSUMER BEHAVIOR

In any field of study there are basic theories and assumptions that experts use to guide their approaches to the subject. Surprisingly, however, these guidelines often become so accepted by the experts that they aren't clearly identified when speaking about the subject matter. Here we will explain and examine seven of the most basic characteristics of consumer behavior as it is viewed by leading persons in this field. As individual points, each is basic and makes sense. When we put them together, moreover, they add up to a rich conceptual structure for the body of knowledge in the field.

The "Seven Keys" are outlined in Figure 1-1. Some students have successfully used the acronym MAP TRIP to help recall the keys and their exact ordering. Of far greater importance than recalling them, of course, is a strong understanding of the nature and implications of each characteristic. The following sections provide brief explanations of each of these key concepts in the field.

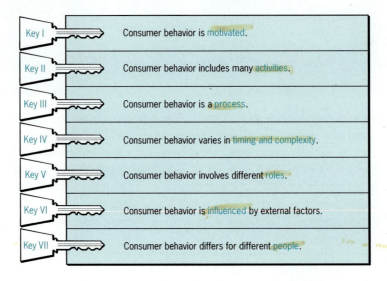

FIGURE 1-1 Seven Keys to Consumer Behavior

Key I — Consumer behavior is motivated.

Key II — Consumer behavior includes many activities.

Key III — Consumer behavior is a process.

Key IV — Consumer behavior varies in timing and complexity.

Key V — Consumer behavior involves different roles.

Key VI — Consumer behavior is influenced by external factors.

Key VII — Consumer behavior differs for different people.

Key I: Consumer Behavior Is Motivated

Probably the most basic question we can ask is, "Why does consumer behavior occur …?" Our definition for consumer behavior provided the most basic answer: "…so as to satisfy needs and desires." This means that, in general, consumer behavior is motivated behavior aimed at achieving particular goals. The behavior itself is a means to an end, with the "end" being the satisfaction of needs and desires.

Note that the consumer quotes of Exhibit 1-2 provide numerous examples of "means-ends" relationships. For example, Anthony Grant will buy tools to build his new room, while Jennifer Anderson's purchase of the vase was a means by which she could express her feelings of friendship for Amanda. In all the cases, products or services were desired to achieve goals held by the person. In addition, however, we should also note that the thoughts and motivations of consumers are usually hidden within them and are not observable by us. This means that theories are especially useful in helping us understand what may be going on, and inferential consumer research methods help us try to actually measure it.

More on Motives.   We cannot delve deeply into the area of motivation in this introductory chapter, but it is useful to recognize three further points. First, some consumer behaviors spring from primarily **functional motives** (an example is Anthony's tool purchase), whereas others can be primarily means of **self-expressive motives** as with Jennifer's gift.

Second, most behaviors have more than one goal, so that a **mix of motivations** is present. Many of us think of detergents as a rather simple product, for example, but let us look again at what Janet Rodgers was saying. While she obviously uses detergents for the functional purpose of obtaining clean clothes, there are strong indications that Mrs. Rodgers also views this product as relating to such goals as being a good mother, having her daughter appear attractive, being seen by others as a worthwhile person, and so forth. Similarly, Scott Campbell's description of his car also suggests a mix of goals, including appearance, performance, and image of the owner.

The third additional point relates to the ease with which we can *identify* motivations. Some motivations are apparent to the consumer and to others, and purchases appear to be fairly straightforward. Anthony's need for tools might exemplify this instance. When decisions are complex or are tied in with heavy self-expression, however, some motivations can be quite difficult to identify. Consider how difficult it would be to identify exactly each motivation operating in Jennifer's case or in Michael Taylor's choice of a college.

Why Marketers Are Interested.   Notice that when multiple motives are present, a consumer is actually buying a **bundle of benefits** in a product. If a marketer can identify the benefits consumers are seeking, he or she can design a product to deliver maximum appeal and satisfaction. This is not an easy task, of course, because different consumers are seeking different mixes of benefits and because some motives are hard to identify. Consumers' motivations are thus of central importance to marketers. We will be discussing more about these topics in our chapter on consumer motivation (Chapter 5). For now, however, it is important that the basic point be reiterated; consumer behavior consists of activities that are goal oriented—it is a *means to an end.*

Means to an end: The concept that consumer behavior is aimed at (the *means* of) achieving particular goals (the *ends*).

Functional motives: Reasons for a purchase that relate to the product's performance insofar as it helps the consumer reach a goal.

Self-expressive motives: Reasons for consumer behaviors that relate to a person's desire to express feelings or something else about himself or herself.

Key II: Consumer Behavior Includes Many Activities

Our definition of consumer behavior focused on activity as a basic characteristic, and now it appears as a key to understanding the topic. Why is there such attention paid to this point? The answer is that *there are many important facets to consumer behavior.* As consumers, we have thoughts, feelings, plans, decisions, and purchases, and the experiences that follow. An observer who looks only at the act of purchase will miss many of the relevant activities. Also, a narrow view of consumer behavior will tend to underrepresent its significance in our daily lives. Finally, marketers must study this range of activities, since it provides marketers with a rich set of possible ways by which to reach, appeal to, and satisfy consumers. Thus an understanding of consumer activities provides a useful basis for developing marketing strategies.

Figure 1-2 summarizes some of the types of activities that make up consumer behavior. Notice that nearly 30 separate activities are shown. Further, think about how many versions each activity on the list might have. "Viewing ads," for example, could include reading ads in magazines, in newspapers, or in the mail; watching them on television; listening to them on radio; or seeing billboards during car travel. Similarly, displays are prominent in supermarkets, in retail stores, and in store windows. Given the number of outlets for ads and displays, and the number of brands using them, imagine what a huge number of marketing stimuli a consumer sees over the course of a week, month, or year!

For activities that are product specific, such as "Deciding to buy," think about how many products and services there are in our marketing economy. Even though you may not personally buy most of these, some consumers *are* thinking about buying and using each product and service available. In total, an enormous amount of time, energy, and money goes into these consumer activities.

As a final note, it is helpful to recognize a distinction between *deliberate* and *incidental* activities. Some of the activities on the list—particularly those near

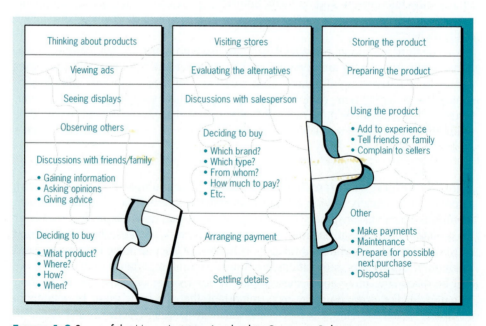

FIGURE 1-2 Some of the Many Activities Involved in Consumer Behavior

the center, such as "Discussions with salespersons" and "Deciding to buy"—are clearly **deliberate consumer behaviors** (that is, we choose to undertake these for a specific purpose involving purchase or consumption). **Incidental consumer behaviors,** on the other hand, usually occur as by-products of other, nonconsumer, activities. For example, few persons turn on the television or radio to catch their favorite commercial! When we stroll through stores, we may have certain products in mind, but we'll also encounter many other products for which we'd not been looking, and we'll often buy some of these. The deliberate/incidental distinction is an important one for marketers who are attempting to gain consumers' attention and interest.

Key III: Consumer Behavior Is a Process

The concept of a *process*, in which a series of related stages occur, has become a major feature of the field of consumer behavior in the last 20 years. Note that the definition referred to "selecting, purchasing, using, and disposing of products." Implicit in these stages is the concept that a consumer's selection would precede purchase, which would in turn precede usage and disposition. Notice that Figure 1-2 also implicitly contains a process orientation: if we were to label the columns, therefore, we might show

$$
\begin{array}{ccccc}
\underline{\text{STAGE } 1} & \rightarrow & \underline{\text{STAGE } 2} & \rightarrow & \underline{\text{STAGE } 3} \\
\text{Prepurchase} & \rightarrow & & & \\
\text{activities} & & \text{Purchasing} & & \\
& & \text{activities} & \rightarrow & \text{Postpurchase} \\
& & & & \text{activities}
\end{array}
$$

This stage relationship represents the **decision process approach** to consumer behavior. By stressing the fact that the actual purchase is only one stage in a series of related stages, the decision process approach helps to analyze *why* a certain purchase will be made by a certain individual. It also helps to clarify what activities are likely to precede a purchase and what effects that purchase might have on later actions of the same consumer (notice, also, that our postpurchase activities for one purchase will feed into prepurchase activities for future purchases). Because of its importance and usefulness, we will examine this approach in detail later in this book.

Decision process approach: A framework that studies consumer behavior as a sequence of activities: stresses that the prepurchase, purchase, and postpurchase stages are all important.

Key IV: Consumer Behavior Differs in Timing and Complexity

Timing refers to *when* the decision takes place and *how long* the entire process takes. *Complexity* refers to the *number of activities* involved in a decision and the *difficulty* of the decision itself. Timing and complexity will typically be correlated. That is, all other factors being equal, the more complex a decision is, the more time will usually be spent on it.

The Inherent Complexity of Consumer Decisions.   In the abstract, many consumer decisions are inherently rather complex and could involve nearly all the activities listed in Figure 1-2. If we consumers were to strive to make the absolutely correct choice, at just the right price, we would have to engage in many **prepurchase activities.** A few purchases are so important, and occur so seldom, that we do come close to doing all of this. Michael Taylor's decision on which college to attend was probably the most complex of our consumer vignettes. He considered a number of alternatives, weighed them on many dimensions, used a number of information sources, and took a long time. Even after enrolling, he is still "consuming" the educational service and making many other decisions related to it (such as which classes to take, which residence to rent, etc.). Finally, notice that his **postpurchase evaluation** is continuing to occur and is not entirely favorable at this time. Most consumers report similarly complex decisions with housing choices, career options, and some major purchases.

Consumers Try to Simplify.   Given that each of us has other things to do with our time, and that complex consumer decisions require effort, there are incentives to find ways to simplify and speed up our decision processes. Some of the major **decision simplifiers** are

- Aiming for a "satisfactory" decision rather than the best one possible.
- Relying on other people's recommendations of what to buy.
- Becoming "brand loyal" for products that we repurchase fairly often.

However, unless we are willing to become habitual purchasers of the same brand every time we buy, some complexity will remain in every consumer decision.

This Leads to a Conflict.   This discussion leads us to recognize an especially interesting conflict that can occur between the forces for simplification and our desires to satisfy positive goals. Let's again take the case of Janet Rodgers as an example. Notice that she can create a fast and easy decision process for herself by merely pulling Tide off the store shelf, regardless of circumstances. If she does this, however, she runs certain risks. For example, she could miss out on a new brand that might be better or miss out on a large price savings or a free gift (premium) from a competing brand that is as good as her favorite brand. In other words, she will not guarantee receiving the best value for her money by pursuing a strict brand-loyalty decision rule. As consumers, we have all experienced this type of conflict. Most of us resolve it by retaining some *flexibility* in our purchasing processes, so that we can take advantage when the situation allows.

This is a key point for marketing managers. Basically, the forces toward simplification can offer a given brand (e.g., Tide) profit opportunities through brand loyalty. Notice the challenge facing Tide's competitors trying to sell to Janet Rodgers, who likely is paying no attention to them! However, consumers' desires for the best overall set of benefits will offer competing brands (Wisk, Cheer, etc.) opportunities through trial purchases and brand switching by even those consumers who favor Tide. In Janet Rodgers's case, the competitors need to somehow capture her interest, and then stimulate a trial purchase.

Key V: Consumer Behavior Involves Different Roles

There are at least three significantly different functions performed within the consumer behavior process. Each of these functions has a **consumer role** associated with it. In brief, a consumer can be an

- Influencer.
- Purchaser.
- User.

A consumer can play different combinations of these roles on any given occasion. Also, for any particular purchase, more than one person may be involved in one or more of

Decision simplifiers:
Heuristics, or rules of thumb, that consumers use to help make decisions more easily.

Consumer role: A part to be played within a consumer decision process.

Topic	Example from Vignette
Influencer, purchaser, and user	Jill Prado
Influencer and purchaser only	Jennifer Anderson
Influencer and user only	Will, Allie, and Jim
Influencer only	Kim Taylor (Michael's sister)
Purchaser and user only	Martha Lindsey
Purchaser only	Father of Will, Allie, and Jim
User only	Daughter of Janet Rodgers

FIGURE 1-3 Combinations of Roles a Consumer Can Play

the roles. Even though we often can overlook the influence of others, when more than one person is involved, the consumer decision process is affected.

Figure 1-3 outlines the basic role combinations. First, a consumer can play all three roles during a purchase: this is particularly common when we are "on our own" and are purchasing for ourselves. Jill Prado's purchase of a blouse is a good example. Even here, however, other influencer roles were active in the process. Those mentioned by Jill were her mother, who suggested the purchase, and the saleslady, who provided reinforcement at the moment of decision.

The remaining combinations all have at least some incompleteness to them, in that one of the normal functions is missing. Jennifer's gift purchase, for example, will not involve personal usage on her part. Will, Allie, and Jim's ages indicate that they may not be purchasers of some products although they already hold strong desires to influence particular purchases, and to consume the products. Kim Taylor, Michael's sister, was not really involved in either purchasing or using Michael's college education, but she did act as an influence on the decision. (This is a relatively common role.)

Martha Lindsey's drug purchases were virtually dictated to her by her physician, thereby removing the "Influencer" role from her. This is relatively common for consumers of professional services, unless they are assertive. The consumer quotes do not provide direct evidence of either of the last two categories. Will, Allie, and Jim's father might act as a "purchaser only" if he gives in to one of the requests and does not exert influence on the actual choice. Similarly, Janet Rodgers's daughter will be a consumer of the detergent's benefits but is not likely to exert direct influence on the purchase.

As we'll see in later chapters, this three-level system of roles can easily be expanded to offer further insights into consumer behavior. And while simple, it has provided us with eight combinations of roles. Further, notice how crucial the exact roles can be in deciding what consumer behavior actually occurs. Jill, for example, could have acted quite differently had the influencers in her case been different: What if her mother had suggested she take in a movie, or splurge on sweets, or come home for a weekend? What if the salesperson had insulted her or had simply suggested a sweater, or jewelry, or something else? There is thus a wide array of possibilities: the actual consumer behaviors we see thus stem from the details of interactions of roles during the process.

More on Roles. Consumer roles arise because of **social interactions.** Think about how frequent and significant these social interactions are in consumer behavior: there are actually very few purchases we make that do not in any way involve anyone else acting in any of these roles. It is also important to note that the roles tend to change over a consumer's lifetime. Young children do not purchase often. Single persons, without the role of child, spouse, or parent to perform, can be individualistic in their buying decisions (though still often influenced by their peers). If and when marriage brings spouse and parental roles, these same persons will become heavily involved in purchasing for family members and in being influenced by their wants and needs.

Why Marketers Are Interested.   For marketers, the fact that *multiple persons* are involved in these roles poses problems and opportunities. For example, frequently there is a need to advertise to the influencers while selling to the purchaser. To do this well, marketers must be able to identify which types of people play which roles for particular purchases. This requires detailed understanding of the workings of social roles, household decision-making patterns, the operation of "buying centers" in organizational purchases, and other topics we'll be examining later in this book.

Key VI: Consumer Behavior Is Influenced by External Factors

Influence: The voluntary alteration of a person's attitudes, preferences, or behaviors by an outside force.

The concept of **influence** deserves special focus because of its importance in understanding consumer behavior. Essentially, this reflects the fact that consumer behavior is *adaptive* in nature: consumers adapt to the situations that surround them. Being influenced, in turn, means that a consumer's decision process has somehow been affected by outside forces. As we'll see, some forms of influence, occur over long time periods, while others work within brief episodes.

Influence is a natural occurrence in the consumer world: influence is not necessarily good or bad. Most people agree that some forms of influence, such as manipulation or coercion, are bad. However, some forms of influence are recognized to be quite beneficial, such as learning about new products and services, learning of price specials, receiving good purchase advice, and so forth.

Numerous Influence Sources.   Many external sources act to influence our consumer behaviors. Figure 1-4 lists the major types. **Culture** refers to the beliefs, values, and views we share as members of a society. It acts on us throughout our lives and has pervasive influence on all our behaviors. One role of culture is to identify boundaries for what we see as acceptable products, services, and consumer activities. **Subcultures** refers to groups of people, within an entire culture, who tend to share particular patterns of values and behaviors. A consumer can belong to several subcultures. Subcultures are defined on bases such as sex, race, nationality, age, and religion. Examples include the black subculture, the Hispanic subculture, the teenage subculture, the Mormon subculture, and so forth. **Social class**, meanwhile, incorporates variables such as occupation, income, and educational level. These variables combine to affect our life-styles, which in turn have great influence on our consumption patterns.

Family helps to develop its children's consumer "personalities" as shoppers and spenders. As adults, although our roles have changed, our family's past continues to exert strong influence on our lives through the values and habits we have internalized. **Reference groups and friends** influence consumer behavior by providing guidelines to appropriate behaviors for those people who identify with them. Fraternities, sororities,

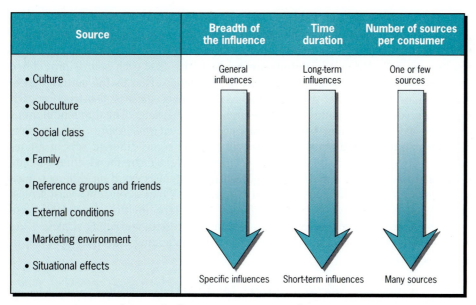

Source	Breadth of the influence	Time duration	Number of sources per consumer
• Culture	General influences	Long-term influences	One or few sources
• Subculture			
• Social class			
• Family			
• Reference groups and friends			
• External conditions			
• Marketing environment			
• Situational effects	Specific influences	Short-term influences	Many sources

FIGURE 1-4 Sources of External Influences on Consumer Behavior

athletes, and career professionals are frequent reference group figures. In addition to explicit discussions with our friends, we are also frequently influenced simply by observing their behaviors and their reactions to our purchases.

External conditions refers to such factors as inflation, unemployment, credit availability, and so forth. They are often, but not always, economically oriented (another form of external condition, such as a long-term illness in the family, could also shift purchase plans). External conditions clearly affect many consumers' decisions on how much to spend and when to buy a given product. In the **marketing environment** we find numerous efforts by marketers to reach and influence our decisions. These efforts include attractively designing the products, advertising, displays, salespersons, prices, and the environment of the store itself. Finally, **situational effects** refer to temporary forces that stem from particular settings in which consumers find themselves for short periods of time. Usually, consumers will adapt to the situational context. For example, a hot dog is fine at a ball game but not as an entree for the boss at dinner.

More on External Influences.   In addition to the list of influences, several points can be gained by considering Figure 1-4. First, the figure is organized in approximate order of *breadth* of influence—from the broadest and most general types of influence to those that are most purchase specific. Culture, for example, may not be a determining factor in our choice of one brand as opposed to another, but it has played an important role in the fact that the product is even available for sale. Second, a difference in *time dimension* is also reflected in the figure. The influence of culture and subculture extends over many years. Even in our adult years we are influenced by cultural factors we internalized as children. At the other extreme, the effect of marketing variables and situations might occur during a very short time and have little lasting impact.

Marketing environment: The setting created by marketers to reach and influence consumer decisions.

Situational effects: Temporary forces that stem from particular settings in which consumers find themselves for short periods of time.

Third, the *number* of influences—for any particular consumer—increases as we go down the list. Most of us belong to only one culture, one social class, and one or two families. At the high-frequency extreme are marketing influences and situations. Finally—not reflected in the figure—we might notice that each source provides a consumer with an *internally consistent* set of guidelines. That is, the culture generally provides the same set of values for every member. This is also true for each subculture, social class, family, reference group, and marketer. The differential influences we see on consumer behavior thus arise from *multiple sources*. For example, different cultures and different families will provide some different sets of guidelines to their members. Similarly, different friends might recommend different cars, restaurants, and so on. Finally, our competitive system is *based on* different marketers recommending different brands. The net result is that a consumer *must develop ways to deal with different sources of influence*. Marketers, in turn, must take these consumer adaptations into account in developing successful marketing strategies. As we'll see, this point is of central importance to understanding consumer behavior in our modern world.

Key VII: Consumer Behavior Differs for Different People

It is obvious that each of us undertakes somewhat different consumer activities and makes somewhat different purchases in line with our somewhat different preferences. The reason that this topic—formally termed **individual differences**—is raised is that to understand consumer behavior, we must understand *why people would engage in different behaviors*. Individual differences make it difficult for us to summarize consumer behavior easily. We need to develop "types" of consumers. This problem is very real for marketing managers who must attempt to predict *who* will respond favorably to a certain program and *how many* of such persons there are in the consumer market. This provides the rationale for **market segmentation**, the process by which we identify key target groups within the consumer marketplace. Much of the material to come in this book will help us to deal with the intriguing puzzle of individual differences.

Individual differences: A formal term referring to the analysis of why each consumer undertakes somewhat different activities, makes somewhat different purchases, and has somewhat different preferences.

FOUR "PITFALLS" IN THE STUDY OF CONSUMER BEHAVIOR

Consumer behavior is a pulsating, interesting topic. At the same time, though, it *is* broad and complex. The Seven Keys will prove to be valuable guides. However, past students in this course have reported four particular difficulties that hindered their learning, and suggested that future students be warned in advance. These four "pitfalls" are listed in Figure 1-5. Each reflects an underlying issue regarding the development of knowledge.

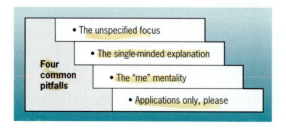

FIGURE 1-5 Four Common Pitfalls in the Study of Consumer Behavior

Pitfall 1: The Unspecified Focus

This issue of **unspecified focus** warns us to check that we are focusing correctly in light of the problem at hand. In scientific terms, the issue stresses the importance of specifying the *level of analysis* that we are using.

Most concepts we'll encounter can exist at various levels of specification. For example, it is often tempting to talk about "the consumer." When we use this term we sometimes mean the total market, while at other times we're thinking of a subgroup. A common possibility is that we're really considering an individual consumer, but are viewing him or her as somehow representative of the target market. It is obviously helpful—both for our own thinking and for communicating with others—to specify at which level we are thinking at the time.

A similar problem is also often found with terms such as "choice" or "purchase." Candidate levels of analysis for these terms include the product class, a particular item (or brand) within the product class, and, sometimes, the store at which the purchase occurs. For each level of analysis the relevant factors can differ. Jill Prado's purchase of a blouse provides a good example of this point. Even though the product, store, and item levels were all related within her purchase process, notice how different are the factors that we'd want to use to best explain: (1) Jill's decision to search for clothes in the first place, (2) her selection of the stores in which to shop, and (3) her choice of the particular blouse that she ended up taking home with her.

At a practical level, this issue assumes particular importance. Marketing managers cannot afford to focus only on the individual consumer level, even though they can gain important insights from it. They must also analyze market segments, as well as market sales statistics. Marketers must also use different variables to predict store choice than to predict product purchase, and then still different variables for brand choice. In general, specifying the target level of analysis will sharpen our insights into consumer behavior.

Unspecified focus: A pitfall that warns us to be specific when we use a common term in this field.

Pitfall 2: The Single-minded Explanation

The **single-minded explanation** refers to the fact that sometimes it is tempting to explain a behavior by pointing to a single factor and viewing it as if it alone "caused" the behavior. However, as was evident in the consumer quotes, there are almost always a number of factors at work, and some of these are not apparent at the surface. A refusal to consider other explanations can thus lead us to miss important insights. For example, a "single-minded explainer" might assert that consumers buy toothpaste to clean their teeth or beer to quench thirst or that consumers purchase on a price basis. None of these explanations is entirely wrong, of course, but all are incomplete. In the case of toothpaste, for example, consumers are also interested in decay prevention, sweet breath, whitening and brightening power, and other important attributes. The recent successes of brands such as Aquafresh® show the power of recognizing combinations of these attributes to appeal to multiple consumer motivations.

Single-minded explanation: A pitfall that warns against the temptation to assume that a single factor alone will cause a consumer behavior.

Pitfall 3: The "Me" Mentality

Much of the appeal of consumer behavior lies in the fact that each of us is a consumer. In learning this field we can use our personal experiences as a means of understanding important consumer concepts. In fact, Chapter 1 has encouraged the use of self-analysis (introspection) for exactly these reasons. What, then, is the problem?

"Me" mentality:
A pitfall that warns against a sole reliance on our own interests, opinions, and experience as being representative of the consumer marketplace.

The **"me" mentality** problem is that a *sole reliance* on our own experience and interests can lead to a nonrepresentative view of consumer behavior. Each of us has limited experience in some consumer behaviors and limited interests in many others. We also have different values from some other consumers and act within different economic and social situations. All these factors limit the power of introspection and can contribute to limiting "selective perceptions."

For example, many readers have not yet had much experience with the purchase concerns of senior citizens or with buying houses. Many males might view Jill's blouse search as a mystery; some readers might also judge this purchase to have been "too extravagant." Many people lack the mechanical background to handle Anthony Grant's tools in the way he plans to. More broadly, many consumers encounter unemployment, mounting debts, and sharp curtailment of purchases, but many readers may not have experienced these setbacks. Thus, because the true scope of consumer behavior is so vast, each of us needs to reach out far beyond our own experience base. This means reading and thinking about matters beyond our personal day-to-day interests. Within the business world, it means gathering as much information as possible about the actual consumer market and applying concepts and techniques as appropriate. Avoiding the "me" mentality, in fact, is the basic reason that marketers use consumer research.

Pitfall 4: Applications Only, Please

Many persons studying consumer behavior are interested in marketing-related careers. Given this career path, there is a natural tendency to look for helpful hints for marketing decisions. This translates into a healthy interest in marketing applications of consumer behavior. This healthy interest can become a pitfall, however, when a short-term stress on **"applications only, please"** becomes a *dominating focus* and begins to drive out appreciation for basic concepts and research methods. This leads to two significant risks. First, the ability to adopt various perspectives is an important asset in a field such as consumer behavior, since these reveal new dimensions of the topic. In an academic sense, then, a stress on "applications only" will risk the loss of a significant degree of learning.

"Applications only, please": A pitfall that warns that our natural tendency to look for helpful marketing hints is taken too far if it drives out an appreciation for learning the basic concepts and research methods of consumer behavior.

Second, this pitfall can turn around to shortchange even the most applications-oriented career in the longer run. This is due to the fact that *the world is rapidly changing: today's theory is tomorrow's practice.* Further, it is important that we recognize that *marketing applications* are by their nature situation specific. What worked for one firm in the past may not work for another firm in the future. If competitors institute changes, the marketing challenge is to search for new ideas, not past examples. The underlying *reasons* for consumer behavior continue across situations and are a valuable help to us in discovering new marketing ideas and understanding human behavior. Thus, while marketing applications are quite relevant, they are not primary. Generalizations and concepts are the key elements of the body of knowledge in consumer behavior: investing in learning these will provide us with the "cutting edge" for the marketing world of the future.

Just as the optimist sees that "the glass is half full," we can also recast the lessons from the four pitfalls to become positive guides for us in mentally approaching this course. In brief, these guides indicate that a strong student of consumer behavior

- Focuses clearly.
- Is flexible in his or her thinking.
- Is open-minded and curious about the world.
- Is interested in understanding that world, as well as in working effectively within it.

EXHIBIT 1-3

Framework for the Study of Consumer Behavior

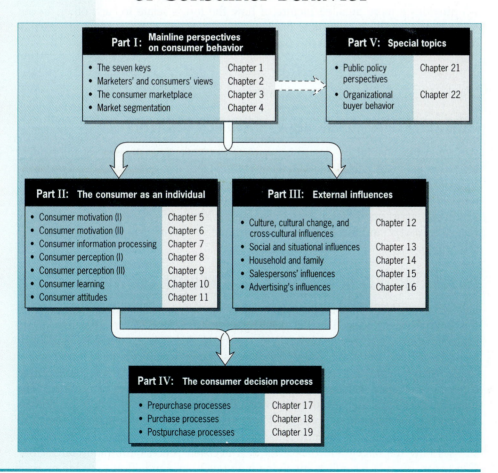

A moment's reflection on these guides can be helpful in preparing for our interesting adventure during the coming weeks.

Where will we be going on this adventure? Essentially, we will be expanding on the Seven Keys, looking more closely into both the ideas and their marketing applications. Exhibit 1-3 shows how this book is organized into five parts, reflecting two fundamental positions regarding knowledge in this field:

- *Position 1: Perspective is important. The perspective we choose will guide what we will discover.* Part I of the book thus presents several "mainline" perspectives on consumer behavior. Here we can perceive new ideas and insights arising from special vantage points. Part V presents additional perspectives of interest to some persons in the field.
- *Position 2: The primary forces that drive consumer behavior stem from the consumer's environment and the personal elements of that consumer.* Thus Part II of the book covers **internal processes** of consumer behavior, while Part III examines **external influences** on consumer behavior. Part IV then combines both elements in examining **consumer decision processes.**

Beyond this basic framework, of course, there are many interesting topics. Exhibit 1-3 provides a more detailed picture of how the topics relate to each other. In our next chapter, we'll examine how marketers and consumers have different views of consumer behavior, and what this means for the field.

■ SUMMARY

CHARACTERISTICS OF MODERN CONSUMER BEHAVIOR

We began this chapter by describing four of the basic characteristics of the field of consumer behavior: that it is *subtle and interesting*, that it is *professionally and personally relevant*, that it is *widespread*, and that it has *great economic and social significance*. The forces that spurred the growth of the consumer behavior field were then identified. Among the most important of these were the *availability of a mass consumer market*, the *marketing concept*, and the *development of computerized methods for studying large samples of consumers*.

MAJOR CONCEPTS IN THE STUDY OF CONSUMER BEHAVIOR

Following our definition of consumer behavior, the central academic concepts in this field were introduced in the *Seven Keys to consumer behavior*. The first key to understanding consumer behavior is to recognize that it is *motivated* by goals that consumers have. Motivations are, however, sometimes difficult to identify, and a single behavior can stem from a mix of motivations. The second key recognizes that consumer behavior includes many *activities* beyond the purchase of products. The third key highlights the view of consumer behavior as a *process*. This decision process approach emphasizes how analysis of prepurchase and postpurchase activities can give us insights into *why* an individual makes a particular purchase. The fourth key stresses how the *timing* and *complexity* of a decision process are important factors. Consumers often face conflicts involving how much time and effort to spend on each decision to achieve the best results.

The fifth key points out the importance that *roles* play in consumer behavior. For example, on any given occasion, a consumer may be an influencer, purchaser, and/or user. These roles flow from social relationships and shift over the course of the consumer's lifetime. The sixth key stresses how consumer behavior is *influenced* by several external factors. Further insights are gained by understanding how consumers adapt to each of these sources of influence. Finally, the seventh key recognizes that consumer behavior *differs for different people*. This means that basic processes and market segmentation—the process by which we identify meaningful target groups within a larger consumer market—are extremely important.

Following the Seven Keys, we engaged in a brief discussion of *four "pitfalls"* in the study of consumer behavior. Pitfall 1, the *unspecified focus*, points out the need to be clear about what we mean when we use such terms as "the consumer" or "purchase." Pitfall 2, the *single-minded explanation*, refers to the fact that there usually are multiple factors at work in consumer behavior. The *"me" mentality*, pitfall 3, points out the dangers of relying too heavily on our own personal views as if they are representative of all consumers. Finally, pitfall 4, *applications only, please*, shows how consumer behavior concepts are important in providing marketers with a solid basis for strong decisions.

WHERE DO WE GO FROM HERE?

Our final brief section of the chapter provided an overview of how we will be addressing the study of consumer behavior in the remainder of this text. The two basic principles guiding our study are (1) perspective is important, and multiple perspectives give us multiple insights, and (2) consumer behavior is determined by the interplay of external influences and internal processes of each consumer. The book is thus organized by important perspectives (in Parts I and V) and by internal processes, external influences, and the consumer decision process (in Parts II, III, and IV). Exhibit 1-3 provides a graphic illustration of this plan.

■ KEY TERMS

As a useful review of your mastery of the concepts in this chapter, you may wish to check your understanding of these key words and terms:

marketing concept	prepurchase activities	reference groups and friends
descriptive consumer research	postpurchase evaluation	external conditions
inferential consumer research	decision simplifiers	marketing environment
consumer behavior	consumer role	situational effects
functional motives	social interactions	individual differences
self-expressive motives	influence	market segmentation
mix of motivations	culture	unspecified focus
bundle of benefits	subcultures	single-minded explanation
deliberate consumer behaviors	social class	"me" mentality
incidental consumer behaviors	life-style	"applications only, please"
decision process approach	family	

■ REVIEW QUESTIONS AND EXPERIENTIAL EXERCISES

[E = **Application extension or experiential exercise**]

1. In its discussion of the characteristics of consumer behavior, the chapter asserts that consumer behavior is "economically and socially significant."

   a. Describe three ways in which consumer behavior is of economic significance. Just how significant is consumer spending in the U.S. economy?

   b. What is the social significance of consumer behavior? In your personal life, how does consumer behavior have social importance for you?

2. For each of the Seven Keys, select three of the consumer quotes from Exhibit 1-2 and explain how that key is represented.

3. What is the text's definition of consumer behavior? How is each phrase represented in the Seven Keys?

4. How does the level of activities involved with consumer behavior differ by type of product or service? Provide examples.

5. Describe your decision process for purchasing the following:

   a. A soft drink   d. A personal computer

   b. A vacation   e. A pair of jeans

   c. An automobile

6. What is the "conflict" referred to in the text's discussion of the issues of timing and complexity in consumer decision making?

7. Assume you are a consumer involved in all three roles in a purchase. In what activities do you engage to fulfill each role? Are these functions continuous during the process?

8. How do the various sources of external influence affect consumer decision making? How might these influences vary for different consumers? How might they vary for different product classes? Provide examples.

9. What are the two basic position statements that have guided the development of this book? How are they reflected in the organization of its chapters?

10. The chapter discusses four common "pitfalls" that some students report having encountered in studying consumer behavior. For each of the four, indicate whether you've observed its occurrence in any other classes. Which, if any, do you think is most likely to occur in this course?

11. [E] Consider a recent large consumer purchase. How does each of the Seven Keys relate to that purchase? Write a brief report summarizing your thoughts.

12. [E] Arrange to interview an acquaintance who is or was involved in marketing to consumers (e.g., store owner, salesperson, advertiser, brand manager). Discuss the Seven Keys with him or her. For each key, ask about marketing implications. Prepare a brief report summarizing the interview and your findings.

■ SUGGESTED READING

■ For a short, interesting look at how American consumers' standard of living has risen as the mass market has grown, go to your library and find Lee Smith's, "How the Average American Gets By," in *Fortune* magazine, October 21, 1991, pp. 52–64. For further interesting readings about how marketers deal with some topics discussed in this chapter, see Note 2 for Chapter 1, which appears on page N-1 near the back of this book.

MARKETERS' AND CONSUMERS' VIEWS

IT WASN'T ALL GRAVY

Some years ago Standard Brands, a major marketer of margarine (Blue Bonnet is its leading brand), decided that one way to sell more margarine would be to use it as an ingredient in a new product. Executives decided to focus on the prepared gravy market, which was valued at almost $100 million and which everyone agreed had enormous growth potential. The resulting product, named Smooth & Easy, was marketed as a refrigerated gravy bar that consumers could slice like margarine, then heat in the pan with water to yield a quality-tasting gravy. Three flavors were offered: brown gravy, chicken gravy, and white sauce. It was priced about 69 cents per bar. One year after introduction—and after spending $6 million to market the new product and having converted a margarine plant to manufacture it—Standard Brands' executives decided to remove Smooth & Easy from the market because of its poor sales performance.[1]

◼ MARKETING DECISIONS AND CONSUMER BEHAVIOR

The Smooth & Easy case is just one of many experienced by marketers each year—new products launched with high hopes but failing to gain acceptance from consumers. Smooth & Easy is, to be sure, a classic example of the risks of a production orientation ("What else can we make with our excess margarine?") rather than adopting the marketing concept ("What do consumers really want and need, and how can we make it available to them?"). Carrying out the marketing concept is not simple, however, as challenges await the marketer who wishes to "know my consumer market."

We will learn more about these challenges in this chapter. Here we will take a closer look at how marketers view consumer behavior, how consumers view their own behavior, and what lessons we can learn from these different perspectives. It is a good idea, therefore, to begin by clarifying exactly what the concept of perspective itself implies.

THE IMPORTANCE OF PERSPECTIVE

Perspective: A mental view of a scene: describes the standpoint from which we choose to analyze something.

Perspective is a term derived from the Latin word *prospectus,* meaning "a mental view of a scene." It is a good term for describing the standpoint from which we choose to analyze something. For example, think about how normal it is that a man or woman looks different when seen from the back than from the front and different yet if viewed from the side. What is actually different, of course, is the perspective we are taking in viewing that person. In general, viewing an object from only one perspective will *highlight* certain characteristics, but will *hide* other characteristics from us. Thus, to understand an important topic well, it is a good idea to adopt several perspectives on it.

Three important sets of persons active in dealing with consumer behavior are marketers, consumers, and public policymakers. *Marketers* and *consumers* are active on a daily basis, each approaching the marketplace for the purpose of making *transactions.* Thus marketers and consumers share certain interests. The transactions themselves, however, involve quite different tasks for the two parties—marketers must *sell,* and consumers must *buy.* These two tasks create quite different perspectives for the two parties.

ಏಖ *A Key Point in Our Market System*

Although often overlooked in textbooks, the fact that marketers and consumers bring different perspectives to the marketplace is a central issue in our market system. In this regard, Adam Smith, the architect of the free market system, said:

> Consumption is the sole end and purpose of all production; and the interest of the producer ought to be attended to, only so far as it may be necessary for promoting that of the consumer.... But in the mercantile system the interest of the consumer is almost certainly sacrificed to that of the producer; and it seems to consider production, and not consumption, as the ultimate end and object of all industry and commerce.   -FROM THE WEALTH OF NATIONS, 1776.[2]

Before moving to our analysis of marketers' and consumers' perspectives, we should also take note of the third set of persons with an important perspective on this field. *Public policymakers,* such as government regulators at the Federal Trade Commission, are primarily concerned that the marketplace function well—that it operate in an efficient fashion and that it be fair for marketers and consumers alike. Our detailed examination of interesting issues in public policy appears in Chapter 20. At this point, however, let's turn our attention to examining how the marketing and consumer perspectives differ, and what this can tell us about the field of consumer behavior. We'll begin with the marketing perspective.

CONTROLLABLE MARKETING DECISIONS: THE 4 P'S

Much of the research in the field of consumer behavior has been undertaken by marketing professors and those working in marketing and advertising jobs in industry. The **marketing perspective** on consumer behavior is thus a dominant viewpoint in the field. The marketing perspective reflects the marketing concept—that every firm needs to match its products and services to meet the needs of potential customers. Understanding consumer behavior is thus crucial for marketing success.

Within marketing, a set of management decisions culminates in what has come to be known as the **marketing mix.**[3] This is basically the entire set of decisions a firm makes in hopes of meeting consumers' wants and needs while making a profit. E. Jerome McCarthy, a leading thinker in the marketing field, pointed out that these **controllable factors** fall into four basic categories, popularly known as the 4 P's:[4]

- Product
- Price
- Place
- Promotion

Although you may already be familiar with the 4 P's, let's review each area briefly to focus on how consumer behavior relates to the decisions that marketers make in developing their marketing mixes.

Product Decisions

Product decisions refer to all aspects of the design, materials, and quality control that are built into a particular product or service offering. Most marketers offer a **product portfolio** that consists of a range of offerings aimed at different consumer preferences in the market. Also, new products are continually being developed, while old products are dropped when they lose consumers' favor. As just one example of the continuing pressures present in product decisions, let's consider the auto industry.

🐋 *Ford Forges Forward*

In 1985, Ford Motor was in trouble. It had just lost over $3 billion in 18 months, and, as chairman Donald Petersen put it, "We had to make some very substantial changes." One change was the creation of "Team Taurus," a group of marketers, designers, engineers, and plant personnel charged with developing a new car to rescue the firm. The team relied heavily on consumer interviews and chose 700 features for the new car from these discussions. In addition, the team bought models of competing cars that were most popular with consumers and then systematically tore them apart to analyze the best product features (over 400 features were reportedly "borrowed" in this process). The results from Team Taurus's efforts? One of the most popular cars ever produced, and a dramatic turnaround for Ford, whose corporate market share rose from 16 percent to 29 percent during the 1980s!

Marketing perspective: The view of consumer behavior from the standpoint of the seller.

Controllable factors: Decisions that a marketing manager makes: these fall into four basic categories, popularly known as the 4 P's.

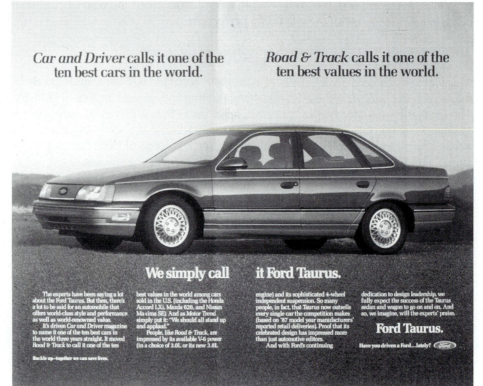

Consumer research played a key role in product design decisions for the original Taurus, then again for its evolutionary changes in the early 1990s.

As of 1992, however, Ford faced a new dilemma: How should it now manage its still successful Taurus model? Competition had intensified, and Honda's Accord had passed the Taurus to become the best-selling model in the marketplace. Should Ford invest moderately ($600 million) to achieve evolutionary styling updates, or should it invest heavily ($1.2 billion) to provide a truly new look for the Taurus? Again, consumer research provided major inputs to the decision. The 2 million current Taurus owners were seen as a key target market for the new models, and they preferred only moderate styling changes. "Our research tells us we have changed it enough," reported Ford's head of marketing (the radical new look is now possible for 1995). Did Ford change its design enough? Early results are given in Note 5 for this chapter, near the back of the book.

Price Decisions

In addition to designing the product or service itself, marketers must also decide on the best **price** to charge consumers. This determination involves many issues, including manufacturing costs, the structure of demand in the marketplace, and competitive factors. Usually, however, pricing decisions are made with considerable uncertainty about what their actual outcomes will be, especially in terms of consumers' responses.

New technology brings change, challenge, and opportunity for marketers and consumers alike. These two grinning scientists, Henry Yuen and Daniel Kwoh, are showing off their invention, VCR Plus. Stimulated by the knowledge that millions of VCR owners had no idea how to program their units to record at particular times (and by the challenge of devising a consumer-friendly system that would do this easily), Yuen and Kwoh based their system on the same principle as dialing a telephone. After perfecting the technical requirements, their new company was in a position to sell their code numbers for every television program (similar to a telephone number for each program) to newspapers and magazines, who would then publish them prominently in their television program listings. The media were enthusiastic, and the firm was in a position to market the $60 remote control device for the consumer to use the system. According to one electronics retailer, "It was one of the hottest products we've seen in years!" Now, several years later, major VCR manufacturers have begun to build VCR Plus into their sets as an additional feature, and are paying royalties to the inventors for each set sold.

New technology also allows for new production processes that can efficiently customize products and services for individual consumers. Here we see the start of personalized bicycle production in Japan: a customer fitting to obtain precise measurements. The measurements are faxed to the factory's computer, which rapidly creates a unique blueprint.

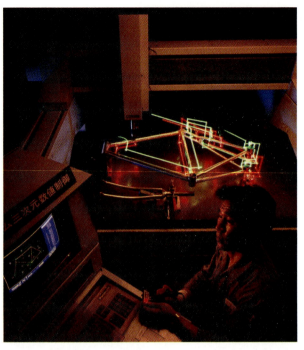

The computer blueprint then guides robots in measuring the frame setting (the colored lights are from a light diode mounted on the robot to trace its measuring paths for us to see).

Once the materials are in place and the sizing is complete, a push of the computer control button begins the customized welding of the frame by the robots.

After skilled humans assemble and decorate the bicycle, it is tested on the "bumpy road" simulator, and then is available for delivery. Total manufacturing time? About 3 hours! Promised delivery time for this personalized bicycle? About two weeks, explains an executive, because "we want people to feel excited about waiting for something special."

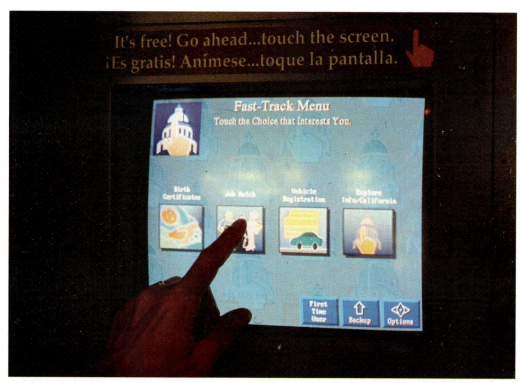

New technology also provides new avenues for marketers to provide information to consumes. Here an interactive "computer kiosk" allows an interested consumer to quickly search for the information most relevant to his needs at the moment. Our discussion of consumer information search appears in Chapter 17.

New technology is also providing new ways for marketers to gain information from consumers through marketing research. Here a participant in an "Information Accelerator" study of a futuristic automobile decides whether to listen to what this woman has to say, or to elect someone else to listen to. Our in-depth discussion of several of these new research methods appears in Chapter 18.

New technology is also increasingly affecting the leisure pursuits of consumers. Simulated experiences are becoming increasingly realistic as "Virtual Reality" technology develops. Here a player ventures forth to conquer new worlds without physically leaving the game room. Virtual reality amusement centers are now starting to appear, and will be common in the near future.

೭ঌ *How Low Can You Go?*

Times were tough for the fast-food industry as the 1990s dawned. Operators were concerned about finding effective means of attracting customers and raising their shrinking profit margins. Then Taco Bell, a unit of PepsiCo, announced that it was going to try slashing its price for tacos by 25 percent (from 79 cents to 59 cents). Would sales increase enough to compensate for this huge cut in margins? Yes, they did. Revenue increased over 50 percent during the next two years. However, competitors such as McDonald's and Wendy's reacted with their own price promotions and value menus. Then, in late 1990, Taco Bell took another big step. It reorganized its menu based on price levels (tiers) rather than food types: consumers were now encouraged to think in terms of 59, 79, and 99 cents. Again customers rolled in, and again competitors retaliated. In the words of the firm's president, "The [tiered price] concept is very, very powerful with the consumer . . . we want to make Taco Bell so strong that it doesn't make sense to eat any place else."

Could Taco Bell go still lower? It could, but one official warned that if prices got down to 39 cents, consumers might not think highly of the product's quality.[6]

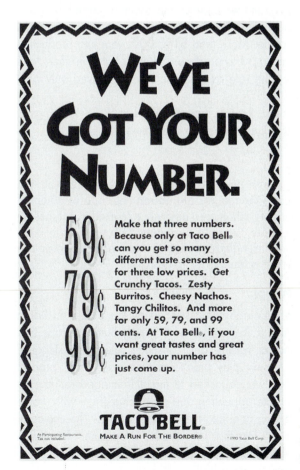

Taco Bell's creative development of the "tiered price" concept has allowed it to prosper in the highly competitive fast-food market of the 1990s.

Place Decisions

Place decisions refer to the manner in which a product or service is made available to customers. In general, the distribution sector is well structured to meet consumers' needs. Occasionally, however, a manufacturer has difficulty in making the right place decision, as described in the following tale:

❧ *Soloflex Needs More Strength*

The recent physical fitness boom helped many firms to achieve success. Soloflex, which markets a home exercise machine, has been one of the most successful. It wasn't always that way, however, recalls Jerry Wilson, president of the firm and developer of this device. At first, Mr. Wilson attempted to use sporting goods stores to sell the machine, but this approach didn't work:

> "I couldn't get the clerks to demonstrate them right," reports Mr. Wilson. "They got all sweaty and didn't understand how it worked."

With his firm's future on the line, Mr. Wilson made a crucial assumption about consumer behavior—that his prospects *had to* watch a demonstration before they would be willing to buy. He then came up with a brave, creative solution: he would remove Soloflex from retail stores entirely and would sell it direct to consumers through a "video brochure." This was a 20-minute videocassette that was closely scripted and designed to create a positive aura for the machine. More than $150,000 went into production of the film. Each cassette cost the firm $6.50 to produce and mail, but consumers who received the cassette bought at twice the rate as consumers who received only print brochures.

As the product became established, the firm moved toward cable TV showings of its brochure and stayed with its direct selling channel to consumers.[7]

Promotion Decisions

The total effect of the product, place, and price decisions is physically to create the opportunity for a transaction to occur. One role for **promotion** is to inform potential customers about the mix and to encourage them persuasively to consider purchasing the firm's product. Promotion is, therefore, the chief communication link between the firm and its customers. Sometimes only friendly reminders and an image touch-up can move consumers to change their buying behaviors, as in this case:

❧ *Dull, Boring, and Wimpy*

These were the findings of consumer research commissioned by the California Raisin Advisory Board into the image of this fruit in consumers' minds. Bumper crops had doubled the supply over the demand for raisins, and consumer sales were sluggish. While consumers liked the taste of raisins, they didn't see them as a "hip" product to buy. Then a promotional campaign was launched to turn this image around. The Claymation technique was used to create appealing, hip raisin characters who would dance, sing, and generally dispense their cool into the consumer world. The choice of theme song was a natural: the classic "I Heard It Through the Grapevine." Results? A memorable campaign, characters licensed for other product tie-ins, and a reversal of the sales decline, with consumer purchases of raisins up![8]

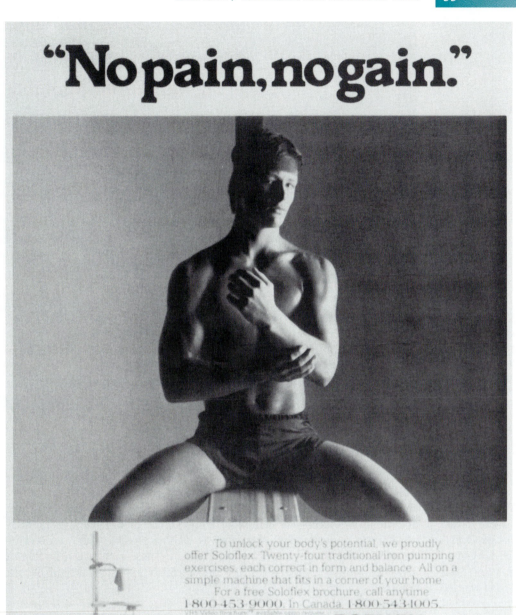

Soloflex management's analysis of consumer decision processes indicated that the machine needed better demonstrations than it was getting from retail stores. This led to development of direct marketing through video brochures.

These hip characters were used to stem a sales decline for raisins by changing the image of the fruit while entertaining the consumers who watched the ads.

UNCONTROLLABLE FACTORS: THE 5 C'S

Notice how important consumer behavior was in each of the 4 P areas. These, however, were all controllable decisions. The real world of marketing also contains a number of factors that a manager does not control. These **uncontrollable factors** can also determine the success or failure of a marketing mix. Thus a marketing manager must try to understand these factors as well as possible, then respond by *adapting* the marketing mix to account best for them. These factors can be summarized in a fashion similar to the 4 P's: the uncontrollable constraints will be termed here the **5 C's.**[9]

Uncontrollable factors: Those forces that a manager does not control, but that help determine success or failure, and which must be accounted for: organized in this text as the 5 C's.

- Competitors
- Company
- Channels
- Conditions
- Customers

The Competitive Constraint

One complicating factor for a marketer is the fact that **competitors** are also striving to make sales and are also devising marketing mixes for this purpose. Thus the search for consumer advantages for our brand becomes an important activity. Also, the presence of competitors serves to reduce realistic options in the 4 P decisions. For example, we often can't price too much above the prices other firms are charging, nor can we easily drop prices without risking price retaliations (and perhaps a "price war") from the competition. Marketing mix decisions are always subject to change depending on competitors' actions. Success is difficult, even for the best marketing mixes, when a marketplace becomes very heavily competitive, as in this report:

❧ More Is Not Better

"It's the end of the world," moaned an auto dealer recently. Across the marketplace, competition has reached red-hot levels. As we enter the mid-1990s, the U.S. market already has over 200 distinct car models competing for consumer attention and purchases. The luxury car segment has 55 competing models alone (up 67 percent in only seven years!). Excess capacity is a serious industry problem; auto plant capacity has now grown to be 50 percent higher than consumer demand.

Thus, although their marketing mixes may have been fine in other times, the competitive constraint has brought hard times to many automakers and dealers. Such status brands as Mercedes-Benz, BMW, and Jaguar saw their sales fall 25–35 percent from the late 1980s levels. Yugo of America filed for bankruptcy, and Britain's Sterling Motor Cars and France's Peugeot announced recently that they were simply leaving the U.S. market behind. "The United States is an inviting and cruel [auto] market," commented one analyst.

What can each marketer do in the future? "Work to appeal to consumers through new combinations of the 4 P's that somehow account effectively for the competitive environment." Thus we are likely to see new forms of auto products and services, new forms of dealerships, and new forms of price promotions, as well as further mergers and strategic alliances to blunt the forces of competition.[10]

The Company Constraint

The **company** constraint is not often encountered in textbook discussions, but it is a key factor in the real world of business. In brief, this constraint recognizes that *companies and their cultures* are different: some marketing mixes are better for some firms than for others. If a firm does not have a strong financial base, for example, it may not be able to invest in a new technology to produce an innovative food product. Similarly, if your company has a low risk-taking profile, as a marketing manager you may not receive approval for attempting certain marketing strategies.

Among the most significant company constraint factors are the *strengths and weaknesses of the people* the marketing manager calls on to help implement the marketing mix. For example, all salespersons don't work as hard as they possibly could: some may be satisfied with their current income and aren't willing to exert further efforts just because you would like them to. Similarly, in your firm the product you develop might encounter quality control problems in production, or the design may be less than perfect, the advertising may not be the best ever done, and so forth. While it is possible to try to improve weaker areas, it is also realistic for marketers to plan on adapting their mixes to feature the company's strengths and work around the areas of weakness. In summary, the company for which you work helps to determine what's best to do, including what can and can't be done in a given situation:

❧ Will Domino's Deliver?

Several years ago Thomas Monaghan, founder and owner of Domino's Pizza, Inc., decided to sell his interests in the firm so as to devote his time to humanitarian works. It was during a recession, however, and no one would meet his asking price. Meanwhile,

As Pizza Hut's development of delivery ate increasingly into Domino's leading share of the market, Domino's responded by offering new flavor combinations at promotional prices, as in this ad. Notice, however, that no comparison with Pizza Hut is made: Domino's founder doesn't believe in this practice.

Domino's had begun to lose some of its dominant market share in pizza delivery, falling from 60 percent to 45 percent, while Pizza Hut had grown from zero to 20 percent in just five years. Mr. Monaghan returned to take charge in 1991 and was searching for ways to reenergize his empire of nearly 6,000 stores (two-thirds are owned by franchises). "We're not setting the world on fire," he remarked. "We're . . . not greatly increasing our sales per store."

One approach was for Domino's to go on the offensive and respond to Pizza Hut's attack ads with a comparative advertising campaign of its own. However, no marketing manager would be able to undertake this option. According to Mr. Monaghan, "As far as knocking the competition in advertising, . . . it may be good business, but I just don't allow it. I don't believe in it."[11]

The Channel Constraint

The third "C" bears a close relationship to the place variable of the marketing mix. Here, however, we explicitly recognize the fact that the **channels** consist of *independent* wholesalers and retailers. While this fact itself is obvious, let's think a bit about its implications for how the marketing mix must be adapted to reflect the reality of channel members' desires. For example, every supermarket has many marketers fighting to get their products on its shelves. To deal with this situation, supermarket chains create buying committees that meet to consider which new items to carry. Presentations from a large number of manufacturers are considered. Decisions are not easy, as the stores are already full. This means that if a new item is added, a current item must be dropped or have its shelf space reduced. The point is that channels will exercise their own best judgments in whether to carry a product and, if so, exactly how the product will be carried. In general, channels are independent businesspersons who can be expected to behave in their own self-interest. A marketing manager must adapt to the desires of his or her channel customers to effectively reach the larger consumer market, as the following case attests.

Roasted Chicken Lays Egg

Holly Farms, excited about the prospects for its new roasted chicken product, spent $20 million to build a plant to produce it. The idea of a more convenient, time-saving alternative to raw chicken seemed on target. Indeed, consumer research in the Atlanta test market showed 22 percent of women tried it, with 90 percent indicating they would buy again. Based on this kind of feedback, Holly Farms began nationwide distribution. However, it soon became apparent that the product wasn't succeeding. The giant Safeway supermarket chain, for example, had dropped the product after only two weeks. What was the problem? It wasn't the product—one Safeway executive even described it as "outstanding." The problem was that Holly Farms had not devoted enough attention to the needs and desires of its retailers. The "shelf life" of the roasted chicken, for example, was conservatively labeled at 14 days in the plant. Unfortunately, it could then take 9 days to get from the plant to a store, which didn't leave grocers much time to sell the products. Afraid of being stuck with out-of-date stock, grocers reacted by waiting until they were out of stock before reordering. No Holly Farms roasted chicken would be sold to consumers until the next shipment was delivered.

What to do? Holly Farms began a three-pronged campaign to win over its channels and achieve success for this product: (1) develop a new nitrogen packing system to add 5–10 days to shelf life, (2) consider a new delivery system separate from raw chicken, and (3) shift substantial consumer advertising dollars to store promotions and incentives for meat department managers.[12]

The Conditions Constraint

The fourth "C" refers to a host of broader economic and social forces that can impact on the success or failure of marketing programs. These include *economic* **conditions** such as inflation, recession, monetary exchange rates, and so on. *Labor* unrest can mean delays in production, which can destroy careful product introduction plans. *Weather* conditions can impact as well. For example, when ski areas have a warm winter period, rentals of equipment, rooms, and so on all drop immediately. *Government* regulations are another source of external constraints on some marketing mixes. Increased product safety requirements, for example, are likely to raise prices of many products.

What can a marketing manager do about these kinds of external conditions? In most cases, he or she must try to *adapt* the marketing mix to the external conditions as well as possible. Sometimes clever new marketing strategies can be designed to overcome consumer problems with a certain external condition. Often, external conditions are extremely powerful and may swamp marketing efforts to adapt. However, the conditions constraint is not always negative, as the following example attests:

ᘓ᠓ *Between Iraq and a Hard Place*

Cable News Network (CNN) experienced "the Mother of all ratings jumps" when the Persian Gulf War broke out in January 1991: in the first 24 hours its ratings increased 2,200 percent! During the entire 100 days of the war, CNN's continuous coverage served to more than double its previous viewer levels, thus obviously changing its attractiveness for advertisers. CNN's rates jumped from $4,000 to over $20,000 for 30-second spots. However, this external constraint also had further impacts: the fact that the war was not perfectly scripted meant that many ad spots had to be shifted and dropped in favor of on-the-spot coverage. Thus CNN had less ad time to sell, and difficult decisions had to be made daily about what time to offer, and when to make it available.

In general, however, advertisers were pleased—especially those who had purchased time in advance. For example, the president of a direct marketing firm, 800 Flowers, reported, "...there was a ninefold or tenfold increase in attempts [to reach our toll-free number]. We couldn't handle it all..." An interesting epilogue: many of the calls were from other countries (since CNN airs worldwide from its satellite), and 800 Flowers is now expanding internationally to meet this unexpected demand.[13]

The Customer Constraint

The fifth constraint represents the actual level at which success or failure is determined. As we saw, each of the other "C's" involves **customer** behavior as a key factor. *Competitors* are trying to appeal to the same market of customers and to take

External conditions can strongly influence consumer behavior and advertising. When the Iraq war broke out in 1991, CNN's live coverage from Baghdad drove its ratings up 2,200%!

the same sales dollars. *Channels* are set up to reach all customers and deliver them products and services. Every *company* wants to sell to a defined group of customers using the resources available. Finally, *conditions* are important because they influence consumers' readiness to purchase products. The key point is that a marketing manager must *understand* his or her customers and must be capable of developing a marketing mix that appeals to them.

As the size of firms and markets has increased, the dollar stakes for both failure and success have risen. Consumer research is now used heavily by marketers, especially at the major consumer goods firms. For example, the president of Lever Brothers reports,

> Understanding ... consumer behavior is our key to planning and managing in the ever-changing environment.

To learn more about consumer behavior, Lever Brothers' researchers talk to 4,000 consumers *every week,* seeking their views of products, new ideas, and trends in their styles of living.[14] In addition to consumer interviews, technology has also offered new ways for marketers to learn about their customers, as described in the following discussion:

🐘 *Scans Make Fans*

Universal Product Code (UPC) scanning systems have revolutionized the world of consumer research. For retail operations, these computer systems offer rapid price changes and strong inventory control. Beyond this, since the systems instantly record consumer purchases, they can provide incredibly valuable information for retailers. *Direct product profits* are now calculated to measure exactly how much each item in the store is contributing: results are used to drop products quickly, to shift shelf space (facings), and to demand higher *slotting fees* from manufacturers for the shelf space.

Further, both manufacturers and retailers face new consumer research horizons with this information. It is now possible to gauge quickly how a sale price, display, coupon, or ad is affecting sales. Special research services such as Infoscan can offer even further insights, by *measuring exactly which consumers are buying what.* They do this by having a sample of households use special credit cards in cooperating stores, so that personal information about the purchaser can be combined with actual purchase information. A brand manager can buy this research to monitor his or her brand's strategies. As one manager who had just saved a brand by modifying its strategy reports, "We expected some problems with trial, but not what we wound up getting. We would never have been able to react in time without scanning data ... we live and die with household panel data."[15]

■ COMPARING MARKETERS' AND CONSUMERS' VIEWS

The 4 P's and 5 C's provide a realistic look into the marketing perspective, showing the various ways in which consumer behavior is important to marketing managers. At this point, we'll want to shift our mental gears consciously and begin to adopt the

Table 2-1 Comparing the Two Perspectives

Characteristic	Marketer's Perspective		Consumer's Perspective
A. Point of view	External ("buyers")	vs.	Internal ("me")
B. Level of interest	Aggregate ("market")	vs.	Individual ("myself")
C. Scope of interest	Product specific ("what I make")	vs.	Across products ("what I buy")
D. "Correct" choice	Brand specific ("my brand")	vs.	Best alternative ("best brand for me")
E. Role of influence	Influence behavior		Handle behavioral influence

consumer's perspective on consumer behavior. This will allow us to *compare* the two perspectives and gain insights into this field of study. The most basic differences are summarized in Table 2-1, which presents extreme positions so that we can identify potential insights.

CONTRASTS BETWEEN THE TWO PERSPECTIVES

External Versus Internal Views

The distinction between **external versus internal views** of consumer behavior stems from the fact that consumers are personally engaging in this activity, while marketers are actually engaged in other activities (e.g., selling, advertising, and so forth). That is, as consumers, most of our behaviors are *internally* focused and driven. We tend to think silently, observe privately, and evaluate according to our own personal dictates. (There are, of course, many external influences—salesperson, friends, or family—on our behavior. Even here, however, we maintain an internal view of our own decisions.)

Marketers, because they are different people playing a different role, must necessarily take an *external* view of consumers' behaviors. To get a better idea of what this means, think about the times that you observe other consumers as they shop in a store. In these instances, you are taking an external view of consumer behavior.

Why is this simple distinction important? Because, by itself, the external view doesn't allow much insight into the underlying reasons for consumer behavior. To gain such insight about others, we need to rely upon *concepts* and *research* that somehow can obtain consumers' internal views from them. Even these assists can't fully tap the richness of each individual's internal perspectives, but they go a long way toward overcoming the inherent shortcomings of the external view. This is the major reason that marketers use consumer research.

Aggregate Versus Individual-Level Views

The contrast inherent in **aggregate versus individual-level views** is closely related to the previous distinction, in that our focus on our own internal needs, desires, and plans brings with it a necessary focus on ourselves as *individual* consumers. (For our purposes here, shared decisions within a household will be treated as individual-level decisions.) As noted earlier, most marketers don't have the luxury of being able to view their markets at the individual person or household level. There are so *many*

Consumer perspective: The view of consumer behavior from the standpoint of the consumer: helpful for marketers in better understanding marketplace behavior and reactions.

External versus internal views: Marketers exist and act in the external world of the consumer, but consumers' thoughts, feelings, and decisions are internal and private. Consumer research is often used to gain a better internal view of consumer behavior.

Aggregate versus individual-level views: Marketers view consumers as part of a market, whereas consumers view themselves as individuals.

consumers that they need to be viewed together (aggregated) somehow if a marketer is to have any chance of comprehending that market. This is why marketers view market segmentation to be so important (in contrast, most consumers have never even heard of this term!).

Turning to consumers again, notice that much of the time we really don't think in terms of a market at all, so individualized is our perspective. Even though our thoughts may sometimes include the popularity of a brand, rarely do they involve an analysis of how many persons in total are in the market, what prices they are paying, and so forth.

Product-Specific Versus Across-Product Views

Product-specific versus across-product views: A consumer purchases items from all important product and service categories, but a marketer specializes in only one or a few categories of products or services.

Whereas the marketer will *specialize* in certain categories of products or services, the consumer cannot afford to do this. Consumers need to purchase from *all* important product and service categories. In fact, if it were not the case that large retailers bring together offerings from numerous manufacturers, the enormous breadth of our consumer interactions with marketers would be even more apparent to us.

The key outcome from this **product-specific versus across-product orientation** is that, as consumers, we *cannot specialize in our buying the way marketers do in their selling. This means that consumers will not be very expert for many of their purchases.* The time and effort it takes to learn about each purchase are costly to consumers. This can lead to consumers making mistakes such as paying too much or selecting products that don't suit their actual set of needs. Each marketer, on the other hand, is expert in his or her product category, and in fact spends most of his or her professional time working on it. However, a product-specific focus can sometimes lead a marketer to overlook the purchase allocation needs of consumers.

Brand-Specific Versus "Best Alternative" Views

Brand-specific versus "best alternative" views: Marketers each act as if the best purchase for a particular consumer were the brand that they are offering, whereas the consumer in interested in obtaining the alternative that is best for himself or herself.

The **brand-specific versus "best alternative"** distinction holds major implications for marketers. From a marketer's point of view, the best brand for a particular consumer should be the brand that he or she is offering to the consumer. As a marketer, the "right" behavior is the purchase of "my" brand, whatever that may be. A consumer, on the other hand, does not enter the purchase process with such a clear-cut answer as to the best choice. As consumers, our desires are to obtain the best alternative for us, regardless of which brand it is or who happens to make it. We are usually confronted with a number of competing brands, each of which is marketed as if it is the best choice for us. *The fact that we are going to choose only one brand thus means that we will be making the "wrong" choice from the point of view of every marketer but one!* As marketers, therefore, we need to take care not to simply assume that our interest is the same as the consumer's interest: we need to work hard to *ensure* that there is a match.

In this regard, we can appreciate the roles that brand names play on behalf of both marketers and consumers. They serve as handy identification tags, enabling the consumer to understand what a particular alternative will be like (if the consumer has had previous experience with that brand). Knowing that a can of soft drink is Coca-Cola, for example, tells us a lot about what the product inside it will be, how it will appear when we open the can, how it will taste, and so on. If the quality control is good, moreover, an established brand name acts as a type of guarantee that we can count on the product performing or tasting exactly as we've learned to expect (imagine how shocked we'd be if a Coke came out tasting like root beer!).

Thus brand names allow consumers to save significant amounts of time and energy in making choices. We can rely on our past experience, as well as on recommendations. Over the longer run, we can develop easy decision rules as to which brands to purchase. Marketers—knowing that there can be severe penalties to future brand sales following a bad consumer experience—work to develop a positive offering before they place a brand name on it and take it to the market. In a broad sense, then, brand names help to communicate the quality and consistency of product offerings to consumers, and their higher prices reflect this.

Influencing Behavior Versus Handling Behavioral Influence

The last dimension—**influencing behavior versus handling behavioral influence**—is an especially interesting distinction that we'll examine at some length. As noted earlier, each marketer's role is to influence consumers to feel favorably toward and buy his or her brand on a regular basis. At any one time, then, we would see marketing managers for Burger King, Ford, Sears, *Newsweek,* and so forth all attempting to influence consumer behaviors for their particular product classes.

How do we, as consumers, react to this continuous array of persuasive stimuli from the marketing system? First, let's consider the fact that *it takes some time and some effort for us to react at all.* We usually have to make some effort to talk with a salesperson, read an ad, or even to attend to a TV commercial. Marketers are, of course, aware of this and try to design their stimuli to be interesting and to require as little extra effort as is reasonable. Nonetheless, the enormous number of marketing stimuli that are competing for our attention means that we consumers *must adapt* somehow. We simply cannot afford the time and effort needed to deal fully with each of the influence attempts of every marketer every time that one appears.

What do we do, then? Basically, *we simply ignore most marketing stimuli* most of the time. For confirmation, take this little test:

Go through today's or yesterday's newspaper and look carefully at each advertisement. How many did you notice when you read the paper the first time? Did you even read that section of the paper the first time? How long would it take you to read and consider carefully all the ads? For what percentage of the products being advertised do you even have an interest?

Sometimes, of course, it is difficult to ignore a particular stimulus. Examples of these **intrusive stimuli** (so-called because they intrude upon our attention) include TV commercials, checkout displays in supermarkets, and so on. When our attention is captured in this way, however, we consumers have developed another means to retain control of our time and effort—we often *don't continue to pay very much attention* to the stimulus. That is, we don't think much about it, and we don't watch it all the way to its conclusion. As one market researcher reported recently, "When we asked consumers last year to tell us the best and worst television commercials, a number told us they simply don't see them anymore.... They don't have to zap them by remote. They have tuned out mentally."[16]

As might be expected, these consumer adjustments to the quantity of marketing stimuli cause severe problems for each marketing manager attempting to influence

Influencing behavior versus handling behavioral influence: Every marketing manager's role is to influence consumers, whereas consumers must find ways to adapt to the enormous number of marketing stimuli, each attempting to influence them in a different direction.

behavior. Thus marketers have had to refine their programs to overcome some of these problems. Examples of marketing mix refinements include

■ Targeting segments of consumers who are most interested in the product. A marketer of rollerblades, for example, will target specific age groups, and will try to focus on likely buyers only.

■ Repeating ads so that consumers may "get the message" the third or fourth time they're exposed. It is too risky to simply assume that an ad will be seen, attended to, and have influence on a single showing.

■ Creating stimuli that are intrinsically interesting for consumers, even though they may not provide a "hard-sell" message for the brand.

■ Ensuring that the stimuli are simple and easy for consumers to handle mentally.

THE MARKETING SYSTEM'S RECOMMENDATIONS

In addition to the basic issue of consumer attention, there is the equally serious question: "How *should* a consumer deal with influence attempts, assuming that he or she is interested and is willing to pay attention?" To address this issue, we need to consider what the entire (macro) marketing system is in fact telling consumers.

Figure 2-1 diagrams the essentials of this issue. Notice how clear and straightforward this situation appears on the left side, reflecting an individual marketer's

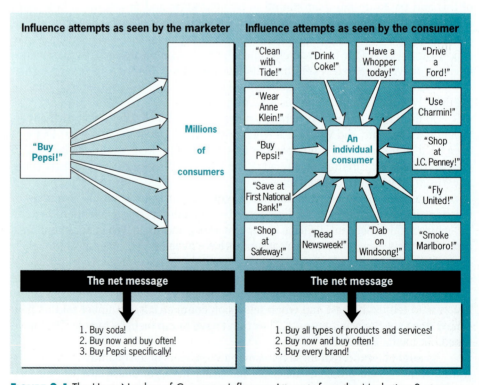

FIGURE 2-1 The Huge Number of Consumer Influence Attempts from the Marketing System

(Pepsi's) perspective. We must recall, however, that the macro "system" really consists of millions of individual (micro) marketers, each providing his or her own influence attempts. This is depicted on the right side, reflecting an individual consumer's perspective. Thus it is clear that the marketing system as a whole is presenting each consumer with three general recommendations:

- Consumers should buy and use products and services.
- Consumers should buy often.
- Consumers should buy brands (i.e., the specific alternative choice is important).

For this reason, we sometimes hear social philosophers—ranging from communists to clergymen—describing the Western nations as **consumerist economies,** in which the pursuit of material goods can become so strong that people may give up some personal and social virtues (family time, volunteering) in a drive for more income and more consumption (the appendix to Chapter 16 discusses this issue further).

Conclusion 1: Consumers Cannot Follow the Marketing System's Consumption Allocation Recommendations

The liquid drink example is a good one to illustrate our first basic conclusion in this discussion: consumers *cannot follow* the set of general recommendations from the marketing system. This is because the total set of recommendations from the marketing system simply proposes too much consumption. As an example, imagine the person who would purchase and consume a can of soft drink each time that he or she came into contact with a marketing influence attempt. Moreover, since the system doesn't confine itself to soft drinks as the only appropriate liquid to consume—milk, beer, wine, bottled water, liquor, fruit juices, coffee, tea, and so on are also heavily promoted for purchase—it is clear that consumers *cannot depend on the marketing system to tell us how to allocate our spending.* As consumers, we *can* rely on the marketing system as a good source of ideas on what we might buy and to provide us with useful information about positive aspects of the alternatives. We cannot, however, rely on it as a guide for what *not* to buy or for suggesting which overall mix of purchases would be best for us.

Conclusion 2: Consumers Cannot Follow All the Brand Recommendations Either

Beyond this, there is another problem for consumers, one that arises from the brand-competitive nature of the marketing system. For this discussion let's refer briefly to the toothpaste market as depicted in Figure 2-2, and again begin by adopting the consumer's perspective. Assume that you're interested in buying toothpaste and that you don't happen to know very much about the brands available. What would we learn from the marketing system's stimuli? Basically, that every brand is good.

However, we need to make a choice: Which one brand should we pick from all the brands available? Which is clearly the best brand for us? Notice that some of the information from the marketing stimuli will prove to be helpful to us, especially if

FIGURE 2-2 A Consumer's View of the Marketing System's Recommendations Within a Product Category

the product class is differentiated enough that the brands are clearly distinguished in terms of features, price levels, and quality levels. Also, we'll learn about different product forms (gels, pastes, etc.), packages (pumps, tubes), and promotional prices and premiums that are available.

Notice, however, that the total set of marketing stimuli presented to us does not itself provide us with the answer to our brand choice problem—each of the brands available is attempting to influence us to accept that brand as the best one for purchase. Since we cannot purchase all of them, we are going to have to make our choice on some other basis than the system's recommendations alone. In terms of the initial topic for this section, therefore, our second basic conclusion is: brand influence attempts from the marketing system are as a set *inherently inconsistent* with a consumer's need to choose one specific alternative for purchase.

Marketing Implications

Alert readers will recognize that the intent of the foregoing discussion was not to paint the marketing system in a bad light. Instead, our analysis explains why consumers exhibit different types of skepticism about marketing efforts. Such skepticism represents an entirely necessary *adaptation* on the part of the consumer. For individual marketers, therefore, *consumers' resistance to persuasion attempts makes success that much harder to achieve.* It heightens the importance of practicing the marketing concept and using consumer behavior knowledge in an intelligent way.

As we will see later in this book, the realities of consumer reactions to marketing recommendations are fairly complex. They include the ways consumers gain information and the strategies they use to reduce risks and make satisfactory choices. It is also the case, however, that more consumer research is needed. If you are interested, you may wish to turn to Appendix 2A for a brief discussion of future research needs in this area.

At this point, however, we need to delve into the final implication that comes from the nature of our marketing system. This implication is that consumers need to do more than simply handle influence attempts well. Consumers also need to *develop their own abilities* to make good consumer decisions. In other words, consumers need to act, as well as react, in their own self-interests.

What does it take to be a wise consumer? What kinds of skills do we need to possess? What storehouse of knowledge should we have available in our heads, to draw upon when needed?

Some future marketers may wonder why this topic is relevant to marketing activity. However, notice that the answers to the questions above represent the state of consumers' knowledge as they approach the marketplace for the purpose of making transactions. A marketer interested in using the marketing concept is keenly interested in discovering consumers' states of mind as they approach the marketplace. This topic begins with the basic issue of what it takes to be a good consumer.

All of us have at least a rough idea of the types of knowledge and skills needed to be a "wise" consumer. However, as we'll see shortly, it is surprising to discover how many topics there are in this area. There is, in fact, so much material that we will be unable to cover it adequately within this book. In this section of the chapter, we'll strive to gain an overall sense for the scope of the issues.

How Skilled Are We?

Just recently the Consumer Federation of America (CFA) teamed up with the Educational Testing Service and the TRW Foundation to give consumers a multiple-choice exam on their knowledge of such practical matters as how to purchase efficiently, how to resolve consumer problems, and how to use products safely. How well did American consumers do? In the words of the CFA, "The study revealed that, overall, Americans are not knowledgeable about consumption. The average score for the entire test was only 54 percent (guessing alone would have produced 25 percent), and in none of the six general subjects did consumers score as high as 60 percent."

The CFA study then recommended that the nation make a stronger commitment to educating its consumers, as health, safety, and billions of dollars in spending are at stake. How do the prospects for such educational improvements appear? Not too bright at present. Several years ago a team of professors of consumer economics gave a test of consumer competency (different from the CFA exam) to over 4,000 prospective teachers of consumer education courses at the grade school and high school level. Of the 55 questions on the test, what was the average score of these prospective educators? Just over 32 items correct, or a percentage of under 60 percent! Thus it appears to be generally true that Americans hold low skill levels as consumers.[17]

WHY ARE SKILL LEVELS SO LOW?

Some explanations are immediately available as to why consumers show low knowledge levels on tests of consumer skills. First, we *do not purchase* some products at all and purchase others only on a very infrequent basis. In these cases it may be more efficient for us to *learn what we need to know at the time we need to know it* and not to worry about it before then. (We will be addressing this possibility in Chapter 17.)

Second, in taking these tests, many consumers discover that there are a number of topics in which they seem to have *little interest* (as well as having little knowledge). This reaction might stem from **life-cycle stages** that consumers pass through as they grow older—for example, many readers have yet to make some of the major consumer purchases personally (such as housing, large appliances, and insurance) or deal much with investment planning or heavy tax payments. Before too long, however, most readers will be active in these areas as well. Life-cycle stages are only a partial answer, however. It is also important that we admit the possibility that much of the material inherent in wise consumer behavior really just *isn't very interesting to most consumers!*

ECONOMICS IS IMPORTANT

In part the surprisingly low interest level in wise consumership seems to be due to consumer behavior's clear economic underpinnings. Significant amounts of money are sometimes at stake, there are sometimes sizable risks associated with decisions that we make, and at times our funds might not stretch as far as we'd like them to. Therefore, there can be considerable *stress* associated with consumer behavior and a clear need for "rational" (as opposed to pleasurable) decision making.

Let's consider briefly the five areas that serve as *background* for most consumer behavior:

- Money management and budgeting
- Consumer protection
- Resource allocation and timing
- Planning for the future
- Investment decisions

Notice that none of the foregoing issues would be considered "fun" by most of us. It is also interesting to note that the marketing system doesn't attempt to help us in these areas (excepting that financial services are available for consumers to purchase). Mastering any of the areas requires much work, and managing our affairs well is a never-ending task. Another factor is that no one (other than possibly family members) monitors our personal behaviors on these topics, and it is easy to let them slide. For all these reasons, it is not surprising that many consumers are not very expert, or even conscientious, in these aspects of their own consumer behaviors. If you are interested in learning more about these topics, your library's reading material on consumer economics is a good place to start. Also, you will find that the *Journal of Consumer Affairs* contains some interesting articles on these issues, while *Consumer Reports* and *Consumers Digest* magazines will offer you timely information on current brands and models.

■ SUMMARY

MARKETING DECISIONS AND CONSUMER BEHAVIOR

The chapter introduced the importance of *perspectives* used to view the field of consumer behavior. *Marketers* and *consumers* are the two major groups who engage in day-to-day activities in the marketplace. Each has a unique perspective on consumer behavior. A third important party is the *public policymaker*, who takes a broader view concerned with how the marketplace is operating.

Marketing decisions are summarized in the marketing mix. The 4 P's—*product, price, place,* and *promotion*—reflect the areas of controllable marketing decisions. The 5 C's reflect the largely uncontrollable constraints. *Competitors* will work to overcome our 4 P efforts. The strengths and weaknesses of the *company* create an important constraint on realistic marketing decisions. The *channels* constraint reflects that wholesalers and retailers are independent businesses, each looking out for their own best interests. Marketing programs are sometimes strongly affected by the *conditions* constraint, which reflects primarily economic events. Finally, the *customer* constraint represents the persons who will ultimately decide whether or not to purchase the offerings of the firm. Examples of each factor were included in these discussions.

COMPARING MARKETERS' AND CONSUMERS' VIEWS

In this section of the chapter the consumer's perspective was contrasted to the marketer's perspective along five specific dimensions. The marketer's perspective is (1) *external*, (2) *aggregate*, and (3) *product specific*, whereas the consumer's perspective is (1) *internal*, (2) *individual*, and (3) *extends across many products*. Further, the marketer has a (4) *specific brand* to sell and (5) *exerts influence* to do so. The consumer, however, is looking to buy (4) *the best alternative*, and (5) must *handle influence* attempts in order to do so. Thus we saw how the overall marketing system advances three general recommendations to consumers:

- Consumers should buy and use products and services.
- Consumers should buy often.
- The alternative chosen is important.

In considering these issues further, we discussed why marketers' recommendations cannot simply be adopted and followed by consumers. Essentially, this is due to the fact that *consumers' needs and marketers' needs are often inconsistent*. It is this inconsistency that leads to much of the consumer resistance to persuasion that makes a marketer's job that much harder. This also means that *consumers need to develop their own abilities to be wise consumers* and to make good decisions in the marketplace.

ON BEING A WISE CONSUMER

In the closing section of the chapter we discussed the fact that consumers and even teachers of consumer education didn't score well on tests of consumer skills (under 60 percent) and considered why consumers seem to have low skill levels. We then examined the important role of economics in a consumer's decisions, pointed to the basic foundations involved in consumption decisions, and indicated where an interested reader might go to learn more about this area. As we close this chapter, please recognize that you may wish also to consider either the brief discussion of future research needs (in Appendix 2A) and/or applying your marketing management skills to solving the "It Wasn't All Gravy" case (entry # 13 in our Review Questions and Experiential Exercises section contains useful guidance for attacking this case, which appeared on the opening page of this chapter).

■ KEY TERMS

perspective	place	external versus internal view
marketing perspective	uncontrollable factors	aggregate versus individual view
marketing mix	5 C's	product-specific versus across-products view
controllable factors	competitors	brand-specific versus best alternative view
4 P's	company	influencing versus handling influence view
product	channels	intrusive stimuli
product portfolio	conditions	consumerist economies
price	customers	life-cycle stages
promotion	consumer's perspective	

■ REVIEW QUESTIONS AND EXPERIENTIAL EXERCISES

[E = Application extension or experiential exercise]

1. [SELF-TEST] Briefly define or describe each of the "key terms" in the list just given. Check your answers by referring to the boldfaced terms through the chapter.

2. Briefly discuss why perspective is important in viewing any field of knowledge. How would this apply to consumer behavior?

3. Describe the purpose and dimensions of the 5 C framework. Relate the key points about each dimension.

4. For each of the following examples from the chapter, indicate the 4 P/5 C dimension it represented, and whether success or failure was at issue.

   a. Ford Taurus   e. Taco Bell
   b. Holly Farms   f. CNN
   c. Soloflex   g. Domino's
   d. California raisins

5. Describe the nature of the trends associated with each of the following. Which 4 P/5 C dimension is represented?

   a. Number of auto models
   b. UPC scanner systems

6. How does the consumer's perspective of the marketplace differ from the marketer's perspective? Be specific.

7. [E] Write a brief report expressing your personal opinions on how marketers view consumers. If you have work experience in marketing, use this as your basis. If you don't have work experience in this field, do a short interview with a salesperson or marketer as your basis.

8. [E] How do consumers handle the huge number of informational messages and influence attempts from the marketing system? Observe your own consumer reactions to the marketing system as described in this chapter; then briefly describe your observations.

9. [E] Choose a product or service for which you feel you have a special level of expertise or insight as a consumer (whether through your own experience or your hobbies and interests). Write a brief report covering

   a. Several common mistakes you feel many consumers make when buying this product or service.
   b. Three tips that would help consumers buy this good more wisely.

10. [E] Conduct one or two personal interviews with a real estate agent, concentrating on the common mistakes that consumers are likely to make when buying a home. Summarize your findings.

11. [E] Think about the consumer behavior patterns exhibited by one relative and two close friends. In which areas do they have high levels of expertise? In which areas do they appear to lack consumer strengths? Write a brief report summarizing your findings (for an interesting follow-up to this exercise, talk with them afterward to gain their own impressions and ask whether or not they desire to change!).

12. [E] Seek out a consumer economics textbook in your library or one or more sources of consumer assistance, such as *Consumer Reports* or *Consumers Digest* magazine. Spend a half hour or more examining its contents. What seems to be the goal and target audience of this publication? How well do you believe it is achieving this goal?

[CASE]

13. Read "It Wasn't All Gravy" again on the first page of this chapter. To gain experience in analyzing this live marketing case, prepare answers for each of the following questions:

   a. Evaluate the 5 C's in this situation.

      (1) Although not much information has been provided, which of the 5 C's do you think were favorable for the success of this product? Which were likely to pose roadblocks?

      (2) Concentrating on the "customer" constraint, what issues in consumer behavior would you suggest are most important for Standard Brands to consider? (You may wish to use the Seven Keys from Chapter 1 to help with this question.)

   b. Consider the 4 P decisions that were reported. For each, discuss your estimates of consumers' reactions. If you feel the decision could be improved, provide your suggested improvements:

      (1) *Product form:* a refrigerated gravy bar
      (2) *Product form:* the flavors offered
      (3) *Product name:* Smooth & Easy. (Also, should the Blue Bonnet name have been used somehow?)
      (4) *Price:* 69 cents per bar
      (5) *Place:* Dairy cases in supermarkets

   c. Assume now that you are a rising young marketing executive with Standard Brands. You are called in and offered the option of taking over the brand management of Smooth & Easy. Assuming that your career will proceed normally if you decline this position, would you accept the job? Why or why not? If so, what marketing mix would you use to turn this brand around, and what arguments would you use to justify further marketing expenditures on this brand?

■ SUGGESTED READING

■ Many interesting reports of marketers' use of consumer behavior knowledge are available in business trade publications such as *Brandweek*, *Advertising Age*, *Business Week*, *Fortune*, *Forbes*, the *Wall Street Journal*, and *Marketing News*. The *Harvard Business Review* also includes occasional longer pieces; see,

for example, Geraldine E. Willigan, "High-Performance Marketing: An Interview with Nike's Phil Knight," *Harvard Business Review*, Vol. 70, No. 4 (July–August 1992), pp. 90–101. See also the references for this chapter in the Notes section at the back of this book, especially those for Note 14.

APPENDIX 2A

RESEARCH IMPLICATIONS FOR THE FUTURE OF CONSUMER BEHAVIOR

Our analysis of the consumer's perspective has raised a number of interesting issues. While some consumer researchers have recognized some of these elements as being significant, surprisingly little formal research has been directed toward many of the points we have been discussing in this chapter. As noted in Chapter 1, consumer research is a relatively young field, and researchers have largely employed the marketing perspective in their research to date. We saw within the present chapter, however, how adopting the consumer's perspective can be a useful way to gain insights to complement those arising from the marketing perspective. In the future, therefore, we might expect to see new research arising from this viewpoint. For example, the following topics appear to be significant and to deserve further attention from researchers in consumer behavior:

■ *The marketing system's impacts.* Here the interest would be on the nature of marketing stimuli as an entire system affecting

consumer behavior. For example, "How do consumers handle the conflicting purchase recommendations they receive from the marketing system as a whole?" "How should consumers be handling these stimuli?" Although the text suggested some answers, this topic has received surprisingly little formal research attention to date.

■ *Low-involvement consumer behavior.* How does consumer behavior occur when consumers become used to ignoring stimuli and otherwise not investing a great deal of effort in many of their decisions? Does it become less "rational"? This topic has received a great deal of attention recently; we'll be looking more closely at it in several later chapters of this text. Even so, there are still many interesting issues that have yet to be studied in this field. For example, "Could low involvement lead to less price sensitivity?" "Could this in turn be partially responsible for price inflation in the consumer sector of the economy?"

3

THE CONSUMER MARKETPLACE

THE FACTS BEHIND PAMPERS

Pampers disposable diapers are considered by many marketing experts to be the greatest new product success in recent marketing history. The idea for the disposable diaper was generated in the 1960s when a man was baby sitting for his first grandchild: "There has to be a better way!" he thought, as he kept changing soggy and soiled cloth diapers. It happened that this man was an engineer at Procter & Gamble, a firm that had considerable experience producing absorbent paper products such as paper towels. He felt the possibility of disposable paper diapers would be of interest to the firm.

The idea did capture P & G's interest, but management first had to develop a preliminary estimate of potential market size. Management decided that the number of U.S. diaper changes per year would be a good starting point. One way to estimate this would involve the following steps:

1. Take the number of babies in diaper-using age groups.
2. Multiply this by the number of days in a year (this yields a "total diaper days" figure).
3. Multiply by the average number of diapers used per day.

Try this yourself (using rough estimates, such as 3.5 million births per year), and see what you calculate as an approximate market size. Does this look large enough to continue with a new product? (If you're interested in seeing what P & G's more sophisticated estimate found, see Note 1 for Chapter 3, listed at the end of the book. This note also cites interesting readings about the current marketplace for disposable diapers.)

Pampers, designed by a doting grandfather, became one of the major new product success stories because of the demographics of its marketplace.

■ MARKET SIZE—A KEY ISSUE

As the Pampers' story illustrates, the *number of potential consumers* for a particular product is a basic piece of information. Learning about the consumer market represents a first step for a host of managerial decisions, ranging from investments in new plants, to hiring workers, to planning advertising campaigns. Thus beyond an estimate of market size, we will also want to know about

- Market composition (*who buys* and who doesn't?).
- Market location (*where are* the buyers?).
- Market trends (*what* will the future bring?).

The **aggregate perspective** on consumer behavior stresses descriptive consumer research on the markets that exist for consumer purchases. In this chapter we'll focus on **demographics,** or the statistical study of human populations. We begin by analyzing our consumer population, how it is growing, and what this growth means. We then assess several key trends that will have major impacts on consumer behavior in the future. At the close of the chapter, we will examine how marketers use demographic data in their decision making.

Demographics: The statistical study of human populations in terms of age, gender, location, and so forth.

POPULATION INFORMATION

The primary source of U.S. population data is the national census, conducted every 10 years. Our most recent census was conducted in 1990; the next will be run during the year 2000. The census attempts to count every person in the country and to gather a few vital pieces of information about them. When all these pieces are assembled, an overall picture of society emerges. The first U.S. census was conducted in 1790, during George Washington's presidency. A total of 3.9 million persons was counted at that time.

Today, the Bureau of the Census is part of the U.S. Department of Commerce, a strong indication of how important population information is for the business community of our nation. Within a business, moreover, the *marketing* function is the primary beneficiary of this information.

Almost all the information we will examine in this chapter is based on the census. To keep up with this area, it is useful to know about *American Demographics,* a monthly magazine with brief, interesting articles about the topics we'll be discussing in this chapter. Another useful source is the *Statistical Abstract of the United States,* published each year by the federal government. The Notes at the end of the book also provide useful specific readings.

PATTERNS OF GROWTH

Past Patterns of Growth

The current U.S. population is nearly 260 million people. This number has been increasing at a rate of less than 1 percent a year and is expected to reach almost 270 million by the year 2000.

Table 3-1 presents some key years and numbers that show the pattern of population growth in our history. Note, for example, that shortly after the Civil War, the United States was home to 50 million persons. This number increased by *50 percent,* to 75 million, in the next 20 years alone—an explosive rate of increase that was fueled by waves of immigrants from Europe coming to the industrializing new country. Massive immigration continued after 1900, and in the 20 years following the turn of

Table 3-1 U.S. Population Trends in Selected Years, 1790–2010

	1790	1880	1900	1915	1950	1968	1990	2010
Millions of people	4	50	76	100	150	200	250	280

	Periods of Growth					
	1880– 1900	1900– 1920	1930– 1940*	1945– 1965	1970– 1990	1990– 2010
Population change	+25 million	+30 million	+10 million	+55 million	+45 million	+30 million
Percentage change*	+50%	+40%	+ 7%	+40%	+20%	+12%

*Note that the 1930–1940 period represents only 10 years.

SOURCE: Author's calculations based on data in the U.S Department of Commerce, Bureau of the Census, *Statistical Abstract of the United States, 1991* (Washington, D.C.: U.S. Government Printing Office, 1991); and "2010," *American Demographics,* February 1989, p. 20.

the century, the population increased by 40 percent. When the Great Depression of the 1930s hit, however, growth slowed substantially, and U.S. population grew only 7 percent in the decade (fewer than 10 million people). This trend continued during World War II, when young men were away in the service and young women were working to support production in the war effort.

When these men and women returned home, however, the pattern of personal lives changed sharply toward work, consumption, and family life. Population again grew rapidly, increasing by almost 55 million people in the next 20 years (representing another 40 percent increase in U.S. population). Unlike earlier periods, when immigration provided the impetus, this period of growth was driven by births of millions of children and came to be known as the "baby boom era" (we'll be discussing its impacts shortly).

For the past 20 years, the total population increase has been only 20 percent, or an average of about 1 percent per year. Even though we have seen a large increase in absolute numbers (up 45 million people), this is still 10 million *fewer* people than were added to the country in the 20-year period from 1945 to 1965. What lies ahead? Projections for the next 20 years show even further slowing, with a gain of only 12 percent. However, the abrupt shifts in growth trends we've seen over the past 100 years provide a sharp reminder that projecting future population growth is difficult.

What are the major factors in population growth? There are three: births, deaths, and immigration. Let's examine each factor briefly.

CAUSES OF POPULATION GROWTH
Birth Rate: Fertility

The birth rate—technically termed **fertility**—has long been the most significant factor for U.S. population growth. As indicated in Figure 3-1 there are currently about 4 million babies born in the United States each year. We can see how the pattern of births parallels the recent overall population trends we've discussed. Note, for example, that by 1960, over 2 million more babies were being born each year than in 1933! This number declined sharply during the late 1960s and early 1970s and then began a slow

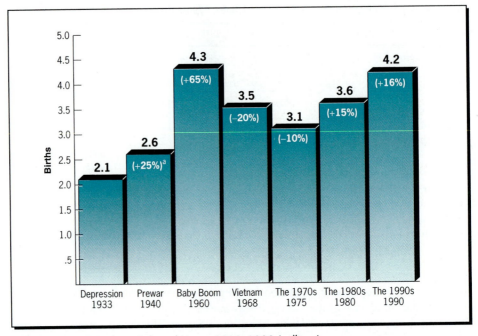

FIGURE 3-1 U.S. Births in Selected Years, 1933–1990 (millions)
SOURCE: See Note 2.

[a]Percentage difference comparison is against previous listed year. For example, 1940s births were 25 percent greater than 1933s births.

rise during the 1980s. Now, the number of births is about 4 million per year, close to the record levels of the baby boom years. These changes in total birth numbers are very important to marketers of many consumer goods and services. Consider, for example, how the 16 percent increase in annual births between the years 1980 and 1990 improved the basic demand levels for diapers, toys, furniture, and other infant and child products during the past decade. This increase in demand will systematically spread to other products over time, as these additional new consumers mature into their teenage years, begin their formation of families, and move on through adulthood. But what does the future hold in store as far as yearly births is concerned? The following report gives us some insights.

🐳 "Fertility Futility," Forecasters Moan

Unfortunately, at this time the experts are confused about future birth trends. They point out that the total population has been rising steadily, so that some increase in annual births is expected from this factor alone. To account for this, the experts chart trends with a key statistic called the **total fertility rate,** or the total number of children the average woman would have in her lifetime. This number is calculated using the birth statistics for a given year, so it can go up and down over time. For example, during the baby boom the total fertility rate reached a high of 3.8 births per woman. During the 1970s, as women's lives changed and new birth control methods developed, this number dropped steeply, to 1.7 children per woman during her lifetime. In the last few

Total fertility rate:
A technical measure representing the total number of children the average woman would have in her lifetime.

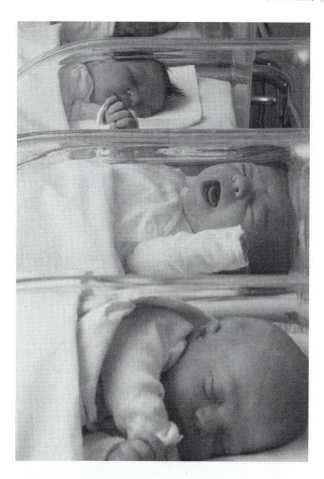

The three basic factors in U.S. population shifts are births (which now add about 4 million babies per year), deaths (now about 2 million people per year), and immigration (which has been adding about 1 million people each year in legal entries and many more people illegally).

years, however, the total fertility rate has turned around and climbed to 2.1 births per woman.

The experts disagree about why this has happened and whether it will continue. One expert honestly admits, "Somewhere along the line, something caused a lot of people to decide to have a child now. That force came into play [just recently]. . . . I can't for the life of me fathom what it is." Another, admitting his frustration, says fertility forecasting is "a miserable job."

Frustrating or not, the future of fertility trends is of major significance to marketers, and at this time we are unable to predict confidently which direction the birth rate will go in the near future. Be sure to watch for new developments in the popular press as they are being reported.[2]

Life Expectancy and the Death Rate

While births are adding to the population, deaths are subtracting from it. **Mortality** is the technical term referring to death. Mortality statistics for the United States show about 2 million deaths per year. This number has been fairly constant for some time. The constant total, however, has resulted from two opposing trends that have balanced each other out: *while the population has been increasing, the U.S. death rate has been decreasing.*

The decreasing death rate reflects primarily the sharp increases in **life expectancy** we have seen during recent years. Between 1970 and 1990, for example, the average American's life expectancy went up by six years, a remarkable jump! This trend is continuing during the 1990s and should lead to an additional three-year increase. Thus the average American born in the year 2000 should expect to live about 79 years. (However, there are differences hidden by this overall figure. For example, the 1990 life expectancy for men was about 72 years, whereas women expected to live nine years longer, on average.)[3]

Immigration

The third factor affecting total population growth is **net immigration**, which reflects people either moving into or out of a country. Although immigration was an extremely important factor in building America, it no longer plays quite as significant a role as do birth and death rates. As with the birth rate, however, trends may be changing in recent years. The number of *legal* immigrants to America was relatively stable between the end of World War II and the late 1980s, at just over one-half million persons per year. In just the past few years, however, legal immigration has jumped to over 1 million persons per year. In recent years, also, *illegal* immigration has been up sharply, reflecting political and economic problems in some other countries. This has had major impacts in the border communities of the West and Southwest, in the coastal areas of South Florida, and in some of the major cities of the nation. (In this regard, you may be familiar with the political disputes over allocations of federal funds based on official census statistics. When illegal aliens are not reflected in these counts, the local communities in which they live must bear additional costs for education, health, and welfare, but these communities are not compensated for such outlays and, thus, have to raise local taxes. As the rate of illegal immigrants has increased, these disputes have become increasingly open and heated.)[4]

AN AGING AMERICA

Not only is the country growing, but its age structure is evolving as well. Some astute marketers have already begun to anticipate the shifts and are altering their strategies to position themselves well for the future. One statistic that's often used to represent the nation's age structure is **median age**, or that point at which half the population is younger and half is older. Figure 3-2 reports some highlights over time. Note, for example, that currently the "average" American is about 33 years old. Due to the sharply increased life expectancies, this is the highest median age in the nation's history and should continue to increase in the future.

Implications of the Shifting Age Structure

Age Groups and Sizes.   Median age is only one summary statistic, and it cannot capture important elements for marketers and others interested in consumer behavior. Another, more useful, breakdown involves the study of separate age groups, as shown in Figure 3-3. Note, for example, how very large the 25- to 34-year-old group is on a relative basis, while the 45- to 54- and 55- to 64-year-old groups are proportionately smaller.

Since age progresses in a very systematic manner, marketers are able to predict almost exactly how the age structure will move in future years. In Figure 3-3, note that by the year 2000, 45- to 54-year-olds will have increased dramatically, up 12 million people over 1990, for an almost 50 percent increase in this age group! However, the 25- to 34-year-olds will actually decrease in number by about 7 million people (down 16 percent from 1990). This surprising shift stems from an amazing social phenomenon—the so-called "baby boom generation."

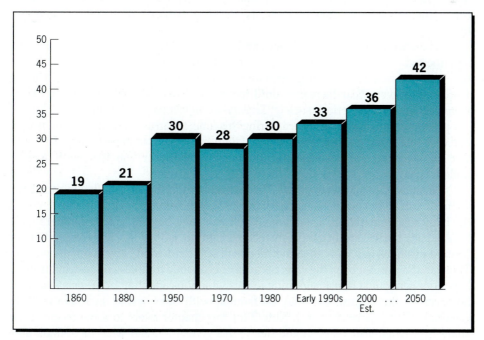

FIGURE 3-2 The Shifting Median Age of the U.S. Population, 1860–2050, Estimated (Selected Years)
SOURCE: See Note 5.

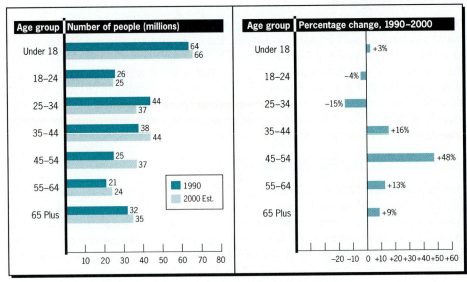

FIGURE 3-3 Shifting Age Segments of the Marketplace, 1990–2000.
SOURCE: See Note 5.

A Special Case: The Baby Boom Tidal Wave

A tidal wave suggests a huge mass moving with inexorable speed and power. It is a good term to describe the baby boom age group as it moves through its lifetime. When the boom arrives at an age, there is an immediate swell of persons that age. When it leaves, there are fewer. While it is there, its effects on all of us—older and younger—are huge.

There were *19 years* of the **American baby boom.**[6] It began in 1946, the first year after the end of World War II. The reasons are not difficult to imagine; millions of young men returned home after having been away at war for several years or more! During 1946, and in every year thereafter until the boom ended in 1964, millions of babies were born into the American society. *Seventy-six million people*—or about one-third of our present population—were born during this time, for an average of 4 million people per year (this from a much smaller population base than we have today). The peak year, in which more babies were born than in any other year, was 1957, with over 4.3 million births.

Many readers of this book may have been born in the years following the baby boom. If you were born between 1965 and 1976, you belong to what has been named the **baby bust generation.** There are 43 million "baby busters." Most demographers believe baby busters are an extremely fortunate group, as they face less competition for favored positions in society than did members of the crowded baby boom generation. Thus far, this has not been the case, because of economic troubles and restructuring of jobs. Your generation is just beginning to receive serious attention from social analysts, however (in this regard, you may be familiar with other terms, such as the "13th Generation" or "Generation X"). Note 7 for this chapter refers to some recent social analysis of what birth years should define this generation and what its outlook may be.[7] We shall return to a discussion of what marketers are doing with baby busters following our review of the massive impacts the baby boom generation has had on our society.

Baby boom generation: The people born in the explosion in births between the years of 1946 and 1964.

Baby bust generation: The people born between 1965 and 1976, when the birth rate was low.

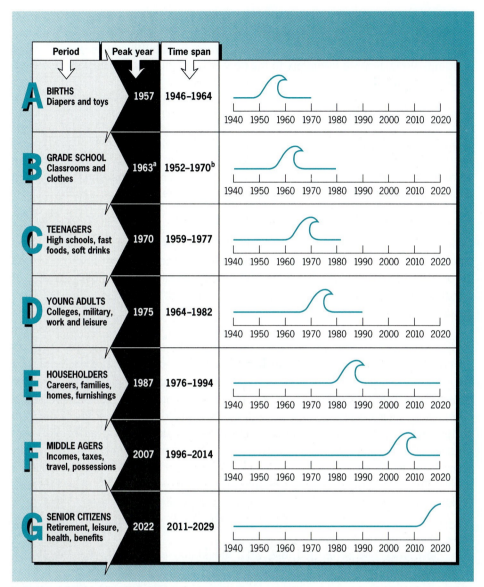

Period	Peak year	Time span	
A BIRTHS Diapers and toys	1957	1946–1964	
B GRADE SCHOOL Classrooms and clothes	1963[a]	1952–1970[b]	
C TEENAGERS High schools, fast foods, soft drinks	1970	1959–1977	
D YOUNG ADULTS Colleges, military, work and leisure	1975	1964–1982	
E HOUSEHOLDERS Careers, families, homes, furnishings	1987	1976–1994	
F MIDDLE AGERS Incomes, taxes, travel, possessions	2007	1996–2014	
G SENIOR CITIZENS Retirement, leisure, health, benefits	2022	2011–2029	

FIGURE 3-4 The Baby Boom Tidal Wave Moves through Life
SOURCE: See Note 10.

[a]"Peak year" represents year at which the highest number of persons entered each stage; 1963 reflects year with the highest number of first graders.

[b]"Time span" represents years during which all baby boom persons entered the stage; first baby boomers entered grade school in 1952; last baby boomers entered in 1970.

Massive Social Impacts.   Figure 3-4 shows some of the social impacts as baby boomers age.[8] Beginning in 1952, baby boomers (age 6) began to arrive at grade schools. Thousands of new teachers, buses, and classrooms were needed, together with millions of pencils, lunches, and other supporting products. Classes became significantly more crowded. The rise in first graders continued until 1970, when the 1964 children began school. Following 1970, enrollments in elementary schools began to drop sharply;

by 1980 there were about 1 million fewer first graders than in 1970, a drop of 22 percent in demand. There was a huge decline in job openings for college graduates who had majored in education. As the tide moved on, closed and shuttered elementary school buildings stood as mute testimony to the tidal wave's effects. Baby busters, however, studied in smaller classes.

Effects were not only felt in terms of size, however. Perhaps in part due to overcrowding, for example, the *SAT scores of high school seniors declined every year for 19 years,* coinciding almost exactly with the passage of the baby boom through the public school system of the country. Similar events occurred with other public institutions as the boom generation arrived. Jails became overcrowded; large new middle and high schools were erected; bowling alleys and movie theaters captured huge crowds of young people and then lost them to other leisure pursuits.

howe *What Should Colleges Do?*

Colleges provide a relevant current case. In 1964 the first members of the baby boom hit college age. Higher education began to grow at almost 10 percent per year and became, by 1970, an industry with more employees than such giants as steel or autos! Universities expanded to take on the huge demand: they added professors, class buildings, and dorms.

Then the boom generation moved on. As shown in Figure 3-4, this happened in 1982, with the last boom class of college freshmen: What does the passing of the boom generation mean for colleges? The number of 18- to 24-year-olds will be decreasing for the rest of this century. In 1994, for example, this age group numbers about 7 million fewer than in 1980, a drop of 23 percent! If we were to assume the same proportion of college enrollments from this group as in 1980, this would mean a decline of over 2.5 million college students nationwide, or about 1 of every 4 students enrolled in 1980. This presents an appalling picture to college trustees. As the president of Boston University pointed out, this loss is the equivalent of the disappearance of 50 universities—one for each state—of 50,000 students each. The picture is very different by state, however. Looking farther ahead, Florida, for example, is expecting a *63 percent increase* in the number of high school graduates by the year 2004, while most northeastern and midwestern states expect decreases.

How have colleges reacted, and what should they do next? Through the 1980s, most were successfully fighting off this trend, and national enrollments were holding steady. Three factors were contributing: (1) more women were pursuing college degrees and became a majority of college students; (2) older persons (age 25 and over) returned to school in large numbers; (3) many students pursued part-time studies while working, so that the average time devoted to achieving a degree moved well beyond four years, and the average age of college students rose considerably. All these factors were assisted by the fact that many colleges discovered *marketing* during this period and put it to work with a vengeance. As the president of Oberlin College relates, "The numbers gave us a good swift kick . . . [we] determined our competitive position in a very quantitative way. It was a fundamental change in the way we make decisions."

As we've seen, though, the numbers are huge, and demographic trends are relentless. As of the early 1990s, though marketing techniques were helping, many colleges were unable to hold off enrollment declines. As the admissions director at the University of Massachusetts said, "There are no more magic buttons. We're all experts at

AUCTION

COLLEGE CAMPUS FOR SALE
ROBERT MORRIS COLLEGE
CARTHAGE CAMPUS
COLLEGE AVENUE, CARTHAGE, ILLINOIS

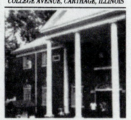

This currently operating private college campus consists of fifteen buildings, totalling approximately 160,000 square feet, on an approximately 20 acre landsite. There are seven residence halls accommodating 484 students, four classroom buildings, a dining hall, a 750-seat auditorium, a learning resource center and an approximately 16,940 sq. ft. recreational center. The town of Carthage is located approximately 210 miles southwest of Chicago, 130 miles north of St. Louis, 85 miles west of Peoria, 20 miles west of Macomb and just 15 miles from the Mississippi River and the Iowa/Missouri border. The campus can be purchased as a whole or in individual parcels and is ideal for a school, corporate training center or redevelopment.
Sugg. Opening Bid: $400,000.

$75,000 CERTIFIED OR CASHIER'S CHECK NEEDED TO BID

AUCTION DATE AND LOCATION:
Thursday, May 18th - 1:00 p.m.
On Site (Earhart Student Center)

VINTAGE SCHOOL BUILDING
REHAB POTENTIAL
HOLY FAMILY ACADEMY
1444 W. DIVISION ST.; CHICAGO, IL

Well located just 2 blocks west of the Kennedy Expressway, this 98,800 sq. ft. classic school building and adjacent 14,000 sq. ft. paved parking lot are in pristine condition. Features include 35 classrooms, 34 sleeping rooms, 4 laboratories, indoor swimming pool, gymnasium, auditorium, 2 classically designed chapels, large kitchen, 2 cafeterias and numerous other features. Ideal for user or rehabber.
Sugg. Opening Bid: $450,000.

AUCTION DATE AND LOCATION:
Sunday, April 9th - 11:30 a.m.
O'Hare Marriott Hotel
8535 W. Higgins, Chicago, IL

**CERTIFIED OR CASHIER'S
CHECK NEEDED TO BID
ON EACH PROPERTY**

For brochure, open house dates, terms of sale and additional information, call:
(312) 630-0915 or
(312) 346-1500

SHELDON GOOD & COMPANY
*Commercial Real Estate Brokers • Auctioneers
through its affiliate Real Estate Auctions, Inc.*
333 W. Wacker Drive • Chicago, IL 60606
Chicago • Dallas • Denver • Ft. Lauderdale
Houston • Los Angeles • New York • San Antonio

As the Baby Boom tidal wave passed its peak schooling years, fewer students were available to enroll in educational institutions. Here are two examples of the fates in store for some private schools.

enrollment management . . . there is no more compensating for the demographic decline." As the decline spread, colleges had to work on reducing costs as tuition dollars fell. Some schools began to close entire departments and lay off staff. Others reduced hiring. At this point everyone involved is looking to the near future for a hoped-for turnaround in applications, as the number of high school graduates is expected to bottom out in 1994, then begin a slow rise for the remainder of the decade. You may wish to check at your own school to learn how enrollment is going, and what marketing efforts and plans are underway. Also, interested readers may wish to consult recent reports on what colleges have been trying to do: some are listed in Note 9 of Chapter 3, near the end of this book.[9]

Settling Down and Settling In. Returning to Figure 3-4, we'll use age 30 to represent the age at which men and women begin to settle into stable household units and purchase housing facilities. Using this age, we see that the nation should be nearing the end of a boom in housing construction. However, this stage is particularly susceptible to economic conditions. Because of high interest rates during most of the past 20 years, and due to the recessions of the early 1980s and early 1990s, the older baby boomers in the householder stage had less than average purchasing in the construction sector. How should we read this result? Do baby boomers want to own homes?

If so, it appears that a huge pent-up demand has been created in this sector, as millions of baby boomers await their chance to buy. When economic conditions are right, then (as they may have become by the time you read this) a major boom is likely in housing. Marketers of building supplies, appliances, real estate, and houses should have bright futures (at least until the decreased number of persons in their twenties arrives at the housing stage). These are the kinds of statistics that create "bulls" on Wall Street. The baby boom market has arrived as adult consumers and promises a booming economy while it's here.

Plenty to Spend.   The next stage of Figure 3-4 uses age 50 to represent a period of settled middle age. Here we see a person's peak level of earnings, fewer demands on the family's money (as children have likely departed), and higher levels of discretionary consumer spending. Note that this era has yet to occur for baby boom members: it is due to begin in 1996, lasting until 2014.

Retirement Time—and Possible Trouble.   Then, beginning in the year 2011, the tidal wave will begin to hit age 65. On average, retirement brings a lower income, lower tax payments, and consumption that is partly funded from savings. What will happen when the baby boom hits retirement age? This will bring numerous marketing opportunities (discussed in the next section). Also, however, there is the difficult question of huge numbers of people moving out of "productive" activities in the economy. The consumer market might be strongly affected, since increased taxation of younger workers might be required to fund the huge increases in payments of such public programs as Social Security and medical care to the baby boom generation. Increased taxes, of course, reduce the discretionary income available (to those people who are taxed) for consumer spending on goods and services. This is an emotional and sensitive dilemma for our society. Forcing us to answer this question may ultimately become the most cruelly divisive impact that the baby boom tidal wave will leave in its historic wake.

Marketing Problems and Opportunities

Beyond the serious social impacts, there are many marketing opportunities and problems associated with the shifting age structure of the consumer marketplace. Many of the opportunities reflect shifts in basic demand for age-related products and services. For example, a continued increase in the senior citizen market segment offers great potential in such diverse areas as gift giving, investment services, specialty housing, health maintenance products, and leisure activities.

Not all age shifts will bring promise, however. For example, recall that the number of 25- to 34-year-olds will drop sharply during this decade. Marketers who target this age group (certain night clubs, housing providers, restaurants, etc.) must adjust their marketing mixes to accommodate this trend or simply face falling demand. In these cases, increased marketing competition is a virtual certainty.

Marketing is, of course, a field that stresses new and creative adaptations to changes in consumers' wants and needs. We can be sure that many marketers will prosper in the years ahead as they respond to the shifting age structure. Exhibit 3-1 indicates some creative strategies that are already being used to address age shifts in the marketplace.

EXHIBIT 3-1

Examples of Marketers Adapting to Age Shifts in the Marketplace

Specific Age Shift	Product/Service/Issue	Examples of Marketing Responses
Increased infants and young children	Hotels/motels	■ Special programs are created for kids (Camp Hyatt, Kids Go Hojo). ■ Special "family weekend getaway" rates are introduced.
	Restaurants	■ "Children's menu" with lower prices, smaller portions is added at various restaurants. ■ Clubs for children are created (BK Kids Club).
	Clothing	■ Sears offers KidVantage program, with 15% discounts after $100 in purchases and warranty against wearout as long as child wears that same size.
	Toys	■ Playskool increases marketing efforts: targets grandparents as toy gift buyers. ■ Mattel introduces younger line of infant and preschool products ($0 to $135 million sales in first 3 years).
Decreased teens and young adults	Fast food	■ Taco Bell cuts prices to spur demand; McDonald's broadens menu, runs price promotions, introduces "cafe" outlets and experiments with fancier "sit-down" restaurants to appeal to older adults.
	Colleges	■ Rider College (N.J.) pays students to cold-call college prospects to introduce them to Rider; enrollment increases by 11 percent. Case Western Reserve U. (Cleveland) begins marketing in South; 34 percent rise in applications.
	Clothing	■ Jeans sales drop 25 percent in United States between 1980 and 1990. Levi's creates *Dockers* looser-cut pants for older men who aren't still slim. Sales are major success ($0 to $500 million in four years); line expands to shirts and sweats, also to women and teens. Side benefit: *Dockers* becomes teen status symbol in some regions. ■ Arizona entrepreneurs buy used Levi's jeans and jackets in United States, ship and sell them in Japan for over $100 apiece.
	Exports	■ Many firms look to huge consumer markets overseas; shift toward export sales as a key growth area.
Increases in middle-aged adults	Autos	■ Mazda designs and introduces the Miata as clear throwback to British sports cars of the 1950s. Smashing success with baby boomer crowd; some baby busters gag. ■ Chrysler introduces minivans; baby boomers buy over 60 percent of them and save the firm from bankruptcy in the 1980s.
	Endorsements	■ Many marketers shift to older athletes. Tennis star Jimmy Connors (39) urges headache sufferers to "Nuke it with Nuprin," while Nolan Ryan (44) pitches Nike's "Just Do It" theme.
	Exercise	■ NordicTrack develops home cross-country ski simulator aimed at middle-age spread. High-quality, high-price pitch: average buyer is 40–45 years old, sales growth is 55 percent per year.
Increases in senior citizens	Autos	■ Buick sells 60 percent of its line to drivers over 55. Dealers begin to offer pickup and drop-off service to retirement communities.
	Housing	■ Hotel chains expand into retirement centers. In addition to advertising to seniors themselves the new centers promote to seniors' adult children. Also, hotels provide cards on pillows in rooms occupied by bankers, doctors, and clergy, who might influence clients' decisions on retirement.
	Leisure	■ Weed tennis racquets are designed for senior players; jumbo face, larger grips. Avid customers can become commissioned salespersons.

SOURCES: See Note 10.

THE EDUCATED AMERICANS

While readers of this book are highly educated, many consumers are not. Therefore, to help avoid the "me mentality," it is wise to consider the issue of basic education in the marketplace. At present, 3 out of every 10 Americans' primary activity is involved with education as a worker or student. Economically, this field accounts for almost 10 percent of the nation's gross national product. Education is a major industry, and, as pointed out earlier, it is affected tremendously by changes in the birth rate in the nation.

Educational Attainment: Rising Rapidly

Rising educational levels represent another important long-term trend in our society, as shown in Table 3-2. The basis for this table is "all adults over 25 years old," reflecting the age at which formal education has been completed for many persons. Notice how the startling effects of our national policy of compulsory education are evident. In 1950, for example, when our parents were young, only about one in three American adults had graduated from high school. By 1990, however, this percentage had increased to 75 percent. Corresponding statistics for the black citizens of our nation show even stronger progress. In 1950, only 15 percent of black adults held a high school degree, while 65 percent of this group does today. Adults of Hispanic origin have a slightly lower level of educational attainment, on average, but one that has climbed as well.

Table 3-2 Educational Attainment of American Consumers in Selected Years, 1950–1990

All Adults (over 25 Years Old)	Completed High School			Median Years of Schooling		
	Total All Races	Blacks Only	Hispanic Origin Only	Total All Races	Blacks Only	Hispanic Origin Only
1950	35%[a]	15%	NA	9.5[b]	7	NA
1970	50%	30%	30%	12	10	9
1990	75%	65%	50%	12.7	12.4	12.0
Young Adults Only, (Aged 25–29)						
1990	86%[c]	82%	61%	12.9	12.7	12.3

Note: All data have been rounded: percentages to nearest 5 percent increment, years to nearest half-year increment (except most recent).

[a]To be read "Of all American adults in 1950, 35 percent had completed their high school education. Considering black adults only, 15 percent had completed this level. Statistics for Hispanic adults were not available for this time."

[b]To be read "Half of all American adults in 1950 had completed less than 9.5 years of school, while half had completed more than this level."

[c]To be read "Considering only adults who were between 25 and 29 years old in 1990, 86 percent had completed high school. For black adults in this age group, the figure is 82 percent, while for Hispanic young adults the figure is 61 percent.

NA—Not available

SOURCE: U.S. Department of Commerce, Bureau of the Census, *Statistical Abstract of the United States, 1991* (Washington, D.C.: U.S. Government Printing Office, 1991), pp. 138–139.

"Educated Americans" celebrate a passage.

The right-hand column of the table represents another way to describe educational attainment. Notice there that the median years of schooling has increased from 9.5 in 1950—that is, half of all adults had less than a tenth grade education in 1950—to 12.7 years—that is, some college—as of 1990. To isolate the most recent trends, the bottom row of the table reports measures for adults between 25 and 29 years old. Notice that about six out of seven of these younger adults hold high school degrees (but only three in five of the Hispanic population of this age). In terms of grades completed, the average young adult now has completed about one year of college. Finally, though not shown in the table, you may be interested in how many persons have completed college degrees. As of 1990, 21 percent of all adults held this distinction. Among younger adults, 25 to 29, about one in four had achieved this level.

Implications for Consumer Behavior

As we know, educational level is a means by which access to particular occupations is granted. This impacts strongly on a person's earning and spending potential. In addition, education allows movement into other social classes (upward social mobility) and helps to determine our consumer life-styles. In turn, these reflect different orientations toward which stores to shop, how much to pay, and so on.

At a more basic level, educational statistics are indicative of the possession (or lack) of skills necessary to be a "good consumer." Rising educational attainment has virtually wiped out basic illiteracy: less than 1 percent of adults in this nation are unable to read and write at all in some language. **Functional illiteracy,** however, remains a serious problem with a large segment of the American consumer population. According to some estimates, at least 25 million adults—that's 1 in 5—lack the reading and writing abilities to handle the minimal demands of daily living in an effective manner.[11] Many of the most basic activities within consumer behavior require such skills. Consider, for example, the basic skills that are required to balance a check-

Functional illiteracy: A condition in which an adult lacks the reading and writing skills necessary for effectively handling the minimal demands of daily living.

ing account, calculate "good buys," figure out interest rates, fend off high-pressure sales presentations, analyze good and bad attributes of competitive products, and appreciate one's rights under a product warranty.

Another look at Table 3-2 indicates the size of the gap still remaining in terms of consumer skills. Even today, 25 percent of all adults have less than a high school degree; this translates to about 40 million people! Although many of these persons are quite capable of handling consumer responsibilities very well, a large number are not and are living less well than they could if they were more skilled as consumers.

AMERICANS ON THE MOVE

Another dimension of importance to consumer behavior is *where* consumers are located and how long they'll stay in one place. **Mobility** is the technical term for change of residence. Mobility statistics for U.S. consumers are surprising! For example, what's your estimate of the answers to the following questions:

1. About how many people move each year in the United States (1 million, 10 million, 23 million, 45 million)?_____

2. Is the average mobility rate increasing sharply, decreasing sharply, or generally remaining about the same?_____

3. How likely is it that the average American consumer will move this year (1 chance in 50, 1 in 26, 1 in 13, 1 in 6)?_____

4. Within the next five years, what proportion of consumers will move at least once (1 of 20, 1 of 10, 1 of 5, 1 of 2)?_____

5. How many times can you, as an average consumer, expect to move in your lifetime?_____

After completing the items, you may wish to turn to Note 12 for Chapter 3 at the back of this book for the answers.[12]

What Does Mobility Mean for Consumption?

Mobility has three major effects on consumer behavior. First, it shifts market locations for retail purchases on local levels. Second, it creates regions of relative growth and regions of relative decline. Third, for consumers who move, it creates demand for certain purchases and for new patterns of patronage.

At an aggregate level, mobility means **shifting local markets,** as some areas grow and others decline. This is particularly important for retailers, as they must plan ahead to be where consumers are going to want to shop. *Most consumer behavior is "local" in nature:* consumers stay fairly close to home for most of their purchases. Until the middle of this century, most localities' population growth was clustered in central urban centers and along railway lines offering easy access to those centers. Following World War II, autos became more available, and the suburbs became prime growth centers. The suburban shopping center emerged as a new concept in retailing. Today suburbs and the small towns outside them have 50 percent more consumers than do our nations' cities. In the Washington, D.C. area, for example, suburban consumers account for 80 percent of the area's drugstore and car dealer sales, 75 percent of food store sales, and almost 90 percent of department store sales![13]

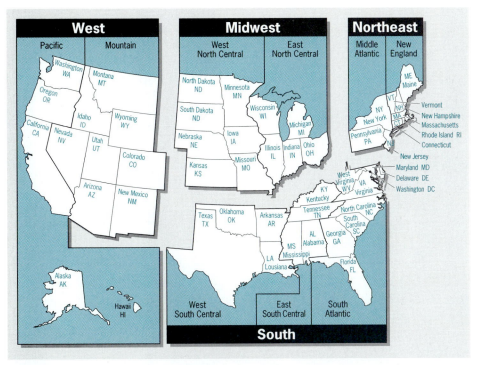

FIGURE 3-5 Map of the United States Showing Census Divisions and Regions
SOURCE: U.S. Department of Commerce, Bureau of the Census, *Statistical Abstract of the United States, 1991*
(Washington, D.C.: U.S. Government Printing Office, 1991).

Growth Regions.   In addition to shifts within local markets, we are all aware of larger trends toward certain regions of the country. Figure 3-5 shows how the Census Bureau defines the largest regions of the United States. Be sure to examine this figure, as these official divisions may not be what you have thought!

The strongest of the regional population trends is the powerful movement of people into the Sunbelt of the United States. Several key facts indicate just how strong is this migration. From 1990 to the year 2000, for example,

- The South will gain the most people (up 10 million).
- The West will have the highest percentage gain (up almost 14 percent).
- The South will stay the most populous region (over 90 million people).
- Just three states will account for over 50 percent of total growth in national population (California, Florida, and Texas). Together with fast-growing Georgia and North Carolina, these five states will be home to 85 million consumers by the year 2000, or about one-third of the entire national market![14]

Mobility Means New Purchases and Patronage.   When a person changes residence, needs for certain products and services arise. Housing must be purchased or leased, representing a major financial commitment. The move itself may also involve thousands of dollars, including possible purchases of moving company services, gasoline, food, and motels. Then, once at their new residence, many consumers

Millions of people move each year, and such mobility has a strong impact on many aspects of consumer behavior.

discover needs for new furnishings, new appliances, and many other items associated with their new life-styles, such as new clothing and leisure products.

In addition to the purchases themselves, an interesting aspect of mobility involves consumers' needs to establish new patterns of **market patronage.** Hundreds of little decisions and questions are involved in this process of settling in: "Where shall I shop for groceries?" "Which doctor should I contact?" "Where should I set up a checking account?" are questions that millions of new arrivals are asking themselves. Notice that in some cases the initial choices made by a newly arrived consumer can be significant since they are difficult to "try out" without making a commitment. Examples include services such as rental housing, insurance, bank, doctor, and dentist, and products such as furniture and appliances. **Word-of-mouth** advice from experienced residents is often a key factor in these decisions. National retail chains (Wal-Mart, Sears, Safeway) provide familiar outlets for the mobile consumer. The local Yellow Pages are often consulted as well, as are retail ads. In addition, organizations such as the Welcome Wagon often contact the new resident to help direct him or her toward using specific marketers in the locality.

Market patronage:
The selection decision of exactly which stores and service providers to use.

EXPLODING HOUSEHOLDS
Most Consumers Share Their Consumption

A substantial proportion of all consumption involves the *shared use of products and services*. Most houses and apartments are shared. In turn, so are many of the products and services consumed therein, such as food, appliances, utilities, and services. According to the U.S. Census Bureau, every occupied housing unit in the nation comprises one **household.** Thus a large family, a husband and wife, a single person living alone, and an apartment with three roommates all count as individual households. Every American except those living within institutional quarters (such as prisons, dormitories, etc.) is viewed as living within one household. There are now about 95 million households, containing 98 percent of the total population.[15]

Household: A technical term referring to an occupied housing unit.

Trends in household statistics reflect **life-style shifts** in our society. For example, the number of households exploded during the 1970s and 1980s. Two key factors were higher divorce rates and persons marrying for the first time at somewhat older ages. The fact that the rate of household formation far surpassed the rate of population growth also means that the average size of household would be dropping. This happened as well—the 1970 average of 3.1 persons per household has fallen to a record low 2.6 as we move through the 1990s. Historically, this continues a long-term trend: our first census in 1790 revealed an average of 6 persons per household. At present, more than half of all households have only 1 or 2 people.

A major distinction in households is between *family* and *nonfamily* categories. Family households have at least two related people living together; the nonfamily category is reserved for persons either living alone (1 in 4 households) or with other people with whom they are not related by family ties (only 5 percent of all households). Thus the family unit is still the dominant form of household.

Families Are Changing

One function that television is said to perform is reflecting the life experiences and aspirations of the average person in the society. It is no accident, then, that the portrayal of families has changed sharply since television's early days in the 1950s. Back then, the "typical" American family was seen to have a father who worked all day, a mother who kept the house clean and running smoothly, and two or three children under the age of 18. Such shows as "Leave It to Beaver," "Ozzie and Harriet," and "Father Knows Best" reflected the family life-styles aspired to in those times. Today, the "ideal" family of the 1950s has given way to various other forms of living: the husband/housewife/two children at home family now accounts for less than 10 percent of all husband-wife families and an even smaller proportion of all households! The average (median) family size is now only slightly larger than three persons.

Why are these numbers so low? There are a number of reasons. First, the portrait itself is age dependent: families whose children have left home would not be counted, nor would younger couples who had not yet had their children. Thus the actual incidence of "typical" families is considerably higher than the 10 percent figure we may hear about in the popular press. Nonetheless, significant societal changes have affected the portrait of a family strongly, including

- Postponing the age of marriage.
- Increasing divorce rates.
- Increasing single-parent families.

An "award winning" family of the 1950s.

A young family today.

An atypical family for either generation!

🐚 *"To Wed or Not to Wed, That Is the Question"*

Approximately 2.5 million couples marry each year, but a major shift masked by this figure is the fact that many young men and women are waiting longer before marrying. Of persons aged 25 to 29 today, for example, about 1 in 3 women and one-half of men have not been married. To recognize the degree of change over time, in 1970, when our parents may have been about this age, only 1 in 10 females and 1 in 5 males between 25 and 29 had not been married.[16] As one alternative to earlier marriages, many young couples have begun to live together outside of marriage. Approximately 2 million people are now living together as unmarried male-female couples in the United States (this is about 5 percent of all male-female couples). This trend is even stronger in some other countries, including Canada and France (where some 10 percent of male-female couples are unmarried) and Sweden and Holland (with about 20 percent in each).[17]

The Deluge of Divorce.   Approximately 1.2 million divorces occur each year, or about one-half the number of marriages. In almost all cases, new household arrangements have to be made. In demographic terms, this often creates both a "single-person, nonfamily" household and a "single-parent family" unit as replacements for the previous husband-wife family unit. It is also typical for *both* households to move to new residences after a divorce. Thus, in addition to the pain and unhappiness involved, the divorce process also stimulates additional consumption needs.

The *rate* of divorce now appears to be declining slightly, after experiencing a rapid increase during the "divorce decade" of the 1970s. At present, about one out of each two couples marrying each year can expect to see that marriage end in a divorce. Remarriages are, however, increasingly common and now account for about half of all marriages. About three-fourths of divorced persons can expect to remarry within five years. Thus, despite the heavy divorce rate, marriage remains the institutional norm for American consumers, with many citizens moving in, out, and back into this state.[18]

Alone Together: Single-Parent Families.   One of the strongest recent social trends has been changes in the internal family unit. Despite our huge increase in population, *the number of two-parent families has actually fallen slightly, while the number of one-parent families has more than doubled since 1970.* Today, one in two American children can expect to spend part of his or her childhood in a one-parent family.

There are many sociological factors associated with **single-parent families.** About 90 percent are headed by a woman. In recent years, three of five black families with children present were in this category, and one in five white families. Both groups had seen sharp increases in recent years. Divorce accounts for about two in five single-parent families, while separation or abandonment accounts for another one-fifth (other important factors are the death of a spouse and nonmarriages).

As we might expect, then, income is a real problem for many of these households. Sharp family income drops occur at the end of a marriage (these average a 30 percent decrease for widows with children, a 40 percent decrease for divorced mothers, and an over 50 percent drop for separated mothers). Most of these women enter the work force, but still many of these families must also rely on other sources of support such as Social Security, child support payments, and food stamps and other social welfare programs. Consumption is often limited to essential purchases and is constrained by the time limitations of a working mother.[19]

Single-parent families have increased substantially.

RISING CONSUMER INCOMES
Economics Affect Spending

Basically, people who have more money also spend more money. The matter of consumer incomes is thus fundamental to consumer purchasing. Most income comes from employment. Employment, in turn, is highly sensitive to the economy's condition. The actual relationship between income and economic conditions is extremely complex, however. Not only do consumer incomes depend on economic activity, but economic activity depends on consumer spending, and consumer spending in turn depends on incomes. Thus there is a circular relationship that is very difficult to disentangle.

Numerous other factors also affect the relationship. *Price inflation,* for example, encourages consumers to spend sooner because their money is losing its purchasing power. *High interest rates* have the effect of raising prices for consumer products purchased on credit. (During the early 1980s, for example, many young consumers were paying more in monthly payments for their cars than their older brothers and sisters were spending for monthly mortgage payments on their houses!) In addition, *taxes* remove money directly from taxpayers' wallets, thus holding down their *disposable income* available for consumption. (Often, however, the government spends the tax money to hire workers, purchase goods and services, or transfer incomes to needy citizens. Such spending can contribute to employment and to later consumer spending on the part of those employed.)

As you can recognize, this description is much too simplified to portray accurately the entire relationship, and it should certainly not be read as an economic policy prescription. There are, however, several very basic relationships that consumer incomes have been found to exhibit, and these should help us to appreciate better the consumer marketplace.

Incomes Differ by Demographics

Looking only at total numbers can hide some major differences that are significant for consumer behavior. The roots of these differences stem from the fact that *consumers have a wide range of incomes*. From the consumer's perspective, then, we face very different situations in terms of our *capabilities* to undertake purchasing. From the marketer's perspective, different income segments offer very different levels of **purchasing potentials.**

A Cautionary Note.   As we're all aware, income differences don't occur randomly. Instead, income differences are systematically related to demographic characteristics. Figure 3-6 graphs five of these relationships, showing just how important they are.

Before briefly examining each one, though, we should note the fact that demographics tend to be correlated with each other. For example, we have already discussed such relationships as age and education (younger people have on average completed more schooling than older people did) and education and race (minority groups have on average completed less schooling than whites have). When we see the very strong effect that education seems to have on income (as we will in Figure 3-6), however, how can we separate out such other related factors as age and race?

This is an extremely sticky task that demonstrates the wisdom behind the adage, "Correlation does not imply causation!" In practice, this analysis would require highly sophisticated statistical techniques (such as those used in a branch of economics known as econometrics). Large marketers employ these techniques, as do government agencies. For our present purposes, however, we will briefly examine the variables one at a time, bearing the cautionary note in mind.

Age and Income.   The first graph in the figure shows a "curvilinear effect" of age on income—household income is low when the household is young, rises rapidly between the ages of 25 and 34, continues to its highest level between 45 and 54, and then declines after the age of 55. Consumer spending, though not shown on the chart, *doesn't vary as much* (that is, it shows a flatter line over the years). On average, younger households (especially those under 25) and the older households (over 65) actually *spend more than they earn*. This is technically termed **consumer dissaving** and represents taking out loans and mortgages, buying on credit, and dipping into savings during retirement. In the middle years of one's life, when income is highest, the reverse is true, resulting in a buildup of savings.

Consumer dissaving: A technical term for spending more than one earns.

Race and Income.   There is a large gap, shown in Figure 3-6, between the average household incomes of blacks, Hispanics, and whites. There are many possible explanations for this statistical finding, including such issues as proportions of single-parent families, age differences, sex differences, and educational-level differences, in addition to questions of job opportunities. At the individual level, the gap is even larger because of more children: the average black or Hispanic American's per capita (per person) income is slightly less than 60 percent of that of the average white American.

Household Size and Income.   Figure 3-6 shows a generally increasing relationship between income and household size, until we reach the largest levels. This finding has many interesting implications for marketers, such as which sizes of households would

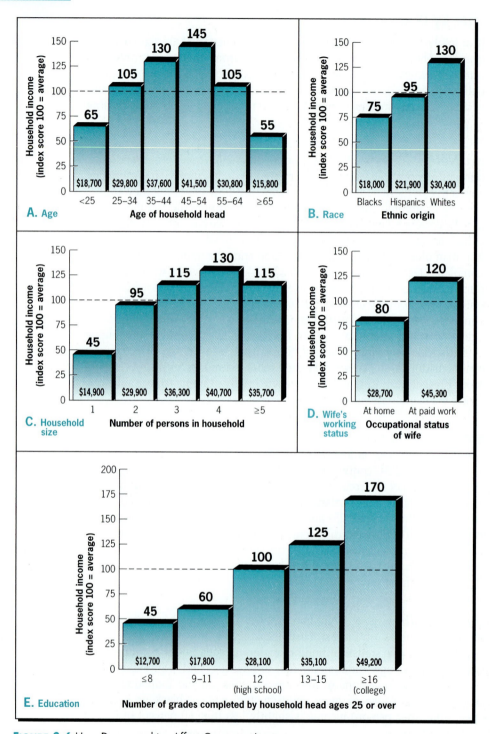

FIGURE 3-6 How Demographics Affect Consumer Incomes

SOURCE: These data have been developed by the author, based on data in the *Statistical Abstract of the United States, 1991*, pp. 424–429. The author has created "income indices" to show relationships. Each index is based on the average income for the six categories shown, unweighted by their representation in the population. Thus the actual "average" income for the population is not shown on these charts, but the average income for each category is shown (at the bottom of each bar), as is its position relative to the other categories. The index numbers have been rounded to the nearest 5 percent level.

be the best prospects for purchasing certain types of products. Of course, marketers of products that are consumed by almost everyone would seem well-advised to pay particular heed to the larger household units as a good way to increase the volume of sales.

Wife's Working Status and Income.   The graph for this relationship shows a definite increase in family income when both husband and wife are working. This is something that we might expect, of course. The dual-earner phenomenon holds strong implications for marketing managers. *Time* is a very important consideration in the consumer behavior of the **dual-earning couple.** And, if the wife is a professional or in a sales capacity, her role may demand more job-related purchases of certain products and services. Finally, the additional income means more money available for consumer spending. In sum, we might expect to see higher demand (and a willingness to pay) for products and services that offer convenience, home work reduction, child care, and a way to "get away" occasionally from the external demands of both work and home.

Education and Income.   The final graph demonstrates an extremely strong correlation between income and educational level. How is consumer behavior affected by educational level? At the start, more highly educated consumers have more money available to spend. College graduates account for less than 20 percent of all households but for almost 30 percent of all income. More broadly, we know that educational level is closely tied to occupation and to life-style. Since *consumption is a means toward living the types of lives we wish to live,* we can expect education to affect which types of products to buy, what kinds of stores to buy them in, and what prices to be willing to pay.

■ HOW MARKETERS USE DEMOGRAPHIC INFORMATION

Three age-old business sayings are

- "Know thy customer."
- "Be there before your competitor."
- "Information is power."

Astute marketers use demographics on a continuing basis. For example, over 4,000 businesses employ the services of the Conference Board, Inc., at annual fees that range up to $100,000. Important elements of the Conference Board's services involve the interpretation of demographics as they relate to consumer behavior. As another example, CACI Marketing Systems, which sells demographic market data keyed to specific geographic areas, has 30,000 clients, including manufacturers, ad agencies, networks, and retailers.[20]

Marketers use demographics in many ways. *Most basically, marketers strive to stay current about the types of trends we've discussed in this chapter, as these reflect the major shifts occurring in the larger consumer marketplace.* In addition, marketers use demographics in their decisions on product characteristics, production levels, retail site locations, assignments of sales territories, and many decisions in advertising. Let's briefly examine a few examples:

৶ৡ *Homing In on Housing Trends*

As the nature of the consumer market changes, astute marketers must adapt the marketing mix to keep pace. For example, consider the following reports from persons in real estate:[21]

> Home builders will face a challenge in 7 to 10 years, when the smaller birth groups from 1971–1974 reach the home-buying age. . . . Immigration will help offset this, however, and may come to account for half of U.S. population growth after the turn of the century. HARVARD PROFESSOR
>
> In 1957 when I started in real estate, we were selling homes to families with four, five, and six children. Today you're talking about families with one or two children being raised in day care centers because the mother and father both have careers. COLORADO REALTOR
>
> We're now building houses with "dual-owner suites" for single people who buy houses together. . . . A variation is a ground-floor master suite for elderly parents or for grown children who've come back home to live. VP, CONSTRUCTION FIRM

৶ৡ *Out of Site, Out of Mind!*

A favorite saying in retailing is

> A store's success depends on three factors: location, location, and location!

This quotation explains why retailers invest heavily to research potential store **site location.** According to one retailing official, a department store may spend up to $50,000 to analyze a potential location. In a typical study, demographic information on an area's local residents is first obtained, then combined with details of consumer expenditure potentials for different product lines. Once a store site has been targeted (and it has been determined that it is not already "overstored" by nearby competitors), the retailer will attempt to identify exactly which customers can be expected to shop there. Through such methods as consumer interviews (or even by monitoring license plates of cars passing by the location), researchers define the size and demographic profile of potential store customers. Since a department store can generate millions in sales per year, good consumer research can contribute substantially to profitability.[22]

৶ৡ *Zip Hits Target*

Demographic profile: A listing of the characteristics of the audience for a particular television show, magazine, or other medium.

Much of the "copy" and "creative" developed for advertising campaigns is based on the **demographic profile** of target consumers for the campaign. Beyond this, the same demographic profile guides media decisions on where to place the advertising. This is often done by a computer program that analyzes how well each magazine, television show, and so on reaches the particular consumer profile, and at what cost.

Another form of advertising—*direct mail*—takes advantage of the fact that our postal system reaches virtually all consumers with individual deliveries. Since people tend to live near others like themselves, there are natural demographic divisions by neighborhoods, and *geodemographic marketers* can target advertising to specific types of households. The U.S. Census Bureau assists business in this task by making available, at low cost, demographic data at several levels of aggregation, beginning with city blocks, then groups of blocks, then census tracts (neighborhoods), then towns

Although many factors are important for retailing success, experienced merchandisers can easily list the three most important ones: location, location, and location! Thus local demographics are crucial for retailing.

or cities, then metropolitan areas. Specialized consumer research firms take these data to create gigantic computer banks of consumers' addresses grouped by demographic characteristics.

For example, a service called PRIZM (Potential Rating Index Zip Markets) rates more than 35,000 zip code areas on 34 different demographic factors, and then groups the areas by demographic similarity. Forty groups of neighborhoods have been identified, including the "blue blood estates," "money and brains," and the "hard scrabble." For each type of neighborhood, PRIZM offers information on over 1,000 types of purchases and preferences that consumers in this type of neighborhood have. We marketers can then send our tailored messages directly to those zip codes with highest potentials for responding to our offers.[23] As you can easily recognize, this example has led us into a high level of market segmentation; we will continue our discussion of these options in the following chapter, which deals directly with the concept and practice of market segmentation.

■ SUMMARY

MARKET SIZE—A KEY ISSUE

An *aggregate perspective* stresses examining the whole of the market. In this chapter we stressed the huge size of the consumer market and the trends that are shaping the future of our society and marketplace. Our focus was on *demographics,* or the statistical study of human populations. We began with the issue of population and population growth. The present size of the U.S. population is about 260 million persons. It has grown in an erratic fashion. It is currently growing at less than 1 percent per year. The major factors affecting population growth are *fertility, mortality,* and *net immigration.*

MAJOR TRENDS IN THE MARKETPLACE

We then discussed the major demographic trends affecting the United States. First, the age structure of the population is shifting to become older. At present the median age for Americans is about 33 years old. This is the highest median age in the country's history, and promises to keep climbing in the future. The structure of different age groups is also shifting. Twenty-five- to 34-year-olds, for example, are declining in number, while the 45- to 54-year-olds are increasing dramatically in number. Senior citizens are also increasing in number. This shifting age structure holds many implications that we examined in this section. We particularly stressed the *baby boom tidal wave,* which is continuing to bring massive changes to our society. We also indicated some implications for the *baby busters* generation.

Next we examined the rapid increases in educational attainment of American consumers. Approximately 75 percent of American adults now hold high school diplomas, for example, versus only 35 percent in 1950. We also saw that education is a major industry in the nation and that it is strongly affected by demographic trends. Among the direct implications of this sector we briefly considered *functional illiteracy* and the presence of minimum consumer skills in some segments of the consumer population. Our further coverage in the chapter considered consumer mobility, households, and incomes. We saw that *mobility* has strong effects on consumer behavior and on consumer markets. We also saw that the number of households is exploding, reflecting *life-style shifts.* This trend has significant implications for consumer behavior as well. As a final major trend, we discussed rising consumer incomes, which bode well for marketers and consumers overall. In this section we noted the general relationships that income holds with other demographic factors.

HOW MARKETERS USE DEMOGRAPHIC INFORMATION

In the final section of the chapter we noted how important demographic trends are for marketers and investigated some ways marketers use demographic information in making decisions such as choosing retail site locations and choosing advertising media. Our next chapter of the book examines market segmentation and continues our discussion of this area.

■ KEY TERMS

aggregate perspective	net immigration	shifting local markets	purchasing potentials
demographics	median age	market patronage	consumer dissaving
fertility	American baby boom	word-of-mouth advice	dual-earning couple
total fertility rate	baby bust generation	household	site location
mortality	functional illiteracy	life-style shifts	demographic profile
life expectancy	mobility	single-parent families	

■ REVIEW QUESTIONS AND EXPERIENTIAL EXERCISES

[E = **Application extension or experiential exercise**]

1. [SELF-TEST] Briefly define or describe each of the "key terms" in the list just given. Check your answers by referring to the boldfaced terms through the chapter.

2. What are the five major trends discussed in the chapter? For any two, what are the major implications for marketers?

3. What are some of the consumer behavior implications associated with marketing the following products to senior citizens:

   a. Grocery products
   b. Banking services
   c. Health care

4. Identify, providing rationale, three products whose purchase and consumption varies directly/inversely with an individual's education level.

5. Given the mobility pattern of Americans, describe direct implications for marketers as individuals seek new homes, new shopping, and new medical services.

6. Indicate, providing rationale, four products or services that would be most affected (positively or negatively) by the following societal changes:

   a. Postponing the age of marriage
   b. Increasing divorce rates
   c. Increasing single-parent families

7. The text discusses the relationship between income and five different demographic variables. Select any two of the five graphs in Figure 3-6, interpret them, and indicate their implications for marketers and for public policymakers.

8. Assume you are the marketing manager for the following products. How specifically could you employ consumer demographic information for any three of them?

   a. Kerosene products (kerosene heaters)
   b. IBM personal computers
   c. American Airlines
   d. Revlon cosmetics

   e. K-mart
   f. Your university

9. [E] Interview an official in the Admissions Department of your college about any changes that have been made in recruiting in response to the population shifts described in the chapter.

10. [E] Visit your local or university library to obtain back issues of *American Demographics* magazine. Read through several issues of this publication. Write a brief report summarizing what you found that is important for marketing managers.

11. [E] Visit your university library to interview the reference librarian about the various means available to learn about demographics, databases, and demographic trends and their implications for marketers. Choose one or more of the following topics and report on your findings.

    a. Households
    b. Baby boom/baby bust
    c. Consumer income
    d. Residential mobility
    e. Age structure
    f. Regional and local markets
    g. Shopping centers; retail site location

12. [E] Visit your local Office for Economic Development (this may be in city or county government or affiliated with the Chamber of Commerce). Interview the chief officer there governing his or her use of demographic data and marketing efforts.

13. [E] Visit a supermarket with the following mission in mind:

    a. Walk through, noting brands, packaging, and products that reflect the changing age structure in society.
    b. Consider what two of these products might be like in 10 years, as the age structure continues to evolve.
    c. As a marketing planner for a grocery retailer, what would you recommend your firm plan to do in these areas? Write a brief report on your findings and thoughts.

■ SUGGESTED READING

■ Because demographic analyses of the consumer marketplace are constantly being updated, the best sources of readings will come from the current search capabilities of your reference library (you will find it worthwhile to learn how to use these options, and help is usually readily available). Also, as mentioned in the chapter, the magazine *American Demographics* provides a regular source of articles aimed at marketers. Finally, for background reading on demographics and marketing, consult any of the three books listed in Note 20 for this chapter, near the back of this book.

4

MARKET SEGMENTATION

GM SHIFTS GEARS

Many consumers are not aware that the giant General Motors Corporation was founded in the 1920s on an elegant but simple segmentation scheme: each of the five GM brands would play a role in consumers' lives. Chevrolet would bring the first-time car buyer into the GM system with a price appeal. As that customer became more affluent, he or she would move up to Pontiac, then Oldsmobile, Buick, and finally, Cadillac. Using this scheme, the company prospered for decades. In the mid-1980s, however, this segmentation scheme was undone by organizational and styling changes: the brands came to look much more like each other, sales dropped dramatically, and archrival Ford's profits drove ahead of GM for the first time in history.

GM then developed a new segmentation strategy for the 1990s. It identified 19 target segments, based on customers' preferences for body styles, size, image, and so on. Buick was to be presented as "the premium American motor car" with a contemporary classic look. Oldsmobile was positioned as a technological leader, while Pontiac was geared for sporty road performance. Chevrolet would continue to go after price-and-value-sensitive consumers, with a special effort to appeal to women. Cadillac, meanwhile, would strive to regain its exclusive image by no longer producing any middle-price market models. The recession of the early 1990s led to sales declines for the entire industry, however, and placed many pressures on GM. As we continue through this decade, it will be interesting to track whether GM will find its segmentation plan to be successful.[1]

As we've seen in Chapter 3, the aggregate marketplace is so huge that any single marketer needs to capture only a small portion of it to be very successful. Market segmentation offers an efficient way for marketers to plan for attaining their desired shares. As you probably already know, market segmentation is among the most popular and important concepts in the entire field of marketing. Professors teach it, students learn it, managers practice it, and researchers examine it—all with interest and enthusiasm. It has become so popular, in fact, that many persons are no longer entirely sure what a market segment really is. In the first section of this chapter, therefore, we'll briefly examine this question.[2] We'll begin by recognizing that market segmentation is something more valuable than taking any possible group of consumers and just giving it a fancy label.

■ BACKGROUND ON SEGMENTATION

Market segmentation was introduced to the marketing field in a classic 1956 article by Wendell Smith in the *Journal of Marketing*.[3] Because market segmentation simultaneously addressed the roles of both marketers and customers, this concept quickly captured the attention of many innovative individuals in the field. Coincidentally, the segmentation concept appeared shortly before the arrival of computers brought about a revolutionary burst of activity in marketing research. During this new era, it became possible to analyze efficiently and powerfully large numbers of variables obtained from large samples in the consumer population. Given its nature, market segmentation became one of the chief beneficiaries of this new technology and quickly became a central topic for marketing researchers and strategists during the decades of the 1960s, 1970s, 1980s, and yet today as we move through the 1990s. It is truly a centerpiece of marketing.

SEGMENTATION AS COMPETITIVE ADVANTAGE

The most basic advantage offered by market segmentation is that it provides us with a structured means of "viewing" the marketplace (which may consist of millions of consumers) confronting a firm. Consider the alternative views of the market depicted in Figure 4-1. At the left, with no segmentation, consumers are all grouped together and viewed as a single market. If there are significant differences within the market (as invariably there are), it becomes difficult to describe the market. As a consequence,

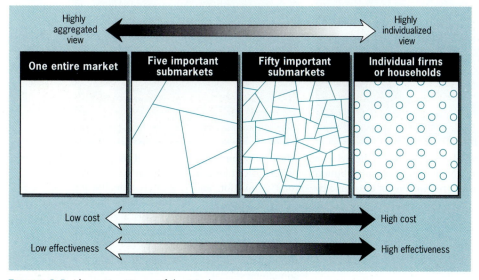

FIGURE 4-1 Alternative Views of the Market

Moving toward the individual as a market becomes more possible through technology. For example, as the era of personalized production dawns in bicycles, we see the start of the process: a customer fitting to obtain precise measurements. These are faxed to the factory's computer, which creates a unique blueprint for the bicycle in only three minutes.

Because robots can measure much faster and more precisely than humans, the computerized blueprint can quickly be translated into frame settings. Here, a light diode mounted on the tip of the robot traces its measuring paths for us to see (over 40 points are included in its stops).

Once the materials are in place and the sizing is complete, a push of the computer control button begins the customized welding of the frame by the robots.

After skilled humans assemble and decorate the bicycle, it can be tested on the firm's "bumpy road" simulator, and it is then available for delivery. Could the bike be available in less than two weeks? "Oh yes," says a company executive: it can actually be manufactured in about three hours with this process, "but we want people to feel excited about waiting for something special."

an aggregate view of the market provides little guidance for strategy development. At the other extreme (the right of Figure 4-1), each consumer is viewed individually. This offers considerable insight into a single customer's behavior and permits the marketer to develop an offering specifically tailored to meet the needs of that individual (or firm). The drawbacks, of course, are the feasibility and costs of dealing with each customer individually (that is, it is expensive for a marketer to customize products, negotiate prices, personally deliver, promote individually, and so forth).

Thus we face a situation—shown in Figure 4-1—in which costs and effectiveness are likely to travel together in the same direction. Viewing the market as a single aggregate is low in cost, but also low in effectiveness. Viewing the market as thousands or millions of individuals, on the other hand, is high in effectiveness but very high in cost. There are so many individual consumers in most markets that they must somehow be grouped together if management is to have any chance of understanding, much less reaching, a sizable portion of the market.

The middle boxes of Figure 4-1 represent moves to segmented views of the market. Notice, however, *how many possibilities there are*, and how differently they will appear to a manager! Until a marketer can decide on the number and membership of target segments, he or she cannot undertake a clean segmentation program. This is usually not an extremely easy task. Thus it is helpful for us to appreciate some of the options available to define market segments. This will be the major topic of our chapter.

A THEORETICAL BASE IN ECONOMICS

Although it is known as a popular marketing concept, segmentation has its theoretical basis in the microeconomic theory of **price discrimination**. This theory points out that a firm with monopoly power can increase its revenues by charging different customers different prices, reflecting the highest level that each is willing to pay.[4] That is, charging a single price to everyone generally means that some customers will be paying less than they would have been willing to pay, while other potential customers will not buy because the single price charged is higher than the maximum they will pay. A quick look at Figure 4-2 shows this point. If the firm charges $1.01, Richard A., Linda A., Rex A., and all others in the "A" group will not buy the product. All the "D" group

Price discrimination: The practice of charging different customers different prices, reflecting the highest level that each is willing to pay.

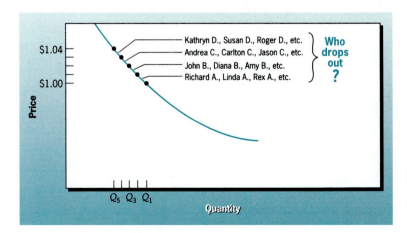

FIGURE 4-2 An Inside Look at the Demand Curve (Or, Who Drops Out When the Price Rises?)

members (Kathryn, Susan, Roger, etc.), however, will be very pleased at the $1.01 price, since they are actually willing to pay even more. Thus we can see that if the firm could somehow approach each consumer set separately and have them pay the most they are willing to, it would maximize its revenues, and each of its customers would still regard his or her purchase as worthwhile (disregarding equity and legal considerations). In today's world of market segmentation, the theory's reliance on price has simply been broadened to now include any combination of the 4 P's marketing mix, including multiple products.

MARKET SEGMENTATION AS A PROCESS

We will define **market segmentation** as a managerial strategy that adapts a firm's marketing mix to best fit the various consumer demand curves existing in a market. It is an *adaptive strategy* that seeks to obtain competitive advantage by doing a better job of satisfying customer requirements.[5]

In practice, market segmentation is a three-stage process, as shown in Figure 4-3:

1. *Identifying segments.*This first stage involves dividing the consumer market into meaningful buyer groups who represent "opportunities" for distinct marketing programs. Consumer research plays the primary role in this stage.

2. *Selecting particular segments to target.* The second stage will differ for each firm depending on a host of strategic and competitive considerations. Marketing management plays the primary role in this stage.

3. *Creating marketing mixes aimed at target segments.* This third stage involves the development of specific marketing mixes, specially designed for target segments. Marketing management also has the key role in this stage.

The first stage—identification of segments—is thus a crucial part of the process. Segmentation usually employs marketing research aimed at classifying customers and providing a detailed understanding of how they differ from each other.

THREE REQUIREMENTS FOR A "TRUE MARKET SEGMENT"

Although the process is flexible, a useful segment must satisfy several requirements, or criteria. Many possible standards have been suggested: you may have already learned

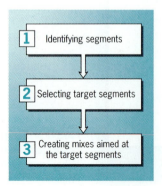

FIGURE 4-3 The Essentials of Market Segmentation

some in an earlier marketing course. In this book, we will rely upon a rich view of consumer behavior, and will therefore adopt the view that there is a set of three basic criteria for market segmentation:

1. *Group identity.* The criterion of **group identity** represents our desire to ensure good groupings. This simply means that members of a segment must be *similar* to other consumers in that same segment and that the members of one segment must be *different* from consumers who are in other segments.

2. *Systematic behaviors.* The concept of **systematic behaviors** refers to consumer behavior itself—members of a segment should behave in a similar manner and be likely to respond similarly to a particular marketing mix. Members of different segments should behave differently and respond differently to a marketing mix.

3. *Marketing mix efficiency potential.* This third criterion—**efficiency potential**—asks the practical question whether or not a marketing mix can be developed to reach efficiently and appeal differentially to the possible segment grouping.

Thus the requirements for a true market segment should now be clear: the search is for a customer grouping that (1) can be identified, (2) will behave differently from other groups, and (3) will be responsive to an efficient marketing mix aimed at it. Our following discussions will clarify what this means for marketing practice.

■ THE START OF A SEGMENTATION STUDY: CLASSIFYING CUSTOMERS

Stage I of the segmentation process—identifying market segments—requires us to pay careful attention to the issue of customer classification. The choices made at this stage not only guide later analyses, but any categories we omit from this stage will not again be available for our segmentation decisions. Thus it is particularly important to appreciate the nature of the options here and to choose intelligently among them.

In the real world of marketing, this task is far from simple. As Ford Motor Company's director of marketing research reported, *"If we want to, we can use 200 or 300 different measuring points to identify our customer."*[6]

THE "THREE LEVELS" OF CONSUMER CLASSIFICATION

As the Ford executive pointed out, there are literally hundreds of ways in which a marketer can choose to classify a customer. Thus we are faced with great opportunities, but also the serious problem of deciding which of the many descriptive bases to use for our segmentation. This decision will depend on our exact situation, of course. In helping us to make a good decision, however, it is fortunate that the possible consumer descriptions actually reflect just three basic levels, or types of classification:[7]

- Personal characteristics of the consumer
- Benefits sought by the consumer
- Behavior of the consumer

LEVEL 1
Personal Characteristics

Mary Winthrop is:

- a 36-year-old female
- unmarried
- an attorney
- a West Side homeowner
- black
- a $75,000-a-year earner
- a convenience-oriented shopper
- interested in obtaining "the better things in life"

Kevin Powers is:

- a 33-year-old male
- unmarried
- an advertising account executive
- a downtown renter
- white
- a $75,000-a-year earner
- an active consumer of travel and entertainment
- a subscriber to *Sports Illustrated*

LEVEL 2
Benefits Sought

Mary Winthrop seeks:

- high quality in clothing
- a business-like image at work
- a stylishly feminine image at leisure

Kevin Powers seeks:

- style in his automobile
- power
- performance
- an image of success and achievement

LEVEL 3
Behavioral Measures

Mary Winthrop:

- prefers status brands such as Anne Klein
- buys fine clothing often
- spends heavily
- tends to be loyal to only a few stores

Kevin Powers:

- buys a new car every year or two
- favors Porsche and Jaguar, dislikes subcompacts
- is not loyal: has switched makes his last four purchases

FIGURE 4-4 The Three Levels of Consumer Classification

Level 1: Personal Characteristics

Personal characteristics: Level 1: measures that describe individuals as people (e.g., age, income, lifestyle, media habits, and so forth).

As Figure 4-4 shows, a particularly useful aspect of this three-level approach is that the levels are themselves related in a systematic way. At the left are the **personal characteristics** of the individual—those can be used to identify or describe particular individuals as people or as consumers. For example, as shown, a consumer named Mary Winthrop might be classified as a female, a 36-year-old, an attorney, an unmarried person, and so forth. These types of descriptions can all be helpful in gaining a general "picture" of this person, her stage and status in life, and her likely areas of interest. Simply put, these demographic and psychographic measures indicate who the consumers are, where they are, what they find interesting, and how they might be reached (Kevin Powers, for example, reads *Sports Illustrated*).

Thus level 1 has a broad orientation toward a person's overall life and applies to all products and brands. Notice that Mary Winthrop's and Kevin Powers's descriptions here will not be affected by what any marketer might do.

Level 2: Benefits Sought

Benefits sought: Level 2: measures of what consumers are seeking in a product or service.

The second level moves to consider explicitly both the person and the product category rather than just the person alone. The title for this level of classification—**benefits sought**—represents an enormously popular approach that is being used by many consumer marketers. Here emphasis is placed on *the nature of consumer demand for various features* of a product or service offering. For example, an automobile maker might classify Mary Winthrop's benefits sought in such terms as importance of price, styling, gas economy, status, size, warranty, and so forth. As shown in Figure 4-4, however, a clothier would need to use a quite different set of benefits to describe Mary, as would other classes of marketers, each depending on the nature of the product or service offering.

In terms of the overall system, three basic assumptions are embedded in this level 2 classification. First, different people will in fact prefer different mixes of features, quality levels, and prices. Second, these preferences will be influenced by personal factors (e.g., age, location, income, type of residence) represented at our first level (personal characteristics). Third, people will *act upon* these different preferences—purchase behaviors will in fact differ depending on the exact mix of benefits a marketer chooses to offer.

Level 3: Behavior

In contrast to the first two levels, this level—**behavior**—classifies each consumer on the basis of his or her *actual behavior* in the marketplace. Many options are available for the precise handling of these measures. Some popular measures of behavior include

Behavior: Level 3: classification of each consumer on the basis of his or her actual marketplace behavior.

- Product ownership or use.
- Quantity used.
- Brand loyalty, supplier loyalty, store loyalty, and so on.

■ USING THE LEVELS FOR SEGMENTATION

Large-scale marketing studies are likely to include measures from all three of our levels of classification. Therefore, we will need to decide how we wish to use the consumer measures that are available in the study. As a practical matter, we will have three basic options in handling them for segmentation.

Figure 4-5 illustrates the three options in the abstract (we will shortly turn to actual examples that will clarify what is done, but for now let's focus on the basic system). Notice in Figure 4-5 that each option starts with one of our levels of classification and *defines* potential segment groups. It then *evaluates* these groups to see if they will meet our criteria as true market segments. This evaluation is done using one or both of our other two classification levels.

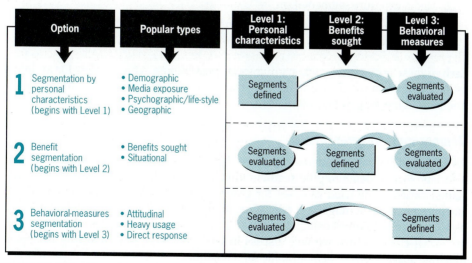

FIGURE 4-5 The Three Primary Options for Segmentation Studies

For example, let's assume we started with the third option in Figure 4-5 and *defined* a possible segment as "heavy users of paper towels." This would provide a basis for group identity and would score well on our systematic behavior criterion (since heavy usage is a behavior). However, we still need to *evaluate* this segment to discover what marketing efficiencies might be possible with this group (for example, what personal characteristics these heavy users have so that we can locate them, understand their interests, and can create appeals for them).

Our discussion to this point has been abstract, but now we will turn to actual marketing practice. We shall examine a number of the more popular segmentation approaches used by marketers, noting examples of applications for each. As Figure 4-5 suggests, we'll organize our investigation in terms of the three basic options, starting with the case in which segments are formed on the basis of consumers' personal characteristics.

SEGMENTATION BY PERSONAL CHARACTERISTICS

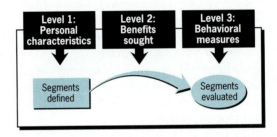

As indicated in the illustration, in this approach our potential segments are first formed using consumers' personal characteristics, then they are evaluated using the behavioral measures from level 3. Four basic approaches are highly popular in marketing today:

1. Demographic segmentation
2. Media exposure segmentation
3. Life-style/psychographic segmentation
4. Geographic segmentation

Each of these approaches contains numerous possibilities, which makes for an interesting menu from which marketers may choose. In the discussions that follow, we'll briefly examine some prime alternatives.

Demographic Segmentation

Demographic segmentation: The creation of segments based on demographic categories such as gender, ethnic group, age, income, and occupation.

As discussed in Chapter 3, demographics reflect the easily measurable vital statistics of a society. Within **demographic segmentation,** demographic and SES (socioeconomic status) variables are used as bases for grouping types of consumers. Differences in age, race or ethnic heritage, sex, education, occupation, and income are all commonly used and are sometimes combined into specific indexes (such as "family life cycle" or "social class," which we will discuss in later chapters). The following examples illustrate applications of demographic segmentation.

🐦 *Segmentation by Gender*

As a basic illustration of our approach, the segments would first be *created* on the basis of a personal characteristic (here, male or female) and then *evaluated* for potential differences in purchasing behavior. For many products, markets have long been clearly segmented either to females or males due to particular differences in personal needs and social roles. Traditional gender segmentation has often successfully included *both* systematic differences in purchasing behaviors (i.e., women bought some products while men bought others) *and* opportunities for marketing efficiency (some magazines, TV shows, stores, etc., geared to either sex, allowing them to be reached more efficiently). Moreover, in recent years, as women's roles have changed, new opportunities for segmentation have arisen.

For example, women now buy about half of all cars sold in the United States (this is a dramatic rise from one in three only 10 years ago: women now constitute the fastest-growing segment of auto buyers). In terms of systematic purchasing behaviors, women also tend to concentrate on certain styles of cars. For example, women account for almost two-thirds of sales of the Nissan Pulsar NX and Toyota Celica models; overall they buy more subcompacts than do men and about as many compacts and small sporty cars. At present, however, they buy only a third or fewer of the luxury and large-car models (although they influence many more purchases in these categories when bought jointly with a spouse).

As gender roles have shifted, new markets have grown for products that formerly were thought of as being for "men only" or "women only." For example, after Smith & Wesson launched its new line of Lady Smith handguns, sales to women jumped from 5 percent to 18 percent of company revenues.

Given its growing significance, auto manufacturers are striving to develop segmented appeals for this huge market segment. Their efforts stretch to all areas of the marketing mix, including car design, credit programs, and special promotions and consumer education materials. One area receiving special attention is the dealers' salesroom. Because over 90 percent of salespersons currently are men, special "sales sensitivity" seminars are being run to improve the interactions salespersons have with the female market segment. Segmented advertising campaigns are also evident. Women's service and professional magazines carry many auto ads, for example, and the design and copy of the ads themselves often reflect research done on this segment (for example, Toyota discovered that women's ad recall scores are higher when a woman is shown driving a car, so its ads were developed accordingly).[8]

ಞ Ethnic and Race Segmentation

In this approach, consumers are first assigned to a potential segment based upon their ethnic or racial group membership; then these segments are evaluated on the marketing efficiency and systematic purchasing behavior criteria. At one time ethnic segmentation in marketing used involved particularly local markets, in which different neighborhood retailers would cater to enclaves of immigrants, or neighborhoods segregated by race. Today, the nature of potential ethnic segments has changed, and there is considerable uncertainty in marketers' minds about when and how ethnic and race segmentation might best be accomplished. Let's briefly consider the following:

■ "Black people aren't dark-skinned white people," states one advertising executive. "We have different preferences and customs, and we require a special effort."[9]

As the ethnic diversity of the United States continues to increase, segmentation opportunities are growing, especially in local market areas. In just 12 years, this Southern California supermarket owner's hard work has taken his immigrant family from poverty to wealth through focus on the Vietnamese submarket.

- A seminar on marketing to Hispanics revealed that in New York City alone, the Hispanic population has surpassed 2.5 million, with a buying power about the same size as the gross national product of the nation of Chile ($19 billion)! Marketers are wrestling with the question of how to most effectively appeal to Hispanics, while minimizing costs. One current marketing controversy, in fact, is whether English or Spanish should be used in ads aimed at Hispanics.[10]

- California, the most populous U.S. state and with a population of trend setters, is experiencing enormous changes in its ethnic makeup. Projections indicate that by the year 2010, that is, within the next 20 years, *every* ethnic group will be a minority in the state. Whites ("Anglos") will fall to 47 percent of the population, while Hispanics will grow to 33 percent and Asian Americans to 12.5 percent (one of eight residents) and blacks will remain at about 7.5 percent.[11]

- Ethnic segmentation is a key factor in other markets around the world as well as in the United States. In Canada, for example, about 45 percent of the citizens are of British origin, about 30 percent are of French origin, and others are from a variety of other nations. Geographically and culturally, these ethnic backgrounds have not entirely assimilated into a single national marketplace. In Quebec, for example, over 80 percent of consumers are of French origin, with only some 10 percent of English origin. The daily languages differ, and a number of customs and preferences differ as well. This has led one Canadian researcher to conclude that "in Canada, cross-cultural studies are not a luxury but a necessity," especially due to government policies aimed at encouraging cultural diversity.[12]

The foregoing points all indicate that large groups of consumers are living daily lives that involve identification with distinct subcultures. In most cases marketing efficiencies are available, such as specialized radio stations, magazines, and retailers. Also, in some cases there are systematic purchasing differences, such as in food preferences. Nonetheless, just as marketers need to guard against stereotyping all women as a single market segment, so do we need to guard against stereotyping any particular ethnic group. Detailed understanding of each potential ethnic market is needed before distinct segmentation is undertaken (if you would like to pursue further reading on issues of ethnic and race segmentation, you may wish to begin with the references in Notes 9–13 for Chapter 4 at the back of the book).

The application examples for gender and ethnic segmentation provide enough illustrations for us to recognize the basic segmentation opportunities for the other demographic and SES variables. *Segmentation by age,* for example, has long been practiced by some marketers for the baby market, teens, young adults, senior citizens, and so on. As we discussed in Chapter 3, the shifting of the huge "baby boom" generation is currently focusing much marketing attention to understanding the 35- to 54-year-old segment for the 1990s. *Segmentation by income* is also frequently studied by marketers, since different consumer spending levels spring from this variable. For example, as a practicing marketer you will find many reports available on the preferences and spending habits of the "affluentials" (a term variously defined as households with incomes over $50,000, $75,000, or other high figures).

Age is a key segmentation variable for many marketers. College students' spring breaks, for example, offer opportunities for producers to promote their wares and for tourism marketers (such as those around South Padre Island, Texas, shown here) to introduce their area to many people who may want to return years into the future, as "winter Texans."

Sometimes, *segmentation by marital status or segmentation by occupation* (e.g., accountants, interior designers) can be very helpful for targeting particular products or services to special interest groups.

In summary, demographic segmentation offers a multitude of possibilities for classifying consumers according to easily identifiable personal characteristics. In each case, the demographic variable is intended to "stand for" special dimensions of these people in how they live their daily lives, what they find to be of particular interest, and how they might behave as consumers.

Media Exposure Segmentation

Media exposure segmentation: The creation of segments based on audience membership for a particular advertising medium.

This approach—**media exposure segmentation**—is much more limited than demographic segmentation, since here the focus is only on choosing effective media (magazines, newspapers, radio and TV stations, etc.) through which to reach desirable consumers with advertising messages. In terms of our segmentation framework, a potential segment here is first *defined* as consumers who are likely to be in the audience for a particular medium. These segments are then *evaluated* by advertisers in terms of their prospective purchasing behaviors.

To assist advertisers in this evaluation (and to help them decide to place advertising dollars with their firm), large media companies employ market research to develop "profiles" of their readers or audience members. These profiles concentrate on who these consumers are (often using demographics) and their purchasing behaviors for particular product types. The media then advertise to marketers and compete for marketers' dollars on the basis of the "fit" of their audiences' consumer profiles and the prices they charge to reach the consumers in that media segment.

In summary, this is a somewhat narrow category of market segmentation. It is, however, frequently used in the daily world of advertising, and does offer marketing mix efficiency through better media decisions.

Segmentation by Life-styles and Psychographics

In contrast to the narrow focus of the media exposure approach, the **life-style/psychographic segmentation** approach can be extremely broad. It was first used in marketing about 25 years ago: before then marketers had relied on general demographic and personality measures for segmentation. As we've seen for demographics (and will see in Chapter 6 for personality), these are general measures that extend to many aspects of a person's life beyond those of interest to marketers. Thus marketers were interested in creating *new forms of measures that would focus more on consumption and less on other aspects of a person.* The two forms of new measurements that emerged were termed "life-styles" and "psychographics." At the start of their development, life-styles and psychographics were *two distinct streams of work,* with life-styles deriving more from demographic bases and psychographics deriving more from personality bases. Let's look briefly at each one to see how they differ, then why they've come to be used together.

Life-style/psychographic segmentation: The creation of segments based on consumers' activities, interests, or psychological measures.

₴ *Consumer Life-styles: "AIO Patterns"*

The concept of "life-styles" has a long and honored place in the annals of social science, including the work of the great German sociologist, Max Weber, in his study of social classes in society (see the appendix to Chapter 12). In general, **life-style** reflects people choosing activities that represent the ways they wish to live. Our life-styles don't just arise and exist in a vacuum. They are largely molded by three factors: (1) the ways in which we were raised, (2) our personal interests and values, and (3) the demands of our daily lives (notice that this suggests that demographic variables such as age or education should be related to different consumer life-styles).

Thus there were good reasons for marketers to expect that life-styles will affect consumer behavior, and therefore would be a useful segmentation variable. The earliest work in marketing developed a large number of "AIO" questions asked of consumers: **AIO** stands for **activities, interests,** and **opinions.**[14] Questions range from work and social activities, through family, food, and media interests, to opinions about oneself, politics, social issues, and the future. Figure 4-6 presents some of the types of questions used in consumer life-style studies, which are given to large, national samples of consumers. Then the data are statistically analyzed to search for groups of people who have similar activities, interests, and opinions. For example, in one famous study U.S. women were classified into five life-style segments whose names tell us quite a bit about what they might be like (the five segments were "Eleanor," the elegant socialite; "Cathy," the contented housewife; "Thelma," the old-fashioned traditionalist; "Mildred," the militant mother; and "Candice," the chic suburbanite). These segments were then *evaluated* by comparing their patterns of consumption behaviors: as we might expect from their names, differences in product and store preferences were found, as were differences in media exposure.[15] Thus an insightful marketer using life-style segmentation can discern which types of consumers are strong prospects for his or her brand, what other things appeal to these prospects, and how they might best be reached through the media.

₴ *Consumer Psychographics*

In an insightful review of this area, William Wells defined **psychographics** as "quantitative research intended to place consumers on psychological—as distinguished

A. Activities

About how many times in the last 12 months have you:	None	Once or Twice	3 to 5 Times	6 to 18 Times	19 to 35 Times	About Once a Week	Almost Daily
Gone to church							
Traveled out of state							
Used a credit card							
Attended a picnic							
Placed a bet							
Gone hunting							
Dialed information							

(and so forth, hundreds of questions are possible.)

B. Interests and Opinions

Please indicate the extent to which you agree or disagree with each statement below. Use the following response scale to record a number next to each statement:

Definitely Disagree   −3 −2 −1   0   +1 +2 +3   Definitely Agree

_____ I live a well-planned life.

_____ My family is the most important thing in my life.

_____ I try to work out physically on a regular basis.

_____ The government should be cut back.

_____ I like parties.

(and so forth, hundreds of questions are possible.)

FIGURE 4-6 Illustrative Questions in a Life-style Study

from demographic—dimensions."[16] Thus the *intention* of psychographic research is quite clear. Marketers were concerned that pure demographics and pure life-style research were not sufficient to capture what was going on in consumers' minds—marketers also strongly desired to have good psychological information available. Unfortunately, the two types of psychological information that were available—motivation research and personality research—faced certain problems. (As we will discuss in upcoming chapters, motivation research was being questioned because of its very small samples and some possibly questionable techniques, while personality research was proving to reveal only low correlations with consumer behavior.)

However, marketers were intrigued with the potentials of *combining the strengths* of these two approaches to form the new consumer psychographics approach. Could new measures be constructed that portrayed consumers' personal fears and desires (as motivation research did), but within large samples that could be statistically analyzed (as personality research did) and that could also reflect the different types of lives that these people were living (as demographics did)? Several groups of researchers thought this was possible and set out to develop psychographics as an area of study.[17]

Now there are many forms of psychographic studies available, so that this approach remains difficult to briefly describe. However, we can easily illustrate the kinds of consumer information obtained by considering a psychographic study that has been reported on the stomach remedy market. This study found that there were basically four psychographic segments of consumers for this category: (1) "severe sufferers" are anxious people who take ailments seriously and believe they suffer more severely than others; (2) "active medicators" are emotionally well-adjusted, but lead demanding lives and use remedies to relieve every ache and pain; (3) "hypochondriacs" are afraid of new ingredients, extra potency, and possible side effects of remedies, but are deeply concerned over their health and seek medical guidance in treatment; and (4) "practicalists" are emotionally stable and little concerned over ailments or remedy dangers, but accept discomforts and use fewest remedies. When these segments were evaluated according to brands used, interesting differences emerged: brands A and B (names were disguised in the release of this study) drew most heavily from the severe sufferer segment, brand C relied on active medicators, brand D relied on hypochondriacs, whereas brand E drew most heavily from the practicalists![18]

Combining Psychographics and Life-styles. Although the backgrounds of these two topics are quite distinct, marketers typically lump their measures together when doing consumer studies (this is not viewed as a problem since the marketer's purpose is to solve managerial problems, not to develop a rigorous theory of psychographics or life-styles). Over time, therefore, the field of marketing has come to view psychographics and life-style research as so intertwined that it is hard to separate the two.

If you are headed for a career in marketing, you should be aware that this intermixing of life-styles and psychographics has led to some serious questioning (by professionals in advertising) as to the validity of this approach. Everyone involved agrees that sometimes this research can offer very useful insights, but also that psychographic/life-style research has moved away from solid grounding in psychological theory. Thus its users must take care in their measurements and interpretations of results if they are to uncover valid information on consumer behavior. (If you would like to read more about this approach, you may wish to begin with the excellent readings listed in Note 19 at the back of the book, under the references for Chapter 4.) In the meantime, you may be interested in how one combination system, VALS (values and life-styles), has been applied to marketing problems.

Why "A Breed Apart"? The VALS System

Within the tradition of this research, the VALS—(values and life-styles)—program is an important development. VALS, created by a consulting firm in California, has been used by many marketers to plan their segmentation efforts. The essence of the VALS program is a classification scheme that assigns each adult American to one VALS segment. The original VALS system had nine segments—in each the people had similar patterns of values and life-style activities. The following application illustrates how the system was used by marketers:

There's an interesting VALS story behind the famous Merrill Lynch advertising campaign showing various scenes in which a lone bull stalks, highlighting the firm's theme, "A Breed Apart." An earlier Merrill Lynch campaign, which ran for a long time during the 1970s, had featured a herd of bulls galloping across the plains, with the theme "Merrill Lynch Is Bullish on America!" With its striking graphics and patriotic overtones, this campaign capitalized on Wall Street's terminology for people who expect increasing stock prices (and profits for investors).

Several years ago, however, the firm changed ad agencies and shifted its campaign to the lone bull, "breed apart" theme. Why? Dr. Joseph Plummer, a leading life-style researcher, and an executive with the new ad agency, explained that the agency's VALS-based research had discovered that the herd photos and the "bullish on America" theme was not appealing to Merrill Lynch's primary target—the Achievers segment, who have money and are heavy stock investors. While it may have appealed well to "Belongers," the idea of a "herd instinct" is not appealing to someone who wants to think of himself or herself as a driving individualist or an entrepreneurial investor. Thus the shift to "A Breed Apart" and the picture of a lone but powerful bull. According to Dr. Plummer, "Our strategy shift was clearly emotionally on track with the Achiever target audience." The results were impressive: the percentage of consumers who noticed and remembered the firm's ads increased from 8 percent to 55 percent and its share of market increased as well.[20]

Thus the combination of psychographic and life-style segments can lead to useful marketing insights, even though it is controversial. The original VALS system has recently been modified into a new system, called VALS-2. If you would like to learn more about the development of VALS-2, exactly what its segments are (there are eight), and how they differ in their consumption behaviors, an overview appears in Appendix 4A.

Geographic Segmentation

Geographic segmentation: The creation of segments based on residential locations.

Although we often don't think of it this way, most consumer behavior is "local" in nature, as individual purchases occur in local retail outlets and through local service providers. Thus there are large potentials for **geographic segmentation.** National marketers can use two key forms of geographic segmentation: **regional segmentation** (in which different mixes are created to satisfy the tastes of different regions) and **geodemographic clustering** (sometimes called *zip clustering,* in which distinct mixes are created for similar types of neighborhoods stretched across the nation). In terms of our segmentation options, in each approach segments are first *defined* based on a consumer's geographic location; then the segments are *evaluated* with regard to the marketing efficiency and systematic purchasing behavior criteria.

Melting Pot or Not? Regions Do Differ...

Historically, many forces have worked to develop regional differences in the United States and other countries. Differences in *climate, geography,* and *natural resources,* for example, led to regional differences in both work and leisure activities, while differences in *immigration patterns* created strong regional differences in cultures. In contrast, the more recent forces of *mobility* and *technology* have worked to reduce regional differences, as people move to new areas, travel widely, and receive a steady stream of communications from various centers around the nation and the world. However, marketers have discovered that a number of regional differences still remain. These have led companies such as Campbell Soup to create special product versions (e.g., spicy soup for the Southwest, more bland for the North) and special sales promotions for each region. Some examples of regional differences are the following: Fifty percent of Southerners report that they "nearly always have meat at breakfast," against only 10 percent of Easterners. Easterners, on the other hand, eat an incredible number of doughnuts, drink 66 percent more hot tea than the national average, and consume the most whisky. Southerners drink the least whisky and wine, but compensate with huge soft drink consumption to wash down all those potato chips they buy. Westerners tend toward a more healthful life-style: they compensate for their high consumption of wine by downing plenty of vitamins, cheese, and fresh fruits and vegetables. Midwesterners are about at the norm for most products, except that their "sweet tooths" for ice cream, candy, and snacks lead them to work off the calories with higher levels of bowling.[21]

As we move to local market areas we find even stronger instances of unique consumer preference patterns. In comparing Los Angeles with Philadelphia, for example, marketers know that cocktail mixes sell very well in Los Angeles (at a rate three times greater than the national average) but at only one-sixth this rate in Philadelphia. In a reversal of this pattern, frozen meat is very popular in Philadelphia (selling at almost four times the national average), while it is almost absent in Los Angeles, selling at a rate only one-fourth of the national rate and only one-fifteenth of that in Philadelphia.[22] With data such as these, marketers can better assess prospects for new entries in related categories.

Consumer preferences differ, of course, even within different neighborhoods in a city. Since neighborhoods are also associated with particular supermarkets, the latest development is **store-specific marketing,** in which major food marketers use data from individual stores' checkout scanners to plan specific promotions for the shoppers in that store. For example, in one city Kraft searched for the 30 stores where customers bought the most from special displays of related products and then installed special coolers to promote favored items for that store's shoppers (for example, for cream cheese, high levels of strawberry in one store, diet in another, and large sizes of plain flavor in a third). How did it work? Sales increased 150 percent over those of the previous year in those stores![23]

ào Zipping Straight to Neighborhood Targets

Geodemographic segmentation is a relatively new approach that concentrates on finding similar types of consumer neighborhoods across the nation and then using the zip codes of these areas to form market segments (thus the nickname "zip clustering").[24] Claritas Corporation, which originated this concept some 15 years ago, is one of the major suppliers of these data today. Essentially, Claritas's approach relies on market research data for huge samples of American consumers, combined with detailed data from the U.S. Census, that has been organized by postal zip codes (in total, over 60 consumer measures are used, for each of the 36,000 U.S. zip code areas). Cluster analysis—a sophisticated form of statistical analysis—is then used to find *patterns of similarity* among zip codes. These are then "clustered" together into segments, or groups of zip codes in which consumers tend to have similar life-styles and consumption behaviors. Claritas's **PRIZM** system offers 40 such segments: you may find it interesting to look at Exhibit 4-1, which illustrates six of these (if you would like to learn more about this approach, you may wish to consult the book cited in the exhibit source line).

EXHIBIT 4-1 _____

PRIZM's Neighborhood Clusters as Market Segments[a]

BLUE BLOOD ESTATES

1.1% of U.S. households

Median household income: $70,307

Age group: 35–44

Wealthy, white, college-educated families; posh big-city town houses

Characteristics: Buy: U.S. Treasury notes; Drive: Mercedes-Benzes; Read: *The New York Times, Gourmet;* Eat: natural cold cereal, skim milk; TV: *David Letterman;* Sample ZIPs: Beverly Hills, Calif 90212; Potomac, Md. 20854; Scarsdale, N.Y. 10583; McLean, Va. 22101; Lake Forest, Ill. 60045

LEVITTOWN, USA

3.1% U.S. households

Median household income: $28,742

Age group: 55 plus

High school-educated white couples; post war tract subdivisions

Characteristics: Watch ice hockey, go bowling; Read: *Stereo Review, Barron's;* Eat: Instant iced tea, English muffins; TV: *Newhart, Sale of the Century;* Sample ZIPs: Norwood, Mass, 02062; Cuyahoga Falls, Ohio 44221; Nashville, Tenn. 37214; Stratford, Conn. 06497; Cheswick, Pa. 15024

MIDDLE AMERICA

3.2% of the U.S. households

Median household income: $24,431

Age group: 45-64

High school–educated, white families; middle-class suburbs

Characteristics: Use domestic air charters, Christmas clubs; Drive: Plymouth Sundances, Chevy Chevettes; Read: *Saturday Evening Post;* Eat: Pizza mixes, TV dinners; TV: *Family Ties;* Sample ZIPS: Marshall, Mich. 49068; Sandusky, Ohio 44870; Hagerstown, Md. 21740; Oshkosh, Wis. 54901; Stroudsburg, Pa. 18360; Elkhart, Ind. 46514

BOHEMIAN MIX

1.1% of U.S. households

Median household income: $21,916

Age group: 18–34

White-collar college graduates; singles, racially mixed

Characteristics: Buy: wine by the case, common stock; Drive: Alfa Romeos, Peugeots; Read: *GQ, Harper's;* Eat: whole-wheat bread, frozen waffles; TV: *Nightline;* Sample ZIPs: Greenwich Village, N.Y. 10014; Dupont Circle, Washington, D.C. 20036; Cambridge, Mass. 02139; Lincoln Park, Chicago 60614; Shadyside, Pittsburgh, 15232; Haight-Ashbury, San Francisco 94117

BLACK ENTERPRISE

0.8% of U.S. households

Median household income: $33,149

Age group: 35-54

Black achievers, intelligentsia; high educational levels

Characteristics: Use cigars, malt liquor; Drive: Yugos; Read: *Ebony, Ms;* Eat; frozen dessert pies: TV: *American Bandstand, Nightline;* Sample ZIPs: Capitol Heights, Md. 20743; Auburn Park, Chicago 60620; Seven Oaks, Detroit 48235; Mount Airy, Philadelphia 19119; South De Kalb, Atlanta 30034; Cranwood, Cleveland 44128

TOWNS AND GOWNS

1.2% of U.S. households

Median household income: $17,862

Age group: 18–34

College-educated, white singles; middle-class college towns

Characteristics: Use civic, country clubs; Drive: Mercury Sables, Subaru DL4s; Read: *Natural History, GQ;* Eat: Mexican foods, canned stews; TV: *Good Morning America;* Sample ZIPs: State College, Pa. 16801; Bloomington, Ind. 47401; Ithaca, N.Y. 14850; Gainesville, Fla. 32606; Corvallis, Ore. 97330; College Station, Texas 77840

---

[a]The "Characteristics" entry indicates products consumed at much higher rate than the average for all Americans

Source: Michael J. Weiss, *The Clustering of America* (New York: Harper & Row, 1988).

How do marketers use this information? There are three primary ways:

1. *Direct marketing.* As you may have experienced, many direct-mail pieces are crafted to appeal to a particular segment's consumers, then sent only to certain zip codes in which these people are likely to be found. As technology develops, moreover, variations on this approach become possible. For example, Buick recently introduced its Roadmaster station wagon by placing ads and a personally addressed, "send for more information" card in special editions of such magazines as *Time, Sports Illustrated,* and *Money,* that were sent only to those zip codes in which the best prospects for this type of car had been found to live. This approach thus reached only 20 percent of the population, but 50 percent of the buyers of large station wagons.[25]

2. *Site selection.* Decisions on where to locate stores, restaurants, and other outlets can be guided by these data. The U.S. Army, for example, found that its top recruits come from the zip cluster called "Shotguns & Pickups," so it opted to place its new recruiting centers in many neighborhoods in this cluster.

3. *Store layout and stocking.* Rather than basing decisions on a specific store's scanner data, as was described earlier, marketers can choose to guide decisions such as what foods to feature or stock heavily in neighborhood supermarkets by using results from other supermarkets located in similar zip codes. Similarly, test promotions that have worked well in a certain zip area can be considered for use in other areas belonging to the same zip cluster.

SEGMENTATION BY BENEFITS SOUGHT

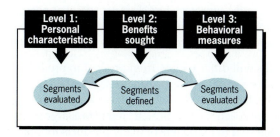

As illustrated, our second major type of segmentation option begins by *defining* segments on the second level of consumer classification—benefits sought from a product or service—and then *evaluates* these segments for differences on *both* personal characteristics and purchasing behavior (levels 1 and 3 of consumer classification). As you may know, **benefit segmentation** is an enormously popular approach. As Russell Haley, the developer of benefit segmentation, explained, "The benefits which people are seeking in consuming a given product are the basic reasons for the existence of true market segments."[26]

Table 4-1 illustrates Haley's classic summary of benefit segments in the toothpaste market. Notice that the four groups are first defined on the basis of the primary benefit they are seeking; then they are evaluated according to differences in some personal characteristics (suggesting potential efficiencies in reaching and appealing to them) and differences in purchase behavior potentials. This type of information can then be used to suggest marketing mix strategies. For example, notice how particular product features, pricing strategies, advertising appeals, and media suggest themselves if we spend a few moments analyzing even the highly summarized information in this table. In addition, further information is usually gathered in a benefit segmentation study to allow us to see how the consumers in each segment feel about competing brands, what

Benefit segmentation: The creation of segments based on what consumer are seeking to obtain from a product or service.

Table 4-1 A Benefit Segmentation Analysis of the Toothpaste Market

	"The Sensory Segment"	"The Sociables"	"The Worriers"	"The Independents"
Principal benefit sought	Flavor, product appearance	Brightness of teeth	Decay prevention	Price
Demographic strengths	Children	Teens, young people	Large families	Men
Special behavioral characteristics	Users of spearmint flavored toothpaste	Smokers	Heavy users	Heavy users
Brands disproportionately favored	Colgate, Stripe	Macleans, Plus White, Ultra Brite	Crest	Brands on sale
Personality characteristics	High self-involvement	High sociability	High hypochondriasis	High autonomy
Life-style characteristics	Hedonistic	Active	Conservative	Value oriented

SOURCE: Russell I. Haley, "Benefit Segmentation: A Decision-Oriented Research Tool." *Journal of Marketing,* July 1968, Table 1, p. 33.

further benefits they might be seeking, and so forth. Benefit segmentation is thus a rich tool for marketing management.

The key to this approach lies in the term "benefits." For consumers, this refers to *positive consequences* they will experience from using a particular product. For marketers, this refers to the *mix of product characteristics* that needs to be designed into the product or service in order to deliver those positive consequences that consumers are seeking. Three key dimensions result from this view of benefits:

1. Specific benefits will differ widely from product to product; thus marketers *need to do customized research studies* for benefit segmentation. We cannot rely on the kinds of syndicated consumer data we have been discussing in the first set of segmentation approaches ("syndicated" refers to a large study done by a research firm that is then sold to marketers of many products for application to their own situations: census demographics, media exposure surveys, VALS, PRIZM, and so forth are all examples of this). In the next section of the book we will be learning more about how to study consumer benefits, so we need not be concerned about research details at this point.

While the total skin care market is growing only 3.5 percent per year, Oil of Olay is targeting the therapeutic benefit segment, growing at 12 percent per year.

2. By definition, benefits are desirable, so most consumers will want most benefits. Opportunities for segmentation arise from *trade-offs* consumers are willing to make among the benefits possible (and the prices paid for them, thus allowing premium products). *Only when different groups of consumers prefer different "packages" of benefits will we have an opportunity for benefit segmentation.* Fortunately, however, this is common in the consumer marketplace. Consider why different types of clothing stores are patronized, different types of automobiles are purchased, and so forth. In fact, when we think about it, we can see this occurring in virtually all aspects of consumer behavior!

3. Because it focuses on product characteristics, *benefit segmentation is particularly suited for product, pricing, or service design decisions.* This in part accounts for its popularity, since it does in a real sense represent "the marketing concept in action"—finding out what consumers want and need and then making it available to them. *It is also appealing in a competitive sense,* as it offers opportunities to distinguish a brand from its competitors by offering a unique set of benefits its target segment of consumers most desire. (In some product categories, technology advances are allowing incredible possibilities for personalized benefit customization. For example, as we saw early in the chapter, the giant Japanese firm Matsushita is now selling its Panasonic brand bicycle on a custom-fitted basis. Using faxed specifications from the consumer's fitting at the store, computerized blueprints from the fax number, and robots to build much of the frame, the firm can deliver any of over 11 million versions within two weeks!)[27] If you would like to read more about benefit segmentation, you may wish to consult Note 28 for Chapter 4 at the back of the book.

Before leaving this topic, we should give special mention to **situational segmentation,** which is related to the traditional benefit segmentation approach and which introduces some further interesting ideas about consumer behavior and marketing strategy. As pointed out by Peter Dickson, consumer demand actually occurs for many products and services because of the situation in which a person finds himself or herself. Shotgun shells, for example, are needed for hunting, special dress clothes are needed for formal social occasions, and so forth.[29]

Situational segmentation: Grouping consumers according to the similarities of the situations they encounter.

🐳 *It Depends on the Situation ...*

Marketers can use the nature of consumers' situational forces in devising special alterations to a marketing mix. For example, researchers for Pizza Hut have discovered that most people in malls have no plans for eating, have no particular outlet in mind, and are generally impulsive in their dining decision in this setting. Thus Pizza Hut's "place" decisions reflect situational factors: its mall units' decor, menu, and promotions are all designed to encourage impulsive purchases from consumers passing by. Advertising is another marketing mix decision that can employ situational factors. For example, technology is now allowing Turner Broadcasting to team with marketers to employ custom-targeted television networks to deliver advertising and promotions to "captive consumers" who are waiting for flights (the Airport Channel), and for the 7 percent of Americans who visit the 8,500 McDonald's stores each day (what else, but McD-TV!). Finally, pricing is perhaps the most obvious of the mix areas to reflect situational opportunities, since consumers are sometimes willing to pay more because of special circumstances. Airlines, for example, have long used a form of situational segmentation

Pizza Hut's recent move into outlets placed in malls involved design, menu, and promotional decisions that reflect situational segmentation. Notice, for example, the extremely open access geared to encouraging impulse purchases from shoppers passing by.

to charge high prices to some travelers whose demand is seen to be inelastic (typically, businesspersons who must travel on short notice, often for only a day or two), and low prices to other travelers (typically those on leisure trips whose situations allow them to plan well in advance, stay over a Saturday night, accept no-refund terms, and so forth).

You should be aware that many thinkers regard situational forces as one of the most important of all factors in consumer behavior. We will be delving further into how situations work in Chapter 13. As our focus here is on segmentation, however, it is important to recognize that the nature of the situation may strongly influence those exact benefits a consumer is seeking at a particular point.

BEHAVIOR SEGMENTATION

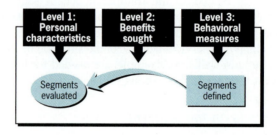

Our third basic approach for segmenting markets, **segmentation by behavior,** is emerging as the "hottest" option for segmentation developments in the 1990s. As illustrated, it begins at level 3 of the consumer system, where we *define* groups of consumers who behave similarly or who hold similar purchase predispositions. Notice that this beginning guarantees that the "systematic behavior" criterion for a market segment is met: our only remaining tasks are to *evaluate* whether the segment's consumers can be identified and the marketing mix efficiency criterion can also be met.

For example, let's assume we begin by grouping together all those consumers in our sample who buy mascara at much higher than average rates: we'll call this the "heavy-user" group. Notice that we know that this group systematically differs in its purchase behavior, but we don't yet know "who" these people are. Thus we need to evaluate the grouping to see which—if any—personal characteristics (demographics, life-styles, media exposure, etc.) actually distinguish heavy purchasers of mascara from the rest of the consumer market. Then, after eyeing this information, we can use it to put the lid on an efficient marketing program that will lash the competition! There are many detailed alternatives possible within behavioral measures segmentation. Let's look more closely at three types.

Attitudinal Segmentation

Attitudinal segmentation is a special form of behavioral segmentation that groups together consumers who hold similar beliefs, attitudes, or preferences within a particular product category. These groups are then evaluated for differences that will distinguish them on personal characteristic measures. In addition, because attitudes do not necessarily reflect actual purchasing behaviors, marketers often attempt to also evaluate these segments in terms of additional measures of how they behave in the marketplace. The following study helps us see how this can be done.

> **Attitudinal segmentation:** Grouping together consumers who hold similar beliefs, attitudes, or preferences about a product.

🐟 *Buying for Frying: Loyal Toward Oil?*

In one recent study of cooking oil, three attitudinal segments were isolated: (1) the *single-brand group,* those consumers who believe that one single brand of cooking oil (regardless of which brand) is the best on the market; (2) the *multibrand group,* those consumers who believe that there is a set of very good brands that they like; and (3) a *parity group,* those consumers who believe that all brands are about the same.

A brief review of some of the study's findings demonstrates how these groups were further evaluated for marketing purposes. For example, the single-brand segment was found to be older and have a lower level of education; the multibrand segment was found to be younger, likely to have attended college, and to live in the Midwest or West; while the parity group seemed to draw from various sectors and had few strong identifying characteristics. In examining other behavioral measures, the multibrand segment was found to use coupons more heavily, and to recall advertising at a higher rate, whereas the parity segment bought more heavily on price specials. At the brand level, Wesson (the market leader) sold well to all three segments, while Mazola, the third-ranking brand, was strongest in the single-brand segment but weak in the parity segment. While this summary is not sufficient to indicate a clear strategic direction, detailed analyses of the entire set of findings would suggest different advertising, promotion, and pricing strategies for different brands in this market.[30]

Heavy-User Segmentation

You may already be aware that many marketers operate by using the "80–20 Rule"— that "80 percent of my business comes from only 20 percent of my customers." While 80–20 is not always accurate, it is often true that the **heavy-user segment** provides a surprisingly high percentage of total product sales, and marketers do search to discover exactly who these heavy users are. This can be done either for an entire product class or for customers of a particular brand, as indicated in the example.

> **Heavy-user segmentation:** Grouping together those consumers who consume a product at rate much higher than the average.

🐟 *Campbell Loves Souper Consumers*

Campbell Soup Company studies its "core customers" carefully and values them highly. The firm has discovered that the top 5 percent of its consumers buy at least 102 cans of soup each year and thus add over $8 each to company earnings. Once the firm

3 customers for Campbell's coming up

Pretty soon now, they'll be good and ready for something good and hot.
Make it Campbell's Soup. Campbell's Tomato Soup, or Chicken Noodle,
or Vegetable. Nothing else takes the chill out of children quite so fast.
Nothing quite so warming tastes so good. And it heats in just 4 minutes.

Soup this good just has to be *Campbell's*

Campbell's Soup ads are designed to emotional bonding appeals for its heavy-user segment of
"core customers," who buy over 100 cans of soup each year.

has identified its heavy users, it further studies them to gauge their brand enthusiasm and emotions. As one executive explains, "We want to understand the brand's essence. These are the people who would put an 'I Love Campbell's' bumper sticker on their car. What makes them want to do that?" Advertising themes are then designed around the emotional dimensions that emerge from the research. (In one ad, for example, mom feeds her chilly little boy a bowl of hot soup and wraps him in a scarf, as the tagline reads "Once a Campbell kid, always a Campbell kid.") Thus the firm is working to appeal to its best customers, and to keep them happy with the relationship. The executive is convinced that emphasis on the core customer is the wave of the future in marketing; "'Value of the Customer' ... has applications to all products and services ... and there are going to be more case studies that show it ... it's going to be the way to do research."[31]

Direct-Response Segmentation

Direct-response segmentation is especially concerned with targeting promotions to consumers who are most likely to react favorably. During its early years, the segmentation literature contained many studies of which types of consumers are most likely to buy on price deals, to use coupons, to switch brands, and so forth. As we move into the 1990s, however, new developments in "database management" are shifting this interest into new areas.

🐚 *Getting to Know You...*

Some marketers are fortunate enough to have natural records that identify their customers by name and address and that keep track of all the purchasing behavior that customer does with the firm. If this is representative of that customer's total activity within the product class, this can become an extremely valuable **consumer database** for segmentation purposes. Airlines, for example, have begun to use their "frequent flyer" program records to identify where and how often their prime customers are flying. Similarly, financial service firms are also developing their database profiles. Imagine, for example, how much VISA and American Express can discover about each cardholder's interests and buying habits if they choose to study the receipts they receive in the course of their business!

Beyond the natural records of transactions, of course, marketers and research firms have the option of requesting consumers' participation in the development of their databases, and are doing so at a dramatically increasing rate. One research firm, for example, is now offering marketers use of its Select & Save database consisting of 25 million households, with 1,000 pieces of detailed information for each (including product usage, brand preferences, demographics, and psychographics). This database has been developed by sending out surveys seeking this information from consumers, in return for a gift, coupons, and the opportunity to receive future promotional offers from marketers who use the service. *Each coupon, however, is encoded to identify precisely which household has received it!* This means that a household's survey information can be used in conjunction with its behavioral responses to the promotions. Thus, over time, the database is updated to record exactly how likely each household is to redeem each coupon or to respond to each type of promotional offer. Since the survey also

Direct-response segmentation: Targeting promotions to specific consumers who can respond directly (e.g., by mail or telephone) with a purchase.

Consumer database: A computerized record of individual households, their addresses, and information concerning their interests or buying histories.

The development of coupons on which each household is identified by a unique code number means that marketers can use databases that target people who are likely to redeem particular types of coupons.

reports which competing brands that household uses, promotions can be targeted on this basis. For example, Folgers might decide to send a very-high-value coupon to heavy coffee-using households that currently purchase Maxwell House or Hills Brothers but send a smaller refund offer to its current users of Folgers. As a measure of the value of this type of consumer information in the huge, competitive American market, we might note that fees for this service are steep: the basic charge to participate is $250,000, with another $50,000 to license the database and additional charges for further services such as tracking household responses to offers.[32]

🐚 A Database Battle Burns in Cigarettes

In addition to several large market research firms, two leaders in the development of database marketing are R. J. Reynolds and Philip Morris, the cigarette giants that have been buying up giant food firms such as General Foods, Kraft, and Nabisco (each of which, interestingly, can also benefit mightily from developments of consumer databases). Within cigarettes alone, RJR reportedly spent $100 million to put together its own giant database of about half of the 55 million Americans who smoke. During the late 1980s Philip Morris reacted to RJR's successes in targeting heavy users of PM's brands and began to mount its own database. Its first effort, which was an insert card in *Time,* asked smokers to fill in some information about their current brands and then mail the card in return for two free packs of a mystery brand. Close to 2 million smokers returned these cards and were rewarded with two packs of Merits, together with a more detailed questionnaire that was entered into the database. RJR later responded with four-page print ads with exploding champagne corks, to call attention to its offer for a free Salem T-shirt: this attracted over 500,000 phone responses and more information for the ever-expanding consumer database. Much more activity than this has continued to go on in the years since and is spreading rapidly to other product classes.[33] As consumers, we may not easily recognize the amount of activity since we are not likely to see it, unless we happen to belong to a specific "response-prone" or "heavy-user" segment and a database marketer wishes to communicate directly with us!

🐚 *Database Drawbacks Sting Some*

Database marketing is clearly a technology of the future that holds great promise for the field. However, this is not a simple area in which to work, and we should be aware that progress has been uneven on several fronts:

1. *Consumer privacy.* Computer technology allows different information banks to be merged, telephone numbers to be monitored, and so forth. Thus it is possible for a considerable degree of information about a consumer's personal life (finances, health, memberships, preferences, etc.) to be sold and used by multiple marketers and solicitors. Public concern about invasion of privacy has emerged and is affecting marketing practices. For example, Lotus Development Corp. recently withdrew a new database it was just about to offer to small businesses after it received 30,000 calls and letters from consumers demanding to have their information deleted, and its executives decided that this was only the tip of an iceberg of future consumer resentment (the Lotus database contained information on 120 million consumers and was to be made available on compact disks for personal computers). Congress has been considering restrictive legislation for some time. (If you would like to read more about the issues and practices involved in the consumer privacy debate, you may wish to begin with the readings listed in Note 34 for Chapter 4 at the end of the book.)

2. *Investment and profitablity.* Database programs can become extremely expensive to develop, and there is no guarantee that they will be profitable. Several firms, including Citicorp and Quaker Oats, have recently reduced their large-scale programs.[35]

3. *Sophistication.* Finally, as one researcher put it, "It's a very statistical business..." Many marketing managers who are not comfortable with advanced statistical methods have experienced some difficulty adapting to this new area. Thus software developments to ease data analysis and presentation have also become extremely important. (If you would like to read some basic material about this business, you may wish to start with the short readings given in Note 36 for Chapter 4 at the end of the book.)[36]

Where Are We Headed?

At the start of our discussion of behavior segmentation, we mentioned that this was becoming the "hottest" area for development during the 1990s. Given our brief summary of the area, it should now be clear why this is the case. This approach is closely related to the explosion of spending on direct promotion in marketing, and it benefits from the increasing sophistication of computer technologies. Although there are some difficulties in using it, its great potentials virtually guarantee that this segmentation option will continue to develop and expand in the future.

Before ending this chapter, a brief comment may be in order. As we've seen, market segmentation is an extremely relevant and valuable concept. However, reading this chapter may have led to a sense that this is a more complex topic than it seemed to be in the introductory marketing course! If this was your reaction, keep in mind that when we dig into market segmentation, we are actually trying to come to grips with the immensity and diversity of the entire consumer marketplace. Despite its attractive appeal, this is not fundamentally an easy task, and all marketers have difficulty with it. However, the great size of the consumer marketplace means that only a small portion of it needs to be captured for a program to be successful. Thus it will pay marketing professionals to have insights about the segmentation options available to them.

As we leave this chapter, we bring the first section of the book to a close. We have now examined various perspectives and can see how segmentation acts as a bridging concept between the aggregate consumer market and the individuals who comprise that market. In Part II of the book we delve more deeply into consumers as individuals and examine why they behave in the ways they do.

■ SUMMARY

BACKGROUND ON SEGMENTATION

In this chapter we examined *market segmentation*, which provides a structured means of viewing the marketplace. The theoretical basis for market segmentation is the economic theory of *price discrimination*, which explains how a monopolist firm can maximize revenues by adapting its price to each customer's willingness to pay. In modern marketing, the concept of segmentation expands this consideration to include any of the marketing mix elements in addition to price alone. Our formal definition of market segmentation is a managerial strategy that adapts a firm's marketing mix to best fit the various consumer demand curves existing in a market.

Segmentation is a three-stage process: (1) identifying segments, (2) selecting target segments, and (3) creating marketing mixes for each target segment. Consumer research plays an especially key role in the first stage, identifying segments. Here there are also three criteria that a true market segment must meet: (1) *group identity*, (2) *systematic behavior*, and (3) *efficiency potential for the marketing mix*. In other words, our search is for a customer grouping that will behave differently from other groups and that will be responsive to an efficient marketing mix aimed at it.

THE START OF A SEGMENTATION STUDY: CLASSIFYING CUSTOMERS

Because an actual segmentation project can involve hundreds of possibilities, a basic framework is helpful for marketing managers and researchers. Our "three levels" framework in the chapter pointed out that every consumer can be classified in three basic ways: (1) according to his or her *personal characteristics*, (2) according to *benefits sought*, and (3) according to his or her *behavior* in actual purchasing. A segmentation study must start by defining groups on one of these levels and then evaluating them on one or both of the other levels.

USING THE LEVELS FOR SEGMENTATION

The remainder of the chapter examined the most popular segmentation approaches in marketing. Within *segmentation by personal characteristics*, we examined four popular approaches. *Demographic segmentation* defines segments on such bases as sex, ethnic group, age, income, and so on. *Media exposure segmentation* is a narrower approach: profiles of a medium's audience detail exactly which types of consumers can be reached by advertising in that medium. *Life-style/psychographic segmentation* is a much broader approach in which activities, interests, and opinions (AIOs) and various consumer psychological measures are used to produce distinct groupings. Our discussion examined the roots of this approach (also a detailed look at VALS 2, a major life-styles/psychographic system, is provided in Appendix 4A). *Geographic segmentation* is the fourth popular type of segmentation by personal characteristics; we saw how this can be done either by *regions,* or by *geodemographic methods* (zip clustering), in which distinct marketing mixes are targeted to similar types of neighborhoods.

Our second major option is *segmentation by benefits sought.* Here the marketer begins by defining groups who are seeking similar mixes of benefits and then evaluates these groups to see if they differ on personal characteristics and purchase behaviors. A subset of this category involves *situational segmentation*, in which consumers desire different sets of benefits depending on their situations at the time. Our third major approach is termed *segmentation by behavior.* Here the chapter examined *attitudinal segmentation*, segmenting by *heavy users*, and *direct-response segmentation*. In each of these cases, consumers are first grouped according to their similarity in attitudes, usage rates, or responsiveness to promotions; then the segments are evaluated according to what personal characteristics they may have in common. These approaches reflect recent developments in creating massive *consumer databases* and using them for direct consumer promotions.

This chapter closes our first section of the book. Given the nature of segmentation, it acts as a natural bridge between the aggregate consumer marketplace (Chapter 3) and the individual level of consumer behavior. In Part II, beginning with Chapter 5, we will be examining the interesting world of individual consumer behavior.

■ KEY TERMS

price discrimination	media exposure segmentation	PRIZM system
market segmentation	life-style/psychographic segmentation	benefit segmentation
group identity	life-styles	situational segmentation
systematic behaviors	AIOs	segmentation by behavior
efficiency potential	psychographics	attitudinal segmentation
personal characteristics	geographic segmentation	heavy-user segmentation
benefits sought	regional segmentation	direct-response segmentation
behavior	geodemographic segmentation	consumer database
demographic segmentation	store-specific segmentation	

■ APPENDIX 4 TERMS

VALS-2	status-oriented consumers	believers	experiencers
resources	action-oriented consumers	achievers	makers
self-orientation	actualizers	strivers	strugglers
principle-oriented consumers	fulfilleds		

■ REVIEW QUESTIONS AND EXPERIENTIAL EXERCISES

[E = **Application extension or experiential exercise**]

1. What are the three criteria or requirements for a true market segment? Explain, using two different examples, why marketers would wish to have both the marketing mix efficiency and systematic behavior criteria satisfied before targeting a particular segment.

2. For three of the products listed, provide descriptions of yourself using the chapter's levels of consumer classification (for each of the three levels, list at least three measures that accurately describe you).

   a. Automobiles   d. Soft drinks
   b. Cereal   e. Fast-food outlets
   c. Music   f. Stock brokerages

3. Choose two of the products or services listed here, and suggest three or four possible types of benefit segments or situations segments you would expect to find in the consumer market.

   a. Automobiles   d. Soft drinks
   b. Cereal   e. Fast-food outlets
   c. Music   f. Stock brokerages

4. [E] Using the chapter notes located at the back of this book, read several classic articles to gain further understanding of market segmentation. Prepare a brief report on your findings. Good options include

   a. Beginnings (Note 3)
   b. Life-styles (Note 14)
   c. Psychographics (Notes 16, 20)
   d. Benefit segmentation (Notes 26, 28)

5. [E] The story at the opening of the chapter reported General Motors' new segmentation strategy. Gather several examples of print ads for each of the GM cars. Also, if possible, monitor television ads for these same cars. In each case, does it appear that this strategy is still being followed? Does it appear that the strategy is working?

6. [E] The story at the opening of the chapter reported General Motors' new segmentation strategy. Use the business periodicals references of your library to locate recent articles on the GM brands. What is currently happening with them? Does this segmentation strategy seem viable?

7. [E] Select two of the personal characteristics bases for market segmentation (age, ethnic background, sex, income, and so forth). Find magazines that are targeted to at least two different groups within each base (e.g., blacks, Hispanics, teens, senior citizens). Analyze the ads appearing in each publication as to the products

and services represented, and the appeals used. Select several ads as representative and include them with a brief report on your findings.

8. [E] Interview a sales representative or marketing manager for an advertising medium concerning the measures of consumers they use to sell their service. Write a brief report on your findings.

9. [E] Interview a salesperson at an auto dealership regarding any differences seen between male and female car buyers. Probe for differences in (a) how the consumers buy and (b) how the salespersons sell. Ask about any ads directed toward females. Does a male-female segmentation scheme make sense here, or is a more detailed breakdown necessary? Write a brief report on your findings.

10. [E] Assume you are a marketing planner for Safeway, Kroger, or another large supermarket chain. Choose four of the "zip cluster" segments from Exhibit 4-1. For each, suggest three specific products that you would consider featuring in special promotions for testing in selected supermarkets in this cluster type. Explain your reasoning.

11. [E] Read carefully the illustrated "zip cluster" segments in Exhibit 4-1; then consider the various types of neighborhoods in your town. Select two supermarkets from different zip codes that you believe are certain to represent distinct types of neighborhood clusters. Interview a store manager in each market concerning the special products, layouts, and policies they use to especially appeal to their customer segment. Write a brief report detailing your findings.

12. [E] Read the book, *The Clustering of America*, by Michael Weiss (Harper & Row, 1988). Prepare a brief written report extending the text's coverage of the PRIZM system and how it is used by members. Be prepared to present this to the class as well.

13. [E] Investigate your library's reference section to discover recent readings on consumer databases used for promotions and segmentation. Write a brief report on your findings.

14. [E] Investigate your library's reference section to discover recent developments on segmentation approaches of interest to you based on the reports in this chapter. Write a brief report on your findings.

15. [E] The book's discussion of database marketing mentioned that consumer privacy has become a hot public issue. Using either the readings given in Note 34 or your library's reference section, read more about what has been happening in this area. Prepare a brief report on your findings, including your opinion about what, if anything, should be done.

■ SUGGESTED READING

■ The topic of market segmentation is so integral to marketing that many good reading sources are available. The Notes for this chapter are thus very useful for locating good readings on particular topics. For general conceptual insights, Notes 3, 14, 16, 20, 26, and 28 contain references to the classic works on this topic. The article that brought market segmentation into the field is Wendell R. Smith, "Product Differentiation and Market Segmentation as Alternative Marketing Strategies,"

Journal of Marketing (July 1956), pp. 3–8. An excellent book that reports how marketers use these ideas is Rebecca Piirto, *Beyond Mind Games: The Marketing Power of Psychographics*. Ithaca, N.Y.: American Demographics Books, 1991. Also, consumer databases are promising to change the future of segmentation strategy and tactics: good readings on this topic are given in Notes 32 and 33.

Appendix 4A

VALS-2: A NATIONAL SEGMENTATION APPROACH

To understand consumer segmentation in the U. S. market better, we can take a look at an example of one large effort—the VALS (values and life-styles) program for segmenting the consumer market. As indicated by its name, this program creates its segments at level 1 of our system: segmentation by personal characteristics. VALS was created by SRI International, a management consulting firm in California, and has been used by hundreds of marketers and advertising agencies, sometimes with success and sometimes not. As we noted in the chapter, it has recently been updated and released in a new version called VALS-2.[37]

The essence of the VALS-2 program is a classification scheme that assigns each adult American to one of eight VALS-2 segments. These segments are determined by both the values and the life-styles of the people in them ("values" here refers to a wide array of an individual's beliefs, aspirations, prejudices, etc.). Thus VALS represents a linkage between the personality orientation of psychographics and the activities orientation of life-style research.

The Essentials of VALS-2

As the decade of the 1980s moved along, it became apparent to SRI management that the original VALS system for segmentation, launched in 1978, would need to be revised and updated. Not only were Americans' life-styles shifting, but marketing researchers were questioning some elements of both the usefulness and the validity of the original VALS system. The planners of VALS-2 thus shifted their emphasis. Readers familiar with the original system will note that VALS-2 places somewhat less emphasis on values and more emphasis on the psychological underpinnings of behavior, influenced by consumer resources. They will also note that the segments are approximately equal in size (thus improving marketing mix efficiency potentials) and that they have been created to ensure that the consumer behaviors actually differ among the groups. In some sense, then, the

new VALS-2 system is less theoretical and more pragmatic in nature. Two national surveys, each with over 2,200 consumers, were used in developing the VALS-2 system. (If you would like to read more about the difficulties some marketers had with the original system, you may wish to consult the works cited in Note 38 for Chapter 4 at the end of this book.)

The two key dimensions underlying VALS-2 are resources and self-orientation. **Resources,** according to VALS-2, refers to the full range of capacities (material, physical, psychological, etc.) consumers have to draw upon. It encompasses education, income, self-confidence, health, and so on and can range from minimal to abundant. With respect to consumer behavior, we would expect that persons with more abundant resources would be able to undertake more purchasing behavior for most product classes. **Self-orientation,** meanwhile, refers to each person's social self-image and the patterns of attitudes and activities that a person undertakes to help reinforce or act out that image. According to VALS, there are three major patterns of self-orientation: **principle-oriented consumers** are guided in their choices by their beliefs, rather than by feelings or desire for approval; **status-oriented consumers** are heavily influenced by the actions, approval, and opinions of others; and **action-oriented consumers** are guided by a desire for social or physical activity, variety, and risk taking. Given such differences in orientations, we would expect consumers in each grouping to be living different types of consumer life-styles. Let's examine this further.

VALS-2: Who Is Who?

Figure 4A-1 shows the network of eight segments defined by VALS-2. Notice that low resources are represented at the bottom, while high resources are at the top. Similarly, each of the three self-orientations occupies one column. Thus the network locations do have meaning: segments shown next to each other have some elements in common and are "closer" than are segments shown farther apart. Brief descriptions of each of the segments follow.

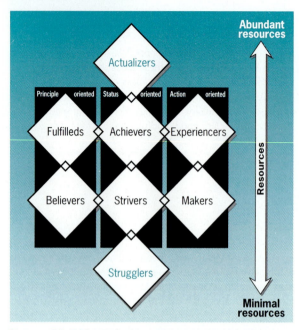

FIGURE 4A-1 The Eight Consumer Segments of VALS-2

Actualizers (8 percent of the population) are successful, sophisticated people with high self-esteem and abundant resources. Actualizers are among the established and emerging leaders in business and government. They have a wide range of interests, are concerned with social issues, and are open to change. Their possessions and recreation reflect a cultivated taste for the finer things in life.

Fulfilleds (11 percent of the population) are people with high levels of resources and who are "principle oriented" (that is, they seek to make their behavior consistent with their views of how the world should be). Fulfilleds are mature people who value order, knowledge, and responsibility. They are well informed about world events. Content with their station in life, their leisure activities tend to center on their homes. They are open-minded about new ideas and social change. Fulfilleds are practical consumers; they look for value and durability in the products they buy.

Believers (16 percent of the population) are the largest segment—one of every six adults belongs to this group. Believers are also principle oriented, but have more modest levels of resources. They are conservative people who hold strong beliefs based on traditional codes. Among the oldest of the segments, they follow established routines, organized around their homes, families, and the social or religious organizations to which they belong. As consumers, believers favor American products and established brand names.

Achievers (13 percent of the population) are the "status-oriented" consumers who have high levels of resources. Achievers are successful career people who feel in control of their lives.

They value structure and stability over risk and self-discovery. Work provides them a sense of duty, material rewards, and prestige. Their social lives are structured around family, church, and business. Image is important to them. As consumers, they favor established products that demonstrate their success.

Strivers (13 percent of the population) are also status-oriented people, but with more modest levels of resources. They are striving to find a secure place in life and are deeply concerned about the opinions and approval of others. Money defines success for strivers, who don't have enough of it, and who sometimes feel that life has given them a raw deal. Strivers are easily bored and can be impulsive. As consumers, many strivers seek to be stylish and emulate those who own impressive possessions.

Experiencers (12 percent of the population) are "action-oriented" people with high levels of resources. Experiencers are the youngest segment and are enthusiastic and impulsive. They seek variety and excitement and are still in the process of forming life values and patterns of behavior. They tend to be politically uncommitted. Experiencers are avid consumers and spend much of their income on clothing, fast food, music, movies, and videos.

Makers (13 percent of the population) are also action-oriented people, but with more modest levels of resources. Makers are practical people who value self-sufficiency. They live within a traditional context of family, practical work, and physical recreation: they have little interest in what lies outside this context. As consumers, makers are unimpressed by material possessions, but do value those that offer practical purposes to assist in daily family life, work, and recreation.

Strugglers (14 percent of the population) are people whose lives are dominated by their very low levels of resources. This is the oldest segment, with the lowest incomes, educations, and work skills. Often concerned about their health, and without strong social bonds, strugglers tend to be focused on meeting the needs of the present. Their chief concerns are for security and safety. As consumers, they are cautious. They represent a very modest market for most products and services but are loyal to favorite brands.

Do VALS-2 Segments Differ in Consumer Behavior?

The short answer to this question is, "Yes, very strongly!" Some illustrative differences are shown in Table 4A-1 and Figure 4A-2. You may find them to be interesting indications of the reality of consumer segmentation in the marketplace. Let's take a closer look at Table 4A-1. The numbers represent indices, in which each segment is compared to the national average for all segments (thus 1.6 indicates 60 percent higher than average, while 0.9 indicates 10 percent lower than average). If we examine Table 4A-1 by each segment, we can see that the product ownership, activities, and media exposure seem to follow the descriptions in our earlier figures and discussion. If

Table 4A-1 VALS-2 Segments and Consumer Behavior (National Average Rate = 1.0)

Segment	Product Ownership				Activities			Media		
	Dish-washer	Fishing Rod & Reel	Color TV	Pickup Truck	Do Wood-working	Do Kids' Activities	Politically Active	Reader's Digest	Watch "Dallas"	Watch "Moonlighting"
Actualizers	1.6[a]	0.9	1.1	0.7	1.2	1.5	3.1	0.6	0.3	0.5
Fulfilleds	1.4	0.9	1.1	1.0	1.0	1.3	1.4	1.4	0.9	0.7
Achievers	1.4	0.9	1.1	1.0	0.6	1.4	0.8	0.9	1.0	1.1
Experiencers	0.5	1.1	0.9	0.9	1.0	0.9	0.8	0.6	0.5	1.4
Believers	1.2	1.1	1.1	1.1	1.1	0.6	1.1	1.5	1.5	0.8
Strivers	0.9	0.8	1.0	1.0	0.5	1.1	0.6	0.6	1.0	1.3
Makers	0.8	1.4	1.0	1.5	2.0	1.2	0.6	0.9	0.7	1.3
Strugglers	0.4	0.9	0.9	0.5	0.5	0.4	0.5	1.3	1.8	0.7

[a]To be read: "Actualizers own dishwashers at a much higher rate than the national average (1.6 or 60% higher than the average). Fulfilleds (1.4), Achievers (1.4), and Believers (1.2) also have higher than average ownership of this appliance. Each of the other segments has a lower than average rate of ownership."

SOURCE: SRI International, Menlo Park, CA. Used with permission.

Actualizers
Enjoy the "finer things"
Receptive to new products,
technologies, distribution
Skeptical of advertising
Frequent readers of a wide
variety of publications
Light TV viewers

Fulfilleds
Little interest in image
or prestige
Above-average consumers of
products for the home
Like educational and public
affairs programming
Read widely
and often

Achievers
Attracted to premium
products
Prime target for variety of
products
Average TV watchers
Read business, news,
and self-help
publications

Experiencers
Follow fashion and fads
Spend much of disposable
income on socializing
Buy on impulse
Attend to advertising
Listen to rock music

Believers
Buy American
Slow to change habits
Look for bargains
Watch TV more than average
Read retirement,
home and garden,
and general interest
magazines

Strivers
Image conscious
Limited discretionary income,
but carry credit balances
Spend on clothing and
personal care products
Prefer TV to reading

Makers
Shop for comfort,
durability, value
Unimpressed by luxuries
Buy the basics
Listen to the radio
Read auto, home mechanics,
fishing, outdoors
magazines

Strugglers
Brand loyal
Use coupons and watch
for sales
Trust advertising
Watch TV often
Read tabloids and
women's magazines

FIGURE 4A-2 Consumer Characteristics of the VALS-2 Segments
SOURCE: From SRI International, Menlo Park, CA. Used by permission.

How Managers Use Segmentation: A "Case" Analysis for Iron City Beer

Stage of Process	What Pittsburgh Brewing Company Did
I. Identifying segments	A. Purchased VALS-2 data (see Appendix 4A description)
II. Selecting particular segment to target	A. (Data analysis) Discovered that current buyers of Iron City were primarily "Makers" and "Believers." In local market, those segments are growing older and consuming less beer.
	B. (Data analysis) Discovered that heavier beer drinkers who were not buying Iron City were primarily "Strivers" and "Experiencers." These two segments are younger, and they consume the most beer.
	C. (Decision) Attempt to retain Makers and Believers, but increase appeal to Strivers and Experiencers.
III. Creating targeted marketing mix	A. (Decision) Rely on new ad campaign to create an image for Iron City that would connect with current users, but *also* reposition the brand in the minds of Strivers and Experiencers.
	B. (Research) Studies were run to learn precisely about ad language and symbols that would appeal to the new segments' interests and self-identities (focus groups, word sorts, projective studies).
	C. (Ad Decision) Ads were designed to switch shots between "Old Pittsburgh" (hard work and determination—civic pride) with "New Pittsburgh" (moving forward and working hard at having fun). Theme music, "Working in a Coal Mine" with new lyrics "Working on a Cold Iron."
	D. (Execution) Campaign began on radio and TV programs appealing to Experiencers and Strivers.
	E. (Results) Early research tracking revealed sales of Iron City were up 26 percent in first month, due primarily to new sales to Strivers.

we examine the table by columns, we can begin to get a picture of which segments present strong and weak prospects for marketing action. Notice that the dishwasher market appears highly segmented, for example. Fishing rods and pickup trucks, meanwhile, have some segmentation in them, with the Makers segment appearing particularly strong. Color televisions, on the other hand, appear not to be very segmented, at least in terms of product ownership (for future purchases, however, further data concerning the number of sets owned, ages of current sets, and styles and price ranges would need to be consulted as well).

With respect to activities, this type of data can be helpful in deciding on useful appeals geared to different segments. For example, notice that Actualizers tend to undertake woodworking activities at higher than normal rates, while Achievers are quite low on this activity. The data on media exposure, moreover, indicate directly how various segments might best be reached. Notice, for example, that *Reader's Digest* has specific appeals to certain groups, as did the television shows "Dallas" and "Moonlighting."

Doing Segmentation: A "Case" Example

At this point all the pieces are in place for actually undertaking a segmentation project. How exactly would a marketing manager proceed? Exhibit 4A-1 outlines how Pittsburgh Brewing Company and its advertising agency (Della Femina, McNamee WCRS, Inc.) recently worked to reverse a sales de-

cline in their flagship brand, Iron City beer, that has long been a major seller in the western Pennsylvania market.[39] Notice that their actions follow the three-stage process for market segmentation we outlined in Figure 4-3. *Stage 1* involves identifying or defining the market segments with which we will work. In this case, the market research director had been working with the VALS system for many years, and chose to adopt these as the primary segments. Thus the project would follow the pattern we discussed under "segmentation by personal characteristics."

Once the segments have been chosen, *stage 2* involves evaluating them to select the precise segments we wish to target with our new marketing mixes. Recall that segmentation by personal characteristics requires that this evaluation involve searching for differences in consumers' attitudes and purchase behaviors. In the Iron City case, the firm was able to obtain this type of purchase data from the Simmons research organization, which cooperates with the VALS program in identifying each consumer in their sample according to both their VALS-2 type and their brand purchase behavior. Statistical analysis of these data showed that the Iron City brand was relying heavily on Makers and Believers for its support, but this segment was growing older (in the local market) and was reducing its consumption levels. The highest volume of beer consumption, meanwhile, was by the Experiencer and Striver segments, but these younger consumers were drinking other brands, not Iron City. The firm then selected these two segments as its primary targets for a new marketing mix.

"Old Pittsburgh": a steel mill along the Monongahela River.

"New Pittsburgh": a high-tech lab.

Stage 3 involves the creation and implementation of the new, targeted marketing mix. For Iron City, management decided that advertising would be used to create a new image for the brand—one that would have to *retain the loyal users from the Makers and Believers segments, but also gain new users from the Strivers and Experiencers segments.* As this could be a risky strategy, further consumer research was used to fine-tune the planning. This involved several types of studies (such as focus groups and projective techniques, which we will discuss in a subsequent chapter) as well as reliance on background information from the VALS-2 suppliers about what kinds of language and appeals work best with each segment type. The emphasis was on themes that would appeal to the self-identities of the new segments (such as status for the Strivers or excitement for the Experiencers), but with language and symbols that would not offend the Makers and Believers. Thus, to accomplish this balancing act, the resulting campaign featured alternating pictures of the "Old Pittsburgh" and the "New Pittsburgh," with pictures of sports, parties, and having fun. In a clever bow to the industrialized past of the region, the hard-driving song "Working in a Coal Mine" was used, with the lyrics changed to "Working on a Cold Iron." The ads were placed on radio and TV programs for which the targeted segments made up a heavy portion of the audience (again, these data are available through the VALS-2 program and for other segmentation bases as well, and help to make the marketing mix more efficient).

What were the results? At the time of this writing, the campaign had been running for only one month, but sales had increased by 26 percent! Initial purchasing research indicated that most of this jump had come from increased purchasing among the Striver segment, while reactions from Experiencers weren't clear yet.

Part II

THE CONSUMER AS AN INDIVIDUAL

IN THIS part of the book—Chapters 5–11—we will view the consumer as an individual. Here we will examine the basic "building blocks" of consumer behavior, the internal processes that guide us in our actions as consumers. In Chapters 5 and 6, Consumer Motivation (I) and (II), respectively, we tackle the question of *why* consumers behave as they do and how marketers can use this understanding to improve strategies. In Chapter 7, Consumer Information Processing, we investigate how understanding consumers' thoughts help us to better understand their behavior. In Chapters 8 and 9, Consumer Perception (I) and (II), respectively, we'll learn about the fascinating area of consumer perception, or how the external world gets translated into the world as we see it. Chapter 10, Consumer Learning, then describes how our experiences shape our behaviors as consumers. In our final chapter of this part of the book, Chapter 11, Consumer Attitudes, we introduce the important roles that consumer attitudes play in guiding our behavior in the future.

As a set, these topics provide us with a powerful base of knowledge. Also as we'll see, each of these topics is interesting and holds significant implications for us as marketing managers and as consumers. So, dig in and enjoy!

5

CONSUMER MOTIVATION (I)
Essentials

WHY, WHY, WHY?

Perhaps the most basic question we can ask about consumer behavior is: "Why do consumers do what they do?" One marketing consultant explains:

> If we believe our overall values drive our behavior, then we should be concentrating on [the important, underlying motives that drive consumers to make product or service choices] rather than simply product attributes.[1]

Another leading consumer consultant provides a similar view:

> The thing to know is "Why." We want to know how to influence behavior, so we must dig below the surface.[2]

Finally, Dr. Ernest Dichter, a famous but controversial Freudian motivation researcher in marketing, relates what happened when a book, *The Hidden Persuaders*, charged that he was helping marketers learn how to discover consumers' true motives, so that they could manipulate consumers' behaviors:

> It was a bombshell... and I was the big villain. So I got calls [from businesspeople] from foreign countries and all over the United States. And the people said, "What you're doing is terrible! How much does it cost?"[3]

The marketing concept says that marketers should try to create products and services that best meet the wants and needs of consumers. As indicated in the opening quotes, this means that marketers must find out what needs consumers have and what

Table 5-1 Key Characteristics of Consumer Motivation

(M)	Consumer motivation has two *major components: energy* and *direction.*
(O)	Consumers' motives are both *overt* and *hidden* and are *multiple.*
(T)	Consumers are driven by *tension reduction.*
(I)	Consumers are motivated by both *internal* and *external forces.*
(V)	Consumer motives have *valence*—they can be positive or negative.
(A)	Consumers are motivated to *achieve goals.*
(T)	Consumers have a *thirst for variety.*
(I)	Consumers' motivations reflect *individual differences.*
(O)	Consumers desire *order* in the world.
(N)	Consumers are guided by the *need hierarchy.*

motivates them to buy. The field of **motivation** seeks to explain *why* behavior occurs. The term "motivation" itself is derived from the Latin verb *movere,* meaning "to move." Basically, then, motivation refers to *the processes that move a person to behave in certain ways.* Motivation deals with how behavior gets started, is energized, is sustained, is directed, and is stopped.[4] Motivation is the basis for all consumer activities.

As consumer motivations tend to be specific to different products and situations, it is important for marketing managers to have a basic foundation of knowledge to draw from when faced with a new situation. In this chapter we will concentrate on an easily remembered framework consisting of 10 of the most significant concepts in the field of human motivation. Our framework is organized as a set of 10 statements in Table 5-1. Notice that a key word or phrase in each statement is in italics— the beginning letters combine to form the acronym MOTIVATION. The separate points of the MOTIVATION framework offer different basic insights into consumer motivations.

Motivation: The processes that move a person to behave in certain ways: how behavior gets started and is energized, sustained, directed, and stopped.

■ KEY CHARACTERISTICS OF CONSUMER MOTIVATION

(M) MAJOR COMPONENTS OF CONSUMER MOTIVATION

There are two major components of motivation: *energy* and *direction.* Energy refers to the fact that *all* behavior—thinking, moving, looking, and so on—requires us to expend an internal supply of energy. Direction, on the other hand, is needed to channel our inner energies into productive, attractive behaviors and to allow us to behave efficiently. All consumer behaviors have both energy and direction as components.

Insights from the Energy Component

Researchers who study the energy dimension often use *physiological measures* of the body's arousal—consumers' pulse rates, blood pressures, brain waves, and skin chemistries can all offer clues to the energy dimension. Within consumer research, these measures are used to gauge consumers' reactions to advertising, brand names, and other marketing appeals.[5]

With any consumer decision process, *intensity,* or the strength of the motivation itself, is an extremely important issue. As consumers, we must constantly deal with questions such as "At how many stores should I shop before buying?" "Is it worth the effort to read the warranty or the instructions?" and so forth. When consumers' intensity is low, marketers face problems in gaining attention for their products and promotions. This **consumer inertia** makes it difficult to stimulate consumers to act—even when the consumers themselves would agree that the action is in their best interests.

Consumer inertia:
The tendency for consumers to continue in the same behavioral mode over time: makes it difficult for marketers to induce changes in behavior.

🐋 *Classic Cases of Consumer Inertia*

Two classic cases of consumer inertia involved recalls of dangerous products. The first million Ford Pintos sold in the United States were later discovered to have defective fuel systems that exposed their passengers to the risk that a rear-end collision could result in a fiery explosion that would kill the driver and occupants. About the same time as this finding by the National Highway Traffic Safety Administration, the same agency also found that over 7.5 million Firestone 500 tires were susceptible to blowouts and other failures that could result in deaths to riders in cars with these tires. Product recalls were ordered in both cases: Pinto owners could have their autos modified free of charge by taking them to a Ford dealer, and Firestone owners could obtain free replacement tires at their dealers. Two years later, despite extensive efforts at reaching and informing consumers with these products, 350,000 consumers continued to drive unmodified Pintos, and over 3.5 million potentially dangerous tires had yet to be returned.[6]

In our next chapter we will return to issues related to the energy component when we investigate recent findings on consumer emotion and consumers' low involvement.

The Direction Component

The direction component refers to exactly *which* behavior is chosen from all those possible, and *why.* In general, motivation theory asserts that the direction taken in a behavior is in large part determined by the particular purposes we are trying to achieve with that behavior (this is technically termed **purposive behavior**). If consumer behavior is purposive, it should be possible to understand *why* a particular direction was chosen. For example, the concept of **primary motives** involves the purposes behind consumers' decisions to use or not to use entire classes of products. Why do some people drink alcoholic beverages, for example, while others do not? **Selective motives,** on the other hand, refer to consumers' decisions as to exactly which stores, brands, and model features will be used or purchased. Why would a patron order a Corona in the bar rather than a Miller?

The directional component thus underlies all consumer decisions to (1) purchase a product at all and (2) choose a particular alternative from that product class. These are, of course, the essential underpinnings of consumer demand in the marketplace and are of crucial importance to the marketing field. The better that marketers are able to understand the purposes being served through consumption, the better they are able to attract consumer patronage and serve consumers' interests well. As consumers, moreover, the better we are able to identify our own goals, the better we should be able to make consumer decisions in our own self-interest.

(0) OVERT, HIDDEN, AND MULTIPLE MOTIVES

Our framework's second statement maintains an emphasis on purposive behavior by turning our attention to **motives.** *A motive is a concept used by researchers to explain the reasons for behavior.* Researchers cannot observe a person's motives, only his or her behavior—from that behavior, they must try to *infer* the exact motives that caused it. One definition of a motive is "a strong and persistent internal stimulus around which behavior is organized."[7] The final statement of our framework, pertaining to the need hierarchy, will address the nature of motives in considerable detail. At this stage, we are only concerned with two basic points—that consumers have **multiple motives** and that some of these motives are **overt** (that is, as consumers we are well aware of these reasons behind our behavior) while others are **hidden** in the minds of consumers (that is, consumers are themselves not aware of what these motives are).

Motive: A concept used by researchers to explain the reasons for behavior.

Multiple Motives, Multiple Acts

It is clear that each of us has many motives that guide our behaviors on a daily basis. Unfortunately, however, marketers have found that the detailed study of motives is quite difficult. Part of this difficulty is due to the fact that *any particular motive can usually be satisfied by several different types of behaviors.* For example, let's assume that Bob Reston has been studying hard and is motivated to break from his work to relax. Notice that there are many options available for this purpose——he could go to a movie, play racquetball, read a novel, and so on. It is also true that *different motives might lead to the same behavior.* For example, suppose we see Bob in a restaurant. He might be there because of a hunger motive, but he might also be there because he wanted to take a break from his studies, he wanted to meet new people, and so forth. Also, of course, several of these *motives might act in combination* to create this behavior.

Simply observing consumer behavior, therefore, will not be sufficient to detect the motives that are at work. Marketers must instead try to measure the motives that are operating with respect to particular purchases. Notice how this was done in a study on shopping:

🐳 *Why Do People Shop?*

It is clear that we shop to make purchases. What else, though, is involved? One interesting study used in-depth interviews with consumers to identify some typical motivations.[8] Among the findings:

- *Role playing.* Shopping is sometimes important to a person's role (e.g., a "provider" feels that it is expected, important, and gratifying to shop for food for the household).
- *Diversion.* Shopping can offer a break from routine and is a form of recreation.
- *Learning.* Shopping allows us to learn about new products and new trends.
- *Exercise and sensory stimulation.* Shopping provides a form of physical exercise, as well as lights, colors, scents, sounds, and so forth, much of which can be pleasant.

- *Peer group attraction.* Shopping can involve affiliating with an important reference group, such as the teen "in group" at the mall.
- *Status and authority.* Some shoppers appreciate the sense of power and attention that flows from being "waited on" by store personnel.
- *Pleasure from bargain hunting or negotiating.* Some shoppers enjoy an "achievement" dimension in their shopping, through searching for "best buys" or attempting to negotiate lower prices with salespersons.

Even with this partial list, we can see that the topic of consumer motivation will encompass a broad range of issues and that some of these will be subtle.

Hidden Motives and the Unconscious Mind

Consciousness levels: A three-part framework for motivation: motives exist at the conscious level, the preconscious level, and the unconscious level.

Until this point, we have assumed that all consumer behavior stems from conscious decisions. When attempting to understand motives, however, researchers have found that much of a person's actions are determined by influences of which he or she is, at the time, completely unaware. Thus the person is *unable* to report some of the true motives for a particular behavior, since he or she is truly not conscious of them. Figure 5-1 shows how many researchers view these different **levels of consciousness,** and why they liken motivation research in marketing to a "fishing expedition." Notice that, at any point in time, a consumer will only be aware of those motivations at level 1, the **conscious level.** Those motives at level 2—the **preconscious level**—are not currently known, but they can be brought to consciousness if they can be located and brought forth. The motives that exist at the **unconscious level,** however, are buried deep beneath the water itself and cannot be expected to emerge at all under the circumstances in which consumer research is conducted, but instead is the area reserved for some specially trained psychologists and psychiatrists. To understand this point better, you may wish to review Exhibit 5-1, which briefly discusses the theories of Sigmund Freud.

Hidden Motives and Marketing Research

Thus we now know consumers are **unaware** of many of their motivations, but that some of these motivations can be brought out if the "fishing" is skillfully done by researchers trained to undertake this type of work. This is the province of

Levels of Consciousness	Similar to:	Motive Status/Consumer Is:
1. Conscious level	Air: Above the surface	Consciously aware of
2. Preconscious level	Water: Beneath the surface	Not consciously aware of, but can be brought to the surface if can be located
3. Unconscious level	Underground: Beneath the water	Deeply embedded/not available to be brought to consciousness

FIGURE 5-1 A Pond Analogy to Depict Levels of Consciousness. Notice that motives exist at all three levels, though consumers are normally aware of only those at level I.

EXHIBIT 5-1

Freud's Psychoanalytic Theory

Sigmund Freud (pronounced "Froyd") worked in Vienna, Austria, during the late 1800s and early 1900s. His controversial theories were stimulated by questions such as, "What do dreams mean?" and "How does hypnosis work?" From these beginnings, Freud evolved a major **theory of unconscious motivation.** This theory is built around three basic systems: the id, the ego, and the superego.

Freud believed that the **id** is the most basic system and is intimately related to a person's physiological system. The id is entirely unconscious, but very powerful. It is the source of our psychic energy behind all behavior. The psychic energy itself is termed **libido** and operates according to the **pleasure principle** (*libido* means "lust" in Latin). Based upon the instincts with which we are born, the id is *entirely geared toward achieving pleasure and avoiding pain.* It is very powerful and demands immediate gratification. Unlike our conscious processes, the id is nonrational and not logical. It is totally internal and has no knowledge of objective reality. The behavior of a newborn baby indicates the id's workings, since the other systems have not yet developed.

The **ego** is the system that is in contact with the external world and that develops to take charge of the person's actual behavior. The ego is governed by the **reality principle**—it seeks to achieve the pleasurable demands of the id in as realistic a way

Sigmund Freud.

as possible. Since many of the id's demands are quite unrealistic, the ego must develop ways to postpone them, deflect them, or substitute feasible gratifications to satisfy the id's cravings. Some of the ego's work goes on at the unconscious level (where it relates to the id) and some at the conscious level (where it relates to the reality of the world). As a child matures, growth stages in the ego can be identified.

The **superego** is the last of the three structures to develop. It has two functions— to *reward* "good" behavior and to *punish* unacceptable actions by creating guilt. Thus the superego represents a person's "conscience" and works *against* the unacceptable impulses of the id (rather than seeking to manage them, as does the ego). The superego is also primarily unconscious: it represents ideal rather than real behavior and strives for perfection rather than pleasure.

Within Freud's theory, the ways these three systems develop in the child are crucial to the different "personalities" that people develop as they become adults. Basically, as the ego develops within each person, it creates systematic ways of dealing with the incredibly strong and conflicting demands coming from the id and the superego. These systematic behaviors form the bases for individual personality traits. Since Freud's emphasis was on the power of the sexual drive from the id, his personality theory reflects a decidedly sexual orientation (in much of his psychiatric work he was dealing with female patients with sexual disorders). Although his theories are extremely controversial, much of the work in psychiatry and clinical psychology has developed directly from his original thinking.

Qualitative research: The use of nonstatistical methods that encourage consumers to reveal their thoughts, feelings, and motivations.

qualitative research. Qualitative research—as opposed to quantitative research—uses nonstatistical, unstructured research methods in which consumers are enticed to reveal what they can about their innermost thoughts and feelings. These approaches are controversial, since they rely heavily on subjective interpretations by each individual researcher. Therefore, their scientific validity and reliability are unknown. That is, they may not yield accurate answers! However, they have come to be widely used in marketing, since there aren't any other ways to try to uncover consumers' hidden motivations.

Qualitative research can be done in either small groups or with individuals. One extremely popular research technique is called the *focus group study*. A typical **focus group** brings 8 to 12 consumers from the target market together, seats them in a conversational setting, and asks them to talk freely about the subject. A trained moderator moves the discussion along, ensuring that the client's (marketer's) questions of interest do get addressed, but also giving freedom to the group members to express their opinions during the one- to two-hour session. **In-depth personal interviews** are also commonly used in qualitative research in marketing.

Qualitative research usually employs some mix of *direct* and *indirect* questions, with the hope that the preconscious level will be tapped as the discussion goes along. Direct questions ask for a consumer's thoughts or feelings in a direct manner, sometimes with answer categories suggested, but usually with some degree of freedom, or "open-endedness." For example, in the Open-Ended Sentence Completion Task ("Lipsticks are . . . ," "Women who wear pink lipstick are . . . "), the consumer is asked to respond quickly with what first comes to mind. Approaches derived from the Thematic Apperception Test, or TAT, are also often used—the consumer is asked to tell a story about a situation depicted in a picture, such as that of a young man standing in front

INTRODUCING A CORPORATE GIFT FOR EVERY CHARACTER.

| Closed circle: Reticent | Full upper loop: Mystical | Initial hook: Acquisitive | Full "d" upper loop: Sensitive to criticism | Full "e" loop: Open-minded | Balanced top & bottom on "f": Organized | Straight downstroke: Loner | No initial stroke: Direct | Closely dotted "i": Attention to details |

| Small loop: Clannish | A large "k" buckle: Defiant | Loop in "l": Philosophical | Rounded "m": Logical thinker | Flourish on "n": Sense of humor | Circle on right side: Secretive | Tall upper "p" stroke: Argumentative | Breakaway stroke: Aggressive | Flat-top "r": Manual dexterity |

| Soft "s" ending: Yielding | Sweeping t-bar: Enthusiasm | Final hook: Tenacity | Sharp "v": Analytical | Short initial stroke: Temper | Firm ending: Decisive | Full lower loop: Imagination | Narrow loop: Selectivity |

Handwriting reveals everything about a person's character. So does their choice of pen. Now you can give a gift that shows good taste, individuality and practicality. The new Parker Insignia Pens. These beautiful writing instruments are designed to fit comfortably in the writer's hand and guaranteed to last a lifetime.

Plus, your company's logo can be placed on the pen with jewelry-quality clip emblems, so it looks like the logo was part of the original design of the pen. With ten distinctive finishes to choose from, there's an Insignia for every personality.

For more information, or for your complimentary copy of the Insignia Corporate Gift Guide, call 1-800-522-3021.

The New
⊕ PARKER INSIGNIA

ASI 76380

This clever ad ties in its product theme—writing—with a basic interest people have in better understanding themselves and others. Not only does this attract attention at the start, but it helps to keep a reader with this ad much longer than usual for a print advertisement. Our discussion of personality begins on page 150 if you're interested....

State Farm Agent

Lynn Seger

on
Life Insurance For Women.

1. Is there a certain kind of life insurance that's best for women?

2. But what if my needs change?

3. So, where do I start?

1. "Actually, the 'best' life insurance program is one that's tailored to your individual needs. And whether you're married or a single working mother, whether your family is large or small, State Farm agents can help you find just the right plan to protect those you love."

2. "That's exactly why you need a State Farm agent. We're there to provide life insurance programs flexible enough to accommodate change. Our goal is to make sure you're getting the right amount of coverage at a price you can afford."

3. "Just call your State Farm agent. Answering your questions, helping you make informed choices — that's what the 'good neighbor' philosophy is all about. And it's what you can expect from every State Farm agent."

Have your nearby State Farm agent answer your questions about life insurance.

Like a good neighbor, State Farm is there.

This ad takes note of the fact that society is changing, that many women are concerned about financial security, and that many women are now considering the purchase of life insurance. Marketing programs are being increasingly designed for this market segment. Our discussion of market segmentation by gender begins on page 93.

Find out what hundreds of researchers already know...

Focus Suites is like no other facility you've ever tried.

- The expertise of our professional recruiters is unsurpassed in this industry.

- We have three separate, totally private 3-room suites.

- These extraordinary suites are available for the same cost or less than that of an ordinary facility.

Call today for a competitive bid on your next qualitative research project.
Once you've tried us, you'll never be satisfied with an ordinary facility again.

The Right People... The Right Price... The Right Place

One Bala Plaza, Suite 622, 231 St. Asaphs Road,
Bala Cynwyd, PA 19004 (215) 667-1110

This ad, aimed at markets, describes the benefits of using this firm's facilities for conducting "focus group" research with consumers. In this photo we see the marketing team seated behind a two–way mirror, watching a group of consumers discussing a grocery product category. The videotape of the session, together with the expert interpretation and recommendations of the researcher, will be used to make marketing decisions on such topics as product name, pricing, packaging, or advertising. Our discussion of the area of "qualitative research" begins on page 128.

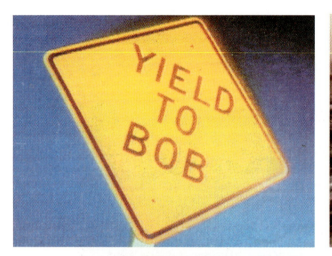

Nissan built its humorous, award-winning TV commercial, "Bob's Road," on a striving for mastery that is shared by many consumers. In it our driver, Bob, is pleased to drive out and find that the streets and highways have been changed to suit his needs above all others! Our discussion of self-concept is quite relevant here: it begins on page 156.

Find out what hundreds of researchers already know...

Focus Suites is like no other facility you've ever tried.

- The expertise of our professional recruiters is unsurpassed in this industry.
- We have three separate, totally private 3-room suites.
- These extraordinary suites are available for the same cost or less than that of an ordinary facility.

Call today for a competitive bid on your next qualitative research project. Once you've tried us, you'll never be satisfied with an ordinary facility again.

The Right People...The Right Price...The Right Place

FOCUS *Suites* of Philadelphia

One Bala Plaza, Suite 622, 231 St. Asaphs Road,
Bala Cynwyd, PA 19004 (215) 667-1110

A backstage view of a marketing focus group facility. Managers and researchers watch from behind the two-way mirror. The session is also taped for later review.

of a ring display in a jewelry store. A TAT-related technique uses cartoons, with the consumer asked to fill in the blank balloons representing thoughts of the characters. Another common technique asks the consumer about *other* people (e.g., "What kind of person drives a sports car?").

The last three methods are termed **projective tests.** Because the situation is deliberately ambiguous or unfinished, it is clear that there are no right or wrong answers. Also, the consumer is not placed in the position of answering personally about himself or herself. The researchers' hope is that the consumers, given a lack of pressure for "acceptable" answers, but pressed for details, will go deeper into their own feelings—and *project* their own preconscious motivations into the answers.

Advertising agencies have increased their use of projective tests in recent years. For example, one major agency gives consumers stacks of photos of people's faces and then asks them to sort out who might be typical users of various brands (each face has been chosen to represent a particular emotional reaction to the product). Another major agency asks consumers to draw shapes expressing their reactions to new product ideas—the twist is that every consumer has to use his or her *left hand* to do the drawing,

Projective tests: A set of research methods that present consumers with unfinished tasks in which right or wrong answers are not possible.

since the researchers believe that the portion of the brain that controls feelings also controls the left hand. A third major agency, searching for consumers' true images of a brand, asks them to assume that a certain brand has "died" and to write a newspaper obituary for it (e.g., a young, virile brand that was the victim of an accident is presumed more healthy than a worn-out brand that finally has died of old age). This agency also favors the use of "stick-figure sketches," as related in the following example.[9]

🐌 Sticking It to Them!

One strange twist that marketing managers frequently encounter is that consumers will say one thing, but will do another. Recently, for example, a major ad agency faced the problem that its client's brand of roach killer (Combat) wasn't selling well with a key segment—low-income women in the South—where the infestation problem means that potential sales are very high. The puzzler: Why weren't sales strong? The agency knew that the *earlier advertising had worked:* these consumers knew about the product—a plastic tray device—and they believed that it did offer the key benefits of effective eradication in a tidy hidden manner. Nonetheless, the women weren't buying, instead staying with the old bug sprays they had used for years. To gain better insight into the reasons, the agency asked some target consumers to draw rough pictures of roaches, then write little stories explaining their sketches. Exhibit 5-2 shows some of the results.

The researchers were surprised to notice that all the roaches pictured were males! According to the research director, many of the women viewed the roach as symbolizing men who had mistreated them in the past. "Killing the roaches with a bug spray and watching them squirm and die allowed the women to express their hostility toward men *and* have greater control over the roaches," she reported.

In summary, there is a broad range of research that falls under the "qualitative research" label. Many managers find that they like some techniques but not others. The area of projective tests is particularly controversial and has gathered groups of supporters and critics. In the words of one supporter (the roach project director), "We're using a whole battery of psychological techniques—some new and some old— to understand the emotional bond between consumers and brands. . . ." The director of advertising research at another major agency agrees: "Brands are not just commercial products we buy and use; they're our companions in life as well." However, the head of the consumer behavior group at a different major agency is critical of this type of research: "I'm really skeptical about these psychoanalysts. . . ."

Much of the debate involves serious scientific research concerns. Since qualitative research can be expensive on a per consumer basis, sampling size and representativeness are often a problem (e.g., do we have any idea what percentage of women actually hold these symbolic views of roaches?). Much of the research is therefore treated as "exploratory" and is used as a source of ideas and insights (notice, however, that if the sample is not representative, these insights could be misleading). The subjective nature of the researcher's interpretations is also a difficulty from a scientific viewpoint—two motivation researchers might well reach different conclusions about what certain answers mean or what should be done about them. Finally, motivation research in marketing is inherently situation specific and not geared toward providing generalizations about all consumer behavior.

For these reasons, the academic field of marketing and consumer behavior has treated motivation research at some distance and has given little attention to this area in recent years. Within the world of marketing management, however, various aspects

EXHIBIT 5-2

Consumer "Picture Stories" About Roaches

The Mind of a Roach Killer

The McCann-Erickson ad agency asked women to draw and describe how they felt about roaches. The agency concluded from the drawings that the women identified the roaches with men who had abandoned them and thus enjoyed watching the roaches-men squirm and die. That's why, the agency figured, that women prefer spray roach killers to products that don't allow the user to see the roach die.

"ONE NIGHT *I just couldn't take the horror of these bugs sneaking around in the dark. They are always crawling when you can't see them. I had to do something. I thought wouldn't it be wonderful! if when I switched on the light the roaches would shrink up and die like vampires to sunlight. So I did, but they just all scattered. But I was ready with my spray so it wasn't a total loss. I got quite a few...continued tomorrow night when night time falls."*

"I TIPTOED *quietly into the kitchen perhaps he wasn't around. I stretched my arm up to the light. I hoped I'd be alone when the light went on. Perhaps he is sitting on the table I thought. You think that's impossible? Nothing is impossible with that guy. He might not even be alone. He'll run when the light goes on I thought. But what's worse is for him to slip out of sight. No, it would be better to confront him before he takes control and 'invites a companion'."*

"A MAN LIKES *a free meal you cook for him, as long as there is food he will stay."*

of the approach are used frequently, because, as we've noted, there just are not many options for discovering consumers' hidden motivations (if you would like to read more about how marketers use these techniques, you may wish to consult Note 10).

(T) TENSION REDUCTION DRIVES CONSUMER BEHAVIOR

This entry is the most basic of all in our framework. It provides the fundamental reason that *any* behavior is undertaken at any point in time. The idea of tension reduction is drawn from studies in biology of the human body's tendency to make adjustments to remain in as steady a condition as possible (equilibrium).[11] For example, we perspire in reaction to a rise in body temperature: it is a natural means of releasing heat and keeping our temperature near normal.

The basic theory is that a nonequilibrium state creates a feeling of tension. When tension gets too high, we experience levels of psychological discomfort, and energy is aroused to reduce this tension. When the body requires nourishment, for example, a tension is created in our systems. We find this mildly uncomfortable, say that we are "hungry," and are motivated to find food to reduce the tension level. Within consumer behavior, tension reduction is inherent in most key concepts. For example, our basic view is that consumers pursue need fulfillment. Need fulfillment, in turn, is based upon desires to reduce tensions brought about by wants that are unsatisfied. In general, then, this entry in our framework stresses that humans are motivated to behave because of tension reduction. We will see many examples of this principle in upcoming chapters.

(I) INTERNAL AND EXTERNAL FORCES IMPACT MOTIVATION

The basic point of this framework entry is that motivation is sometimes sparked internally (e.g., hunger) and sometimes sparked externally (e.g., a friend's suggestion). Once sparked, the direction the motivated behavior will take is also determined partially by internal factors and partially by external factors. For example, a food purchase will be directed in part by a person's product preferences, but also perhaps by what store is nearby and any sale prices there. To understand the foundation for this way of thinking about consumer behavior, let's consider the nature of Kurt Lewin's **field theory.**

Field theory: Lewin's system based on the premise that behavior is a function of both the person and his or her environment.

Professor Kurt Lewin (pronounced "Le-veen" or "Lew-in") has been called the most brilliant figure in recent psychological history and has had a profound impact on thinking in the area of motivation.[12] Professor Lewin worked in Germany until the rise of the Nazi movement caused him to emigrate to the United States in the 1930s. The most famous of his contributions is known as *field theory*, which is a system by which we can visualize and quantify how behavior occurs. Its basic premise is captured in Lewin's famous formula

$$B = f(P, E)$$

This is read, "*Behavior* is a function of both the *person* and the *environment*."

Life space: Also termed "psychological field," represents the totality of all forces acting on a person at a point in time.

The person and environment comprise what is called the **life space** or **psychological field.** The life space is the *totality of all forces acting on a person at a point in time.* This includes all internal forces, together with those external aspects of the environment of which the person is aware. In this theory, therefore, the "environment" does not refer to physical reality itself, but to the psychological reality as each person sees it. Although it may not be clear why yet, as we'll see in our chapters on perception (Chapters 8 and 9), this is an extremely important insight for marketers.

(V) CONSUMER MOTIVATION HAS VALENCE

This framework entry provides a good basis for analyzing the direction behavior will take, and which alternatives consumers are likely to choose. The term **valence** is a *measure of the degree of attractiveness* that a particular object, such as a product, holds for us. A valence is either positive (when the product is attractive to us) or negative (when it is unattractive to us). Valence also reflects the strength of the attraction—it can be low or high, depending on how much we are to attracted or repelled by the product in question. The concept of valence occupied an important role within Lewin's field theory.

Valence: The degree of attractiveness (positive or negative) that a particular object holds for a consumer.

One important application area for the valence concept involves **motivational conflicts.** As we've noted earlier, the typical consumer has multiple motives, is limited in both the time and money that he or she can spend, and has various alternatives from which to choose. This means that *conflicts* will arise on how to allocate attention and purchases. Lewin identified three types of motivational conflicts, each having two forces acting in opposite directions within a given psychological field:

- Approach-avoidance
- Approach-approach
- Avoidance-avoidance

Approach-avoidance conflicts are very common in consumer behavior. They occur when a consumer is considering both positive and negative features of a single alternative. In a motivational sense, the consumer wishes to move *toward* the positive features, but *away* from the negative ones (as an extreme example, consider how you feel about taking a bungee jump... is there some conflict?). Most products and services offer positive benefits to us, engendering approach forces. At the same time, however, there are several types of "perceived risks" that can engender avoidance forces in us. These include performance risks, financial risks, physical injury risks, and social risks. The topic of perceived risk has received considerable attention in consumer research.[13]

The consumer's behavior in an approach-avoidance conflict depends on the relative strength of the opposing forces. However, it is important to realize that *the forces themselves are subject to being influenced by marketers.* For example, advertising people and salespersons can provide information or excitement to strengthen the approach force. Conversely, marketers can use sale prices, easy credit, and product guarantees to weaken the avoidance force.

Approach-approach conflicts are the most pleasant type and are also quite common in consumer behavior. Here we are attempting to decide between two alternatives and are concentrating only on their attractive features. For example, Joan Cohen wants to celebrate a successful semester and is trying to decide between a trip to the seashore and a trip to the mountains. Joan may feel that this is a difficult choice to make and may well think more about each alternative. Since she is moving toward a positive result, though, she will want to make the choice and obtain the benefits from one of the trips.

Avoidance-avoidance conflicts are quite the opposite situation. These are the most unpleasant type of motivational conflict, since they involve a choice between two behaviors with negative valences. The person in this situation is motivated to move *away from* both alternatives and is not likely to purchase at all until his or her perceptions of the situation shift. Fortunately, since most consumer purchases are voluntary on our part (that is, we are rarely *forced* to buy or use products that we don't wish to have), this is not a typical conflict found in brand choice. In areas such as health problems and household maintenance, however, we do often see this conflict arising. For example, many consumers wish to avoid having potentially severe pain and dental problems in the future, but also wish to avoid the task of having to go to the dentist (estimates are that 10 to 12 million Americans will never visit a dentist because of their extreme fears and an additional 35 million put off making appointments because of their anxiety).[14] In these cases, a new product, such as a small pad to numb the mouth, rather than a needle, would reduce the extent of the avoidance forces associated with visiting the dentist.

Approach-avoidance: A class of motivational conflict in which a consumer wishes to move both toward and away from an object.

Approach-approach: A class of motivational conflict that occurs when a consumer is attempting to decide between two attractive alternatives.

Avoidance-avoidance: A class of motivational conflict that occurs when a consumer is choosing between two behaviors with negative valences.

Approach-approach conflict: which will it be, a vacation at the seashore or in the mountains?

Stainmaster became a major new product success by vividly portraying that the consumer could have a high expectancy (*E*) of achieving highly valued (*V*) consequences if accidents should happen with Stainmaster carpets.

(A) CONSUMERS ARE MOTIVATED TO ACHIEVE GOALS

This framework entry offers many useful marketing applications. It represents one of the major schools of motivation theory—the expectancy × value (often called *E* times *V*) approach. **Expectancy × value theory** represents an extension of the key concepts of Lewin's work, together with the work of several other scientists on such topics as learning (Tolman), achievement motivation (Atkinson), and economic decisions (Edwards).[15]

The *E* × *V* approach places great emphasis on how *goals lead to specific behaviors*. Its major proposition is

> The strength of the tendency to act in a certain way depends on the strength of the **expectancy** that the act will be followed by a given consequence (or goal) and the **value** of that consequence to the individual.[16]

Thus we evaluate each possible behavior (such as the purchase of a particular brand) in terms of how desirable we expect its consequences to be for us.

As we might expect, *E* × *V* theory has powerful implications for helping us to understand consumer behavior. It views a consumer as a problem solver, approaching purchasing situations as opportunities to achieve positive goals that he or she may have. Key aspects of *E* × *V* theory are already much used within marketing. We will return to this topic in the next chapter.

Expectancy × value theory The tendency to act is based on expectations that the act leads to consequences and on the value of those consequences.

(T) CONSUMERS HAVE A THIRST FOR VARIETY

This entry expands upon the fundamental idea of tension reduction (the earlier "T" in our framework) by stressing that consumers are *active as well as reactive*. We consumers do not only try to relieve tensions: we also enjoy being stimulated, even though this *increases* our bodily tensions during the event (such as in a movie). In a sense, then, we go through our lives as "tension managers."

Big winners, big losers

A dozen magazines reveal the covers of their best and worst selling issues on the newsstands this year. One moral: Sigourney's hot, Jesse's not

Best

Worst

Best

Worst

Best

Worst

Vanity Fair
Tina Brown, editor
"Our cover image can help circulation by an extra 20,000 or so, but it's really the red 'flash' band on the side that sells at the newsstand.

"The August issue had Sigourney Weaver on the cover but she didn't really do it as much as the red flash about the Shah. We sell on coverlines, and the flash is the hot scoop.

"The Jesse Jackson issue was probably the worst. There's a guaranteed risk putting a politician on the cover—I knew all about that. We did it anyway and it did not work. Also, it was January and that's never a good month. We're definitely spoiled because we've had so many gains at the newsstand.

"The perfect *Vanity Fair* cover is glamo; and class in the image and a hot flash item. It's tough to find that, and sometimes we go for a funny glitz cover and that works, too."

Esquire
Lee Eisenberg, editor in chief
"'Dubious Achievements' is a perennial winner for us. Why that is is self-evident, I think. It's a publishing institution that's talked about and debated.

"The worst issue, Prince Charles, didn't go badly—it wasn't a disaster—but it was the weakest of six strong issues.

"The story itself is something we're proud of but the photo was not particularly warm. It was regal, as befits the prince, but we didn't get the chance to shoot it ourselves. Had we shot the photo it may have played better.

"The men we usually put on the cover must stand for some kind of real character that our readers can relate to. The more emulatable they are, the better. The pool is relatively shallow that we fish from to get our cover subjects."

New England Monthly
Daniel Okrent, editor
"I'm not surprised [at which was the worst and best cover in 1988]. We do best when we feature a place and evoke places of the heart that people in New England love.

"The ones that sell the worst are those with harder journalism. The issues with topics fare poorly compared to those on places.

"No matter how important newsstand sales are, we are overwhelmingly a subscription magazine and the topic issues are important to our readers, our subscribers. If you looked at 12 issues on destinations in New England you wouldn't have a good picture of what the magazine is all about.

Texas Monthly
Gregory Curtis, editor
"There's definitely a different look each month. It's very much a seat-of-the-pants decision. There are no constants. But I try to think what is on people's minds and then try to find some way to do a story about it.

"The trouble is, there might not be a single theme in the air or there is and you don't identify it, but there's a certain amount of luck involved.

"A cover that is perceived as ugly will not sell; but a beautiful cover may not sell either. A cover has to attract people's eyes, but what the cover promises must be what readers want."

Harrowsmith
Thomas H. Rawls, editor
"Our name is nothing but a problem for us on the newsstand. What is a *Harrowsmith*, anyway?

"Where are you going to put us? Do you put us in the H's next to *Hustler*? Do you put us with the home and lifestyle books? Do you put us with gardening magazines?

"Part of the reason we put that positioning statement [The Magazine of Country Life] on there was so that some kid in a convenience store somewhere who's stacking magazines will read it and know where to put us.

"We prefer illustrated covers to photographs even though researchers say photos fare better, and we stay away from a lot of cover copy. Because we don't live or die by the newsstand, we can break some of the rules.

"Historically, January-February is our best issue for a variety of reasons. People like the catalog listing.

"The barn cover will probably sell the least at the newsstand. It's a pleasing piece of art and a good cover but it's less colorful and it's got less pop."

Rolling Stone
Jann S. Wenner, editor & publisher
"What goes into selecting each cover is the newsworthiness of the subject, its appeal to our target audience and the quality of the photograph. A cover story can't be a cover story if there's not a good picture.

"Who's on the cover and how they look is what sells on the newsstand. It's an editorial/circulation decision as to what goes on the cover, what's going to jump off the newsstand."

(Continued on Page S-48)

Best

Worst

Best

Worst

Best

Worst

Magazine sales vary by how curious consumers are about what's inside. Notice how the best- and worst-selling covers differed in their appeals to curiosity and adventure.

Although this point may appear to undercut tension reduction as the basis for motivation, in fact the general theory of tension reduction can incorporate these exploratory behaviors on our part. This can be done by assuming that the optimal level of tension (or stimulation) for our human systems is not zero, but is instead some slight positive level. If the existing stimulation level is too low, then, we will feel a tension (for example, we "feel bored") and will want to raise the level of stimulation ("do something interesting") to reduce the tension level in our system.[17]

This framework entry has a broad array of interesting implications for consumer behavior, including such issues as why consumers are so curious and interested in variety and adventure. These factors work *against* long-term brand loyalty. They underpin consumers' *willingness to try new products and new stores.* Of course, consumers' trial of new products represents the future of most firms (and their managers) and is extremely important to all of marketing.

Consumers' *curiosity* is a key factor. One area of marketing that relies upon consumer curiosity and interest in variety is magazine publishing, where covers are crucial:

🐎 What Appeals to the "Cosmo Girl"?

Cosmopolitan became a highly successful magazine through its glorification of the "Cosmo Girl." According to Helen Gurley Brown, editor, "I knew what she should look like...sexy, gorgeous, friendly....I love lots of hair, cleavage at least every other month....I doubt we will ever do the scrubbed look!" Ms. Brown's husband, David,

Notice how the cover of *Cosmopolitan* follows the guidelines to involve the reader and appeal to curiosity and the thirst for variety.

writes the blurbs for each cover. He explains, "In deciding whether a blurb will attract newsstand buyers, I ask myself whether the subject can involve the reader....I call this the 'you' factor." Among Mr. Brown's tips for top cover blurbs: the use of humor and surprise, recognizing that consumers' desire to learn is one of the most powerful urges (he believes it surpasses sex in the long run); realize that consumers' hope springs eternal; and try to promise something for every problem. Overall, Mr. Brown concludes, "...emotional pull is still the big lure...newsstand sales prove it."[18]

Entire industries are built on the "thirst for variety" motive on the part of consumers. For example, think about the kind of consumer motivations on which television, nightclubs, sports, and tourism are based. Moreover, these industries promise to expand in the future, particularly in the area of "designed experiences."

What Will the Future Bring...Virtual Reality?

In recent years the "designed experience" industry has been booming. Middle-aged athletes now pay $3000 per week to attend adult baseball camps and play against the stars they remember from their childhood. Businesses use designed experiences to reward their sales forces and major clients (one American firm, for example, flew a group of American executives to England, where the firm had prepared the setting for the executives to return to the Middle Ages as Robin Hood and his Merry Men in Sherwood Forest!).

Technology continues to expand possibilities. Already "interactive television" allows consumers in their homes to play the "Wheel of Fortune" game with Vanna White (and to win actual prizes on the show). Also, consumers can shop and order from department stores and supermarkets (J. C. Penney's system is called an "electronic shopping mall" since it allows the viewer to shop and order from 40 different retailers, just as in an actual mall). Beyond this are even more extreme developments in "consumer experiences." Which of the following would you personally like to experience?

- *Total television.* Screens curve around entire rooms, accompanied by authentic noises, smells, and costumes.
- *Virtual reality.* A participant is brought into "another world" through specially designed wired helmets and gloves. Guided by an ultrasophisticated computer program, these devices can provide specific combinations of sights, sounds, touch, smells, and taste to simulate a whole other environment. Sensors detect even the slightest movements, causing the computer to reconfigure the stimuli from the devices. Thus a person can "stroll down a boulevard in Paris, then walk the Great Wall of China, or ski down a treacherous slope in the Alps." According to one noted computer designer, "by the end of this decade, VR will be commonplace." Already, a Japanese appliance marketer is giving its Tokyo customers a chance to "walk through" a basic kitchen, "open" doors, turn on faucets, and so on. The customer can then "place" appliances, cupboards, and other items in different spots to see which is best (the first customer to try this system spent an hour arranging things and then bought $30,000 worth of appliances!). Once a completely customized kitchen has been designed, the plans are transmitted to the factory and the custom-built kitchen is ready in two weeks.

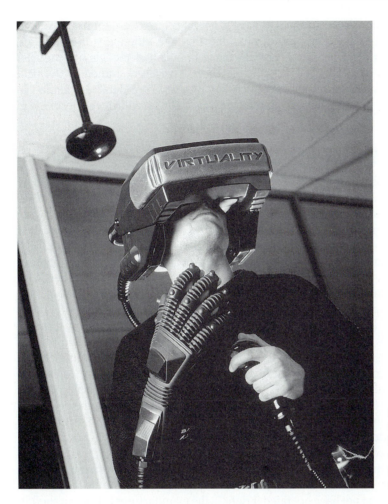

Standard virtual reality gear includes a helmet with built-in video displays, a data glove, and headphones with "3-D" sound. These are all wired to a computer that tracks hand and head movements and adjusts visuals and sound accordingly.

- *"Experience" pills.* Controlled hallucinations might someday allow a consumer to take a pill and then "dream" his or her way through a desired experience, such as climbing Mount Everest as a member of Hillary's expedition.[19]

Most of us have limits as to how far we'd like our curiosity, novelty, and pleasure-seeking motives to take us. Even if all the foregoing possibilities are not attractive, we should recognize from them the power of our motivations in this area. (In recent years consumer researchers have been especially interested in pursuing research on this area; if you would like to learn more about their views and findings, you may wish to pursue the readings listed in Note 20.)

(I) CONSUMER MOTIVATION REFLECTS INDIVIDUAL DIFFERENCES

This framework entry refers to the fact that consumers differ from each other in what, where, and how they buy. If we are to understand buying behavior, we need to understand why these differences occur.

Some of the individual differences we observe are obviously due to external factors, such as income, age, and social pressures. Nonetheless, it also seems that there is a natural inclination for consumers to have different preferences. For example, let's assume that everyone has the same income and that age differences don't matter. Would we then expect everyone to buy the same brands and models of products? Obviously not. Theoretically, individual differences have been studied in the field of personality research. Personality research has received considerable attention in consumer behavior and has yielded some surprising findings, which we'll examine in Chapter 6.

(O) CONSUMERS DESIRE ORDER IN THEIR WORLD

This framework entry stresses that consumers are motivated to do more than simply acquire products and services—all consumers are also motivated to understand (or see order in) their world. In practice, this means that they are constantly estimating what is responsible for, or causes, various events. This process of estimating causes is called *attribution* and is the focus of the broad psychological field of **attribution theory.**[21]

Attribution theory: A theory that people try to estimate the causes for events they encounter.

Attributions occur frequently in consumer behavior, sometimes quite consciously and sometimes not. How many times, for example, have consumers responded, "It's only an ad..." when they see strong positive claims about a product? What they are really doing is *attributing the claim to one cause* (that advertisers exaggerate) *rather than another cause* (that the product really *is* fantastic). Another common example involves purchases of products in which features and quality can be added to each model. In these instances, consumers will often find the salesperson recommending a higher-priced model that offers additional features. In this situation, consumers are confronted with a choice of which attribution to make about the salesperson's recommendations: "Is she trying to sell me the premium model because she believes it is better for me or because her commission will be higher?" Note that this attribution is not only an academic question—the model that we will end up buying depends on which attribution we make!

Consumer attributions are also important *after* a purchase, in evaluating product performance. If consumers are dissatisfied, for example, will they attribute the problem to themselves ("I must not have operated it right"), the manufacturer ("This is a shoddy product"), the retailer or salesperson ("I'll never go there again; they obviously don't care what they sell to the customer"), or some other events ("If Lori hadn't phoned, the pizza wouldn't have burned")? Successful product performance is important as well, since we can attribute it either to ourselves ("I really know how to make a pizza!") or to the marketing system ("This brand makes a great pizza!"). The nature of consumers' postpurchase attributions is obviously a key to marketers' long-run success.

⤵ *"Foot in the Door" and "Door in the Face"*

Self-perception: A theory that people examine their own behavior after they've undertaken it, to help infer their own beliefs and attitudes.

In addition to making attributions about events and other people's behaviors, we also make *attributions about ourselves* and our own behaviors. The area of **self-perception** stresses how we examine our own behavior *after* we've undertaken it. Psychologists have used this theory to recommend two approaches for gaining compliance with requests: the *foot-in-the-door (FITD)* approach and the *door-in-the-face (DITF)* approach. Both FITD and DITF are based on the premise that "two requests are better than one." In essence, the first request is used to "set the stage" for the second by stimulating certain self-perception processes in the mind of the consumer.

The **FITD technique** begins by asking consumers to agree to a small request: once they've done this, their chances of agreeing to a larger request (the one actually desired by the seller) are higher than if the large request alone had been made. The **DITF technique** proceeds in just the opposite fashion. It first asks the consumer to comply with a very large request; after being turned down, it makes a smaller, more reasonable request (the one actually desired by the seller).

The attribution theory explanation for both techniques is that a consumer, after having agreed to or denied the first request, will attempt to explain to himself exactly why he took that action. In the FITD case, the initial small request (for example, putting a sign in the window supporting safety for children) will have led many consumers to agree to the request. However, after having agreed, it is natural for a person to ask himself why he had agreed to the request. One likely (and personally acceptable) answer is that he really does support safety for children. Then, when the representative returns with the second request (for example, to volunteer some time to help get a new playground in the neighborhood), this self-perception will then come to mind—now the consumer is seeing himself as a supporter of the cause and is more willing to do something more to help!

In the DITF case, conversely, the organization tries a different strategy, beginning with a deliberately large request that is likely to be refused (say, may we use your house as a neighborhood playground to keep the children safe?). After the consumer refuses this request, she is again likely to ask herself why. In this case an acceptable attribution is that the request itself was simply too large—although the cause itself is worthwhile and she does support it. Then, when the organization comes back with its second request shortly thereafter, the consumer is not able to employ the same attribution again, since this request (volunteer some time to help get a new playground in the neighborhood) is clearly a reasonable one. She is, therefore, more likely to agree to it than if the first request had not been made.

In closing, we should note that there is considerable theoretical debate in this area. Not everyone accepts that the "self-perception" process is as powerful as suggested: some persons point to a "bargaining" system at work in these situations. (If you are interested in pursuing the debates or research findings, you may wish to begin with the readings listed in Note 22.) As you may have experienced, marketers are well aware of FITD and DITF. These techniques are widely used in selling and fund-raising activities.

(N) CONSUMERS ARE GUIDED BY THE NEED HIERARCHY

This final framework entry shifts our attention to the actual *content* of motivated behavior. Here we will focus on the nature of needs (or motives—we'll use the terms interchangeably in this discussion). In our next chapter we will return to this topic to examine some techniques marketers use to work with this theory.

Maslow's Need Hierarchy

Abraham Maslow was a founder of the school of *humanistic psychology,* a school that has gained popularity in recent years. Maslow felt that too much attention had been given to negative views of people's psyches and not enough to their potentials. This

FITD technique: "Foot in the door": asks consumers to agree to a small request; once they've done this, their chances of agreeing to a second, larger request increases.

DITF technique: "Door in the face": asks consumers to agree to a very large request; after turning it down, they are more likely to agree to a second, more reasonable request.

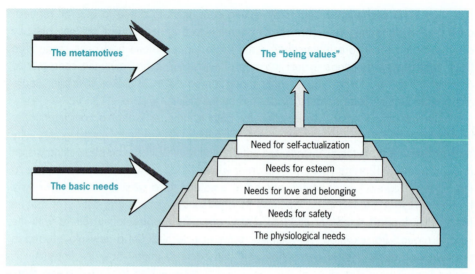

FIGURE 5-2 Maslow's Need Hierarchy.

Need hierarchy:
The concept that some needs will be evoked before others, based upon their level within a system, such as Maslow's.

spirit of personal growth is embodied in the theory of **need hierarchy.** There are several key propositions in this theory. First, the environment is extremely important in establishing which needs will be active within a person at a particular time. Second, when a need has been satisfied, it is no longer active as a need (though it may return later). Third, there is a systematic *order* within the basic needs; a person will not feel a second-level need until the first-level needs have been sufficiently satisfied, and so forth through the five levels of the hierarchy. Therefore, Maslow concluded, if people are able to create a positive environment for themselves, they should be able to move up the need hierarchy toward the higher levels of personal growth, as depicted in Figure 5-2.

Level 1: The Physiological Needs.   These are the demands that our bodies place on us for survival and health. They include air, water, a balance of nutrients, a comfortable temperature, and elimination of bodily waste. These are the *prepotent* needs because they *must* be satisfied before other needs are activated. For example, a starving person needs food. In most modern cultures, these needs are satisfied most of the time. This releases them from active domination of our systems and allows us to proceed to higher-order needs.

Level 2: The Safety Needs.   This set of needs is actually much broader than its title suggests. In addition to physical safety, Maslow referred to psychological security. Thus stability, familiarity, and predictability are important needs. Since our culture is generally designed to provide physical safety and psychological security through organized institutions (religions, schools, families, etc.), these safety needs are usually not active for most of us. When they are, however, they can easily dominate our thoughts and behaviors. Consider, for example, people who are afraid to ride in subways or walk the city streets. In the psychological realm, consider friends you might know who are constant "worriers." Note how their concerns with possible disruptions to their lives can preoccupy their thoughts.

Within marketing, as the proportion of women business travelers has gone to 40 percent (from 1 percent in 1970), major hotel chains have found that "club floors" offering increased security have been a strong selling point.

Level 3: The Needs for Love and Belonging.   If both the physiological and safety needs are fairly gratified, the needs to give and receive love or affection, and to feel the sense of belonging, are likely to emerge. If these needs are not satisfied, a person is likely to feel "lonely" and perhaps depressed. Depending on the situation, a special friend or a small group can help toward resolving this set of needs.

Level 4: The Esteem Needs.   This reflects the general need for an individual to evaluate himself or herself positively. Maslow divided this set into two classes: inward directed and outward directed. The inner-directed needs refer to desires for competence and for confidence as to our own capability. The outward needs refer to the evaluations we receive from others, including recognition and appreciation. If these needs are not satisfied, a person feels inferior, and sometimes helpless. If the needs are satisfied, a person feels self-confident and capable.

Level 5: The Need for Self-actualization.   A person reaching this level will have already achieved much in life—he or she will have physical health, will feel safe and secure, will be loved and belong in a social fabric and will be valued and recognized by others, and will have high self-esteem based upon accomplishments. Not bad! However, since each of these levels has to be maintained, most people are never able to reach the self-actualization phase on a regular basis. Self-actualization means the fulfillment of a person's *unique potential*—the becoming of everything that one is capable of becoming. People in this stage are now motivated by what Maslow calls **metamotives** or ultimate values. These include truth, beauty, "aliveness," goodness, justice, and unity.

Metamotives:
The highest level of Maslow's system: the ultimate values that humans seek, including truth, beauty, "aliveness," goodness, justice, and unity.

Although controversial in some respects, Maslow's hierarchy gives insights into today's consumer culture. For people whose physiological and safety needs are largely satisfied, most focus on social, psychological, and personal growth needs.[23]

Murray's List of Social Needs

Henry Murray was a surgeon, held a Ph.D. in biochemistry, and was the director of the Harvard Psychological Clinic during the decades from the 1920s to the early 1960s.[24] His training in biology and medicine, combined with a deep interest in psychology, allowed Murray to adopt an impressively broad view of motivation. This breadth makes his theory hard to describe in our limited space, but it also allows it to be used in many applications.

Need: A force in the brain that influences a person to perceive and act in ways that would turn unstatisfying situations into more satisfying ones.

The basis of **Murray's inventory of social needs** is that *needs* are the basic motivating forces for people. He defined a **need** as a force in the brain region that influences a person to perceive and act in ways to turn unsatisfying situations into more satisfying ones. Needs can be provoked by either internal or external stimuli and can be weak or strong at any particular time (in fact, Murray further believed that, after observing a person under many conditions for extensive time periods, certain systematic needs would appear, thus accounting for that person's "personality"). Based upon the thousands of investigations by himself and his staff, Murray suggested that there is a limited number of some 20 needs that all humans seem to have in one degree or another. These are listed in Table 5-2.

Table 5-2 An Illustrative List of Murray's Needs

Need	Brief Definition
n Abasement	To submit passively to external force. To accept injury, blame, criticism, punishment. To become resigned to fate.
n Achievement	To accomplish something difficult. To master or organize physical objects, human beings, or ideas. To overcome obstacles and attain a high standard.
n Affiliation	To draw near and enjoyably cooperate. To please and win affection. To adhere and remain loyal to a friend.
n Aggression	To fight. To oppose or punish another.
n Autonomy	To be independent and free to act according to impulse. To be unattached, irresponsible. To defy convention.
n Counteraction	To master or make up for a failure. To overcome weaknesses. To search for obstacles and difficulties to overcome.
n Defendance	To defend the self against assault, criticism, and blame. To conceal or justify a misdeed, failure, or humiliation.
n Deference	To admire and support a superior. To praise, honor, or eulogize. To yield eagerly. To conform to custom.
n Dominance	To control one's human environment. To direct the behavior of others by suggestion, seduction, persuasion, or command.
n Exhibition	To make an impression. To be seen and heard. To excite, amaze, fascinate, entertain, shock, intrigue, amuse, or entice others.
n Harm avoidance	To avoid pain, physical injury, illness, and death. To escape from a dangerous situation. To take precautionary measures.
n Infavoidance	To avoid humiliation. To refrain from action because of the fear of failure.
n Nurturance	To give sympathy and gratify the needs of a helpless object. To feed, help, protect.
n Order	To put things in order. To achieve cleanliness, arrangement, organization, balance, neatness, tidiness, and precision.
n Play	To act for "fun" without further purpose. To like to laugh and make jokes. To seek enjoyable relaxation of stress.
n Rejection	To separate oneself from a negative object. To exclude or remain indifferent to an inferior object. To snub or jilt.
n Sentience	To seek and enjoy sensuous impressions.
n Sex	To form an erotic relationship. To have sexual intercourse.
n Succorance	To have one's needs gratified by the sympathetic aid of an allied object. To be nursed, supported, protected, loved, advised.
n Understanding	To ask or answer general questions. To be interested in theory. To speculate, formulate, analyze, and generalize.

SOURCE: Calvin S. Hall and Gardner Lindzey, *Theories of Personality*, 2nd ed. (New York: John Wiley, 1970), pp. 176–177.

The list of needs is called *instrumental* or *social* because they are often aroused in regard to others and they help us to determine how best to act. They are not independent from each other and often combine ("fuse") together to lead to a particular behavior. For example, let's consider n Sentience, which refers to a need to seek and enjoy sensuous impressions and pleasures (the single "n" is simply used to indicate a specific need). In some situations, for example, n Sentience might fuse with n Affiliation and lead to a desire for romantic love. In other situations, it might fuse with n Achievement, leading to a desire to create works of art, or it may fuse with n Exhibition, leading to a desire to purchase and display erotic or aesthetic products. Also, of course, n Sentience can combine with n Sex.

Although brief, this should be sufficient to give you an idea of the richness of Murray's theory. It has been extremely influential in both psychology and consumer behavior. Murray, for example, was a codeveloper of the Thematic Apperception Test that we described in our earlier "O" framework section on "overt and hidden" motives. He also developed evaluation procedures for the OSS—the U.S. spy agency that operated during World War II. Also, his theory is the basis for one of the most used personality tests in recent times, the Edwards Personal Preference Schedule (EPPS), which some readers of this book have likely taken.

RECAP: THE BASICS OF MOTIVATION THEORY

We have discussed the broad, complex field of motivation at some length, and it may be useful to recap briefly the basic points here. Most consumer behavior experts accept the elements of motivational theory that we have been discussing within our framework. As a check on your understanding of this material, see if the following descriptions, which do not use exactly the same language, make sense. In summary, consumer behavior experts believe that

(M) We need to focus on both energy and direction.

(O) It will be hard to identify all motives in a situation.

(T) The underlying process is drive reduction.

(I) Field theory helps us to recognize factors.

(V) Consumers move toward and away from all marketing stimuli.

(A) Basically, consumer behavior is "goal directed."

(T) Consumer behavior brings stimulation to people's lives.

(I) Consumers will behave differently from each other.

(O) Consumers want to understand their environment and behaviors.

(N) Basic motives drive all human behavior.

■ SUMMARY

KEY CHARACTERISTICS OF MOTIVATION

Motivation refers to the processes that move a person to behave in certain ways. As we'd expect, this is a very broad area. To simplify our task, the chapter was organized around a 10-point MOTIVATION framework:

(*M*) Motivation contains two major components: *energy* and *direction.* Energy is required for any type of behavior to occur, whereas direction is required to channel the energy into specific activities. *Emotion* is closely related to the energy dimension by virtue of its special power to make us want to act (marketers, realizing this, often strive to evoke emotions). Meanwhile, the direction taken in behavior is largely determined by the purposes one is trying to achieve.

(*O*) The second statement in our framework recognizes the distinction between *overt* and *hidden* motives. Discerning a consumer's motivation is almost always difficult, partially because we have multiple motives and partially because people are often unable to report their true motives. This notion of hidden or unconscious motivation was first raised by Sigmund Freud and has been used in marketing by motivation researchers with *qualitative research methods.*

(*T*) This entry stresses the role that *tension reduction* plays in motivating behavior. Basically, a disequilibrium state creates a feeling of "tension." Energy is directed into behaviors that will reduce the tension.

(*I*) Consumers are motivated by both *internal* and *external* forces. Lewin's *field theory* highlighted the view that an individual's behavior at any point in time is a function of both the person and his or her psychological environment.

(*V*) The direction that behavior will take is reflected by the concept of *valence,* a measure of the degree of attractiveness that a particular object, such as a product, holds for us. We can use this type of model to understand which of two desirable alternatives a consumer will be motivated to choose.

(*A*) The *expectancy $\times$ value (E $\times$ V) theory* of motivation is based on the fact that consumers are motivated to *achieve goals.* Its major proposition is that our behavior depends on what we *expect* will happen, and whether we place a positive or negative *value* on each possible outcome. This theory has a strong cognitive orientation and is related to our study of consumer information processing.

(*T*) Consumers have a *thirst for variety.* Sometimes consumers will seek to increase tension rather than to reduce or avoid it. This tendency explains why we consumers are curious, and like to try out new products.

(*I*) Consumer motivation also reflects *individual differences.* While some of these differences are due to observable characteristics (age, sex, etc.), consumers' differences in motivation go beyond their demographic makeup. In our next chapter we examine how individual differences affect consumer behavior.

(*O*) Consumers *seek order* in their world. That is, consumers are constantly attributing causes to the various events that they experience. The attribution the consumer makes regarding the exact reason a salesperson is recommending a high-priced model is very likely to affect the consumer's purchase decision.

(*N*) Our final framework entry stresses that consumers are guided by a *need hierarchy.* Maslow, for example, believed that physiological and lower-level needs must be satisfied before higher needs (such as esteem or "self-actualization") can be activated. A second influential theory—Murray's inventory of human needs—was also introduced in this section.

■ KEY TERMS

motivation	unaware	projective tests	primary motives
consumer inertia	qualitative research	avoidance-avoidance conflict	selective motives
purposive behavior	focus group	expectancy $\times$ value theory	motives
unconscious level	in-depth personal interviews	attribution theory	multiple motives

overt motives	pleasure principle	psychological field	FITD technique
hidden motives	ego	valence	DITF technique
conscious level	reality principle	motivational conflicts	need hierarchy
preconscious level	superego	approach-avoidance conflict	metamotives
theory of unconscious motivation	field theory	approach-approach conflict	Murray's inventory of social needs
id	life space	self-perception	need
libido			

■ REVIEW QUESTIONS AND EXPERIENTIAL EXERCISES

[E = **Application extension or experiential exercise**]

1. Explain the relationship between motivation and consumer activities. What marketing implications come from understanding consumer motivation?

2. Purposive behavior is an important concept in consumer motivation for both consumers and marketers. Explain, citing examples.

3. Individual differences were mentioned as a major aspect of consumer motivation. What exactly does this term mean? Are consumers really so different? Don't we all really want the same things in life? At which levels of motivation do consumers differ? What marketing implications do your answers have?

4. [E] After reading all elements of the MOTIVATION framework, select the three that you believe will be most useful for marketing decisions. Briefly describe your reasoning (together with examples, if possible).

5. [E] Reflecting our discussions of projective techniques, try a sample application for yourself (you may wish to use a market research text or library reference source for detailed guidance). For example, select three brands or stores from a competitive product or service category. Have 10 people write (or relate to you) an obituary for each of the brands or stores (e.g., "Let's pretend that the Tide brand has just disappeared from the market ... what would you write in a brief obituary for Tide?") Do the 10 obituaries show a consistent pattern? What particular implications do these reports have for the competing marketers? Does this seem to be a useful technique, and how might it be improved? Write a report on your study.

6. [E] Interview a market researcher from a company, research firm, or advertising agency. Discuss his or her firm's use of qualitative research. Write a brief report on your findings.

7. [E] Use the references in Note 3 at the back of the book or selections in your library's reference section for further reading on Ernest Dichter's views on hidden motivation (or the views of other researchers). If possible, obtain and read the classic book by Vance Packard, *The Hidden Persuaders.* Write a brief report on your findings.

8. [E] Using some of the readings in Note 19 or selections in the reference section of your library, read about recent developments in marketing planned experiences and in other marketing appeals to consumers' thirst for variety. Write a brief report on your findings.

9. [E] Using some of the readings near the end of Note 21 or selections in the reference section of your library, read more about attribution theory and its recent applications to marketing management (for example, you may wish to read more about the FITD or DITF selling techniques). Write a brief report on your findings.

10. [E] Choose a recent purchase you have made that required shopping and deliberation. Think back over the process, including all your interactions with marketing stimuli and salespersons. Analyze the three stages (your prepurchase process, purchase process, and postpurchase process) in terms of your personal attribution processes. Write a brief report of your analysis, including implications for both the successful and unsuccessful marketers involved in your purchase.

11. [E] What are the levels of Maslow's need hierarchy? For each level, give an example of how consumer behavior relates to it. Overall, what is your estimate of the importance that each level represents in terms of consumers' dollar spending (that is, rank the levels on this measure). Write a brief report summarizing your findings and noting their implications for marketers.

12. [E] Read carefully through Murray's list of needs and the definitions given in Table 5-2. Select any five of the needs and suggest some ways in which each is reflected in typical forms of consumer behavior. Then consider five possible ways in which pairs of these five needs might fuse together to drive particular forms of consumer behavior.

13. [E] One of the examples in this chapter described the findings of a qualitative research study for the Combat

roach killer product. Based on these findings, develop one or several new advertising campaign themes for Combat, with a brief explanation of your reasoning.

14. [E] In discussing the two elements of consumer motivation—energy and direction—the chapter raised the example of recalls for the Pinto automobile and for Firestone tires. Using Table 5-2's listing of Murray's needs as a guide, think about why consumer inertia might exist for these recalls (keep in mind, however, that only some consumers are contributing to the problem). Review the list of Murray's needs to select those that

you believe may be relevant. Create several appeals to these needs that you believe might work to overcome inertia and spark positive consumer reactions to the recalls. Write a brief report on your suggestions.

15. [E] Our discussion of consumers' thirst for variety mentioned the likely appearance of "Virtual Reality" in the next few years. Using either the listings in Note 19 (the *Fortune* magazine piece is particularly helpful) or periodicals in the reference section of your library, prepare a brief report on the marketing uses and implications of "Virtual Reality."

■ SUGGESTED READING

■ A number of interesting books and articles are available. For a well-written and reasonably current look at how marketers are dealing with qualitative research, see Rebecca Piirto, *Beyond Mind Games: The Marketing Power of Psychographics* (Ithaca, NY: American Demographics Books, 1991, pp. 124–141), as well as the references listed in Notes 9 and 10. For a glimpse of the future for "designed experiences" through virtual reality, Gene Bylinsky, "The Marvels of Virtual Reality," *Fortune,* June 3, 1991, pp. 138–150, provides a nice overview (given that developments are rapid here, however, your reference librarian may make a more current suggestion by the time you read this). For any other topic discussed in the chapter, the Notes section should provide some good leads.

CONSUMER MOTIVATION (II)
Applications and Extensions

THE LONGEST RIDE...

Consumer involvement is a matter of degrees. At one extreme is Mr. Philip Miuccio, a 67-year-old Floridian, who went to a Daytona Beach cemetery and requested the construction of a $30,000 marble mausoleum with bulletproof windows to house his remains inside his DeLorean sports car. At last notice, cemetery officials were trying to talk him out of the idea of the windows! According to Mr. Miuccio, "Who says you can't take it with you?"[1]

AND RIGHT IN STRIDE...

Meanwhile, a New York ad agency recently announced that its research showed that different brands of sneakers were appealing to different types of consumers.[2] See if you can match which brand appeals most to consumers who strive for:

1. Winning and status? _____   **a.** Keds
2. Simplicity and family? _____   **b.** L.A. Gear
3. Comfort and stability? _____   **c.** Nike
4. Indulgence and sexiness? _____   **d.** Reebok

In Chapter 5 we learned a great deal about the basics of **motivation**, or "the processes that move a person to behave in certain ways." Our discussion there dealt largely with general topics, however. Here we will get more specific.

Our two opening examples demonstrate that products have meaning for people. Consider, for example, that Mr. Miuccio's case is not newsworthy because he likes his car, but only because his emotional *involvement* appears extreme. The sneaker report, meanwhile, shows how different people, because they have different *values*, will come

149

to prefer different brands of shoes (as an aside, you may be interested to know that the agency's research findings were 1. c; 2. a; 3. d; 4. b).

For many years marketers have been searching for useful, systematic ways to capture dimensions of consumer motivation to improve marketing strategy. In this chapter we will examine four such areas of research and applications: (1) consumer personality, (2) consumer values, (3) consumer involvement, and (4) consumer emotions; then we'll close with a short look at how these can be combined to develop advertising strategy.

■ PERSONALITY AND CONSUMER BEHAVIOR

Personality: Classifications of people, based on consistency in behaviors and reactions to events.

The concept of **personality** is one of the great topics of behavioral science. Thousands of books and articles have been written on this subject over the centuries. The idea in most definitions of personality is to stress a person's *consistency in behaviors and reactions to events* in various phases of their lives. Thus we are interested in classifying individuals into "types" of people.

Sigmund Freud's psychoanalytic theory, described briefly in Chapter 5, provided a starting point for theories of personality. However, Freud's theory was viewed as powerful but restrictive, since he focused so strongly on inner conflicts in childhood. Several of his colleagues broke with him to develop their own broader **neo-Freudian, social views** of personality theory. Although their own theories differed significantly, the neo-Freudian theorists were stressing that people's personalities continued to develop as adults and that the role of interpersonal (social) factors was extremely important. Among the prominent neo-Freudians were Alfred Adler (who invented the term "inferiority complex"), Erich Fromm (who stressed people's loneliness in society and their seeking of love and satisfying human relationships), Karen Horney (whose work is described in our example that follows), and Harry Stack Sullivan (who was especially concerned with people's attempts to reduce tensions through useful interpersonal situations and relationships). While we are unable to detail the specifics of neo-Freudian theory here, the theory is extremely interesting. (For a modern, modified test you can take to classify yourself within the highly regarded neo-Freudian theory of Carl Jung (pronounced "Yoong"), consult the reference in Note 3.)

Trait: A relatively enduring characteristic in which people differ from each other.

More recently, **trait theories** of personality have been developed. While the neo-Freudian work was largely *qualitative*, trait theory has come from *quantitative* studies. A **trait** is a relatively enduring characteristic in which people differ from each other. In developing personality tests with this approach, then, the researchers often begin with people's answers to many questions and then use statistical techniques to identify which answers best distinguish one person from another. This results in a personality test that can be used to classify a person as one "type" or another. (Among the best known of these personality tests is the Edwards Personal Preference Schedule, which is based upon Henry Murray's list of needs that we examined at the end of Chapter 5.) Because these tests have been designed to be readily administered to individuals, they have been frequently used in marketing studies.

Brief though it has been, the foregoing discussion should be helpful in providing a general idea of the nature of personality theories. Each stresses a somewhat different aspect of a person's motivations and interpersonal relations. There are many sources available for in-depth reading in the personality field. One excellent source that reviews all the major theories is the classic text by Hall and Lindzey, whose reference is given in Note 4.

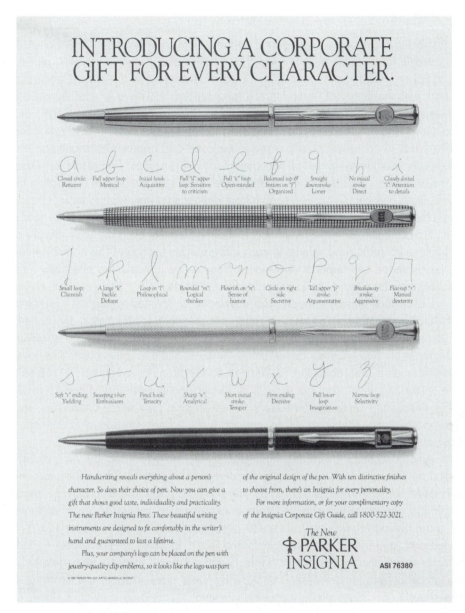

Notice how this ad appeals to people's interest in better understanding their own personality and that of others.

PERSONALITY RESEARCH IN MARKETING

The marketing and consumer research world discovered the computer about 1960. This discovery opened new vistas for research on consumer markets. For the first time it was possible to analyze data on *large samples* of consumers, using *many questions* and sophisticated statistical analyses. Thus began the **quantitative era** of marketing research, which is still in force today.

Consumer personality was one of the first topics to receive attention in this burst of quantitative marketing research. To appreciate the type of research that's been done, let's briefly examine one classic article:

Quantitative era: Still in existence today, refers to the use of large samples, many survey questions, and sophisticated statistical analyses in consumer research.

🐚 *"C," "A," or "D," Which Is He?*

A classic personality study was reported by Joel B. Cohen in the mid-1960s. Cohen was interested in how people behave toward each other and their environments, reflecting the social or "interpersonal" orientation toward personality. In this case, Cohen chose to work with the theory of Karen Horney (pronounced "Horn-eye").[5] Horney classified individuals into three groups: those who move *toward* people (**compliant**), those who move *against* people (**aggressive**), and those who move *away from* people (**detached**). A compliant person wants to be loved and appreciated by others. These individuals seek friendship and an accepted place within groups. Aggressive individuals, on the other hand, desire to stand out and excel. They seek power and admiration from others. Detached people desire freedom from obligations. They wish to be independent from others and are little interested in either influencing them or being influenced by them. Horney believed that, although each of us has some of each tendency, usually one of the three comes to predominate in each individual's personality. This occurs primarily during childhood and depends on which strategy seems to work most effectively for the child attempting to deal with his or her family and peers.

Cohen took Horney's theory and developed a new test called the CAD Scale, reflecting the compliant, aggressive, and detached personality types. He believed, for example, that aggressive persons might prefer products that suggest success or strength. In his study, Cohen administered the CAD Scale to male students at several universities while also obtaining information on the brands they preferred. The results were interesting. In terms of the *strength* of the personality measures, of the 15 product categories Cohen chose as most likely to demonstrate personality differences, seven showed statistically significant differences and eight did not. The size of the differences was not huge in most of the cases.

Among Cohen's interesting findings: *mouthwash* was used by 74 percent of compliant (C) individuals but by only 56 percent of detached (D) persons. C's were also found strongly to prefer *Dial soap* (47 percent), compared with only 31 percent of D's (38 percent of the detached sample expressed no particular brand preference for soap, compared with only about 20 percent in the C and A categories). Within *deodorants*, aggressive men's favorite brand was Old Spice, whereas both C and D types preferred the market leader, Right Guard (of the 8 students who reported no use of deodorants, seven were D's). A's also were more likely to use cologne and after-shave lotion, more strongly preferred manual razors as a shaving method, and were more likely to name Coors as their favorite beer. D's, meanwhile, were more likely to drink tea on a regular basis, but less likely to drink wine than either of the other types. Cohen concluded that his preliminary results were sufficiently strong that the issue of personality's link with consumer behavior deserved much further study in marketing.[6]

SUMMARY OF FINDINGS ON PERSONALITY AND CONSUMER BEHAVIOR

Over 300 studies of personality and consumer behavior have now been reported in marketing literature.[7] This number does not include, of course, the thousands of studies done privately by companies and advertising agencies. The published studies included issues such as

- Do brand-loyal buyers have different personalities?
- Do "innovators" have different personalities?
- Are certain personality types easier to persuade?

If you have an interest in personality issues in consumer behavior, you may wish to read the excellent reviews listed in Note 8.

Overall Findings: Ambiguous

Overall, what have these studies found? As Harold Kassarjian reports in his review of these research studies,

> (They) can be summarized in the single word "equivocal." A few studies indicate a strong relationship. . . . A few indicate no relationship. . . . And the great majority indicate that if correlations do exist they are so weak as to be questionable or perhaps meaningless . . . .

In essence, then, most research has found personality results similar to those obtained by Cohen in our "C," "A," or "D" example. Some personality measures show statistically significant results with consumer behavior, but many do not. Of those that do, the relationships appear to be weak (in statistical terms, they explain only about 10 percent of the variation among consumers). This uncertain or ambiguous pattern of results has left marketers in a somewhat unpleasant position regarding personality research. Does this mean that personality doesn't work? First, we need to understand better why the statistical results seem weak.

Why Are Results Weak?

Why would personality results in consumer behavior explain such a low proportion of variation in the data? In concept, this is not difficult to understand. Let's think about the following cases, using CAD personality types for convenience.

Case 1

Mary Jackson and Kimberly Lane are both aggressive (A) personality types. Mary, however, is 80 years old, and Kimberly is 22. Given such an age difference, we'd well imagine that their tastes in many product classes would be different.

Case 2

Stephen Robbins and Jane Winters both score as compliant (C) personality types. Since Steve is a male, however, he does not even buy many of the products that Jane does, and vice versa. In addition, social factors influence Steve toward certain preferences and Jane toward other preferences.

Case 3

Carter Brown and Ralph Smith are both detached (D) types. Carter, however, comes from an extremely wealthy family, while Ralph's family has faced divorce and welfare conditions for much of his life. Because of their incomes and backgrounds, these two young men shop in entirely different types of stores and search for different quality levels. In total, Carter spends far more money than Ralph does over the course of the year.

These examples could go on and on, of course. The point they are making, however, is that, even if two people share many of the *same personality* traits, they're likely to *differ in many other factors* that are also important in determining actual consumer behavior. Thus, unless these other factors are somehow taken into account, our research on personality wouldn't show terribly strong results.

Unfortunately, this is not the only problem faced by consumer researchers interested in personality's effects. Consider the following examples as well:

Case 4

All the people in cases 1, 2, and 3, except Carter, believe that "soup is good food," and all of them eat Campbell's soup at least occasionally.

Case 5

Kimberly and Ralph each bought a Chevy recently, but for different reasons. Kimberly was sold on the basis of several of her friends' experiences, together with the clear popularity of the car. Ralph, on the other hand, wasn't sure what he wanted, but was talked (driven?) into buying by a skilled salesperson who appealed to his intelligence and achievements.

Case 6

All the people like soft drinks except Mary, who prefers tea. Each person sometimes drinks different brands, though. Carter and Jane happen to prefer Diet Coke, whereas Kimberly likes Diet Pepsi, Ralph prefers Pepsi, and Steve likes 7-Up best.

Cases 4, 5, and 6 show us how reasonable it is that people with *different personalities* might prefer the *same product*, particularly if we are talking about a brand that is frequently purchased and/or quite popular. When consumers exhibit these types of preferences, again we would see very weak personality results emerging in research.

Overall, then, it is clear that there are many reasons why past studies in personality have obtained the results they did. As we've noted, this does not mean that personality exerts no influence on consumer behavior. On the other hand, it does indicate that personality's influence is only one of many significant factors and cannot be expected to dominate all the others.

Recent Trends in Personality Research

Recent work on personality and consumer behavior reveals four distinct trends, each stemming from the lessons learned in the past:[9]

Trend 1: Studying Patterns of Behavior Rather than Single Decisions. Because there are so many factors involved in each specific purchase, and since different brands can be chosen from one time to the next, it is wise to examine more general strategies that consumers use over a set of situations and multiple behaviors. Recent work along this line has shown relationships between personality and types of brand-choice strategies, between personality and patterns of information

Table 6-1 Some Dimensions Used in a Psychographic Study of Premium Cosmetic Buyers

Dimension	Definition
Narcissism	Preoccupied with one's personal appearance (H)
Appearance conscious	Emphasis on looking properly groomed (H)
Exhibitionism	Tendency toward self-display and attention seeking (NS)
Order	Tendency to be compulsively neat, live by rules (NS)
Fantasied achievement	Aspiration for distinction and personal recognition (H)
Capacity for status	Personal qualities that lead to status (L)
Dominant	Need to be in control and in the forefront (L)
Sociable	Need for agreeable relationships with others (H)

SOURCE: See Note 11.

search, and between personality and food behaviors. If we were to think even more broadly, examining such issues as preferences for forms of entertainment, colors, spending versus saving decisions, and so forth, we might uncover further systematic relationships.

Trend 2: Focusing on Consumption Rather than General Needs. Because personality reflects patterns of needs, it should be helpful to concentrate on products or situations especially geared to satisfying these needs in a consumer setting. The rise in popularity of **consumer psychographics** that we discussed in Chapter 4 reflects this trend:

What Types of Women Buy Premium Cosmetics?

The creation and development of "psychographics" by marketing researchers reflects a strong desire to represent personality-type differences in a realistic consumer context.[10] Table 6-1 illustrates some of the psychographic dimensions created by Grey Advertising to study female consumers of premium cosmetics. Looking only at the dimensions in the table, which four would you say will characterize buyers of premium cosmetics? Which two are likely to be irrelevant in distinguishing these people? And on which two dimensions are premium buyers likely to be lower than the average woman? (At the right of each definition, (H) indicates high scores for premium users, (L) indicates low scores, and (NS) indicates no significant difference from other women). Notice how these results can be used in the development of advertising appeals![11]

Trend 3: Shifting Attention to Develop Related Areas As we noted at the start of the chapter, personality is an extremely broad topic. Beyond the "mainline" approaches we've examined, let's take a quick look at two interesting examples of developments in personality-related topics:

It's in My Blood!

Medical researchers have long known that **physiological differences** can cause differences in behavior. Some of this research on the influence of the body's physical characteristics has been extended to consumer behavior. For example, in one highly exploratory study, blood tests showed that consumers with low levels of the enzyme monoamine oxidase (MAO) are more likely than others to make risky investment decisions (this extends earlier research that related low levels of MAO to some people's increased desire to climb mountains and jump out of airplanes). The marketing applications of this finding are not yet entirely clear (and this author is not aware that this issue has been rigorously tested). If this *is* valid, however, it appears that stockbrokers (and insurance firms) would benefit from obtaining blood test results from their prospective clients (sounds vile, doesn't it?).[12]

🐛 Have a Fit!

Self-concept: An area of research based on the premise that products help to express an image of either an "actual self" or an "ideal self."

Another extension, but one that has received more consideration in consumer behavior, is the area of **self-concept.** The belief is that a consumer will prefer those products that help to express that consumer's image of himself or herself. These images, in turn, can reflect either the **actual self** (the "real me") or the **ideal self** (the "person I'd like to be"). Consumer products are useful for both images: we can use them to reflect who we are, and sometimes use them to become more like who we'd like to be. If we think briefly about it, we can recognize this link to store images, to brand images, and to advertising appeals to sophistication, youth, popularity, fashion, and so forth. There is a strong personal component to the self-concept: this is easy to recognize when the actual self and idealized self don't match too well, as mirrored in the following:

Which piece of clothing do women most hate to buy? The runaway winner: the swimsuit! According to Heidi Goldstein, an advertising coordinator, "I really, really hate buying bathing suits. It's humiliating." Cathy Guisewite, the author of the "Cathy" comic strip, says she sometimes breaks down and sobs in the fitting room and is happy to escape with "some shred of dignity." According to a consumer researcher for the swimwear industry, "I didn't find one adult woman in the United States who enjoyed buying swimsuits." Over one-third of consumers described the purchase as "traumatic."

Why is this? According to a fashion sociologist, "it has nothing to do with vanity," but instead reflects consumers' fears about social standards for how they should look in a swimsuit (note: feminist scholars might view this as more complex than described here). She points out that European women don't have these same hang-ups, and they buy more than twice as many swimsuits as Americans. The industry is now attempting to increase sales by clever engineering of new suits, installing pink light bulbs in dressing rooms (to replace the harsh fluorescent lights that create ghastly skin), playing mellow music, and so on. However, they realize that they are up against a powerful self-concept

cathy®   **by Cathy Guisewite**

A.

Oh you are so emotional.

There you are all caught up in your emotions, wearing your heart on your sleeve, wearing your heart on every piece of clothing you own. You cry at the drop of a hat. You cry absolute buckets. You cry me a river.

You're a woman (you can't help it) you're a girl (now don't get me wrong) you're a woman and you're *so emotional* about everything and

even at those times when you're *perfectly* rational and *perfectly* capable somebody somewhere will look at you and shake their head and say (like it's the worst thing in the world)

Oh you are so emotional

and of course that really makes you want to scream.

And then just as soon as you don't weep, which is most of the time anyway, and you're cool and calm and absolutely brilliant under pressure somebody somewhere will say you're too cool and too calm and then, of course, you're suddenly and forever called *insensitive.*

Ah, to be a woman.   (continued)

B.

Somewhere in the middle of all these assumptions and all these labels is the way you really are. You are kind (that's why we have hearts). You are strong (or you wouldn't have made it this far). You are fearless (or you would have hidden your heart long ago). And because you wear your heart so easily sometimes

you know how easily it is broken.

So, through time, you have learned to protect it. You learn to take it out for long walks. You learn to let it breathe deeply. You learn to treat it with respect.

And, through time, you have learned to move it and bend it and shake it and make it accountable, because the best way to keep a heart alive is to be unafraid to use it. And you are so very good at using it.

Listen.

Your heart is beating. This means you are alive. Your body is moving. This means you cannot be stopped. The world and all its labels are calling to you. You'd love to answer. But you're moving so fast you can't hear a thing.

Just do it.

This award-winning multipage ad for Nike was aimed at increasing share of the women's fitness market. Notice the appeals to a person's self-concept, first in A, then in B.

phenomenon. Even women who sell swimsuits can hate buying them! One young sales clerk reported hopefully, "Maybe I'll get sick and lose weight in the next month...or maybe something exciting will happen and I'll be too busy to eat."[13] (Not all aspects of the consumer self-concept are negative, of course. If you would like to learn more about developments in this area, you may wish to consult Note 14.)

Trend 4: Studying How Personality Affects Responses to Advertising.

Recent research has shown that personality affects how consumers respond to advertising. For example, consumers who score high on **need for cognition** enjoy thinking, whereas consumers scoring low on this scale tend to avoid effort in cognitive work. As might be expected, this difference extends to influence how these consumers will process advertising messages. Consumers who are low in need for cognition spend less time thinking about product points made in an ad. Thus they are *less influenced* by the quality of the arguments, but are *more influenced* by the attractiveness of product endorsers than are consumers who have high need for cognition. As we will discuss further in Chapter 16, these findings have implications for how effective ads can be best created.[15]

Self-monitoring: The process of noting how one's actions are being perceived by other people.

Another stream of successful personality research involves **self-monitoring**. For example, some consumers are "high self-monitors"; that is, they strive to be the type of person called for by each situation in which they find themselves: they are adept at tailoring their behavior to social situations (that is, they closely monitor how their actions are being perceived by people around them). By contrast, "low-self-monitoring" consumers are more attuned to their inner concerns about how they wish to act and are usually less sensitive to fitting in with situational concerns. Several studies have shown that—as we would expect—advertising appeals to "image" are more preferred by high self-monitors, while low self-monitors react better to appeals to product quality. For example, in one study high self-monitors reported that they were interested in trying a new shampoo that "usually rates about average in how it cleans your hair, and consistently rates above average in how good it makes your hair look." Low self-monitors, conversely, were not interested in trying this brand, but instead preferred to try the brand that "usually rates about average in how good it makes your hair look, and consistently rates above average in how clean it gets your hair." (Recent research is now clarifying conditions under which self-monitoring seems to work best: if you are interested in learning more about this area, Note 16 lists some good readings.)[16]

CONCLUDING COMMENTS ON CONSUMER PERSONALITY

It is difficult to present a concise conclusion about this area. Given the large number of studies and high hopes held originally, the findings might be characterized as disappointing. However, marketing practitioners have used many insights from the consumer personality area in gaining a "feel" for the consumer marketplace and in devising marketing strategies. As reflected in our Chapter 4 discussion of market segmentation, the development of psychographics has been a significant step, and successful consumer research has recently been conducted in the four trend areas noted here: we expect that this will continue. However, some of the attention that was previously given to personality has now been shifted to other consumer motivation topics. One of these is consumer values, which we discuss in the next section.

Nissan appeals to striving for mastery in this award-winning commercial, "Bob's Road."

■ CONSUMER VALUES AND LADDERING RESEARCH

WHAT ARE CONSUMER VALUES?

While consumer personality research has stressed why people are *different* from one another, consumer values research stresses the *important goals* most people are seeking. In psychological theory, **values** are closely linked to needs, but they exist for us at a more obvious, realistic level. According to Henry Murray (whose list of needs we examined at the end of the last chapter), values are the mental representations of our underlying needs, after they have been transformed to take into account the realities of the world in which we live. In other words, *values are our ideas about what is desirable.* There are two main types of values: (1) terminal and (2) instrumental. **Terminal (or end-state) values** are beliefs we have about the goals or end-states for which we strive (e.g., happiness, wisdom). **Instrumental (or means) values,** on the other hand, refer to beliefs about desirable ways of behaving to help us attain the terminal values (e.g., behaving honestly, accepting responsibility).[17]

Since values are transmitted through cultures and subcultural groups, most people in a society will agree that they are good. What differs, however, is *how important* each value is in each person's daily life and thinking. Some people will stress some values, while other people will stress other values. Also, the prominence of different values can change over time. Figure 6-1 shows how this has happened for college students of the 1960s versus those of the 1980s. Notice how strongly the prevailing values shifted during this time! These results demonstrate why some people

Values: The mental representations of underlying needs after they have been transformed to take account the realities of the world.

Terminal (or end-state) values: The goals or end-states for which we strive (e.g. happiness, wisdom).

Instrumental (or means) values: Desirable ways of behaving to help us attain terminal values (e.g. behaving honestly, accepting responsibility).

Percent surveyed who most wanted to:			% change (from 1967)	Rank	
				1967	1985
Be very well off financially	1985	70%[a]	+63%	4	1
	1967	43%			
Help others	1985	63%	−9%	2	2
	1967	69%			
Have administrative responsibility	1985	43%	+95%	6	3(T)
	1967	22%			
Develop a meaningful philosophy of life	1985	43%	−46%	1	3(T)
	1967	82%			
Keep up with political affairs	1985	38%	−34%	3	5
	1967	58%			
Become an expert in finance and commerce	1985	26%	+100%	7	6
	1967	13%			
Clean up the environment	1985	20%	−59%	4	7
	1967	49%			

0 10 20 30 40 50 60 70 80 90 100

FIGURE 6-1 How College Students' Values Changed over One Generation, 1985 Versus 1967

[a]Numbers show percentage of students who ranked each value as one of the top three in importance to them.

SOURCE: Adapted from "Data Bank Youth Marketing." *Advertising Age*, February 1, 1988. p. S-32.

referred to young people in the 1960s as the "hippie" generation while those in the 1980s were known as the "gimme" generation.

Even so, we should notice also that for each value listed, how very many college students would *not* place it in their three most pressing goals. We can thus see how individual differences (and market segmentation possibilities) are present in the values area as well. Much progress has been reported recently, as indicated in the following example.

ଏ‍ୠ *All We Need Is LOV*

In recent years researchers have been working to develop short lists of values that can be measured in a reliable manner. One contribution, by Lynn Kahle, is simply termed the **List of Values (LOV).** It contains nine terminal values or goals for which we strive:

- Self-respect
- Self-fulfillment
- Security
- Sense of belonging
- Excitement
- Sense of accomplishment
- Fun and enjoyment in life
- Being well respected
- Warm relationships with others

In one exploratory study, researchers found that LOV related well to various aspects of consumer behavior. For example, people who highly value a "sense of belonging" are more heavily involved in leisure activities, particularly those involving groups. Meanwhile, consumers who highly value "fun and enjoyment" preferred more exciting media (*Playboy, Rolling Stone*) and more exciting sports. Conversely, consumers who highly value "security" watched more television and reported more hobby activities.

Recently, LOV has been compared to the VALS system we discussed in the appendix to Chapter 4. The controversy as to which of these is better will likely rage on as developments in methodology continue to be tested. (If you would like to read more about LOV and/or its comparison with VALS as a segmentation device, you may wish to consult the references in Note 18.)

APPLICATION ADVANCE: LADDERING

Switching gears to a different use of values, you may recall that the topic of expectancy-value models arose in the "A" section of Chapter 5's MOTIVATION framework, where we stressed the idea of goal-directed behavior. These models assert that people act to satisfy underlying *needs*. These needs, in turn, are realistically represented by the *values* that we hold. The result is a view of consumer behavior as being a **means to an end:** consumers act in order to achieve the benefits they are seeking. Thus marketers have found it useful to think of products as "bundles of benefits."

In recent years this thinking has been built into a useful marketing approach called **laddering.** Laddering attempts to trace the linkages between a consumer's values and the particular product attributes managed by marketers. These linkages— sometimes called a **means-ends chain**—are shown in Figure 6-2. Notice that the basic **A-C-V model** contains just three steps: (1) products offer *attributes* to consumers, (2) consumers experience *consequences* when they consume the attributes, and (3) the consequences help consumers attain particular *values*. The more tightly a marketer can link the attributes to value attainment, the stronger the attraction his or her product or service will have for consumers.

In the middle of Figure 6-2 we see a slightly expanded A-C-V model. Here distinctions are made between concrete and abstract attributes, functional and psychological or social consequences, and instrumental or terminal values. The sample ladder shown at the bottom of Figure 6-2 helps us see how these various levels interrelate in one consumer's views of the salty snack category. Notice how the concrete attribute of "flavor" in a chip product has meanings and implications that trace back to an important terminal value for that consumer.

Within the real world of marketing, of course, there are many possible concrete attributes for a product or service and many possible ladders moving back toward consumers' values. The relationships for some will be much stronger than relationships for others; thus laddering research can be quite complex. If valid information can be obtained, however, tremendously valuable insights for product development and advertising strategy can become available, as shown in the following example.

🐦 *Why Fool Around with Anyone Else?*

Federal Express has long been known for humorous advertising that helped to make a giant industry out of overnight delivery services. A few years ago, when competition increased significantly, Federal Express turned to the laddering techniques developed by Thomas Reynolds and Jonathan Gutman. The company first determined that one of its prime market segments consisted of executive secretaries. Following a large number of in-depth personal interviews with secretaries, advanced statistical methods were used to generate the "summary hierarchical value map," shown in Figure 6-3. Notice how the two concrete *attributes* at the bottom (availability of convenient places to drop off boxes and on-time delivery) represent the controllable decisions that can be altered by Federal

Laddering: A marketing research technique that traces the linkages between a consumer's values and the product attributes managed by marketers.

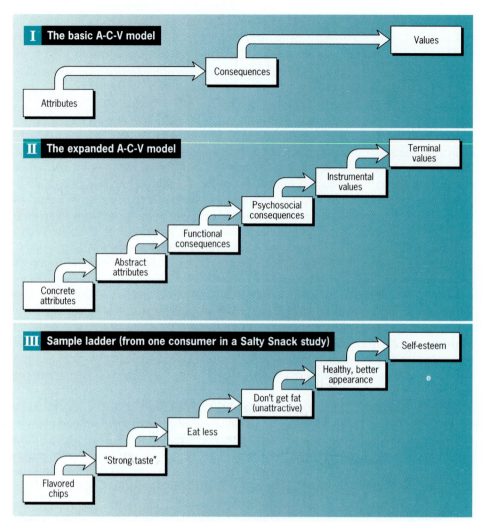

FIGURE 6-2 Means-Ends Laddering. In each case we move from the physical world at the left to the mental world of values at the right. The in-between "steps of the ladder" represent the associations that consumers might make to go from the "means" (buying a physical product or service) to the "end" (helping to attain a particular value).
SOURCE: See Note 19.

Express management. The meanings of these attributes (that is, their *consequences*) are then traced through three different laddering routes in the typical customer's mind, having different lengths and serving different values. (Notice also that the number of levels is different for each ladder—applied work often runs into cases in which consumers reveal shorter or longer ladders.)

Based on these results, together with tests of competitors' advertising, the researchers worked to develop a new advertising campaign using the **MECCAS model** (Means-Ends Conceptualization of the Components of Advertising Strategy). Figure 6-4 outlines the MECCAS approach and summarizes the resulting ad campaign aimed at the secretarial target market. Notice how it stresses the rightmost ladder in Figure 6-3,

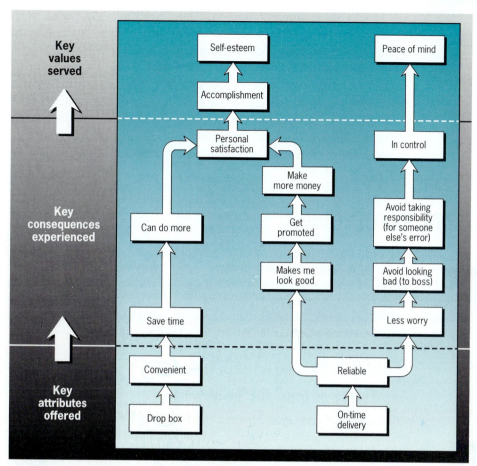

FIGURE 6-3 Summary "Hierarchical Value Map" for the Federal Express Study, Representing Executive Secretaries' Links for Attributes to Consequences to Values. These results were used as the basis for developing a successful ad campaign geared to having the corporate secretaries choose Federal Express for delivery services.
SOURCE: See Note 19.

Target market	Executive secretaries, who decide on which overnight delivery service the company will use, are targeted.
Terminal value	Ad will focus on "peace of mind."
Instrumental value	Ad will focus on the secretary feeling "in control" by using a company in which he or she can place his or her trust.
Executional framework	Execution is humorous, with a secretary working hard at trying to find out where a package is right now. The boss and employee are interrupted and taken by guide to view Federal Express satellite communication system used to track exact status of overnight letters and packages. Secretary realizes the benefits available in using Federal Express.
Customer benefit	Key attribute is reliability/dependability; makes his or her work easier.
Message elements	Superior tracking system; integrated satellite communications network.
Tag line	"Why fool around with anyone else?"

FIGURE 6-4 The Federal Express Ad Strategy (Based on Laddering Research)

aiming to make a strong connection to the "peace of mind" value. Notice also how the execution blends the concrete attributes with a humorous approach to maintain continuity with the past Federal Express ads that the target customers are likely to remember (perhaps you even recall the tag line). Copy test research on the new ads showed that they were strongly communicating the desired messages: executives at Federal Express were quite pleased with the value of this research. Within recent years, many consumer marketers have begun to use this technique to design marketing mixes aimed at achieving consumer satisfaction. (If you would like to learn more about recent developments on laddering and the MECCAS model, you may wish to begin with the readings in Note 19).

■ CONSUMER INVOLVEMENT

Consumer involvement: A concept relating to personal relevance: a state of energy (arousal) that a person experiences in regard to a consumption-related activity.

The third topic in our coverage of extensions and applications of motivational theory concerns **consumer involvement.** In recent years this concept has become a major center of interest in consumer behavior. We will be discussing detailed aspects of its effects in several upcoming chapters. Since involvement is so closely related to individual needs, however, this chapter is an especially appropriate place for us to focus on laying out some of its basic dimensions.

WHAT IS "CONSUMER INVOLVEMENT?"

The Reality of Consumer Involvement

The concept of consumer involvement relates to a sense of personal relevance: let's begin by listening to some typical incidents reported by consumers:

> I'm really involved when I'm getting ready for a date....I care a lot about my appearance—my overall look!...Sometimes I just sit at my dressing table and lose track of the time...to some extent I guess I'm anxious about looking good so my date will be impressed, but it's really more than that usually...I think I really am interested in people's appearance, especially my own!
>
> —Debra Brooks, brand manager

> I enjoy photography and everything about it....I spend hours reading and talking about new developments and testing out new products.
>
> —David Taylor, accountant

> I am very involved with my family life....We just built a new home and I spent months making all the detailed decisions about room arrangements, fabrics, colors, and the like. Now I'm on to the furnishings, and having a ball...if we can afford everything, it's going to be a great home!
>
> —Martha Hook, salesperson

The Theory of Consumer Involvement

Overall, we can define consumer involvement (or CI) as *a state of energy (arousal) that a person experiences in regard to a consumption-related activity.* CI thus includes both major components of motivation: energy and direction. **High involvement** requires that high levels of energy are aroused within the consumer and that this energy is directed toward a particular consumer activity. A person who is *highly involved* is likely to be thinking

High involvement springs from needs that are closely tied to a consumer's self-concept. Many persons, for example, are highly involved in their physical health and appearance and create a huge market for related products. Recently, for example, when TV talk show host Oprah Winfrey revealed that she had lost almost 70 pounds on Optifast's liquid diet program, the firm received 200,000 phone inquiries from consumers in 48 hours.

more, or feeling more strongly. Notice that all of our quotes showed instances of high consumer involvement. We saw consumers highly involved in enjoying experiences (Debra), highly involved in thinking and learning about products (David), and highly involved in making purchase decisions (Martha). (Please note, however, that for some consumers *compulsive behaviors* do cause serious problems.)[20]

Low involvement, on the other hand, occurs when consumers invest less energy into their thoughts or feelings. Theoretically, the CI concept can be traced back to Freud's basic theory that asserts that a person's ego will take control of the id's psychic energy and direct it primarily toward objects (or people, products, activities, etc.) that are most likely to satisfy basic needs that the person is experiencing.[21] Thus involvement is closely related to personality theory and values theory as well, since the same forces are operating.

Several key points are included in our view of CI:

1. *CI occurs within specific consumer-related episodes.* Every type of consumer activity contains some level of CI. The exact CI level will differ by consumer and by occasion, so that each separate episode has its own CI level.

2. *High CI is likely to occur when a person's "self" is closely tied to the consumer activity episode.* A good example is provided by Martha. Notice that she begins by pointing out how important her family is to her. The intensity she is experiencing is closely

tied to her "self-concept" as a wife and mother as well as her "self's" desires to be creative, to build, and to exercise power in decision making.

3. *CI includes both thoughts and feelings.* Both cognitions (thoughts) and emotions (feelings) are present in every instance of CI, although their relative importance may differ. David, for example, clearly experiences pleasurable feelings during his studies of photography. His thinking processes, however, are very important in learning about products and deciding which to purchase.

4. *The study of CI requires difficult research decisions on how to group episodes together, and how to measure energy and direction.* This point addresses advanced research issues, and you may not wish to try to resolve them within an introductory course on consumer behavior. However, it is useful to recognize that these issues pose problems for consumer researchers. (If you would like a sense for these difficulties, see Note 22.)

RESEARCH CONTRIBUTIONS ON CONSUMER INVOLVEMENT

Recent years have seen a number of contributions from researchers toward a better understanding of CI. Entire conferences have been held on this topic, and there have been numerous speeches and articles. Among the interesting and useful insights are:

■ *Different types of involvement.* Researchers have devoted much attention to how best to categorize different types of involvement. For example, one useful distinction is between *product-class involvement* and *brand-choice involvement.* **Product-class involvement** represents the average interest a consumer has in a product category on a day-to-day basis (in our examples, David indicated high product-class involvement for cameras). **Brand-choice involvement** refers to the specific arousal during a purchase process (in our examples, even if Debra had low product-class involvement with cameras, she still might become highly involved during a purchase occasion). Another useful distinction is between the *thinking* and *feeling* dimensions of CI. **Cognitive involvement** refers to the degree of thinking aroused during an episode, while **affective involvement** represents the arousal of feelings and emotions. Another recent distinction of interest points out that *brand commitment* may represent a further type of involvement held by loyal customers. (If you would like to learn more about these and other useful distinctions, Note 23 is a good place to start.)

■ *Measurement of CI.* Useful contributions to theory and measurement have recently been offered and are presently under discussion and extensions. Thus marketers will be able to do even more testing and development on CI in the future.[24]

The Stress on "Low Involvement"

For most people, family, social events, job success, illnesses, and love life are all far more important than is the next purchase of toothpaste or many other products. Thus, while we do care about making "good" purchases, other than for a few purchases (such as a house, car, and so forth) we *don't* usually approach our shopping as if it were a major event in our lives. This affects the ways consumers deal with the marketing environment and make their decisions.

Thus the level of CI that has most intrigued marketers over the past 20 years has been low CI.[25] If we think about it briefly, the reasons behind this interest become clear—marketers may well *not be able to do very much to change the basic levels of involvement* that consumers bring to their encounters with the marketing system. If

Low involvement:
A state of low consumer energy invested in thoughts or feelings concerning an object or purchase.

This award-winning promotion aimed at increasing kids' involvement with Kraft Singles by inviting "outrageous" recipes for sandwiches and sending winners to Disney World. Results? A 21 percent increase in sales, and thousands of new ideas!

this is true, astute marketers are better off to *adapt* their marketing mixes to deal most effectively with the actual levels of CI they encounter.

Thus the interest in low CI has been driven by a need to understand how consumers do make up their minds about purchases when they just don't care very deeply. Some interesting questions typify marketers' concerns with low CI:

- If consumers have low, rather than high, CI with my product class, will it be easier to switch them to my new brand, or will they not even take the trouble to switch?

- Will consumers pay more for my brand because they're not very sensitive about the price of this product, or will they switch away to a lower-priced brand because they're not willing to try to figure out quality differences?

- If I advertise extensively, will consumers with low CI make little or no effort to process my ads, or is constant repetition of my brand name the best strategy, since these consumers won't be thinking much beyond brand names in any event?

We will return to these issues shortly, when we examine a new framework to help plan advertising strategy. First, though, we will discuss a fourth important consumer behavior area that extends and applies consumer motivation concepts: consumer emotion.

■ CONSUMER EMOTION

Emotion is a state of feeling that we experience in reaction to some cause: although it is often sparked by our thoughts, *we experience it through special feelings* in addition to thoughts. Love, joy, surprise, fear, anger, and sadness are some common emotions we experience. Notice how these are primarily *felt* within us and how they have the power to make us *want to act*. If we are angry, for example, we find it difficult to "restrain

Emotion: The state of feeling that we experience in reaction to some cause.

ourselves." Love, on the other hand, leads us to "reach out" to another person, whereas fear makes us want to "get away" from the danger.

Emotion has strong physiological (bodily) elements as well as psychological ones, and produces changes in the state of the person who is experiencing it. For this reason, emotion is difficult to study, but a number of consumer researchers have recently been examining this area.[26]

Hedonic consumption: The sensory, fantasy, and emotive aspects of a person's experiences with products.

The research has covered a number of aspects. For example, Hirschman and Holbrook have looked at what they term **hedonic consumption,** that is, the sensory, fantasy, and emotive aspects of a person's experiences with products, to indicate that people experience many things beyond thoughts when they engage in consumer behavior.[27] Other researchers have been examining the potential uses of **psychophysiological approaches** for consumer research; that is, the use of physiological measures of the body (such as brainwaves, pulse, eye dilation, eye directions, skin response, and so forth) to understand better the emotional and thinking processes that consumers are experiencing.[28] Finally, much of the direct emotion-related research attention recently has been given to the topic of mood and its effects. As defined by Gardner, a **mood** is a feeling state that is subjectively perceived by the individual and that lasts for a relatively short time period (compared to emotions, then, moods are usually less intense, and are less related to a particular stimulus).[29] Moods are interesting in that they affect both how consumers act and how they react. For example, research attention has been given to how different moods affect consumers' receptivity to different kinds of advertising, but also to how different kinds of television programs and different kinds of ads affect consumers' moods.

Mood: A feeling state that is subjectively perceived by the individual and lasts for a relatively short time.

Because of the clear managerial implications for both advertising design and copy testing, researchers are developing and testing scales to measure consumers' moods and emotions; to measure characteristics of different ads in terms of their "warmth," "irritation," and so forth; and to measure consumers' affective, emotional reactions to advertising. (We will be examining some of this research in future chapters, but if you would like to pursue these issues in more depth at the present time, you may wish to begin with the readings in Notes 29 and 30 for this chapter, located at the back of the book.)

■ APPLICATION ADVANCE: A NEW FRAMEWORK FOR ADVERTISING STRATEGY

The motivational concepts we have covered provide a powerful basis for marketers to use in attempting to develop their consumer marketing programs. One recent contribution, by John Rossiter (an Australian marketing professor) and Larry Percy (an ad agency executive), draws directly upon these concepts in a new framework for advertising planning. The entire framework is too large for us to review here, but its essentials are listed in Figure 6-5.

Informational motivations: In the Rossiter-Percy advertising framework, the consumer's desires to relieve negative states.

The heart of the Rossiter-Percy framework involves motivation, emotions, and involvement. Notice at the top of Figure 6-5 that there are two basic types of motivation—a consumer's desire to *relieve a negative state* and a consumer's desire to *achieve a positive state.* These are termed **informational motivations** and **transformational motivations,** respectively. The potential richness of this system can be seen in sections II and III of the figure. Notice that there are five informational motives and that each has emotions associated with it. In the "normal depletion" case, for example, a consumer's supply

CONCEPTS

I. Two types of motivation	A. Relief of a negative state ("informational motivation") B. Achievement of a new positive state ("transformational motivation")
II. Five informational motives (and associated emotional shifts)	A. Problem removal (anger → relief) B. Problem avoidance (fear → relaxation) C. Incomplete satisfaction (disappointment → optimism) D. Mixed approach-avoidance (guilt → peace of mind) E. Normal depletion (mild annoyance → convenience)
III. Three transformational motives (and associated emotional shifts)	A. Sensory gratification (→ elated) B. Intellectual stimulation (→ excited) C. Social approval (→ flattered)
IV. Two levels of involvement	A. Low (consumer does not feel much risk with decision: is willing to "try it and see") B. High (consumer sees decision as risky enough to be worth trying to find out more information)
V. Four types of advertising situations (illustrative product types listed)	A. "Low involvement, informational" (detergents, aspirin, routine industrial products) B. "Low involvement, transformational" (candy, fiction novels) C. "High involvement, informational" (microwave ovens, insurance, new industrial products) D. "High involvement, transformational" (vacation, fashion clothing, car)

GRID

Motivation

	Informational	Transformational
Low	A. *Such products as* ■ detergents ■ aspirin ■ routine industrial products	B. *Such products as* ■ candy ■ fiction novels
High	C. *Such products as* ■ microwave ovens ■ insurance ■ new industrial products	D. *Such products as* ■ vacation ■ fashion clothing ■ car

Involvement

FIGURE 6-5 Some Essentials of the Rossiter-Percy Framework for Advertising Planning
SOURCE: See Note 31.

of bread may have run low (that is, been depleted); the consumer may feel an emotion of mild annoyance, and will be motivated to go out and buy more bread. When this purchase is achieved, the consumer will feel convenienced (or satisfied at having it easily available).

While *informational motives* involve relieving a negative state, *transformational motives* promise to enhance the brand user by delivering a new positive state. That is, in each case the consumer feels positively better (elated, excited, flattered) following the behavior.

Transformational motivations: In the Rossiter-Percy advertising framework, the consumer's desires to achieve positive states.

Involvement is represented at just two levels (high and low) in this framework, each representing a different level of a consumer's "perceived risk" concerning the particular purchase decision. A consumer feeling low involvement would not perceive much risk for a decision, and would simply be willing to make a choice without further mental or emotional activity. Conversely, consumers with high involvement in a decision will perceive risk to be sufficient that they should find out more before deciding what to buy.

The levels of motivation and involvement can then be combined to create a four-cell framework of advertising situations, shown at the bottom of Figure 6-5. Many products can be easily assigned to one of these four categories, depending upon the particular motives and involvement consumers possess. For example, detergents are usually used to relieve a negative state and are often not perceived to be very risky, since most consumers have considerable experience with their favorite brands. Candy, on the other hand, may also not be perceived to be a very risky decision, but the motivation for its purchase is transformational in character and thus would call for some different types of advertising appeals. Similarly, microwave ovens and vacations are both likely to be high-involvement purchases, but the microwave oven is likely to be used to solve some problems, while the vacation is used to enhance one's experiences in life: again, we would expect different types of advertising appeals to be appropriate. (Rossiter and Percy's book goes on to detail many advertising implications of these differences; interested readers may wish to consult the references given in Note 31.)

■ SUMMARY

PERSONALITY AND CONSUMER BEHAVIOR

This chapter examined four areas in which marketers have attempted to extend and apply consumer motivation concepts. The first of these is consumer personality. The term *personality* refers to a consistency in a person's behaviors and reactions to events. We began by discussing two types of personality theories, *neo-Freudian, social theories,* and *trait theories.* The former are qualitative in nature and were developed by followers of Freud who viewed his theory as powerful but too restrictive—their theories stress that personality continues to develop past childhood and that social relationships are important; the latter, on the other hand, came later and were based on quantitative analysis of questions that best differentiated one type of person from another.

Our discussion of personality research in marketing began by pointing out that the widespread availability of computers, beginning about 1960, spurred a great deal of research on consumer personality and psychographics. We then examined a classic study by Cohen that reported a new test called the *CAD Scale.* He classified each consumer as being primarily *compliant, aggressive,* or *detached* and then examined brand preferences where these social traits might be important. Several interesting findings emerged. Over 300 studies of consumer personality have since been reported. Unfortunately, their findings appear to be ambiguous: some are strong, but most are weak. Thus we should not conclude that personality exerts no influence; rather, the evidence indicates that it does not dominate all other factors that bear on consumer behavior. These results have led to four recent trends in consumer personality research: (1) studying patterns of behavior; (2) focusing on consumption-related needs as in psychographic research; (3) shifting attention to related areas such as physiological differences and self-concept; and (4) focusing on how personality affects responses to advertising, where "need for cognition" and "self-monitoring" have been found to be useful personality measures.

CONSUMER VALUES AND LADDERING RESEARCH

The second section of the chapter examined consumer "values," which are our ideas about what is desirable. There are two main types of values, *terminal values*—beliefs about the end-states for which we strive (happiness, wisdom, etc.)—and *instrumental values*—which refer to beliefs about desirable ways of behaving (behaving honestly, accepting responsibility, etc.).

Values tend to be shared within cultures, but can change over time. Our first discussion showed how college students' "most important values" shifted strongly between the 1960s and the 1980s. We then briefly examined the *List of Values (LOV)*, which has received considerable attention recently. We then turned to examine an application advance, a new research technique called *laddering* that allows marketers to use a *means-ends analysis* to link product attributes to consumers' values. A detailed example of the use of laddering by Federal Express was then presented.

CONSUMER INVOLVEMENT

In the third section of the chapter we moved to examine the roots of *consumer involvement, (CI),* which has received much attention in marketing. CI was defined as a motivational *state of arousal* that a person experiences in regard to a consumption-related activity. A person who is highly involved is thinking and/or feeling more strongly about the consumption activity at hand. Among the key points on CI, (1) it occurs within specific episodes, (2) high CI is likely when the person's "self-concept" is closely involved in the consumer activity, and (3) CI includes both feelings and thoughts. We saw why this topic is challenging for marketing researchers and summarized some recent research contributions. We also noted that many consumer behaviors are actually low in CI. Marketers unable to change the basic level of consumers' involvement must adapt to this lower level. Further discussion of CI's impact on consumer behavior will occur in upcoming chapters.

CONSUMER EMOTIONS

The fourth section of our chapter discussed consumer *emotions,* which have also recently received much attention in marketing. An emotion is a state of feeling that we experience in reaction to some cause. Prominent emotions we experience include love, joy, surprise, fear, anger, and sadness. Emotions produce strong physiological (bodily) changes in addition to psychological ones in the person who is experiencing them. This makes it difficult to study, but worthwhile as a subject because of its importance in directing consumer behavior. Recent areas receiving attention include *hedonic consumption* (the sensory, fantasy, and emotive aspects of consumption), *psychophysiological approaches* (use of brainwaves, pulse, eye directions, etc.) for measuring the emotional processes consumers are experiencing, and the affects of *mood* on consumers' reactions, especially to advertising.

APPLICATION ADVANCE: AN ADVERTISING PLANNING FRAMEWORK

The concepts discussed in this chapter, while complex, can offer powerful insights to marketers interested in understanding consumer behavior. As an indication of just how these insights might be combined, we examined another application advance for advertising planning, this one based upon a combination of motivation, involvement, and emotions. The Rossiter-Percy framework first points out that sometimes consumers are motivated to relieve a negative state (termed *informational motivation*)

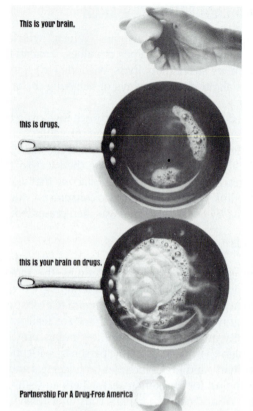

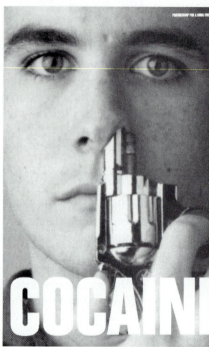

Advertising often uses emotional appeals to help change attitudes. In the case of antidrug advertising, powerful, hard-hitting messages are often used, including some use of fear appeals. About $1 million in media time and space is donated each day to run ads like these, developed by the Partnership for a Drug-Free America. The main goal of the campaign is to reduce demand for drugs by persuading adults, teens, and children that drug use is dumb and dangerous: 92 percent of American teens recall seeing the "fried egg" ("this is your brain on drugs") advertisement.

and sometimes are motivated to achieve a new positive state (*transformational motivation*). The framework details eight types of motives related to this distinction and notes specific emotional changes that are likely to accompany consumer behavior in each case (and which can be used in advertising to stimulate a consumer's interest). However, marketers must also attend to the issue of *involvement*, which Rossiter and Percy measure as the degree of risk a consumer perceives for a particular decision. The importance of both motivation and involvement, therefore, leads the framework to propose four types of advertising situations: (1) *low involvement, informational;* (2) *low involvement, transformational;* (3) *high involvement, informational;* and (4) *high involvement, transformational.* Particular products are likely to be located in each section, and different advertising strategies should work best for each of the four situations.

■ KEY TERMS

motivation	aggressive	actual self	terminal values
personality	detached	ideal self	instrumental values
trait theory	CAD Scale	psychographics	List of Values (LOV)
trait	consumer psychographics	Need for Cognition	means to an end
quantitative era	physiological differences	self-monitoring	laddering
compliant	self-concept	values	means-ends chain

A-C-V model	low involvement	affective involvement	mood
MECCAS model	product-class involvement	emotion	informational motivations
consumer involvement	brand-choice involvement	hedonic consumption	transformational motivations
high involvement	cognitive involvement	psychophysiological approaches	

■ REVIEW QUESTIONS AND EXPERIENTIAL EXERCISES

[E = **Application extension or experiential exercise**]

1. What is "personality"? Do you believe that personality affects consumer behavior? Do the studies reported in this chapter support your opinion?

2. Consider the Cohen CAD study. Was its results roughly equivalent to what you would have predicted? Why are the results called "equivocal" or ambiguous?

3. "Involvement" is an extremely significant concept in the field of consumer behavior. What exactly is it? What implications does low involvement hold for each of the 4 P's?

4. [E] Assume that you had CAD personality scores for a large sample of consumers and were offered the opportunity to ask these consumers four consumer behavior or marketing-related questions. If your goal was to uncover strong relationships between personality and consumer behavior, what four questions would you ask? For each question, briefly indicate the kind of response you expect each personality type would provide.

5. [E] The text discussion of self-concept indicated that consumer products sometimes serve to express the actual self and sometimes to help the consumer feel more like his or her ideal self. Search through magazine ads, looking for examples of these applications. Cut out three examples of each type, attaching brief explanations of your reasoning.

6. [E] Using Note 10 at the back of the book, locate and read William Wells's classic article on psychographics. Write a brief report on your findings.

7. [E] Table 6-1 presented four psychographic dimensions for which buyers of premium cosmetics gave high scores (narcissistic, appearance conscious, fantasied achievement, and sociable). Search through magazine ads for premium cosmetics and perfumes, looking for examples of appeals to each of these dimensions. Cut out at least one example for each dimension, and attach a brief explanation of your reasoning.

8. [E] Locate—in your library or bookstore—the paperback book on personality, *Please Understand Me: Character and Temperament Types*, by David Keirsey and Marilyn Bates, 5th ed., (Prometheus Nemesis Book Company, 1984). Take the personality test included in this book, and score it to identify your own personality type. Then read the interpretations provided, together with the research findings on managerially related topics. Write a brief report on your findings.

9. [E] Use the references in Notes 17 and 18 at the back of this book to find informative discussions on the topic of values. Read through these discussions and prepare a brief report on your findings.

10. [E] Figure 6-1 reports changes in college students' priority values over time. Develop a brief survey in which you ask a number of friends and acquaintances to choose their three highest-priority values from the list provided in the figure. (Note: You may wish to reorder this listing.) Before doing this survey, think about what kinds of consumer behavior differences you might expect from people who would have different value priorities. Include several questions in your survey asking about these consumer behaviors. Administer the survey to at least 30 persons; then analyze the results to determine

    a. Which values scored highest over your entire sample

    b. Whether those who had different value priorities revealed consumer behavior differences as well

11. [E] The chapter's discussion of the laddering system indicated how an advertiser could use consumer research in developing a campaign aimed at consumers' values. As a creative exercise, examine the sample ladder for Salty Snacks shown at the bottom of Figure 6-2. Based on this information, create a proposed magazine ad for a new brand of flavored chips. Accompany your ad with a brief explanation of your reasoning.

12. [E] Using the references in Notes 23, 24, and 25 at the back of the book, select and read some of the recent literature on consumer involvement, its measurement, effects, and implications for marketers. Write a brief report on your findings.

13. [E] Figure 6-5 presents the Rossiter and Percy grid for advertising planning. Read the article by Rossiter and Percy (Note 31 at the back of the book) on how this grid is helpful on planning advertising. Write a brief report on your findings. (Note: You may also wish to read the classic article by Vaughn and the article by Ratchford, also listed in Note 31. This will allow you to assess Rossiter and Percy's claims of superiority for their framework.)

14. [E] Search through magazines for examples of ads suitable for each of the four quadrants in Figure 6-5. (You may use additional products you think would fit in each quadrant.) Develop a large enough sample that you can begin to generalize about the kinds of appeals being used for each quadrant. Cut out good examples (as well as examples that don't fit) and attach a brief report on your reasoning.

15. [E] Using the references in Notes 26–30 at the back of the book, select and read some of the recent literature on consumer emotions. Write a brief report on your findings.

16. [E] The chapter mentioned the following as primary emotions: love, joy, surprise, fear, anger, and sadness. Search through magazines for examples of ads appealing to each of these. Cut out good examples and attach a brief report on your findings.

17. [E] Read the following case. Prepare a brief report on your position, supporting the stand you would take.

ᘓ Should Fear Appear?

Should advertising ever make people uncomfortable? This long-running debate arose again recently when American Health Corporation tried to place ads on TV networks. It seems that of the 12 million diabetics in the United States, half don't know that they have the disease and many others are ignoring some of its dangers. The company, which sells treatment services, discovered that its clients were reporting that they had spent years in "self-denial," refusing to come to grips with having the disease. Accordingly, the firm created a campaign aimed at "getting people off the fence" and into the treatment centers. In one TV spot, for example, a man is shown taking off his shoes, then his socks, then his leg prosthesis, as the announcer says, "If you give diabetes an inch, it'll take a foot." The networks reacted negatively to running this campaign, however: "We don't want to discuss the possible harmful effects of wrong treatment of diabetes...we consider this scare copy," said CBS. The ad agency and the company (which was experiencing both positive and negative reactions from local broadcast stations) indicate that their consumer research studies showed the scare ad outdrawing an ad with a positive appeal ("You can learn to live with diabetes with a little help...") by a 3-to-1 margin. According to an executive from the advertising agency, "The positive campaign gave people a chance to deny the problems of their disease. The negative one didn't. It spurred them to action." About the networks' banning these ads: "We're going to see more health-care advertising everywhere, and these questions are going to keep coming up."[32]

The question is: What goes on with consumers' minds and emotions when they see ads like this? Also, you may someday be in a position to decide whether or not ads like this will be run. What do you think you would do as a broadcasting executive?

■ SUGGESTED READING

■ A diverse set of extensions to motivational topics was presented in this chapter. For a cogent summary of research on personality in consumer behavior, see the Kassarjian and Sheffet article listed in Note 7 (for a fun personal experience with personality itself, try the test and reading suggested in review question 8 above: the paperback book can be ordered from a bookstore if it is not available in your library). For an expanded look at how these topics can meld into a consumer's life, try Russell W. Belk, "Possessions and the Extended Self," *Journal of Consumer Research*, Vol. 15 (September 1988), p. 139–168 (see the critical comment by Joel Cohen and the rejoinder by Russell Belk that appear in the March 1989 issue of this same journal if you are interested in delving deeper into this topic). Relatedly, a look at Ronald Paul Hill's "Homeless Women, Special Possessions, and the Meaning of 'Home': An Ethnographic Case Study," *Journal of Consumer Research*, Vol. 18 (December 1991), pp. 298–310, will introduce many readers to a world apart from their own. For more insight into marketing applications, try (for laddering) Thomas J. Reynolds and Alyce Craddock, "The Application of the MECCAS Model to the Development and Assessment of Advertising Strategy: A Case Study," *Journal of Advertising Research*, Vol. 28 (April–May 1988), pp. 43–54 and (for advertising) John R. Rossiter, Larry Percy, and Robert J. Donovan, "A Better Advertising Planning Grid," *Journal of Advertising Research*, Vol. 31 (October–November 1991), pp. 11–21. Again, for better understanding of any particular topic, the specific Note references are a great place to start.

CONSUMER INFORMATION PROCESSING

NAME THIS BRAND!

I love what you do for me, _____! (Auto)

Be certain, with _____. (Breath mint)

Run for the Border. _____ (Fast food)

M'm m'm good, m'm m'm good, that's what _____ *are . . .* (Soup)

[Pink bunny] *Keeps on going . . . and going . . . and going.* _____ (Battery)

Achieving strong brand-name awareness in consumers' minds is a key goal for marketers. Only a few brands are ever highly successful at this, though. Sometimes consumers recall the ads, but are confused about the brand. In the last example, for instance, almost everyone can picture the bunny banging away, but only 60 percent of consumers name the right brand as the sponsor. Yes, the folks at Duracell have been enjoying this.[1]

This is an important chapter. It is obvious that consumer behavior relies heavily on mental decisions made by consumers. However, what is involved in these mental decisions? In this chapter we will set the stage for answering this question. We will concentrate on two classic frameworks: the first reveals mental stages consumers follow in becoming purchasers, while the second delves into a more detailed look at how consumers' minds actually operate. These two frameworks have had major impacts on marketing thought and can offer key insights for marketing applications.

■ THE HIERARCHY OF EFFECTS MODEL

Hierarchy of effects:
A classic marketing framework outlining a seven-stage process of a consumer moving from an advertising exposure to a brand purchase.

Social scientists have long been interested in the process by which a person comes to behave in a certain way. In 1961, Robert Lavidge, a marketing consultant, and Gary Steiner, a behavioral sciences professor, built on prior theory by describing a new model of how consumers come to purchase a particular brand.[2] This model later came to be known as the **hierarchy of effects.** The original purpose was to assist advertising managers in their decisions. The thinking behind the model went something like this:

> While the ultimate purpose of advertising is to create sales, it is obvious that consumers rarely rush out to buy a brand immediately after seeing an ad. Instead, there seems to be a longer-term impact of advertising. However, for there to be a longer-term impact, there *must* be some kind of short-term effect going on. What kinds of short-term effects are there?

To answer this question, Lavidge and Steiner attempted to outline a logical process of how a consumer arrives at brand purchase. The viewpoint was that of a brand manager looking at the consumer market.

NATURE OF THE HIERARCHY

Hierarchy is a word that refers to any type of organized structure that has a clear beginning, followed by a series of steps in a particular order. Figure 7-1 diagrams the hierarchy of effects model. Note that it consists of seven stages, beginning with "Unawareness" and culminating in "Purchase." Each step provides a foundation for the next step. With respect to a particular consumer, say, Jill Jones, and a particular brand, say, Allure mascara, the model would postulate the following:

> Jill begins by being totally *unaware* that Allure is on the market. At some point she becomes aware of the brand name, but only at a very surface level. At some point later she gains *knowledge* about what Allure has to offer, including its patented "lash lengthener" formula. She then develops a *liking* for Allure, in the sense that she thinks it may be a candidate for purchase. At some later point Jill develops a *preference* for Allure over other brands. This preference then turns into a *conviction* that it will be wise to choose Allure the next time she buys mascara. When that time arrives, the brand *purchase* finally occurs.

Important Characteristics of the Hierarchy

Because this is a relatively formal model, there are several underlying points that we should be sure to understand about it. First, the "hierarchical" nature of the model requires a *fixed order* to the seven stages; unawareness must come first, then awareness, then knowledge, then liking, and so on. This is a strong assumption, although it certainly seems reasonable for many cases. Second, the model allows for *individual differences* in that different people can be at different stages. Some consumers will remain unaware of some brands for their entire lives, while others are happily purchasing and using those same brands. Third, the model allows for *timing differences*. One consumer might, for example, move from unawareness all the way to purchase within a single day's shopping for a small appliance. In contrast, that same consumer might take three months to move from awareness to knowledge of a cosmetic brand, then in only two days move on through to purchase.

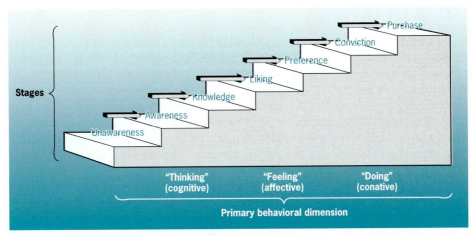

FIGURE 7-1 Stages in the Hierarchy of Effects

The "Think-Feel-Do" View

A fourth assumption embedded in the model is that consumer behavior consists of three major dimensions: cognitive, affective, and conative. This view is widely accepted in the behavioral sciences and in marketing (a popularized description is the "think-feel-do" view of consumer behavior). In brief, the **cognitive component** refers to rational elements involved with mental thought, the **affective component** refers to our emotional or feeling states, and the **conative component** involves the tendency to action or behavior on our part. In terms of fixed order, the model suggests that the cognitive operations come first, followed by affective, then conative.

Controversies and Extensions

Part of the contribution from the hierarchy of effects model comes from the further thinking that its strong assumptions have sparked in the field. Consider, for example, such questions as

- "Do consumers have to go through all the stages?"
- "Do the stages have to occur in the order shown?"
- "What about impulse purchases?"

The answers according to the strict model would have to be, "Yes (unless they don't reach purchase)," "Yes (but they can do so at different speeds)," and "Impulse purchases are those in which the timing is *very* compressed and the stages occur quickly."

Another way to answer these questions is to disagree with the model and respond that "The hierarchy has its limitations, and won't be able to reflect exactly how consumers will proceed in every situation." Professor Michael Ray, for example, has proposed an alternative "think-do-feel" ordering of effects for situations in which consumers have **low involvement** and aren't viewing a purchase to be very serious.[3] Jennifer Huggins, for example, may realize that she's running low on paper towels as she passes the display in the supermarket. She isn't very interested in this product and doesn't have a favorite brand. She does recall seeing some commercials for Brawny, though, and decides to give it a try. Thus Jennifer's purchase really is a trial: not until she actually uses the brand will she have either a positive or negative feeling toward it.

USES OF THE HIERARCHY

As indicated earlier, the original purpose of the hierarchy of effects model was to assist marketers in decision making. One benefit to brand managers, for example, involves a new way to view *market segments* for your brand. This can be done by estimating the proportion of consumers who have reached each of the steps in the hierarchy. Are there a significant number of potential buyers who are still unaware of your brand? Are most persons not very knowledgeable, or is the problem that most consumers are presently not at a level of liking or preference for your brand? Constructing this type of analysis for competing brands as well as for your own can provide useful insights. (This use of the hierarchy, in fact, has been the basis for highly sophisticated "mathematical models" that have recently become popular with marketing managers.)[4] Once you know where consumers stand, you can decide on which step to concentrate and can create programs geared to this stage. Many marketers prefer to try to move one step at a time. For example, special ad campaigns are often created to generate awareness of a new brand and then are replaced by other ads providing more information about the brand.

In addition to its value for business purposes, the hierarchy of effects has provided the field of consumer behavior with a useful basic framework. (If you would like to learn more about the history, controversies, and extensions of this important framework, you may wish to begin with Note 5 at the end of this book under the listings for Chapter 7.) As we move through this text, we will continue to use the hierarchy of effects as a basis for marketing applications of consumer behavior. At this point, however, we turn our attention to a related, even more detailed framework—consumer information processing.

■ CONSUMER INFORMATION PROCESSING

As noted earlier, the consumer information processing (CIP) approach constitutes a different way to consider consumer behavior processes. As with the hierarchy of effects framework, CIP has been enthusiastically received by many marketers. CIP is inherently interesting—it deals with our minds and how they work. Beyond this, CIP holds the potential to contribute new kinds of understanding of consumer behavior.

BENEFITS OF THE CIP APPROACH

Black box model:
Concentrates on external inputs and the consumer behavior outputs that seem to ensue from them.

As shown in Figure 7-2, the traditional approach to studying consumer behavior, called the **black box model,** concentrated on external inputs and the outputs that seemed to ensue from them. For example, dropping the price of Folger's coffee with a 40-cent coupon (external input) might be found to increase sales by 100,000 units (external output). At the individual consumer level, the 40-cent coupon might be found to lead to a purchase by Mark Moore, but not by Laura Jackson. The black box model would record these facts, but would offer no way to trace the internal processes that somehow led Mark to purchase and Laura not to purchase. As we have discussed in earlier chapters, for example, the checkout scanning systems in supermarkets now allow for enormous quantities of this type of black box model information for marketing planners to use.

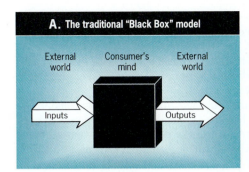
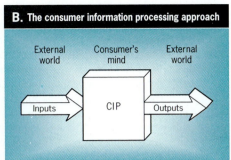

FIGURE 7-2 How the CIP Approach Improves the "Black Box" Model

In contrast, the **CIP approach** would concentrate on the thoughts and reactions that the consumers were having when they received the Folger's coupon. The CIP approach concentrates on the middle of the input-output system. Its contributions lie in illuminating what is going on in consumers' minds. Because of this focus, it is not particularly strong in studying the inputs or the outputs by themselves. This means that CIP will never be a *substitute* for other approaches; it will instead be an important *complement* or addition to our set of approaches to use in understanding consumer behavior.

CIP approach: Concentrates on the thoughts consumers have: not as strong at analyzing inputs and outputs.

WHAT IS CIP?

Consumer information processing *involves sequences of mental activities that people use within consumption contexts.* There are two primary systems involved in CIP: our *sensory system* and our *conceptual system*. The **sensory system** refers to the operations of our five senses—sight, touch, smell, hearing, and taste—the means that each of us uses to contact all aspects of our external world. The **conceptual system**, in turn, is our system for dealing with mental concepts—it is the means by which we think.

Consumer information processing: The sequences of mental activities that people use within consumptions contexts.

CIP relates to an amazingly wide range of consumer activities. CIP relates to our *learning* about and accepting important cultural values, as well as learning the name of a new bubble gum brand. CIP also relates to *evaluative* activities, such as our development of likes and dislikes for products. In addition, CIP relates to our *decision processes*, our *purchasing strategies*, our *usage behaviors*, our *satisfactions*, and any other thoughts we have about products, stores, and so on.

The Computer Analogy

The major force behind the development of information processing models was the invention and growth of computers after World War II. This allowed researchers to conduct studies of very-high-speed operations; such studies had simply been too unwieldy to undertake prior to this time. Because of this heritage, there has been a strong tendency to view CIP as being similar to the workings of a computer.[6]

For example, look back at Figure 7-2 for a moment and consider the following consumer behavior class lecture:

> One way to think of CIP is to view it as being similar to the workings of a computer, where you have input, a central processing unit, and output. The input would be some form of consumption-related stimulus, such as an ad. The information could

come from a number of sources, such as TV or the radio, or it might even arise as you're walking through a shopping center and see someone wearing something you find to be attractive.

The central processing unit is internal. Here your mind will take the input and deal with it in whatever ways you decide are appropriate. The processing might be very brief, or it might be long and involved.

There are many types of outputs that can come from the processing, and these can be either retained privately in your head (for example, you simply decide to buy) or they can also be placed into the external world (for example, telling your girlfriend that you've decided to buy). In more technical language, outputs can consist of an addition of new facts into your memory, changes of a brand attitude, purchases of a new brand, and so on.

There is one important shortcoming of the computer analogy, however, that should be kept in mind. The computer example always seems to start with external information and have the central processor react to those inputs from the outside. In consumer behavior, though, we know that a lot of CIP really begins with *internal* inputs, such as when we begin to think about a particular past purchase or begin to plan for a future one. The computer analogy is helpful, then, but we don't want to fall into the trap of viewing consumers in too mechanical a way. When we talk about consumers, remember that we are talking about ourselves!

General Findings About CIP

Before studying the details of CIP, it may be useful to consider some generalizations about what is involved when we consumers process information:[7]

- *CIP is adaptive.* Since the purpose of CIP is to help us deal effectively with our external world, CIP must be quite flexible. The exact thinking we undertake is highly dependent on the situation we are in at the time: we adapt our thoughts to be most relevant to the situation.

- *Consumers' memories are important.* Processing occurs in, and is guided by, our minds. While external influences can be quite important, we cannot forget the crucial role that our memory plays in guiding our thought processes.

- *Consumers have limited CIP capacity.* We are simply unable to process everything that could be processed at any one time. This means that we must pay attention to some things and ignore others. We must selectively decide what to process and how to allocate our processing resources at any one time.

- *Consumers solve small problems.* Because of our limited CIP capacities, we find it difficult or impossible to reach a decision in one giant "optimal" step. Instead we tend to break larger problems into a series of smaller subproblems, which are more manageable. Taken together, however, these smaller decisions may be less than optimal overall (for example, was our actual spending last month as wise as it might have been had we carefully allocated our budget?).

Each of these four CIP generalizations has been receiving increased attention by consumer researchers. We will be examining their findings in later chapters.

■ STRUCTURE OF THE CIP SYSTEM

[*An Important Note*] Scientists have made tremendous advances in understanding the biochemical and electrical characteristics of the human brain. Their work is not close to being complete, however, and is highly technical. Discussion of the physiology of the brain is beyond the scope of our discussion of consumer behavior and will not appear in this book. In this text we will stress a less technical approach to the mind—one that concentrates on how information processing seems to occur. We should be clear, however, that when the term "structure" is used, we are not talking about a physical model of the mind. Instead, we will be referring to a *functional* representation of the CIP system. In other words, our CIP structure is a good one for explaining how people process information. To get the most out of the following sections, then, try to use the book's discussion to help you think about how you *personally* process information as a consumer. If you are interested in more advanced models or issues, you should find the chapter notes to be useful guides for further reading.

THE SYSTEM'S THREE SECTORS

The **CIP system** is outlined in Figure 7-3. The first important aspect of the figure is that it shows the *outside world* on the left and the *inside world* of the mind on the right. Much of the emphasis of CIP research refers to how the realities of the external world are translated in each person's inner mental world.

    The second important aspect of the figure is that it shows the CIP system as being comprised of three sectors: the sensory register, short-term or working memory, and long-term memory. (As we'd expect with something as complicated as the brain, our CIP system is one of many possible representations.)[8] In the sections that follow, we'll learn much more about each of the three primary sectors of our CIP system.

CIP system: Consists of three sectors: the sensory register, short-term memory (STM), and long-term memory (LTM).

The External World's Many Stimuli

The funnel shown in Figure 7-3 is intended to indicate that CIP deals with relatively *few* of the stimuli present in the external world. For example, think about a fairly quiet classroom and the stimuli that could be attended to by someone in it. There are the sounds of the professor's voice, but other sounds as well—noises from outside, slight squeaking of chairs, turning papers, whispering voices, and so on. There are faint odors, and perhaps breezes or temperature changes hitting your skin. There are also an incredible number of visual stimuli available—even though the room has been designed to have as few distractions as possible. There are *colors* of clothing, hair, and walls; *shapes* of heads, bodies, and furniture; and *movement* in the bodies in the room and the world outside the windows.

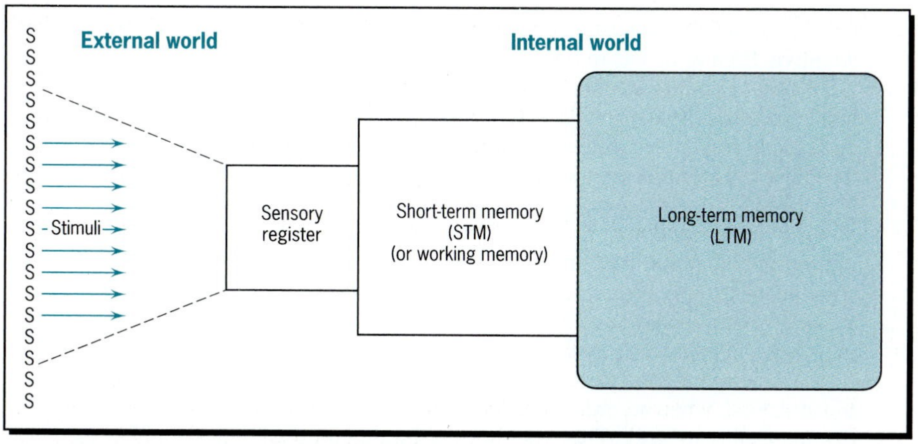

FIGURE 7-3 A Hypothetical CIP System

Despite the large number of stimuli around us, *we do not pay attention to most of them*, especially if we're interested in the lecture (or in the person next to us). Our information processing systems are *choosing* not to deal with most stimuli, so that we can deal better with the stimuli upon which we want to concentrate.

The External World and the Sensory Register

Sensory register:
The CIP sector in which external stimuli are gathered by each of our senses.

The **sensory register** is the CIP sector in which external stimuli are gathered by each of our senses. Here they are "held" for a very brief time in the "front of our mind." Experts in the field of cognitive psychology have had difficulty in pinning down an exact time limit; in general, however, it appears that a sensory impression can be held for something less than 1 second—say, half a second—before it decays in strength and fades out of the sensory register.[9]

This time limit is not as seriously negative as it might first appear, however. Our CIP systems can work at incredibly fast speeds, so that half a second is a fairly long time. (For example, consider how long you focus on any one word while reading a newspaper—try timing yourself for a paragraph, then dividing by the number of words in it.) In addition, we are often able to go back out and *reacquire a particular stimulus* if we desire to do so: we can reread a sentence, look back to a picture or a product label, and so forth. Finally, there are many stimuli that we don't *want* to process at a particular time, and the decay feature of the sensory register handily allows us to dispense with them easily.

Thus the "holding" function of the sensory register is important because it allows us to provide some *order* and *control* to our CIP activities. By combining focused attention on only certain stimuli, and then being able to bring certain of these stimuli into our CIP system on a slightly delayed basis, we are able to insulate or *buffer* ourselves from what would otherwise be an extremely complicated and diverting external world.

SHORT-TERM MEMORY

Short-term memory (STM): The CIP sector that is the working center of the system, where thinking occurs.

You may have noticed that Figure 7-3 denotes the second sector of the system as **short-term memory (STM)** and also as **working memory**. This is because the primary feature of STM is that it is the work center of your CIP system. To appreciate this point more fully, let's listen in on an explanation given in a consumer behavior class:

One important characteristic of our CIP systems is that they have to be so amazingly **adaptive**. Each of us has to be able to deal with a wide range of situations and people. We can't go through the world with specialized approaches that we use regardless of circumstances. Our CIP systems have thus been geared to be highly flexible and able to respond to millions of kinds of external inputs and mental tasks. Such flexibility calls for a special kind of *work system* for our memories. One good analogy is that STM is like an empty production room and LTM is like a warehouse.

To understand this distinction, let's assume that you decided to go into a customized manufacturing business, but—similar to our CIP needs for flexibility—you were unable to specialize in producing any one line of products. Instead, your production system would have to be able to produce many different kinds of products, in as efficient a way as possible.

To design a good system for this business, let's think of some key characteristics. First, when an order comes in, you would need to quickly put your production facility to work. This would mean setting up exactly the right machinery and bringing in exactly the right plans, procedures, and raw materials. You would *not* want your workroom to be cluttered with machinery and materials from other tasks. One efficient way to design your production system would thus be to keep your workroom as *empty* as possible between jobs, but to devise ways for rapid and efficient setup for each new job. Of course, this would also affect the way you would design your warehouse, or storage center.

This analogy provides the basis for our structure of the CIP system. **Long-term memory (LTM)** is the storage center of the CIP system. It contains everything you need to process, except for some special raw materials that are imported from the outside world in the form of external stimuli (information). Short-term memory, conversely, is the work center of the CIP system. To perform its functions most efficiently, *nothing* is stored in STM unless it is related to current work-in-process. All contents of STM have either been imported from the external world or from LTM or created during the work process itself, in STM.

Where do the outputs go? There are three logical routes: contents of STM can decay and fade out of the system, they can be sent to the external world as outputs, and/or they can be sent to LTM to be stored.

Now let's try a math example to demonstrate some of these ideas. First, try to "clear out" your STM to prepare for this little math problem that I'll put on the board:

$$8 + 7 \times 3 = \ ?$$

Notice how your CIP system works in solving this problem. First, you had to read the problem in, through your visual sensory register. The reading itself was quite a process, when we realize that what we've actually seen were some special arrangements of splotches on a surface. For each splotch, we had to bring in the sensory impression and try to give it meaning. For each number and word, this meant that signals had to be sent back to LTM asking, basically, "What is this . . . ?" An extremely rapid search of LTM ensued and likely resulted in a correct identification of each number and word. These were sent to STM, the work center of the system. Also, the process was likely assisted by the fact that I'd indicated that I wanted you to work on a *math* problem. Things should have gone faster because certain parts of your LTM (where you store your math knowledge) were "primed" to be used in STM and thus could be found and retrieved more quickly. That is, you were "ready" for this problem.

Next, notice that the key information you needed from LTM included the basic tables for addition and multiplication, together with specific arithmetic rules to tell yourself exactly what to do. Now, it turns out that this little problem tends to lead to *two different answers, depending on the particular rule* that people take from LTM and use in STM. I won't ask each of you to give your answer here, but my guess is that many of you came up with 29, while most others arrived at 45. The two different answers arise from a slight difference in your *processing* of the problem. The basic difference seems to be that the first group asks LTM if there is a specific math rule to govern the order in which the operations are performed. Their LTM says something like, "Yes, multiplication and division should be done before addition and subtraction, unless parentheses are included. . . . " If you were in this group of students, you then had to shift the problem around in STM and attack it in a different order from how you had read it in initially. It wouldn't be surprising, in fact, if you *took another look or two* at the board to help you reorder the numbers—in reality, you were using your sensory register to relieve some of the pressures on STM's having to remember the exact numbers! Your CIP problem solving then became something like $3 \times 7 = \ . . . 21 . . .$ and $21 + 8 = \ . . . 29$.

If you were in the "45" group, you arrived at a different answer because your *process* was different. Usually, this occurs because you either didn't ask your LTM if there is a special math rule that governs order or you asked about the rule but it wasn't retrieved from LTM. Since *STM always needs to follow some kind of rule*, you probably just used the common cultural rule for English-speaking students. This says, "You should read from the left and take things in the order that they occur, moving from left to right." In this case, the problem becomes $8 + 7 = \ . . . 15 . . .$ and $15 \times 3 = \ . . . 45$.

Long-term memory (LTM): The storage center of the CIP system: contains unlimited capacity for permanent records.

Let me again stress this final point about how important it is that LTM provides *guidance* for our processing activities in STM. Not only does LTM provide interpretations of incoming stimulus patterns, but it also—by sending rules to guide STM—allows us to direct and control our own internal thought processes!

STM's Capacity Limitations

You may recall that one of our four general findings about CIP involved **capacity limitations**. We are all aware that we seem to be limited in the number of separate things we can watch, listen to, or think about at the same time. The CIP system's capacity limitations affect not only how much information we can process at any time, but also how the processing itself occurs. *It is important for us to recognize that most of the capacity constraints exist in STM.* At the front end of the system, the sensory register is capable of detecting huge numbers of stimuli; as we discussed earlier, however, most of them decay rapidly and never enter STM, or working memory. At the other end of the system, long-term memory has a huge, perhaps infinite, capacity for storing information. Many scientists, in fact, believe that we never lose anything that's been stored in LTM.[10] As we go through life, we are constantly adding information to our LTM storage system.

There are two types of STM capacity constraints—time and size. With respect to **time constraints**, information being held in working memory will slowly decay and fade out as its energy is dissipated or lost. Just as with the sensory register, scientists have had difficulty estimating exactly how long STM's time decay might take, but it would clearly be measured in numbers of seconds (say, 10 to 30 seconds) versus the fractions of a second in the case of the sensory register.[11]

The more important STM capacity constraint involves the number of information items that can be processed at any one time. This translates to **size constraints** of the working memory. As with all other estimates, scientists have had difficulty determining STM's exact size limits. A classic article by G. A. Miller proposed "The Magic Number Seven, Plus or Minus Two..." as the basic size limit.[12] This suggested that we are able to retain about seven items of information—the length of a telephone number—in STM. Miller pointed out, however, that this limit would vary somewhat (from five to nine pieces), depending on the person and the nature of the information. Since Miller's paper over 30 years ago, other scholars have also worked on this problem. Their results tend to show a somewhat lower limit for STM, about three or four pieces of information.[13] Our CIP systems are powerful, however, so why is this important?

Why Are Capacity Limits Important?

Since information can come into STM from either the external world *or* from LTM, we usually have a highly active flow of information into STM. However, if there is only room for a limited amount of information, something must happen to the information that's already there. If the earlier information hasn't yet been processed, it probably will be lost from working memory, so the valuable STM capacity can be used by more important information. If, on the other hand, the prior information is being processed with inputs from LTM, it is likely that it will be sent back to LTM and stored there for future reference. Also, if the processing is important and will take a bit longer, STM may simply not accept new inputs from the external environment during this time. A good example of this occurs when we try to *concentrate* and deliberately shut out other stimuli from interfering with our processing.

This clever ad allows us to recognize how our **CIP** system operates when we read the ad. Notice that **STM** tends to slow down while waiting for the proper interpretation of a symbol from **LTM**, then moves to the next symbol, again awaiting a correct answer (given the context) from **LTM**. After getting through it the first time, however, the **CIP** system can work much faster a second time, since **LTM** has been modified by the ad.

Although the inability to define an absolute size limitation is disturbing at first, we should understand that the practical importance of the size limit depends on how well we can *merge the flows between STM and LTM*. As we've already seen with regard to reading and interpreting the math example, our CIP systems can work at amazingly fast speeds. Thus, if we are able to arrange the appropriate transfers between STM and LTM (in a technical process called *rehearsal*), we can use LTM's *huge capacity* to partially overcome problems arising from STM's *limited capacity*. The more easily we can place and retrieve a particular piece of information stored in LTM, the easier the strain on STM capacity.

Scientists have used the concept of **chunking** in relation to this process. Chunking refers to grouping together several pieces of information and treating them as a related set. For example, let's assume that we've just met an interesting new person and want to remember her phone number. We could, for example, treat the telephone number as seven separate digits (9-2-4-1-8-6-3), as two groups of digits (924-1863), or as one group of digits (9241863). The more related the digits are, the easier it is to chunk them (for example, 9876543 is a particularly easy chunk).

Once into LTM, we can think of a chunk as a set of information elements in LTM that are strongly associated with each other. Therefore, once we have brought one of them into STM, it is relatively easy to find others in LTM and bring them into STM in some series that does not overwhelm STM's capacity limits. Marketers strive to achieve this type of LTM "chunk" structure for their brands. Thus, once the brand comes into STM, it is relatively easy for the consumer to go into LTM to come up with further thoughts about the brand and bring them rapidly into STM. To get a better idea

Chunking: The mental process of grouping together several pieces of information and treating them as a set.

of brand chunks, consider how your CIP flows for such names as Reebok, or Heinz, or Toyota. To really understand chunking and its related concepts, however, we need to delve deeper into the nature of long-term memory.

LONG-TERM MEMORY

To obtain a broad sense for LTM, let's listen in again to the consumer behavior class lecture:

> If we step back and think about it a little, we can see that LTM is truly a remarkable center! What is stored in long-term memory very much determines and describes each of us as a person. Long-term memory contains the surviving traces of all that each of us has ever experienced, all that we privately value, and all that we know and feel. LTM is the root of our individual personalities; it holds all the things that we've liked, enjoyed, and feared and all that we aspire to achieve. It is the center from which our thoughts are created.
>
> As consumers, think about what your LTM contains. Here we find a vast number of facts, memories, and opinions about various products, stores, and consumer situations. This mental content plays an extremely important role in determining our future consumer behaviors and our individual reactions to marketing strategies. So, while we think of LTM as a storage center or warehouse, please don't misunderstand this to mean that it is in any way an *uninteresting* part of our CIP system. On the contrary, LTM is fascinating: it is the most important sector for CIP!

Episodic and Semantic Memories

Episodic memory: The picture form in which we remember events or episodes out of our personal life experiences.

One interesting characteristic of LTM is that it seems to include two distinct types of contents: episodic and semantic. **Episodic memories** reflect the way in which we remember events or episodes out of our personal life experiences. These are in picture form, something akin to snapshots from our past. We use episodic memories when we recall special moments in our lives, even though they may have occurred years ago. Also, of course, many episodic memories are less significant, such as browsing at the store yesterday. The other form of LTM contents is known as **semantic memories.** These reflect the facts and other information we refer to when we speak of having "learned something." Semantic memories provide our basis for being able to use language. The field of semantics is in fact the study of signs and word meanings. (One area of research that has received much recent attention in marketing involves this distinction: if you would like to read more about *imagery processing* you may wish to begin with the readings in Note 14.)

Semantic memories: The facts and other information that we store through language.

Networks, Nodes, and Linkages

Node: An LTM center that represents a word, idea, or concept.

Linkage: In LTM, the means of association between two nodes: provides the basis for efficient thinking.

Another important characteristic of LTM is that it appears to have something like a **network organization**. Figure 7-4 shows a much simplified portion of a network that a consumer might have for soft drinks. In technical terms, we see a set of **nodes** connected by **linkages** or arcs into a network of concepts. Each node is a center that represents a word, an idea, or a concept. Nodes are connected to other nodes as a function of whether or not a person associates one idea with the other. Linkages between two nodes refer to the degree of association between them. The stronger we see a relationship between nodes to be, the stronger the associative linkages will be. The more two concepts (nodes) are experienced together, the stronger the link between them will be (notice, for example, that in Figure 7-4, "Water" is not linked to "Sugar" whereas "Sweet" is).

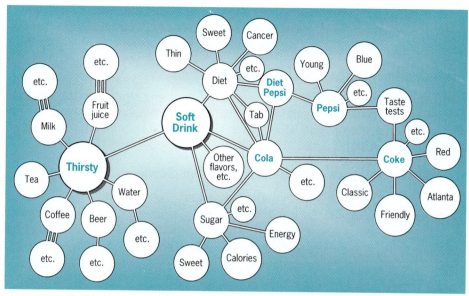

FIGURE 7-4 Portion of an LTM for Soft Drinks

When working memory (STM) calls for certain information to be drawn from LTM, the network organization comes into play. Since some nodes are more prominent than others (because they represent something that is more important or better learned by the consumer), they will tend to be activated first (we can think of **activation** as a kind of energy flow into the areas that are activated). Once the first node is activated, all the other nodes that are connected with it become more available to STM, if the processing continues.[15] Once one node is in STM, those nodes from LTM having the strongest linkages to it are the most likely to be activated next. Let's assume that Tom Mason is a consumer with this particular LTM structure and that Tom becomes thirsty. Notice on the left side of Figure 7-4 that there are many possible nodes linked to "Thirsty," since Tom has considerable past experience with this situation. Let's also assume that the nodes shown in color are those that Tom uses most often these days. However, we need to remember that his choice of a drink on this occasion will depend on which alternatives "come to mind" this time—that is, which LTM nodes are activated and brought into STM.

The "Soft drink" node may or may not be activated; this will in part depend on the situation. Since Tom does often think of soft drinks as reasonable alternatives for satisfying thirst, however, there is a good chance that this node will come into STM. Further, if Tom does process "Soft drinks," his thoughts, and their order, will be heavily influenced by the organization of LTM—which nodes are strong and which connections have been developed in the past. For example, if Tom is concerned about his weight, he might pursue the "Diet" node first. If he is very brand loyal to Coke, conversely, he might go directly to that node.

Pursuing the example just a bit farther, consider what impacts marketing stimuli could have if they were to enter the sensory register just at the time that Tom is considering which LTM nodes to pursue. A big red "Coke" sign might well swing him into the Coca-Cola node system and keep him out of the noncola and Pepsi Cola systems. A Budweiser display might divert his CIP from soft drinks into beers, or a

Activation: An energy flow into particular nodes to bring them into short-term memory.

sale on lettuce could even divert his CIP into an entirely different node system. Given this type of reasoning, we can see why point-of-purchase (POP) materials in stores can so successfully stimulate sales. (We'll be reading more about this in Chapter 18.)

Marketing Implications of LTM's Organization

Creating Content in LTM.   With respect to advertising strategy, marketers face the problem of how to create and strengthen the brand's node in LTM and give it many positive associations with other nodes. The following example allows us to take a much closer look at this issue.

❧ *Who Knows What…Lurks in the Minds of Men? The LTM Nodes…*

LTM nodes become stronger by being "used"—being retrieved from LTM and dropped into STM when a consumer is thinking about brands. Sometimes marketers are successful in creating strong brand name nodes by creating a catchy phrase that consumers store in their LTMs, then using ad repetition to ingrain that phrase deeply. They often use musical "jingles" to help in this process. Listed below are some classic "Blasts from the Past." How many are still in your LTM? (Some may be too old…if so, it's fun to ask older relatives or friends and see how easy it is for them!)

1. "In the valley of the Jolly (Ho, Ho, Ho) _____!"
2. "Hot dogs, _____ hot dogs…what kinds of kids love _____ hot dogs?"
3. "Please don't squeeze the _____."
   (Bonus: Who said this? Mr. _____.)
4. "It's the heartbeat of America, it's today's _____!"
5. "_____ is the place with the helpful hardware man!"
6. "Don't just ask for a light beer, ask for _____!"
7. "You're not fully clean, unless you're _____ -fully clean!"
8. "You deserve a break today, so get out and get away, to _____."
9. "Double your pleasure, double your fun with _____, _____, _____ gum!"
10. "Aren't you glad you use _____? Don't you wish everybody did?"

Grand Bonus Sing-along

"My baloney has a first name, it's _____, my baloney has a second name, it's _____."

Total Score: _____ (Answers to this quiz appear in Note 16 of this chapter if you'd like to check any.)

Beyond the enjoyment this kind of mental exercise brings to people, we are now in a position to also review some key CIP concepts we encountered while doing it. Let's again listen in on the consumer behavior class lecture, now at a point when they've just taken this same little quiz:

Let's think about what happened while we were doing the exercise. Most of you probably noticed that some of the brand names didn't make it into STM at all, others made it with a little difficulty, and some popped in very quickly. Let's look at these options. Why would some *not* make it? There really are two possibilities: either they weren't there at all, or they were there but we couldn't track them down in LTM. According to most CIP theory, the only way these phrases wouldn't be in your LTM is if you never processed them in the first place. If you ever did process these ads, though, their traces should still be in LTM. In this case, your problem in the exercise became one of **retrieval,** or locating the proper LTM nodes and bringing them into STM. So point 1 is "retrieval": what we often think is "forgetting," then, is actually our failure to accurately find and retrieve the proper node.

One important factor in our ability to retrieve a particular node involves **external retrieval cues**. As we just saw in our jingle quiz, external cues (here, parts of the jingle) can be very helpful in retrieving a particular brand node from LTM to STM. Marketers can use this knowledge to improve their campaigns. For example, Quaker Oats' putting a photo of "Mikey" on the boxes of LIFE cereal serves to cue consumers in the supermarket to think of its classic advertising campaign featuring Mikey. Of course, we do live in a competitive environment, and another relevant factor for retrieval is **interference.** Interference refers to the process in which the presence of other, related nodes in LTM seems to block (that is, to interfere with) recalling a particular node from LTM to STM. For example, recent research has found that the advertising done by competing brands creates LTM nodes that interfere with a consumer's ability to recall an ad they have seen for a particular brand in the category.[17]

Point 2 moves from later retrieval to the earlier process called **encoding**.[18] This involves how we categorize a stimulus and then choose a storage location for it back in LTM. If we think a little more about this, we can see that our chances for good later retrieval of a node go up if we've taken care to store it wisely in LTM in the first place. (As an aside, this is why we professors stress that you should "understand" the material and not just memorize it for an exam—"understanding" the material actually means placing each piece of information within the right set of related LTM nodes. Memorization, on the other hand, does work at fixing it firmly back in LTM, but usually doesn't provide a rich network of other nodes to help us retrieve it later, especially after a few days!) The point is that a node's location is a lot easier to find when it is embedded in a cluster of other nodes that are going to be brought to STM either together or one right after another. For example, notice how the first few words of one of the ad themes (acting as external retrieval cues) helped you find the right storage area in LTM. As you went on, your confidence grew that this was the right set of nodes, and the brand name emerged easily into STM. Here you were experiencing the effects of *chunking* in action—the operations of strong linkages between particular nodes!

Point 3—briefly—is that we should take notice of how incredibly helpful the musical jingles were! Our theory is still developing in this area, but it is clear that music not only helped us pay attention and learn the jingles in the first place, but that it also helps us locate the right LTM nodes, provides a rhythm for the retrieval process to STM, and somehow adds pleasure and emotion to our processing experience.[19]

Point 4 involves *mistakes*: some of us thought we had the right name, but somehow got it wrong (and were surprised!). Why would this happen? One possibility is that we encoded wrong originally and now have the wrong brand name actually stored with this theme back in LTM. As we'll see later in the course, marketers have discovered that this is reasonably common among consumers. Another possibility is that we didn't search LTM fully enough. This means that we focused on some part of the ad theme, searched LTM for a strong match on only part of it, then brought the brand name from that network into STM, and announced that as our answer. One good example of this form of interference is the second entry on the list, the hot dog theme—some consumers are likely to first think of the processed meats category, then search back in LTM for nodes relating to branded processed meats, kids, jingles, and so on. Because Oscar Mayer was so successful with its long-running musical kids campaign, many of us will hit that node network quickly and, if we don't check critically, may confidently give that answer (of course, if you didn't do this, you may say my explanation is "baloney"!). Similarly, as we noted at the opening of this chapter, the "pink bunny" battery campaign is frequently misidentified: in a recent study

Retrieval: The process of locating the proper nodes in long-term memory and bringing them into short-term memory.

Interference: The CIP process in which the presence of certain nodes in LTM seems to hinder the retrieval of other nodes.

Encoding: The process of categorizing a stimulus and the choosing a storage location for it in long-term memory.

40 percent of consumers who recall it identify it as a Duracell ad rather than one from Eveready!

So it's time to finish our discussion with point 5, involving **ad repetition**. We should realize that it is rare for such strong node networks to be built up in only one or two CIP episodes. Instead, the linkages between nodes get progressively stronger as they are *practiced* over and over again. This is part of the reason that music sometimes works so well, since kids and adults sing the jingles to themselves and thereby practice locating the node network in LTM, then retrieving it from LTM to STM. This is also the reason that ads are repeated so frequently: each time a consumer does pay attention to an ad, he or she is likely to practice locating the brand's node network in LTM, bringing it to STM, and then perhaps even adding new nodes and linkages to it back in its original storage area.

Creating Attention and Involvement.   One problem marketers face is how to capture consumers' attention and maintain interest. We'll examine this topic in upcoming chapters. But here we can note one special strategy that "tricks" CIP into paying attention by taking advantage of LTM's organization.

❧ *Pedro the Punster on I-95*

We can also detect the operation of STM and LTM by noticing how "puns" operate (a pun is a word or phrase used deliberately with a different meaning or spelling than the listener will expect). We realize we've been exposed to a pun when the contents of STM don't quite "match." We then need to go back and search LTM for the matching meanings and bring them to STM. The "groan" typical from a pun recipient is an acknowledgment that this process has occurred and that the CIP work required wasn't worth the effort! Sometimes puns can work for marketers, since they increase the chances a consumer will pay attention to the message as he or she tries to get it straight. On the other hand, this strategy can backfire if the recipient resents having to undertake the extra mental effort.

Travelers along Interstate 95 have long applied their CIP talents to decoding the messages and puns on billboards for South of the Border, a roadside travel stop along the state line between North Carolina and South Carolina.

▶ **Bulldozing**

If it's out there, it's in here. | **NYNEX** Yellow Pages

Notice how this photo pun causes a reader to return to LTM to clarify the ad's meaning, thereby giving it increased attention.

Travelers along I-95, the Maine-to-Miami interstate route, have long been entertained (frustrated?) by the puns presented on the billboards for South of the Border, a roadside stop located on the border between North Carolina and South Carolina. These are presented by "Pedro," they stretch for 400 miles along the route, and they have made "S.O.B." one of the most successful roadside attractions in the United States, with 6 million visitors annually. How do you react to the following billboard examples?[20]

"Pedro's Weather Report, Chili Today—Hot Tamale!"

"You never sausage a place! You're always a wiener at Pedro's!"

"Pedro's Fireworks! (Does Yours?)"

"Positioning" the Brand in Consumers' Minds.   Marketers strive to have the right kinds of adjectives ("good value," "high quality," etc.) associated with their brands, but also face the challenge of having their brand's name be considered when the consumer is thinking about buying. In marketing terms, the goal is to have your brand be accepted into the consumer's evoked set. The **evoked set** (sometimes termed "consideration set") consists of those brands that are likely to come to mind (enter STM) when a purchase is being considered. Research has shown that this is usually a small number of brands, ranging from one (in cases of brand loyalty) to only three or four under most conditions.[21] Thus there is a major payoff likely for marketers who can achieve this goal.

Evoked set: Those few brands that come to mind (enter STM) when a consumer considers a purchase decision.

🐚 The "UnCola" Campaign

This type of challenge confronted 7-Up brand managers some years ago, when the brand was still a minor factor in the soft drink market. Although consumers liked the product, it did not hold a large market share. The company then tried a new advertising slogan that positioned 7-Up as "the UnCola." Although the people involved had likely never heard of CIP, we can analyze this campaign in CIP terms to see why this was such a clever strategy.

To make sense of the slogan in an ad, a consumer had to search through LTM to locate the "Cola" node and then bring this information to STM. The "Cola" node, though, was already closely tied to "soft drinks," "Coke," and "Pepsi," making these also more likely to be brought to STM. Over time, with repeated exposures to this slogan,

CIP theory is helpful in understanding why 7-Up's "Un-cola" theme is so remarkably memorable. As explained in the text, it has to do with the structure of consumers' long-term memory networks.

many consumers were likely to build linkages between 7-Up and these other nodes. In this way, 7-Up became more a part of the soft drink evoked set for many consumers, and sales responded accordingly.

The story has an interesting postscript. The UnCola campaign had been dropped in the mid-1970s, a new corporate owner took over the brand, and a new ad agency went to work on it. Then, in 1985, the company sponsored a consumer research study that discovered that a large percentage of consumers continued to describe 7-Up as "the UnCola," *even though the campaign had not been run for over 10 years!* In fact, only a current Coke campaign theme scores higher than "the UnCola" tag. According to 7-Up's president,

> I don't care what the competition says. . . . "The UnCola" is the strongest, most singular product identifier in the soft drink business.[22]

Watch for the "UnCola" theme in the future, as the 7-Up company continues to use it on an off-and-on basis. This is an excellent example of the role of LTM and the power that it can display.

■ CIP RESEARCH AND APPLICATIONS

THREE "THINKING" STREAMS OF STUDY

The real power of the CIP framework comes when it is applied in consumer research. Many studies have been undertaken in the past 15 years or so. Special attention has been given to three basic types of CIP research.[23] First, research on **information**

"I wish I'd done that ad."

John Ferrell
Exec. V.P., Chief Creative Officer
Hill Holliday/New York

This is an ad that I know for a fact worked at least once. I was reading a magazine and it caught *my* attention. The idea of a cruise, which had been pretty far back in my thought process, came to the forefront.

And I ended up taking my wife and daughter on the Royal Viking Star.

The ad paints the picture of a never-to-be-forgotten fantasy experience. The agency, Goodby, Berlin & Silverstein, captured the essence of ship travel and appropriated it for Royal Viking.

What first stopped me was the art direction. You see just the very prow of the ship—juxtaposed with the ideal beach. Quite literally, the ship would not come that close to the beach or it would run aground. But that makes it an intriguing, arresting visual.

The copy develops the drama of this kind of vacation in a most elegant way. *"Permit us, for a moment, to indulge your wildest dream."*

Every element supports this idealized vacation concept and appeals to the upscale traveler. The colors are beautiful, the photographs very contemporary. They're surrounded by an elegant, widely-spaced type-face from a bygone era. The ad's border is an interesting touch and conveys all the destinations from Cartagena to Capri.

The brilliance of the campaign is that it lets Royal Viking *own* this kind of experience. The way all the

"The way all the elements come together on the page, you can almost touch and feel the specialness."

elements come together on the page, you can almost touch and feel the specialness.

Of course, because it's in a magazine, you can rip out the ad. Keep it as a reminder. Which, in fact, I actually did.

I cannot envision a campaign of this nature working quite this well in broadcast—no matter how pretty the pictures, no matter how evocative the music. Not even a sixty-second spot would have the power to bring it all together in one place like this.

One thing we believe we have done here at Hill Holliday, where we handle the Irish Tourist Board, is capture the essence of a country—what Leo Burnett used to call the "inherent drama." The Royal Viking ads are among the best examples I've seen of capturing "inherent drama."

As advertising professionals, we tend to be pretty jaded and think that we're beyond being influenced by an ad. But this campaign demonstrates that when everything is right—when every nuance, every detail is correct—we are as persuadable as anyone.

Magazines make things happen MPA

An advertising executive analyzes this ad and explains why the fact that it appears in a print medium helps it to be effective. Our comparison of how print differs from television in terms of consumer information processing begins just after these photos, on page 193.

This clever ad allows us to recognize how our CIP system (described in this chapter) operates when reading the ad. Notice that STM tends to slow down while waiting for the proper interpretation of a symbol for LTM, then moves to the next symbol, again awaiting a correct answer (given the context) from LTM. After getting through it the first time, however, the CIP system can work much faster a second time, since LTM has been modified by the ad.

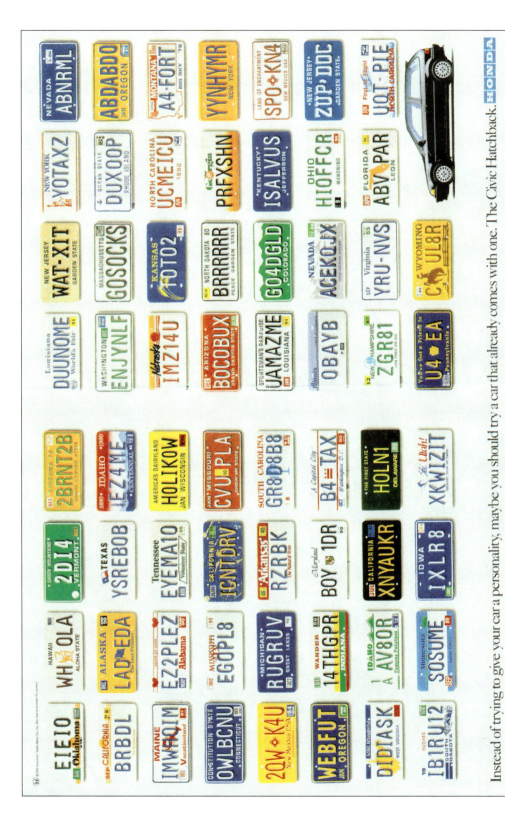

This ad engages our attention with color and variety, then subtly challenges us to correctly "decode" these plates to make sense of each one. Notice how our focus shifts between the external stimulus and our internal store of memory as we work on a tricky one. Notice also how it seems necessary to silently repeat the portion we know so as to "keep it alive" in our short-term memory: this reflects the capacity constraints we discuss in this chapter (7). You may enjoy showing this to friends to see if they get the same ones you did. How well did you do?

Instead of trying to give your car a personality, maybe you should try a car that already comes with one. The Civic Hatchback.

Q. CAN YOU FIND THE HIDDEN PLEASURE IN REFRESHING SEAGRAM'S GIN?

A. If you think this is just a bubble, look again.

As we'll see in Chapter 8, consumers for many years have been concerned that advertisers can manipulate minds through the use of "subliminal advertising." Industry leaders have for years steadfastly denied that anything like this is done, or that it would work. Recently, though, some firms have turned to spoofing the controversy as a way to gain attention and perhaps to deliver a message. Our discussion of the controversy and the evidence on consumers' perceptual processes begins on page 222.

acquisition is keyed to consumers' search for information in the marketplace. It reflects an *active* picture of the consumer, who is seeking to obtain desired inputs for CIP while shopping, talking to friends or salespersons, reading ads, and so on. The second CIP research area, **information integration**, focuses on what happens to information once it has entered working memory. Research here has stressed topics such as how LTM influences treatment of new information, how consumers combine pieces of information to make judgments and decisions, and how consumers' attitudes are formed and changed. The third CIP research area, **initial information processing**, has been particularly focused on how we consumers receive and process advertising. Because of its stress on advertising, this research stream tends to view consumers in a *reactive* light, as recipients of a persuasive message. The central concerns of this research zone must involve *communication* and *persuasion*. We will get a taste for this approach in just a page or two. At this point, however, we should simply be aware that the CIP framework is rich and powerful. We will be examining many of its research findings as we proceed through this book. The next section will give us a taste, however, for the potentials of CIP for marketing applications.

APPLYING CIP CONCEPTS TO ADVERTISING

 *A Demonstration Project*

There is mounting evidence that the broadcast media may have strangely different means of communicating, informing, and influencing people as compared to the printed media (newspapers, magazines, direct mail, etc.). You may wish to try a brief test on yourself to see if you can recognize some of the differences right off:

First, take a few unfamiliar magazine ads and read them through carefully and thoroughly. Now, turn on the television and watch a few unfamiliar commercials carefully and thoroughly. After finishing both tasks, sit down and think about the differences you experienced in your CIP activities. List them briefly in outline form. Also, list any differences you observed in the characteristics of the advertising stimuli in print versus broadcast. What are your findings?

The Dynamics of Television

The differences you have noticed in doing the demonstration project stem from differences between the print and broadcast media themselves. Figure 7-5 lists five such media differences. The first two are apparent when we consider the nature of the television stimulus. Television is *multisensory*; it impacts on both vision and hearing. Print media, on the other hand, impacts only on the visual sense register. Television also portrays *movement* to a much greater degree than does print; it is basically a series of many still pictures shown in rapid succession.

The remaining three differences are apparent if we ask how CIP for television might differ from CIP for print stimuli. First, television is known as an **intrusive medium**—its stimuli force themselves, or intrude upon, our sensory register. While we can obviously find ways to avoid processing a TV ad, we do have to shift CIP to do so. In print media the consumer controls the *CIP timing*: here we are free to spend as much (or as little) time as we wish with each ad. Television's time-controlled property, however, has an upper limit (usually 30 seconds) to the time that we can give to processing a commercial while it's still in front of us. With television, even if we are very interested, we *cannot* have an ad available to us for any longer CIP (we often

Intrusive medium: An advertising carrier that forces itself into consumers' awareness.

Property	Contrast: Print Versus TV		
	Print Ad		*TV Ad*
I. Sensory systems	Single sense (visual)	vs.	Multisensory (audio and visual)
II. Motion	Stationary	vs.	Movement
III. Attention	Nonintrusive	vs.	Intrusive
IV. CIP timing	Controlled by consumer	vs.	Controlled by ad
V. CIP pace	Controlled by consumer	vs.	Controlled by ad

FIGURE 7-5 Special Properties of Television Advertising

choose to spend less time, of course, but do so knowing that we are missing some of the ad).

CIP's *pace* is related to the timing issue. With print ads we can control our own CIP pace, going faster when we wish and slowing down at other points. TV ads, on the other hand, have a pace control built into them. Each commercial is scripted to proceed within the exact time limit. All the contents, *and* the pace or rate at which they appear, are entirely controlled by the advertiser and are fixed on the tape. The flow of stimuli to us, the consumers, has been determined before we are exposed to the stimulus at all. This will have powerful implications for the consumer's CIP during exposure to each type of ad.

CIP for Print Ads

Let's consider what happens when we read an interesting ad in a magazine. First, we can use as much time as we desire for our CIP. Second, we're able to look through the ad in whatever manner we decide is appropriate for us. This could mean, for example, glancing at a picture or two, skipping to the headline, then to the closing tag lines to identify the sponsor, and finally going back to begin to read the paragraphs from top to bottom. Within the process, we'll likely linger over parts of the ad and skim over other parts. Also, we're free to (and often do) look back at something we'd seen earlier, perhaps to check on a certain point. Although the alert advertiser will have designed a natural flow through the ad, each of us is free to set our own pathway and pace for processing it.

CIP for TV Ads

We don't have this freedom with a television commercial. Here we must follow the preset sequence, at the specified rate, or we risk missing some of the ad.

Notice the challenges to our limited CIP capacity! The TV commercial is sending out a constant stream of visual and sound stimuli, over a 30-second period. Our CIP system must maintain a constant interpretation process during each 30-second ad. Processing capacity must be used to decode what the light and sound waves from the TV set are in fact showing and saying. In addition, further STM capacity must be used for us to figure out how the sights and sounds tie together, and still further capacity must be used to decide what meaning the ad has for us personally.

Because we can't control the pace, however, we can't stop or slow down the process to think more deeply about something that has come up (unless, again, we are willing to miss some of the ad). Also, of course, we are totally unable to skip back, say, 12 seconds, to recheck a scene or statement that occurred earlier in the commercial.

"I wish I'd done that ad."

John Ferrell
Exec. V.P., Chief Creative Officer
Hill Holliday/New York

This is an ad that I know for a fact worked at least once. I was reading a magazine and it caught my attention. The idea of a cruise, which had been pretty far back in my thought process, came to the forefront.

And I ended up taking my wife and daughter on the Royal Viking Star.

The ad paints the picture of a never-to-be-forgotten fantasy experience. The agency, Goodby, Berlin & Silverstein, captured the essence of ship travel and appropriated it for Royal Viking.

What first stopped me was the art direction. You see just the very prow of the ship—juxtaposed with the ideal beach. Quite literally, the ship would not come that close to the beach or it would run aground. But that makes it an intriguing, arresting visual.

The copy develops the drama of this kind of vacation in a most elegant way. *"Permit us, for a moment, to indulge your wildest dream."*

Every element supports this idealized vacation concept and appeals to the upscale traveler. The colors are beautiful, the photographs very contemporary. They're surrounded by an elegant, widely-spaced type-face from a bygone era. The ad's border is an interesting touch and conveys all the destinations from Cartagena to Capri.

The brilliance of the campaign is that it lets Royal Viking *own* this kind of experience. The way all the

> *"The way all the elements come together on the page, you can almost touch and feel the specialness."*

elements come together on the page, you can almost touch and feel the specialness.

Of course, because it's in a magazine, you can rip out the ad. Keep it as a reminder. Which, in fact, I actually did.

I cannot envision a campaign of this nature working quite this well in broadcast—no matter how pretty the pictures, no matter how evocative the music. Not even a sixty-second spot would have the power to bring it all together in one place like this.

One thing we believe we have done here at Hill Holliday, where we handle the Irish Tourist Board, is capture the essence of a country—what Leo Burnett used to call the "inherent drama." The Royal Viking ads are among the best examples I've seen of capturing "inherent drama."

As advertising professionals, we tend to be pretty jaded and think that we're beyond being influenced by an ad. But this campaign demonstrates that when everything is right—when every nuance, every detail is correct—we are as persuadable as anyone.

Magazines make things happen MPA

An advertising executive explains how the print medium helps this ad to be effective.

HOW DO CONSUMERS ADAPT?

How do we consumers adapt to this loss of control over our own CIP when we watch television (or listen to a lecture, for that matter)? One type of CIP adaptation involves developing a style we'll call **passive processing.** Here we'll tend to sit back and observe rather than sit up and participate. Although we may enjoy TV ads at one level, we'll not tend to get very involved in thinking about them and may find that our attention tends to wander. This type of consumer reaction has been called **low involvement** and has been charged to be a natural reaction to broadcast media.

Passive processing:
A mode of information processing in which consumers sit back and observe.

Another type of adaptation involves what happens to CIP when TV ads are *repeated*. Each time that we see a familiar commercial, we are capable of exerting a little more control over our own CIP. Because we've already stored some information about the ad in our LTM, we can in effect "play it back" to ourselves at much faster speeds than on TV. Thus we can use this internal LTM to STM process to "hop ahead" easily to find the sponsor's brand name, the punch line, or some other salient aspect of the ad. In this way we can decide which parts of the commercial to watch carefully and which parts to ignore. After some point, however, ads seem to "wear out" and are not able to invoke further responses from the audience. Exhibit 7-1 reports one student's experiences with ad repetition. Does it seem that he is close to "wear out" with this ad?

The topic of low involvement and ad repetition are just two of many interesting issues that can be studied in CIP research. Each will be discussed further in later sections of the book. If, however, you wish to pursue these topics further right now, you may wish to read the articles listed in Notes 24 and 25 at the back of this book, listed under this chapter.

EXHIBIT 7-1

Ad Repetition: Getting the 501 Blues

How does repetition work? Let's hear from one student who reports his experience:

"I picked a Levi's 501 Blues commercial. I don't know if you've seen one, but the commercial is bizarre ... it starts out with a view of a young, extremely attractive woman shown with a rear view from the waist down. Of course, she is wearing 501 Blues. Along with this, there is what sounds like a barbershop quartet singing a very rhythmic tune. The ad continues with a barrage of scenes showing unusual characters wearing 501s ... [they] seem to be having the time of their lives.

The first time I saw the commercial I thought it was very entertaining due to the pretty girls and music. However, I did not really feel an urge to rush out and buy a pair of 501s. The next time I saw the commercial, I did not really anticipate the next scenes, but I did remember them when they were flashed across the screen. I caught myself humming the tune, for the ad is full of energy and excitement. As the repetitions increased I began anticipating and expecting the next scene. I knew exactly when the really shapely girls were going to be flashed, and that was what I was waiting for! By now, I also knew most of the words to the jingle and I was singing along as if I was a player in the commercial. The faces and bodies became incredibly familiar. I can distinctly see and remember many of the details that I did not even notice the first couple of viewings. I also began looking forward to specific parts and began overlooking other parts in anticipation of some of the scenes. I knew exactly what was going to happen, but I still was enjoying it tremendously due mainly to the 501 tune being sung behind each scene.

I felt a yearning to become like the people in the ad. To do that I needed to buy a pair of 501 Blues. The ad gets better with each viewing. I felt a stronger and stronger desire to purchase a pair of those jeans...."

Each of us lives in a symbolic world. All humans use a process of symbolizing to think about and elaborate upon the physical world around us. Understanding symbols provides real insights into the field of consumer behavior.

The report by the student in Exhibit 7-1 shows that his reactions to the Levi's ad were much stronger than mere thoughts produced by an information processing system. To understand these better, the area of *symbolism* is useful. Basically, we can think of a **symbol** as an external object that stands for or represents something else to us. The meaning of a symbol is stored within our CIP system in LTM. Words are one common form of symbol: "tree," for example, represents a certain type of entity in our external world. Numbers and mathematical signs are also symbols. In each case we are easily able to "decode" the sign through the node network (if we have learned it) in LTM. This use of the LTM node network means that symbols can be more than merely words and numbers, however. For example, a particular arrangement of musical notes can become a fight song and symbolize a university, a national flag is much more than a scrap of colored cloth, and a uniform is more than just a piece of clothing.

Symbol: An external object that stands for or represents something else to us.

SYMBOLS ARE HELPFUL

Within consumer behavior, symbols perform two important functions: (1) they improve consumers' *efficiency* and (2) they add to the *enjoyment* of consumer activities. For example, product names and store names serve as symbols that improve efficiency, as consumers are able to learn about the marketplace and to plan future behaviors better (by allowing us to consider where we might shop and what we want to buy when we get there). Prices are also expressed symbolically (that is, through numbers and monetary units). When prices are communicated in ads or on the packages, they help us to evaluate a possible purchase much more quickly than if we had to negotiate with each seller on each item.

Symbols also enliven and enrich our experience as consumers. For example, the products we place on our bodies gain symbolic meaning in our minds; that is, consumers are very interested in how clothing and cosmetics can be used to create a certain image, to create beauty, to commemorate particular events, and so on.

These deeper symbolic dimensions of consumption have recently become the subject of **postmodernism** (sometimes also termed interpretivism) in consumer research. Postmodern writers have generally stressed a much broader view of consumption than has been typical within CIP research or, indeed, in most prior marketing research. For example, postmodernist writers have recently examined what we are consuming when we listen to music or attend a play, the importance of our feelings and attachments to the money we save, the pets we own, or family heirlooms, the underlying themes (e.g., regarding materialism) in comics and movies, and so forth. Thus there is concern with a more holistic view of consumers than marketing's typical focus on what consumers are buying, and many of these articles are written without attempting to draw marketing conclusions about the subject. (If you would like to read more about the emergence of postmodernism and controversies regarding this area, you may consult Note 26.)

Postmodernism: A growing approach in consumer research: stresses a broadened, rich view of consumption.

As we might expect, symbolism plays a prominent role in much of this work. An increasing number of marketers are applying **semiotics** (the study of signs or things with meaning), others are examining *rituals* associated with consumer behavior (for example, think about the various settings in which eating and drinking serve symbolic functions), while other work is stressing the symbolic nature of social interactions. In our discussions concluding this chapter, we will delve more deeply into the relationship of symbols and CIP within a marketing context.

Semiotics: The study of signs and their messages.

SYMBOLS HAVE DIFFERENT LEVELS OF ELABORATION

Basically, something becomes a symbol to us because of how we react mentally to it. Obviously, then, almost everything can be a symbol. An important issue, therefore, is the *level of elaboration* that is stimulated by a particular symbol. It is useful for us to make a major distinction between two extreme levels of elaboration, very low and very high. At very low levels we find **objective symbols**, while at very high levels we find **evocative symbols.**

Evocative symbol:
A symbol that leads a person to bring forth further interpretations or emotions.

Objective symbols are commonly used simply to describe or identify something and thereby to transfer information. Each of the letters on this page, for example, is serving as an objective symbol for you as you read the page. Its function is straightforward: to allow the reader to deal with larger symbols (words, then sentences). In contrast, a symbol is evocative when it leads a person to expand upon the narrow meaning of the symbol itself and somehow to bring to mind ("evoke") further interpretations or feelings during the symbolizing process. Words and sentences can be used for this process (consider, for example, how easy it is to unleash our imaginations upon such words as "furry," "passionate," "evil," and so on, as further nodes, pictures, associations, and feelings flash through STM from LTM). In general, though, the evocative purpose of symbols seems to be expressed better through artistic means that often avoid the use of language. We have all experienced emotions (love, tenderness, anger), tastes (biting into a sweet, ripe cherry, the first taste of a dill pickle), or sensations of touch that have meaning far beyond the realm of language. In fact, these types of experiences are so subjective that they seem to require the artists of the world—the poets, musicians, sculptors, and painters—to symbolize them for us.

❧ *What Does a Prune Symbolize?*

Since both thinking and feeling are involved when we are engaged in symbolic elaboration, it can be difficult for us to assess the total amount of elaboration we are experiencing. From a marketer's perspective, moreover, this problem is even more severe, since consumers' elaborations are private to them and unobservable to us. This means that we need to undertake consumer research to try to find out what's really going on in consumers' minds when they symbolize. One classic marketing case that tried to do this occurred about 30 years ago.[27]

The California Sunsweet Growers Association was attempting to figure out why the per capita sales of prunes had been declining for some time. The association hired a famous motivation researcher, Dr. Ernest Dichter, to suggest what might be done. After studying consumers, using his motivation research methods (we discussed these in Chapter 5), Dr. Dichter reported that *a large segment of American consumers did not dislike the taste of prunes, but seemed bothered by what this fruit symbolized to them.* In particular, six major symbols were causing consumers to shy away from eating this food that they liked on other grounds:

- *Prunes are seen as symbols of old age and sterility.* Many consumers associated prunes with cafeterias, older people, and an older life-style.
- *Prunes are seen as symbols of loss of vitality and natural powers.* Many consumers did not like the look of stewed prunes, lying in their juice, and this vision conjured up further elaborations in their minds.

- *Prunes are symbols of digestive problems.* Prunes were seen as laxatives or medicines. Prunes are good for this purpose, but many consumers evoked images of a person who needed to eat prunes probably also having other health problems.

- *Prunes are symbols of parental authority.* Some consumers had been forced to eat prunes by their parents. These consumers now viewed this product as a symbol of enforced discipline. Now that they were adults and had a choice, they would not choose this product.

- *Prunes are symbols of plebeian tastes and lack of prestige.* Some consumers saw prunes as good basic foods, but not something to serve to others. If they are to be eaten, this should be done in the privacy of one's own kitchen.

- *Prunes are symbols of food for peculiar people.* Many consumers saw prunes as a favored food by "health nuts" and older people with health problems. These consumers did not wish to imitate their behaviors and perhaps become more like these prune users.

The marketing strategists noticed that each of these symbols seemed to have started from accurate observations about the appearance of the fruit, the benefits it offered, and the kinds of persons who consumed it. In each case, however, consumers had apparently gone much farther in their own minds (this is the elaboration process), until they reached the point of having unpleasant feelings about the prune itself. The marketing team was quite unsure about what to do next—should it strive to overcome this negative symbolism by attacking it head-on or should it ignore the negative connotations and try to provide the prune with positive symbolic qualities for consumers to seize upon? After 30 years of trying various approaches, this problem still exists: What would you recommend if you were consulting for the California Prune Board?

SYMBOLS DON'T ALWAYS MEAN THE SAME THING

The levels of elaboration concept also raises another important aspect of symbols: consumers can differ in how they'll react to various symbols. Loyal users of prunes, for example, might be shocked to learn what others think about it! (There are often a few in a consumer behavior class—ask them what they thought when they read the prune story.) For the "objective" level of symbolizing, with very little elaboration, most consumers within the same culture are likely to agree upon the meaning. This is true because we have usually learned the same language, rules, and customs. As a symbol becomes more evocative, the chance that different consumers attach different meanings to it begins to increase. Partially, this happens because of subcultural differences, reflecting differences in our ages, backgrounds, and experiences. Partially, it happens because of our personalities and interests: some people are imaginative, others are observant, some are religious, and so forth.

MARKETERS' USE OF SYMBOLS

With this background, let's briefly consider some of the ways in which symbols are important in marketing strategy. Because symbols can be powerful and because consumers can differ in their reactions, we might expect controversies over how and when marketers should use them. When we stop to think about it, it is clear that marketers try to use evocative symbols in all aspects of the marketing mix. Within the *product* sector, for example, many elements can be extremely important symbols, including the brand name (for confirmation, think of a few bad names for perfumes), the colors available, the packaging sizes and shapes, and so on. Within the *price* sector, consumers frequently assume that higher prices are good signs (symbols) of higher-quality products. Within the *place* sector, the atmosphere and image of the retail store is frequently a very significant factor in consumer purchase decisions. All this also holds for consumer services: many physicians, for example, employ professional designers to create an office atmosphere that inspires confidence and trust and creates tranquility. (Even the framed diplomas on the walls are strategically placed to send a symbolic message to the patients waiting for a consultation in the office.)

Symbols in Advertising

The most obvious symbolic system in marketing occurs, however, within the *promotion* sector of the marketing mix: *all promotion is symbolic communication*. The only questions that remain are (1) to what extent should evocative symbols be used, as opposed to the more objective types of symbolization, and (2) exactly how should the symbols be put together to accomplish best the kind of communication desired by the marketer, given his or her particular situation. The answers to these questions are complex and depend on the situation. For example, an ad need not be beautiful to be effective, nor does it have to evoke powerful emotions within its audience (at times, in fact, evoking strong emotions can lead consumers to ignore the rest of the ad while they emote within themselves and miss the brand's name entirely!). Also, a product or store will often be aiming at the mass market, so its symbols have to be meaningful to most members of its target group and evoke positive reactions from most of them. As one example, however, let's consider how symbols were manipulated in one classic ad campaign:

🐚 *A Marketing Classic: The Symbol of the "Marlboro Man"*

When it was first introduced, the Marlboro brand was advertised as a sleek, sophisticated cigarette for women.[28] Its name seemed derived from English royalty (though its spelling had been changed to reflect the modern times of America), the package was feminine, and the cigarette itself was lipstick red and ivory tipped. After years of this positioning, but without great marketplace success, management decided to change the image of Marlboro and try to sell it to men.

Realizing that this could backfire if the brand's personality wasn't changed to be clearly a "man's" product, the strategists decided to try to place Marlboro as the most masculine brand on the market, even more macho than Camel was at that time. Advertising was the obvious candidate to effect most of this change (the package was changed as well), but the symbolism used in the ads would have to be carefully constructed. Ultimately, several rules were set:

1. No women would ever be shown in the ads.
2. Only very virile men would appear (an early ad had employed an average male model with a manicure, and many consumers wrote in to point out the discrepancy).
3. The men had to appear as forceful as possible and as successful as they wished to be, to inspire admiration from men in the audience.
4. Each man would reveal a tattoo to the audience. This would be seen not only as a symbol of virility, but also hint of a romantic past when he was traveling the world with the U.S. Navy.

Although it wasn't planned this way, the combination of these symbols also evoked strong emotional reactions from many female consumers. Also, the campaign symbols seemed to be tapping some very basic human emotions, because Marlboro was able to move quite successfully into many countries and cultures of the world. The only culture in which it clearly failed was Hong Kong, which is so crowded that the inhabitants couldn't even imagine the open country settings, horses, and so forth. For Hong Kong, then, Marlboro had to create a new campaign featuring a city man with a motorcycle!

With television available for cigarette advertising at that time (cigarette ads were banned from broadcast media in 1971 by the U.S. Congress), Marlboro was able also to use powerful music and sweeping images of cowboys in rugged terrain as further symbols in its repositioning move.

The result? Marlboro moved successfully into its new positioning and found increasing popularity as it moved up in the share of market rankings. About 20 years ago it closed in on and then passed Winston, the previous market leader, and it has been the number one brand since that time. It now holds about 25 percent share of market—one of every four cigarettes sold in the United States—and earns several billion dollars in profit each year for Philip Morris. Advertising remains faithful to the Marlboro code: Talent scouts still search in cowboy country for ranch hands with Marlboro Man potential, since models aren't used. As one female executive explains: "It's how he gets on the horse, how he sits . . . absolutely and exactly macho."

The profile of U.S. Marlboro smokers seems to fit these sentiments: 65 percent are male, 70 percent are between the ages of 18 and 34, 70 percent have high school education or less, and 92 percent are white. Among Marlboro's key sales promotions are sports events and country music events. Thus this classic use of symbols has created a truly powerful brand name. When asked whether we might someday see it used on other products as well, such as Marlboro Beer, an executive replied, "You might."

In addition to the highly evocative nature of the symbols used by Marlboro, it was also necessary that the advertising contain a proper blend of symbols that did not contradict each other (the manicure was perhaps the last contradiction allowed in this campaign). Across the field of marketing, however, there are many examples of ads that *do* contain conflicting symbols, and it should be easy for you to find some cases if you look for them. Why does this happen so often? Primarily, because evocative symbols do result in many consumer reactions, and these can differ among segments of the audience. If the advertising copywriter doesn't happen to have the right target segment in mind, or doesn't know this segment very well, ineffective symbols can easily creep into the ads.

Our goal in this section has been to highlight the importance of symbolism in consumer behavior. In our next two chapters, we shall continue to examine how CIP and symbols work as we move into the topic of consumer perception. Later, we will examine advertising issues themselves in Chapter 16.

■ SUMMARY

THE HIERARCHY OF EFFECTS MODEL

In the first section of the chapter, a key marketing model—*the hierarchy of effects*—was examined. Here we learned how consumers can move in fixed stages from unawareness to purchase of a brand. There are seven stages in the model: unawareness, awareness, knowledge, liking, preference, conviction, and purchase. We discussed the "think-feel-do" view that underlies this model. We also saw how marketers can use this framework to assist their planning and how the framework has some controversial limitations to it. Under low involvement, for example, an alternative "think-do-feel" ordering has been proposed.

CONSUMER INFORMATION PROCESSING

In the second section of the chapter, we discussed the *consumer information processing (CIP) approach* to the study of an individual's consumer behavior. CIP deals with our mind and how it works. It concentrates on the thoughts and reactions we have as we operate as consumers in the marketplace.

STRUCTURE OF THE CIP SYSTEM

In this section we examined the three centers of the CIP system—*the sensory register*, the *short-term memory (STM)*, and *long-term memory (LTM)*. We discussed the functions of the sensory register, the capacity constraints that operate on STM, and the key role that LTM plays within the CIP system. We examined the network model of LTM, noting how associations between concepts enable us to think rapidly and logically. We discussed several ways in which the CIP approach applies to consumer behavior, as in the 7-Up example.

CIP RESEARCH AND APPLICATIONS

We also gained some appreciation for the issues that lie ahead, as we briefly examined three CIP research areas in consumer behavior: *information acquisition, information integration*, and *initial information processing*. Then, we examined how CIP can be applied to better understand how advertising works. Here we compared print versus television as media, and why they affect consumers differently.

CIP AND SYMBOLISM

In the final section of the chapter we broadened our discussion to include symbolism. We saw that a *symbol* is an external object that stands for something in our minds, and that symbols add both efficiency and enjoyment to consumer behavior. We learned that a new research approach, *postmodernism* (or interpretivism), has evolved to explore the breadth of consumer behavior in a variety of ways. We also saw that symbols have different levels of mental elaboration associated with them, ranging from *objective symbols,* which are basically communication devices (letters, words, numbers), to *evocative symbols,* such as flags or songs, which bring further thoughts and emotions to STM. As illustrations of the problems and opportunities symbols bring for marketers, we examined the symbolic images consumers hold of prunes as a product, and how Marlboro cigarettes were skillfully switched from a ladies' smoke into one of the world's most powerful brands through symbolic manipulation.

As we noted at the start, this is an especially important chapter because it presents a number of concepts that we'll continue to use in future chapters, beginning with our next one, on the fascinating topic of consumer perception.

■ KEY TERMS

hierarchy of effects	long-term memory (LTM)	encoding
cognitive component	capacity limitations	ad repetition
affective component	time constraints	evoked set
conative component	size constraints	information acquisition
low involvement	chunking	information integration
consumer information processing (CIP)	episodic memories	initial information processing
black box model	semantic memories	intrusive medium
CIP approach	network organization	passive processing
sensory system	nodes	low involvement
conceptual system	linkages	symbol
CIP system	activation	postmodernism
sensory register	retrieval	semiotics
short-term memory (STM)	interference	objective symbols
adaptive	external retrieval cues	evocative symbols
working memory		

■ REVIEW QUESTIONS AND EXPERIENTIAL EXERCISES

[E = **Application extension or experiential exercise**]

1. Indicate at what stage of the hierarchy of effects model you are currently located for the following products/services. Provide rationale.

   a. Video games
   b. Ivory soap
   c. Sanka
   d. Club Med
   e. IRA
   f. Cellular telephones

2. Consider the market for Olive Garden restaurants:

   a. How would you analyze the market in terms of the hierarchy of effects model?
   b. What percentage of consumers are at each stage?
   c. What are the characteristics of these consumers?
   d. What are the marketing implications of your analysis?

3. What are the advantages to the marketing manager of employing a CIP approach versus a black box approach? What are the advantages of the black box approach? Is it possible to apply both approaches?

4. Capacity limitations were discussed in the CIP section of the chapter:

   a. What exactly are these? To which system sectors do they apply?
   b. Think about your own consumer behavior. Have you ever run into capacity limitations? What were their effects?

5. [E] From your LTM structure, map individual network organizations for two of the following (see Figure 7-4):

   a. Pizza
   b. Personal grooming
   c. Education
   d. Travel
   e. Beer

6. [E] Leaf through several popular magazines, examining the ads as you go. Choose one example each of ads that appear to be aimed primarily at each stage of the hierarchy. Clip them out and attach brief explanations of your reasoning.

7. [E] The 7-Up example demonstrates how marketers can try to use the LTM network to "associate" a brand name with some other concepts that consumers hold in their minds. Look for other good examples of this strategy in current ads. Find two ads that attempt this, briefly analyze how they go about it, and indicate whether you believe they are successful.

8. [E] Using the relevant Notes for this chapter at the back of the book or reading material in the reference section of your library, read in more depth about a CIP topic of interest to you. Write a brief report on your findings.

9. [E] Using Notes 24 and 25 for this chapter (in the back of the book), locate further readings about CIP and advertising. Write a brief report on your findings.

10. [E] Using Note 21 for this chapter, locate further readings on the concept of evoked set. Write a brief report on your findings.

11. **[E]** Conduct the demonstration project suggested at the start of our section "Applying CIP Concepts to Advertising." Write a brief report on your findings.

12. **[E]** Try to observe CIP in action within the marketing-consumer environment. Go shopping with a friend or relative. Do not inform your shopping companion about the nature of your exercise, but do make a special effort to observe and monitor his or her CIP. Encourage your companion to voice thoughts as you move along. What stimuli are being processed, and which ones are being missed? What seems to attract your companion's attention? How strong a role is LTM playing versus external stimuli? Does CIP seem to be as rapid a process as the book claims? Write a brief report summarizing what you observed here.

13. **[E]** The chapter mentions that CIP is likely to change as consumers see repetitions of any particular advertisement. If you have access to a VCR, try taping an ad and then replaying it for a total of four to six repetitions (such as every half hour or each time other commercials appear during a regular TV program). Try to watch this ad as naturally as you normally would. Notice whether the relative roles of the ad itself and your LTM change over the repetitions. Notice also whether your pace, timing, and reactions to the ad change or not. Write a brief report summarizing your findings.

14. **[E]** Look through a number of magazine ads, noting how symbols are used in each. Clip out one example of each of the following.

   a. An ad that has, in your opinion, a use of symbolism that led to *positive* emotions or reactions on your part.

   b. An ad that has a *negative* use of symbolism in your opinion (i.e., it led to negative reaction on your part).

   c. An ad that seems to have *conflicting* symbols within the ad itself.

   d. An ad that uses symbols in a way likely to be *controversial.*

   Briefly explain your reasoning related to each example.

■ SUGGESTED READING

■ This chapter covers many key issues, so a large number of excellent articles are available in the Notes' references. For better understanding of one useful marketing concept, see the classic Lavidge and Steiner article proposing the hierarchy of effects (cited in Note 2) and the excellent review of work on the hierarchy by Berry (cited in Note 5). For interesting examinations of advertising's impacts from an information processing perspective, see the MacInnis and Jaworski article (cited in Note 24). For a number of interesting perspectives on postmodern consumer research, the volume by Hirschman (cited in Note 26) is useful. Another good bet for this chapter, though, is to browse through the Notes to identify articles that speak directly to issues of personal interest.

CONSUMER PERCEPTION (I)
Attention to Marketing Cues

THE "COCKTAIL PARTY" PROBLEM

A classic example demonstrates the power of selecting stimuli in our perceptual process. See if you've experienced something close to it. Imagine that you're standing in a crowded room while friends and acquaintances are socializing all around you. The sounds of conversations, laughter, glasses clinking, and music are loud and confusing. You are attempting to carry on a reasonable conversation in your little circle but are having trouble hearing the others speak. All of a sudden, from across the room, you hear your name mentioned. Immediately, *selective attention* operators spring into overdrive. You now find it easier to screen out other stimuli, pick out the discussion of interest, and overhear it.

Scientists studying attention pose an interesting question that arises in this setting, however: How were you able to recognize your name, given all the other stimuli so confusing just the moment before? Further, how are you now able to screen them out so effectively?

■ DEFINING CONSUMER PERCEPTION

In a broad sense, the topic of **perception** is concerned with the translation from the external, physical world to the internal, mental world that each of us actually experiences. Although we don't often think about it, we are able to experience only a limited degree of the total physical world, and our mental experiences are themselves usually biased to a greater or lesser extent. Since shopping, purchase, and use activities all require interactions with the external world, the topic of perception is crucial to our understanding of consumer behavior. Furthermore, it is important to note all marketing stimuli exist only in the external world: they *must be perceived by consumers* to have any impact at all. Thus marketers are keenly interested in understanding consumer perception.

In reading this chapter, it will be helpful to think in terms of our CIP framework from Chapter 7. The basic system is reproduced in Figure 8-1 (you may wish to refresh

Perception: The process of sensing, selecting, and interpreting consumer stimuli in the external world.

205

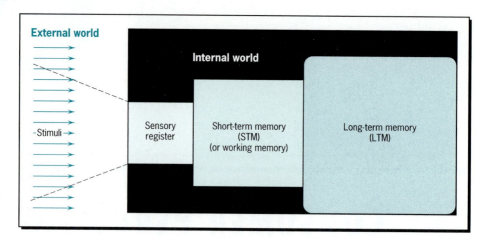

FIGURE 8-1 The Consumer Information Processing System

your understanding of each sector at this point). We will define consumer perception as *the process of sensing, selecting, and interpreting consumer stimuli in the external world.* Thus all sectors of our CIP system are involved—the sensory register, the short-term memory (STM), and our long-term memory (LTM).

TWO KEY FACTORS IN PERCEPTION

As we saw in the CIP chapter, our human information processing system is capable of dealing with a remarkably wide array of stimulus inputs and works at extremely rapid speeds (in thousandths of seconds). Thus our perceptual processes are at work continuously, dealing with many stimuli at great speeds. This presents a serious challenge to researchers: a basic framework is quite helpful in appreciating what goes on.

The most basic point of our framework is that there are two key factors that determine what will be perceived and how it will be perceived:

- Stimulus characteristics
- Consumer characteristics

Since consumers are subject to capacity constraints in their CIP systems, we know that they will be incapable of—and uninterested in—fully perceiving and processing all aspects of their environments. **Stimulus characteristics,** a wide-ranging set such as color, size, photos, story, scent, loudness, design, music, and so forth, help us to understand which properties of a stimulus will cause it to receive attention. Since marketers control stimulus characteristics, they are interested in understanding how this factor affects consumer perception.

Consumer characteristics, on the other hand, refer to the influences that our CIP system has on what we perceive. For example, let's consider what really goes on while we are watching TV and an ad comes on. The screen itself will contain many dots emitting light waves of varying magnitudes. Our sensory system picks up those light waves and delivers them to the sensory register, where they are briefly held available for interpretation and any further processing by our CIP system. *Notice, however, that we are unable even to begin to interpret these signals without using our prior knowledge of the world that is stored in LTM.* Without using LTM, we could not know that the dots were portraying a mountain scene, or a laughing surfer, or a miraculous new cleanser for the home.

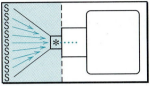
Stage 1: Sensing

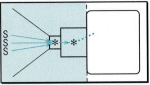
Stage 2: Selecting and attending

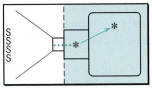
Stage 3: Interpreting

FIGURE 8-2 A Simplified Form of the Three Functions (Stages) of Perception

Scientists who study perception usually make a choice as to which perspective to take on this process. Those who stress the role of the external stimuli emphasize a "bottom-up" or **data-driven view** of the perceptual process. Those who stress the role of personal characteristics employ a "top-down" or **theory-driven approach.** It is not important to pursue detailed distinctions at this point: because of our interest in marketing applications, we will find both approaches useful in helping us appreciate this topic.

Data-driven view: A perception research approach that stresses the influence of stimulus characteristics on perception.

BREAKING DOWN THE PROCESS OF PERCEPTION

Because of the incredible speed of the perception process, it is very difficult to break it down into discrete stages. There are, however, three basic functions that are contained in our definition of perception (see Figure 8-2):

Theory-driven view: A perception research approach that stresses the influence of a consumer's characteristics, such as expectations.

- *Sensing* a stimulus in the external world
- *Selecting* and *attending* to certain stimuli and not others
- *Interpreting* the stimuli and giving them "meaning"

As a set, these functions move from the early stages of a perceptual episode (when it is concentrated on the external environment) to the later stages (when it is concentrated on dealing with the new information in STM). In our discussions we will treat these as isolated stages and examine them separately. In the first half of this chapter, therefore, we concentrate on consumers' sensory processes: how we become aware of consumer stimuli in our environment. In the second half of this chapter, we shift our focus to consumers' selectivity operators, emphasizing the role that attention plays within the perceptual process. Then, in Chapter 9, we'll examine the topic of consumers' interpretive processes. As we discuss each topic we'll see applications that reflect the importance of consumer perception in the real world of marketers, consumers, and public policy.

■ CONSUMER SENSATION

THE FIVE SENSES

Most humans rely on the **five senses** to bridge the gap between the external world and their mental worlds. That is, we see, we hear, we taste, we smell, and we touch the world around us in order to sense it. Our **sensory receptors** are our organs—eyes, ears, mouth, nose, and skin—that receive inputs from the environment. All five of our sensory receptors are employed in consumer behavior.

Sensory receptors: The human sense organs—eyes, ears, mouth, nose, and skin—that receive inputs from the environment.

Marketing Applications of Sensation

As we noted earlier, marketers are extremely interested in perception because they know that all elements of the marketing mix must be perceived by consumers before they can have any impact at all. Thus an understanding of sensory processes, the first step in perception, is an important issue for marketers. The following examples indicate some of the value of this area:

🐚 Taste, Smell, and the Science of Food

In the English language there are only four words to describe what one tastes. Something will be *sweet, bitter, sour,* or *salty* or some combination of these. Food marketers know that the chemistry of sourness and saltiness is quite simple, while sweetness and bitterness are more complicated. Food producers know that the tastes we perceive are really the result of a complex interaction of two senses—taste and smell. As a simple test to detect this interaction, try taking a sip of liquid (wine, soft drink, liquor, etc.); then hold your nose. The flavor will probably seem to diminish. Then release your nose and the flavor will come up again.

Marketers know that the sense of smell is much more complex than the sense of taste. That is why most of us have a very difficult time using specific terms to describe smells. Instead, we tend to use the names of objects that possess the scent—something "smells like a rose," or pine, or a skunk, and so on. Food producers know that humans have 10 million olfactory receptors for sensations of smell, while the number of taste receptors is only one-tenth to one-hundredth as large. They also know that consumers can indeed smell something inside the mouth, and it is likely that smell contributes more to consumers' perceived taste of food and drink than the taste sense itself![1]

🐚 The Strange Case of Tab

Marketers also know that heredity plays a role in a person's sense of taste and that about 7 of every 10 consumers will find the chemical PTC to be bitter, while the other 3 will not. Those who find PTC bitter are likely to dislike the taste of saccharin, which they also taste as bitter.

The differences in consumers' taste of PTC and bitterness may have accounted for the strange case of Tab's reception by consumers during its first 20 years on the market (when it used a distinctive taste relying on saccharin as a sweetener). According to the senior vice president of marketing for Coca-Cola, Tab "turned off more people than it turned on. A lot of people took a sip, made a face, and said, 'Yuk!' They never tried it again. It was a brand that polarized people very much." However, there was another market segment in which Tab did very well—the so-called "Tab fanatics." These consumers spent over $100 million each year that Tab was relying on saccharin as its major sweetening ingredient. It was not until consumer taste tests showed greater preference for Tab containing NutraSweet that the company reformulated the brand to include both NutraSweet and saccharin. Today, the marketers of Tab are attempting to increase the soft drink's market share by testing a clear version, by "reminding consumers of Tab's crisp taste" and are wondering whether it might become "the Virginia Slims of the Colas."[2]

🐚 Vanity, Impaired Sensation, and Package Design

A typical large supermarket now stocks about 20,000 different items, and marketing competition to gain attention from shoppers who pass by in the aisles is fierce. Package design and color are important factors in this competition, as we'll discuss in a further section of the chapter. With respect to the topic of consumers' use of their sensory systems, however, consider what marketers should do with the knowledge that many consumers are shopping with impaired sensory systems. Specifically, package designers know that *one out of every six shoppers* who needs eyeglasses doesn't wear them while shopping. In designing packages to appeal to consumers and to sell the product effectively, therefore, marketers must also allow for less efficient sensory receptors on the part of a significant portion of the market.[3]

✒ *I'll Bet You Didn't Know...*

Retailers and service providers are very sensitive to the stimuli that consumers encounter in their stores and offices. For example, fast-food chains have designed their plastic seating not only to be durable, but also to be somewhat uncomfortable. This is done so that consumers will not linger over their meals and cause seating problems for new arrivals.

Several years ago, a major hotel-casino in Atlantic City signed a $7 million contract with an interior design firm to remodel and "create an environment that relaxes the morality of people." Among the changes:

1. Lobby windows replaced by sheets of marble, so "people won't relate to time" by having daylight changes to serve as a sensory cue.
2. Materials added to increase casino noise because "noise creates excitement."
3. Lighting for the blackjack tables designed to extend out to envelop the player but not far enough to include spectators, since this may interrupt the player's sense of security.
4. In the free hotel suites used by "high rollers," decor in bold, contrasting colors with very bright lighting and enhanced noise materials. The intent was to have the gamblers wish to spend as little time as possible in their rooms.[4]

CONSUMER "SENSITIVITY"

Psychophysics is the science that studies how the actual physical environment gets translated into our personal psychological environments. One basic question involves the limitations that we humans have in our abilities to sense everything that actually exists in the world. In other words, what are humans *not able* to perceive, because their sensory systems are not sensitive enough?

A **threshold** is a level at which an effect begins to occur. Within the field of sensation, the **absolute sensory threshold** is defined as the minimum amount of energy that can be detected by a particular sensory receptor. For example, sounds below the absolute threshold cannot be heard or billboards that are too distant cannot be seen. Most of us are naive enough simply to assume that our sensory system is providing us with a complete record of the outside world. If we consider all the waves (radiation, television bands, etc.) around us in the atmosphere, however, we can easily begin to recognize limitations to our sensory systems. If we compare our sensory abilities with those of other animals, the lesson becomes even more clear.

Dogs have a sense of smell that is as much as 1 million times more sensitive than that of a human, birds can sense magnetism from the earth, dolphins employ sonar, and some moths can smell each other from a mile away. By comparison, then, we humans could easily be described as "somewhat insensitive" creatures. Our strong suits are in sight and touch, our hearing is fair, and our sense of smell and taste are very weak in comparison to those of other living species.[5] At a practical level, of course, we have adapted our world to living within our absolute sensory thresholds.

Psychophysics: The science that studies how the physical environment is translated into our personal psychological environments.

Threshold: The level at which an effect begins to occur.

Moths can smell each other from a mile away.

Birds can sense magnetism from the earth.

Dolphins use sonar to monitor their underwater world.

Dogs have a sense of smell that is 1 million times more sensitive than a human's.

By comparison, we humans are somewhat insensitive creatures! We are at our strongest in sight and touch, fair in hearing, and weak in taste and smell.

The **differential sensory threshold** refers to the ability of our sensory systems to detect *changes* or *differences* in stimuli. Differences that are too small will not be recognized as differences at all. For example, we're all aware that quality control can't be perfect. This means that all packages of a given brand will have minute differences in shapes and colorings, yet these are usually undetectable to us. The very slight variations in taste, smell, and consistency within a package also often go undetected.

"JNDs" and Weber's Law

Another term for differential threshold is the **just noticeable difference,** or **JND.** This is defined as the minimum actual change in a stimulus that can be detected as a change. Well over 100 years ago, the German scientist Ernst Weber discovered a systematic process involving JNDs: *as stimulus intensities get larger, it takes more of a change in the stimulus to be detected as a change*—a 1-pound change in weight will be much easier to detect in a 3-pound bag than in a 75-pound bag, a whisper is easier to hear in a silent room than in a noisy one, and so forth. (Note 6 discusses some technical details of Weber's law for those readers interested in pursuing it further.)

> **Just noticeable difference (JND):** Another term for the differential sensory threshold: the minimum amount of change in a stimulus that can be detected.

✌ *"Downsizing" and the JND*

Despite some limitations, Weber's law remains an important generalization for marketing. There are two basic situations in which the JND concept comes into play: (1) those in which marketers want a difference to be detected and (2) those in which they do not want a difference to be detected. An example of the first case might involve a soft drink firm that believes that its sales will increase if it can achieve a taste that consumers will perceive as sweeter. Adding sugar will yield a sweeter taste. As sugar costs money, however, the managers realize that this change will increase production costs. Thus they want to add as little additional sugar as possible, consistent with consumers being able to detect a sweeter taste to the drink.

The second case—changes not to be detected—frequently involves lowering costs while maintaining prices at a constant level. This is known as **downsizing.** For example, when most gins dropped their alcoholic contents from 90 proof to 80 proof, distillers saved 15 to 21 cents a fifth in federal taxes, as well as saving on ingredient costs. It is not likely that many consumers were able to detect the difference in taste. Package changes are also sometimes made because of squeezes on costs, and sometimes they are done in such a way as to minimize the noticeable differences in quantity. When Procter & Gamble reduced the contents of its Sure spray deodorant from 9 ounces to 8, for example, it did not change the price or size of the cans. In total, savings from downsizing can be considerable for a firm: after StarKist removed 1/8 ounce of tuna from its cans, it used *1.7 million fewer pounds* of tuna to fill the same number of cans the next year.[7]

> **Downsizing:** Decreasing contents or ingredients, often while maintaining constant prices.

Beyond Sensory Processes

A careful analysis of our examples might well lead to the question,

> Wait a minute! Are we talking about *capability* of sensing a difference, or are we really asking whether consumers will *actually notice* that a change has occurred? There are probably a lot of cases in which consumers *could* detect changes that had been made in a brand, but they just don't try.

Sensory threshold concepts refer to *capability* of sensory detection. These concepts do not say that changes in stimulus intensity *will* be noticed, but only that they *can* be noticed if the consumer chooses to try to do so.

Although sensory thresholds are important, in most practical applications marketers are interested in how likely it is that consumers *will* perceive changes or differences in stimuli. Lawry's Seasoned Salt, for example, wanted to change its somewhat stodgy package and "L" symbol, but did not want to lose its fine reputation with loyal customers. The firm decided to introduce very minor packaging changes over a series of years. As its president explained,

> When we started, we were sensitive to the damage that a too radical change in packaging graphics could do to consumer recognition of Lawry's. So we changed all the individual elements, but left the overall look—colors, proportions..., positioning of the elements—sufficiently similar to ease the transition in the marketplace...in all, it took us 12 years to get where we wanted to go from the beginning.[8]

In this case consumers could easily see that the new label was different from the old one, if asked to compare them on a side-by-side basis. The question of interest, however, was whether consumers would choose to make this sort of comparison on their own.

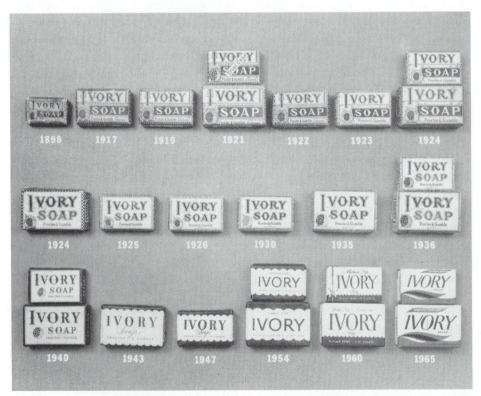

Examples of the changes in labeling in the early years of Ivory soap. Notice how consumers might have been unlikely to notice some of the changes, such as those in the early 1920s.

New!
Half the strength!

A Connecticut reader alerted us to this NEW! IMPROVED bottle of *Triaminic Syrup*, a children's cold medicine. The new bottle looks similar to the old one, although it comes encased in a cardboard box. And it costs the same—about $8 for eight ounces. But our reader noticed a big difference: The amount of active ingredients has been cut in half, and the dosage, accordingly, has risen from one teaspoon to two. She wondered if this wasn't the same as doubling the price. We asked Sandoz Pharmaceuticals Corporation, *Triaminic's* maker, to clear things up.

A Sandoz spokesman emphasized the positive. "We've improved the flavor," he told us, "and changed the dosing regimen." (Meaning you take twice as much.) Furthermore, he pointed out, "We didn't raise the price when we brought out the new product line."

Thank goodness for small favors. But we'd be happier if the price had been cut along with the active ingredients.

Consumer Reports magazine takes issue with a case of downsizing in this editorial from its November 1992 issue (p. 739).

The more similar the new label was to the old, Lawry's management believed, the less likely consumers would be to notice any difference at all.

The downsizing examples raise this question even more clearly. Although consumers may not have been able to detect a change in the *taste* of the gin, for example, they could easily have used their sight sense to detect the alcoholic content on the label. Similarly, although P&G did not highlight the quantity change in Sure's can, the labels did accurately depict the amount of Sure in the can. This is why labeling laws require that information be made available that would otherwise be difficult or impossible for a consumer to sense.

🐚 *Sensory Discrimination in "Blind Taste Tests"*

To this point in our discussion we've focused on sensory discriminations *within* the same brand. In marketing, however, considerable attention is also paid to *comparisons between brands*. Consumers are encouraged to believe that there are substantial differences between brands, and to become loyal to a certain brand that appeals most to their tastes. Most of us do exhibit such beliefs and loyalties and are confident that we "know what we like and what we don't." In many cases there *are* significant differences between brands, and we are able to perceive them accurately. However, the nature of certain food and drug categories leads to them being known within marketing as **parity products,** indicating that the actual differences among brands are very slight:

Parity products: A term indicating that the actual differences between brands are very slight.

they are on a par with each other. Examples include analgesics (headache remedies and pain killers), soft drinks, cereals, cigarettes, and beer. It is no accident that these product classes have among the highest ratios of dollars spent on advertising to dollars in sales—the cigarette industry, for example, spends over $2 billion per year to differentiate its brands.

EXHIBIT 8-1

Debbie Loves Pepsi

Let's listen to Debbie Strednak as she takes a blind taste test for colas. After trying four unidentified cups (nibbling a cracker between each taste), Debbie doesn't even ask about the real brands—they're so *obvious*. She prefers the second cup: "It's Pepsi," she confides. "I guess I'm just used to the taste." She wrinkles her nose with distaste for the first cup, and ranks it last.... "I can't drink Coke, it gives me a headache...it has an aftertaste. I have Pepsi with everything."

In fact, Ms. Strednak has gotten it all wrong. Her favorite was Coke Classic. She wasn't even given Pepsi in the test. She expressed shock: "No!" she shrieks, slapping her forehead. "Are you sure? Oh, that is horrible!"[9]

As Debbie Strednak illustrates in Exhibit 8-1, many consumers find it difficult to accept that brands are really all that similar in these categories. "Maybe some other people can't tell the difference," they say, "but I certainly can." Most of us are likely to feel, for example, that we prefer our favorite brand of beer or soft drink because it really does taste better to us. The interesting question, however, is whether this better taste arises from our sensory system or from the associations we make from the brand image that we hold in LTM. Producers of these products know that sensory reality is subtle and that either factor can be at work. Considerable private testing goes on within the industry. The literature, moreover, presents mixed results.

In one classic study, for example, a beer company teamed up with a professor to conduct an experiment with beer drinkers, who were provided with a six pack of mixed brands, all in identical containers that did not disclose their identities. As the people consumed each bottle (the study was conducted over weeks of time!), they rated the contents on a tag. These ratings were based only on sensory stimuli. During the next period, the firm provided similar six-packs, but this time with the labels present. How did the ratings compare?

Basically, consumers appeared unable to distinguish their favorite brand from the others when no label was provided. When loyal users of each brand rated all five brands without labels, in no case was their favorite brand rated significantly higher than

SHOE

all the other brands. Two of the brands did receive some higher ratings, one brand's users rated all five equal, and two brands were rated significantly lower by their own users! When labels were provided, of course, these ratings changed back to reflect the brand preferences stated at the start of the test. The brewing company concluded that

> physical product differences had little to do with the various brands' relative success or failure in the market . . . [instead, success was due to] various firms' marketing efforts, and, more specifically, . . . the resulting brand images.[10]

Further research in this area has shown that the method used in a study can make the discrimination task easier or more difficult for consumers (for example, had the beer company asked consumers to taste small amounts of two or three beers at a time, the consumers likely would have done better in discriminating among them). Also, some consumers are better able to discriminate among brands than others. Expert "tasters," for example, are retained by companies because of their highly developed sensory palates. What about the "average" consumer, though? According to the head of a large consulting firm's flavor science unit, beer drinkers appear to be split into three equal-sized segments:

1. Those who can't tell taste differences well at all
2. Those who can detect taste differences, but buy beer on a price basis or other reason
3. Those who can discriminate between brands and buy what tastes best to them [11]

SUMMARY: SENSORY PROCESSES

Our discussion to this point is helpful in indicating the basic role that sensory processes play in the larger process of consumer perception. If there are objective differences in the external world, consumers may or may not actually notice them. A necessary but not sufficient requirement is that they be *capable* of detecting the difference—that the stimulus intensity be above the relevant sensory threshold. Beyond this, consumers need to employ their CIP systems to detect such differences as may exist in the world. Many consumers likely did not take this step in either the gin or Sure examples, cases in which marketers themselves may not have desired to highlight the changes made. Even when marketers do wish to highlight changes, however, consumers often still do not choose to take notice. Thus the issue of which stimuli consumers *choose to perceive* becomes a key question. We'll take this up in our next section, which examines consumer selectivity and attentional processes.

■ SELECTIVITY AND ATTENTION

Recall the cocktail party example at the start of this chapter? It indicates several important points about consumer attention.[12] For example, it shows how both stimulus and personal factors are important in capturing and guiding attention. A stimulus with particular properties (in this case, our name) is quite capable of interrupting our other CIP processes and capturing attention from our system. At the same time, this attention was selectively focused because our personal factors were geared to that type of stimulus.

The example also shows how *attracting* attention and *maintaining* attention are really quite different processes. The maintenance of attention is much more determined by personal factors than by stimulus characteristics. In this case, for example, we might have already heard the story being told about us. If so, we might shift our attention to the listeners, to monitor their reactions, or we may decide to ignore that conversation and again focus our attention on our attractive partner for the evening.

As consumers, consider how many packages we pass on a store shelf without consciously perceiving them, how many ads we fail to process, and so forth. Our sensory system makes a wide range of stimuli from the external environment available to us. To live our lives in a rational manner, however, we must choose to "perceive" some elements and ignore other elements of that world. Thus the issue of *selectivity* is crucial. For marketers, of course, understanding how consumers' selectivity operators work offers guidance for designing ads that "break through the clutter" to gain attention, packages and displays that attract attention in the store, and so forth.

THE SELECTIVITY OPERATORS

Consumers use four types of **selectivity operators** in helping to order our lives and the mental world in which we live them. These are

- *Selective exposure.* Consumers use **selective exposure** to decide to which situations and stimuli they'll be exposed at all. In general, we expose ourselves to situations we view as interesting or necessary and avoid others with unpleasant characteristics (political strategists have long known, for example, that audiences for candidates' speeches are largely comprised of people who have already decided to support that candidate). In marketing, selective exposure is extremely important in both the "place" and "promotions" elements of the marketing mix. Store location decisions, for example, are based largely on where consumers are likely to be driving. Similarly, measures of selective exposure such as ratings points for TV and radio determine what shows advertisers will support.

- *Selective attention.* While selective exposure vastly reduces the range of stimuli available to a person, it does not decide which remaining stimuli will be perceived. This is determined by **selective attention,** which we'll analyze in this chapter.

- *Selective interpretation.* Once an external stimulus receives attention from us, the material we bring from long-term memory (LTM) is crucial to determining exactly how that stimulus is categorized and interpreted by us. We'll examine **selective interpretation** in more detail in the next chapter.

- *Selective retention and retrieval.* In many cases we choose to stress some aspects of a person or brand and play down other aspects. We may remember a date as being "wonderful," for example, although the early part of the evening actually dragged a little. We may even have had some dates a few years ago that we actually cannot remember. This element of **selective retention and retrieval** is quite common in consumer behavior as well.

Television networks have to sell against loss of viewers who use remote controls to rapidly switch channels ("surf") during commercials. Notice how this cable network uses its higher levels of selective exposure.

ATTENTION!

The scientific treatment of **attention** is very similar to the way in which most of us normally think of this concept. That is, *attention refers to the momentary focusing of our information processing capacity on a particular stimulus.* It thus involves an allocation of processing capacity to one stimulus and, by implication, away from other possible stimuli to which we might have attended during that brief period of time.

Attention: The momentary focusing of our information processing capacity on a particular stimulus.

It is useful to distinguish three types of attention in consumer behavior:[13]

- Planned attention
- Spontaneous attention
- Involuntary attention

Planned attention is the strongest form of selective attention. It occurs when consumers use their attentional processes to help with their consumption activities. Much of "information search," for example, relies upon planned attention prior to purchase. However, planned attention is actually at work in even the most routine consumer activities: when we set out for the gas station, for example, we used planned attention to locate our car, find the ignition, turn at the right spots, identify the station, and so forth. Notice how important LTM is in this example—for many of us, the entire "picture" of the process already resides there (as we'll discuss later, this is termed a perceptual "script").

At the other extreme, **involuntary attention** occurs when an external stimulus literally forces its way into our consciousness. A loud "BANG!" a flashing light, or a tap on the shoulder are usually sufficient to capture the attention of most of us.

Between these extremes lies **spontaneous attention**, a combination of the other two types. Here we are not concentrating too narrowly and are ready to attend to new stimuli. On the other hand, no particular stimulus is forcing its way into our consciousness. Our attention, therefore, is "spontaneous" in that it simply arises at that point in time. This appears to be the most common case in consumer behavior, as our attention moves from object to object, sometimes sparked by our mental interests and sometimes by features of the stimuli.

STIMULUS CHARACTERISTICS THAT ATTRACT ATTENTION

Consumer attention is a powerful and important area. Before turning to marketing implications, let's consider a classic "snapshot" that indicates how powerful attentional processes are:

 *A Classic Olympic Moment…*

In preparation for the 1996 Olympic Games to be held in Atlanta, marketers engage in bidding wars for the right to be called an "official product" of the Olympic Games. During the 1980s, when the Olympics were held in Los Angeles, two sets of "official" rights were sold—one for the U.S. trials (held earlier to determine the U.S. team members) and one for the games themselves. In the film product category, the Japanese firm, Fuji, was named the official brand for the games, while the American firm, Kodak, was named the official brand for the trials. Upon arrival in Los Angeles, Fuji sent its blimp up for a test run over the Los Angeles Coliseum. However, it happened that at this time the U.S. trials were in progress. True to the exclusive marketing agreements signed with Kodak, U.S. officials were perturbed at this sight. What should they do to minimize this disruption? An amazing decision was reached—over the loudspeakers boomed the following announcement: "WE WOULD APPRECIATE IT IF YOU WOULD NOT LOOK AT THE BLIMP PASSING OVERHEAD." At this point, of course, everyone shifted his or her attention to the sky and watched the Fuji blimp being driven away by a helicopter (whether it was the official helicopter of the trials is unknown).[14] The point, for our purposes, is that the audience's attentional processes work *so quickly* that there was

The Fuji blimp soars over the Olympic Games. Despite their best intentions, officials were powerless to stop the audience's attentional processes from seeing the wrong brand's blimp at the trials!

no hope for this strategy to work, especially since it also attempted to have consumers ignore their natural motivations involving curiosity!

Within the typical world of marketing, managers work hard on efforts to attract the attention of consumers. There are two key dimensions that they can use to attract attention: *position* and *contrast*.

How "Position" Attracts Attention

Position works because there is a higher probability that a consumer's sensory system will encounter the stimulus. *Size,* for example, is one position characteristic that works this way. Larger ads and larger signs are likely to receive more attention, in part because a consumer is simply more likely to see them.

Placement in the stimulus field is another important position factor. In cultures that read from left to right, for example, consumers' eyes have been trained to proceed in a systematic manner across a page. This training carries over into our casual scanning as well. For example, our eyes are most likely to drift to the top left as we turn a magazine page. It is not surprising, therefore, that an ad placed on the upper half of a page tends to receive greater attention than does one on the lower half or that it is likely to receive greater attention on the left-hand side than on the right. "Readers are ignoring at least 50 percent of advertising in magazines," reports the president of a research firm. "Without a good position, the odds are that people will turn the page without even seeing your brand name."[15]

Similarly, consumers' eyes travel along certain paths in supermarkets and discount stores. Brands that sit along those paths are more likely to receive attention from the consumer: *"eye level is buy level"* is a marketing adage that reflects the importance of positioning to gain consumer attention. This is backed up by the findings of consumer research firms that use sophisticated cameras to track the movements of consumers'

Many sales are determined by in-store purchase decisions, so marketers must battle hard to gain attention on the shelf. "Eye level is buy level" is one marketing adage that reflects the importance of consumer attention.

eyes as they shop (special cameras are also used to learn the exact patterns used in reading ads to find which copy elements attract the most attention). Findings of one such store study showed that

- Brands on an upper shelf received 35 percent greater attention than did those on a lower shelf.
- Increasing the number of rows of a brand (called "facings") from two to four resulted in a 34 percent increase in attention from consumers.
- An ideal shelf position can result in a 76 percent increase in visibility.[16]

With these kinds of impacts, it is little wonder that competition is fierce for improved shelf positions in stores!

Retailers are also stressing attention principles in store layout decisions. One former marketing professor, for example, has built a very profitable business helping chains to redesign their stores. Among the strategies he recommends are

- Dropping long aisles in favor of short aisles and arranging them as a honeycomb. This way, shoppers are often encountering aisle ends or "windows" that are eyecatchers and attract increased attention.
- Installing more interior walls to organize products and attract attention to them.
- Eliminating fixtures and signs to emphasize the products themselves.

This perceptually based system seems to work. As a manager of a client store said, "We've had comments from customers who thought we had brought in new merchandise or improved our lines of merchandise. But we haven't." According to an executive of the chain, "If we judge success by the bottom line [profits], we'd have to give [the professor's firm] high marks."[17]

How "Contrast" Attracts Attention

Adaptation theory: Consumers become accustomed to constant levels of stimuli and pay less attention to them over time.

Contrast: A change in the environment: activates sensory receptors and stimulates attention.

One important insight into attention processes is called **adaptation theory.** This states that consumers tend to adapt to constant levels of stimuli and pay less attention to them over time. When we enter an air-conditioned store on a hot summer day, for example, we're very likely to pay attention to the temperature change. After a few minutes, however, our sensory system has adapted to the new temperature, and we are much less likely to notice it. This reflects the physical characteristic that our sensory receptors fire in response to change rather than to constant conditions. **Contrast,** then, because it represents a change to our sensory systems, will activate our sensory receptors and stimulate our attentional processes.

Intensity of the stimulus is one basic means of creating contrast and drawing attention. Stronger scents, louder noises, and brighter lights are all commonly used by marketers for this purpose. *Movement* is another device that creates a variability contrast for the sensory receptors and sparks them to send impulses. Moving signs and store displays, for example, are employed to help that stimulus stand out, while much of the greater success of television is due to its ability to portray movement to our eyes.

Color is another means of creating contrast in our sensory system, since the light waves are recognized as different by our sensory receptors (warm colors such as red have longer wavelengths, while cold colors such as blue have shorter wavelengths). Interestingly, there is also evidence that attending to different colors has physiological effects on our bodies. For example, blood pressure increases under red lights and decreases under blue, as does eye-blink frequency, and brain waves are slightly different depending on the color being sensed.

CONSUMER CHARACTERISTICS THAT DIRECT ATTENTION

Underpinnings of Attention

Of our three types of attention, both planned and spontaneous attention require inputs from a person. However, as we have seen in our discussion of sensory processes, much of perception is extremely rapid, and we are not entirely conscious of every step that is taking place. The concept of **automaticity** is helpful in our recognizing how attention operates when it is not at a conscious level: this refers to processes that are performed with minimal effort and without conscious control. As an example, let's consider a consumer who has been loyal to Tide for many years. Notice that this consumer would have repeated a specific visual detection task many times—sensing a Tide box and recognizing it. This particular task has now been practiced so often that it is "overlearned" and will continue to occur whether the consumer desires it to or not. When in the grocery store, then, this consumer will automatically detect the Tide box, even without conscious effort or control. (Note: The consumer may not be consciously aware that he or she has attended to the box, but will notice that it is very easy to recognize if he or she desires to do so!) When consumers' automatic attention processes are sparked by the Tide box, the Coca-Cola sign, or the Golden Arches, these marketers benefit strongly from this type of **preconscious attention.**[18]

The conscious level of attention is much easier to understand, as we are aware of it, and have a considerable degree of control over it. Our discussions of motivation in Chapter 5 covered the primary personal factors that direct attention. Our *needs* and *goals* cause us to be more sensitive to potential stimuli that might satisfy them. For example, we are more sensitive to food odors when we're hungry. Similarly, consider how many gasoline stations we begin to notice when we're on a trip and our gauge begins to drift toward the "empty" mark!

Novelty and *curiosity* can also cause us to direct our attention toward an interesting stimulus. Marketers have long used such words as "New!" "Improved," and "Free!" to play upon this factor in attracting attention from potential customers. Finally, our *moods* and emotions also influence our attentional processes. When we're tired, for example, we seem generally less alert to external stimuli; when we are rushed, the field of our attention seems to narrow; and so forth.

Maintaining Attention

Because our perceptual systems work at such incredible speeds, the issue of *maintaining attention* is equally as important as, or even more important than, attracting attention.

Automaticity: Attentional processes that are performed without conscious control and with minimal effort.

Preconscious attention: Another term for attentional processes that occur without conscious control.

Primary Goal	Possible Ad Strategy	Examples
I. Attract initial attention	■ Use prominent cues	■ Loud music ■ Pictures ■ Size ■ Color ■ Motion ■ Celebrity endorsers
	■ Use novel stimuli	■ Unusual photography ■ Large number of scenes ■ Changes in voice, silence, movement
II. Attract/maintain attention	■ Appeal to hedonic needs (feeling good)	■ Sexual themes ■ Appetite themes
	■ Enhance ad complexity	■ Complex pictures ■ Many edits and cuts
III. Maintain attention	■ Enhance relevance to self	■ Use similar spokespersons ■ Ask rhetorical questions ■ Employ "dramas" in ad
	■ Enhance curiosity about brand	■ Open with suspense or surprise ■ Use humor about brand ■ Withhold some information

FIGURE 8–3 Some Attention-Getting Tactics for Advertising

SOURCE: Adapted from a portion of the discussion in Deborah J. MacInnis, Christine Moorman, and Bernard Jaworski, "Enhancing and Measuring Consumers' Motivation, Opportunity, and Ability to Process Brand Information from Ads," *Journal of Marketing*, Vol. 55 (October 1991), pp. 32–53. Interested readers will want to consult this article for further discussion and citations.

The natural course of attentional processes is to move rapidly from stimulus to stimulus. To maintain our attention on a particular stimulus, then, we must usually concentrate on it and use some degree of will power to keep our attention from drifting elsewhere. Whether or not we will *choose* to concentrate depends primarily on our motivations, interests, and how well the stimulus seems to be satisfying them. This has important implications for marketers. In advertising, for example, the very stimuli that may be highly successful in *attracting* attention to an ad (such as sex or music) might then hinder *maintaining* attention to the brand and its message (since the viewer is now enjoying his or her further thoughts about the sexual or musical stimulus that attracted interest). For this reason many ads are "scripted" to assist the consumer in moving along with the message. There are many possible ways for marketers to work on attention-related issues. Figure 8-3 supplies some "tips" that advertisers might wish to consider.

THE PUZZLING CASE OF SUBLIMINAL PERCEPTION

During a six-week period in 1956, a New Jersey movie theater was reported to have flashed the subliminal messages "Hungry? Eat Popcorn" and "Drink Coca-Cola" during the popular movie *Picnic*. Over 45,000 people attended the theater during this period and apparently were influenced by the subliminal ads. Compared with previous sales records, the sales of popcorn increased 58 percent and sales of Coca-Cola increased 18 percent during this time. When this story hit the press, a popular uproar

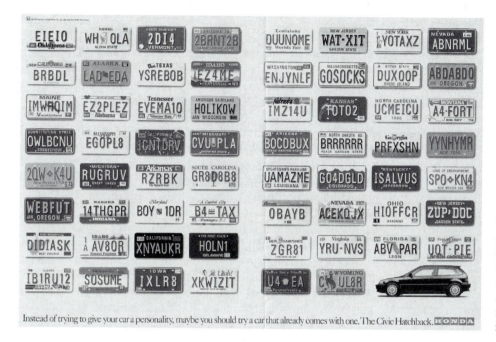

This ad captured attention initially with its size (two pages), color, and variety. It relies on the reader's **LTM** to maintain attention, however. (How many stump you and your friends?)

arose. Angry charges of "sinister plots," "breaking and entering people's minds," and the like were freely raised. But what exactly is subliminal perception? What was all this furor about?

The Concept of Subliminal Stimulation

Contrary to what some consumers believed, **subliminal perception** does not refer to an "invisible" stimulus. Strictly speaking, "subliminal" means "below the threshold" (*limen* is the technical term for a threshold). A subliminal stimulus, therefore, is one that cannot be discriminated by our conscious perceptual processes. To "stimulate" us, however, it must be capable of being sensed by our sensory system. The two major types of subliminal stimulation, therefore, are (1) visual stimuli presented so briefly that we cannot consciously detect them (this was the method reportedly used in the movie theater study) and (2) sound messages that are presented very rapidly and at such a low volume that we cannot detect them.

> **Subliminal perception:** The perception of a stimulus that is presented below the threshold of conscious awareness.

Is subliminal perception possible? The answer seems clearly to be "Yes." A number of well-controlled studies in psychology shows results that would have occurred only if the subjects had been perceiving the subliminal stimuli in the study.[19] After reading this chapter, this should not be surprising to us, since it is clear that our sensory system has strong powers and can work at extremely high speeds. The truly controversial issues in this area deal with the *effects* that subliminal stimulation might have.

Subliminal Advertising and Persuasion

The 1950s furor really concerned possible abuses of subliminal stimulation for *persuasive purposes*. Brainwashing was feared, in which consumers would be manipulated by forces that they could not consciously perceive or even know about. This raises the question, "How effective is subliminal stimulation in the area of persuasion?" Note that this question introduces a further step in the process—not only must the subliminal stimulus be perceived, but a consumer's behavior must also be affected.

The evidence on this question is mixed. Most studies indicate that such "hidden persuasion" is unlikely to occur. The original results claimed in the movie theater, for example, have been strongly criticized. There were no scientific controls in the theater test, and the results could have been due entirely to other factors, such as consumer reaction to the movie's scenes of eating and drinking, the summer weather, or the types of customers. It is notable that the theater results have not been repeated (replicated) in later studies (and there is some question as to whether the study was even actually performed).[20] Also, a more controlled study on TV ads in Indianapolis was conducted shortly thereafter and showed no evidence of even the slightest effects in persuading the mass audience.[21] Within marketing, some significant effects have been reported, but other studies have found no significant effects of subliminal ads. A recent complex study of subliminal self-help audiotapes came to a surprising conclusion: consumers *did improve* after using these tapes for one month, but it appears that the improvement was due to *expectations* rather than the tapes themselves, as the researchers had switched labels on the real tapes! (That is, consumers who thought they were listening to an "improve self-esteem" tape were actually listening to the "improve memory" tape: their scores on improving self-esteem improved substantially, but not their scores on improving memory. A similar lack of results occurred for the tapes labeled "improve memory," which were actually designed to be subliminal "self-esteem" tapes.) The researchers thus concluded that consumers' expectancies of improvement actually accounted for the improvements, similar to the "placebo" effect found in many medical studies.[22]

On balance, then, the evidence seems to suggest that subliminal advertising will not be very effective in persuading consumers to buy. Many leaders in the advertising community, moreover, view this as an unethical technique and would likely support legislation to ban it if it were found to be effective.

As to a scientific judgment of its effectiveness, however, the jury is still out. Given our analysis of the powers of the sensory system and the CIP system, we must maintain an open mind to the possibility that subliminal messages could be effective under some conditions. (For mass marketing, the issue is further clouded, however, by the fact people differ in the sensitivity of their sensory and CIP systems. That is, what is subliminal for one person may be consciously perceived by someone else: this means that making a stimulus subliminal for everyone would require it being weakened substantially.) The evidence to date within marketing settings does not suggest that the effects would be powerful, if they were to occur at all. We can at this point conclude, therefore, that persuasion is not likely.

Persuasion Without Awareness

Persuasion without awareness: Consumers' evaluations are influenced by a stimulus that was not consciously perceived.

As we just noted, a subliminal stimulus is one that we cannot consciously perceive. A much broader issue, however, concerns stimuli that we *can* consciously perceive if our attention is directed to them but that *will not be* consciously perceived by most or all consumers in their normal activities. When these stimuli affect our feelings and evaluations without our realizing why, a case of **persuasion without awareness** occurs. Although little formal work has been done on this topic, it would seem possibly to occur frequently in advertising (recall our brief discussion of automaticity and preconscious attention in the prior section). For example, various cues in the background of a picture might affect our feelings and evaluations, without our realizing that they are doing so.[23] As we've already seen, colors can have this effect as well.

This area is just beginning to be investigated in published research on consumer behavior, so there are still many unresolved questions in it. However, you may be interested in briefly reviewing some issues in this area:

🐌 Key's Erotic Implants

Although he termed his work *Subliminal Seduction,* persuasion without awareness is in fact the primary basis for the sensationalist writings of Wilson Bryan Key. Key (whose work has found its way into many high school and college courses studying other subjects than marketing and consumer behavior, where it does not receive a professional analysis) claims to have found numerous erotic stimuli and messages in ads. He further asserts that they've been deliberately placed there by malicious advertisers and that they have significant effects on consumers in the audience. A recent survey, moreover, revealed that over half of American consumers (60 percent) believe that this is being done by advertisers.[24] Many leaders in the advertising industry became irate at these charges, viewing them to be irresponsible and without foundation. On the other hand, it certainly is possible that a few isolated advertising people might have done this on a few occasions—this is an issue that's virtually impossible to determine with certainty.

Beyond his chilly reception by ad professionals, Key's arguments have not been met with much acceptance by consumer researchers either. Several recent marketing studies have attempted to test Key's contention that ads that "embed" sexual symbols do create a subconscious receptivity to the suggestions in the ad. These studies compared normal ads against the same ads in which sexually oriented **embeds** (sometimes called *implants*) had been added. Although consumers could recognize the embeds after they'd been pointed out to them, they did not report recognizing them when viewing the ads the first time. The question for these studies: "Did ads with the implants affect consumers differently than those without?"

One study analyzed verbal reactions to the ads and did find significantly more consumer comments that suggested that the erotic implants had had an effect on people's feelings. This study did not, however, contain any measures of effects on brand attitudes

Embeds: Symbols placed in advertising to influence evaluations subtly with low or no conscious awareness.

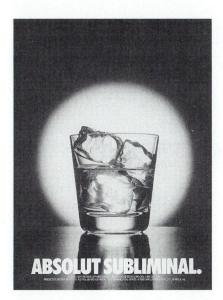

Some advertisers have seized on the subliminal seduction flap by spoofing it to gain attention to their ads.

PEOPLE HAVE BEEN TRYING TO FIND THE BREASTS IN THESE ICE CUBES SINCE 1957.

The advertising industry is sometimes charged with sneaking seductive little pictures into ads.

Supposedly, these pictures can get you to buy a product without your even seeing them.

Consider the photograph above. According to some people, there's a pair of female breasts hidden in the patterns of light refracted by the ice cubes.

Well, if you really searched you probably *could* see the breasts. For that matter, you could also see Millard Fillmore, a stuffed pork chop and a 1946 Dodge.

The point is that so-called "subliminal advertising" simply doesn't exist. Overactive imaginations, however, most certainly do.

So if anyone claims to see breasts in that drink up there, they aren't in the ice cubes.

They're in the eye of the beholder.

ADVERTISING
ANOTHER WORD FOR FREEDOM OF CHOICE.
American Association of Advertising Agencies

The advertising industry's leaders are angry about Wilson Bryan Key's charges of erotic implants in ads.

or purchase behavior and, therefore, gives no evidence on the issue of whether consumers were at all persuaded by the embeds.[25] The other studies did examine persuasion measures, but again the results are mixed. In general, their evidence suggested no systematic persuasion effect. However, some evidence did emerge to suggest that under certain conditions, some form of persuasion *might* occur. This tentative conclusion will be further examined in Chapter 10.[26]

SENSATION, ATTENTION, AND MARKETING ETHICS

The topics we've covered in this chapter deal with the first two stages of consumers' perceptual systems. They show tremendous speed and power in our sensory and conceptual systems, yet some of it is beyond our conscious control as consumers. We have also seen that marketers control some of the stimuli consumers encounter and are attempting to influence consumers with those stimuli. Not surprisingly, therefore, at times questions have arisen regarding the ethics of some marketing practices. We will not try to resolve these at this point, since further issues will arise in our next chapter. How do you feel about these examples? Which, if any, do you believe might be unethical?

- *Rigged demonstrations in advertising.* In most ads there are numerous details that never come to a consumer's conscious attention. Volvo's ad agency had to resign after the news came out that it had artificially braced the roof of the Volvo with lumber and steel and had weakened the roof support posts of competing cars in an ad depicting a "monster truck" crushing the other cars as it rode roughshod over all but the Volvo. The driver was quoted in the ad as saying, "I tried everything. The darn thing just wouldn't give." Volvo's dilemma: it hadn't approved these actions, and its cars really are made to be safe. Nonetheless, the Texas Attorney General forced Volvo to run "corrective" ads in 19 newspapers and to pay over $300,000 in legal costs.[27]

- *Artful photography to enhance appeal.* Some professional "food stylists" make over $100,000 per year for artfully preparing food to be used in advertising shots. "Our job is to make food so luscious and appealing you want to dive into the page and eat it!" explains one stylist. Some secrets: (1) never use milk in cereal—use Elmer's glue or Wildroot hair tonic; (2) angel food cake can be substituted for a souffle, which will never hold up under the lights; (3) mashed potatoes are a good substitute for ice cream; and (4) if a plate of chicken pot pie is to be featured, bake at least a dozen, then hunt through for the best peas, carrots, and chicken chunks (in the proper proportions) to create the featured pie.[28]

- *Downsizing as a means of raising prices.* Sometimes consumers *can* sense a fact, but marketers are confident that they *won't do so.* Our earlier discussion of downsizing in this chapter explained this practice, but didn't fully indicate how controversial it is. Although it is legal as long as weight or volume labels are accurate, state and local officials have recently begun investigations into downsizing as a possible deceptive practice: "It's a surreptitious way of raising price without having to actually put a new price tag on the product. I regard it as sneaky and misleading," steamed one official.[29]

- *Subtle packaging and product alterations to encourage faster use.* Many creative variations of downsizing are possible, again relying on consumers not noticing changes. For example, some marketers of condiments (such as catsup) have enlarged bottle openings so more product would flow out at one time: children might then use up a bottle more quickly, leading to more frequent household repurchase rates. Similarly, several paper companies have lengthened each sheet of paper towels by over an inch: while the total roll is the same length, fewer sheets are sold, again leading to more frequent repurchase rates.[30]

■ *Futuristic issues: manipulation by smell, color, and a "sixth sense."* Part of the power of odors and colors stems from the physiological ties of the sense organs and the emotional and glandular systems in the human body. For example, sight of the primary color red stimulates the pituitary gland to command the secretion of epinephrine (adrenaline), which causes the body to go into a state of arousal. (Thus it is no accident that red has long been used for lipstick or blush colors or that marketers have discovered that it works so well in the decor of a restaurant.) Similarly, researchers have just discovered that hundreds of genetic blueprints for odor receptors guide our sensory processes and that the nerves from these receptors reach back into the portions of the brain that deal with both memory and emotions. (This is why certain smells evoke such powerful memories and pleasant or unpleasant reactions from us.) In the future it should be possible to design "individualized" scents for people, based on their pattern of receptor characteristics.

Finally, a "sixth sense" has recently been discovered as well: found inside the nose is an organ that scientists had thought was inactive in humans, but just recently has been discovered to detect "pheromones," behaviorally controlling substances that stimulate sexual activity in animals. These receptors connect to a nerve system to the brain that parallels the olfactory system for smells, and stimulates "good feeling" responses. The scientist who discovered this has now formed two companies to develop and market consumer applications: Erox will market new perfumes, while Pherin will explore ways for dieters to control hunger with a nasal spray.[31]

Results such as these are indicative of the fascinating and subtle ways in which our perceptual systems can work. To this point we have focused only on the early stages of the perceptual process. In the next chapter we'll examine further interesting processes within perception, as we turn to how consumers *interpret* the stimuli in our marketing-consumer environment.

■ SUMMARY

DEFINING CONSUMER PERCEPTION

Perception is defined as "the process of sensing, selecting, and interpreting consumer stimuli in the external world." This chapter focused on the sensory and selectivity processes of consumer perception (the following chapter concentrates on interpretation).

CONSUMERS' SENSORY SYSTEMS

We first examined some instances to illustrate how an understanding of *sensation* can be useful to marketers. Each of the five senses—sight, sound, smell, taste, and touch—is used in marketing to communicate to consumers. We then discussed key terms and concepts. An *absolute threshold* defines the minimum amount of energy that can be detected. *Differential thresholds* refer to a person's ability to detect changes in stimuli: this concept has been generalized into *Weber's law,* which quantifies the notion of the JND, or *just noticeable difference.*

SELECTIVITY AND ATTENTION

Our discussion of selectivity began by pointing out that attracting attention and maintaining attention are different processes. Consumers must cope with the wide range of stimuli that are in the environment. Thus the *selectivity operators*—exposure, attention, interpretation, and retention/retrieval—are of crucial importance. The concept of *attention* refers to the momentary focusing of our information processing capacity on a particular stimulus. Attention may be planned, spontaneous, or involuntary. With respect to marketing applications, we saw how *stimulus factors* such as position and contrast can be used to attract attention, whereas *personal factors* such as motivation and interest have a stronger impact on maintaining attention. Tips for advertisers on gaining attention were also given.

We next briefly examined the controversial topic of *subliminal persuasion.* Available evidence here suggests that its effects would not be powerful, if they occur at all. Our discussion noted some subtle issues in this area, including *persuasion without awareness,* which may occur frequently in the consumer's world and is worthy of further investigation. In our final section of this chapter, we noted that questions of marketing ethics sometimes arise in the area of consumer perception, in part because of the nature of our sensory systems, and in part because marketers are attempting to influence consumers through the stimuli they present. Examples of possible ethical questions were then provided. The further aspects of perceptual processes are the subject of our next chapter.

■ KEY TERMS

perception	just noticeable difference (JND)	involuntary attention
stimulus characteristics	downsizing	spontaneous attention
consumer characteristics	parity products	position
data-driven view	selectivity operators	adaptation theory
theory-driven approach	selective exposure	contrast
five senses	selective attention	automaticity
sensory receptors	selective interpretation	preconscious attention
psychophysics	selective retention and retrieval	subliminal perception
threshold	attention	persuasion without awareness
absolute sensory threshold	planned attention	embeds
differential sensory threshold		

■ REVIEW QUESTIONS AND EXPERIENTIAL EXERCISES

[E = **Application extension or experiential exercise**]

1. Discuss the general topic of consumer perception:
   a. Define the process of consumer perception.
   b. Explain the two key factors in consumer perception.
   c. Describe how the sectors of the CIP system are involved.

   d. Indicate why an understanding of consumer perception is important for marketers. Is it important for consumers as well? Why or why not?

2. What is involved in consumers' sensory systems? Which human senses are relatively the strongest and the weakest? Briefly evaluate print versus radio versus television in terms of their impacts on consumers' sensory systems.

3. What is the subject matter of psychophysics? Compare and contrast the concepts of absolute and differential thresholds. Discuss what types of implications these concepts hold for marketers. Provide examples.

4. For each of the five senses, cite an actual marketing example of how to appeal to consumers using this sensory receptor.

5. Why make a distinction between attracting consumer attention and maintaining consumer attention? Which is likely to be more difficult for the marketer? Why?

6. The text describes three types of consumer attention. Define each of these, providing examples. In what ways is this distinction helpful to marketers?

7. Describe the four types of selectivity operators consumers use to help order their lives. Provide illustrations of each as they occur in consumer behavior.

8. [E] The text stated that a significant number of consumers shop without wearing their eyeglasses. In exactly what ways would this affect their shopping behaviors? In your opinion, have retailers and manufacturers adjusted for this factor adequately? Go to a supermarket and look for evidence regarding marketers' responses. Write a brief report on your findings.

9. [E] Conduct a "blind taste test" for various brands and types of soft drinks. Write a brief report summarizing your findings. What implications do they hold for the marketing mix of any particular brand you tested?

10. [E] Use the *Consumer Reports* article in Note 9 plus the *Business Periodicals Index* (or other reference source) to locate articles allowing you to trace the recent history of the Pepsi-Coke marketing war. What role did blind taste tests and other concepts from this chapter play? Write a brief report on your findings.

11. [E] Assume that you were given the power to rule on the following questions. How would you rule, and what would your explanation be?

a. Should subliminal messages be allowed in broadcast advertising? Should they be allowed on sound systems or point-of-purchase materials in stores?

b. Should "embeds" be allowed in advertisements? Should they be allowed on sound systems or point-of-purchase materials in stores?

12. [E] As a consultant for a marketer in each of the categories listed, suggest some ways in which each of the major topics in this chapter can improve the marketing mix.

a. A family restaurant

b. A new dentist

c. A candy bar manufacturer

d. A golf equipment and apparel firm

13. [E] The chapter noted some difficulties with the demonstration used in a recent Volvo campaign. Using the references in Note 27, read about how this happened and why people were upset. Write a brief report on your findings and your reaction.

14. [E] The chapter noted several examples of possible questions about marketing ethics. For each case, provide your opinion about whether you would personally engage in this behavior as a marketer. Create several convincing arguments supporting your stand for each case.

15. [E] The chapter noted that there are some potentially powerful future developments involving color, smell, and a new "sixth sense." Using the references in Note 31, or others available in your library, learn more about these possibilities. Write a brief report summarizing your findings.

16. [E] This chapter contained a number of interesting speculations about consumer behavior. Listing several of these (e.g., downsizing, blind taste tests, shelf-level attention), interview a supermarket or discount store manager. Ask about his or her experiences with consumers on these kinds of topics. Write a brief report on your findings.

■ SUGGESTED READING

■ A useful reference for applications of concepts from this chapter is Deborah J. MacInnis, Christine Moorman, and Bernard Jaworski, "Enhancing and Measuring Consumers' Motivation, Opportunity, and Ability to Process Brand Information from Ads," *Journal of Marketing*, Vol. 55 (October 1991), pp. 32–53. For pursuit of specific issues, consult the relevant Notes for some good leads.

CONSUMER PERCEPTION (II)
Interpreting Marketing Cues

NOTHING BUT THE BEST...

"Is it rich Co-REEN-thee-an leather?" Actor Ricardo Montalban asked this question for years in his commercials for Chrysler's luxury cars. Then he answers, "Of course. We wanted the best." But (1) What is Corinthian leather? (2) Is it from the ancient city in Greece? (3) Is it really the best?

Answers: (1) It's a name dreamed up by the marketers at Chrysler to suggest both elegance and the Mediterranean image of its Cordoba model. (2) The leather comes from various U.S. suppliers, including one in Newark, New Jersey. (3) It's good, but since it gets heavy wear on car seats, it can't be the highest grade of leather. "It's just a name, really," reported Mr. Montalban when asked. "That's all."[1] For millions of consumers, though, that isn't all. In this chapter we'll step further into the world of consumer perception, now to concentrate on how consumers interpret cues from marketers.

Up to this point in our analysis of consumer perception, we have stressed the sensation and attention stages of the perceptual process and have placed emphasis on external stimuli in the consumer's world. In this chapter we move further into the perceptual process and further into the consumer's mind. We will encounter many marketing applications of this material in such areas as advertising, packaging, pricing, and store design.

■ THREE ACTIVITIES IN CONSUMER INTERPRETATION

When we "perceive" something, we make efforts to "interpret" it. Interpretation refers to the *meaning* that a consumer will attach to a particular stimulus. Three basic processes—organization, categorization, and inference making—are involved. To appreciate the nature of these processes, let's begin at the sensory stage. Although some of us (the author included!) are always surprised when reminded of the fact, it is the case that *people don't sense the real world directly*. Instead, we sense the real world through molecular intermediaries such as light waves, sound waves, scents, and so on.

The first stage in interpreting external stimuli, therefore, is to determine which of the huge numbers of molecules in our environment actually *belong together*. This activity is termed **perceptual organization**.

Once a stimulus has been sensed, the problem becomes one of identifying it, so that we "know" what it is. This activity is termed **perceptual categorization.** After a stimulus has been categorized, however, we are able to think more about it. This process involves **perceptual inference.** In the sections that follow, we examine each process in greater detail, indicating implications for marketers, consumers, and public policymakers.

■ ACTIVITY ONE: ORGANIZATION

THE GESTALT SCHOOL

Perceptual organization: The first stage in interpreting stimuli: determines which molecules belong together.

The basic principles of perceptual organization have been developed by scientists of the **Gestalt school** of psychology, which began about 75 years ago in Germany.[2] The primary principle is that of *organized wholes*—the belief that people perceive entire objects rather than just the separate parts of them (the German term *Gestalt* is roughly translated to mean "whole" or "pattern"). This suggests that the whole has an identity beyond the sum of its parts. When a consumer drives into a shopping center parking lot, for example, Gestalt theory suggests that he or she is much more likely to perceive stores rather than just glass windows, bricks, and a sign—the total arrangement is more important than the parts individually.

Gestalt psychologists also believe that people strive to have **good Gestalts.** That is, people desire to have perceptions that are simple, complete, and meaningful. Most of these processes are not carried out consciously, but they have a strong impact on our perceptions. Based on this desire for a good Gestalt, most of us will perceive our worlds as being consistent with the following principles (illustrated in Exhibit 9-1 and in Figures 9-1 and 9-2):

1. *Figure and ground.* Perception tends to feature one object at a time and to view the remaining stimuli as background, which is less important and which is not

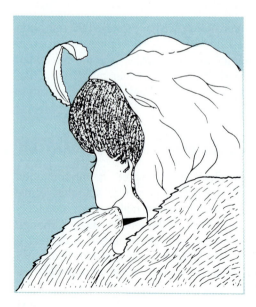

FIGURE 9-1 An Interesting Woman

Gestalt Principles of Organization

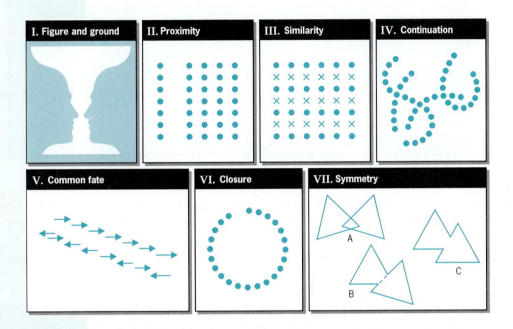

Focused upon. Perception can be rapidly reorganized, however, so that the part of the ground becomes the new figure, while the old figure moves into the ground. In Exhibit 9-1, for example, notice how difficult it is to see both the vase and the people at the same time. Instead, when you see the vase, it is the "figure" and the faces are the "ground": when your perception is reorganized to focus on the faces as "figure," the vase moves to become the "ground." Now shift your attention to Figure 9-1, how old would you say the woman is? What if you were told you're way off, what would your next guess be? (This is a more challenging puzzle, since the two women have some overlap in the picture. Again, however, it is virtually impossible to see both of them at exactly the same time.)

2. *Proximity.* Elements that are close together in space or time are seen as belonging together, to form a unit. In Exhibit 9-1's example of proximity effects, notice how natural it is to perceive rows going down, as opposed to across the figure.

3. *Similarity.* Elements that are similar in appearance seem to form a unit. For example, notice how the substitution of "x" for "o" in some positions of the exhibit's illustration now leads us to see rows across the figure.

4. *Continuation.* Elements that together form a line or a curve seem to form a unit. If we look carefully at the illustration, we will notice that these are simply blots of ink on the page. However, we're likely to find our eyes "crossing" lines as we follow the curves. This will lead us to see four separate figures as opposed to 44 independent dots.

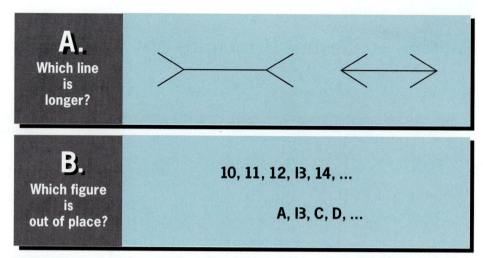

FIGURE 9-2 Two Instances of Perceptual Context Effects

5. *Common fate.* Moving elements traveling in the same direction seem to form a unit. Notice how much easier it is for us to follow the top figure than it is to follow the bottom arrows.

6. *Closure.* Perception favors a complete or closed figure. For example, as shown in the exhibit, a 320-degree arc is perceived by most people to be a circle even though it's not complete.

7. *Symmetry.* Perception favors a symmetrical form over an irregular one. In Exhibit 9-1, drawing A will lead many of us to see separate triangles rather than the overall form. In drawing B, we may focus more on the top triangle than the irregular four-sided shape. In drawing C, however, we'll tend to see the more regular overall outline and may even "shape it" to the more symmetrical form of an arrow.

Notice how helpful these basic principles are in considering how to design aspects of a package, product, or advertisement so as to be pleasing to consumers' eyes, to attract their attention, or to guide their attention toward specific cues.

The Importance of Context and Constancy

This set of principles leads to two further insights into consumer perception: the notions of perceptual context and perceptual constancy. The following sections briefly introduce each of these important concepts.

🐌 *Do Our Eyes Play Tricks?*

Perceptual context:
The principle that various stimuli will affect our perceptions, even if we are not conscious of this happening.

The concept of **perceptual context** states that, because we are concerned with perceiving a "well-organized" whole, various stimuli will affect our perceptions, even if we are not conscious of this happening. Figure 9-2 contains some simple illustrations of how context affects even our simplest perceptions. In panel A, for example, which line is longer? Most of us will miss this question unless we've been warned to expect a trick. To check, try taking the edge of a sheet of paper, mark the length of one line

This ad, which is run only during the holiday season, cleverly plays on consumers' tendencies to have a "good gestalt"—one that is complete and meaningful. Here the consumer must use the principle of closure (by using the initials of the brand's name) to form the meaningful words and holiday phrase.

on it, and then compare it to the other. You'll easily see how objective reality can differ from subjective reality: in this case the flow of the arrows (as we took them into account) actually intruded on our perception of the horizontal lines themselves.

Panel B of Figure 9-2 extends the topic of context effects into the area of "meaning." Notice that most of us would say that "13" and "B" both belong where they've been placed. Notice, however, that to make that form into a number we had to subtly interpret distance between the line and the curves. Then, to fit the alphabetic context, we had to subtly ignore the small gaps and employ closure for this context.

Notice how the use of context helps us to interpret these figures and perceive the advertising message. Upon closer inspection, notice how the other Gestalt principles, such as figure and ground, operate within this ad. Finally, give your back a pat!

𐑟 *How Much Does the World Change?*

Perceptual constancy is also a very powerful concept. This concept points out how strongly our past experience influences our perceptions of the present. Perceptual constancy refers to the fact that we strive to perceive our world as a relatively unchanging environment, even though our sensory receptors are providing us with changing sensory impressions. Looking at panel A of Figure 9-2 again, for example, many students have confidently predicted that both lines were the *same length,* since they had seen this example in an earlier course. Notice, however, that their reliance on long-term memory (LTM), reflecting perceptual constancy, overruled their dealing with this new problem: when encouraged to take the measurements, they "got the point"!

Let's also consider a simple marketing example. If we know the approximate height and width of a box of Tide, we'll tend to "perceive" that size even as we walk toward the shelf from the other end of the aisle (at the sensory level, however, the box is much larger at 2 feet away than at 30 feet). Similarly, we'll continue to perceive the box as rectangular, even though its retinal image from all but a 90-degree angle is in fact trapezoidal. Finally, we'll see the same orange, yellow, and blue colors on the box, even if they are physiologically closer to brown under poor lighting conditions. Perceptual constancy works on all other products as well. Imagine what it does to our perceptions of the taste of Coke or Pepsi, or the words of a salesperson!

Perceptual constancy: The concept that we strive to perceive our world as a relatively unchanging environment.

The Concept of Perceptual Set

In a related area of work, Gestalt scientists investigated "problem solving," a vast area of study that has significant implications for consumers and marketers. The following story illustrates their approach:[3]

𐑟 *Monkey See, Monkey Do?*

One of the most influential of the Gestaltists, Wolfgang Kohler, conducted studies of perception while trapped on the Canary Islands by a British blockade during World War I. A typical study would confront an ape named Sultan with a problem, such as how to obtain a basket of fruit hanging from the top of the cage. Various tools would be available, but only one would allow him to be successful. Observation of Sultan's actions clearly showed that *his perception of the situation was a key to his solving the problem or not.* If he were trying unsuccessful methods, he would have to *reorganize his perceived situation*—to shift his figure-ground relations—to see the answer. In one study, after collapsing against the walls of the cage to rest from his energetic failures trying to bash the fruit down with various sticks, Sultan happened to glance at a box on the floor. After a short pause (during which the box moved from background to figure in his perceptions), he jumped up, moved the box under the fruit, and easily reached his goal.

Across the series of studies Kohler discovered that perceptual constancy was a powerful force, leading to the apes finding it difficult to change their perceptions of a problem situation. Thus "fixed" perceptions hindered problem solving. This led to the concept of **perceptual set,** which is defined as *a readiness to perceive or act in particular ways in a situation.* After Sultan had learned about the boxes, for example, he was able to use this "set" the next time he confronted a problem to structure his figure-ground relations, find the boxes rapidly, and solve the problem quickly. When the

Perceptual set: The readiness to perceive or act in particular ways in a situation.

problem required a different solution from piling the boxes, however, his "set" interfered with a solution, and Sultan had a hard time shifting away from it. As humans, we experience similar problems in our attempts to arrive at good consumer decisions.

APPLICATIONS OF GESTALT PRINCIPLES IN MARKETING

The Gestalt principles of perceptual organization have many implications for marketing practice. Marketers have long been aware of these principles and have used them in many areas of the marketing mix. Consider these examples:

୧ଌ *Physical Design*

Looking back at Exhibit 9-1, notice how a sweater designer could use such principles as proximity (here to make a person appear taller), similarity (here to make a person appear wider or stronger), or continuation (to create an interesting, flowing design). Many products are designed with a view toward the perception of their forms. The chrome and painting of autos and boats, for example, use such principles as common fate and symmetry to provide perceptions of speed and movement. Also, store signs are often created using principles of common fate, continuation, and closure to direct the consumer's eyes to the displays and the product.

୧ଌ *Problems with Perceptual Sets—Off to a Fresh Start!*

The concept of perceptual set relates to consumers' expectations about where to shop, what to buy, and how to use products. This may have special implications for innovations, when their use may deviate from existing sets consumers hold. We are currently experiencing an interesting market test of this issue in the case of "superconcentrated" detergents, which have been introduced on a large scale in the 1990s. There are many advantages of this product: (1) it uses *less packaging,* thus appealing to environmental concerns; (2) it uses less *chemical filler,* so is cheaper for producers to make; and (3) retailers love the smaller boxes, since they free up *valuable shelf space* to stock other products that carry higher profit margins. In summary, the new products are equally effective and offer other important advantages.

However, soap marketers were extremely concerned that the new concentrates might not be well received by consumers, due to three likely perceptual sets: (1) "That small box doesn't give me as much detergent for my money" (this would limit pricing flexibility for marketers, thus killing the success of these products); (2) "If I use less, it can't possibly clean as well" (this perceptual set would inhibit consumer trial); (3) "I know how much detergent to use . . . I've been doing it for years!" (some consumers might use just as much as before and then become unhappy with either the performance or the number of washloads per box).

Marketers realize that consumers' existing perceptual sets are powerful: in the detergent category, Colgate's superconcentrated *Fresh Start* detergent had been introduced in 1980, yet struggled into the 1990s with less than a 2 percent market share, as most consumers stayed away from using it. To overcome these potential problems with their new entries, the giant soap companies have used heavy advertising, delivered many free product samples, relied on large price discounts and coupons, and included plastic measuring scoops inside the boxes to help with proper usage. Even with these

The recent launch of many "superconcentrated" detergents represents an over $100 million bet by marketers that they can overcome negative perceptual sets held by American consumers.

programs, marketers have been fearful of the power of perceptual sets and have made interesting command decisions to go slow on *how* concentrated the products would be: for example, Super-Concentrated Cheer was designed for a consumer to use half a cup per wash, while technology could have allowed a quarter-cup size.[4]

■ ACTIVITY TWO: CATEGORIZATION

As the sensory stimuli are being perceptually "organized" (activity one), they are also becoming available for our second interpretive activity, **perceptual categorization.** This is the process we go through to translate sensory inputs into a mental "identification" of a particular stimulus, such as a product (car), a brand (Tylenol), and so on. This process works extremely rapidly, and usually not at a conscious level (recall our discussion of automaticity in the previous chapter). When we've encountered the external stimulus previously and have a strong category for it in long-term memory (LTM), the process is similar to "recognizing" the stimulus pattern and calling forth the right node from LTM. When we've not encountered this particular external stimulus before, however, the categorization process must rely on using cues from the stimulus to "figure out" which identity seems right for it.

Categorization: The second stage in interpreting stimuli: translating sensory inputs into an idenfitication of a stimulus.

CATEGORIZATION'S IMPORTANCE IN CONSUMER BEHAVIOR

This process is extremely important in consumer behavior. Our categorization of a stimulus affects how interested we'll be in it, what we'll expect from it, whether we'll evaluate it positively or negatively, and so forth.

In most cases, a consumer's categorization of a new brand is a private event that goes unnoticed by the rest of the world. Occasionally, however, enough consumers miscategorize a brand to reveal an underlying problem. The following cases demonstrate such instances: when consumers are (1) *unable* to categorize a new offering,

Notice that, because of their plain labels, the ability to read English is required to correctly categorize these generic products.

(2) *unwilling* to change their categorization of a brand offering, and (3) *misled* into miscategorizing the new offer, with negative outcomes as a result.

(1) Unable to Categorize: What You See Is What You Get!

"Generic" food products originated in France in the 1970s and became a phenomenal success in the United States, until dropping in popularity in recent years. Retailers find them to be quite profitable because their costs are lower. Consumers who buy them pay 30 to 40 percent less than for major advertised brands and about 20 percent less than for a supermarket's private labels. Consumer studies showed, however, that the group *most* expected to buy generics—those on low incomes for whom the savings are most substantial—tended not to be purchasing these items. Further investigation revealed one major reason: a significant proportion of low-income persons are "functionally illiterate" and cannot read well enough to perform everyday shopping tasks. Because generic products were wrapped in plain labels, these persons *could not categorize* the product in the can or box. Since they didn't know whether the generic can would contain peas or beets, these shoppers stayed with higher-priced brands having pictures on the contents of the package.[5]

(2) Unwilling to Categorize: "Gerber Is for..."

Gerber Products, which claims about 70 percent of the baby food market, was interested in expanding its base into the teenage consumer group as well. "We know there are closet users out there in the 15–22 age bracket," said one Gerber executive. The firm launched a major promotional campaign to teens with the theme: "The secret's out. Gerber isn't just for babies!" Teen consumers, however, thought otherwise and just wouldn't swallow it. Evidently, the name "Gerber" was a strong cue to the LTM category "baby food." Millions of teens would not change this perceptual categorization and purchase a product perceived to be in this category. Gerber has now given up on teens: Gerber's mid-1990s strategy is to go global (where 95 percent of babies are), with a product line of baby foods, kids' clothing, and baby care items.[6]

🐃 (3) Misled into Miscategorizing: Sunlight's Not Right!

In launching its new Sunlight brand of dishwashing liquid, Lever Bros. designed a major product sampling campaign in large metropolitan areas. Sample plastic bottles were delivered by mail. The brand was attractively packaged in a bright yellow bottle, with a picture of a sun and lemon prominent on the label (highlighting its new feature of lemon juice as an ingredient). When sampling began in Baltimore, however, a totally unexpected development occurred—local medical facilities and the Poison Control Center reported receiving many frantic phone calls from frightened consumers who had drunk the contents of the bottle before realizing that they had miscategorized it as a new lemon drink! Just as this news made its way into the national press, a similar outbreak was reported in Tampa Bay, the second area to receive the mail samples. No deaths or serious injuries were reported, but the phenomenon was widespread. When pressed for a reaction, a company person defended the package, pointing out that it clearly stated that this was a dishwashing liquid. He also indicated that the company did not make a practice of marketing brands through the poison control centers![7]

The Role of "Schemas"

As the generic food and Sunlight examples show, consumers use cues from the stimulus as a basis for categorizing. However, LTM is also important, and categorization is actually a *very rapid* two-way process, depending both on the features of the external stimulus and on the consumer's available categories in LTM. Thus, as the Gerber example demonstrates, categorizations are themselves strongly influenced by the prior expectations that a consumer brings from LTM.

Prior expectations can combine into a **schema** that acts to guide the overall perceptual process. There are many theories about schemas, but in general, we can define a schema as *a cognitive structure that represents a person's knowledge about a given object or behavior.*[8] One good way to think of a schema is to recall our network diagram of LTM that we examined in Chapter 7 (Figure 7-4). A schema would consist of those particular beliefs (nodes) that are most likely to be brought into short-term memory (STM) when a consumer begins to think about a topic. When a schema is strong—as when we know a lot about a topic, or have engaged in a particular act many times before—it can take over to guide our perceptual processes and physical activities.

One form of special schema is a **script,** or an organized sequence of behavioral events, much like a movie script or cartoon series. Figure 9-3 summarizes some familiar steps in this type of script. To see just how powerful these are, close your eyes and imagine going to your favorite supermarket to buy milk or fruit. Notice how you can visualize so easily, and how the process is so strongly structured! This indicates the potential power that LTM has to guide our categorization processes. Of course, not all categorization occurs from LTM: the stimuli being categorized ought to play a strong role as well! Let's look briefly at what this means for marketers.

Schema: A cognitive structure that represents a person's knowledge about a given object or behavior.

Script: A form of schema: an organized sequence of behavioral events.

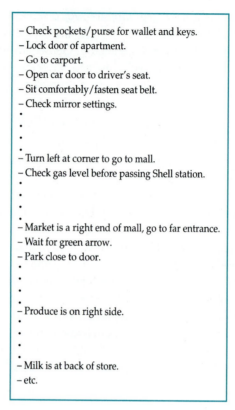

– Check pockets/purse for wallet and keys.
– Lock door of apartment.
– Go to carport.
– Open car door to driver's seat.
– Sit comfortably/fasten seat belt.
– Check mirror settings.
•
•
•
– Turn left at corner to go to mall.
– Check gas level before passing Shell station.
•
•
•
– Market is a right end of mall, go to far entrance.
– Wait for green arrow.
– Park close to door.
•
•
•
– Produce is on right side.
•
•
•
– Milk is at back of store.
– etc.

FIGURE 9-3 A Script Type Schema for Going to the Store

Implications for Marketers

Marketers are able to *influence* consumer behavior by influencing how consumers categorize brands and stores. This process can be interesting and subtle, however. Let's take a brief look at some of the possibilities:

🐟 *What Shall I Sell? Food for Thought...*

Marketers are interested in categorization to ensure that target consumers will view their products in the desired ways and will act accordingly. For example, let's assume that we have developed a new food product to be aimed at the "kids' after-school snack" market. Our initial consumer research has indicated that kids want sweet taste, while some mothers want healthy products. We are in the midst of a meeting discussing how to position our product so as to have it categorized in the most positive light. Our discussion has covered the following marketing implications so far:

■ Consumers are likely to seize upon cues immediately, in an effort to "place" products and stores in their minds. Thus, if we advertise our product as "sugar sweet, and crunchy too!" we can expect to have it categorized as a "junk food," competing against candy bars or cookies. If we advertise it as "packed with vitamins, and crunchy too!" it may be seen more as a fruit-based substitute for apples or carrots. We can strongly affect which competitive arena we will be in by how we lead consumers to initially categorize. *Thus marketers need to choose their cues with care.*

Last night, I performed for the Metropolitan Ballet.

W.E. ANDREWS CO.

"I was just about to lift my prima ballerina up in triumph when I noticed she didn't look so good.
The varnish I used wasn't trapping to the photo like it should. It was passable. But it wasn't perfect. And nothing leaves my press until it's absolutely perfect."

I knew what I had to do. And I did it. Lucky for my ballerina I'm quick on my feet."
If you want it perfect, you want W.E. Andrews. We can handle any sheet fed, half web or full web job. 140 South Road, Bedford, MA 01730, (617) 275-0720/ 1-800-343-4061. In Connecticut, 206 Murphy Road, Hartford, CT 06114, (203) 527-5570
W. E. Andrews Co., Inc.

This ad deliberately (and cleverly) creates a categorization mismatch between the headline and the photo. This will then lead many readers to look below (maintaining attention to the ad) to clarify the situation.

- The categorization process is extremely rapid, and "perceptual sets" can take over quickly. For example, once our new product is categorized as "sugar sweet," it is more difficult for consumers to also see it as "packed with vitamins." *Thus marketers need to choose the order and presentation of their cues with care.*

- For new products that are close to existing products, marketers can use an **exemplar strategy.** This can involve associating our product with an already well-known, well-liked example: if our product were a cereal, for instance, we might advertise it with "If you like Honey-Nut Cheerios, you'll love...". Notice how the exemplar approach helps consumers to quickly and easily categorize our offering.

Exemplar strategy:
A marketing approach to help consumers categorize a new product by associating it with one already well known.

Feature-based strategy: A marketing approach to help consumers categorize a new product by stressing its special attributes.

- Marketers can also use a **feature-based strategy** to help consumers categorize. This strategy is quite popular, since it allows marketers to stress their product's special appeals (features). However, for categorization, a feature-based strategy is *especially useful for a new product* that doesn't quite fit into an existing category (since consumers are expected to have some difficulty in categorizing the new entry). For example, if our product is outside existing categories, we might try advertising, "For a new treat, try . . . ! It is sweet, healthy, and crunchy too!" (Notice that the features are helpful, but, because it is entirely new, it is still somewhat difficult for us to "imagine" this product: this indicates that the right category simply isn't yet available in LTM, and still must be created after we try the product.)

- Consumer categorization provides the basis for competition in the marketplace. *It will determine in which kinds of "evoked sets" our product will appear* as a candidate for purchase (for example, we might want to rethink possible use situations for our new product: Do we want consumers to consider it in their evoked sets for a snack, or a dessert, or a breakfast item, and so forth?).

- As noted earlier, consumers' categorizations are quick and private: whether they are right or wrong, favorable or unfavorable, no one will know unless we make special efforts to find out. Thus *marketers will highly benefit from conducting consumer research on this topic,* including research to learn how consumers categorize and how advertising appeals work for new products.

Perceptual categorization has received a great deal of attention from psychologists.[9] In recent years consumer researchers have also begun to focus on categorization. (If you would like to read more about this complex but interesting topic, you may wish to begin with the readings in Note 10.) However, the categorization process is not only important in itself, but also because it sets the stage for consumers to have *further* thoughts about a stimulus. This is the topic of our concluding section of the chapter, dealing with consumers' *perceptual inferences*.

■ ACTIVITY THREE: PERCEPTUAL INFERENCES
THE CONCEPT OF PERCEPTUAL INFERENCE

Once a stimulus has been categorized, the issue turns to how much—if any—further attention we'll give to that stimulus. Most objects we perceive in our environment will not receive much further attention from us, and the perceptual episodes for these uninvolving objects simply end. For example, think of all the occasions we are driving along, sense a new object, categorize it as a car, and then turn our attention back to the highway.

Inference: A belief we develop based on other information. The third stage in interpreting stimuli: a tentative conclusion about an object.

When we're *interested* in an object, however, we're very likely to go on to make further interpretations about it. These interpretations are termed **inferences.** An inference is defined as *a belief that we develop based on other information* (e.g., if a person's name is Sue, we infer that the person is likely to be a girl; if a product has a high price, we infer that it is likely to be higher quality). Not all inferences will be correct, though we'd like them to be. In a strict sense, all our thought processes require inferences. Here, however, we'll focus on perceptual inferences that stem directly from stimulus cues. Again, the incredible speed of our consumer information processing (CIP) system means that many of these inferences will be made at an unconscious level—we can view these as "subtle" inferences, since consumers may not be aware that they've made them. Other perceptual inferences will be at the conscious level, however, and we will know we're making them (we'll term these "conscious inferences").

🐚 *Illustrating the Concept of Perceptual Inference*

Returning to our car example, let's assume that we've taken an interest in a car that's on display as we drive by and decide to pay further attention to it. In this case we're almost certain to begin to make inferences about it. Conscious inferences might include whether it's a new or old model, expensive or not, and a domestic or foreign make. More subtle inferences might include estimates of whether it is prestigious or not, or stylish or not. These inferences might then contribute to a further conscious inference that it is "my kind of car" or not. Perceptual inferences thus play a major role in directing consumer behavior. Because they stem from consumers' processing of cues from the stimulus, inferences can be encouraged or discouraged by marketing mix decisions.

SENSORY CUES AND CONSUMER INFERENCES

In an earlier discussion of sensory cues, we stressed their role in triggering sensory receptors, thus starting the perceptual process. However, sensory cues can also lead to consumer inferences about what characteristics products are likely to have. The following cases illustrate some of the many ways in which sensory cues work on inferences.

🐚 *Sight: A Cheery Blue*

Many years ago, Procter & Gamble introduced Cheer as a new product that was "good for tough-job washing." Consumers apparently perceived it to be just another detergent, however, and it was not particularly successful. Then P & G changed its color, made it into a blue powder, and continued its promotion as a "tough" detergent. This color change altered consumer perceptions of the brand. Apparently, the blue color allowed inferences that this detergent was capable of powerful cleaning. Cheer became a major national success.[11]

🐚 *Sounds Abound*

Consumers often use sound as a cue to make inferences about the quality of particular products. In motorcycles and lawn mowers, for example, a loud engine may be believed to be more powerful than a quiet one. Marketers who try to sell well-muffled models that purr may find their brands spurned by most of the market. On the other hand, for other purposes quiet is perceived as indicating better quality. For example, a quiet car inside is perceived to be better built and more luxurious than a noisier one. Consumer inferences about sound are taken into account within marketing programs. For example, many salespersons in stereo stores set controls heavy on bass, as they believe that consumers infer this to be a higher-quality sound.

🐚 *Touch: Which Tastes Better?*

Many consumers use touch to allow inferences about the freshness of foods, including fruits and bakery products. For packaged goods, however, the wrapping can also contribute to the perception of freshness. For example, in one study, identical potato chips—all very fresh—were placed in two types of bags, an easy-to-open wax-coated paper bag and a hard-to-open polyvinyl bag. Supermarket shoppers were asked to take a bag, open it, and taste the product. Most consumers had real difficulty opening the polyvinyl bags—reactions included biting the bags, yanking them apart and spilling the contents on the floor, and giving up in despair. Even though the contents of the bags had identical tastes (this was established in a separate taste study), shoppers overwhelmingly reported that they preferred the chips in the polyvinyl packages. These chips were perceived as being both "crispier" and "tastier." When asked about which package they preferred, 93 percent of the shoppers indicated the polyvinyl bag, despite the difficulty in opening it.

An interesting question emerges from this study: Did consumers perceive a taste difference because (1) they inferred that a difficult-to-open package contains better contents, or (2) they inferred that it protects its contents better, or (3) they knew that polyvinyl bags offer longer shelf life to products and inferred that these bags had been on the shelf a long enough time for their contents to have been affected? In any of these cases, of course, an inference to the current taste and crispiness still had to be made and consumers showed themselves quite willing to make this perceptual inference.[12]

❧ Smell: The Nose Knows Hose

A classic study of how sensory cues can affect inferences of product quality was conducted over 50 years ago by a professor and students at Colgate University. In the study 250 women in the local community were asked which of four pairs of hosiery was highest in quality and why they thought so. In reality, the hosiery was from the same manufacturer and was selected to be as identical as possible. The only difference was that a faint scent had been added to three of the four pairs—the intensity of this scent was controlled to be at the same level as the normal scent of the fourth pair, which arose from the manufacturing process. Of the three scents, one was a fruity type, one a sachet, and one a narcissus. In making their judgments, only 6 of the 250 housewives mentioned noticing the scent differences. After making their choice as to the highest quality, they explained that their choices were based on such product attributes as texture, weave, durability, shine, and weight.

But which hose did the women choose? Given the form of this study, if scent did not have an effect, we would expect that each pair should randomly receive 25 percent of the choices. In reality, however, the "natural" hose received only 8 percent of the choices, while the narcissus hose was favored in 50 percent of them. Thus it is clear that the sensory cues did affect quality inferences made by these consumers, even though the consumers were not aware of the correct reason for their judgments. (As a student of consumer behavior, you may find this postscript to the study of interest: the study was originally planned for a larger sample, but it had to be suspended when a housewife became suspicious that the interviewer was not trying to sell his product and suspected a potential robbery. She called the police, and their investigative report was featured in the Utica, New York, newspaper. The report explained the nature of the study and the use of the scents.)[13]

■ MARKETING IMPLICATIONS OF CONSUMERS' PERCEPTUAL INFERENCES

Our discussions to this point make it clear that consumers are engaging in inferential processes on a very regular basis. This means that marketers have opportunities to influence sales by learning about these inferences and designing programs for them. Within this section we'll briefly examine implications for each area of the marketing mix.

PRODUCT DECISIONS AND CONSUMER INFERENCES

Because products and packages are complex, tangible stimuli (that is, they can be sensed with our sensory systems), virtually all decisions on a product's physical characteristics can affect consumers' perceptual inferences. We've already noted examples in which a product's color, scent, noise, and feel have impacted. Here we'll examine how other aspects can be employed.

✑ *Names Can Be Seductive*

In general, a **brand name** offers an opportunity to gain ground in consumers' minds by suggesting special qualities or characteristics of the product or its owner. Consider, for example, what inferences are sparked in your mind by such names as "Senchal" perfume, "Craftsman" tools, "Ultra-Brite" toothpaste, "Sunkist" fruits, and "Whirlpool" washers. As one marketer explained, "Naming is a form of seduction." One paint firm believes this. Its color "Ivory" was in twentieth place in sales when the name was changed to "Oriental Silk"—two years later it had risen to sixth place in sales.[14]

✑ *Ayds, X-LAX, and Fried Food*

Brand names can also cause problems, however, when consumers draw negative inferences from them. For example, consider the plight of Ayds dietetic candy, which found its sales sinking as the AIDS health epidemic continued to spread. The firm didn't want to lose the long-term benefits from its successful brand name, but knew that consumers' inferences were hurting sales. The solution: try a compromise name—"Diet Ayds,"—to see if that would be enough different (meanwhile the name "Aydslim" began testing in a foreign market).

At least consumers weren't laughing at Ayds as they were in the Georgia test market of LAX beer from Anheuser-Busch. "The company should have known consumers would put an "X" in front of the name!" snickered one stock market analyst.[15]

A slightly different problem faced the Toro Corporation when it proudly introduced its new lightweight but efficient snow thrower. To highlight its lightweight feature, Toro named it the Snow Pup. When sales were far below expectations, consumer research was undertaken to discover why. The research indicated that the name Snow Pup had to go—consumers were inferring that the product lacked power and was not durable. When the name was changed to Snowmaster, sales increased significantly.[16]

Finally, several fast-food firms have become quite concerned about their names in light of the recent trends toward "healthy eating." It is no mistake that Kentucky Fried Chicken has shifted its name to KFC: as its vice president of advertising explained, "The name 'Fried' is very limiting...we want to...fit into consumers' lifestyles." Similarly, Burger King has begun to downplay the first word of its name by relying more on its initials "BK" and heavily promoting such items as the "BK Broiler."[17]

As consumers' health interests have changed, firms have modified their offerings and appeals. Here we see the shift from Kentucky Fried Chicken (which might lead to a negative health influence) to KFC, which offers more menu options.

🐚 *It's All in the Family*

Family branding is another strategy firms often use to stimulate specific perceptual inferences by consumers. Here a firm such as General Electric or Campbell will use some of its "brand equity" (a term indicating the special value attached to a brand name) by lending the established name to a new product it will be marketing. The expectation is that consumers will use the firm's name in their categorization process; thus inferences such as "tested," "high quality," and "dependable" are more likely to be made.

Family branding is a useful means for capturing further efficiency from a well-developed brand name in the marketplace, through "brand extensions" or other efforts to "leverage" the strong brand name. This strategy can sometimes backfire, however, if the perceptual inferences required of consumers seem to cross natural categories. When this happens, consumers may find the inferences to be *contradictory* and react negatively. For example, what perceptual inferences might arise for these new products?

- Sara Lee Chicken & Noodles au Gratin
- Listerol, a household cleaner from Listerine
- Bic Perfume
- Arm & Hammer Antiperspirant
- Clorox Super Detergent

All these were new product entries that faced a rocky reception in the consumer marketplace. In the Clorox case, for example, as one supermarket manager commented, "People see Clorox, and they think bleach...they don't want all their clothes to turn white."[18]

PLACE DECISIONS AND CONSUMER INFERENCES

Consumer inferences in this area pertain primarily to the retail store. Retailers are increasingly sensitive to the various cues that consumers encounter while shopping. This concern extends across store layout, displays, merchandise, salespersons, and service. In general, the physical considerations fall within a topic known as **atmospherics.** Atomsperics leads to the creation of a planned environment in which cues are used by a marketer to stimulate particular perceptions and behaviors on the part of consumers.

🐚 *Perceptual Inferences of the "Bargain Hunters"*

From the consumer's point of view, a retail store presents many individual stimulus cues from which perceptual inferences can be made. Experienced retailers are aware of many of these types of inferences and adjust their environments accordingly. Sometimes, however, the consumer inferences are not immediately obvious. Once, for example, a famous Harvard professor of decision sciences was retained by a retailer to suggest ways to improve sales efficiency in its store. When he arrived, he became especially concerned with the women's blouse subdepartment in the "bargain basement." This area seemed to be extremely inefficient. Blouses were strewn about in a jumble, and shoppers wasted many minutes attempting to find their correct size. Upon mentioning this to management, the professor was invited to return the next morning to observe the entire process from scratch. He noted that prior to the store opening hour, employees neatly arranged all the blouses by size. Then, however, they threw them on the counter

Family branding: Placing a strong brand name on a number of products to stimulate positive inferences by consumers.

Atmospherics: Creation of a planned retain environment: cues are managed to stimulate particular perceptions by consumers.

and thoroughly mixed them up! The first shoppers had to spend more time than usual to locate their correct size. This created a small crowd of women searching for the correct sizes in a style they liked. This small crowd, in turn, seemed to serve as a magnet for other shoppers, who seemed to be inferring that special blouse bargains were available since so many other shoppers had already been attracted to this area.[19]

ADVERTISING DECISIONS AND CONSUMER INFERENCES

Because advertising is a communication form, the issue of which perceptual inferences consumers are led to make is crucial to an ad's success or failure. Perceptual inferences have substantial impacts on how much attention is paid to an ad, and what types of *thoughts* might be stimulated. We should, however, recognize that advertisements are complex stimuli, their effects will differ depending on the medium in which they appear, and that the perceptual process for them can easily extend over a 30- to 60-second time period. During this time the precise stimulus being perceived will shift as the consumer proceeds further into the ad. Perceptual inferences will shift as well, and will continue as long as attention is being paid to the ad.[20]

🐋 *Size and Subtle Inferences: "The Giant and the Sprout"*

Subtle perceptual inferences are often called forth by the detailed stimuli contained within ads. The following case provides a good example. The Jolly Green Giant is one of the most successful characters in advertising history. In his early years his fame led his firm to change its name from the Minnesota Valley Canning & Packing Co. to the Green Giant Company (and, advertising students might be interested to know, the Green Giant's fame also launched the stunning success of Leo Burnett and his ad agency, since this was his first client). At his peak, a national poll showed that more people could correctly identify the Jolly Green Giant than they could the president of the United States. After some years, however, consumers began to pay less attention to ads featuring him doing his same "stand up and smile" routine, and the firm began to look for new ad strategies.

Consumer research revealed, as expected, that viewers enjoyed the Giant's "Ho-ho-ho" at the end of each commercial. However, consumers were very sensitive to how the Green Giant acted within the commercial—this sensitivity was due to perceptual inferences they were making beyond the actual scenes. For example, if ads showed the Giant walking around his valley, consumers reacted negatively—it seems that the thought of his walking raised images of happy little helpers and crops being stepped on by giant green feet. When close-up views of the Giant's face were used, consumers also reacted negatively, indicating that he was no longer friendly—it seems that a giant is only jolly if he is far away from us! As a result of these consumer inferences, the ad agency (Leo Burnett, Inc.) then developed a set of rules for use of the Green Giant in ads: (1) he is always in the background, (2) his features are obscure, (3) he only says "Ho-ho-ho," (4) he moves very little, (5) he doesn't walk, and (6) he never leaves his valley. These rules are followed in all countries where the advertising is run.

To give itself more advertising flexibility, the agency decided to develop a new character who would provide most of the benefits of the Giant, but who wouldn't pose these special problems. Finally, the "Little Green Sprout" was born. When he was introduced, special cues were given so that consumers' *categorizations* would be correct but their *inferences* would not be negative. Specifically, the Sprout's name and song clearly indicated a small size ("not very big, about the size of a twig") but a direct relationship to the Jolly Green Giant himself ("that's how Jolly Green Giants start out").[21]

🐋 *Bush League Brushbacks?*

We are all aware that U.S. presidential politics is a high-stakes, "hardball" affair. We may not be aware, however, of some of the tricks that are used to influence voters' perceptual inferences in subtle ways. During the primaries of the late 1980s, for example, the following story came out. George Bush had been trounced by Senator Robert Dole in the Iowa primary election and desperately needed to win in New Hampshire if he was to capture the Republican party's nomination and go on to win the presidency. His key TV commercial—one that attacked Senator Dole for "straddling" on the big issues—was credited by both observers and Dole advisors as turning the tide away from Dole and toward Bush. An interview with the video editing artist who "touched up" the commercial gives us some insights:

- Why did Senator Dole look so strange in this commercial? "I do believe we might have flipped his photo around," laughed the editor, "It's nothing one would notice, but the senator's hair is parted on the wrong side and his face looks awkward."

- Why did Mr. Bush look so good? One reason was the thin "halo" of light that appeared around his head in each photo of him.

- In other ads, similar techniques were used. Mr. Bush's photos were always outlined in blue, Mr. Dole's in black. Any people in Mr. Bush's background were colorfully dressed (Mr. Dole's fans were washed out). Enthusiastic cheers from a soundtrack were added to crowd scenes for Mr. Bush (in one slip-up, the camera showed the audience with all mouths closed while the cheers rang on). Finally, each time a Dole position was typed on the screen, it would be underlined in red ("hot tempered"), while the Bush positions were underlined in a calm, cool blue.

This type of editing wasn't used just for Mr. Bush, of course. According to the editor, "Political commercials are now filled with special effects . . . what we do one night in an editing room in New York can have such a big effect one day later."[22]

PRICE DECISIONS AND CONSUMER INFERENCES

The pricing area presents us with an interesting set of issues. First, as compared to product, place, and promotion cues, price is usually a much simpler stimulus cue. Because of this, researchers have a more manageable task in attempting to study perceptual inferences consumers make in response to price cues. Second, as compared to all the other marketing mix areas, price would seem to represent a cost rather than a benefit to consumers—price measures what we must *give up* in a transaction to receive the benefits we desire. If price is only a cost, though, what kinds of perceptual inferences would it stimulate? The brief discussions that follow explain some of these:

"You Get What You Pay For!"

If we think briefly about this common phrase, we'll see that consumers don't always view price as only a cost. Instead, we also can view price as an "extrinsic" or external cue

Perceived quality inference: A tentative conclusion about the quality of a product in the absence of direct quality information.

that helps us judge the quality of the product itself. This **perceived quality inference** may be grounded in reality. It might, for example, stem from a recognition that higher quality often requires higher production costs, which in turn produce higher prices. It might also stem from elements of perceived status or prestige, or even from inferences that the higher prices represent a scarcity of the good.

Considerable consumer research has been conducted on this type of inference. In general, this research has shown that consumers *do* infer product quality from the price charged for the product. They are more likely to rely on the price cue when other information to help with the quality inference is not available and when they have less personal experience with the product itself. While further research remains to be done, we can conclude at this point that the price-quality perceived inference is active in the consumer marketplace.[23]

🐋 *How Good Is It?*

In practice, the perceived quality inference can sometimes lead to unexpected results. A store's prices can be perceived as being "too low," and consumer demand for a product may actually decrease because it is perceived as lacking in desired quality. In one case, for example, a discount chain received a large shipment from the Orient of teen jewelry costing a few cents per unit. It was shipped to its stores and priced at 19 cents per unit, allowing a large percentage profit on each sale. However, the jewelry received little interest from shoppers. At this point an experienced retailing executive proposed that prices be raised dramatically. A few weeks later, the new promotional plan went out from headquarters, repricing these items at 59 cents per unit, and featuring this price with in-store posters. Sales picked up immediately, and the shipment sold out in a short time!

Reference Pricing and Price Lining

Reference price: A benchmark "expected" or "normal" price: can be porvided by a consumer's memory or by a marketer.

In many cases consumers are not entirely confident about what price to expect and are quite willing to rely on other external cues to help with this judgment.[24] Thus many retailers use **reference prices.** For example, sales are often announced with both a reference price and the special sales price ("Regularly $29.95, now $18.95!"). The reference price provides a "normal" price for consumers and encourages perceptual inferences of special savings. Reference prices are also used by some outlets to project an image of more value for the money, especially when the product is not a well-known brand ("Compare to products costing $50, here priced at only $34.95!"). In many instances reference prices do help consumers accurately perceive special price savings. However, reference prices can be used for unscrupulous purposes as well, when they are artificially inflated to deceive consumers as to the actual value of the offering.

Price lining: The retail practice of pricing at the top of several price ranges that consumers see as reasonable for a product.

Price lining is a legitimate retail practice stemming from consumers' inferences about price ranges. Here the seller stocking several grades (lines) of a good will try to price each at the top of the price range that consumers are willing to pay for that good. For example, let's assume that Kathryn Alexander comes to a store wanting to pay about $25 for a gift item, but knowing that she may end up paying a little less (perhaps as low as $22) or a little more (as much as $28). How can the retailer increase profits? By pricing the item at $28, which Kathryn will still infer represents the grade level she desires and is not so distant from $25 that she reacts negatively. The retailer might then establish another price line at $18 (Kathryn will infer this product as being below the grade she desires for her gift and will not buy it). To plan this strategy with precision, of course, requires taking all customers' preferences into account: consumer research may be necessary.

"Why Do So Many Prices End in '9'?"

This question refers to *odd-even pricing practices* that lead to most prices ending in either a "9" or a "5." No one knows exactly how this custom has arisen. Some speculations are interesting, however:

- *Speculation 1.* It leads to consumer inferences that the product costs less than it actually does. Consumers' perceptions focus on the larger-digit positions, so the ending number (which represents pennies) gets rounded down. Since it is the larger-digit positions that are recalled accurately, a good priced at $28.59 will be recalled as being "about $28" rather than "about $29."

- *Speculation 2.* The circles in double nines ("99") attract attention to the object.

- *Speculation 3.* Odd endings force the store to give the consumer change, and consumers like to receive change when they check out.

- *Speculation 4.* Discount stores use odd pricing because it connotes savings, but prestige or fashion retailers use even pricing because it connotes status.[25]

What do you think?

SUMMARY: THE MARKETING MIX AND CONSUMERS' INFERENCES

We have now examined many examples of marketing applications within each of the 4 P's. Before closing, however, we should note that an especially powerful treatment occurs when a marketer is able to use **image management** to *coordinate* each of the elements of the marketing mix to work together to influence consumer inferences. For example, notice how carefully Procter & Gamble has managed the image of Ivory Soap: its purity positioning is conveyed by the *product's* color, brand name, the fancy lettering but simple packaging, the *promotional* slogan of "99 and 44/100% pure," and the use of the Ivory girl in advertising. Notice also that the Ivory girl wears no makeup, stands by a white picket fence in a pastoral setting, rides a 3-speed girls' bicycle, and wears a simple white shirt and jeans. (Readers wishing to pursue this issue of image management for a strategic brand concept should consult Note 26 for this chapter, located at the back of this book.)

In closing this section, we should also note that a considerable amount of advanced consumer research has recently been undertaken to more closely assess how consumers' inferences affect memory, judgments, and purchase decisions (see Note 27 for citations). We will be returning to those topics in upcoming chapters. At this point, however, let us briefly consider how consumers' perceptual inferences can sometimes raise public policy difficulties.

Image management: The coordination of the elements of the marketing mix to work together to influence consumer inferences.

■ PUBLIC POLICY AND CONSUMERS' INFERENCES

In its role as regulator of the setting for transactions between marketers and consumers, public policy frequently must deal with mistaken perceptual inferences. Often these involve advertising stimuli that tend to lead to mistaken inferences on the part of consumers. For example, in bait and switch advertising (in which the retailer does not intend to sell the advertised item, but is instead attempting to get a consumer to visit the store for a high-pressure sales pitch), consumers are likely to infer that, if a product is advertised by a store, it will be available for sale. Because these consumer inferences can be expected, marketers are prohibited from engaging in bait and switch advertising. Policymakers also believe that consumers infer that a product is safe if no warning to the contrary appears—when a product does have health or safety hazards, then, warnings of these are required. Similarly, descriptions of products can lead to mistaken inferences. Recently, for example, much attention has been given to setting standards for using such claims as "Light," "Diet," "Low-Fat," "Fresh," and other food descriptions, so that consumers will not be misled in their inferences about a food's benefit. In general, in the area of deceptive advertising, it is a concern with mistaken inferences by consumers that leads to regulatory actions.

In addition, competition plays an extremely important role in what consumers perceive about the marketplace and options in it. One interesting public policy problem in this regard concerns the law toward trademark protection. Once a marketer has legally gained the right to use a brand name to consumers, what actions can competitors employ and still be within the boundaries of the law? Within this area, consumers' perceptual processes of categorization and inference often become key issues in disputes:

🐋 Trademark Infringement: "Tide" Versus "Tibe"

Consumers' perceptual processes are usually the target of competitors who enter a market with imitations of successful brands. Confused consumer inferences might then shift sales and profits from the established brand to the imitator. In these instances the successful brand has a right to sue for trademark infringement and to try legally to recover monetary damages to its sales and reputation. In recent years many cases have been brought in this area. For example, how would you vote in each of the following trademark infringement cases, in favor of the original brand (listed first) or the new competitor (listed second)?

Case 1: Pampers versus Rumpers diapers?

Case 2: Vantage versus Advance cigarettes?

Case 3: Opici wine versus Amici wine?

Case 4: Duet bottled cocktails versus Duvet brandy?

Case 5: McDonald's hamburgers versus McBagel restaurant?

Case 6: McDonald's hamburgers versus McSleep Inns?

Case 7: Jordache jeans versus Lardashe jeans?

If you're interested in how the cases came out, you may wish to turn to Note 28.

Sometimes these cases result from honest mistakes rather than deliberate infringement, and often there are good arguments on both sides of the issue. In many of these cases, advanced consumer research can be used to study the perceptual inferences made by consumers with respect to these products and can contribute to a wise decision in the case.

In some cases, however, the infringement strategy is obviously deliberate and can cause serious difficulties. At one time, for example, P & G filed suit to seize more than 100 tons of detergent products made in Singapore—the brand names used included Tibe, Tike, Tile, and Tipe. None of the copycat detergents was sold in Singapore or the United States—all were exported to Arab countries, a fact that raised further legal problems for P & G.[29]

■ SUMMARY

THREE ACTIVITIES IN CONSUMER PERCEPTION

In our framework for perceptual processes, sensation and attention (the topics of our previous chapter) are followed by *perceptual interpretation*. Here the consumer identifies the meaning of a stimulus. Three key activities are involved in interpretation: (1) organization, (2) categorization, and (3) inference making.

PERCEPTUAL ORGANIZATION

The chapter's first section examined *perceptual organization*. Here we discussed *Gestalt theory*, which holds that people perceive entire objects (not just individual parts)—that we strive for perceptions that are simple, complete, and meaningful. The major Gestalt principles are figure and ground, proximity, similarity, continuation, common fate, closure, and symmetry. We also discussed how *context* and *perceptual constancy* affect consumers' perceptions.

PERCEPTUAL CATEGORIZATION

The second section turned to *categorization*, which is the process of *identifying* a stimulus. Here we are interested in how a stimulus is recognized and tentatively classified from our LTM. Categorization will strongly influence our further CIP processes (e.g., interest in a stimulus and positive or negative evaluation of it). Expectations (such as in "shopping scripts") also play an important role in categorization. Researchers are now studying this area in detail.

PERCEPTION AND CONSUMER INFERENCES

Our third section of the chapter discussed *perceptual inferences*. These are beliefs we form based on other information, such as stimulus properties. Since all thinking involves some form of inferences, this topic is crucial. Product, place, promotion, and price-related consumer inferences were all examined, and numerous marketing applications were discussed.

PUBLIC POLICY AND CONSUMERS' PERCEPTUAL INFERENCES

The final section of the chapter turned briefly to some broader issues that arise when consumers develop mistaken inferences based on marketers' stimuli. We also noted that legal problems can crop up with product imitations.

■ KEY TERMS

perceptual organization	perceptual set	family branding
perceptual categorization	schema	atmospherics
perceptual inference	script	perceived quality inference
Gestalt school	exemplar strategy	reference prices
good Gestalts	feature-based strategy	price lining
perceptual context	inferences	image management
perceptual constancy	brand name	

■ REVIEW QUESTIONS AND EXPERIENTIAL EXERCISES

[E = **Application extension or experiential exercise**]

1. What three factors influence how consumers attach meaning to a particular stimulus? Explain. How can marketers apply these factors to their activities?

2. Describe the principles that determine whether or not a specific perception will qualify as a "good Gestalt."

3. Explain figure and ground. What are the implications for marketers?

4. Provide examples of how a "perceptual set" may work as an advantage and as a disadvantage for marketers.

5. Describe briefly, giving examples;
   a. A schema
   b. A shopping script

6. What is an inference? How are subtle inferences different from conscious ones?

7. [E] Provide examples (different from those in the text) of how consumers form quality inferences based on
   a. Sound   c. Smell
   b. Touch   d. Color

8. [E] How can "reference pricing" either help or mislead consumers?

9. [E] Consider the text's examples of family brand names for products that did not do well, perhaps because of poor perceptual inferences (e.g., Sara Lee Chicken...). As a creative exercise, propose three further examples of possible new products for which a family branding strategy would create negative perceptual inferences (one winner in a recent contest, for example, was Hellman's Mayonnaise Creamsicles!).

10. [E] Give examples of current products using a family branding strategy well. Suggest three further brands you think should try this strategy for a new product (that is, you suggest the product and the name).

11. [E] Choose a local retailer with which you are familiar. Discuss the implications of consumer perceptions of product quality for this retailer's decisions regarding
   a. Store layout
   b. Logos
   c. Price

12. [E] Using the Notes for this chapter, choose an interesting topic in perception and read more about either recent research or marketing applications involving this topic. Write a brief report on your findings.

13. [E] Interview an "expert" in a particular product category (product engineer, store manager, experienced salesperson) concerning the price-quality inferences made by most consumers. How do prices and quality actually compare? How do reference prices work? Summarize your findings.

14. [E] Search magazine ads for examples of the perceptual topics discussed in this chapter. Cut out two or three examples of each of the following and attach a brief explanation of your reasoning.
   a. Gestalt principles in ads
   b. Possible problems with categorization
   c. Possible problems with perceptual inferences

15. [E] Visit a supermarket with which you are very familiar, on a normal shopping trip. This time, however, be sure to monitor your schemas and scripts from the time you enter the store. If you were a consultant for a minor brand in each of these categories, what would you recommend it consider doing?
   a. Pickles
   b. Frozen pizza
   c. Soup
   d. Gravy mix
   e. Paper towels

■ SUGGESTED READING

■ This chapter has been filled with fairly basic research concepts that have significant implications for marketing programs. For an interesting piece that integrates some of these concepts, see C. Whan Park, Bernard J. Jaworski, and Deborah J. MacInnis, "Strategic Brand Concept-Image Management," *Journal of Marketing*, Vol. 50 (October 1986), pp. 135–145. For some surprising findings in the area of objective price-quality relations, see

Ruby T. Morris and Clare S. Bronson, "The Chaos in Competition Indicated by Consumer Reports," *Journal of Marketing*, Vol. 33 (July 1969), pp. 26–34 (the subsequent references at the end of Note 23 can then bring you up to date with more advanced analyses). For good readings on a particular topic of interest, the Notes are an excellent place to start.

Where do you suppose they keep the Range Rover?

A Range Rover is quite at home in weather that would keep other luxury cars, well, at home.

After all, with its permanent 4-wheel drive and powerful V-8 engine, you can plow through unplowed roads.

Tool along slushy streets.

Make it up sleet-covered hills.

And easily cope with conditions that would discourage a sled dog.

In fact, the Range Rover County even comes with an anti-lock braking system considered by many to be the most sophisticated one on four wheels.

RANGE ROVER

Which not only means you can drive with a reassuring amount of control.

You can stop with it too.

So why not call 1-800-FINE 4WD for the name of a dealer near you?

Granted, with Range Rovers starting at just under $39,000, it's not the sort of thing one should take lightly.

But then, neither is a ton of snow.

This clever ad invites the reader to use the Gestalt principles of continuation and common fate in order to interpret it correctly. In so doing, it gains attention and interest as it makes its point. To learn more about this topic, see our discussion at the start of Chapter 9, page 232.

Your package leads to many possible consumer inferences, and can gain or lose sales for you. Here are four success stories from package changes:

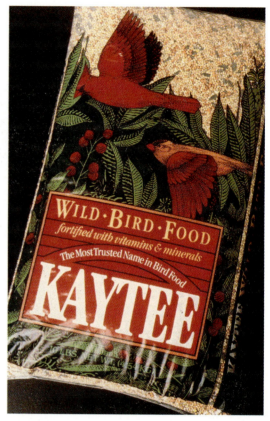

(a) Kaytee Birdseed redesigned to suggest quality and status. This allowed it to enter new outlets as well. Sales increased from $10 million to $90 million per year.

(b) Rayovac redesigned to stand out better on the shelf (70% of battery purchases are impulsive), and to suggest power. Market share increased 5% in the first year.

(c) Sutter Home wine wanted to offer low price but to also suggest that it is a quality wine. Its subtle redesign reduced the size of the name and increased the sized of the seal (a quality cue). Sales increased 15% in the first six weeks.

(d) Jergens lotion had a strong brand name, but management wanted a more expensive look. Changes to both the bottle shape and the label assisted in a 30% gain sales dollars in the next year

In a famous recent case against Volvo for running a "rigged demonstration" ad, the Texas attorney general used these photo exhibits showing how the demonstration was actually designed and run (two bystanders took the photos and turned them over to the government office). In the finished TV version, a monster truck, called Bear Foot, rides over the tops of a line of cars, crushing all but the Volvo. For more details see the story at the end of Chapter 8, page 227.

State exhibit 2: worker shown cutting apart the roof support pillar in a Ford Maverick, one of the cars to be crushed.

State exhibit 4: The steel structural support placed inside the rear of the Volvo station wagon (note the crushed competitor to the left).

State exhibit 9: As the cameras record the scene, workers manually roll only a tire across the Volvo's front.

CONSUMER LEARNING

HAVE A COKE AND A SMILE...

Coca-Cola has acknowledged that it has developed a new ad-testing procedure based on Ivan Pavlov's famous theories of learning. A high-ranking executive at Coke said, "We nominate Pavlov as the father of modern advertising. Pavlov took a neutral object and, by associating it with a meaningful object, made it a symbol of something else... that is what we try to do in modern advertising." The specifics of Coke's test are secret, but it is known to involve the measurement of how well a positive image can be transferred to the product and then to sales. According to one report, in three years of testing, ads that scored high on this measure almost always resulted in higher sales of a soft drink... (excerpted from the chapter).

This is one of many examples of ways in which learning theory has been applied to consumer marketing. In this chapter we'll delve further into this fascinating subject.

■ WHAT IS CONSUMER LEARNING?

In this chapter we'll examine how consumer learning occurs. First, though, let's examine carefully what learning really is. It is not just what we normally think it to be. Unless you have already studied psychology, our opening discussion may contain some surprises!

Broadly speaking, **learning** refers to *relatively permanent changes in behavior, feelings, and thoughts as effects of information and experience*. The scope of consumer learning is very broad. All our environment and internal processes (e.g., perception) *contribute* to consumer learning. In addition, however, all consumer behavior *depends on* learning from our prior experience. This topic is so broad, in fact, that experts have long disagreed about the best way to study it.[1] The result is that there are now two different "schools" of learning, each of which has much to offer us.

Learning: Relatively permanent changes in behavior, feelings, and thoughts as effects of information and experience.

THE TWO SCHOOLS OF LEARNING

As we noted, learning reflects the effects of experience. When we think further about this point, we can recognize five major factors that are involved:

- (S) Stimuli or conditions
- (K) Knowledge or memory (long-term memory, LTM)
- (I) Internal thought processes
- (R) Responses or behaviors
- (T) Time or "experience episodes"

An overall model of learning (SKIRT, for short), would include each of these factors as important. For example, the appearance of a particular stimulus (S) sparks a consumer to draw on her knowledge (K) from LTM, to guide internal thought processes (I) on the part of a consumer. Then she responds (R) in some fashion, perhaps by a physical action such as talking or buying, or perhaps by a mental action to update her knowledge. The next time (T) a similar stimulus (S) appears, she can call on her updated knowledge (K) to guide new internal processes (I) toward new responses (R).

Although this example seems simple enough, it hides a key fact for researchers who want to study learning: *there are too many variables* to be studied in any one research effort. This crucial point has had an enormous impact on the history of research on learning. It forced experts to face the question: "Since I can't study every aspect of learning, what shall I stress, and what shall I ignore?" Their answers led to two quite different approaches to research on learning, each of which offers useful insights for consumer behavior.

☜ *Behavior versus Knowledge*

The two approaches can be termed the **learning as behavior (LAB)** view and the learning is knowledge (LIK) view. The LAB approach concentrates on the stimuli (S) and the response behaviors (R) made over time (T). This research stream has thus focused on the *external world of learning*. Because of its stress on behavior as representing learning, this approach is sometimes called **behaviorism**.

In contrast, the LIK approach stresses knowledge rather than behavior as the best measure of learning. This approach emphasizes the *internal world of learning*, stressing the role of memory and knowledge (K) and internal thinking processes (I). In the spirit of the CIP perspective, LIK has achieved great popularity recently. However, we should recognize that by concentrating on these internal sectors, the LIK view gives up strength in studying stimuli and conditions (S), behavioral responses (R), and the role of time (T) in learning.

While it is true that either school is capable of introducing some improvements in its weak areas, their differences are quite real. In the remainder of this chapter we'll take a closer look at each of these approaches and some current marketing applications. We'll begin our analysis with the LIK view of learning, since this is the basic approach we have been taking in the textbook to this point.

■ THE LEARNING IS KNOWLEDGE (LIK) VIEW

The LIK perspective on learning focuses on internal characteristics rather than on behavior. Almost all our coverage in the earlier chapters of the text has reflected this LIK view, since LIK learning processes are forms of consumer information processing

(CIP). The **LIK** school stresses a consumer's memory as the center of learning. The LIK school thus views "learning" to be *the development of the LTM "node network,"* that is, the creation of new nodes and new linkages (to refresh your understanding of the node network concept, you may wish to look again at Chapter 7's Figure 7-4). *Thus we've already examined a number of significant issues related to the LIK approach.* In this chapter, therefore, we'll restrict our further discussion of LIK learning to three topics that aren't covered elsewhere in the text.

Learning is knowledge (LIK): A major approach to learning: emphasizes the role of memory and thinking.

I: CONSUMER LEARNING IN CHILDREN

Some marketers are extremely interested in children as consumers, for reasons that are easy to understand! This is a large market, with over 40 million children under the age of 12 in the United States alone. These children spend over $4 billion themselves each year, in addition to influencing multiples of this amount in household purchases made by relatives. In addition, these are the adult consumers of the future. However, marketers who sell to children are also concerned about what reasonable limitations ought to be applied to this area. Such limitations spring from the special characteristics of children as "limited learners."

Children form an important group from an LIK perspective, since they are building so much basic knowledge during this time. Childhood is also the period in which we form our individual consumer values and buying styles. Beyond this is the fact that there are systematic barriers in children's learning. In this section we'll briefly examine why this is so.

Childhood Learning Stages

Research on stages of development has been inspired by the work of the Swiss psychologist Jean Piaget, beginning about 60 years ago.[2] Piaget discovered that children pass through four stages of cognitive growth. Within each stage, the child is limited in what and how he or she learns and thinks. Table 10-1 provides a brief description of Piaget's stages. Notice that in the early years up to age 2, a baby's lack of language ability restricts abstract thought. When language has developed, however, young children are still restricted in their learning abilities. In a famous experiment, Piaget

Table 10-1 Piaget's Four Stages of Child Development

Stage Name	Characteristics
Sensorimotor Stage (from birth to age 2)	The infant is not capable of abstract thought since language ability is only slowly beginning. Behavior is mainly physical (motor), driven by stimuli (sensory inputs).
Preoperational Thought Stage (from ages 3 to 7)	The young child is developing the ability to use symbols (language, mental images). However, most thinking is still driven by stimuli in the outside world. Attention spans are very short, and thinking focuses on only one dimension of a problem at a time.
Concrete Operational Stage (from ages 8 to 11)	The child's internal thought processes are becoming stronger, so he or she is better able to "think about" objects. Such thinking is "concrete," however, in that the objects need to be physically present.
Formal Operational Stage (from age 11 up)	At about this age the child begins to think more like an adult, especially in the sense of being capable of abstract thought. Ideas and logical systems take on more meaning, perception is less crucial for thinking, and the child can consider multiple characteristics of a problem.

I. The Sensorimotor Stage (birth to two years old): Behavior is mainly physical and is in response to stimuli. Here the shiny pots have attracted interest, and the bangs and flying objects sustain it.

II. The Preoperational Thought Stage (ages three to seven): Language is developing, but thinking is still stimulus driven. Attention spans are short, and focus is on one dimension at a time.

III. The Concrete Operational Stage (ages 8 to 11): Internal thought processes are developing, but are still "concrete." Here the fingers and thumb really do help with addition!

IV. The Formal Operational Stage (age 11 and up): Adult-like thought processes are possible—more abstract and multidimensional.

demonstrated how "perceptual boundedness" restricts a "preoperational" (ages 3–7) child's reasoning: he first showed children two identical glasses, tall and thin, that were filled to the same level. He then poured the contents of one of the glasses into a short broad jar; the children at this stage refused to believe that the two containers had the same amount of liquid, but insisted that the tall glass contained more. By the time they move to the next (concrete operational) stage, at about age 8, the children are easily able to answer this question correctly.

The "KidVid" Issue: Advertising to Children

Piaget's theories hold many significant implications for consumer behavior. For example, because of reading deficiencies, children receive much of their consumer information from television advertising. The average child spends about 25 hours per week watching television and thus is exposed to about 20,000 ads in a year. As we'd expect from Piaget's work, however, younger children lack certain skills necessary to process ads very well. They are likely to focus on only a limited amount of available information and to have difficulty in using reasoning processes. Preschoolers, for example, often believe that advertising is "real" and that there are little people inside the television. Even when outgrowing this perspective, children may think that a person speaking from the set is addressing them personally and may have difficulty in understanding the difference between an ad and the program itself.[3]

Research in consumer behavior has consistently shown age differences in children's ability to process television advertising. These differences stem from developmental differences in children's abilities to (1) *store* information in the proper nodes in LTM and (2) successfully find and *retrieve* the proper information with which to interpret TV messages. (Much research has been done recently on this topic in the consumer behavior field. If you are interested in reading more about it, you may wish to start with the readings listed in Note 4.)

One interesting summary of research findings points up the special aspects of the children's advertising area:

1. *Types of ads directed to kids.* Foods—particularly cereals and snacks—are the most frequently advertised products, followed by toys. Message appeals tend to be emotional and emphasize fun themes. Ads tend to be fast paced and light rather than discuss the product. Premium offers are featured.

2. *Kids' understanding of advertising.* Sophistication about advertising increases with age. Children below age 8 display low understanding of selling intent and make little distinction between programming and advertising.

3. *Belief in TV ads.* Few children below age 8 exhibit any generalized distrust of advertising. Kids are skeptical about claims for toys they already own, but readily accept claims of medical or nutritional nature. Heavy viewers of commercials are more likely to believe ads than are light viewers.

4. *Influence of ads.* Exposure to advertising increases consumption desires: children who watch much TV are far more likely to request parents to buy food and toy products for them. Parents reject between one-third and one-half of children's requests for products—this leads to conflicts in about half of all families, although such arguments are reported to be mild.

5. *Parental guidance.* Parents do not play a strong direct role in educating children about advertising. Most do not watch the ads with their children, and fewer than half of the mothers say they teach their children about advertising.[5]

Given these types of findings about children's learning processes, everyone—marketers, parents, and public policymakers alike—agrees that the children's advertising area deserves special attention. There is disagreement, however, about how this should best be handled.

🐚 *Self-regulation in Children's Advertising*

One option is for marketers to police themselves. About 15 years ago advertising trade associations developed guidelines for marketers to follow in creating ads aimed at children. Shortly thereafter, the National Advertising Division (a self-regulatory body) established its Children's Advertising Review Unit (CARU). CARU monitors advertising directed to children under 12 years of age and, within a self-regulatory process, seeks modification or discontinuance of ads it finds to be inaccurate or unfair. CARU has also developed detailed guidelines for advertisers in this area. (In one recent CARU study, during 600 hours of programming, over 10,000 commercials directed to children appeared. Only 4 percent failed to meet CARU voluntary guidelines.)[6]

🎣 Government Regulation: Get Rid of KidVid?

In spite of the careful attention given to children's advertising by the industry's leaders, many consumer groups and parents remain distrustful of the practice. Occasionally proposals arise to restrict it further. For example, prior to the deregulatory era of the 1980s, the Federal Trade Commission's staff recommended that the FTC enact rules that would

1. *Ban* all TV advertising directed to young children (under 8 years of age).
2. *Ban* TV advertising for sugared food products directed to older children (ages 8 to 12).
3. Require all other TV advertising for sugared food products seen by significant proportions of older children to be balanced by health messages paid for by the advertisers.

Reaction to this proposal was massive and heated. Companies and advertising agencies banded together to fight any regulations resembling those suggested. They charged that the FTC was attempting to become a "National Nanny" and was willing to ride rampant over the right of free speech accorded to businesses in this country. They also charged that the FTC staff's descriptions of children's limitations were overstated and that children could learn more about commercials if appropriate education were provided. During the hearings extensive lobbying was being undertaken in Congress, against the FTC issuing rules of any type. Congress reacted against the FTC, and this children's rule-making issue was dropped in the United States. (However, the Canadian province of Quebec did prohibit all commercial advertising aimed at children under 13 years of age.)

In 1990, Congress passed the Children's Television Act, which placed mild restrictions on advertising to children: ads are limited to 10.5 and 12 minutes per hour on weekends and weekdays, respectively, and stations are required to carry educational programs for children. However, there is still considerable political pressure on children's advertising: for example, the head of ACT (Action for Children's Television) described the new time limits as better, but "still disgusting."[7] Given the research on children's learning, should there be further restrictions on kids' advertising, in your opinion?

II: LEARNING ABOUT WHAT CONSUMERS ARE LEARNING

A second topic arising from the LIK approach moves to the question of how to measure consumer learning itself. One of the most interesting aspects of our current marketing-consumer environment is that *no organization is engaged in the overall measurement of what consumers learn.* Put another way, apart from the limited test of consumers' skills used in a few consumer education classes, we simply do not know what consumers do or do not know. As we saw in Chapter 2, part of this problem is due to the wide range of topics about which consumers learn—everything from money management skills to individual brand jingles.

Academic researchers have begun to consider the nature of consumer knowledge, but little descriptive information is presently available in the literature.[8] The primary reason is that marketers specialize in particular product categories. Individual marketers study what consumers have learned and what they are learning from current promotional strategies, but only for the product being sold. These firms do not release their findings, of course, because of their profit implications. Thus there is no general source available on consumer learning.

Marketing Research Techniques

As noted, however, marketers do carry out many individual studies involving consumer learning. The primary technique for measuring consumer learning is the consumer survey. Consumer surveys allow marketers to discover which products consumers do and do not use, what they know about those products, what they view the strengths and weaknesses of each brand to be, and so forth. This information is then useful for designing new marketing programs. Surveys of consumer knowledge can yield valuable insights for public policymakers as well. In recent years, for example, such surveys have allowed assessments of consumers' diets, health knowledge, insurance coverage, and so forth.

Cognitive Responses to Advertising

Marketers also invest considerable money in studying exactly what consumers learn from individual advertisements (we will be discussing communication research in Chapter 16, but here we stress the issue of measuring consumer learning). Advertising research often takes the form of **copy testing**, to help advertisers choose which ad ideas to run and how the ads might be modified. "Day-after" recall tests and ad recognition tests are both efforts to measure some of what consumers have learned. In recent years ad researchers have given much attention to **cognitive responses** as a method of measuring how consumers are reacting to an ad and what they are learning from it. Cognitive responses are ideas that are evoked by material in the ad.

Cognitive responses: Thoughts that consumers have in response to a message.

Basically, researchers would like to monitor all the thoughts that a consumer has while watching an ad. This is an extreme challenge, given that consumers' CIP systems work at such remarkable speeds and can't be directly observed by the researcher. However, considerable work has been done. Among the interesting findings are (1) in general, print ads yield more cognitive responses than broadcast ads and (2) some cognitive responses stem from the message itself, while others reflect the receiver's own life. To appreciate better what is involved, let's assume we've just run a test ad for a household cleaner and have asked people for the thoughts they had while watching the tape. We can then use a basic system of classifying cognitive responses to provide us with useful insights. This system contains three types of cognitive responses that are of most interest to an advertiser. **Support arguments** are cognitive responses in which a consumer is agreeing with the points being made by the ad ("I agree with what the ad said, that cleaner will probably get my house white and bright."). **Source derogations** are responses in which a consumer disagrees with the ad, but does so by reacting to its source rather than its message ("What would we expect a company to say anyway . . . ? They're just trying to sell it."). **Counterarguments**, on the other hand, are responses in which a consumer disagrees with the message claims themselves ("The ad was wrong; I tried that cleaner and it just spread the grease around in a larger area . . . it's terrible!").

Not surprisingly, ads that evoke more support arguments have been found to yield positive attitude change by consumers, whereas those that spark more negative responses are less persuasive. Of particular value to managers, however, are the insights into the kinds of reactions consumers are having to the message of the test ad and how it is being delivered. If you're interested in learning more about this area of consumer research, you may wish to begin with the readings listed in Note 9. (We will also be examining closely related issues in our next chapter, and in Chapter 16.)

III: "MISLEARNING" ISSUES IN CONSUMER BEHAVIOR

Mislearning: An instance in which what a consumer learns about his or her environment is incorrect.

A third interesting topic reflecting the LIK view of learning involves "mislearning." **Mislearning** refers to cases in which what consumers learn about their environment is incorrect. Sometimes this is the consumer's own fault, through lack of effort, overgeneralizing, or just plain ignorance. On other occasions, it may have been aided by certain marketing practices, such as outright fraud or deception, or the use of ambiguous terminology. In general, mislearning represents a cost to the efficiency of the marketplace, a cost to honest marketers, and a cost to consumers themselves.

Deceptive Advertising

It is often difficult for a consumer to know when he or she has mislearned something. For this reason each year there are many efforts made to ensure against misleading ads. Most of these are removed by businesses themselves—within the advertising approval systems of companies, agencies, and the media—before the ads are run. Some misleading ads do survive this process, however, and are presented to consumers. In some instances, cases are brought within the self-regulatory system; in other instances, cases are brought within the formal regulatory system, which involves state governments, or especially the Federal Trade Commission. Traditionally, the FTC has moved against ads that had a "tendency or capacity" to mislead or deceive consumers. Within the law, however, deception has not been specifically defined. This provides regulators with flexibility for their decisions in individual cases. (An FTC policy statement on deception has pointed to elements that would guide decisions in this area, but even these are subject to interpretation. Interested readers may wish to consult Note 10.)

In recent years many consumer researchers have become interested in measuring deceptive advertising. David M. Gardner, a marketing professor, provided a classic description of three basic types of deceptive ads.[11] The **unconscionable lie** reflects an ad that contains statements that simply are not true ("Regularly sells for $250" or "Guaranteed to last 10 years" when these are untrue). In a **claim-fact discrepancy**, the ad's description needs some further information to avoid misleading implications. For example, in one case the FTC ruled that showing various television sets together might well lead consumers to the inference that all the sets were available at the advertised price—to avoid this, the prices of the other sets could have been listed, or they could have been removed from the photo. The **claim-belief interaction** occurs when all the information in the ad is literally correct but might be expected to be interpreted in a misleading way by consumers because of their existing knowledge and beliefs. In another FTC case, for example, a carpet retailer had featured very attractive prices in his ad but had expressed these as price *per square foot* rather than the normal price per square yard. Because the commission felt that consumers would expect to see such prices in square yard units, it ruled the ad to be deceptive.

In general, then, ads can be deceptive when they are either literally false or potentially misleading. To gauge falsity, we need only to examine the ad itself, together with objective background facts. To gauge "misleadingness," however, we need to consider how consumers will interpret the ad and what they will learn from it. Consumer researchers have stressed what consumers learn from ads as the basis for studying deception. (If you would like to read more about advances in this area, you may wish to pursue the readings given in Note 12.)

Consumer Miscomprehension of Ads

Miscomprehension results when the receiver of a message extracts either an incorrect or confused meaning from it. This topic is much broader than deception, since the marketer may not have played any active role here. *Frequently, in fact, marketers suffer from consumer miscomprehension of their claims:*

🐚 *Say What?*

For example, the Food and Drug Administration (FDA) has recently relaxed some rules about prescriptions, so that certain products that had been sold only by prescription could now also be sold "over the counter" ("OTC" products are those displayed on drugstores' shelves and sold directly to consumers). This was expected to shake up market shares, since the newly available OTC products would be stronger medicinally, and therefore likely to be the most effective in treating consumers' symptoms. However, a study showed that a new advertising claim for the products ("now available without a prescription") was being miscomprehended by over half of consumers! Over 43 percent of consumers thought the phrase meant that the drug was "the same ingredients at a weaker strength." Another 20 percent thought that it meant "it's now a different product." However, the products are exactly the same as they had been as prescription items; what had changed was the government's restrictions on selling directly to consumers.[13]

🐚 *What's Right and What's Wrong?*

Surprisingly, the general topic of consumer miscomprehension has simply not been much studied. In this regard, research on adults and teens has raised striking questions about what consumers *are* learning in our society.

An important association of advertisers, concerned that ads might be charged as being deceptive whenever some consumers misunderstood what was being said, decided to fund a large-scale study to discover what the "normal" rate of miscomprehension might be. Twenty-seven hundred consumers across the United States participated. Three types of communications were used: (1) TV commercials, (2) public service announcements (PSAs), and (3) program excerpts from TV news and entertainment shows. In total, 60 different communications, each 30 seconds long, were studied. Each consumer saw two of the communications. After viewing the first, a six-item true-false quiz was given to the participant. This procedure was repeated after the second viewing as well. Each quiz was designed to have two correct statements and four false statements.

Results were surprising. The *average consumer missed 3.5 of the 12 items, for a miscomprehension rate of 30 percent!* Less than 4 percent of the people were correct on all 12 quiz questions (12 percent missed 1 question). Education wasn't a strong factor: those with college and graduate degrees still had miscomprehension rates over 25 percent! Turning to the communications, the researchers found that all three types fared badly. This indicates that miscomprehension seems to be rampant as we watch all forms of TV.[14]

Miscomprehension: A state of mislearning: results when a message receiver extracts an incorrect or confused meaning.

This study proved to be controversial and sparked several comments from critical marketing professors associated with the FTC, together with replies by the study's authors, who stood behind their findings. (Note 15 provides a list of readings in this controversial research area.)

This completes this chapter's discussion of the LIK approach to consumer learning. However, many of the topics in later chapters will continue to build on this view, so our learning about LIK is not complete. At this point, though, we will turn to a consideration of the LAB approach for the remainder of this chapter.

■ THE LEARNING AS BEHAVIOR (LAB) VIEW

Learning as behavior (LAB): A major approach to learning: concentrates on stimuli and response behaviors made over time.

This approach defines learning as *a relatively permanent change in behavior that occurs as a result of experience.* "Behaviorism" has a long history in studying learning and applying this knowledge to the real world. In fact, the founder of behaviorism, John B. Watson (a famous professor and president of the American Psychological Association) moved to an advertising agency in 1920, where he worked for many years.

Perhaps the most distinguishing characteristic of the behaviorist approach is its emphasis on the external world (as opposed to internal mental processes). *Behaviorist scientists emphasize objective control of the external environment*—in their research we find that stimuli, responses, and time are rigorously manipulated and monitored. Experimental methods are employed to study how precise changes in stimuli would produce precise changes in response—external facts and evidence are of utmost importance to behaviorists.

Many of the founders of this field were trained in physiology and were comfortable with measurements of slight body movements and other changes in body measurements. To achieve control in their studies, they often used animals as subjects (this gave rise to the term "rat psychology"). When animals were used, of course, verbal reports of reactions were lost, so the entire emphasis was placed on overt behaviors as representing learning. (In this regard, Watson did suggest that human subjects be placed in the same-style "discrimination boxes" that delivered either bread or electric shocks to hungry rats penned within, but was rebuffed on the grounds that this was demeaning to humans).[16]

Through its rigorous studies, the LAB approach has developed several key concepts of learning. In the discussions to follow, it will help us to have a basic understanding of these:

- *Conditioning.* This term refers to the acquisition of new behavior relationships with stimuli and thus represents the learning process.
- *Practice.* This term refers to repeated learning episodes.
- *Contiguity.* Meaning "close together," contiguity refers to having stimuli or responses designed to occur closely together so as to increase learning.
- *Reinforcement.* This term refers to the strengthening of learned associations between stimulus and response. A positive reinforcer increases the probability of learning a behavior when it appears.

Within the LAB approach there are two traditional theories: classical conditioning and instrumental conditioning. Before examining recent extensions, let's briefly look at each of these, together with some applications for marketing.

CLASSICAL CONDITIONING

The key figure in **classical conditioning (CC)** is Ivan Pavlov. The son of a Russian priest, Pavlov was trained in physiology and pharmacology (his work on the physiology of digestion, in fact, won him a Nobel Prize in 1904).

🐚 *The Tune and the Fork*

Given his background, Pavlov's approach to the study of learning is understandable. His famous experiments used dogs as subjects and showed how new response behaviors could be created simply by manipulating stimuli, contiguity, practice, and reinforcement. In brief, a dog would be harnessed into a still position and a tuning fork rung. The fork's tone (the stimulus to be conditioned) led to normal responses of the dog hearing the sound. Shortly thereafter (that is, with high contiguity), a dry meat powder was given to the dog, whose normal physiological reaction to this food included salivation. This procedure was repeated over a number of episodes, representing "practice." As the episodes progressed, the food began to be associated with the tone and served as a *reinforcement*. Finally, the dogs reached the point at which the ringing of the tone alone would bring salivation, whether or not meat powder was provided later. At this point the new stimulus-response behavior (tone causes salivation) had been *conditioned*.

Several points should be noted regarding classical conditioning. First, in this case the learner is *reactive*—the learning takes place in response to arrangements of stimuli from the external environment. Second, the learning is based upon an *already existing* stimulus-response (S-R) relationship (here, food induces salivation). Thus classical conditioning potentially places power in the hands of someone who can discover such already existing stimulus-response relationships and then mold the stimulus environment to use them to advantage. (For a discussion of modern developments in Pavlovian psychology, the interested reader may wish to consult Note 17.)

Classical Conditioning and Marketing

Curiously, until recently the formal topic of classical conditioning received little research attention in the marketing and consumer literature. Learning in this fashion tends to occur naturally in consumers' everyday lives, of course. Consider, for example, how certain stimuli often tend to "go together" in our daily lives (such as picnics, fun, and certain foods). These relationships, over time, lead to our "learning" new associations and response behaviors. Symbols, visuals, and music come to have meaning for us and seem able to evoke strong emotional reactions at times.

From the marketing side, however, while more interest has been shown recently, little systematic effort seems to have been given to studying how exactly to manipulate stimuli so as to strongly condition consumers in the Pavlovian style (this may be due to the fact that the individual marketer *lacks significant control* over much of his or her customers' lives and cannot present stimuli to them as they are harnessed into a fixed position). While this does not place a marketer in a powerful position vis-à-vis the consumer (which may be a good thing from an ethical point of view), there are a number of occasions in which marketers do have opportunities to present stimuli in contiguous fashions and attempt to create classical conditioning. Let's look at two examples:

Classical conditioning (CC): New reponse behaviors are created by repetitively pairing a neutral stimulus with a stimulus known to evoke the desired response.

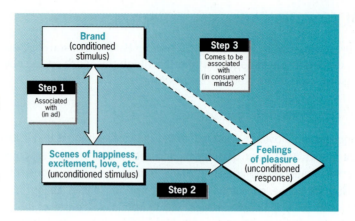

FIGURE 10-1 Using a Classical Conditioning Approach in Advertising. (Step 1) The advertiser pairs the brand with a positively-valued scene in the ad. (Step 2) The consumer derives feelings of pleasure from the scene. (Step 3, after some repetitions of steps 1 and 2) The consumer comes to associate feelings of pleasure with the advertised brand.

🐚 Have a Coke and a Smile…

As shown in Figure 10-1, one common advertising strategy is to place a brand close to other stimuli that are known to evoke strong and favorable emotional responses from consumers in the target audience. Recent research is beginning to indicate that classical conditioning can work in advertising, and firms are paying more and more attention to this area. For example, Coca-Cola has acknowledged that it has developed a new ad-testing procedure based on Pavlov's behavioral principles. A high-ranking executive at Coke said, "We nominate Pavlov as the father of modern advertising. Pavlov took a neutral object and, by associating it with a meaningful object, made it a symbol of something else…that is what we try to do in modern advertising."

While this statement doesn't emphasize the behavioral responses stressed by Pavlov, apparently the company's tests are concerned with this link. The specifics of Coke's test are secret, but it is known to involve the measurement of how well a positive image can be transferred to the product and then to sales. According to one report, in three years of testing, ads that scored high on this measure almost always resulted in higher sales of a soft drink.[18]

🐚 Grease Pens Outdraw Indian Ink

A well-known study by Gerald Gorn helps us to see how classical conditioning might work. In this research, preference for a pen color was conditioned by music during an advertising exposure. In prior testing, it was discovered that light-blue and beige pens were each evaluated as "neutral" by most students. It was also discovered that music from the movie *Grease* provoked a positive emotional response, whereas classical East Indian music produced a negative emotional response by most of the sample.

Four groups were used. Two of the groups viewed an ad picturing the pen while the "liked" music was playing (a light-blue pen was used in one group and a beige pen in the other). The other two groups saw the same pen visuals, but paired with the "disliked" music. All groups had been told that an ad agency was trying to select music for use in a commercial for a pen. No attention was drawn to the color of the pen. After viewing the ad, the students provided brief ratings on the music they'd heard. They were then told that the agency wanted to thank them by giving them one of the pens and that two colors were available. The blue pen box was on the left side of the room; the beige pen box was on the right side. According to the classical conditioning hypothesis, if the music

Coca-Cola pairs a positive phrase and photo with its brand name in order to have consumers develop an association between Coke and fun.

was liked, the pen color should also be liked, whereas if the music was disliked, that pen color should likewise become disliked. Thus the experiment was cleverly designed to predict that in *two groups* the blue pen should be chosen (once when advertised with liked music, the other when not advertised but disliked music had been used for the beige pen). In the other two groups, however, the beige pen should be chosen if conditioning had taken hold.

Results supported the hypothesis: when "liked" music was played, the color of the pen in the ad was chosen by a 3.5:1 ratio over the color that had not appeared. When "disliked" music was played, however, the color that had *not* appeared was chosen 2.5 times more often than the "advertised" color! This effect occurred for both the blue and beige colors, so they were not the cause. Moreover, when asked for the reasons for their choice of a color, only 2 percent mentioned the music. Over half indicated simply that they "liked" the color they'd chosen (if this were the real reason, the experiment would not have worked), while others could give no particular reason for their choice. Thus Gorn's results strongly suggested that classical conditioning can work within even a single exposure and that consumers will not necessarily be aware that it is at work.[19]

As we have seen before, however, whenever consumer unawareness is at issue (as with hidden motives in Chapter 5 and subliminal perception in Chapter 8), *strong disagreements* will crop up among researchers concerning the exact explanations for the effects that are found. Thus it is not surprising that research following Gorn has pointed to further questions on the nature of these effects. Later studies have shown mixed results for classical conditioning: some studies with only slight differences from Gorn's have not discovered his results, while other studies have found positive effects. For example, in one carefully done study, rather than using music, a pairing of pictures of attractive water scenes with a new brand of toothpaste was shown to condition more favorable purchase intentions for the new brand.

At this point, therefore, it appears that classical conditioning does offer significant potential for application in marketing, but not in simplistic fashion. Currently, consumer researchers are developing more sophisticated concepts and research in this area. (Readers interested in pursuing the latest developments and debates about classical conditioning in marketing might wish to begin with the readings in Note 20.)

INSTRUMENTAL CONDITIONING

Instrumental conditioning (IC) is a theory developed to explain learning that is goal directed. The term "instrumental" refers to the fact that the appropriate behavior is viewed as an instrument by which we can attain our goal. It has two distinctive differences from classical conditioning (CC):

- Whereas CC has a *reactive* learner, IC has an *active* learner.
- Whereas CC depends primarily on *contiguity* (the pairing of stimuli and responses), IC depends primarily on *reinforcement.*

In essence, IC shifts the focus from the stimulus side to the behavior side. For example, while the appearance of a can of 7-Up might lead us to pick it up and drink it, we won't do so *every* time we see it, but only those times when this behavior is instrumental to us—we wish to take a drink to help quench our thirst.

🐚 *Buying by the Peck*

Instrumental conditioning (IC): Goal directed: a new behavior is learned as a result of reinforcements of earlier trials.

The key figure in instrumental conditioning theory was B. F. Skinner, a famous professor at Harvard. His basic point was that people and animals behave in "purposive" ways all the time—we buy products in order to receive benefits, ask questions in order to receive answers, and so on. Although Skinner accepted that some learning might be of the CC variety, he viewed this as relatively unimportant—most human behavior, Skinner believed, is instrumental and depends upon the reinforcements we've received in the past.

Since reinforcement is the key to this form of learning, it is important that the rat, pigeon, or human figure out which response produced the reinforcement. Once the cause is identified, the actor will be able to reach his goal by producing the proper behavior: he will have *learned* how to get something he wants.

Skinner's major contributions went well beyond this simple point. In particular, he showed how reinforcements could be varied to produce certain forms of behavior. By providing *intermittent reinforcement* (that is, the subject's behavior is not rewarded on every occasion, but only sometimes), Skinner was able to show strong forms of learning that would persist for long periods of time. By varying his reinforcements for different forms of behavior, he was able to produce *shaping* of behavior. For example, a new pigeon might first be rewarded whenever he moved to the right side of the box, then rewarded only when he moved toward the bar, then only when touching the bar, then only when touching the bar three times, and so on. Eventually, the pigeon's behavior can be shaped into a very precise sequence of activities.

The many years of research by Skinner and his followers has had enormous impact. The stress on the importance of manipulating external stimuli has led to many applications of IC. In education, for example, Skinner was primarily responsible for the creation of *programmed learning*. In medicine, *biofeedback* and *behavior modification* programs are both drawn from his principles. Skinner believed that his principles could work to improve society as well: he wrote a novel, *Walden Two*, which takes place in a Utopian community built along Skinnerian principles. This stress on external control made Skinner a major and controversial figure in our society.[21]

Instrumental Conditioning and Marketing

As consumers, the operation of this form of learning in the marketplace is obvious to us. On a daily basis we learn which products and stores bring positive reinforcement to us and which ones do not. We "learn from our experience," avoid repeating purchases that disappoint us, and return to buy again the products that have rewarded us, at the stores from which we have obtained these rewards.

For marketers, however, the challenge is to control the external environment in order to create IC learning in their target markets. Three areas of application of IC in marketing include **reinforcement schedules, shaping**, and **discriminative stimuli.**[22] The normal case for marketers is to strive for consumers to receive *continuous reinforcements*—each time they buy and use the brand, they will be satisfied. Rebates and premiums can also serve reinforcement functions. In some promotional situations *intermittent reinforcement* can also be used—sweepstakes, games, and lotteries are examples of these strategies.

Shaping involves the reinforcement of a series of behaviors that will gradually bring the consumer to the desired final behavior. For example, positioning of sale items in a particular corner of a store can, over time, shape the path that some consumers will use as they shop there. Finally, *discriminative stimuli* are those that, when present, increase the probability of purchase behavior. Marketers strive mightily to achieve this status with logos, brand names, and in-store signs. For example, the sight of the "golden arches" on a billboard or at roadside has led many a driver to veer off in that direction. Similarly, a "Clearance Sale!" sign on a display can serve as a discriminative stimulus to attract special purchase probabilities from many retail shoppers.

A "discriminative stimulus" is one that increases the probability of purchase behavior. McDonald's "golden arches" sign has achieved this status for many consumers.

❧ Customer, You're a Gem...

A small jewelry store in Texas experimented with simple forms of reinforcement on its clientele. Names and phone numbers of over 400 customers were divided into three groups. Those in the "control" group received no contact. The other groups were contacted by phone: in one, the caller simply introduced himself (herself) and said, "I would like to thank you for being one of our customers." In the second group, the customer was thanked and also told about an upcoming diamond sale during the next two months. What were the results of this reinforcement? Store salespersons reported an immediate increase in store visits, with many persons from the first contact group stopping in to comment about "that nice person who called." Apparently, the simple "thanks" was seen as being more sincere than the call mentioning the special sale (this topic involves "attribution theory," which we examined in Chapter 5). Although sales for the year to date had been down, sales that month went up 27 percent over the prior year! Purchases by customers in the control group were unchanged—the entire increase came from customers who had received the reinforcing calls. Seventy percent came from customers in the first group, who had received only the simple "Thank you."[23]

FURTHER LAB APPROACHES TO MODIFYING CONSUMER BEHAVIOR

In addition to the basic CC and IC theories, more recent LAB developments also have many implications for marketing and public policy. In this section we'll take a brief look at three such approaches:

Using Modeling to Guide Consumer Behavior

Modeling: Learning achieved by having a consumer observe the actions of others (the models).

Modeling can be important in modifying behavior. Modeling is achieved by having a person observe the actions of others (the models) and the consequences of the models' behaviors. There are three ways in which marketers can use modeling:

- *Educating consumers in new behaviors.* Advertising can present models demonstrating how to use products. Thus, before ever performing an actual behavior, consumers are able to have mentally practiced it.

The antidrug forces use negative modeling in this ad: as the viewer imagines what will happen to the model, he or she also begins to imagine what could happen personally.

- *Increased purchase probabilities.* Modeling can also be used to focus on the consequences of behaviors, thereby representing a form of **vicarious reinforcement.** For example, when we see the pleasure that a model receives from a loved one's telephone call, we can easily feel that pleasure for ourselves. The probability of such a behavior on our part increases.

- *Discouraging negative consumer behaviors.* Modeling is also useful for discouraging consumers from behaviors such as smoking, drinking, and littering.[24] Here consumers will see a model experiencing negative outcomes from his or her actions and may be led to change the behavior rather than encounter the same consequences personally.

Ecological Design

Behavior modification is also apparent in the area called **ecological design** (sometimes termed "atmospherics" in marketing), which refers to the deliberate design of environments and stimuli to modify human behavior.[25] There are many ways in which this can be applied, some obvious and some not. For example, some retail stores use subliminal messages as a means of reducing negative customer behavior. Messages such as "Stealing is dishonest...," "I won't steal...," "I am honest...," and so forth are played on the store's sound system, but at a volume below the conscious threshold. According to one unconfirmed report, a large decline in shoplifting occurred during the nine months following the introduction of these stimuli.[26] (Notice that LAB does not claim that thinking does not occur here, but simply is interested in changing the shopper's environment so that desired behavior does occur.) Results from another study, this time involving music, are indicative of the potential power of this area in modifying customers' behavior:

🐂 Buying Beets by the Beat

Consumers and store managers like having music in the store—it makes shopping a more pleasant experience and it may encourage customers to spend more money. This suggestion was tested over a two-month period in a medium-sized supermarket in the southwest United States. Each day, one of three randomly chosen treatments was used in the store: no music (the control condition), "slow" music (averaging 60 beats per minute), or "fast" music (averaging 108 beats per minute), with the volume set to soft background music. Measures were taken of shoppers' awareness of the music, walking speed, and sales. Results showed that consumers paid little attention to the music itself—when asked if music had been playing in the store they'd just left, customers were equally likely to report "Yes," "No," or "Don't Know." Whatever effects might occur, then, would seem to be happening without conscious control by consumers.

And interesting behavioral effects were found. The average consumer walked 17 percent faster with the fast music than with the slow music (when no music was playing consumers walked at a pace about midway between the two). Most important from the marketers' point of view, the days in which slow music was played had *38 percent higher dollar sales* than when fast music had been playing—this amounted to an almost $5,000-per-day increase in sales for that store! (Again, the days without music averaged sales that were midway between the music figures.) This would seem to call for marketers to use soft, slow music to retain customers in their stores, where they'll buy more. However, in other situations, such as fast-food outlets at lunch time, management may want to switch on the rock n' roll to move business through the store. As a consumer,

Vicarious reinforcement: Learning achieved when a consumer observes positive outcomes of behaviors undertaken by others.

Ecological design: The deliberate design of retail environments to modify human behavior.

moreover, the next time you hear "Muzak" in a store, you may want to step up your pace if you want to save money![27]

All aspects of a store are potential targets for ecological design. Among some other interesting reports,

- J. C. Penney developed *walking lanes* through its stores to route people past many more items than if they were allowed to go directly. (Why don't you visit a nearby store and take this tour sometime?)

- K-mart is testing the use of *infrared light beams* to track consumers through areas of their stores. This would allow more timely management of marketing actions. For example, when certain areas have few shoppers, "blue-light specials" can be added as discriminative stimuli to draw people there.

- *Smells* are being tested for their sales effects. In one jewelry store study, both a floral and a spicy aroma held men longer in certain store sections, while only the floral aroma worked for women.

- Even *parking lots* aren't off limits. The firm that operates a number of 7-Eleven and Hoagy's Corner stores, for example, dealt with young people hanging out around the stores by installing outside speakers and playing Mozart, Mantovani, and 1960s folk songs. Result: "They hated it. . . . A lot of kids . . . are looking for another place to hang."[28]

Ethical Considerations in Behavioral Modification

Consumers are obviously quite responsive to stimuli in their environments. Marketers control some aspects of these stimuli (especially within a store and within an ad). Since LAB learning theory has stressed how behavior can be shaped and controlled, it is a natural force for marketers to use. In so doing, however, we cannot escape questions of responsible behavior. Nord and Peter, in proposing that attention be given to behavior

FROM NOW ON, SHOPLIFTING IN THE U.S. IS A VERY, VERY DIRTY BUSINESS.

An ad aimed at reducing shoplifting. The product is a special tag attached to apparel in retail stores. When a garment is shoplifted, the thief is likely to find it ruined by the burst of dye that emerges when the tag is incorrectly removed. Thefts reportedly dropped 70 percent to 90 percent in European stores that used this tag.

modification, recognized that "there are major ethical/moral issues involved" in its use in marketing:

> We maintain that behavior modification is not, in itself, immoral or unethical, but that valid ethical/moral concerns stem from (1) the ends to which the technology is used and (2) the process by which these needs are determined. The application of these techniques in marketing seems ethically vulnerable on both these counts. Efforts to market products rarely include the subject whose behavior is modified, as a full participant in determining either the use of the technology or the ends to which it is put. There are, of course, examples...which many people believe are socially desirable (reduction in littering, pollution, and smoking and consumer education efforts). However, there appear to be many other applications which have few redeeming social benefits....Since it is clear that the type of emotions often labeled "needs" or motives can be developed through conditioning and modeling processes, the defense that marketing satisfies needs is not fully adequate.[29]

There are no easy answers in this area. In the abstract, we need to address complex systems of philosophy and ethics, about which persons of good will can disagree. At a practical level, answers will depend on how effective various techniques actually are. At this stage consumer researchers have few answers to this question. For example, several years ago a chief official of the FTC charged that cigarette companies were running ads showing background scenes whose message was health, freshness, and well-being (for example, scenes of mountain lakes or young handsome men and women). Is it likely that CC would work to influence consumers' actual views of cigarettes in this way? Should such scenes be banned? (If you are interested in pursuing further thinking in this area, you may wish to begin with the readings listed in Note 30.)

UNDERSTANDING CONSUMER PURCHASE PATTERNS

As a final topic within the LAB perspective, let's switch our focus to strictly purchase behaviors and briefly examine **consumer purchase patterns.** These are measures of a consumer's (or household's) exact brand purchases over a certain time period. The notion of a "pattern" arises because the purchases are rarely random: usually one or several brands will dominate, but only rarely will exactly the same brand be bought on every single purchase. Further, the reason that this is "learning" in the LAB view is that these purchases are seen as *responses to stimuli*: researchers are interested in seeing what stimulus factors can assist the development of a pattern of brand loyalty or can change a pattern by stimulating a brand-switching response.

Consumer purchase patterns: Regularities in a consumer's brand purchases over a time period.

Within the real world of marketing, moreover, for many products, it is the patterns of consumers' purchases over time that make the difference between success or failure. Marketers purchase **consumer panel data** from research firms. These firms gather samples of consumers who agree to provide records of all their purchases over a long time. If a panel is representative, its results can be projected to the marketplace as a whole, to provide marketers with insights as to "what's going on out there."

Consumer panel data: Information from consumers who provide records of all their purchases over a time period.

Using the LAB perspective, marketers are interested in how their promotional, product, or price decisions will affect purchase patterns, and how brands compete with each other. The chances that a particular brand will be bought at a particular time are hard to predict with certainty, because considerable brand switching goes on. This means that the topic of probability becomes central to research on purchase patterns.

Probability models:
Mathematical systems
that represent market-
place behavior.

Marketers for some time have been interested in developing quantitative **probability models** (technically termed *stochastic* (stō-kas-tic) models) of purchase behavior, based on the probability that a consumer will purchase a particular brand.

Once purchase patterns are modeled as probabilities, consumer researchers can investigate a number of strategic issues. For example, we are able to assess which consumers are loyal users, which are "switchers" among brands, and which are not using the product at all. We can also easily see which consumers are "heavy users" and which are "light users." Since the panel data also contain information about each consumer's demographics (age, income, etc.), we are able to evaluate who is in each segment and how easy it may be to reach them.

Beyond segmentation strategy, information on consumer purchase patterns can be used to study the effects of specific marketing mix decisions. In one study, for example, researchers discovered that the effects of coupons were different between margarine and flour, with margarine the more sensitive product for coupon use. Distinct effects on consumer purchase patterns were measured—normally about 40 percent of consumers switch their margarine brand purchase, but when a coupon was included, 65 percent of consumers switched brands.[31]

These kinds of analyses can be conducted for many forms of promotion-price deals, displays, coupons, and advertising simply by tracing their effects on consumers' purchase patterns. With the advent of new technologies, the study of brand loyalty and brand switching is growing even more rapidly. For example, the Universal Product Code **scanners** at supermarket checkout counters have revolutionized the study of consumer purchase patterns. Consumer panel research firms now use these devices to register every brand and purchase as it occurs at the checkout. The members of these panels use special credit cards to make their purchases, so all information is immediately available in the computer. Also, in some panels, the consumers' television sets at home are arranged (via "split cables") to receive different versions of TV commercials. These consumers' purchases can be analyzed to discover which type of advertising produces more sales. Thus new technology means that very fast feedback on effects of special promotional campaigns is now possible through studying consumer purchase patterns.

Scanners: Comput-
erized devices that
register every brand
and price as sold at
checkout: provide mar-
keters with instanta-
neous information on
consumer behaviors.

Stability in Purchase Patterns: Brand Loyalty

Consumer behavior has a large component of stability to it. This stability reflects consumers having learned specific purchase behaviors and having found these to be rewarding. The term we apply to the class of repeated brand purchases is **brand loyalty.** Brand loyalty can bring positive benefits to both consumers and marketers.

For a consumer, brand-loyal behavior offers (1) savings in time, (2) savings in decision-making effort, and (3) lowered risks of buying an unsatisfactory product. On the other hand, it may mean paying higher prices, and it also carries the risk of missing new improvements available from other brands in the market. For the marketer, brand loyalty is also beneficial, since it provides a solid base of customers into the future. Within the competitive market, of course, this is a double-edged sword, since consumers who are loyal to other brands are difficult to attract away.

In a research vein, we should note that brand loyalty is a more difficult phenomenon to define in detail than we might first expect. For example, one insightful overview reports that over 50 different definitions of brand loyalty have been offered in the consumer literature![32] Whatever the research difficulties in brand loyalty, though, the fact is that marketers are striving to achieve it for their brands.

Brand loyalty: A
favorable attitude to-
ward, and consistent
purchases of, a particu-
lar brand.

At the present time there is also considerable uncertainty about the extent to which consumer brand loyalty might be changing. The 1980s brought significant retail industry changes (increased retailer power, increased promotional price dealing, increased store brands) that began to pull consumers away from loyalty to nationally advertised brands. This decline in loyalty appears to have leveled off, but the situation is still in flux due to continuing changes in the retailing environment.[33] Despite changes in the larger environment, of course, most marketers are continuing to strive for as much loyalty as possible. In this regard, new "frequency marketing" programs have become an important option, as the following discussion shows:

🐚 Rewarding the Loyal: Treat Them Royal!

The airline industry has traditionally faced difficult marketing problems, since prices can easily be met by competitors, as can in-flight services. Time is an important factor for many travelers, and scheduled departures will often override all but the strongest brand preferences in this market. A few years ago, however, the airlines developed a unique program to "create" brand loyalty among their most important class of passengers—the "frequent flyers." Frequent flyers (typically businesspersons, often marketers) are the 20 percent of airline passengers who account for about 80 percent of an airline's revenues because they fly so often. As a frequent flyer flew a particular line more often, he or she would build up more points, which could then be cashed in for such rewards as upgraded seating to first class, free tickets, or, if many miles had been accumulated, free vacations at international resorts.

Consumer response was so positive that the idea spread rapidly, first to all the airlines, then to their travel partners (major hotel chains, car rental firms, etc.), then to a host of other businesses. Food products ("The Kool-Aid Club"), department stores (Dallas-based Neiman-Marcus provides its "In Circle" members rewards in exchange for minimum purchases of $3,000 per year), restaurants, and dog foods are among those with programs. There is now even an industry newsletter to help marketers keep up. It defines **frequency marketing** as an activity " . . . to identify, maintain, and increase the yield from Best Customers, through long-term, interactive value-added relationships," and provides details on successful ideas and programs around the country.[34] According to a senior vice president of Hyatt Hotels, "[Frequency-marketing] is the way companies will market themselves in the 1990s and for years to come." Might this go too far, though? The continuing decline in hard liquor sales led several brands—Cutty Sark and Dewar's White Label among them—to create "Frequent Drinker" programs for their customers![35]

Frequency marketing: Activities that encourage long-term, interactive value-added relationships with a firm's best customers.

■ SUMMARY

WHAT IS CONSUMER LEARNING?

Learning is concerned with the effects of *experience*. There are five key factors involved in consumer learning: (1) stimuli, (2) knowledge or memory, (3) internal processes, (4) responses, and (5) time. The fact that all these factors cannot be studied at the same time has led to two distinct approaches to research on learning: *learning as behavior (LAB)* and *learning is knowledge (LIK)*. Both views offer useful insights into consumer behavior.

THE LEARNING IS KNOWLEDGE VIEW

The chapter devoted less space to the learning is knowledge view, since this has been the dominant approach taken in earlier chapters in this text. The LIK view is based upon consumer information processing theory. The LIK approach emphasizes the "internal world" of the consumer and has enjoyed great popularity in recent years: *it stresses that knowledge, rather than behavior, is the best indicator of learning*. Within the LIK view of learning, long-term memory (LTM) provides the storage center for our knowledge—increases in this knowledge base constitute learning. Three LIK application areas were examined. First, we examined *learning in children*, looking at why cognitive limitations can cause controversy over advertising aimed at kids. We then turned to the issue of *measuring consumer learning*, including the study of cognitive responses to advertising. Our third topic concerned *consumer mislearning*, including both deceptive advertising issues and some surprising findings about consumers' miscomprehension of broadcast messages.

THE LEARNING AS BEHAVIOR VIEW

The second half of the chapter examined the learning as behavior approach. The LAB approach is associated with behaviorism: *it views learning to be a relatively permanent change in behavior that occurs as a result of experience*. Our discussion of LAB proceeded in three sections, covering two primary LAB theories of learning plus many recent extensions and developments in this area. We first discussed Pavlov's famous *classical conditioning (CC)* experiments, which taught dogs to salivate at the sound of a tuning fork. We noted applications of this conditioning approach in the real world of marketing, including the design of Coke's advertising and an experiment involving pens and music. We then examined the different approach taken by Skinner's famous *instrumental condition (IC)* experiments, which were developed around the idea of goal-directed learning. An experiment in a jewelry store indicated the positive effects *reinforcement* can have.

Our third section on LAB discussed recent developments within the LAB perspective. These include modeling effects and ecological design (example: music in the supermarket). Both reflect the emerging practice of *behavior modification*, in which an environment is structured to develop certain types of consumer behaviors. We also noted that this practice has raised some ethical questions for marketers to address in the future. We then discussed the marketing importance of understanding consumer purchase patterns, including both *brand switching* and *brand loyalty*.

■ KEY TERMS

learning	source derogations	instrumental conditioning (IC)	consumer purchase patterns
learning as behavior (LAB)	counterarguments	reinforcement schedules	consumer panel data
learning is knowledge (LIK)	mislearning	discriminative stimuli	probability models
behaviorism	unconscionable lie	continuous reinforcements	scanners
CARU	claim-fact discrepancy	modeling	brand loyalty
copy testing	claim-belief interaction	vicarious reinforcement	frequency marketing
cognitive responses	miscomprehension	ecological design	
support arguments	classical conditioning (CC)	brand switching	

■ REVIEW QUESTIONS AND EXPERIENTIAL EXERCISES

[E = Application extension or experiential exercise]

1. Compare and contrast the two basic research approaches to learning.

2. The text discussed childhood as the period in which we form our individual structures of consumer values and buying styles. It also stated that children are a "vulnerable segment." What does this mean? What are its implications?

3. Comment on the "miscomprehension" results presented in the text. What do you think are some reasons why consumers miscomprehend TV ads? What if anything can or should be done about this?

4. Explain, providing examples, the differences between classical conditioning and instrumental conditioning.

5. Consumer research concludes that consumers are responsive to environmental stimuli that lead to their behavior being shaped and controlled. What are the ethical implications for marketers? For public policymakers?

6. Assume you were arguing in favor of stronger controls on behavior modification attempts by marketers. What would your key arguments be? If you were opposed to such controls, what would your key arguments be?

7. Explain why marketers should be interested in learning about consumers' purchase patterns for their products.

8. Brand-loyal behavior offers advantages and disadvantages for both consumers and marketers. Explain. Is "proportion of purchases" a good measure of brand loyalty? What might a better one include?

9. [E] Learn more about the issues surrounding the "children's" television debates. Choose one of the following options and write a brief report on your findings:

   a. Use the references in Notes 3 to 5 to locate readings on the subject.

   b. Use the reference section of your library to locate recent articles on the subject.

   c. Arrange to watch several hours of Saturday morning television with children at different age stages of Piaget's system. Observe their reactions and interview them if possible.

10. [E] Create a "Word Game" quiz, listing 15 product categories. Ask a sample of 20 people to list the first and second brands that come to mind. Summarize your findings in a brief report. Here are some possibilities:

   a. Tires
   b. Tissues
   c. Pizza
   d. Toilet paper
   e. Catsup
   f. Cameras
   g. Running shoes
   h. Soft drinks
   i. Bacon
   j. Dress shoes
   k. Polo shirts
   l. Business suits

11. [E] Show four ads to at least five different friends. Ask them to write down all thoughts that came to mind while reading each ad. Classify these thoughts as support arguments, source derogations, and counterarguments. How do the patterns of these thoughts relate to your friends' preferences for the products advertised?

12. [E] Use the listings in Notes 9 through 15 to locate readings on recent developments on *one* of the following topics that most interests you. Write a brief report on your findings.

   a. Cognitive responses to advertising

   b. Deceptive advertising

   c. Miscomprehension of advertising

13. [E] Search through magazines to locate efforts by advertisers to pair positive stimuli with their brands. Provide three generalized statements about what you discovered, and cut out examples of each.

14. [E] Use the listings in Notes 19 through 36 to locate readings on *one* of the LAB-related topics in marketing. Write a brief report on your findings.

15. [E] Interview a local store manager concerning LAB-related topics such as music in the store, efforts to combat shoplifting, planned reinforcements, placement of strategic stimuli, and so forth. Are consumers responsive to particular types of stimuli? Write a brief report on your findings.

■ SUGGESTED READING

■ This chapter ranges across topics, so no single article will cover most of its material. For a good basic discussion of the children's area, see the classic article by Scott Ward, "Consumer Socialization," *Journal of Consumer Research*, Vol. 1 (September 1974), pp. 1–14; the references in Notes 4–7 then bring us up to date on this interesting area. For insights on why deceptive advertising is such a challenging area, see Gary T. Ford and John E. Calfee, "Recent Developments in FTC Policy on Deception," *Journal of Marketing*, Vol. 50 (July 1986), pp. 82–103. The references in Note 12 provide further extensions on this issue. For a retailing perspective related to our conditioning discussions, you may enjoy Mary Jo Bitner, "Servicescapes: The Impact of Physical Surroundings on Customers and Employees," *Journal of Marketing*, Vol. 56 (April 1992), pp. 57–71. Finally, for a practical look at managing brand loyalty, you may enjoy Terry Vavra, *Aftermarketing: How to Keep Customers for Life through Relationship Marketing*, Homewood, IL: Business One Irwin, 1992.

11

CONSUMER ATTITUDES

BRANDS WORTH MANY GRANDS

During recent years, powerful forces have been changing the face of consumer marketing. *Megamergers*—in which one giant firm would buy another and capture its markets—have swept the United States. For example, Philip Morris, Inc., gobbled up the giant General Foods corporation and then turned and "creamed" Kraft, while RJR, another tobacco giant, crunched Nabisco into its spreading empire.

According to the new buyers, these firms were giant bargains sitting on the stock market shelf. One high-level dealmaker explained that a key factor was that the concept of *brand equity* was missing from the accounting assets for these firms: "Brand equity, being an off-balance-sheet item, [underlies] undervalued or bargain companies." The president of Canada Dry stated: "Brand equity is driving all of Wall Street."

What is "brand equity"? Simply, it is the extra value that belongs to a brand name. As one market manager put it, *"A petroleum jelly factory is much more valuable if its output can be called 'Vaseline.'"* In reality, brand equity is based upon the *attitudes* that consumers hold about a particular brand. In this chapter we'll learn more about what consumer attitudes are, how they can be measured, and what they mean for marketers.[1]

■ WHAT ARE CONSUMER ATTITUDES?

Of all the concepts in consumer behavior, many experts believe that attitudes are the most significant. Why are attitudes such a key concept? What do they represent? Basically, *attitudes represent our summary evaluations* of various elements in the world around us. "I like Pepsi" is the type of attitudinal statement that we make every day.

Because their purpose is to summarize a consumer's evaluation of a particular product, attitudes can offer tremendously important information to marketers. By knowing what consumers' attitudes are, a marketer should be able to (1) *understand* why current sales are strong or not and (2) *improve* the marketing mix to improve consumer's attitudes. For these reasons marketers are continuously monitoring con-

"Attitude" originally referred to a person's physical position. Now it refers to a person's mental position, or evaluation.

sumers' attitudes and working to influence them. Besides sales themselves, attitudes may well be the most measured aspects of consumer behavior.

ATTITUDES DEFINED

The term **attitude** is derived from the Latin words for "posture" or "physical position." The general notion was that a body's physical attitudes suggested the type of action in which a person would engage. The famous statue of the Greek discus thrower, for example, presents a striking attitude that leaves little doubt of the movements that are to come. In recent times, the concept of attitude has been broadened to reflect a person's mental position or evaluation of an object. Gordon Allport's classic definition is

> Attitudes are learned predispositions to respond to an object or class of objects in a consistently favorable or unfavorable way.[2]

Several aspects of the definition help us to understand this topic. The fact that attitudes are *mental positions* means that marketers must try to infer them through research measures—they cannot be observed directly. The fact that attitudes are *learned* means that they will be affected by information and experiences. While attitudes are relatively enduring (that is, we tend to hold them for rather long periods of time), *attitude change* is possible. For obvious reasons, great attention is given to the topics of attitude formation and attitude change by marketers.

Attitude: A learned predisposition to respond to an object in a consistently favorable or unfavorable way.

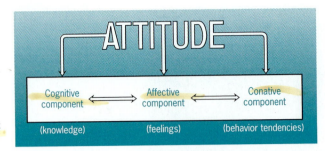

FIGURE 11-1 The Three Components of Attitudes

The fact that attitudes are **predispositions to respond** indicates their relationship with consumer's *actual behaviors.* Knowing a consumer's attitude toward a particular brand should help us to understand how he or she will react to that brand in the future. For example, if Jean does not like Cheer, we would not expect to see her buying it. Finally, the term *object* in our definition has a broad meaning. Consumers have attitudes toward entire product categories ("I never did care for squid"), stores (K-mart), brands (Pepsi), styles, and so forth. Thus it's clear that consumers have a vast array of attitudes. These attitudes are important reflectors of what we think, how we feel, and how we will behave.

ATTITUDES HAVE THREE COMPONENTS

Cognitive component: Knowledge or beliefs about an attitude object.

Affective component: Feelings about an attitude object.

Conative component: The tendency to act toward an attitude object.

Cognitive consistency: Striving for harmonious relationships among thoughts and feelings.

The primary view of human behavior, at least since the time of the early Greek philosophers, has been that all behavior is actually a combination of mental, emotional, and physical dimensions (popularized as the "think-feel-do" perspective we've seen elsewhere in the text). This perspective resulted in the classic "three-component" view of attitudes, depicted in Figure 11-1. The **cognitive component** refers to the knowledge or beliefs the person has about the attitude object (e.g., "The Mercedes is an expensive automobile"). "Affect" is a technical term for positive or negative feelings; thus the **affective component** reflects feelings regarding the attitude object (e.g., "I like the Mercedes"). The **conative component** reflects behavioral tendencies toward the attitude object (e.g., "I would like to buy a new Mercedes").[3]

The three components are not entirely independent from one another, of course. **Cognitive consistency**—the concept that consumers strive for harmonious relationships in our thoughts and feelings—is a key concept underlying consumer attitudes. As we saw in our chapter on motivation, a psychic tension is likely to arise when we have inconsistent thoughts. For example, how would you feel if you held the following thoughts: "I really like that Mercedes (affective)... it is an ugly car (cognitive)." Most consumers would feel somewhat uneasy with these two thoughts representing their current state of affairs together, and would likely revise one of them to be slightly more consistent with the other (that is, I would either like it a little less or would come to think of it as not quite so unattractive). Thus we expect to see a basic consistency among the components of a consumer's attitude.

This point holds several key implications for marketers. Regarding *attitude formation,* for example, it suggests that marketers should be able to use already favorable attitudes to help create a new favorable attitude. Product endorsement ads are a common example of this strategy. Having our favorite celebrity endorse a new product increases our chances of developing a positive attitude toward that product. Regarding *attitude change,* the forces toward cognitive consistency indicate that marketers will need to plan for some possible resistance to their persuasive attempts if consumers already have some negative elements in their attitude components. For example, consumers who have been dissatisfied in the past are often difficult to regain as customers.

ATTITUDES ARE USEFUL TO CONSUMERS

Why are consumers motivated to form and maintain their attitudes? Basically, because *attitudes are useful* to them. This raises the issue of the motivational basis for attitudes. Four key functions that attitudes serve are:

- **Adjustment function.** Attitudes sometimes help consumers to adjust their likes and dislikes to the realities of their external environment. Examples of the adjustment function are all around us. Consumers who have a positive first experience with purchases from The Gap are likely to adjust their overall attitudes to be positive toward shopping again at this store. Also, in supermarkets, some consumers believe that private labels offer more "value for the money" and hold positive attitudes toward them. In each of these cases, the attitudes that are held provide a way of simplifying a consumer's decisions on a daily basis.

    Adjustment function: Attitudes help consumers adapt to the marketplace.

- **Ego-defense function.** Sometimes attitudes are helpful in protecting consumers' egos from threats to their self-identities: "I guess I'll die someday, but not now," "I'm socially acceptable," and so on are common attitudes that people have that help in ego defense. Within marketing, ego-defense attitudes are likely to be operating in such areas as sex appeal, social attractiveness, and physical fears of injury or death. Marketers of such personal care products as deodorants or diets can expect this attitude function to be at work in a large segment of their target markets.

    Ego-defense function: Attitudes help in protecting consumers from injury to their self-identities.

- **Value-expressive function.** In some cases, consumer attitudes allow strongly held personal values to be expressed in consumer behavior. For example, if Richard Smith has a strong need for power, he may develop quite favorable attitudes toward products that help him feel powerful, such as motorcycles. If Linda Taylor places a high value on personal success, she'll be likely to have positive attitudes toward products that allow her to express her own success—Cross pens, a designer briefcase, and other status goods.

    Value-expressive function: Attitudes enable personal values to be expressed in consumer behavior.

- **Object-appraisal function.** Sometimes termed the "knowledge function," this refers to the fact that attitudes also help consumers to organize and add structure to their perceptions of the external world. For example, if Peter Franklin sees the new box-shaped Porsche driving by, his attitude toward this new car will help to quickly remind him that he likes it, as well as some things he knows about it. As a summary evaluation, therefore, his attitude helps him deal efficiently with familiar objects in his environment. Thus the object appraisal of attitudes helps to govern consumers' *selective perception* processes.[4]

    Object-appraisal function: Attitudes help consumers to organize their knowledge about the marketplace.

Any particular attitude may perform more than one of the functions. Thus attitudes are extremely helpful to consumers. In addition, awareness of the attitudes consumers hold can be extremely helpful to marketers.

■ CONSUMER ATTITUDES AND BRAND MANAGEMENT

Before turning to a detailed examination of consumer attitudes themselves, it may be useful to highlight some key points about why marketing managers are so interested

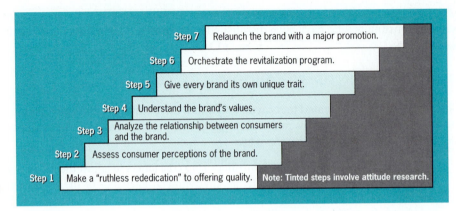

Step 7	Relaunch the brand with a major promotion.
Step 6	Orchestrate the revitalization program.
Step 5	Give every brand its own unique trait.
Step 4	Understand the brand's values.
Step 3	Analyze the relationship between consumers and the brand.
Step 2	Assess consumer perceptions of the brand.
Step 1	Make a "ruthless rededication" to offering quality.	Note: Tinted steps involve attitude research.

FIGURE 11-2 How One Major Ad Agency Revives a Brand

Brand attitude: The feelings and evaluations consumers hold about a brand.

in consumer attitudes. Traditionally, this interest has been centered on **brand attitudes**, or the feelings and evaluations consumers hold about a brand. Measurement of brand attitudes is a truly basic part of the management of a brand.

Figure 11-2 demonstrates this point well. It outlines the program that a major advertising agency recommends to marketers for a brand that is not doing well. According to Ogilvy & Mather's president, "If you're in charge of a brand which is in need of revitalization, then you're in charge of a brand/consumer relationship which is no longer healthy, which is no longer working. You need to find out what's gone wrong with the relationship." Notice the significance of consumer attitudes in this proposal: each tinted step in Figure 11-2 involves decisions based upon the measurement of consumer attitudes.[5]

Brand equity: The value of a brand name for the company that owns it.

In this regard, you may recall the opening vignette for this chapter indicated that **brand equity** has become a key issue in corporate takeovers. Brand equity refers to the value of a brand name for the company that owns it. In one study, for example, *Financial World* magazine reported that the name "Marlboro" is the world's most valuable brand name, worth an estimated $31 billion, or about twice its annual sales revenue.[6]

In this section, however, let's look at the marketing implications of brand equity. Do marketing managers see brand equity as important? When the Marketing Science Institute polled its members—comprised of many of the world's most prominent marketing companies—on priority issues, brand equity was the runaway winner as top research priority. "We buried brand equity in the middle of the deck to see what would happen, and all of the groups pulled it out and put it on top," reports MSI's president. Recently, for example, Colgate-Palmolive Co. hired a director of "equity management" to guard the value in Colgate-Palmolive brands.

Market researchers are now at work to try to measure brand equity. According to the president of a major research firm, "There are four factors you must measure. First is *prominence*, which is easy. Just ask people what name comes to mind. Second is how favorable the *associations* are—also easy...third is the *"portrait"* enlisted by a brand or image...fourth is the *flexibility* of the brand—can the brand be generalized or used on other things? [Then] the task of weighing the various factors and pulling the techniques together remains to be done."[7]

Exhibit 11-1 gives us some insight on how U.S. consumers view certain brands. You might enjoy seeing how well you can predict the "Top 10" brand names, then see if you can even name the product or service offered by those at the bottom. Beyond these listings, you may want to test your insights into the competitive battles given at the end of the exhibit.

EXHIBIT 11-1

America's Top (and Bottom) Brands

Listed below are the product categories for the 10 "most powerful" brand names, according to surveys of American consumers, who were asked about both their *recognition* of the name and their *opinion* or *esteem* for the brand. This listing is followed by the 10 brand names that finished at the bottom of a similar survey. See how well you can do in guessing the name of the most powerful brands, then in guessing the product or service of the least powerful brands' names. The answers are given in Note 9.

I.   THE "TOP 10"

PRODUCT/SERVICE	BRAND NAME	MY ATTITUDE TOWARD THIS BRAND IS:
1. Soft drinks	_____	_____
2. Soups	_____	_____
3. Entertainment	_____	_____
4. Soft drinks	_____	_____
5. Cameras, film	_____	_____
6. Television network	_____	_____
7. Household tools	_____	_____
8. Breakfast cereals	_____	_____
9. Hamburgers	_____	_____
10. Chocolate	_____	_____

II.   THE "BOTTOM 10"

PRODUCT/SERVICE	BRAND NAME	MY ATTITUDE TOWARD THIS BRAND IS:
663. _____	Export "A"	_____
664. _____	Klipsch	_____
665. _____	Primerica	_____
666. _____	Bang & Olufsen	_____
667. _____	Asahi	_____
668. _____	Blue Mountain	_____
669. _____	Daewoo	_____
670. _____	Gaggenau	_____
671. _____	Ricola	_____
672. _____	Exide	_____

III. COMPETITIVE STRUGGLES: WHICH BRAND NAME IS MORE POWERFUL?[*]

     1. Duracell versus Energizer? _____

     2. Burger King versus Wendy's? _____

     3. Nike versus Reebok? _____

     4. Federal Express versus UPS? _____

     5. Folgers versus Maxwell House? _____

[*] "Power" reflects a combination of consumers' *recognition* of the brand name and their *opinion* of the brand.

The Marriott Corporation estimates that adding its name to a new lower-priced line, Fairfield Inn, increased the line's occupancy rate by 15 percent. (Note the lower-left portion of the roadside sign.)

🐦 Brands Borrow on Equity

Brand extension: A new product offering that uses an existing brand's name.

When a brand name has high brand equity, one natural way to capitalize on it is to offer **brand extensions,** in which the brand's name is also given to a new product. Consumers should respond more positively to the new product because of their positive attitudes toward the existing brand name. This worked well for Dole, which recently retained a research firm to investigate the nature of brand equity for its name. The firm's president reports: "Dole had a readout that went way beyond pineapple. It was all about health, sunshine . . . and health foods." These results guided Dole to its new logo, a bright yellow sunburst, and to market Dole Fruit Juice Bars, which were highly successful. Similarly, Marriott estimated that adding its name to its new lower-priced line, Fairfield Inn, increased occupancy rates by 15 percent.[8]

🐦 Cadillac Loses Equity and Interest

While brand extensions can be extremely lucrative, they are subject to limitations based upon the exact nature of consumers' images of the brand. For example, a Walt Disney Co. study found that consumers would not accept Disney movies for adults—Disney meant children's and family entertainment. Rather than try to fight this consumer image, Disney launched Touchstone Films.

Cadillac wasn't so fortunate in the 1980s when it introduced the Cimarron model, a small car that was a relative of the Pontiac 2000 and Chevrolet Cavalier models. The Cimarron was aimed at a less affluent buyer who would not be likely to buy a Cadillac. "The decision was . . . shortsighted," reflects a General Motors executive.

"Financial analysts would argue that . . . any sale would be one we wouldn't have gotten otherwise . . . the bean counters said, 'We'll get this many dollars for every model sold,' [but] there was no thinking about brand equity . . . a horrible mistake."

The Cimarron was dropped in 1988. Although there is no precise estimate of its cost to Cadillac's brand equity, the survey reported in Exhibit 11-1 gives us some interesting insights (not shown in the exhibit). In 1988, Cadillac ranked 16th in *public awareness* of the brand name—a very strong showing. On the other component of the power index, *opinion* or *esteem* for the brand, however, Cadillac landed in 84th place! A General Motors analyst mused, "Even though brand equity may sometimes be hard to [precisely] define, it's pretty clear when you've lost it."[10]

Although a number of advances have recently been made on the topic of brand equity (interested readers may wish to pursue the recent citations in Note 11), our major point here is to appreciate the central role that consumers' attitudes play for marketing decisions. Our next section delves into the nature of these attitudes and how marketers obtain measures of them.

■ THE ATTITUDE REVOLUTION: MULTIATTRIBUTE MODELS

A little over 20 years ago, the marketing world discovered the area of multiattribute attitude models and reacted with an explosion of research studies. Within this section we'll briefly examine the nature of these models and how they can help to provide marketing insights into the dynamic consumer marketplace.

THE BASIC MULTIATTRIBUTE MODEL

At this point you may be wondering why marketers don't just ask consumers, "How much do you like or dislike Tide?" In other words, if an **overall evaluation** is what we're after, why not just measure it directly? The answer is that marketers do measure it directly and do use the overall measure for certain purposes. Notice, however, that such a simple measure of attitude *doesn't tell us why* the consumer feels the way he or she does, nor does it suggest anything that we might be able to do about changing that attitude. It is precisely in this area that multiattribute attitude models offer their strongest benefits.

Basically, a **multiattribute model** views an attitude object (brand, store, etc.) as possessing *many attributes* (characteristics) that provide the basis on which consumers' attitudes will depend. Thus *the attitude a consumer has toward a brand will depend on the beliefs that consumer holds about what the brand has to offer*. Each belief pertains to one attribute, thus leading to the designation as a multiattribute model. The major advantage of multiattribute models over the simpler overall evaluation measure of attitude is in gaining understanding of attitudinal structure. *Diagnosis* of brand strengths and weaknesses on relevant product attributes can suggest specific changes in a brand and its marketing support.

To gain a clear understanding of the nature of these models, we'll begin by stressing one basic form that has been much used within marketing. (Note: Some researchers in marketing prefer other forms of this model: our Notes will inform you where you can learn about your options. For now, however, we'll begin with this basic

Overall evaluation: A single measure of how much a consumer likes or dislikes an attitude object.

Multiattribute model: Consumers' attitudes depend on attribute importance and beliefs about how well a brand provides each attribute.

one because it is especially easy to learn and use.) The basic formula for a multiattribute model is

$$A_j = \sum_{i=1}^{n} B_{ij} I_i$$

where

i = attribute or product characteristic

j = brand

such that

A = the consumer's *attitude* score for brand j

I = the *importance weight* given to attribute i by this consumer

B = the consumer's *belief* as to the extent to which a satisfactory level of attribute i is offered by brand j

Although the formula may appear complex, in fact it is not, and with a little practice you'll easily see how this type of model works. Since this model is a compositional one, we will begin with the separate attributes and together "compose" them into the larger measure of overall attitude. Exhibit 11-2's example helps with the discussion. **To learn the model best, enter your personal ratings into Exhibit 11-2 as we go along and then calculate your attitudes toward these outlets.**

Attributes (i)

Attributes provide the basic dimensionality of this model and are of crucial importance. Notice that the left-hand column contains five attributes that consumers might associate with the fast-food product category. To understand the model better, it is a good idea for you to add some further attributes to the listing, in the space below "Price."

Importance (I)

Although all the attributes are relevant, we'd not expect them to be equally important. Thus the "importance weight" element of the model allows us to vary the impact that different attributes will have on consumers' attitudes. Within our example, we've included one consumer's—Andy Taylor's—ratings for discussion purposes, using a 1 to 7 scale (with 1 = unimportant and 7 = very important). Notice that Andy is quite concerned with location, "atmosphere," and taste and reports that price is relatively unimportant to him. (We'll expect other consumers to have different patterns of importance.) You should enter your own weights at this point on the empty lines, using the additional attributes you've added as well as the ones listed here.

Beliefs (B)

In our form of the model, the belief measure represents the extent to which each fast-food restaurant offers satisfaction on the attribute in question. Andy's ratings of his local Watta-Burger are shown in the exhibit (again on a 1 to 7 scale, with 1 = very poor and 7 = very good). Notice that Andy views Watta-Burger to have good-tasting food at very low prices, but to offer little atmosphere and little nutrition and to be in a somewhat inconvenient location. Continuing with your own example, fill in *your* belief ratings for each attribute for McDonald's, Burger King, Wendy's, and any other fast-food outlets you'd like to assess.

Multiattribute Attitude Model Calculations

Attribute (i)	Importance (I)	Beliefs (B)				
		Watta-Burger	McDonald's	Burger King	Wendy's	(Other)
"Atmosphere"	(6) ———	(2)	———	———	———	———
Location	(6) ———	(4)	———	———	———	———
Taste	(7) ———	(6)	———	———	———	———
Nutrition	(4) ———	(3)	———	———	———	———
Price	(2) ———	(7)	———	———	———	———
———	———		———	———	———	———
———	———		———	———	———	———
———	———		———	———	———	———
Attitude score: (A) =		(104)	———	———	———	———
Overall preference (ranking)		———	———	———	———	———

Scales: Importance: 1 = (unimportant) through 7 (very important)
Beliefs: 1 = (very poor) through 7 (very good)

Model Calculations

Model structure refers to the ways in which the ratings are combined and calculated within the model. In our basic model, the multiplicative relations between importance and beliefs, the summation over all attributes, and the nature of the ratings all suggest that this is a *linear compensatory* attitude model. Within an attribute, notice that each rating unit is assumed to provide equal marginal utility to consumers—this allows high scores on one attribute to "compensate" for low ratings on another attribute.

With respect to the modeling of your personal attitudes in Exhibit 11-2, you should at this point move to the bottom of the exhibit and provide a ranking of the fast-food outlets you will be rating. That is, give a "1" to the outlet you most prefer, a "2" to your next favorite, and so forth. In Andy's case we're now ready to calculate his attitude score toward Watta-Burger by simply following the form given in our basic model's formula. That is, we'll take each attribute in turn, multiplying the importance weight that Andy gives it times the belief that Andy has for Watta-Burger on this attribute. Once all the attributes have been multiplied, we'll add up their scores to arrive at a total attitude score that Andy holds toward this fast-food restaurant. In our example, this means that

$$\text{Attitude score} = (6 \times 2) + (6 \times 4) + (7 \times 6) + (4 \times 3) + (2 \times 7)$$
$$= 12 + 24 + 42 + 12 + 14$$
$$= 104$$

This score has little meaning in itself until it is compared with Andy's attitude scores toward other fast-food outlets. Notice, however, how these patterns of scores can give us marketing insights into Andy as a potential Watta-Burger customer. First, it doesn't look as if there's a very good match here. For example, even though Andy's belief rating is "very good" for Watta-Burger's price, this doesn't add very much to his attitude score (only 14 points) because Andy's importance rating for this attribute is quite low—price is just not very important to this consumer. Watta-Burger's lack of atmosphere, on the other hand, hurts it considerably with Andy—although it could have added 42 points to its attitude score with a very good atmosphere rating (that is, if Andy had given a belief rating of 7), the current store draws only 12 points. Overall, then, we would expect that Andy does not patronize Watta-Burger very often.

Now proceed with your multiplication and summation processes to arrive at your total attitude scores for each outlet. Use your overall scores from the model to rank the outlets and compare this ranking with your simple preference ranking given at the bottom. How do the two rankings match up? That is, does your favorite outlet have the highest attitude score, does the second favorite have the second highest score, and so forth? Finally, go back through the calculations to conduct your *marketing diagnostics* exercise—what attributes is each outlet strong on and in what areas does it need help? What proposals would you suggest to the management of the various fast-food marketers?

ISSUES IN USING THE MODEL

The exercise we've just presented should be helpful in appreciating why the multiattribute model approach is so widely used by marketers. It clearly allows us to see what is important to consumers, how well our brand does in providing the attributes that are important, and how we stack up against our competitors.

Because of these benefits to marketers, you may well find yourself using a multiattribute model to help you with business decisions in the future. You should know that there is a large literature available in the multiattribute area. As you'll discover if you attempt your own study, there are many challenging decisions you'll have to make, but if the stakes are high, you'll want to make sure the model is done right. At that point, you'll be pleased to discover that efforts to create the best models possible have led consumer researchers to examine many key questions. (Readers interested in pursuing further research issues with this and related multiattribute attitude models may wish to begin with the readings listed in Note 12.)

■ APPLICATIONS OF MULTIATTRIBUTE CONCEPTS

The fundamental purpose of the multiattribute model is to provide an insight into the structure of a consumer's attitude—to tell us why consumers like certain brands, for example, and why they dislike others. But what can marketers do about what

J.C. Penney is engaged in a long-term program to raise consumers' beliefs (Strategy 1) that it is an upscale, national department store chain.

they find out? In this section we'll examine the amazing potential of this approach for understanding consumer behavior and offering inputs to marketing strategy.

APPLICATION ADVANCE: FIVE STRATEGIES FOR ATTITUDE CHANGE

In the marketing arena we are interested in *how to improve consumers' attitudes* toward the enterprise we are managing. As Boyd, Ray, and Strong pointed out, the multiattribute approach offers useful guidance to us. Let's return to our basic model to see how

$$A_j = \sum_{i=1}^{n} B_{ij} I_i$$

where

i = attribute   and A = attitude score

j = brand B = belief

I = importance weight

If we work logically through the model, we'll locate five prime marketing strategies to raise the relative attitude scores consumers hold for our brand.[13]

Strategy 1: Increase Belief Ratings for Our Brand

This is the most common strategy used by marketers. If it is attainable, it is a surefire way to improve consumer attitudes for us. Unfortunately, almost all our competitors also recognize this strategy. And consumers have seen it so often that they have come to expect it. Thus we're likely to need more than just a promotional program (unless our product or service isn't very well known yet). An actual *product improvement* and an offer of *better value for the money* (perhaps through special prices) are two actions that can yield increases in consumer belief ratings. However, sometimes other versions of this strategy are called for:

🐋 *Fire over Six Flags*

Several years ago a funhouse fire killed eight people at Six Flags Great Adventure amusement park in New Jersey. Consumers reacted swiftly: attendance that had been running 6 percent ahead of the prior year's suddenly dropped off to 15 percent behind. Consumer research helped to clarify the problem. As the park's marketing director explained, "We found that . . . safety in theme parks in general was a big concern . . . we decided that the best approach was to speak out . . . and tell people we were making our park as secure as possible." To do this, a direct mail campaign was sent to 650,000 households in the area. The cover letter, written to parents, stressed the safety attribute. It explained how all the park's rides are inspected several times daily and that a new multimillion-dollar fire and safety program had been instituted. Included with the letter was a certificate good for two free admissions to the park, inviting the parents to come for themselves and see how safe it really is. Within the month, 10,000 certificates had been redeemed. Management felt that this strategy had turned around the volume decline.[14]

Strategy 2: Increase the Importance of a Key Attribute

This strategy involves the selection of an attribute in which our brand is stronger than the competition, then stressing to consumers that this attribute deserves higher weighting in their views of the product category. Low price and *value for the money* are related attributes for which this strategy is often used, as by Suave grooming products and Purex home care products. *Health* and *safety* provide other attributes that often lend themselves to this strategy, as marketers stress the importance of better nutrition, more protection, and so forth. Meanwhile, retailers can use *warranties* and *money-back guarantees* to stress the attribute of a consumer's reducing risk if he or she buys from that store. As a final example (this may "hit home" with some readers), a group of former Domino's Pizza executives have started a Chinese food chain, Ho-Lee-Chow, that is stressing the convenience of home delivery for this type of food.

Strategy 3: Add an Entirely New Attribute

This is the most exciting marketing strategy, as it usually involves the creation of a new benefit. When successful, this strategy can lead to major profit increases. About 30 years ago, for example, P & G added fluoride to its Crest toothpaste and won the only Seal of Approval from the American Dental Association. Almost immediately, its share of the market jumped from 10 percent to over 33 percent! Again recently, when it introduced the new attribute of tartar control, its share moved from 29 percent to 39 percent of the huge market. (And, as we discussed in Chapter 3, P & G experienced a similar success with Pampers, when it introduced the new attribute of disposability into the baby diaper market.) In an entirely different sphere, a new airline, "Smokers Express," has announced that it will allow smokers to puff away to their heart's content on its flight from the Florida coast (the airline plans to get around the government ban on smoking on commercial air carriers by registering as a travel club).[15] In addition to adding a new attribute, a closely related strategy is introducing new uses for an existing product:

🎀 *Arm & Hammer's Knockout Punch*

One of the classic examples of introducing new uses for an existing brand is the Arm & Hammer baking soda story. Until 1969, Arm & Hammer was a sleepy, one-dimensional brand of sodium bicarbonate. In that year, the company hired a new marketing vice president who undertook a policy of promoting new uses for this brand name. Based

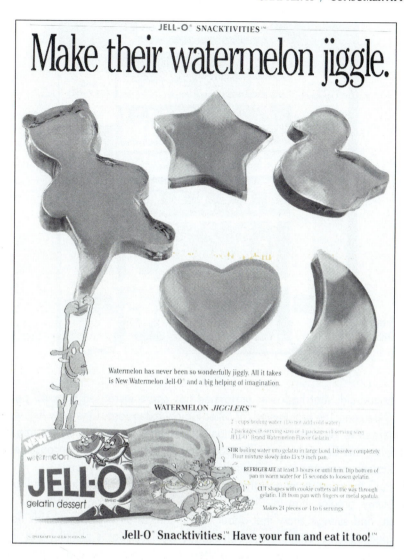

Strategy 2: Jell-O sold 50 million more boxes (up almost 20 percent) after it launched its "Jell-O Jigglers" campaign that stressed the value of the product's "jiggling" attribute, showing how kids (and parents) could have fun with Jell-O.

on consumer research, the firm determined that many housewives felt guilty about not cleaning their refrigerators often enough. Since one attribute of baking soda is that it is an excellent deodorizer, the firm ran a West Coast advertising test promoting this attribute as a new use for the product. Faced with phenomenal success (out-of-stock conditions in all the states where the product was tested), the company went national with this campaign. Sales increased 72 percent, and research showed that consumer behavior had indeed been changed—the percentage of households that had ever used baking soda as a refrigerator air freshener went from less than 1 percent in 1972 to over 90 percent by the end of the decade!

However, once the box was in the refrigerator consumers showed a tendency to forget about it, thus reducing repeat purchases. How could this be combatted? The answer: suggest yet another usage for Arm & Hammer—once it's done its job in the refrigerator (a box should last about two months), consumers were exhorted to remove it and pour its contents down the kitchen drain to deodorize that also. Within a two-year

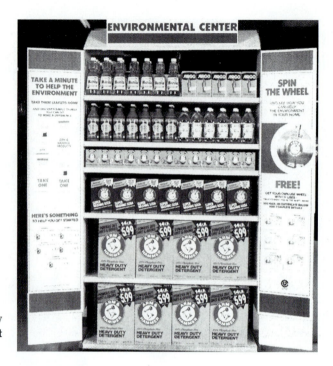

Arm & Hammer promotes entirely new uses for its baking soda, noting also that it is environmentally sound.

period, households that had ever performed this chore increased from 40 percent to almost 70 percent! The firm looked for other logical extensions. One easy link was from the refrigerator to the freezer. A campaign suggesting an extra box for the freezer was run in the late 1970s, and was again successful. Research showed that consumer usage for this purpose increased from 12 percent to 28 percent in four years!

What's the current status of this brand? The firm's sales have increased to a level over 10 times greater than in 1969. The brand name is recognized by 97 percent of women, and surveys show that about 95 percent of all U.S. households have one or more packages currently in their homes. The raw material is plentiful and cheap to produce, there are no strong brand competitors, and there are many other possible uses. Each year the firm receives letters from thousands of consumers suggesting new uses that they personally have encountered. Since the 1980s, for example, Arm & Hammer has been launched as a baking soda carpet cleaner (that's gained over 30 percent share of market), a toothpaste (that has captured fourth place and is moving toward third) and a cat litter deodorizer. The firm has also moved into industrial markets, where it offers significant environmental advantages as an industrial cleanser for printed circuit boards (name: "Armakleen") and a key ingredient in sandblasting and paint removal (the Statue of Liberty was recently cleaned with "Armax"). Also, the company has begun to sell its products to cities as an additive to municipal water supplies, since it neutralizes acids that can leach lead from old pipes!

What lies ahead? The company is now investigating *co-branding*, in which other marketers will feature the fact that they include Arm & Hammer as an ingredient, similar to the strategy used successfully by NutraSweet and Intel. Some recent co-branding efforts involved Stayfree Pads and bottled water. What happened to the marketing vice president? He became president of the company![16]

Strategy 4: L'Oreal deals effectively with its weaker attribute of higher price by stressing its value: "I'm worth it. So are you!"

Strategy 4: Decrease the Importance of a Weak Attribute

Under this strategy if we find that we have an attribute on which we *do not* rate as highly as our competitors, we might suggest to consumers that this attribute is not as significant as they may otherwise think. Many marketers of high-priced goods face this problem: one way to employ this strategy is to stress a trade-off of a strong attribute for the weak one. L'Oréal hair tints, for example, acknowledge that they "cost a little more" but that their users believe "I'm worth it." The promotional theme for fine jewelry— "Diamonds Are Forever"—stresses many years of pleasure and downplays initial concern over price. Price is not the only attribute that may have to be downplayed, of course. The U.S. military, for example, faces difficulty deciding how to treat the reality of combat: its director of advertising for recruiting reports, "We don't want to be misleading, but too much combat footage interferes with the long-term attributes of Army service that we want to portray: money for college, skills training, and relevance to a civilian career."[17]

Strategy 5: Decrease Belief Ratings for Competitive Brands

This strategy has been used for years by salespersons in retail settings. When a consumer asks for advice, a salesperson will often indicate both positive and negative aspects of different brands and stores. It was not a strategy often used in advertising, however, until the advent of *comparative ads* about 20 years ago. The strategy is sometimes very successful—Schick, Inc.'s controversial comparative ad campaign for its Fleximatic electric shaver, for example, was credited with a rapid increase from an 8 percent to a 24 percent share of the market, a gain of almost $30 million in sales.[18]

We should note that this strategy is risky, however, and can become unfair to competing firms. Many persons in the advertising industry dislike the practice of comparative advertising: they stress that the technique lends itself to disparaging competitors. Indeed, much of the caseload of the advertising self-regulatory system is concerned with comparative ad cases, and many lawsuits have been filed in court as well. In one of the earliest, Alberto-Culver won a large settlement from Gillette because Gillette claims about its "Balsam" hair conditioner had driven the brand out of the market. Recently, the long-distance telephone market has been a center for this strategy, especially on the part of MCI and AT&T. In summary, this strategy is risky and somewhat unpleasant, but it can be quite effective.

Summary Comments: Multiattribute Marketing Strategies

The multiattribute attitude model thus suggests five different strategies that a marketer can pursue to raise consumers' attitudes toward his or her brand. There is also the possibility of *staging the strategies* in a particular sequence. Mazola's marketing program demonstrated how this can be done. First, the firm pursued strategy 3 by introducing the new attribute *(i)* of 100 percent corn oil in margarine. Then, once consumers were aware of the attribute, Mazola shifted its stress to strategy 2. To increase the importance *(I)* of this attribute in consumers' minds, Mazola's advertising extolled the health virtues of corn oil as compared to the other vegetable oils that had been used in margarines. Finally, after having established corn oil as a very desirable attribute, Mazola shifted to strategy 1. Here the stress was on brand beliefs *(B)*—in this campaign the firm used comparison ads to clarify that, among the three leading brands, only Mazola contained 100 percent corn oil.[19]

Our discussion in this section has thus indicated the basic set of strategies the multiattribute approach can offer marketers who wish to change consumers' attitudes (we will also be discussing how advertising can influence consumers' attitudes in our advertising chapter, Chapter 16). Here, however, we will turn our attention to further developments related to the multiattribute approach, involving *product positioning* decisions. Our next section presents a nontechnical discussion, with applications, of this important area.

APPLICATION ADVANCE: PRODUCT POSITIONING

Positioning: The design of a marketing mix to lead consumers to perceive a distinctive brand image.

Bundle of attributes: The set of charactersitics offered by a product to consumers.

A number of years ago two marketing men, Ries and Trout, trumpeted the message, "The Positioning Era Cometh."[20] Since that time marketers have had an enormous interest in this area. **Positioning** *refers to a managerial process of deliberately designing a marketing mix that will lead consumers to perceive the brand as having a distinctive image in comparison to brands offered by competitors.* Multiattribute concepts are at the core of this approach, since the key to the approach is to view a product as a **bundle of attributes**. The positioning itself will depend on which attributes *(i)* are most important *(I)* to the target segment of consumers, at what levels they will be offered, and what brand beliefs *(B)* consumers will be encouraged to have.

Since multimillion-dollar markets are often at stake in brand positioning, actual marketing programs can be very detailed. Aaker and Shansby,[21] however, have suggested six basic positioning strategies for marketers to consider:

- *Strategy 1. Stress a specific performance attribute:* Volvo offers "durability," Fiat offers "craftsmanship," and so on.

- *Strategy 2. Offer a specific balance of price and quality:* Saks offers high quality at high prices, Sears is moderate on both bases, Zapper Stores is low on both, and so on.

- *Strategy 3. Stress specific use occasions:* Gatorade satisfies athletes' thirst, Arm & Hammer is positioned for use in a refrigerator, and so on.

- *Strategy 4. Stress the types of product users:* Baby shampoo is directed toward infants and toddlers, *Seventeen* is designed to appeal to teen and preteen girls, Charlie fragrance is marketed to socially active young women, and so on.

- *Strategy 5. Positioning as a new product variation:* Imperial margarine features the taste of butter, Caress is "bath oil" soap, and so on.

- *Strategy 6. Associate with or compare against a well-known competitor:* Consider Sabroso versus Kahlúa, Avis versus Hertz, Pepsi versus Coke, and so on.

Consumer Research for Positioning

Since the stakes are high, several hundred thousand dollars might be spent on advanced consumer research methods within a positioning project. This research will try to determine exactly what our positioning options are and then to estimate quantitatively and model how consumers (and competitors) are likely to react to various options we might choose for our brand.

Shocker and Srinivasan[22] have outlined the process as a sequence of five stages:

- *Stage 1. Determine the relevant product market:* This stage answers the questions, "Which brands compete with each other and which consumer segments are involved."

- *Stage 2. Identify the determinant attributes for each submarket:* This stage isolates **determinant attributes,** namely, those particular product characteristics that are most crucial in determining which exact brand a consumer will choose. Determinant attributes must be *both* important *and* ones in which brands are seen to differ.[23]

- *Stage 3. Create an abstract representation of each submarket:* This stage involves the development of a perceptual map of the relevant market (we'll look at perceptual mapping following this list of research steps).

- *Stage 4. Develop consumer models to predict preference and choice:* These models often take the general form of our basic multiattribute attitude model, but are extended in a different direction. Interest here is in obtaining the best quantitative estimates of parameters within the model (for example, the specific regression coefficient for each brand belief). These models involve advanced statistical methods.[24]

- *Stage 5. Evaluation of product positions to find the best options:* This step involves several quantitative estimates, namely, (1) the consumer sales appeal of each positioning strategy, (2) the profit implications of each strategy (including required investment and cost factors), and (3) possible competitive reactions. Close work with a firm's management is likely to be needed to obtain these judgments. Based on predicted profits from each positioning option, the firm then begins to develop its marketing mix to achieve the desired "niche" in the marketplace.[25]

Determinant attributes: Those product characteristics most crucial in deciding the exact brand chosen.

Even though the heavy mathematical emphasis in the later stages of this process may be beyond the scope of our treatment, our earlier discussions of the multiattribute model should allow us to understand what the researchers are trying to achieve. For the stages to be even more clear, let's take a closer look at how a *market map* can be developed and used.

Mapping Markets and Minds

Perceptual mapping is a particularly interesting approach to studying consumer attitudes and can easily be visualized. For example, Figure 11-3 displays two related maps of the Chicago beer market some years ago. These were produced by Richard Johnson,

Perceptual map: A graphical depiction of how competing brands' attributes are perceived by consumers.

Preference map: A graphical depiction of the preferences that consumers have for various bundles of attributes.

Multidimensional scaling (MDS): An analysis program that produces a perceptual map based on the "best fit" of consumers' brand ratings.

Ideal point: A consumer's most preferred combination of available attributes.

a market researcher who was working on a project for one of the local brewers (note that the four local brands are not identified by name).[26]

The first map describes the *product space* for beer, as consumers perceive it. It is thus known as a **perceptual map.** It shows where each brand is "located" in consumers' minds (we shall return to this point!). The second map represents the preferences that consumers have for various attributes and is thus known as a **preference map.** (We should note that a product space actually exists in as many dimensions as there are independent key attributes, but is most easily seen when simplified to two-dimensional space and graphed out. If three dimensions were noted, a Tinkertoy model might be built.) The shaded circles represent different segments of consumers, in terms of what they want in a beer (the larger the circle, the larger the number of consumers in that segment).

The general research approach in producing these maps is easy to understand, though the actual mathematical techniques can be complex. Basically, the perceptual map in Figure 11-3 was produced by asking beer drinkers how similar the eight beer brands were to each other. ("Similarity" can be measured in several ways. In this study, Johnson asked for brand belief ratings on the 35 attributes, some of which are shown in the map. Another popular approach would simply present consumers with the names of three of the brands, say, Miller, Bud, and Coors, and then ask which two are the most similar.) After all different combinations of brands were used, the similarity ratings could be put through some form of a special analysis called **multidimensional scaling (MDS).** This computer program then produces the perceptual map that best fits the ratings that the consumers have provided. Johnson's approach to this step yielded the first map in Figure 11-3.

For the second map, consumers are asked now to rank the brands in their order of preference. These rankings are analyzed within the confines of the perceptual map to define the **ideal point** for each consumer, that is, his or her most preferred combination of attributes available. According to this analysis, each consumer has only one ideal point located somewhere on the preference map. The closer a brand comes to a consumer's ideal point, the more that consumer will like what the brand has to offer. The ideal points from the various beer drinkers were then grouped together into the numbered *preference circles* shown on the map. Since these represent consumers having similar ideal points, each preference circle is akin to a *market segment* of beer drinkers in Chicago.

These points can easily be understood by examining the details of the two maps. For example, notice that the perceptual map indicates that the two key dimensions appear to be (1) a *price-quality* dimension on the horizontal, with lower-priced brands to the left and premium brands to the right, and (2) a *mildness* dimension on the vertical, with mild beers toward the top and heavy beers toward the bottom. Each brand's current positioning can easily be located on the perceptual map. Miller High Life, for example, showed up as a relatively mild beer that was seen to be popular with women.

But where are the best places to be? The *preference map* on the bottom of the figure can allow us to answer this important question. Notice that nine consumer segments seem to exist here, representing different ideal points for these dimensions. Segment 1, for example, is a large group that is not very price sensitive and wants a slightly heavier brew. Budweiser and Schlitz were likely to have been appealing to these drinkers. Segment 2 is another large group that is also willing to pay premium prices, but which is looking for a "lighter" beer such as Hamm's and Miller were seen to be. Segment 4, on the other hand, is seeking a heavier, "filling" beer at a lower price. No brand was ideally positioned for this segment at the time, though local brand D was closest.

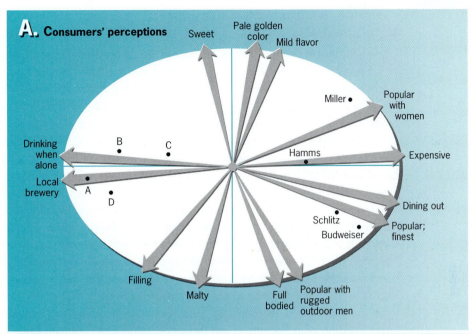

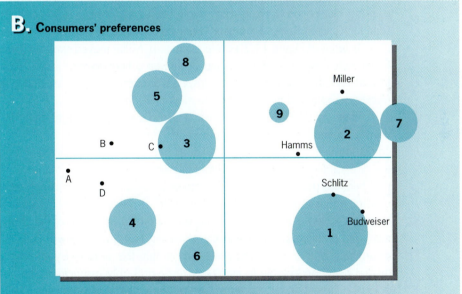

FIGURE 11-3 A "Market Map" for Beer in Chicago some years ago. In panel A, we see that consumers perceived Miller Beer to be popular with women, Budweiser as popular and "the finest," and Brand A as local and "good to drink when alone." In panel B, we see market segments' preferences for the types of beer they desired, with 1 being the largest segment and 9 the smallest. (Further discussion is in the text.)

SOURCE: See Note 26.

✑ *"Welcome to Miller Time"*

Assuming that these maps are accurate, what strategies should the different brands follow? To answer this question in reality, we would have to proceed through the types of analyses suggested for stages 4 and 5 of the positioning process, drawing upon much more detailed information from the particular firm for which we're working. To see the potentials for this type of approach, however, we can look back at several actual developments with Miller Beer and note how they relate nicely to Johnson's study.

About the time the maps in Figure 11-3 were developed, the Miller Brewing Company was purchased by the cigarette giant, Philip Morris, Inc. At the time, Miller's prime brand was Miller High Life, which was being promoted as "The Champagne of Bottled Beers." Overall, the firm held only about 3 percent of the national beer market. When Philip Morris took over, it introduced the aggressive promotional techniques of the cigarette industry to the beer market, striving to increase sales sharply and gain market share. As a key part of this strategy, the flagship Miller brand was *repositioned* away from being a "woman's beer." Studies showed that although this segment was potentially large in numbers, its members didn't actually consume very much beer. The heavy beer drinkers instead were blue-collar working men who would not respond well to the female-oriented positioning of the Miller brand. Accordingly, Miller placed huge advertising expenditures behind a repositioning of its flagship brand, now promoting it as a rugged brew for the heavy-drinking blue-collar working man. Such themes as "Welcome to Miller Time . . ." were used in this effort to move the beer "from the champagne bucket into the lunch bucket."

In terms of Figure 11-3's preference map, Miller moved strongly toward segment 1, thereby challenging Budweiser and Schlitz on a head-to-head basis. Shortly thereafter, in part for other reasons, Schlitz dropped dramatically in sales and popularity, while Miller passed it and moved in on the market leader.

Then, in 1975, Miller successfully introduced its new "Lite" beer. In this effort, the brewer teamed the claims "Tastes Great!" and "Less Filling!" in a famous advertising campaign that featured rugged ex-sports heroes to endorse this new type of beer. The use of these men clearly signaled that this was a macho brew (retired stars were used in part because active athletes don't endorse beers due to their position as role models for children and teenagers). Notice that the "Lite" strategy does not fit as nicely on our map, since it involved at least three distinct sectors on the right side of the chart (light, rugged men, and premium price). It is likely, however, that Miller Lite was able to capture much of segment 2. It is also worthwhile to note that this brand—by making the concept of a "diet beer" acceptable to many drinkers—probably *restructured* the beer market into at least a three-dimensional map. Overall, how did these programs fare for Miller? Not bad—its new positionings for Miller and Miller Lite shot its share of the national beer market from 3 percent to 25 percent over a 10-year period.[27]

ATTITUDE RESEARCH IN PUBLIC POLICY

Thus far our discussion has stressed how marketing managers can use this important information. Before leaving this topic, we should note, however, that consumer attitude concepts are also quite useful for public policy decisions. For example, periodic surveys of beliefs and attitudes toward cigarette smoking have been used to track the remarkable shifts occurring in this area of consumer behavior during the past 30 years. Broader-scale surveys are also run on consumers' attitudes toward their economic well-being (e.g., the Index of Consumer Sentiment) and of consumers' buying intentions for major purchases in the near future. Since consumer purchases are so important to the economic vitality of our system (you may recall that they account for about two-thirds of the U.S. GNP), these surveys provide important information for both government and private business.

Consumer attitude research is also useful in the regulatory area of public policy. The author was involved in one case, for example, in which Hawaiian Punch was required to run a corrective disclosure on its label until consumer surveys would show that high proportions (67 percent, 80 percent, or 95 percent, depending on which market segment was being surveyed) of consumers no longer held a mistaken brand belief about the amount of fruit juice actually in Hawaiian Punch. A number of recent developments, in fact, suggest that the role of consumer attitude research is likely to increase in public policy in the future.[28]

■ LINKING ATTITUDES TO BEHAVIOR

Up to this point we have examined the link between the cognitive and affective ("thinking" and "feeling") components of Figure 11-1. Now let us briefly turn our attention to the next linkage in the figure—that between affect and conation ("feeling" and "doing"). Typically, we assume that knowing about a consumer's attitude will allow us to predict that consumer's behavior at a later time. While this is not a bad assumption for us to make, it turns out that this issue is more interesting than it might first appear.

ATTITUDES AND BRAND PURCHASES: EMPIRICAL RESULTS

One good way to examine the relationship between attitudes and behavior is to take measurements of the same consumers at several points over a time period. Once a brand has been purchased, the researcher can look back to see what types of brand attitudes that consumer held prior to the purchase. In one famous marketing report, Alvin Achenbaum reported that in numerous studies of specific brands his ad agency had found strong relationships between consumer attitudes and brand purchase behaviors.[29] Figure 11-4 shows a typical form of this relationship for one brand of a dental product. Notice that of all those consumers who rated the brand as "Excellent," 78 percent are current users of the brand. At the other extreme, of all those who rated the brand as "Not So Good" or "Poor," only 8 percent were users of the brand during the period measured. If we look toward the attitudes of *former* users of the brand, however, an almost mirror image emerges—of those rating it "Excellent," only 8 percent have stopped using it, while of those consumers rating it to be "Poor," a full 76 percent no longer purchase the brand. In his more detailed analyses of these types of data, Achenbaum also discovered that consumers whose attitudes changed positively toward a brand were more likely to purchase that brand in the future, while those whose attitudes changed negatively were less likely to purchase the brand in the future. Thus this basic evidence supports our general assumption that there is a strong relationship between attitudes and behavior.

So what's all the fuss about? Why are we reading a special section on this topic?

If we look again at Figure 11-4, we can see the answer to this quite reasonable question. Note that while the relationship itself is obviously positive, there are quite a few consumers who don't seem to be behaving according to our assumption. For

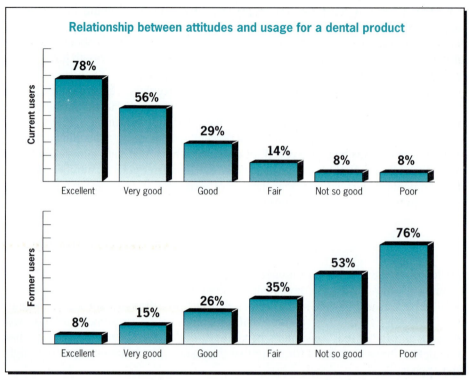

Relationship between attitudes and usage for a dental product

Current users

78%   Excellent
56%   Very good
29%   Good
14%   Fair
8%   Not so good
8%   Poor

Former users

8%   Excellent
15%   Very good
26%   Good
35%   Fair
53%   Not so good
76%   Poor

FIGURE 11–4 Achenbaum's Findings on Attitudes and Behavior for a Representative Product

example, why would those 22 percent of consumers (i.e., 100%− 78%) who rate our brand as "Excellent" not be buying it, and why would 44 percent of those rating it to be "Very Good" not buy it either? At the other extreme, why in the world would any consumer who thinks our brand is "Poor" go out and buy it? Thus the answer to the question, "Why all the fuss?" is that when we actually measure consumers, *we find that the correlations between their attitudes and their behaviors are far from perfect.* This lowers the predictability of our models, increases our uncertainty as marketers, and might lead to reduced profits from our decisions. Thus we're quite interested in finding out why the correlations aren't higher than they are.

As a first step, we can look at other factors that may be at work. For example, Achenbaum's analyses showed that **product use experience** was a significant factor in changing people's attitudes toward a brand. This poses another issue: *Which comes first, the attitude or the behavior?* In other words, are we better off to assume that positive attitudes are needed before a product will be purchased or, to the contrary, that product use behavior is needed before any meaningful attitudes can be formed?

The correct answer is "Both statements can be true," which means that we must look further into the conditions under which either is more likely. Many researchers now believe that the key to disentangling these paths lies in understanding the nature of **consumer involvement** with a particular product purchase. When consumers are *highly involved* with a purchase, marketers can expect *attitude change preceding behavior.* When consumers have *low involvement,* however, attitudes will play a *weaker role* in determining purchase behavior. Instead, once behavior has occurred, the product use experience is then likely to have a strong impact on developing the consumer's attitude.[30]

COMPLEXITIES IN THE RELATIONSHIP

But even if we're not sure about the direction of causality between attitudes and behavior, why aren't the correlations higher than they'd seem to be in Figure 11-4?

This is another good question, one that has received considerable attention already. Among the key explanations are the following:

- *Not all attitudes are tied closely to behavior.* Consumers hold many attitudes toward people we'll never meet, brands we never buy, and so on. For example, many consumers hold positive attitudes toward Harvard University, Rolls-Royce autos, and large homes with sweeping lawns. Usually these attitudes are not held with the idea of a purchase in mind, due to other factors such as income limits. If these other factors were favorable, however, such attitudes might become predictors of behavior.

- *Consumers have positive attitudes toward multiple brands.* In most product categories, consumers are favorable to a number of the brand alternatives. If we measure "behavior" by single-time purchases, obviously many of the brands with favorable attitudes will not be purchased at that time.

- *The role of time and change is important.* Attitudes can change after they've been measured in a study, and this might easily affect the correlations we obtain. Achenbaum found, for example, that about 75 percent of the consumers in his study changed their attitude ratings during a six-month period. (We should note that some of this apparent change might simply reflect the fact that some attitudes are not very precise, leading a consumer to be somewhat uncertain about which single rating (e.g., "good" or "very good" or a "5, or 6, or 7") to give the brand. In a later second rating, that consumer may choose a different rating from the same set of options: this would give an appearance of change when none has actually occurred (this is technically termed response unreliability, or instability). Whether the differences in attitude ratings reflect true change or response unreliability, there is a lot of it, which means that correlations with behavior are likely to be lowered (in this regard, we should also note that behavior change tends to occur less frequently than attitude change: in Achenbaum's study only 20 percent of consumers switched brands during the six-month period).

- *Situational effects can alter purchase plans.* Many situational factors can intercede between a person's attitude and his or her actual purchase behavior. Special price deals, out-of-stock conditions, new brands to try, or a usage situation calling for a prestige type of brand are all fairly common occurrences.

- *Personal and economic factors can affect purchase behavior.* Purchases of expensive products, for example, are strongly affected by the dollars we have available to spend. Similarly, diets can alter our food-buying behaviors, although underlying attitudes haven't changed at all. Inputs from the marketplace, such as salespersons' recommendations, or sales prices, or in-store displays, can change our purchase away from our earlier attitude ratings. Also, some consumers will have a higher consistency than others: research has shown that more knowledgeable consumers and those with a higher "need for cognition" are likely to hold attitudes more predictive of their behaviors.[31]

- *Social factors can affect purchase behavior.* For many types of purchases, the opinions of other people such as friends and family, and the norms of social organizations and groups can influence a consumer to take a purchase away from his or her personal favorite, to a different alternative that is more socially popular or acceptable.[32]

Attitude accessibility: The extent to which an attitude is likely to "come to mind" (move from LTM to STM) when a purchase is being made.

■ *CIP factors are important as well.* Recent research has shown that **attitude accessibility** is also a key factor in attitude-behavior relationships. That is, an attitude needs to "come to mind" (i.e., be accessed, and move from LTM to STM) when a purchase is being made, or it will not in fact influence that purchase. Although we might at first think that it is natural for attitudes to "come to mind," research has shown that when a decision is low in involvement, or a consumer has only a weak attitude about a brand, or when an outside factor such as a sales display is sending a powerful message to "give me a try!" attitudes may not actually be factored into the purchase behavior. In one study, for example, consumers having high-accessibility attitudes were more likely to search further on the shelves to find their favorite brands, while other consumers (whose brand attitudes were less likely to come to mind) were more likely to buy an item that was prominently placed in a front shelf position (indicating that their attitude had played less of a role in the behavior).[33] More broadly, given marketing's brand-competitive setting, this entry suggests that the attitude for one brand might come to mind during a purchase, but not the attitudes for some other brands. If this is the case, the brand whose attitude comes to mind (a concept similar to "evoked set") is much more likely to be purchased. In this regard, notice that all the brands in Exhibit 11-1's listing of the "most powerful brand names" would score highly on accessibility in most consumers' minds.

These entries provide ample evidence that the attitude-behavior relationship is a complex one. However, in recent years there has been considerable research done by social psychologists and marketing professors on these questions. The general conclusions are quite positive—it does seem that attitudes offer a considerable potential for understanding consumer behavior. At the same time, there have been some heated debates about concepts and measures, as well as new ideas that offer potential improvements in the approach. (If you would like to read more about developments in this research area, you may wish to pursue the readings listed in Note 34. Also, Chapter 16 of this text presents considerable discussion of recent research on how advertising can be used to change consumer attitudes and influence behavior.)

■ SUMMARY

WHAT ARE CONSUMER ATTITUDES?

In this chapter, the important *role of attitude in consumer behavior* was discussed. The chapter was divided into four major sections. The first began with a *definition of attitudes* as "learned predispositions to respond to an object…in a consistently favorable or unfavorable way." Several *key theoretical perspectives on attitude* were discussed, including the traditional model that viewed attitudes as a composite of three elements: *cognitive, affective,* and *conative.* We also said that *cognitive consistency* is at work among the components of an attitude, and we examined the four key functions that attitudes serve to make them useful to us: the *adjustment function,* the *ego-defense function,* the *value-expressive function,* and the *object-appraisal function.*

CONSUMER ATTITUDES AND MARKETING MANAGEMENT

The second section of the chapter examined why marketers are so interested in measuring consumer attitudes, particularly in brand management activities and in the emerging area of *brand equity.* Here we saw that consumer attitudes offer useful measures of how a brand or store is regarded by consumers, and thus supply insights about both what the future will bring and also what a manager might do to improve it, including offering *brand extensions* that take advantage of the strengths of a brand's name with consumers. We also took a quiz on the strongest (and weakest) brand names in the United States.

THE ATTITUDE REVOLUTION: MULTIATTRIBUTE MODELS

The third section focused on the links between the cognitive and affective components—between beliefs and attitudes. Here we discussed *multiattribute attitude models*, an approach that has achieved great popularity in marketing, and we examined the structure of the *marketing model*. To best understand this complex-appearing model, we worked through an example, and discovered that it was quite straightforward. We then saw how these models provide insights into the dynamics of consumer behavior. We then analyzed an application advance consisting of a set of five model-based strategies for changing consumer attitudes: (1) *increase belief ratings*, (2) *increase importance of a key attribute*, (3) *add a new attribute*, (4) *decrease importance of a weak attribute*, and (5) *decrease beliefs for competitive brands*. We then discussed another multiattribute application advance: the key area of *product positioning*. Here we noted, in a nontechnical fashion, the importance of high-level consumer research to develop such analyses as *perceptual maps* and *preference maps* of the marketplace. We showed how these worked for one city's beer market and how Miller's progress could be understood using these maps.

HOW DO ATTITUDES RELATE TO CONSUMER BEHAVIOR?

The chapter's concluding section focused on the *relationship between consumer attitudes and consumer behavior*. A brief review of the research evidence here showed that the attitude-behavior link is generally positive, but is often not as strong as one might expect. We examined a number of logical reasons for this gap indicating just how complex this area can be. Fortunately, however, considerable research has been done on this issue, and can be quite helpful to a marketer who is trying to use consumer attitude measures to improve his or her market position.

■ KEY TERMS

attitude	object-appraisal function	determinant attributes
cognitive component	brand attitudes	perceptual map
affective component	brand equity	preference map
conative component	brand extensions	multidimensional scaling (MDS)
cognitive consistency	overall evaluation	ideal point
adjustment function	multiattribute model	product use experience
ego-defense function	positioning	consumer involvement
value-expressive function	bundle of attributes	attitude accessibility

■ REVIEW QUESTIONS AND EXPERIENTIAL EXERCISES

[E = **Application extension or experiential exercise**]

1. Why is "attitude" considered a central concept in consumer behavior? Consumer attitudes toward products may be one of the most monitored aspects of consumer behavior by marketers. Why is this so? Provide examples.

2. What is "brand equity," and why has it been important in financial takeovers of consumer marketing firms?

3. What is the basic rationale behind a multiattribute attitude model? Discuss the formula for this model, pointing out each of the key components.

4. Evidence appears to support the basic assumption that there is a relationship between attitudes and behavior, but that it sometimes can be distressingly low. Discuss six basic reasons for this, using an example for each.

5. [E] Administer the "most powerful brand" quiz (from Exhibit 11-1) to 10 persons. As they take it, listen to their comments, then discuss their answers with them. Your goal: to discover other significant elements of consumer attitudes that were pointed out in the chapter (for example, are there indications of cognitive consistency at work? Does a conative component appear? Is "accessibility" an issue for some attitudes? What is the evidence for an attitude-behavior linkage? and so forth). Write a brief report on your findings.

6. [E] Consider the five multiattribute marketing strategies for changing consumer attitudes. Analyze a number of advertisements, searching for instances of each strategy. Clip out one example of each. Briefly explain your rationale.

7. [E] Using either the relevant Notes for this chapter, or the reference section of your library, investigate recent developments in one of the following:
   a. Brand equity/brand extensions
   b. Product positioning

8. [E] If you are interested in learning more about technical approaches, using either the relevant Notes for this chapter or the reference section of your library, investigate recent developments in one of the following:
   a. Conjoint analysis (a positioning technique)
   b. Multidimensional scaling (MDS)

9. [E] As the 1990s move along, some of the upscale "yuppie" brands of the 1980s have become concerned about protecting their brand equity. Indicate what you would recommend for four of the following:
   a. Häagen-Dazs ice cream
   b. Filofax organizers
   c. BMW autos
   d. Corona Extra beer
   e. Coach bags
   f. Club Med

   (Tip: If you wish assistance, consult the article by Kathleen Deveny in *The Wall Street Journal*, December 20, 1990, p. B1.)

10. [E] Using either the relevant Notes for this chapter, or materials in the reference section of your library, investigate one of the following topics in greater depth:
    a. The multiattribute model
    b. Attitude accessibility

11. [E] Using Figure 11-3 (a market map for beer in Chicago), identify what positioning strategies you would have recommended for Miller beer based on Aaker and Shansby's product strategies. Write a brief report summarizing your analysis.

12. [E] Conduct a multiattribute attitude project for a local retail outlet (e.g., fast-food restaurant, bar, grocery store). The following steps might prove helpful:
    a. Outline the essential elements as shown in Exhibit 11-2.
    b. Create a consumer questionnaire to obtain actual measures for each element (the cited references in the notes may be helpful here).
    c. Pretest your questionnaire and revise it to ensure that consumers can answer it appropriately.
    d. Survey 10 consumers (this size will be too small for strategic purposes, but it will provide you with insights into the model).
    e. Perform the essential calculations.
    f. Interpret the results and offer marketing strategy recommendations using the five options from the multiattribute model. Write a report summarizing your project, results, and recommendations.

13. [E] Interview members of two local health clubs you believe to be appealing to different consumer segments. Try to identify the relevant product attributes, then try to determine whether the members differ in their importance weights for these attributes, and what their belief ratings are for the two clubs. Are both clubs seemingly competing successfully? Write a brief report on your findings and any recommendations you have.

14. [E] Interview the managers of two or three local bars (or restaurants, or clothing stores) you believe are offering different levels of attributes to consumers, such as sports bars, dance clubs, jazz clubs, neighborhood bars, and so forth. Identify the views each manager holds about his or her consumer market, the key attributes for the bar's customers, and the present strong and weak points of the marketing strategy. How might the concepts from this chapter help to improve the marketing strategy for one of these establishments? Write a brief report on your findings.

15. [E] Interview an executive of a market research firm as to the types of consumer attitude studies his or her firm offers to marketing and advertising managers. Obtain literature if available, and ask about sample sizes (and selection), operational issues, timing, and costs. Learn also about how the results can be used, and any cases in which they were clearly helpful. Write a brief report on your findings.

■ SUGGESTED READING

■ As indicated at the start of the chapter, attitudes are a mainstream topic for both consumer behavior and marketing. Thus many good applied readings are available. For an interesting look at brand equity, for example, see James C. Crimmins, "Better Measurement and Management of Brand Value," *Journal of Advertising Research*, Vol. 32 (July–August 1992), pp. 11–19. For a good book on the topic, see David A. Aaker, *Managing Brand Equity* (New York: Free Press, 1991). For recent reading on the rise of private labels and the challenge to brands, see Julie Liesse, "Private Label Nightmare," *Advertising Age*, April 12, 1993, p. 1; or "Brands on the Run," *Business Week*,

April 19, 1993, p. 26. As realistic marketing decisions will (at least in large companies) rely upon sophisticated measurements of consumer attitude-type concepts, you may wish to pursue some good advanced readings. Two to try are Paul E. Green and V. Srinivasan, "Conjoint Analysis in Marketing: New Developments with Implications for Research and Practice," *Journal of Marketing*, Vol. 54 (October 1990), pp. 3–19; and Abbie Griffin and John R. Hauser, "The Voice of the Customer," *Marketing Science*, Vol. 12 (Winter 1993), pp. 1–27. Again, for pursuit of any particular point of interest, consult the Note of interest.

Part III

EXTERNAL INFLUENCES ON CONSUMER BEHAVIOR

I n the first chapter of the book, our "Seven Keys to Consumer Behavior" highlighted the fact that external factors play key roles in influencing consumer behavior. Now, in Chapters 12–16, we will examine these key external factors in some detail. In Chapter 12, we begin by examining the subtle but powerful forces of *culture*, noting how consumer behavior differs across international cultures, how cultural trends affect consumer behavior, and (in Appendix 12A) how people's daily lives are influenced by the social classes to which they belong. Chapter 13 then narrows our focus somewhat, as we examine how *social* and *situational influences* operate on consumer behavior. Chapter 14 strikes even closer to home, as we focus on *families* and *households*.

Each of the first three chapters contains many insights for marketers. However, in our final two chapters of Part III, we turn specifically to the issue of how marketers influence consumer behavior: Chapter 15 examines *salespersons' influences*, and Chapter 16 analyzes *advertising's influences* on consumer behavior. Throughout Part III, you'll encounter some influences that are obvious, but many that are not, and you'll see many implications for yourself as both a marketer and a consumer. So turn the page, and let's get started!

12

CULTURAL INFLUENCES

TWO WOMEN

Seeta Singh wiped her brow and sighed softly. It was a hot, humid day in the rural village of Rampur, India, and Seeta was very tired. She was a pretty, 20-year-old brunette and was now in her seventh month of pregnancy with her second child. Her family had arranged her marriage to Deepak some four years earlier, when she had reached the age of 16 and Deepak had been 24. Their son, Ram, was now 3 years old and was a chore for Seeta to handle when she was tired and the days were so hot. Deepak would be home in a few hours, however, and could help out with Ram that evening. Meanwhile, a continent away to the west, Revital Ofir was also wiping her brow and sighing softly. She had just come in from mock combat maneuvers and was very tired. Already it was hot and dusty outside—it looked to be a long day ahead. Revital was a pretty, 20-year-old brunette who was looking forward to the end of her stretch in the Israeli army. She had already been accepted into the university, where she planned to study hard and enjoy an active social life!

What neither woman knew, however, was the fact of their biological similarity—they were identical twins, born to Iranian parents hours before the catastrophic earthquake had destroyed many of the settlements in the eastern foothills. During the ensuing tumult, their mother had perished, and the twins had been inadvertently separated by the workers of the humanitarian agencies who had been flown in to help. Their paths had diverged, one to the east and other to the west, as they had been taken in by new families and raised in new cultures.

■ WHAT IS CULTURE?

The story of the two young women is certainly not typical, but it does serve as dramatic evidence of the powerful forces contained within culture. Imagine how *different* the twins are from each other—their (1) languages, (2) religions, (3) clothing,

(4) appearance, (5) housing, (6) family relationships, (7) daily activities, (8) memories, (9) values, (10) views of the world, (11) possessions, and (12) entire futures are all different because they have been determined by different cultures. There are, of course, also some similarities between these women, some of which are due to their common heredity and some because their cultures do have some elements in common.

Culture has the broadest of all the external influences on consumer behavior: in this chapter we'll analyze several of its key effects on consumers and marketers. Our first section introduces the concept. The second section looks at consumer behavior *across different cultures*—the major challenge (and opportunity) for marketers in our increasingly globalized marketing world. The subsequent sections look at *cultural change:* this provides the basis for new product success for marketers and improved daily lives for consumers. Finally, Appendix 12A returns to the culture concept again for a close look at how societies are structured into social classes. Altogether, then, this chapter contains much important, interesting material to help us understand the world around us, and it all begins with the concept we call "culture."

Slightly over 100 years ago, just after the U.S. Civil War, Sir Edward B. Tylor, an Englishman, introduced the scientific concept called *culture.* Tylor was one of the early leaders of the field of anthropology, which was just beginning to formalize its study of human beings and their life-styles.[1]

Tylor's original 1871 definition of **culture** still stands as a classic statement:

> **Culture** is that complex whole which includes knowledge, belief, art, morals, custom, and any other capabilities and habits acquired by man as a member of society.[2]

Culture: That complex whole acquired by a person as a member of society.

This definition presents a *descriptive view* of culture—it concentrates our attention on the way of life of a society. As is true for most really important concepts, there are many different facets that might be recognized in a definition. One of the most basic divisions is between (1) external, material culture and (2) internal, mental culture.

THE COMPONENTS OF CULTURE

External, Material Culture

External, material culture refers to the *tangible* objects of our world—the things that we can see, touch, and use in our day-to-day living. Our material culture allows us to express ourselves aesthetically (as, for example, in art and music), protect ourselves (with clothing, buildings, etc.), and enjoy our leisure (with books, sports equipment, etc.). It includes the means by which we make ourselves more attractive, and it allows us to perform bodily functions (eating, sleeping, shaving) more safely. Material culture also provides a means for division of labor, so that each of us can exchange the products of our work for the output of others and thereby raise the living standards of all parties. Much of the difference we see in the lives of Revital Ofir and Seeta Singh is a result of differences in the external, material dimensions of their cultures.

External, material culture: The tangible objects of our word.

Internal, Mental Culture

Internal, mental culture refers to the ideas and points of view that are shared by most members of a society. The most prominent of these include *knowledge systems* (such as

Internal, mental culture: The ideas and points of view that are shared by most members of a society.

language, sciences, and objective descriptions of the material culture), *belief and value systems* (such as religious, political, or social philosophies), and the *social normative system*. When there are differences in knowledge systems or in belief and value systems, people actually "see the world" differently (we will discuss this point further in the next section of the chapter).

Let us now consider the idea of a "social normative system," something we may not have thought about before. The most basic concept is that of a norm.[3] **Norms** are guides or rules for behaving in certain situations or for adopting a particular role. **Sanctions** are used to enforce norms; these consist of some form of reward for behavior in keeping with the norm and some sort of punishment for behavior in violation of the norm. Norms can be classed into four basic categories: fads and fashions, folkways, mores, and laws. **Fads**, which come and go very quickly, and **fashions**, which have only a little longer existence, are the least significant of the norms because they do not persist for long times in the culture. Both fads and fashions have certain interesting characteristics, however. They are associated with enthusiasm and intensity. The social forces for conforming with a fad or fashion can be quite powerful, and a person who refuses to conform risks being labeled "out-of-date," an "oddball," or worse. We should also recognize that *fashion* does not only apply to the clothing field; politics, entertainment, literature, and management are all subject to "fashionable" views and practices.

Folkways refer to norms for most routine activities in our everyday life; they define what is socially correct and are subject to only informal sanctions. Every culture has thousands of folkways. Examples include how to greet someone you know only slightly ("Is it expected that I kiss him or her?") and how to dress in a business setting ("Can I wear my running shoes?"). An important aspect of folkways is that over time we accept these behavioral rules as the way we personally do act. As they become a part of us, we tend not to question them or even recognize their existence.

Mores (pronounced mor-ays) are more significant behavior norms than folkways and are subject to more intense sanctions if violated. Mores tend to be associated with moral and religious values in a culture and are treated as being absolute rules for behavior. Consider how you react to cannibalism, nudity on the street, or killing babies of an undesired sex. Each of these taboos would receive strong negative sanctions in the culture of the United States, but we should realize that all have been accepted at one time or another in some cultures in the world. Finally, **laws** are specific rules of behavior created and enforced by some type of special power in the culture. They allow for the formal imposition of sanctions against prohibited behaviors and, thus, are used to enforce the mores of the dominant sector of the society.

In terms of our personal mental development, we should recognize that cultural influences build up over our lives. They strongly affect what we "know" about our world and thus account for a substantial portion of our beliefs and opinions in long-term memory (LTM). Cultural influences also help us interpret external events. This is why, for example, many readers in their twenties would be surprised to have a 56-year-old show up as their blind date, or why most of us would be surprised to see a store paying its customers to take away the merchandise or an ad telling consumers to buy a competing brand because it's really better! These events don't occur in our culture, and they are not in accord with the beliefs and expectations we have in our minds.

As noted, over time we *internalize* the prevailing cultural values into our own personal values. This process is termed **enculturation,** or the learning of a person's

Norms: Social guides or rules for behaving in certain situations: range includes fads, folkways, mores, and laws.

Enculturation: The learning of a person's own culture.

own culture. The learning of a different culture, as when a person might immigrate or be transferred to work in a different land, is known as **acculturation** (for marketing purposes, this topic becomes very important in international business).

Acculturation: The learning of a different culture.

In summary, because of its powerful presence in every person's mind, cultural influence is a powerful force in our external social world. Social norms, in fact, are actually beliefs and rules that are held in people's minds in exactly the same ways. Because of this, there is a pervasive force toward *conformity* arising from cultural influences in the external consumer environment, since each of us agrees about these particular aspects of the world. In the main, this is a stabilizing force that helps people to adapt to their world, and for the culture to run smoothly.

CULTURAL UNIVERSALS

The notion of **cultural universals** springs from an interest in the *similarities* between cultures or the search for "the universal pattern" that all cultures share. The results are worth taking a short time to think about.[4]

Cultural universals: Elements that are common to all known cultures: represent the nature of human life.

For example, according to leading anthropologists, all the cultures ever known have created some type of system to deal with such topics as language, cooking, housing, hygiene, law, medicine, education, and kinship and marriage. "Of course," someone might object, "What's so surprising about that? All those things are related to important needs that we all have." What is really interesting is that the list doesn't stop there. Figure 12-1 lists 21 elements that were found to be present in all known human cultures (and this is only a partial listing). It is interesting to read the entries in a leisurely fashion. Think, for example, what it means that virtually every person in the entire history of the world has been involved in each of these activities!

In summary, when we stress the similarity of cultures we are dealing with the nature of humans. George Murdock, an anthropologist, summed it up well:

> This basis (for a universal cultural pattern) cannot be sought in history, or geography, or race, or any other factor limited in time or space, since the universal pattern links all known cultures, simple and complex, ancient and modern. It can only be sought, therefore, in the fundamental biological and psychological nature of man and in the universal conditions of human existence.[5]

If you would like to read more about these types of cultural characteristics and their implications for marketing, you might wish to pursue the excellent article in Note 6.

All cultures known in history have possessed or engaged in some form of		
Athletics	Feasting	Magic tricks
Body decoration	Forbidden foods	Music
Calendar making	Funeral ceremonies	Myths and legends
Courtship	Games	Personal names
Dancing	Giving of gifts	Supernatural beings
Dream interpretation	Hair styling	Religious rituals
Etiquette	Joke making	Status and prestige ranks

FIGURE 12-1 A Partial List of Cultural Universals

■ CONSUMER BEHAVIOR ACROSS CULTURES

 Cross-Cultural Customs Quiz

The rapid growth of international business means that many readers will be dealing across cultures in the future. When they do, they will discover many interesting points of similarity and of difference. The following quiz raises just a few of these:

1. True or false: Direct eye contact is considered rude in Europe.
2. True or false: In China, it is a good idea to present a clock to a business associate.
3. True or false: In Hungary, be careful about asking about buses.
4. Which brand of Australian beer probably won't be imported to the United States?
5. Which Anheuser-Busch subsidiary in Europe probably won't export its brand name for bread to the United States?

Answers: (1) False, it is a sign of sincerity; in the Far East, however, it does border on rude behavior. (2) False, since a clock symbolizes death. (3) True, the English pronunciation means fornication. (4) Fourex (a name already used in the United States by a condom brand). (5) Bimbo, a market leader of premium baked goods!

It is interesting to realize that people living in other cultures have experienced differing life-styles, events, norms, and customs in their cultures. Of course, over time, with international trade, travel, satellite communication, and immigration, cultures have come to have increasing effects on one another. Even so, the fact remains that *cultural differences* in consumer behavior are extremely important to marketers. What are some primary dimensions of these differences?

ECONOMIC, TECHNOLOGICAL, AND POLITICAL DIFFERENCES

Why does consumer behavior differ in different countries? Some of the answers are obvious, while others are less clear on the surface. Let's consider some of the most obvious dimensions leading to differences in consumer behavior:

- *Consumer incomes.* In most instances within the U.S. culture, a consumer exchanges money for products or services. In some other cultures of the world, though, money is a less used medium for exchange simply because a large number of consumers do not possess enough money income to be able to purchase their basic needs for living. Of all the countries of the world, only a relatively few would qualify as consumer economies that are basically similar to that of the United States.

- *Economic infrastructures.* This refers to the financial and physical (roads, power, buildings, etc.) resource systems available to support economic activities. Differences in **economic infrastructures** mean that many products considered a necessity in the United States may not be functional in large sections of other cultures. Electricity, for example, is not readily available in many rural areas of the world: this presents an obvious barrier to use of household appliances. Supplies of gasoline, refrigerant, and other specialty commodities may not be readily available, or the routine supply of repair parts and trained repairpersons may be a problem.

Economic infrastructure: The physical and financial resource systems available to support economic activities.

- *Government policies.* Finally, governments in all nations have adopted policies that have the effect of encouraging different forms of consumption in their countries, while discouraging other forms. For example, most nations have erected trade barriers against certain imported products, such as autos and foods, to protect their home-based industries against possibly ruinous competition. (This practice usually has the effect of raising consumer prices for the products in question, but protects the jobs of domestic workers in the affected industries, thus shielding their personal

314

incomes and consumer spending.) At the extreme, some governments have for many years controlled the production of consumer products to be able to allocate national resources to particular economic sectors (for example, power plants, steel mills, railroads, and armaments). And in many countries, certain goods—for example, cigarettes, liquor, and jewelry—are singled out for "luxury taxes" to raise their actual prices to consumers and perhaps to discourage their use (in many U.S. states and cities, for example, these "sin taxes" are popular alternatives to increasing property taxes or income taxes).

An important point for us is to realize that *the greater the degree of differences in consumer incomes, economic infrastructures, and/or government policies, the less we are able to use marketplace behavior as a guide to knowing the true desires of consumers.* All these factors act to change the material elements of culture and serve to enlarge the differences we see in consumer behavior across cultures.

LIFE-STYLE, LANGUAGE, AND BELIEF DIFFERENCES

Beyond the economic and material realm, other cultural differences in consumer behavior occur because of the ways that different people have learned to want to live their lives. Consumer behavior springs from the value systems and daily life-styles of a people and generally serves to support their preferred ways of living and of viewing the world. Before turning to comparisons across cultures, let's briefly examine some dominant traits of the U.S. culture.

Traditional American Values

At a cultural level, values are reflected by widely held beliefs about what is desirable. However, the attempt to identify the major values of the American culture is extremely difficult. Most of us do not talk about our values—indeed, they do not even seem to enter our consciousness in any neat and clean form (also, not every American subscribes to every dominant value in the culture, and some values are becoming less strong in the current generation, while other values are becoming stronger today). Recognizing these difficulties, one of the most impressive attempts to isolate key American values was made by Robin Williams, a sociologist who proposed *six summary propositions* representing the traditional American culture (some students have found it useful to employ the acronym "MERCER" to aid in recalling them: key words for this are in bold in the headings). Let's look at each of these six propositions:[7]

1. *Attempts at active **mastery**.* Americans stress power, approve of assertiveness, encourage expressions of desire, and refuse to accept temporary setbacks. Active mastery falls at the other extreme from passive acceptance of what the world may bring.

2. *Focus on the **external** world.* American culture is interested in objects and current events more than inner experiences involving meaning or feeling. The American genius is in manipulation rather than contemplation.

3. *A **rationalist** faith.* In keeping with their openness to the future and their willingness to entertain change, Americans stress scientific approaches to the daily world. Tradition is not as important as in some other cultures, but orderly planning for the future is quite important.

4. *Acceptance of a **changing** world.* Americans welcome an open view of the world— one that provides for change, growth, and movement. The American personality

As globalization of trade expands, citizens in many cultures are increasingly concerned about jobs and incomes, due to plants moving to other countries. These consumers, for example, may well check to see if this clothing is "Made in the USA."

is outgoing and adaptive and expects things to be different tomorrow from what they were yesterday.

5. *Belief in* **equality** *of opportunity.* American culture shows a strong belief in equality of opportunity for all, and a universalist ethic, in which laws are meant to apply to everyone equally. Also, there is relatively more emphasis on peer relations than on superior-subordinate relationships.

6. *Respect for the Lone Ranger.* Americans retain an underlying respect for the individual pursuing his or her own vision in the world and have somewhat less regard than other cultures for group identity and responsibility to a group.

Although it may be difficult for Americans to recognize, each of these characteristics differs from the traditional values of many other cultures of the world. As they experience other cultures through travel, discussions, or postings in international business, they will increasingly encounter contrasts with these traditional beliefs. (In addition, Appendix 12A provides a related discussion of social stratification in cultures, which will further address some of the reasons for differences both among and within the cultures of the world.)

Life-style and Belief Differences

Figure 12-2 summarizes some of the major life-style and belief bases that underpin differences in consumer behavior across cultures. Marketers need to be aware of each of these and check to see how they may apply to a particular situation. First, **differences in cultural values** can be a key factor in understanding cross-cultural consumer behavior. For example, some American marketers have found that a good way to sell to consumers in Southeast Asia is to stress the previous success

Basis of Difference	Example
Cultural values	Marlboro in Hong Kong
Cultural conventions	Detergent box in Middle East
Climate and geography	Vehicles in rough terrain
Physiological characteristics	Powdered milk in South America
Needs and use environment	Toothbrushes in Vietnam
Perceptions of product need	Deodorant usage
Past product experience	Campbell's soup in England
Product usage customs	Detergent in Peru
Existing product preferences	Cornflakes in Japan

FIGURE 12-2 Dimensions of Differences in Cross-cultural Life-styles and Beliefs

of the product being offered. The reason: Asian people prefer to be harmonious with their social group rather than stand out through individual choice. As an illustration, Phillip Morris has been very successful with its Marlboro brand in Hong Kong by citing the brand's dominant market share in the United States. Each time a new report on cigarette brand market shares is issued, the results are beamed by satellite to Hong Kong consumers and announced on TV.[8]

Cultural conventions are a second important factor. These reflect the normal ("conventional") ways that consumers of a given culture have learned to think and act. For example, a well-known marketing story concerns the large detergent manufacturer that shipped a new set of print ads to its Middle East subsidiary. The ads showed, left to right, pictures of a laundry sequence: a picture of soiled clothes, followed by a picture of the soap box, followed by a picture of clean clothes. The firm's headquarters forgot, however, that consumers in these countries had learned to read *from the right to the left.* Their logical interpretation of the package, therefore, was that this product would actually soil clothes![9]

Climate and geography raise a third set of important considerations for consumer behavior. Many vehicles are simply not engineered for operation in very cold climates, for example, or in rugged terrain. **Physiological differences** also exist between cultures and can sometimes be very significant. In one case, a foreign aid program sent huge quantities of powdered milk to natives in South America. Claiming that it made them ill, the natives instead used it to whitewash their houses! It later turned out they were right: an enzyme needed to break down the product is present in the digestive systems of North Americans and Europeans, but not in most South American adults, who were unable to digest this product. Novel product uses can also occur when the **cultural need and use environment** is quite different. Some years ago, for example, a U.S. firm was very pleased with its high toothbrush sales in South Vietnam. It later found out that the sales spurt had been due to the Vietcong soldiers using the product to clean their guns as they fought the American forces!

Perceptions of product need can also differ across cultural boundaries. For example, should everyone use a deodorant? Almost all American consumers agree with this premise (89 percent), but only half of Australians do (53 percent), and only three of five French consumers agree (59 percent), according to surveys conducted by a major advertising agency. In addition, **past product experience** also is likely to be different across cultures. Campbell's soup initially failed because of this factor, when it first tried to enter the British market for soup. It turned out that English consumers had never seen "condensed" soup before and interpreted the size of the can as providing them with far too little soup for the money. In this case, Campbell's chose to modify its product by adding water rather than attempting to teach the public the difference in soup styles.

Product use customs, when unnoticed by marketers, can sometimes cause real problems for a firm. A foreign detergent maker, for example, introduced its new stain-removing enzyme product in Peru. After a good trial rate was achieved, sales dropped off quickly. The reason: The local consumers had always boiled their wash to kill germs. Such boiling, however, happened to destroy the enzymes in this product, so that the detergent became useless and did not perform as advertised!

Existing product preferences is the final factor in our list, and it reminds us that the consumers of another culture were managing to get along for many years before our product became available to them. During this time, they have developed their own sets of preferences, which can naturally be hard to overcome. Food is often a problem in this regard, especially when our product type has not previously appeared in the local culture. An American cornflake manufacturer, for example, failed miserably in introducing its product to the Japanese market: the Japanese were not used to breakfast cereals and were simply not interested in them. Similarly, a large U.S.-based catsup maker failed in its attempt to enter the Japanese market: it forgot that soy sauce was a dominant feature of the Japanese culture. Rather than quit, however, the firm was flexible: it began to import the Japanese soy sauce to the American market!

Thus there are many aspects to the life-style and belief system differences across cultures. Unfortunately, even these are not all the factors that need to be considered. In particular, a host of additional problems stems from language barriers across cultures.

Language Differences and the Troubles They Cause

Written and spoken language serves the fundamental purpose of allowing humans to communicate with each other. Within a given culture, language serves to provide continuity and an opportunity for consensus to emerge. Based on our language, we share many concepts in our minds with others in our culture. Across different cultures, however, language differences can set up distinct barriers and sometimes can create aggravating problems. This property of language has affected marketers as they have attempted to cross cultural boundaries and has made it more difficult to develop standardized marketing strategies that can be transferred efficiently from one country to another. Sometimes the results have been amusing: Exhibit 12-1 lists some classic language-based marketing social blunders.

EXHIBIT 12-1 _____

Classic Marketing Mistakes with Language

■ The same word often has different meanings in different languages. One major detergent manufacturer decided to check on this before marketing a new brand name. It found that the brand's name, which meant "dainty" in English, meant "song" in Gaelic, "horse" in an African language, "dimwitted" in the Mideast, and "out of one's mind" in Korea. In the Slavic languages, moreover, the name was obscene and offensive.

- Automakers, for some reason, seem to have had more than their share of these problems. For example, Ford's difficulties with the Spanish language are widely discussed. It introduced a low-cost truck, the "ugly old woman" (Fiera), into some less developed countries. Its Caliente model did not do well in Mexico, perhaps because this is a slang term for a streetwalker there. Finally, in Brazil, the Pinto was changed to the Corcel after its initial introduction: this meant that the "small male appendage" became a "horse" in Portuguese.

- Similarly, the foreign firm selling Evitol shampoo in Brazil was embarrassed to discover it was claiming to be a "dandruff contraceptive."

- Pet Milk has problems with French-speaking consumers, since this word can be translated as "to break wind." Similarly, Fresca soft drinks appeared to be aiming at a specialized market segment in Mexico: the word there is slang for lesbian. And a new airline trying to enter the Australian market chose EMU as its symbol: unfortunately, the emu is an Australian bird that cannot fly.

- Other types of problems can occur when there is no similar collection of letters in another language, so that some translation must occur into different words. When Coca-Cola was attempting to enter China in the 1920s, it developed a group of Chinese characters that sounded like Coca-Cola. Unfortunately, when these characters were placed on the bottles, they translated as "bite the wax tadpole."

- When Hunt-Wesson attempted to introduce its Big John brand into French-speaking Canada, the translation Gros Jos turned out to be slang for a woman with large breasts. The brand sold well, however.

- General Motors, touting its "body by Fisher" to Belgian consumers, found that the phrase was interpreted there as "corpse by Fisher."

- The famous Pepsi-Cola slogan "Come alive with Pepsi!" was translated in Germany as "Come out of the grave!" and in Taiwan as "Bring your ancestors back from the dead."

- Oregon-based Taco Time decided to expand into Japan, when management learned that "tako" can mean either "octopus" or "idiot" in the Japanese language. The company's president commented, "Well, we'll have to do a bit of marketing."[10]

- Sometimes there are problems with high illiteracy rates, when written language cannot be used. One food company maintained its normal practices in selling baby food in Africa. The local population, most of whom could not read, looked at the labels with pictures of infants and interpreted them to mean that the jars contained ground up babies!

- American marketers are not the only ones with language problems. A popular chocolate candy in Europe, for example, did not sell well in the United States. Its name: Zit.

- Similarly, a large Japanese industrial firm entered the United States market with ads promoting its new specialty steel named Sumitomo High Toughness steel. Rather than writing this out each time in the ads, the firm used the acronym in bold capitals throughout the advertising, which closed with a claim that this product "was made to match its name."

- Finally, to attract American tourists, a dress shop in Paris featured the sign: "Come in and Have a Fit!"

Source: These examples are given in an interesting book by David A. Ricks, *Big Business Blunders: Mistakes in Multinational Marketing* (Homewood, Ill.: Dow Jones-Irwin, 1983).

Cross-cultural Hidden Languages

In addition to the overt use of language, people use a variety of other means with which to communicate with each other, including:

- Body movement
- Eye contact and avoidance
- Type of clothing
- Body posture
- Voice tone and pace
- Use of touch

Fa shower Gel is a very high quality German product, and is the number 1 seller in 42 of the 51 countries in which it is sold. When it was brought to the United States, however, some consumers were confused by the packaging and began to request applicators from the company (*douche* is known to mean shower in Europe, but not throughout the U.S.). A special promotional package (bottom photo) clarified the product type and generated substantial trial from American consumers.

Humor is international. This ad was run in the United Kingdom by a famous beer brand from New Zealand. Do you think it would have gone over well if it were run in Australia, though?

This ad is one in a famous series of puns run by NYNEX in the United States. In light of our stories of language problems in this chapter, however, what do you think a consumer in another culture, who does not understand English, might make of it?

A policeman at the accident, Officer Jimmie Boylan, thought, "She's lucky to be alive." Cheryl had just stepped out of her totalled Saturn coupe. Upon impact, her shoulder harness and lap belt held her tight as the spaceframe of her car absorbed most of the collision. He watched as Cheryl's sport coupe and the other cars were towed away.

The following week, Cheryl made the return trip to Saturn of Albuquerque and ordered another SC, just like her first. And then we started noticing some rather unconventional "referrals."

A few days later, Officer Boylan came into the showroom and ordered a grey sedan for himself. Then a buddy of his, also a policeman, did the same. And shortly thereafter, Cheryl's brother, more than a little happy that he still had a sister, and needing a new car himself, bought yet another Saturn in Illinois.

But the topper came when a very nice young woman walked into the showroom to test drive a sedan. She said she just wanted to know a little more about what our cars were like. Not that she was going to buy one right away, or anything. She'd just never seen a Saturn up close until she'd rear-ended one out on the highway several weeks earlier.

A DIFFERENT KIND OF COMPANY. A DIFFERENT KIND OF CAR.
If you'd like to know more about Saturn, and our new sedans and coupe, please call us at 1-800-522-5000.

CHERYL SILAS had a highway collision, was hit twice from behind, and then sold three cars for us.

© 1991 Saturn Corporation. Cheryl Silas is pictured with a 1991 Saturn SC.

In the next chapter we will take up the topic of social and situational influences on consumer behavior, including a discussion of referral networks and consumer word–of–mouth. The workings of these factors is well captured in this powerful story from Saturn, which at the time was still developing its brand image in the minds of consumers.

How to Put Your Product on the Road to Success.

Targeting Consumers at the Crossroads of Their Lives

LIFESTAGE MARKETING

MATURE COUPLES
TEENAGE HOUSEHOLDS
NEWLYWEDS
YOUNG SINGLES
YOUNG COUPLES

MRI
MEDIAMARK RESEARCH INC.

Identifying the consumers who are right for your product is no longer a matter of what *age* they are, but what *stage* in life they occupy.

As adults move through transitions in their lives, their needs and priorities change as consumers. *Lifestage Marketing* is the fascinating new booklet from Mediamark Research Inc. that points you in the direction of increasing your product's chance for success by discovering which "lifestage" it appeals to.

Using product purchase and usage information drawn from Mediamark's Survey of American

Consumers, the most widely used database of its kind, *Lifestage Marketing* takes you step-by-step through five adult lifestages and the consumer patterns each represents.

Call For Your Free Copy

For a free copy of *Lifestage Marketing,* call Evelyn Carter at (212) 599-0444, or contact the Mediamark office nearest you. Additional copies are available on request.

So call today. After all, the road to success starts with the first step.

MRI

© Mediamark Research Inc. 1990

MEDIAMARK RESEARCH INC.
708 THIRD AVENUE, NEW YORK, NY 10017
500 NORTH MICHIGAN AVENUE, CHICAGO, IL 60611
690 MARKET STREET, SAN FRANCISCO, CA 94104
12001 VENTURA PLACE, STUDIO CITY, CA 91604
A member of the MAI Information Group

Here is an ad aimed at marketers, explaining how this research firm's studies of consumers at different lifestages can help to target marketing strategy. Our discussion of the "consumer life cycle" begins on page 406, in Chapter 14.

Edward T. Hall, the noted anthropologist, has termed these **hidden languages** referring to the fact that people in a culture learn to communicate with each other through these other means as well as through spoken language.

Within a culture, we share an implicit understanding of what these hidden languages mean. We are comfortable with them and know how to use them, even if we are not always conscious of doing so. This point is especially apparent when we encounter someone who does not understand the hidden language the same way we do.

For example, the *use of space* is one of the hidden dimensions of culture, and very strict (albeit unspoken) rules develop as to how space is to be handled in personal interactions. As a simple example, consider how you feel when someone you don't know well stands very close to you while talking and breathes directly into your face. In some cultures this is the accepted mode of communication: to do otherwise is to insult the person with whom you are trying to talk. In other cultures, as in the United States, this is extremely uncomfortable, as it is perceived to violate a person's "private space."

As a second example, consider how the context or situation must be understood similarly by both parties in a particular communication. For example, the same action (e.g., staring into another's eyes) can mean very different things depending on the other person's relationship to you, his or her status or role, and the general situation. Within consumer behavior, these topics have particular importance for communication situations such as salesperson-customer interactions and in reaching business sales agreements. (This is a broad, interesting area that has become increasingly important as international business has grown. Good references are available, listed in Note 11.)

CROSS-CULTURAL DEVELOPMENTS IN CONSUMER POLICY

The development of specific public policies toward marketers and consumers provides one of the clearest areas for cultural differences to emerge. Here, the primary focus is within a single country, reflecting the question of which policies are most appropriate for that culture. As we'd expect, different countries have arrived at different answers, with religious forces and political philosophies playing an important role in these decisions. Several years ago in Indonesia, for example, the president abruptly announced a ban on all television advertising. He explained that he did so because advertising stirs materialist wants and acts to retard development of the nation.[12] In Norway, a Singapore Airlines ad to business travelers was banned by the consumer ombudsman. The ad, which stressed an attractive Oriental stewardess bringing a pillow and serving brandy to a tired male passenger, was intended to focus attention on the gracious service offered by this airline. The ombudsman, however, said that women are not pleasant, smiling servants and cannot be used to sell airline flights.[13]

The development of consumer policy is often difficult when there are strong differences in subcultures within a country. Here we find pressures arising from different groups of consumers (and from the marketing community) who are attempting to operate according to their views of what is best. In the United States, for example, a key issue involves the balance of marketer freedoms against consumer protection. In many other cultures, however, religious values are placed on a much higher level than are individual freedoms. For example, one-fourth of the world's consumers are Moslems. Some countries with Moslem majorities have at various times simply banned products or marketing practices that conflicted with tenets of the religion. Even when this was done, however, the policymakers had to deal with the forces for economic growth and consumer subcultures that wanted to see Westernized practices in the country.

Hidden languages:
The ways people communicate with each other not including spoken language.

Pakistan, for example, is an Islamic country that had been a rather freewheeling consumer nation under both democratically elected governments and military dictatorships since its formation by the partition of a British India in 1947. Then, about 20 years ago, a strongly religious military dictatorship took over the country. The new government instituted traditional Moslem punishments for serious violations of social laws—a thief's right arm is severed and an adulteress is sentenced to death by stoning, for example. Within the consumer sphere, while dancing, lingerie, and alcohol were banned as representing decadent behavior, television advertising was allowed to continue for other products. However, an influential national commentator then took to the air to complain that Pakistani women were being exploited and commercialized and that these practices were in clear violation of God's will that women have a position of sanctity in the society. His solution: The government should ban all women from appearing in advertising. This sentiment received strong support from the dominant subculture in the nation. Another subculture, however—represented by the All-Pakistan Women's Association—immediately staged an angry demonstration against both the premises and proposal of the commentator. What should the public policymakers do in this instance?[14]

Thus the making of consumer policy is a controversial and complex process in most cultures. Since most of us live within only a single culture, we cannot easily see just how very differently cultures deal with the same types of issues. For marketers engaged in international business, however, such differences are crucial. Let's briefly examine a few facets of this issue.

THE "GLOBAL VILLAGE": IMPLICATIONS FOR MARKETERS

Our discussion to this point has indicated how significant economic, political, and lifestyle dimensions are in determining consumer behavior across cultures. Each of these also impacts marketing managers in many specific ways, depending on the product and country in question. Therefore, it is virtually impossible to generalize about a single "international picture" for most marketing situations. For example, one recent study of promotional laws found that a marketer considering an international promotional campaign in 42 countries would find 42 different sets of regulations! The regulatory differences, moreover, are not minor: in some countries coupons are restricted or banned, in some countries gifts are restricted or banned, while in some countries sweepstakes or games are banned. Further, the specific regulations are continually changing in various directions.[15] The result is that *marketers must approach each country individually* to undertake this effort.

Despite these types of barriers, the rapidly increasing importance of international business is introducing significant changes into the courses offered by business schools and executive training institutes. Thus a number of managerial tips and techniques are available in current courses, books, and articles in this area. Beyond the managerial specifics, however, there are several broader issues that deserve our attention.

■ *Huge differences in population trends.* Consumer markets fundamentally depend upon population. A glimpse at trends indicates a global future quite different from our past. As you may know, *growth has virtually stopped in the most affluent countries, but is continuing rapidly elsewhere.* For example, at recent rates, Canada's population will not double for 90 years, the United States's for 100 years, Japan's and France's for 150 years, Britain's for 300 years, and Italy's for 2,300 years! In contrast, at current rates India—which already has the world's second largest population—will double its population in just over 30 years, as will many smaller countries. Overall, in 30 years

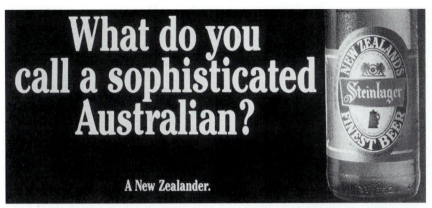

International humor is at work in English transit poster advertising a beer made on the other side of the world.

(about the time when many of this book's readers should be enjoying successful senior executive positions), we can expect the entire population of the affluent markets of the world today to have a combined population only about half that of either China or India alone![16] Of course, this simple analysis does not account for many other important factors. It does, however, indicate where the massive future growth in the world will be occurring, and it has clearly captured the attention of business and government planners around the globe!

■ *The key for marketers: subcultures and segments.* Within international marketing, it is important to note that *each marketer will be concerned with only a portion of each relevant market.* This will usually be sufficient for profitability and can make matters easier when natural segments exist. According to a European manager, a Paris business executive will likely have more in common with business executives from Oslo or Rome than with a small-town French café-owner: "Once you have identified the same group in different markets, you can develop a strategy that appeals cross-culturally." Benetton, for example, has done this by appealing to young people in different countries who all want stylish, affordable clothes. Even so, the local campaigns are likely to be modified to work more smoothly within each culture.[17]

■ *Fundamental changes in economic and political systems.* As a final point in our cross-cultural analysis, we must consider *cultural change.* It is difficult to express the incredible degree to which our futures are likely to have been altered by the events across cultures in just the past few years. Although we may not recognize it on a day-to-day basis, *we are living in a remarkable period:* it now appears that the decade of the 1990s (together with the 1980s) will prove to be one of the most important periods of *fundamental restructuring* in our world's history! As we move toward the Year 2000, we see the massive populations of China, the former Soviet Union, and Eastern Europe still in the process of working toward some form of economic and political equilibria, with complex pressures at work, and much uncertainty facing the participants. At the same time, we see "economic miracles" developing in some smaller nations of the "Pacific Rim," but continuing warfare and severe starvation conditions elsewhere in the world. Altogether, the picture is rapidly changing—fraught with danger, but pregnant with opportunity for a better world. As a marketer, it is imperative that you will keep informed about these international developments as they occur in the future.

Change in China: consumers clamor for TV sets in Shanghai.

■ CHANGES IN CONSUMER CULTURES

As we have just seen, there is an *extremely high rate of change* in some aspects of modern cultures. The topic of cultural change is an extremely important issue for marketers, who must adapt to survive, and who will prosper if they anticipate and handle cultural change well.

All of us have lived during a period of constant flux, so that, without thinking much about it, we tend to accept and expect change in our lives. We share these types of changes with huge numbers of people—these are the cultural shifts that have the major impacts on consumer behavior in the marketplace. Changes in the consumer environment sometimes occur suddenly, as in the case of fads, but more often they tend to move slowly into the lives of more and more people until they are recognized as having "arrived." This process of acceptance across a society is known as *diffusion*, and it will be discussed in an upcoming section. For the present, however, let's consider some examples of changes that have occurred in some very different areas of consumer behavior in the recent past. These are listed in Exhibit 12-2.

EXHIBIT 12-2

Recent Changes in Consumer Markets

Where Do We Shop?

The typical business executive will work for 40 years (perhaps in several different fields). What kinds of changes can he or she expect to see, based on our recent past experience? For example, some 30 years ago, there were fewer than 1000 shopping centers in the entire United States. None were enclosed, climate-controlled "malls" as we know them today. Altogether, shopping centers accounted for only 7 percent of retail purchases. Today, there are about 20,000 shopping centers in the United States, *accounting for half of all consumer retail purchases in the nation.* Thus have shopping centers become a key element in the life-styles of millions of American consumers today. However, purchasing by TV and computer is now beginning to spread: what will the shopping picture be twenty, thirty, or forty years from now?[18]

Cosmetics and Style Changes

In 1940, Charles Revson revolutionized the cosmetic field by matching lipstick to his Revlon nail care line. Stylish lips matched fingertips for the first time, and Revlon's sales increased 50 percent! Vibrant red was the decade's color, and rouge, cake mascara, and leg makeup (nylon was being rationed for the war effort) accompanied the heavy use of lipstick and nail polish. The 1950s saw a shift to the eyes, as eyeliner was introduced and mascara became available in different colors. In the 1960s, hair moved to center stage, first with elaborate beehives and pageboy fluffs, then with wigs, falls, and fake eyelashes. Then flower children and the women's liberation movement moved to the fore. The long hair and natural ingredients that dominated the late 1960s and early 1970s were replaced by short cuts and natural looks. As the beauty industry moves through 1990s, the cultural changes that had taken hold over the years are causing harder times for marketers. Total sales are huge (over $10 billion), but are almost flat from year to year. The industry is looking harder at males as their main target for future sales growth. Will men be willing, though, to increase greatly their use of cosmetics and beauty aids?[19]

In Touch with the Media

Consumers' access to media technology stands out as one of the major changes in our history. In 1950, for example, 40 percent of U.S. households did not have their own telephones. Television had just appeared, and less than 10 percent of households owned this new communications marvel, which offered its programs in living black and white! If we consider these figures today, we can quantify the incredible change in consumers' life-styles. Telephones are now in over 96 percent of all homes, radios in 99 percent (with six sets per household), and television in 98 percent (with almost two sets per household). Cable systems are rapidly penetrating our daily lives, as are home computers and cellular telephones. Reading, however, is an activity on the decline. Today, about half of all American adults almost never read a book or magazine. Newspapers are also on a decline: today, one newspaper is being printed for every four American consumers, down from one for every three in 1950.[20]

Paying Less in a World of Inflation

During the past 25 years the consumer price index has soared: goods costing $100 in 1967, for example, cost over three times that much today. Did you know, though, that in the 1960s the famous Neiman-Marcus catalog was offering a home video recorder for $34,000? Or that ballpoint pens were introduced after World War II for $12.50 for a utility version? Or that a portable calculator used to weigh 3 pounds, while a portable dictating machine tipped the scales at 8 pounds and cost $650? Many other examples exist, but those given indicate how strongly technological advances and mass production have brought affordable changes to the consumer culture of our modern world.[21]

Fitness as a Consumer Life-style

During the last 25 years the proportion of American adults who report exercising regularly has increased from 24 percent to almost 50 percent. So what, you say? During this same time, there has been a 25 percent decline in deaths from coronary heart disease and a 33 percent drop in the incidence of strokes. There have been booming markets in various food and recreation product categories aimed at fitness, whereas marketers of products associated with health risks have seen declines in their total demand levels. Milk, cream, butter, and egg consumption have all declined. Cigarette and cigar smoking by adults has fallen also. Finally, hard liquor marketers are concerned about their products' declining sales: the average consumption is dropping each year, especially in brown liquors. Distillers are now trying to sell lower-proof mixed drinks, such as Bacardi Breezer and Tennessee Tea, to prop up this sagging market.[22]

American Consumers' Discovery of Wine

Some years ago, a market research firm asked Americans who they thought drank wine. The three answers were "foreigners," "rich people," and "bums." This attitude had persisted for many years, as few consumers even considered using this product. In 1960, for example, the U.S. market was still small. Red wine was by far the consumers' favorite, accounting for 75 percent of all sales. By the 1990s, however, the situation had changed markedly. Not only were millions of consumers drinking wine, but their tastes had changed as well. White wine was now the favorite, with rose and blush varieties in second place. Red wines were now the least favored, with only 15 percent of sales.

As we move into the 1990s, wine seems to be slipping slightly from consumers' favor, with U.S. sales beginning a slight decline. Of further importance to marketers, the current market is highly segmented. For example, a mere 5 percent of the U.S. consumers account for 50 percent of the wine consumed! About one-third of American adults drink wine, while another third refuse to do so for health and religious reasons. The wine industry is viewing the remaining third as its huge potential growth market and would like to know how to convert them to regular usage. Any suggestions?[23]

While reviewing the examples in the exhibit, notice how each set brings with it new *challenges* for some marketers (as markets move away from their product offerings and profits fall) and new *opportunities* for other marketers alert enough to "be there" with a marketing mix to fit the new consumer behaviors. These are just a few examples of the massive shifts that continually occur in the consumer marketplace. Even though these are just a few examples, notice what they say about how a person's consumer behavior will have shifted over recent years. Consumers have changed where they shop, what they view as being in style, what they watch and read, and what they can afford. Modern consumers have also changed what they eat and what they avoid, what they do for fitness, and how they spend their leisure time. From a marketer's perspective, if a shift similar to one of these occurs, it can mean either huge rewards or bankruptcy. *It is clearly important to adapt the marketing mix appropriately.* To do this best, we need to understand what forces are behind the changes and to identify what trends are likely in the future.

MONITORING CULTURAL TRENDS

Cultural trends are broad and sweeping: No one of us can possibly be exposed enough in our personal life to discern each trend as it is developing. There are, however, some research-based approaches that can be used in the attempt to discern key trends.

One method is to use content analysis, a technique refined during World War II by America's spy agency, the OSS (now the CIA). **Content analysis** is a systematic method of objectively studying what is contained in a given set of communications.[24] The best known user of content analysis to study cultural trends is John Naisbitt, author of the best-seller *Megatrends,* which sold over 5 million copies, in 17 languages. Naisbitt's firm monitors each issue of 200 daily newspapers in the United States. Every local news article is coded into a massive data bank, which is analyzed to discover the total amount of attention that is being devoted to any particular topic. The results are tabulated in a *Trend Report* sent to subscribing firms and agencies on a regular basis. In general, topics receiving greater attention are used as signals of future developments, and as possible themes for new product developments, ad campaigns, and so forth.[25]

Content analysis represents an indirect research approach to assessing cultural trends. A *direct* approach is to use survey research techniques. Here the researcher simply asks people about their current views about the world around them and their places in it. If the sample is selected well, if the questions are appropriate and worded well, and if people answer them honestly, this survey-based approach can yield valuable insights into our culture. Such an undertaking is no small matter, however, as it might involve in-depth interviews (1 to 2 hours long) with a nationally representative sample of over 2000 consumers. Since these measures are relevant to many marketers, however, they can be sold similarly to the content analysis reports, on a subscription basis to marketers, who pay $15,000–35,000 for the findings.

In terms of current trends, listed next are eight major changes as seen by such leading trend-watchers in the marketing research field as Joseph Smith, Florence Skelley, Judith Langer, Faith Popcorn, and Daniel Yankelovich. Let's take a brief look at each, to clarify the nature of the trend:[26]

- **"Nobody's Old Anymore"** refers to the fact that more people are living longer and are active during most of this time. Many of these people genuinely don't feel old, and they don't want to be forced to live as if they were.

- **"Time Is Precious"** is a feeling that results from the expanded number of obligations and options faced by a number of people today. For these persons, there simply doesn't seem to be enough time to do everything they have (want) to do. If they can gain time by sacrificing some money (as by paying more for a convenience product) they are very pleased to do so.

- **"Money Is for Pleasure"** refers to a change in consumers' views about the value and purpose for this asset. In past generations, money was seen as a security guarantee, to protect against bad times or an unforeseen event. More recently, people have been shifting their views toward seeing money more as a tool for achieving pleasure and less as a protective device.

- **"A Return to the Home"** reports a shift back to the home as a place to relax, entertain, or be entertained. Driven by the increase in the number of working women (for whom a night out is not always a pleasant prospect), and by new entertainment technologies (VCRs, cable TV, and computer games), this shift, sometimes called *cocooning,* is also reflected in an increase in "do-it-yourself" home projects.

- **"A Growing Concern for Health"** deals with fitness ("feeling healthy and looking good") as well as avoidance of disease. This trend should soon clash with the rising costs of the U.S. health system (now over 10 percent of the gross national product) to produce changes in the nation's medical practices.

Content analysis: The objective study of what is contained in a given set of communications.

- **"Rise of the Two-Earner Family"** contributes to several of the other trends in terms of changes in time pressures, life-styles, and incomes. For some of these families, the incomes are moderate, but for others—households in which two professionals are bringing home paychecks—this trend is resulting in the creation of a new class of "rich" consumers whose problems lie in finding the time to spend the money they have!

- **"A Return to Tradition"** may be related to the middle-life stage of the baby boom generation. Proms are back, as are ceremonial, social-event weddings. Organized religion is increasing again. Nostalgia is rising on the radio, and the sexual revolution is moving back toward more monogamous relationships.

- **"Visible Virtue"** reflects a desire to give toward the improvement of society. During the 1990s, citizens' increasing concerns about the "3 E's"—education, ethics, and the environment—will lead to some major changes during this decade.

These trends have already led to some significant changes for marketers, and they will continue to drive shifts in marketing mixes in the years to come. In addition to reacting to cultural change, however, some marketers also help to create changes, by introducing innovations to the society. Our next section examines this important topic.

■ INTRODUCING CHANGE TO A CULTURE: THE "DIFFUSION OF INNOVATIONS"

WHAT IS DIFFUSION?

Innovation: An idea, invention, or process that is new and different.

Diffusion of innovation: The process by which new ideas, products, or practices spread through a culture.

An **innovation** is something that is new. It can include new ideas, new inventions, new ways of doing things, and so on. The term **diffusion,** meanwhile, comes from the Latin word meaning "to spread out." Diffusion is exemplified by the way that gases or vapors slowly expand and spread out through available space. Thus the general topic of **diffusion of innovation:** refers to *the manner in which new ideas, products, or practices spread through a culture*. It represents the fundamental manner in which entire societies change and grow.

Diffusion Is Not Automatic!

This topic is challenging because experience has shown that the diffusion process is not an automatic one—*most new ideas (and new products) do not diffuse through the population. Instead they are rejected and disappear from view.* This often happens even when a new idea or product is clearly an improvement over current practices (recall the many times you've heard a "build a better mousetrap" analogy). Thus, in addition to humans' willingness to change, the *reluctance* of human beings to change their views and behaviors is also an important facet of diffusion theory.

🐦 *The "Black Holes of Marketing"*

Recalling the black holes in outer space, into which matter disappears, marketers sometimes call new product development "The Black Hole of Marketing" into which their dollars disappear. While exact numbers vary, most marketers accept that 80 to 90 percent of new products fail, at enormous costs to the firms that launched them. In the food industry, for example, it is estimated that the costs of launching a new product run $15–20 million and that over *$300 billion* was lost in new product failures over a recent seven-year period. The launching of thousands of new food products each

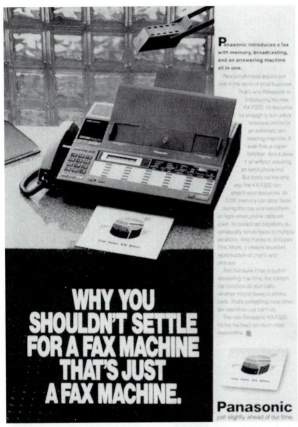

High relative advantage helped fax machines to diffuse more quickly.

How do cordless telephone/answering machines rate on the six diffusion characteristics?

year "is sheer lunacy!" exclaimed the executive vice president of Nabisco Brands, Inc. "[Food marketers] would have done much better had we just taken our new product dollars...and put them in an ordinary passbook savings account." His basic message: Marketers *must* introduce new products, but they must manage this process better than in the past.[27]

TYPES OF INNOVATIONS

When marketers begin to dig into this area, one of the first questions to arise is, "What exactly do we mean by 'an innovation'?" This is important, since the speed and pattern of diffusion will depend on the type of innovation itself. There are three major types of innovations:

■ A **discontinuous innovation** is the most significant type. This is a new product or service that represents a *major change* in the benefits offered to consumers and in the behaviors necessary for them to use the product (i.e., consumers must in some way "discontinue" their past patterns to fit the new product into their lives). Examples include the automobile, airplane, radio, telephone, television, personal computer, and microwave oven. Major technological changes create these types of innovations.

Discontinuous innovation: The strongest category: consumers must discontinue their past patterns to fit the new product into their lives.

NEVER BEFORE SEEN ON TELEVISION!

ON JANUARY 16TH, THANKS TO A LANDMARK FCC DECISION AND TV ANSWER, TELEVISION BECAME A 2-WAY MEDIUM.

Soon you'll be able to . . . preview a whole day's worth of programming and automatically set-up your VCR

play along with live sporting events

participate in your favorite game show

. . . instantly request product information or coupons

. . . order direct response merchandise without using your phone

. . . even order a pizza!

On January 16th, the Federal Communications Commission authorized the use of radio spectrum for the application of 2-Way Interactive Video and Data Services. This decision set the stage for the creation of a network of independent FCC licensees nationwide and with it, the creation of a new communications industry . . . 2-Way Television.

This exciting new technology allows viewers to use their regular TV set to do everything from actively participate in their favorite game shows and sporting events to paying their bills. They can even order a pizza . . . all from the comfort of their favorite chair!

The implications are immense: for consumers it means a whole new way to interact with the world. For advertisers . . . including retailers . . . it means a whole new way to generate immediate/direct response. For TV producers it means achieving levels of viewer interest and involvement never before possible. For educators it means turning the television into a classroom. For banks it means a branch office in every home with a TV set. And for potential local FCC licensees, it could mean the opportunity of a lifetime.

TV Answer pioneered the development of 2-Way TV, championed its authorization by the Federal Communications Commission and is now building a nationwide interactive service network to support local FCC licensees. If you're interested in participating with TV Answer as a potential FCC licensee, network service provider or strategic partner, write: TV Answer, Inc., PO Box 3900, Merrifield, VA 22116-3900. Or call us today at 1-800-222-3584 (fax 1-800-915-7733).

TVAnswer®
AMERICA'S LEADER IN 2-WAY TV

A discontinuous innovation is one that calls for distinct changes in a consumer's behavior in order to use the product or service. Notice that now, at very early stages, two-way television presents challenges to a consumer. Using Figure 12-4, decide how two-way TV stacks up. What early marketing strategies might work best?

Dynamically continuous innovation: A moderately strong category: consumers have to alter their behaviors somewhat.

- **A dynamically continuous innovation** is a moderate-level category, in that consumers have to alter their behaviors somewhat for this type of product, but not too greatly. Examples of this type of innovation include electric toothbrushes, telephone answering machines, voice mail, electric blankets, the Sony Walkman, and VCRs.

- **A continuous innovation** change from current consumer practices (that is, consumers can "continue" their present behaviors, with only minor changes in product benefits). Examples here include new models of automobiles, new flavors of soft drinks, most of those new product failures in foods, and so on. This category contains by far the most new products brought to the consumer market.[28]

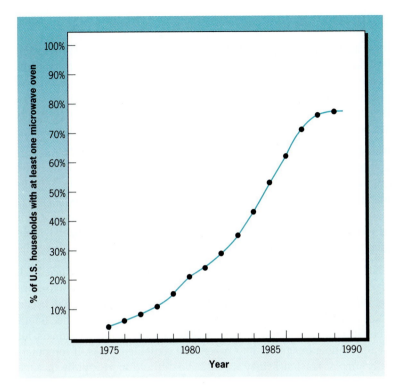

FIGURE 12-3 The S-shaped diffusion curve represented by microwave oven ownership (percentage of U.S. Households owning a microwave oven), 1975–1990

SOURCE: Adapted from Sonia L. Nazavio, "Microwave Packages That Add Crunch to Lunch may Also Pose Chemical Risks," *The Wall Street Journal*, March 1, 1990, p. B1.

THE S-SHAPED DIFFUSION CURVE

What represents the least degree of pattern are we likely to see in the process of diffusion of an innovation across a marketplace? Over many studies of diffusions, it has been found that an **S-shaped diffusion curve** tends to emerge. The case of microwave ovens provides an excellent example: Figure 12-3 depicts the proportion of households at each point in time who had adopted the innovation (own a microwave). Notice that the resulting curve is roughly in the shape of an "S." This carries important implications for a marketing strategist. The essential message is that we can expect a successful innovation to start out rather slowly in terms of its market acceptance, then begin a more rapid growth, then to continue its growth, but at a slower rate, until everyone who will adopt now has done so.

The S-shaped diffusion curve is extremely important for *market forecasting and corporate planning purposes*. When we are talking about a discontinuous innovation, marketers face a situation in which entirely new plants need to be built, new employees hired, and many other business investments made, all before a single item of the new product is even produced. These decisions can involve spending millions of dollars. Since we are talking about a discontinuous innovation, however, there is bound to be considerable uncertainty about how consumers are going to respond to it. This makes the role of advanced consumer research and the development of "marketing models" to estimate future sales especially important (if you would like to learn more about this advanced research area, you may wish to begin with the references in Notes 28 and 29).

Continuous innovation: A weak category of innovation: here a product is modified or improved.

S-shaped diffusion curve: The cumulative adoption of an innovation is likely to be slow at the start, then increase rapidly, then slow again as a ceiling is reached.

HOW FAST WILL DIFFUSION BE?

The potential success and speed of diffusion will depend on both the innovation itself and on the culture into which it is being introduced. Three characteristics of cultures that are more receptive to innovations are (1) a positive view of change as a good aspect of life, (2) members who interact frequently with other social systems, and (3) a positive view of science and education.[30] With respect to innovations themselves, six characteristics have been found to affect speed and success rates:

- **Relative advantage:** the degree of improvement that the new innovation represents over existing alternatives. In general, the greater the relative advantage possessed by an innovation, the faster it will be accepted. Classic marketing examples include the first fluoridated toothpaste (Crest shot to the market leadership position when it was endorsed by the American Dental Association for its decay preventive benefits for children) and the first disposable diapers (the incredible success of Pampers). More recent examples include fax machines and 35mm self-focusing cameras.

- **Complexity:** the inherent difficulty associated with the new idea or product. High levels of complexity can make it more "expensive" for a consumer to try to learn about the innovation and increases the chances that misunderstandings will occur. The converse of complexity is simplicity: simple innovations will, all other things being equal, be diffused faster through a population. Many potential consumers, for example, had a hard time imagining how a personal computer works. If computers were inherently simpler machines, they would have diffused more rapidly through the consumer market.

- **Communicability:** the ease with which the essence of the innovation can be conveyed to potential adopters. New products that lend themselves to usage demonstrations, as automobiles, telephones, and VCRs did, are highly communicable, even though complex. In these cases many consumers were willing to adopt the innovation because they could easily perceive its benefits for them. *Visibility is a related aspect, when consumers are able to see adopters using and benefiting* from the new product. The Sony Walkman, for example, benefited greatly from being highly visible to others. Conversely, innovations with long-term benefits that are difficult for consumers to detect (such as improved nutritional practices, health maintenance practices, and energy-saving appliances) are apt to diffuse more slowly.

- **Compatibility:** how well the innovation fits with the existing beliefs and practices of potential adopters. Sometimes compatibility refers to beliefs or values. In Moslem or Hindu nations, for example, many new products from the West will diffuse slowly (if at all) because their implicit message is incompatible with the cultural beliefs or customs. At other times compatibility refers to consumers' existing ways of using the products themselves. Crest, Gatorade, and Pampers were all compatible with prior consumer use patterns, as are cellular telephones. Automobiles and home computer systems, on the other hand, had to overcome problems of incompatibility, as consumers needed to invest considerable effort to learn how to use these products.

- **Divisibility:** sometimes termed "trialability," this refers to an innovation's capability of being "tried out" in smaller doses by potential adopters. Within the product realm, some innovations lend themselves easily to consumer trial (again, the famous examples of Crest, Gatorade, and Pampers are relevant), while others offer some problems on this (in general, durable goods such as solar energy systems, microwaves, and sonar pest machines can be demonstrated, but their full use cannot easily be experienced by a consumer prior to purchase). The result is that an initial purchase can be a major event, and the diffusion process overall is slowed.

■ **Perceived risk:** consumers' judgments about the adoption of the innovation, especially in terms of possible negative social, economic, or physical consequences. In social settings, for example, ownership of certain innovations (birth control pills or minidresses in conservative cultures, for example) may carry considerable social risks to the potential adopter. Economic and physical perceived risks tend to increase as the cost of an innovation rises, if breakdowns can be a problem, or if repair service may be hard to obtain. Similarly, the pace of innovation itself can be a problem: many consumers perceived that immediate purchases of personal computers were risky in that more options would soon appear and prices would fall as well. Thus there are many reasons that perceived risks can arise to slow the diffusion of an innovation.[31]

Perceived risk:
A consumer judgment of negative social, economic, or physical consequences possible with a purchase.

■ IMPROVING PROSPECTS FOR DIFFUSION SUCCESS

Once marketers are able to discern which of the six key characteristics may hinder the diffusion of a particular innovation, a host of strategies is available to enhance the prospects of success. Some of these are summarized in Figure 12-4. If we examine each problem in turn, we can see how particular weaknesses can be addressed. If we look across the categories, moreover, several interesting issues arise. First, notice that product redesign pops up several times: many innovations have been *technology driven*, and careful attention to *consumer-driven* design issues can pay large dividends. Second, product trials or demonstrations are also frequently mentioned: because innovations adopters. Third, are by definition new to consumers, these marketing tools help to familiarize potential notice that the options use all "4 P's" of the marketing mix: marketers control many means of attracting consumer adoption behaviors. Fourth, the final entry under "low relative advantage" recognizes that many new products—while new for the firms offering them—really do not offer significant new benefits to customers. As the Nabisco executive pointed out, most of these "me-too" products are not really "innovations" and have no real basis for market success. Fifth, two of the entries mention targeting consumer segments. This reminds us that a closer attention to the consumers who will adopt our innovation is extremely important.

THE CONSUMER ADOPTION PROCESS

Up to this point, we have been looking at innovations entirely from the marketer's perspective. However, across a society, the diffusion of an innovation develops from a series of adoption decisions made by individuals, families, or company managers. In attempting to understand these adoption decisions, let us consider the process they undertake. Figure 12-5 depicts our modification of the hierarchy of effects model to reflect adoption decisions in the **adoption-process model.** Notice that the flow of the model is from left to right, across time. **Awareness** of the innovation is the first step toward eventual adoption. Once awareness is achieved, if there is no strong external influence at work; the route goes to **knowledge.** Here the consumer is beginning to learn about the new idea or product and gradually comes to understand its characteristics, and strong and weak points. As knowledge increases, **liking** (or **disliking**) begins to develop as well. The nature of the like/dislike attitude will in part depend on how well our consumer feels the innovation will meet his or her needs.

Adoption-process model: A modified hierarchy of effects model for an innovation: adds "trial" and "use evaluation" stages.

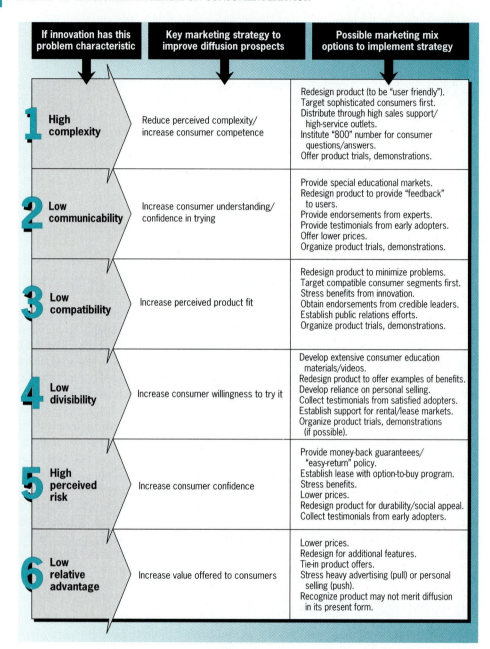

If innovation has this problem characteristic	Key marketing strategy to improve diffusion prospects	Possible marketing mix options to implement strategy
1 **High complexity**	Reduce perceived complexity/ increase consumer competence	Redesign product (to be "user friendly"). Target sophisticated consumers first. Distribute through high sales support/ high-service outlets. Institute "800" number for consumer questions/answers. Offer product trials, demonstrations.
2 **Low communicability**	Increase consumer understanding/ confidence in trying	Provide special educational markets. Redesign product to provide "feedback" to users. Provide endorsements from experts. Provide testimonials from early adopters. Offer lower prices. Organize product trials, demonstrations.
3 **Low compatibility**	Increase perceived product fit	Redesign product to minimize problems. Target compatible consumer segments first. Stress benefits from innovation. Obtain endorsements from credible leaders. Establish public relations efforts. Organize product trials, demonstrations.
4 **Low divisibility**	Increase consumer willingness to try it	Develop extensive consumer education materials/videos. Redesign product to offer examples of benefits. Develop reliance on personal selling. Collect testimonials from satisfied adopters. Establish support for rental/lease markets. Organize product trials, demonstrations (if possible).
5 **High perceived risk**	Increase consumer confidence	Provide money-back guaranteees/ "easy-return" policy. Establish lease with option-to-buy program. Stress benefits. Lower prices. Redesign product for durability/social appeal. Collect testimonials from early adopters.
6 **Low relative advantage**	Increase value offered to consumers	Lower prices. Redesign for additional features. Tie-in product offers. Stress heavy advertising (pull) or personal selling (push). Recognize product may not merit diffusion in its present form.

FIGURE 12-4 Marketing Strategies to Improve Diffusion

Up to this point, Figure 12-5 is identical to the basic hierarchy of effects we discussed in Chapter 7. However, in the special case of an innovation, a consumer is likely to perceive uncertainty and risk. Our model thus suggests that some form of a trial will occur next. Here our consumer will attempt to "try out" the product, but without making a long-term commitment in case it doesn't work out too well. Since the purpose of the trial is to provide the consumer with more information, the **use evaluation** stage is crucial. If this result is positive, **adoption** of the innovation is likely. If not, the liking level will be revised downward, and future adoption is not likely, at least until the situation changes.

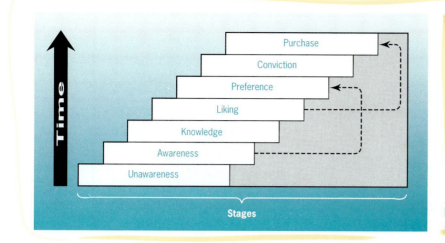

FIGURE 12-5 A Modified Hierarchy for the Adoption Process

The figure also makes it clear that *time* is a variable factor in the process. For example, some people might move through the entire process very rapidly, within a day or two. Other persons may take months to complete the same process. Others, of course, will stop at some point and may never adopt the innovation.

Finally, the dashed arrows in Figure 12-5 address the question of whether a consumer would have to experience the series of steps in exactly the order shown in the figure. Under some conditions we might find slightly different processes. If friends apply social pressures to try a new food product, for example, we might be willing to go right from awareness to trial without knowing very much about the new product (on the other hand, notice that our chances of trial do go up if our friends tell us about it and reassure us that "You'll like it!"). Marketers can attempt to stimulate this awareness-to-trial linkage by providing free trials (e.g., test drives of cars), free samples, and valuable coupons. Sometimes a true trial might be unreasonable, such as with a new surgical procedure or a custom-built home. In these instances the link must go from liking to adoption, as indicated by the second dashed arrow. As we noted earlier, in our discussion of the "divisibility" characteristic, this situation is likely to slow down the adoption process, extending it over a longer time period.

Notice how well the new "Can up" storage trays score on the dimensions of Figure 12-4. Now that it has been patented and trademarked, we can look for it in the canned foods section of supermarkets.

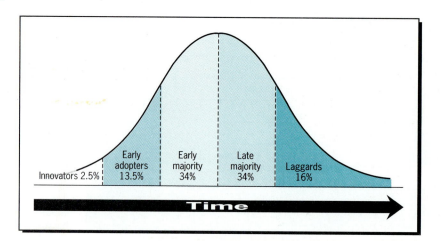

FIGURE 12-6 Adopter Categories

THE FIVE CATEGORIES OF ADOPTERS

Different people proceed through the adoption process at very different rates. This means that some consumers are—psychologically speaking—"in the market" for a new product at a given time, while other consumers will arrive in the market later. Marketers are interested in finding "who" each of these types of people is, so that the group can be targeted with the appropriate marketing mixes at the appropriate times.

If we take an individual-level perspective on the adoption process, it is useful to classify consumers in terms of how soon they are likely to adopt a particular innovation. Figure 12-6 shows the classification, developed by Everett Rogers, a leading figure in diffusion theory. After reviewing over 500 research studies, Rogers proposed a simple but powerful scheme that divides the market into five "types" of consumers, ranked from those who first adopt the innovation to those who come last to the adoption phase.[32]

His fundamental assumption is that the numbers of people falling into each category will approximate a *normal distribution* (which is also related to the S-shaped diffusion curve). This means that, starting from the time that the innovation is first introduced, most people will adopt at some "average" length of time (the mean of this distribution). A few people will adopt very early—these are the **innovators.** Rogers assigned the first 2.5 percent of adopters to this category, representing those who are more than two standard deviations away from the mean time taken for all adopters. Notice that this is a very small portion of the market and that it consists only of those persons who are very early purchasers of the new product. The innovators are soon followed by a somewhat larger group of **early adopters,** who comprise 13.5 percent of the adopting population. This group is followed by the **early majority,** a sizable group comprising just over one-third of all those who will end up adopting the innovation. At this point we have reached the average time for all consumers who will eventually adopt this innovation. Another large group—**the late majority**—now enters the market. Finally, about one-sixth of the target population is seen as trailing in at later points in time (beyond one standard deviation past the mean time for adoption). These are the **laggards.**

Innovators: Adopters of an innovation at a very early time: the first 2.5 percent of adopters.

LOCATING THE CONSUMER INNOVATORS

A substantial number of studies have been done on identifying the kinds of consumers who are the *very first* people to try and buy new products and services.[33] What, in general, has been learned?

We're All Innovators at Heart . . .

We should begin by reminding ourselves that almost everyone is interested in novelty—in new ideas, new stores, and new products. What would our lives be like if nothing new ever entered? Each of us, therefore, is a potential innovator in the sense that we are likely to be interested in trying something that is new to us.[34] To qualify for this title within the consumer marketplace, however, we have to be among the *first consumers to adopt a particular innovation.* Thus the issue is not simply the adoption of something that's new *to us,* but something that's new to the entire market. Also, early *consideration* of an innovation is not enough either: in the research literature those people who were interested but then decided not to adopt are termed **rejectors.** Rejectors have been little studied at all.[35]

Continuous Innovations Bring Out Product-Specific Innovators

With this brief background, we can easily appreciate why, for *continuous* types of innovations, there does *not* seem to be a general innovative consumer. Recall that innovations are those that follow along existing product lines, usually representing new features, styles, and so forth. Purchases of these types of innovations are thus driven by a person's specific interest in a product category. For example, all of us know some people who are very interested in cars, and these are precisely the people we would expect to be first in trying new automotive tools or new accessories. At the same time, we may know others who are caught up with personal computers (though we may not see them often!) and yet others who love music or fashionable clothes. As long as the new products for these categories represent relatively minor modifications, our friends who specialize in each category will likely be the first to learn of the innovations, as well as having the most interest in trying them.

This product-specific nature of innovativeness can be traced to constraints we all face in our lives. Since none of us has unlimited time or unlimited funds, we simply *cannot* innovate across very many categories. In fact, we often are not even aware of the continuous-type innovations until after they have already been adopted by the very first set of consumers! Across all products and services, therefore, *different people tend to act as innovators in different product classes,* very much in keeping with their personal interests.

Innovators Exist for Discontinuous Innovations, Though

In contrast, when a major new innovation arrives, anyone adopting will have to change drastically some elements of his or her consumer life-style. Are there some people who seem to do this systematically more than others?

Within consumer behavior, some of the most prominent findings relate to the *ability to afford* the high prices associated with the initial appearance of prototypes in the market. Innovators have been found to be persons with higher income levels, higher occupational status, and higher levels of education (whether education plays an independent role in creating an innovator, or whether its presence is due to its role in providing the higher income level, is not clear).

Another set of characteristics relates to interests in learning about new products and their opportunities to do so. Innovators have been found to be more cosmopolitan and to travel and read magazines extensively. Thus they are more *socially mobile,* come into contact with many groups, and are exposed to a high level of communications about the world around them. A third set of characteristics reflects *psychological traits.* As we might expect, innovators are less rigid than the average person in dealing with change, and they are *risk takers* and are more *venturesome* than most of the rest of us.

Interestingly, though, the true innovator tends not to be very well integrated into his or her social groups. Instead, these are *inner-directed individuals* who do not wish to rely on others' judgments of which products are good ones to own and use. Somewhat surprising, therefore, is the conclusion that marketers and public policymakers are not wise to rely *too* heavily on innovators as targets for their marketing efforts. This segment is by definition small—only the very first adopters of the innovation—which can make it somewhat inefficient to reach through mass promotional techniques (since the true innovator actually *wants* to buy new ideas and products, however, he or she doesn't require much promotion to create a purchase). The more significant characteristic is the lack of close relationships with social groups. Since innovators tend not to be guided by the norms of their groups, the other members of the groups tend not to be very influenced by the innovators either! Although it is important to have the innovators buy so as to get the process started, they should not be counted on to be the influential "opinion leaders" who will *really* create the burst of adoption interest across the broad consumer market.

THE REMAINING ADOPTER CATEGORIES, IN BRIEF

Early adopters:
Those persons who adopt just after the innovators, but before the rest of the population: the next 13.5 percent of all adopters.

Early adopters represent the next 13. 5 percent of consumers and, together with the early majority, constitute the key targets for marketing and public policy strategists. Early adopters bear some similarities to innovators, in that they are interested in change and are willing to take risks. These people have been found to be very different from innovators in some other significant respects, however. Early adopters tend to be much more integrated with their social groups—they believe in the group norms and are guided by them in their lives. As such, they are less cosmopolitan than innovators, preferring to focus their attention within their local community. Because they are so well tied to their groups, other consumers are well aware of their purchases, and become more likely to view purchase as an acceptable step to take. Thus the early adopter serves as an **opinion leader:** an example for the other consumers in their social systems.

Opinion leader: A consumer who offers advice and has influence on others in his or her social system.

Members of the *early majority* enter the market next, often after having been influenced by an early adopter that they know and respect. These people, who constitute a large and important market segment, tend to be less willing to take risks, although they are interested in acquiring new products. Their shopping may take longer, therefore, as they search for the best alternative available.

Early majority Those persons who adopt after the innovators and early adopters, but before the rest of the population: just over one-third of all adopters.

As time goes on, and more and more consumers adopt the innovation, its "newness" declines, as do the risks associated with owning it. The *late majority*, therefore, is not really buying a new product on the market. In part, this may be due to their financial circumstances: these consumers have somewhat lower incomes than average and tend to be older. They may also be less directly influenced by others in their social group and tend to be more influenced by advertising and other mass media information about the product and its benefits.

Late majority: Those persons who adopt just following the median time for adoption: over one-third of all adopters.

Finally, the *laggards* enter the market after the innovation has been well accepted in general and when few risks are present. At times, in fact, these people are buying the original innovation while early adopters are moving on to a new innovation that offers further improvements, but at higher prices and with greater risks. When it appears that a product's future prospects are not bright, an alert marketer may choose to target this market segment for special promotional efforts, since the laggards may still be good candidates for an initial purchase if the price is right. Laggards have generally not been studied within the field of marketing, so our information about them is sketchy. In other fields, however, a fairly clear picture emerges: laggards are relatively isolated

Laggards: Those consumers who are the last to adopt an innovation: one-sixth of all adopters.

from their community social groups (preferring to communicate within their families) and are not very influenced by others' views. They tend also to be older, to have lower incomes, and to be traditionalists in their outlook on life.[36]

Our brief summary of research findings on the adoption process is sufficient to point out how powerful are the effects of social influences on consumer behavior. We will continue with this thought in our next chapter. At this point, however, we will conclude the present chapter with some broader points about marketing and culture.

CLOSING COMMENTS: MARKETERS AND DIFFUSION

Marketers have an obvious and keen interest in diffusion research because it deals so closely with the topic of new products and their success or failure in the marketplace. Within the broader topic of culture, however, we should realize that marketing was not the first discipline to study diffusion of innovation.

Rural sociology, for example, is a field that has long dealt with this area. Such serious problems as how to persuade farmers to adopt new strains of crops or new methods of cultivation have been studied here. (When we recall that in many areas of the world the failure of a year's crop means literal starvation for a farm family, we can appreciate better why they are reluctant to switch from time-proven methods.) Other fields also have strong interests in diffusion, including *medicine* (how do doctors come to adopt or reject new medicines and treatment methods, given the demands on their time?), *education* (how do teachers learn themselves, and how do they adopt new teaching methods?), and a large number of subject areas associated with *modernization* in developing countries (why are new methods of family planning or sanitation practices, for example, so hard to infuse into these societies?). Finally, in the realm of ideas, the field of *communication research* has long been interested in how people come to change their views of what is correct, what is popular, what is "out," and so forth (many nations have followed on the Nazi example of World War II in stressing centralized communications agencies to work on achieving agreement among citizens on key social questions).

Marketing is a key discipline for the diffusion of innovation, however, even for the other fields just mentioned. For example, marketers sell the new seeds, farm equipment, pharmaceuticals, and so on that are purchased in developing countries. In our modern world, therefore, private marketers are a major force for change and progress. In addition, the subfield of **social marketing** employs advanced techniques to market new ideas and social practices. Sometimes this work is done on behalf of governmental agencies, sometimes for charitable organizations (for example, encouraging people to have blood pressure checks), and sometimes for educational, religious, or civic groups.

Social marketing: The marketing of new ideas and social practices on behalf of not-for-profit organizations.

The Role of Persuasion

We should also recognize that marketing often stresses *persuasion*, attempting to have people change their present beliefs and behaviors. In this sense marketing tends to be **pro-innovation:** it assumes that the change involved is good and that people *should* adopt it. In many cases, of course, almost everyone would agree that this is true—blood pressure checks are good things to do, and so is improving the nutritional level of poor children, be they in the United States or in some other country.

In other cases, however, there is a clash between the innovation's meaning and one or more cultural values within a society. Recently, for example, young mothers in Indonesia were targeted for nutritional education: it was believed that many babies in Indonesia were not receiving enough nourishment because of a custom of mothers breastfeeding only with the left breast. This was based on Islamic religious beliefs relating to use of the hands: "the right hand is for food and the left hand is for toilet." A busy mother whose right hand was involved with cooking, therefore, would be unable to feed the infant according to the baby's needs. According to the marketing consultant involved in this project, "[t]hese resistance points were obstacles to effective education, and the messages had to concentrate on effectively challenging them."[37]

Marketers as Advocates of Change

Thus marketers find themselves in the position of generally advocating changes in peoples' behaviors and views of the world. Sometimes there are strong forces *against* such change, and marketers are viewed with suspicion and even disfavor. Those Indonesians who believe deeply in the customs would not like to think of them as "obstacles to effective education," for example. On the other hand, marketers are also responsible for successfully bringing many positive, noncontroversial innovations to the consumers of the world. In ending our analysis of the diffusion literature, then, we should be aware that *marketing is an important force in cultural change.* However, our theory tends to assume that innovations are valuable and should be adopted. It does not ask the hard questions posed by the attempts to break down and replace longstanding cultural values, beliefs, and customs. (If you are interested in reading further on these issues, you may wish to consult the excellent sources in Note 38.) In this regard, Appendix 12A provides a deeper analysis of how cultures are organized, which will help clarify why this issue is significant.

■ SUMMARY

WHAT IS CULTURE?

This chapter begins Part III's study of external influences on consumer behavior. We began with the broadest of all these influences—the impact of culture. *Culture* refers to the way of life of a society. It is a very powerful force in shaping people's lives. Two major components of culture are *external, material culture* and *internal, mental culture.* *Cultural norms* range from fads and fashions (that may come and go very quickly), to folkways (everyday practices), to mores (moral or religious values), to laws (strict codes of behavior). *Cultural universals* refer to the patterns of similarities that cultures share.

CONSUMER BEHAVIOR ACROSS CULTURES

In our discussion of cross-cultural comparisons, we noted that consumer behavior is different in different cultures for many reasons. *Consumer incomes* and *economic infrastructures* help to determine what products are viable within a culture. *Government policies* also have major impacts through such instruments as trade barriers, tax policies, and production controls. Another major set of differences stems from *cultural values beliefs,* and *life-styles.* We examined some traditional American values, as well as some cross-cultural differences in beliefs and life-styles. We then noted some humorous problems marketers have had with language differences and pointed out that there are further *hidden dimensions* of culture such as the use of space, time, and color. Our closing discussion of cross-cultural topics dealt with implications for marketers. Here we noted differences in population trends of affluent versus developing societies, the importance of subcultures for marketing success, and the major changes that are occurring in political and economic fronts around the world. (Appendix 12A also provides a more detailed discussion of social class across cultures.)

CHANGES IN CONSUMER CULTURES

Our third section was based in the fact that the rapid rate of *change in the consumer marketplace* has enormous implications for which marketers will succeed and which will fail. Here we noted that within a manager's career, he or she would have seen large changes in where consumers shop, cosmetics and styles, health and fitness, and technological advances, as just a few examples. We then examined how marketers and policymakers attempt to monitor cultural changes and briefly reviewed eight current trends as diagnosed by leading market researchers.

INTRODUCING CHANGE TO A CULTURE: "DIFFUSION OF INNOVATIONS"

We then moved to the topic of *diffusion of innovations,* or the spread of new ideas or products through a culture. Innovations are of three main forms. Those that cause major shifts in accompanying consumer behaviors are labeled *discontinuous innovations. Dynamically continuous innovations* are more moderate in the changes that they bring, and *continuous innovations* bring little changes in the way that consumers use them. Mathematical models, used to forecast the pattern of new product sales, usually rely on the S-shaped *diffusion curve.* Marketers must examine six characteristics of innovations: *relative advantage, complexity, communicability, compatibility, divisibility,* and *perceived risk,* since they will determine the speed with which a particular innovation will diffuse through a consumer market.

IMPROVING PROSPECTS FOR DIFFUSION SUCCESS

We then moved to a discussion of how marketers can influence the speed and success of diffusion. We noted that the adoption of innovations tends to follow specific patterns and that consumers can be divided into five categories—*innovators, early adopters, early majority, late majority,* and *laggards*—based on the time they take to adopt an innovation. We then summarized how each type of adopter category can be identified and understood. Among the interesting points here was that marketers usually don't (shouldn't) target the *innovators;* instead it is the *early adopters* who usually comprise the key group of "opinion leaders" for a new product offering. Our chapter then concluded with some brief comments concerning marketing's important role in bringing change to a culture, but also pointing out that a pro-innovation bias sometimes makes marketers unpopular. This point is further clarified in Appendix 12A, which discusses how social classes exist in different cultures, and what this means for marketers.

■ KEY TERMS

culture	acculturation	cultural conventions
external, material culture	cultural universals	climate and geography
internal, mental culture	economic infrastructure	physiological differences
norms	attempts at active mastery	cultural need and use environment
sanctions	focus on the external world	perceptions of product need
fads and fashions	a rationalist faith	past product experience
folkways	acceptance of a changing world	product use customs
mores	belief in equality of opportunity	existing product preferences
laws	respect for the lone ranger	hidden languages
enculturation	differences in cultural values	content analysis

"nobody's old anymore"	continuous innovation	trial
"time is precious"	S-shaped diffusion curve	use evaluation
"money is for pleasure"	relative advantage	adoption
"a return on the home"	complexity	innovators
"a growing concern for health"	communicability	early adopters
"rise of the two-earner family"	compatibility	early majority
"a return to tradition"	divisibility	late majority
"visible virtue"	perceived risk	laggards
innovation	adoption-process model	rejectors
diffusion	awareness	opinion leader
diffusion of innovation	knowledge	social marketing
discontinuous innovation	liking or disliking	pro-innovation
dynamically continuous innovation		

■ APPENDIX 12A TERMS

social stratification	life chances	open system	functionalist theory
property	social change	social mobility	marketplace theory
prestige	inherited status	caste systems	privilege level
power	earned status	class systems	American mainstream
life-styles	closed system	estate systems	lower Americans

■ REVIEW QUESTIONS AND EXPERIENTIAL EXERCISES

[E = **Application extension or experiential exercise**]

1. The cross-cultural differences between versus within countries have different implications for marketers than public policymakers. Comment.

2. Exhibit 12-2 summarizes six examples of recent shifts in consumer behaviors and markets. Which of these would you say is the most important for consumers? Which would you say is the *least important?* Rank the examples in their order of importance. Explain your ranking.

3. What is a cultural trend? How do the methods to measure these trends differ? As a marketing manager, why is it important to be aware of new trends as they arise?

4. What are the six basic dimensions associated with the speed and success rates for diffusion of an innovation? Are they of equal importance? Comment, using examples.

5. "An individual's adopter category remains unchanged across products." Do you agree with this statement? Why or why not? Provide examples.

6. Define the three bases of social inequality described in the appendix. Which of the three seems to be most easily acquired? Which seems most important in the culture of the United States?

7. [E] Select one of the following areas as a topic for a "current developments in marketing" research project. Use the reference section of your library to locate recent articles. Prepare a short summary of your findings.

   a. China
   b. Soviet Union
   c. Western Europe
   d. Eastern Europe
   e. Japan or South Korea
   f. Other nations

8. [E] Use the reference section of your library to discover recent articles reporting how a company is developing its strategy for international consumer markets. Write a brief report on your findings.

9. [E] Use the Note listings for Chapter 12 at the back of the book to locate good references for learning about "hidden languages" across cultures. Write a brief report summarizing good lessons for international marketers to learn.

10. [E] Arrange for an informal interview with one or two people (including fellow students) who have been raised in other cultures than your own. Ask about contrasts and similarities across the cultures (a good ice-breaker is, "What things did you find most surprising or different when you moved into my culture?"). During the interview try to cover such topics as family, education, economic system,

politics, social classes, economic infrastructure, values, media, shopping, marketplaces, and so forth. Write a brief report summarizing your findings.

11. [E] Interview a friend or relative from an older generation about the changes he or she has seen in the consumer culture (you may wish to use the examples in Exhibit 12-2 as a starting point). Write a brief report on what you learned from this interview.

12. [E] Use the business reference section of the library to locate recent articles on cultural trends and changes in the consumer marketplace. Write a brief report on your findings.

13. [E] Interview a department or specialty store manager about his or her experience with innovative new products. What types of consumers are interested in them? What are the typical problems with them? Select two or three current examples and have the manager classify them according to the six characteristics affecting diffusion rate (Figure 12-6). What, if anything, are the marketers doing about the problem areas? Write a brief report on your findings.

14. [E] Interview a supermarket manager about his or her experience with new product entries. How do they get on the shelf? How well do they sell? What are two or three examples of success? Of failure? What recommendations would the manager offer to a marketer with a new food product to introduce?

15. [E] Use the business reference section of your library to locate detailed analyses, reports, or overview articles about specific innovations (e.g., cellular telephones, fax machines, health maintenance organizations, new music technologies). Select one of these innovations as the basis for a report.

16. [E] Consumer trends, innovations, and new product development are all crucial to future business success. The general business press contains many interesting articles on these subjects. Choose option (a) or (b) to complete this assignment:

a. In your library, look up and read at least three of these articles from a few years ago. Write a brief report on your findings:

(1) "We Had to Change the Playing Field," *Forbes,* February 4, 1991, pp. 82 ff.

(2) "Winning Over the New Consumer," *Fortune,* July 29, 1991, pp. 113 ff.

(3) "Why 'New' Is Old Hat," *Forbes,* July 22, 1991, pp. 302 ff.

(4) "Business plans for the Millennium," *Forbes,* October 21, 1991, pp. 86 ff.

(5) "Closing the Innovation Gap," *Fortune,* December 2, 1991, pp. 56 ff.

(6) "The Bundle Book," *Financial World,* January 5, 1993, p. 34 ff.

b. In your library, find a set of recent issues of *Forbes* or *Fortune* magazines. Skim through them to find articles dealing with the themes of this chapter (international markets, changing market conditions, and/or new product management). Write a brief report summarizing the lessons of the articles you find.

17. [E] How would you react as a McDonald's executive? In Finland, you have just run a TV commercial that shows a bored (depressed? lonely?) young boy walking around an apartment that his parents are going to rent. When he glances out the window, however, he spies a McDonald's on the corner and noticeably brightens. The ad ends with the happy lad munching away in the restaurant. The Finnish authorities contact you with a request to stop the ad immediately: they feel that it wrongfully suggests that eating in McDonald's can relieve loneliness or substitute for having friends. If you will not stop this ad, they may take your firm to court, with possible fines of $50,000 if future ads use these types of themes that exploit children. How would you respond if you were the company manager in charge of this decision?[39]

■ SUGGESTED READING

■ This chapter presents many excellent reading extensions. For interesting in-depth looks at cross-cultural differences important to a marketing manager see, for example, Roger E. Axtell, *Do's and Taboos around the World* (New York: John Wiley & Sons, 1993); and Edward T. Hall and Mildred R. Hall, *Hidden Differences: Doing Business with the Japanese* (Garden City, N.Y.: Anchor Press/Doubleday, 1987). For a short recent account of one marketer's experiences in Russia see Valerie Reitman, "P&G Uses Skills It Has Honed at Home to Introduce Its Brands to the Russians," *Wall Street Journal,* April 14, 1993, p. B1.

■ For an interesting look at cultural change and our future, see John Center, "Where America Was a Century Ago," *The*

Futurist, January/February 1990, pp. 22–28; and United Way Strategic Institute, "Nine Forces Reshaping America," *The Futurist,* July/August 1990, pp. 9–16. Warnings to marketers are given in Herb Brody, "Great Expectations: Why Predictions Go Awry," *Journal of Consumer Marketing,* Vol. 10, No. 1, 1993, pp. 23–27.

■ Again for leads on topics of particular interest, the specific Notes contain excellent places to start. Further, for this chapter in particular, your reference librarian should be a fine source of advice to learn about current developments on these topics.

Appendix 12A

SOCIAL CLASSES ACROSS CULTURES
The Concept of Social Stratification

How Are Societies Structured?

Just as culture is the key concept for describing an entire society, social stratification is the key concept for analyzing the structure or internal organization of that society. The term **social stratification** refers to groups (or strata) of people who are arranged in some sort of ranked order, much like different layers of a pyramid. People who are ranked within the same stratum or level will tend to view each other as social equals. They will tend to feel comfortable with each other, spend time together, and share interests and activities. When we begin to look at *different* strata, however, we come up against the root characteristic of social stratification—*inequality*. People within any one stratum will tend to view those in other classes as being either socially superior or socially inferior to themselves.

Stratification is found in some form or other in every society in the world. Stratification is in essence a social agreement about what should be looked up to versus what should be looked down upon. It derives its support from a culture's values and social institutions. Whatever its details, however, *stratification has important implications for the lives of every group and individual in a society.*

The Bases of Inequality

One of the great sociological thinkers, Max Weber, developed an extremely influential theory of social stratification.[40] Weber, a German writing at the turn of the century, was particularly interested in the performance of capitalism as an economic system. This led him to ask why inequality seemed always to spring up within societies. In his theory, Weber first recognized that *social inequality is not a simple concept.* It exists in many forms, each with a different basis. Weber isolated three bases as being most important: property, prestige, and power.

Property differences, according to Weber, are the key basis for the creation of *classes* in a society, whereas **prestige** differences generate *status levels*, and **power** differences create *parties* or political interest groups. The importance of the three separate bases lies in the fact that they each constitute a distinct form of social stratification. Some people, for example, are *respected* because of their property holdings (land, wealth, products owned, etc.). Other people are *obeyed* because of the power that they command (such power might flow from an organizational position, personal strength, leadership abilities, etc.). Still other people are *admired* because of their abilities or accomplishments, reflecting the prestige of the roles that they can play within the society.

Also, however, the three bases tend to correlate with each other. Whichever resource (property, prestige, or power) a person acquires first, it can help to achieve the other two. Wealth, for example, can allow access to prestige—a wealthy person can buy "the right" products and services, join "the right" clubs and churches, and so on. Wealth can also provide an entry to the *corridors of power*, through heavy financial support of political parties or control of such corporate decisions as where to locate a new plant, from whom to purchase equipment or services, and so on. In like manner, prestige can open doors to gains in property and power, whereas power can be effectively used to improve an individual's property and prestige.

Life-styles and Life Chances

Max Weber also made a second important contribution when he pointed out that social stratification has two significant types of *consequences* for the lives of members of a society: different life-styles and different life chances. The term **life-styles** refers to overall patterns of living. This term is meant to include almost every aspect of our daily lives—where we live, what we do with our time, what we eat, how we talk, and so forth. Weber pointed out that people within each social stratum tended to associate more with each other (and less with those from other strata). In this process of daily associations, each stratum develops different life-styles. In contrast to life-styles, the term **life chances** stresses the inequality that is present in social stratification. People are provided with differential advantages and disadvantages in their lives. Those born into upper strata receive greater material rewards within the system and find good prospects for their futures. In contrast, children born into lower social strata face more barriers in their futures. These generalizations tend to hold true across societies and across history.

Consumer Behavior Reflects Life-styles One contribution in isolating these two types of consequences lies in the fact that each one provides substantial ground for study. Marketers and consumer behavior professionals have concentrated almost entirely on the life-style dimension, as this reflects most directly the purchasing patterns of different social classes. We have continued this stress within this text, particularly with our analysis of market segments in Chapter 4. However, it is important that we also briefly consider the types of attention that other fields give to the life chances dimension.

Life Chances and Marketers The topic of life chances is extremely complex. Its importance bears notice if you are planning a career in business. This is the topic that feeds the fires of social critics and political activists. The business community is often a target of criticisms. Easy answers to its questions are not to be found. Good people disagree about such issues as why some people are at the top while others are at the bottom, whether or not inequality is a necessary social condition, and what, if anything, should be done.

Several fields of study have long been involved in this topic, including sociology, philosophy, economics, and political science. A vast literature on life chances exists. We should realize, however, that this literature is often *not neutral* in its approach (a national survey of sociology professors, for example, showed that 5 percent rated themselves as "Conservative," 12 percent as "Middle-of-the-Road," 63 percent as "Liberal," and 20 percent as "Leftist").[41] While these figures may no longer be quite accurate, they do indicate the prevailing orientation of persons writing in this area. Businesspeople are often viewed as supporting the current stratification system, since they hold wealth and wield power in it. They are also seen as being generally insensitive to the plight of people in the lower social strata. There is a particular mistrust of marketers and advertisers. Questions are raised, for example, about pricing in poor neighborhoods, credit restrictions, and many other marketing practices that affect the poor. Much of this literature calls for more government regulation of business and involvement in redistributing property and power in society.

Different Cultures, Different Systems

Inherited versus Earned Status Across international cultures, a key distinguishing factor in stratification systems is the extent to which they rely on inherited versus earned status.[42] **Inherited status** is automatically assigned to individuals without any control on their part or any possibility of their influencing the process. This happens at birth, and high or low status is immediately assigned to the infant. The parents' and family's position, the sex of the child, the nationality, and the religion are important factors in the assignment of inherited status. **Earned status**, on the other hand, is based on a person's actions and performance. It is typically assigned in late childhood and in adulthood.

Some amount of inherited status is present in every stratification system. The *degree* to which it dominates earned status,

however, can differ dramatically. Cultures in which inherited status dominates tend to be **closed systems**; those in which earned status is dominant tend to be **open systems**. Open systems allow for high degrees of **social mobility**. People are able, through their own effort, to move up or down within the system. In closed societies, people born into one stratum can virtually never leave it.

Since a person in a closed system must be assigned to his or her level at birth, the basis for assignment must be *very* clear. Closed systems thus have sharp boundaries between their social classes. Tradition is very important. Socializing between classes is always discouraged and is sometimes prohibited. In open systems, on the other hand, the greater social mobility means that the initial assignment to a social class is less important, class distinctions are less important, and class boundaries are blurred. This occurs because some people are moving up in class, while others are moving down; each type of person is bringing some characteristics from his or her original class into the other class.

Caste Systems and Class Systems Caste and class systems are the two basic models for social stratification in our present world. **Caste systems** are very rigid structures, with social inequality as the core value in the society. Their social classes are called *castes*. Caste systems rely on inherited status, have no social mobility, and reflect very sharp boundaries between the castes. The best example of a true caste system can still be found in parts of the rural society of India, where it has served for several thousand years. There are many fascinating differences between the Indian caste system and the set of cultural values we saw for the United States at the start of the chapter. You might enjoy reading the summary of such characteristics provided in Exhibit 12A-1.

Aspects of the Caste System in India

The Nature of the Caste System

Every Hindu in India belongs to one and only one caste, or *jat*.[43] Membership is hereditary and permanent. At one time, the caste system provided a basis for the division of labor in an area. All men in the same caste had to pursue the same occupation, with defined duties to perform and other duties to avoid. Within a living area such as a village, therefore, all tasks

were assigned by birth. In total there were over 3,000 subcaste groupings in this very complex, highly structured society. These subcastes were derived, however, from four major castes:

- Priests and scholars   *Brahmins* (pronounced 'brahm-en)*
- Warriors and princes   *Kshatriyas* (pronounced 'cha-trē)*
- Merchants and artisans   *Vaisayas* (pronounced 'vish-uh)*
- Laborers and servants   *Sudras* (pronounced 'soo-draah)*

---

*Because the language sounds are different, these terms are difficult for many non-Indians to pronounce correctly. For example, *Webster's Dictionary* indicates a pronunciation of "(ke)'sha-tré-l(y)e" for the warrior caste.

Beneath the four castes there was another group of persons, estimated at 20 percent of the population, who were known as *Outcasts* or *Untouchables* because they were considered to be outside the spiritual community.

In terms of Weber's three bases, the caste system was designed to provide high status to one caste on each basis. Brahmins were very high on prestige; they were viewed as almost godlike and deserving of all respect. Kshatriyas were very high on power, as befitted their occupational roles as warriors and princes. Vaisayas were very high on property, as they specialized in business and economic matters. Over time, however, each of the high castes was able to use its strong base to raise its levels on the other bases—Brahmins gained power and wealth, Kshatriyas gained prestige and wealth, and Vaisayas gained power and prestige.

The Importance of the Hindu Religion

The caste system was so powerful that it dominated almost every aspect of people's lives in India. How could such a strong system be accepted, especially by those assigned to low status for all of their lives? One key factor was the power of the Hindu religion and its teachings. Basically, in Hinduism, unlike many Western religions, a person's soul lives an endless existence on earth. When someone dies, his or her soul is reborn (reincarnated) into a new and different body. Any one person's lifetime is thus just a short time in the soul's existence. For that short time, the soul is assigned its duties on earth (*dharma*) by being born into a particular caste. If the soul performs its duties faithfully, it will be rewarded by being assigned to a higher caste

in its next life. There is *no social mobility* possible in the present life, however, since the soul's duties have been assigned at birth.

This strong religious backing resulted in Hindus accepting that some people were spiritually "better" than other people, since their souls were being highly rewarded while the souls of others were being punished for their performance in earlier lives. Over time, though not a part of the religion itself, a complex set of social codes arose for each caste to follow. For example, if a Brahmin were to be touched by (even by the shadow of) an Untouchable, he or she must go immediately to wash off. If requested to provide a drink of water by a member of a lower caste, a Brahmin felt compelled to provide it (as a holy act), but could not allow the cup to touch the other person. The Brahmin therefore had to pour the water into the other person's cupped hands. If by chance the person touched the cup, the Brahmin would have to throw the cup away as forever unclean.

Impacts of the Industrial Revolution

In modern India the caste system is less powerful, due to such forces as industrialization, radio and television, education, the growth of a national government, and other modernizing influences in the society. It still is, however, a basic framework for many members of the society and is ingrained in their lives. As an example, you might be interested in some recent advertisements appearing in a U.S. newspaper that serves Indians now living in America. These ads were run for the purpose of arranging suitable marriages. Note the presence of status appeals in the descriptions given.

MATRIMONIAL, FEMALE

Parents invite suitable medico or well-settled professional match, under 29, for tall, slim, beautiful, 23, immigrant Punjabi Hindu Kshatri woman, from a status family with exceptional merit. Convent school education in India and college in U.S.A. from a known university. Reply (box number).

Brother invites matrimonial correspondence for his sister, Gujarati Brahmin, 35, . . . nice personality. Caste no barrier.

Correspondence invited from immigrant Punjabi Agarwals for beautiful, homely, 22, 5'3", sister in India. Write with returnable photographs.

Kerala Iyer, Vadama family seeks match for very beautiful daughter, 28, 5'4", fair, slim, convent educated, B.Sc., L.L.B. (Bombay), from handsome, non-Kaushika Tamil Iyer professionals under 34.

MATRIMONIAL, MALE

Medico, 27, 5'7", handsome, fair, Green Card holder, seeks exceptionally beautiful and fair woman. No dowry. No caste barrier. Preferably Kashmiri, Himachili Brahmin, B.Sc. medical or nursing.

U.S.A. settled professional, 34, 5'11", slim, handsome, youthful, Kerala Iyer, Vadama invites matrimonial correspondence from non-Kaushika Tamil families. Women should be a graduate, beautiful, slim, under 26.

Physician, American citizen, invites correspondence from tall, attractive, educated Telugu Brahmin women, early 20s, for his tall handsome brothers, engineer (28) and physician (26), both immigrating to U.S. shortly. Respond with recent photograph and horoscope.

Correspondence invited from parents of extremely beautiful, cultured, well-educated young ladies, 20–23, preferably settled in North America, for very handsome, 25, successful MBA, Hindu young man.

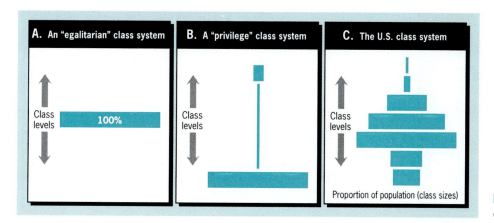

FIGURE 12A-1 Patterns of Social Stratification

Class systems conform in most respects to open systems. They rely on a mixture of inherited and earned status, have moderate opportunities for social mobility, and are found in the United States, Russia, and other industrialized societies. Class systems arose with the Industrial Revolution about 200 years ago. They replaced the **estate systems** in which a few nobles (kings, dukes, barons) held high status and almost everyone else (peasants, serfs, etc.) held low status.[44] The estate systems were based on land holdings. The Industrial Revolution, with its development of transportation and factories, shifted the center of society from rural estates to new large cities. Lower-class citizens found that they could earn money and live better by working in production rather than agriculture. New classes of merchants, bankers, and traders emerged and gained wealth, while government bureaucrats began to gain power. Political thinking began to change also. By the late 1700s, the French and American revolutions represented the shift of social ideals toward personal freedom for all citizens.

One result of these changes was a dramatic increase in a person's social mobility. New people could gain property and power (especially industrialists), while others could gain prestige by developing specialized knowledge and skills. Over time, emphasis shifted more and more toward economic success as a means for improving one's status. During the 1900s, the class system has evolved in new directions as well. Workers formed unions to improve their power standing and raise their incomes and working conditions. Education was made compulsory in many countries: this allowed millions of people to prepare for new occupations (another route toward social mobility). Finally, the entire standard of living has risen dramatically. Almost everyone is living better than their ancestors did, whether or not their relative social standing is higher.

A class system, however, can still reflect substantial inequality. As we all know, different countries have chosen to handle this situation in quite different ways. Karl Marx had a major influence in the course of history with his writings in *The Communist Manifesto*.[45] In terms of social stratification, Marx believed that social inequality was *not* necessary and should not exist in any society. He argued that a society could be arranged to have everyone at the same level. At the opposite extreme from Marx stands the **functionalist theory** of social stratification. In brief, the functionalists argue that at least two of the three bases—prestige and property—*must* be handed out unequally for a society to function well. Their position is that human nature requires extra incentives for someone who must work especially hard or receive special training to do his or her job well. If society does *not* allow extra wealth or prestige, these jobs won't be done well. Thus the functionalist position supports the **marketplace theory** of capitalist systems. (Our brief summary here obviously does not cover many key issues. If you wish to read more, the reading in Note 46 is a good place to begin.)

The result of different cultural decisions about stratification is that our modern world has a wide range of stratification systems. As shown in Figure 12A-1, the type of egalitarian system desired by Marx would have a long, narrow shape. (Under communism, modern Russia utilized to some extent this form for property but reflected clear differences on power and prestige: as it moves toward capitalism, we may see increasing class differences on property.) At the other extreme, Panel B of the figure shows a variant of the *privilege* society found in many developing nations of the world. Here we see a small number of extremely powerful and wealthy families at the top, virtually no middle class at all, and then a huge class of peasants and who spend their lives supporting the rich and powerful. Finally, Panel C of the figure shows that the U.S. system is roughly in the form of a *diamond* (in which the middle classes are by far the largest). In the closing section of this appendix, let's turn to consider the social classes of the United States.

Social Classes in the United States

The Social Class Structure

Because it is a young society that has emphasized earned status, immigration, and growth, describing social class in America is a complex, judgmental activity. There is no single answer for the number of social classes or their exact nature. Some people may see 20 social classes while others see 6. Here we will choose

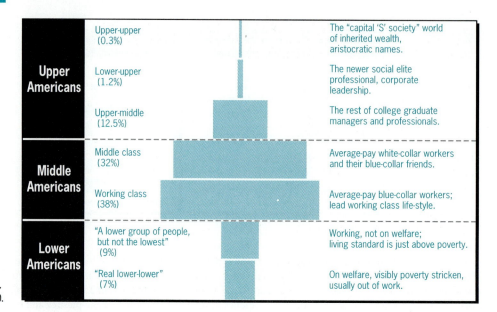

Figure 12A-2 Social Classes of the United States
SOURCE: Adapted from Richard P. Coleman, "The Continuing Significance of Social Class to Marketing," *Journal of Consumer Research,* December 1983, pp. 265–280.

to discuss a seven-level structure that is generally accepted in marketing circles. Figure 12A-2 presents the conclusions of one expert in this area, Richard Coleman. (If you would like to see a guide that measures consumers' social classes, Coleman's article presents an actual questionnaire: see Note 47). Notice that seven social classes are present, ranging from the "lower-lower" class to the "upper-upper" class. Notice also that the two uppermost classes are tiny in terms of population: it is the fact that they are so high on power, property, and prestige that makes them so important. Finally, we can see that it is the three classes in the center (the upper-middle class, middle class, and working class) that really define the mainstream, where five out of six people live.

As a final point about class structure, Coleman has contributed the concept of **privilege level** within each class into the marketing field.[48] This concept recognizes that within each social class, income levels can vary widely. For example, some middle-class households earn $42,000 per year, whereas others are at $18,000. Coleman would label the first household as an *overprivileged family* and the second as an *underprivileged family.* A *class average family* here would have an income at about the average for the class, say, $30,000 in this case.

Since income provides a basis for consumer spending, there are some behavioral differences between privilege levels. In cars, for example, it is the overprivileged in each class who tend to buy expensive autos (in the working-class or lower-class levels, the choice is often a used model of one of the expensive lines). In leisure spending, we can expect to see an underprivileged upper-middle (UM) family making very different purchases from our earlier overprivileged middleclass (MC) family, even though both may have incomes of $42,000. The overprivileged MCs are much more likely to own motor boats, campers, and backyard pools. The underprivileged UMs,

on the other hand, are much more likely to spend their money on club memberships and private school tuitions.

Thus income and social class are actually different concepts. While there is a general increase in average income as we move from lower to upper levels, the statistical correlation between social class and income is only modest, at about +0. 40. Thus marketers can choose both measures to use in predicting consumer spending for various products.[49]

Our closing discussion of this chapter summarizes aspects of each of the primary social classes outlined in Figure 12A-2. We'll do so in two parts: first, we'll concentrate on the American mainstream; then, we'll move to the extreme social classes.[50]

The Classes of the American Mainstream

The **American mainstream** consists of three social classes: the upper-middle (UM) class, the middle class, and the working class. Taken together, these three classes account for five of every six citizens, about 83 percent of the population. Because some households will shift class levels over time, because the sons and daughters of one class can move into another class (especially through education and occupational choices), and because there is some overlap in incomes, it is sometimes difficult to distinguish these three groups clearly. On the other hand, each class has some distinguishing characteristics, as summarized next.

The Working Class (38 percent of the population) This is the single largest social class, accounting for two of every five citizens. People here typically occupy blue-collar or manual jobs, perceiving themselves as hard working and honest. Job security is a threat, however. Income is about at the same level as spending (so that savings are hard to accumulate). Perhaps because of the nature of the work, many members sharply separate their workplace from the social sphere of their lives. When off the job, they do not think much about it, and the spouse is unlikely to know the coworkers very well.

WC Americans are "family folk." One study found, for example, that about half of WC people live within a mile of a relative, against only one of five MCs and only one in eight UMs. In television news, WCs prefer local segments rather than national or world news, and WC vacations are often spent either at home or within a two-hour drive. WC persons are also highly patriotic and supportive of American industry. For example, WCs' ownership of foreign cars is only one-third to one-fifth the rate found in the MC and UM classes. In summary, the WC world is closer to traditions. Family, neighborhood, long-time friends, and a stress on "enjoying today" are all important elements of this life-style.

The Middle Class (32 percent of the population) MCs constitute the other very large segment of the American population. These are white-collar workers in average pay brackets and skilled blue-collar craftsmen. Many MCs have college backgrounds. Unlike most WCs, who are living their lives on an immediate day-to-day basis, many MCs are interested in "investing" time and effort today so they can improve their lives in the future. In this regard there is some attention paid to what those in the UM class are doing and some effort to engage in similar behaviors. Money and high morals are important to MC Americans. Among important purchases are nice homes in nice neighborhoods, college educations for the children, and good brand names. There is a strong interest in being seen as "respectable" by others: the appearance of the "public areas" in a home—those that are seen by visitors—is quite important, for example.

The Upper-Middle Class (13 percent of the population) UMs are characterized primarily by high levels of education and the expert knowledge associated with it. Many lawyers, accountants, engineers, and managers fit into this class. Not only are incomes higher here, but UMs are usually more secure economically because they can transfer their knowledge from one setting to another. In contrast to most WCs and to many MCs, the work center and coworkers are likely to play a major role in a UM's life while on the job and off it.

The UM class is usually visible and respected in a community. They value money for both the status it brings and the comfortable life-style it can buy. UM children tend to be enrolled in the public schools and are pointed toward gaining higher education from an early age. UM parents are likely to be involved in self-interest and voluntary "cause" associations such as the school PTA and Chamber of Commerce. UMs often belong to country clubs. They watch less TV than WCs or MCs, and read more books and newspapers. In general, UMs are interested in prestige brands and stores and spending "with good taste." As their incomes increase, many UMs seek to travel more, to add more "help in the house," and to gain prestigious educations for their children.

The Extreme Social Classes in America

Most Americans can easily relate to the life-styles of the WC, MC, and UM social classes. There are, however, three social classes that occupy the extreme positions of social status in America—the upper-upper, lower-upper, and lower-class Americans—with whose lives we may be less familiar. These three classes are often not considered to be key sectors of the mass market to which many large marketers cater. Because they are extreme, however, they are useful in highlighting some subtle aspects of social class and are quite interesting in themselves. Thus we will devote slightly more attention to them in our coverage here.

The Upper-Upper Class (less than one-half of 1 percent of the population) These are the "aristocrats" of the society. Family background, or "breeding," is very important. *Inherited, old wealth* is the key to membership in the Blue Blood society. In America, this wealth came from land holdings and corporate fortunes, most of which were amassed about a century ago, during the "robber baron" business era (you may be familiar, for example, with names such as Rockefeller, Mellon, Vanderbilt, Carnegie, Whitney, and so on). Thus the upper-upper (UU) class of America is different from that of most other countries—it is not based on royalty bloodlines (from the Estate class). Its business heritage instead represents both the relative youth of the United States as well as the national stress on business success. As we would expect, the UU class holds tremendous power behind the scenes of business and government.

The UU class is a closed society unto itself. It has erected many barriers to entry for persons not born into this select grouping. Members of this class are well buffered from the mainstream of society. Their privacy is guarded by social secretaries, security personnel, and exclusive clubs. The UU class in America is largely Protestant, especially belonging to the Episcopalian and Presbyterian denominations. There is pressure to marry within the class; a wedding here represents the joining of one family with another much more so than in other classes. UU children are educated at elite preparatory schools, followed by attendance at the best universities. (Dick Cavett, the television personality, was a non-UU scholarship student at Yale. One day, when asked where he had "prepped," Cavett supposedly replied, "I didn't 'prep,' I 'highed' out in Nebraska.")

With respect to their life-styles, the UU class is an interacting group. Its members tend to know each other either personally or by reputation. They engage in elite leisure pursuits, including fox hunts, polo matches, and tennis. They are active in charity balls and social visits. In addition, they actively support major arts activities. Most members of this group do not need to work, but many choose to do so; they occupy important positions in business, the professions, and philanthropic organizations. In this regard, it is fairly common that the family name be memorialized through charitable foundations.

In terms of overall consumption in the United States, the UU class is not a significant factor due to its very small size. With respect to wealth and power, however, there is quite another story—it is estimated that the top 200,000 households in the United States (less than one-half of 1 percent of the population) control about 22 percent of the personal wealth of the country! The UU class's consumption expenditures per person are quite large, and it can be a significant market for a few specialty marketers of products and services.

Because its members are comfortable and feel well established in their social positions, this class tends not to engage in "conspicuous consumption" to the extent that some other classes do. Their life-style tends to be mannered and genteel; their purchases tend to be conservative and tasteful. UU women, for example, appear to be relatively independent of the changing fashion in clothing; they avoid the "daring styling" of Paris fashions, instead staying with the woolens and tweeds that distinguish the well-bred British woman. There are retailers who cater exclusively to this class and to whom an introduction is needed before a new customer can attempt to undertake a purchase. Finally, UUs serve as an "aspirational reference group" for some members of less prestigious classes: these people are watching carefully to see what the UUs are purchasing so they can attempt similar consumer behaviors.

The Lower-Upper Class (1 percent of the population) These are the very high achievers in the American society—those with extremely successful careers in business, the professions, and entertainment. These people can be *extremely* wealthy; it is not uncommon for LU families to be more wealthy than many members of the UU class. The distinction, however, is that the LU family wealth was not passed down through family generations. In social terms, this represents "new" money—these people are the *nouveau riche*.

This class is characterized by high ambition and excellent performance. Many of its members, however, have to confront a conflict after their success has been achieved. At that point, they *must seek a new balance* between the genteel, cultured life-style to which they aspire and their strong personal drives for more achievement, power, and success. Since many of these persons have just entered the LU class during their own lifetimes, they lack the established family traditions and support that are available in the UU class. Even as adults, many LU persons are having to learn new values and behavior norms.

Unlike the UUs, LUs often feel that they have less impressive family pasts to look back on. They are more geared to the present and future. LUs are *not* accepted into the UU social elite, but their children and grandchildren *may* be, if they are sent to the "right" schools, develop the correct social graces and viewpoints, and are able to marry wisely. This, of course, places even more pressure on an LU family's behavior patterns. Many LUs are *very* active in civic, charitable, and philanthropic causes.

As there is usually no shortage of money, consumption can become an important outlet for LUs. They can use consumption to reward themselves and to show others that they have both succeeded and know what to do with their success. At times they will be addressing those in the UU class; at other times, they will be aiming at those in less prestigious classes.

Accordingly, many LUs spend freely on products that are visible to others and that can serve as status symbols of success and power. Success and high-style living are represented by purchases of large, plush homes, second and third residences and retreats, luxury automobiles, expensive forms of adornment (fine furs, jewelry, and clothing), custom services (tutors, interior designers), large boats, and so on. This is the class that supports high fashion from Paris; a designer name serves a very important communication function so that the purchaser of the clothing can ensure that other people see just what a fine purchase it is.

Because power is so often important to their success, many LUs strive to acquire and employ power symbols. This can reach an art form in itself. For example, consider the following power symbols:

- *Highly polished shoes.* Many power people have their shoeshine person visit their offices twice a day, once early in the morning and again after lunch.

- *The right type of shoe.* These come from the right shoemakers. Recently, for example, Gucci loafers were acceptable, but the terms under which they could be acquired were demanding. Reportedly, one man was overheard to tell another (who had just asked him to visit Gucci with him to help him buy the right loafer), "I will, but if you need help, maybe you're not ready for Guccis. You can't put Guccis on Florsheim feet, you know."

- *Limousines.* Even better than a Rolls-Royce was a Mercedes 600 with its chrome painted black and with tinted windows so that no one could see inside.

- *Briefcases.* The slimmer and more elegant, the better. Best of all, of course, is being able to walk around empty-handed; this demonstrates that you are able to command others to do all the work![51]

Similarly, furniture, decorations (original works of fine art), watches, and other objects are commonly used to advantage by accomplished LUs, as well as by striving members of the UM class. Overall, the lower-upper class is too small to be an important target for mass marketers. It can, however, be a significant market for specialized, high-quality goods and services.

The Lower-American Class (16 percent of the population) At the other extreme of the U.S. class structure are the two groups of **lower Americans**. Also termed the *poverty class*, this is a very diverse set of people whose major common characteristic is the fact of their very low incomes. Included here are those subject to continuing unemployment, plus low-paid service workers, the elderly poor, illegal immigrants, abandoned families, and some people with deviant life-styles. There are many minorities in this class, although the majority of its members are white persons born in the United States. As a group, these people could be viewed as the "outcasts" of society rather than being an integrated class within the social structure. Their lives do not come close to reflecting the ideals of the American society, and many mainstream members of the other classes have a tendency to regard all L-As as disreputable persons, and worse.

Other attributes of life in the L-A class are closely tied to the low income levels. Members of this class represent unskilled labor and the lowest educational levels and are more likely than those in other classes to have physical or mental handicaps. Many are recipients of government welfare and subsidy programs. If they live in urban areas, they reside in slums or poor neighborhoods; very few own their own homes. Average family sizes are larger than in the other social classes, and there are many more single-parent households; these factors combine to limit the per capita income and to stretch its use over more children.

These factors contribute to a highly *insecure* existence, especially for lower-lower class members. With respect to the three bases of stratification, these people have no prestige, wield little or no power, and possess almost no property. Several reactions typify their adjustments to this sort of insecurity. They are more likely than other classes to rely on relatives for social and financial support; they are less likely to participate in community functions. Over time, many L-As exhibit a distrust of others, a pessimism about the future, and a feeling that they themselves have virtually no control over what their lives will bring (this is termed *fatalism,* suggesting that fate and luck are extremely important forces in a person's life). In turn, these beliefs can lead to low expectations, reduced feelings of personal responsibility, little ambition, and a short time horizon, so that the person tends to "live for today" and "enjoy what's available." These mental outlooks not only contribute to antisocial behaviors in the short run (for example, juvenile delinquency, crime, drug dependency) but almost guarantee a continuation of the poverty cycle in the long run. These descriptions surely do not typify every L-A. However, these issues are at the heart of the heated debates over government social policy in the United States, and the lower-American class is the target for most government social assistance programs.

There are several interesting aspects of the consumption practices of the L-A class. First, it is a large group of people, accounting for about one out of every six persons in the United States. Given its low average income, however, its overall importance for consumer spending is much less—perhaps representing only $1 of every $12 to $15 spent. For this reason, many marketers do not stress this class in their planning. If, however, a product tends to be a necessity, and doesn't easily fit into the resale (used) market, the L-A class can emerge as a significant

factor. Groceries, for example, fit these criteria, and government food stamp programs assist in making this a large market for retail foodstuffs.

Consumer research has also indicated that the L-A class behaves in some ways that we might not expect from a strictly economic point of view. For example, L-As often engage in what Rotzell has termed *compensatory consumption*[52]—they purchase appliances at a fairly high rate and were among the early adopters of color television sets. They tend not to buy the cheapest items available, but instead rely on name brands more than do some other classes. L-As also spend higher proportions of their incomes on personal appearance items and on personal gifts. Finally, L-As on average watch much more television than any other social class. They must surely gain ideas about consumption from the ads there, and some frustration must result from the realization that they are unable to afford many of the products advertised or the life-styles glamorized on the air.

A final topic that bears mention has to do with pricing and selling practices, credit policies, and consumer protection. Many L-As are *vulnerable consumers.* Some are functionally illiterate, others do not speak the English language. Many are unable to perform simple arithmetic. The availability of credit is important in allowing them to obtain expensive merchandise, but these are exactly the people who are more likely to be poor credit risks. Transportation is a problem for many people in this class, so they tend to shop close to their homes. They are also often poorly informed about what alternatives they have in terms of products, prices, and retail outlets.

The net result is that a subset of marketers has come to serve these clients. While most of the marketing mainstream is available to them, it is not patronized as often. If a retailer chooses to cater to this market, he or she can expect to incur higher costs through shoplifting and vandalism and to work in less pleasant surroundings. Often this means that retail prices will be higher, that bad debts will raise interest rates for credit, and that an attitude of mistrust between retailers and customers may develop. Unfortunately, this negative outlook can cause some honest businesspeople to decide not to serve the lower-class communities. While many honest retailers choose to remain, there is also an opportunity for the unscrupulous operator. Thus we find many of marketing's "shameful practices" (perpetuated by only a small percentage of all marketers) occurring here. These include misrepresenting merchandise, overpricing, deliberately inflating the totals obtained by addition, selling shoddy and defective goods, high-pressure selling, hiding exorbitant interest rates by misleading pricing schemes, and so on. Overall, the marketing and consumer behavior issues in the lower-American social class are not pleasant to think about, but they are a real part of life in the United States and cannot simply be ignored in our coverage of this society. (If you would like to read more in this area, the references in Note 53 for this chapter provide a good starting point.)

13

SOCIAL AND SITUATIONAL INFLUENCES

"HAVE YOU HEARD ABOUT TROPICAL FANTASY?"

According to *The Wall Street Journal*, after years of trying, Brooklyn Bottling finally hit it big in 1990, when it introduced Tropical Fantasy into the small grocery stores in poor inner-city neighborhoods of the Northeast. Priced at about 50 cents for a 20-ounce bottle, the new brand took away large chunks of business from Coke, Pepsi, and other popular brands that were sold at 80 cents for a 16-ounce bottle. After six months, as sales continued to climb, a strange flier appeared in New York City. Addressed to blacks and minority groups, it charged that, according to the TV show "20/20," Tropical Fantasy sodas were "Being manufactured by the Ku Klux Klan [and] contain stimulants to sterilize the Black Man ... they are only put in stores in Harlem and minority areas, you won't find them downtown ... look around ... you have been warned."

The charges were untrue, and the district attorney began an investigation (included in the investigation were the rival soft drink companies, bottlers, and distributors, and their workers' union—Brooklyn Bottling is not unionized: all denied any responsibility). What happened to consumer behavior? Despite strong statements of safety from the company, the mayor of New York, and others, consumers spread the story to one another and changed their behavior immediately. *Sales dropped 70 percent*, and showed little sign of turning around. As one consumer commented, "It sounds kind of far-fetched, but this goes to the heart of race and the system. The 49-cent sodas can't be chanced." As another approached the counter with a Tropical Fantasy in hand, she stopped, said, "I forgot ... it's made by the KKK to poison blacks," and turned back to get a Sprite.[1]

This devastating rumor was successful only because it worked its way through the social system, through consumer word–of–mouth. This is one of the forms of social influence that we will examine in this chapter.

As we've just seen in Chapter 12, cultural effects on consumer behavior are very powerful. These effects are usually transmitted through the social fabric of the society, as people interact with one another. When we analyze these interactions as involving individuals or groups (rather than entire cultures), we enter the area of social and situational influences.

Social and situational influences work in all phases of consumer behavior—they affect which products we aspire to own, which styles we prefer, at which stores we'll shop, and so forth. They work when other people are present or even when they're absent (if we think about their reactions). These are broad and powerful forces in the consumer world. Within this chapter we will examine a number of ways in which these forces work, including consumer "word–of–mouth," conformity and social pressure in consumer behavior, how group influence works, and how situational influences work as well. In each case we will see many applications for astute marketers to consider. At the start, however, let's briefly look at the connection between culture and social influences—the process of "socialization."

■ SOCIAL INFLUENCES BEGIN EARLY

THE SOCIALIZATION OF CHILDREN

Socialization is the process by which each individual learns to live and behave effectively as a person among other people.[2] Socialization occurs throughout our lives, beginning in childhood. Here the baby makes the basic discovery that people and objects are separate from himself or herself and that he or she must learn to *interact* with them. As time goes on, the young child learns that there are *rules* for such social interactions. Children learn that certain behaviors are expected when they have a certain *social role* (e.g., a baseball outfielder should not laugh and point when the ball is hit to him, nor should she throw it over the fence!). Children also learn that the rules of organized social structures apply to everyone, not just them, and that they need to be accepted to participate. Finally, the thousands of social interactions during childhood also help each child to find what works well and what does not: through this social process each of us develops our unique identity within our world.

Socialization: The process by which each individual learns to live and behave effectively as a person among other people.

KEY SOCIALIZING INSTITUTIONS

Socialization processes are heavily controlled by a few powerful agents or **socializing institutions** in our society.[3] For many people, the **family** is the first, and most powerful, socializing institution. The values and life-style of the other family members are internalized by the child as he or she forms a personal identity: although these may change through the years, a basic part of ourselves is formed here. The onset of **schooling** introduces much formal socialization of the child into the culture of the society, including learning the bases for written communication, calculation, history, societal governance, and so forth. Increasingly, **mass media** has become a potent socializing force in society. Messages from the media convey much information about the world beyond our doorsteps: these messages can challenge or reinforce our current values and teach us about new forms of behaviors.

Socializing institution: An organization having a strong influence in socializing the members of a society.

The three remaining socializing institutions have more diverse impacts across the society. People who are active in **organized religions** can experience strong socializing influences on their lives, but many persons are not active in a religion and are not subject to these direct influences. The same comments hold for **work centers**, since many persons are not exposed to daily socializing influences from this source. Those who are exposed, however, can be strongly affected in dress, speech, and leisure activities and life-styles. **Social groups**, meanwhile, are highly diverse and can have very strong influences. We shall return later in the chapter to consider their impacts on consumer behavior.

CHANGES OVER TIME

Role transitions:
Shifts that take place as a person changes roles, as in moving from childhood to adulthood.

As we move through our lives, socialization continues, but its nature changes. *Adolescence* is a difficult bridging time as a child becomes an adult. Part of the difficulty stems from physical changes, but part also stems from three difficult social **role transitions:** (1) a shift from being submissive to being independent, (2) a shift from nonresponsible to responsibility roles, and (3) a move from inhibited sexuality to acceptable sexual roles.[4] For many teenagers the major socializing institutions, including the family, do not provide clear guidance on how to make these difficult changes, and the teenage subculture and friendship groups emerge to help with them.

In adulthood, because people have more freedom than during their school years, they tend to pursue their personal preferences to a greater extent and experience widely differing socialization experiences. Much adult socialization involves the learning of new roles and appropriate behaviors for them. For example, many readers can still look forward to learning the roles of a parent, spouse, in-law, rising executive or entrepreneur, manager of others, community leader, appliance buyer, and so forth.

In this regard, there has recently been great interest in "adult growth stages" in which every American adult is seen as passing through a sequence of psychosocial periods, each of which is 5 to 10 years long. During each period some "predictable crises" are likely to occur, and the person needs to develop ways to cope with them. For example, the period from ages 23 to 28 (the *entering adult world* stage) is viewed as a stressful time, as men and women search for goals to which they can commit themselves. (If you would like to read more about this area, you may wish to refer to Note 5.) We will examine the concept of consumer life cycle in our next chapter: at this point, let's turn to look more directly at social influences in our day-to-day world.

■ SOCIAL INFLUENCES THROUGH "WORD-OF-MOUTH"

At this point we will turn to a direct focus on social influences in the consumer marketplace. We know, of course, that marketers are actively trying to influence consumers, but we sometimes overlook the fact that consumers are in frequent communication with each other and that much influence occurs here as well. Let's take a closer look.

THE "WEB OF WORD-OF-MOUTH"

The phrase **web of word-of-mouth** comes from a classic marketing study by William H. Whyte, published in *Fortune* magazine about 40 years ago.[6] Room air conditioners had just been introduced to the consumer market, and Whyte had noticed that this had led to an interesting pattern in the diffusion of the innovation. In urban neighborhoods, because conditioners were used in front windows, adoption could easily be traced. Whyte found that even within the same neighborhood, air conditioners appeared in clusters rather than in random fashion. For example, six houses in a row might each have an air conditioner, while the three houses on either side would not. From this simple observation, Whyte expanded on his notion that the purchase of these goods reflected *patterns of social communication* within the neighborhood: the people who talked together about the products were the people who bought them. (Television was

Notice how the pattern of backyard swimming pools is not random: this suggests that a "web of word-of-mouth" has been operating among neighbors.

becoming very popular at that time as well, and similar patterns could be observed with TV antennas. Also, you can still see these patterns when flying over urban areas in an airplane and noting how home swimming pools are clustered, even in the same neighborhoods.)

This observation shows how powerful an influence consumer **word-of-mouth communication** can be. Most consumer word–of–mouth seems to be of an *approach* nature. That is, we enter freely into these discussions and enjoy them for their sake, whether or not they influence our behaviors. Through consumer discussions, we learn about product and service options. We also have the chance to tell others about our opinions and experiences.

Analyzing Consumer Networks

Although the study of social networks has long been of interest in sociology, there has recently been some very interesting work done in consumer research.[7] Figure 13-1 provides a portion of a certain type of consumer word-of-mouth network called a **referral network,** in this case reflecting the recommendations for a physician in a university town. Notice that this research begins with the choice of that physician (G) by a new professor (A) at the university. To create the network shown, it basically works backward in time, discovering who had issued each recommendation, and to which other persons referrals had also been offered.

In reality, the physician's entire word-of-mouth referral network would of course include many other people who use her and would be much more complex to create and to analyze. Even in Figure 13-1, though, we can identify some typical characteristics of consumer word-of-mouth networks. For example, (1) the consumer referral network (arrows) is a subset of a larger social network (both arrows and bars) and largely depends on it in order to function, (2) neighborhoods, work centers, and social organizations are all important sources for consumer word-of-mouth activity, (3) these networks tend to operate as almost independent smaller clusters (for example, notice that if it hadn't been for the single discussion at church, the entire

Word-of-mouth communication: Discussions among consumers regarding marketplace phenomena: can be a powerful influence.

Referral network: A pattern of word-of-mouth discussions recommending a new product or service provider.

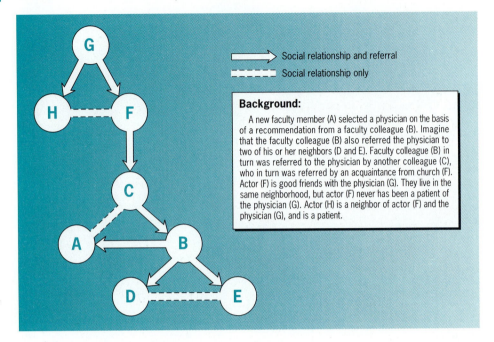

Social relationship and referral

Social relationship only

Background:

A new faculty member (A) selected a physician on the basis of a recommendation from a faculty colleague (B). Imagine that the faculty colleague (B) also referred the physician to two of his or her neighbors (D and E). Faculty colleague (B) in turn was referred to the physician by another colleague (C), who in turn was referred by an acquaintance from church (F). Actor (F) is good friends with the physician (G). They live in the same neighborhood, but actor (F) never has been a patient of the physician (G). Actor (H) is a neighbor of actor (F) and the physician (G), and is a patient.

FIGURE 13-1 Portion of a Referral Network for a Physician   SOURCE: Adapted from Peter H. Reingen and Jerome B. Kernan, "Analysis of Referral Networks in Marketing: Methods and Illustration," *Journal of Marketing Research*, Vol. 23, no. 4, November 1986, p. 371.

professor cluster might well be seeing a different physician), and (4) some consumers play the role of opinion leaders within a social network, as indicated by B's importance in influencing the decisions of others in the group.

The Power of Consumer Recommendations

We all know how powerful consumer word-of-mouth discussions can be in influencing our consumer behaviors, but why is this so? The power of consumer recommendations appears to stem from three key factors: First, consumer communications usually have **high source credibility.** Most of our discussions are with either friends or family. We enter them with a feeling of trust and openness. Also, the discussions tend to be friendly and can offer us support for trying certain behaviors. (If we are providing information to others, we can also receive some support for our own views or behaviors when they accept our advice.)

Second, unlike the one-way flow of communication from television advertising or consumer reporters, consumer word-of-mouth employs a two-way flow. The power of the **two-way flow of communication** stems from the fact that we can ask questions, obtain clarifications, follow up on issues that interest us, and also spend as much time as we desire on the communication. Thus the word-of-mouth process itself is conducive to a successful learning situation and can lead to better brand recall and stronger attitudes.

The third strength of consumer word–of–mouth comes from its **vicarious trial** attributes. (The word *vicarious*, from Latin, means an "imagined" experience or substitute for an actual experience.) We can gain some of the experience of having tried a movie, for example, and have a better idea of how much we might like it, simply by asking a friend who has seen it already. If his or her recommendation is negative, our chances of actual product trial can go down dramatically, whereas a strong positive recommendation might well create a new customer for that movie. Similarly, we can gain some idea of how a hair style holds up, how a suit "wears," and so forth, without actually having personally to buy and use it.

Two-way flow: Communication in which each party can both give and receive information.

Consumers' Social Integration

We all know that some people are "more sociable" than others. Some of us are extroverts, some are introverts. Some of us have many friends, some of us have few close friends. Do these factors influence our word-of-mouth communications?

Yes, they do. The concept of **consumer social integration** is a useful framework for understanding word-of-mouth behavior.[8] The basic nature of consumer social integration is depicted in Figure 13-2. Note that there are four "types" of consumers in this framework:

- Socially integrated
- Socially dependent
- Socially independent
- Socially isolated

These categories take into account the two-way flow of word-of-mouth communication, and thus represent an improvement over earlier stress on "opinion leadership" alone, which took a one-way flow look at word-of-mouth influence. To use the two-way flow, consumers need to be classified in terms of both opinion giving (to other consumers) and information seeking (from other consumers).

Consumers who score high on both opinion leadership and information seeking are classed as **social integrateds.** Those who score high on influencing others, but low on being influenced themselves, are classed as **social independents.** These two groups comprise the **opinion leader** segment of the market. **Social dependents**, on the other hand, are those who score low on influencing others but high on being influenced by others. **Opinion follower** might be a good term for these consumers. Finally, **social isolates** score low on both types of influence: they are simply less involved in the web of word-of-mouth for a given product or service.

It is important to recognize that these assignments are product class specific. Every consumer is interested in some products but not in others. Being classed as a social isolate for personal computers, for example, does not mean that a consumer is a hermit, but only that he or she is not very involved in consumer word-of-mouth for this product category. Most college students, for example, would probably be classed as social isolates for baby furniture, yachts, or retirement homes, but be placed in one of the other three categories for music or restaurants.

Interesting research has continued to shed light on consumer word-of-mouth. For example, one study sorted word-of-mouth comments about automobiles into four

Consumer social integration: A four-category framework for consumer word-of-mouth behavior in a product class.

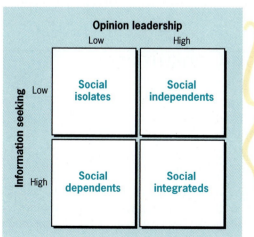

FIGURE 13-2 The Basics of Consumer Social Integration

categories: (1) *advice giving* about which cars to buy or where to shop, (2) *product news* about cars' characteristics and new features available, (3) *positive personal experiences* about one's own car or how it was purchased, and (4) *negative comments* about either cars or a consumer's experiences. The study found that the higher a consumer's basic interest (enduring involvement) in automobiles, the more likely he or she is to serve as an opinion leader: opinion leaders are more likely than other consumers to give advice, provide product news, and tell other consumers about their positive automotive experiences. Meanwhile, those consumers who have bought a car recently (high situational involvement) were not found to be more likely to serve as opinion leaders, but they did share their positive experiences at a higher than average rate. Finally, an interesting result appeared for negative comments in this study—*none* of the foregoing factors (enduring involvement, opinion leadership, or situational involvement) correlated significantly with it![9] This suggests that negative word-of-mouth is a different type of phenomenon: it may be that consumers only relate negative comments if they've had negative experiences, but the timing of the negative experience doesn't matter too much—consumers have long memories for bad experiences!

Consumer Folklore Is All Around Us

Consumer folklore:
The total set of consumer beliefs, opinions and stories across a society or subculture.

Across our society there are millions of general consumer beliefs, opinions, and stories. The total set of these beliefs, opinions, and stories has been termed **consumer folklore.**[10] Consumer folklore ranges from accurate beliefs to wildly inaccurate—and even bizarre—myths and rumors. It includes old kernels of wisdom passed down through families for generations ("Feed a cold, starve a fever," "Chicken soup and bed rest are the best cure for almost any ailment," "The whiter the bread, the quicker you're dead," and so on). It also includes the latest in important and interesting information.

New rumors about popular stores and products are especially favored in some consumer circles, and are passed along with enthusiasm. Exhibit 13-1 summarizes a few recent rumors that were reported by consumers in a recent study, as well as some reported by marketers. You may have heard them yourself.

*E*XHIBIT 13-1

Rumors by Consumers

Rumors as Reported by Consumers

- "I remember hearing about McDonald's supposedly putting worm meat in their hamburgers . . . Burger King may have started that."
- "I heard that a guy bought a bucket of Kentucky Fried Chicken, . . . he and his girlfriend were eating it in the dark at the drive-in. She noticed it tasted funny, so they turned on the light, and she saw she had been eating a rat. She . . . supposedly died."

- "A certain baby formula was deemed unsafe by the USDA for consumption in the United States...caused cancer or something...they just kept manufacturing it and sold it overseas, mainly in the Third World countries."

- "Procter & Gamble's corporate symbol looks like a half moon, with an old man's face, and thirteen stars. Supposedly the reason that Procter & Gamble's so successful is that it's in with devil worshippers and all that. If you...connect the thirteen stars in a certain way, it would come out to 666—that's a symbol for the devil. The half moon looks like the devil."

- "This...candy called Space Dust, or Pop Rocks...you put it in your mouth and it starts crackling...that kid 'Mikey' on the commercial for Life cereal...put some of the candy in his mouth and had a lot of Coca-Cola, and he died from that!"

- "This 17-year-old girl won a trip to Hawaii and wanted a nice tan for the trip. She went to a tanning parlor, and they would only allow her to stay in for a half hour. Well, she wanted a great tan fast, so she went to seven places for a half hour each. Now she's in the hospital, she's totally blind, and she has cooked herself from the inside out, like a microwave. There's nothing they can do for her, she has only 26 days to live."

Rumors Reported by Marketers

- Corona Extra became the second most popular beer in the United States during the late 1980s, based largely on extremely favorable consumer word-of-mouth. Then a false rumor began, that the Mexican beer was contaminated with urine. Sales, which had been up over 80 percent, began to drop sharply in many key markets.

- A restaurant in a midsized Illinois town became the subject of a false rumor that one of its employees had AIDS. According to one businessperson who dined there, "Leo's was virtually empty at lunch."

- Rumors have international appeal as well, with similar dangers for marketers. For example, an anonymous list of 60 products said to contain pork fat appeared in Indonesia. Word began to spread rapidly among the country's 160 million Moslems, since this would mean that such brands are not *halal*, the Moslem equivalent of kosher. The rumor wasn't true for many leading brands on the list, but sales dropped sharply anyway (e.g., Indomie noodles sales were off over 30 percent, while Bango, the nation's leading catsup, had to close its plant for one week after the rumor began).

SOURCES: See Note 11.

MARKETING IMPLICATIONS FROM WORD-OF-MOUTH

Consumer word–of–mouth can be extremely important for marketers. Figure 13-3 shows four strategies that can be used, depending on the situations. Let's look at them in sequence.

Strategy 1: What Can Marketers Do About Rumors?

As we know, word–of–mouth can be either positive or negative. One of the most serious classes of marketing problems arises for firms that are hit with negative rumors. As we saw at the opening of the chapter, Tropical Fantasy's sales dropped 70 percent when

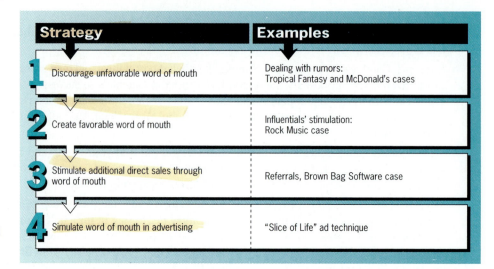

Strategy	Examples
1 Discourage unfavorable word of mouth	Dealing with rumors: Tropical Fantasy and McDonald's cases
2 Create favorable word of mouth	Influentials' stimulation: Rock Music case
3 Stimulate additional direct sales through word of mouth	Referrals, Brown Bag Software case
4 Simulate word of mouth in advertising	"Slice of Life" ad technique

FIGURE 13-3 Marketing Strategies for Word-of-Mouth

the deceptive rumor spread. Similarly, the McDonald's worm rumor (see Exhibit 13-1) reportedly caused sales drops of up to 30 percent in areas where the rumor circulated. General Foods was hit hard by the Pop Rocks rumor, as were Procter & Gamble with the Satanic story, Corona beer, Leo's restaurant, and a number of brands in Indonesia.

The key question confronting a marketer when a negative rumor begins is, "How do I combat it?" In McDonald's case, management took a *refutational approach* and tried to mount arguments to refute, or overcome, consumers' beliefs that the rumor may be true. For example, the company posted a letter from the Secretary of Agriculture that stated that McDonald's products met all government standards. It also modified its TV and magazine ads to emphasize the phrase "100 Percent Pure Beef" and issued information pointing out that worm meat was so much more expensive than hamburger meat that substitution would not be a cost-effective approach in any event. Very little guidance was available to McDonald's as to what strategy might work best. What do you think might have been better? (If you are interested in reading more about this, see Note 12.)

Strategy 2: Creating Consumer Word-of-Mouth

Influentials' stimulation: A marketing strategy that promotes a new product to opinion leaders and then relies on them to advise others.

In a more positive vein, marketers can use consumer word–of–mouth in various ways to promote brand sales. One possible marketing approach involves **influentials' stimulation** to try to create consumer word-of-mouth. This strategy involves locating the socially integrated and socially independent consumers for a particular product category and promoting the product especially to them, even giving it to them free, and then encouraging them to promote the product to others.

🐋 *The Rock Music Experiment*

An interesting test of this approach has been reported in the rock music category. There are hundreds of new songs released each week, and the marketing challenge—to create a hit using unknown artists—is severe. The typical promotional program employs a *push strategy*, attempting to sell radio and TV stations, disk jockeys, and record outlets, hoping that they will in turn influence consumers to buy the records.

In this marketing test, however, no push strategy was used. Instead, a *pull strategy* was employed in a special way. The high school population in a number of trial cities

Reebok reacted strongly against rumors that it manufactured shoes in South Africa, where the government had the racial policy of *apartheid*. Concerned that it would be seen as racist by its black customers, Reebok ran this ad campaign in more than 200 newspapers as well as such major magazines as *Ebony* and *Jet*.

DRIVE CONCORDE
THE ARCHITECTURE OF THE AUTOMOBILE IS CHANGING.

To have a new Chrysler Concorde

delivered to your home or office

by a Chrysler Corporation representative,

please complete this card,

place it in the postpaid envelope provided

and drop it in the mail.

Or call

1-800-XXX-XXX

Please have the Chrysler Corporation representative contact me concerning a driving evaluation of the 1993 Chrysler Concorde.

My phone number is:

( )   ( )
Work   Home

Best time to call   Best time to call

Today's date

Chrysler employed an "influential stimulation" strategy to introduce its new line of LH models in 1993. Invitations to try the car for a weekend were sent to influential community leaders and businesspersons: results were "nothing short of phenomenal," as 98 percent reported they'd recommend the car to friends. A web of word of mouth had been jump-started!

was targeted as the key consumer market due to their heavy purchase rate for rock music. The researchers then obtained the names of various types of student leaders in each school in each city. Each of these students was sent a letter inviting him or her to join a "select panel" of leaders that was being formed to evaluate rock songs. Each week for a period of several months, the students received packets of free songs. They were asked to return their evaluations, plus the opinions of any friends and acquaintances who might care to give them.

The results? Several of the recordings hit the "top 10" in the cities with the panels. In all other cities in the nation, where normal promotions had been used, not a single one of these records ever reached the hit lists! This effect was achieved without any contacts with either radio stations or music stores in the trial cities: the new hits had been "pulled" through the channels by the power of consumer word-of-mouth![13]

This rock music application represents a case in which marketers could rely on the strong interests of opinion leaders to help create word-of-mouth, once the opinion leaders knew about a particular product's benefits. A variation of this approach is to contact trusted opinion leaders, but *not* in their roles as consumers. For example, food manufacturers have begun to provide physicians with detailed information regarding the nutritional benefits of foods sold to consumers in supermarkets. According to one industry executive, "Patients are now asking doctors about diet and nutrition, and doctors are now contacting companies to get more information. A company can run all the ads it wants, but if a consumer doesn't understand what saturated fats are, or why they're important, the message is wasted. Doctors can explain that, and suggest ways for their patients to cut down."[14]

Strategy 3: Stimulate Additional Direct Sales

Consumer word-of-mouth operates perhaps most frequently in terms of local market retailing and services. So far, we have discussed this as an entirely voluntary activity on the part of consumers, operating independently of any marketer involvement. Word-of-mouth can be *so valuable* to manufacturers, stores, and salespersons, however, that sometimes they become more active in attempting to stimulate this activity directly. Various approaches are possible, ranging from a salesperson simply asking a customer to "Spread the word if you're satisfied with the service you've gotten from me" to providing payments for successfully directing new purchasers to the marketer. In many cases the term **referral fee** is used, in which the person providing advice about where to seek service will receive a payment from the marketer (lawyer, doctor, stockbroker, contractor) who has received the new client or customer. While many word-of-mouth referrals do not have payment involved (Figure 13-1's referral network, for example, did not), within business and the professions this practice is fairly common. In this regard, a recent creative variation merits our brief attention:

🐚 *Brown Bag Feasts as Pyramid Builds*

The Brown Bag Software Company was in serious financial trouble a few years ago, because it couldn't provide software dealers with sufficient incentives to learn its systems and sell them against industry giants such as Lotus or Microsoft. Out of desperation, Sandy Schupper, chairman of the firm, decided to employ some consumer research that had shown that 95 percent of working professionals were willing to pay a reasonable price (about $100) for software they had been given free, but liked well enough to continue using. "What made that 95 percent figure so hard to swallow is the fact that our biggest problem in this industry is consumer theft," Schupper explains. "We're not talking about sampling here either, because once they've got it, they've *got* it. They don't have to come back to you and buy it again."

As a hedge against total trust in a computer honor system, Brown Bag decided to reduce its cost of goods to a minimum and to introduce incentives for users to pay up. Rather than using diskettes, it placed the software on over 1000 local on-line "bulletin boards," so that computer enthusiasts could simply download the program to their personal machines and use the self-contained, working Brown Bag program. The firm then offered two different incentives for the consumer to send in a payment. One was a product improvement (upon payment, the consumer would be sent a diskette with additional features and a manual).

The other incentive was the prospect of future financial rewards if the consumer was willing to engage in favorable (and successful) word-of-mouth for Brown Bag's programs. This worked as follows: each diskette sent out had a personalized serial number. The buyer was encouraged to make as many copies as he or she desired and give them to friends to try. If any friends liked the program and wanted to buy a diskette for themselves, they had to send in that serial number, and the original buyer would receive a 10 percent commission. The friend's new diskette, however, would have a new serial number for him or her, and she could begin to copy it for other friends and begin to earn commissions as well. How has this approach worked? Brown Bag now has a commission-only sales force that numbers in the thousands, it has expanded into international markets, and it is planning the introduction of six new software products each year, which will allow its past customers to continue with their referral activities. In contrast to the bleak times, Mr. Schupper now reports, "I make millions giving software away free!"[15]

Strategy 4: Advertising Appeals Using Word-of-Mouth

Our fourth strategy uses an indirect approach, by simulating consumer word–of–mouth in a commercial. The **slice-of-life approach** in advertising, for example, often depicts two or more normal-appearing consumers conversing about a typical consumer problem (this varies by the product and target audience, of course). After the nature of the problem is made clear, one of the consumers will pass on the key information as to how successful he or she was when using the sponsoring brand to solve the problem.

If the ad is successful in getting the audience to relate to the actors as normal consumers, the effect is to obtain something similar to a *consumer testimonial* in a word-of-mouth context. In terms of our dimensions of word-of-mouth for automobiles, a slice-of-life commercial can show any or all of the four types: advice giving, product news, and/or positive personal experiences are typical, while even negative comments (about competitors) are possible if done in a tasteful and legal manner.

FOCUS GROUPS IN MARKETING RESEARCH

Before turning to discuss social influence theories in marketing, we should briefly address one remaining issue about word-of-mouth. Consumer word-of-mouth represents such a powerful force in the consumer marketplace that—if they could—marketers would listen in on every consumer conversation about their particular product or service category. After hearing them, the marketer would try to adjust the marketing mix accordingly. In reality, "listening in" would, of course, represent invasion of consumers' privacy in addition to being a very inefficient process. The point is, though, that the information contained in these discussions is extremely valuable to marketers.

In place of the real discussions, therefore, marketing researchers have developed several research forms to try to capture consumer word-of-mouth characteristics in a research setting. One extremely popular research technique, for example, is called the *focus group study*. A typical **focus group** brings 8 to 12 consumers from the target market together, seats them in a manner conducive to easy discussion, and asks them to talk freely about their opinions. A trained moderator keeps the discussion flowing and ensures that the key topics for the marketer are covered within the session, which lasts from one to two hours.

Focus group: A popular research technique that brings together 8 to 12 consumers for discussion about the product.

One purpose of this research method is to try to obtain exactly the sort of information that consumers pass along to each other freely in their daily discussions, but to do so on behalf of a sponsoring marketer (often, these studies are held in special rooms with two-way mirrors, so that researchers and sponsors can sit in the next room and monitor the session). The groups are tape recorded and then interpreted by researchers to pull out significant themes and results from the sessions in formal reports to the sponsors of the research.

Because of its low cost, fast turnaround, and insights into actual consumer opinions and language, focus group research is extremely popular across all facets of the marketing field. If you are interested in learning more about this technique, as well as some drawbacks of it, you may wish to begin with the sources listed in Note 17.

Consumer word-of-mouth represents an activity through which social influence operates. As we have all experienced, however, there are a number of subtle (and powerful) aspects involved in social influence itself. Within this section we will examine five key topics in understanding social influences on consumer behavior (each has been the subject of an extensive literature in itself):

- The main types of social influence
- The nature of social interactions
- The importance of symbolism
- The power of groups
- Questions about "consumer conformity"

Within each discussion we'll examine typical forms of marketing applications.

THE TWO MAIN TYPES OF SOCIAL INFLUENCE

It is helpful to recognize that there are two basic forms of consumer social influence: normative and informational.[18] Essentially, **normative social influence** occurs when there is a heavy weighting of social pressure in the decisions that consumers make. For example, if Stacy Phillips buys Reebok shoes only because she is interested in gaining approval (reward) from others or avoiding disapproval (punishment), we are seeing normative social influence at work on her decision.

There is also, however, another common way in which social influence can occur in consumer behavior. Consumers often learn relevant information about products, movies, restaurants, and so on from other people and from groups. When they are influenced by the contents of this new knowledge (but do not feel pressured to behave one way or another), **informational social influence** is at work. *The key difference is whether we are primarily influenced by the pressure we perceive (normative) or by the contents of the new knowledge (informational).* While some decisions will reflect both types of influence, one type will usually dominate.

Certain characteristics of effective influencers for each type have been identified. *Normative* influences are stronger when the influencing person or group is important to the consumer, when they are able to deliver clear rewards or punishments (including social disapproval) to the consumer, when their desires are clear, and when the consumer's behavior is public.

Informational influences respond to a quite different set of characteristics: expertise, trustworthiness, and empathy. **Expertise** refers to the quality of the information offered to a consumer by someone else. The person need not be an expert in a technical sense, but the more that we believe his or her information is important and true, the more likely we are to be influenced by it. **Trustworthiness** relates to the presence or absence of a manipulative intent on the part of the influencer. Can we trust what we are hearing, or is the information likely to be biased toward the benefit of the information source? **Empathy**, on the other hand, refers to how closely the other person is able to relate to our personal position. The more similar their value judgments are to ours, the more relevant the information is likely to be for our personal needs. Marketers can benefit from an understanding of these different source characteristics, as indicated by the application that follows.

Normative social influence: A heavy weighting of social pressure on a consumer.

Informational social influence: The influence of knowledge gained from other people on a consumer.

🐳 *Life's Precious Gift*

There are certain products and services in which consumers are "squeamish" and influence is particularly difficult. Blood donation is an example. Even though most people say they support the idea of donating blood, the turnouts for most blood drives are quite low, and blood banks must rely heavily on "regular" donors. Organizational drives (which involve heavy doses of normative influence) are also effective.

LaTour and Manrai report an interesting experiment with a Chicago-area blood center to see if they could directly employ the concepts of normative and social influence to increase donations of blood during a drive. In the first of several tests, they divided area citizens into four groups: (1) the *control group* received no special influence attempts; (2) the *information group* received a direct mail piece explaining that blood donations help other people, and that the blood donation process is short, painless, and not likely to result in tiredness. Examples of blood needs in the area, and a picture of a child whose life was saved by blood donations were included in an enclosed brochure. The letter then requested that the person come and donate blood; (3) the *normative group* received a telephone request from another community member, and was asked personally to agree to come and donate blood; and (4) the *combined group* received first the direct mailer and then the telephone call.

The results were very interesting. The control group turned out 2 percent of its members for the blood drive (representing what was expected if no special influence attempts were made). The information group, having received the direct mailing, turned out over 4 percent of its members. The normative group responded even better to its phone requests and turned out over 7 percent of its members. However, the combined group's response was overwhelming—about 22 percent of its members poured out to fill the blood center's vessels! In accord with the predictions of the researchers, the staged application of an informative strategy followed by a normative social influence attempt was much more effective than was a single application of either approach by itself.[19]

WHAT REALLY GOES ON IN SOCIAL INTERACTIONS?

Social influence operates when people interact. Social interaction has been studied by philosophers, sociologists, and psychologists throughout history. There are many ways to analyze social interactions. Although we may not be consciously aware of it, four important elements are often found in social interactions:[20]

- Social exchange
- Power
- Cooperation
- Conflict

Any particular interaction can contain some or all of these.

Social exchange is a basic element in many interactions. It occurs when one person provides benefits of some sort to the other, usually with the expectation of some reciprocal benefits that will be returned. In purely economic exchanges, the obligations of the seller and buyer are likely to be quite formalized by contracts or by law. In social interactions, however, the "obligations" are often less clear. This leads to such dimensions as personal liking, trust, gratitude, and so on being extremely important in social exchanges. *Cooperation* is another element often found in social interactions. It refers to two participants joining together to accomplish a common goal. Within consumer behavior, a salesperson and customer often work together to find the most suitable purchase, and a husband and wife will strive to cooperate in reaching their important purchases. Word-of-mouth advice among friends also reflects this element.

Power reflects a difference in the authority levels (or other power sources) between the participants. A salesperson who knows a great deal about stereo systems, for example, possesses certain power in an in-store discussion. If the customer also knows a great deal, the seller's power is reduced, while if the consumer feels inadequate, the seller's power is increased. *Conflict* interactions are those of the "I win, you lose" variety: competition, either overtly or hidden, is active here. Within consumer behavior these issues often arise when we are forced to allocate resources (money, time, effort) in a joint decision situation. Within a family setting, for example, common instances can include which vacation to choose, which car to buy, or even which movie to see.

The Situation as an Element in a Social Interaction

Social interactions also depend on the situation. Consider how differently most of us act when we are at a wild party, compared to a formal dinner. Some of our behavioral difference is due to the other people with whom we are interacting. Most of the variation, though, is due to *the overall situational context.* Within each specific situation, we turn to our expectations of what "is supposed to happen," and how the other people present will act themselves and will expect us to act (this is one major reason that new environments are often difficult for us to adjust to: our long-term memories do not contain "scripts" for these, and we are simply not very certain about what to expect or how to behave). Thus situational influence on social interactions is closely related to the subject of social roles and expectations.

The Importance of Social Roles

A **role** can be defined as a set of accepted rules for appropriate behaviors in a particular situation.[21] Social interactions are greatly assisted by the presence of roles, since they help us to predict something about the behavior of others with whom we will interact. For example, imagine the following scene as it might unfold in a play:

> Pat and Lee strolled casually through the entrance of the exclusive shop in the mall. Chris, turning around, saw them coming and . . .

Role: A set of accepted rules for appropriate behaviors in a particular situation.

How did you cast this scene? What was Chris going to do? This little example allows us to see how important are the roles that we assign to people. For example, would it have made much difference if Pat were a father, Lee were his son, and Chris were Lee's mother? What if Chris was a salesperson, and Pat and Lee were teenage girl shoppers? Or if Pat and Lee were police officers and Chris were a criminal? Notice that all three names could denote a male or female. Did your view of the scene depend on this at all? The essential point of the example is that, just as in a play, *the role that one occupies really helps to define the actions we expect.* However, roles do not specify everything; this allows for some individual freedom, as long as the behavior is within the accepted boundaries of the role. For example, Chris, as a salesperson, can rush over to wait on Pat and Lee, or can simply look over at them with a friendly, inquiring appearance. If the behavior is outside the boundaries of the role, however, the social interaction is likely to suffer, since the expectations of the other person are not being met. For example, Chris cannot refuse to look at Pat and Lee, or order them to leave the store, and still expect a smooth sales interaction.

Role repertoire: The set of all roles that an individual possesses.

We all adopt many roles during our daily lives. A **role repertoire** refers to the set of all roles that an individual possesses. A young woman, for example, might have such roles as rising young executive, wife, mother, daughter, sister, jogger, shopper, club member, and friend to various others. As we move through our lives, we are likely to add new roles and give up some past roles. Most of the roles that we add are our choice, and we enjoy carrying them out.

The impact of roles has received some degree of attention in consumer research and more is likely in the future. We'll see more about this topic in Chapter 14 (when we examine household decision making) and Chapter 15 (when we focus on salesperson influences on consumer behavior).

SYMBOLISM IS IMPORTANT TOO

Symbolic interaction theory: The study of how individuals interact with symbols and how products play symbolic roles.

As we learned in Chapter 7, a "symbol" is something that stands for something else: it *signifies* something to us and to others. Within the consumer behavior literature, Belk has pointed out that consumers use possessions as symbols that help them to create, maintain, and extend *meaning* in their lives through different life stages.[22] More broadly, **symbolic interaction theory** in consumer behavior studies how individuals interact with the symbols in their environment, and how products play symbolic roles. For example, notice that while a Rolex watch, Brooks Brothers suit, and BMW auto have nothing in common on the surface, many consumers would easily group them together as a symbolic unit.[23]

COMMUNICATING WITH SYMBOLS THROUGH CONSUMER BEHAVIOR

In keeping with our discussions elsewhere in the book, Figure 13-4 shows a basic framework for understanding the communication process between two people. Notice that much of this process occurs within the inner worlds of our minds and cannot be observed. Three processes are involved: encoding, transmission, and decoding. **Encoding** refers to the choice and arrangement of symbols to represent the intended meanings of person 1. Transmission refers to the actual movement (through light waves, sound waves, TV systems, etc.) of the message from the sender to the receiver. **Decoding** then requires the receiver to take the message and interpret the symbols so as to take away meaning from it. When person 2 responds, the process works in the opposite direction.

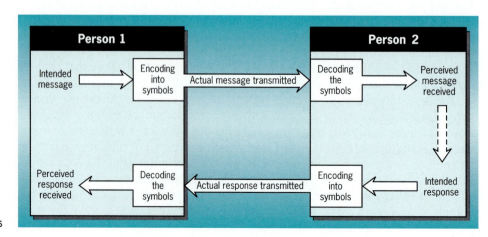

FIGURE 13-4 Outline of a Communication Process

Decoding Symbols from Others

A number of research studies have found that consumers make inferences about others based on their use of many types of products and services. But how does this really happen? To begin to analyze this process, try jotting down the first brief impressions you have about each of the following people:

- Ted Marston drives a red Camaro and smokes Marlboros._____
- Mark Abelson drinks Tab._____
- Ann Fleming bought her new dress from Sears._____
- Jennifer Dawson wears her Tri-Delt pin frequently._____

If you had no particular impression based on any of these short descriptions, it is likely that the product involved does not have a strong symbolic meaning for you, even though it may for others. Try giving this exercise to a few of your friends and see what their impressions are. Do they seem to agree? In either event, are the inferences that we're making fair to the consumers involved? Are they fair to the brands? If you were a marketing manager for each, would you be pleased with these results?

🐌 *A Marketing Classic: Symbolism and Nescafé*

The marketing field contains its share of "war stories" that are useful to demonstrate certain fundamental points about consumer behavior. One of the best known has been passed along in classrooms for years and demonstrates how consumers use products as symbols that they decode to make judgments about other consumers.

Shortly after World War II, the Nestlé Company, headquartered in Switzerland, attempted to introduce the new form of soluble (instant) coffee into the huge U.S. market. No longer would consumers have the problems of cleaning old grinds, waiting for the coffee to perk, or making an entire pot of coffee when all they needed was a single cup. No more would they be tempted to drink a stale cup because it was "left over" from the morning's brew. Although the new instant coffee would surely not replace drip grind entirely, it was likely to be a smashing success, especially since it tasted good in addition to being convenient. Thus was Nescafé launched to the American public.

But something went wrong. After achieving a strong rate of trial purchases, consumers seemed to stop buying the brand. When asked why, they responded that they didn't really like its flavor. *The brand's managers knew, however, that this couldn't be the real reason,* based on the company's own consumer taste tests, taken when consumers didn't know what kind of coffee they were drinking. Instead, there appeared to be something about this product itself, perhaps its name, that symbolized something negative to potential purchasers. Mason Haire, a professor, began some research to discover the real problem.

Haire conducted a test to see what the use of Nescafé seemed to be symbolizing in the minds of consumers. He presented a shopping list to participants in the study, and then asked them to write a brief description of what they thought the woman would be like (her personality and character) who had brought home these groceries. The twist was that there were actually two shopping lists used, and half of the participants got one list while the other half responded to the other list. The lists included seven typical items, ranging from meat and bread to canned peaches, with brand names included. The lists were identical except for a single change in one entry—one list had Nescafé

Instant Coffee listed in the fifth position while the other listed Maxwell House Coffee (Drip Grind) in that position.

The results were surprising, as it was clear that the single little change in type of coffee had led the participants to *infer two very different types of women shoppers.* Those receiving the Maxwell House list, with its common coffee form, did not have any particular image in mind of the shopper, though the adjectives they used were generally positive. The two most common descriptions were "Good Wife" and "Thrifty." The consumers who had received the Nescafé list, however, showed strong agreement about their shopper: the most common descriptions were "Lazy" and "A Poor Planner," with each coming from half of all the participants who saw this list!

From these results, the firm decided to change its advertising approach, now to show consumers that using Nescafé was something good to do, since it gave a busy and active woman more time to devote to her real chores as a wife, mother, and guardian of the household. Following this shift in emphasis, and as more brands entered the market, instant coffee became increasingly popular in the U.S. market, and Nescafé became a major brand. (A follow-up study conducted in 1968 found no differences in participants' responses to the two shopping lists, indicating that the negative symbols that had been so strong for instant coffee in 1950 had disappeared from consumers' minds a few years later.)[24]

Sending Messages to Others

It stands to reason that the same consumers who are decoding symbols from others will begin to wonder about possible messages *they* may be sending—inadvertently or not—to others who may be decoding them. As a person begins to think about the signals that he or she may be sending out, it is just a short step to then realize that it is possible to "manage" these signals to create symbolic messages about oneself (the theoretical term for this process is **impression management,** or *self-presentation*).[25] Notice, however, that our culture has already taught us the "proper" ways to appear neat and clean, or alert, or confident, or attractive. For consumer behavior purposes, this reasoning is simply extended to focus on how products might enhance the impression management process, serving as "props" of a sort.

For example, assume that each person in the list that follows is an acquaintance who has asked you for some good advice. In each case, what would you advise?

- Bob Johnston wants a good social life. What kind of car should he think about driving? What kinds should he avoid?_____

- Todd McNeill wants to be seen as sophisticated. What should he order at the bar?_____

- Diana Carry has taken a new position in which she will manage a bank branch with 25 employees. What colors and styles of clothing should she buy? What colors and styles should she avoid?_____

Again, the extent to which it was easy or difficult to answer each question is an indication of how closely you associate symbolism with each of the product areas. Notice, however, that this time the process was slightly different: we *first* had to take the perspective of the encoder of the message, *then* look out to possible decoders to anticipate their reactions and find the product that brings out the best anticipated reaction, and *then* pass this information along to the encoder. In this regard, notice

Impression management: The theory that people manage the signals they send out in order to create symbolic messages about themselves.

Not everyone sees a symbol the same way: a group of American Indian parents in Minnesota used this poster to sway high schools to change their nicknames.

how very important the particular social group is that will be decoding the symbolic messages (that is, the answers for Todd McNeill might differ for executives and college students, and even within each population the answers might differ for certain subgroups). This reflects the concept of reference groups, which we will examine shortly.

Status Symbols and Conspicuous Consumption

Before leaving the topic of how consumers use products to send symbolic messages, a brief mention of status symbols is appropriate. **Status symbols** are products that serve to send others a message about the elevated social status of a person. Often, they also serve to tell the person internally that he or she "has arrived" or has personal value: thus status symbols can combine the characteristics of private and public symbolic expressions.

Status symbols are no recent phenomenon in the consumer marketplace. In 1899, for example, Thorstein Veblen published his famous book, *The Theory of the Leisure Class*, in which he strongly questioned the "conspicuous consumption" and "conspicuous waste" that he saw all around him.[26] Veblen's ire was directed to a narrow band of upper-class society (one social couple, for example, spent $370,000 to convert the interior of the Waldorf-Astoria Hotel in New York City to a replica of the palace at Versailles—for one evening's party).[27]

Status symbols:
Products or possessions that serve to send others a message about the elevated social status of a person.

The world has changed in many ways since Veblen wrote, but the essential nature of status symbols has remained much the same. A long list of social critics have observed the stress on status symbols throughout this century. Some have been favorable, but most have not.[28] Today, given the much higher standard of living, and the marketing of credit to the general consuming public, most consumers are able occasionally to engage in "status seeking" through consumption. What are some products or services that serve as status symbols for you?

🎋 Marketing Application: Grey Poupon Cuts the Mustard

As a "gourmet" mustard, Grey poupon had for years commanded a 2 percent share of market. It seemed to be appropriately advertised in *Gourmet*, the *New Yorker*, *Smithsonian*, and other upscale publications. Its owners realized, however, that it might be possible to expand sales into the larger consumer segments if somehow they could identify the brand as having a "sense of bigness." They decided to test a new TV campaign that relied on symbols of "bigness," including Rolls-Royce autos, chauffeurs, expensive clothing, upper-crust accents, and so forth. By using understated humor, they hoped to make the drama easy for the mass audience to accept (and to be willing to now pay $2.00 as compared to 79 cents for competing brands).

The ad that emerged became a classic. In it, one Rolls-Royce drives up beside another at a stop light. The dignified occupant asks out the window, "Pardon me, would you have any Grey Poupon?" The commercial closes with a jar of this premium brand being passed across for other sophisticates to enjoy.

The firm tested this ad in two local markets hoping for a sales increase of about 10 percent. It was shocked to find that sales more than doubled immediately! The ads were then rolled out nationally, and the campaign continued, with modifications, for the next 10 years. The net impact of this successful use of advertising symbolism? Grey Poupon's sales are now over $50 million per year, compared to $1.5 million before the use of status symbol advertising.[29]

GROUPS CAN BE POWERFUL SOCIAL INFLUENCERS

Each of us belongs to many groups during our lives. Groups can give us friendship, security, and opportunities to express ourselves. A company, a sales department, a civic organization, a church committee, a family, and a friendly club all represent groups to which a marketer might belong. Understanding group processes is important for marketers who sell to company buying committees, to institutions, or to households.

The clever mix of symbolism and humor helped spice up Grey Poupon's sales through a classic advertising campaign.

The formal term **group** refers to two or more individuals who (1) share a set of norms, values, or beliefs; (2) have certain role relationships; and (3) experience interdependent behaviors.[30] Therefore, a group is more than simply a collection of individuals who happen to be in the same place at the same time. It usually has a continuing life, and its members share a sense of belonging to it. There are many types of groups, each with some different characteristics.

Group: Two or more individuals who (a) share a set of norms, (b) have role relationships, and (c) experience interdependent behaviors.

Why a Group Has Social Power

Social power is defined as the potential influence that an individual or group can have over a person.[31] Each of us is subject to social power and also possesses it over others. Five types of social power are

Social power: The influence an individual or group can have over a person.

- Legitimated power
- Coercive power
- Expert power
- Reward power
- Referent power

Each type reflects a different reason for an individual to "go along with" someone else's recommended behavior.

In brief, **legitimated power** stems from a person's belief that another person has the right to suggest (or even order) a particular behavior. For example, a junior executive might carry out the assignment from her boss. In general, this type of power reflects group organizations, when a member accepts his or her role within the group. **Expert power**, on the other hand, reflects the belief that another person "knows what she's talking about," perhaps through long experience or intensive studies of a particular issue. Here a recommendation is seen as good because of the expert background involved. **Referent power**, meanwhile, reflects a person's desire to feel that he or she "belongs" with another individual or group and wants to act so as to express this identity (this is a key topic for consumer behavior, which we'll examine again shortly). The final two types of social power represent more activity on the part

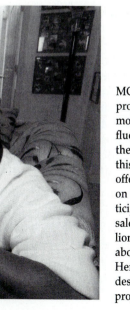

MCI's "Friends and Family" program was successful in motivating consumers to influence other members of their groups to sign up with this long-distance carrier by offering 20 percent discounts on calls made from one participant to another. Estimated sales gains for MCI: 2.5 million new subscribers, worth about $500 million per year! Here one satisfied member describes her reaction to the program.

of the other person or group. **Coercive power** rests on the threat, real or imagined, that the group can punish the member if he or she does not comply with the recommended behavior. For example, a group might ridicule the member, remove some privileges, or even expel the person from membership. **Reward power**, conversely, is the other side of the coin: in this instance a person will comply because he or she expects to receive material benefits, praise, or other positive recognition if the group members like what he or she has done.

Group Influence Processes: Kelman's View

Social power theory helps us see *why* groups are influential, but not exactly how the process might work. Herbert Kelman has helped us with this question by identifying three types of **group influence processes** that focus on the individual being influenced:[32]

- Compliance
- Identification
- Internalization

> **Compliance:** A person goes along because of the group's power to reward or punish.

> **Internalization:** A person goes along because he or she agrees with the group's values.

> **Identification:** A person goes along because he or she desires to be related with the group.

The first case, **compliance,** represents a response to the group's power to reward or punish a person (either physically or socially). In this case, a person is likely to go along with the group whether or not he or she believes in the norm, because of the external power the group has to reward or punish.

The other two cases are different in that the person is more internally motivated. **Internalization** is directly related to the group norms being accepted by the individual. In this case the individual discovers what the group believes and personally agrees with these values for himself as well. **Identification,** on the other hand, represents a social response: the individual desires to create a close relationship with the group, but has little interest in the group's norms. To attain this closer relationship, he will adopt the behavioral norms of the group, even though the norms themselves may be of little importance to him.

Marketing Applications Using Group Power and Influence

Because social groups are self-contained, marketers must generally adapt strategies to account for the characteristics of each. Understanding the power sources and influence processes at work within business organizations and government buying centers is particularly important for salespersons in industrial marketing. Within consumer marketing, opportunities for strong manipulations of group power are rare, but they do exist. For example, the employment of typical consumers as sales agents—selling to their friends—has been quite successful. The fabled Tupperware party (at its peak, one of these parties began every 10 seconds somewhere in the world) is one instance of this technique.

❧ *Group Pressure: I Really Ought to ...*

A typical Tupperware party involves a relatively small group (of 10 to 20 people, usually women) invited as guests to a friend's house for a party of games and refreshments. Near the end of the party, the dealer demonstrates each of the Tupperware items and passes out order forms. While doing so, however, the dealer informs the guests that their friend, the hostess, will only win a big prize if two of the guests agree to hold future parties in their homes. Also, a strong flow of orders from the guests will be needed for their hostess to be rewarded. The social pressure and sense of obligation of each of the guests is quite strong in this environment! Over the years, millions of household items have found their ways home with the departing customers. In recent years, with women moving increasingly to the workplace, Tupperware office parties have been designed for lunch hours: these now account for over $60 million in sales each year.[33]

Marketing Simulations of Group Pressure and Influence

The personal presence of other consumers within the sales context obviously contributes much of the power to the Tupperware case. Even when other consumers are not present, however, marketers can try to *simulate their social pressures through "hard-sell" sales techniques or through various advertising themes.* In so doing, however, the possibility of **psychological reactance** must also be considered. This refers to the fact that consumers will sometimes resent receiving social pressures (because of a perceived loss of freedom), and marketers can experience a "boomerang effect" as people resist the influence attempt and even begin to move against the desires of the influencer.[34] Thus the tactical questions are not always simple.

The simulation of group pressure in advertising usually attempts to raise *anticipations of how other consumers will react if a certain product is or is not purchased.* Usually, the approach is a "positive" one, stressing how purchase of a particular brand will impress others (that is, act as a status symbol) or in some way will lead to acceptance by them because of the superior—sometimes even magical—qualities of the brand. We are all familiar with the man who dabs on the aftershave and fights off the females, the man who drives home his new car and watches the neighborhood gather round in admiration, the woman who wins admiring glances as she strolls down the sidewalk in her custom-look business suit, and so forth.

Sometimes, however, a social influence advertising theme is a negative one—stressing that embarrassing social consequences lie ahead if a certain product is not used. This is termed **social fear advertising.**[35] Social fear is a theme that is used frequently in certain product categories, particularly those that involve the body's functions, such as deodorants, feminine hygiene sprays, dandruff shampoos, mouthwash, and so forth. The prime reason that these claims are effective, of course, is that we really *do* expect that others would react the way they are portrayed in the ads and that our reputation would actually suffer. In this sense, then, the ads are realistic, even though they are playing upon areas sensitive to us. One of advertising's "classics" was built on this theme:

🐌 *"Ring Around the Collar!"—An Advertising Classic*

"That's a really obnoxious ad" is a description marketing professors heard for years, as their students have reacted to various television commercials. One ad campaign probably earned this description more than any other, however—the "Ring around the Collar!" commercials for Wisk, a liquid detergent marketed by Lever Bros.

Wisk was introduced about 30 years ago as the first liquid detergent. It initially experienced success in the intensely competitive detergent market, but by the mid-1960s its share had fallen to less than 3 percent. Lever's focus group was used to search for possible new ad themes. Within the studies, dirty shirt collars were frequently mentioned by housewives who were heavy users of detergents. Based on the focus group research, the new ad campaign was built around the schoolyard "Ring Around the Rosie" chant, an evocative symbol of other peers chanting in unison around the person in the middle.

Psychological reactance: Consumers sometimes resent social pressures and may resist an influence attempt.

Social fear advertising: Use of themes that suggest that embarrassing social consequences lie ahead if a certain product is not used.

The commercials used adult settings, of course, but relied heavily on social embarrassments as their theme. The early commercials placed the blame clearly on the housewife, who had apparently been responsible for laundering her husband's shirts. One ad showed the happy couple arriving in Hawaii, bending down to receive their honorary lei's, when the beautiful native girl shrinks back in disgust at what she discovers, and loudly points it out to everyone in the vicinity. The wife is mortified. However, the commercial ends with the couples reunited in bliss: the woman has obviously followed the announcer's advice and used Wisk to remove the ring. In the late 1970s and through the 1980s, the campaign was toned down somewhat: the blame for the rings was taken off the wife's shoulders and placed more squarely on competitive brands that had not done the job they should. After 20 years of "Ring around the Collar," Wisk was a powerful brand in the huge detergent market. As the 1990s began, however, Lever Bros. announced that it was moving the account from the ad agency that had created this classic campaign. This meant that it was almost certain that the obnoxious "ring" would finally disappear. What happened? The new ad agency appointed the *son* of the man who developed the original "Ring around the Collar" ad to head the new advertising effort! The result? The new campaign warned viewers that "Ring around the collar was just the beginning," followed by shots of embarrassing food spills ("Tsk, tsk, tsk!") and the detergent's removing them ("Wisk, Wisk, Wisk!"). What did the father think of the new campaign? "I love the notion." And what about the original campaign? "... I'm a devout believer ... it sold the bejesus out of Wisk."[36]

Reference Groups and Referent Others

As a final topic in groups, it is appropriate that we raise the subject of reference groups, as these can be extremely important in influencing consumer behavior. The term **reference group** has come to mean a group to whom we look ("refer to") for guidance for our own behavior.[37] Reference groups can be large or small, formal or informal. We do not even need to be a member of the group or to be in physical contact with it. When an individual is very important to us and serves this function, he or she is called a **referent other**. Reference groups are especially important because we identify with at least some aspects of that group. *Normative reference groups* provide us with values and standards for our behavior. Our family is our first normative reference group. Some groups serve as *negative reference groups*: these represent norms or behaviors that we do not admire or seek for ourselves. On the other hand, some groups serve as *aspirational reference groups*, positive groups that we hope to join in the future, such as successful business executives.

> **Reference group:** A group to which a consumer looks for guidance for values and behavior.

Reference Groups and Product Differences. Interesting research has been done on *how products differ in their susceptibility to reference group influences*. Marketers of some products need not concern themselves very much with this area, since consumers are not likely to respond to reference group influences when buying their products. Marketers of other products, however, would be very wise to pay careful attention to developments in this field of study, since reference group effects should be strong.

In brief, reference group influence depends on two characteristics of a product: how *visible* it is to other persons and how *exclusively* it is owned (if everyone already owns a product, it is much less exclusive than if only a few persons own it). Since products can be either high or low on each of these dimensions, four combinations are

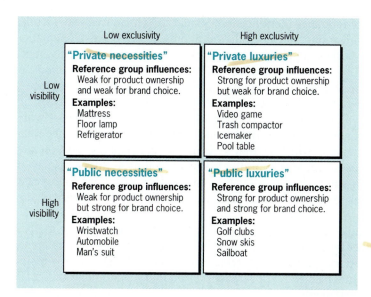

FIGURE 13-5 How Reference Group Influence Differs by Product SOURCE: Adapted from William O. Bearden and Michael J. Etzel, "Reference Group Influence on Product and Brand Purchase Decisions," *Journal of Consumer Research,* September 1982, p. 185.

possible (high on both, low on both, high-low, and low-high). Figure 13-5 depicts the framework proposed by William Bearden and Michael Etzel to summarize findings on this topic.[38] In Figure 13-5, low visibility is denoted by "private goods," while high visibility is denoted by "public goods." Similarly, low exclusivity is denoted by "necessities," while high exclusivity is represented by "luxury goods." As we'll see, exclusivity reference group influences will be centered on whether a *product* should be owned, while visibility-type reference group influences will stress that *particular brands* or *styles* should be chosen. Thus the particular impacts depend on which cell of the table into which a product falls. For example,

- For **private necessities**, reference group influences are expected to be weak. These products are required by almost everyone and are not easily visible to others.

- For **private luxuries,** in the upper right, fewer people own these, so having the product will provide an exclusivity benefit. However, since it will not be easily seen by others, the brand or style chosen should be less influenced by reference groups.

- For **public necessities,** reference group influences will not be very strong for product class ownership, since almost everyone already believes that they need this product. Because the product is visible, however, reference group influences on the brand or style chosen will be strong.

- For **public luxuries,** in the lower right, reference groups should be strong influences on both (1) owning the product at all and (2) which style or brand should be obtained. Since fewer people own these, having the product will bring an exclusivity benefit. Also, since the product is visible, the brand or model will be noticed. Thus the potential for reference group influence is very high.

ENDORSEMENTS AND TESTIMONIALS

A major contribution of the reference group/referent other concept is that it can extend the social influence far beyond the membership groups with whom we physically interact. Fantasies, heroes, stars, and other models can enter the analysis, as they stimulate the process of **reference identification.** Similar to Kelman's view of identification with respect to any group, reference identification reflects a positive orientation of the consumer, who wishes to identify himself or herself with a desirable reference person or group. Because consumer products can easily serve as external symbols of this association, they are especially susceptible to the reference identification process. Thus an ordinary pair of basketball shoes can convert the wearer to a vicarious life as "Air Jordan," while a few lines sewn on the back pocket of a pair of jeans—when coupled with the right advertising and right name—can allow a tripling of the retail price compared to a similar product without these identifying symbols. (As you may know, this phenomenon seems to be worldwide—many youths in Russia display an avid desire for Western jeans, whether or not they have design affiliations: in this case, the identification seems to be with freedom and another culture rather than with any particular fashion figures.)

Marketers are able to employ reference identification rather easily in their marketing mixes, either by showing the product being used by the relevant reference group or person or even more directly by having it endorsed by them.[39] In advertising there are two types of endorsements: appearance-only endorsements and testimonials. **Appearance-only endorsements** are those in which a celebrity acts as a spokesperson for the brand, but does not pretend to offer any special expertise with the product. In this case, the ads are likely using the celebrity for attention getting and pleasant advertising overtones. The **testimonial** is the more powerful form of endorsement. Here the celebrity has personally used the product in his or her field of expertise and is attesting to its quality and usefulness. Testimonials are so effective for sports equipment, for example, that stars and coaches are "signed" to endorsement contracts just as they are to playing contracts. The battle for visibility of sport shoes, for example, recently led Nike to sign Duke's basketball coach, Mike Krzyzewski, away from

Testimonial: An ad in which a celebrity is attesting to personal use of a product in his or her field of expertise.

Before the campaign, Lean Cuisine was outselling Weight Watchers frozen entrees by a three-to-one margin. After four years of a testmonial ad campaign featuring actress Lynn Redgrave (who had successfully used the brand to reach her weight goals), Weight Watchers was in a virtual tie for the first place position.

Reebok and McDonalds each paid golfer Greg Norman $500,000 per year to wear their logos on televised golf tournaments.

Adidas, with a $1 million signing bonus, an annual salary of $375,000, plus stock options![40] (Although each player is free to wear any brand of shoe, it is likely that we will now see the Nike "swoosh" emblem when the Blue Devils' games are televised in the future.)

Usually, the exact value of endorsements and testimonials for a marketer are hard to calculate. Occasionally, however, the value of stimulating consumer reference identification processes becomes clearly apparent, as in the following example:

🐋 Ray-Bans Are Exposed, Take Off

The Bausch & Lomb company developed Ray-Ban (antiglare) sunglasses during the 1930s, with some considerable success. During the 1950s it created its "Wayfarer" model of Ray-Bans, also with considerable success. By 1981, however, the Wayfarer line was seen as old and tired and was scheduled to be killed at the end of the year. Suddenly, however, sales began to spurt on the West Coast, and Wayfarers sold out the entire inventory in a short period of time. The company, shocked by this reversal of trend and the almost 600 percent increase in sales, checked into what had happened. It turned out that *Gentlemen's Quarterly* magazine had used the sunglasses in a feature on a male supermodel and that several other fashion magazines had then also used the line in their spreads.

Seeing the light, the firm began a deliberate strategy of "planting" the sunglasses in visible, positive settings. The next year Tom Cruise wore them in the movie *Risky Business*, and sales increased another 300 percent. During the next five years Ray-Ban models were deliberately placed in scores of television shows (e.g., "Miami Vice") and movies, including the megahit *Top Gun*, which featured numerous close-ups of Tom Cruise and the other pilots wearing their Ray-Ban "Classic Metal" aviator glasses as they dispensed their cool into the world. Demand continued to soar, with worldwide sales of Ray-Bans flying from 18,000 to 8 million pairs in only seven years.

The movie appearance emphasis continues today (Ray-Bans have appeared in as many as 160 films in one year), but further public exposure is now also a key part of the Ray-Ban promotional program. Another 10,000 pairs have been given away to leading rock stars, movie stars, and athletes, with the hope that they would wear them in MTV videos and during other appearances. Obviously this is not a tightly controlled promotional activity, but just how valuable is this type of public exposure for the Ray-Ban line? As designer competition and cheaper imitations have sprung up, reference identification for the pricy line has become even more important. According to one executive, "As far as we're concerned, if we give away 1000 sunglasses and 1 gets into a movie, it's worth the other 999."[41]

WHAT ABOUT "CONSUMER CONFORMITY"?

As a final topic in our examination of social influences on consumer behavior, let's briefly consider the issue of "consumer conformity." This has long been a subject of intense debate among marketers and social critics. Many critics believe that consumer conformity is bad. They point to consumers "acting like sheep" and striving to be accepted by buying only socially approved brands and styles. For us to appreciate these issues better, however, we first need to consider the concept of a conforming behavior.

A **conforming behavior** is that which follows and is similar to the behavior of others. If we think briefly about it, we can see thousands of examples of conforming behaviors in the everyday world around us. Almost all of us drive cars, watch TV, and wear clothes that fall into a relatively few categories. Our hair styles are similar to those of our peers, we wear similar-looking watches and rings, and we eat similar kinds of foods. An outsider looking at our society thus could easily decide that consumer conformity is indeed very high here.

This may not be true, however. There are in fact a number of reasons for such similarity in our consumer behaviors. For example,

Conforming behavior: An action that follows and is similar to the behavior of others.

- *Availability.* Consumers face a restricted range of product and style alternatives. The products available for purchase tend to reflect the preferences of large numbers of consumers, as mass marketers seek to maximize profits.
- *Cost.* The marketing system's stress on a restricted range of alternatives is also associated with *economic incentives* for consumer conformity. Mass production offers dramatically lower costs, thereby bringing many products into affordable price ranges.
- *Product performance.* In addition, many products are popular for *functional reasons*—they simply serve our needs very well. For example, consumers enjoy watching TV, walking in well-cushioned soft shoes, and keeping cool with shorts or warm with sweaters.

Thus we can see that there are many conforming behaviors about which the critics would not complain. Their concern is thus not with similarity itself, but with (1) the *social pressures* that are sometimes placed on consumers' shoulders by other consumers and with (2) the fact that products can come to symbolize certain values (materialism, worthiness through possessions, social superiority, etc.) that the critics feel are actually harmful to people. Further, (3) because marketers sometimes try to stimulate social influences so as to obtain desired behaviors from consumers, the critics point to marketing as a cause of these problems.

Each reader, of course, should arrive at his or her own opinions about the appropriateness of the various marketing themes and strategies that might be used to stimulate social influence processes in the marketplace. However, by recalling the numbers from such examples as Grey Poupon, Tupperware, Brown Bag Software, or Ray-Ban, we can see that sales gains in the hundreds or thousands of percents are possible when the huge consumer market begins a socially influenced response to a brand. Thus, whether we agree with a particular approach or not, it is hard to ignore the sheer size and power that social influences have on consumer behavior.

■ SITUATIONAL INFLUENCES

Within the final section of this chapter we'll shift our emphasis slightly to examine the impacts of situations on consumer behavior. **Situational influences** are immediate forces that do not come from within the person or from the product or brand being marketed. Instead, these temporary forces stem from particular settings or conditions in which consumers find themselves, usually for short periods of time. Situational influences *do* often involve social influences, but, as we'll see shortly, they *need* not involve them. (See Note 42 if you are interested in pursuing further details about the definitional question.)

Situational influences: Immediate forces that stem from particular settings or conditions, and not from within the person.

Situational influences pose an interesting question for consumer researchers. If we focus only on consumers and the products they buy, we implicitly are assuming that situations do not influence consumer behavior. On the other hand, we know that situational influences *do* affect consumer behavior. The problem is that *all* consumer behavior might be affected by situational influences. The challenge for consumer researchers, then, is to figure out which situations are *most likely* to affect consumer behavior on a regular basis. As a marketer, your problem will be somewhat simplified, since you can focus only on those situations most likely to affect *your product*.

HOW DO SITUATIONS AFFECT CONSUMER BEHAVIOR?

As an indication of the wide range of possible situational influences, let's consider the following quotations (we'll be referring back to these):

> I have a big date coming up Saturday night with Mike, and I need to start planning now. Should I get my hair done, or can I make it with the way it is? Which outfit shall I wear? Does the pink dress need to be cleaned? What color fingernail polish should I use?
>
> —Jennifer Holmes, student

Procter & Gamble just called and asked if I would interview with them next week. Wait 'til I call my folks! I'd better learn what's expected of me. Maybe there's a book that lays all this out ... I think I'll look at a new suit and maybe a good pair of dress shoes.

—Steve Smith, student

Oh no! Jim, come here! ... The refrigerator isn't working, and the freezer section is dripping all over the floor! Do you think we should call the repairman now, or just go and look for a new one? ... No it can't wait!

—Janet Meyer, realtor

The baking business runs on a daily basis—consumers demand fresh baked goods. Demand fluctuates daily. For example, if it's raining or snowing, bread sales drop off immediately. The days of the week are important too, depending on when the food ads are published. Thursday, Friday, and Saturday are usually the big days. Many chains run special promotions for the slow days to even out demand patterns, though, so we have to stay on top of this too.

Then there are seasonal changes—people's diets change in the summer and bread sales are down generally. On really hot days, bread sales just die! ... Holidays are big sale times, except in ethnic areas where people bake for themselves at these times. Specialty products increase a lot because of holiday parties, and sandwich bread is big after the holidays since it is used with the leftover turkey or ham.

Finally, time of the month is important ... The first week of the month usually has much higher sales because the welfare checks, Social Security checks, and paychecks are all available at this time ... Yes, based on my experience I'd say that situational influences play a major role in my marketing planning!

—John Meehan, plant manager

These quotes provide many insights on situational influences. In each case, notice how consumers are adapting their behavior to their situation. For example, consumers' *personal economic* situations, if temporary, can be considered situational influences. These can vastly restrict consumption or stimulate purchases at particular times (as John Meehan reports). Our *physical environment* (weather, season, geographic location) can also affect what we consume, and when. And *product failures* can literally force unanticipated purchases to occur, as Janet and Jim Meyer just discovered with their refrigerator! In addition, *social factors* also play strong roles with many situations. Specific situations often lead us to want to play a certain role or to make a particular kind of impression on others, and consumer purchases help our impression making. Steve Smith, for example, feels that he needs a specific appearance to do well in his interview.

MARKETING APPLICATIONS OF SITUATIONAL INFLUENCES

As consumers, we have all felt some of the pressures described in our quotes, and can easily recognize that situations affect our behaviors. Surprisingly, however, there is little formal research available on situational influences in consumer behavior. In fact, much *less* research has been done on situational influences than on person or product variables. The research that has been done, however, shows a *very significant impact* of situational influences. The following sections briefly highlight how significant four types of situations are

- Temporary economic situations
- Product depletion and failure
- Usage situations
- The special case of gift giving

Impacts of Temporary Economic Situations

Consumers can find themselves in **temporary economic situations** that can dramatically affect consumption. In economic terms, the presence of funds does not *cause* purchases, but the absence of funds can prevent or postpone them. Thus we say that economic situations *enable* consumer purchases to occur.[43]

In Figure 13-6, notice how consumer purchases can vary from one year to the next. The purchase obviously shown did not arise because consumers or products were very different from year to year—instead they arose largely from the temporary economic situations in which millions of consumers found themselves at particular times (since this figure reports yearly data, timing of purchases within a year are not reflected here, thus understating actual situational effects). We should also note that the figure reports percentage changes in consumer purchases from one year to the next (adjusted for price changes). Consumer purchases in the durable goods, nondurables, and service categories range from $250 billion to $1 trillion per year. These markets are huge—a change of only a few percentage points in sales thus translates to several billion dollars per year!

Marketers are very interested in the actual percentage changes shown in Figure 13-6. On the left side, we can see that *nondurables* (food, household products, etc.) have

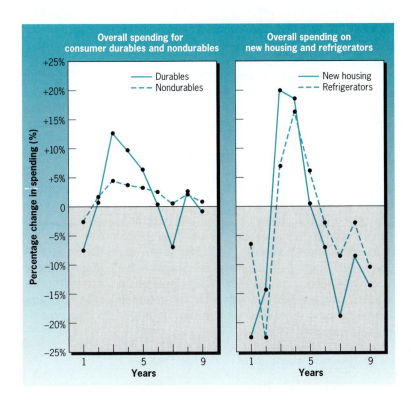

FIGURE 13-6 Variations in Consumer Purchases over a Nine-Year Period   SOURCE: See Note 44.

a general consistency in purchases—changes from one year to the next were always below 5 percent. This suggests that, as a group, nondurables are not very sensitive to economic situations, probably because many purchases are treated by consumers as necessities.

Durable goods (automobiles, houses, appliances, etc.), on the other hand, show high volatility from year to year. Within durable goods, moreover, there are certain product categories for which consumers are especially sensitive to temporary economic situations. The right side of Figure 13-6 graphs consumer purchases of two of these: new housing and refrigerators. Notice that, not only did purchases *decline* often, but by very large amounts—down as much as 23 percent in each category. When times were good, however, consumers could and did respond, with purchase *increases* by as much as 20 percent in one year. These drastic swings in consumer behavior were caused by temporary changes in such economic situations as money available (employment, personal income) and interest charges (mortgage costs). Having now seen how strongly consumers respond to economic factors, we can better appreciate the special challenges marketing managers face in the "boom or bust" industries of consumer durable goods!

Product Depletion and Product Failures

As we've noted, a person's temporary economic situation does not force purchases to occur, even when it is positive. There are some situations that do precipitate (stimulate or cause) consumer purchases directly, however. Two of the prime categories of **purchase precipitators** are *product depletion* and *product failure*.

Depletion: The using up of a product during consumption.

Product depletion refers to the using up of a product during consumption. Food, for example, is depleted through eating, and gasoline is depleted through driving. The situational influence stemming from product depletion, then, occurs at the point in which we realize that we are "out of stock" and need to repurchase the particular item. Viewed in this manner, it is obvious that product depletion situations precipitate a *massive amount of consumer spending* in our society.

The second category—**product failure**—constitutes a special form of depletion. Product failures occur most often in durable goods and are also extremely important in stimulating consumer spending. Each failure forces a consumer to choose from among losing the product's service, making a repair purchase to restore service, or making a replacement purchase of a new or used product.

How important are product failures in precipitating consumer purchases? In one national study, Wilkie and Dickson found that 60 percent of buyers of major home appliances (refrigerators, freezers, clothes washers, and dryers) had been stimulated by a breakdown or a need for repair of the existing appliance in the home. This translates to about 10,000 new refrigerators being sold each day to U.S. consumers who are shopping directly because they have had a breakdown or repair need at home! Over a year's period, some 3.5 million units, worth $3 billion, are sold because of this situational influence. (This figure does not, moreover, include the additional money spent by consumers who choose to repair their refrigerators or purchase used units.) When we recall that product breakdowns also occur for automobiles, TVs, washers, dryers, ovens, and many other products, we can see the huge importance of this situational factor in consumer behavior.[45]

The Importance of Usage Situations

In a sense, economic situations, product depletion, and product failures have relatively straightforward effects on consumer behavior. Each of these operates to precipitate, prevent, or postpone new purchases. None of them operates, however, to direct the specific *type* of product purchase that might be made.

The situational category that does this, and that has drawn the most attention from consumer behavior experts is **usage situation**.[46] This refers to the exact purposes, settings, and conditions under which a consumer expects to be consuming the product. In general, consumers see different product subtypes as being appropriate for different usage situations. For example, our choice of clothing is often strongly affected by usage situations, as evidenced in the quotations from Jennifer Holmes and Stephen Smith earlier in the chapter. When this effect is strong—as for beverages—we see consumers choosing orange juice for certain situations (e.g., breakfast) but not others (e.g., weddings), beer for certain situations (e.g., parties) but not others (e.g., breakfast), and so forth. One strategy for marketers, then, is to position a brand as being just right for a particular usage occasion. When Lunch Bucket microwaveable meals were introduced with taste sampling at 135 Jewel supermarkets, for example, the stores sold over 400,000 containers in two days: there was obviously a situational need in the marketplace that this new product could meet![47]

Thus consumers who are likely to be in a particular situation will be especially interested in products geared especially for that situation: the majority of Lunch Bucket meals, for example, are eaten in work centers that make microwave ovens available. Lunch Bucket's marketing strategy is an example of a more general approach advanced by Peter Dickson, who calls it *person-situation segmentation.* Dickson points out that when conditions are right, marketers can benefit from the approach in designing their marketing mixes. For example, heavy users of shotgun shells tend to have the personal characteristics of being young males from the rural South, having lower educational levels and blue-collar jobs. Situationally, of course, the shells are used in hunting. Beyond this, we can identify *related activities* in which people engage within hunting situations, such as camping, playing cards, drinking, and cooking out. These related activities can suggest both product development opportunities and advertising themes that are likely to appeal to this person-situation market segment.[48]

The Special Case of Gift Giving

Our final situational topic returns to a heavy weighting of social influences. **Gift giving** is a special type of situation and a very important activity in our economy—*gifts are estimated to account for about 10 percent of all retail sales.* Many retailers experience one-third to one-half of their total yearly sales volume during the months of November and December alone. Given retailers' fixed costs of operations, the fourth quarter (October, November, and December) often contributes 60 percent of their profits for the entire year! These astounding figures are due primarily to heavy gift buying during the holidays, of course.[49]

In addition to economic significance for marketers, gifts also present us with interesting insights into consumer behavior. For example, Russell Belk has noted that gifts perform four important functions.[50]

1. *Gifts serve as forms of symbolic communication.* When we give a gift, we are conveying symbolic messages as well as the physical product. Much of the time and energy we spend in searching for a gift in fact is usually devoted to our concern with delivering the correct message. This is sometimes difficult to achieve, since we run the risk that the message we intend to send may not be properly represented by the product we choose and may be misinterpreted by the receiver of the gift. This may be the primary reason that traditional products

Usage situation: The exact purposes, settings, and conditions under which a product is used.

are used so often as gifts—they are safe to give because the people receiving them understand their messages already.

2. *Gifts help to establish and maintain social relationships.* There is a curious characteristic inherent in much of gift giving—it helps to define a relationship between one person and another. Gifts can reflect intimacy of relationships (lingerie), compassion (charitable presents), gratitude for services (tips to hairdressers), congratulations (baby showers, weddings, etc.), friendship, and so forth. Underlying much of the ritual of gift giving, moreover, is the notion of **reciprocity,** or "I'll scratch your back if you'll scratch mine." As many astute consumers know, giving a gift can place the receiver in a position of owing the giver something in the future.

3. *Gift giving provides economic value.* In addition to symbolic messages and social dimensions, gifts can also satisfy functional needs of the receiver. For example, a baseball glove can help in catching the ball, and flowers provide beauty.

4. *Gift giving provides a socializing function.* This occurs primarily in the case of children. Consider, for example, how the gifts they receive (e.g., dolls, guns) might impact a child's development of his or her identity (female versus male) and how gifts are used as a means for encouraging good behavior (millions of children have believed that Santa Claus was endowed with magical powers to monitor good and bad behavior just before Christmas Day).

Gift giving is also interesting because the giver must often consider what the receiver already expects. Sometimes a buyer's concern about these anticipated judgments becomes more important than the gift itself, the thought behind it, or the occasion that produced it! Thus, *product cues* acquire a special significance in gift giving. Product quality, appearance, brand name, and the store from which the gift is purchased can all be important considerations to the prospective buyer. In addition, *price* assumes special importance within a gift purchase. Consumers frequently search for the "right" price to spend rather than a "best value for the money" purchase. If the correct messages are to be sent, the gift giver should spend an appropriate amount—neither "too much" nor "too little." Spending too little might connote, for example, that the giver does not value the person receiving the gift or that he or she is having financial difficulties or is just cheap. Spending too much, on the other hand, could be seen as reflecting that the giver is insecure. When the gift is purchased in a reciprocal exchange situation (as during holidays), the search for appropriate price is often even more serious, since usually neither party wishes the other to feel awkward after the exchange.

Because gift giving has been a ceremonial aspect of human existence since prehistoric times, many interesting analyses of this practice are available in anthropology, sociology, psychology, and marketing. (If you are interested in reading more about the hidden dimensions of gift-giving behavior, you may wish to refer to the references in Note 51.)

Reciprocity: The principle that a person who receives something from another should in some manner repay the other.

■ SUMMARY

SOCIAL INFLUENCES BEGIN EARLY

This chapter presented an overview of the broad and important topics of social and situational influences on consumer behavior. *Socialization* was defined as the process by which individuals learn to live and behave effectively in the larger society. Socialization is most crucial during childhood, where the child is introduced to the world of social roles, organizations, and other social concepts. Socialization continues throughout our lives. There are five key *socializing institutions:* the family, the educational system, religious institutions, mass media, work centers, and social groups. Adolescence is a trying period because many role transitions occur at this time. During adulthood, socialization experiences continue, but differ greatly among people.

SOCIAL INFLUENCES THROUGH "WORD-OF-MOUTH"

The second section of the chapter examined consumer *word-of-mouth.* An early study of the *web of word-of-mouth* was first reviewed together with the idea of consumer referral networks. We then noted the power of consumer recommendations. Three elements behind this power are *high credibility,* a *two-way communication flow,* and the *chances for vicarious learning.* The pattern of consumer word-of-mouth is related to the concept of *social integration,* which reflects the extent to which—for each product category—a consumer both gives influence to others and is influenced by them. Marketers can have a difficult time dealing with consumer word-of-mouth, as we saw in our discussion of consumer folklore and rumors. We also saw, however, how marketers can try to create favorable word-of-mouth, stimulate direct sales by consumers, and simulate word-of-mouth in "slice-of-life" advertising. We also discussed how research using focus groups offers a way for marketers to try to tap into the contents of consumer discussions.

HOW DOES SOCIAL INFLUENCE OPERATE?

Our discussion of *social influence* began by making the point that we both influence others and are influenced by them. There are two basic types of social influences, *normative* and *informational:* we saw how these could be combined in a study of blood donations. *Social interactions* provide a basis for social influence. Power, conflict, social exchange, and cooperation are elements often found in social interactions. Social roles are extremely important in understanding social interactions.

We next discussed the fact that much of consumer behavior is *symbolic.* Consumers use products to communicate with others through consumption behaviors (the Nescafé case illustrated how significant this process can be). Impression management studies how an individual will manage symbols to create certain impressions in the minds of others: status symbols are used in this fashion.

Social groups were then considered. The *power* that a group may have over a person can arise from different bases—legitimate, expert, reference, coercive, and reward power. Three types of *group influence processes*—compliance, identification, and internalization—were then explained. Several means by which marketers apply these concepts were presented. We then briefly examined the theory of *reference groups and referent others,* which act to extend social influences far beyond our daily social interactions. Here we saw that some products are quite susceptible to reference group influence, while others are not: we also examined why endorsements and testimonials can be so effective.

Our last discussion of social influence then examined the broad topic of *consumer conformity,* which sometimes serves as a focal point for social critics. Here we saw that there are many factors contributing to *conforming behavior,* including economic incentives and functional reasons, in addition to social influences. The social criticisms actually relate to social pressures, and to some marketing techniques that attempt to use them.

SITUATIONAL INFLUENCES ON CONSUMER BEHAVIOR

In our final section we turned to *situational influences,* which represent immediate forces that do not come from within the consumer, or from the product or brand being marketed. This is a broad, important topic, but has not been heavily researched in consumer behavior. Our discussions here focused on four types of important situational influences: (1) *temporary economic situations,* which especially impact on durable goods sales; (2) *product depletion and product failures,* which fuel many replacement purchases; (3) *usage situations,* which offer key possibilities for segmentation strategies; and (4) *gift giving,* which has a heavy social influence component and which accounts for 10 percent of all retail sales.

■ KEY TERMS

socialization	informational social influence	identification
socializing institutions	expertise	psychological reactance
role transitions	trustworthiness	social fear advertising
web of word-of-mouth	empathy	reference group
referral network	social exchange	referent other
high source credibility	role	private necessities
two-way flow of communication	role repertoire	private luxuries
vicarious trial	symbolic interaction theory	public necessities
consumer social integration	encoding/decoding	public luxuries
social integrateds	impression management	reference identification
social independents	status symbols	appearance-only endorsements
opinion leader	group	testimonial
social dependents	social power	conforming behavior
opinion follower	legitimated power	situational influences
social isolates	expert power	temporary economic situations
consumer folklore	referent power	purchase precipitators
influentials' stimulation	coercive power	product depletion
referral fee	reward power	product failure
slice-of-life approach	group influence processes	usage situation
focus group	compliance	gift giving
normative social influence	internalization	reciprocity

■ REVIEW QUESTIONS AND EXPERIENTIAL EXERCISES

[E = Application extension or experiential exercise]

1. Consider how adolescent and adult socialization can impact on how consumers buy, and what they buy. List three impacts you recall from your adolescence. Also discuss three impacts you currently are experiencing.

2. Discuss examples of how each of the four dominant elements of social interactions (power, conflict, social exchange, and cooperation) occur in

   a. Household consumer discussions

   b. Consumer word-of-mouth discussions

   c. Salesperson-consumer discussions in an appliance store, stereo shop, or other major purchase setting

3. Do you believe that the symbolic "impression management" view accurately reflects typical consumer behavior? Discuss three ways in which it does and three ways in which it does not.

4. Consider the following consumer purchases. Indicate what types of social influences (i.e., normative, informational, or both) are likely to be operating and in which ways they would operate.

   a. A new automobile   e. A vacation

   b. An air conditioner   f. A pair of theater tickets

   c. A candy bar   g. A tube of toothpaste

   d. Designer jeans   h. A case of beer

5. Employing the Bearden and Etzel matrix (Figure 13-5) provide two additional product examples per quadrant. Include reasons why. For those products high in "visibility," identify particular brands that would benefit from reference group influences.

6. Consider how situational influences can affect the purchase of the following goods and services. In thinking about these, be sure to consider each of the four types of situations identified in the text.
   a. Life insurance
   b. Stereo systems
   c. New car
   d. Beer
   e. Perfume or cologne

7. Gift giving offers a unique situation that is specific to consumer behavior. Explain the four functions of gift giving, using examples from your personal experience. Finally, briefly discuss the best gift you've ever given and why.

8. [E] Interview an official of your local blood bank concerning its sources of supply and the psychological barriers it faces in stimulating donations. Discuss topics of normative and informational social influence with the official. Write a brief report summarizing what you've learned.

9. [E] Consider carefully the consumer behaviors of one relative and one friend. For each person, choose a product example for which he or she is in each one of the four categories of social integration. That is, for what product or service is your friend a "social independent"? For what product is he or she a "social isolate"? And so forth. Finally, classify yourself for each category.

10. [E] Interview the creative director of an advertising agency concerning his or her views of symbolism in advertising. Try to gain several specific examples. Write a brief report on your findings.

11. [E] List five current consumer status symbols in your subculture. For each, briefly describe the symbolic meaning being communicated to others and the types of consumers possessing the status symbol.

12. [E] As a creative exercise in symbolic management, select three of the following entries listed. For each, propose (a) a bad symbolic *name* for a client firm to use in this product or service category, (b) a bad symbolic *color* to adopt, (c) a bad symbolic *package design or logo*, (d) bad symbolic *theme music*, and (e) a bad *advertising theme*.
   a. A new perfume
   b. A new bank
   c. A new automobile model
   d. A new fast-food restaurant
   e. A new women's basketball team
   f. A new housing development
   g. A new clothing shop
   h. A new stomach remedy

13. [E] Using some references in Note 17 (located at the back of the book, under Chapter 13's listings), read several reports on the advantages and problems with focus group research. Write a brief report on your findings.

14. [E] Conduct an interview with a focus group researcher and, if possible, sit in and watch a focus group study (names of researchers might well be available from a local advertising agency or market research firm). Write a brief report on your findings.

15. [E] Conduct an interview with a manager or experienced salesperson in a gift shop, concerning Belk's dimensions of gift giving. Write a brief report on your findings.

16. [E] Select a recent consumer recommendation you have received. Trace back and diagram the referral network behind this.

■ SUGGESTED READING

■ For an interesting article on focus groups and a famous marketing decision, see Robert M. Schindler, "The Real Lesson of New Coke: The Value of Focus Groups for Predicting the Effects of Social Influence," *Marketing Research*, Vol. 4, No. 4 (December 1992), pp. 22–27. A recent overview of findings on reference group influence is available in Terry L. Childers and Akshay R. Rao, "The Influence of Familial and Peer-based Reference Groups on Consumer Decisions," *Journal of Consumer Research*, Vol. 19, No. 2 (September 1992), pp. 198–211. For an examination of how marketers can use celebrity endorsers, see Mary Walker, Lynn Langmeyer, and Daniel Langmeyer, "Celebrity Endorsers: Do You Get What You Pay For?" *The Journal of Consumer Marketing*, Vol. 9, No. 2 (Spring 1992), pp. 69–76. For a critical look at the social status given to shoes, see Bill Brubaker, "The Cultural Foothold of Sneakers," *Washington Post National Weekly Edition*, April 6–7, 1991, pp. 8–11. Finally, for an interesting look at gift giving, you may enjoy David Glen Mick and Michelle DeMoss, "Self-Gifts: Phenomenological Insights from Four Contexts," *Journal of Consumer Research*, Vol. 17, No. 3 (December 1990), pp. 322–332. Again, for specific readings on a given topic, try the relevant Notes for this chapter.

14

HOUSEHOLD INFLUENCES

DID YOU KNOW THAT IN THE UNITED STATES...

- The number of single-person households has doubled in the last 20 years?
- Three of every 10 unmarried adults ages 25 to 29 are living with their parents?
- About one in four children lives with just one parent and one in two kids will do so at some time while growing up?
- Over one-fourth of today's male and female executives with children turn down job promotions or transfers because it would mean sacrificing family time?
- Over 90 percent of American adults marry at least once?
- Over 40 percent of families have three or more TVs?
- Women buy more subcompact cars than do men?
- There is a systematic pattern of spending related to the "consumer life cycle"?
- There are key strategies households use to reduce conflicts over purchases?
- "DWM, 28, is ISO S/DWF, 22-32"?

All this, and more, lies ahead in this chapter!

Although we've tended to emphasize either the consumer market or consumers as individuals in our discussions to this point, in reality many consumption decisions—especially the "big-money" ones—*are made within a household context.* Many changes have been occurring in household structures recently—divorce and remarriage, living together or waiting longer before marriage, having fewer or no children, establishing single-parent families, and women pursuing careers are just some of these (the aggregate statistics for these changes were discussed in Chapter 3).

Within this chapter we will discuss four key topics to help us understand household influences on consumer behavior:

1. *Household types.* The market data on household purchases are based on a strict set of definitions by the Census Bureau. It is important that we interpret these correctly to understand best the overall picture of our modern society.

2. *Consumer socialization.* The family household unit is one of the most important socializing institutions in our culture. Lessons learned here are likely to influence a person's consumer behavior for the rest of his or her life.

3. *Household decision making.* Within a household, many products and services are consumed by more than one person. The exact decisions on what to buy, therefore, are subject to intimate influences from various members. These reflect *joint decision making,* which is far more complex than the decisions made personally by individuals. For marketers selling these products, an understanding of the flows of influences is essential.

4. *The consumer life cycle.* Much consumer spending is *systematic*—it stems from natural needs that change as a consumer goes through typical stages of life. Understanding these life stages adds insights about consumer markets.

■ WHAT ARE HOUSEHOLDS?

HOUSEHOLD TYPES

We should begin our discussion by understanding that the U.S. Census Bureau bases its household data on *residential units* rather than on love, affection, or any other dimension we might find important. According to the Census, therefore, every occupied housing unit in the nation comprises one **household**. Thus an apartment with three roommates, a single person living alone, and a large family is each one household. As we noted in Chapter 3, every American except those living within institutional quarters (prisons, nursing homes, dormitories, etc.) is viewed as living within one household. There are now almost 100 million households, containing 98 percent of the total population.[1]

Household: A technical term referring to an occupied housing unit.

Figure 14-1 displays the relative proportion of various types of households in our society. Notice that the three largest categories are "Married couples without children present," "Married couples with children present," and "People living alone." "Single parents with children present" and "other family units" comprise reasonably large segments, with "people with roommates and unmarried couples" constituting the smallest major grouping.

Statistically, one major division used by the Census concerns "family" and "nonfamily" households. A **family household** is defined as having at least two people—related by blood or marriage—living together. As we can see in Figure 14-1, 70 percent of all households are defined as family households.

Family household: A living unit having at least two people related by blood or marriage living together.

HOUSEHOLD SHIFTS AND FORMATIONS

Further examination of Figure 14-1 can help us see how natural it is for people to shift from one household category to another. "People with roommates," for example, often shift to either living alone, or into a married couple unit. Similarly, "people living alone" may move into the "roommate" category, or into a married couple state, while divorce moves people from the married couple category into one or two of the other categories (and in the process creates an extra household).

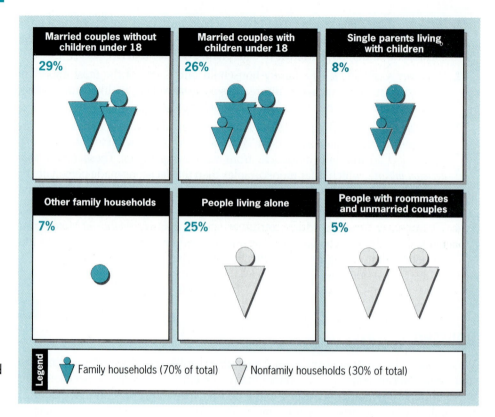

FIGURE 14–1 Household Types According to the Census

"DWM, 28, ISO S/DWF, 22–32"

These abbreviations ("divorced white male, 28, in search of single or divorced white female, between the ages of 22 and 32") reflect the mate-matching efforts found in many magazines and newspapers. While other motives are strong, to be sure, many of these ads represent new households formed through divorces, and the potential for further new households with remarriages (46 percent of marriages are remarriages for one or both partners). In either event, most Americans want to marry, and over 90 percent will at some point in their lives. However, more young Americans are putting off this step, as the average age for first marriage is now the highest in our history: 24 years old for women and 26 for men.[2]

Career, Family, and the Future

There is no question that different sets of living arrangements and different forms of family life are evolving throughout society. Some serious social problems (child poverty, for example) are becoming more serious as household forms change, but new opportunities for personal growth are emerging as well. In the main, however, there is considerable continuity: national surveys have consistently documented that, while some values change, others remain the same. For example, famous pollster Lou Harris reports that 63 percent of adult women said they want to "Combine marriage, a career, and children," whereas 26 percent prefer "marrying, having children, and no career" (as a measure of continuing change, these numbers were 52 percent and 38 percent just 10 years earlier). Similarly, in a poll conducted for the Conde Nast publishing group (*Vogue, Glamour, Self*, etc.), 82 percent of adult women said that they felt that "all women have a part of them that wants to stay home with their family," but 92 percent say a woman can have a job and still be a good mother. In an interesting split, 59 percent say marriage has always been their primary goal, whereas 21 percent opt for their career as the primary goal. Finally, in a poll of 18- to 34-year-old women, the Census Bureau asked how many children each woman expected to have. The winning numbers? Two (48 percent) and three (20 percent); 14 percent expect one child, 9 percent expect none, and 9 percent expect four or more.[3]

■ CONSUMER SOCIALIZATION IN THE HOUSEHOLD

As we saw in the last chapter, socialization occurs throughout our lives, but its greatest impacts are during childhood. As one form of socialization, **consumer socialization** is defined as "the process by which young people acquire skills, knowledge and attitudes relevant to their functioning as consumers in the marketplace."[4] Several aspects of the family's role are of interest. Basically, *consumer socialization seems to occur in subtle ways*—families usually do not "teach" a child how to be a consumer. They do not prepare lectures to be memorized. Instead, within the household,

Consumer socialization: The process by which young people acquire consumer skills, knowledge, and attitudes.

- *The parent acts as a model* for the child on numerous occasions. Here, the child learns through observation, usually silently, and without the parent's conscious awareness or intention to teach.

- *Parent-child discussions* also occur about consumer activities. These often involve either requests from children or explanations from parents about particular products (why they are good for you, why they are not, of what they're made, etc.). Other socializing influences such as TV ads and friends often stimulate these family discussions, from which parents learn as well.

- *Child-child interactions* can also be important socializing influences within a family. These influences can be especially important for younger children as they learn from and emulate their older siblings.

- *The child begins to handle money* as he or she becomes older. Thus, through gifts and "allowances," the family provides opportunities for a child to become more experienced as a consumer.[5]

WHAT IS LEARNED IN CONSUMER SOCIALIZATION?

Most children live in a family setting for all their childhood (and some of their early adulthood)—*imagine the enormous amount of consumer learning that occurs* during this time! This learning falls into one of two basic categories:[6]

1. *Directly relevant consumer skills.* These are basic skills necessary to carry out actual consumer behaviors. The ability to budget money, to understand prices or contracts, and to develop shopping strategies are all examples of direct consumer skills required in today's world. A child raised in a family with good consumer budgeting and buying skills is much more likely to possess these than is a child from a family having consumer skill deficiencies.

2. *Second-order consumer knowledge.* These are not direct skills in actually performing shopping functions, but are indirect skills related to the social sphere. For example, what types of clothes are appropriate for which occasions? Which stores are to be

patronized and which types should be avoided? During childhood, consumers develop awareness of these social dimensions and begin to learn how to cope with them. The family starts out to be very important, but as the child begins to interact more outside the home, at school, and with friends and media, the family gradually loses its significance in this area.

INTERGENERATIONAL CONSUMER INFLUENCES

Intergenerational influences: Consumer socialization through time within a family: from grandparents to parents to children.

Intergenerational means "between the generations"; **intergenerational influences** refers to what is passed along from parents to their children.[7] Figure 14-2 outlines the sense of this passage of influences over time, from grandparents to parents, from parents to children, and from the children to their children in the future.... Many forms of influences are passed along, including religious values, voting preferences, and attitudes toward education, sports, and social life. Our interest here is in the role that intergenerational influences play in forming product preferences.

How strong are intergenerational influences? This is an interesting question that has not yet received a great deal of attention within consumer research. Its potential effects, however, are very powerful, as was found in a study in the insurance industry:

🐳 *The Case of Auto Insurance*

There are over 600 firms offering auto coverage in the United States, and the 20 largest firms account for only 60 percent of the market. Despite this basic fact, a study conducted by the State Farm Insurance Company found that *almost 40 percent of families held auto policies with the same company as the husband's parents did!* Statistically, it is obvious that consumer choice here is not random and that family intergenerational influences are very strong in this product class. But how long do these influences last? We would expect the effects to decline over time, since each family has more opportunities to change its buying behavior. In the State Farm study, when the 40 percent overall figure was broken out by age, it was found that almost *65 percent of the husbands in their twenties held the same auto policy as their parents.* This number fell to 55 percent for husbands in their thirties and on down to only 25 percent for those over 50 years old.[8]

FIGURE 14-2 The Concept of Intergenerational Carryover. As time moves along, knowledge, values and consumer preferences are transmitted within families. In the past, the grandparents transmitted these to the parents of today, who are now transmitting some of them to their children. In the future these children, as parents, will transmit their knowledge, values, and consumer preferences to the generation to come.

Intergenerational influences can be extremely important to marketers, since they mean that every year a new generation of consumers goes out on their own, to continue using products they had been socialized to use while living at home. *Seventeen* magazine stresses this point strongly in selling advertising space to the marketing community. According to research commissioned by *Seventeen*, for typical cosmetic products, almost half the women ages 20 to 24 are still using the same brand they decided upon when they were teenagers. Although this percentage drops to 25 percent when the women reach the 30 to 34 age group, this is still a major advantage for the marketers capitalizing on such loyalty. (In case you're interested, the women in this study were most loyal to their original brands of mascara and mouthwash and least loyal to their first brands of bras, panty-hose, and bath soap.) At the other end of the life span, funeral homes also benefit from intergenerational influences: on average, 80 percent of an operator's business is from families served in the past.[9]

❧ U.S. Automakers Pursue the "Lost Generation"

However, intergenerational influences can work *against* marketers as well as for them, if for some reason switches in brand loyalties occur. U.S. automakers, for example, are extremely concerned that the present generation of parents—in distinct contrast to *their* parents—has come to view the purchase of foreign cars as highly desirable, even the norm (lower quality and higher prices of U.S. autos in the 1970s and early 1980s led to this change). A recent survey, for example, showed that 86 percent of auto buyers who were over 65 years old bought a domestic (U.S.) model, compared to only 54 percent of buyers between the ages of 25 to 34. According to one, a 26-year-old graphic designer who just bought her first new car (a Mitsubishi), "I never really considered buying an American car. . . . I guess buying a foreign car has been kind of ingrained in me."

The U.S. automakers view these younger consumers as the industry's "lost generation." According to the president of Chrysler, "If Detroit is not successful in getting these buyers back, market share will experience further, gradual erosion." Current marketing strategies reflect this long-term concern. According to one advertising executive for Cadillac and Pontiac, "The car makers have to try to go after the very young . . . by the time you get into your 40's it's too late to win you back." In fact, General Motor's Saturn division was conceived and developed with the "lost generation" in mind: during its first year of sales, early in the 1990s, it was extremely successful in this goal: half the people who purchased Saturns said they would have bought a foreign car if they hadn't chosen the Saturn.[10]

Further Findings

Recent research suggests that intergenerational carryover effects are stronger for convenience goods than for products that involve much shopping, that they are equally strong for men and women, and that they decline with age and time away from home. Also, because of their high rate of residential moves, U.S. consumers tend to reside in **nuclear family** households, those with only parent(s) and children residing together. In other cultures, however, the **extended family** household, with grandparents and perhaps other relatives present, is more common. In these situations, intergenerational influences are likely to be even stronger.[11]

Nuclear family: A household with at least one parent and children residing together.

Extended family: A family structure in which grandparents or other relatives are also present.

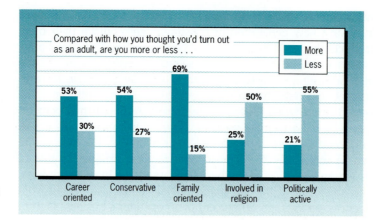

FIGURE 14-3 *Rolling Stone's* Survey Results of Changes in Adult Years

As we delve deeper into this topic, we can see that it is also possible that we should add some *reverse* arrows to Figure 14-2: in many families children influence some of the parents' consumer behaviors, interests, and preferences over time. For example, a surprising result emerged in a recent survey of households with children under age 18 present: one-third of American parents reported they have recently changed their shopping, buying, or disposal habits because of pressure and information from their children about environmental concerns.[12]

As noted at the start of this section, we should be clear that the socialization process continues into adulthood and through the rest of our lives. Figure 14-3, for example, summarizes some interesting results from a survey by *Rolling Stone* magazine.[13] "Here the "postwar generation" of younger adults (18–44) were asked what they were like as adults—and how this compared to what they thought they'd be like! Notice that many people are more "career-oriented" and more "conservative" than they had expected to be, but are less involved in religion and less politically active. Most significant for our purposes, however, is the dramatic change shown in the center of Figure 14-3: a large majority of adults are more "family oriented" than they had expected to be when they were younger. We'll return to this topic in our closing section on the consumer life cycle. For now, however, let's turn to focus on how households make consumer decisions.

■ HOW DO HOUSEHOLDS MAKE DECISIONS?

The topic of how households reach their purchase decisions is among the most important of all areas for marketers to understand in planning their strategies. At the same time, it is among the most challenging of all consumer behavior topics on which to do research. (Almost all the research in this area has been done with families, so we will focus on this form of household in this section. Many of the points made can pertain to other household types as well, however.)

SIX CHALLENGES TO CONSUMER RESEARCH ON THE FAMILY

One of the most puzzling aspects of the topic of household decision making is that, although most of us easily relate to the issues that are involved, this remains one of the most formidable research areas in the entire field of consumer research! Why is this the case? Let's think about the following characteristics of families, the most common form of households:

1. *Families make and spend money continuously, day after day, for many years.* The sheer number of decisions is so large that it is almost impossible to measure them all or to generalize about them accurately.

2. *Family decisions are made within a private, intimate, social group.* They are therefore not easy to observe and may depend upon past personal histories within the family of which the researcher is unaware.

3. *Family consumption decisions are often not independent from one another.* Thus they are difficult to study in isolation. In most families, limited income is exceeded by members' needs and desires for purchases. Allocation of resources is thus necessary, and trade-offs among alternative products and services occur. College for Sue, for example, might compete with a new Pontiac for the family, or with that long-awaited trip to Europe for the parents' twenty-fifth anniversary. The possible combinations are enormous, and they continue to be handled by families on a continuing basis over the years.

4. *Families have multiple decision makers.* Decisions range from individual choices made by members within the home, to truly joint decisions that may involve any combination of members. The husband and wife might be deciding about a bed, for example, while the wife and daughter are thinking about a dress, and so on. Capturing what actually goes on when multiple decision makers are involved, of course, adds a special research challenge to this area of study.

5. *Family decision making differs by the type of product or service being studied.* Most marketers are interested in family decision processes for "their" particular product or service. Unfortunately, what is true for one marketer may not be true for another. Family decisions on a new computer will likely differ from those regarding which restaurant to use for a special celebration. Specific studies thus need to be done for each type of product.

6. *Families differ significantly from each other.* In addition to individual personalities, families differ in wealth, age, social standing, life-styles, goods already owned, and so forth. In addition, decision styles vary. Some families are patriarchies, in which the father exercises influence over major consumer decisions; other families are matriarchies, in which the mother rules supreme; still others are more egalitarian, where the power is more equally shared, with the children perhaps weighing in with considerable influence of their own. Further, within each family the styles may shift over time, as spouses' work situations change, the children mature, divorce intervenes, and so forth.

Overall, then, it is difficult to generalize about how families make decisions. This does not mean, however, that the topic should be overlooked. The marketing community, then, must strive to understand as much as possible about this area.

❧ *The Family Purse String Study*

"The woman of the house controls 80 percent of the money that's spent, so go after her hard!" This marketing adage controlled the marketing planning of many firms for years. It led to many products being advertised exclusively to housewives. It caused sales managers at men's magazines (e.g., *True* and *Field and Stream*) and at general interest

Seventeen magazine provides advertisers with consumer reasearch describing how influential female teens are in purchase decisions made in their households, and for which products their influences are strongest.

magazines read by both men and women (*Look, Life, Time*, etc.) to tear their hair out trying to entice advertisers to aim at husbands as well as their wives.

These magazines commissioned many studies aimed at understanding who was actually involved in family purchase decisions. Their results showed, again and again, that the true picture of family decisions was much more complex than marketing managers of that time thought that it was. Wives did in fact make most purchases in most categories, but the involvement level of husbands and other family members often turned out to be very high as well. These magazines' message to advertisers: don't overlook either husbands or wives—advertise to them both! (*Seventeen* magazine has taken a similar approach, offering advertisers consumer research showing products for which teenage girls exert considerable purchase influence within families.)

Finally, the source of the original "80 percent finding" was tracked down. It turned out that this "marketing truth" had been based on a "study" that had counted the number of shoppers in a department store one day and had found that 80 percent were women![14]

Thus, for many years, marketers have been studying the issue of how family households make their purchasing decisions. How many members are involved in each decision? How are they involved? What roles do they play?

HOUSEHOLD ROLES AND BUYING BEHAVIOR

Much of the consumer behavior exhibited by families and many group households results from a well-developed **role structure**. For example, two basic functions needed by all families are leadership in instrumental behaviors and expressive behaviors.[15] **Instrumental behaviors** are aimed at successfully completing the basic tasks of the group, whereas **expressive behaviors** stress family affection, pleasure, and lower levels of tension. Families also require **external leadership** and **internal leadership.** In traditional families, the father played most of the instrumental and external roles, while the mother performed most of the internal, expressive roles. These distinctions can easily be recognized in the marketplace. For example, men have traditionally been important consumers for automobiles, repair services, tools, and mechanical products. Women, on the other hand, have constituted the dominant market segment for expressive and nurturance products. This has been true even for products worn exclusively by husbands: women still buy over 70 percent of men's colognes, sweaters, sport shirts, and socks.[16] In recent years, of course, these distinctions have become more cloudy as both men's and women's roles have shifted toward external careers in the workplace and as households have shifted in their makeup. Even so, role structure theory requires that someone in the household adopt each role or that several persons share these responsibilities.

Role structure: A relatively fixed organizational arrangement in which particular persons perform specific functions.

Consumer Roles within the Household

There are multiple roles enacted within a household's buying process. Depending on the product and situation, some roles will be more important than others. Also, it is possible for the same person to play all the roles (in which case, it is really an individual decision within a household context) or for many members to be involved at various stages. Seven of the most important buying roles are

- *Stimulator*. This person first brings up the idea of the purchase.
- *Influentials*. These are the members whose opinions have either direct or indirect influences on the final purchase decision.
- *Experts*. These members contribute information about the product, the options possible, where it can be bought, and so on. Often, this person or persons will shop around, talk to friends, or consult *Consumer Reports* to obtain the information that will be passed on to other members.

- *Decision maker.* In a joint decision, several persons will perform in this role, which decides exactly what to buy (or not buy). In other purchases only one of the members will actually make the final decision, often while in the store.

- *Buyer.* This person actually purchases the product, pays for it, and either takes it home or arranges for delivery. At times, this person is acting as the decision maker, but at other times as a purchasing agent for another member, as when a roommate wants a particular cereal or the father needs razor blades.

- *Consumer.* This is the person who actually uses the product. Since many products are jointly consumed within the household setting, the set of persons likely to consume is a good indicator of who may be involved in the other roles as well.

- *Caretaker.* This is the person or persons who undertake various tasks to store the product, prepare it for use, and maintain it in operating condition.

Gatekeeper: A role in which a person controls the flow of information about products.

These roles can be enacted either openly or through nonverbal means. Several lend themselves to a **gatekeeper** activity. This means that a person can decide either to "let in" certain information or products if he or she is in control of the "gate" through which it would enter. A father, for example, could decide not to act as a stimulator and not mention a party dress he saw on sale at the department store. Or he might ask Aunt Carolyn to bring up the subject of a vacation when she comes for dinner. Similarly, a mother acting as an expert for furniture might easily decide not to mention that the Scandinavian Shop is having a sale if she's already decided that she'd like to buy a colonial style for the living room.

Because many households are so close, moreover, members can play roles even when they are not aware of the fact. Marketers' private studies of women food shoppers, for example, have shown that traditional homemakers are very sensitive to each family member's preferences. Women from small families, for example, tend to think about each member's food preferences while shopping at a supermarket. They try to give everyone (except themselves!) a turn at having their favorite foods at mealtimes, and this goal is extremely important in their shopping decisions. They are also willing to allow any family member to veto foods they dislike, especially the fathers at dinner (in general, then, once the spouses are aware of the mate's preferences, the mates can often indirectly influence the family's consumption). Related to this stream of in-store thinking the wives preferred to go shopping alone: their children, on the other hand, liked to go along and use the opportunity to act as purchase stimulators and influencers![17]

The general role structure just presented pertains to all households. Differences between households occur in terms of how much attention is given to various roles and who actually performs them. For example, recent social changes in women's roles, dual-earner families, one-parent families, "latch-key" children (children whose parents are at work when they arrive home from school, so that they have to carry their own keys to gain admission into the home), house husbands, and so on have all had dramatic effects on exactly who performs each of the roles.[18] In general, children, teens, and husbands have become more active as buyers and consumers.

PURCHASE INFLUENCES AND ROLE SPECIALIZATION

Most household research in marketing has focused on an overall measure of purchase influence and has usually restricted attention to the husband and wife part of a family. Within this framework, surveys of family purchase influence have been completed and have often classified purchases as being *husband dominant, wife dominant,* or *joint.* When

Decision stage	Laundry (washer)			Television set		
	Husband	Joint H/W	Wife	Husband	Joint H/W	Wife
1 Brought up idea*			70%	55%		
2 Decided on type and size			50%	45%	45%	
3 Decided on brand		40%	40%	45%	45%	
4 Decided how much to pay		45%		45%	45%	
5 Visited stores		65%			60%	
6 Actually made purchase	40%	40%		50%		

FIGURE 14-4 Marital Role Specification in Several Product Decisions. Consumers were asked to name who was the most influential family member at each decision stage, the husband, the wife, or both equally (joint H/W). Responses were given for every category, but only the most frequently given appear here. To be read, In 70 percent of the families, the wife brought up the idea of purchasing a washer . . . for decisions on type and size of television sets, on the other hand, in 45 percent of families the husband was the most influent. While in another 45 percent, the husband and wife had equal influence.

SOURCE: See Note 20.

either partner is dominant for a particular product, that product decision is said to be attributed to **role specialization:**[19]

As we would expect, family members tend to specialize in products for which they have particular interest. Also, however, the influence of various members differs depending on the stage of the decision-making process.

Role specialization: One spouse acting as the dominant factor in purchases of a particular product.

🐚 Roles on the Stage

In one representative study, Woodside and Motes asked 200 couples to describe their purchase processes for three different products.[20] The results, summarized in Figure 14-4, allow us to reach several general conclusions:

- *Interesting patterns* emerge as the decision moves from initial consideration stages toward final purchasing. In general, one or the other spouse will tend to dominate the early stages; then the process will shift toward joint decision making, with the husband making the actual purchase in many families.
- *Product differences* are evident, with the wife's influence stronger for clothes washers, while the husband's influence is stronger for television sets.
- By looking at the numbers we can see that, for each of the products and for every subdecision listed, there are many families reporting a different influence pattern. This indicates that *market segmentation* is likely to exist in many marketing situations.

HOW ARE JOINT DECISIONS MADE?

Among his significant contributions to the literature on household decisions, Harry Davis has discussed the two basic conditions that a household can face when making a syncratic (joint) decision—*either everyone agrees about the goals (desired outcomes) or*

Joint decision making characterizes important household purchases, such as an automobile.

they do not. This leads to two types of joint decisions: consensual and accommodative. For example, if everyone feels that "getting away and relaxing" would be fine use of vacation time, the family would be undertaking a **consensual decision:** the goals are agreed upon, but the exact destination still remains to be decided. If, on the other hand, Suzanne wants an exciting visit to a large city, Bob wants to relax, Mark wants to surf, and Donna wants to stay home to be near her new boyfriend, this family is headed for an **accommodative decision** in which *conflict resolution* has to occur: the goal differences have to be resolved in some manner. How, then, do these decisions actually occur? Table 14-1 outlines the major strategies.[21]

Decision Strategies Under Goal Consensus

Consensual decisions: Family members share the same goal, but the details need to be settled.

When household members agree about goals, the burden on the decision is considerably lightened. As shown in Table 14-1, several useful strategies are available. Within a given area of decisions, such as food shopping, a **role structure strategy** is feasible: here one member can simply assume the role of a *specialist* and handle most decisions on a routine basis. Alternatively, **rule strategy** can be set up by members, and someone can act as a *controller* to see that the rules are followed. For example, a child can be told, "You know we all want a healthy family, so only one box of cookies allowed." Notice that the rule can be applied on an impersonal basis, thus avoiding hard feelings directed at any one person.

In other cases, a **problem-solving strategy** can also be used for particular decisions. Many tactics are possible here. For example, *experts* can be relied on for good advice, or family discussions can be held to discover a *better solution.* Also, *multiple*

Table 14-1 Different Types of Family Decisions

Problem Type	Strategy	Ways of Implementing
Goal consensus (family members agree about goals)	Role structure Rule strategy Problem solving	The specialist The controller The expert The better solution The multiple purchase
Goal conflict (family members disagree about goals)	Persuasion	The irresponsible critic The astute timer Shopping together Coercion Coalitions
	Bargaining	The next purchase The impulse purchase The procrastinator

SOURCE: See Note 21.

product purchases sometimes solve particular issues—second cars, several TV sets, and additions to the house are all common means of lessening tensions and achieving goals that all members agree are good ones.

Decision Strategies When Goals Conflict

When household members *disagree* about goals, decisions are much more difficult to reach without bringing out the inherent conflict in the situation. Davis called this an "accommodative" decision because one or more members will have to adjust their desires to allow (accommodate) a decision to move forward. The two basic ways to deal with goal conflict situations are a persuasion strategy and a bargaining strategy. The basic distinction between these two related processes is that, under a **persuasion strategy**, a member is led to make a decision that he'd rather not make, while a **bargaining strategy** tries to create conditions under which the member will want to make the decision. Let's see some ways these can be undertaken:

- *Persuasive strategies.* Since there is conflict inherent in these situations, strategies range from openly recognizing the conflict, to trying to minimize and avert it. The *irresponsible critic*, for example, already knows that he or she will not be making the final decision (and perhaps doesn't even want to) and so feels free to "snipe" at the person(s) who will be responsible for it. If the decision turns out well, the critic will benefit along with everyone else; if not, he or she can always say, "I told you so...". *The astute timer*, on the other hand, reflects an ability to sense exactly when other members are susceptible to being persuaded and employs well-designed persuasion only at those times. *Shopping together* is done in the hope that additional influences from a salesperson and/or actual experience with the product itself can sway the reluctant member into a positive purchase decision. *Coercion*, on the other hand, is the use of power or authority simply to announce that a decision will be made (this is not "persuasion" in the normal sense of the term!). Finally, *coalitions* are often formed when some members agree on the decision and put pressure on other members by banding together to present their viewpoint.

Accomodative decisions: Family members have different goals; thus conflict resolution must occur.

Persuasion strategies: A broad set of approaches in which a family member is led to make a decision he or she would rather not.

Bargaining strategies: A broad set of approaches that involve "give and take" in order that family members want to make the decision.

■ *Bargaining strategies.* These involve more "give and take" within the household than do the persuasion strategies. A *next purchase* strategy allows one member to have his or her way in a decision, with the understanding that another member will have the choice next time. An *impulse purchase* strategy isn't as friendly—it involves one member racing out to buy the product. A husband, for example, might buy a new remote-control wall system with the hope that his wife will be less likely to argue that he should take it back. Finally, *procrastination* represents delaying a purchase in the hope either that something better will come along that everyone favors or that some members will change their minds. Given, in our society, that many purchases represent desires rather than immediate needs, this strategy is frequently employed as a means of reducing conflict.

Consumer Research Findings

In general, research has found that underlying decision conflict is common in household decisions, but that most households work hard to minimize its appearance and effects. This is a natural outgrowth of the family's strong thrust toward intimacy and maintenance of pleasant relations.

How Partners Handle Disagreements

When Spiro asked a sample of husband-wife pairs about a recent household durable purchase decision, *88 percent* of the couples reported that they had encountered disagreements and had to undertake accommodative strategies. The husbands and wives completed separate questionnaires. Among the questions asked were items involving the "strategies" that each partner used on the other when the disagreement occurred. Results were interesting. Most of the sample reported only low or moderate attempts to influence their partners. Those who reported high use of influence attempts, moreover, seemed to try "every trick in the book" rather than rely on only one or two techniques. When the partners were asked about what their spouses had tried on them, their answers did not come close to matching what their spouses reported they were trying![22]

To learn more about the types of approaches used, Nelson surveyed 284 households (only one consumer per household responded in this study) about a recent purchase conflict. She found four general approaches:

1. Use of negative emotion, punishments, and so on (e.g., "I refused to do something expected of me, for example, chores").
2. Use of positive emotion and subtle manipulation (e.g., "I was especially pleasant, helpful, or charming before bringing up the subject").
3. Use of withdrawal (e.g., "I clammed up and refused to discuss the issue").
4. Use of persuasion and reason (e.g., "I tried to convince or persuade the other person that my way was best").[23]

The "Muddling-Through" Study

Muddling through: A decision-making process that is not well planned; instead, the spouses work to avoid conflict.

Another interesting study was reported by C. W. Park, who analyzed how couples went about buying a house. He found that avoiding conflicts was an extremely important part of the overall process. In fact, rather than a highly rational, well-planned procedure (called *synoptic decision making*), Park found a process he described as **muddling through.** Here, each spouse is not quite sure of his or her own preferences in a house (since it is such a complex decision). Beyond this, they have little or no idea of what

House buying is often a "muddling through" process.

their partner prefers until they are actually going through the process. Park describes the resulting experience as "groping" while striving to avoid conflict. In his terms, the family "believes that it 'makes' a decision jointly, when in fact it 'reaches' a decision through a disjointed, unstructured, . . . strategy."

How did couples avoid conflict? First, for objective house characteristics (price, number of bedrooms, etc.), the partners tried to find out which ones they agreed upon early in the process, and these were set as goals. Second, for characteristics in which one partner had expertise (kitchen, plumbing, etc.), he or she was assigned the major decision responsibility. Third, when differences arose on other characteristics, the spouse who felt less strongly about that characteristic made a concession to the other about it ("Well, I don't really care for the idea of a fenced yard, but if you really want it . . . .").

In terms of the partners' decision plans themselves, both the husband and wife thought they had approached the decision in a similar way, when in fact their approaches had been quite different! As was found in Spiro's study, the family members were not very successful in identifying relative influence by their spouse, nor did they seem to know about the other's actual decision strategy. To improve performance in the actual decision, therefore, Park recommends that spouses sit down beforehand, have each lay out his and her plan for making the decision, and then discuss them together.[24]

Thus we have seen two important lessons in the consumer research conducted in this area: families encounter *considerable conflict* in their joint decisions, and the partners seem to have *much less insight* into their mates' goals and strategies than they think they have. In another study, over 200 married couples were asked to respond to a number of concepts for new products and services. Not only did their reactions to the concepts not match very well, but they again showed very little ability to predict how their spouse was reacting to the same concept. In fact, the results were only slightly greater than if husbands and wives had been randomly thrown together![25] These kinds of results present a major challenge to consumer research in the future, particularly the most efficient types of studies in which one of the members of a household is surveyed, and provides answers for the household as a whole.[26] Given its importance, this is one research field that bears watching for the future.

■ THE CONSUMER LIFE CYCLE

Consumer life cycle (CLC): A framework of stages a consumer passes through in life: reflects systematic effects of age, marital status, and the presence of children.

The concept of **consumer life cycle (CLC)** represents a belief that there is a systematic basis for much of consumer behavior, and that this primarily relates to the passage of time. Some consumer behavior impact comes simply from *age*—as we grow older, our activities and preferences change and evolve. Some of the effects come from *income*—as we grow older, our incomes tend to rise until retirement, when they fall again. Some of the effect also comes from *stock of goods*—once we own durable goods, we are not in the market again until it is time for replacements. A major portion of the effects, however, comes from *changes in our family situation*. For this reason the early work on this topic was termed the "family life cycle" (FLC). With the recent changes in households and life-styles, however, it is now appropriate to think of this as a more general "consumer life cycle."

The earliest work on life cycles occurred in the field of sociology, with emphasis on such issues as life stages of poverty and the impact of children on a nuclear family. Within consumer behavior, interest in the CLC concept began when economists began carefully to analyze the patterns of income and expenditures by age groups.[27] Then, in 1966, a very influential paper was published by Wells and Gubar. Based on some new analyses of consumer spending data, the authors proposed an eight stage framework for a consumer-oriented "family life cycle." Table 14-2 outlines these. We'll now take a brief look at each stage to gain a better understanding of the entire CLC concept and its implications for consumer spending.[28]

THE EIGHT STAGES OF THE CONSUMER LIFE CYCLE
The Young Single Stage

About 10 percent of the adult population falls into the **young single stage**, which consists of single people under the age of 35. Although their incomes are relatively lower since they are starting out in their careers, young singles have fewer financial burdens than do most other adults, and thus have considerable discretionary funds to spend on consumption. On average, this group spends less money on products that might restrict their mobility and more money on cars, convenience products, entertainment, and other "mating game" products and services.

The Newly Married Stage

People in the **newly married stage** are young and married but do not yet have children in the family. In total, this group is small, accounting for less than 5 percent of the U.S. population. However, marriage requires substantial adjustments, and there is an *incredible burst of spending activity*. In a recent year, for example, about 2 percent of the U.S. population got married for the first time: this group, however, accounted for a total of 13 percent of all service and retail sales! In one recent year, they spent over $6 billion on home furnishings.[29]

Table 14-2 The Eight Stages of the Traditional Consumer Life Cycle

Stage	Definition	Approximate Population Proportion	Defining Characteristics
1. Young single	■ Unmarried, under 35	10%	■ Below-average incomes, high discretionary spending, considerable freedom
2. Newly married	■ Young, married, no children	5	■ Good financial situation, creation of a new household, new obligations and activities
3. Full nest I	■ Married, youngest child under 6	25	■ Arrival of children, parents' loss of freedoms, new focus on home, incurring financial debt
4. Full nest II	■ Married, youngest child 6–12	15	■ Increase in freedoms of parents, improvement in financial situation, continuing focus on home
5. Full nest III	■ Married, youngest child in teens	15	■ Increase in freedoms of parents, improvement in income, but pressure on saving for college, focus moving outside of home
6. Empty nest I	■ Married, children have left home	5	■ Increase in freedoms of parents, improvement in finances (income up, spending down), focus shifting to outside of home and extended family
7. Empty nest II	■ Married, retired from work, children have left home	5	■ Drop in income and possible stress on finances due to medical concerns, substantial freedoms, possible focus on extended family
8. Solitary survivor	■ Widowed, retired from work, children have left home	2	■ Lower income, possible health and loneliness problems, substantial freedoms and possible focus on extended family

During this time, both partners are likely to keep working, so that the overall financial situation of the family is quite good. Many of the purchases made during this time are symbolic, as the couple attempts to shift into a new family situation. Housing and its adornments can be important as are leisure activities and vacations that the couple can take together.

The Full Nest I Stage

When children arrive, the couple moves to the **full nest I stage**, which is characterized by having the youngest child under 6 years of age. This stage has a much larger number of consumers in it, accounting for about 25 percent of the population. Beyond the thrill of parenthood, powerful new pressures arise on the family. Increased expenses put a squeeze on the incomes of many families. (For example, one study estimates that it costs over $30,000 to raise a child to age 5.)[30] Also, young mothers and fathers lose much of their former freedom, and the husband-wife pair loses some of its former social companionship. With respect to consumption, this stage has the highest level of debt associated with it, as housing, appliances, and insurance are purchased at high

Newlyweds represent 2 percent of the population, but 13 percent of all retail and service sales!

rates. In addition, the baby brings with it a host of required purchases, ranging from medical expenses through toys, cribs, and baby foods.

The Full Nest II Stage

In the **full nest II stage,** the house still has children, but the youngest is now over 6 years old. As a group, this stage accounts for almost 15 percent of the population. The family's financial position is better, since the spouses' careers are improving with more experience and some of the wives have returned to their careers as the children are in school. These families begin buying larger-sized packages and multiple-unit deals. The children are heavy influences in certain categories, such as bicycles, pianos, dental care, and sports equipment.

The Full Nest III Stage

The **full nest III stage** is characterized by children still at home, but in their midteen years. This group accounts for about 15 percent of the population. Here, the family's financial position is continuing to improve, with the children beginning to earn money outside the home as well. These families have higher purchase rates for durables, due to a combination of necessary replacement purchases, and multiple purchases for spouse and teen use (cars, stereos, etc.).

The Empty Nest I Stage

In the **empty nest I stage** the children have left the home and are not usually dependent on the parents for support anymore. The parents are still working, with career earnings at a high level. This group accounts for just over 5 percent of the population, but it is a very lucrative consumer market because of the combination of higher income and lower expenses for required purchases. As a result, this group engages in travel and recreation, gifts, and luxuries.

The Empty Nest II Stage

In the **empty nest II stage,** the couple has retired from active participation in the labor force and experiences a sharp drop in income (many couples are still well off, of course, due to pensions and accumulated savings). This group accounts for about 5 percent of the population. It is a strong market for such types of goods as medical products and services. Many consumers in this stage will also move from their former homes to a smaller home, perhaps in a retirement community.

The Solitary Survivor Stage

On a proportional basis, the **solitary survivor group** is the smallest, accounting for only about 2 percent of the population. These persons are likely to have even lower incomes and increasing medical needs. In addition, they have special needs for attention, affection, and security.

ISSUES AND USES OF THE CLC CONCEPT
Current Issues with the CLC

Researchers agree that there is a large systematic component to consumer behavior and that the CLC is a useful concept for capturing this. At the same time, however, researchers disagree as to exactly how the CLC should best be defined. The eight-stage framework is probably still the most commonly used.

At the same time, however, the dramatic social changes of recent years suggest that some improvements are needed in that framework. This framework was developed before most of these changes had occurred and may need some alteration to reflect current living and spending patterns. For example, note that the proportions of the population given for each of the stages do not total 100 percent. This is because some people simply cannot be classified in the current CLC framework. This has always been true, of course, but in recent years, the proportion has been increasing, due to

- *Fewer children per family.* Couples have been waiting longer to have their first child and have been having fewer children. In total, then, this means that the newly married stage is stretched longer than in the past and that the full nest I stage is shorter. Also, more families are choosing not to have children at all; and there is no stage to handle these persons once they pass the age of 35.

- *Divorce.* The divorce rate has risen sharply, but there is no provision in the current framework for single parents with children. Since these families often have lower incomes due to only a single paycheck, we would expect their consumption behaviors to differ in some important respects.

- *Unmarrieds.* More people are choosing to remain single for longer periods of time. This group includes both persons who have never married and persons who have divorced, but are without children. The eight-stage CLC handles these persons well while they are young but makes no provision for them once they reach middle age.

The result of these changes has been a movement toward modifying the current structure. Patrick Murphy and William Staples, for example, have proposed a "modernized family life cycle" that adds stages to account for divorce and the absence of children in a marriage: their framework contains 13 stages and is able to assign 6 percent more of the population than our basic framework.[31] Another proposal, by Mary Gilly and Ben Enis, removes marriage as a requirement for assignment to life-cycle stages, in recognition of increasing proportions of children born out of wedlock and couples living together without marriage. Their framework is able to assign all but 3 percent of the U.S. population.[32]

Which framework is the best? This is a considerably more complex issue than it first sounds. First, simplicity does have the benefit of more easily representing the basic idea of a "life cycle" (this is the primary reason we have stayed with the eight stage version in this text). Second, to decide what's "best," the exact purpose for which we're using the CLC needs to be taken into account. Assigning larger proportions of the population is one indicator, to be sure, but we must also be concerned with the ability of the categories to distinguish meaningfully among the consumption behaviors of consumers. These obviously differ for different products and services: it is possible, therefore, that different CLC schemes might perform better in different categories and for different countries and cultures. In one test of clothing expenditures, for example, the Wells-Gubar (8 stages) and Murphy-Staples (13 stages) frameworks performed at about comparable levels. In another study, across a number of product and service categories, the Gilly and Enis framework performed more strongly. Thus there is still useful work to be undertaken.[33]

Marketing Applications of the CLC

The essence of CLC analysis employs some of the key demographics used in market segmentation—age, marital status, and size of household. As we saw in Chapters 3 and 4, government statistics are easily available for each of these measures. Thus it is quite feasible for marketers to use the traditional CLC concept to estimate segment sizes and to forecast demand shifts in the future. This process can become quite refined, since marketers also have available to them syndicated research services that measure exactly which products are purchased by which types of consumers.

₰ *"Lifestages" as Market Segments*

Some market research firms have created their own versions of CLC segments (these are hard to describe succinctly, since their makeup can be changed to best reflect the product of interest in a particular study). To gain a basic understanding of this approach, for example, let us consider the case of MediaMark Research, Inc. This firm surveys 20,000 adults each year, gathering information about their personal traits, product purchases, and media habits (radio, TV, magazine exposure, etc.). This extensive database then allows for special analyses comparing "lifestage" (this firm's name for a CLC-like framework) segments as to their marketing potentials.

One analysis of financial services, for example, discovered that "young couples" (childless, ages 30 to 39) and "mature couples" (40 to 54, no children at home) had roughly equal incomes, but bought very different types of luxury items and financial instruments. In brief, the "young couples" were *below the average of all American adults* in their ownership of money market funds, certificates of deposit, and common stock, whereas "mature couples" were far above average for all these. Related analyses

How to Put Your Product on the Road to Success.

Identifying the consumers who are right for your product is no longer a matter of what *age* they are, but what *stage* in life they occupy.

As adults move through transitions in their lives, their needs and priorities change as consumers. *Lifestage Marketing* is the fascinating new booklet from Mediamark Research Inc. that points you in the direction of increasing your product's chance for success by discovering which "lifestage" it appeals to.

Using product purchase and usage information drawn from Mediamark's Survey of American

Consumers, the most widely used database of its kind, *Lifestage Marketing* takes you step-by-step through five adult lifestages and the consumer patterns each represents.

Call For Your Free Copy

For a free copy of *Lifestage Marketing*, call Evelyn Carter at (212) 599-0444, or contact the Mediamark office nearest you. Additional copies are available on request.

So call today. After all, the road to success starts with the first step.

MRI

MEDIAMARK RESEARCH INC.
708 THIRD AVENUE, NEW YORK, NY 10017
500 NORTH MICHIGAN AVENUE, CHICAGO, IL 60611
690 MARKET STREET, SAN FRANCISCO, CA 94104
12001 VENTURA PLACE, STUDIO CITY, CA 91604
A member of the MAI Information Group

© Mediamark Research Inc. 1990

This advertisement, aimed at marketers of consumer products, summarizes some of the benefits of "lifestage" research, closely related to the consumer life cycle (CLC). (Note: the five stages shown on the booklet's cover are a part of the entire system.)

helped to explain why: the "young couples" are spending their money on fine wines, entertainment, foreign travel, and investments in art and coin collections. Notice that, armed with this type of information, a marketer of, say, a mutual fund is in a position to decide whether to pursue the "young couple" segment (trying to convince them to shift some of the types of purchases they are making to a new form for them) or to pursue the "mature couple" group (trying to switch some of their future purchases to her fund, confident that they already know about this general category of investment).

Once the strategy is decided, the research firm can again be very helpful in how to best reach the chosen lifestage group, since detailed information is available as to the media habits of each. (On TV, for example, the "mature couples" segment are heavy watchers of golf and prime-time films, while the "young couples" opt for baseball and pro basketball. News specials, on the other hand, can reach both groups in an efficient manner.[34]) As a final twist on the marketing options, the strategist may instead search for the older members of the "young couples" and the younger members of the "mature couples," since each of these will be moving into the years in which they are likely to be putting large amounts of money into financial investments.

Beyond this database example, the CLC concept can also be used to develop simpler but useful insights for marketers. For example, several studies have found that joint decision making *decreases* as families move through the life cycle. That is, young married couples tend to engage in high levels of joint decision making, but as time goes on, one or the other begins to take over particular decision areas—an instance of increasing role specialization.[35] Also, CLC-related research can be undertaken by marketers on specific product areas. For example, one study found that a mother yields to a child's *cereal* request almost 90 percent of the time, but for *clothing*, whether or not the mother yields depends on the child's age (clothing agreements go from 20 percent when children are ages 5 to 7, to almost 60 percent when they are 11 to 12 years old).[36] Notice that this means that cereal makers such as Kelloggs and General Mills can confidently direct their promotion for kids' cereals directly to the children themselves. Sears, on the other hand, would need to take life-cycle stages into account and direct some of its promotions for kids' clothing at mothers and other promotions at older children.

■ SUMMARY

WHAT ARE HOUSEHOLDS?

This chapter began with an examination of the nature of *households*. We saw that this is actually a technical term of the Census Bureau, and refers to residential units. We noted that there are now almost 100 million households in the United States, about 70 million of which are *families*. We also saw how typical it is for people to shift types of households, and how new households are formed through both divorce and marriage.

CONSUMER SOCIALIZATION IN THE HOUSEHOLD

Consumer socialization refers to the process by which we "learn" to become consumers, from the time we are young children. This occurs in subtle ways, being affected by parental models and discussions between family members. Children learn *directly relevant consumer skills* like budgeting and buying, but also *second-order skills* that involve an awareness of the social dimensions of consumption. Researchers are beginning to examine how product and brand preferences are transmitted through *intergenerational influences* from grandparents to parents to children. We saw, for example, how auto insurance coverage shows marked brand preferences within families.

HOW DO HOUSEHOLDS MAKE DECISIONS?

The area of *decision making* is very important, but it poses strong challenges for consumer researchers. Within a household, there are different *consumer roles* that have to be filled by members. In addition, there are different modes of decision making. At times family members agree in their goals and can use *decision strategies of the consensus type.* At other times the goals differ, and *strategies of accommodation* are called for to reach decisions. Consumer research for very important decisions (such as houses) has shown that most couples seem to *muddle through* to reach their decisions. That is, they work hard to avoid conflicts, but they do not seem to know very much about what their partners really desire in the purchase. As pointed out later in this section, this lack of spousal awareness poses a difficult issue for future research on the household.

THE CONSUMER LIFE CYCLE

In the last section of the chapter we turned to the topic of the *consumer life cycle (CLC)*. This concept has been of interest within consumer behavior for many years, since it represents a series of typical stages of life that a person will experience. As these stages change, so do the demands for certain types of goods and services, and the income available to buy them. We examined a traditional *CLC framework* consisting of eight stages: (1) *young single,* (2) *newly married,* (3) *full nest I,* (4) *full nest II,* (5) *full nest III,* (6) *empty nest I,* (7) *empty nest II,* and (8) *solitary survivor.* Recently shifts in family structure and life-styles have raised the issue of whether this framework is still sufficient in today's marketplace. We reviewed some of the evidence on this issue, which is still a question. In the final section we saw how the CLC concept is flexibly employed by marketers to assist in their segmentation strategies.

■ KEY TERMS

household	expressive behaviors	rule strategy	full nest I stage
family household	external leadership	problem-solving strategy	full nest II stage
consumer socialization	internal leadership	persuasion strategy	full nest III stage
intergenerational influences	gatekeeper	bargaining strategy	empty nest I stage
nuclear family	role specialization	muddling through	empty nest II stage
extended family	consensual decision	consumer life cycle (CLC)	solitary survivor group
role structure	accommodative decision	young single stage	
instrumental behaviors	role structure strategy	newly married stage	

■ REVIEW QUESTIONS AND EXPERIENTIAL EXERCISES

[E = **Application extension or experiential exercise**]

1. Despite major shifts in sex roles and life-styles in recent years, polls concluded that these changes have not had a major impact on women's desires to be part of a family. How would you account for these seemingly inconsistent phenomena?

2. Consider the four primary ways in which family influences are transmitted. What is the relative impact of each on the consumer socialization process?

3. The text lists six challenges to consumer researchers who are trying to understand consumption decisions in households. Relate these characteristics to reference group influences on consumer behavior (Chapter 13). Are these challenges limited to the family influence, or can some/all apply to reference groups as well? Comment.

4. Consider the family buying process for the following goods or services. Indicate, providing rationale, who "normally" would play the most important buying roles:

   a. A summer vacation
   b. Breakfast foods
   c. A wedding present
   d. An automobile

5. Describe the primary distinctions among the three decision strategies in which consensus exists as to the goals (role structure, budgets, and problem solving). Provide an example of each of the five ways of implementing

these strategies as you've experienced them in your own family.

6. Describe the primary distinctions between the two decision strategies that have accommodation as the goal (persuasion and bargaining). Provide an example of each of the eight ways of implementing these strategies as you've experienced them in your own family.

7. Describe the consumer behavior-related effects of age, marriage, and the presence of children as one goes through life.

8. [E] Marketers of what kinds of goods or services would be most uncomfortable with the traditional eight-stage CLC framework? Why?

9. [E] Identify two products whose marketing strategy would be heavily influenced by the CLC. Identify two products whose marketing strategy might be almost independent of any stage in the CLC.

10. [E] Interview a person with experience in selling to couples or families making joint decisions (e.g., a salesperson in real estate, appliances, automobiles). Focus on the pertinent issues as raised in the text, such as conflict, disagreement as to goals, use of influence strategies, insights into the partner's preferences, the role that children play, and so on. Write a brief report summarizing your findings.

11. [E] Reflect on the question "How has my family influenced my consumer behavior?" Write a brief report summarizing your thoughts on this, providing specific examples.

12. [E] Using the reference sources in your library, locate discussions of how marketers are using data on households and families for marketing mix decisions. Write a brief report summarizing your findings.

13. [E] Using either reference sources or the Notes for Chapter 14 at the back of this book, read more about the consumer life cycle (family life cycle or consumer lifestages). Write a brief report on your findings.

■ SUGGESTED READING

■ To gain insight into the life-styles of modern households see, for example, Louis S. Richman, "The New Middle Class: How It Lives," *Fortune*, August 13, 1990, pp. 104ff; and Lee Smith, "How the Average American Gets By," *Fortune*, October 21, 1991, pp. 52ff. For a somewhat different look at intergenerational influence, see William Strauss and Neil Howe, "Generations," *American Demographics*, April 1991, pp. 25ff. For an (advanced) analysis of competing CLC frameworks, see Charles M. Schaninger and William D. Danko, "A Conceptual and Empirical Comparison of Alternative Household Life Cycle Models," *Journal of Consumer Research*, Vol. 19 (March 1993), pp. 580–594. In general, your reference library is an excellent source of current articles describing the changing nature of households (as is *American Demographics* magazine). Again, the Notes provide good leads by which to pursue specific topics.

SALESPERSONS' INFLUENCES

A CANDID INTERVIEW WITH AN APPLIANCE SALESPERSON

Q. Can you recall any particular advice or "rules" that your sales manager would stress during your early time as a salesman?

A. He tried hard to teach me how to sell in that setting and gave me a lot of "advice." My first few weeks, I tried to sell the product on benefits alone. I spent hours and hours reading the brochures from the manufacturers and really stressed the product benefits when I talked to a customer. People walked out on me, however; I wasn't doing well.... So I started to listen to my boss and brought his "laws" into my sales presentations. As a result, sales doubled over what they were at the start.

Q. What were some of his "laws"?

A. He had a bunch of them.... The one I'll never forget, though, was about "Be-Backs." He'd tell me about three times a day for the first few months on the job, "Bill, Be-Backs don't exist! Before a customer leaves this store, I want a yes or no from them. Before you let someone hit the door, I want you to have every salesperson in this store talk to the guy, including myself! That's because when they say they'll be back, they won't. Be-Backs don't exist!" He also had a lot of other strong beliefs. (Interview continues in Exhibit 15-2.)

"What was your most useful source of information for a major purchase recently?" A national sample of consumers answered: "My salesperson," by a 3-to-1 margin over the next closest source, friends and relatives![1]

In this chapter we focus on another important source of influence on consumers—the role and impacts of the salesperson. Although not all aspects of consumer behavior are affected by salespersons (vending machines and self-service stores, for example), many types of purchases—especially the major ones—are conducted through sales representatives. In total, there are over 11 million consumer salespersons in the United States, with another 9 million salespersons in the industrial marketing area.

How important are salespersons? The quotation gives some indication of how consumers rate salespersons' significance when product purchase stakes are high. Marketers also rate this function as extremely important, especially in industrial marketing, where businesses deal with businesses. One study, for example, found that executives of industrial firms rated the sales function as *5 times more important than advertising* in their marketing mixes; for consumer durables marketers, sales was rated 1.8 times as important as advertising; while for consumer nondurables, advertising and personal selling were rated as about equally important.[2] Our primary interest in this chapter is in the nature of the external social influences that salespersons have on consumer behavior. We thus begin by focusing on the nature of a sales transaction itself.

■ WHAT GOES ON IN A SALES TRANSACTION?

SOME INSIGHTS INTO SALES INFLUENCES

Sales influences are quite different from the others we've examined so far, primarily because they are *marketer controlled and they occur close to the point of transaction.* Salespersons are the closest representatives of marketers to consumers. In addition, salespersons perform the *transaction,* or **exchange function,** between marketers and consumers—they provide the means by which actual purchases are made. The sales transaction allows marketers to be paid for their efforts, and for consumers to receive the benefits they seek from the goods. Most salespersons do more than ring up transactions, of course. Particularly with important consumer purchases, they inform consumers about the options available and help consumers decide which option best fits their needs, desires, and ability to pay.

Within this process, both objective and subjective information is used. Personal selling frequently involves *influence* and *persuasion* along these subjective lines. Consumers usually know that these elements are present and often welcome them as an aid to making purchase decisions. Of course, some salespersons sometimes engage in inappropriate selling techniques. In the main, however, personal selling serves as a basic means by which consumers are able to serve their wants and needs through purchases of goods and services in our society.

ANALYZING THE "INTERACTION DYAD"

Interaction dyad: A pair of individuals engaged in a common activity, such as a salesperson and consumer.

A marketing professor, Franklin B. Evans, had a strong impact on the field when he proposed that to understand the nature of personal selling, it is necessary to focus on the **interaction dyad.** A dyad is a pair of individuals engaged in a common activity. Within the selling situation, this perspective helps us to see that *both* the salesperson and consumer are involved and that the result of the contact depends on how the two parties view and react to each other. It is not enough that we concentrate on either the salesperson or consumer alone.[3]

Surprisingly, there are relatively few studies that have focused on the salesperson-customer interaction process itself. In one famous study, Willett and Pennington monitored over 200 different consumer transactions for large-ticket home appliances. Each interaction was recorded by a hidden microphone placed in the salesperson's clothing. The tape recording of the entire sequence was then analyzed using a technique known as *interaction process analysis.*[4]

Their results are interesting. The average transaction lasted 23 minutes, and within that time, almost 200 separate transaction "acts" were performed by either the salesperson or the consumer. This averaged about 10 acts per minute. Most of these involved trading opinions and explanations. As we would expect, the customer asked more questions (four times as many as the salesperson) and provided fewer answers (only one-third as many as the salesperson). The study also showed, interestingly, that the *customer* contributed more of the *positive* statements made in a sales interaction, by a 3-to-2 ratio (some were likely in response to prompts from the salesperson). Relatively few *negative* statements were made, but of these, *salespersons* contributed eight times more than customers (likely these were intended to point out deficiencies of certain models and guide the customer toward a satisfactory match). Overall, the authors noted that it appeared that salespersons held considerable power (control) as to the direction that the sales process would take.[5]

Salesperson Power in the Interaction

The issue of **salesperson power** was further investigated by Richard Olshavsky, who reanalyzed the original tapes of these transactions. He characterized the sales interaction process as a three-stage sequence:

1. **Orientation phase.** Here the salesperson is learning about the consumer's interests and the consumer is learning about the store's offerings.

2. **Evaluation phase.** Here the alternative products are examined.

3. **Consummation phase.** Here the consumer decides either to buy or not. If a positive decision is reached, payment, credit, and delivery are discussed.

In his analysis of the tapes, Olshavsky arrived at several interesting conclusions. First, he found that the *orientation phase was usually very brief:* over half the appliance salespeople did not ask any questions of the customer, and no salesperson asked more than two. Most customers, moreover, volunteered very little information: they mentioned only one or two product characteristics in which they were particularly interested. (These findings appear to contradict most marketing textbooks on selling, which emphasize the need for the salesperson to learn about customer wants and

Salesperson power: The control a salesperson exerts over the sales interaction and item chosen.

A sales transaction involves a multistage process that has three basic phases: orientation, evaluation, and consummation.

needs before offering choice alternatives. However, we might find that these results would differ in another product category or culture.)

As a result, the process moved into the evaluation phase very quickly, and on the basis of little information having been shared. The evaluation phase accounted for most of the time spent in the transaction. Here, *the salespeople were found to dominate the evaluation process:* they selected the order and the number of product alternatives that would be evaluated and used their semiprepared presentations to guide the customers' attention to each model. In many cases, in fact, the customer simply gave up his or her power in the interaction and asked the salesperson for a recommendation, which was then followed.

The key result of this study is that the salesperson often plays an extremely powerful role in influencing the customer's actual choice and purchase.[6] Rather than assuming that salespersons strive to first learn about, and then cater to, customers' wants and needs, it would seem that salespersons are much more active in guiding customer choices toward the brands and models favored by the salesperson. This is, of course, only one study concerning a limited sample of salespersons, customers, and products. If its findings hold up across the marketing-consumer environment, the way such sales power is managed by marketers becomes an important and interesting issue.

■ THE MARKETING PERSPECTIVE ON PERSONAL SELLING
MULTIPLE VIEWS ON SELLING

The preceding section provided us with several basic concepts: a *sales transaction process*, occurring within an *interaction dyad*, with considerable *salesperson power* during the transaction process. At this point, let's examine what this might mean from a marketer's prospective.

The personal selling situation is one that calls for extra care in our analysis of the marketing perspective. In a channel of distribution, each level—manufacturer, wholesaler, and retailer—is normally an independent business. When we think of "the marketer," therefore, we must realize that *several* marketers are involved—the manufacturers, the wholesalers, the stores, and the salespersons—and that each has a somewhat different interest.

Retail salespersons work at the end point of the entire channel and are actual contact points with consumers. To do well, the retail salesperson often needs to earn commissions on purchases: commissions increase either by selling more products or by selling products with higher prices and profit margins.

Thus, a brand manufacturer may have one set of goals, such as serving the needs of target consumers. At the other end of this channel, however, this firm will be represented by thousands of salespersons (who also represent other brands sold in their store). These sales personnel have their own personal needs to be met by the sales interaction; a key one of which is to earn income through successful sales to consumers. *In practice, therefore, salespersons usually represent themselves and their stores rather than the manufacturer.*

Exhibit 15-1 provides examples of these different perspectives. It contains quotations from college students who were asked the question, "How does the marketer view the consumer?" The first set of quotations comes from students who have never worked as salespersons and who answered this question from the viewpoint of the initial marketing course. The second group of quotes is from students who have worked as salespersons and who reported from their personal experiences. Notice how strongly the quotes differ in how they view the consumer! While certainly not a representative sampling of marketer views, these statements do indicate the different perspectives that are found in the real world of selling.

EXHIBIT 15-1

How Do Marketers View the Consumer?

Students Who Have Not Yet Worked in Marketing

Jim L.   "Consumers are the lifeline to profits and the sole route to success. Therefore, everything we do in business is related to consumer satisfaction. . . . The customer has the right to be sold a quality product. . . . Personal attention and friendliness are qualities that have immeasurable value. Gearing to their customer's needs is what sets the most successful businesses apart from their competitors."

Lisa S.   ". . . today, the marketer views the consumer in a totally different light. He realizes that the consumer knows what kinds of product he wants. The consumer demands good quality and will accept nothing less."

Marie K.   "As a beginner, without having any marketing experience in working with the so-called consumer, it seems obvious enough. . . . The consumer will vote with his or her money, and the marketer must listen and care about the product's users in order for any system to work. Through this two-way communication . . . the marketer must always listen and react according to the needs of the consumer."

All these comments are true and offer useful insights about marketing and consumer behavior. Because these students had not experienced work as a salesperson, however, their reports were necessarily more abstract, reflecting the exposure they had received in their marketing courses to this point. For some students who had worked as salespersons, however, the responses to this question were quite different:

Students Who Have Worked as Retail Salespersons

Dawn F.   "In my personal experience as a retailer, I merely viewed the consumer as the object of my salesmanship technique. It did not matter what I sold . . . each person was a potential buyer and would be instrumental in boosting my sales record or quota for the day. . . . It is the marketer's duty to sell anyone his product. It is of no importance whether he is interested in the product at that time or merely browsing. A good marketer can often arouse a need for that particular good.

"My memories of retail clothing . . . my sole intent was a quick, expensive sale . . . the store I worked at was a high-pressure fashion boutique complete with swirling lights and disco music. Employees had only one thing on their minds, and that was to sell, sell, sell! We had hourly sales quotas, and sometimes fought over who would wait on a customer . . . if you were low on your hourly quota, you would tell a customer anything. . . . Marketing is a strange business, but it is an art in and of itself. I feel marketers view customers as merely a means to an end, with that end being a sale of the product and another chalk-up on your sales record."

J.R.   "I have done some buying, selling, and advertising for about six years. My general opinion of a consumer is that he is out there waiting to be taken advantage of . . . there just is not enough time in the day to research each item, and he must trust the promises of the seller when he goes to market. He does not want the seller to think he is ignorant, so often he will not ask the questions necessary to protect himself from a bad deal . . . he will also tend to pay a higher price for an item due to either his lack of knowledge or his demand for a status symbol . . . the consumer wants to be one of the crowd . . . a good marketer will convince the consumer to buy his product by exploiting the buyer's shortcomings. To paraphrase an old saying, 'Never give a consumer an even break!' "

Wendy O.   "Working as a salesperson in a retail clothing store provided an excellent opportunity to interact with consumers and to be on the other side of the fence as a seller—a marketer. When business was slow, the owner of the store would complain about profits being too low. Then we would see customers as prey, or targets. Our goal was to sell to anyone and everyone, the idea being to move the merchandise! The consumers lost their individuality in the eyes of the salespeople and were simply means to increase sales and please the owner. When sales were good, though, the tension lightened . . . customers were seen as family, friends, and new faces to meet. Selling was not only to generate dollars, but was fun and sociable."

❧ *Auto Salespersons "Brake" Away*

Manufacturers are well aware of the distance that separates them from the salespersons who represent their products to consumers. In the highly competitive world of automobiles, for example, some salespersons are compensated entirely by commissions on what they sell. One good performer, Tony, earns 20 percent—about $200—of the gross profit on each Toyota he sells, and expects to make about $50,000 per year on this basis. This does not lead to loyalty to Toyota, however: this is his fourth auto dealership in the last year! Tony changes dealerships as customers' brand preferences shift during the year: he wants to be offering what customers want to buy. Dealers are happy to have him, and both the dealer and manufacturer are sorry when he leaves. As an Audi executive put it, "If you lose a guy who's worth a hundred cars a year, it's like losing a whole dealer." In an effort to combat turnover—and to improve salespersons' interests in developing long-term consumer loyalty to a brand and a dealer—*manufacturers* are experimenting with delayed bonus programs and with bonuses for salespersons who score high on consumer satisfaction surveys.[7]

TRACING THE FLOW OF A SALES INTERACTION

Apart from motivational issues, it is useful for us to realize that both the salesperson and the customer are acting in specific roles within a sales transaction. Of the two, the salesperson's role is generally more structured. For example, a salesperson generally has commanding knowledge of the brands and also has a well-thought-out, heavily practiced set of approaches to guide him or her through each customer interaction. The

Tony Salcido, a successful auto salesman, moves from dealer to dealer in pursuit of the latest "hot" car to sell.

customer, on the other hand, generally has much less detailed product knowledge, less sales interaction experience, and a less developed interaction strategy than the salesperson.

The Flow in Life Insurance Selling

An interesting study by Taylor and Woodside reports on the structure of life and health insurance sales interactions between agents (all men, in this study) and prospects.[8] They found a six-stage process of selling effort, as follows:

1.	Contact initiation/"prospecting"	5 percent of all acts
2.	Building rapport/"common ground"	5 percent of all acts
3.	Information swaps/"clarify needs"	40 percent of all acts
4.	Persuasive attempts/"selling"	30 percent of all acts
5.	Attempts to "close" the sale	15 percent of all acts
6.	Ending discussion/"follow-up"	5 percent of all acts

Notice the logical, "stylized" nature of the progression from beginning to end. Since this product category is one in which the salesperson must work hard to create consumer motivation to buy, the analysis of the kinds of acts that occur within each stage is especially interesting. Most of the salesperson's references to mutual acquaintances, his similarity to the customer's situation, and his expertise with insurance occurred during the rapport building stage. Most of the questions occurred during the information exchange stage, which is also when most of the price limits were discussed.

During the persuasion stage, attention was focused on the alternative policies themselves, and almost all the mention of potential catastrophes occurred here. The average sales presentation then contained *three* attempts to get the prospect to say "yes" during the closing attempt stage. The salesman also made all efforts to have the customer increase the amount spent at this stage. Then, during the last stage, conversation returned to a social level, with the salesperson attempting to lay the groundwork for a long-term relationship with this customer.

Considerable research has been done on salespersons' knowledge about the process of "how to sell." Emphasis has been given to studying salespersons' **scripts**, which we learned in Chapter 9 (see Figure 9-3 for a refresher) are organized memory (long-term-memory, LTM) structures that describe a particular sequence of activities.

Scripts: In selling, organized memory structures used by salespersons to plan and carry out effective sales presentations.

In life insurance selling, creating consumer motivation to buy is a challenge: one study showed that almost half of all the discussion acts involved persuasive attempts and "closing the sale."

In a sales interaction context, a salesperson's scripts provide the detailed plans and expectations he or she has for carrying out the role (and for the customers acting out their roles as well). If you would wish to pursue further readings on this topic, Note 9 is a good place to begin.

The ISTEA Model of Effective Sales Interactions

The Taylor-Woodside study concentrated on describing the sequence of events during a sales interaction. This sequence is primarily the result of a preplanned strategy on the part of the well-trained salesperson. What does this strategy look like, however?

To understand how a salesperson can best blend preplanning with necessary flexibility during a sales interaction, let's briefly examine Figure 15-1. This displays a

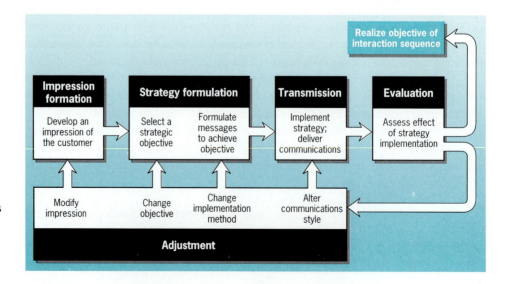

FIGURE 15-1 The Sales Interaction as Seen by the Salesperson: The ISTEA Model. SOURCE See Note 10.

Table 15-1 Some Practical Tips for Stages 1 and 2 of ISTEA

Impression of Customer Type	Tips on Strategy Formulation
The "Silent Prospect"	Get a response, ask questions. Be more personal.
The "Procrastinator"	Summarize benefits customer will lose by failing to act. Be positive, self-assured. Suggest that the customer has the ability to make decisions. Use showmanship.
The "Talker"	Keep leading this prospect back into the sale. This person sells you, but he doesn't seem to buy. Say, "By the way, that reminds me, ..." Keep on the track–be brief.
The "Slow and Methodical" Type	He appears to weigh every word, so slow down and amplify on details. Adjust your tempo to his.
The "Chip-on-the-Shoulder" Type	Usually insincere and tries the salesperson's patience. This customer type is a difficult type to deal with but sincerity and respect on the salesperson's part create respect.
The "Timid" Type	Take it slow and easy. Reassure on every point. Use logic, but make it simple.
The "Suspicious Customer"	Acknowledge the customer's background, stay with facts, be conservative in statements.
The "Grouch"	Ask questions to ascertain real problem. Listen and let the customer tell his or her story.
The "Flighty Buyer"	Be rapid, speed up, concentrate only on important points, omit details when possible.
"Mr. or Ms. Opinionated"	Give them rope. Flatter them. Cater to their whims. Listen attentively. Take the cash and let the credit go.

SOURCE: See Note 11.

model developed by Barton Weitz.[10] Weitz calls his model **ISTEA** (pronounced "iced tea"), an acronym for the five stages the salesperson experiences in a customer-sales interaction. In the first stage, the salesperson develops an **impression** of the consumer: this results from combining past information, stereotypes about similar consumers, and whatever information is available at the time of the interaction. The second activity—**strategy formulation**—depends on the customer impression that was formed. Here, the salesperson decides on his or her basic plan for persuading the customer to buy and which exact messages would be best. Table 15-1 summarizes some sales experts' ideas the first two stages of ISTEA: forming an *impression* about the type of customer and then developing a *strategy* that will work for this type of person.

The third stage of the ISTEA model—**transmission**—then involves the actual delivery of these messages to the customer. In the fourth stage—**evaluation**—as the salesperson delivers the message, he or she watches and listens carefully for even minor reactions from the customer, to see how the message is working. Customer reactions can range from clear statements down to flickers of the eyes, shifts of body posture, or other signs of heightened interest, displeasure, or other emotions.

Referring to Figure 15-1, we can see that after the evaluation stage, the flow of the model diverges. If the customer agrees to purchase the product, for example, the upper branch is taken and the sales interaction draws toward an end. If, on the other hand, the interaction is still in its early stages, we move along the bottom arrow to stage 5—**adjustment.** *Adjustment is the key factor in Weitz's model.* It suggests that the salesperson should continually "customize" his or her presentation during the sales interaction. There are many types of adjustments possible: modifying the initial

ISTEA: A five-stage model of adaptive selling.

impression of the customer, changing your strategic objective, and changing your types of selling messages and/or the way in which they are delivered.

THE MARKETING LITERATURE ON SALES EFFECTIVENESS

Given the importance of personal selling in the field of marketing, it is no surprise that there is a huge literature on this topic. Part of this literature focuses on personal sales techniques and part on how to manage a sales force. These issues are the subject of entire marketing courses and numerous company training efforts. Our interest here, however, is in the nature of the influence process as it affects consumer behavior. For example, we noted earlier that the salesperson often seems to have considerable power over the flow of the consumer interaction. How does this power arise?

Two theoretical sources of power are expert power and reference power. **Expert power** arises when the consumer believes that the salesperson has superior knowledge or skills in regards to the product or service. **Referent power** on the other hand, comes from a consumer's feelings of identification with the salesperson. In general, it is believed that the more a consumer *likes* a salesperson, the more positive he or she is likely to be toward following the recommendations. Characteristics related to *similarity* are important here: these include race, age, sex, and interests. An interesting study on these factors was reported by Woodside and Davenport.[12] They were interested in finding out whether it was more important for a salesperson to be similar to his or her customer (that is, to serve as a "referent other") or for the salesperson to possess knowledge and expertise about the product class.

Expert power: A source of selling influence based on superior knowledge.

Referent power: A source of influence based on a consumer's identification with the salesperson.

ठ﹖ *The Stereo Kit Experiment*

The Woodside and Davenport study dealt with the purchase of a new type of cleaning kit for stereo tape players. Customers who came to the checkout counter of a music store with tapes were presented with one of five conditions: some received no sales presentation about the new product, but could purchase it from a display set up next to the cash register. This was the "control" condition, and it resulted in 13 percent of the consumers buying the product.

The other four conditions were combinations of the saleswoman appearing to be "high" or "low" on the expertise and similarity dimensions. High expertise meant that her brief sales talk indicated that she knew what she was selling ("Here is a device ...will clean the dirt and tape oxide from the guides..."), while the lower expertise talk admitted that she did not ("...they tell me it will keep your tape player clean. I don't really know how it works, but you can read the directions right here...this thing is supposed to help the tape player a lot. It's only $1.98. Would you like one?"). In the high similarity condition, she noted the kind of tapes being purchased, and praised them, and indicated that she owned the same songs and enjoyed them very much: in the low similarity condition she indicated personal preference for an opposite kind of music, but wished the buyer enjoyment with the tapes. The results of the experiment:

- When the saleswoman was low on both dimensions, only 13 percent of the customers purchased the new kit (the same rate as in the control condition).
- When high on similarity but low on expertise, 30 percent purchased.
- When low on similarity but high on expertise, 53 percent purchased.
- When the saleswoman was high on both, 80 percent purchased.

Of course, this was one study with specific kinds of treatments, and for a specific kind of product, so we must be careful of generalizing too far from its results. If you are interested in pursuing other literature in this area, you may wish to begin with the suggested readings listed in Notes 12 and 13.

 What Goes on Behind the Scene?

As a final element in our analysis of salesperson-customer interactions, you may be interested in reading Exhibit 15-2, which presents the candid observations and explanations of one former salesperson, identified here as Bill B. There are many kinds of marketers, salespersons, and selling situations, and we do not present Bill's experiences as being representative of most of them. If you have experience as a salesperson, you may find yourself agreeing with some of his observations and disagreeing with others. If you do not have experience as a salesperson, you may wish to show the exhibit to friends with experience, to see their reactions. In either event, the practices that Bill reports *are* relatively common in retail selling, and some of them may be new to you.

EXHIBIT 15-2

A Salesperson's View of Consumer Behavior

The following is a candid discussion with Bill B., a former salesman in a medium-sized appliance store. While his experiences will not be true for all selling situations, neither are they atypical. To begin, we asked Bill about his training period:

I. LEARNING TO SELL:

Q. *Can you recall any particular advice or "rules" that your sales manager would stress during your early time as a salesman?*

A. He tried hard to teach me how to sell in that setting and gave me a lot of "advice." My first few weeks, I tried to sell the product on benefits alone. I spent hours and hours reading the brochures from the manufacturers and really stressed the product benefits when I talked to a customer. People walked out on me, however; I wasn't doing well. If they did buy, they tended to buy the low-margin items that I wasn't supposed to sell...when you get paid on the quantity you sell, and the margin you sell at, the old sayings about the "customer always being right" and "fitting product benefits to customer wants" soon go by the wayside. So I started to listen to my boss and brought his "laws" into my sales presentations. As a result, sales doubled over what they were at the start.

Q. *What were some of his "laws"?*

A. He had a bunch of them.... The one I'll never forget, though, was about "Be-Backs." He'd tell me about three times a day for the first few months on the job,

"Bill, Be-Backs don't exist! Before a customer leaves this store, I want a yes or no from them. Before you let someone hit the door, I want you to have every salesperson in this store talk to the guy, including myself! That's because when they say they'll be back, they won't. Be-Backs don't exist!"

He also had a lot of other strong beliefs...he used to say, "I'll take one salesman who knows people over five who know products."

Q. *Did he give you tips on how to sell?*

A. Definitely. For example, "Don't ask customers 'Can I help you?' Ask 'What do you need to buy today?'" He also said, "Act like your customer. If he works with his hands, you work with your hands; if he's a bank executive, act like a bank executive!" He also gave me some good advice about selling to couples. "If you're selling to a group, pick the person most supportive and let them sell the product....Reinforce any positive comment he or she makes."

II. "READING" THE CUSTOMER:

Q. *What about your own views of consumers...did you see many differences?*

A. That's the point, after a while you can really tell...the type of customer that you can dictate what they were going to buy. And those would be the most desirable customers because you can take them to the most expensive pieces of merchandise, or if they can't afford the expensive piece of merchandise, you can at least steer them to a piece of merchandise that has the highest margin. They just have a look about them, it's hard to explain, probably not as self-assertive, the type of people that need to be told what to buy.

Q. *Did you have a fairly fixed process you went through in selling a customer?*

A. For every line of merchandise we had in a store, whether it was refrigerators or TVs, there was a set procedure. We'd go to the same TV first, or the same refrigerator, and the refrigerator we would go to first would be stripped, the lowest-selling model. It would be the one that would go in the newspaper at $398. It wouldn't have crispers and it wouldn't have dividers in the freezer; it wouldn't have things that people look for. We'd do our best to show them it didn't have those things most wanted.

Q. *Why did you go to it first?*

A. Because it was a tool to make them feel we were trying to get them the best deal possible. They'd walk in and we'd say, "Oh, would you like to see our sale model first?" and I'd open up the door and say, "...it's on sale for $398 this week. Do you like crispers in your refrigerator? Oh, you do, well this one doesn't have that...maybe you'd like to see something else?"

Q. *Were there any consumers that seemed to give you more trouble than others?*

A. Definitely! Landlords and apartment owners were the worst...apartment building owners would come in not caring what they got as long as they got something for their tenants and then we would be in a mess because we would actually lose commission by selling the leader items. Their margin was so low; they bring down our average margin for the week.

Q. *Were you allowed to give price concessions to customers?*

A. The first two or three months I had to get the sales manager's approval on everything: any time I lowered it below the retail price....By the time the manager got to know me, and I had a good sales record, I could lower it on my own accord, but I would tell the customer that I had to ask the sales manager. What I would do is walk into the other room and get a Coke or something and sit down by myself for two minutes and then come back out and say that I talked to the sales manager and he'll give you this price, a special deal for you today only.

III. SPIFFS AND SUCH:

Q. *You said earlier that your store did not do bait-and-switch selling, is that right?*

A. Legally, we didn't. In a true bait-and-switch operation, the sales merchandise is never sold. We'd avoid selling to the point of lying about the durability of the refrigerator to get a point across, saying, "Well you might spend $300 for this sale model, but it's only going to last you 2 years. You're going to come back in 2 years from now and spend another $300, when you could spend $500 on this refrigerator here, and it will last 10 years."

Q. *What about "spiffing," did you ever get involved with that?*

A. Yes, definitely! The best way to get a salesman's attention is to offer a **spiff.** When a spiff is offered that product will suddenly become what every consumer needs....Generally, it would be the sales representative from a manufacturer who would come in and announce that a spiff was on for a certain product. And every month we would get a spiff check from the company, based on how many spiff items we had sold that month.

> **Spiff:** An added bonus paid to a retail salesperson by a manufacturer if a particular model is sold; also termed "push money."

Q. *As I understand it, a spiff is an added bonus on certain items, is that right?*

A. Yes, it comes directly from the sales rep, and it supplements your commission.

Q. *How much is an average spiff worth?*

A. That depended on the price of the item. For economy models, the spiffs were usually low, or they didn't have them.... For a midrange model that would sell for maybe $400, the spiff might be $15, and for the expensive model, the spiff might be $25, to give you incentive.

Q. *How common were the spiffs, would you say?*

A. There were some periods when no spiffs were on, but usually one out of every three or four lines would be offering spiffs to us...some companies didn't offer them very much, but others seemed to have it as part of their marketing strategy.

Q. *How sensitive would you say sales were to these spiffs?*

A. I'd say 35 percent of the customers that came in didn't have a clear idea of what they wanted and they didn't have a clear knowledge of the product. They are very malleable people and I could steer them to any spiff item I wanted. I would only highlight the great parts of the product and the true advantages it had over other products. I wouldn't lie about it, but the next day if that line lost its spiff, and the other line that I was saying wasn't so great offered a spiff, I could change the story making the new spiff line appear superior. Again, this was not lying, but it would be a distortion of the picture, and I would certainly be creating the want.

Q. *How valuable was a spiff to you as a salesman, in terms of your commission on each sale?*

A. Hard to say, since our commissions depended on how well we did over a time period. I guess...the spiff would about double the amount we got from a particular sale.

Q. *And the store didn't seem to take a position about the spiff, is that right?*

A. Not unless things really got out of line, and we were only selling the spiff items. Sometimes, then, the reps from the other lines would complain, but this didn't happen very often.

Q. *Wasn't there a temptation for you to cut the price on the spiff items to up your income?*

A. Certainly. But that's something the sales manager can control. We were never supposed to lower a price until the customer was ready to walk. We would only cut price if we had to—if the customer knew what she was doing in negotiating with us. I never, ever, would lower the price unless it was clear that I had to, to make the sale. It's a timing thing, if you wait too long they might walk on you, and you lose the sale, but if you don't wait long enough, you may be selling . . . at a price below what you could have gotten . . . there's also a matter of credibility involved—if you offer a discount right off, they may think that the product is low quality.

Q. *One last thing about spiffs . . . were they usually for lower-quality products?*

A. (Pause) It's hard to generalize, but I wouldn't say so. They were used by most of our lines, and certainly for the higher-priced, good models that needed a strong selling pitch.

IV. MANAGING PRICE WITHIN A SALE:

Q. *What about pricing, did your store have a policy of meeting competitors' lowest prices?*

A. Yes, but it wasn't a major marketing element. We'd run it in ads every once in a while, and that would stimulate some more consumers coming in with competitive offers.

Q. *About what percentage of your consumers would you say would bring competitive prices to their negotiations with you?*

A. Surprisingly, only about 30 to 40 percent, when we ran an ad, would come in with a competitor's quote.

Q. *What about Sears?*

A. Sears did a lot of damage, especially its washers and dryers, because its prices were quite a bit lower than any of the independent brand names. We would have to be good at overcoming the higher price objection because Kenmore was also real big at putting a lot of gadgets on its washers and driers.

Q. *So if a customer came in and said that, "I can get a Kenmore for $150 less than what you're trying to sell me. . . ."*

A. It wouldn't matter; we'd say, "Well sure, and you can buy a Volkswagen cheaper than a Mercedes . . . you are comparing apples and oranges here."

Q. *But what if the customer was ready to walk out and buy that Kenmore?*

A. That's when you would definitely go into price cutting: "Let me talk to the sales manager." You have to. In that case it was necessary to convince the person that quality-price trade-offs exist between a Kenmore and GE or Amana, because there is no way you are going to get the price down to be compatible. You have to take an argument, "Look, I'll cut the price 15 percent; dollar for dollar you're getting a much better deal with this Amana. . . . Plus, we have our own service department and plus, plus . . . ". If he's still going to walk, you usually try to bring the sales manager out in person to talk to the guy, you might try to bring other salespeople in . . . get as many guns as possible.

V. SELLING STRONGLY:

Q. *What about browsers?*

A. We had a store policy not to allow browsers to roam the store unattended. If they said "just browsing," we would let them be for a couple minutes, then ease our way into a conversation. This was in response to another of our laws: "Browsers Don't Buy!"

Q. *Was there anything else you sold that was different from what we've already talked about?*

A. Yes, extended warranty plans, and that was a big money maker for salesmen. First, we would sell somebody, whether it was a TV, a refrigerator, washer, dryer, it didn't matter, then we would start offering extended service plans: You get a one-year warranty on this, Mrs. Jones, but if you pay a little more, we'll give you five years' parts and labor, everything. You'll never have to worry about this again. I'm selling you a good piece of equipment, but you never know, even the best manufacturers occasionally make a lemon, so you can protect yourself." A big pitch, and they're great because we would get about 25 percent commission on those deals.

Q. *How much do they cost?*

A. A washer and dryer might cost $150, a TV might cost a little more than that, and a refrigerator might be $175 for the full five years. But they had the option to buy one extra year, two extra years, three extra years, or four extra years also. We had a contest because nobody was ever selling these things and the sales manager finally got down and arranged an incentive: whoever could sell $2000 in warranties first would get another $150 bonus."

Q. *What—$2000 of these warranties?*

A. Yes. And the first one to get there would get a $150 bonus, plus all the commissions on the warranties themselves. I really blew everybody away on that one! (laughter). I got to $2000 before anyone else was at $400...because I was practicing and practicing....At home I made little charts, trying to figure out how to approach every possible contingency.

Q. *What proportion of consumers bought the service warranty, would you say?*

A. Before the contest maybe 1 out of 20: it was something the salespeople just didn't like to bring up, because when you work real hard, oftentimes, by the time the sale has been made, both parties are tired, and the buyer is a little intimidated by the amount of money he or she is about to pay. At this point we found it difficult to say, "Well, for $150 more you get this..."—especially when you've been haggling over $20 for the last 15 minutes. It's just hard to approach the person on that, so we did really poorly. But during the contest, I'd say maybe 1 out of every 3 bought it. It was just breaking through the barrier of being hesitant and cautious.

VI. CONSUMER INSIGHTS:

Q. *What about consumers, is there any way you can characterize the classic "sucker"?*

A. Yeah, I'm ashamed to say it, but I would say the poor working-class people. They would come in and they would buy on credit and they would buy just about what you told them to buy. Now none of the salesmen got to the point of really exploiting them and making them buy something that was really not what they came in for, but they were always easy sales, because they had very little product knowledge and I don't think they understood a lot of the pitch if you went down to product features a lot. I think they just pretty much wanted to be reassured what they were buying was good.

Q. *Could you characterize what type of consumer seemed to be at the other extreme and get the best deal possible from you?*

A. A middle-aged professional...they would come in and they would know everything....At least they thought they knew everything....Many times they had misinformation, but they would hardly allow me to go through a pitch; that would be a very rational sale.

Q. *What about family decision making...did this present any special challenges for you?*

A. I was extremely worried selling to a young couple if only the wife or husband was present. Sometimes they would come back and sometimes they wouldn't. There was nothing I could do to close the sale. I think either the husband or the wife would go out on a fact-finding mission and go to maybe five or six stores, and then they would make a narrowing-down process at home. Then both would go to perhaps the final two or three alternatives and make the decision together. With older couples, on the other hand, I got the distinct impression that one person had the authority to make the decision and that when they did leave, using the reason, "I need to talk it over with my husband/wife," it was an excuse. They generally didn't come back. Older couples also engaged in joint decision making, but to a lesser degree.

Q. *What percentage of your sales, would you say, were to joint purchasers?*

A. There were a lot of young couples moving into that area, and it was almost always a joint decision because they were buying a household of appliances.

Q. *Did they know coming in that they could get 35 percent off?*

A. That was one of the first things we told them. If I ever saw a couple coming in, I would ask if they were building a house, and if so, I would offer them contract pricing. If you didn't, you usually ended up dead, because anybody who is going to be buying six or seven appliances will shop in more than one place and the other place will offer contract prices.

Q. *And with the younger couples, did there seem to be specific roles for the man or woman?*

A. It seemed that it was a true joint decision in most of the cases, and it was definitely the case if both had a job, and there wasn't anything like clear role definitions.

Q. *Did you see more of that with the older consumers?*

A. With the older people, the refrigerator, washer/dryer decisions would tend to be made by the women, TVs were joint, and air conditioners were usually handled by the men.

■ THE CONSUMER'S PERSPECTIVE OF A SALES INTERACTION

To this point we have focused on only one side of the interactive dyad, the salesperson. Now we shall turn to the side on which consumer behavior actually occurs, the consumer. In contrast to the large literature on the marketing perspective of sales interactions, there is almost no literature on the consumer perspective on this same topic. As we discussed in Chapter 2, there are many books dealing with "how to be a better consumer" in such fields as consumer economics. However, the specific topic of dealing with sales interactions is not much discussed in these books either. There are, however, several *principles* that experts recommend for consumers. Here are a few of the most important (as you read them, think back to the points made by Bill B. in his interview):

PRINCIPLE I: KNOWLEDGE IS POWER

As we've noted, there is often an imbalance between the knowledge of the salesperson and the knowledge of the consumer. The salesperson works daily with the products or services offered, knows the terms at which they can be offered, understands principles of influence and persuasion, and has been trained to use effective techniques to work with his or her customers. However, most consumers know little about many of the larger products and services they buy, little about the range of offers that the store might make to them, and little about persuasive techniques and bargaining methods.

According to experts in consumer economics, the more that a consumer can do to learn something about each of these topics, the better off he or she will be when venturing out for a major purchase. As one old saying goes, *"If you're in the market for a car, the best place to start shopping is your local library."* Here you can learn, not only about product qualities and alternatives, but also the prices that dealers are paying for the models, their common forms of price markups, and the type of deal you can probably get if you bargain well. There are other good sources of information as well, an issue we'll discuss in Chapter 17, when we take up consumer information search. However, the key point is that a consumer who wants to buy the best product at the best terms needs to learn important facts about the product, its prices, and how it is sold.

PRINCIPLE II: UNDERSTAND THE MARKETING THEORY OF PRICE DISCRIMINATION

What Goes on behind the Scene?

To serve consumers over the long term, marketers have to attain profits from their operations. In theory, marketers can maximize revenues by selling to each customer at the highest price he or she is willing to pay, assuming that the sale is profitable to the marketer. This approach to selling is known as **price discrimination,** and is not intended to be a negative term. Usually, a price discrimination strategy involves personal selling, to obtain the best price offer possible from each consumer. Recall, for example, that Bill B.'s store would cut prices, but only at the last moment, and only when the salesperson recognized that a sale depended on doing so. In addition to those retailers who practice price discrimination as a strategy with their sales force, there are also many retailers who choose *not* to practice price discrimination. Their reasons usually involve the store's overall marketing strategy (high-volume outlets, for example, may wish to have people spend as little time on any one item as possible, so as to shop for a large variety of products) and sometimes legal restrictions.

Price discrimination: The theory that revenues are maximized by charging each customer the highest price that he or she is willing to pay.

Taking a Shot

Two friends were looking at a used lens priced at $150 in a camera store. "Too much," said the first. "Offer $75," advised the second. The offer was rejected: "I really want the lens," whispered the first friend. "Never mind," whispered the second, "Follow me out of here . . . just follow me." They were almost to the door when the salesman called out, "Ninety dollars." The second friend shot back, "Tax included?" The sale was done.

According to the well-known consumer finance writer Sylvia Porter, American consumers are almost illiterate when it comes to bargaining and negotiation. Thus the story just related is not especially common in the United States.[14]

When Consumers Should Negotiate

When a price negotiation approach is taken by a retailer, a consumer who doesn't understand that this is happening will almost always end up paying more for the product. According to Scott Maynes, a leading consumer economist, consumers can expect to find negotiable prices *most of the time* for

- Used items
- Appliances
- Purchases involving trade-ins
- Houses
- Automobiles
- Home repairs and improvements

Fees for professional services (doctors, lawyers, decorators, brokers, etc.) are sometimes negotiable, while those for mail-order goods are almost never negotiable.[15]

PRINCIPLE III: HAVE A STRATEGY FOR THE TRANSACTION

To make the most advantageous sales arrangement, a consumer should know how to adopt a negotiating approach and have a **transaction strategy**. By understanding the role and needs of the salesperson—just as the salesperson attempts to do with customers—the consumer will carry more "clout" into the sales interaction, as evidenced by the lens purchase in the camera store. Research has shown that the major reasons that some consumers pay less than others for the same brands and models are (1) they know more and (2) they use greater bargaining strength.[16] Personal characteristics can help or hinder a customer within the interaction. Who are the most successful "bargainers" in sales transactions? In one of the rare studies in this area, it was discovered that the most successful people in bargaining within a sales interaction were those with dominant personalities—who were highly efficient and not very tolerant of others. Other descriptions of successful bargainers include people who have "high levels of aspiration" and those who "are more flexible," "look out for themselves," and "are psychologically assertive."[17]

If a consumer has these tendencies, he or she will certainly want to use them in a purchasing situation. If a consumer does not have these traits, however, it may be overly dramatic to try to change his or her entire personality just to save a few dollars! They can, however, work to develop purchasing strategies that will improve their performance and with which they do feel comfortable. For example, *comparison shopping* is a useful way to learn about alternatives and gain price concessions. In this case, "walking out" on the salesperson does not represent rejection, but part of a planned shopping experience. Some consumers, however, do not wish to shop around, either because they don't enjoy it or because it is costly in terms of time and effort. In these cases, some consumers use a variant of the *Dutch auction technique*, in which the auctioneer *begins at a high price and reduces it slowly;* the first person who accepts the current price wins the bidding. These consumers simply inform the salesperson that they do not wish to haggle, but want his or her best price and terms so that they can either accept them or go elsewhere to buy. In another simple strategy, the consumer decides beforehand what he or she is willing to pay and then goes to the store and proposes exactly those terms. If they are accepted, the sale is made; if not, the consumer leaves and tries elsewhere.

In recent years some automakers, such as Saturn, and some dealers have introduced *no-dicker stickers.* Here consumers are informed that no negotiation is possible—the *sticker price* is the price. The new prices were as much as several thousand dollars lower, and many consumers have responded positively.[18]

As we have noted several times already, consumers typically do not enter sales interactions with clear strategies aimed at minimizing the prices they will pay. Scholars in the fields of marketing, economics, and psychology have long had strong disagreements about why this seems to be the case. Would you say that this description applies to your behavior? If so, why? Would you shift your sales interaction strategies if you were in a position to do so easily? To gain further realistic appreciation for these issues, consider how each of the three principles in this section applies to the following report:

🐚 *Pleas for Fees...Omissions on Commissions*

When the stock market drops, small investors usually cut their transactions. Recently, industry volume was down over 20 percent, and pressures increased on retail brokers to sell harder. But which financial products would they recommend?

Although many investors do not realize it, commissions and other sales charges are generally unregulated in the investment world, and are used as incentives for brokers to sell particular products. This can pose problems. According to one former broker, "the broker's incentive to sell lies with the varied products that may provide the least investment benefit to clients." Making recommendations based on a commission rate "isn't...occurring only at second-rate firms...it provides a temptation so great it represents a whole new level of investment risk."

Commissions can vary widely depending upon the type of investment—for a client investing $10,000, for example, a financial advisor could earn $0 (if a no-load mutual fund is purchased), $50 (if a Treasury bond is bought), $200 (if it is common stock), $600 (if it is a new mutual fund with load), or $1000 or more (if it is limited partnership or similar venture). Often, the riskiest, most complicated financial investments offer salespeople the greatest compensation, because these are the hardest products to sell. According to officials of the Securities and Exchange Commission (SEC), clients—whether out of embarrassment, ignorance, or misplaced courtesy—almost *never* inquire about the compensation brokers receive from investment recommendations. Explains one broker, "If people really understood what they were paying sometimes, they wouldn't pay it."

Of course, many good brokers rely on long-term relationships with their valued clients and base their recommendations on the investment strategy worked out with the client. Even so, many clients are not aware that commissions on many transactions are in fact highly negotiable. As a rule, more attention by clients to the issue of commissions is clearly appropriate. As an SEC official comments, "We could use a little paranoia in this area [on the part of consumers.]"[19]

■ THE PUBLIC POLICY PERSPECTIVE

Our discussion to this point has made it clear that personal selling is important for both marketers and consumers. The personal selling function helps to deliver many of our most prized possessions as consumers—homes, automobiles, and products with which we live our daily lives and entertain ourselves. Further, salespersons and customers usually have goals in common. Usually, the customer *wants* to make a purchase, and the salesperson *wants* him or her to make that purchase. The conflicts that arise concern exactly *which* purchase should be made, under *what terms*, and *from which source*. These are the issues that sometimes challenge public policy.

THE CHALLENGES TO PUBLIC POLICY

The key role for public policy is to act to protect consumers' rights while preserving the benefits and freedoms that are associated with marketing in our society. From the public policy perspective, the staggering size of the economy presents a real problem. As we noted, there are *over 11 million salespersons working with consumers every day* (with several billion dollars in customer purchases daily). Most of these individuals do not cross the line from legal to illegal sales activity or from scrupulous to unscrupulous sales behavior. However, if only 1 percent of these individuals, for whatever reason, acts to mislead or pressure consumers to act against their best interest, a problem of staggering proportions would exist. According to a former prominent U.S. senator, Warren Magnuson (D., Wash.),

> Deceptive selling by the unscrupulous few in the business underworld is, in fact, our most serious form of theft. It cheats Americans of . . . more than is lost through robbery, burglary, larceny, auto theft, embezzlement, and forgery combined. . . . Today's modern bandits of the marketplace are the masters of the light touch . . . these men can reach even deeper into our pockets without producing a rustle to disturb the law, or often the victim himself.[20]

HIGH-PRESSURE SALES TECHNIQUES

Our discussion to this point has concentrated on salesperson-consumer interactions in a retail setting. In most of these cases, the customer has *chosen* to come to the store and is likely to have some advanced interest in making a purchase. There are, however, other instances in which the sales interaction begins with *no* purchase interest on the part of the customer. Telephone soliciting and door-to-door selling are the best examples of this. When a consumer has not even thought about purchasing a particular product or service, two characteristics are likely to govern aspects of the encounter. First, the consumer's knowledge—which we noted in Chapter 2 is often low in general—is likely to be especially low with no prior planning or development of a shopping strategy for the sales interaction. Second, the consumer has a low motivation to buy, at least in the sense of having planned to purchase. Thus the salesperson's major task is creating a purchase motivation. In these instances, "high-pressure" selling is often used. Various tactics are brought into play, including both product promises and plays upon the customer's emotions. High-pressure selling is not in itself deceptive, of course, but the temptations are much heightened in this setting.

⌇ *Frauds by Clods*

Consumer activists have a long list of tales concerning fraudulent practices in high-pressure selling. "Creating a consumer want" has a much more cynical meaning here.

It includes such actions as altering the customer's product in a hidden manner and then pointing out the problem. Gas stations on interstate highways, for example, have been caught plunging ice picks into tires and placing foreign chemicals into batteries to cause adverse reactions. "Termite inspectors" have been caught placing the bugs in houses and then informing the frightened residents of the imminent collapse of their structure. Traveling "tree surgeons" have thrived by pointing out undetectable diseases in large trees overhanging a house, and then removing them at high prices. The classic case in using this type of fear sell, though, is that involving the Holland Furnace Company, which at one time employed 5000 persons in its 500 offices around the United States. Its primary sales method was for the employees to introduce themselves to housewives as "safety inspectors," go to the furnace and dismantle it, and then condemn it as "so hazardous that I must refuse to put it back together—I can't let myself be an accessory to murder!" According to Senator Magnuson, the salesmen were merciless. One elderly woman was sold *nine new Holland furnaces in six years, costing over $18,000!*[21]

MISREPRESENTATIONS OF SELLING INTENT

Other situations involve lowering the consumer's defenses against a sales pitch. A telephone consumer might be told that he or she has "just won a valuable prize in our contest" or that the caller is "taking a survey and would appreciate your answers to a few brief questions." Once the ice is broken, and the discussion becomes more relaxed, the salesperson's prepared script calls for a gradual shift into the sales presentation. At this point, the consumer may feel some social obligation to consider the discussion, and in fact may be enjoying it.

ᘓ *Selling Knowledge, by the Book?*

Some years ago an important Federal Trade Commission (FTC) case against the Encyclopaedia Britannica Company included a number of charges concerning this initial description by the firm's sales representatives. According to sworn testimony during the trial, the sales representatives were provided with an introductory speech to memorize and a letter from a senior company official stating that the person is an "interviewer" who is studying the effectiveness of the company's advertising. According to one salesman who testified,

> The two most common objections were, "Are you selling anything?" We were specifically told to say, "No, I am not selling anything, but may I come in?" Then we were supposed to start to go in. The other one was, "Well, how long will it take?" And we were supposed to say, "Only a couple of minutes. May I come in?" [22]

In fact, a full sales presentation would take at least an hour and sometimes over two hours. The FTC then went on to find a number of further deceptive and misleading selling practices throughout each stage of the sales presentation, contract signing, and debt collection activities of the firm. After four years of investigation and trial, the FTC issued a lengthy order aimed at fixing these practices in the future. Among the order's terms:

- In advertising used to gain the names of sales prospects, offers of contests or free gifts must include a clear statement that Britannica's salespersons may call.
- In door-to-door sales, the Britannica salesperson must, at the start, hand the consumer a 3- by 5-inch card stating that the purpose of this call is to sell encyclopedias.

The company sharply criticized this order and appealed it to the federal court system. After considerable controversy, the FTC announced that it had modified its order to allow the salesperson to present a business card rather than the larger card. The business card had to have the term "sales representative" on it, but did not require a statement concerning the purpose of the call, nor was the salesperson required to tell the consumer to read the card. The two major reasons behind these modifications were (1) the First Amendment's freedom of speech for marketers and (2) the fact that the FTC had not done consumer research to test whether its original requirement would work with consumers!

BAIT AND SWITCH AND OTHER DECEPTIVE PRACTICES

Bait and switch: An illegal combination of advertising and personal selling.

You may recall that Bill B. mentioned that his firm did not engage in true bait and switch, although it did come close. Bait-and-switch practices stem from the retailer's need to get customers into the store where they can be persuaded by salespersons to make purchases. One good way to do this, of course, is to use advertising that is effective in bringing "traffic" to the store. **Bait and switch,** then, is a clever combination of advertising and personal selling. The advertising sets the "bait," and the consumer takes the bait and comes to the store, where the salesperson "switches" the consumer from the advertised item to a more expensive, more profitable model.

It is important to recognize that there is a distinction between the salesperson's natural desire to "trade up" a customer (thereby obtaining a higher price and higher profit contribution) and the practice of bait and switch. Trading-up is legal and can be seen as a natural part of the retail selling process. In a trading-up situation, the customer is free to purchase whichever item he or she desires. In bait and switch, however, the store has never intended to sell the advertised item! The salesperson is typically under orders *not* to sell that item and is often fined if he or she does sell the item. In salesroom parlance, the bait model is "nailed to the floor." A variety of tricks are used: from not having the item on the floor at all ("Our latest shipment hasn't come in yet...") to the use of a truly unattractive model that the customer is almost certain to find unappealing when he or she inspects it ("Isn't that ugly! I don't know why they would make something like that, but that is the one we have on sale today.... Maybe you'd like to see this one over here...").

There are, of course, many variations on this theme, some of which are legal and some of which are not. Even such large and reputable retailers as Sears, Roebuck have been charged with instances of this practice. In the Sears case, the FTC charge concerned sewing machines, and the company *did* have a policy of selling the advertised machines at the low price. The FTC, however, was moving against the in-store sales practices of some of Sears' salespersons: they would routinely advise customers that the advertised model was noisy, came without a standard guarantee, and might take a long time to deliver. According to Sears' chairman,

> The incidents which came to light in recent FTC hearings were violations of Sears' policy as well as FTC standards. We regret that even one such case occurred in our annual transactions of some 9.5 million major home appliances.[23]

In many other cases of bait and switch, however, the retailers involved have been more clearly guilty of illegal and fraudulent practices. Since the appeal is primarily geared to low price, this technique hits hardest at low- and moderate-income consumers often with smaller retail operations in local markets. Monitoring and enforcement by local officials is therefore extremely important.

Despite the fact that the FTC stresses national cases in its regulatory activities, its files are packed with fraudulent personal sales examples. In three related cases in the Washington, D.C., area, for example, the FTC moved against carpet retailers who were advertising incredible bargains, plus free gifts, in their local advertising. As a remedy for the bait and switch practices of these retailers, the FTC ordered them to include, in each ad, the following statement:

> The Federal Trade Commission has found that we engage in bait and switch advertising; that is, the salesman makes it difficult to buy the advertised product and he attempts to switch you to a higher priced item.

This notice had to be ringed with a black border and set off in a conspicuous place in the ad. The firms were ordered to run it for a period of at least one year. If they had changed their selling practices by that time, the remedy was open for revision.[24]

INDUSTRY AND GOVERNMENT RESPONSES TO PERSONAL SELLING ABUSES

Even though the kinds of abuses we have been discussing are not typical of most marketers, they do cause severe problems for both the marketing community and for consumers in our society. For public policymakers, a great deal of the difficulty arises from special characteristics of the salesperson-customer interaction itself. Consider, for example, how this differs from either print or broadcast advertising: (1) Much advertising occurs on a national or regional level: personal selling always occurs on a local level; (2) the number of instances that need to be monitored is much higher with personal selling than with advertising; (3) advertising leaves a record of what was said, whereas personal selling almost never leaves a record; (4) advertising is typically brief, with only a few basic points being made, while personal selling usually includes many more points, within an interactive discussion framework; and (5) if an advertising order is issued, future advertising can easily be checked to see whether or not it has complied with the terms of the order. If a personal selling order is issued, however, future sales interactions are still extremely difficult to monitor for compliance.

For these reasons, regulation of deceptive selling practices is extremely difficult. As noted earlier, state and local agencies are heavily involved in this process. In addition, the creation of laws that specify consumers' rights become especially important. **Cooling-off laws,** for example, allow consumers three business days in which to obtain a full refund if they decide they do not wish to carry through a purchase (greater than $25) they had agreed to with a door-to-door salesperson. The intention here is to protect consumers against caving in to slick, high-pressure selling techniques; the regulation requires the salesperson to provide a consumer with a "notice of cancellation" that can be returned within the three-day period to void the sale. Notice that this regulation makes door-to-door selling less efficient. It is designed, however, to overcome the regulatory limitations brought about by the nature of personal selling itself. The presence of these types of laws is intended to help consumers to protect themselves. We will return to this topic in Chapter 19, when discussing postpurchase consumer behavior.

Cooling-off laws:
Allow three days for consumers to cancel purchases made under high-pressure selling conditions.

Businesses' Reactions to Selling Abuses

It is particularly important that we recognize that fraudulent and deceptive practices by some sellers are also injurious to the marketing community of reputable businesspersons. Not only does the credibility of marketing suffer in general, but *honest retailers in the community lose business each time that a customer is misled by a deceptive operation.* And retailers are not the only persons to suffer: the manufacturers of lines sold in the reputable stores also suffer losses of sales and profits. For this reason, many businesspersons support codes of conduct for their industries and such local organizations as the Better Business Bureau.

☜ *Marketers Are Angry*

Another interesting—and damaging—effect of unscrupulous sellers has been felt by the marketing research community. Because so many firms have used "Hello, I'm taking a market survey..." as their openers for sales solicitations (either by telephone or in person), consumers have naturally reacted with suspicion and anger. This has made the legitimate consumer research task considerably more difficult (and more expensive), as "refusals" to participate in legitimate surveys have risen. In addition, at the time of this writing the U.S. Congress is considering a bill that would have the effect of further hurting survey research, though its purpose is to protect consumers from high-pressure telephone selling. Thus the American Marketing Association, a professional group with over 30,000 members, developed a Research Code of Ethics that addresses this practice directly:

> No individual or organization will undertake any activity which is directly or indirectly represented to be marketing research, but which has as its real purpose the attempted sale of merchandise or services....

Beyond the issue of selling abuses there are other interesting questions involved in the ethics of conducting marketing and consumer research. If you are interested in these questions, you may wish to pursue the references listed in Note 25.

■ SUMMARY

WHAT GOES ON DURING A SALES TRANSACTION?

Unlike other social influences we've encountered, *salesperson influences* are marketer controlled and occur close to the point of transaction. Both these factors render the salesperson of utmost importance to the marketer. Moreover, a plurality of a national sample of consumers who had recently purchased a consumer durable named the salesperson as their most useful source of information. With over 11 million consumer salespersons in the United States, it is evident that salespersons exert a pervasive and important influence upon consumer behavior. The first section of the chapter was devoted to the *sales transaction* itself. We saw here how research focuses on the *consumer-salesperson interaction dyad.* In the few studies that have been done, one of the surprising results is how powerful a position the salesperson is often in during these interactions.

THE MARKETING PERSPECTIVE ON PERSONAL SELLING

In our next section we examined salesperson influences from the marketing perspective. The *ISTEA model* of effective sales interactions was introduced. This model describes how a salesperson can blend preplanning with the flexibility necessary to achieve his or her objectives. We then examined some key dimensions of salesperson effectiveness.

Expert power and *referent power* are two key factors: a record shop study demonstrated how they can vary. This section closed with a candid interview with Bill B., a former appliance salesman.

THE CONSUMER'S PERSPECTIVE OF A SALES INTERACTION

The third section examined the *consumer's perspective on salesperson influences.* Here we saw how a general lack of knowledge concerning products, persuasive techniques, and bargaining methods hinders many consumers. In this light, *three principles* were reviewed: (1) recognize that knowledge is power, (2) understand the theory of price discrimination, and (3) have a strategy for the transaction. Even the consumer who may not be psychologically assertive will benefit from adopting a reasonable prepurchase strategy.

THE PUBLIC POLICY PERSPECTIVE

In our final section we examined some of the *public policy issues* in this area. The basic issue involves how to protect consumers' and competitors' rights while preserving the benefits and freedoms associated with personal selling in our society. Given the hundreds of millions of sales transactions each day, if only a tiny percentage of sales behaviors are illegal or unscrupulous, the magnitude of the resulting loss to consumers is staggering. In this regard we reviewed some examples of fraudulent *high-pressure selling, misrepresentation of selling intent,* and *bait-and-switch advertising.* We also examined the difficulty involved in regulating personal selling, since it occurs at a local (versus national) level, it seldom leaves a record of what was said, and it is hard to monitor compliance with orders when they are issued. Thus preventive actions such as consumer protections (e.g., cooling-off laws), industry codes of conduct and self-policing, and consumer vigilance are all important.

■ KEY TERMS

exchange function	evaluation phase	impression	adjustment	transaction strategy
interaction dyad	consummation phase	strategy formulation	expert power	bait and switch
salesperson power	scripts	transmission	referent power	cooling-off laws
orientation phase	ISTEA	evaluation	price discrimination	

■ REVIEW QUESTIONS AND EXPERIENTIAL EXERCISES

[E = **Application extension or experiential exercise**]

1. Compare and contrast salespersons' influences on consumer behavior with reference group and family influences. Be specific.

2. Compare the salesperson's view and customer's view of the sales transaction.

3. Relate the six-stage processes of selling developed by Taylor and Woodside to the ISTEA model developed by Weitz.

4. Consider the results of the stereo kit experiment. Identify two other products that might generate comparable effects of the expertise and similarity dimensions of the salesperson. Identify two products you believe would have opposite effects: high similarity more significant than high expertise.

5. Summarize the key points concerning salespersons' influence that you learned from the Bill B. interview. Which of these had you already known? Did he make any statements with which you disagree?

6. Describe exactly how a wise consumer should follow the text's three principles for dealing with sales interactions in this situation: "Your broker, whom you've recently met, calls and offers you 1000 shares of a secondary stock issue of Marsea Corp., a small company with which you are not familiar. The stock is offered at $10 per share. He says it will sell fast, and he needs to know your decision."

7. Why might a public policymaker prefer to regulate advertising as opposed to personal selling?

8. [E] Over 20 years ago the magazine *Consumer Reports* issued a brief report on "spiffs" (also termed "push money") and then petitioned the Federal Trade Commission to ban this practice. Read this report (*Consumer Reports,* January 1971, p. 24), and reread the discussion in our interview with Bill B. (Exhibit 15-2). Write a brief report explaining why you would or would not support a ban on spiffing.

9. [E] A few years ago a law professor raised the question of whether the civil rights laws were adequate to protect blacks and women against discrimination as consumers (see *Harvard Law Review,* February 1991). It seems that a study of 90 car dealers compared the prices negotiated by experimenters on a car whose sticker prices was about $13,500 (dealer's cost about $11,000). White males were able to buy the car for an average price of $11,362; white females, $11,504; black males, $11,783; and black females, $12,237. A further study was planned to better examine this issue. Based just on this report, plus the material in this chapter, do you believe there is likely to be a problem? Why or why not? If so, what—if anything—should be done about it?

10. [E] Conduct a brief interview with an experienced salesperson to learn about consumer behavior in a sales interaction (you may wish to use the Bill B. interview as a guide). Write a brief report summarizing your findings.

11. [E] Accompany a friend or relative on a shopping trip in which an interaction with a salesperson will occur (do not inform your partner of your purpose before the trip). Listen and watch the interaction closely, relating it to the concepts in this chapter. Did the stages proceed similarly? Where did most of the acts occur? Write a brief report summarizing your findings.

12. [E] Based on the notes listed for Chapter 15 at the back of the book, select several research studies likely to be of interest to you. Write a brief report on your findings.

13. [E] Locate the book, *Influence: The New Psychology of Modern Persuasion,* by the psychologist Robert B. Cialdini (New York: William Morrow/Quill, 1984). Read the portions pertaining to salesperson activities. Do you agree with his assertions? Write a brief report summarizing your reactions.

14. [E] Locate two books aimed at salespersons to assist them in selling more effectively. As you review their contents, select several insights concerning (a) consumer behavior and (b) effective selling techniques. Write a brief report summarizing your findings.

■ SUGGESTED READING

■ Cialdini's book (cited in question 13 above) is a highly readable discussion of various influence strategies. For the observations of an anthropologist concerning the roles and processes involved in salesperson influence, try Robert Prus, *Making Sales* (Newbury Park, Calif.: Sage Publications, 1989). For managerial insights, see Saul W. Gellerman, "The Tests of a Good Salesperson," *Harvard Business Review,* No. 3 (May/June 1990), pp. 64–69; and Karl Boedecker, Fred Morgan, and Jeffrey Stoltman, "Legal Dimensions of Salespersons' Statements: A Review and Managerial Suggestions," *Journal of Marketing,* Vol. 55, No. 1 (January 1991), pp. 70–80. Again, reference to specific Notes is helpful for specific topics, and the huge literature on selling effectiveness is helpful if you have no experience in this area.

ADVERTISING'S INFLUENCES

"DOES SHE OR DOESN'T SHE?"

" . . . Only her hairdresser knows for sure," was a daring headline for Clairol hair colorings during the conservative 1950s. It connected with consumers' hopes: sales increased 400 percent in the next six years, and almost half of U.S. women tried tinting their hair. This campaign created an industry and became an advertising classic.[1]

"HERB DEFINITELY DOESN'T"

The mid-1980s saw another classic ad campaign, but this time in the other direction. Burger King, which had been extremely successful until then, was searching for a campaign that would capture the public's fancy. It chose to feature "Herb the nerd" and spent $40 million pointing out that he'd never been to Burger King. The advertising trade press still loves to discuss this campaign: marketing blunders are called "Herb marketing," while failure to understand consumers is evidence of a "Herb gap." Even the folks at Burger King admit the fiasco. One executive reports that history there is marked "B.H." and "A.H."—Before Herb and After Herb: it's "When Kennedy was shot and when Herb was launched, where were you?"[2]

Every year an incredible amount of money is being spent on advertising and sales promotion aimed at consumers: in the United States alone, over $130 billion is spent on advertising each year, with many billions more being spent for other types of sales promotion (sweepstakes, displays, coupons, etc.). Advertising is a major industry in the United States, accounting for about 3 percent of our gross national product. Almost every business firm advertises, as do many nonprofit institutions (churches and hospitals, for example). Although it sounds obvious, we should remember that everyone who advertises does so in the belief that he or she will benefit by putting these dollars into advertising. Thus it appears that advertising must be highly influential in terms of impacts on consumer behavior. In this chapter we'll delve more deeply into this interesting issue.

As we saw in Chapter 2, the two primary actors bring quite different perspectives to the topic. Marketing managers *create* and *distribute* advertising: conversely, consumers primarily *react* to advertising. As consumers, however, our reactions are highly affected by the fact that we are exposed to *so many ads* for so many competing products and brands. It is estimated that the average American is exposed to about 300 ad messages each day, or *over 100,000 ads in one year.*[3] Thus most consumers have to ignore most ads most of the time, either because they're for products of little or no interest or because the consumer is busy with other matters (on the other hand, sometimes a certain ad captures our attention and evokes strong responses).

Of most significance for our text is the fact that consumers are both *informed* and *influenced* by advertising. In fact, over the course of the average advertising campaign, enough consumers are informed and influenced that managers continue to invest in advertising during future periods. Moreover, advertising is so visible and so interesting that all of us are already "experts," in the sense that we've reacted to and talked about it for years. Thousands of articles about advertising appear each year. Many books are available, and many universities offer courses (and even majors) in advertising.

Given the scope of the subject, we must limit our goals and coverage in this chapter. We'll do this by focusing on several basic frameworks about how advertising works with consumers. We'll begin with a brief overview of what's involved in advertising decisions. Our second—and largest—section focuses on the persuasive element of advertising (the origin of the word *advertise* meant "to turn someone . . ."). Our third section then briefly highlights some approaches used in controlling this sprawling, brawling, exciting field. In addition, two appendices are available for interested readers: Appendix 16A summarizes the major economic and social debates about this field, and Appendix 16B summarizes some managerial factors involved in successful ads.

■ WHAT'S INVOLVED IN ADVERTISING DECISIONS?

This section provides a brief overview of advertising decision areas in order to broaden our appreciation of the marketing perspective on advertising. As we'll see later in this chapter, it is clear *that the average ad, by itself, is not likely to have a major impact on consumer behavior.* This means that, from the marketer's perspective, it is the overall program that is most important. If the product is not very appealing, or is not received well by consumers when they use it, it is doubtful that even the best advertising campaign can influence consumers to purchase this brand over any extended period of time.

At the same time, *most marketers and consumers would agree that advertising does have an impact on consumer behavior* and that for most brands it returns a profit on the money invested. As we saw in our opening quotes, provided the remainder of the marketing mix is of reasonable quality, advertising holds the potential to tip the "bottom line" toward great success, moderate profitability, or even failure. In assessing advertising's influences, then, we need to keep the paradoxical question, "Is advertising's impact really strong or really weak?" in mind. Although it is a frustrating issue, this is the question with which advertising experts have been wrestling for years.

THE 7 M'S OF ADVERTISING

At the very start, we should recognize that there are many aspects within any ad campaign that will determine its impacts on consumers. Consider, for a moment, the almost infinite number of detailed decisions that are made in creating any ad. Most of these are very subtle. For example, we need to decide whether the model should be sitting or standing, wearing red pants or blue, facing to the right or the left; whether the music should be soft or loud; and on and on (notice, by the way, that our example assumed that we had already decided to have a model and music and had already chosen which person and which tune).

When we think of entire advertising *campaigns,* the scope of the decisions widens even farther. One useful framework for advertising decisions, for example, is known as the **7 M's** of advertising management.[4]

- *Merchandise.* What is it that we have to promote?
- *Markets.* To whom are we advertising?
- *Motives.* Why do these consumers buy?
- *Messages.* What appeals will work best?
- *Money.* How much should we spend, and when?
- *Media.* Where and when should we reach our audience?
- *Measurement.* How do consumers respond to our ads?

7 M's: A framework of seven factors in advertising management.

Notice the first six factors contribute to the impact of every ad campaign, and since each of the six has many subfactors within it, we can see how difficult it is to single out any one variable and generalize about its true impact on advertising effectiveness. The seventh factor, measurement, refers to the use of consumer research within advertising. Because of the large gains possible from a significant improvement in an advertising campaign, consumer research is commonly used to provide insights and help with advertising decisions in the first six areas.

Figure 16-1 diagrams a basic model of advertising: notice that it is shown as a **one-way communication flow.** Here the **source** of the communication develops a **message,** and then delivers it to the **receiver** through a **channel** (personal contact, letter, television). The flow of the system is from left to right, and the communication ends when the message has been received: there is no flow of communication back from the receiver to the source.

ADVERTISING IS ONE-WAY COMMUNICATION

As a one-way communication form, advertising holds both advantages and disadvantages. Let's consider a few of these.

Disadvantages of One-way Communication

Two-way communications between persons offer some distinct advantages that advertising cannot offer to us. As consumers, for example, when we discuss a product with a salesperson, we can ask for *clarification* of the message points that may not be clear.

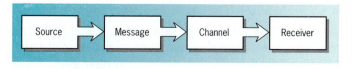

FIGURE 16-1 Advertising as a One-Way Communication Flow

Also, we can *tailor* the discussion to matters of specific interest. Finally, we are not required to communicate within a tight *time* limit—the discussion can extend out until one or both parties wish it to end.

Two-way communications also afford significant advantages to marketers. First, unlike advertising and other one-way modes (such as class lectures!), two-way communication situations are much more likely to command *attention* from customers (since they bear some responsibility within the communication itself). Second, the message sender is able to obtain immediate *feedback* on how well the message is being received. If the receiver is not understanding or is receiving a meaning different from that which we intend (this is technically termed "distortion"), there is an opportunity for us to try to *clarify* our message. Finally, if we see that the customer is not reacting positively to the persuasive aspects of our message, we are able to *alter the message* (or our presentation style) to try to improve our effectiveness. As we saw in the ISTEA model (Chapter 15), an astute salesperson is constantly interpreting verbal and body signals from customers and adjusting accordingly.

Advantages of One-way Communication

The situation is not entirely bleak for advertising, however. Since advertising is a one-way mode, the source can concentrate on a single message that can be sent to any number of receivers if the channels are available. *Cost per thousand customers*, for example, is a common term that captures the efficiency with which advertising can contact the mass consumer market. In comparison, a salesperson-customer interaction involves only one or two consumers at a time.

Hypodermic needle approach: A term to describe a one-way flow of communication.

A one-way flow is sometimes described as the **hypodermic needle approach** to communication, bringing to mind a picture of a needle through which the source injects the audience with his or her message. This model is most appropriate for those situations for which the audience is "captive" and *must* receive the message (e.g., prisoner-of-war camps, schools, consumer behavior classes). In the real world of advertising, on the other hand, few consumers feel that they must sit still for such injections. The hypodermic analogy does, however, help us to see how an advertiser controls all aspects of the message's contents and timing in a one-way communication. It indicates the potential to create highly *efficient* messages and helps us recognize why consumer research on messages can be very helpful to advertisers.

■ THE PERSUASIVE ASPECT OF ADVERTISING

⌘ *Spuds Sells Suds As Night Falls*

Not so long ago, a national poll of consumers showed that the "Spuds MacKenzie" ad campaign was one of the most popular of recent years. It worked on purchases, too, as Bud Light sales increased 20 percent in one year with the English bull terrier. His bosses at Anheuser-Busch were pleased with this success, but puzzled with the performance of their "The Night Belongs to Michelob" campaign featuring Genesis's catchy rock music. It also scored as one of the country's most popular campaigns in the consumer poll, but Michelob's sales dropped 5 percent that year.[5]

WHY IS ADVERTISING COMPLEX?

What do these reports tell us about advertising? The experiences of Bud Light and Michelob (and Clairol and Herb at the chapter opening) are examples of the successes and failures with which advertising is associated on a regular basis. It can succeed, sometimes strikingly, but it can also fail, sometimes spectacularly! And, because advertising is but one of the elements of the overall marketing mix, its actual contributions to a product's success or failure are often difficult to isolate, as indicated by this classic advertising quotation:

> I know that half of the money I spend on advertising is wasted, but I can never figure out exactly which half it is!

The quotation is attributed to John Wanamaker, a Philadelphia merchant whose department stores became one of the most successful businesses in America at the turn of the twentieth century. The quote remains a classic even today because it captures two of the essential characteristics of advertising: (1) businesses use advertising because it *does* work but (2) no one is yet quite sure *how* it works.

Because advertising costs money, and because that money could be pocketed as profits if not spent in this way, the concept of "wasted dollars" is important. For example, if Procter & Gamble were able to discover a way to achieve equal sales while spending only 10 percent less on advertising, the firm would add over $100 million to its profits before taxes! The issue of *how advertising works* is thus a major question for marketers in the quest for efficiency and profit.

ADVERTISING AS AN IDEAL PERSUASIVE SYSTEM

Although we've seen that advertising is supposed to be complex, we've yet to see why this might be the case, or what might be done about it. Let's start with Figure 16-2, which portrays an expanded version of our one-way flow model of advertising communication. Notice that the figure now shows six stages in the system, arrayed three on the advertiser's side and three on the consumer's side.

Stage I, **advertising goals,** represents management's aims for the upcoming advertising campaign. These goals depend on many factors, including current share of market, profit status, competition, and nature of the *target audience*. Four common types of advertising goals are (1) **persuasion** (for example, convincing consumers of a brand superiority claim), (2) **reinforcement** (e.g., assisting favorable consumer evaluation following a purchase), (3) **reminder** (e.g., for consumers favorable to the brand, to "keep it alive" in their evoked sets), and (4) **purchase precipitation** (e.g., encouraging

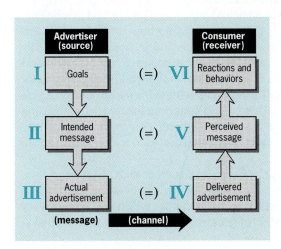

FIGURE 16-2 The Ideal Advertising Persuasive System

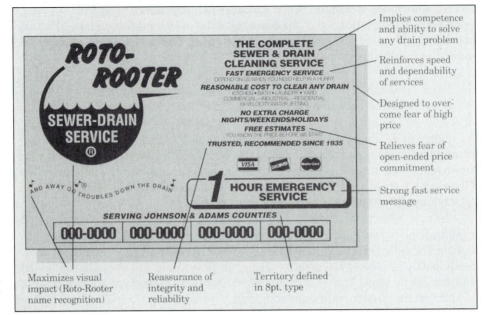

Here is a useful analysis of how the design of an ad helps to achieve its purposes. In this case, the ad will appear in a telephone directory.

consumers to "buy now").[6] Notice that all these ad goals depend on consumer reactions to be effective: in Figure 16-2, the equal sign between "Goals" and "Reactions and behaviors" indicates that a perfect operating system (from the advertiser's viewpoint) would result in consumers behaving exactly in accord with the goals of the advertising campaign.

Stage II, **intended message,** begins campaign planning. After settling on specific goals for the campaign, brand managers and the advertising agency must decide on their strategy by which these goals are to be attained. In essence, they must decide on their intended message to be sent to their consumer audience. In making this decision, they may be guided in part by research findings about consumers' interests and present behaviors, as well as by their past experience about what types of advertising messages seem to work well.

Stage III, **actual advertisement,** involves the "encoding" of the message. This stage reflects the "art" of advertising, as the ad agency converts the mental strategy for the campaign into the physical reality of an actual ad, using symbols and symbolism. As we noted earlier, literally thousands of interacting decisions need to be made in this stage, including the exact words, models, colors, actions, music, timing, and so forth. (If you've never had to analyze advertisements from this perspective, you might find it interesting and worthwhile to do so. The next time you're reading a magazine or watching TV, analyze the likely strategy the firm had in mind for the ad, and speculate what each ad might have been like had different decisions been made when converting the strategy into the ad itself.) In conjunction with all these decisions, managers need to select and purchase time or space in specific **channels** (media) to deliver the ads to the target consumer market.

Stage IV, **delivered ads,** turns our attention to the other side of the figure—to consumer reception processes. The first stage here concerns delivery of the ad from the channel to the consumer, including the conditions under which it is received—or whether it is even received—by the target consumer.

Stage V, **perceived message,** concerns the fact that physical delivery of an ad is either accompanied by (in the case of radio or TV) or is followed by (in the case of print) the consumer's mental processing of the ad to yield a perceived message. As we've already discussed in earlier chapters, the mental processes involved in the "decoding" (perception) of an external communication can be quite complex. The *equal sign* between "Intended message" and "Perceived message" indicates that the advertiser wishes consumers to take away exactly the same message as was originally intended to be sent.

Stage VI, **reactions and behaviors,** involves any later thoughts or behaviors that consumers might undertake because of the ad. As we noted earlier, this is an ideal communication system from a brand manager's viewpoint when a consumer's reactions and behaviors match perfectly with the goals that the managers had at the first stage of the system.

ADVERTISING IN REALITY—THE STAIR SYSTEM'S GAPS AND PITFALLS

In reality, of course, advertisers face communication situations that fall far short of the ideal system we just examined. One problem is that it is too inefficient to try to communicate only with a small number of consumers. Instead, the advertiser must strive to communicate effectively with a very large audience comprised of different types of people with different levels and types of interests. Thus an ad that is perfect for Jim Hunt might be neutral for his sister, and even disliked by his parents. Paying to send that ad to Jim's parents and sister is an inefficient step—and one to be avoided if possible.

When we think about the vast differences that exist between consumers, we can see that communication efficiency is a very significant issue for advertisers. It is for this reason that the concept of **market segmentation** is so significant. If the market can be segmented into large subgroups that are appropriate for the product in question, the marketer can create special product versions and advertising campaigns aimed especially at each subgroup and can more directly tailor messages to that group's key interests. Even though segmented advertising can offer major efficiencies, there are still significant challenges that confront our ideal system. In our **STAIR** system, therefore, we highlight five *potential gaps or pitfalls* that can occur: these are depicted in Figure 16-3 (as indicated there, past students have found the acronym "STAIR" to be helpful in recalling the general nature of each challenge).

STAIR system: A framework that highlights five potential gaps, or pitfalls, that can occur in advertising.

Potential Gap 1: Strategic Problems

The **strategy problem pitfall** represents an instance in which *the advertising strategy is not capable of achieving the goals that have been set for the campaign.* This could occur because the goals have been set at an unrealistically high level, because the goals have not been set clearly, or because the strategy chosen (in other words, the intended message) just isn't effective enough to achieve the goals.

Several years ago, for example, Burger King introduced a campaign featuring the theme, "Sometimes You've Gotta Break the Rules," intended to reflect a commitment to going out of its way to provide great service. Franchisees rebelled against the theme of this campaign, however, as they did not feel it would be successful with consumers. As one Burger King operator reported,

The consensus among franchisees is 'Why bother?'.... [it] isn't worth saving, so let's kill it and move on.[7]

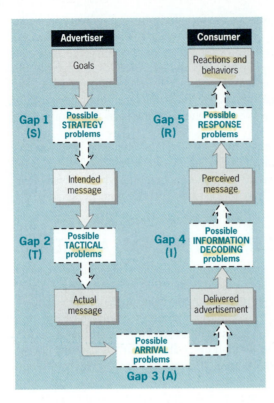

FIGURE 16-3 Advertising's Potential Gaps: The Stair System

Shortly thereafter the executives responsible for this campaign moved to new jobs, and Burger King shifted to a different campaign theme.

Potential Gap 2: Tactical Problems

The **tactical problems gap** recognizes *the thousands of tactical decisions that go together to make up the actual advertising campaign.* This potential gap occurs when the actual advertising does not capture the intended strategy for the campaign, or where there is some type of mistake made in the ad itself. Another Burger King executive commented on this gap as it occurred with an earlier (different) campaign:

> Frankly, I think those commercials may have gotten a bit off track.... Our overall strategy was based on food quality, but you didn't see a lot of food presence in those last commercials.... It's very easy to get off track.[8]

Exhibit 16-1 presents another, pictorial, example of the reality of this gap.

Potential Gap 3: Arrival Problems

The **arrival problems gap** reflects *any difficulties that may occur in the physical transmission or delivery of an ad to the consumer for whom it's intended.* One type of potential problem is whether the physical ad is transmitted in its original form. Static, or audio or video problems, for example, sometimes occur for television ads. Print smears or faulty color reproduction sometimes occur with print ads. In any of these cases (or others,

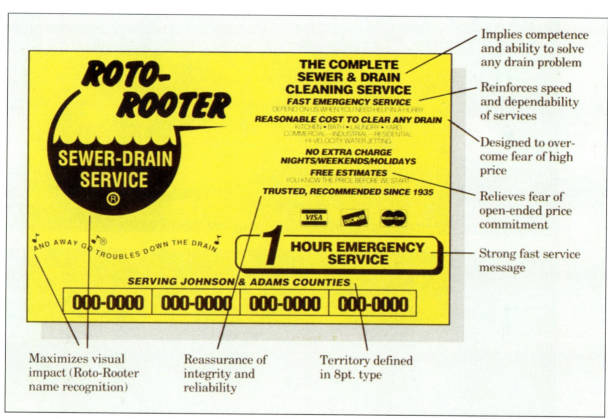

Advertisers should design their copy to achieve particular goals and to address issues that are important to consumers. Here is an interesting research–based analysis of a Roto–Rooter ad prepared by the company for its local affiliates to use in the Yellow Pages for their city.

Advertising campaigns can take quite different paths to success, depending on their circumstances. In the case of raisins, the problem was that many consumers held an image of the fruit as "dull, boring, and wimpy." The development of the "California Raisins" group singing the mega-hit, *Heard it through the Grapevine,* entertained enough consumers that sales reversed their decline and began to "climb." In the case of Stainmaster, the product was a revolutionary improvement, and the problems was to get consumers to pay enough attention to learn about it. Once they did, Stainmaster became one of the all-time new product success stories, as DuPont "cleaned up."

3 customers for Campbell's coming up

Pretty soon now, they'll be good and ready for something good and hot. Make it Campbell's Soup. Campbell's Tomato Soup, or Chicken Noodle, or Vegetable. Nothing else takes the chill out of children quite so fast. Nothing quite so warming tastes so good. And it heats in just 4 minutes.

Soup this good just has to be *Campbell's*

More than 30 kinds
(M'm! M'm! Good!)

Emotion is a powerful consumer motivator. Campbell's research into their "core customer" group—people who love the product—is described on page 107, and explains why this type of approach is so successful in its advertising.

In recent years, spending on promotions has increased at a far faster rate than spending on advertising. Here we see a karaoke display sponsored by Pepsi in a supermarket. Notice that it has garnered a huge amount of display space for the product in a prime floor spot in the store. It's also gaining attention (and product notice) from everyone passing by. It's hard to know exactly what those expressions of the shoppers indicate, however....

An Example of Gap 2 of the System

If This Is Their Best...!

Sometimes advertising deadlines cause problems in local media as well. This happened in one ad run by a car dealership that had the bold headline "Here's Our Best To You!" Obviously an untrained assistant had handled the art, which showed no wheels on the right side of the luxury auto (a different brand than in our mock-up shown here), and some tires on the left that give a new meaning to the term "flat tire" How many autos do you think that ad might have sold?

such as newspapers left out in the morning rain, or children changing channels partway through an ad), the ad that is "delivered" is something less than the ad that was sent. A general term for this phenomenon is *noise,* indicating that the system is not operating in a trouble-free manner.

The other major problem in this sector is whether the ad is actually delivered at all—that is, is there a consumer at the other end who actually receives it? We're all familiar with the days that we're too busy to read some sections of the newspaper, the times our attention is diverted and we miss a highway billboard, and so forth. Studies have shown that this problem can be serious for television ads as well, during program breaks, as viewers get up and leave the room, turn to discussions, and so on. Furthermore, remote controls have aided consumer **zapping,** the practice of flipping channels to check on other programs when a commercial break begins. Research estimates indicate that zapping might be costing a 10–15 percent loss in viewership between programs and commercials, and is especially heavy in wealthier households, those with cable, and during sports event time periods.[9] **Zipping,** or running the VCR on fast forward through commercials, is a less serious problem at present. Overall, we can see that arrival of an ad is not the automatic process that it at first might appear to be. Part of the reason that ads are repeated with such frequency is to overcome the problems with ad delivery.

Zapping: The consumer practice of switcing channels when a commercial begins.

Zipping: The consumer practice of running the VCR on fast forward through commercials.

"We'll be right back after these messages"

Our system's Gap 3 refers to problems in delivering advertising to the consumer audience. TV rating services have trouble measuring actual viewership from minute to minute: one study estimated an audience drop of 20 percent to 40 percent during commercial breaks.

Potential Gap 4: Information Decoding Problems

The **information decoding gap** refers to *any problem that may occur during consumers' perceptions of each ad as it is delivered to them.* Recall that the advertiser's objective here is that the consumer's perceived message be equivalent to the advertiser's intended message. In reality this potential gap stands as a major stumbling block to advertising effectiveness. The first difficulty involves attention: as we noted at the start of the chapter, consumers are exposed to over 100,000 ads in one year, which makes it very hard to gain attention for any one ad. Thus experts are concerned about how an ad can cut through the "clutter" to gain a consumer's attention.

Beyond attention, of course, a successful ad must be processed correctly by the recipient. To decode and interpret a message correctly, for example, consumers must be able to understand its language and symbols as they've been used (encoded) by the sender. (In this regard, you may have heard advertising criticized as being "written for 12-year-olds"; this simplicity of thought, language, and symbolism is largely due to advertisers' wishing to ensure that almost all the mass audience is able to perceive the intended messages correctly.) In addition to *capability* of understanding the message, *motivation* to process it is also important (as we will discuss shortly, consumer low involvement is a common problem). Finally, of course, each consumer's interpretation of the message will depend on exactly which nodes in long-term memory (LTM) are triggered by the ad and are brought into short-term memory (STM) for processing. *Perceptual processes* are thus also central to this area.

Within the working world of advertising, there is daily evidence of this gap. The "miscomprehension" results we explored at the end of Chapter 10 indicate that a shocking 30 percent of communication messages are being misunderstood regularly.

Thus an astute marketer must be aware that there often will be a serious gap between the "ad that's delivered" and the "ad that's perceived" by a consumer.

Potential Gap 5: Response Problems

The **response problems gap** refers to *the advertiser's goal that the perceived message lead to particular reactions on the consumer's part*. This gap involves three distinct and important processes. First, consumers need to *retain* the message after the ad exposure is over. This can be done either by recalling the message itself (that is, by having it stored in an accessible location in LTM) or by having formed a more favorable impression of the brand itself and maintaining this favorable impression in LTM. Second, consumers need to be *influenced* or *persuaded* by the advertising. As we noted in our discussion of ad goals, there are some occasions in which consumers have already been persuaded, and the ads are geared to reminders or purchase precipitation goals. In most cases, however, strong competitive brands are a fact of life facing the advertiser, and consumer persuasion toward your brand is a necessary component of advertising. Third, consumers need to at some point *behave* in the manner advocated by the advertising, usually by purchasing the product. As we saw in Chapter 11's discussion of the attitude-behavior relationship, there are many good reasons why desired consumer response behavior is difficult to achieve.

Thus all advertisers know that effective consumer persuasion and behavior change is a difficult challenge. We can recall (from Chapter 2) that much of this difficulty stems from the nature of our marketing system, which delivers a *total set of ads* that proposes that a consumer buy *all* competing products and services: as consumers, we realize that we thus cannot allow ourselves to be persuaded to buy most of the goods being advertised to us. Further, if an ad attempts to shift us toward a brand or store we already dislike, we're likely to be "hard to sell" on the notion that we should change our behaviors to those recommended by the ad. Across the field of advertising, then, advertisers must expect to encounter *consumer defensiveness* at this stage as a normal course of affairs. The key for a marketer is to restrict these problems to the minimum possible and strive for effective communication with specific target segments.

THE HIERARCHY OF ADVERTISING EFFECTS

As a set, the five potential advertising gaps in our STAIR system present a major challenge for marketers. Notice that slippage at each stage can add up to a large difference between the advertiser's original goals and the actual consumer behavior that ensues. This point can be seen even more clearly if we consider another framework on how advertising works. This was developed by William McGuire, an eminent social psychologist with considerable experience in advising advertisers. It is depicted in Figure 16-4. This system is similar to the general hierarchy of effects model we discussed in Chapter 7 in that the steps are assumed to occur in a specified sequence and failure to achieve any step means that the next step cannot be reached. In brief, McGuire's **hierarchy of advertising effects** requires that (1) the ad be *presented* to a consumer, (2) he or she then *pay attention* to it, (3) it be *comprehended* or understood, (4) it lead to the consumer *yielding* or being persuaded as to the ad's conclusions and recommendations, (5) the persuasion or influence be *retained* over some time span, and finally (6) the overt *purchase behavior* the ad desires is actually taken by the consumer.[10]

Hierarchy of advertising effects: A six-stage framework of the process of advertising influence.

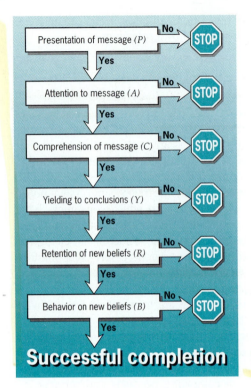

FIGURE 16-4 McGuire's Hierarchy of Advertising Effects

The system is based upon the notion of a **probabilistic linkage** between the stages. This means that success at each stage will occur only for some fraction of consumers in the market and that only these people are still available to move to the next stage. For example, 50 percent of consumers may have a newspaper ad message presented to them: only these 50 percent are then available to the next stage, to pay attention to the ad. Then if the probability of paying attention is also 50 percent, the "probabilistic linkage" of the first two stages will mean that only (0.5 × 0.5 = 0.25) or 25 percent of consumers are available to move on to the third stage in the sequence.

Calculating the Level of Ad Impact

Continuing our example of probabilistic linkage, we simply need to continue to multiply the probabilities for each stage if we want to calculate the overall impact of a *single showing* of the ad on consumers' purchase behavior. To simplify, let's just continue to assume that each stage's probability is 0.5 (that is, that each stage has a 50-50 probability of success with each consumer who gets to it). What is the overall impact of this advertisement? The formula to calculate this is

$$P(\text{purchase}) = P(P) \times P(A) \times P(C) \times P(Y) \times P(R) \times P(B)$$
$$= 0.5 \times 0.5 \times 0.5 \times 0.5 \times 0.5 \times 0.5$$
$$= 0.0156$$

In this example, then, the ad would have a probability of only 1.6 percent of leading to the desired behavior. As several commentators have remarked, this view of advertising leads one to question how it has any effect at all!

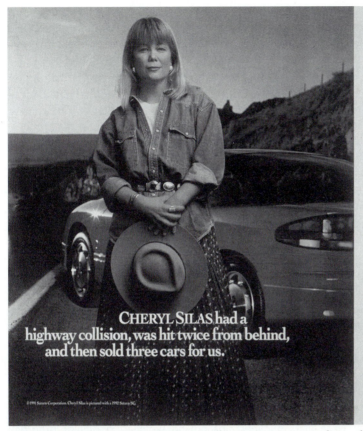

An award-winning caption for the Saturn tells an interesting story, but makes its safety point as well!

Analyzing the Level of Effect

Before leaping to any conclusions, let's recall that our estimate of a 1.6 percent impact resulted from a simplistic assumption of a 50 percent success rate at each stage. Let us consider, however, the following points:

- *The probabilities for the system will differ by product.* For example, we all realize that it's much easier for a consumer to buy a box of cereal than it is to buy a car. This difference means the role of advertising in each product category will differ as well. Ford, for example, is likely to use its ads to stimulate potential buyers to look for Fords on the road and appreciate their better points and to want to visit the Ford dealer to investigate further. The dealers, meanwhile, use local newspaper ads and limited-time offers to stimulate immediate shopping visits. Few sales occur directly from the ads themselves, however, since the role of the salesperson is crucial to "closing" many sales.

- *Our initial assumption of a 0.5 probability for each consumer who reaches a stage is quite unrealistic—it is probably too high.* Thus the realistic probability for the overall system in most product classes is much, much lower than the 1.6 percent we've just calculated. (If you find this hard to accept, try calculating the sales that Ford would get from a single showing of an ad for a $15,000 model if the ad reached 10 million adults. Then extend your analysis by multiplying your results for only 10 showings of this ad and apply these results to all ads for all models of all brands of automobiles.)

- *The probabilities for the system's stages are almost certainly not equal.* It is much easier for an advertiser to obtain consumer exposure than consumer attention, for example, and either of these stages is much easier to obtain than consumer purchase behavior. Further, the probability for a stage's success depends on the ad itself.

- *Repetition's effects will change some of the probabilities within the system.* During the second, third, and subsequent times we are exposed to an ad, we are able to draw upon our LTM to help recall parts of it and to anticipate what will be coming. In this way a consumer might move through the hierarchy's stages over time, as probabilities for later stages slowly increase. (Of course, repetition won't continue to work positively forever.)

- *Finally, these probabilities need to be applied to the huge consumer market.* This means that even a small probability can lead to a large sales volume and high profits. Thus, if we are able to improve the probabilities by even a few percentage points, this can mean very large increases in sales and profits.

HOW STRONG ARE ADVERTISING'S IMPACTS?

Our coverage of both the STAIR system gaps and McGuire's hierarchy of advertising suggests that ads may not actually be nearly as powerful on one exposure as we may have thought. In this section we'll briefly examine two important studies on what actually happens with consumer ads.

The Starch Study of TV Commercials

A number of years ago a leading advertising research firm, Daniel Starch, Inc., made waves in the advertising community when it publicized the results of a special research study it had run on what consumers take away from commercials. Within this study, consumers were first "qualified" as having watched particular programs within two hours before being questioned in the study. All consumers had thus had their ads "delivered" in the terms of our ideal system and were "presented" according to McGuire's framework. Out of every 100 audience members, how many would you think remembered having seen the average commercial?_____ With respect to the intended message, what percentage could correctly answer "What brand was advertised?"_____ How frequently did a consumer come up with an incorrect brand name to this question?_____ After providing your estimates, you may wish to check the brief description of the study's findings in Note 11 in the listings for Chapter 16 at the back of the book.

The Gallup & Robinson Study of Ad Effectiveness

Gallup & Robinson (G & R), another leading advertising research firm, examined its research findings for several years on all ads in five different product categories (autos, tires, men's colognes, television sets, and insurance). For each ad, consumers were again qualified as having either read the magazine or viewed the TV program within which the test ad was contained. Rather than two hours after exposure, however, G & R conducted its interviews the day following ad exposure (this technique is often termed **24-hour recall**).

Results varied widely based on which ad was studied. One key measure, for example, is *registration of the featured idea* in an ad. This measure ranged from 0 percent for several ads (that is, not one consumer could remember any point from a particular ad to which they'd been exposed a day earlier) to a high of 39 percent registration for one auto ad that had appeared in a magazine. The highest average rate was 10 percent for television ads in the cologne product class, while the lowest rate was for insurance ads appearing in magazines, which averaged only 3 percent registration. In numbers, these findings indicated, for example, that of 5462 viewers of a TV commercial for tires, an average of only 300 (5.5 percent) would recall the key point of the commercial by the next day.[12]

CONTROVERSY: IS THE HIERARCHY THE ONLY WAY?

Before leaving the topic of advertising's persuasive aspects we should note that controversies exist in this area. As we discussed, no one entirely understands how advertising works its influences on consumer behavior. It is not surprising, therefore, that the hierarchy will have some limitations in its explanations.

One area in which this point is particularly raised is in respect to low involvement, which we've discussed earlier in the book. Michael Ray, a recognized expert on marketing communication, has suggested that low-involvement situations change the order of the hierarchy's stages from a "think-feel-do" order into a "think-do-feel" ordering.[13] In terms of Figure 16-4, this would mean that consumers won't pay enough attention to ads to *yield* to their conclusions. Instead, ads in low-involvement situations work by skipping the yielding stage and focusing their low-intensity effects on the retention and behavior stage probabilities. Rather than having an immediate impact within a single exposure, moreover, these effects build up slowly over a long time period and many repetitions of the ad. Toward the end of this longer time frame, the consumer knows the brand name and knows it's heavily advertised, but doesn't feel strongly one way or another about the brand itself.

How would the alternative think-do-feel hierarchy work in the real consumer setting? Let's assume that Donna Smith, as she stands in a drugstore, sees a display for Creemo face cream, recalls that she's seen this brand advertised a lot, and decides to "try it" and see how it works. Only after she brings it home and uses it will she commit herself to a positive or negative feeling about the brand and either "yield" or "not yield" to the Creemo ad's statements about the brand.

When the low-involvement situation is operating, implications for advertising strategy will be different from those when the traditional hierarchy is at work. According to Ray, some conditions leading to the low-involvement situation are (1) little differences in the brands of the product class (a so-called "parity product" situation), (2) a mature stage of a product life cycle (that is, most brands have been in the market for quite a while, and consumers are aware of this fact), and (3) heavy use of advertising in the mass media.

Recent research has investigated several interesting aspects of the low-involvement hierarchy approach. According to Andrew Ehrenberg, a leading researcher in England, advertising is usually "a weak, reinforcing influence on consumers rather than a strong persuasive influence." It increases awareness and interest, suggests trial, and reinforces the feelings of satisfaction after purchase.[14] William Wells, a senior advertising research executive, points out that advertising can also have a special type of **transformational effect** on consumers: it can help them to look for certain effects from a brand and can thereby change (transform) the experiences they have following purchase and use.[15] For example, this is often the case with a status symbol or with a performance automobile.

In addition to these insights, a significant amount of recent research attention has been given to two frameworks on how advertising works: the "elaboration likelihood model" and "attitude toward the ad." We shall discuss each briefly.

Transformational effect: One possible ad impact: consumers anticipate and thereby change the use experiences they have.

THE ELABORATION LIKELIHOOD MODEL (ELM)

Elaboration likelihood model (ELM): An advertising effects framework featuring two paths of persuasion: the central route and the peripheral route.

The **elaboration likelihood model (ELM),** developed by John Cacioppo and Richard Petty, has had a major impact on recent research on consumer behavior and advertising.[16] This interesting model stresses the view that *the process of persuasion will be fundamentally different when consumers elaborate on an ad than when they do not.* **Elaboration** in this model refers to *thinking about the information* provided in the advertising message.

Figure 16-5 presents a simple version of the basic ideas in this model. Notice that two basic paths to persuasion are possible, the *central route* and the *peripheral (or outside) route.* The **central route to persuasion** reflects the consumer who pays attention to the major points or arguments made by the ad, thinks about (*elaborates on*) the ad, and strengthens or changes his or her attitude toward the brand (notice that this is exactly the type of process we have been assuming in our earlier discussions of attitude models, hierarchy models, and high-involvement processes).

Often, however, a consumer is not motivated to think very much about what an ad has to say about a brand, or may not be able to devote careful attention (because of distractions in the room, for example). Interestingly, the ELM suggests that this ad still might be effective, but in a different way—through the **peripheral route to persuasion.** As shown in Figure 16-5, the peripheral (or "outside") route involves little or no thinking about the ad's arguments about the brand: instead the consumer attends to other aspects of the ad, including the scenery, music, and so forth. In addition, other elements also can act as *cues,* such as the credibility of the source, his or her attractiveness, the number (not quality) of the arguments presented, and so forth. The result is that the consumer may have some positive attitudinal change toward the brand, but it is not likely to be as strong or persisting as that formed by the central route.

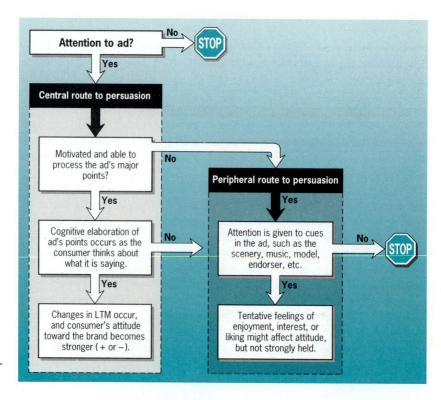

FIGURE 16-5 Central versus Peripheral Processing: A Basic Look

As we noted earlier, one of the major determinants of which route—central or peripheral—will be taken is consumer involvement. When involvement is high, the central route is more likely, but when it is low, the peripheral route is more apt to be operating. Since ads can be successful with either route, it is important to learn which mode is likely to be operating for our ads. If an advertiser knows that most consumers will be in low-involvement states when they're exposed to ads for his or her brand, wouldn't he or she be better off *to design ads to appeal specifically to this peripheral mode of processing?* If so, what would these ads contain? Perhaps lots of action, color, sound, sex appeal, and fast movement, with rapid cuts from one scene to the next to preserve attention? Music and dancing? Moods and appeals to emotions? As you think about these issues, you may wish to turn on the TV and observe how commercials for low-involvement products are being constructed these days! (If you would like to read more about the extensive research on ELM, you may wish to begin with the readings in Note 16.)

"ATTITUDE TOWARD THE AD"

This term designates a separate but closely related stream of research to ELM. The concept of **attitude toward the ad (A/ad)** was proposed in 1981 by Terence Shimp and, in a separate article, Andrew Mitchell and Jerry Olson.[17] Their major point was that, when watching or reading an ad, *consumers have reactions to the ad itself.* Thus there are two attitudes of interest related to advertising: the attitude toward the brand and the attitude toward the ad. For example, it is quite possible for a consumer to enjoy an ad greatly but to have a neutral attitude toward the sponsor's brand.

> **Attitude toward the ad (A/ad):** A consumer's evaluations of a particular advertisement.

The concept of creating ads that consumers will enjoy is of course nothing new—ad agencies have been measuring detailed viewer reactions to ads for years. Recently, moreover, a major industry study revealed that "liking" an ad is a strong predictor of its effectiveness.[18] What is important about the A/ad approach, however, is that it asks, "What *exact role* does a consumer's affective reaction to a commercial play in his or her larger intentions to purchase the product?" That is, does A/ad affect the attitude toward the brand, or does A/ad affect buying behavior directly? If the first explanation is true, we're likely to like brands more because we like their commercials. If the second explanation is true, we're more likely to buy brands because we like their commercials.

In each case there are further issues that are important to advertisers. Research in this area is quite complex, as it attempts to "tease out" subtle forms of effects, such as which exact aspects of ads lead to effective changes in brand attitudes or purchasing behavior. As we might expect, early research on A/ad has indicated that its impact is likely to be greatest when consumers are in low-involvement processing modes. In these instances (which reflect ELM's peripheral persuasion route), consumers are likely to process little of the substance of an ad's message about a brand, but are more attuned to other aspects that might capture their casual attention and interest. (If you would like to read more about developments in this topic, you may wish to begin with the readings in Notes 17 and 18.)

THE GROWING ROLE OF PROMOTIONS AND "INTEGRATED MARKETING"

One key message from our discussion of advertising's influence is that a single ad exposure is apt to have only a low-level impact on the audience. Over time and repetitions, however, advertising does seem to "cumulate" its effect. Thus there appears to be a *long-term impact from advertising* to consumers. In recent years, however, U.S. business has faced increased pressures for *short-term impact*. Stock investors want increased profits. New brand managers want to make their mark quickly. How do we attain short-term impact on consumers? "*Use sales promotions* !" is the increasing answer.

Coupons, refunds, premiums or gifts, samples, cents-off specials, and sweepstakes are all popular forms of consumer promotion. Because they are aimed directly at short-term impacts on consumers' buying behavior, sales promotions can offer advantages in measuring effectiveness and in creating a quick jump in business for the successful firm. Also, of course, they are popular with consumers:

❧ *Raisin' Their Sales at Hardee's*

"It was beyond our wildest dreams," reports the executive in charge of the California raisin figurine promotion run by Hardee's hamburger chain. Each of four Claymation "grapevine" dancers was sold for 99 cents to customers at Hardee's. The tie-in was with the firm's cinnamon and raisin biscuits for breakfast, an area in which Hardee's wanted higher sales. The campaign's goal was for a 5 percent sales increase for the promotional month. The results: sales increased by 18 percent, with some outlets reporting 30 percent jumps. The figurines have become collectibles and are now commanding hefty prices on resale![19]

While many promotions work well with consumers, some marketers are concerned about putting too heavy a reliance on them. When auto brands offer rebates, sales go up, but when the rebate ends, sales drop as consumers wait for the next round. Similarly, sweepstakes may make an impact, but do not build consumer loyalty. Also, couponing—which actually represents price competition—may threaten to

As detailed in the accompanying story, the Hardee's Raisin promotion was a grape success!

If You Know The Code, You Can Double Your Volume In Days.

0-65779-76943

Looking for an instant sales spike? Checkout Coupon turns the UPC code into your own exclusive volume-building tool. First, our retail merchandising tie-ins let shoppers know about your Checkout Coupon promotion. Store ads, shelf talkers, and in-store posters alert consumers before the purchase to the special offers, and motivate them to buy now. Using scanner data from the checkstand, Checkout Coupon identifies those shoppers buying your product. Only then do we reward them. Guaranteeing you performance before you provide the incentive.

When you control the code, you reach over 80 million shoppers at the nation's best retailers. Let us show you how the Catalina Marketing Network can do volumes for your brand. Call Catalina Marketing Corporation, (800) 955-9770.

CHECKOUT COUPON
FROM CATALINA MARKETING CORPORATION

© 1993 Catalina Marketing Corporation.

An ad directed to marketers, explaining the ways a promotional program can help them.

lower average prices for branded products. In the longer run, "brand equity" might be threatened. In general, then, marketers are seeking a proper balance between the short run and the long run: it appears that both promotions and advertising have important roles to play. According to Procter & Gamble's chairman,

> Think of advertising and promotion as exercise and recreation. Advertising is exercise. It's something you need and it provides long-term benefits, but it's awfully easy to either cut or postpone because there's no immediate penalty for not exercising...[but] if you want your brand to be fit, it's got to exercise regularly.[20]

Integrated marketing: A planned program that unifies all activities in promoting a product.

These developments have led to an increasing stress on **integrated marketing,** which actually refers to creating promotional programs that integrate traditional advertising, packaging, in-store promotions, direct mail, direct response, database marketing, consumer promotions, and so forth. This has been a hotly debated topic recently in the advertising industry, as agencies have begun to change their organizational structures around this new approach. Further, the availability of detailed data from computerized checkout scanning systems has begun to allow specific tests of how well both advertising and sales promotions work. To learn more about developments in this fast-moving area, you may wish to begin with the readings in Notes 21 and 22.

■ CONTROLLING THE INSTITUTION OF ADVERTISING

As we noted at the very start of this chapter, advertising is a huge and important institution in our society. At the same time, since millions of private businesses are active in placing their ads into the larger environment, *advertising in our society is ultimately an uncontrollable activity.* This will continue to be the case unless government would begin to engage in the types of widespread censorship and restrictions that are viewed as unacceptable in a market-based economic system that prizes freedom of speech. Appendix 16A details many of the key issues and debates concerning the social and economic roles of advertising. In this section we will concentrate on how the institution itself is monitored.

GOVERNMENT REGULATION OF ADVERTISING

In Chapter 20, we discuss in some detail the nature of government regulation of marketing, especially that by the Federal Trade Commission (FTC). As noted there, the FTC has long been criticized for being either too harsh or too soft in its regulatory activities and has shifted directions several times. Recently, for example, we saw an era of deregulation in which the FTC and other agencies cut back significantly on their regulatory efforts. Marketers realize, however, that if advertising abuses become widespread, or if opponents of advertising become sufficiently powerful, the government is likely to turn around and move against the advertising industry with restrictions and regulations.

The threat of governmental interference provides one reason for leaders in advertising to seek ways to control the quality of advertising. Beyond this, advertising leaders realize that negative practices breed consumer cynicism and lead to lower effectiveness of all advertising. Finally, many people in the industry are personally angered by ad practices that they believe are at or beyond the edge of ethics, fairness, or taste (for example, an industry trade publication, *Advertising Age,* frequently includes an "Ads We Can Do Without" feature in its "Letters to the Editor" column). For all these reasons, the advertising industry has sought to supplement government regulation with its own programs of self-regulation.

SELF-REGULATION IN ADVERTISING

Advertising industry codes: Guidelines and standards for advertising practices.

Advertising industry codes represent a common basis for industry self-regulation. It is helpful to have guidelines for developing advertising campaigns. Industry trade associations representing advertisers, agencies, media, and research firms all regularly publish codes of ethics and guidelines for their members to follow voluntarily. Many firms also publish their own policies for advertising.

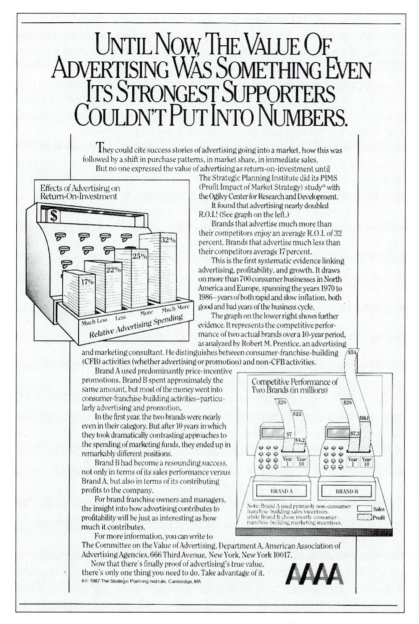

Increasing pressures for short-term sales increases from consumer promotions have led the advertising community to expend further efforts to study and publicize how advertising works. This ad, aimed at the marketing community, explains advertising's contributions to a firm's return on investment (ROI).

Advertising approval processes often also exist for each advertising campaign. Most large advertisers and ad agencies, for example, follow a formal "approval" process for ads after the storylines have been developed by the marketing department and ad agency (but before expensive production has taken place). This process usually includes approval, in writing, by the public relations department, technical departments, and top management. In addition, the legal department will typically go over the ads carefully and ask for revisions when they feel they may be needed.

Media clearance procedures follow the internal reviews at the agency and firm. Advertising must be submitted to the media for "clearance" before it will be accepted. Television networks are probably the most severe in attempting to adhere to high standards in clearing their commercials. The broadcast standards department at CBS,

Advertising approval processes: Internal steps at firms and ad agencies to review, modify, and approve ads prior to release.

Media clearance procedures: Review and modification requests by media before acceptance of an ad.

for example, reviewed over 30,000 commercials in a recent year and raised objections to over 11,000 of them, primarily on the basis of poor taste or lack of substantiation. When this occurs, the advertiser must reach agreement with the network on changes to be made before the ad will be cleared to be run. Some magazines also take pride in their standards and clearance procedures (*Good Housekeeping* employs a seal of approval for products advertised in its pages, for example), while others are more lax. Newspapers, on the other hand, often face short lead times because of the specific dates for retail sale ads and must employ clearance processes that are less comprehensive.[23]

The **advertising self-regulatory system** was created as a further check by the business community since the three prior stages are not sufficient to remove all potential difficulties from a huge market-based activity with competitive and persuasive aims. If problems arise after an ad has appeared, the logical alternatives are that it be handled either through public means (either the courts or the government's regulatory system) or private means (an agreement is reached between a consumer and a firm, or between two competitors, or the firm decides to modify its advertising with the help of a neutral third party). When an industry sets up a continuing arrangement to encourage such private means of dispute settlement, it is said to be engaging in self-regulation. Self-regulation must be voluntary and, therefore, depends on the cooperation of the firms in the industry.

🐚 *The NAD/NARB System*

NAD/NARB system: A very successful program of industry self-regulation: companies agree to have complaints about their ads heard by two groups.

Since 1971, the advertising industry has had its own **NAD/NARB system**—a very successful program of self-regulation. The system consists of two agencies—the National Advertising Division (NAD) and the National Advertising Review Board (NARB). NAD is the first stage of the system and acts as its investigatory arm. The NAD collects and evaluates data concerning the ad, and arrives at an initial decision as to whether the claims in the ad have been substantiated or not. If the NAD feels the ad is not satisfactory, it negotiates with the advertiser to have the campaign modified or discontinued. Cases that cannot be resolved at the NAD are appealed to the NARB and are heard by a panel of five "judges" from firms, ad agencies, and the public sector. If the NARB then cannot resolve the matter (an extremely rare event), the case may be referred to the government or court system.

Self-regulatory cases arise from several sources. The NAD has its own monitoring program, which initiates many inquiries to firms about their advertising claims. Local Better Business Bureaus also forward complaints to the NAD: these account for about one in every six cases. Individual consumers may, and do, institute complaints to the NAD: these account for about one in eight cases. Finally, competitors may complain about advertising they perceive to be harmful to their interests. In recent years this has increased dramatically, to about 40 percent of the cases. Several thousand cases have now been heard by the self-regulatory system. In about half these cases the NAD determined that the ad claims are reasonable and had been substantiated. In almost all remaining cases, the advertiser voluntarily agreed to either modify or discontinue the campaign. Only 2 percent of the cases were appealed to the NARB, sometimes by the NAD (because it could not reach agreement with the advertiser) and sometimes by the original complainant, who was displeased with the NAD's decision in the matter.[24]

According to industry observers and government regulators alike, the advertising self-regulation program has been extremely successful. It has shifted many cases from the antagonistic setting of government proceedings and has speeded up the processing of these cases (the average case concludes in six months, as opposed to several years in government proceedings). While not solving all the problems that advertising faces on its social dimensions, this system should be credited with helping to improve the character of consumer advertising in our society.

■ SUMMARY

WHAT'S INVOLVED IN ADVERTISING DECISIONS?

This chapter has dealt with the influences of advertising on consumer behavior. Advertising is a major industry in our nation, comprising about 3 percent of GNP. The two chief actors—marketers and consumers—are here arrayed as *senders and receivers of messages.* Marketers control the basic decisions about the advertising that is distributed, while consumers control their reactions to it.

In the first section of the chapter we briefly examined the complex nature of advertising decisions. The *7 M's framework* is useful in this regard. The first six factors—*merchandise, markets, motives, messages, money,* and *media*—all contribute to the overall impact of an ad, while the seventh factor—*measurement*—attempts to monitor and refine this impact through research.

We then examined a basic model of advertising as a *one-way flow* of communication. Four elements are present in the simple model: the *source* of the communication develops a *message* and then delivers it through a *channel* to the *receiver.* Unlike most other communications, advertising as a one-way communication flow has certain disadvantages and certain advantages.

THE PERSUASIVE ASPECT OF ADVERTISING

The second section focused on the *persuasive nature of advertising impacts.* Here we examined a staged "ideal" framework. First, marketers need to set advertising goals. Possible goals could be to persuade, to reinforce, to remind, or to stimulate an immediate purchase. Next, the advertising goals must be translated into an intended message, or a strategy for the ad campaign. Third, the intended message must be developed into an actual advertisement. Designing the actual ad entails going through thousands of interacting decisions on art and execution. Fourth, the ad must be delivered to the consumer, via planned channels. Fifth, the consumer takes away a perceived message from the communication. In the final stage, the consumer's reactions and behaviors occur.

We noted, however, that in reality the system does not work so smoothly. Here we introduced our *STAIR system* of potential gaps or pitfalls with advertising. These involved possible (S) strategy problems, (T) tactics problems, (A) arrival problems with message delivery, (I) information decoding problems by consumers, and (R) response shortfalls in terms of the actual reactions and behaviors consumers exhibit in response to our ad. Thus we see that advertising is indeed complex and challenging!

The chapter next presented a related *hierarchy of advertising effects model* that concentrates on consumers' reactions to advertising. A consumer must first be *exposed* to an ad, must *pay attention* to it, and must *understand* it. The ad must lead to the consumer being *persuaded,* and such persuasion must be *retained* over time and should lead to *purchase behavior* as advocated by the ad. According to this model, an effective ad must take the consumer through all these stages. Our analysis showed that the probability of success with a single advertisement is indeed very small. However, we need to remember that these probabilities depend on the type of product and amount of repetition and may differ for each stage of the model. Further, in a mass consumer market, even a minute probability translates into a large volume of sales dollars. We also noted why the "low-involvement" (think-do-feel) hierarchy may be a better model for some product classes.

Our next analyses focused on two recent research topics about persuasion. First, the *elaboration likelihood model (ELM)* points out that some ads are effective through their arguments about the brand (the *central route to persuasion*), while others are effective through other cues they contain (e.g., music, scenery, favorable endorser), to which consumers respond favorably: this is the *peripheral route to persuasion.* A second recent research topic—*attitude toward the ad (A/ad)*—relates to this by studying exactly how a consumer's liking of an ad will translate into more favorable buying behavior. Our final topic in this section discussed the major shifts recently in the role of advertising in consumer marketing. Basically, we saw that the stress of short-term influences on consumer behavior has increased *sales promotions* by marketers and has led to a growing trend toward *integrated marketing.*

CONTROLLING THE INSTITUTION OF ADVERTISING

The chapter concluded with a discussion of the various organizations and codes that have been created to control the institution of advertising. Some are governmental, but most have arisen within the industry itself. We saw how these programs have helped to improve the character of advertising directed to consumers in our society.

Appendix 16A moves beyond this coverage to present a broader look at the subject of advertising's influence on consumers. The economic and social roles for advertising are topics of heated debates. The basic positions are summarized in this interesting and thought-provoking appendix. Meanwhile, Appendix 16B should be consulted by readers interested in learning more about advertising decision making, as it summarizes some findings and provides useful guides for further reading.

■ KEY TERMS

7 M's
one-way communication flow
source
receiver
channel
hypodermic needle approach
advertising goals
persuasion
reinforcement
reminder
purchase precipitation
intended message
actual advertisement
channels

delivered ads
perceived message
reactions and behaviors
market segmentation
STAIR system
strategy problem pitfall
tactical problems gap
arrival problems gap
zapping
zipping
information decoding gap
response problems gap
hierarchy of advertising effects
probabilistic linkage

24-hour recall
transformational effect
elaboration likelihood model (ELM)
elaboration
central route to persuasion
peripheral route to persuasion
attitude toward the ad (A/ad)
integrated marketing
advertising industry codes
advertising approval processes
media clearance procedures
advertising self-regulatory system
NAD/NARB system

■ APPENDIX 16A TERMS

barrier to entry   market power school   information school

■ APPENDIX 16B TERMS

source credibility   trustworthiness   expertise   attractiveness   receivers   comparison advertising

■ REVIEW QUESTIONS AND EXPERIENTIAL EXERCISES

[E = Application extension or experiential exercise]

1. Compare/contrast how the one-way model of communication (Figure 16-1), if applied to family or salesperson influences on consumer behavior, would change the nature of these communications. Which is a more effective marketing tool, advertising or salespersons?

2. Consider the four basic types of advertising goals described in the text. Analyze a number of ads, searching for two examples of each type of goal.

3. Consider the "potential gaps" in the STAIR system of advertising (Figure 16-3). Which would you say is the most frequent? Which is most serious?

4. Humor is an approach used in advertising. How frequently is this employed? Do you believe it is effective? Why or why not?

5. Indicate at what stage of the "hierarchy of advertising effects" model (Figure 16-4) you are currently located for the following products or services. Provide rationale.

   a. Charmin   d. Gerber pudding

   b. Rolling Rock   e. Subaru

   c. Butter Buds   f. American Express

6. One of the basic propositions in Appendix 16B states that advertising effects depend on source, message, and media factors as well as on the receiver. Of the first three, which would you judge is usually the most significant? Why? Provide examples.

7. How do the two major schools of economics (discussed in Appendix 16A) differ in their answers to the questions of advertising's effects on prices and on competition (as an entry barrier)? Which side do you tend to favor?

8. Many social criticisms of advertising are listed in Appendix 16A. Which, if any, do you find to be either completely in error or lacking justification? Which, if any, do you find you agree with?

9. [E] During recent years movements arose to ban advertising for certain products. Develop a brief, well-designed set of arguments either for or against the following proposal: "Broadcast advertising for beer and wine should be banned."

10. [E] Use your library to locate back issues of the *Journal of Advertising Research* and the *Journal of Advertising*. Write a brief report summarizing the topics discussed and a few of your best findings from the articles.

11. [E] Refer to the citations listed in Notes 16, 17, and 18 to locate recent articles on the elaboration likelihood model and/or "attitude toward the ad." Read several of these and write a brief report on your findings.

12. [E] Using the listings in Notes 21 and 22 or the business reference index at your library, locate and read several articles on such topics as the increasing use of sales promotions, returns to advertising, or the growth of "integrated marketing." Write a brief report on your findings.

13. [E] Select one of the four factors—source, message, media, and receiver—discussed in Appendix 16B. Using the relevant note listings at the back of this book or material in the reference section of your library, read several key articles on the subject. Write a brief report on your findings.

14. [E] Review a series of magazine ads, analyzing each in terms of the advertising systems shown in Figures 16-2 and 16-3. Cut out several examples of what you believe are especially good or bad ads. For each, present a brief analysis of your position, pointing out any "gaps" that you may have found.

15. [E] Interview a manager or copywriter for an ad agency. Discuss, in detail, the process of creating and placing an ad. Write a brief report on your findings.

16. [E] To gain a better understanding of your local advertising scene, arrange to interview a manager or a sales representative for a local television or radio station, newspaper, or Yellow Pages directory. Ask about their views of how advertising works in their medium versus their competitors, what the relative costs are, which businesses get best results from which type of media, and what trends are occurring in the market. Write a brief report summarizing your findings.

■ SUGGESTED READING

■ Because advertising and promotion is such a huge area, there is a wealth of material available in trade publications, in the general business press, and in journals devoted to this area. It is worthwhile to ask your reference librarian for a brief introduction to what sources are actually available: if you haven't yet done this, you'll be shocked! With respect to specific suggestions, this author would recommend a leisurely scan through the Note listings for this chapter: this alone will go far in indicating the many interesting issues in this field, as well as highlighting some specific articles on topics of interest. Beyond this, you may find the article by Deborah J. MacInnis, Christine Moorman, and Bernard J. Jaworski, "Enhancing and Measuring Con-

sumers' Motivation, Opportunity, and Ability to Process Brand Information from Ads," *Journal of Marketing,* October 1991, pp. 42–53 to be helpful in integrating a number of consumer behavior concepts into managerial implications. For background, see Josh McQueen, "The Different Ways Ads Work," *Journal of Advertising Research,* Vol. 30, No. 4 (August/September 1990), pp. RC13–RC16. For results of a significant industry project on ad effectiveness, see Russell I. Haley and Allen Baldinger, "The ARF Copy Research Validation Project," *Journal of Advertising Research,* Vol. 31, No. 2 (1991), pp. 11–32. Again, however, the Notes will provide many fine leads for further reading on topics of special interest.

Appendix 16A

ECONOMIC AND SOCIAL ISSUES IN ADVERTISING

As we've stressed throughout the chapter, advertising is essentially a business function. It is planned and run as an integral part of the marketing mix. The benefits that flow from advertising are typically economic and are planned to go to the sponsor of the ads. As potential business managers of advertising, this is the proper view for us to take of this topic. However, when we move *beyond the single firm* to consider advertising from a broader viewpoint, we find debates about its social and economic character in our society. Within this appendix we'll begin with the economic dimensions; then we'll turn to social criticisms.

Economic Debates on Advertising

Prominent economists, advertising leaders, and public policymakers are divided on how well advertising performs its economic roles. Among the questions that are debated are:

■ Is advertising a barrier to entry?

■ Does advertising raise or lower prices?

Advertising and Barriers to Entry

A **barrier to entry** is something that hinders a potential competitor from entering a product class and competing for sales in it. Large plant investments, lack of access to raw materials, or inability to gain retail shelf space are examples of entry barriers. With respect to advertising, the barriers to entry debate concerns the effects that advertising has on competition within a product class. The data are clear that (1) firms with higher shares of market tend also to have higher shares of advertising expenditures and (2) firms with higher profits also tend to advertise more. The question is "Why?" Does advertising by large firms act to keep out other, smaller firms who may have

superior products? If so, advertising would be acting in an anticompetitive manner.

It is important to note that this need not be a result of a conscious effort by a large company to act in an anticompetitive manner. For example, the economics of advertising tend to work in favor of size, as fixed costs of production can be spread over more exposures and volume discounts are typically available from the media. Also, for some media (especially national television), the lowest levels of money necessary to gain exposure can be quite high (e.g., $300,000 for a 30-second spot in prime time). These amounts are well within the ability of large firms to afford but may be risky for the financial health of a smaller firm.

The actions of channel members and consumers might also serve to make advertising a barrier to entry by new firms. For example, since retailers are interested in giving their valuable shelf space only to brands they are confident will be quickly purchased, a smaller firm may be less able to convince wholesalers and retailers that the new product will be in demand. Consumers, of course, lie at the heart of this issue, as a function of how receptive they are to trying new entries to the market. If consumers are willing to buy only heavily advertised brands, for example, new firms will have a more difficult time in successfully offering their products.

Economists who believe that advertising has these types of effects often belong to the **market power school** of thought. They stress advertising's *persuasive aspects* and believe that successful advertising often contributes to increasing industry concentration in which a few firms come to form an oligopoly to dominate production and sales. In the brewing industry, for example, hundreds of local and regional beer brands have gone out of business as Budweiser, Miller, and a few other major brands have come to dominate the market.

Economists who reject these effects from advertising often belong to the **information school** of thought. They argue that the situation is just the opposite—that advertising actually acts to ease the path of a new competitor's entry into the market. They stress that advertising offers *information* to consumers, who are free to choose whether to buy or not. If the product is worthwhile, consumers will try it and will return for more in the future. Advertising is an efficient way of informing consumers about new offerings and can offer handsome returns to firms that are willing to invest in it, even if they have to borrow to do so. The fact that firms with a higher share of the market advertise more, then, indicates to this school that these firms are offering a product that the public values.

As you may know from a course in economics, detailed answers to the questions raised in these debates require advanced quantitative analyses of the special conditions of each case. Even then, the opposing sides are likely to continue to disagree. (If you are not familiar with these types of arguments, or would like to read more about them, Note 25 provides a good place to begin.)

Advertising's Effects on Prices

"Does advertising raise or lower prices to consumers?" This interesting question again raises arguments among the experts. Here the data are clear that consumers pay higher prices for advertised brands than for those not advertised, that retailers also pay higher prices for these brands, and that advertisers have to pay to create and place their ads. For all these reasons, it would appear that advertising would act to *raise* consumer prices, since "Someone has to pay for it!"

Members of the market power school support this concern about higher prices coming from heavy advertising in an industry. Because they stress advertising's persuasive aspects, they see advertising as creating an inelastic demand curve for a brand (through consumers' building a preference and loyalty for that brand and being willing to pay higher prices for it). If this is based on "image" rather than performance factors—as it may be in the case of some beer brands, for example—then consumers would be paying more than they otherwise would have to if advertising were less significant in the industry.

Also, when primary demand (total unit sales for the entire product class) is dropping, logic indicates that high advertising expenditures cannot be returning increased unit sales to all advertisers. The cigarette industry, for example, spends over $2 billion per year in promotional activities, even though its sales are falling as more people quit smoking for health reasons. For at least some of the brands, then, advertising represents an added cost in the losing fight for increased sales and helps to keep prices higher than they otherwise would be.

Members of the information school again hold just the opposite views. They point out that advertising is often a very efficient means of creating a mass market for a product, by communicating with large numbers of consumers at a low cost per person. When successful, this affords a much larger sales base for the firm. This larger base usually lowers per unit costs for materials, production, distribution, and overhead because of efficiencies associated with higher volumes. In turn, these lower costs allow the firm to *lower* the price for the product, even though the advertising's cost is included in the selling price. Also, since this school believes that advertising helps new competitors to enter the market, it sees markets with heavy advertising to be quite competitive, with constant competitive pressures to either lower prices or improve products to gain market share and increase profits.

Implications for Public Policy

Thus each side has strong grounds for holding its positions, and the debates continue. These are not just irrelevant debates, however. Depending on the answers, public policymakers should take different positions on how advertising should be treated. For example, should there be certain conditions under which advertising should not be tax deductible as a business expense? Are there market conditions under which a cap should be placed on the amount of advertising that an industry is allowed? Should utilities be allowed to charge customers for the advertising they do? These debates occur at both the federal and state government levels and are often very heated. Since millions of dollars are typically involved in these decisions, the stakes are high, and economic debates on advertising are sure to continue far into the future.

Social Dimensions of Advertising

Almost everyone has opinions about advertising, ranging from aspects that we like to those that we dislike most intensely. Some of the most important opinions relate to broader social and economic concerns about advertising. Within this section we'll briefly examine some of the questions and controversies involving advertising's role in our society.

What Do Consumers Like and Dislike About Advertising?

In a famous study of advertising in America, two leading experts, Raymond Bauer and Stephen Greyser, asked consumers about their views of this institution, including what they liked and disliked. When asked why they like advertising, many points emerged:

The Consumers' View: Pros and Cons

1. A majority of consumers mentioned first the *information* that advertising provides. Consumers reported that ads help them to understand products better, learn about new products and services, and help them to stay current about prices and specials.

2. *Economic* reasons were also mentioned by about one in five persons—these reflect appreciation of the roles that advertis-

ing plays in providing employment to many workers and in contributing to lowering prices for mass-market products.

3. *Entertainment* was also recognized, in two ways. First, some consumers mentioned that they liked some of the humorous, warm, and exciting ads themselves. Second, some consumers expressed appreciation for advertising subsidizing television, radio, newspapers, and magazines and lowering the costs of these media.

When asked what they disliked about advertising, consumers in the Bauer and Greyser study also raised a number of criticisms:

1. The most frequently mentioned objection was the *intrusiveness*—advertising was seen as "intruding" on our lives too often and too strongly. People mentioned that they felt there are simply too many ads and that some ads are repeated far too often. Concern was also expressed that TV ads are recorded at higher volumes and are too loud.

2. *Falsity* and *exaggeration* were also frequently raised points, with consumers registering a belief that some ads don't present quite a true picture of the product or service and might be misleading.

3. Among the list of other dislikes mentioned was *silliness*, reflecting a belief that ads talk down to people and are sometimes irritating.[26]

Broader Social Criticisms: The Seven Sins of Advertising

A series of broad criticisms of advertising in modern society have been raised by serious observers, primarily persons outside of the business community. If you are not already familiar with these charges, you may wish to stop and think about how you feel about them. How generalizable is each, and how accurately does it reflect legitimate concerns? What—if anything—do you feel should be done about each of the "seven sins" charged by advertising's critics?[27]

Charge 1: Advertising Persuades People to Do Things They Otherwise Wouldn't
This is the broadest attack on advertising. It raises fundamental questions about the nature of commercial persuasion, the use of sophisticated theories, research, and technologies to make this persuasion as effective as possible and the ends toward which the persuasion is directed. Among the specific questions that arise in this area are

1. Under what conditions, if any, is it appropriate *to try to create new desires* in consumers for no reason other than profits to the advertiser?

2. Under what conditions, if any, is it appropriate to *play on people's emotions* for no reason other than increasing profits for the advertiser? Why not simply deliver only factual product information that accurately portrays the benefits of products and services, including any drawbacks?

3. What are consumers' *true needs?* Are there such things as "bad" wants or needs? What would people desire to buy if there were no advertising?

Charge 2: Advertising Propagandizes in Favor of a Materialistic Life
This charge shifts focus to the fact that advertising is used to encourage people to consume more and more. Several key questions arise in this area, such as

1. Does advertising cause people to *judge themselves and others* on the basis of their possessions rather than their personal qualities?

2. Does advertising *stress conformity* with others as a goal to be sought by consumers?

3. Does advertising encourage consumers to *use, then throw away*, rather than care for and maintain products?

4. Does advertising advocate that people obtain more and more possessions even if they can't *afford* them?

Charge 3: Advertising Lowers the Values and Ethical Standards of Society
This charge continues the issues raised in charge 2, but now concentrates on what may be lost if a person or society pursues a materialistic life-style. Some questions here include

1. Does advertising encourage people to feel that they badly need more money, so that they come to *change what they think about, feel, and do* on a daily basis? For example, does advertising lead people to take on more work (e.g., a part-time job) or neglect their families as they strive to increase their material possessions?

2. Does advertising glorify possessions to such an extent that some persons even *engage in crime* (e.g., shoplifting or writing bad checks) to obtain more material possessions?

3. Does advertising *discourage people from noneconomic activities* such as volunteer work, religious devotion, or appreciating the arts, because of its emphasis on buying more?

4. Does advertising *encourage a desire for instant gratification?*

Charge 4: Advertising Employs Bad Taste and Questionable Morals
This charge moves attention to what is included in ads. Among the issues arising here are

1. Does advertising *embarrass* sectors of the audience by discussing and portraying products, such as those used for feminine hygiene? What, if anything, should advertisers do about this, or do they have an absolute right to act as they see fit?

2. Does advertising use social fear techniques to *make people feel inferior or inadequate* for no reason other than to increase the profits of the advertiser?

3. Does advertising *use sexual themes and innuendoes* to make products seem desirable? What effects might this have on various members of the audience?

4. Does advertising *stress youth and beauty* in selling its products? Everyone is getting older, and most audience members are much less physically attractive than the models used in ads. Does this constant stress on youth and beauty have the effect of making people uneasy and dissatisfied with themselves? For example, is advertising a major factor behind so many young women having anorexia nervosa and bulimia?

Charge 5: Advertising Employs Negative Stereotypes This charge stresses the ways in which particular types of people are represented in ads and what effects this might have. Some key questions in this area include

1. Does advertising portray *blacks or Hispanics* in roles as members of lower classes in society, but not as doctors, professors, or successful businesspersons? If so, what effects does this have on whites' views of minority persons' competencies and roles in society? What, if anything, should advertisers and the media do about this?

2. How should advertising portray *women* in modern society? Is it demeaning to use the "housewife slice-of-life" ad to sell detergents, waxes, and household cleaning products? Is it demeaning to portray women in slinky gowns to sell perfume and other cosmetics? What about using women in slinky gowns to sell cars or industrial machinery?

3. How should advertising portray *older citizens*? Should they only appear in ads for denture products and medical supplies? Why aren't they portrayed as having the wisdom of experience and as having much to offer society in general and younger persons in particular? Why isn't this stage of life portrayed in a positive light in advertising, or is it actually portrayed with accuracy?

4. Overall, should advertising portray life as an *ideal* or as *reality*? Should advertising try to help *lead* societal trends or *reflect life* as it still is in society's mainstream?

Charge 6: Advertising Has Strong Adverse Effects on Society's "Underdogs" This charge continues the thrust of charge 5 but now focuses on possible effects of advertising on certain groups and persons who are less able to participate fully in the consuming society. The basic question in this area is as follows:

1. Over a period of years, what effect does advertising have on *poor persons* in our society? Do they consciously realize that they'll probably never possess the glamorous houses, clothes, or trips offered in some ads? Do the ads inspire them to achieve more or serve to remind them of their prospects and thereby act as a depressant? Does constant exposure to ads make these persons feel less worthwhile?

Charge 7: Advertising Exploits the Innocence and Immaturity of Our Children This charge has led to years of controversy and regulatory battles in Washington, D.C., as consumer groups have fought for further restrictions on advertising aimed at children. We examine these issues in Chapter 10, but the general nature of the questions is

1. Do advertisers *take advantage of limitations in children's abilities* to persuade them to want products for no other reason than to increase profits of the advertiser?

2. Does advertising *stress impulsive purchases* of toys at inflated prices, without regard to their durability or likelihood of delivering enjoyment over a period of time? Why is plastic stressed so much and why does it crack so easily—is this a case of planned obsolescence to increase industry sales?

3. Does advertising *push sugared products and junk foods* on children and thereby contribute to lifelong problems with dental caries, obesity, and unbalanced diets? Why don't fresh fruits and vegetables get advertised as much as candy and snacks?

4. Does advertising *contribute to family problems* by encouraging kids to want too many products and in particular certain brands that are overpriced because of the advertising?

Given the subjective nature of all these charges, it seems apparent that most of the issues will never be fully resolved. As citizens, consumers, and professionals in marketing, however, they pose significant questions for us to consider and debate. If you wish to read more about this topic, you may want to begin with the extensive list of possible readings in Note 27.

Appendix 16B

KEY FACTORS IN ADVERTISING'S IMPACTS

In this appendix we will combine the concepts from our chapter frameworks to investigate key factors in advertising's impacts on consumers. Within this section we briefly examine two key advertising propositions and then illustrate them using the case of comparison advertising. Our first proposition reflects the essentials for Figure 16-1 at the start of the chapter.

Proposition 1: Effects Depend on Source, Medium, Message, and Receiver

Source Factors

Persuasive communications are affected by who presents them—some sources are better at communicating than are others. As a source, advertisers face a special problem, since consumers know their purpose to be self-serving. At the same time, of course, consumers are interested in making good purchases, so there is a potential for successful communication to occur.

One special characteristic of advertising is the flexibility as to who should be identified as the source. The next time you see an ad, for example, notice that the ad agency's name is probably not presented. Often, in fact, the name of the manufacturer is not even provided—only the brand name is given (particularly in broadcast commercials, where time is at a premium). There is no single "rule" for how best to handle the question of identifying the ad source. Since most consumers will provide their own inferences about the source, however, advertisers want to provide sufficient clues that the inferences will be positive.

Conceptually, the answer lies in achieving **source credibility.** Source credibility refers to believability, the extent to which consumers feel that they can believe and act upon what the source is telling them. Low source credibility evokes feelings of distrust and suspicion, thus hindering prospects for persuasion to occur. Studies have shown that two key dimensions of source credibility are trustworthiness and expertise. **Trustworthiness** means that the source can be relied upon—that he or she is basically honest and is not trying to manipulate the audience. **Expertise,** on the other hand, refers to the qualifications of the source to make knowledgeable recommendations about the product or service being advertised.[28] Another important source factor is **attractiveness,** namely, the consumer's perceptions of how prestigious the source is, how empathic (similar to the consumer) the source is, and how physically attractive he or she may be. In all these instances, the more attractive source is likely to bring forth more positive reactions from the audience, assuming that the attractiveness does not detract from the message itself.[29]

Advertisers have several options in creating source identifications. One is to use the company or brand name prominently, especially if it holds a strong reputation. A related technique is to identify the company with an attractive slogan, such as "Panasonic—We're Just Slightly Ahead of Our Time." A third option is to use a seal of approval, such as *Good Housekeeping's* or *Parent's Magazine,* or test results from independent research organizations. Finally, an advertiser can employ a special "spokesperson" in the ads, to benefit from the goodwill or trust that the public has for the speaker. (If you would like to learn more about research findings on source effects, Notes 28 and 29 contain a number of references.)

Media Factors

Beyond delivering messages, media can also enhance or hinder special characteristics of those messages. For example, television allows the advertiser to use demonstrations of a product that may be otherwise difficult to describe in use. Television also allows excitement to be created, through its combination of sight and sound. Print, on the other hand, allows the consumer to spend a longer time with an ad, thus allowing the advertiser to explain more concepts, in more detail. Print also offers a longer time frame within which the advertising may be read, since a particular ad may be seen a week after the magazine arrives at a home. Several media offer immediacy: ads can be quickly inserted in local newspapers or on local radio stations. Finally, an advertiser using specialized media can obtain an extra "tone" for his or her ads. *Cosmopolitan,* for example, adds the sense of the product being modern, *The New Yorker* lends sophistication, and *Road & Track* lends an air of expertise.

Message Factors

The message comprises the heart of most ads. There are two general considerations in this area: (1) *what is said* in the message and (2) *how it is said.* The first depends on the consumer's interests, the properties of the seller's brand, and the ads being run by competitors. The second, however, is much more open to various decisions. For example, should an ad use one-sided appeals only (that is, say only positive things about the brand), or should it try a two-sided appeal (which might recognize some areas in which a brand isn't so strong)? Should emotional appeals, such as fear or humor, be used? Unfortunately, there is no simple answer to these kinds of questions, because of the many variables that interact within the ad itself.

In fact, in the real world of advertising, creators of messages usually do not rely on generalized rules and research findings. Instead, each ad is developed as a whole, and research (if undertaken) will be directed to that specific message, to see whether or not it is working well. As a result, the theories that appear in the literature are only used as general guides, and not as "the final word." Unfortunately, because advertisers want to protect their insight into what works and what doesn't, most advertising research is treated as proprietary in nature and is kept secret. If you have a special interest in learning more about message factors, however, you will find some useful articles appearing in the advertising trade publications, as well as in the extensive listing in Note 30. In this regard, you may also wish to pay special attention to the rapid developments in computerized "expert systems" that rely on knowledge about what works well in advertising.[31]

Receiver Factors

The **receivers** of an ad actually determine whether or not it will succeed in its mission. The most significant receiver factors involve needs for the product, interest in the messages about it, and the prior attitudes and brand loyalties that consumers bring to the advertising exposure.

All these factors are usually available to advertisers through marketing research and are taken into account in designing messages and choosing media schedules. Beyond this, there has been some general research on receiver's personal characteristics and how they relate to *persuasibility*. For example, an ad using high fear appeals will work best for receivers who have high self-esteem, who try to "cope" with their problems, who are not normally "anxious" individuals, and who presently see the product as low in relevance for them. Persons who do not hold these characteristics are more likely to resist ads with high fear appeals: for these people, either low-fear or no-fear appeals would be a better advertising approach. Thus insurance companies might find that fear appeals are appropriate for groups who see themselves as not needing insurance at this time. And fear appeals may be particularly appropriate for advertisers attempting to break into new market segments. A number of studies have examined additional receiver factors such as consumers' mood states and commitment to particular brands. (See Note 32 for a guide to readings in this area.)

Proposition 2: Ads Affect Different Stages Differently

This proposition refers to the different levels in the hierarchy and points out that different types of ads are aimed at different levels of effects. The point is quite straightforward but very significant in helping us to analyze how an ad is likely to work at the consumer level. Assume, for example, that you were asked for *three ideas* for an ad that would *capture attention*. What might you suggest?_____, _____, _____. What might you suggest for an ad that would maximize the probability of having its message *comprehended*? _____. What about increasing its ability to *persuade*? _____. Notice that these techniques might work *against* each other—a very simple message might be more easily comprehended, for example, but consumers might be less likely to be persuaded by it, and may even find it less interesting. As a general rule, then, an advertiser needs to decide which level of effect he or she wishes to achieve and design the message accordingly.

Example: Comparison Advertising

As just one example of how our frameworks can be applied, let's briefly consider the case of comparison advertising. **Comparison advertising** is defined as advertising that (1) compares two or more specifically named (or recognizably presented) brands of the same product class and (2) makes such a comparison in terms of one or more specific product attributes.

Until the early 1970s, almost no comparison ads had ever been run in the United States. The advertising industry's codes prohibited this practice, and most media refused to accept ads in which competitive brand names appeared. Then the Federal Trade Commission pushed for the removal of these bans, so that advertisers could use this method if they so desired. Many advertisers did desire to use it, and the practice spread rapidly. Estimates of its use range from 7 to 25 percent of all ads in recent years. As you may know, many of these ads have proven to be controversial. A number of lawsuits have been filed, as competitors named in ads have claimed that their brands have been misrepresented.

Our interest in this section, however, lies with *comparison advertising as a message strategy* and how it might work at the consumer level. One analysis of this issue was conducted by William Wilkie and Paul Farris and is summarized in Table 16B-1. Notice that column A of the table reflects strategic (source and message) factors, whereas column B stresses receiver factors and effects. In column A we see some of the message strategy questions that an advertiser needs to decide in creating a comparison ad. To gain a better appreciation for these issues, take two recent comparison ads from a magazine (one that you feel is good and one that is not) and see how each one handled this list of issues in column A. For the ad you liked less, does the list suggest some ways it might have been improved?

Column B lists some of the effects Wilkie and Farris expected the typical comparison ad to have on consumers. Notice how these effects are divided into three categories that correspond to *sections of our hierarchy framework: attention* to the ad, *understanding* the message, and *yielding* to its conclusions. As you read through column B, see whether you agree with each of the hypotheses listed. Be aware that these statements pertain to the "average" case, and not to every ad. Since the Wilkie-Farris article appeared, much research has been done on comparison advertising. It has offered mixed results as to whether or not it is more effective than other types of ads, together with many insights on how it can be effectively employed. If you are interested in reading more about comparison advertising, you will find the references listed in Note 33 to be a good starting point.

Table 16B-1 The Wilkie-Farris Assessment of Comparison Advertising

A Message Strategy Questions	B Possible Consumer Effects
1. Brand comparisons and positioning *How many and which brands* should be used for comparisons? What role should brand positioning play? Would, for instance, a desired economy car image be best achieved by a sharp contrast with a luxury car or less stark comparisons with compacts?	**1. Attention** The novelty of a comparison ad will cause it to receive more attention than will a standard ad. Comparison ads will receive more attention from users of competing brands mentioned than from users of brands not mentioned. Increasing the prominence of competing brands will increase attention from their users, but will also increase misidentifications of the sponsoring brand. Aggregate recall levels of comparison ads will be higher than those for standard appeals.
2. Product dimensions for comparison *Which product attributes* should be used? Might use of a "trivial" attribute be considered deceptive? *How many* attributes should be used? Should the advertiser's brand "win" on *every* attribute?	**2. Comprehension** Exposure to a comparison ad will lead to a "clearer brand image" than exposure to a standard ad. Consumers will rate comparison ads as more "informative" and more "interesting" than standard ads. Users of a named competing brand are more likely to admit the sponsor brand into their evoked set than are users of brands not mentioned. Users of the sponsored brand are more likely to *reduce* the size of their evoked set when exposed to a comparison ad than when exposed to a standard ad.
3. Use of tests Should tests be *stressed* or *avoided*? How *conclusive* should tests be before including the results? How restrictive should conditions be? Should competitors receive the results before or after campaign launch, or not at all?	
4. Brand identification How should a comparison ad be *constructed* to reduce audience misidentification of the sponsoring brand? Will some media be better than others for this problem?	**3. Message acceptance** Claims made in a comparison ad are more likely to be accepted as "correct" than are those in a standard ad. Naming a competing brand will tend to increase support arguments by users of the sponsoring brand and counterarguments by users of the competing brand. The level and duration of counterarguing will be negatively related to changes in brand preference.
5. Product/market factors *Which product/market factors* are important? Is a highly segmented market most appropriate for this tool? Are shopping goods special candidates because consumers often compare two or more brands before purchasing— or, for the same reasons, are these poorer prospects for comparison advertising? Will, as some fear, minor brands use comparison advertising to trade on the images of the market leaders?	Comparison ads will yield higher variance (i.e., increased polarity) in postexposure brand preferences than will standard advertisements. On the average, comparison ads are *more effective* in improving consumer preference for the sponsored brand than are standard advertisements.

SOURCE: See Note 33.

Part IV

CONSUMER DECISION PROCESSES

PART IV of this book consists of three chapters and focuses on the *consumer decision process*. Consumer decisions can range widely in time (from split-second choices to deliberations taking months or even years) and in the amount of effort given to the choice. Thus we can learn a great deal by examining the basic stages that distinguish most consumer decisions. In Chapter 17, we will look at the starting stages of consumer decisions—problem recognition and information search. These are known as *prepurchase processes*: they are very significant in determining *which* product and services consumers will buy at all and *when* they will do so. In Chapter 18, *purchase processes*, we focus on the final decision and actual purchase. Finally, in Chapter 19, we turn our attention to *postpurchase processes*. Here our interest is in what happens after a purchase is made, both for consumers and for marketers.

Since much of this book has been written from a decision process perspective, the topics in Part IV mesh well with topics in other chapters. If you are reading this part at the end of your course, it can serve as a useful synthesis and extension of many familiar issues. If you are reading it early in the course, it can serve as a framework into which other topics will fit. In either event, there is some very interesting material in the chapters ahead, so let's move forward!

17

CONSUMER DECISIONS (I)
Prepurchase Processes

SEARCHERS REPORT ON PREPURCHASE PROCESSES

In-depth interviews with consumers provide helpful insights for marketers. Let's listen in on different consumers talking about their prepurchase activities when buying a car in Chicago (some key prepurchase issues are noted in parentheses):

(*Time and effort*) "Every spare minute that we had we spent at a car lot. We went to at least 12 to 15 dealerships . . . "

(*Social influences*) "It seems whenever I've got a decision I talk to friends and people and just get their general opinion . . . to me if you talk to enough people eventually you can find the right key . . . "

(*Sources of information*) "I went to one of the bookstores. They have books there that tell you how much the dealers pay for them, how much they're marked up."

(*Important attribute: Safety*) "But I think the baby was the biggest concern. He kept talking about a smaller car and I don't want to drive the baby around in a little car. If we were hit, I want . . . a car that would back us up."

(*Learning*) " . . . the more I looked into it, the more I wanted to keep investigating, trying to know as much as possible, (so I would be) able to go from one dealer to the next and basically say, listen, this is the kind of deal I can get, what can you do for me?"

(*Source*) "I was trying very hard to buy an American-made car . . . I had real difficulty feeling that I was slightly undermining the economy by buying a Japanese car . . . in a way I resent it because I want the best for my money and I don't like to feel that I am buying something to save America and screwing myself at the same time! And that's what I felt I did to a certain extent. I really did! When I saw what the Toyota Camry had to offer, it killed me! I love my Buick Somerset, but for the little bit of price difference—and there's not much—it was very hard to do . . . "

(*Price*) "I would have went to Indianapolis if I could get a better deal. If I would have broke $1000, I would have went to Indianapolis!"[1]

■ SHOCKING NEWS AND CONSUMER REACTIONS

Do you remember reading any headlines like these?

> "Sales of Tampons Dip 20%."
>
> "Sales of Aspirin Soar."

Occasionally a major breakthrough occurs, or something serious goes wrong with a consumer product. When either happens, we see almost instantaneous consumer reactions in the marketplace. The two headlines, for example, appeared in recent years. Let's examine what happened to consumers' decision processes in each case.

ᘒ TSS and P & G

The tampon headline arose from a medical connection with toxic shock syndrome (TSS), a virulent blood-related disease that began striking females about 15 years ago. As experts tracked down the cases, a pattern began to appear. The pattern related to extended use of superabsorbent tampons, a new entry into the market. Procter & Gamble had built a very strong brand—Rely tampons—that had been reportedly used by many of the victims. When the news broke, Rely, which held a 20 percent share of the market, was simply withdrawn from distribution at a cost of millions to P & G. Tampon sales of all types dropped 20 percent immediately thereafter, with gains going to sanitary napkin brands. P & G planners studied the pattern of earlier product crises such as the botulism found in canned tuna and the cancer announcement associated with cyclamates in soft drinks. In each case, it took about one year for consumers to return fully to earlier behavior patterns.[2]

ᘒ Heart Report Pumps Profits

Several years ago the prestigious *New England Journal of Medicine* reported a study showing that daily aspirin use by healthy men may lower the risk of heart attacks. Aspirin sales, which had been on a downward trend (down 7 percent) shot up between 35 and 50 percent in the next month. According to a researcher, "There's no doubt . . . that study had a big impact on consumers!"[3]

In Chapter 1, the concept of a *consumer decision process* was introduced as one of the "Seven Keys" to understanding our field. Since that chapter, we've repeatedly discussed how difficult consumer decisions are for marketers to influence. The shocking news examples, however, demonstrate that consumer decisions can change rapidly. In each case a single new input into the decision process had a startling impact on consumer behavior—millions of consumers changed their prior purchase and use patterns almost instantaneously! Although these examples are certainly not typical, they do demonstrate the inherent flexibility of consumer decision processes and further suggest that these processes are worth understanding.

■ WHAT DO CONSUMERS DECIDE?

Consumers make many types of decisions in their day-to-day lives. In analyzing them, we can stress two dimensions: the **type of the decision** (that is, what is decided) and the **complexity of the decision process** (that is, how important or complicated is the decision process).

FOUR BASIC TYPES OF DECISIONS

There are four primary types of decisions that consumers must make:

- Budget allocations
- Product purchase (or not)
- Store patronage
- Brand and style choice

Budget allocation: Choices of how and when to spend (or save) available funds and whether to borrow.

Budget allocation involves our choices of how to spend (or save) our available funds, how to time our spending, and whether to borrow in order to buy. Rather than one giant overall budget allocation decision, consumers make many "yes-no" purchase choices continuously. In this manner each household allocates spending into many product and service categories. Consumers differ in how much consideration they give to the budget constraints. A few consumers are highly deliberative, using much preplanning. For some other consumers, budget constraints rarely enter their decision processes. Most consumers, however, are somewhere in between. In these cases, some budget will be given to necessities, with the remainder of funds (viewed as **discretionary**) available for spending or saving as occasions arise.

Product purchase or not: The choice of buying or not buying in each product or service category.

The second category of decisions—**product purchase or not**—reflects choices made with respect to each product or service category itself. Often choices must be made between two or more competing product purchases: if we buy a new set of contact lenses, for example, we might not buy that new outfit we'd been considering. However, in some cases, such as household appliances, purchases are often ordered into *priority acquisition patterns*. The Ronsell family, for example, might have started with a TV set and a vacuum in their rented apartment, then added a washer/dryer, and then a microwave. When moving to their home, they needed to buy a refrigerator and range, and they are now saving for a dishwasher. This type of decision has a great impact on the *size of consumer markets*. From a consumer research viewpoint, we are also interested in how these decisions get made—how are they influenced, how consciously are nonpurchase decisions made (that is, how many consumers decide not to buy a given product or service versus never even considering the purchase in the first place?)—and related issues.

Store patronage: The choice of at which sources to shop to obtain a product or service.

Once a consumer has decided to purchase something in a product or service class, the remaining two types of decisions come into play. Both introduce direct competition into our consideration. **Store patronage** refers to the decision of which source to use to obtain the product. Usually this is a retail store, although in recent years direct-response and catalog shopping have been increasing in popularity.

Consumers' store patronage decisions are of vital interest to retailers, since these decisions determine where their money will be spent.

Brand and style decisions refer to the details of exactly which items are purchased. This choice acts to reward marketers for strong performance by stimulating a larger dollar flow back to those firms creating better products and marketing mixes. Not surprisingly, given marketers' interest in maximizing profits, this decision has received by far the most attention by consumer researchers: most of the consumer marketing literature is geared to exploring consumers' brand and style decisions.

Brand and style decisions: Choices as to the details of exactly which items are purchased.

SOME DECISIONS ARE COMPLEX, SOME ARE NOT

Some decisions are rather simple and easy to make, whereas others are complex and difficult. This means that the nature of the decision process is different in these cases. Two very useful perspectives are available to help us better appreciate the processes that occur at different levels.

Involvement and Effort

As we've already discussed at several points in the text, the **level of involvement** is a crucial determinant of the type of decision process a consumer will undertake. High involvement suggests that the order of decision making will follow our hierarchy of effects model in the think-feel-do sequence—beliefs will be formed, attitudes will develop, and purchase behaviors will follow. Consumers will put effort into the decision, will treat it as important, and will likely compare brands, stores, styles, and prices. With low involvement, on the other hand, the consumer decision process will be quite different. Much less effort will be given prior to a purchase. Consumers may be less attentive to marketing stimuli and the arguments they present. Less effort will be given to the overall decision, with perhaps less concern about which brand is purchased. Even the order of the decision process may change—we may see decisions being made impulsively or for trial purposes, with little in the way of beliefs or attitudes having been formed before the purchase itself has been made.

Time, Learning, and Complexity

Another important perspective stresses the fact that some products are purchased time and time again, whereas others are purchased only infrequently. Repeat purchasing allows consumers to *learn* what is available and what they like. Consumers are thus

Retailers have long relied upon new or interesting window displays to bring new shoppers into stores to investigate.

able to make choices from a position of strength. John Howard has captured this point in his definition of three types of processes:

- **Extensive problem solving.** This mode of decision making requires much effort, can take a long time, and is complex. Many consumers face this process when making their first purchase in an important product category. Here they must learn about important attributes and which brands offer which benefits (at what costs). They must also develop their own criteria to evaluate which option is best for them. House buying, choice of a university, and purchase of a car are three cases where this form might be adopted.

- **Limited problem solving.** This is an intermediate type of decision making in which the consumer knows about the product category, but is unfamiliar with the exact brand, style, and price options that are currently available. For example, if a consumer had already purchased one or more suits, but was now in the market again, this might well be the mode of decision making. Emphasis will be primarily on search for a suitable alternative, with less concern given to learning about the product itself (since this is a broad category that lies between the extremes of extensive problem-solving and routinized-response behavior, it is the most difficult to characterize). Most consumer decisions are probably of this type.

- **Routinized-response behavior.** In this least complex mode of decisions, the consumer has purchased the product frequently in the past, knows what it can do, and has clear likes and dislikes among the brands available. Thus there is no perceived need for external search, and decisions can be made quickly and easily. Many purchases in supermarkets and drugstores are of this variety.[4]

FURTHER THOUGHTS

We should note several subtleties that are important in understanding these perspectives on the complexity of consumer decision processes. Don't miss, for example, the *importance of long-term memory (LTM)*. As our LTM develops (that is, learning occurs) with respect to a product category, we are able to move toward less demanding forms of decision making. For example, there is often a marked shift from relying on external sources of information to a stress on our own internal knowledge, experience, and brand preferences.

Another subtlety concerns *how good a decision needs to be*. As we've noted before, consumer behavior theory has increasingly had to recognize that consumers do not seek to "optimize" the purchase itself—this would require that too much effort be devoted to search and evaluation each time a purchase is made. Instead, **satisficing** appears to describe the goal for most consumer purchases—we wish to obtain a product with which we will be pleased, which is "good enough", even if it does not represent the absolutely best buy that might be available if we work hard enough to find it.

Given this background, we can begin to appreciate that Howard's framework of the three decision types can become quite complex as we begin to analyze real decisions. Some decisions are made very quickly—in flashes of a second—while others extend over months or even years. Some decisions are backed up by much thought, careful analysis, and even great worry, while others are made in the most flippant and casual of manners. The underlying order in which cognitive, affective, and behavioral aspects occur is not always the same. In some consumer decisions, external influences are extremely important, while in others they are not. Marketing programs are success-

Extensive problem solving: The most involved decision mode: requires effort.

Limited problem solving: The intermediate decision mode: the consumer already knows the product, but needs to find a suitable alternative.

Routinized-response behavior: The least complex decision mode: the consumer has purchased the product frequently and has clear brand preferences.

Satisficing: A common consumer purchase goal: obtain a product that is "good enough," even if not the best buy anywhere in the market.

Since recent research has confirmed that many consumer decisions are made on an impulsive basis in the store, promotional displays have become increasingly important means by which to attract consumer dollars.

SHATTER YOUR CURRENT REDEMPTION RATE

IT'S THE INSTANT COUPON MACHINE... NOW AVAILABLE NATIONWIDE IN 10,000 FOOD AND DRUG STORES.

After extensive testing by more than 70 major brands, the Instant Coupon Machine has proved its success.

- Drives high redemptions averaging 17%
- Quickly builds brand share by increasing brand penetration
- Average volume increases of 35%
- Creates high impulse purchases, trial and brand switching - 55% of purchases are unplanned

The Instant Coupon Machine is a dynamic new marketing tool that will change the way you build your business. It rewards shoppers in the store, at the shelf where most of all brand purchase decisions are made. In short, it can help you dominate the shelf and your category 24 hours a day, seven days a week. The Instant Coupon Machine. Finally, someone put coupons where they count.

For more information call:

- William Cargill, Headquarters, (203) 845-6206
- Jim Irish, Los Angeles, (714) 939-9200
- Ron Perchik, Chicago, (708) 699-4050
- David Pittman, Atlanta, (404) 422-1476

ACTMEDIA
THE IN-STORE MARKETING NETWORK

Creative suppliers are offering marketers numerous new ways to appeal to consumers in the store, and to stand out from the competition on the shelf. Notice how this ad presents consumer research evidence to back up its claims.

If You Know The Code, You Can Double Your Volume In Days.

0-65779-76943

Looking for an instant sales spike? Checkout Coupon turns the UPC code into your own exclusive volume-building tool. First, our retail merchandising tie-ins let shoppers know about your Checkout Coupon promotion. Store ads, shelf talkers, and in-store posters alert consumers before the purchase to the special offers, and motivate them to buy now. Using scanner data from the checkstand, Checkout Coupon identifies those shoppers buying your product. Only then do we reward them. Guaranteeing you performance before you provide the incentive.

When you control the code, you reach over 80 million shoppers at the nation's best retailers. Let us show you how the Catalina Marketing Network can do volumes for your brand. Call Catalina Marketing Corporation, (800) 955-9770.

CHECKOUT COUPON
FROM CATALINA MARKETING CORPORATION

This competing coupon system relies on a different stage of the consumer's decision process, and is based on the scanner system's immediate information about what a consumer is buying at checkout.

The U.S. government is also trying to influence consumers' decisions, but not toward any particular brand. Instead these new food labels, mandated to appear in May 1994, are intended to more clearly highlight the positive and negative nutritional qualities of different foods. Do you think they'll have any impact?

ful in changing the course of some decisions, while others remain immune to even the most expensive and sophisticated advertising and selling efforts. Because the real world is complex and has many factors at work, the decision process perspective we will learn about in the remainder of this chapter can offer many useful insights for us.

■ THE CONSUMER DECISION PROCESS

Figure 17-1 depicts the four essential stages of the consumer decision process.[5]

1. **Problem recognition** represents the start of a decision process. This stage occurs when we first begin our move toward a purchase decision. As we'll see, this step is extremely important to marketers and consumers alike.

2. **Information search and alternative evaluation** represent the second stage of the process. Here the necessary information is gathered and used to evaluate mentally the options that are open to us.

3. **Purchase processes,** the third stage, represent the activities that occur during the final decision making and actual purchase of the product or service. The shaded overlap in the figure indicates that often this stage is hard to disentangle from the second stage (as when a salesperson helps us to decide which tape player to buy, then writes out the order and arranges the payment). In other decisions, however, the prior stage may be carried out over an earlier period, with the purchase stage occurring at a later point (for example, when we decide to order from a catalog after searching many stores).

4. **Postpurchase processes** represent the final stage of the decision process. Here our interest is in what happens *after* a purchase is made. This stage can be of critical importance to future marketing sales potentials, since a consumer's usage experience with a product leads to new attitudes that will come into play during the next consumer decision process for a similar product. Thus, in an important way, postpurchase processes cycle into future decision processes and strongly influence them.

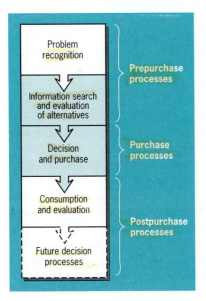

FIGURE 17-1 The Major Stages in a Consumer Decision Process

Within the remaining sections of this chapter, we'll examine the first two stages of the consumer decision process: problem recognition and information search.

■ STAGE 1: PROBLEM RECOGNITION

❧ *In Plain Sight, but out of Contact*

A national survey recently showed that 65 percent of American adults wear eyeglasses. Age is a factor, with this figure ranging from 30 percent of those 18 to 24 years old to 93 percent of those over age 50. But only about 10 percent of all consumers wear contact lenses (although 30 percent have considered doing so, and young consumers are much more likely to wear them than are their parents). Marketers of contact lenses realize that there is a huge market potential if only consumers can be persuaded to begin purchase decision processes. These marketers are wondering how best to go about stimulating increased problem recognition.[6]

❧ *POP Contests Spark Sales Gains*

As a means of increasing the "push" from retailers to consumers, manufacturers frequently run sales promotion campaigns and contests. For example, the American Dairy Association once offered $100,000 in prizes for the best point-of-purchase (POP) displays created by retail store employees. The theme for the displays was "Cheese Adds a Slice of Life." ADA officials estimated that employees of over 4,000 stores built displays. The effect was quite noticeable—during the three-month promotion, 90 million pounds more cheese was sold (an increase of 16 percent in sales). Some of the winners did much better: a Dutch windmill display, for example, led to a 100 percent sales increase for a California market.[7] Successful displays are not limited to cheese, of course. In an Arm & Hammer promotional contest, a POP display suggesting "1001 Uses" increased a store's sales from the normal level of 3 cases a week to over 70 cases a week![8]

THE CONCEPT OF PROBLEM RECOGNITION

The foregoing examples show what marketers and retailers have known for years—*the consumer decision process can be triggered into action* by the right forms of external stimuli, and large sales increases can result. On the other hand, this process does not always occur, as the makers of contact lenses have discovered. Within this section we'll take a structured look at why this occurs.

Problem recognition: The first stage of a decision process: the consumer perceives a need and becomes motivated to act.

Problem recognition represents the beginning of a consumer decision process. It is here that the consumer *perceives a need and becomes motivated* to solve the "problem" that he or she has just recognized. Once the problem is recognized, the remainder of the consumer decision process is invoked to determine exactly how the consumer will go about satisfying the need. Figure 17-2 diagrams the process of problem recognition and summarizes some of its key determinants. Conceptually, *problem recognition occurs when the consumer perceives a gap or discrepancy* between his or her **current state** and his or her **desired state.** Notice that the term "problem" is not intended to be negative in this definition—it actually represents the recognition of a goal that the consumer wishes to achieve. While a "problem" could be somewhat unpleasant, it might also represent an opportunity, such as the chance to obtain heart protection with aspirin or good savings on a product.

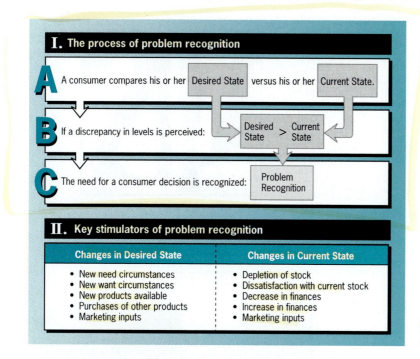

FIGURE 17-2 Determinants of product recognition

CAUSES OF PROBLEM RECOGNITION

As noted, the dynamics of problem recognition occur when a large enough discrepancy is recognized. Basically, a discrepancy can arise from one of two sources: a change in the desired state or a change in the consumer's current state.

Changes in the Desired State: Major Causes

- *New "need" circumstances.* As we encounter changes in our daily lives, we often find that entirely new categories of consumer needs arise. The consumer life cycle captures many such events. A young single, for example, is unlikely even to imagine problem recognition for diapers, baby furniture, or pediatricians, but in several years may well be in the midst of these decision processes.

- *New "want" circumstances.* Noting some distinction between wants and needs, new circumstances can create problem recognition of a "want" variety. For many students, for example, the move away to college opens new possibilities: travel to other countries, classical books, music, or art might appear on one's horizon, as might attendance at new types of functions.

- *New product opportunities.* The marketing world is constantly providing consumers with new options for purchases. Prior to our becoming aware of a new product, we're unlikely to experience problem recognition for it. Once the product has been explained to us—perhaps through advertising or by friends—we can experience a substantial increase in our "desired state" for it.

- *Purchases of other products.* Sometimes problem recognition is sparked by having purchased a different product. Once having bought a computer, for example, consumers are likely to recognize opportunities for using certain software packages and other accessories. A VCR purchase similarly affords prospects for problem recognition for tapes, movie rentals, and cameras.

This ad stimulates problem recognition by reminding women of a possible gap between current state and desired state for shoe comfort (and proposing a solution!).

Changes in the Current State: Major Causes

- *Depletion of stock.* This refers to running down the available supply of products or services, usually through consumption. When gasoline is used to power a car, for example, its current state becomes depleted as the needle moves toward "E." At some point, the discrepancy between the current amount of gasoline and the desired amount of gasoline becomes sufficiently large that we recognize there is a problem. Similarly, our shoes wear down, some items break, and food and household supplies are used up in our daily lives. Thus depletion is probably the most frequent single cause of consumer problem recognition.

- *Dissatisfaction with current stock.* This change occurs when we perceive that the products that we currently own are insufficient to continue to serve their purpose (even though they may not have been depleted). Clothing and fashion are a common example, with both males and females perceiving that their older-style clothing is no longer suitable for current social demands and triggering search for new clothing.

- *Decrease in finances.* When funds run low (whether due to unemployment or other uses of the money), consumers will recognize problems that require a *reduction* in spending. Discretionary purchases are usually the ones to go, such as cutting down on movies or concerts or repairing durable goods rather than replacing them.

EXHIBIT 17-1

Problem Recognition
Opportunities in Fitness

According to one expert, one in five adults exercises at least once a week, two in five don't exercise at all, and two in five feel they should exercise but don't. "That's 40 percent of the adult population that's an untapped market...the trick for marketers is to find the button that gets them to overcome that barrier." (See Note 10.)

Consumer research is useful for suggesting where the prime opportunities are, since fitness options show sharp segment differences. Here are some results from a recent Gallup Poll:

Activity	Percentage Participating	Percentage by Age			Percentage by Gender	
		18–34	35–54	55+	Male	Female
Walking	54%	42%	59%	65%	39%	68%
Biking	10	11	10	7	9	10
Weightlifting	10	18	9	2	16	5
Aerobics	8	12	7	4	3	13
Running	6	11	5	1	10	3
Ball teams	4	9	2	—	6	2

SOURCE: See Note 10.

- *Increase in finances.* An unexpected increase in finances, through a new job, bonus, or gift, can lead the consumer to rethink the desired state to spend the money. Investments and luxury items are among the uses that may arise from this type of problem recognition.

THE ROLE OF MARKETING

Without considerable activity by marketers to stimulate and direct problem recognition, they would face possibly lower sales and certainly great uncertainty about sales patterns.[9] Analysis of Figure 17-2 shows that marketers can influence consumer problem recognition through either side of the equation. Relatively less marketing attention seems directed to the current state, however (perhaps because this will vary so much among consumers). The most likely form of marketing strategy aimed at the current state seems to be to try to induce some dissatisfaction with the current stock of goods. Examples include asking whether a husband is underinsured or stressing the social punishments that await someone who is out of step with the current styles. While these types of *fear appeal strategies* can sometimes be effective, they do carry a negative tinge, which might lead the consumer to react *against* the marketer.

Most marketing inputs seem to be aimed at affecting the levels of the desired state. Presentation of products as problem solutions can thus lead to consumers recognizing the problems in the first place! As a result we see new products marketed as ways to achieve more convenient, safer, or more exciting experiences for consumers. And we see *bundling strategies,* that is, secondary products (e.g., VCR supplies) being marketed in terms of added benefits from the primary product. Finally, we see many products marketed essentially through reminding consumers of their basic desires for satisfying wants and needs.

¿❧ *"Problem" Means Marketing Opportunity*

Consumer research can play an important role in helping marketers to identify opportunities for strategies to stimulate problem recognition by consumers. Exhibit 17-1, for example, summarizes some findings about American consumers' recent preferences for different fitness activities (notice the large potential markets: where would you start?). Similarly, research by Owens-Corning, which produces home insulation, shows that fewer than one in six U.S. homes meets the new standards for house insulation: two-thirds of homes have less than half of the suggested 12 inches, while 7 percent have no insulation at all. Over half of all homeowners, moreover, don't know how much insulation they have. (It will be interesting to watch if and how the firm uses the "Pink Panther" in ads to stimulate this problem recognition process, probably through "dissatisfaction with the current state.")

Likewise, the auto industry is aware that depletion is at work on the cars consumers now own. Some research figures for a recent year: 20 percent of cars on the road are at least 12 years old, 36 percent are nine years or older (the average life for a car is 12 to 13 years). Further, the boom years for auto sales were in the mid-1980s. All these facts taken together indicate that the mid- to late 1990s should see plenty of depletion-related problem recognition opportunities for the auto industry![10]

■ STAGE 2: INFORMATION SEARCH AND ALTERNATIVE EVALUATION

In the decision process framework the problem recognition stage activates a goal and motivates the consumer to act. In our next stage—information search and alternative evaluation—the consumer moves toward achievement of the goal. To reach the goal of matching the levels of actual and desired states, consumers need to discover what their options are, process information about them, and decide which alternative to choose. There are many interesting issues hidden within this simple stage structure, however. For example, let's consider the following tale:

¿❧ *Coupon Fanatics Hit Supermarkets*

David Carlisle's wife was hospitalized and he was unemployed when, in desperation, a partial solution to his problems came to him in a dream—to use cents-off coupons to reduce his food spending. After great preparation, he called his local IGA store to explain his plan and ask for their cooperation. He arrived on a Friday morning at

9:30 with coupons and list. After nine hours in the store, he checked out at 6:30 with 15 grocery carts packed with food and household goods. The total value was over $1800, but with his coupons Mr. Carlisle paid only $125! Since then he has continued this practice—his wife, now home, spends six hours per day cutting coupons from home publications, while he sorts and organizes them. Similar results were reported by an Indiana woman who won a national "Longest Tape" contest. Cindy Dorgan's cash register tape measured nearly 37 feet! She purchased $1287 worth of goods, but with 18 feet, 3 inches of coupon deductions, she paid only the sales tax of $25.30. "When that first $1.00 refund check arrived in the mail, I was hooked!" she said.[11]

We should notice that Mr. Carlisle's story received special treatment in news reports *not* because he behaved as an irrational consumer, but because most of the rest of us don't behave this way. Given the huge potential savings, however, why don't more of us follow Mr. Carlisle's and Ms. Dorgan's leads? How much information search do we undertake and why?

UNDERSTANDING SEARCH AND EVALUATION

The classic discussions of "information" refer to its ability to *reduce uncertainty* about the state of nature. That is, as we gain information, we learn more about a particular issue. The phrase **consumer information search,** therefore, refers to a deliberate attempt to gain knowledge about a product, store, or purchase. Here we are especially interested

A comparison ad aimed at travelers' prepurchase planning.

Consumer information search: The deliberate attempt to gain knowledge about a product, a store, or purchase terms.

in how information search impacts on the decision. This raises several subtle but important implications:

■ First, information search can sometimes lead to *increases* in uncertainty as we learn more. This is because our relevant "uncertainty" is often about which purchase we should make rather than only about understanding more about the alternatives available.[12] Because of this, consumer information search can become "psychologically costly," which means that we might do less of it than otherwise expected.

■ Second, the information relevant for a consumer purchase decision might come either from inside our LTM or from the external world.

Two Basic Types of Information Search

Incidental learning: Gaining information when not actually making a consumer decision, as in browsing through a mall

Directed search: The conscious search for information to help make a particular consumer decision.

There are two primary modes of consumer information search. The first mode, **incidental learning,** refers to gaining information when we're not actually making a consumer decision. Each of us, for example, engages in considerable information search each time we browse through shops at the mall.[13] This form of information acquisition leads to increases in long-term memory (LTM) for use later when an appropriate purchase occasion might arise.

A second primary mode—**directed search** and evaluation—refers to conscious search for information to help us make a particular purchase decision. Within this area there are three basic types of purchases:

1. *Internal search-only purchases.* These decisions employ the simplest form of "search"—here we recognize a problem, invoke our LTM to help consider it, and end by making the purchase. There are, however, two different varieties of internal search decisions: loyalty decisions and impulse decisions. **Loyalty decisions** occur when our LTM has strong experience and a single strong brand preference to guide it. The decision is made in a well-practiced manner and is quite deliberate. **Impulse decisions,** in contrast, represent very little impact from LTM. In these instances, an external stimulus display stimulates problem recognition, but no deliberate external search is undertaken to look for options. Instead, the remaining search is internal and brief; then the purchase is made. Checkout aisles at supermarkets are stocked to stimulate impulse purchases: you may enjoy observing these the next time you are in line![14]

2. *Purchases employing both internal and external search.* In these cases a consumer first engages in an internal search of LTM. If she finds LTM's current information to be insufficient, she turns to the external world to gain assistance. Her purchase-directed external search can involve stores, friends, and other appropriate information sources. As new alternatives arise, they are evaluated using both internal and external information.

3. *"No-purchase" decisions.* These are decision processes that lead to nonpurchase outcomes—the products we don't buy and that never appear in any formal records of consumer behavior. All of us have frequently experienced these episodes. Sometimes purchase is postponed, and we vow to make it later, while other times we simply decide not to buy. In either instance, of course, we have engaged in information search. "No-purchase" decisions represent lost opportunities for marketers.

Table 17-1 Factors Likely to Affect External Information Search

	Factors Associated with	
	Lower Search Levels	High Search Levels
Overall	High perceived costs of search, with low perceived benefits	High perceived benefits from search, low perceived costs
Psychological factors	Low involvement Much past experience Current satisfaction Dislike of shopping Brand loyalty	High involvement Little relevant experience Enjoyment of shopping Curiosity Favorable attitudes toward several stores/brands
Situational factors	Social pressure for a particular choice High time pressure Physical constraints Special price offer Easy return guarantees Low cost/low risk Effective selling	Social pressures to search (e.g., husband and wife "team") Easy to shop Many sources Long time horizon for purchase Long product life High price/high risk Significant differences exist in prices and/or quality levels Technological improvements in the product
Information processing factors	Inability to understand information Lack of confidence with salespersons	Desire to learn more Confidence in ability to use information Higher number of evaluative criteria (key attributes)

KEY FACTORS IN EXTERNAL INFORMATION SEARCH

The overall theory of information search is based on *costs versus benefits*. A consumer will search more when he or she perceives either high benefits from the search or sees the costs of search to be low. When opposite conditions exist, consumers should undertake less external information search. There are, however, many factors that combine to affect costs and benefits. Table 17-1 summarizes a number of these.[15]

Within the table, note the three general types of influences—psychological, situational, and information processing factors. Note also that the entries are often not identical on the left and right sides: the table reports influences that tend to either encourage or discourage further searching by consumers. Thus there are a number of factors relevant to this area of consumer behavior. A few minutes spent looking through Table 17-1 will help us to appreciate better what these are.

Type of Good Affects Search

Several distinctions among types of goods and types of characteristics relate to consumer search behavior. You may recall (from your introduction to marketing textbook) that marketers often speak of three types of products and services—convenience goods, specialty goods, and shopping goods—based upon consumers' typical search patterns. **Convenience goods** are those consumers will tend to purchase where available: they will not go to another store to obtain a different brand. Many foods and household supplies are of this type. Marketers of convenience goods, therefore, strive to obtain extensive distribution aimed at being available in virtually every store in which a con-

Convenience goods: Products that consumers purchase where available: they will not go to another store to obtain a different brand.

Window-shopping at Bloomingdale's (New York City): much incidental learning occurs this way.

Specialty goods: Products for which consumers have a strong brand or type preference: they will seek out a particular outlet for these.

Shopping goods: Products for which consumers engage in prepurchase search at several stores.

Search characteristics: Product attributes or claims that consumers can evaluate through search and shopping, such as the style of a dress.

Experience characteristics: Product attributes or claims that the consumer can evaluate only after purchasing the good and trying it out, such as the taste of a food product.

sumer may shop. **Specialty goods**, on the other hand, are those for which consumers have a strong brand or type preference, and for which they *will* search for a particular outlet from which to buy. Marketers of such products as musical instruments, art supplies, some clothing lines, and other specialty items seek to have relatively few outlets, but to ensure that their brands are sold well to consumers looking for them. **Shopping goods**, meanwhile, are those for which consumers are expected to engage in prepurchase search at several stores, to learn about products, options, and prices. Appliances and some audio equipment are often in this category: marketers of these products seek to have them in a moderate number of outlets, again with a strong selling push available to consumers engaged in prepurchase search.

Found in the field of economics, another useful distinction is made among search characteristics, experience characteristics, and credence characteristics. **Search characteristics** are those which consumers can evaluate through search and shopping (such as the style of a dress). **Experience characteristics** are those for which the consumer must purchase the good and try it out before the consumer is able to evaluate its quality (e.g., the taste of a food product). **Credence characteristics**, meanwhile, are those that typical consumers will never be able to evaluate precisely, even after purchase and use (e.g., the quality of internal stitches during an operation). For credence characteristics, consumers must rely on marketers' assurances and reputations.[16]

One common division in marketing separates the categories of nondurables, durables, and consumer services. **Nondurables** are products that are consumed quickly and are often repurchased on a frequent basis. They usually do not inspire high levels of external search by consumers. Their prices are often low, and the consumer's risks from a bad purchase are low as well. The frequent repurchases provide an LTM base of experiences with various brands and types. This allows us to often use *internal information search* as a replacement for external information search in nondurable product categories.

The information search picture for **services** is less clear. Services are often intangible and are "customized" for each consumer. In addition, many services are infrequently purchased and are often high in price. Thus they would seem to be natural candidates for high levels of external information search. However, because services *are* customized and intangible, and because they often reflect the "credence characteristics" noted earlier, it can be difficult for a consumer to assess the information he or she gains during external search. (How does Sandy Bender really know, for example, whether one dentist will be better than another for her?) Such characteristics of services often lead consumers to rely heavily on either the reputation of the service provider or word-of-mouth recommendations from friends. Other forms of external information search for services are often low.[17]

CONSUMERS' INFORMATION SEARCH AND SHOPPING FOR DURABLE GOODS

Most research on consumer information seeking has studied **durable goods**—products that provide benefits over long time periods, such as houses, autos, and appliances. In glancing back through Table 17-1 we can see many reasons why higher levels of information search should occur in durables purchases. For example, there is often very high consumer involvement with durables purchases. Since durables are not purchased often, little recent information may be available in LTM for internal search to rely upon, and new product features are likely to be available that had not been encountered before. Also, since a consumer will have to live with the product for a long time, the benefits from a good durable purchase are higher, and risks of buying a "lemon" are also higher. Finally, as we noted earlier, many durables are considered "shopping goods," so the marketing system for durables often has different brands sold through different stores. For all these reasons we would expect to see high levels of information search for durable goods. What do we actually find however? To appreciate this area more fully, let's examine highlights from a research study of a national sample of consumers:

🐚 The Wilkie and Dickson Report on Search and Shopping

Peter Dickson and William Wilkie have reported the results of a national survey on consumer information search and shopping behavior.[18] This research focused on recent purchasers of refrigerators, freezers, and clothes washers and dryers. Their study was conducted under the auspices of the Marketing Science Institute and was financially sponsored by four major corporations—Sears, General Electric, Whirlpool, and Frigidaire—whose managements were interested in using the findings to improve their marketing mix decisions. Table 17-2 presents a subset of the results, in the same form you will be receiving research findings as a marketing manager in the future (although the table at first may look confusing, it is actually easy to follow, as we'll see shortly). In examining these findings, you might usefully consider two questions:

1. Why would the results have come out this way—what explanations are appropriate?
2. What implications do the findings have for a marketing strategist?

The first results reported in the table reflect *purchase circumstances*. In part A of the table, note how significant the situations of "failure," "repair problems," and "household moves" are in stimulating the purchases of these particular appliances. Parts B, C, and D then report further background descriptions of the purchasers. Note that women represent the major portion of the market for these products, although about half

Credence characteristics: Product attributes or claims that typical consumers will never be able to evaluate precisely, even after purchase and use, such as the quality of internal stitches during an operation.

Table 17-2 Summary Findings From the Wilkie and Dickson Study of Information Search and Shopping for Durables

A. Purchase Circumstances

Appliance failure	36%
Replacement of working unit	
Needs some repair	24
Working well	14
Residential move	18
Other	8

B. Who Participated in the Decision?

Homemaker solely	29%
Homemaker primarily	11
Joint effort w/spouse	52
Spouse primarily/solely	8

C. Previous Purchase Experience

None	35%
One prior purchase	33
Two or more purchases	32

D. Familiarity with Local Stores

None	4%
One to three stores	24
Four or more stores	72

E. Total Time Spent Considering the Purchase

Same-day purchase	9%
Within first week	24
1-4 weeks	33
1-3 months	11
3-6 months	11
Over 6 months	13

F. Total Number of Stores Visited

One	37%
Two	19
Three	19
Four or more	25

G. Total Number of Brands Considered

One	32%
Two	26
Three	26
Four or more	16

H. Total Time Spent Shopping

Less than two hours	45%
Two to four hours	28
Five to eight hours	14
More than eight hours	14

I. Types of Stores Shopped

1. Appliance store[a]	59%
2. Sears	57
3. Department store	27
4. Discount store	25
5. Wards	18
6. Furniture store	15
7. Penney	12
8. K-mart	9
9. Other type	13

[a]To be read, "Fifty-nine percent of the purchasers shopped in at least one specialty appliance store during their decision process, while 57 percent shopped at Sears, and so on."

J. Number of Information Sources Used

1. Number of "independent" source types (friends and relatives, *Consumer Reports*):

Zero,	52%	Range = 0 to 2 sources used
One,	37%	Mode = 0 sources used
Two,	11%	Mean = 0.58 sources used

2. Number of marketer source types (of the seven listed in part K, following):

Zero,	15%	Four,	6%	Range = 0 to 7 sources used
One,	27%	Five,	5%	Mode = 1 source used
Two,	25%	Six,	2%	Mean = 2 sources used
Three,	19%	Seven,	—	

K. Ratings of Source Usefulness

Information Source	Buyers Who Consulted	Buyers Who Found Source Useful	Buyer's "Most Used" Info Source
1. Appliance salesperson[b]	59%	49%	41%
2. Newspaper ad	39	28	13
3. Friend or relative	38	31	13
4. Catalog	35	28	9
5. Brochures/labels	28	25	9
6. *Consumer Reports*	20	18	9
7. Appliance repairperson	14	10	5
8. Magazine ad	12	7	1
9. TV ad	10	5	1

[b]To be read, "Fifty-nine percent of the buyers reported having consulted a salesperson as an information source. Almost all these people (49 percent of the total sample) reported finding the salesperson to be a 'useful' source of information. When asked which source had been the 'most useful,' 41 percent of consumers reported that the salesperson had been."

Table 17-2 (*Continued*)

L. Consumer's Search Interests

(Forced choice: pick one or the other)   "I was most interested in learning:
- "As much as possible about the appliance."   69%
- vs.
- "Just enough to make a choice."   31%

(Forced choice)   "I was most interested in:
- "Enjoying the search...because it was interesting."   32%
- vs.
- "Spending as little time as possible."   68%

M. Consumer's Search Strategies

(Forced choice)   "During my decision process I primarily relied on:
- "Past experience and knowledge."   69%
- vs.
- "New information from search."   31%

(Forced choice)   "During my decision process I primarily relied on:
- "Past experience and knowledge."   68%
- vs.
- "Knowledgeable others' advice."   32%

N. Where Purchased

Store Type	Share of Market	Bought on Sale	Negotiated Lower Price	Bought at First Store
Specialty appliance	37%	51%	28%	34%
Sears	30	89	4	46
Wards	9	92	8	22
Furniture	6	41	22	48
Discount	5	80	20	30
Department	4	69	13	38

O. Purchase Behavior

Bought at a special low price	76%
a. On sale	70%
b. Negotiated with salesperson	17%[c]
Brand loyalty	31%

[c]Some consumers both bought on sale and negotiated a special low price; thus, the total exceeds 76 percent.

P. Postpurchase Satisfaction with New Appliance

Very satisfied	71%
Satisfied	24
Neutral	3
Dissatisfied	2
Very dissatisfied	—

SOURCE: See Note 18.

the purchases are made as a joint effort with husbands. There is an interesting range of experience available from past purchases, and most consumers are familiar with some local stores from which they might buy.

Parts E, F, G, and H of the table report typical measures of consumers' information seeking behavior before buying their appliances. "Total time," for example, reflects the total elapsed time between *first thinking about making the purchase* until the actual purchase itself. Notice how wide the range is here—some consumers purchase the same day the thought arises, while others wait over three months before the actual buy! The other statistics here provide measures of the shopping activity itself. In reviewing them, you may find yourself to be somewhat surprised—notice that the largest groups of consumers report that they considered only one brand, visited only one store, and spent less than two hours in total time (including traveling) shopping for their purchase!

Parts I, J, and K move us further into the details of store search and information source usage. Of particular note here are (1) the *dominant position occupied by Sears* as a seller of appliances—it appears that over half of all consumers in the United States shop at Sears when in the market for one of these products—(2) the low number of information sources used, and (3) the surprisingly dominant position of the *salesperson* as the "most useful" information source encountered by the largest group of consumers. Parts L and M report findings on the primary forces within consumers' search interests and strategies. Again, the results may be somewhat different from what we might predict. Notice, for example, the potential conflict between "Learning as much as possible" and "Spending as little time as possible." In the area of search itself, it is clear that "past experience and knowledge" (which probably represents internal search) clearly dominates both measures of external search during shopping.

Part N of the table provides insights into the nature of retail competition. Again the performance of Sears is noteworthy—it appears to sell about one of every three machines in the nation. Its policy against its salespersons negotiating against posted prices comes through clearly in the data (along with Ward's). Finally, the statistic "bought at first store" suggests that Sears's marketing mix is inordinately successful in converting consumers from "searchers" to "buyers" during their store visit; its rate on this measure is approached only by the furniture stores, which account for a much smaller market.

Parts O and P of the table report key measures of the purchase itself. Most of these appliances are purchased at a sale price, but negotiation is not used often (some consumers both negotiated and bought on sale, which accounts for the fact that the numbers do not add to 76 percent). Brand loyalty—the purchase of the same brand as that owned previously—was surprisingly low in these product categories. Finally, part P reveals consumers' reports of how satisfied they were with their purchases after having owned them for up to a year. Notice the extremely strong results—95 percent of the participants in this survey reported that they were "Satisfied" or "Very satisfied" with their appliance. This level is so high that it is obvious that the wide range of consumer differences in information search and shopping behaviors does not lead to systematic differences in early consumer satisfaction, since virtually everyone is satisfied.

The results reported by Wilkie and Dickson are quite consistent with findings of earlier major studies in this area. (If you are interested in reading more of the findings, you may wish to consult the discussion in Note 19.)

CONSUMER SEARCH SEGMENTS

The findings by Wilkie and Dickson are useful in describing overall information search behavior. In reviewing the results, however, we can see that there is high variation for almost every measure taken—some consumers seem to search very little before they buy, while others search a great deal. Notice, however, that Table 17-2 did not tell us whether one type of search might be substituting for another type. To discover whether this is the case, we need to examine the "patterns" of a consumer's search behaviors. Also, Table 17-2 did not tell us *who* the various consumers were who were searching a little or a lot. Fortunately, research on consumer search segments has addressed each of these areas:

❧ *Patterns of Search*

Several interesting studies have investigated patterns of information search for durable goods.[20] In one study, for example, Westbrook and Fornell used advanced statistical analysis and discovered four primary search segments for major household appliances.[21]

- *Personal advice seekers.* This segment comprised about 20 percent of all consumers. They relied heavily on the advice and opinion of friends and family members, did not use much other information, and visited an average of only two stores.

- *Store intense shoppers.* Representing about 30 percent of consumers, this segment primarily relied on store visits to learn about and evaluate their alternatives. On average, this segment visited four to five stores before buying.

- *Objective shoppers.* This segment made up about 20 percent of consumers. These persons did not use personal sources at all, but made heavy use of objective sources such as *Consumer Reports*, brochures, magazine articles, and so on. This group also shopped extensively, visiting between three and four stores on average.

- *Moderate shoppers.* Comprising 30 percent of the sample, this segment visited only one store, tended not to rely on friends or relatives, and used only a moderate amount of other forms of information before making their purchases.

Who Are the "Information Seekers"?

In an interesting set of studies, Hans Thorelli and associates examined persons who subscribe to reports of product testing agencies (e.g., *Consumer Reports*) in the United States, Norway, and West Germany.[22] They found the same type of people in all three cultures—information seekers have higher income and higher education and read more magazines and newspapers than does the average consumer. Their beliefs are also different—they have high expectations for product performance, are less favorable toward advertising, and are not likely to be innovators (although they are opinion leaders).

Recent research by Duncan and Olshavsky and by Muncy has examined consumers' "beliefs about the marketplace." Consumers who held the following beliefs were found to *search less* for information before buying their products:

- "Most store salespersons are well informed about the products they sell."

- "The best brands are usually the ones that sell the most."

- "I am a poor judge when it comes to evaluating products that are mechanical."

- "Competition . . . tends to keep the prices of different brands about the same."[23]

■ APPLICATION AREAS: CONSUMER INFORMATION PROVISION

MARKETING APPLICATIONS

When we think of the marketing mix, we can see what a large portion of the mix is devoted to appealing to customers at the prepurchase stage. The *product* must be designed, packaged, and named so as to attract the interest of the potential buyer. *Place* decisions are crucial in bringing the product and the buyer together so that a transaction may actually occur—if Kathy Fitzgerald is shopping at the Northway Mall while

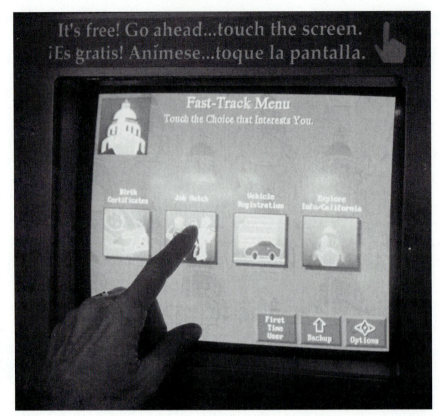

As marketers search for new ways to deliver consumer information, kiosks are becoming increasingly popular, especially those that enable consumers to use touch screens to obtain information from computers. One researcher estimates that the number of kiosks will grow from 60,000 to 2 million in four years (which would make them more numerous than gasoline pumps!).

our product is being offered elsewhere, we run the risk of losing a sale. *Price* decisions are also important, since these might define our product out of further consideration if we're seen as being "too high" or "too low." And *promotion* decisions are aimed right at buyers in the prepurchase stage. One of the key options that marketers have, of course, involves *providing consumers with useful information.* The field of consumer information has many issues that have been recently addressed. Let's take a look at three interesting reports.

🐌 *Shopping for a Home? Head for the Library!*

Consumer Housing Libraries, Inc. (CHL), is changing the way many consumers buy homes in the Washington, D.C., area. House-hunters are free to browse through the housing information displays: included is a wealth of information on residential developments, home builders and lenders, facts on schools, zoning, transportation, and so on. The CHL charges businesses $1000 a month for the right to set up promotional displays. According to the founder of CHL, the appeal to advertisers is the high-quality prospect who visits the library: "A developer can buy a quarter page ad in the Saturday *Washington Post* for $3000," he explains. "That same amount will get them 3 months with us . . . and our ratio of buyers to visitors is much better." The average visitor spends about 1 hour looking at the various exhibits and takes away as much print information as he or she desires. Once the visitor leaves, however, CHL faces a problem—how to track the later purchase behavior of its visitors (this information is obviously of great interest to prospective exhibitors at CHL). As one effort, CHL's managers asked visitors to return an information postcard after they buy and promised a CHL house-warming gift in return for this feedback![24]

How Nice Is the Price?

One area in which consumer research can contribute involves the form ("format") in which information is provided to consumers. Improved formats can attract attention, assist comparisons, decrease the chances of miscomprehension, and aid in retention of the information. As an example, J. Russo and his associates have reported on several studies involving the provision of unit pricing information by supermarkets.

In unit pricing a store provides shelf tags that present prices in a product category on a common "per unit" weight or volume basis, such as cents per ounce for catsup, cents per pound for sugar, and so forth. Unit pricing was originally proposed to help shoppers who might want to compare prices of different sizes of packages. This can be a very difficult task—several studies challenged consumers to select the most economical buys in various categories and found error rates of about 50 percent.[25] Many grocery chains introduced unit pricing as a convenience for their patrons. Following introduction, there was great interest in how many consumers were using this new tool, and how they were reacting to it.

The initial consumer research reports were surprisingly mixed. The studies that asked consumers, "What do you think of unit pricing!" showed that consumers were very favorable and reported using it often to help them buy better. Those studies that examined consumers' actual purchase behavior, however, revealed very little evidence that consumers were buying any differently then they had before. Russo, speaking from a consumer information processing (CIP) perspective, suggested that this disparity might exist because it was still difficult for a consumer to compare unit prices of different brands and sizes: since the tags were up and down along the shelves, a consumer would be placing some strains on short-term memory (STM) to keep the other prices in mind while searching out new ones to compare. His solution: reduce the strain by placing *all the unit prices* for a product class in the same spot for easy reference. This could be done by posting a product list, ranking the brands from lowest to highest unit prices, in a prominent location amid the shelf display.

One retail chain tested this idea for several product categories over a five-week period (typically, private labels offer higher profit margins to the retailer—thus if a unit pricing program were to shift sales toward private labels, the store's overall profits should increase). The results of the trial showed a significant shift in sales toward the lower-priced brands, averaging a 2 percent decrease in the average prices paid for purchases for the test product categories while the posted lists were in operation.[26]

More Is Better, or Is It?

Every marketer faces the decision of the amount of information to attempt to convey. The space available on package labels and in ads is limited. Normally, however, we would expect that more information is desirable, since it can cover more aspects of the product and can present different elements of appeal to consumers. Before leaving the topic of marketing applications, we should mention that one of the most interesting debates in the consumer behavior field concerns the topic of **consumer information**

**Consumer informa-
tion overload:** A po-
tential danger from too
much information: the
CIP system is stretched
beyond capacity, pos-
sibly leading to confu-
sion or the avoidance of
available information.

overload. This issue was originally raised by Jacob Jacoby and his coworkers. They were concerned that some people were making the assumption that "if some information is good, then more information must be better." For example, at that time there was a movement to place nutritional information on package labels. But how much of this information should be provided? Is there any danger from providing higher amounts of information?

Jacoby proposed that such a danger might well exist. As you'll recall from our discussions of the CIP system, STM (the work center of the system) is subject to severe capacity constraints. If too much information is forced upon STM, it is possible that it will become "overloaded." If overload occurs, the consumer can become confused and could make worse decisions than would have been made without the extra information. Alternatively, many consumers might simply ignore some information they would have used if so much hadn't been provided. However, supporters of more information argue that if information isn't made available, it *can't* be used. Also, they point out that some consumer segments will wish to use different information than other segments, so having more available is positive.

A number of interesting empirical studies have been undertaken to try to clarify these issues, with further debates on how the findings should be interpreted. If you would like to learn more about this interesting area, you may wish to consult Note 27.

PUBLIC POLICY APPLICATIONS

In addition to marketing's interest in consumer information, this topic is also a primary center of interest for public policy's regulatory activities. Three characteristics are key for public policy's interests in this area:

1. *Fully informed consumers.* Our market-based economic system rests on a theoretical assumption that consumers are fully informed about the alternatives they have when making their purchases. Being fully informed (according to the theory), consumers are able to allocate their resources in the most efficient manner. Although we know that consumers are not *actually* fully informed, policymakers have an obligation to work toward having all important information as available to consumers as possible.

2. *Choice-neutral information.* Unlike a marketer's stress on providing information to *influence* the consumer's choice of a brand, public policy is interested in providing information to allow a consumer to make the best choice for him or her, which might be any brand available. Thus the emphasis is on knowledge rather than choice, and the information should be objective rather than subjective.

3. *Cost and freedom trade-offs.* When regulators consider which forms of information should be made available, they need to consider the costs involved, the benefits likely to accrue to consumers, and the extent to which the provision of the information might restrict legitimate freedoms of marketers.

Key Questions About Consumer Information Programs

In all, over 30 federal agencies and many state and local offices are currently engaged in disseminating information to consumers. You may have seen, for example, ads for the Consumer Product Information Center in Pueblo, Colorado, which serves as a distribution center for many government publications. Many citizens do not expect the

New Look: The proof is in the pudding

Nutrition Facts

Serving Size: ½ cup (113 g)
Servings Per Package 4

Amount Per Serving

Calories 100* Calories from Fat 10	
	% Daily Value*
Total Fat 1 g	2%
Saturated Fat 0 g	0%
Cholesterol 0 mg	0%
Sodium 140 mg	6%
Total Carbohydrate 19 g	6%
Dietary Fiber 0 g	0%
Sugars 13 g	
Protein 2 g	

Calcium 6%	•	Iron 0%

Not a significant source of Vitamin A, and Vitamin C

*Percent Daily Values are based on a 2,000 calorie diet. Your Daily Values may be higher or lower depending on your calorie needs:

		Calories	2,000	2,500
Total Fat	Less than		65 g	80 g
Sat Fat	Less than		20 g	25 g
Cholesterol	Less than		300 mg	300 mg
Sodium	Less than		2,400 mg	2,400 mg
Total Carbohydrate			300 g	375 g
Dietary Fiber			25 g	30 g

Calories per gram:
Fat 9 • Carbohydrate 4 • Protein 4

*Regular Pudding 150
© 1993 DISTRIBUTED BY DEL MONTE FOODS.

The new nutrition label (left) differs a great deal from the old one (right). These labels are from Del Monte vanilla flavored Lite Pudding Cup. Here's how to read the new one.

• **Calories.** The new label is based on a 2,000-calorie-a-day diet. A serving (1/2 cup) of this product has 90 calories; 10% of those are from fat.

• **% Daily Value.** This new term gives the consumer an idea of what percentage of the nutrient comes from this food. For instance, a serving of this product contains 190 milligrams of sodium, which is 8% of the day's sodium limit for someone on a 2,000 calorie diet.

• **Total fat.** A serving of this product has 1 gram of fat—2% of the day's limit for a 2,000 calorie diet.

• **Other information.** This product has no fiber, 14 grams of sugar and a gram of protein.

Some products, like this one, will offer a general guide for how much of each key nutrient you should have—or limit yourself to—each day based on a 2,000 and a 2,500 calorie intake. You can use it as a quick reference to see how the product fits into your overall diet.

For instance, this label tells you that a person eating 2,000 calories a day should consume less than 65 grams of total fat. (This is based on the widespread recommendation that no more than 30% of calories in the diet come from fat.) It also tells you that you should consume at least 25 grams of fiber and no more than 20 grams of saturated fat.

CALORIE COMPARISON
SERVING SIZE 4-1/4 OZ.
LIGHT PUDDING 100
REGULAR PUDDING 150

NUTRITION INFORMATION –
PER 4-1/4 OZ. SERVING
SERVINGS PER PACKAGE – FOUR
CALORIES 100
PROTEIN 2g
CARBOHYDRATE 19g
FAT 1g
   SATURATED 0g
CHOLESTEROL 0mg
SODIUM 85mg
POTASSIUM 140mg

PERCENTAGE OF U.S.
RECOMMENDED DAILY
ALLOWANCES (U.S. RDA) PER
4-1/4 OZ. SERVING
PROTEIN 6
VITAMIN A .... *
VITAMIN C .... *
THIAMINE (VIT. B₁) ..... *
RIBOFLAVIN (VIT. B₂) ... 8
NIACIN .... *
CALCIUM 8
IRON .... *
PHOSPHORUS 2
*CONTAINS LESS THAN 2% OF THE
U.S. RDA OF THESE NUTRIENTS.
INGREDIENTS: SKIM MILK, WATER, SUGAR SYRUP, FRUCTOSE, MODIFIED FOOD STARCH, COCOA POWDER PROCESSED WITH ALKALI, HYDROGENATED SOYBEAN OIL, CARRAGEENAN, SALT, ARTIFICIAL FLAVOR, SODIUM STEAROYL-2-LACTYLATE, YELLOW 6.
© 1991 DISTR. BY DEL MONTE FOODS SAN FRANCISCO, CA 94105

Copyright 1993, USA TODAY. Reprinted with permission.

As of May 1994, the U.S. government's required changes in food labels will be on the market. Notice how the new labels (on the left) are aimed at better informing consumers about nutritional aspects of purchase choices as compared to the old labels (on the right), which provided more informational items, but less basis for understanding their role in a person's diet.

government to carry the burden (and costs) of developing all consumer informational and educational materials. Since marketers are reaching consumers directly every day, and are engaging in information programs themselves, these citizens suggest that marketers should be either asked or required to provide certain types of information as a necessary part of their programs.

While most experts would agree that consumers should be as fully informed as possible, they disagree—sometimes heatedly—over how this best should be accomplished. Four key questions that arise again and again are

1. *What* information should be provided?

2. *How much* information should be provided?

3. *In what form* should the information be provided?

4. Will consumers *use* the information?

We already have a good basis for appreciating the types of issues raised by these questions. The rights of consumers have to be balanced off against the rights of marketers; unwise government regulations can work against a fair and efficient market system. Also, our previous coverage of such topics as "low involvement," social influences, and impulse purchasing has warned us that consumers may not always use information when it is made available. For these reasons the debates in this area are especially sharp, since no one is really certain of the answers to the four questions just posed. Also, since all information programs present some costs, questions of which exact information to provide are often controversial. Information programs can have several types of goals. These range from helping consumers to compare brands and prices, to informing consumers about contents and possible hazards, to clarifying terms of sale and contracts. To gain a better feel for some issues that can crop up, let's take a look at a program involving energy efficiency.

🐌 *Energy Tags Lack Power, but LCC Adds Punch*

In response to the energy crisis some years ago, the U.S. government decided to encourage consumers to demand more energy-efficient products. Special tags would be placed on each machine for sale in a store. These tags would inform consumers of the costs to operate that appliance for one year, with the hope that consumers would shift their purchases toward the machines that cost less to run. In the government's plan, a bright yellow and black label would be prominently posted on each new appliance. This label would provide (1) the estimated annual electricity cost to run the appliance and (2) the range of costs offered for similar-sized machines on the market, thus offering a baseline for comparing that model with the other options a consumer would find if he or she shopped around. A consumer research study conducted by Dennis McNeill and William Wilkie indicated, however, that the government's plan—although likely to be successful in informing consumers of actual costs—wasn't likely to affect consumers' appliance purchasing behavior.[28] As a policy aimed at reducing energy consumption, therefore, it seemed likely to fail.

Life-cycle cost (LCC): Rather than purchase price, the expected total cost of ownership of a product.

R. Bruce Hutton and William Wilkie then suggested that a *large part of the problem was the type of information the government was trying to convey*. Instead of telling consumers about yearly operating costs, they argued that a new form of information—**life-cycle cost (LCC)**—be used instead. LCC has been routinely used for years by financial analysts and engineers in business when planning large projects. Rather than equating "cost" with selling price, as many consumers are used to doing, LCC considers all the costs we can expect to encounter. With most appliances, these consist of purchase price, service, and energy costs. Refrigerators, for example, typically require more spending for electricity during their 10 to 15 years of life than they do for the original purchase price.

When Hutton and Wilkie studied the impact of giving LCC information to consumers, they found that appliance buyers did change their behavior in a significant manner. The LCC labels (although presenting the same basic type of information as the government energy labels) highlighted the fact that energy savings occur for many years (not just one) and should be added together (and discounted to a present value) to compare best the options available. When consumers saw this, they shifted their purchases toward their own financial interests and rewarded manufacturers of the more energy-efficient machines with increased purchases. The shift in purchases in this study was so strong, in fact, that when the authors extrapolated their results to the entire nation, they calculated that, for refrigerators alone, LCC tags would save the nation's consumers over $4 billion every year in energy costs. If you were a judge with responsibility for consumer energy information, would you order a move toward LCC labels? (If you'd like to read more about this possibility, you may wish to pursue the readings in Note 29.)

APPLICATIONS FOR CONSUMERS

In closing our discussion of prepurchase processes we should return briefly to the topics of Chapter 2, in which we recognized that much of the material in a consumer behavior book has important implications for individual consumers. In this regard, you may wish to review briefly the contents of this chapter from your own personal perspective as a consumer. In so doing, consider how an understanding of problem recognition processes might be helpful, for example, or how you might benefit from a fuller appreciation of the nature of information search. In the next chapter we will focus on what research has found about consumer purchase processes.

■ SUMMARY

TYPES OF CONSUMER DECISIONS

In this chapter we began our examination of *consumer decision processes* by concentrating on *prepurchase processes*. Our introductory vignettes stressed the importance of understanding consumer decision processes and showed how flexible they can be—just a single new input can have a profound effect on how consumers will make their decisions, what they will buy, and even whether they'll buy at all.

Four basic types of consumer decisions were identified in the chapter's first section: *budget allocation, product purchase, store patronage,* and *brand choice.* Complexity variations in these decisions was also examined—we discussed how consumer involvement affects the effort and order of a decision process and how time, learning, and complexity differ among such decision processes as *extensive problem solving, limited problem solving,* and *routinized-response behavior.*

THE CONSUMER DECISION PROCESS

A model of consumer decision processes was presented in the chapter's second section. This model consists of four stages: (1) problem recognition, which leads to (2) information search and alternative evaluation, which is followed by (3) the purchase itself, which is followed by (4) postpurchase processes. In this chapter, the first two stages—problem recognition and information search—were discussed, with the remaining stages examined in the two following chapters.

STAGE 1: PROBLEM RECOGNITION

The *problem recognition* stage begins a decision process. Problem recognition results from a discrepancy between a consumer's "current state" and "desired state." Several key causes for such a discrepancy were described, and the role that marketing plays in this process was analyzed.

STAGE 2: INFORMATION SEARCH AND ALTERNATIVE EVALUATION

Our discussion of the *information search and alternative evaluation* stage pointed out the two major types of search that consumers employ: incidental learning and purchase-directed search. We then focused on the many factors that combine to affect the amount and nature of search. These factors can be classified into three general categories:

psychological, situational, and information processing factors. Finally, we discussed detailed findings from a recent national study of how consumers shop for major appliances.

APPLICATION AREAS: CONSUMER INFORMATION PROVISION

In our final section, we examined several applied issues of consumer information provision. These addressed such questions as: "Will consumers use unit price information?" "What is information overload and is it a problem for marketers?" and "What information can move consumers to conserve energy?" In each area we saw that consumer research provides useful marketing insights.

■ KEY TERMS

type of the decision
complexity of the decision process
budget allocation
discretionary
product purchase or not
store patronage
brand and style decisions
level of involvement
extensive problem solving
limited problem solving
routinized-response behavior
satisficing

problem recognition
information search and alternative evaluation
purchase processes
postpurchase processes
current state
desired state
consumer information search
incidental learning
directed search
loyalty decisions
impulse decisions

convenience goods
specialty goods
shopping goods
search characteristics
experience characteristics
credence characteristics
nondurables
services
durable goods
consumer information overload
life-cycle cost (LCC)

■ REVIEW QUESTIONS AND EXPERIENTIAL EXERCISES

[E = Application extension or experiential exercise]

1. Consider the four primary types of substance variations in decisions.

   a. Indicate the nature and extent of the relationship(s) to one another.

   b. Address the issue of ordering of these decisions. Is it fixed or variable?

2. Identify three recent purchases classified as "low-involvement" goods or services.

   a. Indicate the rationale for the "low-involvement" classification.

   b. Note any changes in the order of the decisions from that presented in the hierarchy of effects model.

   c. Comment on the type and level of effort expended in the overall decision.

3. Based on John Howard's definition of the three different types of behavior processes, identify two additional

examples of each. What are the marketing implications associated with these behavior processes?

4. [E] Figure 17-2 lists the key determinants of problem recognition.

   a. Consider three of your recent durable goods purchases and five recent nondurable purchases. Identify the key determinant(s) of your problem recognition.

   b. For each purchase, analyze the nature and extent of marketing's influence on the problem recognition stage for you.

5. [E] Interview a recent purchaser of a durable good (as a guide, you may wish to use the items contained in Table 17-2). Try to probe for further explanations of the nature and reasons for the particular search pattern. Write a brief report to summarize your findings.

6. **[E]** Answer for the following products: shampoo, video disk, VCR, bank.

   a. What primary sources of information are consumers likely to consult?

   b. How are the types of information used likely to vary by individual based on experience, for example? Importance of the decision?

   c. For any one of the foregoing, detail three marketing implications.

7. **[E]** Why do some marketers supply limited, if any, information regarding their brands in advertising? For example, consider the typical ad for soft drinks or pain remedies. If you were a brand manager in one of these product categories, how would you regard an approach that supplied more information?

8. **[E]** What are the characteristics of the four primary segments in the Westbrook and Fornell analysis? As a consumer, where would you place yourself?

9. **[E]** Choose any four products or services. For each, give two actual examples of how marketers attempt to

   a. Minimize the cost of information.

   b. Enlarge the consequences of nonsearch.

   c. Alter the weight attached to different information sources.

10. **[E]** Consider the three issues (for example, fully informed consumers) associated with the public policy-maker's perspective on the information search stage.

    a. Are these issues independent?

    b. In an effort to ensure that consumers are fully informed, is it possible for such information to remain choice neutral and not restrict the freedom of marketers? Comment, using examples.

11. **[E]** Consider two major household purchases in which you have been involved. Address the question, "How does information search vary in a multiperson unit, such as a family!" (You may need to conduct interviews to answer this.) Write a brief report on your findings.

12. **[E]** To gain some insight into the nature of browsing as a form of incidental learning, conduct two interviews with consumers just as they return from a shopping trip. Ask them what they learned during the trip, then probe for new thoughts/information they had while browsing. (*Tip:* You may want to have them "replay" the trip slowly to capture more of these.) If time is available, monitor your own or a friend's reactions *during* a trip. Write a brief report on your findings.

13. **[E]** Interview an experienced automobile salesperson concerning consumers' prepurchase processes. (*Tip:* You may want to begin by asking about the quotes opening this chapter.) Also ask about marketing and sales techniques he or she and his or her agency use to influence consumers at this stage. Write a brief report on your findings.

14. **[E]** Interview an experienced manager or salesperson in a stereo, appliance, or upscale clothing store concerning how consumers shop, the role of consumer information, and what techniques he or she finds useful for the problem recognition/information search stages of the decision process. Write a brief report on your findings.

15. **[E]** Use Notes 19–29, or the reference section of your library, to locate recent readings on a prepurchase topic of personal interest to you. Write a brief report on your findings.

■ SUGGESTED READING

■ This set of topics lends itself to studies of consumers that tend to be interesting and readable: thus our Note references are especially attractive for this chapter. For 10 good short cases of firms having to deal with crises similar to the toxic shock syndrome case at the start of this chapter, see Paul Holmes, "Pride Before a Fall," *Inside PR,* May 1990, pp. 8ff. For closer analysis of the results in Table 17-2, together with marketing implications and a suggested model of consumer shopping that ties the results together, see William L. Wilkie and Peter R. Dickson, "Consumer Information Search and Shopping Behavior," in H. Kassarjian and T. Robertson (eds.), *Perspectives in Consumer Behavior,* 4th ed. (Englewood Cliffs, N.J.: Prentice Hall, 1991), pp. 1–26. For a short, interesting look at car buyers' stories similar to those in our chapter's opening quotes, see Micheline Maynard,

"New Wheels: An Annual Rite for Some," *USA Today,* February 8, 1993, p. 6E. For an applied look at how firms are battling to intervene in consumers' prepurchase decision processes, try Stephen Kindel, "Cutting through the Clutter," *Financial World,* April 13, 1993, pp. 36ff. Finally, for three recent looks at how technological innovations may change the future of consumers' prepurchase processes, see James H. Snider, "Shopping in the Information Age," *The Futurist,* November–December 1992, pp. 14–18; Robert E. Widing and W. Wayne Talarzyk, "Electronic Information Systems for Consumers: An Evaluation of Computer-Assisted Formats in Multiple Decision Environments," *Journal of Marketing Research,* Vol. 30 (May 1993), pp. 125–41; and "Retailing Will Never Be the Same," *Business Week,* July 26, 1993, pp. 54–60.

18

CONSUMER DECISIONS (II)
Purchase Processes

BUYERS REPORT ON AUTO CHOICES

Let's listen in again on the interviews with Chicago auto buyers. This time, we'll cover some aspects of their purchase decision processes (relevant dimensions are noted in parentheses for each one):

(*Purchase timing*) "Then when the $2000 rebate came up...I said if we're ever going to do this, this would be the time."

(*Evaluation*) "And we test drove the same car—two Corsicas—one was a four-cylinder, one with a six-cylinder just to see the difference...and the six-cylinder just won!...She didn't care...I liked the performance."

(*Time pressure*) "We couldn't wait [because of the wife's new job] for a car coming in on order; that was out of the question. So we had to buy."

(*Desire for benefits*) "No, I could have taken three months...I wanted what I wanted and would do whatever I had to do."

(*Negotiation*) "The thing that gets me is, when you go in...they'll say, what are you looking to pay. So you tell them...He goes in and he talks to the manager and you sit there. And then he comes back and says, 'This is the best I can do.' You say, 'No, I know you can do better than that.' So he goes back in, and watch, the manager is going to come. Sure enough, the manager comes and says, 'Listen, this is the best we can do.' Usually Dick is the one who says no...and they keep playing this game back and forth. I think you're just wasting your time, but they're not going to come down to what you want right then and there. Just say, 'If this is just not feasible, fine, let's go!'"

(*Choice*) "It was 2.6 percent financing, four years, $500 down. Actually, to be perfectly honest between you and me, it wasn't the car I wanted. I wanted the other one. But because the financing was so good, we thought OK, for four years we'll take this one and then maybe in four years we'll get the other one."

(*Choice*) "Part of that probably was the $2000 rebate...In the paper it said that for a Cadillac it was just a terrific deal. We bought a couple of cars over the years, and I'm thinking my Dad spent $8000 for a car and if he knew I was spending $22,000 he'd roll over in his grave. I said, "What the hell, we got a nice car."[1]

504

Supermarket cooling cases are overrun with products trying to get placed there, then to attract a purchase decision from consumers. For example, over 700 ice cream products are available. A Haagen-Dazs executive reports, "It's very difficult.... There are too many products and not enough freezers." But so much choice makes it difficult on consumers as well. According to one industry researcher: "People are just standing in front of freezers, staring.... They don't know what to pick."[2]

From the marketer's perspective, the purchase stage is particularly crucial, since it is here that the money flow back to the business is generated. Consumer purchases serve as a ratification of a brand's marketing mix, whereas purchases of other brands may signal a need for change in the mix. From the consumer's perspective, the purchase phase is also very important. Not only is this the point at which we give up money in return for a product, but the choice of only one brand means that we must depend on it to deliver the benefits we're seeking.

In our first chapter on consumer decisions we focused on the early stages of the process: problem recognition and information search. As we saw, these two stages pose a number of significant issues. Within the overall decision process, however, they merely "set the stage" for purchase processes, where alternatives are evaluated and decisions are made. In this chapter we'll discover some frameworks that help us to understand consumer decision processes. *We'll see that just a slight shift in the process can change the purchase decision itself, which makes this area extremely important for marketing managers to understand.* We'll see how researchers go about studying these processes and what challenges they face in this task. We'll analyze the basic "decision strategies" that consumers use. Finally, we'll explore some interesting recent marketing developments influencing consumers' purchasing behaviors in stores.

■ MONITORING CONSUMER DECISION MAKING

Since a consumer's decision making is a personal mental process, it can be difficult or even impossible for a marketing researcher to measure directly. Also, the fact that decision making can operate at extremely high consumer information processing (CIP) speeds only makes matters worse. How, then, *do researchers study the consumer decision-making process? Two basic approaches are generally used: input-output and process monitoring research.

INPUT-OUTPUT RESEARCH

Input-output approach: Research that provides a stimulus input to consumers and then observes their behavioral responses as outputs.

The **input-output approach** usually employs some form of experimentation. Here the researcher provides a certain stimulus *input* to consumers' decisions (e.g., a special price) and then observes how consumers' behaviors—the *outputs*—change from what they were before. Often several types of inputs are pitted against each other to discover which works best. Input-output research does not, however, measure the decision process itself. For example,

🐘 *How Do Soap Sales Stack Up?*

In one simple but interesting input-output experiment, Safeway Supermarkets teamed with Procter & Gamble to study how the in-store display of bar soap affects consumer purchases. Specifically, P & G executives were wondering if hand-stacking of its bars in a bin display would increase sales, as compared to just having them dumped in the bin. Thus the *stimulus inputs* that were varied included some stores with hand-stacked displays, and others with bin dumping (in accord with good marketing research practice, a large number of stores should be used, with random selection of which stores receive which treatment and perhaps other "controls" such as comparison with sales in prior time periods). Since this was an "input-output" study, no consumers were interviewed or specially observed. Instead, the *outputs*, in the form of sales of the test brand of bar soap, were carefully tabulated through the scanning computer system. Results? The soap brand's sales increased by 5 percent when hand-stacking was used for the display. Managerial action? Since labor costs are a key issue for supermarkets, P & G would try to seize this opportunity by developing a delivery process that would take the soap to the retailer in pre-stacked piles![3]

Marketers frequently use input-output methods before committing themselves to large expenditures in their marketing mixes. Sometimes these are conducted on small samples of consumers in "laboratory" conditions that are carefully controlled. Advertising is frequently studied this way, through special forms of "copy tests." In this form of test, for example, alternative Jell-O ads would be used to see which themes work best with the target audience for these commercials.

Further, as our Safeway example shows, the "real world" can also be used for input-output research, in a *field experiment*. While the conditions cannot be as carefully controlled, field experiments have the advantage of providing results under realistic conditions. These kinds of tests are run on other aspects of the marketing mix besides shelf displays, of course. For example, you may have noticed publishers testing different covers for the same book or magazine to see which ones "draw" best at the newsstand, and marketers often test different prices in different cities. And, as in our Safeway example, **supermarket scanners** now allow for considerably more in-store testing—coupons, ads, price changes, shelf spacing, and so forth can now be tested using computerized sales figures that provide rapid results for input-output experiments.

Input-output designs are also crucial in academic research that studies the nature of consumer decision making. Here we find lab experiments developed to test theories of how consumers make decisions. These studies challenge the researcher's ingenuity, since the researcher must develop a set of stimuli and conditions that will allow the consumer's decision outputs to identify which process the consumer had followed. The theory testing work of academics is very likely to be carried out in lab experiments, often using college students as participants in the studies. Although a quite technical area, this approach has received considerable attention in the field and has contributed much to our understanding.[4]

PROCESS MONITORING RESEARCH

The second approach to studying consumer decision making places less emphasis on stimuli and decision outcomes themselves. Instead, **process monitoring** *focuses on trying to capture the reality of the decision process itself, as it occurs*. Three types of process monitoring methods have been popular: verbal (Exhibit 18-1), physical, and observational.

Process monitoring: Research that focuses on measuring the decision process itself, as it occurs.

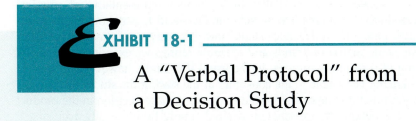

EXHIBIT 18-1

A "Verbal Protocol" from a Decision Study

Mike, a consumer, is choosing a hand-held calculator based upon product information presented to him in the form of a multiattribute matrix of brands and their characteristics. The information display is similar to that shown in Figure 18-1, except that the brand names have been disguised and the attributes are those for calculators.

Mike's Discussion As He Makes His Choice

"The first thing I'm going to do is look for size," he said. "I like smaller ones better than a real big one. And I've got a large one and it's a hassle carrying it to class. So let's check, let's check out the compacts first. . . . OK, versatility would be the first thing. Medium, very high, and uh . . .

(Pause) "OK, so far Brand F has got compact size, and very high versatility, easy to use, very convenient. Brand F's looking pretty good. And battery life really doesn't matter, it's 6 hours and the warranty's 9 months. . . . The highest warranty is 12, this one's 9. It's got . . . not a bad battery.

"Brand F looks to be the best, I'm going to check out brand E 'cause that's still in a compact size. It's got medium versatility, it's fairly convenient, 3 hours, 3 months, and it's standard size, so forget that one.

"Brand C, very high versatility, fairly convenient, 6 hours, 12 months, credit card size...hmm...

"Ok, Brand D, another credit card size, it's got high versatility, it's fairly convenient, 6 hours, 3 months.

"I, I'm going to go with Brand F....Yes, Brand F, definitely!"

SOURCE: Courtesy of Dipankar Chakravarti.

Verbal monitoring methods simply ask the consumer to verbalize his or her thinking about the decision as it occurs (or sometimes to "play it back" to the researcher after the decision has been made). For example, a researcher may accompany a consumer while shopping in a supermarket. Observations the consumer is making are taped by the researcher, who may also ask occasional clarifying questions. When the recording is analyzed, a *verbal protocol* of the purchase decision process is available, and several types of analyses can be run to compare the strategies used by different consumers. Sometimes, a *decision net* is also developed. This is a formal map that traces the process from the beginning to the end and notes all steps along the way. Exhibit 18-1 demonstrates a verbal protocol recording the thoughts of one student in a recent decision-making study.[5]

Information display boards (IDBs) are a popular representative of **physical monitoring methods**.[6] A sample IDB is shown in Figure 18-1, as it would appear to a consumer participating in an IDB study. Note how this array of information is similar to the multiattribute matrix of brands and attribute ratings we examined in Chapter 11's discussion of consumer attitudes. In the usual IDB study, however, the specific cells' ratings are not yet visible to the consumer at the start of the study. Instead, the consumer is informed that he or she should make a purchase decision in the product category and can obtain any information desired simply by physically acquiring it from the appropriate cell in the matrix.

ὲ🐚 How Does an IDB Work?

To see more clearly how an IDB can work, let's assume that Marilyn Hart is a new transfer student entering her junior year at the university. She needs to find an apartment as soon as possible and has Figure 18-1's IDB available to her. Let's also assume that she decides to start her decision process by finding out the prices for rentals at the Whispering Willows complex, since she's intrigued by the name. Her exact instructions for using the IDB would depend on the nature of the IDB's design, but if the IDB were in the form of a honeycomb of boxes (similar to the rental boxes at a post office), Marilyn would

1. Reach in to the third box in the top row.
2. Remove one of the cards having Whispering Willow's rates on it.
3. Examine the information and use it for her decision making.
4. Place the card face down in another container that holds the physical record of the information she is acquiring.
5. Decide which piece of information she'd like next and repeat the process of acquisition.

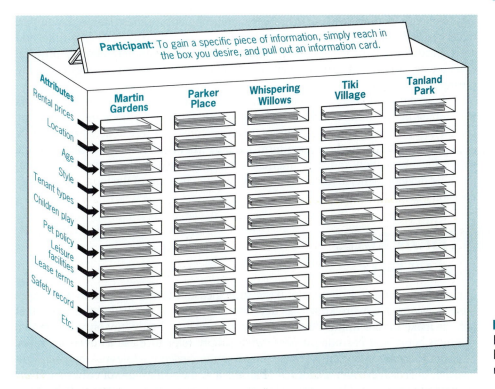

FIGURE 18-1 A Sample Information Display Board for Local Apartment Complexes

If the IDB is on a computer terminal, Marilyn needs only to push the appropriate button representing that position in the array. In any of the methods, if she wants to look at the information again later, she can do so by repeating the process.

Why go through all this? Researchers are interested in how many tabs Marilyn will turn, and in what order, before she makes her decision. From this, they are able to infer the types of decision processes that are being used. For example, Marilyn might pursue either a **processing by attributes (PBA)** strategy or a **processing by brands (PBB)** strategy. As an example of the PBA case, she might start by pulling information all across the price attribute row to find out which apartments are most expensive and which are cheapest. She might then eliminate a few (because they're too high priced or seem too low priced) and move to the location attribute row, to compare the remaining apartments on how convenient they'll be. In general, then, a PBA strategy will have Marilyn moving across the rows of the table.

The PBB process is quite different. What if Marilyn has heard that Whispering Willows is "the place to be" and that she should try to get in there if at all possible? Here it would be natural for her to find out more about this complex before she looks at the competition, and we might expect her to begin by pulling information down the Whispering Willows column of Figure 18-1. In general, then, a PBB strategy will have Marilyn moving down the columns of the table as she learns more about each apartment's features.[7]

Observational monitoring methods have also been used in consumer research. *Eye cameras,* for example, detail exactly where consumers' eyes travel as they are confronted with product labels or IDB displays. Based on this information, researchers can infer what information is being considered and what is being ignored, as well as the timing of information usage.[8] In general, however, observational methods are used

Processing by attributes (PBA): A consumer compares brands based on one attribute, then on another, and so on.

Processing by brands (PBB): A consumer learns about one brand across several attributes before moving across the attributes of another brand.

less frequently than are the other process monitoring approaches. This is due in part to cost considerations (it is hard to observe more than one consumer at a time, and specialized equipment is sometimes required). Also, if we merely observe physical movements, we are not learning very much about the thinking processes occurring during the same time.

In recent years there has been an increasing tendency for consumer researchers to combine both the input-output and process monitoring methods into even more complex studies. With careful designs of this type, consumer researchers have recently been able to investigate how long-term memory (LTM) affects consumers' internal search for information and how internal search affects external search.[9] We'll examine these developments in more detail following our coverage of the topic of consumer decision rules.

■ CONSUMER DECISION RULES

WHAT ARE THEY?

Decision rules: Also termed "decision heuristics," the strategies that consumers use to provide guidance while making decisions.

Experts have defined a number of basic strategies consumers can use in arriving at their decisions. These are known as **decision heuristics** or the "rules of thumb" that help us make up our minds. "I always buy the best" or "I only buy on sale" are two common heuristics. For our purpose, we'll simply refer to these as **decision rules**. Decision rules are important because they provide *guidance* while making decisions. Usually, in fact, they offer a shortcut to a decision: they allow use of only part of the available information. Of course, using less information makes it more likely that a consumer won't make the optimal purchase, but most people are willing to settle for a "satisficing" purchase (one that is "good enough") when the mental or physical costs of evaluation are high.

Consumer researchers have identified three basic types of decision rules. The basis for differentiation is *how many attributes* are used in a brand comparison and *how* the attributes are chosen and used by the consumer. Using Exhibit 18-2 will help us appreciate how the three rules operate.[10] Let's assume that three people close to graduation are interested in buying new sets of luggage. We'll also assume that they'll be using the exhibit's multiattribute ratings for their decision making and that each person will use a different decision rule. Then we'll see how this leads each to buy a different product.

THE COMPENSATORY RULE

Compensatory rule: The consumer selects the best overall brand: a brand's overall score is calculated as in the multiattribute model.

The **compensatory rule** requires the most effort of all the decision rules, since it is not a "satisficing" rule: it is aimed at discovering the best overall brand of luggage (or maximizing the purchase). The rule itself is identical to the calculations we undertook within the multiattribute attitude models. That is, the consumer must use a PBB strategy and work down the columns in turn. For each brand, the consumer must calculate the product of the importance weight and the attribute rating for each attribute and then sum these over all the attributes to arrive at a total brand score. Paul, who prides himself on his analytical bent, adopts this rule. After working through to his decision, he is pleased with the outcome. However, in analyzing his decision rule, he notices that it didn't matter in what order he took things: as long as he used every piece of information in the table (in the correct manner!), he would arrive at the same decision every time. In reviewing his calculations, he's also struck by the way

EXHIBIT 18-2

Luggage Ratings[a]
for Decision Rules[b]

Attribute	Importance	Brands[c]			
		A	B	C	D
Style	40	6	8	8	3
Price	30	7	7	8	7
Covering	20	7	4	1	8
Durability	10	6	7	3	9

[a] Belief rating scale = 1 to 10, with 10 most favorable.

[b] Assume Ed's conjunctive cutoff = 5.0.

[c] Brands are A = Air Attache, B = Beauty Brief, C = Comfort Case, D = Downtowner.

in which a high rating on one attribute had the effect of compensating for a low rating on another attribute and can understand how his decision rule got its name! What brand did Paul buy?

THE LEXICOGRAPHIC RULE

The importance weights play an even more significant role in this decision rule than they did in the compensatory model. This is fine with Sandy, since she knows what she wants and is willing to work to ensure that she gets it! In effect, the **lexicographic rule** says, "I want to ensure that I buy the brand that is best on the attributes that are the most important to me, even if I have to give up something on some of the lesser attributes." To use this rule, Sandy must first rank the important attributes in order, from most to least important (notice that this ranking is shown on Exhibit 18-2). Then she must evaluate all the brands on the most important attribute. If one stands out, this is chosen. If two or more tie, they remain as candidates for purchase while all the other brands are dropped from further consideration. The consumer then takes the remaining candidates on to the second most important attribute, where they are again compared to find the best performer. If two or more remain tied, they remain as candidates as the consumer moves to the next most important attribute. The process continues until a single brand survives and is chosen. Sandy is very pleased with her purchase and notices that it didn't take her nearly as long to make it as it took Paul. Unlike Paul, however (who understands why his rule is compensatory), Sandy still has no idea why her rule is called lexicographic. (If you'd like to know, see Note 11.) What brand did Sandy buy?

Lexicographic rule: The consumer ranks the attributes according to importance and then selects the brand that is superior on the most important attribute.

THE CONJUNCTIVE RULE

Conjuctive decision rules are quite commonly used by consumers as a means of eliminating a number of alternatives in a fast and simple manner.[12] In our earlier example of Marilyn's use of the IDB for apartments, she employed a conjunctive type

Conjunctive rule: The consumer sets a minimum standard for each attribute: if a brand fails to pass any standard, it is dropped from consideration.

of rule when she dropped some apartments from further consideration because they were priced too high for her budget or located too far from the university. In a formal sense, a consumer using the conjunctive rule must create a *minimum level of performance* that is acceptable on each important attribute. Each brand is evaluated only in terms of whether or not the minimal levels are reached. If a brand falls short on *any* attribute, it is rejected. If a brand passes all the standards, it remains a candidate for purchase.

Thus it is possible either for multiple brands to remain after the rule has been invoked or for no brand to survive all the levels. In either case, the consumer is likely to go on to use another decision rule to make the final choice or to reset the minimum levels so that a choice can be made.

For our luggage example in Exhibit 18-2, let's consider Ed's case. Ed is a conservative shopper who knows little about luggage. His major concern is avoidance of a bad mistake. Therefore he decided to use the conjunctive rule, which he'd heard tends to weight negative information about a brand more heavily and helps the consumer avoid a brand that has any glaring weaknesses. To be reasonable, Ed decided to require a minimum level of 5.0 for each attribute. When his decision was over, he was surprised at how easy it had been and was pleased that only one brand had remained, so the final choice had been easy. What brand did Ed buy? (If you're interested in checking your answers for these consumers' choices, they're in Note 12.)

■ BEYOND THE BASIC DECISION RULES

THE CONCEPT OF "MIXED STRATEGIES"

Mixed strategies: The use of several consumer decision rules in a sequence.

It is obvious that consumers rarely use one of the basic decision rules in its pure form to make a decision. They often, however, use mixed strategies—or combinations of the rules in a sequence. Conjunctive rules, for example, are often used first, since these are good ways to eliminate options quickly and reach a manageable number of brands (all of which possess desired attributes to some extent). At this point the consumer can move to another decision rule to use on the remaining brands. In recent years much research on consumer decision making has moved to consider the nature of mixed strategies. Among the findings are that task factors have strong effects on the decision strategies consumers use: that is, consumers adapt their decision making to fit the situations they are in at the time. For example, *time pressure* can be an important task factor, as can be the *amount of information* (number of attributes) available to the consumer. The *number of alternatives* he or she has to choose from is also a key task factor—as we've already noted, when the number of alternatives gets high, a consumer is likely to use a screening rule (such as conjunctive or lexicographic) first, then use a compensatory strategy for the remaining few brands.[13]

Task factors: Aspects of the setting or problem to which the consumer must react.

For example, in our earlier case of Marilyn considering apartment complexes, she is likely to eliminate some options early, perhaps because of price or location (thus using conjunctive or lexicographic kinds of rules). After she works down to her last several options, she is likely to look at how they compare on a number of attributes (thus using something like a compensatory decision rule). As to effects of task factors on her decision process, Marilyn will be more likely to eliminate alternative complexes quickly if she has, say, 20 to choose from than if there are only 3 or 4. If she is under great time pressure, she may not even consider some complexes at all, or may change her set of relevant attributes to, say, looking for which complex has an apartment available for her to move in this weekend, with price and location being much less important to the decision.

MEMORY'S IMPACT ON DECISION STRATEGIES

Sometimes consumers rely on specific decision strategies they've used many times before and have stored in memory (e.g., "I always buy whichever paper towels are on sale"). More often consumers need to think somewhat about how they will make their choice at the time they are deciding: they need to "construct" a decision strategy for that purchase. Whether the strategy is already stored or needs to be constructed, though, memory (LTM) will play a very important role.[14] Peter Wright, for example, highlighted this point when he proposed a special decision rule—called **affect referral**—that consumers may use when purchasing a product they know very well.[15] In these cases, rather than evaluating much external information at all, the consumers may simply call back (refer to) their "affect" (attitude) for one of the brands (e.g., "I always buy Tide . . . it's the best."). Much of the recent research in this area has focused on the role that a consumer's *prior knowledge* plays during a decision. What does a well-developed LTM do for us while we're buying?

Affect referral: A special decision rule: the consumer chooses a familiar brand simply by recalling his or her favorable attitude.

 "Prior Knowledge—Sew What?"

In an award-winning study, Merrie Brucks examined the effect of knowledge on how consumers search for information. A notable aspect of her study featured a computerized information method designed to overcome some drawbacks in the traditional IDB study. Glancing back at Figure 18-1, we can see that an IDB presents a consumer with an *already selected* set of attributes and brands set into a *tabular (matrix) format*. These factors can affect the way a participant in a study will begin the decision process.

Brucks changed this procedure by having each participant type in a request for the information she desired, using a computer terminal (the participant's task was to "shop" for a sewing machine). The researcher sat in another room, received and interpreted the questions, and then sent back prespecified messages with the proper information via the computer terminal. Through this means the participants were able to "phone" stores with simple questions, "visit" stores for detailed shopping, and ask for a salesperson's advice. Among the findings were the following:

- When the decision task was a difficult one, consumers who had more knowledge about sewing machines searched for more information than did less knowledgeable consumers (who likely expected that they might not be able to understand some of the information). When the decision task was easy, however, both groups searched at the same level.
- When the decision task was difficult, more knowledgeable consumers searched more efficiently (that is, they screened out bad models more quickly).
- Consumers who had more confidence in their own knowledge about sewing machines asked for fewer salesperson evaluations and relied more on their own judgments.[16]

Along the line of the Brucks study, much research has been undertaken in recent years on the role that LTM plays. This research addresses four key questions:

1. Which of the available brands or stores will be considered, and why?
2. Which information is processed in evaluating each brand?
3. How are these inputs combined to reach a decision?
4. How do the memories of past decisions affect the new decision?

Thus we can see how the CIP orientation can address a number of issues to help us understand better the nature of consumer decision making as well as various subtle influences on it. (If you are interested in reading advanced reviews of this work, three excellent sources are listed in Note 17.) So far, we've concentrated on LTM's effects: Now let's look at some other key factors.

OTHER KEY FACTORS AFFECTING DECISION MAKING

Beyond LTM, other important factors can obviously also influence consumer decision processes. We have already discussed some of these earlier in the book. For example, *joint decisions,* such as those made in households or in social contexts, can profoundly affect consumer decision processes, as can social and situational influences. The *format* in which information is provided to consumers can also have significant effects (we've just reviewed some of these effects in our last chapter, in the unit price posting study and in the life-cycle costs study, as well as in the many examples of perceptual processes in Chapters 8 and 9). In addition, however, we should take note of two newer topics that also appear to strongly affect decision processes: the concepts of (1) problem framing and (2) start point.

Problem Framing Changes the Picture

Frame of reference: The mental perspective from which a consumer subjectively evaluates a decision problem.

Recent studies indicate the subtle power that our mental **frame of reference** has in even simple choices that we make. For example, what would most consumers do if, after prepurchasing a play ticket for $10, they discover that they've lost the ticket as they enter the theater? If they are unable to prove they had bought it earlier, would they pay another $10 for another ticket? Most consumers say *they would not*—the idea of paying a double price for the same performance is quite negative.

Prospect theory: A theory built on the concept of frame of reference: stresses the process by which a consumer forms subjective estimates of decision alternatives.

What if their frame of reference changes slightly, however? Another group was asked what they would do if they were going to a theater to see a play and upon arrival discovered that they'd lost a $10 bill. Would they go ahead and buy a $10 ticket to the play? Almost all consumers said *they would.* This research, one of a stream of studies by Amos Tversky and Daniel Kahneman on **prospect theory,** indicates how sensitive consumers can be to the way in which they *perceive* a problem and in the connections they make.[18] Even slightly different framings of problems can change choices quite substantially.

Recent work by consumer researchers is now investigating such issues as whether the problem is framed in positive (gain) or negative (loss) terms. *In one study, for example, consumers expressed higher satisfaction with ground beef when it was described as "percent lean" rather than "percent fat" (actual price and quality were equal).* The key role of "reference point" is also being examined. According to Thaler, for example, this explains why a man lying on the beach would be willing to give his friend more money for a can of beer if the friend is going to buy it from a resort hotel bar rather than the grocery store (although the exact reason is subtle, we all see that this does occur).[19]

These issues have major implications for marketers. In pricing, for example, a "SALE!" or "CLEARANCE" sign helps to create certain frames for consumers. Reference prices ("An $89.95 value, now only $49.95"), coupons, and rebates are other popular forms. Although marketers obviously already recognize the value of these approaches, this work provides a strong framework by which their effects can be better understood. (If you are interested in learning more about this area, you may wish to begin with the readings in Notes 18 and 19. Because this area lends itself to manipulation of consumers' perceptions, you may wish also to examine especially the article on ethics cited at the end of the second note.) As consumers, how can we protect ourselves against inconsistent reasoning and outside manipulation? The researchers suggest stepping back, trying to "reframe" the decision in other ways, and testing whether or not our preferences remain the same.

Pathways to Purchase

As a final point in our coverage of consumer decision rules, we should reiterate the importance of the concept of **start point** in the direction and outcome of a decision process. Earlier in the book, for example, we examined the concept of **evoked set,** or those few brands that come to mind when a consumer considers his or her purchase decision. If decision time is short and no other factors intervene in the process, the chances that a purchase will be made from the evoked set are very high.

For any particular brand, then, gaining entry to consumers' evoked sets means higher probabilities of purchase. In an award-winning study, for example, Nedungadi showed how (1) asking consumers to answer several background questions about a brand at the start of the session (simply to make that brand name more "accessible" or likely to be retrieved from LTM) could (2) make these brands more likely to be in the evoked set in a later choice task and (3) raise the probabilities they would be chosen. Grey's Poupon mustard, for example, increased its choice probability from 3 percent to 22 percent with those early questions, Vlasic pickles increased theirs from 0 percent to 22 percent, whereas Tropicana orange juice moved from 22 percent to 47 percent in this laboratory study.[20]

This research has strong implications for marketing practice. For example, it indicates that some brands are likely losing sales, not because they are not liked by consumers, but *because they never come to mind during the consumer's (often rapid) decision process: they are simply never considered!* Other brands, conversely, are considered, but are not chosen because they are not preferred, at least for this purchase. Thus the appropriate marketing strategies will differ for different brands (and, likely, for different segments). For brands with strong consumer liking, but low initial consideration (Grey Poupon, Vlasic, and Tropicana in this study), reminder advertising and point-of-purchase displays would seem to be very powerful possibilities. For brands that were in consumers' evoked sets but were not purchased, however, persuasive advertising and/or cents-off coupons would likely be required to shift the final choice the consumer will make.

Of course, brands are not the only elements that might be evoked in a consumer decision process. *Stores are also likely candidates for evoked set contents, as are sources of information.* In the Wilkie and Dickson report we examined in Chapter 17, for example, appliance buyers were questioned about the first information source they consulted in their decision process. From this start point, the pathways to purchase were calculated. Considering only buyers at Sears and specialty appliance stores, how much impact did their source first consulted (start point) have on the final purchase decision? A great deal, as shown by the following findings. Of those who began their search by consulting

- *Consumer Reports*   81% purchased at specialty stores
- Repairpersons   73% purchased at specialty stores
- Salespersons   63% purchased at specialty stores
- Friends/relatives   50% or so purchased at each type
- Newspaper ads   61% purchased at Sears
- Catalogs   72% purchased at Sears

Start point: Concept that stresses that the first step taken is an important determinant of which purchase will be made.

Evoked set: Those few brands that come to mind when a consumer considers a purchase: also termed "consideration set."

In some respects, these results reflect the marketing mixes of these types of stores.[21] The role of start point remains, however. *What a consumer does first will have a strong impact on the remainder of his or her consumer decision process.*

FUTURE RESEARCH METHODS

Our discussion to this point in the chapter has presented a number of basic concepts that help us to understand consumer decision making. These concepts and theories are necessarily abstract, as they pertain to basic processes. Don't be misled into thinking that they are not important or useful for marketing managers, however. To the contrary, they have formed the basis for many advanced marketing analyses and decisions. In this regard, you may find Exhibit 18-3 of special interest: it describes two futuristic consumer research systems marketers are using today!

EXHIBIT 18-3

The Future of Marketing Research: "The Information Accelerator" and "The Visionary Shopper"

The academic concepts we have discussed so far in the chapter are now being combined with advanced computer capabilities to allow marketers to conduct new forms of "simulation" market tests. Let's take a quick look at two of the most sophisticated new systems.

The "Information Accelerator"

California has established a 1998 deadline: any automaker wishing to sell cars in the state must offer (in at least 2 percent of the line) some cars that have *zero pollutant emissions*. Other states are working on similar deadlines. The message to automakers is clear: you must bring electric or other alternative fuel cars to the market soon! Thus GM faces the question: Exactly how should such cars be designed? Will consumers buy them?

General Motors is presently using a consumer research system—the "Information Accelerator"—designed by Professor Glen Urban of the Massachusetts Institute of Technology to guide its key decisions in this area (the system is available to other firms as well, through the firm Market Technology Interface in Cambridge, Massachusetts). Because it is designed to study real innovations to which consumers must adjust, the name of the "Information Accelerator" system represents its goal of moving people into a future time frame where they will react to the kind of information they'll receive at that time. This is challenging, as consumers don't yet clearly understand many of the concepts of alternative fuel vehicles: thus the system needs to educate them gently in ways similar to how they will learn in the marketplace.

One project concerns a new 1997 car model, the Synergy, "Made in America by General Motors . . . a hybrid sedan for those who feel personally responsible for the

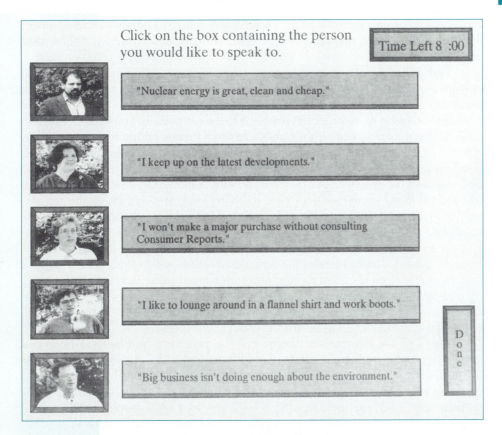

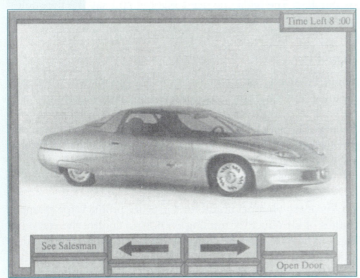

Two features of the Information Accelerator research method: choosing which (if any) consumers you'd like to hear from and taking a look at the outside of the car before "getting in" to examine the interior.

environment." (Note: The term "hybrid" refers to a car that will run on electric batteries, but that will also occasionally use a small gasoline engine to power a generator that will recharge the batteries.) A consumer participating in the study can spend up to two hours considering the $17,000 Synergy, plus other alternatives. During that time he or she will read some future news stories to set the scene for these types of cars and then begin a decision process with any of four start points—word-of-mouth from other consumers, magazine articles about the cars, advertising, or a showroom visit.

Each of these options offers many computer-controlled alternatives: as a GM executive explains, "We basically leave it up to the respondent to go after whatever information they want to see, depending on what they value most." For example, a participant seeking word-of-mouth reactions to the car can select tapes from different kinds of consumers (a man who studies *Consumer Reports* faithfully, a woman who distrusts big business, and a man who prides himself on keeping up with auto developments are three of the many options here) and then probe for their likes and dislikes about the Synergy. A participant choosing a showroom visit, meanwhile, can use a menu to ask numerous questions, receiving voice answers. He or she can also use the video controls to view the car, move inside, and learn the interior, all on the computer.

The study then allows an actual test drive in a model Synergy, followed by some research questions on opinions of the car on many attributes, together with a series of preference questions (e.g., less driving range for a lower price, or more driving range for a higher price) that will help with the design of the final models. These questions are also computer-controlled, so that the answer a consumer gives to one question will trigger a specific follow-up to learn more about that response.

Although the Information Accelerator is expensive, it represents a huge cost savings for GM, which traditionally would have had to build full-sized fiberglass models of every car type being tested, plus arranging to have all the competitors' cars also present in a huge consumer research building. Further, consumers enjoy participating. A GM executive reports: "On the way in, a lot of people say they would never have come if they had known computers were involved. But on the way out, they say it was great, it was painless. The techie people come out and say it's the coolest software they've ever seen."

"The Visionary Shopper"

As we've seen throughout the book, consumer decisions for low-priced, frequently purchased products are quite different from those for one-time, large-ticket purchases such as the Synergy automobile. Thus there is a need for futuristic research systems to differ as well. "The Visionary Shopper" is a system developed by Professor Raymond Burke of the Harvard Business School that is based on virtual reality computer principles. It is presently being used by several major consumer product firms (it is also available for use by other firms, through the MarketWare Corporation in Atlanta).

A participant in a Visionary Shopper study for a grocery product, for example, receives about five minutes of introductory training on how to control the computer software through menus and then is "turned loose" in portions of a supermarket to go about his or her shopping. Improved graphics makes the computer display of shelves lifelike. Seated at the screen, consumers can move along the aisles, noting price tags or display markers. A consumer can then remove a package from the shelf (through something like progressive zoom-ins that bring it in larger forms to the front of the screen) to read the label and can rotate it to examine the sides and the back. Another command can put it in the shopping cart for purchase or return it to the shelf if not purchased. The shopper can then move along the aisle to another product category. An entire research sitting may last about 30 minutes.

A participant in a Visionary Shopper study views part of an "end of aisle" display for Bounty paper towels. Notice that her menu of options is on the right screen and that she is controlling the simulation with her right hand. At this point she may decide to move down the aisle, to stop and examine the display, or to just place a Bounty package in her shopping cart as she passes by.

The system thus offers significant potentials for both manufacturers and retailers to study a host of issues, such as pricing, price specials, couponing, shelf markers and displays, shelf spacing and product placement, packaging changes, size changes, labeling, premium offers, and so forth. As Professor Burke refines the technical aspects of the simulation, he is also developing entirely new applications, including one for retailers, in which a shopper can stroll through an entire mall in "virtual reality"!

SOURCE: See Note 22.

■ CONSUMERS' IN-STORE PURCHASING BEHAVIOR

Up until this point in the chapter we have focused our attention on the mental operations that underpin decision making. However, as we've seen earlier in this book—and have surely experienced in our own lives as consumers—there are many external influences also at work in the real world of consumer behavior. How do these translate into actual decision processes when we're at the point of sale? Let's first look at one study that examined how much time consumers spend in making their supermarket purchases.

ぞ Search in the Supermarket

One interesting consumer research study, by Kendall and Fenwick, timed over 200 supermarket shoppers as they chose specific items. Some interesting findings emerged. Over all consumers and products, the decision times obtained ranged from almost instantaneous (less than 1 second) to 5.5 minutes (yes, one consumer did stand in front of the display this long, trying to make up her mind!). Almost all purchases were at the low end of the time range, of course.

It turned out, however, that consumers spent much longer in choosing some products than others. This would indicate either that the decisions were more difficult or that less LTM was available for the choice, requiring some reading of the product labels while standing in the aisle. For products such as canned meat, tuna, and powdered soup, the typical consumer spent about half a minute on the purchase (within the study this was classed as a "label reader"). For products such as rice and spaghetti, on the other hand, the most common consumer was classed as a "grabber" who spent *less than 1 second* standing in front of the shelf—many buyers didn't even stop but simply reached out and "grabbed" the package they desired as they swung on by![23]

Other research (also listed in Note 23) has given similar findings. Thus we can see why consumer researchers have been concentrating on CIP-oriented studies of decisions. It is clear that internal search of LTM plays an extremely important role in many consumer purchases and that for some consumers there is very little else that goes on for many of the purchases they make in the supermarket.

This does not tell the entire story, however, since we have thus far looked at only a small sampling of all the purchases that consumers make. Let's next look at the findings of a famous study that, while still on supermarkets, has a much broader base of products.

🐋 *The POPAI/DuPont Study*

A classic set of studies undertaken by the Point-of-Purchase Advertising Institute (POPAI) and the E. I. du Pont de Nemours Company has alerted marketers to the consumer dynamics of decisions within the supermarket. In one study of the buying practices of over 4000 consumers across the United States, *the researchers found that most purchases consumers make are not planned in advance—that in-store decision making is the norm rather than the exception.*

To examine this issue, the researchers categorized each purchase into one of four classes:

1. *Specifically planned.* Here the consumer had plans to buy the item before entering the store. This category accounted for 34 percent, or one out of every three purchases made in this study.

2. *Planned in general.* Here the consumer had the general intention to buy something in the product class but did not have a specific brand in mind when entering the store. This category, which we might expect would be the most frequent of the types, accounted for only 11 percent, or about one out of every nine purchases.

3. *Substitute purchases.* Here the consumer changed his or her mind while in the store and substituted a related product or different brand. Only 3 percent of the purchases were of this type.

Pepsi sponsored over 3000 Karaoke events, such as this one in a Wichita, Kansas, Alberton's store, during a two-month period recently. Based on the Japanese practice of singing along with a recording, amateurs were able to sing a song (and the Pepsi "Uh-Huh" jingle with Ray Charles). Results? Nationally, 20 million consumers watched and listened while Pepsi's sales soared. The stores did well also: this one's sales increased 20 percent that week!

4. *Unplanned purchases.* Here the consumer did not report a plan to buy the item at the time he or she entered the supermarket. Instead, the entire decision process—from problem recognition to actual purchase—occurred while in the store (some may have been "reminder" purchases, in which the consumer used packages or displays as a reminder that the product could be needed, while others may have been truly impulsive purchases).[24] Over half of all the purchases recorded in the study (53 percent) were of this type.

Thus (adding together the three last categories), 67 percent of purchase decisions were found to be made in the store. As we would expect, however, there were distinct *product differences* in terms of the way they fit into the categories just listed. (This information is particularly important to marketing managers, who of course are most concerned with the consumer decision process for their particular product categories.) Product-specific analysis showed that products likely to be subject to a "depletion" type of problem recognition were least likely to be subject to unplanned purchases: examples here included coffee, milk, and baby foods. At the other extreme, almost all "general merchandise" (nongrocery) products provided high levels of unplanned purchases. As you may know, these products often carry high profit margins for the stores, and it is not hard to imagine why they've been receiving more space in the latest supermarket designs! Many of us can also easily relate to some of the other "high-flier" products in impulsive purchasing by considering our taste buds: these included baking mixes, relishes and mustards, almost all frozen foods, fresh cakes, pies, and doughnuts, and all categories of candies, crackers, cookies, and snacks![25]

MARKETING IMPLICATIONS

What implications do the POPAI findings hold for marketing managers? They indicate that, for certain products especially, *consumer demand is not fixed but is likely to be quite responsive to various forms of promotional efforts.* At the start of the last chapter, for example, we saw how point-of-purchase displays for cheese were able to boost sales substantially. Studies over broader ranges of products have shown similarly strong results:

- One scanner study of in-store displays in supermarkets showed sales increases ranging from 60 percent (for dog food, toothpaste, orange juice) to over 200 percent (for frozen dinners and detergents) while the products were on a display.[26]

As marketers have learned more about consumers' in-store decisions, aisles and shelves have become a battleground to gain attention from shoppers at the point of purchase.

■ Another study, this time focusing on newspaper ads for groceries, also reported finding very substantial effects. If the item was advertised in small type in a list, sales were 80 percent higher than when not advertised, while if the item was advertised in a separate section (i.e., not in a list), the increase was 800 percent. For items advertised in large type, the sales changes were even more dramatic—ad weeks' sales for items in a large print list were over 1000 percent higher, while a large-type, separate section led to average sales almost 1700 percent higher than in nonadvertised weeks![27] (However, we should recall the nature of newspaper advertising for foods and be careful not to attribute all these effects to the promotions themselves—advertised items are often priced at special low levels.) Thus it seems reasonable that advertising, displays, and prices work in an interactive fashion: the ad or display helps bring a brand into the evoked set; then the price appeal helps to "close the sale."

In terms of our current interest in purchasing processes, these numbers are significant in helping us recognize just how flexible consumer decision processes can be. *Thus there are significant opportunities for marketers to appeal successfully to consumers both prior to the shopping experience (with advertising, direct mail, and coupons) and during shopping itself (with point-of-purchase displays, shelf placement, packaging appeal, and personal salespersons).* Exhibit 18-4 describes some high-tech possibilities we can expect to see in the near future. (If you are interested in learning more about these options, you may wish to consult the sources listed in Note 28.)

EXHIBIT 18-4

What Will the Future Hold In-Store?

In recent years evidence has continued to accumulate as to just how flexible consumer purchase decisions really are, and how effective in-store promotions can be. This trend is probably accelerating, moreover, as dual-career households struggle to find free time in their lives. For example, the POPAI study also discovered these significant changes: 70 percent of grocery consumers did not prepare a shopping list (up from 61 percent in 1977); 75 percent ignored newspaper ads before shopping (up from 62 percent), 90 percent of shoppers did not look at store circulars, and 80 percent did not redeem coupons. While each of these measures relates only to one shopping trip, the message is clear: *Consumers are waiting until they are in the store before they make many final decisions.*

These results have begun a revolution in marketing—the future will see even more promotional effort directed at consumers in the stores. Retailers will begin to charge directly for store space, and high-tech methods of influencing consumers will appear. For example, here are a few interesting developments we can expect to see in the near future (perhaps you've already experienced some of them!).[28]

"Sniff-Teaser" Spends Scents

As we've seen earlier in the book, consumers can be highly responsive to subtle stimuli (colors, music, etc.). A **sniff-teaser device** is now available that emits a product's smell into the store aisle near its display and is expected to raise sales of detergents, coffee, baked goods, and so on. Sound devices are now available that will broadcast a brief message when a consumer passes by ("Psst...over here" supposedly generated a 300 percent increase in sales for a TV set, and other sound messages have been reported to show sales increases over 100 percent.) Also, holograms are likely in special settings: Don't be surprised if the 3-D image of George Washington or another famous figure beams into an aisle to talk to you about a purchase!

Radio Wendy's Is on the Air!

Drive-through customers at certain Wendy's stores see signs telling them to tune their radios to a particular FM frequency to hear "Radio Wendy's." This station, with a broadcast range of only a few blocks, discusses the menu, special deals, and new products. The idea, according to a Wendy's spokesperson, is to increase the use of drive-throughs and to get customers thinking about the menu before they order, thus speeding up the flow and perhaps increasing sales as well. The radio message delivers a "secret word," and if the customer uses the secret word while ordering, he or she receives a special discount.

Muzak Rocks While the Smart Cart Rolls

You've likely heard Muzak's product plenty of times: it's that soft background music piped into elevators, dentists' offices, and retail stores all over the country. Muzak's system has 200,000 special telecommunication receivers in businesses across the land. Its clients choose from 12 channels with different music types: these are then sent by satellite to the business and are broadcast on the sound system. Following the POPAI study, however, Muzak has moved strongly into including in-store advertising messages in with the musical programming. Thus, beyond music, customers hear commercial announcements as they shop. Advertisers have been extremely pleased with their early results. For example, at Maybelline, the product manager for Shine Free cosmetics said she was "amazed" at the difference that the in-store audio ads made: *"We were seeing double-digit increases on every single Shine Free product in stores that had the ads,"* she reports. According to the vice president of A&P, one participating

POP sales assistance for Clarion Cosmetics.

This ad, aimed at marketers, offers a program that delivers coupons right at the store shelf.

retailer, the firm "has done excellent research" and the consumer response has been "tremendous."

And while hearing Muzak ads, we will also be seeing computers at work around the store. For example, the new **Checkout Coupon computer system,** hooked to a supermarket's scanner display, analyzes a customer's purchases as they are being made and spits out coupons tailored to that buyer. For example, if a shopper buys diapers, the machine may issue a coupon for those diapers, or perhaps for a competing brand, attempting to induce a trial purchase. (In early tests of this system, 8 percent of these competitor coupons have been redeemed.) In another system, backed by Procter & Gamble, discounts are shown on the screen at the checkouts. In one test, for example, shoppers who bought four of six designated P & G products received a 10 percent discount ($3 maximum) on their grocery bill. Another test created a "frequent shopper program" that adds up a member's purchases from particular brands and stores to give special prizes at different levels.

Finally, we'll soon be piloting **VideOcarts** through the aisles if the founder of Information Resources, Inc., has his way. IRI is the nation's third largest market research company, based on its specialty work in gathering and analyzing supermarket scanner data. Its new company, now an independent firm, is putting the equivalent of laptop computer displays on shopping carts. *Triggered by infrared sensing devices, these displays offer product information and electronic "paperless" coupons as consumers reach the brand's specific shelf space in the store.* An advertiser is thus able to gain the customer's attention at exactly the point of purchase and to offer any special promotions at that

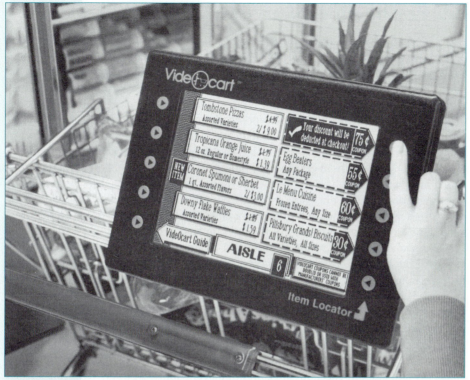

The sophisticated system sends ads to the display, so that each sponsor's ad will come up on the screen as the shopper nears that shelf space! Price specials, coupons, or other information can also be supplied.

time. Further, the cart computer will record the exact path of each shopper through the store and the time spent in each aisle, tell the host computer if the cart leaves the parking lot, show *USA Today* while waiting in the checkout line, and so forth.

The relationship between promotions and consumer response is not a simple one, however.[29] As the "search in the supermarket" study showed, most consumers make most of their purchases in a very rapid manner and do not seem to be very sensitive to point-of-purchase materials. In a related study, in fact, Peter Dickson and Alan Sawyer found that only slightly over half the buyers of four common purchases (margarine, coffee, toothpaste, and cold cereal) *even checked the price* in the store before they bought the item. As we might expect, less than 50 percent of buyers were then able to give the correct price of their choice right after putting it in their shopping cart (most of those who hadn't checked indicated that the price just wasn't important to them). Even so, almost 30 percent of the brands purchased in this study had been bought at a special low price. (Of these buyers, however, only about half—15 percent of the total sample—knew that this was a price special, while another 7 percent had bought an item they thought was on special when it was not.)[30]

Thus it is apparent that considerable slippage occurs in the real in-store purchasing environment. At the same time, impressive sales gains can be chalked up by marketers who are successful in shifting only a relatively small proportion of the (huge) total consumer market. Again we see why "market segmentation" is such a key topic in the marketing field.

■ OTHER ASPECTS OF THE PURCHASE TRANSACTION

As the decision process moves through information search, alternate evaluation, and decision making, *we finally reach the point at which the actual purchase is made.* Since we've all made thousands of purchases in our lives, the mechanics of this process are quite clear. In simple store purchases, there is a direct transfer of money for product, with the consumer departing in physical possession of his or her new property. Notice that money, ownership, and physical possession are all exchanged during this basic form of transaction. None of these elements *has* to be exchanged at this time, however. In some purchases consumers pay in advance (e.g., some direct mail, telephone, or catalog orders), while in others credit or financing arrangements allow for payment at later times. Similarly, physical possession (delivery) can be moved forward (e.g., by shipping a product and enclosing a bill to be paid later) or backward (e.g., by paying for an item and arranging for delivery at a later time). Legal ownership, on the other hand, tends to be tied to payment of the full purchase price.

As we've noted since the early stages of this book, *the purchase transaction is the key point at which marketers and consumers come together in our economic system.* Its fundamental purpose is positive for both parties–marketers gain the revenues they need to continue profitable operations in the future, while consumers gain the product or service they seek to gain the benefits offered from its consumption. One outstanding attribute of modern marketing-consumer environments is the emphasis given to *easing the act of purchase.* Salespersons are trained to move the consumer into the purchase stage and "close" a sale. If self-service is involved, arrangements aimed at speedy and smooth checkout are commonplace, with items likely to be impulsively purchased strategically placed near the purchasing area. The rise of bank credit cards (VISA, MasterCard) has also eased the act of purchase for consumers, by making an independent form of credit available for the store to accept. The fact the stores are willing to pay significant fees (of about 3 percent) for card charges is a good indication of the extent to which they wish to ease the purchase transaction for the consumer.

Within the decision process perspective, the act of purchase serves as a culmination of sorts, since all the search, evaluation, and choice activities now reach a single resolution for the consumer. In another sense, however, *the act of purchase serves as a bridge for the consumer, who can now shift his or her attention to postpurchase activities,* which include consuming the product and enjoying the benefits that have been sought all along. Accordingly, we too will now turn to examine the postpurchase phase in our next chapter.

■ SUMMARY

MONITORING CONSUMER DECISION MAKING

In this chapter we focused on the middle stages of the consumer decision process—consumer decisions and in-store purchasing behavior. Given that much material relevant to these topics has already been covered in earlier chapters, here we concentrated on research approaches, decision strategies, and in-store purchasing behavior. The first section of the chapter covered methods to monitor consumer decision making. Because this is a personal mental process, it can be difficult for marketing researchers to measure. Two basic approaches are generally used: *input-output research* and *process monitoring research.* Input-output research usually employs some form of an experiment in which the researcher provides a special stimulus to consumers (special price, new advertising theme), then observes how consumers react to it (the outputs of the process). Advertising copy tests are a common form of this approach. Process monitoring, on the other hand, places less emphasis on the stimuli and the outcomes but more emphasis on trying to capture the reality of the decision process itself, as it occurs. Three methods used here are verbal protocols, physical monitoring methods (such as an information display board, IDB), and observational monitoring methods (such as eye cameras). In recent years, researchers have begun to combine several of these methods in the same study.

CONSUMER DECISION RULES

Decision rules are the strategies consumers use to help make up their minds when choosing from a set of alternatives. We examined three basic decision rules in this chapter, using luggage information from an IDB as the basic for our example. The *compensatory rule* requires the most effort and is aimed at discovering the best overall brand. It is similar to the multiattribute model we discussed in Chapter 11. The *lexicographic rule* relies on attribute importance as its key; the brand that stands out on the most important attribute will be chosen here. The *conjunctive rule,* on the other hand, is frequently used to eliminate many alternatives in a fast manner. A minimum level of performance is set for each important attribute, and each alternative is judged by whether or not it meets this minimum level. If it falls short on any attribute, it is rejected; if it passes all the standards, it remains a candidate for purchase.

BEYOND THE BASIC DECISION RULES

In extending our discussion on the decision rules, we noted that *mixed strategies* are likely to be found in the actual consumer world. Sometimes consumers construct decision rules as they go along; other times they rely on their LTM to supply stored rules. *Affect referral,* for example, is one such stored decision rule. We also noted that the degree of expertise or prior knowledge will affect decision strategies, as will joint decisions, information format, *problem framing,* and the *start point* at which consumers begin their search and shopping activities.

CONSUMERS' IN-STORE PURCHASING BEHAVIOR

The final section of the chapter examined several studies of in-store purchasing behavior. Our major finding was that *consumer demand is not fixed: it responds to external cues beyond price.* Here we noted that most consumers in supermarkets seem to shop very quickly. We also reviewed the POPAI/DuPont study, which concluded that *in supermarkets in-store decision making is the norm rather than the exception.* In accordance with this finding, we saw that *in-store displays can increase sales* dramatically and that many consumers are not aware of the exact price they are paying. Thus in-store behavior and stimuli are extremely significant factors in consumer behavior. Our review of how marketers are using new technology indicates what we can expect to see in future years.

■ KEY TERMS

input-output approach	verbal monitoring methods	processing by brands (PBB)
supermarket scanners	physical monitoring methods	observational monitoring methods
process monitoring	processing by attributes (PBA)	decision heuristics

decision rules	task factors	evoked set
compensatory rule	affect referral	sniff-teaser device
lexicographic rule	frame of reference	Checkout Coupon computer system
conjunctive decision rules	prospect theory	VideOcarts
mixed strategies	start point	

■ REVIEW QUESTIONS AND EXPERIENTIAL EXERCISES

[E-Application extension or experiential exercise]

1. Briefly explain the input-output method in consumer decision research, citing specific examples to illustrate.

2. What significance do flexibility and affect referral have for the decision-making process? Cite examples of each from your experiences as a consumer. What implications do they hold for marketers?

3. What generalization was drawn from the Wilkie and Dickson study concerning the start point of a decision? Do their data support this?

4. Two futuristic consumer research methods—the "Information Accelerator" and the "Visionary Shopper"—were described in Exhibit 18-3. In what ways are these methods similar? In what ways are they different? Prepare a short list of possible marketing applications for each method; identify any potential weaknesses you would be concerned about as a marketing manager considering the use of either method.

5. Some of the studies in the chapter suggest that consumers make their supermarket purchases very quickly, with many people not looking at either prices or alternatives. Other studies suggest that most decisions are made in the store. Still others show that ads and displays can have large impacts. How can all this be true? Prepare a logical series of points that explain all of this.

6. [E] As an interesting project to link the prepurchase and purchase chapters together, select a recent decision you (or a friend or relative) have made. Think back (or interview) through the stages of the decision process as shown in Chapter 17. Create the brands-attributes matrix (similar to Figure 18-1 or Exhibit 18-2) as it was *at the problem recognition* stage of your purchase. Then, as you replay the decision process, *modify* the matrix by adding alternatives, dropping alternatives, adding attributes, adding information, and so forth, as you did when you went through the search, evaluation, and final decision stages. Write a brief report on your findings.

7. a. [E] Accompany a friend to the supermarket and observe his or her behavior there: the time it takes to shop, the time spent pondering alternatives, and the number of products purchased. Summarize your findings.

   b. At the conclusion of the shopping trip (back at home or apartment) determine the extent to which the purchase of each item was planned or unplanned. Compare your results with the findings of the POPAI/DuPont study.

8. [E] Stroll through a supermarket or discount store, noting the placement, design, and appeals of the special displays. Predict which three you believe will be most effective and three that might be ineffective. Then interview a store manager about the displays, their effectiveness, and the marketing process involving point of purchase. Write a brief report summarizing your findings.

9. [E] Conduct an observational study of shoppers in a supermarket, similar to those reported in the chapter. Compare your findings with those reported in the chapter, in a brief report. (*Hint:* You may wish to use the references in the Notes to locate details of how a study was done.)

10. [E] Refer to Note 19 for some interesting readings concerning the impacts and applications of "problem framing." Write a brief report on your findings.

11. [E] If you are interested in learning more about the study of decision rules and decision-making processes, excellent (but technical) references are available in the Notes listed for each specific decision topic in the chapter. Write a brief report on what you have found.

12. [E] To help gain a manufacturer's view of in-store behavior and the revolution in supermarket retailing, arrange to interview a sales representative for a major grocery manufacturer (your local supermarket manager should be able to provide names of possible people). Based on the material in this chapter, ask about how shelf space is gained, how new products are introduced, promotions are run, and so forth. Probe for insights on consumers' responsiveness to marketing programs, and for which types of marketing techniques seem to work best. Write a brief report on your findings.

■ SUGGESTED READING

■ The topics discussed in the first half of the chapter represent much of the best work in academic consumer research. The three references in Note 17 provide excellent, advanced overviews of recent work in these areas. For applications related to consumers' in-store behaviors and marketing actions see, for example, Harry Levinson and Nan Stone, "The Case of the Perplexing Promotion," *Harvard Business Review*, No. 1 (January–February 1990), pp. 11–21; Robert D. Buzzell, John A. Quelch, and Walter J. Salmon, "The Costly Bargain of Trade Promotion," *Harvard Business Review*, No. 2 (March–April 1990), pp. 141–149; and John Philip Jones, "The Double Jeopardy of Sales Promotions," *Harvard Business Review*, No. 5 (September–October 1990), pp. 145–152. For more detailed findings and discussion of consumer shopping itself, see Peter R. Dickson and Alan G. Sawyer, "The Price Knowledge and Search of Supermarket Shoppers," *Journal of Marketing*, Vol. 54, No. 3 (July 1990), pp. 42–53. For a brief and fairly recent update of the successes and failures of the new in-store promotional methods described in Exhibit 18-4, see Ronald Grover, "Big Brother Is Grocery Shopping with You," *Business Week*, March 29, 1993, p. 60. For more recent developments on these topics, your reference librarian should be helpful, as many articles are carried by the business trade press. For further depth on specific topics of interest, this chapter's Notes present excellent sources.

19

CONSUMER DECISIONS (III)
Postpurchase Processes

THE OWNERS SPEAK

Let's listen again to the Chicago-area car buyers, now as they describe some aspects of their postpurchase experiences (some underlying concepts are given in brackets):

[*Changes over time*] "...two years ago I wouldn't be caught dead in a four-door...the statement it makes. [Now] even when...I don't have the little guy in the car, it's like I'm a family man now."

[*Cognitive dissonance*] "People...do not admit they made a bad decision unless it's fairly obvious...the minute you buy something you start an internal process of convincing yourself that this was the right thing."

[*Social feedback and reinforcement*] "I've had a tremendous number of compliments on its appearance, which makes me feel so good...I know in GM...it's one of the top-level cars, which made me feel better...it was a Buick, and hopefully it was a better car."

[*Status and self-satisfaction*] (Wife): "I'm a Cadillac person."

(Husband): "...When Karen gets on her nice diamonds and puts on her big fur, and she gets in her Cadillac, and goes to the women's club...she looks as good as anyone."

(Wife): "It's real special. When I get in the car and turn the stereo on where I have the tape in there, you feel good. And I didn't realize you got a gold key...there's a special gold one. I thought, 'A gold key!' it's just kind of those little touches."

[*Uncertainty/evaluation*] "I won't be comfortable that we got our value until maybe a year from now...to see how it performs...I'm a little insecure. But any decision where you're spending that amount of money, you're going to be a little insecure...so far we're happy with it."[1]

◼ WHY IS POSTPURCHASE IMPORTANT?

In this chapter we'll explore the interesting world of postpurchase processes, or what goes on after the consumer makes a purchase. If we think briefly about the *consumer's perspective*, we can see that *the goal of the consumer's decision lies in consumption and consumption occurs during the postpurchase phase.* Purchases are only "means to an end,"

530

with the end being the attainment of benefits from consuming the product or service. We benefit from our purchases of Tide and Chrysler not when we purchase them, but during the postpurchase phase, when our clothes become fresh and clean and we're traveling in comfort and style. The postpurchase phase is extremely important for the *marketing perspective* as well: it is here that consumers' wants and needs are satisfied. *It is here that long-term profits are built, since a favorable postpurchase experience is needed for a repurchase to occur.* During the postpurchase phase, consumers evaluate the brand they've purchased. Marketers who stress favorable *post*purchase evaluations are the ones likely to receive favorable *pre*purchase evaluations in future consumer decisions.

■ A FRAMEWORK FOR POSTPURCHASE

To help us begin our analysis of the postpurchase phase, let's consider a few subtle points contained in the framework in Figure 19-1. First, notice that the postpurchase phase accounts for two of the three major activities in an overall consumption system. This is in contrast to the overwhelming emphasis that the field of consumer behavior research has given to the "Acquisition" stage. In the bottom of Figure 19-1, note the role that *time* plays. The total time for the postpurchase phase can vary widely, ranging from only a few seconds (as in consuming a piece of candy) through several hours (attending a movie) to a number of years (as with a piano). Figure 19-1 also shows a **support system:** *storage* is often required to cushion the period between purchase and use; *service* (maintenance and repair) and *energy* (e.g., gas for an auto) are often needed as well. Thus *further expenditures* are also involved in a postpurchase system. Finally, some *means* for *disposing* of the product is usually needed when consumption is complete.

Support system: A set of postpurchase resources: can include storage, servicing, and energy.

THE CONSUMPTION OF PRODUCTS AND SERVICES

The analysis of how consumers consume products and services can provide marketers with useful insights. The following dimensions of consumption were suggested by Philip Hendrix: notice the many marketing implications that emerge.[2]

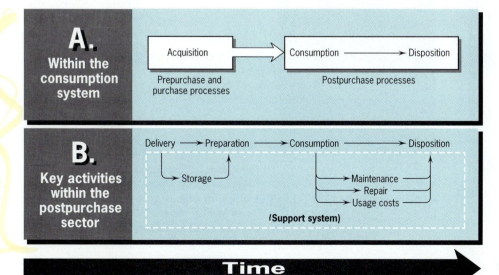

FIGURE 19-1 The Postpurchase Phase

ℰ❧ *Consumption Amount*

A product's total demand is comprised of the frequency of use times the **average amount consumed**. Strategies to *increase the average amount consumed* thus translate directly into higher sales. Marketers recognize this when they use special pricing plans that reduce the marginal cost of additional units' consumption. Many home carpet cleaning firms, for example, price their offerings so that each additional room costs less to have cleaned, thus encouraging more carpet cleaning during a home visit.

ℰ❧ *Consumption Frequency*

A focus on **consumption frequency**—how often a product is used—can offer useful insights about the market for our product or service. Consumption of a few products and services is essentially *continuous,* as with housing, electricity, and insurance. For most products, however, consumption is *discontinuous*—it occurs on discrete occasions. One way to increase demand, therefore, is to increase consumers' frequency of **perceived use occasions** for your product. Sometimes this option can be handled through the concept of product storage. For example, millions of American consumers enjoy the taste and wiggle of Jell-O and are happy to buy it in the supermarket. Recently, however, the company discovered that sales levels were falling short of potential for the simple reason that consumers tended to "forget" about the product once it was put away in the cupboard. A new promotion strategy was thus born—ads reminded consumers how good Jell-O is and suggested that it was probably already "right there in the cupboard."

BUTTONS FROM HELL THIS OLD REMOTE HAS ROW UPON ROW OF CLOSELY SPACED BUTTONS OF THE SAME SMALL SIZE AND SAME DARK COLOR. SONY'S MINIMALIST REMOTE DOES ALL YOU REALLY WANT

Consumers' difficulties in using advanced technological features have opened market opportunities for brands to capitalize on by offering "user-friendly" designs, features, and instructions. Designers who formerly put in all possible options are now being reined in: "Who in the world programs three weeks of TV ahead of time? . . ." asks one design consultant. "Why do we need those functions in a VCR? . . ." Sony's new simple design on the right does all that most users want.

COMM'L NO.: FCOJ 1328   LENGTH: 30 SECONDS

(SFX: THUNDER)
MAN: What a day!

Let's see...what should I get?

Hey! That looks good—

a burger and

a big glass of Florida Orange Juice!

That's it—

ice-cold orange juice would sure taste great.

Oh, yeah!

(MUSIC UP)

CASHIER: For here or to go?

MAN: I'll drink it right here!

ANNCR (VO): 100% pure orange juice from Florida.

Order it anytime, anywhere.

It isn't just for breakfast anymore.

Storyboard for the "Isn't just for breakfast anymore!" advertising campaign to change consumers' patterns of consumption intervals for orange juice. Notice how this would expand potential sales!

Consumption Intervals

New opportunities can arise by examining the nature of the **intervals between consumption occasions**. In some categories there may be an option to replace storage with a new product form that will offer *continuous service*. This was the case in the introductions of "stick-up" room deodorizers, continuous-release toilet bowl cleaners, and time-release capsules for medicines. The *pattern* of consumption intervals can also be a key factor in restricting demand. For example, many products face time-dependent use patterns. Orange juice manufacturers elected to fight their restrictive image with the "...isn't just for breakfast anymore!" campaign, while Stove Top stuffing mix decided to position this product against potatoes to expand the types of meals at which consumers would see the product as appropriate.

Finally, the *regularity* of use can also be a significant factor. Consumption of electricity, for example, has a large irregular component determined by the temperature each day. Utilities would very much like to smooth out this pattern, and they are experimenting with "time-of-day" pricing, in which consumers are charged less for electricity if they use it during the less busy times of day and are charged premium rates for use during busy times (this is similar to the pricing for long-distance telephone service, which was adopted for much the same reason). Other marketers have also designed successful strategies along this line. Prince Spaghetti, for example, has long promoted Wednesday in the Northeast as Prince Spaghetti Day.

❧ *Consumption Purposes*

A final key consumption dimension for marketing concerns the exact **consumption purposes** that consumers perceive as appropriate for the brand. Some brands have been notably successful with narrow and precise positionings. Woolite, for example, has carved out a unique niche for itself by restricting its consumption purposes. On the other hand, Coke, Pepsi, and most other soft drink entries suggest that they are appropriate for many occasions and settings. The classic example of extending consumption purposes, of course, remains Arm & Hammer baking soda, which was able to raise its sales dramatically by extending perceived consumption purposes, first to the refrigerator, then to the freezer, and on to further new uses over the years, as we discussed in Chapter 11.

PRODUCT DISPOSITION

Product disposi-tion: The final stage in a product's life with a particular owner.

Following consumption, the final stage in a product's life occurs when the consumer *disposes* of it. There are three major options in **product disposition**:

- Trash it!
- Save it (either store it or repair it).
- Sell it or give it away.

There are substantial product differences in disposition modes. At one extreme, some products (especially foods) are disposed of during consumption itself. At the other extreme, products that are used over periods of time usually do face disposition decisions. It is likely that almost all product packaging, and most products themselves, ultimately find their ways to the trash bins of the nation. This can differ by product type, however. In one study, for example, consumers reported throwing away used toothbrushes but storing high proportions of wristwatches and phonograph records. Used stereos and bicycles, on the other hand, were most likely to be given away, traded, or sold to others. For some of our possessions that are central to our self-identities, such as the family home, pet, or heirloom, the act of disposition can be a deeply emotional experience.[3]

In the Aggregate, a National Concern

Because everyone disposes of products and packages as a matter of daily living, at the aggregate level several national problems arise. The sheer volume of garbage in our country presents problems of safe disposal. For example, when Oakland, California, decided that it would no longer serve as the garbage repository for San Francisco, matters got so severe that the daily trash from the "City by the Bay" was mounted on huge barges and carted far out to sea to be dumped. Product disposition decisions pose special problems with respect to hazardous materials and threats to ecology. As another example, the volume of our national laundry became evident to consumers some years ago, when several rivers began to "suds up" due to heavy concentra-tions of detergents that weren't breaking down in the sewer systems! Marketers reacted by changing the nature of the product ingredients to lessen such problems. Finally, disposable diapers were found to pose a long-term disposal threat, since they did not biologically degrade in the trash disposal system. Manufacturers went to work to try to remedy this problem also. In general, marketers' actions in this area are important for the future:

🐚 Marketers Improve Their Disposition through "ECO-LOGIC"

As landfills continue to close and governments are seeking solutions, the fact that product packaging is a major contributor to consumer trash has brought new challenges and opportunities for marketers. Here are some steps alert marketers are taking to contribute to improving the environment (organized in an "Eco-logic" framework):[4]

- **E** *Environmental materials.* Many marketers—from greeting cards to plastic soda bottles—now use recycled materials to help keep trash out of landfills. Most report little negative consumer reactions and positive consumer responses from some market segments.

- **C** *Content reduction.* Using less materials in the first place can save money as well as trash. Procter & Gamble undertook this step when it eliminated its boxed packaging for Sure and Secret deodorants, saving 3.4 million pounds of packaging trash each year.

- **O** *Overtime product use.* Replacing disposable products with reusable products or refillable containers provides new opportunities as well. Returnable soda bottles and reusable diapers are two products on the way back to popularity.

- **L** *Longer-lasting products.* Higher-priced, more durable products can sometimes replace throw-aways, as the success of Gillette's Sensor shaving system shows.

- **O** *Ordinary repairs or recycling made easy.* Products can be designed for ease of repair, as with Electrolux vacuum cleaners, or for ease of recycling, as with Heinz' squeezable plastic bottles.

- **G** *Gathering products for recycling.* Profitable and promotable programs are possible, if used products can supply a low-cost source of recycled materials. For example, Exide (the largest maker of auto batteries) has teamed with K-mart to pay consumers for old batteries: it thereby gains a source of lead while helping to save the environment, consumers get something back, and K-mart gains new battery sales.

- **I** *Incinerator-safe packages and products.* Ensuring that disposed products are safe for burning (or for landfills) directly helps. Everready batteries, for example, were redesigned with this in mind.

- **C** *Compostable packages.* Biodegradability is an achievable goal for many types of papers and plastics, including Warner-Lambert's new form of plastic packaging, Novon.

These are all options: the basic logic is that a concerned marketer will ask, "What would I want to do environmentally if I had to dispose of the products and packages myself?" and then, "How can I develop a workable marketing plan to achieve that end?"

As this field has grown in significance, however, many issues have been unclear, so that a significant potential for deceptive marketing claims exists. Following numerous disputes, cases, and state and local regulations, many marketers joined with environmentalists to ask the national government to provide some uniform guidance for what marketers can and can't claim about environmental effects. Accordingly, in July 1992, the Federal Trade Commission issued a set of marketing guidelines based on extensive testimony and submissions: these are intended to assist marketers in making legitimate environmental claims, while restricting deceptive or misleading claims. This is a potentially important step for the future of "green marketing," and bears watching in the future.

﹖ﻬ *But Will Consumers Bash Trash?*

Marketers' actions on products and packages are obviously crucial, but much will depend on how consumers act on disposition issues in the future. Two of the key areas for consumer behavior are

- *Willingness to purchase "green" products and packages.* If consumers are willing to "buy green" (that is, try to choose products that in some way—including packaging—are good for the environment), marketers will have incentives to invest in a range of new options. If consumers will not support these initiatives, however, only those that provide marketers with cost savings, or those that are mandated by law, are likely to remain.

- *Willingness to engage in recycling and other positive disposition behaviors.* This is an area in which consumer behavior has been changing recently: the amount of trash that is recycled or composted has roughly doubled in the last five years. However, problems and barriers remain: the "sorting" done by some consumers is often so poor that entire shipments have to be rejected at recycling centers!

A study conducted for the S. C. Johnson Company by the Roper Organization showed that consumers' awareness of these issues has risen considerably, but consumers are *highly segmented* as to their actual behaviors. Only 10 percent of adults were identified as **True Blue Greens,** people who try to "buy green," recycle, and support new initiatives (interestingly, this is not a partisan political issue: these people are both liberals and conservatives and demographically tend to be female, with higher income and education, residing in the Northeast or West). Another 10 percent, the **Greenback Greens**, indicated a willingness to pay more for environmentally safe products, but are not willing to change their own disposition behaviors much. Another 25 percent of adults (termed "Sprouts" in this study) may become more environmentally aware in the future, if good options present themselves. The remaining portion of the population—over half of U. S. adults—are not positive prospects yet, however. Basically, they are either indifferent about the environment, or they feel that individuals can't do much to solve the problems. Beyond new government requirements, therefore, the types of green marketing programs offered by marketers under the Federal Trade Commission guidelines, and the response by the first three consumer segments, will largely determine environmental progress in the United States in the near term.[6] (If you are interested in reading more about this area, Notes 4 and 5 present some excellent references.)

Product Disposition, Time, and Market Potentials

As a final topic in our coverage of product disposition, let's again think briefly about the concept of time. *When* do people decide to dispose of their products? As we saw in the shopping study conducted by Wilkie and Dickson (reported in Chapter 17), most

One way for consumers to contribute to composting is by sorting their trash. Here the photo series shows the following: (1) A worker removes nondegradables from trash arriving at the Recomp Inc. plant in Minnesota. (2) The remaining trash is composted for one month in a great digestor and then emerges for a last sifting (3) and inspection (4).

large-appliance purchases were sparked by breakdowns or operating problems with the existing machine. This suggests that consumers wait until their present product breaks before moving to dispose of it and undertake a new purchase. In this sense, an existing product, late in its life, presents a *barrier* to a new purchase the consumer might otherwise be willing to make. Alert marketers may be able to overcome this barrier and increase overall product demand by attempting to move the disposition decision to an earlier point in time. This would seem especially likely for products that can be "traded up" for better features or new advances, such as computers and stereos.

Second, you may also recall that Wilkie and Dickson found that brand loyalty seemed quite low for these products. Could this be due to the fact that consumers are displeased with their product after it has broken down? That is, Sears might have a much higher chance of selling another refrigerator to Jo Ann Abraham if she disposes of it in the twelfth year (while it's still working well) as opposed to the thirteenth year, after it has broken down. This does not mean, of course, that a consumer is necessarily better off to dispose of old products earlier. On some occasions, however, this could well be the case. New energy developments, for example, can offer increased operating efficiencies in newer models of appliances, new tires can offer increased safety in a person's automobile, special price deals at slow periods can offer substantial dollar savings, and so forth. Thus, for both marketers and consumers, the issue of changing the timing of product disposition bears increasing attention.

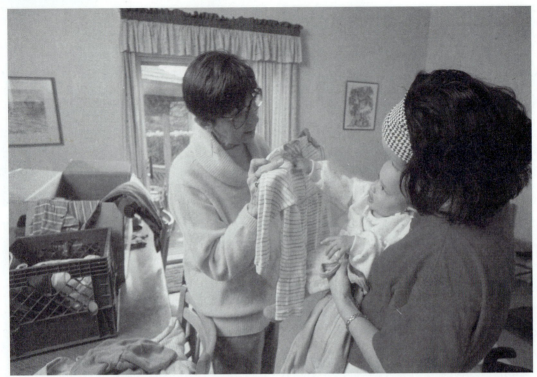

An Oregon-based direct mail marketer of children's clothes, the Hanna Anderson Company enhanced both its quality image and its contributions to the community through its "Hannadowns" Program, which gives a customer a 20 percent credit for mailing back their used Hanna clothes once their kids have outgrown them. The clothes are then laundered and given to needy families and women's shelters. The reaction from one customer: "It makes you feel like spending your money with them."[5]

■ PSYCHOLOGY IN POSTPURCHASE

Postpurchase learning: New knowledge about a product following its purchase, often through use or storage experience.

One of the most interesting aspects of the postpurchase phase involves the several forms of psychological processes consumers can experience following a purchase. One key psychological process is **postpurchase learning.** Here the consumer discovers something of objective reality about a product or service, stores this new knowledge in LTM, modifies relevant attitudes, and is ready for the next decision process with an improved base of knowledge. Since we've already discussed this, we need not delve into it further here. There are, however, two other psychological topics relevant to postpurchase that we've not discussed earlier, *cognitive dissonance* and *consumer satisfaction/dissatisfaction (CS/D)*.

COGNITIVE DISSONANCE

About 30 years ago Leon Festinger, a Stanford University psychology professor, propounded what was to become one of the most popular and controversial theories in all of psychology: cognitive dissonance.[7] Cognitive dissonance belongs to the family of cognitive consistency theories we've already discussed in our chapter on consumer motivation. Let's first examine the theory, then its implications.

Basics of the Theory

Each person has many cognitions (beliefs or opinions) about himself or herself, other people, and the decisions he or she makes. Any two cognitions can be *unrelated* (e.g., "I like fresh green peas" and "Ward sells Buicks") or *related*. If they are related, their relationship can be described as either *consonant* ("I like Ward" and "Ward sells good cars") or *dissonant* ("I don't like Dan" and "I'd like to buy a Buick from Dan."). That is, elements are **consonant cognitions** if one follows logically from the other, whereas they are **dissonant cognitions** if there is a logical inconsistency between them. For any consumer decision we're likely to have many cognitions (e.g., our Buick purchase would produce many elements involving ourselves, the car, the dealer, and the decision itself). The thrust of **cognitive dissonance theory** is that (1) dissonance is likely to occur *after* a choice has been made and (2) it will reflect a natural occurrence *because* the choice has been made.

In terms of postpurchase processes, it is the *total amount of dissonance* that we experience that is important. The more dissonant cognitions we have about the decision, and the more important these are to us, the higher our dissonance will be. And, since dissonance produces unpleasant feelings, we'll be motivated to act to *reduce* the amount of dissonance we are experiencing.

We should recognize that cognitive dissonance is not a significant factor in all situations. Basically, dissonance should be higher (1) when a choice was a close decision and (2) when the purchase was important to us. But why is this? Let's examine a typical case.

🐌 Carrie's College Choice

Carrie Parker is due finally to make up her mind as to which school she'll attend next year. Her decision is down to two universities (we'll call them X and Y so as not to offend anyone). Each school has a number of points in its favor. University X is closer to home, is a little less expensive, and has many course options and a number of Carrie's friends are already there and urging her to join them. University Y, on the other hand, is slightly more prestigious, has a strong marketing department, and has a pretty campus with ivy-covered walls, and Carrie's mother is an alum who loves the school.

Let's consider what happens if Carrie chooses University X. All the positive aspects of Y will now become dissonant elements in her decision—Carrie has given up some prestige, a beautiful campus, and a top-flight major in marketing, and she has a slightly disappointed Mom. Of course she's also gained the positive elements of X, and these produce consonant cognitions for her. Unless X is perfect, though, there will also be a few drawbacks to it (parking problems, several bad teachers, etc.) that will add some further dissonant elements to her total consideration. Overall, since the decision is important to her, and since University Y did offer a number of attractive attributes, Carrie will experience at least a moderate amount of dissonance after making her decision.

What will Carrie do to handle this dissonance? In theory, she'll be attempting to reduce her total dissonance score by (1) reducing the number of dissonant elements, (2) reducing the importance weights she attaches to the dissonant elements, and/or (3) raising the number of consonant elements. For example, she may decide that ivy-covered walls are actually irrelevant to the quality of a college experience and that the school her mother knew 25 years earlier isn't the same place today. She might also be pleased to hear that the star professor at University Y has left the school for greener pastures

Consonant cognitions: Beliefs that are related and that fit logically.

Dissonant cognitions: Beliefs that are related but are logically inconsistent.

Cognitive dissonance theory: An influential theory that posits that dissonant cognitions cause discomfort and motivate consumers to act to minimize this discomfort.

at A&M. Finally, she may not seek out too many supporters of University Y over the next week or so, not wanting to hear any new points that could create new dissonant elements for her.

With respect to University X, Carrie will strive to increase the number and importance of the consonant elements. She may reread the materials from the school, stopping to linger over the attractive photographs of student life and campus landscapes. She'll notice the story in the paper about the rising academic prestige of the university and may well point this out to her parents after dinner. And she'll seek out her friends from the university to let them know of her decision and receive their congratulations and assurances. Over time, Carrie will feel somewhat more favorably toward her chosen school and will be somewhat less favorable toward the school she almost chose. This "spread of attitude" between Universities X and Y will help to ease the dissonance Carrie has experienced and will allow her to set off with enthusiasm for her college life ahead.

Marketing Implications of Dissonance

The special contribution of cognitive dissonance theory rests in its explicit stress on the consumer's motivation to reduce tension following an important purchase decision. From this basis, a number of predictions emerge:

1. *Attitude spread.* As in Carrie's case, one likely outcome is that consumers will strive to see their chosen brand as significantly better than the rejected ones.

2. *Selective information seeking.* Promotional materials and ads provide very favorable information about a brand, as do satisfied owners of the product. For this reason we'd expect consumers to seek out such information as a means of reducing their dissonance. Some marketers believe that consumers read more ads (for the brand they've chosen) *after* they purchase than they had before they bought!

3. *Motivated opinion giving.* More acceptance by others can also serve to reduce dissonance. Thus—especially for innovations, which most consumers haven't yet accepted—we'd expect to see early adopters wanting to bring about further acceptance by engaging in favorable influence attempts on their friends.

These predictions suggest some useful strategies for marketers. For example, some marketers *provide reassurance* through congratulating recent buyers and reviewing strong product attributes in the manuals provided to new purchasers. Several automakers publish special editions of magazines geared to recent purchasers, provided free of charge to them. In addition, some advertising appeals can be geared to recent purchasers as well as potential buyers—the auto ads featuring recent buyers leaping in the air beside their new Toyotas are incorporating this feature. Also, salespersons of "big-ticket" items are often instructed to call their recent buyers within a day or so after purchase, to offer further information and assurances.

These are examples of the many interesting speculations that the theory of cognitive dissonance offers us. Before leaving the topic, however, we should note that scientists have been debating for years the precise nature of dissonance theory and its explanations. These debates do not mean that dissonance does not occur or that it cannot lead to significant impacts on consumer behavior. The debates do, however, suggest caution in accepting dissonance explanations too easily or expecting that the results will always occur. (For our purposes we need not delve into the detailed arguments here. If you are interested in pursuing this further, Note 8 provides a summary of issues and a good set of readings.)

CONSUMER SATISFACTION/DISSATISFACTION ("CS/D")

Consumer satisfaction *is a topic in which marketers and consumers have common interests.* Marketers strive to have satisfied customers—this makes the daily business more pleasant, provides a good base for repeat purchases, and sets the stage for favorable word-of-mouth to potential customers. On the other side of the transaction, consumers enjoy being satisfied. Not only does this indicate that they are obtaining the benefits they seek, but satisfaction also provides a pleasant feeling in itself.

Consumer dissatisfaction *brings quite different reactions, and often serves to set marketers' interests in opposition to those of consumers.* Dissatisfaction is unpleasant for consumers and indicates problems with a product, store, or service provider. It is also bad for the marketer, who risks the loss of future business, negative word-of-mouth, and the prospect of some unpleasant encounters with dissatisfied patrons.

Recently, other business areas have discovered this topic as they have begun to stress "total quality management." Marketers and consumer researchers have been studying it for years, however. In fact, the topic of CS/D is one of the most studied issues in the field of consumer behavior (the acronym "CS/D" was devised by Keith Hunt). There have been over 700 papers written on this topic in the last 15 years. Special CS/D conferences are held so that researchers can report their latest findings and stay current on the work of others and a new journal has now been started on this topic. (If you are interested in reading collections of papers on CS/D, Note 9 explains how to locate them.)

The Concept of Satisfaction

Satisfaction/dissatisfaction refers to an emotional response to an evaluation of a product or service consumption experience.[10] In Figure 19-2, notice that a time dimension underlies this process, which has five key elements:

1. **Expectations.** The seeds of consumer satisfaction are planted during the *prepurchase* phase, when consumers develop "expectations" or beliefs about what they expect to receive from the product. These expectations are carried forward into the postpurchase phase, when they are again activated at the time of consumption.

2. **Performance.** During consumption we experience the actual product in use and perceive its performance on the dimensions that are important to us.

3. **Comparison.** After use, the availability of both the prepurchase expectations and actual performance perceptions allow us to conduct a comparison between them.

4. **Confirmation/disconfirmation.** The comparison results in either a "confirmation" of the consumer's expectations (when the two performance levels are equal) or a "disconfirmation" of expectations (when actual performance is *either* greater than or less than the expected level).

5. **Discrepancy.** If the performance levels are not equal, a discrepancy measure indicates how different one is from the other. For negative disconfirmations—those in which actual performance falls below expected levels—larger discrepancies should produce higher levels of dissatisfaction.

Thus the basic process of CS/D is reasonably straightforward: consumer satisfaction is likely to result when actual performance levels either meet or exceed expected levels (notice that satisfaction thus occurs with both confirmation and positive disconfirmation outcomes). Dissatisfaction occurs when a *negative disconfirmation* is present—when actual outcomes fall below the expected levels of performance.

Consumer satisfaction: A positive emotional response to an evaluation of a consumption experience.

Consumer dissatisfaction: A negative emotional response to an evaluation of a consumption experience

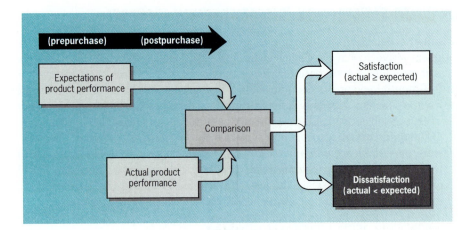

FIGURE 19-2 CS/D as a
Comparison Process

In reality, of course, matters can be more complicated. For example, if a consumer is quite *inexperienced* with a product, his or her expectations of performance are likely to be uncertain. In this case, using the product for the first time provides information for the consumer. One outcome can be to revise the earlier expected levels (during the comparison process) up or down toward the actual performance level. Thus a dissatisfaction outcome is less likely to occur in this instance, as compared to a case in which a consumer has had more experience on which to base his or her initial expectations. Similar revisions of judgments can occur on the actual performance side. This usually happens when a consumer has a hard time judging actual performance. For example, consider how well most of us are able to judge the actual performance of such products as vitamins, modern art exhibits, and new roofing. Thus, when we know we aren't too accurate in our appraisal of performance, our judgments might be selectively nudged toward our earlier expectation levels. As we pay the roofer for our new roof, for instance, we notice that it looks all right, and we're happy to believe it's fine, in part because we expected (and desired) that it would be fine.

How Satisfied Are Consumers?

The Overall Level Is High.   In general, the results of many CS/D surveys—by academics, government agencies, and businesses—show that the overall level of consumer satisfaction is high. For example, a mail survey of Sears, Roebuck customers found that four out of five customers (81 percent) reported that they were "completely satisfied" with their most recent Sears' purchase, whereas only 3 percent were "not too satisfied" (the remainder was "fairly satisfied").[11]

🐚 *We've Got the Power!*

"There isn't a car manufacturer around that can ignore a J. D. Power report," says one auto news chief. "It is an extremely credible source, and its data carries quite a bit of weight." The report in question is the automobile Consumer Satisfaction Index issued annually by the Power firm. Power waits a year and then sends out over 100,000 questionnaires to owners of new cars and trucks. Questions focus on the quality of the car and the service received. Over 130 different models are rated in the survey. Power charges clients an average of $35,000 to examine the CSI report and also uses its expertise to conduct private surveys for interested clients. As you scan auto ads, you will

The J.D. Power firm has slowly been expanding beyond automobiles for its influential studies of consumer satisfaction. When it first tackled personal computers, Dell Corporation was obviously pleased with the results!

probably notice some (high-ranking) cars featuring the Power rating results. According to Mr. Power, "By measuring consumer satisfaction...auto makers now see how they fare against the competition. That always wakes a business up...and we all benefit from their awareness."[12]

But Problem Areas Do Exist.   Although the overall level of consumer satisfaction is high, this doesn't mean that all products and services are trouble free. Are there certain sectors in which consumer *dissatisfaction* is a particular problem? To see if this was the case, the White House Office of Consumer Affairs sponsored a major investigation a few years ago:

ટ્ર The White House/TARP Study of Consumer Problems

A Washington-based consulting firm, TARP, conducted the research for the White House office.[13] Over 2500 consumers across the United States were interviewed. Each respondent was shown a list of possible consumer problems and asked if any had been experienced in the past year. For each problem mentioned, follow-up questions were asked to learn details of the problem, how consumers reacted, and the ultimate outcome. We should note that the TARP study concentrated only on dissatisfaction and is therefore unable to address the overall question of how satisfied consumers are. It is significant, however, that *two-thirds of the consumers reported that they had not experienced any consumer problems during the past year.* While this does not strictly mean that these consumers had no dissatisfaction at all, it does suggest that they would have experienced only mild forms at most.

The *other one-third of the TARP sample did report experiencing consumer problems* (at a rate of almost two problems per household over the year). Table 19-1 lists the types of problems they most frequently reported. In examining this list, it is interesting to see that product performance, while sometimes a difficulty, doesn't account for most consumer problems. Instead, the *service elements* of the marketing mix (availability, repair, delivery, etc.) more frequently cause problems for consumers. When TARP analyzed the problems in terms of the products/services involved, this point became even more clear—*automobile repair and appliance repair are the two major individual sources of consumer problems.*

Table 19-1 Consumer Ratings of CS/D

Type of Consumer Problem	Households Having This Type Problem
1. Store did not have product advertised for sale	25%
2. Unsatisfactory performance/quality of product	22
3. Unsatisfactory repair	20
4. Unsatisfactory service (unrelated to repair)	16
5. Long wait for delivery	10
6. Failure to receive delivery	10
7. Overcharge or excessive price	10
8. Distasteful or offensive advertising	9
9. Product/service not as ordered/agreed on	9
10. Incorrect/deceptive or fraudulent billing	9
11. Deceptive advertising/packaging/pricing	8
12. Goods received in damaged condition	8
13. Manufacturer/dealer didn't live up to guarantee/warranty	7
14. Dealer/salesperson misrepresented product/service	7
15. Failure to receive refund	5
Others (all less than 5%)	

$N = 814$ households in the survey experienced consumer problem(s); there were 1,582 incidences of problems.

SOURCE: See Note 13.

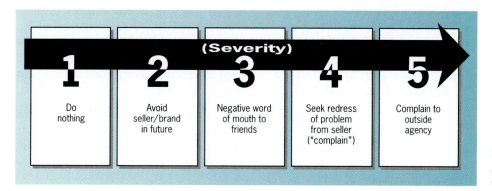

FIGURE 19-3 Alternative Actions in Response to Consumer Dissatisfaction

How Do Consumers Respond to Dissatisfaction?

What can a consumer do when dissatisfied? Figure 19-3 displays five options. Notice that they are roughly arrayed in order of increasing severity and that a consumer might decide to undertake several of the options. How many of these have you employed? In examining the figure, note that those listed are only some of the options a consumer might choose. How often do consumers undertake each response shown? No data can answer this question entirely, but some findings are suggestive. *First, most consumers do not move into the right side of Figure 19-3 in most instances of dissatisfaction.* One major survey, conducted by Alan Andreasen and Arthur Best, covered many product categories and found that 70 percent of dissatisfied consumers did not voice a complaint into the marketing system.[14] The TARP study did, in contrast, find more than a majority of consumers report having either sought "redress" (a product exchange, money return, repair, etc.) or complained to an outside agency. TARP, however, had asked only about the *most serious* problem that the consumer had experienced and found that almost 70 percent of consumers had sought redress for these (even here, however, 30 percent of consumers did not complain).

What influences a consumer's decision to complain or not?[15]

- *Level of dissatisfaction.* For a mild form of dissatisfaction, it may not be worthwhile. The world is not perfect. When a high level of dissatisfaction occurs, however, the likelihood of consumer responses increases.

- *Importance.* Products or services that are more important to us are more likely to generate complaints when unsatisfactory experiences occur. A face lift that goes bad or a new car that won't run is likely to generate redress actions.

- *Costs/benefits of actions.* We are more likely to complain when our expected benefits are high and our expected costs of complaining are low. A defective purchase made on vacation 2000 miles away may not yield a return to that store, while that same purchase around the corner is likely to be returned.

- *Personal characteristics.* Studies have shown that some people are more likely to complain than others. Highly educated persons are more likely to seek redress, as are people with more time available. Personality characteristics such as aggressiveness also determine whether a person complains or not.

■ *Attribution of blame.* If Dee Sequin has a problem, but believes that she could possibly be at fault, she's less likely to complain than if she attributes the cause of the problem to the manufacturer. One common source of difficulty for marketers occurs because of this attribution process, when the seller and the buyer each attribute the problem to be the other party's fault! This situation is made even more difficult because emotions are involved and the persons may not communicate clearly.

In regard to consumer attributions—and as a reward for reading this far into the chapter—you may enjoy reading the quotes in Exhibit 19-1. These are actual statements from insurance policyholders reporting how the auto accident had occurred. While not exactly complaint reports, they do demonstrate forms of blame attributions and give a sense for what it's like in the real world!

XHIBIT 19-1 _____

Consumer Attributions of Accident Causes: A Biased Sample

"Not My Fault!"

- "No one was to blame for the accident but it never would have happened if the other driver had been alert."

- "A pedestrian hit me and went under my car."

- "I had been shopping for plants all day....As I reached an intersection a hedge sprang up obscuring my vision. I did not see the other car."

- "I was on my way to the doctor with rear end trouble when my universal joint gave way causing me to have an accident."

- "As I approached the intersection, a stop sign suddenly appeared where no stop sign had ever appeared before. I was unable to stop in time...."

- "My car was legally parked as it backed into the other vehicle."

- "The indirect cause of this accident was a little guy in a small car with a big mouth."

- "The telephone pole was approaching fast. I was attempting to swerve out of its path when it struck my front end."

- "An invisible car came out of nowhere, struck my vehicle, and vanished."

"It Was My Fault, But..."

- "I pulled away from the side of the road, glanced at my mother-in-law, and headed over the embankment."

- "In my attempt to kill a fly I drove into a telephone pole."

- "The accident occurred when I was attempting to bring my car out of a skid by steering it into the other vehicle."

- "I had been learning power steering. I turned the wheel...and found myself in a different direction going the opposite way."

- "I was taking my canary to the hospital. It got loose and flew out the window. The next thing I saw was his rear end and there was a crash."

- "When I saw I could not avoid a collision, I stepped on the gas and crashed into the other car."

- "The pedestrian had no idea which way to go, so I ran over him."

"I'm Still Dazed by It All..."

- "I collided with a stationary truck coming the other way."

- "I told the police that I was not injured but on removing my hat, I found that I had a fractured skull."

- "I saw her look at me twice, she appeared to be making slow progress, then we met on impact."

- "A guy was all over the road, I had to swerve a number of times before I hit him."

- "I was thrown from my car as it left the road. I was later found in a ditch by some stray cows."

SOURCE: These quotes were abstracted from information submitted to the FTC project on consumer life insurance information disclosure and reflect actual policyholder reports.

What Happens When Consumers Complain?

When consumers do seek redress (complain), most go directly to the store. This means that *retailers* receive most complaints about a given product, while the manufacturer receives relatively little direct feedback from consumers. This can be undesirable, since considerable information can be lost if not fully passed along. What about consumers contacting outside agencies, such as the Better Business Bureau, Federal Trade Commission, local agencies, or newspapers? Outside agencies are the *least* likely to be contacted: they accounted for less than 10 percent of the complaints in the TARP study and only 1 percent in the Best and Andreasen research.

How successful are consumers in having their dissatisfaction handled well? The TARP research found that 40 percent of the complaining households obtained either "completely satisfying" or "acceptable solution" responses from the business. Another 13 percent got "something" but were not completely satisfied, while another 40 percent were "not at all satisfied" with the way in which their complaints were resolved. The TARP research team concluded that serious difficulties exist with actions to resolve consumer problems. They pointed out that, adding the 30 percent of consumers who did not complain at all to the 40 percent who were displeased with the resolution of their complaints suggests that about 70 percent of serious consumer problems are not being satisfactorily remedied. As we'll see in the next section, this poses some serious problems (and opportunities) for marketers.

■ MARKETING APPLICATIONS
OF POSTPURCHASE CONCEPTS

John Czepiel succinctly described the tasks of marketing as follows:

> In any organization, marketing bears the responsibility for three key tasks: (1) *design* of an offering to meet consumer needs, (2) *attraction* of clients to that offering, and (3) *monitoring and control* of results to ensure the continued meeting of customer needs in a changing environment.[16]

This perspective reminds us that marketers should consider *all* aspects of the consumer's decision process—activities at the prepurchase stage, during purchase, and during postpurchase—when designing their management system. Alert marketers have already recognized some useful guidelines from the consumption and satisfaction dimensions of consumer behavior. Let's briefly examine five examples of these insights.

𝒆🐚 Insight 1: Consumer Use Can Guide
New Product Positioning

Alert marketers monitor how consumers are using various products. Procter & Gamble, for example, in monitoring consumers' laundry behaviors, discovered that households were washing more frequently and using cooler water to wash new artificial fabrics. Based on this information, the firm developed Cheer detergent to wash effectively in all water temperatures. P & G takes consumer use problems seriously: when it learned that people in high-altitude regions were having difficulty preparing baked goods, the firm added special "high-altitude baking" directions to its Duncan Hines packages. The product disposition stage also offers opportunities for enterprising marketers. For example, a new machine that accepts empty soda and beer cans, crushes them, and returns a nickel to the consumer is now on the market. These machines are rented to retailers in states with "bottle laws."[17]

𝒆🐚 Insight 2: Don't Overpromise—Consumer
Dissatisfaction Can Be Costly

As Czepiel's quote reminded us, marketing involves the distinct processes of both *attracting consumers* and *satisfying them*. Glowing promises are useful ways to attract purchasers, but marketers should bear in mind that these promises may form the basis for consumer expectations. Since consumer dissatisfaction springs from negative disconfirmations of these expectations, some instances of dissatisfaction could be avoided if consumers simply expected less in the first place. Thus marketers are wise to strike a reasonable balance between performance promised and that consumers are likely to experience.

How costly can dissatisfaction be? According to a TARP study on automobiles, *disgruntled auto owners are likely to vent their frustration to 16 additional people!* On the other hand, a satisfied owner provides positive word of mouth to 8 other people, plus being likely to buy four more cars of the same make over the next 12 years![18] Similar results were also uncovered in a TARP study conducted for Coca-Cola. In this research, consumers who complained and were not satisfied, typically told 9 or 10 friends about their experience, and 30 percent of these persons said they stopped buying Coke products altogether (another 45 percent said they'd buy less in the future). However, when the complaint was resolved satisfactorily, the average consumer told 4 or 5 people about the positive experience.[19]

🐚 *Insight 3: See If a Guarantee of Postpurchase Satisfaction Is Possible*

It would be naive to assume that a firm should always strive to obtain the highest possible level of consumer satisfaction. Many factors need to be considered. For example, *some consumers may be wrong* when they complain (repairpersons report that one of their most common experiences is the discovery that the appliance the consumer believes to be defective has in fact become unplugged from the wall socket!). Also, increasing the probability of consumer satisfaction is likely to bring *higher costs* into the system, and in some cases there is an *inherent uncertainty* in the product. This uncertainty means the costs of guaranteeing consumer satisfaction may be too high and the consumer is better off to assume some risk of being dissatisfied. *Used cars* provide a classic case of this point. Most of us recognize that used car dealers hold one of the lowest reputations for consumer satisfaction guarantees in all of marketing, but we may not have thought why this would tend to occur. Note that part of the used car dissatisfaction syndrome is due to inherent uncertainties about the product itself. What is the history of the car, how much abuse has it already suffered? What will happen in the car's future—how will it be driven, and what will break down? Thus, if it were possible to guarantee complete satisfaction, the costs of doing so would raise the prices of used cars for all buyers, and some consumers might find this undesirable. In a sense, then, the consumer is choosing either to pay for "satisfaction insurance" when buying a used car (by buying from a reputable dealer who offers warranty protection) or to bear the risks personally and buy from a dealer who offers "as-is" cars at lower prices.

There are, of course, many situations in which strong guarantees can work to a marketer's advantage. The famous Zippo lighter, for example, was marketed with an ironclad guarantee that any consumer problem would be promptly corrected, free of charge, at the factory. Similarly, many finer retailers offer "Free Return If Not Completely Satisfied" policies to guarantee their customers' postpurchase satisfaction. And Domino's shot to its powerful position in pizza by guaranteeing delivery within 30 minutes, or a $3 refund. Nationally, Domino's hits this time on 92 percent of its pizzas (for this to work, an efficiency system was developed that prepares a pizza from phone order to delivery truck in 7 minutes).

When firms become serious about this idea, they sometimes learn some interesting facts about their market. Xerox, for example, discovered that they should definitely rush a replacement model copier into service rather than offering a firm its money back. The reason? A money-back return signals that the purchasing agent had made a bad decision, while a good replacement validates his or her choice of Xerox as a supplier that cares about its customers! Similarly, Thomas McAndrews, president of the Mannington flooring company, discovered that the industry and customers had for years been miscommunicating about "no wax" flooring. Consumers thought that it meant that the floors never had to be waxed, while industry knew that they meant that the floors could be mopped without having to be waxed each time. Mr. McAndrews reports that

There's *only* one hotel chain that guarantees your complete satisfaction with every visit—Hampton Inn. If you're not 100% satisfied with your Hampton Inn stay, we don't expect you to pay. It's just our way of doing business.

And at Hampton Inn, your clean, comfortable room comes with value-added extras you're sure to enjoy. Like a complimentary continental breakfast, free local calls, a free in-room movie channel and your choice of smoking or non-smoking rooms—all at rates usually 20-40% less than at traditional hotels.

One stay with us and you'll see why 9 out of 10 guests say they would go out of their way to come back to a Hampton Inn. Plus, with over 200 hotels nationwide, you'll find us conveniently located wherever you travel.

So stay with Hampton Inn...the *only* hotel chain where your satisfaction is always guaranteed.

Smart Style. Smart Price. Smart Choice.®

For reservations or a free directory call: 1-800-HAMPTON or your travel agent.

Call: 1-800-451-HTDD

©1989, Hampton Inns, Inc.

Hampton Inns tells guests that if they aren't happy, they don't have to pay. In the first year of this program, 7000 guests invoked the guarantee, costing the firm about $350,000 in sales. However, 99% of these people said they'd try again in the future, and over one-third had within the year. In addition, research indicates that another 2% of guests chose Hampton because of the guarantee. In total, therefore, the firm estimates that it receives $8 for every $1 paid out under the guarantee program!

these misperceptions had built up a huge wave of consumer resentment: "We were stunned by what we heard...people were broadly dissatisfied with the industry, and with us." His response was strong and risky: drop the term from advertising and offer a one-year "no questions asked" guarantee for its top-line Mannington Gold brand—if a consumer wishes (for whatever the reason), the company will rip out the floor and replace it free of charge! The results? Consumers responded strongly. In a depressed market, Mannington moved its production from two shifts a day, five days a week to three shifts a day, seven days a week![21]

🐚 Insight 4: Stay in Contact with Consumers during Postpurchase

The prevailing attitude at the best consumer marketing companies is to encourage consumer complaints and questions after purchase—to view these as an opportunity rather than a problem. Tom Peters, author of the best-selling book *In Search of Excellence,* quotes Joe Gerard (the highest-volume auto salesman in the country) as saying that he "likes to sell a lemon...then he can show the customer how well he'll perform on after-sales service." Similar reactions were voiced by representatives of IBM and other major firms: "This gives us a chance to convert a dissatisfied customer into a positive supporter of our firm and our products. Also, the word-of-mouth is terrific." As the head of P & G's Consumer Services Department put it, "If people have a problem with one of our products, we'd rather they tell us about it than switch to a competitor's product or say bad things about ours over the backyard fence."

With this in mind, many firms have introduced toll-free "800" telephone lines for consumers to use in contacting the firm. Surprisingly, most of the calls *don't* reflect complaints. General Electric's "GE Answer Center" is generally considered the best of all: it receives 60,000 calls per week! About 25 percent are asking for information about a GE product they are considering, 35 percent are seeking help in caring for their appliances, and the remaining 40 percent have a problem with the appliance and want diagnostic help. Only 15 percent of all calls are actual complaints. Internal studies indicate that an average call costs $2–5 but that service is highly profitable: 700,000 callers are referred to dealers, 95 percent of callers are satisfied with the outcome of their call, and many of these become more loyal to GE. According to the center's manager, "Most businesses don't understand that customer service is really selling."

Along with contact from customers, keeping in touch with consumers after purchase also means contacting them to *measure consumer satisfaction/dissatisfaction (CS/D).* Stimulated by the Total Quality Management movement, measurement of CS/D by companies has grown rapidly in recent years and now represents about $100 million in research spending. The major advantage of this type of study is that it can be "benchmarked," so that a firm's improvements, or decreases, can be tracked across time (by doing periodic surveys, then comparing results). Specific problems spots can be identified and remedied, and sometimes useful new ideas emerge from the customers. Finally, CS/D measures can be used as an incentive to improve customer service: Infiniti, for example, offers its dealers a bonus for each period that their CS/D scores beat 87 on a scale of 100 (the bonus is $10,000 each month, plus $25,000 each quarter, for a total of $220,000 per year!).[22]

🐚 Insight 5: Manage Your System Well

Consumer postpurchase satisfaction involves more than abstract systems, information, and technical product quality. *People* are involved, on both the business and consumer sides. Recognizing this fact, many marketers have found that paying closer attention to their own internal management systems can pay handsome dividends. The Bell Telephone System, for example, has taken pride in maintaining high customer service levels for over 30 years. When it examined its program carefully, however, the firm discovered that it was using internal operating criteria (the number of seconds required to locate a customer's record) rather than consumer-based criteria to guide the program. As a

Nissan recently completed a $5 million consumer satisfaction study, covering everyone who used its warranty service.

spokesperson explained, "It became apparent that customers don't particularly care whether it takes 15 seconds or 45 seconds, or even longer, to find customer records. *What they do care about is courteous, accurate service.*"

Many postpurchase problems are unique, and both the business representative and the consumer are operating in an uncertain situation. How can a marketer know whether the firm's representatives are making the best decisions? One approach (used in a study conducted for a home products manufacturer) asked a sample of consumers and managers from the company to judge five consumer complaint letters. The consumer respondents were asked to take the role of the letter writer, while the managers were to indicate how they would normally respond to that letter. Results were surprising. *In general the managers gave more to consumers than the consumers themselves expected to receive!* The average cost of consumers' expectations in this study was $135, whereas the average cost for the managers' responses was $167. Managers with over 10 years of experience were much more liberal in their complaint resolutions, while less experienced managers tended to be more inflexible and less likely to please the customer. Are these results good or bad? A more liberal complaint resolution is more likely to please the customer, but also represents a higher commitment of corporate resources. It thus appears that the firm would benefit from developing a more streamlined system.

As a final point, we should again note that many instances of consumer dissatisfaction arise from the nature of the interaction with the firm or store's representatives. To handle this problem, most firms have developed systems and procedures to aid their employees in dealing with customers. This can be challenging, however, especially for firms whose employees are either low paid or who work under stressful conditions. This pressure will increase in the future, moreover, as many new entrants to the low-wage sector of the service work force will have low education levels and possible English language problems. Thus one phrase that has been recently accepted as a rule for consumer businesses is "customer retention and employee retention go together." Thus marketers are increasingly willing to raise pay and prospects for their strong performers with customers, to keep these key employees happy.

Further, however, these firms must train and organize for *both* efficiency and customer satisfaction. Notice, for example, the extreme emphasis that many well-run organizations (retailers such as McDonald's, service providers such as the police force, and highly automated, time-dependent operations such as United Airlines) place on operating procedures for their employees to follow when interacting with consumers. In all these cases, the operation is geared to providing a maximum service for the customer or citizen, but with minimal extra social interactions. Those interactions that must occur, moreover, are highly programmed, even to the point of requiring memorized statements and smiles on cue. While these procedures may at first appear "cold," it is interesting to understand why they are deemed necessary by managers charged with achieving both work efficiency and customer satisfaction.[23]

■ POSTPURCHASE ISSUES IN PUBLIC POLICY

Marketers are not the only parties with a keen interest in the postpurchase phase. Public policy is also highly involved, as we saw in our coverage of "green marketing" and the environment. More broadly, public policy often gets involved in postpurchase issues because *it is usually at this stage of the process when problems arise between consumers and marketers.* There are two basic issues we'll briefly examine in this section: *postpurchase remedies* and *product liability.*

POSTPURCHASE REMEDIES

Postpurchase remedies, or **PPRs,** is an area of regulation that poses many difficult issues: product safety can provide us with just one brief illustration.

❧ *What to Do About Product Safety?*

One question in this area is how to minimize problems consumers will face when they use various products. Let's consider insecticides—most of these chemicals are toxic (poisonous) and can cause serious health problems or even death. Why is this issue difficult? First, insecticides perform a function that millions of consumers seek. In this sense there are *clear benefits from these products.* Unfortunately, there are also *clear risks* associated with using insecticides. It is these risks that bring public policy into the picture. In considering regulatory options, several key characteristics complicate matters. For example, not all insecticides are equally toxic: some have much more severe effects than others. Also, some are more effective than others, and there is likely to be a *correlation* between toxicity and effectiveness—insecticides that are more effective are also likely to be more toxic.

The problem is further complicated when we consider the consumers who are involved. Most consumers *don't know* very much about chemicals and poisons and can't be counted on to use them as experts would. Also, many potential users are *not able to read* very well (this group includes those with vision difficulties, the estimated 25 million persons who are functionally illiterate, and any young children who may come into contact with the insecticides at home). In addition, some insecticides have *long-lasting traces* on the surfaces of carpeting, walls, or furniture—many households have young children and pets who roam through the house with curious hands and tongues. Even though they may not be the purchasers or even the users of the product, there is a danger that they'll be "consumers" of it! Finally, we know that many consumers are "low involved" and don't make much effort to listen carefully to ads or read package labels

Postpurchase remedies (PPRs): Public policies aimed at minimizing or resolving problems that arise after purchase of a product or service.

and use instructions. And the *conditions of use* don't encourage careful thought and reading, as when consumers use the product on an intruder such as a mosquito.

What *should public policy be toward the packaging, labeling, and advertising of various insecticides?* Notice that our options range from doing nothing to requiring only minimal information (warnings, detailed instructions for safe use, etc.), to outright product bans (for example, if a new insecticide is found to kill people, the best remedy may be to ensure that it's not available for use by the general public). As we move toward stronger remedies, however, note that we are restricting marketing freedoms and depriving consumers of effective products that some might possibly desire.

In the area of postpurchase remedies, the role of public policy is to provide a system that (1) minimizes postpurchase problems and (2) provides for corrective actions when serious problems do occur. In creating this system, it is important that public policymakers clearly recognize both the *rights of the consumer* and the *freedoms of the marketer.* The system should be fair to both parties, and it should support other desirable goals, such as economic growth, innovation, and efficiency.

Types of Postpurchase Remedies

There are three basic approaches that public policymakers can employ in the PPR area: (1) informational remedies, (2) enforcement remedies, and (3) mandatory PPRs.[24] **Informational remedies** aim at having consumers know about products and how to use them. The care labels we find in clothing, for example, are aimed at reducing unsatisfactory postpurchase experiences by informing consumers of the proper cleaning procedures for that particular garment. In another sector, *vocational schools* are now required to inform prospective students of the job placement rates of recent graduates. Also, considerable attention has also been given to the informational aspects of *warranties.* Historically, many firms had their warranties drawn up by attorneys who used the instrument as a means of limiting the responsibilities of the firm. Millions of consumers thus grew up with little hope of even *attempting* to read a product warranty—they knew that it would only befuddle them. Because consumers were not attempting to read the warranties, firms that sold more durable products were finding it difficult to compete effectively on this basis. Thus the U.S. Congress led a movement to improve warranties and relied mostly on informational remedies. Clear and simple disclosure of warranty conditions was required, and the act also required that consumers be informed of the step-by-step procedures to follow to obtain redress of a postpurchase problem.

Enforcement remedies ensure that the rights of consumers are protected if they encounter postpurchase problems. One option is for private mechanisms to resolve disputes, such as *arbitration boards* consisting of independent persons. Such boards are low in cost, provide speedy decisions, and are designed for easy consumer access. Other enforcement remedies have involved regulations for the timely *delivery* of mail-order merchandise (some sellers were not sending out the goods for long periods after receiving payment), *refunds* for defective products, and *repairs* for defective automobiles. Of course, each case has its own set of facts. In the auto case, for example, Ford had found that in some small cars the pistons were scuffing cylinder walls, necessitating major engine repairs. Even though the warranties on some cars had expired, the firm was opting to make free repairs for those customers who came in to complain. The FTC, however, argued that these adjustments were actually "secret warranties" that the firm should make known to all buyers, not just to those

Informational remedies: Public policies that aim at having consumers know about products and how to use them.

Enforcement remedies: Public policies that ensure that consumers' rights are protected if they encounter postpurchase problems.

who complained about it. The firm then notified about 2 million owners about the program.

Mandatory PPRs constitute the strongest form of postpurchase remedy; here the government steps directly into the terms and conditions for contracts. This step is usually taken reluctantly. *Product bans*, such as those we discussed with insecticides, are one form of mandatory PPR. *Cooling-off laws* reflect another form of mandatory remedy, giving the buyer a right to cancel the sale within a certain time, usually three days to two weeks. These laws were passed in response to the complaints of thousands of consumers that they had been "pressured" into buying magazines, land, and other products. When they thought it over or discussed it with their spouses, they found that they were bound by the contract they had signed and now owed hundreds or even thousands of dollars for something they no longer wished to own. Since in most cases the goods have not yet been delivered, the intention of these laws is clear: to give the buyer enough time to reconsider the purchase in the absence of high-pressure selling.

Required trial periods are another, stronger form of mandatory remedy. In one case the FTC required a reducing salon to offer consumers the option of canceling a long-term contract after their first visit. In another case a land sales company was required to offer its customers the option of canceling the purchase after they had a chance to visit the land they were contracting to buy. This is not the general rule, however: the FTC created these orders in response to the high-pressure sales tactics used by the firms in the cases. Since all mandatory remedies restrict freedoms and are likely to raise the costs of selling, they are the most controversial form of postpurchase remedy.

THE PUZZLING CASE OF PRODUCT LIABILITY

Before leaving public policy applications, we should briefly examine a puzzling problem area that crops up primarily in the state court systems—the issue of **tort liability** for injuries caused by products. Tort law is concerned with what *compensation* is due one party for the wrongs committed by another party. For example, how would you rule in these three cases?

🐚 Torts in the Courts

Case 1.

A teenager attempted to scent a candle by pouring perfume (made by Fabergé) over it. The candle, however, was already lit, and the perfume ignited. A friend nearby was burned in the neck region. The friend sued Fabergé, claiming that no warning had been given that the perfume was flammable. Should the consumer win? If so, how much compensation should be awarded?

Case 2.

A Florida high school student was paralyzed due to a head injury suffered while playing football with the school team. He sued the maker of the helmet, Riddell, Inc., claiming that the helmet did not adequately protect him from severe physical injury and that this was intended to be its major function. Should the student win? If so, how much compensation should be awarded?

Mandatory PPRs: The strongest category of postpurchase remedy: the government steps directly into the terms for product sale, including bans.

Tort liability: Compensation due an injured party for the wrongs committed by another.

Case 3.

The classified ad in *Soldier of Fortune* magazine read: "Ex-marines–'67–69 'Nam vets. Ex-DI, weapons specialist, jungle warfare, pilot, M.E., high-risk assignments, U.S. or overseas (phone #)." Mr. Black saw the ad, contacted the men who placed it, and four months later hired one of them to kill Mrs. Black. Mrs. Black's family sued the magazine for negligence in running the ad. Should the family win? If so, how much compensation should be awarded?

While there is not enough detailed information on the cases to allow firm conclusions as to the proper verdict, thinking about them allows us to recognize some of the basic principles involved in this area of public policy and the law. (If you're interested in the outcomes, they are briefly described in Note 25.)

Types of Product Defects

As noted, product liability law is concerned with compensating consumers who have been wrongfully injured. Judges and juries are called upon first to decide whether the manufacturer is *liable* for the injury and then to decide on the appropriate amount of *damages* to award. There are three basic ways in which a product can be judged to be defective:[26]

1. *A quality-control problem.* This occurs when the item in question does not meet the manufacturer's own standards for quality or safety. The famous "mouse in the soft drink bottle" is an example, and injured consumers are likely to win.

2. *Inadequate warnings or instructions.* This concerns the seller's responsibility to provide buyers with information that allows them to use products properly and warns them of special risks. (The Fabergé case reflects this category.)

3. *Product design defects.* In these instances the firm is charged with having built a problem into the product. When the design has been repeated on a mass-production basis, this category lends itself to "class action" suits that represent large numbers of consumers and can run into multimillion-dollar damage levels. In the *Grimshaw* v. *Ford Motor Company* case, the company was charged with having designed a defect into the gas tanks of its Pinto line of cars, causing the tanks to explode when the car was hit in the rear.

The "Strict Liability" Controversy

In recent years marketers have been bemoaning the development of the *doctrine of strict liability.* To appreciate exactly what this is and why marketers are so concerned, let's go back to see how it came about.

✒ *How "Strict Liability" Developed*

Negligence doctrine: The former rule, under which an injured consumer had to prove that a marketer had acted negligently in order to recover.

For years the traditional rule in liability law was the **negligence doctrine.** Under this doctrine, injured consumers could only recover for product-related injuries when the seller failed to exercise reasonable and prudent care in design, quality control, and informational decisions affecting the consumer. However, while the *principle* of negligence may have been appropriate, its *practice* raised serious problems for consumer rights. To understand why, let's briefly consider the fundamental nature of our court system.

Essentially, our courts are ruled by *the principle of evidence*. As we all know, a person (or firm) is "innocent until proven guilty." This means that factual evidence establishing guilt is necessary. Under the negligence doctrine, "guilt" meant negligence, and it was necessary for a court to have solid proof that the firm had acted in a negligent manner before it would rule in behalf of an injured consumer. This meant that the entire burden of proof fell on the injured consumer. He or she not only had to show that an unreasonable injury had occurred, but also to prove that the seller had been negligent (and that this negligence had led to the injury).

The result of this doctrine was that in many cases consumers who had been severely injured were unable to recover, while many others were advised not to even bring a case. In both instances the injured party either didn't have access to the materials needed to prove negligence or the records simply didn't exist. The courts recognized that this situation was unfair, and ways were sought to provide consumers with more of an equal footing.

In recent years courts have experimented with other types of doctrines and now seem to have settled on **strict liability.** This doctrine does require proof that the product was in a "defective condition" (or was "unreasonably dangerous") when sold, but does not require that the consumer prove that the marketer was negligent in any way. This would appear to be reasonable in terms of what might be reasonable for the injured party to prove.

When we consider the marketer's viewpoint, however, the strict liability doctrine becomes a real threat. In brief, it means that a seller can be held liable for damages even when he or she has exercised all due care in the manufacturing, designing, and packaging of a product. Many marketers are outraged, since this seems to say that they can be sued even when they've done nothing wrong that they can control.

The Current Controversy. The result of the changing doctrines has been a dramatic increase in the number of consumer product injury lawsuits and in the size of damage awards as well. Critics claim that consumer prices have to increase to cover the risks of the new system and that product innovation is stifled, since firms fear possible suits arising from new, less tested products. As we'd expect, insurance costs for product liability suits have skyrocketed in recent years. Riddell, the helmet maker, lost the football case and now spends 14 percent of the cost of its helmets on insurance and litigation (compared to only 1 percent prior to the suit). Many firms cannot even obtain insurance coverage and are searching for ways to band together to insure themselves.

Consumer Research May Provide Answers. It does seem obvious that modifications in the strict liability doctrine will have to be made in future years. Several are essentially legal in nature (e.g., a firm's compliance with appropriate industry standards might be used as a defense against liability judgments). Our interest, however, lies in modifications that involve increasing attention to the consumer behaviors in these cases. If consumers have altered the product (as in gas emission devices for autos), have not read warnings or instructions, or have misused the product (as in underinflating tires, then suing when they blow out), they might well not deserve to collect huge damage awards. Some states have begun to recognize this stance and are moving toward a **comparative–fault doctrine** in which damages would depend upon the extent to which the injured party contributed to the creation to the problem. To resolve these issues, further participation by consumer behavior experts will be

Strict liability doctrine: Allows consumers to recover for injuries with proof that a product was unreasonably dangerous or in defective condition when sold.

Comparative-fault doctrine: An emerging compromise rule: here damages depend on the extent the injured party contributed to the problem.

needed to establish reasonable baselines for consumer information processing and use behaviors. As a marketer, you may be called upon to defend your practices in this arena. As a consumer and a citizen, your inputs into the system can be significant. The legal system does face frustrating problems in trying these cases, and in turn poses frustrating problems for marketers and consumers who must deal with it.

The fact remains, however, that dangerous and defective products are sold on a regular basis in our economy, some quite innocently and some with a negligent disregard for potential users. Some consumers do misuse these products, while some do not. Tragic injuries do occur, and some people are forced to live with the aftermath of those accidents. *Although infrequent at the individual level, in the aggregate this is a huge problem area.* As an indicator of its magnitude, the Consumer Product Safety Commission was involved in recalling over 1200 products during its first six years of existence, with millions of individual items being recalled because of product hazards. (If you would like to read further about product liability, you may wish to pursue the readings in Note 27.)

■ CONSUMER APPLICATIONS OF POSTPURCHASE CONCEPTS

Our previous sections have covered many topics pertinent to the consumer's perspective of the postpurchase phase. Two of the important points are (1) *many marketers have a primary interest in long-term consumer satisfaction.* They wish to have loyal patrons and will work to achieve consumer satisfaction within the bounds of reasonable decisions. While they don't like to have problems arise, they'd rather hear about them and have a chance to resolve them than lose the goodwill and future purchases of dissatisfied customers and their friends. And (2) *many public policymakers have an interest in seeing that consumers are able to exercise their rights within our system.* They focus primarily on minimizing dissatisfaction in the system. There are several types of remedies available to consumers experiencing postpurchase dissatisfaction.

HOW TO AVOID CONSUMER PROBLEMS

Although consumer problems can't be avoided entirely, there are several clear steps that consumers can take to minimize the probability that they'll crop up. The best place to start is during the prepurchase stage. Consumers have the right to be informed, but this right brings with it a responsibility to inform themselves. They should seek information. They should shop comparatively. The more capable consumers recognize that sellers are motivated to make sales and that often negotiation is possible. Also, a little effort at the library can yield substantial benefits from a better purchase.

The choice of a seller *does* make a difference. It is primarily important to avoid disreputable or fraudulent sellers. A simple telephone call to the local Better Business Bureau is one way to screen for this possibility. This agency is supported by local merchants; it maintains complaint records from consumers and will indicate the status of a seller's complaint record to consumers who call to inquire. Also, we know that retailers pursue different strategies. Some offer higher prices but high levels of postpurchase services and guarantees. These sellers may not seem as attractive when only initial selling prices are considered, but if postpurchase aggravation is factored in, they may actually be quite competitive. Moreover, a number of these high-service retailers are willing to "meet competitive prices." If so, our willingness to ask about this policy can result in both buying at a lower price *and* obtaining better guarantees of postpurchase satisfaction.

Finally, experts know that a buyer's leverage is much higher *before* the purchase is made than it is right afterward. It is at this time that many potential postpurchase problems can be minimized. Speedy deliveries can often be arranged, trial periods can often be arranged, and, for large purchases, inspections are an intelligent option. We've all experienced postpurchase problems that are our own fault. Reading and following instructions, taking reasonable precautions, and otherwise avoiding foreseeable problems are responsibilities for consumers that mirror the product liability responsibilities of marketers.

HANDLING POSTPURCHASE PROBLEMS

The options that consumers have for redress have been noted at various points in the chapter. The most typical first step is to return to the seller to explain the difficulty and try to arrange for a satisfactory resolution. In many cases of defective products, the fault lies with the manufacturer rather than the retailer, and the retailer deserves the right to resolve the problem rather than lose the customer's future business. A consumer who approaches this step with a strategy in mind (e.g., asking for certain actions that are easy for the seller to take) is more likely to achieve a reasonable resolution at this stage.

When the problem cannot be resolved directly, several options exist. If a defective product is involved, direct contact with the manufacturer is a good option. If the firm has a toll-free consumer number (a consumer can inquire by calling 1-800-555-1212 and asking whether a toll-free number is listed), there is likely to be a well-developed system available to handle consumer problems. Also, letters to high-level company executives can sometimes bring speedy results. The names and addresses of executives are listed in Standard & Poor's *Register of Corporations*, available in most libraries.

If problems exist with local retailers or service providers, complaints to the local Better Business Bureau can be worthwhile. Another option in many localities is a local media-sponsored "consumer action line" that specializes in resolving such problems. There may be local consumer groups available, and many universities have legal service offices. Finally, a good source to contact is often the city, county, or state office of consumer protection (these operate under a variety of names, so consumers are advised to call the information office of the government unit to locate the appropriate office). Since these officials deal with consumer problems daily, they often have excellent contacts by which to satisfy disputes on a voluntary basis.

Sometimes, when all voluntary avenues have been exhausted, the only remaining recourse is to enter into some form of system that will enforce compliance with the law (consumers can, of course, lose their cases as well as win them). As discussed earlier in the chapter, consumer arbitration is emerging as a reasonable option for dispute resolution, since the system is being designed precisely to offer easy-access, low-cost routes for consumers to follow. For other circumstances, such as when dollar amounts at issue are less than $1000–2000, small claims courts are a good option to investigate, since these are designed for consumers to represent themselves, without attorneys, to hold down costs. ("The People's Court" television series, featuring Judge Wapner, depicts a small claims court.) When dollar amounts are larger, the advice of an attorney is likely to be the best alternative for the consumer to pursue.

A CLOSING NOTE

It is unsatisfying to close this chapter with a discussion of contacting an attorney, going to small claims court, or otherwise engaging in disputes with marketers. As we all know, these occurrences are not typical, and while we consumers should be aware of our options, we should also not be planning to have to exercise them very often. As we noted at the start, it is in the postpurchase phase that consumers experience the benefits offered by our highly developed, sophisticated consumer marketing system. All parties involved in this system—marketers, public policymakers, and consumers alike—face complicated decisions that need to be made in the face of uncertainties about the future. As we've seen, all three parties make some mistakes and could improve. At the same time, it seems appropriate to close by noting that the overall marketing consumer system is working rather well!

■ SUMMARY

WHY ARE POSTPURCHASE PROCESSES IMPORTANT?

The *postpurchase phase* can actually be the most important stage in a decision system. From the consumer's perspective, this stage represents the point at which consumption actually occurs and when benefits are received. From a marketer's perspective, long-term success flows from having consumers experience satisfaction during the postpurchase phase. Finally, postpurchase processes account for two of the three major activities within the overall consumption system: consumption and disposition.

A FRAMEWORK FOR POSTPURCHASE

The chapter began by noting *four key dimensions of consumption:* (1) frequency, (2) amount, (3) consumption intervals, and (4) consumption purposes. Each presents implications and opportunities for marketing managers. We next discussed the *process of disposition* and saw that it is more complex than we may first imagine. Product disposition, in the aggregate, raises serious *ecological questions:* we discussed some ways in which marketers can use an "Eco-logic" framework to address these. The FTC has introduced new guidelines for "green marketing," which should impact the future of this area. We also noted that the consumer market is highly segmented as to environmental concerns, with about half of all adults having little or no interest. Finally, we noted that the question of when people decide to dispose of their products also raises important issues for marketers.

PSYCHOLOGY IN POSTPURCHASE

In the next section of the chapter we examined *two key psychological processes* that operate during the postpurchase stage. *Cognitive dissonance theory* suggests that consumers experience tension following a difficult decision and may behave in some "strange ways" in an effort to reduce the dissonance. *Consumer satisfaction/dissatisfaction* (CS/D) is determined by five elements: (1) consumer expectations, (2) actual performance, (3) the comparison between expectations and performance, (4) confirmation or disconfirmation of expectations, and (5) the size and direction of the discrepancy score. The chapter then presented data on actual levels of CS/D. Although problem areas exist (notably in automobile repair and appliance repair), overall levels of consumer satisfaction are quite high. Next we examined the *alternative actions available to a dissatisfied consumer.* The range was from doing nothing to complaining actively. Consumers usually do not take action when dissatisfied: very few voice complaints back into the marketing system. Marketers, however, generally *do* want to receive complaints.

MARKETING APPLICATIONS

The final section of this chapter discussed *application issues.* Among the implications for marketers are (1) study of consumer use patterns can guide positioning, (2) over-promising performance may lead to dissatisfaction, (3) marketers should explore means to guarantee satisfaction after purchase, (4) consumer complaints can be viewed as an opportunity, and (5) the consumer satisfaction system should be managed well.

POSTPURCHASE ISSUES IN PUBLIC POLICY

Problems between marketers and consumers often occur in the postpurchase phase: these introduce a role for public policy. Three basic approaches are employed: (1) informational remedies, (2) enforcement remedies, and (3) mandatory remedies. Another public policy issue—"product liability"—concerns the compensation due to a consumer for wrongful damage caused by product defects. Our final section of the chapter discussed why consumers should take an active interest in resolving their postpurchase problems and examined a number of pointers for how to do this successfully.

■ KEY TERMS

support system	consonant cognitions	discrepancy
average amount consumed	dissonant cognitions	postpurchase remedies (PPRs)
consumption frequency	cognitive dissonance theory	informational remedies
perceived use occasions	consumer satisfaction	enforcement remedies
intervals between consumption occasions	consumer dissatisfaction	mandatory PPRs
consumption purposes	expectations	tort liability
product disposition	performance	doctrine of strict liability
True Blue Greens	comparison	negligence doctrine
Greenback Greens	confirmation/disconfirmation	comparative–fault doctrine
postpurchase learning		

■ REVIEW QUESTIONS AND EXPERIENTIAL EXERCISES

[E = **Application extension or experiential exercise**]

1. What are the roles of time, support system, and disposal in postpurchase?

2. Explain the five key elements in the consumer satisfaction/dissatisfaction process depicted in Figure 19–2. Which is probably the most important?

3. Consider how each of the following aspects may influence the nature of postpurchase evaluation (whether or not evaluation occurs and if so, how). For each, give an example in which the aspect has influenced the postpurchase evaluation of products or services you have consumed.

    a. Importance of benefits sought from consumption
    b. Strength of beliefs/expectations prior to purchase
    c. Complexity of product
    d. Nature of consuming unit—individual or group
    e. Product consumed alone, or with other products
    f. The degree to which desired benefits are social
    g. The (in)tangibility of the good—(professional services, dry-cleaning)
    h. Time span of use

4. What are the five factors influencing a consumer's decision to complain or not? Provide examples from your own experience.

5. Discuss the concepts of informational remedies, enforcement remedies, and mandatory PPRs, including examples of each.

6. Why are marketers so opposed to the concept of strict liability? Why does this concept exist? Can you suggest a better option?

7. [E] To gain a better appreciation for the depth and challenges of problems with product disposition, read George C. Lodge and Jeffrey F. Rayport, "Knee–deep and Rising: America's Recycling Crisis," *Harvard Business Review*, September–October 1991, pp. 128–139. Write a brief report on your findings.

8. [E] Four dimensions of consumption proposed by Hendrix were reviewed. Explain each one, in each case providing an example of a new strategy you would propose to Procter & Gamble as a consultant for their consumer product groups.

9. [E] Explain the distinction between consonant and dissonant cognitions. Using "Carrie's College Choice" from the chapter as a guide, analyze your own decision to join your present university (the harder that decision was, the more interesting this will be). List the primary alternatives, the major positive aspects and drawbacks of each, and the manner in which you handled your choice. Would you say you experienced (any, some, large) cognitive dissonance? Did you engage in any symptomatic postchoice behaviors? Write a brief report on your analysis.

10. [E] Consider a product or service with which you were dissatisfied. How was your dissatisfaction manifested? To what extent was the marketer responsible for your dissatisfaction? What steps would you recommend this marketer take to avoid creating dissatisfied consumers in the future?

11. [E] To gain a better appreciation for managerial challenges in satisfying consumers, read and consider the excellent case study in Dan Finkelman and Tony Goland, "The Case of the Complaining Consumer," *Harvard Business Review*, May–June 1990, pp. 9ff. After consider-ing the comments by the experts, decide on your own position and present it briefly.

12. [E] Interview five friends or relatives about memorable cases of consumer dissatisfaction. Try to learn exactly what they did or did not do about it. As part of the interview, learn exactly how many others they told about it, and what they had to say. Write a brief report on your findings.

13. [E] Conduct an interview about CS/D, consumer complaining, and marketers' responses with a representative of your local newspaper's "Action Line" or with a local government consumer representative.

14. [E] Use Note 27 or the reference section of your library to locate readings on recent developments in product liability. Write a brief report on your findings.

15. [E] Use the relevant notes for this chapter or the reference section of your library to locate recent articles on how marketers are handling customer service, consumer affairs, and so forth. Write a brief report on your findings.

16. [E] Using the relevant notes from this chapter or materials in the reference section of your library, read more about current issues and developments in "green marketing." Prepare a brief report on your findings.

17. [E] Interview the manager of a local retail store, auto repair shop, hospital, or other interesting enterprise concerning their typical experiences with the topics in this chapter. What are the major problems they face? What policies do they follow? Are the laws very important? Prepare a brief report on your findings.

18. [E] (Bonus Question) Choose your favorite report from Exhibit 19-1. Explain what, if anything, this has to do with attribution theory and the topic of this chapter.

■ SUGGESTED READING

■ There are many managerial readings associated with the topics in postpurchase processes. For insights on one topic we did not discuss much in the chapter, consumer use of a product and how this relates to product design and development, see Bruce Nussbaum, "I Can't Work This Thing!" *Business Week*, April 29, 1991, pp. 58ff. For an interesting overview of environmental concerns, see the Lodge and Rayport article cited in Question 7 above. For a look at how some marketers react to the J. D. Power ratings, see Larry Armstrong, "Who's the Most Pampered Motorist of All?" *Business Week*, June 10, 1991, pp. 90ff. For a recent overview of CS/D research, see Mary L. Carsky and Margery S. Steinberg, "Customer Satisfaction—Where Are We Going? Where Have We Been?" *American Marketing Association's Winter Educators' Proceedings* (1993), pp. 362–369. For description of an effort to provide health consumers with case outcome ratings of Cleveland–area hospitals, see Zachary Schiller, "A Consumer's Guide for Health-Care Shoppers," *Business Week*, May 3, 1993, pp. 52ff. And for a managerial puzzler, try the Finkelman and Goland article listed in Question 11 above. Finally, the Notes for this chapter contain many excellent sources for readings in specific topics.

Chapter Twenty
Public Policy
and Consumer Behavior

Chapter Twenty-one
Organizational
Buying Behavior

Part V

SPECIAL TOPICS IN CONSUMER BEHAVIOR

THIS VERY short part of the book consists of two chapters that deal with topics that are out of the "mainstream" of consumer behavior, but are quite important in our daily world. Chapter 20, "Public Policy and Consumer Behavior," introduces the areas of government regulation and industry self-regulation as they affect the way marketers actually deal with consumers in a marketplace system. As both a marketer and a consumer, you will likely find it interesting to consider how the rights and responsibilities of both parties interact. Chapter 21, "Organizational Buying Behavior," then shifts emphasis to consider how buying behavior occurs within organizations, and what implications this has for marketers who are attempting to sell to these buyers. As we'll see, most of the concepts we've examined for consumer behavior are also useful in this context, but there are some new considerations as well. Because most readers of this book are likely to be involved in this area at some point in their careers, the contents of this chapter should have professional value in the future.

Thus these two chapters introduce us to two different and important contexts. They contain many interesting facts and insights, so let's begin!

PUBLIC POLICY AND CONSUMER BEHAVIOR

BUSINESS HATES GOVERNMENT REGULATION, OR DOES IT?

A former editor of *The Wall Street Journal*, Vermont Royster, once said:

> The cry of our time is for "deregulation." Deregulate everything. The airlines. The banks. Stockbrokers. The drug companies. The theory behind this is that the marketplace will do the regulating.... Much of this cry for deregulation is justified....
>
> [But] I shudder at the thought of a wholly deregulated society. I prefer knowing my pharmacist has to be licensed and that someone checks on him.... We shouldn't forget that a great deal of the regulation we encounter today in business...arose from a recognized need in the past.... As society (our way of life) gets more complicated there will be newer areas calling for some kind of regulation...genetic manipulation ...surrogate motherhood...organ transplants...trade in human tissue....
>
> We the people must collectively decide not only what should be regulated but how.... But...we should never make the mistake of thinking that "regulation" is a dirty word.[1]

■ ESSENTIALS OF PUBLIC POLICY

In spirit, this chapter is most similar to Chapter 2, where we examined the marketing perspective and the consumer perspective on consumer behavior. However, since most students of consumer behavior have less background in the public policy area, in this chapter we'll stress an introductory look at the public policy perspective.

The public policy sector is the center of heated debates and controversial decisions. Unlike the consumer and marketing perspectives, the public policy perspective does not focus on transactions themselves. Instead, the public policy perspective

Table 20-1 Comparing the Three Perspectives

	Characteristic	Marketer's Perspective		Consumer's Perspective		Public Policymaker's Perspective
A.	Point of view	External ("buyers")	vs.	Internal ("me")	vs.	External ("buyers and sellers")
B.	Level of interest	Aggregate ("market")	vs.	Individual ("myself")	vs.	Aggregate ("affected groups")
C.	Scope of Interest	Product specific ("what I make")	vs.	Across products ("what I buy")	vs.	Across products ("all products and services")
D.	"Correct" choice	Brand specific ("my brand")	vs.	Best alternative ("best brand for me")	vs.	Neutral ("maximize utility")
E.	Role of Influence	Influence behavior ("please buy this")	vs.	Handle behavioral influence ("what should I really buy?")	vs.	Neutral ("must be fair and not deceptive")

stresses the setting within which consumer transactions occur. This setting is termed the **marketing-consumer environment.** The basic question confronting public policy is: "What exactly should the marketing-consumer environment look like in our society?" Given the massive scope of the economy, there are many issues related to this question. However, the *primary goal of public policy is to have a marketing-consumer environment that is efficient but fair for marketers and consumers alike.*

You may recall that our early discussions in Chapter 2 indicated that consumers, marketers, and public policymakers were the three primary groups involved in the marketing-consumer environment. Table 20-1 reintroduces Table 2-1 in which the consumer's perspective was contrasted with the marketer's perspective. Our table now adds a third column to represent the public policymaker's perspective. Notice that the **public policy view** reflects an interesting combination of the marketer and consumer viewpoints. Similar to the marketer, the public policymaker takes an *external* view (but applies it to both marketers and consumers), which is primarily *aggregate* in nature. Similar to the consumer, the public policymaker adopts an *across-products* scope of interest (but this extends to all products and services).

In the last two dimensions public policy must depart from both of the other parties. While interested in seeing that consumers be able to buy "the best brand for them," the public policymaker is usually unable to determine what that brand is—a **neutral view of actual choice** must be adopted in our free society. Instead, the policymaker places stress on the *setting* within which those choices are made, assuming that if buyers are fully informed and free to act in their own best interests, they will in fact do so. This applies to marketers as well: those sellers offering the best alternatives are assumed to prosper when the marketplace is working freely. Thus, with respect to the role of influence, the public policymaker is again *neutral*, stressing that the setting must be open and the information presented be fair and not misleading.

MARKETING FREEDOMS

All societies face the questions of how their economic systems will be formed and allowed to function in the best interests of the citizens of that society. As we discuss in Chapter 12, some nations have chosen to stress centralized planning and control for the economy. One result of this type of system is that consumers may not be able to

Marketing-consumer environment: The setting within which consumer transactions occur: should be efficient but fair for both marketers and consumers.

Public policy view: The perspective of the consumer marketplace: external, aggregate, across products, and choice-neutral.

Neutral view of actual choice: In a free market, the government does not discriminate on behalf of some consumer purchases over others.

purchase as much as they wish of any type of good, since the production of that good may have been restricted in the economic plan.

Western nations have generally opted for more of a **market system**, in which the desires of consumers play a much more important role in determining what is produced in the economy. For this type of system to work, marketers must have considerable freedom to anticipate and react quickly to consumer desires.

In fact, when we stop to think about it, we can see that *the basic freedoms granted to marketers are quite remarkable!* In the United States, for example, a person can choose to go into virtually any type of business (with the exception of those few that have been deemed illegal or that require licenses) at any time and in any location. He or she can produce any kind of product or service, in any quantity, and can offer it for sale under almost any conditions the seller desires. Prices, product characteristics, locations, and promotional devices are all up to the individual marketer.

Market system: An economy in which marketers are granted freedoms to produce and sell and consumers are free to buy.

CONSUMER RIGHTS

On the other side of the transaction, the society of the United States has also agreed that consumers have certain rights that must be respected by the economic system. In 1962 President John F. Kennedy sent the U.S. Congress a now famous message concerning the **Consumer Bill of Rights** in our society. In that message, the president summarized consumer rights as shown in Figure 20-1.

Several important points are implicit in the Consumer Bill of Rights. First, these are closely related to the fundamental basis for our economic system. As you may recall from introductory economics, *our society is assumed to prosper when consumers are able to make good purchase decisions*—decisions that reward marketers of good products and do not reward marketers of inferior or defective goods. Thus the **right to be informed** and the **right to choose freely** are key underpinnings of our system.

The **right to safety**, meanwhile, is geared more toward the use of products. It asserts that consumers should not be exposed to some undue hazards at all (such as cancer-causing additives in foods) and, for other potential hazards, should be sufficiently warned and instructed prior to purchase (many household chemicals fall into this category). The consumer right to safety has become increasingly important as technology has made new substances available.

The **right to be heard** raises a third implicit message: that the government should play a major role in interpreting consumer rights and in ensuring that they are protected in the marketplace. This was the most controversial of President Kennedy's statements, since in practice, this means more regulation of marketers. Not surprisingly, marketers tended to view such moves as governmental interference in the marketplace. On the other hand, many consumer advocates, led by Ralph Nader, viewed such programs as ways to create a proper balance in the marketplace that would allow consumers to buy wisely. Thus came controversy.

Our society did see dramatically increased governmental programs during the 1960s and 1970s, reflecting strong increases in the regulation of marketing practices. *For example, in just 10 years, between 1970 and 1980, spending for federal regulatory activities in consumer health and safety increased over 500 percent!* During the 1980s, under Presidents Reagan and Bush, the pendulum swung back toward deregulation, with government showing less desire to restrict marketer freedoms. However, late in the decade pressure began to build among marketers and consumers alike for more regulation in a number of areas (including stock and bond markets, savings and loans, marketing solicitations by telephone, and so forth). Under the Clinton administration, the 1990s have seen a further swing back toward more government involvement.

Consumer Bill of Rights: Four basic consumer rights recognized by President Kennedy: the right to be informed, the right to choose freely, the right to safety, and the right to be heard.

I. The Right to Safety
Consumers have the right to be protected against products and services that are hazardous to health and life.

II. The Right to Be Informed
Consumers have the right to be protected against fraudulent, decietful, or misleading advertising or other practices and to be given the facts they need to make an informed choice.

III. The Right to Choose
Consumers have the right to be assured, wherever possible, access to a variety of products and services at competitive prices. In those industries in which competition is not workable, government regulation is substituted to assure satisfactory quality and service at fair prices.

IV. The Right to Be Heard
Consumers have the right to be assured that consumer interests will receive full and sympathetic consideration in the forumulation of government policy and fair and expeditious treatment in its administrative tribunals.

FIGURE 20-1 The Consumer Bill of Rights

SOURCE: Executive Office of the President, *Consumer Advisory Council, First Report* (Washington, D.C.: U.S. Government Printing Office, October, 1963).

In addition to President Kennedy's list of four basic rights, several others have been proposed more recently and are worthy of note. President Richard Nixon, for example, proposed that citizens have a **right to consumer education**. Esther Peterson, who ran the White House Office for Consumer Affairs, suggested that the path of much legislation reflected a **right to consumer recourse and redress**, that is, a right to have a fair settlement of problems that consumers encounter. Finally, another, broader, consumer right also emerged during the 1970s: the consumer's **right to an environment that enhances the quality of life**, reflecting increased concern for ecology, pollution, and hazardous waste issues.[2]

Consumer research has come to play an increasingly important role in public policy matters. Notice how the right to be informed, for example, raises issues of consumer knowledge, learning, shopping, advertising, and so forth, while the right to be heard raises issues of how, and when, consumers complain.

INHERENT RESPONSIBILITIES FOR ALL SECTORS

There is another side to rights and freedoms—the **inherent responsibilities** that are associated with them. For marketers, there are responsibilities to conduct business in accord with the spirit and laws of our system. Consumers have responsibilities as well; these include informing themselves about products, purchasing within the bounds of their finances, and abiding by the terms of the contracts they sign.[3] For government, meanwhile, there is the major responsibility to strive to preserve freedoms while protecting rights and to be fair and judicious in the exercise of its power.

Inherent responsibilities: The other side of rights, power, and freedoms: the requirements that marketers, government, and consumers behave in the spirit of our system.

Slippage in the Marketing Sector

Most marketers, of course, have chosen to abide by the rules and meet their responsibilities to consumers by offering good products at fair prices. Over the long run, these businesspersons feel that ethical behavior is in their own best interest as well as that of their customers. Unfortunately, however, a small percentage of marketers have opted to engage in illegal and/or unethical practices as a way of business. Even though these cases don't characterize most of marketing, we should realize that this type of behavior has generated citizen support for more government regulation of marketing. It has also had the unfortunate consequence of lowering the credibility of all marketers as the following examples demonstrate:

🐚 High-Pressure Selling to Vulnerable Groups

Some sellers focus on elderly, or poor, or lonely consumers because they can be talked into deals that most consumers would turn down. Among the many examples are the firm in Chicago that convinced a widow to pay thousands of dollars to replace "cancerous bricks" on her house, the "dance studios" that extract thousands of dollars from lonely oldsters for dance lessons, and the "home repair" representatives who deliberately create a problem while "inspecting it" (for example, dumping some termites under the carpet), and then pointing out the problems in anguished tones to the fearful homeowner. In the classic case of the Holland Furnace Company, for example, inspectors would dismantle the homeowner's furnace, condemn it as hazardous, and then refuse to reassemble it because they "wouldn't be an accessory to murder." This firm, which had 50 offices around the country, operated for 30 years, with many of its salesmen practicing this technique. One elderly New England woman, in fact, was sold nine new furnaces over a six-year period![4]

🐚 Mail Frauds

The *sting artists* in this area cause problems for honest direct-response marketers as well as for the consumers they "hook" with their schemes. Some play with language, such as when Solardry, Inc., offered a solar clothes dryer, a "new innovation developed by space-age technology," guaranteed to work, to lower utility bills, to make clothes brighter." The price was only $36.99, and a special aid kit of "solar stabilizers" was available (at $9.99, down from $25). Or when the Mar-Dee Corporation offered its "scientifically tested" miracle liquid, W-L-40, that would attack body fat and expel it through the pores of the skin. As proof, an unnamed client attested to having lost 61 pounds in only five 15-minute baths in the miracle product, which was offered for $9.98. What were these products? A clothesline kit and a bottle of bubble-bath![5]

Sometimes several marketers link up in questionable activities. Dream-Away diet pills, for example, were advertised on 160 TV stations for over a year, offering 42 tablets for $19.95. The claim: consumers would lose weight while they slept. In a California court case, the company was ordered to stop selling the product and to pay $162,000 in penalties. It was also revealed that some of the TV stations carrying the ads had been receiving commissions on each bottle sold over their stations.[6]

🐚 Bolar Went Too Far

Recently, the Bolar Pharmaceutical Company entered a plea of "guilty" to charges of illegally distributing adulterated drugs and obstructing government attempts to investigate. Bolar had been the nation's largest distributor of a number of generic drugs—those made without a patent and sold for lower prices than brand names. In addition to 20 criminal charges, a competitor also filed a civil lawsuit. Here, Bolar was charged with having taken the competitor's brand-name blood pressure drug, stripping its name, and then submitting it for Food and Drug Administration (FDA) testing as a Bolar generic product that could be sold for lower prices. After receiving FDA approval, Bolar produced and sold its (untested) version for three years, bringing in $140 million in sales (meanwhile, the competitor's brand lost $167 million in sales during this time). What penalties do you think might be appropriate?[7]

Slippage in the Consumer Sector

Almost all consumers also abide by the rules and generally meet their responsibilities. There are, however, enough examples of bad consumership all around us to lend support to critics who question whether consumers really deserve increased protection by government programs and/or whether such programs can really work. As we've discussed in Chapter 2, there are good reasons why consumers don't make perfect decisions all the time. Further, this is a free society, and we citizens are free to spend our money as we desire.

Nonetheless, the theory of our economic system is important. Our system does require that consumers try to choose wisely if the system is to work and marketers are to be given correct signals as to what to offer in the marketplace. Some serious commentators, for example, view many consumers to be not as price conscious as would be desirable for the economy as a whole. They suggest, for example, that this characteristic was a major factor in fueling the inflationary pressures of recent times, which then led to recession and enormous deficits in the 1980s. Their reasoning: if the vast majority of consumers don't stop buying when prices are increased on a given item, there is no pressure on suppliers to reduce costs or price levels. Instead, alert retailers should raise prices even more! Also, consumers who don't pay their bills, who abuse physical property, switch price tags, or file false insurance claims cause problems for marketers and undermine the marketing-consumer environment.

🐚 *Cheats with Cleats*

One hallmark of the marketing concept in retailing is to provide consumers with satisfaction after the sale. Some consumers abuse this practice, however, as the following report attests: "Mark is a soccer player who needs new shoes frequently and has developed a system to get them from a local store that will take back 'defective' shoes. Once or twice a season, Mark will remove the sole on a shoe, slice off a cleat or two, or place a rip in the tongue, in each case in a way that is hard to detect. He then brings the shoes to the store in exchange for a new pair. At last count he had received eight pairs this way! Mark is sure to go to a different clerk on each visit, and unless someone carefully checks records for returned items, Mark probably won't get caught in the near future."

🐚 *Coupon Misredemptions Increase to Epidemic Proportions*

Most coupons promise the retailer the face value plus a small handling charge as reimbursement. Note that this policy provides no incentive for retail stores to monitor closely the coupons they accept. In fact, the more coupons accepted, the higher the payment a store will receive from the manufacturer. Many consumers, aware of this fact, have recently been redeeming coupons for either the wrong brand or for products they didn't buy at all. How widespread is this practice? One study using "scanners" at checkout counters showed that some brands—Diet Pepsi, Keebler cookies, Cheez-its among them—had misredemption rates higher than 40 percent! (This means that the makers of these brands were paying bonuses for consumers to buy competing brands

As one way to fight coupon misredemptions by persons who photocopy large numbers of coupons, Comark Merchandising is offering coupons marketers this printing process, in which the word "Void" cannot be seen on an original coupon, but appears on a photocopy.

or nothing at all, almost half the time!) In total, coupon fraud—partially from dishonest consumers and partially from dishonest retailers and "clipping gangs"—is costing manufacturers over half a billion dollars per year, or about one-quarter of the total worth of consumer coupons redeemed.[8]

Slippage in the Government Sector

Public policy problems almost always involve disputes regarding the balance of competing interests and points of view. It is difficult, therefore, to find areas in which everyone would agree that a particular step was entirely good or entirely bad. This does not mean, however, that the issue of slippage in public policy decisions is not a very serious one. In particular, policymakers can make two types of errors: errors of omission and errors of commission. **Errors of omission** refer to a lack of activity when activity is warranted. Examples include a failure to act quickly against problems such as a nuclear plant leaking radioactive dust or a deceptive ad campaign luring customers to a useless purchase, or this startling case:

Errors of omission:
A lack of activity when activity is warranted.

🐦 *We'll Get Around to It Later*

As an example of errors of omission, New York City's health department discovered that a dispute between two laboratory managers had led to *delays of up to a year* in reading cancer test results for women of limited means using city clinics. Among the 3,000 delayed Pap smear readings, 11 were definitely malignant, 93 appeared to be, and nearly 500 more showed abnormalities that called for immediate follow-up. The new health commissioner denounced his department for "outrageous insensitivity" and "betrayal of the public trust," as he demoted or transferred four officials (apparently, none could be fired!).[9]

Given the nature of bureaucratic organizations, lengthy delays and periods of inactivity in public agencies are relatively common. Since salaries are being paid during the time, and since attorneys are likely to be involved on both sides of a controversial issue, dollar costs from time delays can be very large. Beyond this, civil service is often a "safe" job in which there is little reward or incentive to act quickly or to take risks. The more this is the case, the more likely that errors of omission will occur.

Errors of commission, on the other hand, occur when policymakers commit unwise or bad actions. Much of the public policy decision-making system is geared to the reduction of errors of commission by offering various levels of appeals to regulatory rulings. It is not atypical, for example, to find an appeals court modifying some aspects of regulatory rulings that were appealed. To appeal, however, a citizen or company needs to be able to afford high-priced legal talent.

In general, then, public policy faces situations in which **cost-benefit analysis** is needed—the benefits of a particular action must be compared against the costs involved in the action, including indirect costs to marketers and consumers. Given the size of our economy, the aggregate benefits from government actions can be large. According to the Consumer Product Safety Commission (CPSC), for example, its product recalls have prevented over 1 million consumer injuries. Similarly, the CPSC worked out some voluntary product standards with industry in some dangerous areas: it estimates that these prevent 200 deaths and 200,000 injuries each year.[10]

Cost-benefit analysis is frequently complex and highly subjective. Consider, for example, how often benefits will not be easy to measure in dollar terms. What, for example, is the value of a person's life? If a product recall would be likely to save three people's lives in the next year, but would cost $6 million, should that recall be ordered? These are some of the types of decisions that confront agencies such as the Food and Drug Administration (FDA):

> ### 🐋 *The Thalidomide Tragedy*

One long-debated topic concerns the FDA and its role as the government watchdog for pharmaceutical products in the United States. As noted in our Bolar example, before a product can be sold on a prescription basis, the FDA must examine tests for its effectiveness and safety. These tests are arranged and conducted by the sponsoring firms.

However, many times it is not possible for the tests to be absolutely foolproof, especially if harmful side effects might take years to develop. Further, the new drug might offer significant relief to U.S. citizens suffering from a particular ailment. One such drug emerged in the early 1960s and provided a serious disagreement in the United States, between persons who wanted it approved as soon as possible and those who wanted to wait for further tests. The drug was known as thalidomide. It was designed as a sedative, to be used in sleeping tablets. After testing on animals, it had been routinely approved for use in some European countries and became a popular sleeping pill. Encouraged by this success, marketers began to combine thalidomide with other medicines to treat coughs, colds, headaches, and asthma. A liquid form was made for West German children. Pregnant women found one version useful for combatting the nausea of early pregnancy and another version helpful for a good night's sleep. Soon, thalidomide was being sold at the rate of 20 million tablets per month in Germany alone, and many other countries approved the drug for sale. In the United States, the Merrell Company applied to the FDA for a license to market it under the brand name Kevadon. Included with the firm's application were reports on animal tests and the several years of human use in Europe. All indications were that the drug had no side effects. The firm pressed the FDA's project officer for a speedy approval to sell it in the United States.

Errors of commission: Unwise or mistaken actions undertaken by policymakers.

Cost-benefit analysis: All the direct and indirect costs of an alternative are compared against all direct and indirect benefits.

The FDA's project officer was Dr. Frances Kelsey, who had only recently joined the agency. In reading the testing reports, she was puzzled to discover that the drug had not been effective as a sedative for the animals. With humans, however, it worked well as a sedative. She decided to ask Merrell for more test evidence to discover why thalidomide seemed to affect humans differently from animals. This FDA request would mean a lengthy delay, which not only would reduce profits for Merrell, but would also mean that American consumers would not benefit from the superior performance of the drug. Dr. Kelsey's insistence on further test evidence resulted in thalidomide being kept off the U.S. market for almost two years. During this time the company increased its pressure on her—Dr. Kelsey was contacted over 50 times, and her senior FDA officials were also approached in efforts to obtain approval.

Then, in early 1962, Merrell suddenly withdrew its application. At this point it had become clear that thalidomide had been responsible for over 10,000 deformed babies born in West Germany. The type of deformity was striking and sad—babies were born without arms and legs or with short, flipperlike hands or fingers attached to the shoulders. Many died at birth. Several mothers committed suicide, and one was charged with a mercy-killing of her child. Hundreds of others required psychiatric help.

Upon publication of these facts—together with pictures—in national magazines, it became clear to millions of U.S. citizens that the doctor at the FDA had almost singlehandedly prevented a national disaster. (If you'd be interested in reading more about this case, you may wish to pursue the readings listed in Note 11.)

The thalidomide case is a striking, but not typical, illustration of the stakes that are involved when dealing with health and safety of consumers. This tragedy did not come about because marketers were negligent; it took scientists a long time to link the deformities to the drug, even after the epidemic appeared. Nor is delay or refusal to license a new drug a good rule to follow for every case; new drugs can save lives and relieve human suffering when they are available for use. Recent and current issues concerning new drugs for cancer, AIDS, and other diseases reflect the same kinds of tradeoffs today. Thus there is a great need for public policymakers to strike a sound balance between risk and innovation. Slippage in public policy occurs when government employees lose sight of this goal. (If you would like to read more about recent issues and problems the FDA has faced in this regard, consult the readings in Note 12.)

■ THE INSTITUTIONS OF PUBLIC POLICY

GOVERNMENT INVOLVEMENT

Within the federal government, the executive, legislative, and judicial branches are all active in consumer behavior issues. In the executive branch, most recent presidents have made public statements about consumer rights similar to President Kennedy's. They have arranged for the government departments to carry out consumer programs consistent with the current administration's beliefs about the best forms of government presence. In the legislative branch, the U.S. Congress has traditionally been very active with respect to consumer matters, although the directions taken have again differed as a function of the prevailing political climate. The Congress has passed consumer laws, has over the years created our structure of regulatory agencies, and each year appropriates increases or decreases in support for consumer-related programs.

The judicial branch of government is also active in consumer policy matters, primarily through decisions as to the legal powers of government agencies. A major means for the judicial branch to become involved is to have significant cases appealed into the court system. In recent cases, for example, actions by the U.S. Supreme Court have given doctors and lawyers the right to advertise and supported the government's authority to order marketers to run "corrective advertising." (Appendix 20A contains a review of this interesting program.)

State and local governments are also active in consumer matters. Many cities have personnel available to help with consumer disputes, and a *small claims court system* is available when negotiation fails. Similarly, local agencies work to control fraudulent business operators, monitor the accuracy of scales used in stores and gasoline stations, and enforce sanitation codes in restaurants.

MARKETER AND CONSUMER INVOLVEMENT

Not all the activity in public policy is conducted by government. Many marketers have developed company and industry codes of behavior: Exhibit 20-1 displays the American Marketing Association's Code of Ethics for Marketers. (You should read it carefully to see if there are any surprises there, or if there are any norms that appear to be troublesome given what you see your future to be.)

In addition, in some areas, marketers have chosen to undertake **industry self-regulation.** For example, an extensive advertising self-regulatory system has heard several thousand cases. It has been successful in having many ad campaigns modified and others voluntarily stopped and has taken the place of much government regulation. (Chapter 16 examines this system in more detail.) In addition, individual marketers sometimes encounter other situations that call for public policy perspectives. Sometimes these involve lobbying, and sometimes use of the court system.

Industry self-regulation: Rather than submit disputes to government agencies or courts, marketers develop a voluntary system of resolution.

 *"Miami Vice" Isn't Nice*

Product counterfeiters pirate an estimated $20 billion a year from marketers of strong brand names such as Gucci, Microsoft software, and General Motors auto parts. In a typical case, bogus goods are imported from unauthorized plants overseas and are sold to businesses and consumers as the genuine articles. Sometimes the customers are aware of the "scam" and sometimes not. Sometimes the products are of adequate quality, but sometimes not (auto brakes and birth control pills are among the long list of defective items sold). In every case, the original marketer is losing rightful sales, since the counterfeit name and package is instrumental to the sale.

However, branders are now fighting back. Under the Trademark Counterfeiting Act of 1984, companies get search warrants and hire groups of private detectives for raids on pirate firms. "We're the 'Miami Vice' of civil law!" brags one raider. Merchandise and business records are seized in these raids, and the business pirates can be turned over to criminal authorities for indictment and sentencing.[13]

 *Two Firms in a Lather*

As a way to settle a court case, the Gillette Company and its advertising agency agreed to pay the Alberto-Culver Company over $4 million. The case involved a Gillette ad

EXHIBIT 20-1

The Ethics Code for Marketers*

Members of the American Marketing Association (AMA) are committed to ethical professional conduct. They have joined together in subscribing to this Code of Ethics embracing the following topics:

Responsibilities of the Marketer

Marketers must accept responsibility for the consequences of their activities and make every effort to ensure that their decisions, recommendations, and actions function to identify, serve, and satisfy all relevant publics: customers, organizations, and society.

Marketers' professional conduct must be guided by

1. The basic rule of professional ethics: not knowingly to do harm.
2. The adherence to all applicable laws and regulations.
3. The accurate representation of their education, training, and experience.
4. The active support, practice, and promotion of this Code of Ethics.

Honesty and Fairness

Marketers shall uphold and advance the integrity, honor, and dignity of the marketing profession by

1. Being honest in serving consumers, clients, employees, suppliers, distributors, and the public.
2. Not knowingly participating in conflict of interest without prior notice to all parties involved.
3. Establishing equitable fee schedules including the payment or receipt of usual, customary, and/or legal compensation for marketing exchanges.

Rights and Duties of Parties
in the Marketing Exchange Process

Participants in the marketing exchange process should be able to expect that

1. Products and services offered are safe and fit for their intended uses.
2. Communications about offered products and services are not deceptive.
3. All parties intend to discharge their obligations, financial and otherwise, in good faith.
4. Appropriate internal methods exist for equitable adjustment and/or redress of grievances concerning purchases.

*SOURCE: "AMA Adopts New Code of Ethics," *Marketing Educator*, Fall 1987, pp. 3 ff.

576

As we discuss in Chapter 19, consumers' disposing of tons of products and packaging each day has caused a massive problem for our society. One role for public policy is to provide laws or program incentives by which marketers and consumers can participate in solving this problem. These photos show one recycling success, in which the empty plastic bottles (before) are converted to the bright plastic park benches (after).

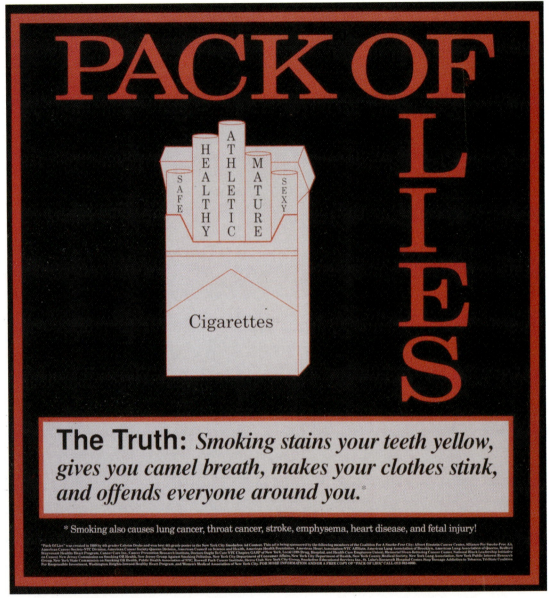

One aspect of the regulation of marketing deals with the so–called "marketplace of ideas," the notion that opposing points of view should be expressed even if one party has no economic resources or will not benefit from people agreeing with his or her view. Public service announcements reflect this position, for example. In the case of controversial products, however, the debate can get heated. Here is a recent winner in a poster contest sponsored by antismoking forces.

Another arena of controversy concerns where promotions for potentially dangerous products should appear. Shea Stadium, for example, has been a center of debate because of the large, strategically placed sign for Marlboro cigarettes. Since advertising on television is banned for this product in the United States, opponents argue that its signs should not be appearing on television each time the camera pans by that spot.

These three baseballs, signed by Hall–of–Famers Willie Mays, Mickey Mantle, and Stan Musial, figure prominently in one of the most clever sales promotions of recent years. Read about it in our chapter on Organizational Buying Behavior on page 598.

It is understood that the above would include, *but is not limited to,* the following responsibilities of the marketers:

In the area of product development and management,

- Disclosure of all substantial risks associated with product or service usage.
- Identification of any product component substitution that might materially change the product or impact on the buyer's purchase decision.
- Identification of extra-cost added features.

In the area of promotions,

- Avoidance of false and misleading advertising.
- Rejection of high-pressure manipulations or misleading sales tactics.
- Avoidance of sales promotions that use deception or manipulation.

In the area of distribution,

- Not manipulating the availability of a product for purpose of exploitation.
- Not using coercion in the marketing channel.
- Not exerting undue influence over the reseller's choice to handle a product.

In the area of pricing,

- Not engaging in price fixing.
- Not practicing predatory pricing.
- Disclosing the full price associated with any purchase.

In the area of marketing research,

- Prohibiting selling or fund raising under the guise of conducting research.
- Maintaining research integrity by avoiding misrepresentation and omission of pertinent research data.
- Treating outside clients and suppliers fairly.

Organizational Relationships

Marketers should be aware of how their behavior may influence or impact on the behavior of others in organizational relationships. They should not demand, encourage, or apply coercion to obtain unethical behavior in their relationships with others, such as employees, suppliers, or customers. Marketers should

1. Apply confidentiality and anonymity in professional relationships with regard to privileged information.
2. Meet their obligations and responsibilities in contracts and mutual agreements in a timely manner.
3. Avoid taking the work of others, in whole, or in part, and represent this work as their own or directly benefit from it without compensation or consent of the originator or owner.
4. Avoid manipulation to take advantage of situations to maximize personal welfare in a way that unfairly deprives or damages their organization or others.

Any AMA member found to be in violation of any provision of this Code of Ethics may have his or her Association membership suspended or revoked.

comparing its brand of hair conditioner (Tame) to the Alberto Balsam brand. According to Alberto-Culver, the ads had "disparaged" its brand by inaccurately showing that it left a greasy, oily residue on the hair. At the time the campaign had begun, Alberto Balsam was highly successful, holding a 12 percent share (Tame had 17 percent). In only five months, Alberto Balsam's share had dropped to 6 percent and was continuing to shrink. After it fell to under 3 percent, the company removed its brand from the market.[14]

Consumers and consumer groups are also active in this arena, though not nearly so well organized. In addition to dealing with government agencies and businesses, consumers have also employed the court system, sometimes as individuals and sometimes in class action lawsuits. In summary, there are a number of institutions involved in various aspects of the marketing-consumer environment. The backbone of the public policy perspective is our system of laws—both in the courts and in the administrative agencies.

What public policy actions, if any, do you believe are appropriate to protect the teenagers of our society?

The period from 1968 to the present has been a turbulent time in marketing regulation. *Activism* and *deregulation* have each held center stage during the period. The question "What is the proper way to regulate marketing?" has been continually addressed. The answers to this question have reflected different weightings of how to balance marketer freedoms against consumer rights. The Federal Trade Commission is our nation's key regulatory agency for most of the marketing-consumer environment. In this section, therefore, we'll focus on the FTC and take a look at some of its consumer protection programs.

THE FTC'S VAGUE MANDATE

The Federal Trade Commission was established in 1914 as the government's chief economic regulatory agency. As such, it is broadly charged with the responsibility for providing a *fair competitive environment* for the nation's economic system. Its actual responsibility (or mandate) is, however, surprisingly vague. Section 5 of the FTC act originally declared "unfair methods of competition in commerce" to be unlawful. In 1938, this was amended to add "unfair or deceptive acts or practices" to this category.

Thus there are two basic types of issues. One type involves one firm's dealing with other firms; these issues fall in the area of competition and reflect **antitrust regulation**. The other category involves a firm's interactions with its consumers: the regulatory area of **consumer protection**.

One effect of the FTC's vague mandate is uncertainty as to its authority to undertake various programs. This uncertainty must usually be resolved by either the Congress or the courts. Thus it is normal for the FTC to propose new programs, without having a complete assurance that it has the legal authority to carry them out. Throughout its history, in fact, the FTC has been roundly criticized by both liberals and conservatives, sometimes because it has not advocated enough new regulatory efforts and sometimes because it has advocated too many!

THE POLITICAL SETTING

Any overview of public policy would be incomplete if it did not note that politics and political philosophies play an extremely important role. For example, the stage was set for 25 years of FTC controversy by Ralph Nader and followers, known as Nader's Raiders. Following a critical report of the FTC by this group in 1969, the president of the United States requested the American Bar Association (ABA), a prestigious professional organization of attorneys, to investigate the FTC's activities. The ABA's committee returned with a conclusion similar to the Nader group's report. Both reports urged the FTC to increase its efforts to protect consumers and regulate marketers. President Nixon and the Congress appeared to support such changes during the early 1970s. The FTC received larger budgets each year, as it became more activist in its regulations. (If you are interested in reading more about these programs, you may wish to pursue the reading in Note 15.)

Following a brief respite in the mid-1970s, liberal Democrats gained control of the FTC when President Jimmy Carter was elected. The FTC's activism was renewed. By 1980, this had sparked a major backlash from the business community, which went to its legislative representatives. The Congress began to subject the FTC to harsh scrutiny, and in 1980 it cut the budget and programs of the agency, after threatening to disband it entirely. These congressional actions were in part the result of a massive lobbying effort by businesses across the country. Funeral directors, for example, were incensed at FTC proposals for requiring changes in funeral marketing practices. Insurance companies and agents were upset over FTC-proposed rules that would have required each insurance salesperson to give a consumer information as to whether or not there were better prices available than the agent was offering them! Auto dealers were also angry at the FTC: the agency wanted stronger regulations regarding guarantees for used cars. In terms of the political setting, notice that all three of these businesses are well represented in thousands of communities across the land. Their members are usually involved in civic affairs and are respected town citizens. When these people (and their local Chambers of Commerce) contact their legislative representatives to complain, they receive serious consideration.

Beyond lobbying in Congress, the political nature of consumer policy is particularly evident with the election of a new president. When this happens every four (or eight) years, the top officials of many of the regulatory agencies are replaced, some programs are dropped, while others are expanded. Priorities change drastically, as do spending levels for specific programs. When a Republican administration came into office in 1981, for example, it undertook **deregulation**. Deregulation is the deliberate reduction of government control of business activities, based on the belief that the marketplace works best when individuals are most free to operate in their own self-interests. Most policymakers accept that this theory is strong in the abstract, but there is much disagreement about where to draw the line in the real world (especially over possibilities that some powerful persons will take advantage of smaller businesses and consumers).

Deregulation: The reduction of government activities, based on the belief that the marketplace works best when it is most free.

ஜ Are the States Fed Up?

U.S. deregulatory policy, during the 1980s, hit hard at consumer protection agencies, especially at the Consumer Product Safety Commission and the Federal Trade Commission. The staff at each agency was cut almost in half (to 500 and 900 persons, respectively), while dollar budgets were slashed also. These efforts have won both supporters and critics, but the critics of deregulation appear to be winning. The American Bar Association convened another blue-ribbon committee to investigate the FTC in 1989, 20 years after its last report. This committee returned with a number of suggestions aimed at making the FTC more active and more effective (see Note 16 for detailed readings on this report).

Thus the 1990s are a time for increased marketing regulation, being held in check largely by the huge government deficit that has been tightening budgets. According to one Republican at the CPSC: "...*conservatives will now live to see the day [of] doubling budgets and bringing things back...they were overzealous, and now we're going to get in trouble for that.*" Meanwhile, an FTC commissioner warned that by the end of the 1980s the FTC had been cut back to its size in 1961 and was in danger of becoming a "stealth agency—one whose presence would elude detection" by anyone looking for it! "If there is no change," he warned, "the states will continue to take on more responsibility."

Indeed, this has been happening in recent years. As federal regulation decreased, the state attorneys general (each U.S. state elects its own) have become much more active. In recent years they banded together to force $16 million in payments from Chrysler to certain purchasers of its cars (odometer tampering), and $4 million in payments from

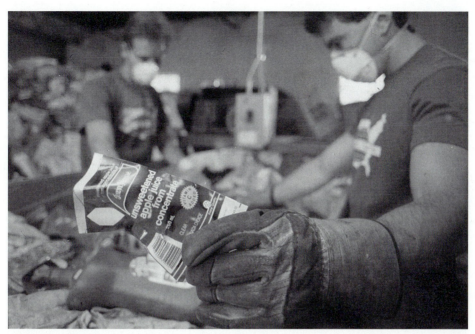

As environmental concerns have increased, public policy has become concerned about the packages used by marketers. The state of Maine, for example, outlawed aseptic juice boxes because they were so difficult to recycle. In a strange twist, these boxes had been winning design awards from nutritionists and parents because they retard spoilage of food inside ("aseptic" means "germ-free").

Minolta for camera pricing manipulation, and challenged several advertising practices, including those featuring airline fare specials but without indicating the restrictions. Indeed, some of the state officials appear to be quite antimarketing. One Texas official, for example, charged that Kellogg "constantly lies about its products," and then explained that his time spent working in New York City had had an impact: "I'm a Texan with a New York spin. . . . I'm mean as hell and I'm not very nice." Since different states creating different sets of requirements is such a major threat to managers trying to plan national programs, the marketing community is also interested in seeing the federal government be more effective in setting national regulations.[17]

NO EASY ANSWERS

The 1990s present an especially challenging time in marketing regulation in the United States. The administration, the Congress, the regulatory agencies, and the independent state attorneys general all must deal with the conflicting forces toward regulation and deregulation. As shown in Table 20-2, the American public supports government efforts to find a proper balance.[18]

It is fair to summarize by saying that public policy issues are almost always interesting, are often important, and are invariably controversial. The people involved in a particular matter are usually highly committed to one side or the other, and personal interests and philosophies are usually involved as well. For those of us who

Table 20-2 What Do the People Think?

Issue	Percentage of Public Who Respond That		
	"Business Will Do"	versus	"Government Must Watch"
Invest in new products/services	65%		31%
Advertise honestly	29		65
Make safe products/services	25		71
Not engage in price fixing	15		79
Clean up air and water pollution	11		85

SOURCE: See Note 18.

are not personally caught up in the public policy battle, however, it is easy to see that there are two sides to most questions and that both sides can raise good arguments. In our dual roles as consumers and as marketers, we have a stake in seeing regulation handled in the best possible manner. Toward that end, we'll now examine a basic framework that captures many dimensions of the regulatory settings.

■ A BASIC FRAMEWORK FOR REGULATION

Consumer information: A category of programs aimed at having pertinent facts available for consumers.

Consumer information, because of its significance in the Consumer Bill of Rights and its relatively nonrestrictive nature (that is, consumers can still buy freely when an information program is in effect), has long been a favorite option for marketing regulation. To learn more, let's look at an interesting framework by a team working with the Federal Trade Commission.[19] The essentials of the framework are outlined in Figure 20-2. Note that there are three stages for analyzing a possible consumer information program.

STAGE 1: IS THE REMEDY WORTHWHILE?

The first stage asks whether any program at all seems to be needed. This involves a comparison of costs and benefits. In the consumer information area, there are three types of costs that can be significant to consider:

1. *Compliance costs.* These are the additional costs to the marketers for supplying the information, including testing, space, and personnel costs.

2. *Enforcement costs.* These are the costs to the government for enforcing the information remedy. They can include personnel, travel costs, and court costs.

3. *Unintended side effects.* These are additional costs to either marketers or consumers that crop up as an unforeseen by-product of the remedy. For example, forcing TV commercials to include too much detailed information might lead consumers to ignore them entirely or might lead marketers to shift to less efficient forms of promotion to get their messages across.

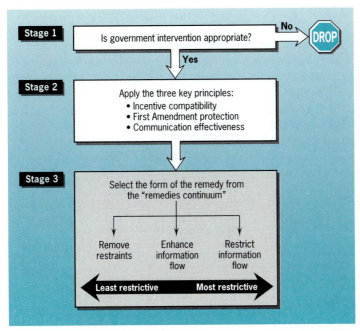

FIGURE 20-2 A Framework for Consumer Information Regulation   SOURCE: See Note 19.

There are also three classes of benefits that could flow from increased consumer information:

1. *Improved consumer decisions.* These would flow from consumers being better informed about the strengths and weaknesses of each alternative.

2. *Enhanced product quality.* In some cases, increased consumer information can cause marketers to upgrade the performance of their brand, if they believe that consumers will now recognize quality better and reward it with purchases.

3. *Lower prices.* In some cases, increased advertising can use lower price to attract new customers. A high-quality new brand, for example, can advertise a low price to gain trial. Its larger competitors might then match these prices.

In deciding on a potential public program, the likelihood and size of each type of cost and benefit needs to be estimated. If the costs are likely to exceed the benefits, the program will be dropped. If not, consideration will move to stage 2.

STAGE 2: THE THREE PRINCIPLES

There are, of course, many ways in which a program can be designed. Stage 2 suggests that three "principles" be followed. **Incentive compatibility** refers to an attempt to create regulations that marketers would *like* to comply with rather than those they will fight against. For example, the FTC used to prohibit cigarette manufacturers from making claims about low-tar and nicotine content in their brands. When it lifted its ban, the marketing landscape immediately lit up with "tar derby" advertising. Competing brands outdid themselves to suggest how low they were on this measure, while many new brands were created to take advantage of a low-tar positioning. Consumers in turn became more sensitive to tar and nicotine content and rewarded low-tar brands by

Incentive compatibility: Regulations constructed so that marketers desire to comply with them.

purchasing them. Overall, the average level of these ingredients dropped dramatically within a few years.

The second principle, **communication effectiveness**, reflects that consumer information be designed to communicate effectively to the target market for whom it is intended (this point seems natural to marketers, but is a good reminder for many attorneys and economists who are often involved in creating these programs). At a minimum, consumers should be able to understand what is being said. Beyond this, the disclosure should also be interesting, noticeable, and so forth. The third principle, **First Amendment protection**, reminds regulators to strive to maintain freedom and not simply order marketers around by whim. This principle reflects a belief that consumers will benefit most when the marketing-consumer environment has a free flow of marketing information in it.

First Amendment protection: Reminds regulators to strive to maintain freedom of speech for marketers to the extent possible.

STAGE 3: SELECTING FROM THE "REMEDIES CONTINUUM"

Public policymakers can take quite different approaches toward handling consumer problems. The arrows at the bottom of Figure 20-2 suggest that the regulator should consider different levels of "restrictions" with these remedies. Let's look at three representative levels.

Little or No Restrictions

At the left side of the figure, notice that some policy alternatives are *not very restricted at all* and could even remove restraints rather than impose them.

❧ *I Can See Clearly Now...*

The case of eyeglasses and contact lenses provides a good example. Until about 15 years ago, most states banned eyeglass advertising on grounds of health, safety, and quality assurance. This meant that doctors were the source for most eyeglasses, acting as intermediaries for the labs where they were made to order. A few states did allow eyeglass advertising, however, and retail eyeglass shops were operating in these states. Several consumer research studies showed that consumers were paying substantially higher prices (by 25 to 40 percent) in the states that restricted the advertising.[20] Policymakers decided that the states' ad bans were keeping marketers from informing consumers about prices and thus not allowing price to be used as a competitive tool. The FTC moved *against the bans*, freeing marketers to advertise and compete on price bases in all states. Prices dropped substantially as the competitive market began to work more freely.

Following the eyeglass rule, regulators moved into cases in the *professions*. Societies of doctors, dentists, attorneys, and accountants had created codes that banned most forms of marketing to potential clients. Since the professions deal largely in intangible *services* rather than more standardized products such as eyeglasses, the issues are more debatable, and this area has experienced much controversy. Quality, for example, is a key issue; price advertising might be used to sell lower-quality legal, dental, surgical, or other services. On the other hand, these services *are* expensive, and it would seem that prices would decrease if price competition were fostered. At present, the competitive information flow view seems to have won the battles.

Representing the least restrictive type of remedies in Figure 20-2 (stage 3), the government's removal of state advertising bans spurred the growth of this optical outlet, which features price specials.

Most professional societies have changed their codes to allow advertising, at least in certain forms. However, many professionals have staunchly refused to engage in active marketing to consumers, and they continue to view (and treat) those who do as outcasts. (If you know one of these professionals well, you may find a discussion of this topic most interesting.)

Moderate Restrictions

Moving toward the center of the remedies continuum in Figure 20-2, there is a range of possible ways to enhance the flow of consumer information. One option is to give the consumer *more time* to make a decision. **Cooling-off laws**, for example, often allow three days for a consumer to cancel sales agreements that they may have made under high-pressure selling conditions (as in door-to-door sales or telephone solicitations). Another option involves the *separation of "diagnosis" from "treatment."* As part of the eyeglass regulations, for instance, the eye examiner was required to inform a consumer, in writing, of his or her exact prescription (diagnosis). Now that the consumer has this information, he or she would have the option to shop elsewhere for the lenses and frames (the "treatment," in this case). Notice that similar possibilities exist in such areas as automobile repairs, medical records, and so on. Two other forms of enhancing consumer information flow are (1) *setting information standards* and (2) *requiring certain disclosures* by the marketer. Since both forms are frequently used, let's look briefly at each:

Standards Are All Around Us.   Standard setting allows all marketers to communicate using a similar basis and affords consumers the chance to compare different brands on a comparable basis as well. Although we don't often think about it, **product standards** are a necessary part of the marketing-consumer environment. In the area of food, for example, the calorie, pound, U.S. RDA (recommended daily allowance), and grades of meat (Prime, Choice, etc.) are all standards that have been decided in public policy. There are tens of thousands of standards currently in use. Current public policy

Cooling-off laws:
Moderately restrictive: allow consumers three days to cancel sales agreements that they may have made under high-pressure selling.

Product standards:
Required measures, ingredients, sizes, and so on used to identify products and quality levels.

questions involve *what new standards should be set (if any) and at what levels*. For example, should there be specific requirements that have to be met before a food can be sold as a "natural food" or "hypoallergenic" cosmetic?

Affirmative disclosures: Programs that require marketers to disclose certain information to consumers.

Requiring Marketers to Disclose.   As another way to enhance information flow, albeit a more restrictive one, policymakers can consider **affirmative disclosures,** which *require* marketers to disclose certain information to consumers. Familiar examples include cigarette warnings, food ingredient listings, warranty descriptions, and mileage ratings for cars. Notice that these affirmative disclosures are required by *all marketers* in a product class. Other affirmative disclosure orders pertain only to a *particular marketer* and usually occur as a result of consumers having been misled because certain important facts about the product had not been provided to them. The FTC has used this type of remedy quite often: Wilkie reports over 200 such orders in a seven-year period.[21]

Heavy Restrictions

The final zone of the remedies continuum moves toward the strongest form of government regulation—*restricting information flow*. **Free speech** is a right guaranteed for both consumers and marketers by the First Amendment, so any restrictions of free speech must be approached with great care. Most public policy experts agree that these remedies should probably be reserved for only those cases that cannot be sufficiently handled by any of the less restrictive options we have been discussing.

There are, however, some situations in which restrictions might receive wide support. The U.S. ban of cigarette advertising on TV and radio, for example, was enacted in 1970 and seemed to enjoy majority support from consumers.[22] Many industrial countries also ban some or all advertising for cigarettes. Recently, the Canadian Parliament has gone even further—it banned all tobacco ads, free samples, and sponsorship of events, and it raised taxes significantly (recently the price per pack was about $5.50, versus about $2.00 in the United States). Together, these actions resulted in a decline in smoking of 25 percent in three years.[23]

A variety of other options are possible, depending on the situation. Sometimes the *type and style* of information might be restricted in preference to banning it entirely (this has happened with advertising to children, for example, and with advertising prescription drugs to consumers). Sometimes consumer policy restricts the *timing* of information. For example, increasing pressures to restrict telephone marketers from

Controversy over product safety and marketing practices has led to "counter-advertising" against certain products. Here is a winner in the New York City transit (bus and subway) Smokefree Ad Contest.

Alcohol and cigarettes are two product categories in which public policy has been willing to pursue significant restrictions. Are further restrictions on the way? Should they be?

As of the mid-1990s this huge Marlboro logo continued to adorn left-center field at Shea Stadium, much to the vocal displeasure of antismoking activists. They point out that it is strategically placed to show up in typical TV coverage of batters and baserunners, thus forming a type of "ad" on television, even though cigarettes are banned from broadcast advertising in the United States.

"cold-calling" homes at dinner time or late in the evening make these restrictions likely in the near future. Similarly, the discovery that credit-checking firms are selling mailing lists to direct marketers will also likely bring restrictions on the *distribution* of such information as personal finances, medical histories, and group memberships. When one marketer told a consumer, "I see you have been making a lot of phone calls to Newark and Wilmington...," she joined the movement to change the laws that allow the sale of information such as this. Consumer concerns about privacy have led to many recent changes in marketing practices. American Express, for example, settled a case with the New York State attorney general by agreeing to disclose to its 25 million cardholders that for years it had been studying transaction patterns, then sorting out members with particular purchases and renting their names and addresses to marketers of those products. While this practice may not be offensive, it was being done without the members' knowledge or consent and signaled the possibilities of further intrusions into consumer privacy in the future (public attention was focused on this topic in 1988, when the U.S. Senate's review of Judge Robert Bork's nomination to the Supreme Court included the public release of a list of videos he had rented for private viewing).[24]

Finally, we should be aware that restrictions are sometimes *lifted* as well. This has recently happened in the cases of TV advertising for feminine hygiene products and for condoms.

CONCLUDING NOTE ON THE FRAMEWORK

There are many ways in which public policy can tend to its mandate of encouraging and ensuring a fair competitive and consumer environment. Each option will probably have strong points and drawbacks, and most are quite controversial. It is difficult to apply a simple rule to cover every case. You will encounter more issues of this type in our other chapters. If you are interested in learning a little more about some of the issues that arise in the world of public policy, however, you may wish to read the material in Appendix 20A, which describes the FTC's program of corrective advertising.

■ SUMMARY

ESSENTIALS OF PUBLIC POLICY

This chapter is an optional companion to Chapter 2 (marketing and consumer perspectives). Here we introduced the public policy perspective on consumer behavior. The first section focused on how the overall character of a society and its economic system broadly determines the environment for consumers and marketers. In the *market system* of the Western nations, for example, marketers and consumers are awarded significant freedoms to act in their own self-interest. As a part of these freedoms, consumers hold certain rights. The *Consumer Bill of Rights* asserts consumers' rights to be informed, to choose freely, to be heard, and to safety. In addition to rights and freedoms, however, marketers and consumers also have *responsibilities*. For marketers there are responsibilities to conduct business in accord with the spirit and laws of the system. Consumers are responsible for informing themselves, purchasing wisely, and abiding by contracts. The government is granted certain powers, but also has the responsibility of preserving freedoms and acting fairly in the exercise of its power. We saw how these aspects of the system are often quite controversial and are heavily influenced by the political climate.

THE INSTITUTIONS OF PUBLIC POLICY

In our next section we examined the various institutions of public policy—the involvement of the executive, legislative, and judicial branches of government, as well as industry self-regulatory boards, consumer groups, and the Code of Ethics of the American Marketing Association.

REGULATING THE MARKETING-CONSUMER ENVIRONMENT

The following section centered on consumer protection regulation itself, with special emphasis on the Federal Trade Commission (FTC). Here we examined its history, its vague mandate, and its controversial political setting. We saw how the pendulum has swung between activist regulation and deregulation. After a decade of deregulation, we are now apparently in a period of increasing regulation of marketing.

A BASIC FRAMEWORK FOR REGULATION

As one guide for regulatory options, we then examined a framework for consumer information regulation. This included three stages. In the first stage, the potential value of a remedy is considered using a cost-benefit analysis. Stage 2 involves three principles: *incentive compatibility*, *communication effectiveness*, and *First Amendment protection*. At stage 3, different potential remedies are considered along a dimension of relative restrictiveness. The least restrictive forms of remedies involve the removal of present restraints on information flow. At a moderately restrictive level we find remedies such as "affirmative disclosures," in which marketers may be required to disclose facts about the product or service. At the most restrictive level we see government banning certain advertising. Thus there are many options available in attempting to achieve a "fair and efficient environment" for marketers and consumers alike. In Appendix 20A we look more closely into the FTC regulatory program of corrective advertising.

■ KEY TERMS

marketing-consumer environment
public policy view
neutral view of choice
market system
Consumer Bill of Rights
right to be informed
right to choose freely
right to safety
right to be heard
right to consumer education

right to consumer recourse and redress
right to an environment that
   enhances the quality of life
errors of omission
errors of commission
cost-benefit analysis
industry self-regulation
antitrust regulation
consumer protection

deregulation
consumer information
incentive compatibility
communication effectiveness
First Amendment protection
cooling-off laws
product standards
affirmative disclosures
free speech

■ REVIEW QUESTIONS AND EXPERIENTIAL EXERCISES

[E = **Application extension or experiential exercise**]

1. Contrast the viewpoints of marketers, consumers, and public policymakers.

2. What prompted the Consumer Bill of Rights? What prompted the additional rights to be added later? Indicate the general effects of each of the rights on marketers, consumers, and government agencies.

3. Discuss, with examples, how slippages in marketer, consumer, and government responsibilities affect a market-based economic system.

4. "One cannot separate politics and political philosophies from public policy issues." Is this true? Is this desirable? Comment.

5. Describe briefly the shifts in perspective that occurred at the FTC between the 1960s and the 1990s. What are the implications for marketing practices? What is your regulatory prediction for the climate of the 1990s?

6. Briefly describe the concept and history of corrective advertising (see Appendix 20A). Do you believe this type of remedy should be used?

7. [E] Because of its role in health and safety, the Food and Drug Administration is a particularly interesting agency. Use the articles in Note 12 to gain a quick insight into some of its issues. Then use the reference area of your library to consult more recent readings about this agency. Write a brief report on your findings.

8. [E] Recent years have seen dramatic changes occurring in the public policy perspectives taken in Eastern Europe, China, and Russia. Use the library reference facilities to learn more about these events. Summarize your findings.

9. [E] Many interesting books have been written about problems with marketing practices, government regulation, and consumer protection. Locate this section in your library and review the materials there. Summarize your findings.

10. [E] Detailed coverage of public policy topics can be found in the *Journal of Public Policy & Marketing, Journal of Consumer Affairs, Journal of Marketing*, and *Journal of Advertising* (see the Notes for this chapter for examples). Locate one or more of these sources as well as *Regulation* magazine and the *Antitrust Bulletin* in the library and review its contents. Summarize your findings.

11. [E] One of the massive failures of public policy in this century involved the breakdown and government bailout of the savings and loan industry. Excellent reviews of this debacle are listed in Note 25. Consult these and prepare a brief report on your findings.

12. [E] An excellent overview of social issues in marketing has been prepared by Andreasen (Note 26). Consult this source and prepare a brief report on your findings.

13. [E] How do state and local governments involve themselves in consumer matters? Call or visit a local government agency dealing with these matters. Interview an official regarding the agency's activities and priorities. Write a brief report summarizing your findings.

14. [E] Monitor your local advertising media to locate advertising by local professionals (doctors, dentists, lawyers, accountants, etc.). Arrange a brief interview to examine their experiences with this practice, and how consumers and other professionals have responded.

15. [E] Read carefully "The Code of Ethics for Marketers" in Exhibit 20-1. Do you see any problems with it? Discuss this code with friends or acquaintances who work in retailing, purchasing, advertising, sales, research, or industrial marketing jobs. What realistic reactions do they have?

■ SUGGESTED READING

■ An excellent, readable overview of academic work on the broad topic of social issues in marketing is available in Alan Andreasen, "Consumer Behavior Research and Social Policy," in T. Robertson and H. Kassarjian (eds.), *Handbook of Consumer Behavior* (Englewood Cliffs, N.J.: Prentice Hall, 1991), pp. 459–506. The story of botched regulation in the savings and loan scandal is well presented in "Hall of Shame," *Wall Street Journal*, November 2, 1990, pp. 1ff; and Alan Farnham, "The S&L Felons," *Fortune*, November 5, 1990, pp. 90–108. As ethics is moving to the forefront of interest to business persons, you may be interested in reading Jerry R. Goolsby and Shelby D. Hunt, "Cognitive Moral Development and Marketing," *Journal of Marketing*, Vol. 56, No. 1 (January 1992), pp. 55–68; and Gene R. Laczniak, "Marketing Ethics: Onward toward Greater Expectations," *Journal of Public Policy & Marketing*, Vol. 12, No. 1 (Spring 1993), pp. 91–96. Finally, to gain insight into the many considerations that appear in public policy matters, see William L. Wilkie, Dennis L. McNeill, and Michael B. Mazis, "Marketing's Scarlet Letter", *Journal of Marketing*, Vol. 48 (Spring 1984), pp. 11–31.

Appendix 20A

CORRECTIVE ADVERTISING

Corrective advertising is a regulatory program that can force a marketer, who had run deceptive advertising in the past, to run new advertising to correct any deceptions still existing in consumers' minds. This remedy is a special form of the FTC's affirmative disclosure program. It has always been very controversial, since it represents a clear government intrusion into a marketer's control of its own promotional strategies.

On the other hand, it may bring real benefits to consumers and competitors. There is much complexity in this area. Our coverage will focus on some of the highlights (if you wish to learn more, Note 27 provides an excellent list of sources).

A "Brief" History

The Soup Case

The seeds for corrective advertising were planted by a small group of law students from George Washington University. As part of a course project, these students banded together under the acronym SOUP (Students Opposed to Unfair Practices) and tried to intervene in a case against Campbell Soup Company. That case involved ads that showed bowls of vegetable soup with the vegetables piled above the liquid level, suggesting ample portions. A complaint had been lodged with the commission (rumored to have come from the H. J. Heinz Company, which manufactured many stores' private-label soups, but which has for years had trouble gaining a strong position for its own soup brands). After an investigation, the FTC found that the ad agency had achieved the vegetable piling effect by placing clear glass marbles in the bottoms of the soup bowls before filling them with the soup and forcing the solid ingredients to the top. As a remedy in the case, the FTC intended to issue a cease-and-desist order against Campbell. This order would require the company to stop showing these types of ads and never to engage in such a practice again in the future.

The law students, however, did not believe that this was the best remedy for FTC to use. Instead, they proposed that a *corrective* message be ordered, to inform consumers who may have been misled by the false ads. Otherwise, SOUP argued, a deceived consumer might never become aware that he or she had been misled!

FTC did not accept SOUP's argument in this case, since it is obvious that a person who buys the soup would soon see the actual ingredient quantities. Thus, the chances of a continuing deception were low in this case. The commission also noted, however, that the *concept* of a correction was interesting, and perhaps would be appropriate in more serious cases. Thus was corrective advertising born.

A Spurt of Activity

Over the next few years, the FTC announced many corrective advertising investigations that it intended to consider. These received great attention in the press, and in business circles. Supporters of corrective advertising saw it as a boon to consumers and to competitors, in which a wrongdoer would be rightly "denied the fruits of a violation." Also, of course, there was a feeling that this stronger remedy would cause other advertisers to think twice before engaging in deceptive ads—thus the potential *deterrence* effect might also be large. Opponents of corrective advertising raised a series of objections. They argued that the remedy was beyond the FTC's powers and represented further intrusion by government bureaucrats into the market system and a further attack on marketing freedoms.

Interestingly, most of the early corrective ad complaints issued by the FTC did *not* lead to actual corrective advertising orders. Most of the orders that *were* issued, moreover, seemed to be weak. Exhibit 20A-1 shows the text of four of the earliest corrective ads. What do you think about each of them?

Beyond the corrective ads themselves, however, most of the marketing community's anxiety dealt with the threat of further government intrusion into marketers' freedoms. For this reason, a legal test of the FTC's powers was important.

EXHIBIT 20A-1

Texts of Four Early Corrective Ads

I. Profile Bread

"Hi (celebrity's name), for Profile Bread. Like all mothers, I'm concerned about nutrition and balanced meals. So, I'd like to clear up any misunderstanding you may have about Profile Bread from its advertising or even its name.

"Does Profile Bread have fewer calories than any other breads? No. Profile has about the same per ounce as other breads. To be exact, Profile has 7 fewer calories per slice. That's because Profile is sliced thinner. But eating Profile will not cause you to lose weight. A reduction of 7 calories is insignificant. It's total calories and balanced nutrition that count. And Profile can help you achieve a balanced meal because it provides protein and B vitamins as well as other nutrients.

"How does my family feel about Profile? Well, my husband likes Profile toast, the children love Profile sandwiches, and

I prefer Profile to any other bread. So you see, at our house, delicious taste makes Profile a family affair."

(To be run in 25 percent of brand's advertising, for one year)

II. Ocean Spray

"If you've wondered what some of our earlier advertising meant when we said Ocean Spray Cranberry Juice Cocktail has more food energy than orange juice or tomato juice, let us make it clear: we didn't mean vitamins and minerals. Food energy means calories. Nothing more.

"Food energy is important at breakfast since many of us may not get enough calories, or food energy, to get off to a good start. Ocean Spray Cranberry Juice Cocktail helps because it contains more food energy than most other breakfast drinks.

"And Ocean Spray Cranberry Juice Cocktail gives you and your family Vitamin C plus a great wake-up taste. It's...the other breakfast drink."

(To be run in one of every four ads for one year)

III. Amstar

"Do you recall some of our past messages saying that Domino Sugar gives you strength, energy and stamina? Actually, Domino is not a special or unique source of strength, energy and stamina. No sugar is, because what you need is a balanced diet and plenty of rest and exercise."

(To be run in one of every four ads for one year)

IV. Sugar Information, Inc.

"Do you recall the messages we brought you in the past about sugar? How something with sugar in it before meals could help you curb your appetite? We hope you didn't get the idea that our little diet tip was any magic formula for losing weight. Because there are no tricks, or shortcuts, the whole diet subject is very complicated. Research hasn't established that consuming sugar before meals will contribute to weight reduction or even keep you from gaining weight."

(To be run for one insertion in each of seven magazines)

The Listerine Case: A Legal Test

The first case to test the FTC's legal power to order corrective advertising involved the Warner-Lambert Company's Listerine brand of mouthwash. Warner-Lambert had advertised—for over 50 years—that gargling with Listerine helped prevent colds and sore throats because Listerine killed the germs that caused these illnesses. This marketing program had been extremely successful—Listerine was by far the dominant brand of mouthwash (at one time holding over a 60 percent share of market) and was believed by many consumers to be an excellent safeguard for their families' health.

The FTC's staff believed that the advertising was erroneous and that corrective advertising was needed to rectify the mistaken beliefs held by so many consumers. Warner-Lambert, on the other hand, argued that the advertising was *not* erroneous and, further, that FTC did not have the power to order corrective advertising in any event. After four months of hearings, covering 4000 pages of testimony, the commission *did* order corrective advertising. The company then took the FTC to court, appealing its decision. The circuit court of appeals upheld the FTC in general (it did, however, remove part of the required corrective phrase).

Listerine's corrective campaign was run for a period of 16 months, stretching from late 1978 until early 1980. As ordered, just over $10 million was spent on these ads, almost all of it on television. The required disclosure was placed midway in the commercial, taking up about 5 seconds of the 30-second spot. Consumer research (based on our multiattribute attitude model discussed in Chapter 11) showed an interesting pattern of results from this corrective campaign. A study by the FTC showed that many consumers did change their beliefs about Listerine and cold prevention. Also, however, many consumers did *not* get the message or else did not believe it. Over 40 percent of Listerine users, for example, still believed (at the end of the campaign) that Listerine continued to be promoted as effective for colds and sore throats. Almost 60 percent of Listerine users continued to say that cold and sore throat effectiveness was a key for their purchasing. Given these results, would you say that the Listerine corrective ad campaign was a success (from a public policy perspective), or not? If not, what should the FTC or Warner-Lambert do now?

Lessons Learned

Since the Listerine campaign, there was little activity on corrective advertising through the 1980s and thus far in the 1990s. The political backlash from Congress and the administration's deregulation program reduced the chances of further use of this remedy at the time. At present, however, the FTC retains the power to order corrective advertising. It may well be, therefore, that we will see it return in the future. Exhibit 20A-2 outlines 10 conclusions about corrective advertising, as reported by three marketing professors who conducted an in-depth analysis of the program. What is *your* general position regarding corrective advertising? Would you like to see it return as a remedy that the FTC is using, or would you prefer to have it never arise again?

EXHIBIT 20-A2

Summary Conclusions on Corrective Advertising

1. The FTC is empowered to order corrective advertising as a remedy against deceptive advertising campaigns.
2. There are important legal constraints as to when and in what manner the FTC can employ this remedy form.
3. Corrective advertising holds the potential to yield beneficial effects for consumers.
4. Corrective advertising appears to hold the potential to affect the sales and/or image of the advertised brand.
5. There is little evidence of a systematic FTC program for corrective advertising:
   a. Bursts of case activity have been followed by long periods of inactivity.
   b. Philosophical and personnel changes occurred throughout the 1970s and early 1980s, at both the staff and commissioner levels.
   c. Past orders have used a wide range of requirements for corrective advertising.
6. Consent negotiations between FTC staff members and company representatives have played a key role in the exact requirements in almost every case to date.
7. Consumer effectiveness of corrective advertising has not been the primary concern of the orders issued to date.
8. In communication terms, past corrective advertising orders against major advertisers appear to have been weak.
9. In terms of consumer impacts, the major corrective advertising orders appear *not* to have been successful in remedying consumer misimpressions across the marketplace.
10. If corrective advertising is to continue as an FTC remedy, some changes in the form of the orders will be required.

SOURCE: William L. Wilkie, Dennis L. McNeill, and Michael B. Mazis, "Marketing's Scarlet Letter: The Theory and Practice of Corrective Advertising," *Journal of Marketing*, Spring 1984, p. 26. Reprinted with permission.

21

ORGANIZATIONAL BUYING BEHAVIOR

(Because this is a specialized field of study, this chapter was prepared by Dr. Darrel Miller, Queens College, Charlotte, North Carolina, in conjunction with Dr. Wilkie so that it fits well with the spirit and content of the other chapters.)

MILLIKEN CLEANS UP AS BUSINESS PARTNER

The world of industrial buyer behavior is in the midst of a major change, as marketers have discovered "relationship marketing." In essence, this shifts attention away from making a single transaction with a customer toward making a series of sales over a long time period. The famous marketing professor Philip Kotler points to Milliken & Company as a good example of "benefitizing" its customers. Milliken sells shop towels to laundries, which in turn supply them to factories. Milliken's towels are pretty much like everyone else's, but laundries willingly pay 10–15 percent more. Why?

Because Milliken says to the laundries, "If you buy from us, you're our Partner for Profit. We will give you special software to help you route your laundry trucks, as well as special software for accounting. We'll train your sales force to sell more effectively; we'll do market research for you and supply new customer leads. Finally, we'll put together Customer Action Teams to solve problems." Thus Milliken's business customers are getting much more than towels when they form a business relationship with this marketer.[1]

This chapter focuses on a special context for buyer behavior—purchasing done by organizations rather than by individual consumers. If we think briefly about it, we can see that organizations buy many products and services, including plant and equipment, raw materials, supplies, insurance, and so forth. In fact, *in actual dollars, organizational buyers spend substantially more money than do the individual consumers in our economy.* Not only are purchases typically for larger amounts of money, the total is much greater as well. Many readers of this book are likely to work in organizational buying or selling sometime during their careers. It is thus important for us to look more closely at how "organizational" consumers make purchases. We will examine three primary topics in this chapter: (1) the organizational context, (2) the process of organizational buying, and (3) relationships between buyers and sellers.

■ BACKGROUND ON ORGANIZATIONAL BUYING

Organizational buying refers to the purchasing processes and decisions within organizations. Organizations can be industrial firms, government agencies, retail businesses, service establishments, and so forth. Organizational purchases can be made by a single individual or any number of individuals in a variety of subunits within the organization. In some ways organizational buying is similar to consumer buying, but in other respects it is different.

SIMILARITIES TO CONSUMER BUYING

Leading the list of similarities is that *organizations and consumers use the same basic decision processes* we discuss throughout this text. Organizations also have needs. Their purchase processes involve searching for information about alternative products. External factors also influence their choice, including social influences, salespersons, and advertising. Once a purchase decision is reached, it is also later evaluated to see if the purchase performs to expectations.

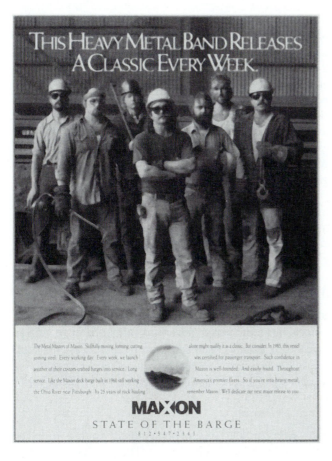

Businesses may use humor to attract attention and gain readership, but the ad's copy usually has to address the benefits that buyers are seeking.

Table 21-1 Selling to Organizations through "Benefits"

One marketing consultant uses consumer behavior concepts in advising his clients on how to sell to industrial buyers. His ideas, which revolve around the acronym "Benefit," list seven possible appeals for a marketer to use:

- *B = Benevolent results:* Describe how much better their employees will perform or feel with your product at work.
- *E = Economics:* Present the product in terms of the money that the customer will either save or make because of it.
- *N = Nobility:* Present the product in a light that appeals to a customer's sense of right and fair play, as in "Buy American" in the United States.
- *E = Ego:* Show how buying the product will enhance the customer's image to others, in terms of appearing to be wiser, richer, or more "state of the art."
- *F = Fear:* Show how the firm's purchase will provide increased safety from physical or competitive forces.
- *I = Information:* Present the product as an answer to questions that are likely to arise in the near future, or as a means toward progress.
- *T = Time savings:* Demonstrate how the purchase of your product will free up resources for other productive uses.

Notice how similar these appeals are to those that might be used in a consumer marketing setting.

SOURCE: See Note 2.

Some consumer behavior experts believe that the models marketers use for understanding individual consumer behavior are also useful for organizational buyer behavior. One recent study, for example, focused on the effects of an organizational buyer's previous purchasing experience. The researchers found that the more experienced the buyer, the broader the set of alternatives he or she would consider. More experienced buyers also needed less *external* information, because they were able to draw upon their prior experiences with the product category. These types of findings allowed the researchers to conclude that organizational buyers use the same basic cognitive purchasing strategies as individual consumers.[3] Table 21-1 shows how one marketing consultant adapted consumer behavior concepts to "benefit" his clients engaged in selling to organizations.

Further evidence of similarities involves the *increasing use of advertising and promotional techniques* by organizational sellers. Some of this may be due to the increasing number of consumer products marketing managers taking jobs in industrial products firms, but increased competition is the chief reason organizational marketers are finding consumer-selling techniques so useful.

ಇಲ *Psychedelic Machines Speed Sales*

Rather than focusing on product specifications, some mature products are advertised with an extra twist. Sumitomo Machinery Corporation advertises its variable-speed drives [small machines] painted in psychedelic colors, candy stripes, and other styles. The copy gives product specifications and offers to paint any machine to the customer's desires for an extra charge. An executive with the company attributed a 20 percent sales increase to this campaign.[4]

A third similarity between consumer and organizational buying involves the *number of people who participate* in the decision process. The purchase in either the consumer household or the organization can be made by one individual or by multiple persons. For example, just as family members and friends may influence a purchase by a consumer, the organizational buyer may consult with colleagues who will use the product or who may have expertise about it.

DIFFERENCES FROM CONSUMER BUYING

There are, however, some significant differences to consider. One major difference between an individual consumer purchase and an organizational purchase is that *the organizational buyer is usually not the end user* of the product. When an individual consumer makes a purchase, the end result is that the product is taken home and used or consumed in some fashion. The organizational buyer, however, is buying the product for use in the manufacturing process, to maintain the business, or for reselling to other customers. Thus the role of the organizational buyer is different from that of the individual consumer. (It is somewhat similar to the role played by the person in a household who is charged with doing all the shopping. The "buying agent" for the household makes some purchases on behalf of the household as a whole, and others according to the needs and wants of individual household members.)

A second major difference involves the *roles of people who participate* in the decision process. An organizational purchase is entrusted to a **decision-making unit (DMU).** Depending on the structure and internal dynamics of the organization, the decision-making unit's makeup is flexible. For example, a manufacturing firm purchasing prefabricated parts might employ a DMU with representatives from the engineering and production departments. Each department, again depending on the organization, may have a greater or lesser degree of participation. The possibilities are limitless and can change with personnel changes within the organization.

A third difference is that the *quantities involved in organizational purchases can be enormous.* For example, an individual shopper seldom purchases more than one or two dresses on a shopping trip. A department store buyer, on the other hand, often purchases hundreds of dresses (and mistakes may be very costly).

Decision-making unit (DMU): The center for organizational purchasing: can consist of one or many individuals.

An organizational DMU (decision-making unit) in deep discussion concerning a significant purchase for the organization. Representatives from production, engineering, finance, accounting, marketing, and personnel are all present, together with the director of purchasing.

The CIT Group smacked a home run with its creative program to provide executives with a collection of autographed baseballs in return for appointments to discuss its services.

How to Reach a CEO

At times a marketer will find itself with only a few prospective customers, but each of extremely large size. For example, the CIT Group—a financial services company that makes large loans to large corporations—faced the problem of how to reach a small set of decision makers with the power to approve a multimillion-dollar deal. In conjunction with its promotion agency (the Direct Marketing Group), CIT developed an award-winning plan that targeted only 96 executives in the entire country (each person was a chairman, president, or chief financial officer of one of the 96 giant corporations, well protected from contacts by eager marketers). How could CIT gain access to these potential clients?

The strategy: the 96 executives were first sent a letter from CIT's chairman, together with a baseball autographed by baseball Hall of Famer Willie Mays (who played at about the time many of these executives would have been young fans) and a specially designed display case with room for two more baseballs. Those who responded then received a letter from their CIT representative requesting an appointment, along with a baseball signed by another Hall of Famer, Stan Musial. Those who granted an appointment received a hand-delivered third ball from the sales representative, autographed by the great Mickey Mantle.

Results? A grand slam in any league: 89 of the 96 executives (93 percent) responded, and all made deals with CIT, totaling $120,000,000. The cost of the promotion: less than $18,000![5]

Specifications: The basis for buying by bids from competing suppliers: these detail the exact product to be purchased.

A fourth way in which organizational decisions differ from consumer decisions is that *they more frequently rely on highly structured processes,* in which bids from competing suppliers are invited, and are to be based on a complex set of **specifications.** Such "specs" detail the exact product to be purchased and are designed by the buyer's DMU to reflect precisely the role the new machinery, for example, will perform in the production process. When complex purchases are being made, other provisions may also be built into the organization's purchase process. If a business purchases a new computer system, for example, employee training and service contracts are just two of the special postpurchase specifics likely to be agreed upon formally.

Exhibit 21-1 provides excerpts from an interview with Linda H., a buyer for a major discount department store chain. Her experiences are not meant to be representative of all buyers, but they do offer some interesting illustrations of overall purchasing experiences. As you read it, think about how organizational buying is similar to and different from consumer buying behavior.

An Organizational Buyer Reveals Her Secrets

The following is an excerpted interview with Linda H., a buyer of women's clothing for a major discount department store chain. Linda earned her undergraduate degree in education, then took her first job as a secretary in a prestigious department store. As she "became interested in the business," she took further college courses and store training programs. She now has 13 years of experience as a buyer, in three chains.

Q. *What were your impressions the first time you went out as a buyer?*

A. The first time I went as an associate buyer in infants' wear. The children's market is very conservative. People are nice, there's not a lot of pressure. Then I moved to ready-to-wear dresses. In ready-to-wear, the competition is much greater. People are a lot more aggressive . . . a lot more pressure filled, a lot crazier, a lot funnier, a lot more exciting. There's nobody like the dressmaker! You can have one dress resource or you can have five dress resources making the same dress—all within the same price range. And who you buy from is really the person with whom you develop a relationship.

Q. *Did you frequently have "straight rebuys"?*

A. Yes, in children's I'd say probably 70 percent was on straight rebuys [editor's note: a "rebuy" is a simple reorder of a particular item]. But not in ready-to-wear. Here, by and large, it's a new buy. You could buy 10 items and maybe 2 are reorder and you buy 8 new things. This means in ready-to-wear, you travel to market every month; in children's you travel only four times a year.

Q. *Where's the market?*

A. New York and California.

Q. *What types of dress marketers do you deal with?*

A. With the brand-name labels, the people are corporate types. It's when you're dealing with people who aren't labeled where you get the characters. And they can be wackos!

Q. *How do you deal with the wackos?*

A. Most of the wackos are probably very good. They're out to make money and that's what we're all in business for. But, generally, they're willing to do anything you need to get business. And I'd say that 90 percent of them, as wacko as they are, are reliable and trustworthy. And 10 percent are not reliable—not somebody you would trust.

Organizational buyers select and purchase the clothing sold in department stores, but as our interview with Linda H. explains, the buyers' influences don't always extend to how the clothes are displayed!

Q. *Is change in the retail structure creating a disruption?*

A. Oh, yes! For instance, when you have mergers, like when Jordan Marsh and Maas Brothers merged, vendors say they don't make a buck. Say you were a manufacturer selling to both companies involved in the merger, your business will drop off afterward because the dress buyer isn't going to be accustomed—she used to buy for 20, now she's buying for 60 stores—she's not going to buy three times more than she bought before. It's frightening to a buyer.

Q. *What is a "garmento"?*

A. I define the garmento as a sleaze who will do anything to get a sale. Will promise you anything.

Q. *Have you had experience with one?*

A. I've not done business with them, but I've met a couple. I wouldn't trust them. I have a very difficult time dealing with somebody I feel that way about. And sometimes you have to. Sometimes they have something that you need, so you have to interact with them.

Q. *How do they talk? Is it a line they have?*

A. Yes. "I've got the hottest thing," "It's on fire around the country," "You gotta get into it," "Maybe I can steal you some so you can get into it immediately." You know the type.

Q. *Does this immediately clue you?*

A. Yeah. If it's so hot, they're not going to steal me any. And they're not going to be able to get it to me immediately. Like the phone call I just received. He had something real hot that he could ship right now, would I be interested?

Q. *I take it there are buyers out there, or these guys wouldn't continue this approach?*

A. I don't know who would. I can't see very many buyers doing this. But I'll tell you what *does* happen in retail organizations. A lot of these garmentos become friendly with merchandise managers and vice presidents and presidents, so they don't have to deal with the buyers. They can dial up a merchandise manager and say, "My merchandise is really hot, can I ship some?" Some divisionals will say yes, and write up the order. So they get accustomed to succeeding in certain ways if they have a friend in the organization. It doesn't happen here, but it does happen in a lot of department stores.

Q. *As we've been talking I get a sense that dealing with sellers can be exciting . . .*

A. I really feel that you learn from everybody. You can get a lot of good ideas from these people. They deal with your business everyday, thousands of retailers they deal with. They get ideas, merchandising ideas, so it's not only just shopping their line but listening to what they have to say. For example, when I bought sportswear, an old friend told me of a successful advertising event his firm did. I applied it to sportswear, and it was like record sales for our firm! It came from this angle I received from a vendor that I don't even do business with because he's not in my line. But he came up with a good idea.

Q. *If you had to deal with only the corporate people . . .*

A. That would not be real swift. Not that you can't learn from the corporate people, but it's a different type of learning. When I started I knew very little about buying dresses. I dealt with a substantial dress company, and the president of that company—a corporate-type person, a "don't buy if you don't want to" type—he sat me down and I learned dresses from him. Every month I would visit and learn something from him and I was a success. He actually taught me how to buy dresses. So I've had to rely on different resources, corporate, wacko, whatever, to learn and to grow.

Q. *Is buying different with other product lines like hardware, domestics, or electronics?*

A. I think so; they have different situations. Their business is so planned out, they almost have to *marry* their resource. Also, I don't think that every buyer approaches things in the same way, even in ready-to-wear. I'm just giving you my approach to business.

Q. *Your job is one link in providing products to your firm—how do you see yourself in this chain?*

A. Middle portion of the chain. I look to give directions below. I look for certain types of direction from above. Not so much for the details of my assortment, but direction about how are we going to sell what I buy—the advertising, pricing strategy, what kind of fixtures I am going to have for my merchandise. All that will affect how I approach the market and what I buy. And then it's also my job to inform my divisional manager of what I see is important to market and what I think we could sell. And then it's actually his job to make sure the people under and over are aware of it.

Q. *So there's a smooth flow from top to bottom . . .*

A. No, it's not. There are many advantages working in our chain, but the flow is smoother in the major department stores. We run into a product presentation difference. In a department store atmosphere, the people working in the store—the link under me—it's their job to merchandise the product and to sell it. In a department store, those store people are striving to get to a higher position in the company. They're generally the best that college had to offer, and they want to become a buyer and to go up the corporate ladder. They take a little bit of training and they know what they're doing. They know stock turnover, they know on-order, they know markdown, markups, all this. Those people do a better job. When you go into our stores, there's not as much help as in the major department stores. They don't know what to do when the goods come in. And a lot of what I perceive it looking like when it hits the floor . . .

Q. *Is fiction?*

A. Right, it's definitely in my head. I can't go into a store and see that. So, going into a store in my organization is not the bright spot in my day . . . and it really whips me for a couple of days. . . . We spend a lot of time tracing my sell, going over assortments, what's it gonna look like in a C store, B store, and A store and you're all excited about it and then all of a sudden, when I see it, any similarity is purely coincidental!

Q. *What about price?*

A. Price is the bottom line in all negotiations. But there's something more important than price, and that is *value*. If that $70 item in our store is similar to what's carried in another store for $140, that's value. As far as negotiating for the lowest price, yes. I will fight and negotiate. And to do that intelligently, you have to know the market and what it's actually worth.

Q. *How do you judge quality? Higher price, higher quality?*

A. Not necessarily. That's how it should be, but not necessarily. You can go into a Fifth Avenue store and spend $1000 on an outfit and get it home and see how it's made. I have merchandise at $24 that's made better than the $1000 outfit. The price should dictate the quality of the garment, but it's not what's happening in ready-to-wear. In fact, there have been many articles in magazines about that right now.

Q. *So how do you judge a product?*

A. On a new buy, it's almost a stab in the dark. I go out and shop better stores every week. I read fashion magazines and as many women's wear publications as I can get. I look and see what I could utilize from this information, then I go to market and look for it. I might not be able to do it in silk, but I may be able to do it in crepe-de-chine and give the customer the same look. So, there's a lot of things that go into it. It's not just an off-the-wall stab in the dark. Price is very important, quality is important, value is important.

A RANGE OF ORGANIZATIONS

The term **organization** refers to a group interacting together on the basis of shared identity and goals. In this regard, you may have heard the term "industrial buying" used synonymously with organizational buying. For our purposes, there is no major difference in terms, except that we must be clear that we are referring to many types of organizations, including (1) industrial firms; (2) governmental agencies; (3) nonprofit organizations, such as hospitals; (4) the service sector—banks, restaurants, and so on—and (5) retail stores. All have DMUs or centers that make purchasing decisions for their organizations. They often purchase in large quantities and fulfill other definitional characteristics of organizational buying outlined earlier.

Organization: A group interacting together on the basis of shared identity and goals.

TYPES OF BUY SITUATIONS

One important distinction in organizational buying distinguishes three types of purchases, depending on the amount of past experience available for a purchase:[6]

- The **straight rebuy** is a largely routine purchase. It involves frequently purchased items that have been purchased before by the organization. Information search and concern with specifications are minimal.

- The **modified rebuy** is also a routinized purchase; however, the organization has decided to change product specifications or suppliers.

- The **new buy** is not a routine purchase. Since the item has never been purchased before by the organization, information search is high. Specifications must be researched and developed, and vendors must be evaluated.

After the new buy, if the vendor performs well and the product continues to meet needs, rebuys require very little further input by either the buyer or supplier. *Thus, in the rebuy stages it is difficult for competitors to dislodge an established vendor.* For this reason a new buy usually becomes the focal point for salespeople as they analyze the organizational buying process.

■ THE PROCESS OF ORGANIZATIONAL BUYING

ROLES IN THE BUYING CENTER

The process of organizational buying encompasses a number of actors on both the buying and selling side. On the buyer's side, the decision-making unit is often referred to as the **buying center.**[7] Webster and Wind have identified a number of functional roles associated with the buying center:

Buying center: Another term for the decision-making unit (DMU).

1. *Initiators*—those within the organization who first identify the need for a service or product

2. *Influencers*—those who affect a purchase decision either indirectly or directly

3. *Gatekeepers*—those who control the flow of information into the buying center

4. *Users*—those within the organization who will use the product or service.

5. *Buyers*—those who will actually make the purchase

6. *Deciders*—those who have the authority to decide which supplier will provide the product or service

This large number of roles within an organization can be a serious complicating factor for a new supplier or vendor. For example, notice that the buyers and deciders are at the bottom of the list. This suggests that they may enter the process at a later stage. When a supplier's salesperson contacts a purchasing agent (buyer), it is even possible that the supplier may have already been eliminated as a possible vendor because of decisions or preconditions set by other executives or scientists in the earlier stages of the purchasing decision process. Coupled with these various roles, the supplier must also deal with a formal organizational structure as exemplified by the traditional corporate organizational chart. In fact, this formal organizational chart may be all the supplier has when first contacting an organization in a new buy situation.

❧ Tech Reps: An Innovative Sales Approach

According to one sales research firm, salespeople often reach only 3 out of 10 "influentials" involved in the average purchasing process. In addition, often purchasing

Baxter International, a huge hospital products company, has moved into relationship marketing with its largest hospital customers. A Baxter executive explains, "Hospitals are there to administer care, not to worry about managing inventory." Here, a Baxter representative helps Herman Hospital in Houston keep tabs on its inventory: savings to the hospital are expected to reach $8 million over five years. Results for Baxter: a greatly increased share of the hospital's business, plus a fee for these additional services.[8]

agents themselves are not aware of some purchases by departments (especially in the case of research and development departments, where this information might lag for more than a year!).[9] To overcome these constraints, AmCast Industrial Corporation replaced its traditional sales force with college-educated technical representatives. The job of the new "tech reps" is to get involved in the decision-making process of their potential customers as early as possible. They are to contact engineering and design personnel at the target companies and find out what assistance they can give in designing new products. They are to try to get to know *everyone* within the organization and try to become "quasi-members" of the customer's team.[10] This is one step toward **relationship marketing,** in which suppliers and customers cooperate for long-term advantages for each. This approach led to the design of a new disk brake for General Motors and a substantial contract for AmCast.

Relationship marketing: An arrangement in which suppliers and customers cooperate for long-term advantages for each.

THE "BUYGRID–BUYPHASE" MODEL

Because of the complexity of organizational purchasing, marketers have relied on models for helping to identify roles, stages, and influences within the organizational purchasing process. One of the most widely used models is the Buygrid framework.[11] It relates the three types of buy situations discussed earlier—new buy, straight rebuy, and modified rebuy—to eight key "Buyphases." These are shown in Figure 21-1. Let's examine the framework briefly.

The process begins with the identification of the need for an item. This usually occurs in the using department, which provides a statement of the problem and a general description of the need to the buying center. Marketing research indicates that the sooner a supplier can get involved in the process, the more likely he or she will be selected to supply the needed item. For a new buy situation, it is difficult for the

		BUYCLASSES[a]	
BUYPHASES[b]	*New Task*	*Modified Rebuy*	*Straight Rebuy*
1. Recognition of a problem (need)			
2. Determination of characteristics and quantity of needed item			
3. Description of needed item to potential suppliers			
4. Qualification of potential sources			
5. Acquisition of proposals			
6. Evaluation of proposals and selection of supplier(s)			
7. Selection of an order routine			
8. Performance feedback and evaluation			

FIGURE 21-1 Buygrid Framework for Organizational Buying

[a]The most complex buying situations occur in the upper left portion of the BUYGRID matrix. Thus, a New Task in its initial phase of problem recognition generally represents the greatest difficulty for management.

[b]As Buyphases are completed, moving from phase 1 through phase 8, the process of "creeping commitment" occurs, and there is diminishing likelihood of new vendors gaining access to the buying situation.

SOURCE: See Note 11.

supplier to become involved at this stage unless one is already an "in" supplier. In that case, previous contacts and sales calls within the organization may help. The "in" supplier usually has an even greater advantage in the rebuy situations.

In stage 2, the using department puts together a description of the item and defines parameters. In stage 3, the buying center seeks information from outside sources, including suppliers. In these two stages, the "out" supplier (one currently not selling to the organization) has greater opportunities to affect the decision process in all three buy situations. In stage 4, the search for potential sources, the buying organization decides which suppliers can meet the needs set forth in the previous stages. A marketer's reputation and any previous contact that the buying organization might have had with the supplier are important.

Once the possible suppliers are identified, specific proposals and price quotations are sought in stage 5. In stage 6 the proposals are evaluated, and a final decision is made. In stage 7, selection of an order routine, the buyer monitors the sending of the purchase order, the vendor's progress in filling the order, and internal reporting to the using department of progress by the vendor. Finally, in stage 8, the buying organization evaluates the performance of the purchased item. Service and other follow-up activities by the supplier are also evaluated. Satisfaction at this stage determines a supplier's future opportunities with the purchasing organization.

AN EXPANDED MODEL

The Buygrid model is helpful in laying out basic stages, but it does not detail some realistic influences and considerations. When we add these, the model appears to be more complex, but it is actually much more realistic. Let's consider Figure 21-2, a more general model developed by Webster and Wind. Notice that its major components (reading down) include the *environment*, the *organization*, the *buying center*, the *individuals*, and then the *decision process* itself.

As shown, there are many types of possible **environmental factors** that might impact organizational buying. Environmental factors are external to the organization yet impact the purchase decision process, such as labor unions, governmental regulations, or the number of business competitors. In many respects, **organizational determinants** are the internal equivalents of environmental factors. These are unique to each organization and consist of relevant technology, structure, goals, and actors. As those with business experience can testify, "organizational cultures" do exist: managers must make specific adaptations to work effectively within any given organization.

Within the buying center, **interpersonal determinants** are at work. These reflect social influences on the buying center's group activities, interactions, and feelings (sentiments) as members undertake buying tasks and other actions. Notice that the social influences do not just involve the entire group, but that subgroups (e.g., engineers versus accountants or friends versus a new manager) can also be extremely important. As shown in component IV, exactly who the **individual participants** are can also be extremely important. For example, Sherry Oliver might react positively to the technical presentation by Ajax Engineering, whereas George Wratney might push for a different supplier.

In sum, the process of organizational buying is complex. It includes individuals and small groups of people. Knowing how these people interact and what external and organizational constraints are affecting a decision is important. (If you would like to learn more about recent research in this area, please see Note 12.)

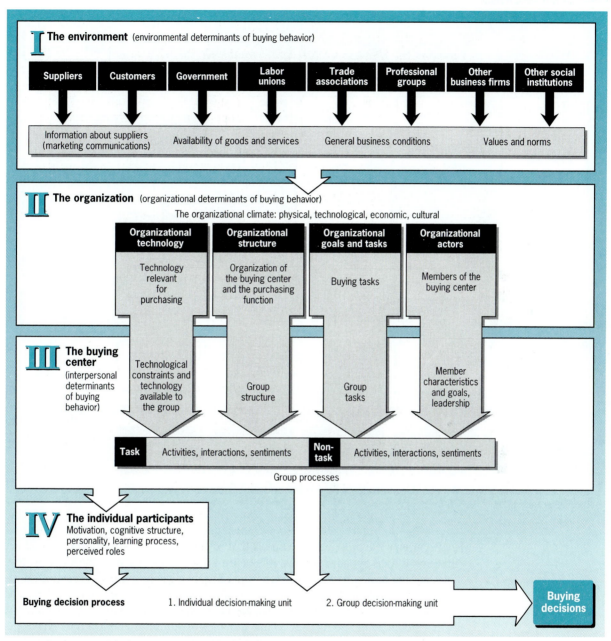

FIGURE 21-2 A Model of Organizational Buying Behavior
SOURCE: See Note 7.

■ ORGANIZATIONAL BUYER AND SELLER BEHAVIOR

THE ORGANIZATIONAL BUYER

What about the person who is designated as a "buyer" for an organization? Our models to this point have stressed the overall buying center's decision-making process. There are, however, also *models that center on the behavior of the individual organizational*

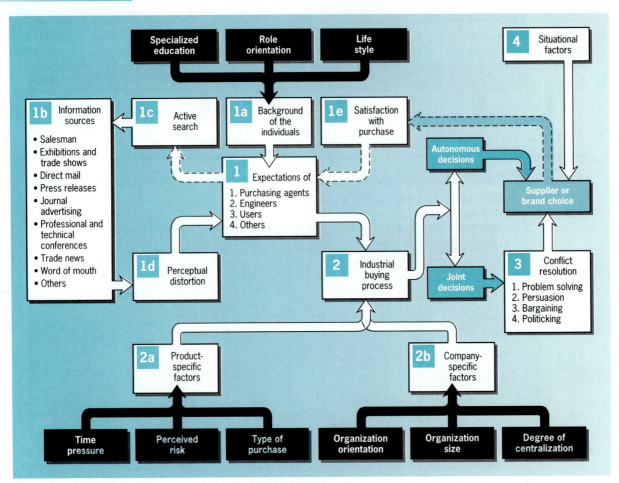

FIGURE 21-3 An Integrative Model of Organizational Buying Behavior
SOURCE: See Note 13.

buyer. Perhaps the most widely used is that of Jagdish Sheth, shown in Figure 21-3.[13] Although it does appear complex, it is helpful if we concentrate on the basic process. Note that the basic process consists of the central stages numbered: (1) expectations, (2) industrial buying process, and (3) conflict resolution. Significant substeps and influences are designated at each stage as (1a), (1b), (1c), and so forth. The strength of Sheth's model is that he focuses on the variables or stimuli that affect the behavior of individuals involved in the decision-making process.

INDIVIDUAL DIFFERENCES IN THE BUYING CENTER

Research has shown that individuals within any buying center are looking for different things when they are deciding about a purchase. For example, for a particular piece of machinery, the firm's purchasing agent's most important product attributes might be low price and economical delivery, while the engineer might seek high quality and standardized design, and the plant's operating department may be stressing durability, energy efficiency, and ease of servicing. This is the reason that stage (3), conflict resolution, occupies such a key role in Sheth's model (Figure 21-3).

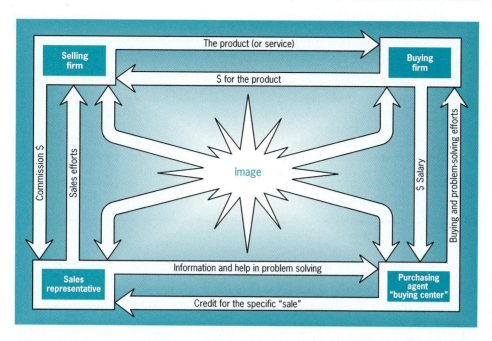

FIGURE 21-4 The Industrial Buying Process as an Exchange
SOURCE: See Note 14.

Notice, however, that the seller isn't shown as having a very prominent role in Sheth's model, appearing only as one player in (1b). To focus more on the seller's role, let's examine the "**exchange model**," developed by Thomas Bonoma, Gerald Zaltman, and Wesley Johnston, shown in Figure 21-4.[14] This model focuses on the *exchanges* taking place between the buying organization and the selling organization. Exchange takes place at the primary level of the **buyer-seller dyad.**

Focusing on the dyad rather than the individual demonstrates the interrelationships that are an integral part of the purchase process. As Figure 21-4 illustrates, the purchasing agent and sales representative are (1) each part of their respective organizations (exchanging work for money) as well as (2) separate entities who negotiate help and credit among themselves. In addition, they arrange for the top flows in Figure 21-4, in which different departments of the organizations actually deliver goods and services and payments for them. Notice how this look at the process allows us to appreciate how the details of transactions (e.g., price) are influenced by other factors at work within the dyad.

Buyer/seller dyad:
The pairing of salesperson and purchaser, whose interrelationships are studied with respect to the exchanges taking place.

THE SELLER

What are the key issues that affect the salesperson in the organizational buying context? Many of the points presented in Chapter 15, "Salespersons' Influences on Consumer Behavior," are also appropriate for the organizational context. The major difference is that in this case the *customer's perspective* is that of an organizational buying center, and the salesperson needs to adapt to this.

The importance of the types of customers on the selling task is nicely illustrated in Table 21-2.[15] This summarizes a study of which sales skills are most important, according to industrial salespersons themselves. Notice that the priorities given by salespersons who work for manufacturers are different from those who work for industrial distributors. This is due to the differences in the sales tasks that each type of sales-

Table 21-2 How Priority Sales Skills Differ by Customers

Priority Skills for Distributors' Salespersons	Priority Skills for Manufacturers' Salespersons
1. Time management habits	1. Skill in listening
2. Tempering optimism with reality	2. Ability to establish goals
3(T). Skill in solving customer problems	3. Effective communication
3(T). Ability to field questions	4. Develop continuing rapport
3(T). Develop continuing rapport	5. Time management habits
3(T). Effective communication	6. Apply judicious judgment
3(T). Courteous communication	7. High ethical standards
3(T). Skill in listening	8. Ability to field questions

SOURCE: See Note 15.

person performs and the customers on whom he or she calls. The manufacturer's salesperson will typically be selling to either larger businesses or distributors, sometimes with customized products. Order quantities can be high, and time may stretch out before a decision is made by the buyer. A distributor's salesperson, on the other hand, is likely to represent many more products (maybe in the thousands), produced by many manufacturers. He or she contacts many more customers, perhaps every factory in a given geographical area. Customers may order from catalog books, especially for smaller items of a standardized nature. For many distributor salespersons, then, the emphasis is more on "servicing" accounts than on "selling" to them.

❧ *Premier Relay Without Delay Saves the Day*

One afternoon the phone rang in the offices of Premier Industrial, a parts distributor in Los Angeles. An emergency request came from the manager of a Caterpillar tractor plant in central Illinois: a $10 electric relay had broken, idling the entire assembly line. Could Premier find a replacement and get it there as soon as possible? Yes: part located, rushed onto a plane, flown to St. Louis, driven across Illinois, put in place, assembly line back in operation by 10:30 that same evening. In the words of a grateful Caterpillar executive, "You can't build tractors if you can't move the line...they really saved us a whole lot of money." According to Premier's chairman, whose firm stocks 250,000 industrial parts and charges up to 50 percent more than its competitors, "To us, customer service is the main event."[16]

The Value of Trust

Customer trust: A willingness to rely on a seller to serve the best interests of the buyer: a key determinant of the long-term success of a salesperson.

Swan and Trawick have examined how industrial salespeople gain the trust of their customers.[17] As indicated by the high ranking of "develop continuing rapport" in Table 21-2, the issue of trust is a key determinant of success in establishing long-term relationships between buyers and suppliers. **Customer trust** develops from five attributes of a salesperson: *dependability, honesty, competence, customer orientation,* and *likability.* The more a salesperson exhibits these five characteristics, the more he or she is perceived as trustworthy. Salespeople report that when they are perceived as trustworthy, the relationship with customers is more open and less strained. This is especially helpful for "accessibility," as in making appointments or making product suggestions to the purchasing agent.

Establishing trustworthiness takes time and occurs over a series of sales calls. Also, after an initial sale, the postsale follow-up allows the salesperson to prove his or her trustworthiness by ensuring timely delivery of an order or by making sure that the customer's order is not "short-shipped" (shipping a lesser quantity than ordered). These kinds of concrete demonstrations of trust can be beneficial to both buyer and seller by turning a new buy situation into a less time-consuming (and less competitive) rebuy situation.

Since many organizational purchases turn into rebuy or repeat purchases, the establishment of a trusting relationship can save time and money for both the buying and selling organizations.[18] For the buyer, for example, it can reduce the risk of purchasing a large quantity of a product which is inferior or not delivered on time. *Risk reduction* on large purchases can be a significant factor in the decision process.

Let's listen in again on the retail clothes buyer, Linda H., and see what she reports about trust in buyer-supplier relationships:

> **Q.** *What are the characteristics of a trustworthy supplier?*
>
> **A.** *Honesty.* He's up-front. *Follow-through.* He takes an interest in the account and how it's performing. He's interested in us because we're partners and it's profitable for both companies. He *services the account.* He makes sure that reorders are available if the item sells well. He fights for deliveries on time and for me to get the lowest possible price.
>
> **Q.** *What do you do to encourage "trust" from a supplier?*
>
> **A.** I lay my cards on the table. Since I'm not locked into a resource [supplier] structure, I have a free hand with resources. When you're talking to a resource, you sense that honesty is present in the relationship. Trust is a growing process and through experience you learn who you can't trust.

Ethics: A Serious Concern

Related to the issue of trust is concern for **ethical behavior** among organizational buyers. Ethical behavior refers to actions that are carried out in accordance with a personal code of justice and morality—a code that also does not violate acceptable standards of society as a whole.

In any exchange relationship, we should recognize that both the buyer and the seller hold certain *expectations*. Basically, the buyer trusts the seller to deliver a product or service in a timely fashion and to bill at the price agreed upon. The seller also trusts the buyer to honor negotiated prices and to keep confidences about the purchase negotiations.

Because of severe competition, however, many questionable practices can arise on the part of both sellers *and* buyers. In one survey, for example, an overriding concern about problems was discovered.[19] Purchasing managers and sales managers alike expressed an interest in ethical practices. Padding expense accounts and giving gifts to make a sale were two issues of concern to both sides.

Trust and ethical issues thus are critical to the purchase process; however, in the actual course of conducting business, there are often no clear and easy solutions to the problems that arise concerning these issues. Awareness of the possibility of problems and practice in resolving hypothetical situations is clearly important for

Ethical behavior: Actions carried out in accordance with a socially acceptable personal code of justice and morality.

business professionals. (If you would like to read more about these issues, you may wish to begin with Note 20.)

■ SUMMARY

BACKGROUND ON ORGANIZATIONAL BUYING

Although organizational buying behavior displays both similarities and differences when compared to individual consumer buying behavior, it has been treated in this chapter as primarily a separate activity. A key characteristic of this topic is that the organizational buyer acts within the context of a larger group—the organization—that affects how and why decisions are made. The primary objective of this chapter was to understand and characterize organizational buying, both as a process and as buyer behavior.

The first section of the chapter defined organizational buying in terms of similarities and differences with consumer behavior as represented in the rest of this text. Similarities included the meeting of needs through the purchase process and the search for information about products that would satisfy that need. The key differences noted were that the organizational buyer is not usually the end user of the product and that the purchase decision within an organization is often made by a group of people. This section also reviewed the types of organizations that make purchases and, in effect, provided a possible segmentation scheme for the market. We then examined the three types of buy situations: (1) new buy, (2) straight rebuy, and (3) modified rebuy.

THE PROCESS OF ORGANIZATIONAL BUYING

In the next section, we discussed the various models that are used to describe what goes on within the decision-making unit in a buying center. They ranged from a description of the roles and stages in the process and how they are affected by the buying situation, Buygrid-Buyphase, to a more complex model by Webster and Wind that included variables both internal and external to the organization. Other more recent models were also discussed to focus on the personal social networks within the organization that may affect the buying process.

ORGANIZATIONAL BUYER AND SELLER BEHAVIOR

The organizational buyer and seller were highlighted in a separate section. The psychology of the decision maker was cited as a fundamental factor in an organizational purchase decision, much as it is in an individual consumer purchase decision. Again, however, the joint nature of the decision process causes a variety of other influences to come into play. A model was presented to illustrate the process from the individual perspective. A second model included the seller as a part of the purchase or buying dyad and focused on the nature of the exchanges that are taking place. In the final section of the chapter, we examined the role of the seller. Here we noted some of the priority skills needed for selling to organizations, and then discussed the need for trust in the relationship between the members of the dyad and ethical behavior in organizational buying.

■ KEY TERMS

organizational buying	modified rebuy	environmental factors	"exchange model"
decision-making unit (DMU)	new buy	organizational determinants	buyer-seller dyad
specifications	buying center	interpersonal determinants	customer trust
organization	relationship marketing	individual participants	ethical behavior
straight rebuy			

■ REVIEW QUESTIONS AND EXPERIENTIAL EXERCISES

[E = Application extension or experiential exercise]

1. Summarize the major similarities and differences between consumer buying and organizational buying.

2. Suggest examples of the three types of organizational purchases—straight rebuy, modified rebuy, and new buy. Indicate the product, the purchasing agency, and any situational circumstances that might cause the purchase to be classed in one category and not in another.

3. Discuss how environmental factors—those outside of the organization—can affect an organizational purchase.

4. Why is the behavior of individuals such an important part of understanding what goes on within the buying center? Discuss in terms of both individuals and dyads.

5. How does trust enter into a typical organizational buying situation?

6. Can you identify organizational buying situations in which ethical issues might arise? Such situations often appear in the media; can you think of a recent prominent case?

7. [E] In your library find the *Standard Industrial Classification Manual* and list the major divisions. Then locate the *Census of Manufacturers* and choose five products that might be sold in an organizational buying situation. List the value of product shipped and other geographic (for your region) information about those products.

8. [E] Consult the following articles about DMUs and prepare a brief report about the main points of each article:

   a. Anita M. Kennedy, "The Complex Decision to Select a Supplier: A Case Study," *Industrial Marketing Management*, Vol. 12 (1983), pp. 45–56.

   b. Jim Holden, "Selling to Buying Committees: Separating the Rubber Stamps in a Politically Charged Environment," *Business Marketing*, December 1983, pp. 30–36.

9. [E] Interview a purchasing agent or organizational buyer in your community. They can be employed by manufac-turing, service, or retail entities, but don't forget governmental organizations such as schools, county-city agencies, or hospitals. Concentrate your questions on whom they consult when making buying decisions, what kind of information they collect and from where, and how a final decision is made.

10. [E] Locate a formal organizational chart for a business or agency. Your own college or university might be an interesting example. Select a particular purchase situation and try to decide where you might find initiators, influencers, gatekeepers, users, buyers, and deciders within the organization. Identify and interview a salesperson who calls on this organization. Write a brief report on your findings.

11. [E] Use your library's reference section to locate articles on business ethics written within the past few years. Read several that are likely to deal with issues that arise between organizational purchasers and salespersons (alternatively, you may wish to consult the Laczniak and Murphy book referenced in Note 20 as a source for this reading). Prepare a brief report on your findings.

12. [E] A competitor's disgruntled employee has just mailed you plans for what looks like a promising new product. Do you

   a. Throw the plans away?

   b. Send them to your research department for analysis?

   c. Notify your competitor about this?

   d. Call the FBI?

   For more details, and one case answer, see Kevin Kelly, "When a Rival's Trade Secret Crosses Your Desk," *Business Week*, May 20, 1991, p. 48.

13. [E] As we noted in Chapter 12, the fact that customs and laws differ around the world makes for a challenging ethical environment for marketers selling in the international marketplace. Using your reference library, locate some recent articles on this topic. Write a brief report on your findings.

■ SUGGESTED READING

■ For two excellent real-world looks at aspects of this topic, see Harvey B. MacKay, "The CEO Hits the Road (and Other Sales Tales)," *Harvard Business Review*, Vol. 68, No. 2 (March–April 1990), pp. 32–44; and Benson P. Shapiro, V. K. Rangan, and J. J. Sviokla, "Staple Yourself to an Order," *Harvard Business Review*, Vol. 70, No. 4 (July–August 1992), pp. 113–122.

■ For a look at the effects and ethics of providing gifts to industrial purchasers, see Richard F. Beltramini, "Exploring the Effectiveness of Business Gifts: A Controlled Field Experiment," *Journal of the Academy of Marketing Science*, Vol. 20, No. 1 (Winter 1992), pp. 87–92.

■ For a discussion of the expanding status of women as organizational sellers and buyers, see Patrick L. Schul and Brent M. Wren, "The Emerging Role of Women in Industrial Selling: A Decade of Change," *Journal of Marketing*, Vol. 56, No. 3 (July 1992), pp. 38–54.

■ For good readings on specific issues, see the Notes.

NOTES

Here it is—the section you have all been waiting for! Welcome to the fascinating world of Notes! Here you will find the references from which the findings and reports in the book have been drawn. Beyond this, however, you will also find pathways for further reading in areas that may be particularly interesting to you. At some points you will be offered brief extensions of text discussions, at some points specific answers to questions raised in the text, and at some points extensive reading lists that trace the development of thought and findings on key topics in consumer behavior. Therefore, if you are able to spend some time looking through the relevant notes for each chapter, you will see numerous opportunities for customizing your learning experience by reading further about both concepts and marketing applications.

Please be aware that this Notes section is organized by chapters, so be sure that you have the correct chapter heading when searching for a particular note number. Please note also that the references have been listed with the assumption that you will have access to a college library that possesses the source materials. Two of the most commonly cited sources are *Advances in Consumer Research*, which is published on a yearly basis, and *AMA Educators' Proceedings* which is published twice a year, identified as *Winter* or *Summer* in the citations. If your library wishes to order any volumes, the former is published by the Association for Consumer Research, with offices in Provo, Utah (telephone 801/378-2080); the latter is published by the American Marketing Association, with offices in Chicago (telephone 312/648-0536).

As you will find if you search, this section holds the keys to hours of thrills, fun, mild pleasure, productive reading, and engaging thought. Enjoy!

Chapter 1
The Fascinating Field of Consumer Behavior

1. GNP and consumer spending are estimated from figures provided by the U.S. Department of Commerce. Calculations were performed by this author. Readers should note that these numbers do not include spending for purchases of used goods.

2. For some further readings on relevant topics, see David W. Stewart, "From Methods and Projects to Systems and Process: The Evolution of Marketing Research Techniques," *Marketing Research*, Vol. 3, No. 3 (September 1991), pp. 25–36; J. Walker Smith, "Beyond Anecdotes: Toward a Systematic Model of the Value of Marketing Research," *Marketing Research*, Vol. 3, No. 1 (March 1991), pp. 3–14; Ajay K. Kohli and Bernard J. Jaworski, "Market Orientation: The Construct, Research Propositions, and Managerial Implications," *Journal of Marketing*, Vol. 54, No. 2 (April 1990), pp. 1–18; Stephen Barlas, "Researchers Rally 'Round Customer Focus," *Marketing News*, January 2, 1989, pp. 46–47; and Ruth Ann Smith and Davis

S. Lux, "Historical Method in Consumer Research: Developing Causal Explanations of Changes," *Journal of Consumer Research*, Vol. 19, No. 4 (March 1993), pp. 595–610.

Chapter 2
Marketers' and Consumers' Views

1. "The Gravyest?" *Sales & Marketing Management*, February 6, 1979, p. 19; Nancy Giges, "Smooth & Easy Brand's Short Life Was Anything But . . .," *Advertising Age*, September 10, 1979, pp. 3ff.

2. Adam Smith, *The Wealth of Nations*, 1776 (quoted from 1937 reprinting), as cited in Dick Berry, "The Marketing Concept Revisited," *Marketing News*, July 18, 1988, p. 26.

3. The concept of the marketing mix was proposed by James Culliton of the Harvard Business School, then developed and presented to the field in a classic article by Neil H. Borden, "The

Concept of the Marketing Mix," *Journal of Advertising Research*, Vol. 4, June 1964, pp. 2–7.

4. The "4 P's" framework is another classic presentation in the field. Developed by E. Jerome McCarthy, it appeared in the first edition of his best-selling text, *Basic Marketing: A Managerial Approach* (Homewood, Ill.: Richard D. Irwin, 1960), pp. 45–48. For a recent proposed extension, see Walter van Waterschoot and Christopher Van den Bulte, "The 4P Classification of the Marketing Mix Revisited," *Journal of Marketing*, Vol. 56, No. 4 (October 1992), pp. 83–93.

5. Ford's Taurus design decision, based on extensive consumer research, turned out very well: The Taurus passed the Honda Accord to recapture the title of America's hottest-selling car in 1992. See Jacqueline Mitchell and Neil Templin, "Ford's Taurus Passes Honda's Accord," *The Wall Street Journal*, January 7, 1993, p. B1; Neil Templin, "Ford Bets Its New Taurus Will Thrive with Old Look," *The Wall Street Journal*, September 4, 1991, p. B1; and Kim Foltz, "Marketer of the Year: Ford's Donald Petersen," *Adweek*, August 3, 1987, pp. 12–13.

6. John P. Cortez, "Taco Bell Cooks Up Superbrand," *Advertising Age*, May 24, 1993, p. 44; Stuart Elliott, "Taco Bell Sounds New Round in Price War," *USA Today*, October 29, 1990, p. B1; and Dan Koeppel, "Taco Bell Drops Prices to 39 Cents," *Marketing Week*, June 17, 1991, p. 5.

7. David Arnold, "Video Puts Muscle into Sales Efforts," *Advertising Age*, October 11, 1984, pp. 48–49; and Cara S. Trager, "Video Catalogs a Moving Experience," *Advertising Age*, October 26, 1987, p. S3.

8. Alice Cuneo, "FCB Creativity Bears Fruit," *Advertising Age*, July 6, 1987, p. 25.

9. William L. Wilkie, "A New Framework for Assessing the Context of Marketing Decisions—The '5C's'," Graduate School of Business, University of Florida, Gainesville, Fla., 1985.

10. Krystal Miller, "European Luxury Auto Makers Resort to Discounts in Drive to Jump Start Sales," *The Wall Street Journal*, April 29, 1991, p. B1; "Sterling Motor Leaves USA," *USA Today*, August 12, 1991, p. B2; Ralph Gray, "Future Shock: Too Many Autos, Not Enough Buyers," *Marketing Week*, June 22, 1987, p. 17; and Cleveland Horton and Raymond Serafin, "Automotive Doomsday?" *Advertising Age*, February 22, 1988, p. 36.

For good academic discussions of this topic, see also C. Whan Park and Daniel C. Smith, "Product Class Competitors as Sources of Innovative Marketing Strategies," *The Journal of Consumer Marketing*, Vol. 7, No. 2 (Spring 1990), pp. 27–28; and Peter R. Dickson, "Toward a General Theory of Competitive Rationality," *Journal of Marketing*, Vol. 56, No. 1 (January 1992), pp. 69–83.

11. Alan Adler, "Domino's Founder Fights Contrast of Image, Beliefs," *South Bend Tribune*, October 27, 1991, p. B1.

12. Arthur Buckler, "The Holly Farms' Marketing Error...," *The Wall Street Journal*, February 9, 1988, p. 36.

13. Joanne Lipman, "CNN Ads Get Extra Mileage During the War," *The Wall Street Journal*, February 27, 1991, p. B1; Wayne Walley, "The Mother of All Ratings Jumps," *Advertising Age*, April 8, 1991, p. 35; Wayne Walley, "Popularity Sparks Ad Turmoil at CNN," *Advertising Age*, February 4, 1991, p. 42.

14. "Marketing-Oriented Lever Uses Research to Capture Bigger Dentifrice Market Shares," *Marketing News*, February 10, 1978,

p. 9. For a useful overview of terms and practices, see Vincent P. Barabba, "The Market Research Encyclopedia," *Harvard Business Review*, No. 1 (January–February 1990), pp. 105–116. For recent discussions and examples, see Horst Stipp and Nicholas Schiavone, "Research at a Commercial Television Network: NBC 1990," *Marketing Research*, Vol. 2, No. 3 (September 1990), pp. 3–10; Sabra Brock, Sara Lipson, and Ron Levitt, "Trends in Marketing Research and Development at Citicorp/Citibank," *Marketing Research*, Vol. 1, No. 4 (December 1989), pp. 3–8; Mary Jane Burns and Robert B. Woodruff, "Delivering Value to Consumers: Implications for Strategy Development and Implementation," *AMA Winter Educators' Proceedings* (1992), Vol. 3, pp. 209–216; Mary T. Curren, Valerie S. Folkes, and Joel H. Steckel, "Explanations for Successful and Unsuccessful Marketing Decisions: The Decision Maker's Perspective," *Journal of Marketing*, Vol. 56, No. 2 (April 1992), pp. 18–31; and Lori Mitchell Dixon and Debbera Diehn, "The Challenged Marketing Concept: A Repositioning Strategy for a Concept in the Decline Stage," *AMA Winter Educators' Proceedings* (1992), Vol. 3, pp. 432–440.

For a different style of consumer research, see, for example, Deborah D. Heisley, Mary Ann McGrath, and John F. Sherry, Jr., "'To Everything There Is a Season': A Photoessay of a Farmers' Market," *Advances in Consumer Research*, Vol. 17 (1990), pp. 39–40.

15. David Kiley, "Small Firms Grow Strong on Steady Diet of Data," *Marketing Week*, May 16, 1988, pp. 17ff.

16. Lena Williams, "Decisions, Decisions, Decisions: Enough!" *New York Times*, February 14, 1990, p. B1. For related discussions, see also Kathleen M. Rassuli and Gilbert D. Harrell, "A New Perspective on Choice," *Advances in Consumer Research*, Vol. 17 (1990), pp. 737–744; Amna Kirmani, "The Effect of Perceived Advertising Costs on Brand Perceptions," *Journal of Consumer Research*, Vol. 17, No. 2 (September 1990), pp. 160–171; Horacio Soberon-Ferrer and Rachel Dardis, "Determinants of Household Expenditures for Services," *Journal of Consumer Research*, Vol. 17, No. 4 (March 1991), pp. 385–397; and Mary Frances Luce, "Buying More Than We Can Use: Factors Influencing Forecasts of Consumption Quantity," *Advances in Consumer Research*, Vol. 19 (1991), pp. 584–588.

17. Stephen Brobeck, *U.S. Consumer Knowledge: The Results of a Nationwide Test* (Washington, D.C.: Consumer Federation of America, September 1990); T. O. Stanley, E. T. Garman, and R. D. Brown, "Test of Consumer Competencies," in *Manual of Directions* (Bensenville, Ill.: Scholastic Testing Service, 1976). See also Robert O. Herrmann and Rex H. Warland, "Consumers' Use of Recommended Food Buying Practices," *The Journal of Consumer Affairs*, Vol. 24, No. 2 (Winter 1990), pp. 307–325.

Chapter 3

Demographics and the Consumer Marketplace

1. The story of the development of Pampers is told in "Consumer Choice, the Driving Force of a Market Economy," published by Procter & Gamble, Inc., Cincinnati, Ohio, 1977. The company's estimate of the size of the market was that there were more than 15 billion diaper changes per year in the United States! How successful was the new product? Within six years after its national introduction, Pampers were being worn by half the babies in the United States!

As of the 1990s, the disposable diaper market is worth $3.5 billion, with P&G holding about 50 percent through its Pampers and Luvs brands (Huggies, by Kimberly-Clark, is the leader with a 33 percent share). The average child uses some 7800 diapers during his or her first two and one-half years. One major issue that has emerged, however, is the environmental impact of these products (some 18 billion disposable diapers end up in landfills each year). If you would like to read more about this issue and what P&G has done, see Laurie Freeman, "Procter & Gamble: Case Study," *Advertising Age*, January 29, 1991, p. 16; and Kathleen Deveny, "States Mull Rash of Diaper Regulations," *The Wall Street Journal*, June 15, 1990, p. B1. Your reference librarian can also be helpful in locating recent articles tracking new developments in this area.

2. "Baby Boomlet Seems to Be Letting Up," *The Wall Street Journal*, June 2, 1993, p. B1; Joseph Spiers, "The Baby Boomlet Is for Real," *Fortune*, February 10, 1992, pp. 101–104; Barbara Vobejda, "Keep Those Booties Coming...," *Washington Post National Weekly*, January 28, 1991, p. 39; Thomas Exter, "Birthrate Debate," *American Demographics*, September 1991, p. 55.

For an interesting sidelight discussion on birthdays (did you know that more than normal are in August and September, and are on Tuesdays?), see Judith Waldrop, "The Birthday Boost," *American Demographics*, September 1991, p. 4. For further background on fertility and issues in forecasting it, see Jane Newitt, "How to Forecast Births (and Be Right)," *American Demographics*, January 1985, pp. 30 ff. The data presented in Figure 3-1 represent calculations by the author from data appearing in the *Statistical Abstract of the United States, 1991* (Washington, D.C.: U.S. Government Printing Office, 1991), and "Projections of the Population of the United States, by Age, Sex, and Race, 1983–2080," Current Population Reports, Series P-25, #952.

3. Kim Painter, "Life Expectancy Increases for Blacks, Infants," *USA Today*, August 29, 1991, p. D1; Randolph E. Schmid, "Statistics: National Death Rate Drops to Record Low," Associated Press Wire Service, February 8, 1985.

4. Judy Keen, "Immigration Fast Becoming Issue for '92," *USA Today*, January 3, 1992, p. 4A; *Statistical Abstract of the United States, 1991* (Washington, D.C.: U.S. Government Printing Office, 1991).

5. Figure 3-3 contains author's calculations based upon data presented in the *Statistical Abstract of the United States, 1991*.

6. The following discussion is based on a number of sources discussing population and aging statistics. See, for example, Bickley Townsend, "Boomers Facing 50," *Marketing Research*, Vol. 4, No. 2 (June 1992), pp. 48–49; Joseph O. Rentz and Fred D. Reynolds, "Forecasting the Effects of an Aging Population on Product Consumption: An Age-Periods-Cohort Framework," *Journal of Marketing Research*, Vol. 28 (August 1991), pp. 355–360; Richard C. Leventhal, "The Aging Consumer: What's All the Fuss About Anyway?" *The Journal of Consumer Marketing*, Vol. 8, No. 1 (Winter 1991), pp. 29–34; Louise B. Russell, *The Baby Boom Generation and the Economy* (Washington, D.C.: The Brookings Institution, 1983); and Conrad Taeuber, "A Changing America," *American Demographics*, January 1979, pp. 9–15.

7. Social analysts have not yet agreed upon a single name, birth span, or size for the generation of Americans who have followed the baby boom. For some interesting recent discussions, see "Postboomers: History's Clean-up Brigade?" *USA Today*, May 6, 1993, p. 13A; Scott Donaton, "The Media Wakes Up to Generation X," *Advertising Age*, February 1, 1993, pp. 16–17; "Move Over, Boomers," *Business Week*, December 14, 1992, pp. 75–82; Paul Herbig, William Koehler, and Ken Day, "Marketing to the Baby Bust Generation,"

The Journal of Consumer Marketing, Vol. 10, No. 1 (1993), pp. 4–9; and Bryant Robey, "Busters Will Be Wealthier and Wiser Than Boomers," *Marketing Week*, October 3, 1988, p. 16. For broader implications, interested readers may wish to consult Louis Richman, "The Coming World Labor Shortage," *Fortune*, April 9, 1990, pp. 70ff.

8. Figure 3-4 is adapted from Taeuber, "A Changing America," p. 11.

9. Your reference librarian should be helpful in finding current literature on this topic. In general, *The Chronicle of Higher Education* contains frequent interesting reports on how colleges are trying to deal with enrollment shortfalls, and what marketing techniques have been successful. In this publication see, for example, Michele Collison, "Acceptance Rate Up for This Semester at Many Colleges," November 19, 1991, p. A1; and "Applications Down at Private Campuses, Up at Public Colleges," March 6, 1991, p. A1; and Julie Nicklin, "Liberal-Arts Colleges Face Up to Cost-Saving Measures...," January 30, 1991, p. A25. See also Alan Deutschman, "Why Universities Are Shrinking," *Fortune*, September 24, 1990, pp. 103ff; Brad Edmondson, "Colleges Conquer the Baby Bust," *American Demographics*, September 1987, pp. 27ff; and Ian R. Stewart and Donald G. Dickason, "Hard Times Ahead," *American Demographics*, June 1979, pp. 12–24.

10. Marketing trade publications contain many examples of creative strategies that companies are using to adapt to age shifts in the marketplace. The examples in this exhibit are drawn from Christy Fisher, "Wooing Boomers' Babies," *Advertising Age*, July 22, 1991, p. 3; Elaine Underwood, "Marketing the Halls of Ivy," *Marketing Week*, March 18, 1991, p. 26; "Those Aging Boomers," *Business Week*, May 20, 1991, pp. 106–111; Stuart Elliott, "New Wrinkle in Endorsing...," *New York Times*, October 1, 1991, p. C15; Mariann Caprino, "Middle-age Spread Trims Jeans Sales," *South Bend Tribune*, July 22, 1990, p. D5; Elaine Underwood, "Three Strategies for Reaching Older Consumers in the 1990s," *Marketing Week*, December 3, 1990, pp. 30–31; and Cyndee Miller, "Nostalgia Makes Boomers Buy," *Marketing News*, November 26, 1990, p. 1.

11. Diane Chun, "Can You Read This?" *Gainesville Sun*, August 1, 1982, p. H1.

12. The answers to the mobility questions are (1) 45 million; (2) the average mobility rate has been roughly constant for the past 35 years; (3) about 1 in 6 American consumers will move in any 1 year; (4) 1 out of every 2 consumers will move at least once in any 5-year period; and (5) the average person will move about 12 times in his or her lifetime. For further reading, see Robin A. Higie, Linda L. Price, and Julie Fitzmaurice, "Leaving It All Behind: Service Loyalties in Transition," *Advances in Consumer Research*, Vol. 20 (1993), pp. 656–661; Cathy Goodwin and Murphy Sewall, "Consumer Socialization Associated with Relocation to a New Community: A Framework and Pilot Study," *Advances in Consumer Research*, Vol. 19 (1991), pp. 532–540; and three articles in *Advances in Consumer Research*, Vol. 16 (1989): John Gottko and Paul Sauer, "Toward Development of a Model of the Mediating Effects of Household Geographic Mobility on Consumption, Patronage, and Social Status Mobility," pp. 81–84; John Gottko and Paul Sauer, "Household Geographic Mobility and the Impact on Macro Market Segments," pp. 85–92; and James N. Morgan, "A Conditional Analysis of Movers' Housing Responses," pp. 93–104.

13. Ben Simon, "Success Comes in Numbers," *Advertising Age*, July 20, 1981, pp. S18ff.

14. *Statistical Abstract of the United States, 1988,* p. 20; see also Bryant Robey, "Smaller Populations Expected for Industrial States," *Marketing Week,* February 13, 1989, p. 48.

15. Data in this section are based on *Statistical Abstract of the United States, 1991.*

16. *Statistical Abstract of the United States, 1991,* p. 44.

17. "USA's Changing Households," *USA Today,* June 24, 1993, p. 10A; and Spencer Rich, "Unmarried, with Children," *Washington Post National Weekly,* July 2, 1990, p. 38.

18. "Shifting Marriage and Divorce Patterns," *USA Today,* December 9, 1992, p. 12A; and Carlee Scott, "As Baby Boomers Age, Fewer Couples Untie the Knot," *The Wall Street Journal,* November 7, 1990, p. B1.

19. "People Patterns," *The Wall Street Journal,* November 12, 1990, p. B1; *Statistical Abstract of the United States, 1991,* p. 45; Pamela L. Kiecker, Shelby D. Hunt, and Lawrence Chonko, "Gender, Income Differences, and Marketing: Examining the 'Earning Gap' in Three Areas of Marketing," *Journal of the Academy of Marketing Science,* Vol. 19, No. 2 (Spring 1991), pp. 77–82; Rose M. Rubin, Bobye J. Riney, and David J. Molina, "Expenditure Pattern Differentials between One-Earner and Dual-Earner Households: 1972–1973 and 1984," *Journal of Consumer Research,* Vol. 17, No. 1 (June 1990), pp. 43–52; and Peter Francese, "One-Parent Families Joining a Crowd," *Advertising Age,* August 2, 1984, p. 36.

20. "Ready to Zero In on Census Data," *Advertising Age,* January 28, 1991, p. 16; see also "Inside the Board," *American Demographics,* September 1981, pp. 38–39. For detailed marketing discussions, see Louis G. Pol, "Demographic Contributions to Marketing: An Assessment," *Journal of the Academy of Marketing Science,* Vol. 19, No. 1 (Winter 1991), pp. 53–60; Peter A. Morrison, "Applied Demography: Its Growing Scope and Future Direction," *The Futurist,* Vol. 24, No. 2 (March–April 1990), pp. 9–15; and John W. McCann and David J. Reibstein, "Forecasting the Impact of Socioeconomic and Demographic Change on Product Demand," *Journal of Marketing Research,* Vol. 22 (November 1985), pp. 415 ff.

In addition, there are several books that interested marketers may wish to consult in order to learn more about the role of demographics in marketing decisions. See, for example Diane Crispell, *The Insider's Guide to Demographic Know-How,* 2nd ed. (Ithaca, N.Y.: New Strategist, 1990); Peter Francese and Rebecca Piirto, *Capturing Consumers: How to Target the Hottest Markets of the 1990s* (Ithaca, N.Y.: New Strategist, 1990); and Margaret Ambry, *Consumer Power: How Americans Spend Their Money Today* (Ithaca, N.Y.: New Strategist, 1991) For methodological insights, see also Leslie A. Miller and Theodore Downes-Le Guin, "Reducing Response Error in Consumers' Reports of Medical Expenses: Application of Cognitive Theory to the Consumer Expenditure Interview Survey," *Advances in Consumer Research,* Vol. 17 (1990), pp. 193–197; Barbara A. Bickart, Johnny Blair, Geeta Menon, and Seymour Sudman, "Cognitive Aspects of Proxy Reporting of Behavior," *Advances in Consumer Research,* Vol. 17 (1990), pp. 198–206; and E. Marla Felcher, "Cognitive Models for Behavioral Frequency Survey Questions," *Advances in Consumer Research,* Vol. 17 (1990), pp. 207–211.

21. See Ann Mariano, "This Old House Just Doesn't Cut It Anymore," *Washington Post National Weekly,* August 5, 1991, p. 37; and "The Changing American Family and Its Effect on Real Estate," *Real Estate Today,* June 1981, pp. 52–55.

22. For a current debate, see Jeffrey Trachtenberg, "Largest of All Malls in the U.S. is a Gamble . . . ," *The Wall Street Journal,* October 30, 1990, p. A1. See also Richard Dearworth, "Setting Your Sites," *American Demographics,* February 1979, pp. 21–23; and Martin L. Cohen, "Getting to Know You," *American Demographics,* January 1979, pp. 17–21.

23. See, for example, Marilyn Melia, "Census Bureau Targets Data Users to Help Them Target Their Markets," *Marketing News,* March 4, 1991, p. 14; Hugh M. Cannon and Amir Rashid, "When Do Demographics Help in Media Planning?" *Journal of Advertising Research,* Vol. 30, No. 6 (December 1990/January 1991), pp. 20–26; Patricia Strnad, "Count on Cartography," *Advertising Age,* December 10, 1990, p. 46; and Christy Marshall, "PRIZM Adds Zip to Consumer Research," *Advertising Age,* November 1980, p. 22.

Chapter 4
Market Segmentation

1. Raymond Serafin, "How GM Is Shifting Gears," *Advertising Age,* January 4, 1988, pp. 1 ff.

2. Much of the material in this chapter is based on longer discussions in other works by the author and his colleagues. See especially William L. Wilkie and Joel B. Cohen, *An Overview of Market Segmentation: Behavioral Concepts and Research Approaches* (Cambridge, Mass.: Marketing Science Institute Report 77105, June 1977); and Dipankar Chakravarti, Philip E. Hendrix, and William L. Wilkie, *Market Segmentation Research, Volumes I and II* (Palo Alto, Calif.: EPRI, 1987).

3. Wendell R. Smith, "Product Differentiation and Market Segmentation as Alternative Marketing Strategies," *Journal of Marketing,* Vol. 20 (July 1956), pp. 3–8. For an interesting further discussion, see also Peter R. Dickson and James L. Ginter, "Market Segmentation, Product Differentiation, and Market Strategy," *Journal of Marketing,* Vol. 51 (April 1987), pp. 1–10; David W. Stewart and Michael A. Kamins, "Segmentation in Consumer and Market Research: Applications, Current Issues and Trends," *Advances in Consumer Research,* Vol. 18 (1991), pp. 176–178; and Peter J. Danaher and Roland T. Rust, "Linking Segmentation Studies," *Journal of Advertising Research,* Vol. 32, No. 3 (May/June 1992), pp. 18–23.

4. For an interesting look at the broader topic of consumers and price discrimination, see E. Scott Maynes, "Price Discrimination; Lessons for Consumers," *Advancing the Consumer Interest,* Vol. 2, No. 1 (1990), pp. 22–27. See also Wagner A. Kamakura and Gary J. Russell, "A Probabilistic Choice Model for Market Segmentation and Elasticity Structure," *Journal of Marketing Research,* Vol. 26 (November 1989), pp. 379–390; and Joseph Kamen, "Price Filtering: Restricting Price Deals to Those Least Likely to Buy without Them," *The Journal of Product & Brand Management,* Vol. 1, No. 3 (Summer 1992), pp. 45–51.

5. Nelson Foote, "Market Segmentation as a Competitive Strategy," in Leo Bogart (ed.), *Current Controversies in Marketing Research* (Chicago: Markham, 1969), pp. 129–139. Segmentation is also an important issue in public policy; see, for example, Christine Moorman and Linda Price, "Consumer Policy Remedies and Consumer Segment Interactions," *Journal of Public Policy & Marketing,* Vol. 8 (1989), pp. 181–203.

6. John Koten, "Upheaval in Middle-Class Market Forces Changes in Selling Strategies," *The Wall Street Journal*, March 13, 1987, p. 21 (italics added).

7. For further discussion of the classification system, and of undertaking research to operationalize this system, see the Wilkie and Cohen, and the Chakravarti, Hendrix, and Wilkie references given in Note 2 above.

8. Dennis H. Tootelian and Ralph M. Gaedeke, "The Teen Market: An Exploratory Analysis of Income, Spending, and Shopping Patterns," *The Journal of Consumer Marketing*, Vol. 9, No. 4 (Fall 1992), pp. 35–44; James Cox, "Automakers Now Turn to Women," *USA Today*, June 17, 1988, p. B1; Janet Neiman, "Infiltrating the Women's Market," *Adweek*, July 6, 1987, pp. 18–22. For additional research, see Robin Widgery and Jack McGaugh, "When Men and Women Buy Cars," *AMA Summer Educators' Proceedings (1992)*, pp. 117–118; Joan Meyers-Levy and Brian Sternthal, "Gender Differences in the Use of Message Cues," *Journal of Marketing Research*, Vol. 28 (February 1991), pp. 84–96; Lynn J. Jaffe, "Impact of Positioning and Sex-Role Identity on Women's Responses to Advertising," *Journal of Advertising Research*, Vol. 31, No. 3 (June/July 1991), pp. 57–64; Julia M. Bristor, "Insider versus Outsider: Reflections of a Feminist Consumer," *Advances in Consumer Research*, Vol. 19 (1991), pp. 843–849; Suzana de M. Fontenelle and George M. Zinkhan, "Gender Differences in the Perception of Leisure: A Conceptual Model," *Advances in Consumer Research*, Vol. 20 (1993), pp. 534–540; and Basil G. Englis and Greta Pennell, "Candidates as Engendered Products: Prototypes in Political Person Perception," *Advances in Consumer Research*, Vol. 20 (1933), pp. 565–569.

Age is another demographic measure frequently used for segmentation. For recent research findings on older consumers, for example, see Lisa D. Spiller and Richard A. Hamilton, "Senior Citizen Discount Programs: Which Seniors to Target and Why," *The Journal of Consumer Marketing*, Vol. 10, No. 1 (1993), pp. 42–51; Paula Fitzgerald Bone, "Identifying Mature Segments," *The Journal of Consumer Marketing*, Vol. 8, No. 4 (Fall 1991), pp. 19–32; George P. Moschis, "Marketing to Older Adults," *The Journal of Consumer Marketing*, Vol. 8 No. 4 (Fall 1991),pp. 19–32; George P. Moschis, "Marketing To Older Adults," *The Journal of Consumer Marketing*, Vol. 8, No. 4 (Fall 1991), pp. 33–42; John J. Burnett, "Examining the Media Habits of the Affluent Elderly," *Journal of Advertising Research*, Vol. 31, No. 5 (October/November 1991), pp. 33–41; Rajshekhar G. Javalgi, Edward G. Thomas, and S. R. Rao, "Targeting the Elderly in the Financial Services Marketplace," *AMA Summer Educators' Proceedings* (1991), pp. 749–759; and Ronald E. Milliman and Robert C. Erffmeyer, "Improving Advertising Aimed at Seniors," *Journal of Advertising Research*, Vol. 29, No. 6 (December 1989/January 1990), pp. 31–36. For related discussions, see Robert E. Wilkes, "A Structural Modeling Approach to the Measurement and Meaning of Cognitive Age," *Journal of Consumer Research*, Vol. 19, No. 2 (September 1992), pp. 292–301; and Rose L. Johnson, "Age and Social Activity as Correlates of Television Orientation: A Replication and Extension," *Advances in Consumer Research*, Vol. 20 (1993), pp. 257–261.

9. Douglas M. Stayman and Rohit Deshpande, "Situational Ethnicity and Consumer Behavior," *Journal of Consumer Research*, Vol. 16, No. 3 (December 1989), pp. 361–371; Laurie P. Cohen, "Slowdown in Advertising to Blacks Strains Black Ad Firms and Media," *The Wall Street Journal*, March 23, 1988, p. 27; and Laura Bird, "Most Marketers Missing Out on Black Buyers," *The Wall Street Journal*,

April 9, 1993, p. B1. For further findings, see Ronald E. Goldsmith, J. Dennis White, and Melvin T. Stith, "Values of Middle-Class Blacks and Whites: A Replication and Extension," *Psychology & Marketing*, Vol. 4 (Summer 1987), pp. 135–144; Judy Cohen and Carol Kaufman, "Consumption Choice within the Black Extended Family Network," *Advances in Consumer Research*, Vol. 19 (1991), pp. 338–345; Thaddeus H. Spratlen, "Targeting Blacks in Cigarette Advertising: Knowledge of Externalities Using Secondary Research," *AMA Winter Educators' Proceedings* (1992), Vol. 3, pp. 517–524; Jerome D. Williams, "Reflections of a Black Middle-Class Consumer: Caught between Two Worlds or Getting the Best of Both?" *Advances in Consumer Research*, Vol. 19 (1991), pp. 850–856; and Jerome D. Williams, "Alcohol Promotion & Ethnic Minority Target Marketing: A Review of Policy & Research Issues," in *Proceedings of the 1993 Public Policy and Marketing Conference* (East Lansing: Michigan State University, Eli Broad Graduate School of Management, 1993), pp. 69–70.

10. "Monitoring Hispanic Minds," *Marketing Week*, March 14, 1988, p. 29; Jack Fuerer, "To Segment or Not to Segment?" *Marketing Week*, April 11, 1988, p. 17; and Jose deCorboa, "More Firms Court Hispanic Consumers—But Find Them a Tough Market to Target," *The Wall Street Journal*, February 18, 1988, p. 25. For related analyses and discussions, see Humberto Valencia, "Developing an Index to Measure Hispanicness," *Advances in Consumer Research*, Vol. 12 (1985), pp. 118–121; Joel Saegert, Robert Hoover, and Marye T. Hilger, "Characteristics of Mexican-American Consumers," *Journal of Consumer Research*, Vol. 12 (June 1985), pp. 104–109; Sigfredo A. Hernandez and Carol J. Kaufman, "Marketing Research in Hispanic Barrios: A Guide to Survey Research," *Marketing Research*, Vol. 2, No. 1 (March 1990), pp. 11–27; Van R. Wood and Roy Howell, "A Note on Hispanic Values and Subcultural Research: An Alternative View," *Journal of the Academy of Marketing Science*, Vol. 19, No. 1 (Winter 1991), pp. 61–68; Jerome D. Williams and Francis J. Mulhern, "Using Retail Scanner Data to Analyze Effects of Price Promotions on Hispanic Purchasing Behavior," in C. Haugtvedt and D. Rosen (eds.), *Proceedings of the Society for Consumer Psychology* (Knoxville: D. W. Schumann, 1991), pp. 25–26; Geraldine Fennell, Joel Saegert, Francis Piron, and Rosemary Jimenez, "Do Hispanics Constitute a Market Segment?" *Advances in Consumer Research*, Vol. 19 (1991), pp. 28–33; Naveen Donthu and Joseph Cherian, "Hispanic Consumption: The Impact of Strong and Weak Ethnic Identification," *AMA Summer Educators' Proceedings* (1992), pp. 339–340; and Blanca N. Fuertes and Ruth B. Smith, "Research Challenges: Are Conventional Data Collection Methods Adequate for Hispanic Elderly?" *AMA Winter Educators' Proceedings* (1993) Vol. 4, pp. 71–77.

11. Bryant Robey, "California's Growth Now Comes from Abroad," *Marketing Week*, May 22, 1989, p. 44.

12. Michel J. Bergier, "Predictive Validity of Ethnic Identification Measures: An Illustration of the English/French Classification Dilemma in Canada," *Journal of the Academy of Marketing Science*, Vol. 14, No. 2 (Summer 1986), pp. 37–42. See also Charles Schaninger, Jacques Bourgeois, and W. Christian Buss, "French-English Canadian Subcultural Consumption Differences," *Journal of Marketing*, Vol. 49 (Spring 1985), pp. 82–92; Chankon Kim, Michel Laroche, and Brenda Lee, "Development of an Index of Ethnicity Based on Communication Patterns among English and French Canadians," *Journal of International Consumer Marketing*, Vol. 2, No. 2 (1989), pp. 43–60; and Annamma Joy and Ruby Dholakia,

"Ethnicity and Consumption: South Asians in the Canadian Mosaic," *AMA Winter Educators' Proceedings* (1992), Vol. 3, p. 363.

13.   For a brief overview, see Cyndee Miller, "Researcher Says U.S. Is More of a Bowl Than a Pot," *Marketing News*, May 10, 1993, p. 6. For general background research on race and ethnic groups, see Milton J. Yinger, "Ethnicity," *Annual Review of Psychology*, Vol. 11, pp. 151–180. For historical background in marketing, see Frederick D. Sturdivant, "Subculture Theory: Poverty, Minorities and Marketing," in S. Ward and T. Robertson (eds.), *Consumer Behavior: Theoretical Sources* (Englewood Cliffs, N.J.: Prentice Hall, 1973), pp. 469–520. For recent reports on specific topics, see the listings in Notes 9 through 12 above, and Chankon Kim, Michel Laroche, and Annamma Joy, "An Empirical Study of the Effects of Ethnicity on Consumption Patterns in a Bi-Cultural Environment," *Advances in Consumer Research*, Vol. 17 (1990), pp. 839–846; Nejdet Delener and James P. Neelankavil, "Informational Sources and Media Usage: A Comparison between Asian and Hispanic Subcultures," *Journal of Advertising Research*, Vol. 30, No. 3 (June/July 1990), pp. 45–52; Michel Laroche, Annamma Joy, Michael Hui, and Chankon Kim, "An Examination of Ethnicity Measures: Convergent Validity and Cross-Cultural Equivalence," *Advances in Consumer Research*, Vol. 18 (1991), pp. 150–157; Geraldine Fennell and Joel Saegert, "'Ethnic Segmentation' and Marketing Analysis," in C. Haugtvedt and D. Rosen (eds.), *Proceedings of the Society for Consumer Psychology* (Knoxville: D. W. Schumann, 1991), pp. 16–24; Wei-Na Lee and Koog-Hyang Ro Um, "Ethnicity and Consumer Product Evaluation: A Cross-Cultural Comparison of Korean Immigrants and Americans," *Advances in Consumer Research*, Vol. 19 (1991), pp. 429–436; Bruce de Pyssler, "The Cultural and Political Economy of the Indian Two-Wheeler," *Advances in Consumer Research*, Vol. 19 (1991), pp. 437–442; Johanna P. Zmud and Carlos H. Arce, "The Ethnicity and Consumption Relationship," *Advances in Consumer Research*, Vol. 19 (1991), pp. 443–449; Wei-Na Lee, "The Cultivation Effects on Consumer Perception of Affluence: A Cross-Cultural Comparison among Taiwanese Americans, Korean Americans, and Anglo Americans," *AMA Winter Educators' Proceedings* (1992), Vol. 3, p. 364; and Corliss L. Green, "Ethnicity: Its Relationship to Selected Aspects of Consumer Behavior," in Robert L. King (ed.), *Marketing: Perspectives for the 1990s* (Richmond, Va.: Southern Marketing Association, 1992), pp. 106–109.

14.   For excellent overviews of this approach, see Joseph T. Plummer, "The Concept and Application of Life Style Segmentation," *Journal of Marketing*, Vol. 38 (1974), pp. 33–37; and William D. Wells and Stephen C. Cosmas, "Life Styles," in R. Ferber (ed.), *Selected Aspects of Consumer Behavior* (Washington, D.C.: U.S. Government Printing Office, 1977), pp. 299–316; W. Thomas Anderson, Jr., and Linda L. Golden, "Lifestyle and Psychographics: A Critical Review and Recommendation," *Advances in Consumer Research*, Vol. 11 (1984), pp. 405–411; William D. Wells, "Attitudes and Behavior: Lessons from the Needham Life Style Study," *Journal of Advertising Research*, Vol. 25 (February–March 1985), pp. 40–44; and Ernest Dichter, "Whose Lifestyle Is It Anyway?" *Psychology & Marketing*, Vol. 3 (Fall 1986), pp. 151–164.

For more recent discussions and findings, see John L. Lastovicka, John P. Murry, Jr., and Eric Joachimsthaler, "Evaluating the Measurement Validity of Lifestyle Typologies with Qualitative Measures and Multiplicative Factoring," *Journal of Marketing Research*, Vol. 27 (February 1990), pp. 11–23; Stephen W. McDaniel and John J. Burnett, "Targeting the Evangelical Market Segment,"

Journal of Advertising Research, Vol. 31, No. 4 (August/September 1991), pp. 26–33; Susan Fournier, David Antes, and Glenn Beaumier, "Nine Consumption Lifestyles," *Advances in Consumer Research*, Vol. 19 (1991), pp. 329–337; and Martha T. Moore, "Courting the Gay Market," *USA Today*, April 23, 1993, p. B1.

15.   A detailed description of these findings is provided in Sunil Mehrotra and William D. Wells, "Psychographics and Buyer Behavior: Theory and Recent Empirical Findings," in A. Woodside, J. Sheth, and P. Bennett (eds.), *Consumer and Industrial Buying Behavior* (New York: Elsevier/North Holland, 1977), pp. 54–55.

16.   William D. Wells "Psychographics: A Critical Review," *Journal of Marketing Research*, Vol. 12 (May 1975), pp. 196–213. See also Jack A. Lesser and Marie Adele Hughes, "The Generalizability of Psychographic Market Segments across Geographic Locations," *Journal of Marketing*, Vol. 50 (January 1986), pp. 18–27.

17.   Two early papers credited with laying the foundations for psychographics research were written in 1966, one by Edgar Pessemier and Douglas Tigert and the other by Clark Wilson, a research director at a major advertising agency. See Sunil Mehrotra and William D. Wells, "Psychographics and Buyer Behavior: Theory and Recent Empirical Findings," in *Consumer and Industrial Buying Behavior*, pp. 49–65.

18.   Joseph Pernica, "The Second Generation of Market Segmentation Studies: An Audit of Buying Motivations," in W. Wells (ed.), *Life Style and Psychographics* (Chicago: American Marketing Association, 1973), pp. 277–313.

19.   See especially an interesting book, Rebecca Piirto, *Beyond Mind Games* (Ithaca, N.Y.: American Demographics Books, 1991); and the fine discussion in William D. Wells, "Psychographics: A Critical Review," *Journal of Marketing Research*, Vol. 12 (May 1975), pp. 196–213.

20.   James Atlas, "Beyond Demographics," *Atlantic Monthly*, October 1984, pp. 49–58.

21.   These findings are reported in Marion Long, "Food for Thought," *Family Weekly*, June 10, 1984, p. 22. For recent research findings on geographic segmentation, see, for example, Lynn R. Kahle, Ruiming Liu, and Harry Watkins, "Psychographic Variation across United States Geographic Regions," *Advances in Consumer Research*, Vol. 19 (1991), pp. 346–352; Lynn R. Kahle, "The Nine Nations of North America and the Value Basis of Geographic Segmentation," *Journal of Marketing*, Vol. 50 (April 1986), pp. 37–47; U. N. Umesh, "Transferability of Preference Models across Segments and Geographic Areas," *Journal of Marketing*, Vol. 51 (January 1987), pp. 59–70; and James W. Gentry, Patriya Tansuhaj, L. Lee Manzer, and Joby John, "Do Geographic Subcultures Vary Culturally?" *Advances in Consumer Research*, Vol. 15 (1988), pp. 411–417.

22.   Alan B. Miller, Jr., "L. A. Consumer Thinks Rice Is Nice but Nixes Bacon Mixes," *Advertising Age*, March 22, 1982, pp. M22–25; and Alan B. Miller, Jr., "They Like Their Tea Iced, Their Waffles Frozen," *Advertising Age*, May 31, 1982, pp. M6–27.

23.   Michael J. McCarthy, "Marketers Zero In on Their Customers," *The Wall Street Journal*, March 18, 1991, p. B1.

24.   The examples provided here are given in Stuart Elliott, "Marketers Say Clusters Are Us," *USA Today*, March 16, 1989, pp. B1 ff.

25.   Raymond Serafin and Cleveland Horton, "Buick Ads Target ZIP Codes," *Advertising Age*, April 1, 1991, p. 1.

26. Russell I. Haley, "Benefit Segmentation: A Decision-Oriented Research Tool," *Journal of Marketing*, July 1968, pp. 30–35.

27. Susan Moffatt, "Japan's New Personalized Production," *Fortune*, October 22, 1990, pp. 132–135.

28. The literature in this area tracks research developments well. Some good articles include Haley (Note 26 above); Russell I. Haley, "Beyond Benefit Segmentation," *Journal of Advertising Research*, Vol. 11 (August 1971), pp. 3–8; Russell I. Haley, "Benefit Segments: Backwards and Forwards," *Journal of Advertising Research*, Vol. 24 (February–March 1984), pp. 19–25; Richard M. Johnson, "Market Segmentation: A Strategic Management Tool," *Journal of Marketing Research*, Vol. 8 (February 1971), pp. 13–18; Paul E. Green, Yoram Wind, and Arun K. Jain, "Benefit Bundle Analysis," *Journal of Advertising Research*, April 1972, pp. 31–36; William L. Wilkie and Joel B. Cohen, "An Overview of Market Segmentation: Behavioral Concepts and Research Approaches," Working Paper Series, Marketing Science Institute, Cambridge, Mass., 1977; Roger J. Calantone and Alan G. Sawyer, "The Stability of Benefit Segments," *Journal of Marketing Research*, Vol. 16 (August 1978); pp. 395 ff; Girish Punj and David W. Stewart, "Cluster Analysis in Marketing Research: Review and Suggestions for Applications," *Journal of Marketing Research*, Vol. 20 (1982), pp. 134 ff; and Russell I. Haley, "Benefit Segmentation—20 Years Later," *The Journal of Consumer Marketing*, Vol. 1, No. 2 (1984), pp. 5–13. For recent applications and methodological advances, see also Ronald Hoverstad, Charles W. Lamb, Jr., and Patrick Miller, "College Benefit Segmentation Analysis: Approach and Results," *Advances in Consumer Research*, Vol. 16 (1989), pp. 332–338; James W. Harvey, "Benefit Segmentation for Fund Raisers," *Journal of the Academy of Marketing Science*, Vol. 18, No. 1 (Winter 1990), pp. 77–86; Paul E. Green and Abba Krieger, "Segmenting Markets with Conjoint Analysis," *Journal of Marketing*, Vol. 55 (October 1991), pp. 20–31; and James B. Wiley, "A Strategy for A Priori Segmentation in Conjoint Analysis," *Advances in Consumer Research*, Vol. 20 (1993), pp. 142–148.

29. This concept is introduced in Peter R. Dickson, "Person-Situation: Segmentation's Missing Link," *Journal of Marketing*, Vol. 46 (Fall 1982), pp. 52–64. The examples provided are drawn from Kathy Wussler, "McDonald's, Turner Team for McD-TV," *Marketing Week*, November 18, 1991, p. 5; Allison Cowan and Edward Gargan, "Mirage of Discount Air Fares Is Frustrating to Many Fliers," *New York Times*, April 22, 1991, p. A1; and Stephanie Goodman, "Dinner is Served—at the Mall," *Marketing Week*, July 24, 1989, pp. 30ff. See also Joel S. Bubow, "Occasion-based vs. User-based Benefit Segmentation: A Case Study," *Journal of Advertising Research*, Vol. 32 (March/April 1992), pp. 11–18.

30. "A Pilot Study of Brand Differentiation" (Mamaroneck, N.Y.: Starch INRA Hooper, 1988). For a detailed review of related managerial options and developments in the retail sector, see David J. Curry, "Single-Source Systems: Retail Management Present and Future," *Journal of Retailing*, Vol. 65 (Spring 1989), pp. 1–20. See also Michelle A. Morganosky, "Cost versus Convenience-Oriented Consumers: Demographic, Lifestyle, and Value Perspectives," *Psychology & Marketing*, Vol. 3 (Spring 1986), pp. 35–46; James B. Hunt and Mark G. Dunn, "The Impact of Demographics and Usage Variables on Perceptions toward Emergency Care Clinics," *AMA Summer Educators' Proceedings* (1987), pp. 76–81; and Rajiv Grover and V. Srinivasan, "An Approach for Tracking Within-Segment Shifts in Market Shares," *Journal of Marketing Research*, Vol. 26 (May 1989), pp. 230–236.

31. Rebecca Piirto, *Beyond Mind Games* (Ithaca, NY: American Demographics Books, 1991), pp. 229–231. For related topics of studies in the academic literature, see Ken Kono, "Are Generics Buyers Deal-Prone? On a Relationship between Generics Purchase and Deal-Proneness," *Journal of the Academy of Marketing Science*, Vol. 13 (Winter 1985), pp. 62–74; Kapil Bawa and Robert W. Shoemaker, "The Coupon-Prone Consumer: Some Findings Based on Purchase Behavior across Product Classes," *Journal of Marketing*, Vol. 51 (October 1987), pp. 99–110; David M. Szymanski and Paul S. Busch, "Identifying the Generics-Prone Consumer: A Meta-Analysis," *Journal of Marketing Research*, Vol. 24 (November 1987), pp. 425–431; E. W. Boatwright, J. Steven Kelly, and William Haueisen, "Off-Price and Outlet Malls: A Profile of 'Heavy' Shoppers," *AMA Summer Educators' Proceedings* (1988), pp. 237–241; and Lucille Pointer, "A Profile of the Deal Prone Consumer: The Role of Moderating Factors," in Robert L. King (ed.), *Marketing: Perspectives for the 1990s* (Richmond, Va.: Southern Marketing Association, 1992), pp. 65–69.

32. Examples are from Kathleen Deveny, "Segments of One," *The Wall Street Journal*, March 22, 1991, p. B4; and Nancy Youman, "Getting to Know You: Data-Base Age Dawns," *Marketing Week*, February 8, 1988, pp. 1 ff. See also David C. Schmittlein, Lee G. Cooper, and Donald G. Morrison, "Truth in Concentration in the Land of (80/20) Laws," *Marketing Science*, Vol. 12, No. 2 (Spring 1993), pp. 167–183; S. Ram and Hyung-Shik Jung, "The Conceptualization and Measurement of Product Usage," *Journal of the Academy of Marketing Science*, Vol. 18, No. 1 (Winter 1990), pp. 67–76; David W. Stewart, "Consumer Self-Selection and Segments of One: The Growing Role of Consumers in Segmentation," *Advances in Consumer Research*, Vol. 18 (1991), pp. 179–186; and Arch G. Woodside and Praveen K. Soni, "Direct-Response Advertising Information: Profiling Heavy, Light and Nonusers," *Journal of Advertising Research*, Vol. 31, No. 6 (December 1991), pp. 26–36.

33. Gary Levin, "Package-goods Giants Embrace Databases," *Advertising Age*, November 2, 1992, p. 1; Judann Dagnoli, "PM Has New Unit for Database Functions," *Advertising Age*, April 6, 1991; and Stan Rapp, "Cigarette Giants Pioneer Data-Base Marketing in Package Goods," *Marketing News*, December 5, 1988, p. 17.

34. There are a number of interesting articles available in the popular press concerning facets of the consumer privacy debate. See, for example, Alan Radding, "Consumer Worry Halts Data Bases," *Advertising Age*, February 11, 1991, p. 28; Scott Hume, "Consumers Target Ire at Data Bases," *Advertising Age*, May 6, 1991, p. 3; Michael Miller, "Coming Soon to Your Local Video Store, Big Brother," *The Wall Street Journal*, December 26, 1990, p. 9; Daniel Mendel-Black and Evelyn Richards, "They Know Your Name, Bank, and Cereal Number," *Washington Post National Weekly*, January 28, 1991, p. 23; Ellen Schultz, "Worried about Your Financial Life Being Shared? Here's Some Advice," *The Wall Street Journal*, April 25, 1991, p. C1; Evan Schwartz, "Equifax' Exit May Not Tame the Consumer Backlash," *Business Week*, August 26, 1991, p. 30; and Jeffrey Birnbaum, "Curbs on Unsolicited Phone, Fax Messages Clear House," *The Wall Street Journal*, November 19, 1991, p. B1. The Lotus story is further described in Laura Bird, "Amid Privacy Furor, Lotus Kills a Disk," *Marketing Week*, January 28, 1991, p. 9; and Lawrence M. Fisher, "New Data Base Ended by Lotus and Equifax," *New York Times*, January 14, 1991, p. C3. For academic discussions of these issues see, for example, Kevin F. McCrohan, "Information Technology, Privacy, and the Public Good," *Journal of Public Policy*

& Marketing, Vol. 8 (1989), pp. 265–278; Mary Gardiner Jones, "Privacy: A Significant Marketing Issue for the 1990s," *Journal of Public Policy & Marketing*, Vol. 10, No. 1 (Spring 1991), pp. 133–148; Cathy Goodwin, "Privacy: Recognition of a Consumer Right," *Journal of Public Policy & Marketing*, Vol. 10, No. 1 (Spring 1991), pp. 149–166; and Ellen R. Foxman and Paula Kilcoyne, "Information Technology, Marketing Practice, and Consumer Privacy: Ethical Issues," *Journal of Public Policy & Marketing*, Vol. 12, No. 1 (Spring 1993), pp. 106–119.

35. Laura Bird, "Citicorp POS Abandons Coupon Program," *Marketing Week*, December 3, 1990, p. 5; and Laurie Petersen, "Quaker Sues Partner in Aborted Coupon Venture," *Marketing Week*, April 15, 1991, p. 6. See also Mario A. Abate, "Applications and Analyses in Single-Source Data: Experiences of the American Chicle Group Warner Lambert," *Journal of Advertising Research*, Vol. 29, No. 6 (December 1989/January 1990), pp. RC3–RC6.

36. For some short and basic readings about database marketing developments, see Gary Levin, "Data Bases Loom Large for 90s," *Advertising Age*, October 21, 1991, p. 22; Cyndee Miller, "Magic Wand," *Marketing News*, January 7, 1991, p. 48; Howard Schlossberg, "Marketers Moving to Make Data Bases Actionable," *Marketing News*, February 18, 1991, p. 8; Michael Miller, "Data Mills Delve Deep to Find Information about U.S. Consumers," *The Wall Street Journal*, March 14, 1991, p. A1; and Susan Caminiti, "What the Scanner Knows about You," *Fortune*, December 3, 1990, p. 51. For longer, more detailed discussions, see Melvin Prince, "Some Uses and Abuses of Single-Source Data for Promotional Decision Making," *Marketing Research*, Vol. 1, No. 4 (December 1989), pp. 18–22; J. Walker Smith, "The Promise of Single Source—When, Where, and How," *Marketing Research*, Vol. 2, No. 4 (December 1990), pp. 3–5; Blair Peters, "The 'Brave New World' of Single Source Information," *Marketing Research*, Vol. 2, No. 4 (December 1990), pp. 13–21; Verne B. Churchill, "The Role of Ad Hoc Survey Research in a Single Source World," *Marketing Research*, Vol. 2, No. 4 (December 1990), pp. 22–26; Gale D. Metzger. "Single Source: Yes and No (The Backward View)," *Marketing Research*, Vol. 2, No. 4 (December 1990), pp. 27–33; James M. Sinkula, "Some Factors Affecting the Adoption of Scanner-based Research in Organizations," *Journal of Advertising Research*, Vol. 31, No. 2 (April/May 1991), pp. 50–55; and Henry Assael and David F. Poltrack, "Using Single Source Data to Select TV Programs Based on Purchasing Behavior," *Journal of Advertising Research*, Vol. 31, No. 4 (August/September 1991), pp. 9–17.

37. The descriptions and statistics presented in Appendix 4A's discussion of VALS-2 were provided by SRI International, Menlo Park, California.

38. An interesting overview of the history of VALS and the thinking behind the development of VALS-2 is given in the book, Rebecca Piirto, *Beyond Mind Games* (Ithaca, N.Y.: American Demographics Books, 1991). For detailed arguments from marketers and researchers about the usefulness of VALS (original version) see, for example, Sonia Yuspeh, "Syndicated Values/Lifestyles Segmentation Schemes: Use Them as Descriptive Tools, Not to Select Targets," and the response from Brooke Warrick, "SRI's Response to Yuspeh: Demographics Aren't Enough," both in *Marketing News*, May 25, 1984, p. 1; see also Aimee Stern, "Tired of Playing Mind Games," *Marketing Week*, July 13, 1987, pp. 1ff; Marcia Harlik, "A Standing Ovation for VALS," *Marketing Week*, October 12, 1987, p. 12; Lynn R. Kahle, Sharon E. Beatty, and Pamela Homer, "Alternative Measure-

ment Approaches to Consumer Values: The List of Values (LOV) and Values and Life Styles (VALS)," *Journal of Consumer Research*, Vol. 13 (December 1986), pp. 405–409; Sharon E. Beatty, Pamela M. Homer, and Lynn R. Kahle, "Problems with VALS in International Marketing Research: An Example from an Application of the Empirical Mirror Technique," *Advances in Consumer Research*, Vol. 15 (1988), pp. 375–380; Thomas Novak and Bruce MacEvoy, "On Comparing Alternative Segmentation Schemes: The List of Values (LOV) and Values and Lifestyles (VALS)," *Journal of Consumer Research*, Vol. 17 (June 1990), pp. 105–109; Wagner A. Kamakura and Jose Afonso Mazzon, "Value Segmentation: A Model for the Measurement of Values and Value Systems," *Journal of Consumer Research*, Vol. 18, No. 2 (September 1991), pp. 208–218; and Thomas P. Novak, Jan de Leeuw, and Bruce MacEvoy, "Richness Curves for Evaluating Market Segmentation," *Journal of Marketing Research*, Vol. 29, No. 2 (May 1992), pp. 254–267.

39. This report is based on information provided in Rebecca Piirto, *Beyond Mind Games* (Ithaca, N.Y.: American Demographics Books, 1991), pp. 92–94.

Chapter 5

Consumer Motivation (I): Essentials

1. Al Ries and Jack Trout, *Bottom-Up Marketing* (New York: McGraw-Hill, 1989), as quoted in "Turning Marketing Upside-Down," *Advertising Age*, November 28, 1988, p. 36.

2. Burleigh B. Gardner, "The Consumer Mind," *Advertising Age*, July 27, 1981, p. 42.

3. For an entire book describing Dichter's views of the hidden meanings in common consumer products, see Ernest Dichter, *Handbook of Consumer Motivation* (New York: McGraw-Hill, 1964). For shorter descriptions, see Rena Bartos, "Ernest Dichter: Motive Interpreter," *Journal of Advertising Research*, Vol. 17 (June 1977), p. 8; and Katherine Barrett and Richard Green, "Work Motivates Psychoanalyst," *Advertising Age*, November 1, 1984, pp. 43–45. For a classical critical view, see Vance Packard, *The Hidden Persuaders* (New York: Pocket Books, 1957).

4. M. R. Jones, *Nebraska Symposium on Motivation* (Lincoln: University of Nebraska Press, 1955).

5. For an advanced review of this topic, see Richard P. Bagozzi, "The Role of Psychophysiology in Consumer Research," in T. Robertson and H. Kassarjian (eds.), *Handbook of Consumer Behavior* (Englewood Cliffs, N.J.: Prentice Hall, 1991), pp. 124–161.

6. "Recalls: Why So Many Are Flops," *Changing Times*, October 1980, pp. 29 ff.

7. J. Jung, *Understanding Human Motivation: A Cognitive Approach* (New York: Macmillan, 1978); and M. H. Marx and T. Tombaugh, *Motivation* (San Francisco: Chandler, 1967). See also Michael E. Hyland, "Motivational Control Theory: An Integrative Framework," *Journal of Personality and Social Psychology*, Vol. 55, No. 4, pp. 642–551.

8. Edward M. Tauber, "Why Do People Shop?" *Journal of Marketing*, Vol. 36 (October 1972), pp. 46–59. For further readings on related topics, see also Dennis W. Rook, "The Buying Impulse," *Journal of Consumer Research*, Vol. 14 (September 1987), pp. 189–199; Emin Babakus, Peter Tat, and William Cunningham, "Coupon

Redemption: A Motivational Perspective," *The Journal of Consumer Marketing,* Vol. 5 (Spring 1988), pp. 37–44; Lew G. Brown, "The Strategic and Tactical Implications of Convenience in Consumer Product Marketing," *The Journal of Consumer Marketing,* Vol. 6 (Summer 1989), pp. 13–20; William M. Strahle and E. H. Bonfield, "Understanding Consumer Panic: A Sociological Perspective," *Advances in Consumer Research,* Vol. 16 (1989), pp. 567–573; Pay McIntyre, Mark A. Barnett, Richard Harris, James Shanteau, John Skowronski, and Michael Klassen, "Psychological Factors Influencing Decisions to Donate Organs," *Advances in Consumer Research,* Vol. 14 (1987), pp. 331–334; Richard P. Bagozzi and Paul R. Warshaw, "Trying to Consume," *Journal of Consumer Research,* Vol. 17, No. 2 (September 1990), pp. 127–140; Michelle M. Bergadaa, "The Role of Time in the Action of the Consumer," *Journal of Consumer Research,* Vol. 17, No. 3 (December 1990), pp. 289–302; Brent G. Goff and Rajan Nataraajan, "Shopping-Buying Interface: A Typological Exploration," *AMA Winter Educators' Proceedings* (1991), pp. 286–293; Miriam Tatzel, "On Not Liking to Shop for Clothes," in C. Haugtvedt and D. Rosen (eds.), *Proceedings of the Society for Consumer Psychology,* (Knoxville: D. W. Schumann, 1991), pp. 46–53; and Felicia G. Lassk, Rosemary R. Lagace, and Paul J. Solomon, "Emotional Profiles in the Volunteer Market: An Exploratory Study," in Robert L. King (ed.), *Marketing: Perspectives for the 1990s* (Richmond, Va.: Southern Marketing Association, 1993), pp. 366–371.

   9. Ronald Alsop, "Advertisers Put Consumers on the Couch," *The Wall Street Journal,* May 13, 1988, p. 17. For a related discussion, see J. H Flynn, "Qualitative Research in Advertising: When to Do What," *Advances in Consumer Research,* Vol. 18 (1991), pp. 280–283.

   10. For two interesting readings on marketers' use of qualitative research, see Rebecca Piirto, *Beyond Mind Games: The Marketing Power of Psychographics* (Ithaca, N.Y.: American Demographics Books, 1991), pp. 124–141; and Bernice Kanner, "Mind Games," *Marketing Insights,* Spring 1990, pp. 50–58. For related implications for consumer research, see Martin Weinberger, "Seven Perspectives on Consumer Research," *Marketing Research,* Vol. 1, No. 4 (December 1989), pp. 9–17. For recent analyses and proposals, see Deborah D. Heisley and Sidney J. Levy, "Autodriving: A Photoelicitation Technique," *Journal of Consumer Research,* Vol. 18, No. 3 (December 1991), pp. 257–272; Geraldine Fennell, "The Role of Qualitative Research in Making What the Customer Wants to Buy," *Advances in Consumer Research,* Vol. 18 (1991), pp. 271–279; Jeffrey Durgee, "New Product Ideas from Focus Groups," *The Journal of Product & Brand Management,* Vol. 1, No. 3 (Summer 1992), pp. 24–32; Peter Tuckel, Elaine Leppo, and Barbara Kaplan, "Focus Groups under Scrutiny," *Marketing Research,* Vol. 4, No. 2 (June 1992), pp. 12–18; Naomi R. Henderson, "Trained Moderators Boost the Value of Qualitative Research," *Marketing Research,* Vol. 4, No. 2 (June 1992), pp. 20–23; Janet R. Day and William R. Gombeski, Jr., "Short-Notice Focus Groups," *Marketing Research,* Vol. 4, No. 4 (December 1992), pp. 4–7; Terry Bristol and Edward F. Fern, "Using Qualitative Techniques to Explore Consumer Attitudes: Insights from Group Process Theories," *Advances in Consumer Research,* Vol. 20 (1993), pp. 444–448; and George W. Hunt and Wayne D. Hoyer, "Action Identification Theory: An Examination of Consumers' Behavioral Representations," *Advances in Consumer Research,* Vol. 20 (1993), pp. 449–454.

   11. W. B. Cannon, *The Wisdom of the Body* (New York: W. W. Norton, 1932). For recent overviews, see Richard P. Bagozzi, "The

Role of Psychophysiology in Consumer Research," in T. Robertson and H. Kassarjian (eds.), *Handbook of Consumer Behavior* (Englewood Cliffs, N.J.: Prentice Hall, 1991), pp. 124–161; and James A. Muncy, "Physiological Responses of Consumer Emotions: Theory, Methods, and Implications for Consumer Research," *AMA Summer Educators' Proceedings* (1987), pp. 127–132. For related discussions, see Kevin G. Celuch and Linda S. Showers, "It's Time to Stress *Stress.* The Stress-Purchase/Consumption Relationship: Suggestions for Research," *Advances in Consumer Research,* Vol. 18 (1991), pp. 284–289; Dana-Nicoleta Lascu, "Consumer Guilt: Examining the Potential of a New Marketing Construct," *Advances in Consumer Research,* Vol. 18 (1991), pp. 290–295; Lawrence R. Lepisto, J. Kathleen Stuenkel and Linda K. Anglin, "Stress, an Ignored Situational Variable," *Advances in Consumer Research,* Vol. 18 (1991), pp. 296–302; and Robert Cameron, "Everyday Behavior Theory: Activation Based Behavior Originating Systems," in T. J. Page, Jr., and S. E. Middlestadt (eds.), *Proceedings of the Society for Consumer Psychology,* (Clemson, S.C.: CtC Press, 1992), pp. 19–22.

   12. This section is based on discussions in Harold H. Kassarjian, "Field Theory in Consumer Behavior," in S. Ward and T. Robertson (eds.), *Consumer Behavior: Theoretical Sources* (Englewood Cliffs, N.J.: Prentice Hall, 1973), pp. 118–140; and Bernard Weiner, *Human Motivation* (New York: Holt, Rinehard & Winston, 1980), pp. 141–177. For a recent related discussion, see Nancy M. Ridgway, Scott A. Dawson, and Peter H. Bloch, "Pleasure and Arousal in the Marketplace: Interpersonal Differences in Approach-Avoidance Responses," *Marketing Letters,* Vol. 1, No. 2 (June 1990), pp. 139–148.

   13. Ivan Ross, "Perceived Risk and Consumer Behavior: A Critical Review," *Advances in Consumer Research,* Vol. 2 (1975), pp. 1–19; Mark G. Dunn, Patrick Murphy, and Gerald Skelly, "The Managerial Implications of a Consequence-chaining, Conditional Probability View of Perceived Risk," *AMA Educators' Proceedings* (1984), pp. 72–75; G. R. Dowling, "Perceived Risk: The Concept and Its Measurements," *Psychology & Marketing,* Vol. 3 (Fall 1986), pp. 193–210; Janet E. Oglethorpe and Kent B. Monroe, "Risk Perception and Risk Acceptability in Consumer Behavior: Conceptual Issues and an Agenda for Future Research," *AMA Winter Educators' Proceedings* (1987), pp. 255–260; Robert N. Stone and Frederick W. Winter, "Risk: Is It Still Uncertainty Times Consequences?" *AMA Winter Educators' Proceedings* (1987), pp. 261–265; and Uger Yavas, Glen Riecken, and Emin Babakus, "Efficacy of Perceived Risk as a Correlate of Reported Donation Behavior: An Empirical Analysis," *Journal of the Academy of Marketing Science,* Vol. 21, No. 1 (Winter 1993), pp. 65–70.

   14. Daniel Pearl, "Miami Firm Hopes to Take Out Pain of Going to the Dentist," *The Wall Street Journal,* November 29, 1990, p. A6; see also John S. Hulland and Bonita G. Guther, "The Impact of Information Valence and Congruency on Product and Service Evaluations," *AMA Winter Educators' Proceedings* (1992), pp. 499–504; and Mai Neo and Audrey J. Murrell, "Valenced Emotions in Satisfaction: A Look at Affect in Shopping," *Advances in Consumer Research,* Vol. 20 (1993), pp. 667–672.

   15. For good basic reading in this topic, see John W. Atkinson, *An Introduction to Motivation* (Princeton, N.J.: D. Van Nostrand, 1964); and Joel B. Cohen (ed.), *Behavioral Science Foundations of Consumer Behavior* (New York: Free Press, 1972), pp. 52–58. For discussions closer to the consumer behavior context, see William J. McGuire, "Psychological Motives and Communication Gratification," in J. Blumer and C. Katz (eds.), *The Uses of Mass Communications* (Beverly

Hills, Calif.: Sage, 1974), pp. 167–196; and James R. Bettman, *An Information Processing Theory of Consumer Behavior* (Reading, Mass.: Addison-Wesley, 1979), pp. 43–72.

16. Atkinson, *An Introduction to Motivation*, p. 274.

17. See, for example, Daniel E. Berlyne, *Conflict, Arousal, and Curiosity* (New York: McGraw-Hill, 1960); M. Venkatesan, "Cognitive Consistency and Novelty Seeking," in S. Ward and T. Robertson (eds.), *Consumer Behavior: Theoetical Sources* (Englewood Cliffs, N.J.: Prentice Hall, 1973), pp. 354–384; L. McAlister and E. A. Pessemier, "Variety Seeking Behavior: An Interdisciplinary Review," *Journal of Consumer Research*, Vol. 9 (December 1982), pp. 311–322; R. A. Mittelstaedt, S. Grossbart, W. Curtis, and S. Devere, "Optimal Stimulation Level and the Adoption Decision Process," *Journal of Consumer Research*, Vol. 3 (September 1976), pp. 84–94; P. S. Raju, "Optimum Stimulation Level: Its Relationship to Personality, Demographics, and Exploratory Behavior," *Journal of Consumer Research*, Vol. 7 (December 1980), pp. 272–282; Russell G. Wahlers and Mark G. Dunn, "Optimal Stimulation Level Measurement and Exploratory Behavior: Review and Analysis," *AMA Winter Educators' Proceedings* (1987), pp. 249–254; William J. Havlena and Susan L. Holak, "The Influence of Variety on the Demand for Bundles of Musical Performances," *Advances in Consumer Research*, Vol. 15 (1988), pp. 22–26; Russell G. Wahlers and Michael J. Etzel, "A Structural Examination of Two Optimal Stimulation Level Measurement Models," *Advances in Consumer Research*, Vol. 17 (1990), pp. 415–425; Denise D. Shoenbachler, Mary Boguslaw and Monica Ganas, "Sensation Seeking Dimensions and Attention to Anti-drug PSAs," *AMA Summer Educators' Proceedings* (1991), pp. 210–218; Debra Treise and David Schumann, "Sensation Seeking as a Moderator of Fear Appeal Effects: The Danger in Living Dangerously," in T. J. Page, Jr., and S. E. Middlestadt (eds.), *Proceedings of the Society for Consumer Psychology* (Clemson, S.C.: CtC Press, 1992), pp. 34–39; and Jan-Benedict E. M. Steenkamp and Hans Baumgartner, "The Role of Optimum Stimulation Level in Exploratory Consumer Behavior," *Journal of Consumer Research*, Vol 19, No. 3 (December 1992), pp. 434–448. For discussions that focus on consumers' pruchase of a variety of brands, see, for example, Itamar Simonson, "The Effect of Purchase Quantity and Timing and Variety-seeking Behavior," *Journal of Marketing Research*, Vol. 27 (May 1990), pp. 150–162; Fred M. Feinberg, Barbara E. Kahn, and Leigh McAlister, "Market Share Response When Consumers Seek Variety," *Journal of Marketing Research*, Vol. 29, No. 2 (May 1992), pp. 227–238; and Itamar Simonson and Russell S. Winer, "The Influence of Purchase Quantity and Display Format on Consumer Preference for Variety," *Journal of Consumer Research*, Vol. 19, No. 1 (June 1992), pp. 133–138.

18. "Creators Keep Cosmo Cookin'," *Advertising Age*, October 24, 1988, pp. S-36–S-38.

19. Virtual reality presents some extremely interesting possibilities for the future. For a good picture, you may wish to begin with Gene Bylinsky, "The Marvels of Virtual Reality," *Fortune*, June 3, 1991, pp. 138–150. See also Cindee Miller, "Interactive Marketing Hits Surrealistic High," *Marketing News*, November 25, 1991, p. 6; Philip Kotler, "The Marketing of Designed Experiences," Working Paper, Northwestern University, Evanston, Ill., April 1984; Blayne Cutler, "Anything for a Thrill," *American Demographics*, August 1988, pp. 38 ff.; and Lenore Skenazy, "Interacting with Your TV," *Advertising Age*, August 29, 1988, p. 52.

20. See, for example, E. C. Hirschman, "Innovativeness, Novelty Seeking, and Consumer Creativity," *Journal of Consumer Research*, Vol. 7 (December 1980), pp. 283–295; M. B. Holbrook and E. C. Hirschman, "The Experiential Aspects of Consumption: Consumer Fantasies, Feelings, and Fun," *Journal of Consumer Research*, Vol. 9 (September 1982), pp. 132–140; E. Hirschman and M. Holbrook, "Hedonic Consumption: Emerging Concepts, Methods and Propositions," *Journal of Marketing*, Vol. 46, No. 3 (Summer 1982), pp. 92–101; O. T. Ahtola, "Hedonic and Utilitarian Aspects of Consumption Behaviors: An Attitudinal Perspective," *Advances in Consumer Research*, Vol. 12 (1985), pp. 7–10; L. A. Hudson and J. B. Murray, "Methodological Limitations of the Hedonic Consumption Paradigm and a Possible Alternative: A Subjective Approach," *Advances in Consumer Research*, Vol. 13 (1986); Elizabeth Cooper-Martin, "Consumers and Movies: Some Finding on Experiential Products," *Advances in Consumer Research*, Vol. 18 (1991), pp. 372–378; Basil Englis, "The Willing Suspension of Disbelief and Its Importance in Understanding Advertising Effectiveness," *AMA Winter Educators' Proceedings* (1992), Vol. 3, pp. 203–208; Timothy B. Heath, "The Reconciliation of Humanism and Positivism in the Practice of Consumer Research: A View from the Trenches," *Journal of the Academy of Marketing Science*, Vol. 20, No. 2 (Spring 1992), pp. 107–118; John Deighton, "The Consumption of Performance," *Journal of Consumer Research*, Vol. 19, No. 3 (December 1992), pp. 362–372; Richard L. Celsi, Randall L. Rose, and Thomas W. Leigh, "An Exploration of High-Risk Leisure Consumption through Skydiving," *Journal of Consumer Research*, Vol. 20, No. 1 (June 1993), pp. 1–23; and Eric J. Arnould and Linda L. Price, "River Magic: Extraordinary Experience and the Extended Service Encounter," *Journal of Consumer Research*, Vol. 20, No. 1 (June 1993), pp. 24–45.

21. Useful overviews of attribution theory and related concepts as applied to consumer behavior are available in Valerie S. Folkes and Tina Kiesler, "Social Cognition: Consumers' Inferences about the Self and Others," in T. Robertson and H. Kassarjian (eds.), *Handbook of Consumer Behavior* (Englewood Cliffs, N.J.: Prentice Hall, 1991), pp. 281–315; Valerie S. Folkes, "Recent Attribution Research in Consumer Behavior: A Review and New Directions," *Journal of Consumer Research*, Vol. 14 (March 1988), pp. 548–565; Richard W. Mizerski, Linda L. Golden, and Jerome B. Kernan, "The Attribution Process in Consumer Decision Making," *Journal of Consumer Research*, Vol. 6 (September 1979), pp. 123–140; and Harold Kelley, "The Processes of Causal Attribution," *American Psychologist*, Vol. 28 (1973), pp. 107–128. See also W. R. Swinyard and M. L. Ray, "Advertising-Selling Interactions: An Attribution Theory Experiment," *Journal of Marketing Research*, Vol. 14 (1977), p. 509–516; R. M. Sparkman and W. B. Locander, "Attribution Theory and Advertising Effectiveness," *Journal of Consumer Research*, Vol. 7 (December 1980), pp. 219–224; J. M. Hunt, T. J. Domzal, and J. B. Kernan, "Causal Attributions and Persuasions: The Case of Disconfirmed Expectancies," *Advances in Consumer Research*, Vol. 9 (1982), pp. 287–292; Valerie S. Folkes and Barbara Kotsos, "Buyers' and Sellers' Explanations for Product Failure: Who Done It?" *Journal of Marketing*, Vol. 50 (April 1986), pp. 74–80; Mary T. Curren and Valerie S. Folkes, "Attributional Influences on Consumer's Desires to Communicate about Products," *Psychology & Marketing*, Vol. 4 (Spring 1987), pp. 31–46; and Robert Baer, "Overestimating Salesperson Truthfulness: The Fundamental Attribution Error," *Advances in Consumer Research*, Vol. 17 (1990), pp. 501–507.

22. For a basic discussion of self-perception theory, see D. Bem, "Self-perception Theory," in L. Berkowitz (ed.), *Advances in Experimental Social Psychology*, (New York: Academic Press, 1972), pp. 1–62. For readings on FITD and DITF studies in consumer behavior, see, for example, P. H. Reingen and J. B. Kernan, "Compliance with an Interview Request: A Foot-in-the-Door, Self-perception Interpretation," *Journal of Marketing Research*, Vol. 14 (1977), pp. 365–369; C. A. Scott, "The Effects of Trial and Incentives on Repeat Purchase Behavior," *Journal of Marketing Research*, Vol. 13 (1976), pp. 263–269; C. A. Scott, "Modifying Socially-Conscious Behavior: The Foot-in-the-Door Technique," *Journal of Consumer Research*, Vol. 4 (1977), pp. 156–164; A. M. Tybout, "Relative Effectiveness and Three Behavioral Influence Strategies as Supplements to Persuasion in a Marketing Context," *Journal of Marketing Research*, Vol. 15 (1978), pp. 229–242; J. C. Mowen and R. B. Cialdini, "On Implementing the Door-in-the-Face Compliance Technique in a Business Context," *Journal of Marketing Research*, Vol. 17 (May 1980), pp. 253–258; P. H. Reingen, "On Inducing Compliance with Requests," *Journal of Consumer Research*, Vol. 5 (September 1978), pp. 96–102; P. H. Reingen and J. B. Kernan, "More Evidence on Interpersonal Yielding," *Journal of Marketing Research*, Vol. 16 (November 1979), pp. 588–593; Edward F. Fern, Kent B. Monroe, and Ramon A. Avila, "Effectiveness of Multiple Request Strategies: A Synthesis of Research Results," *Journal of Marketing Research*, Vol. 23 (May 1986), pp. 144–152; Cynthia Fraser, Robert E. Hite, and Paul L. Sauer, "Increasing Contributions in Solication Campaigns: The Use of Large and Small Anchorpoints," *Journal of Consumer Research*, Vol. 15 (September 1988), pp. 284–287; Kathleen Debevec, Harlan E. Spotts, and Jerome B. Kernan, "The Self-Reference Effect in Persuasion: Implications for Marketing Strategy," *Advances in Consumer Research*, Vol. 14 (1987), pp. 417–420; Kathleen Debevec and Easwar Iyer, "Self-Referencing as a Mediator of the Effectiveness of Sex-Role Portrayals in Advertising," *Psychology & Marketing*, Vol. 5 (Spring 1988), pp. 71–84; Ian Brennan and Kenneth D. Bahn, "Door-In-The-Face, That's-Not-All, and Legitimizing a Paltry Contribution: Reciprocity, Contrast Effect and Social Judgement Theory Explanations," *Advances in Consumer Research*, Vol. 18 (1991), pp. 586–590; and Rohini Ahluwalia and Robert E. Burnkrant, "A Framework for Explaining Multiple Request Effectivess: The Role of Attitude towards the Request," *Advances in Consumer Research*, Vol. 20 (1993), pp. 612–619.

23. Abraham H. Maslow, *Motivation and Personality*, 2d ed. (New York: Harper & Row, 1970). For consumer-oriented applications see George Brooker, "The Self-actualization Socially Conscious Consumer," *Journal of Consumer Research*, Vol. 5 (September 1976), pp. 107–112; and William E. Kilbourne, "The Self-actualizing Consumer vs. the Class Cage," *AMA Winter Educators' Proceedings* (1987), pp. 312–315.

24. This section is based upon discussions in Desmond S. Cartwright, *Theories and Models of Personality* (Dubuque, Iowa: William C. Brown, 1979), pp. 2–25; and Calvin S. Hall, Gardner Lindzey, John Loehin, and Martin Manosevitz, *Introduction to Theories of Personality* (New York: John Wiley & Sons, 1985), pp. 309–339. For advances in working with this listing, Paul T. Costa and Robert R. McCrae, "From Catalog to Classification: Murray's Needs and the Five-Factor Model," *Journal of Personality and Social Psychology*, Vol. 55, No. 2 (1988), pp. 258–265.

Chapter 6

Consumer Motivation (II): Applications and Extensions

1. "He'll Die with His Driving Gloves On," *Marketing Week*, November 23, 1987, p. 62.

2. Alison Fahey, "BBDO Studies Brand Images," *Brandweek*, July 27, 1992, p. 7.

3. David Keirsey and Marilyn Bates, *Please Understand Me: Character and Temperament Types*, 5th ed. (Del Mar, Calif.: Prometheus Nemesis, 1984); Stephen J. Gould, "Jungian Analysis and Psychological Types: An Interpretive Approach to Consumer Choice Behavior," *Advances in Consumer Research*, Vol. 18 (1991), pp. 743–748.

4. Calvin S. Hall and Gardner Lindzey, *Theories of Personality* (New York: John Wiley & Sons, 1987).

5. See, for example, Karen Horney, *New Ways in Psychoanalysis* (New York: W. W. Norton, 1939); and Karen Horney, *Our Inner Conflicts* (New York: W. W. Norton, 1945).

6. This description is based upon Joel B. Cohen, "Toward an Interpersonal Theory of Consumer Behavior," *California Management Review*, Vol. 10 (Spring 1968), pp. 73–80; and Joel B. Cohen, "An Interpersonal Orientation to the Study of Consumer Behavior," *Journal of Marketing Research*, Vol. 4 (August 1967), pp. 270–278. Another classic study that helped to stimulate interest in this topic (and many commentaries) was by Franklin B. Evans, "Psychological and Objective Factors in the Prediction of Brand Choice," *Journal of Business*, Vol. 32 (October 1959), pp. 340–369. For a comprehensive listing of articles debating Evans's results and conclusions, see Note 8 in William L. Wilkie's *Consumer Behavior*, 2d. ed. (New York: John Wiley & Sons, 1990), p. N15.

Since the time of the original studies, Cohen's CAD instrument has been further tested and used within the marketing field. See, for example, Jerome Kernan, "Choice Criteria, Decision Behavior, and Personality," *Journal of Marketing Research*, Vol. 5 (May 1968), pp. 155–164; Joel B. Cohen and Ellen Golden, "Informational Social Influence and Product Evaluation," *Journal of Applied Psychology*, Vol. 50 (February 1972), pp. 54–59; Jon P. Noerager, "An Assessment of CAD—A Personality Instrument Developed Specifically for Marketing Research," *Journal of Marketing Research*, Vol. 16 (February 1979), pp. 53–59; Arch Woodside and Ruth Andress, "CAD Eight Years Later," *Journal of the Academy of Marketing Science*, Vol. 3 (Summer–Fall 1975), pp. 309–313; Michael Ryan and Richard Becherer, "A Multivariate Test of CAD Instrument Construct Validity," *Advances in Consumer Research*, Vol. 3 (1976), pp. 149–154; Pradeep K. Tyagi, "Validation of the CAD Instrument: A Replication," *Advances in Consumer Research*, Vol. 10 (1983), pp. 112–118; and Mark E. Slama, Terrel G. Williams, and Armen Tashchian, "Compliant, Aggressive and Detached Types Differ in Generalized Purchasing Involvement," *Advances in Consumer Research*, Vol. 15 (1988), pp. 158–162.

7. Harold H. Kassarjian and Mary Jane Sheffet, "Personality and Consumer Behavior: An Update," in H. H. Kassarjian and T. S. Robertson (eds.), *Perspectives in Consumer Behavior*, 4th ed. (Englewood Cliffs, N.J.: Prentice Hall, 1991), pp. 281–303.

8. Ibid., pp. 281–303; Joseph T. Plummer, "How Personality Makes a Difference," *Journal of Advertising Research*, Vol. 24, No. 6

(December 1984–January 1985), pp. 27–31; and Paul Albanese, "Personality, Consumer Behavior, and Marketing Research: A New Theoretical and Empirical Approach," *Research in Consumer Behavior,* Vol. 4 (1990) pp. 1–49.

9. See, for example, Charles Schaninger and Donald Sciglimpaglia, "The Influences of Cognitive Personality Traits and Demographics on Consumer Information Acquisition," *Journal of Consumer Research,* Vol. 8 (September 1981), pp. 208–216; Chin Tiong Tan and Ira J. Dolich, "Cognitive Structure in Personality: An Investigation of Its Generality in Buying Behavior," *Advances in Consumer Research,* Vol. 7 (1980), pp. 547–551; Lawrence A. Crosby and Sanford L. Grossbart, "A Blueprint for Consumer Behavior Research on Personality," *Advances in Consumer Research,* Vol. 11 (1984), pp. 447–452; Benoy Joseph and Shailesh J. Vyas, "Concurrent Validity of a Measure of Innovative Cognitive Style," *Journal of the Academy of Marketing Science,* Vol. 12 (Spring 1984), pp. 159–175; Ram Kesavan and Oswald Mascarenhas, "An Alternate Measure of Cognitive Complexity and Its Comparison with the Bieri Measure," *AMA Summer Educators' Proceedings* (1986), pp. 46–49; Scott Dawson and Nancy Ridgway, "The Relationship between Need for Uniqueness and Fashion Opinion Leadership: A Motivational Approach," *AMA Winter Educators' Proceedings* (1987), pp. 225–228; Gordon R. Foxall and Ronald E. Goldsmith, "Personality and Consumer Research: Another Look," *Journal of the Marketing Research Society,* Vol. 30, No. 2 (1988), pp. 111–125; John L. Lastovicka and Erich A. Joachimsthaler, "Improving the Detection of Personality-Behavior Relationships in Consumer Research," *Journal of Consumer Research,* Vol. 14 (March 1988), pp. 583–587; Meera P. Venkatraman, Deborah Marlino, Frank R. Kardes, and Kimberly B. Sklar, "Effects of Individual Difference Variables on Responses to Factual and Evaluative Ads," *Advances in Consumer Research,* Vol. 17 (1990), pp. 761–765; William D. Harris III and David J. Moore, "Affect Intensity as an Individual Difference Variable in Consumer Response to Advertising Appeals," *Advances in Consumer Research,* Vol. 17 (1990), pp. 792–797; James M. Munch, Paul Albanese, Michael A. Mayo, and Lawrence J. Marks, "The Role of Personality and Moral Development in Consumers' Ethical Decision Making," *AMA Summer Educators' Proceedings* (1991), pp. 299–308; and James T. Strong, Michael F. d'Amico, and Khalid M. Dubas, "Personality as a Moderator of the Threat-Persuasion Relationship: A Conceptual Discussion and Research Propositions," in Robert L. King (ed.), *Marketing: Perspectives for the 1990s* (Richmond, Va.: Southern Marketing Association, 1992), pp. 89–93.

10. For an excellent analysis of the beginnings of psychographics and its strengths and weaknesses, see William D. Wells, "Psychographics: A Critical Review," *Journal of Marketing Research,* Vol. 12 (May 1975), pp. 196–213.

11. Shirley Young, "The Dynamics of Measuring Unchange," in Russel L. Haley (ed.), *Attitude Research in Transition* (Chicago: American Marketing Association, 1972), pp. 49–82.

12. "A Blood Sample for Your Broker," *Fortune,* August 15, 1988, p. 12.

13. This is an interesting area that poses some challenging problems for consumer researchers. For an early overview of research in this area, see M. Joseph Sirgy, "Self-concept in Consumer Behavior: A Critical Review," *Journal of Consumer Research,* (December 1982), pp. 287–300. Among the interesting papers in this area are the following: Edward L. Grubb and Harrison L. Grathwohl, "Consumer Self-concept, Symbolism, and Market Behavior: A Theoretical Approach," *Journal of Marketing,* Vol. 31 (October 1967), pp. 22–27; Ira J. Dolich, "Congruence Relationship between Self-image and Product Brands," *Journal of Marketing Research,* Vol. 6 (February 1969), pp. 80–84; Ivan Ross, "Self-concept and Brand Preference," *Journal of Business,* Vol. 44 (1971), pp. 38–50; Laird Landon, "Self-concept, Ideal Self-concept and Consumer Purchase Intentions," *Journal of Consumer Research,* Vol. 1 (September 1974), pp. 44–51; Danny N. Bellenger, W. W. Stanton, and F. Steinberg, "The Congruence of Store Image and Self-image as It Relates to Store Loyalty," *Journal of Retailing,* Vol. 52 (Spring 1976), pp. 17–32; Terrence V. O'Brien and Humberto T. Sanchez, "Consumer Motivation: A Developmental Self-concept Approach," *Journal of the Academy of Marketing Science,* Vol. 4, No. 3 (1976), pp. 608–616; Bruce L. Stern, Ronald F. Bush, and Joseph F. Hair, Jr., "The Self-image/Store Image Matching Process: An Empirical Test," *Journal of Business,* Vol. 50 (January 1977), pp. 63–69; George F. Belch, "Belief Systems and the Differential Role of the Self-concept," *Advances in Consumer Research,* Vol. 5 (1978), pp. 320–325; James W. Gentry, Mildred Doering, and Terrence V. O'Brien, "Masculinity and Femininity Factors in Product Perception and Self Image," *Advances in Consumer Research,* Vol. 5 (1978), pp. 326–332; Linda L. Golden, Neil Allison, and Mona Clee, "The Role of Sex-Role Self Concept in Masculine and Feminine Product Perception," *Advances in Consumer Research,* Vol. 6 (1979), pp. 595–605; Neil K. Allison, Linda L. Golden, Gary M. Mullet, and Donna Coogan, "Sex, Sex-Role Self Concept and Measurement Implications," *Advances in Consumer Research,* Vol. 7 (1980), pp. 604–609; J. Michael Munson and W. Austin Spivey, "Assessing Self Concept," *Advances in Consumer Research,* Vol. 7 (1980), pp. 598–603; Joseph M. Sirgy and Jeffrey Danes, "Self-image/Product Image Congruence Models: Testing Selected Mathematical Models," *Advances in Consumer Research,* Vol. 9 (1981) pp. 556–561; Warren S. Martin and Joseph Bellizzi, "An Analysis of Congruous Relationships Between Self-images and Product Images," *Journal of the Academy of Marketing Science,* (December 1982), pp. 473–488; Bernd H. Schmitt, France Leclerc, and Laurette Dub-Riox, "Sex Typing and Consumer Behavior: A Test of Gender Schema Theory," *Journal of Consumer Research,* Vol. 15 (June 1988), pp. 122–128; Barbara B. Stern, "Sex Role Self-concept Measures and Marketing: A Research Note," *Psychology & Marketing,* Vol. 5 (Spring 1988), pp. 85ff; Jeffrey E. Durgee, "Quantitative Methods for Developing Advertising That Makes Consumers Feel, 'Hey, That's Right for Me,'" *The Journal of Consumer Marketing,* Vol. 7, No. 1 (Winter 1990), pp. 15–21; Dong H. Lee, "Symbolic Interactionism: Some Implications for Consumer Self-concept and Product Symbolism Research," *Advances in Consumer Research,* Vol. 17 (1990), pp. 386–393; Michael R. Solomon, "The Imperial Self," *Advances in Consumer Research,* Vol. 17 (1990), pp. 68–70; C. B. Claiborne and Julie L. Ozanne, "The Meaning of Custom-made Homes: Home as a Metaphor for Living," *Advances in Consumer Research,* Vol. 17 (1990), pp. 367–374; Clinton R. Sanders, "The Animal 'Other': Self Definition, Social Identity, and Companion Animals," *Advances in Consumer Research,* Vol. 17 (1990), pp. 662–668; David Glen Mick and Michelle DeMoss, "To Me from Me: A Descriptive Phenomenology of Self-Gifts," *Advances in Consumer Research,* Vol. 17 (1990), pp. 677–682; Kelly Smith and Anil Mathur, "'Dependency' as a Stigmatizing Label Influencing the Elderly's Participation in the Food Stamp Program," *AMA Winter Educators' Proceedings* (1991), pp. 245–246; M. Joseph Sirgy, J. S. Johar, A. C. Samli, and C. B. Claiborne, "Self-Congruity versus Functional Con-

gruity: Predictors of Consumer Behavior," *Journal of the Academy of Marketing Science*, Vol. 19, No. 4 (1991), pp. 363–375; Susan Fournier, "A Meaning-based Frameword for the Study of Consumer-Object Relations," *Advances in Consumer Research,* Vol. 18 (1991), pp. 736–742; John W. Schouten, "Selves in Transition: Symbolic Consumption in Personal Rites of Passage and Identity Reconstruction," *Journal of Consumer Research,* Vol. 17, No. 4 (March 1991), pp. 412–425; Raj Mehta and Russell W. Belk, "Artifacts, Identity, and Transition: Favorite Possessions of Indians and Indian Immigrants to the United States," *Journal of Consumer Research,* Vol. 17, No. 4 (March 1991), pp. 398–411; George M. Zinkhan and Jae W. Hong, "Self-concept and Advertising Effectiveness: A Conceptual Model of Congruency, Conspicuousness, and Response Mode," *Advances in Consumer Research,* Vol. 18 (1991), pp. 348–354; Jean B. Romeo and Kathleen Debevec, "An Investigation of Self-Referencing's Influence on Affective Evaluations," *Advances in Consumer Research,* Vol. 19 (1991), pp. 290–295; Newell D. Wright, C. B. Claiborne, and M. Joseph Sirgy, "The Effects of Product Symbolism on Consumer Self-concept," *Advances in Consumer Research,* Vol. 19 (1991), pp. 311–318; Reid P. Claxton and Robert E. Stassen, "Comparative Measures of Extended Self: An Exploratory Study," *AMA Winter Educators' Proceedings* (1991), Vol. 3, pp. 354–362; Susan L. Holak and William J. Havlena, "Nostalgia: An Exploratory Study of Themes and Emotions in the Nostalgic Experience," *Advances in Consumer Research,* Vol. 19 (1991), pp. 380–387; Barbara B. Stern, "Nostalgia in Advertising Text: Romancing the Past Abstract," *Advances in Consumer Research,* Vol. 19 (1991), pp. 388–389; Alan R. Hirsch, "Nostalgia: A Neuropsychiatric Understanding," *Advances in Consumer Research,* Vol. 19 (1991), pp. 390–395; Robert E. Kleine, Susan Schultz-Kleine, and Jerome B. Kernan, "Mundane Everyday Consumption and the Self: A Conceptual Orientation and Prospects for Consumer Research," *Advances in Consumer Research,* Vol. 19 (1991), pp. 411–415; Jerome B. Kernan, "Self Examination," *Advances in Consumer Research,* Vol. 19 (1991), p. 416; Morris B. Holbrook, "Patterns, Personalities, and Complex Relationships in the Effects of Self on Mundane Everyday Consumption: These are 495 of My Most and Least Favorite Things," *Advances in Consumer Research,* Vol. 19 (1991), pp. 417–423; Beth Ann Walker, "New Perspectives for Self-Research," *Advances in Consumer Research,* Vol. 19 (1991), pp. 664–665; Stephen J. Gould and Robert N. Stinerock, "Self-Fashioning Oneself Cross-culturally: Consumption as the Determined and the Determining," *Advances in Consumer Research,* Vol. 19 (1991), pp. 857–860; Ronald Paul Hill, "Homeless Women, Special Possessions, and the Meaning of 'Home': An Ethnographic Case Study," *Journal of Consumer Research,* Vol. 18, No. 3 (December 1991), pp. 298–310; Maureen Morrin, "Advertising and the Self: Is Negative Affect Effective?" *AMA Summer Educators' Proceedings* (1992), pp. 64–71; Cathy Goodwin, "A Conceptualization of Motives to Seek Privacy for Nondeviant Consumption," *Journal of Consumer Psychology,* Vol. 1, No. 3 (1992), pp. 261–284; and the following chapters in Robert L. King (ed.), *Marketing: Perspectives for the 1990s* (Richmond Va.: Southern Marketing Association, 1992): Paulette Marino, "You Are What You Own: The Creation of Self through Possessions," pp. 1–5; Tanuja Srivastava and Paul J. Hensel, "Self-concept in Marketing: An Integrated Theoretical Update," pp. 6–9; and Brian D. Till, "Consumer-Object Relationships: Stages of Development and Dissolution," pp. 10–15.

14.   Francine Schwadel, "The Bare Facts Show a Suitable Swimsuit Is Difficult to Find," *The Wall Street Journal,* July 5, 1988, pp. 1ff.

15.   See, for example, Curtis P. Haugtvedt and Richard E. Petty, "Need for Cognition and Attitude Persistence," *Advances in Consumer Research,* Vol. 16 (1989), pp. 33–36; Ayn E. Crowley and Wayne D. Hoyer, "The Relationship between Need for Cognition and Other Individual Difference Variables: A Two-Dimensional Framework," *Advances in Consumer Research,* Vol. 167 (1989), pp. 37–43; Curtis P. Haugtvedt, Richard Petty, and John Cacioppo, "Need for Cognition in Advertising: Understanding the Role of Personality Variables in Consumer Behavior," *Journal of Consumer Psychology,* Vol. 1 (1992), pp. 239–260; Douglas Stayman and Frank Kardes, "Spontaneous Inference Processes in Advertising: Effects of Need for Cognition and Self-monitoring on Inference Generation and Utilization," *Journal of Consumer Psychology,* Vol. 1 (1992), pp. 125–142; Sucheta S. Ahlawat and Harlan E. Spotts, "Need for Cognition in Advertising Research: A Reexamination," *AMA Winter Educators' Proceedings* (1992), Vol. 3, pp. 247–353; and Elizabeth Cooper-Martin, "Individual Differences in Choice Processes: The Role of Ability and Motivation," in T. J. Page, Jr., and S. E. Middlestadt (eds.), *Proceedings of the Society for Consumer Psychology,* (Clemson, S.C.: CtC Press, 1992), pp. 12–18.

16.   Mark Snider and Kenneth G. DeBono, "Appeals to Image and Claims about Quality: Understanding the Psychology of Advertising," *Journal of Personality and Social Psychology,* Vol. 49, No. 3 (1985), pp. 586–597; and the following chapters in C. Haugtvedt and D. Rosen (eds.), *Proceedings of the Society for Consumer Psychology* (Knoxville: D. W. Schumann, 1991): Chae Un Lim, Masaaki Kotabe and Alan J. Dubinsky, "Relationship between Self-monitoring and Salesperson Performance: A Cross-cultural Investigation," pp. 116–117; Kenneth G. DeBono, "Advertising and Self-monitoring: From Attitudes toward the Ad to Attitudes toward the Product," pp. 118–120; and Leslie M. Fine and David W. Schumann, "The Role of Self-monitoring in Judgments of the Buyer/Seller Relationship," p. 121. See also William O. Bearden, F. Kelly Shuptrine, and Jesse E. Teel, "Self-monitoring: Relationships to Different Advertising Appeals," *AMA Summer Educators' Proceedings* (1991), pp. 204–209; and Sharon Shavitt, Tina M. Lowrey, and Sang-Pil Han, "Attitude Functions in Advertising: The Interactive Role of Products and Self-monitoring," *Journal of Consumer Psychology,* Vol. 1, No. 4 (1992), pp. 337–364.

17.   Milton Rokeach, *Understanding Human Values: Individual and Societal* (New York: Free Press, 1979); see also Milton Rokeach, *The Nature of Human Values* (New York: Free Press, 1973); Ronald E. Goldsmith, J. Dennis White, and Melvin T. Stith, "Yeasaying and the Rokeach Value Survey: Interactions with Age and Race," *AMA Summer Educators' Proceedings* (1987), p. 238; and J. Michael Munson and Edward F. McQuarrie, "Shortening the Rokeach Value Survey for Use in Consumer Research," *Advances in Consumer Research,* Vol. 15 (1988), pp. 381–386.

18.   For recent methodological developments in analyzing LOV, see especially Wagner Kamakura and Thomas P. Novak, "Value-System Segmentation: Exploring the Meaning of LOV," *Journal of Consumer Research,* Vol. 19 (June 1992), pp. 119–132; and Wagner Kamakura and Jose A. Mazzon, "Values Segmentation: A Model for the Measurement of Values and Value Systems," *Journal of Consumer Research,* Vol. 18 (September 1991), pp. 208–218. For reading on the LOV versus VALS controversy, see Note 38 of Chapter 4. For information on the basic nature of LOV itself see especially Sharon Beatty, Lynn R. Kahle, Pamela Homer, and Shekhar Misra,

"Alternative Measurement Approaches to Consumer Values: The List of Values and the Rokeach Value Survey," *Psychology & Marketing*, Vol. 2 (Fall 1985), pp. 181–200. For additional recent findings, see also Lynne R. Kahle and Patricia Kennedy, "Using the List of Values (LOV) to Understand Consumers," *Journal of Consumer Marketing*, Vol. 6 (Summer 1989), pp. 5–12; and Lynn R. Kahle, Basil Poulos, and Ajay Sukhdial, "Changes in Social Values in the United States during the Past Decade," *Journal of Advertising Research*, Vol. 28 (February–March 1988), pp. 35–41. For further related readings, see L. J. Shrum, John A. McCarty, and Tamara L. Loeffler, "Individual Differences in Value Stability: Are We Really Tapping True Values?" *Advances in Consumer Research*, Vol. 17 (1990), pp. 609–615; Pierre Valette-Florence and Alain Jolibert, "Assessing the Structure of Social Values: An Exploratory Study of Alternative Methods via a Two-Stage Approach," *AMA Winter Educators' Proceedings* (1991), pp. 263–274; May Jane Burns and Robert B. Woodruff, "Value: An Integrative Perspective," in C. Haugtvedt and D. Rosen (eds.), *Proceedings of the Society for the Consumer Psychology*, (Knoxville: D. W. Schumann, 1991), pp. 59–64; Robert E. Pitts, John K. Wong, and D. Joel Whalen, "Consumers' Evaluative Structures in Two Ethical Situations: A Means-End Approach," *Journal of Business Research*, Vol. 22 (1991), pp. 199–130; John A. McCarty and Patricia M. Hattwick, "Cultural Value Orientations: A Comparison of Magazine Advertisements from the United States and Mexico," *Advances in Consumer Research*, Vol. 19 (1991), pp. 34–38; John Paul Fraedrich, Neil C. Herndon, Jr., and O. C. Ferrell, "A Values Comparison of Future Managers from West Germany and the United States," *Journal of International Consumer Marketing*, Vol. 4, Nos. 1/2 (1991), pp. 7–38; Jungki Lee and Sharon E. Beatty, "A Review and New View of Personal Values," *AMA Winter Educators' Proceedings* (1992), Vol. 3, pp. 251–257; Jeff Allen and Duane Davis, "An Investigation of the Effects of Individual Values and Professional Ethics on Consulting Behavior," *AMA Winter Educators' Proceedings* (1992), Vol. 3, pp. 399–406; Three articles in T. J. Page, Jr., and S. E. Middlestadt (eds.), *Proceedings of the Society for Consumer Psychology*, (Clemson, S.C.: CtC Press, 1992): Fredrick G. Kropp, "Changing Values and the Pardigm Shift: A New Approach to Analyzing Change," pp. 40–45; Fredrick G. Kropp, Malcolm C. Smith, Gregory M. Rose, and Lynn R. Kahle, "Values and Lifestyles of Pet Owners," pp. 46–49; and Robert Madrigal, "Social Values and American Tourists in Scandinavia," pp. 50–56; and Penelope Prenshaw, "The Dimensions of Values: A Measurement Approach for International Marketing Research," *AMA Winter Educators' Proceedings* (1993), pp. 62–70. In addition, the Winter 1985 issue of *Psychology & Marketing* is devoted to this topic.

For recent research on the related topic of materialism, see, for example, Scott Dawson and Gary Bamossy, "Isolating the Effect of Non-economic Factors on the Development of a Consumer Culture: A Comparison of Materialism in the Netherlands and the United States," *Advances in Consumer Research*, Vol. 17 (1990), pp. 182–185; Guliz Ger and Russell W. Belk, "Measuring and Comparing Materialism Cross-culturally," *Advances in Consumer Research*, Vol. 17 (1990), pp. 186–192; Marsh L. Richins, Kim K. R. McKeage, and Debbie Najjar, "An Exploration of Materialism and Consumption-related Affect," *Advances in Consumer Research*, Vol. 19 (1991), pp. 229–236; Seth Ellis, "A Factor Analytic Investigation of Belk's Structure of the Materialism Construct," *Advances in Consumer Research*, Vol. 19 (1991), pp. 688–695; Marsha L. Richins and Scott Dawson, "A Consumer Values Orientation for Materialism and Its Measurement: Scale Development and Validation," *Journal of Consumer Research*, Vol. 19, No. 3 (December 1992), pp. 303–316; Aaron C. Ahuvia, "The Role of Intrinsic Motivation/Concern in Materialism and Love," *AMA Winter Educators' Conference* (1993), p. 52; and Susan Fournier and Michael Guiry, "An Emerald Green Jaguar, a House on Nantucket, and an African Safari: Wish Lists and Consumption Dreams in Materialist Society," *Advances in Consumer Research*, Vol. 20 (1993), pp. 352–358.

19. For a summary discussion of the basic laddering approach, see Thomas J. Renolds and Jonathan Gutman, "Laddering Theory, Method, Analysis, and Interpretation," *Journal of Advertising Research*, Vol. 28 (January–February, 1988), pp. 11–31. For further discussion of the MECCAS model and the Federal Express case, see Thomas J. Reynolds and Alyce Craddock, "The Application of the MECCAS Model to the Development and Assessment of Advertising Strategy: A Case Study," *Journal of Advertising Research*, Vol. 28 (April–May 1988), pp. 43–54. Figures 6-2 and 6-3 are adapted from working papers by these authors: detailed results are available in the references above. See also Geraldine Fennell, "Context for Action = Context for Brand Use = Source of Valued Attributes," in C. Haugtvedt and D. Rosen (eds.), *Proceedings of the Society for Consumer Psychology* (Knoxville: D. W. Schumann, 1991), pp. 73–79.

20. See, for example, Ronald J. Faber and Thomas C. O'Guinn, "A Clinical Screener for Compulsive Buying," *Journal of Consumer Research*, Vol. 19 (December 1992), pp. 459–469; Alain d'Astous and Sylvie Tremblay, "The Compulsive Side of 'Normal' Consumers: An Empirical Study," Working Paper, University of Sherbrooke, Quebec, 1989; Gilles Valence, Alain d'Astous, and Louis Fortier, "Compulsive Buying: Concept and Measurement," in K. Blois and S. Parkinson (eds.), *Proceedings of the 17th Annual Conference of the European Marketing Academy* (Bradford, England: University Management Centre, 1988), pp. 601–624; Thomas C. O'Guinn and Ronald J. Faber, "Compulsive Buying: A Phenomenological Exploration," *Journal of Consumer Research*, Vol. 16 (September 1989), pp. 147–157; George P. Moschis and Dena Cox, "Deviant Consumer Behavior," *Advances in Consumer Research*, Vol. 16 (1989), pp. 732–737; Alvin C. Burns, Peter L. Gillett, Marc Rubinstein, and James W. Gentry, "An Exploratory Study of Lottery Playing, Gambling Addiction and Links to Compulsive Consumption," *Advances in Consumer Research*, Vol. 17 (1990), pp. 298–305; Alain d'Astous, Julie Maltais, and Caroline Roberge, "Compulsive Buying Tendencies of Adolescent Consumers," *Advances in Consumer Research*, Vol. 17 (1990), pp. 306–312; Howard T. Tokunaga, "Use and Abuse of Credit Cards: Application of Psychological Theory," in C. Hougtvedt and D. Rosen (eds.), *Proceedings of the Society for Consumer Psychology* (Knoxville: D. W. Schumann, 1991), pp. 2–9; Stephen J. Hoch and George F. Loewenstein, "Time-Inconsistent Preferences and Consumer Self-control," *Journal of Consumer Research*, Vol. 17 (March 1991), pp. 492–507; Elizabeth C. Hirschman, "The Consciousness of Addiction: Toward a General Theory of Compulsive Consumption," *Journal of Consumer Research*, Vol. 19 (September 1992), pp. 155–179; and Ronald A. Fullerton and Girish N. Punj, "Choosing to Misbehave: A Structural Model of Aberrant Consumer Behavior," *Advances in Consumer Research*, Vol. 20 (1993), pp. 570–574.

21. The definition is adapted from that given by Joel B. Cohen, "Involvement: Separating the State from Its Causes and Effects," paper delivered to the Conference on Involvement in Marketing,

New York University, June 1982. The theoretical basis for CI stems from the concept of object cathexis in Freudian theory. This concept later evolved into the concept of ego involvement, reflecting the fact that individuals would perceive some objects and issues as more personally involved with the self. One subset of this concept concerns commitment to a position, as reflected in the oft-cited work by Sherif and others. See, for example, M. Sherif and M. Cantril, *The Psychology of Ego Involvement* (New York: John Wiley, 1947).

22. In all our quotations, for example, our consumers *already* grouped together many distinct episodes for us and presented us with an overall description of high CI. Can low-CI episodes so easily be grouped together and described, however? Also, how can different types of thoughts or feelings be compared as to energy level—is Debra more involved than Martha? Further, should we say that Debra is highly involved with the *products* she uses in her beauty sessions (lipstick, blush, perfume, etc.), or are these merely accompaniments to the *beauty sessions* themselves? Although all these are advanced questions, to study CI, consumer researchers have to decide how to treat them.

23. For overviews of this research, see Carolyn L. Costley, "Meta Analysis of Involvement Research," *Advances in Consumer Research,* Vol. 15 (1988), pp. 554–562; and Blair T. Johnson and Alice H. Eagly, "Effects of Involvement on Persuasion: A Meta-analysis," *Psychological Bulletin,* Vol. 106 (1989), pp. 290–314. For debates on the latter article, see Richard E. Petty and John T. Cacioppo, "Involvement and Persuasion: Tradition versus Integration," and Blair T. Johnson and Alice H. Eagly, "Involvement and Persuation: Types, Tradition, and the Evidence," both in *Psychological Bulletin,* Vol. 107 (1990), pp. 367–374 and 375–384 respectively. For conceptual discussions, see also Marsha L. Richins and Peter H. Bloch, "After the New Wears Off: The Temporal Context of Product Involvement," *Journal of Consumer Research,* Vol. 13 (September, 1986), pp. 280–285; Banwari Mittal and Myung-Soo Lee, "Separating Brand-Choice Involvement from Product Involvement via Consumer Involvement Profiles," *Advances in Consumer Research,* Vol. 15 (1987), pp. 43–49; Sharon E. Beatty, Lynn R. Kahle, and Pamela Homer, "The Involvement-Commitment Model: Theory and Implications," *Journal of Business Research,* Vol. 16 (March 1988), pp. 149–168; Richard L. Celsi and Jerry C. Olson, "The Role of Involvement in Attention and Comprehension Processes," *Journal of Consumer Research,* Vol. 15 (September 1988), pp. 210–224; James A. Muncy, "Involvement and Perceived Brand Similarities/Differences: The Need for Process-oriented Models," *Advances in Consumer Research,* Vol. 17 (1990), pp. 144–148; Lee D. Dahringer, Charles D. Frame, Oliver Yau, and Janet McColl-Kennedy,"Consumer Involvement in Services: An International Evaluation," *Journal of International Consumer Marketing,* Vol. 3, No. 2 (1991), pp. 61–78; Ronald E. Goldsmith, Janelle Emmert, and Charles Hofacker, "A Causal Model of Consumer Involvement: Replication and Extension," *AMA Winter Educators' Proceedings* (1991), pp. 330–338; and Marsha L. Richins, Peter H. Bloch, and Edward F. McQuarrie, "How Enduring and Situational Involvement Combine to Create Involvement Responses," *Journal of Consumer Psychology,* Vol. 1, No. 2 (1992), pp. 143–154.

24. For interesting developments, see Gilles Laurent and Jean-Noel Kapferer, "Measuring Consumer Involvement Profiles," *Journal of Marketing Research,* Vol. 22 (1985), pp. 41–53; Judith Lynne Zaichkowsky, "Measuring the Involvement Construct," *Journal of*

Consumer Research, Vol. 12 (December 1985), pp. 341–352; Edward F. McQuarrie and J. Michael Munson, "The Zaichkowsky Personal Involvement Inventory: Modification & Extension," *Advances in Consumer Research,* Vol. 14 (1987), pp. 36–40; Raj Arora, "Involvement: Its Measurement for Retail Store Research," *Journal of the Academy of Marketing Science,* Vol. 13 (Spring 1985), pp. 229–241; Raj Arora and Robert Baer, "Measuring Consumer Involvement in Products: Comment on Traylor and Joseph," *Psychology & Marketing,* Vol. 2 (Spring 1985), p. 59ff; Mark B. Traylor and W. Benoy Joseph, "Reply to Arora and Baer's Comment on Measuring Consumer Involvement in Products," *Psychology & Marketing,* Vol. 2 (Summer 1985), p. 127ff; Marya J. Pucely, Richard Mizerski, and Pamela Perrewe, "A Comparison of Involvement Measures for the Purchase and Consumption of Pre-recorded Music," *Advances in Consumer Research,* Vol. 15 (1988), p. 37–42; and three papers in *Advances in Consumer Research,* Vol. 16 (1989): Thomas D. Jensen, Les Carlson, and Carolyn Tripp, "The Dimensionality of Involvement: An Empirical Test," pp. 680–689; Robin A. Higie and Lawrence F. Feick, "Enduring Involvement: Conceptual and Measurement Issues," pp. 690–696; Banwaari Mittal, "A Theoretical Analysis of Two Recent Measures of Involvement," pp. 697–702; Elizabeth C. Hirschman and Priscilla A. LaBarbara, "Dimensions of Possession Importance," *Psychology & Marketing,* Vol. 7 (Fall 1990), pp. 215–233; Kapil Jain and Narasimhan Srinivasan, "An Empirical Assessment of Multiple Operationalizations of Involvement," *Advances in Consumer Research,* Vol. 17 (1990), pp. 594–602; Judith L. Zaichkowsky, "Issues in Measuring Abstract Constructs," *Advances in Consumer Research,* Vol. 17 (1990), pp. 616–618; Joseph Cherian and Barbara Harris, "Capricious Consumption and the Social Brain Theory: Why Consumers Seem Purposive Even in the Absence of Purpose," *Advances in Consumer Research,* Vol. 17 (1990), pp. 745–749; J. Craig Andrews, Srinivas Durvasula, and Syed H. Akhter, "A Framework for Conceptualizing and Measuring the Involvement Construct in Advertising Research," *Journal of Advertising,* Vol. 19, No. 4 (1990), pp. 27–40; Edward McQuarrie and J. Michael Munson, "A Revised Product Involvement Inventory: Improved Usability and Validity," *Advances in Consumer Research,* Vol. 19 (1991), pp. 108–115; A. Dwayne Ball and Lori H. Tasaki, "The Role and Measurement of Attachment in Consumer Behavior," *Journal of Consumer Psychology,* Vol. 1, No. 2 (1992), pp. 155–172; and Victoria Seitz, Leon Kappelman, and Tom K. Massey, Jr., "Measuring Involvement: Another Look," *AMA Winter Educators' Conference* (1993), pp. 292–298.

25. Harold H. Kassarjian, "Presidential Address, 1977: Anthropomorphism and Parsimony," *Advances in Consumer Research,* Vol. 5 (1978), pp. 13–14; see also H. H. Kassarjian, "Low Involvement—A Second Look," *Advances in Consumer Research,* Vol. 8 (1981) pp. 31–34; George M. Zinkhan and Claes Fornell, "A Test of the Learning Heirarchy in High- and Low-Involvement Situations," *Advances in Consumer Research,* Vol. 16 (1989), pp. 152–159; Jacques E. Brisoux and Emmanuel J. Cheron, "Brand Categorization and Product Involvement," *Advances in Consumer Research,* Vol. 17 (1990), pp. 101–109; Simeon Chow, Richard L. Celsi, and Robin Abel, "The Effects of Situational and Intrinsic Sources of Personal Relevance on Brand Choice Decisions," *Advances in Consumer Research,* Vol. 17 (1990), pp. 755–760; Scott A. Hawkins and Stephen J. Hoch, "Low-Involvement Learning: Memory without Evaluation," *Journal of Consumer Research,* Vol. 19, No. 2 (September 1992), pp. 212–225; and Dev S. Pathak, Suzan Kucukarsalan, Deepak Sirdeshmukh, and Richard Segal, "The Vulnerable Consumer in the High Blood Pressure Drug Market: Bothered but Satisfied?" *Advances in Consumer Research*, Vol. 20 (1993), pp. 245–252.

26. For excellent, advanced discussions of affect and emotions in consumer behavior, see Joel B. Cohen and Charles S. Areni, "Affect and Consumer Behavior," in T. Robertson and H. Kassarjian (eds.), *Handbook of Consumer Behavior* (Englewood Cliffs, N.J.: Prentice Hall, 1991), pp. 188–240; and Barry J. Babin, William R. Darden, and Mitch Griffin, "Some Comments on the Role of Emotions in Consumer Behavior," *AMA Summer Educators' Proceedings* (1992), pp. 130–139. See also Harold H. Kassarjian, "Consumer Research: Some Recollections and a Commentary," *Advances in Consumer Research*, Vol. 13 (1986), pp. 6–8; Robert B. Zajonc and Hazel Markus, "Affective and Cognitive Factors in Preference," *Journal of Consumer Research*, Vol. 9 (September 1982), pp. 123–131; Carl Obermiller, "Varieties of Mere Exposure: The Effects of Processing Style and Repetition on Affective Response," *Journal of Consumer Research*, Vol. 12 (June 1985), pp. 17–30; Y. Tsal, "On the Relationship between Cognitive and Affective Processes: A Critique on Zajonc and Markus," *Journal of Consumer Research*, Vol. 12 (December 1985), pp. 358–362; R. Zajonc and H. Markus, "Must All Affect Be Mediated by Cognition?" *Journal of Consumer Research*, Vol. 12 (December 1985), pp. 363–364; James A. Muncy, "Physiological Responses of Consumer Emotions: Theory, Methods, and Implications for Consumer Research," *AMA Summer Educators' Proceedings* (1987), pp. 127–132; Punam Anand, Morris B. Holbrook, and Debra Stephens, "The Formation of Affective Judgments: The Cognitive-Affective Model versus the Independence Hypothesis," *Journal of Consumer Research*, Vol. 15 (December 1988), pp. 386–391; Robert A. Westbrook and Richard L. Oliver, "The Dimensionality of Consumption Emotion Patterns and Consumer Satisfaction," *Journal of Consumer Research*, Vol. 18 (June 1991), pp. 84–91; Mary T. Curren and Ronald C. Goodstein, "Affect and Consumer Behavior: Examining the Role of Emotions on Consumers' Actions and Perceptions," *Advances in Consumer Research*, Vol. 18 (1991), pp. 624–626; Debra A. Laverie, Robert E. Kleine III, and Susan Schultz Kleine, "Linking Emotions and Values in Consumption Experiences: An Exploratory Study," *Advances in Consumer Research*, Vol. 20 (1993), pp. 70–75; Francis Piron, "A Comparison of Emotional Reactions Experienced by Planned, Unplanned and Impulse Purchasers," *Advances in Consumer Research*, Vol. 20 (1993), pp. 341–343; and Hyongoh Cho and Patricia A. Stout, "An Extended Perspective on the Role of Emotion in Advertising Processing," *Advances in Consumer Research*, Vol. 20 (1993), pp. 692–697.

27. Elizabeth C. Hirschman and Morris B. Holbrook, "Hedonic Consumption: Emerging Concepts, Methods and Propositions," *Journal of Marketing*, Vol. 46 (1982), pp. 92–101. For other interesting examples of these issues, see William J. Havlena and Morris B. Holbrook, "The Varieties of Consumption Experience: Comparing Two Typologies of Emotion in Consumer Behavior," *Journal of Consumer Research*, Vol. 13 (December 1986), pp. 394–404; Roberto Friedmann, "Psychological Meaning of Products: Identification and Marketing Applications," *Psychology & Marketing*, Vol. 3 (Spring 1986), pp. 1–15; Kathleen T. Lacher, "Hedonic Consumption: Music as a Product," *Advances in Consumer Research*, Vol. 16 (1989), pp. 367–373; Morris B.Holbrook, "The Role of Lyricism in Research on Consumer Emotions: Skylark, Have You Anything to Say to Me?" *Advances in Consumer Research*, Vol. 17 (1990),

pp. 1–18; Brian Lofman, "Elements of Experimental Consumption: An Exploratory Study," *Advances in Consumer Research*, Vol. 18 (1991), pp. 729–735; William J. Havlena and Susan L. Holak, "'The Good Old Days': Observation on Nostalgia and Its Role in Consumer Behavior," *Advances in Consumer Research*, Vol. 18 (1991), pp. 323–329; Morris B. Holbrook and Robert M. Schindler, "Echoes of the Dear Departed Past: Some Work in Progress on Nostalgia," *Advances in Consumer Research*, Vol. 18 (1991), pp. 330–333; Stephen J. Gould, "The Self-Manipulation of My Pervasive, Perceived Vital Energy through Product Use: An Introspective-Praxis Perspective," *Journal of Consumer Research*, Vol. 18, No. 2 (September 1991), pp. 194–207.

28. For an advanced reading in this area, see Richard P. Bagozzi, "The Role of Psychophysiology in Consumer Research," in T. Robertson and H. Kassarjian (eds.), *Handbook of Consumer Behavior* (Englewood Cliffs, N.J.: Prentice Hall, 1991), pp. 124–161.

29. Meryl Paula Gardner, "Mood States and Consumer Behavior: A Critical Review," *Journal of Consumer Research*, Vol. 12 (December 1985), pp. 281–300. See also Thom Srull, "Memory, Mood and Consumer Judgment," in *Advances in Consumer Research*, Vol. 14 (1987), pp. 408–410; Ronald P. Hill and Meryl P. Gardner, "Product Evaluation: Effects of and on Consumer Mood States," *Advances in Consumer Research*, Vol. 14 (1987), pp. 408–410; Meryl P. Gardner and John E. Scott, "Product Type: A Neglected Moderator of the Effects of Mood," *Advances in Consumer Research*, Vol. 17 (1990), pp. 585–589; David Kuykendall and John P. Keating, "Mood and Persuasion: Evidence for the Differential Influence of Positive and Negative States," *Psychology & Marketing*, Vol. 7 (Spring 1990), pp. 1–10; Haim Mano, "Emotional States and Decision Making," *Advances in Consumer Research* Vol. 17 (1990), pp. 577–584; Carl Obermiller and April Atwood, "Feelings about Feeling-State Research: A Search for Harmony," *Advances in Consumer Research*, Vol. 17 (1990), pp. 590–593; Rajeev Batra and Douglas M. Stayman, "The Role of Mood in Advertising Effectiveness," *Journal of Consumer Research*, Vol. 17, No. 2 (September 1990), pp. 203–214; Steve Smith and David R. Shaffer, "Mood, Peripheral Cue Positioning and Persuasion," in C. Haugtvedt and D. Rosen (eds.), *Proceedings of the Society for Consumer Psychology* (Knoxville, D.W. Schumann, 1991), pp. 30–32; Patricia A. Knowles, Stephen J. Grove, and Gregory M. Pickett, "The Role of Mood in Consumers' Responses to Service Encounters: Review and Propositions," *AMA Winter Educators' Proceedings* (1992), Vol. 3, pp. 140–141; K. Douglas Hoffman, "A Conceptual Framework of the Influence of Positive Mood States on Service Exchange Relationships," *AMA Winter Educators' Proceedings* (1992), Vol. 3, pp. 144–150; Paul W. Miniard, Sunil Bhatla, and Deepak Sirdeshmukh, "Mood as a Determinant of Postconsumption Product Evaluations: Mood Effects and Their Dependency on the Affective Intensity of the Consumption Experience," *Journal of Consumer Psychology*, Vol. 1, No. 2 (1992), pp. 173–195; Meryl P. Gardner and V. Carter Broach, Jr., "Mood-Product Interactions: An Exploratory Study," in *Proceedings of the Society for Consumer Psychology* (1992), pp. 1–6; Jacquelyn L. Twible and Stacey B. Frank, "The Construct Validity of Mood: An Assessment of Convergent and Discriminant Dimensions," *AMA Winter Educators' Proceedings* (1992), Vol. 3, pp. 17–22; Daniel J. Howard, "Gift-wrapping Effects on Product Attitudes: A Mood-biasing Explanation," *Journal of Consumer Psychology*, Vol. 1, No. 3 (1992), pp. 197–224; and Patricia A. Knowles, Stephen J. Grove, and W. Jeffrey Burroughs, "An Experimental Examination of Mood Effects on Retrieval and

Evaluation of Advertisement and Brand Information," *Journal of the Academy of Marketing Science,* Vol. 21, No. 2 (Spring 1993), pp. 135–142.

30. Useful outlines of current thinking and approaches are given in Carolyn Yoon, *Tears, Cheers, and Fears: The Role of Emotions in Advertising: Conference Summary* (Cambridge, Mass: Marketing Science Institute Report 91-112 (May 1991); and John R. Rossiter and Larry Percy, "Emotions and Motivations in Advertising," *Advances in Consumer Research,* Vol. 18 (1991), pp. 100–110. This topic has received a considerable degree of recent attention in the field. For interesting overviews, see Rajeev Batra and Michael L. Ray, "Affective Responses Mediating Acceptance of Advertising," *Journal of Consumer Research,* Vol. 13 (September 1986), pp. 234–249; and Deborah J. MacInnis and Bernard J. Jaworski, "Information Processing from Advertisements: Toward an Integrative Framework," *Journal of Marketing,* Vol. 53 (October 1989), pp. 1–23. For a variety of further insights and findings, see, for example, David A. Aaker, Douglas M. Stayman, and Michael R. Hagerty, "Warmth in Advertising: Measurement, Impact, and Sequence Effects," *Journal of Consumer Research,* Vol. 12 (March 1986), pp. 365–381; Richard W. Mizerski and J. Dennis White, "Understanding and Using Emotions in Advertising," *Journal of Consumer Marketing,* Vol. 3 (Fall 1986), pp. 57–70; Marvin E. Goldberg and Gerald J. Gorn, "Happy and Sad TV Programs: How They Affect Reactions to Commercials," *Journal of Consumer Research,* Vol. 14 (December 1987), pp. 387–403; Morris B. Holbrook and Rajeev Batra, "Assessing the Role of Emotions as Mediators of Consumer Responses to Advertising," *Journal of Consumer Research,* Vol. 14 (December 1987), pp. 404–420; Julie A. Edell and Marian Chapman Burke, "The Power of Feelings in Understanding Advertising Effects," *Journal of Consumer Research,* Vol. 14 (December 1987), pp. 421–433; Chris T. Allen, Karen A. Machleit, and Susan S. Marine, "On Assessing the Emotionality of Advertising via Izard's Differential Emotions Scale," *Advances in Consumer Research,* Vol. 15 (1988), pp. 226–231; David A. Aaker, Douglas M. Stayman, and Richard Vezina, "Identifying Feelings Elicited by Advertising," *Psychology & Marketing,* Vol. 5 (Spring 1988), pp. 1–16; Thomas J. Page, Jr., Patricia J. Daugherty, Dogan Eroglu, David E. Hartman, Scott D. Johnson, and Doo-Hee Lee, "Measuring Emotional Response to Advertising: A Comment on Stout and Leckenby," *Journal of Advertising,* Vol. 17 (November 1988), pp. 49–52; Patricia A. Stout and John D. Leckenby, "The Nature of Emotional Response to Advertising: A Further Examination," *Journal of Advertising,* Vol. 17 (November 1988), pp. 53–57; Mark A. Pavelchak, John H. Antil, and James M. Munch, "The Super Bowl: An Investigation into the Relationship among Program Context, Emotional Experience, and Ad Recall," *Journal of Consumer Research,* Vol. 15 (December 1988), pp. 360–367; Judy I. Alpert and Mark I. Alpert, "Background Music as an Influence in Consumer Mood and Advertising Response," *Advances in Consumer Research,* Vol. 16 (1989), pp. 485–491; Ellen Day, "Share of Heart: What Is It and How Can It Be Measured?" *Journal of Consumer Marketing,* Vol. 6 (Winter 1989), pp. 5–12; and Marian Chapman Burke and Julie A. Edell, "The Impact of Feelings on Ad-based Affect and Cognition," *Journal of Marketing Research,* Vol. 26 (February 1989), pp. 69–83; Rajeev Batra and Morris B. Holbrook, "Developing a Typology of Affective Responses to Advertising," *Psychology & Marketing,* Vol. 7 (Spring 1990), pp. 11–26; and Jeremy D. Pincus, "Interpreting Perceiver Reactions to Emotional Stimuli," *Advances in Consumer Research,* Vol. 19 (1991), pp. 245–250.

31. For a summary description of this framework, see John R. Rossiter, Larry Percy, and Robert J. Donovan, "A Better Advertising Planning Grid," *Journal of Advertising Research* Vol. 31, No. 5 (1991), pp. 11–21. For further details, see J. R. Rossiter and L. Percy, *Advertising and Promotion Management* (New York: McGraw-Hill, 1987). This grid is competitor to another well-known framework, which is described in Brian T. Ratchford, "New Insights about the FCB Grid," *Journal of Advertising Research,* Vol. 27, No. 4 (1987), pp. 24–37. For applications of the grid model, see Richard Vaughn, "How Advertising Works: A Planning Model," *Journal of Advertising Research,* Vol. 20, No. 5 (1980), pp. 27–33; and Richard Vaughn, "How Advertising Works: A Planning Model Revisited," *Journal of Advertising Research,* Vol. 26, No. 1 (1986), pp. 57–66. For further related readings, see Richard E. Petty, John T. Cacioppo, and David Schumann, "Central and Peripheral Routes to Advertising Effectiveness: The Moderating Role of Involvement," *Journal of Consumer Research,* Vol. 10 (September 1983), pp. 135–146; Anthony G. Greenwald and Clark Leavitt, "Audience Involvement in Advertising: Four Levels," *Journal of Consumer Research,* Vol. 11 (June 1984), pp. 581–592; Gordon W. McClung, C. Whan Park, and William J. Sauer, "Viewer Processing of Commercial Messages: Context and Involvement," *Advances in Consumer Research,* Vol. 12 (1985), pp. 351–355; James D. Gill, Sanford Grossbart, and Russell N. Laczniak, "Influence of Involvement, Commitment and Familiarity on Brand Beliefs and Attitudes of Viewers Exposed to Alternative Ad Claim Strategies," *Journal of Advertising,* Vol. 17 (November 1988), pp. 33–43; Herbert E. Krugman, "Point of View: Limits of Attention to Advertising," *Journal of Advertising Research,* Vol. 28 (October–November 1988), pp. 47ff; Russell N. Laczniak, Darrel D. Muehling, and Sanford Grossbart, "Manipulating Message Involvement in Advertising Research," *Journal of Advertising,* Vol. 18 (November 1989), pp. 28–38; Brian T. Ratchford and Richard Vaughn, "On the Relationship between Motives and Purchase Decisions: Some Empirical Approaches," *Advances in Consumer Research* Vol. 16 (1989), pp. 293–299; James A. Muncy, "Discussion: Involvement and Perceived Brand Similarities/Differences: The Need for Process Oriented Models," *Advances in Consumer Research,* Vol. 17 (1990), pp. 144–148; William K. Darley and Jeen-Su Lim, "Personal Relevance as Moderator of the Effect of Public Service Advertising on Behavior," *Advances in Consumer Research,* Vol. 18 (1991), pp. 303–309; Robin A. Higie, Lawrence F. Feick, and Linda L. Price, "The Importance of Peripheral Cues in Attitude Formation for Enduring and Task Involved Individuals," *Advances in Consumer Research,* Vol. 18 (1991), pp. 187–193; Blair T. Johnson, Cynthia S. Symons, and Barbara C. Newman, "The Ephemeral Nature of Impression-Relevant Involvement," in C. Haugtvedt and D. Rosen (eds.), *Proceedings of the Society for Consumer Psychology* (Knoxville: D.W. Schumann, 1991), pp. 21–28; Jin K. Han, "Involvement and Advertisement Size Effects on Information Processing," *Advances in Consumer Research,* Vol. 19 (1991), pp. 762–769; Deborah J. MacInnis and C. Whan Park, "The Differential Role of Characteristics of Music on High- and Low-Involvement Consumers' Processing of Ads," *Journal of Consumer Research,* Vol. 18 (September 1991), pp. 161–173; and Arjun Chaudhuri, "A Theoretical Framework for Advertising," *AMA Summer Educators' Proceedings* (1992), pp. 442–446.

32. David Kiley, "Cutting the Fat," *Marketing Week,* March 13, 1989, pp. 20ff.

Chapter 7
Consumer Information Processing

1.   Joanne Lipman, "Too Many Think the Bunny is Duracell's, not Eveready's" *The Wall Street Journal,* July 31, 1990, p. B1. The answers to the chapter-opening quiz: (1) Toyota; (2) Certs; (3) Taco Bell; (4) Campbell's; (5) Eveready Energizer.

2.   Robert J. Lavidge and Gary A. Steiner, "A Model for Predictive Measurements of Advertising Effectiveness," *Journal of Marketing,* Vol. 25 (October 1961), pp. 59–62. See also Lawrence F. Feick, "Latent Class Models for the Analysis of Behavioral Hierachies," *Journal of Marketing Research,* Vol. 24 (May 1987), pp. 174–186.

3.   Michael L. Ray, *Advertising and Communication Management* (Englewood Cliffs, N.J.: Prentice Hall, 1982).

4.   See, for example, Glen L. Urban and John R. Hauser, *Design and Marketing of New Products,* 2d ed. (Englewood Cliffs, N.J.: Prentice Hall, 1994).

5.   For an interesting review and discussion of the history of the hierarchy of effects framework, see Thomas E. Berry, "The Development of the Hierarchy of Effects: An Historical Perspective," in J. Leigh and C. Martin (eds.), *Current Issues & Research in Advertising,* Vol. 10 (Ann Arbor: University of Michigan Press, 1987), pp. 251–295. For extensions, see also Hugh McGinley and Douglass Hawes, "Verbal and Affective Cognitions and Their Application to Advertising," in C. Haugtvedt and D. Rosen (eds.), *Proceedings of the Society for Consumer Psychology* (Knoxville: D.W. Schumann, 1991), pp. 105–108; and Esther Thorson, Annie Chi, and Clark Leavitt, "Attention, Memory, Attitude, and Conation: A Test of the Advertising Hierarchy," *Advances in Consumer Research,* Vol. 19 (1991), pp. 366–379.

6.   See, for example, Herbert A. Simon and Allan Newell, "Information Processing in Computer and Man," *American Scientist,* Vol. 53 (1964), pp. 281–300; and Allan Newell and Herbert A. Simon, *Human Problem Solving* (Englewood Cliffs, N.J.: Prentice Hall, 1972).

7.   Each of the four CIP generalizations has recently received considerable research attention from consumer researchers. Citations for many of these studies are included in conjunction with our discussions of the detailed topics to which they are most pertinent in Parts Two, Three, and Four of this book. For a further overview and more extended discussion of the generalizations and their consumer behavior contexts, see William L. Wilkie, *How Consumers Use Product Information: An Assessment of Research in Relation to Public Policy Needs* (Washington, D.C.: National Science Foundation, 1974). See also James R. Bettman, *An Information Processing Theory of Consumer Choice* (Reading, Mass.: Addison-Wesley, 1979); and John G. Lynch and Thomas K. Srull, "Memory and Attentional Factors in Consumer Choice: Concepts and Research Methods," *Journal of Consumer Research,* Vol. 9 (June 1982), pp. 18–37.

8.   The essentials of this system are presented in R. M. Shiffrin and R. C. Atkinson "Storage and Retrieval Processes in Long-Term Memory," *Psychological Review,* Vol. 76 (1969), pp. 179–193.

9.   George Sperling, "The Information Available in Brief Visual Presentations," *Psychological Monographs,* Vol. 74, No. 11 (1960); C. J. Darwin, M. T. Turvey, and R. G. Crowder, "An Auditory Analogue of the Sperling Partial Report Procedure," *Cognitive Psychology,* Vol. 3 (1973), pp. 255–267.

10.   See, for example, Elizabeth Loftus and Geoffrey R. Loftus, "On the Permanence of Stored Information in the Human Brain," *American Psychologist,* Vol. 35 (May 1980), pp. 409–420. For a closely related "workbench" analog to the work center/warehouse sectors description, see Roberta Klatzky, *Human Memory: Structures and Processes* (San Francisco: W. H. Freeman, 1975).

11.   For an appreciation of these issues, see L. R. Peterson and S.T. Johnson, "Short-Term Retension of Individual Verbal Items," *Journal of Experimental Psychology,* Vol. 58 (1959), pp. 193–198. See also B.B. Murdock, Jr., "The Retention of Individual Items," *Journal of Experimental Psychology,* Vol. 62 (1961), pp. 618–625.

12.   George A. Miller, "The Magical Number Seven, Plus or Minus Two: Some Limits on Our Capacity for Processing Information," *Psychological Review,* Vol. 63 (1956), pp. 81–97.

13.   See, for example, Herbert A. Simon, "How Big Is a Chunk?" *Science,* Vol. 183 (February 1974), pp. 482–488.

14.   E. Tulving, "Episodic and Semantic Memory," in E. Tulving and W. Donaldson (eds.), *Organization of Memory* (New York: Academic Press, 1972). For related discussions, see Eleanor Rosch, "Cognitive Representation of Semantic Categories," *Cognitive Psychology,* Vol. 104, pp. 192–233; and Edward J. Shoben, "Semantic and Episodic Memory," in Robert S. Wyer and Thomas K. Srull (eds.), *Handbook of Social Cognition* (Hillsdale, N.J.: Erlbaum, 1984), pp. 213–231. Recent research in consumer behavior has also given considerable attention to "imagery" and related topics. See, for example, Terry L. Childers, Michael J. Houston, and Susan E. Heckler, "Measurement of Individual Differences in Visual versus Verbal Information Processing," *Journal of Consumer Research,* Vol. 12 (September 1985), pp. 125–134; Jolita Kisielius and Brian Sternthal, "Examining the Vividness Controversy: An Availability-Valence Interpretation," *Journal of Consumer Research,* Vol. 12 (March 1986), pp. 418–431; Deborah J. MacInnis and Linda L. Price, "The Role of Imagery in Information Processing: Review and Extensions," *Journal of Consumer Research,* Vol. 13 (March 1987), pp. 473–491; Keren Johnson, Mary Zimmer, and Linda Golden, "Object Relations Theory: Male and Female Differences in Visual Information Processing," *Advances in Consumer Research,* Vol. 14 (1987), pp. 83–87; Ann L. McGill and Punam Anand, "The Effect of Vivid Attributes on the Evaluation of Alternatives: The Role of Differential Attention and Cognitive Elaboration," *Journal of Consumer Research,* Vol. 16 (September 1989), pp. 188–196; Deborah J. MacInnis and Linda L. Price, "An Exploratory Study of the Effect of Imagery on Expectations and Satisfaction," *Advances in Consumer Research,* Vol. 17 (1990), pp. 41–47; Joan Meyers-Levy and Durairaj Maheswaran, "Exploring Differences in Males' and Females' Processing Strategies," *Journal of Consumer Research,* Vol. 18, No. 1 (June 1991), pp. 63–70; Jacquelyn L. Twible and James S. Hensel, "Vivid Information in Services Advertising: The Mediating Role of Prior Knowledge," *AMA Winter Educators' Proceedings* (1991), pp. 378–384; Charles E. Young and Michael Robinson, "The Visual Experience of New and Established Product Commercials," *Advances in Consumer Research,* Vol. 18 (1991), pp. 545–549; Linda M. Scott, "Playing with Pictures: Postmodernism, Poststructuralism, and Advertising Visuals," *Advances in Consumer Research,* Vol. 19 (1991), pp. 596–612; Laurie Babin, Alvin Burns, and Abhijit Biswas, "A Framework Providing Direction for Research on Communications Effects of Mental Imagery-evoking Advertising Strategies," *Advances in Consumer Research,* Vol. 19 (1991), pp. 621–628; H. Rao Unnava and Robert E.

Burnkrant, "An Imagery-processing View of the Role of Pictures in Print Advertisements," *Journal of Marketing Research,* Vol. 28 (May 1991), pp. 226–231; Susan E. Heckler and Terry L. Childers, "The Role of Expectancy and Relevancy in Memory for Verbal and Visual Information: What Is Incongruency?" *Journal of Consumer Research,* Vol. 18, No. 4 (March 1992), pp. 475–492; and Paula Fitzgerald Bone and Pam Scholder Ellen, "The Generation and Consequences of Communication-evoked Imagery," *Journal of Consumer Research,* Vol. 19, No. 1 (June 1992), pp. 93–104.

15. As we can appreciate, the distinction we make in this chapter among the three "stores" (sensory register, STM, and LTM) is a functional one; we are attempting to stress three different and important functions that are carried out during information processing. Experts in this area have also developed alternative ways of dealing with these functions. Some more advanced models of information processing do not use an STM sector, but instead view LTM to be the center for both storage and processing activity; one popular model, for example, relies on the concept of "spreading activation" as processing energy moves through the network system of LTM nodes to move from one thought to the next. For the purposes of this text, we do not need to move into this level of model. If you are interested in more advanced work in information processing, however, you should read more about these alternative models. See, for example, A.M. Collins and E.F. Loftus, "A Spreading Activation Theory of Semantic Processing," *Psychological Review,* Vol. 82 (1975), pp. 407–428; and John R. Anderson, *The Architecture of Cognition* (Cambridge, Mass.: Harvard University Press, 1983).

For discussions of some of the many implications of these and related issues for consumer behavior, see, for example, Thomas K. Srull, "A Model of Consumer Memory and Judgment," *Advances in Consumer Research,* Vol. 13 (1986), pp. 643–647; Joseph W. Alba and J. Wesley Hutchinson, "Dimensions of Consumer Expertise," *Journal of Consumer Research,* Vol. 13 (March 1987), pp. 411–454; George M. Zinkhan and Abhijit Biswas, "Using the Repertory Grid to Assess the Complexity of Consumers' Cognitive Structures," *Advances in Consumer Research,* Vol. 15 (1988), pp. 493–497; Joan Meyers-Levy, "The Influence of a Brand Name's Association Set Size and Work Frequency on Brand Memory," *Journal of Consumer Research,* Vol. 16 (September 1989), pp. 197–207; C. Whan Park, Robert Lawson, and Sandra Milberg, "Memory Structure for Brand Names," *Advances in Consumer Research,* Vol. 16 (1989), pp. 726–731; Dawne Martin and Pamela Kiecker, "Parallel Processing Models of Consumer Information Processing: Their Impact on Consumer Research Methods," *Advances in Consumer Research,* Vol. 17 (1990), pp. 443–448; Naresh K. Malhotra, "Mnemonics in Marketing: A Pedogogical Tool," *Journal of the Academy of Marketing Science,* Vol. 19, No. 2 (Spring 1991), pp. 141–149; Ehsan Ulhaque and Kenneth D. Bahn, "A Spreading Activation Model of Consumers' Asymmetric Similarity Judgement," *Advances in Consumer Research,* Vol. 19 (1991), pp. 782–786; and Thomas K. Srull, "Toward Articulating Theories, Triangulating Concepts, and Disambiguating Interpretations: The Role of Converging Operations in Consumer Memory and Judgment," *Advances in Consumer Research,* Vol. 19 (1991), pp. 23–27.

16. The answers to the jingles are as follows: (1) Green Giant; (2) Armour; (3) Charmin, Whipple; (4) Chevrolet; (5) Ace (Hardware); (6) Bud Light; (7) Zest; (8) McDonald's; (9) Doublemint; (10) Dial. **Bonus: Oscar Mayer.

17. See John G. Lynch and Thomas K. Srull, "Memory and Attentional Factors in Consumer Choice: Concepts and Research Methods," *Journal of Consumer Research,* Vol. 9 (June 1982), pp. 18–37; and Kevin Lane Keller, "Memory Factors in Advertising: The Effects of Advertising Retrieval Cues on Brand Evaluations," *Journal of Consumer Research,* Vol. 14 (December 1987), pp. 316–333. See also Julie A. Edell and Kevin Lane Keller, "The Information Processing of Coordinated Media Campaigns," *Journal of Marketing Research,* Vol. 26 (May 1989), pp. 149–163; Stephen J. Hoch and John Deighton, "Managing What Consumers Learn from Experience," *Journal of Marketing,* Vol. 53 (April 1989), pp. 1–20; Raymond R. Burke and Thomas K. Srull, "Competitive Interference and Consumer Memory for Advertising," *Journal of Consumer Research,* Vol. 15 (June 1988), pp. 55–68; Kevin Lane Keller, "Memory and Evaluation Effects in Competitive Advertising Environments," *Journal of Consumer Research,* Vol. 17, No. 4 (March 1991), pp. 463–476; Diane Halstead, Thomas J. Page, Jr., and Cornelia Droge, "Shaping Processing Mode through Forced Focus on Attributes: From Category to Piecemeal Processing," in C. Haugtvedt and D. Rosen (eds.), *Proceedings of the Society for Consumer Psychology* (Knoxville: D.W. Schumann, 1991), pp. 27–34; and Bernd H. Schmitt, Nader T. Tavassoli, and Robert T. Millard, "Memory for Print Ads: Understanding Relations among Brand Name, Copy, and Picture," *Journal of Consumer Psychology,* Vol. 2, No. 1 (1993), pp. 55–82.

18. Recent research has contributed interesting insights into the process of encoding. See, for example, David J. Bryant, "Implicit Associated Responses Influence Encoding in Memory," *Memory & Cognition,* Vol. 18, No. 4 (1990), pp. 348–358; Abhijit Sanyal, "Priming and Implicit Memory: A Review and a Sythesis Relevant for Consumer Behavior," *Advances in Consumer Research,* Vol. 19 (1991), pp. 795–805; and Marian Friestad and Esther Thorson, "Remembering Ads: The Effects of Encoding Strategies, Retrieval Cues, and Emotional Response," *Journal of Consumer Psychology,* Vol. 2, No. 1 (1993), pp. 1–24.

19. A considerable degree of consumer research attention has been given to this topic. See, for example, Wanda T. Wallace, "Jingles in Advertisements: Can They Improve Recall?" *Advances in Consumer Research,* Vol. 18 (1991), pp. 239–242; Gail Tom, "Marketing with Music," *The Journal of Consumer Marketing,* Vol. 7, No. 2 (Spring 1990), pp. 49–54; Linda M. Scott, "Understanding Jingles and Needledrop: A Rhetorical Approach to Music in Advertising," *Journal of Consumer Research,* Vol. 17, No. 2 (September 1990), pp. 223–236; Gary L. Sullivan, "Music Format Effects in Radio Advertising," *Psychology & Marketing,* Vol. 7, No. 2 (Summer 1990), pp. 97–108; Judy I. Alpert and Mark I. Alpert, "Music Influences on Mood and Purchase Intentions," *Psychology & Marketing,* Vol. 7, No. 2 (Summer 1990), pp. 109–134; David W. Stewart, Kenneth M. Farmer, and Charles I. Stannard, "Music as a Recognition Cue in Advertising-Tracking Studies," *Journal of Advertising Research,* Vol. 30, No. 4 (August/September 1990), pp. 39–48; Gordon C. Bruner II, "Music, Mood, and Marketing," *Journal of Marketing,* Vol. 54, No. 4 (October 1990), pp. 94–104; Judy I. Alpert and Mark I. Alpert, "Contributions from a Musical Perspective on Advertising and Consumer Behavior," *Advances in Consumer Research,* Vol. 18 (1991), pp. 232–238; James J. Kellaris and Robert J. Kent, "Exploring Tempo and Modality Effects on Consumer Responses to Music," *Advances in Consumer Research,* Vol. 18 (1991), pp. 243–248; James J. Kellaris and Moses B. Altsech, "The Experience of Time as a Function of Musical Loudness and Gender of Listener," *Advances* *in Consumer Research*, Vol. 19 (1991), pp. 725–729; Deborah J. MacInnis and C. Whan Park, "The Differential Role of Characteristics of Music on High- and Low-Involvement Consumers' Processing of Ads," *Journal of Consumer Research*, Vol. 18, No. 2 (September 1991), pp. 161–173; Brian Wansink, "Listen to the Music: Its Impact on Affect, Perceived Time Passage, and Applause," *Advances in Consumer Research*, Vol. 19 (1991), pp. 715–718; Hans Baumgartner, "Remembrance of Things Past: Music, Autobiographical Memory, and Emotion," *Advances in Consumer Research*, Vol. 19 (1991), pp. 613–620; James J. Kellaris, "Consumer Esthetics outside the Lab: Preliminary Report on a Musical Field Study," *Advances in Consumer Research*, Vol. 19 (1991), pp. 730–734; and James J. Kellaris and Robert J. Kent, "Using Music to Influence Consumers' Experience of Duration: *Does* Time Fly When You're Having Fun?" *AMA Winter Educators' Proceedings* (1992), Vol. 3, p. 346.

20.   Roy Furchgott, "You'll Never Get Bored Driving to South of the Border," *Marketing Week*, April 11, 1988, pp. 20–22. For a related discussion, see David Tanner, "Applying Creative Thinking Techniques to Everyday Problems," *The Journal of Consumer Marketing*, Vol. 9, No. 4 (Fall 1992), pp. 23–28.

21.   Prakash Nedungadi, "Recall and Consumer Consideration Sets: Influencing Choice without Altering Brand Evaluations," *Journal of Consumer Research*, Vol. 17, No. 3 (December 1990), pp. 263–276. The concept of evoked set (or consideration set) is one of the most interesting ideas that link CIP to applied marketing issues in consumer behavior. For background readings in this area, see John A. Howard and Jagdish N. Sheth, *The Theory of Buyer Behavior* (New York: John Wiley & Sons, 1969); Lance P. Jarvis and James B. Wilcox, "Evoked-Set Size—Some Theoretical Findings and Empirical Evidence," *Combined Proceedings American Marketing Association* (1973), pp. 236–260; C.L. Narayana and Rom T. Markin, "Consumer Behavior and Product Performance: An Alternative Conceptualization," *Journal of Marketing*, Vol. 39 (October 1975), pp. 1–6. For findings and discussions, see, for example, Michael Reilly and Thomas L. Parkinson, "Individual and Product Correlates of Evoked Set Size for Consumer Package Goods," *Advances in Consumer Research*, Vol. 12 (1985), pp. 492–497; Joseph W. Alba and Amitava Chattopadhyay, 'The Effects of Context and Part-Category Cues on the Recall of Competing Brands," *Journal of Marketing Research*, Vol. 22 (August 1985), pp. 340–349; Susan Spiggle and Murphy A. Sewall, "A Choice Sets Model of Retail Selection," *Journal of Marketing*, Vol. 51 (April 1987), pp. 97–111; David B. Klenosky and Arno J. Rethans, "The Formation of Consumer Choice Sets: A Longitudinal Investigation at the Product Class Level," *Advances in Consumer Research*, Vol. 15 (1988), pp. 13–18; John R. Hauser and Birger Wernerfelt, "An Evaluation Cost Model of Consideration Sets," *Journal of Consumer Research*, Vol. 16, No. 4 (March 1990), pp. 393–408; Wayne D. Hoyer and Steven P. Brown, "Effects of Brand Awareness on Choice for a Common, Repeat-Purchase Product," *Journal of Consumer Research*, Vol. 17, No. 2 (September 1990), pp. 141–148; Paul W. Miniard, H. Rao Unnava, and Sunil Bhatla, "Investigating the Recall Inhibition Effect: A Test of Practical Considerations," *Marketing Letters*, Vol. 2, No. 1 (January 1991), pp. 27–34; John H. Roberts and James M. Lattin, "Development and Testing of a Model of Consideration Set Composition," *Journal of Marketing Research*, Vol. 28 (November 1991), pp. 429–440; Ayn E. Crowley and John H. Williams, "An Information Theoretic Approach to Understanding the Consideration Set/Awareness Set Proportion," *Advances in Consumer Research*,

Vol. 18 (1991), pp. 780–787; David B. Klenosky and W. Steven Perkins, "Deriving Attribute Utilities from Consideration Sets: An Alternative to Self-explicated Utilities," *Advances in Consumer Research*, Vol. 19 (1991), pp. 657–663; Prakash Nedungadi and Vinay Kanetkar, "Incorporating Consideration Sets into Models of Brand Choice," *Advances in Consumer Research*, Vol. 19 (1991), pp. 251–252; John S. Hulland, "An Empirical Investigation of Consideration Set Formation," *Advances in Consumer Research*, Vol. 19 (1991), pp. 253–254; Stephen J. S. Holden and Richard J. Lutz, "Ask Not What the Brand Can Evoke; Ask What Can Evoke the Brand?" *Advances in Consumer Research*, Vol. 19 (1992), pp. 101–107; Juanita J. Brown and Albert R. Wildt, "Consideration Set Measurement," *Journal of the Academy of Marketing Science*, Vol. 20, No. 3 (Summer 1992), pp. 235–244; and Frank R. Kardes, Gurumurthy Kalyanaram, Murali Chandrashekaran, and Ronald J. Dornoff, "Brand Retrieval, Consideration Set Composition, Consumer Choice, and the Pioneering Advantage," *Journal of Consumer Research*, Vol. 20, No. 1 (June 1993), pp. 62–75.

22.   Patricia Winters "7UP Logs 'Un'-usual Gains in Market Share," *Advertising Age*, November 16, 1992, p. 43; Jennifer Lawrence, "Uncola Spotlight," *Advertising Age*, September 30, 1991, p. 4; Scott Hume, "An Un-Happy Seven-Up Returns to Old Theme," *Advertising Age*, March 11, 1985, p. 10.

23.   This classification was developed by G. David Hughes and Michael L. Ray, *Buyer/Consumer Information Processing* (Chapel Hill: University of North Carolina Press, 1974).

24.   For basic discussions of media differences and low involvement, see Herbert E. Krugman, "The Impact of Television Advertising: Learning without Involvement," *Public Opinion Quarterly*, Vol. 29 (Fall 1965), pp. 349–356; Herbert E. Krugman, "The Measurement of Advertising Involvement," *Public Opinion Quarterly*, Vol. 32 (1968), pp. 583–596; Herbert E. Krugman, "Brain Wave Measures of Media Involvement," *Journal of Advertising Research*, Vol. 11 (February 1971), pp. 3–9; and Peter L. Wright, "Analyzing Media Effects on Advertising Responses," *Public Opinion Quarterly*, Vol. 38 (1974), pp. 192–205. For recent developments, see Herbert E. Krugman, "Point of View: Limits of Attention to Advertising," *Journal of Advertising Research*, Vol. 28 (October–November 1988), pp. 47–50; Deborah J. MacInnis and Bernard J. Jaworski, "Information Processing from Advertisements: Toward an Integrative Framework," *Journal of Marketing*, Vol. 53, No. 4 (October 1989), pp. 1–23; Chris Janiszewski, "The Influence of Print Advertisement Organization on Affect toward a Brand Name," *Journal of Consumer Research*, Vol. 17, No. 1 (June 1990), pp. 53–65; Michael L. Rothschild and Yong J. Hyun, "Predicting Memory for Components of TV Commercials from EEG," *Journal of Consumer Research*, Vol. 16, No. 4 (March 1990), pp. 472–478; Daniel J. Howard and Robert E. Burnkrant, "Question Effects on Information Processing in Advertising," *Psychology & Marketing*, Vol. 7, No. 1 (Spring 1990), pp. 27–46; James Ward and William Gaidis, "Metaphor in Promotional Communication: A Review of Research on Metaphor Comprehension and Quality," *Advances in Consumer Research*, Vol. 17 (1990), pp. 636–642; G. David Hughes, "Studies in Imagery, Styles of Processing, and Parallel Processing Need Realtime Response Measures," *Advances in Consumer Research*, Vol. 17 (1990), pp. 461–466; Paul W. Miniard, Sunil Bhatla, Kenneth R. Lord, Peter R. Dickson, and H. Rao Unnava, "Picture-based Persuasion Processes and the Moderating Role of Involvement," *Journal of Consumer Research*, Vol. 18, No. 1 (June 1991), pp. 92–107; Jeffrey J. Stoltman, "Advertising Effectiveness: The Role of Advertising Schemas," *AMA Winter Educators' Proceedings* (1991), pp. 317–318; Gregory W. Boller and Jerry C. Olson, "Experiencing Ad Meanings: Crucial Aspects of Narrative/Drama Processing," *Advances in Consumer Research*, Vol. 18 (1991), pp. 172–175; Amna Kirmani and Youjae Yi, "The Effects of Advertising Context on Consumer Responses," *Advances in Consumer Research*, Vol. 18 (1991), pp. 414–416; Youjae Yi, "The Influence of Contextual Priming on Advertising Effects," *Advances in Consumer Research*, Vol. 18 (1991), pp. 417–425; Esther Thorson, "Moment by Moment Analyses of TV Commercials: Their Theoretical and Applied Roles: Summary of the Panel," *Advances in Consumer Research*, Vol. 18 (1991), pp. 538–539; Mark Polsfuss and Mike Hess, "'Liking' through Moment-to-Moment Evaluation: Identifying Key Selling Segments in Advertising," *Advances in Consumer Research*, Vol. 18 (1991), pp. 540–544; Linda F. Alwitt, "Analysis Approaches to Moment by Moment Reactions to Commercials: Discussion for Special Session on Moment by Moment Analyses of TV Commercials," *Advances in Consumer Research*, Vol. 18 (1991), pp. 550–551; Ida E. Berger, "Toward a New Understanding of the Effects of Advertising: A Look at Implicit Memorial Processes," *Advances in Consumer Research*, Vol. 18 (1991), pp. 688–692; Stephen J. Gould, "Parallels between Hypnotic Suggestion and Persuasive Marketing Communications: Insights for New Directions in Consumer Communications Research," *Advances in Consumer Research*, Vol. 19 (1991), pp. 56–61; Thomas Boyd and G. David Hughes, "Validating Realtime Response Measures," *Advances in Consumer Research*, Vol. 19 (1991), pp. 649–656; Hugh McGinley and Douglass K. Hawes, "Verbal and Affective Cognitions and Their Application to Advertising," in C. Haugtvedt and D. Rosen (eds.), *Proceedings of the Society for Consumer Psychology* (Knoxville: D. W. Schumann, 1991), pp. 105–108; Scott A. Hawkins and Stephen J. Hoch, "Low-Involvement Learning: Memory without Evaluation," *Journal of Consumer Research*, Vol. 19, No. 2 (September 1992), pp. 212–225; and Ronald C. Goodstein, "Category-based Applications and Extensions in Advertising: Motivating More Extensive Ad Processing," *Journal of Consumer Research*, Vol. 20, No. 1 (June 1993), pp. 87–99. Further related references are provided in the Notes for Chapter 16, which deals specifically with advertising.

25. For basic discussions of a CIP view of advertising wearout, see G. David Hughes, "Realtime Response Measures Redefine Advertising Wearout," *Journal of Advertising Research*, Vol. 32, No. 3 (May/June 1992), pp. 61–77; Bobby J. Calder and Brian Sternthal, "Television Commercial Wearout: An Information Processing View," *Journal of Marketing Research*, Vol. 17 (May 1980), pp. 173–186; C. Samuel Craig, Brain Sternthal, and Clark Leavitt, "Advertising Wearout: An Experimental Analysis," *Journal of Marketing Research*, Vol. 13 (November 1976), pp. 365–372; and R. C. Grass and Wallace H. Wallace, "Satiation Effects of T.V. Commercials," *Journal of Advertising Research*, Vol. 19 (1969), pp. 47–57. Further related findings are referenced in the Notes of Chapter 16, which deal specifically with advertising's influences on consumer behavior.

26. The rise of postmodern consumer research has raised many new issues and many new possibilities for the field of consumer behavior. The proceedings of the annual conference of the Association for Consumer Research (*Advances in Consumer Research*) and the *Journal of Consumer Research* have had a large number of postmodern articles recently, together with debates. An excellent overview is available in John F. Sherry, Jr., "Postmodern Alterna-

tives: The Interpretive Turn in Consumer Research," in Thomas Robertson and Harold Kassarjian (eds.), *Handbook of Consumer Theory and Research* (Englewood Cliffs, N.J.: Prentice Hall, 1991), pp. 548–591; in the same volume see the related discussion by J. Paul Peter, "Philosophical Tensions in Consumer Inquiry," pp. 533–547. See also Elizabeth C. Hirschman (ed.), *Interpretive Consumer Research* (Provo, Utah: Association for Consumer Research, 1989).

For interesting reading in this area, see, for example, Morris B. Holbrook, "Seven Routes to Facilitating the Semiological Interpretation of Consumption Symbolism and Marketing Imagery in Works of Art: Some Tips for Wildcats," *Advances in Consumer Research*, Vol. 16 (1989), pp. 420–425; Craig J. Thompson, William B. Locander, and Howard R. Pollio, "Putting Consumer Experience Back into Consumer Research: The Philosophy and Method of Existential-Phenomenology," *Journal of Consumer Research*, Vol. 16 (September 1989), pp. 133–146; Thomas C. O'Guinn and Russell W. Belk, "Heaven on Earth: Consumption at Heritage Village, USA," *Journal of Consumer Research*, Vol. 16 (September 1989), pp. 227–238; Barbara B. Stern, "Literary Criticism and Consumer Research: Overview and Illustrative Analysis," *Journal of Consumer Research*, Vol. 16, No. 3 (December 1989), pp. 322–334; Craig J. Thompson, "Eureka! and Other Tests of Significance: A New Look at Evaluating Interpretive Research," *Advances in Consumer Research*, Vol. 17 (1990), pp. 25–30; A. Fuat Firat, "The Consumer in Postmodernity," *Advances in Consumer Research*, Vol. 18 (1991), pp. 70–76; Ruth Ann Smith, "Methodical Diversity in Consumer Esthetics Research," *Advances in Consumer Research*, Vol. 18 (1991), pp. 379–380; Jean Umiker-Sebeok, "Meaning Construction in a Cultural Gallery: A Sociosemiotic Study of Consumption Experiences in a Museum," *Advances in Consumer Research*, Vol. 19 (1991), pp. 46–55; Mary Ellen Zuckerman and Mary Carsky, "Feminist Theory and Marketing Thought: Toward a New Approach for Consumer Research," *Advances in Consumer Research*, Vol. 19 (1991), pp. 464–471; Russell W. Belk (ed.), *Highways and Buyways: Naturalistic Research from the Consumer Behavior Odyssey* (Provo, Utah: Association for Consumer Research, 1991; Alladi Venkatesh, "Postmodernism, Consumer Culture and the Society of the Spectacle," *Advances in Consumer Research*, Vol. 19 (1991), pp. 199–202; Ahmet Suerdem, "What Are You Doing after the Orgy? or Does the Consumer Really Behave ('Well')?" *Advances in Consumer Research*, Vol. 19 (1991), pp. 207–212; and Edward F. McQuarrie and David Glen Mick, "On Resonance: A Critical Pluralistic Inquiry into Advertising Rhetoric," *Journal of Consumer Research*, Vol. 19, No. 2 (September 1992), pp. 180–198; Russell W. Belk, "Moving Possessions: An Analysis Based on Personal Documents from the 1847–1869 Mormon Migration," *Journal of Consumer Research*, Vol. 19, No. 3 (December 1992), pp. 339–361; Julia M. Bristor and Eileen Fischer, "Feminist Thought: Implications for Consumer Research," *Journal of Consumer Research*, Vol. 19, No. 4 (March 1993), pp. 518–536; and Barbara B. Stern, "Feminist Literary Criticism and the Deconstruction of Ads: A Postmodern View of Advertising and Consumer Responses," *Journal of Consumer Research*, Vol. 19, No. 4 (March 1993), pp. 556–566.

The postmodern approach has also sparked serious debates about the basic nature of consumer research. See, for example, Morris B. Holbrook, "What Is Consumer Research?" *Journal of Consumer Research*, Vol. 14 (June 1987), pp. 128–132; Jerome B. Kernan, "Chasing the Holy Grail," *Journal of Consumer Research*, Vol. 14 (June 1987), pp. 133–135; Bobby J. Calder and Alice M. Tybout, "What Consumer Research Is . . . ," *Journal of Consumer Research*, Vol. 14 (June 1987), pp. 136–140; Eileen Fischer, "Regularities, Rules and

Consumer Behavior: Tangencies between Positivist and Interpretive Approaches to Research," *Advances in Consumer Research*, Vol. 17 (1990), pp. 19–24; Shelby D. Hunt, "Positivism and Paradigm Dominance in Consumer Research: Toward Critical Pluralism and Rapprochement," *Journal of Consumer Research*, Vol. 18, No. 1 (June 1991), pp. 32–44; Douglas B. Holt, "Rashomon Visits Consumer Behavior: An Interpretive Critique of Naturalistic Inquiry," *Advances in Consumer Research*, Vol. 18 (1991), pp. 57–62; Craig J. Thompson, "May the Circle Be Unbroken: A Hermeneutic Consideration of How Interpretive Approaches to Consumer Research Are Understood by Consumer Researchers," *Advances in Consumer Research*, Vol. 18 (1991), pp. 62–69; Jeff B. Murray and Julie L. Ozanne, "The Critical Imagination: Emancipatory Interests in Consumer Research," *Journal of Consumer Research*, Vol. 18, No. 2 (September 1991), pp. 129–144; William Val Larsen and Newell D. Wright, "A Critique of Critical Theory: Response to Murray and Ozanne's 'The Critical Imagination,'" *Advances in Consumer Research*, Vol. 20 (1993), pp. 439–443; A. Fuat Firat, "Fragmentations in the Postmodern," *Advances in Consumer Research*, Vol. 19 (1991), pp. 203–206; J. Paul Peter, "Realism or Relativism for Marketing Theory and Research: A Comment on Hunt's "Scientific Realism,'" *Journal of Marketing*, Vol. 56, No. 2 (April 1992), pp. 72–79; George M. Zinkhan and Rudy Hirschheim, "Truth in Marketing Theory and Research: An Alternative Perspective," *Journal of Marketing*, Vol. 56, No. 2 (April 1992), pp. 80–88; Shelby D. Hunt, "For Reason and Realism in Marketing," *Journal of Marketing*, Vol. 56, No. 2 (April 1992), pp. 89–102; Elizabeth C. Hirschman, "Ideology in Consumer Research, 1980 and 1990: A Marxist and Feminist Critique," *Journal of Consumer Research*, Vol. 19, No. 4 (March 1993), pp. 537–555; and Shelby Hunt, "Objectivity in Marketing Theory and Research," *Journal of Marketing*, Vol. 57, No. 2 (April 1993), pp. 76–91.

27. This report is based upon discussions in Ernest Dichter, *Handbook of Consumer Motivations* (New York: McGraw-Hill, 1964); "Algonquin Advertising Agency," in Edward C. Bursk and Stephen A. Greyser (eds.), *Advanced Cases in Marketing Management* (Englewood Cliffs, N.J.; Prentice Hall, 1968), pp. 1–18; and Erik Larson, "Admen Try to Make Juice-loving World Swoon for a Prune," *The Wall Street Journal*, February 15, 1983, pp. 1ff.

28. This report is based upon information in Fara Warner, "M'Boro Moves," *Brandweek*, April 5, 1993, p. 1; Anthony Ramirez, "The Marlboro Man's Dominance," *New York Times*, March 8, 1990, p. C1; Christine Donahue, "The World's Most Powerful Brand," *Marketing Week*, May 9, 1988, pp. 32ff; and especially Pierre Martineau, *Motivation in Advertising* (New York: McGraw-Hill, 1971).

Chapter 8

Consumer Perception (I): Attention to Marketing Cues

1. Harold M. Schmeck, "To Appreciate Flavor, Taste with Your Nose," *The New York Times News Service*, June 24, 1982.

2. Alison Fahey and Cathy Taylor, "New Tab Spots Coming Regionally," *Brandweek*, August 10, 1992, p. 3; Kyle Chadwick, "Coke Gives Tab a Second Chance," *Marketing Week*, July 17, 1989, p. 17; and Nancy Giges, "Why Coke Delayed on Reformulating Tab," *Advertising Age*, May 21, pp. 2ff.

3. Bill Abrams and David Garino, "Package Design Gains Stature as Visual Competition Grows," *The Wall Street Journal*, August 6, 1981, p. 25.

4. Stephen Morin, "Interior Design Sets Out to Make Casino That Relaxes Your Morality," *The Wall Street Journal*, January 10, 1983, p. 31.

5. Anthony Smith, *The Mind* (New York: Viking Press, 1984), pp. 175–201. See also Fairfid M. Caudle, "An Ecological Perspective: Implications for Consumer Psychology," in C. Haugtvedt and D. Rosen (eds.), *Proceedings of the Society for Consumer Psychology* (Knoxville: D. W. Schumann, 1991), pp. 12–18.

6. The formula for Weber's Law is

$$JND = K \times I$$

which read, "The just noticeable difference in a given stimulus is equal to a constant of proportion (K) times the original intensity (I) of the stimulus." Subsequent scientific research has established that the value of the constant of proportion, K, differs for each type of sensory receptor, that it can differ slightly for each person, that it holds better for normal circumstances than for those cases in which intensities are very high or very low to begin with, and that the relationships are slightly more complicated than the simple multiplication shown in our formula. See Bernard Berelson and Gary A. Steiner, *Human Behavior—An Inventory of Scientific Findings* (New York: Harcourt, Brace & World, 1964). For controversial extensions of this sensory principle to broader perceptual areas in marketing, see Steuart Henderson Britt, "How Weber's Law Can Be Applied to Marketing," *Business Horizons*, February 1975, pp. 21–29. See also Elizabeth J. Wilson, "Using the Dollarmetric Scale to Estimate the Just Meaningful Difference in Price," *AMA Summer Educators' Proceedings* (1987), p. 107.

7. David Kiley, "Shrinking the Brand to Fit the Hard Times," *Marketing Week*, November 26, 1990, p. 6; an interesting discussion of strategic marketing issues is presented in Anthony Adams, C. Anthony diBenedetto, and Rajan Chandran, "Can You Reduce Your Package Size without Damaging Sales?" *Long Range Planning*, Vol. 24, No. 4 (August 1991), p. 86–96; see also A. Kent MacDougall, "The World Is Becoming a Much Smaller Place in More Ways Than One," *New York Post*, June 17, 1978.

8. "Packaging Design Seen as Cost-effective Marketing Strategy," *Marketing News*, February 20, 1981, pp. 1ff.

9. For an interesting general reading on the cola marketing wars and blind taste test, see "Who's Got the Right One!" *Consumer Reports*, August 1991, pp. 518–525. See also Betsy Morris, "In This Taste Test, the Loser is the Taste Test," *The Wall Street Journal*, June 3, 1987, p. 33; Bruce Buchanan, Moshe Givon, and Arieh Goldman, "Measurement of Discrimination Ability in Taste Tests: An Empirical Investigation," *Journal of Marketing Research*, Vol. 24 (May 1987), pp. 154–163; and Bruce Buchanan and Pamela W. Henderson, "Assessing the Bias of Preference, Detection, and Identification Measures of Discrimination Ability in Product Design," *Marketing Science*, Vol. 11, No. 1 (Winter 1992), pp. 64–75.

10. Ralph I. Allison and Kenneth P. Uhl, "Influences of Beer Brand Identification on Taste Perception," *Journal of Marketing Research*, Vol. 2, No. 3 (August 1964), pp. 36–39. See also Gary A. Mauser,

"Allison and Uhl Revisited: The Effects of Taste and Brand Name on Perceptions and Preferences," *Advances in Consumer Research*, Vol. 6 (1979), pp. 161–165; and John G. Lynch, Jr., and Thomas K. Srull, "Memory and Attentional Factors in Consumer Choice: Concepts and Research Methods," *Journal of Consumer Research*, Vol. 9, No. 1 (1982), pp. 18–37.

11. William Copulsky and Catherine Marton, "Sensory Cues: You've Got to Put Them Together," *Product Marketing*, January 1977, pp. 31–34. See also Jacob Hornik, "Tactile Stimulation and Consumer Response," *Journal of Consumer Research*, Vol. 19, No. 3 (December 1992), pp. 449–458.

12. E. Colin Cherry, "Some Experiments on the Recognition of Speech, with One and Two Ears," *Journal of the Acoustical Society of America*, Vol. 25 (1953), pp. 975–979. For related discussion, see Armen Tashchian, J. Dennis White, and Sukgoo Pak, "Signal Detection Analysis and Advertising Recognition: An Introduction to Measurement and Interpretation Issues," *Journal of Marketing Research*, Vol. 25 (November 1988), pp. 397–404.

13. These terms are adapted from the original tripartite classification presented by Magdalen D. Vernon, "Perception, Attention, and Consciousness," in K. K. Soreno and C. D. Mortensen (eds.), *Foundations of Communication Theory* (New York: Harper & Row, 1970, p. 138). For marketing applications, see, for example, Scott B. MacKenzie, "The Role of Attention in Mediating the Effect of Advertising on Attribute Importance," *Journal of Consumer Research*, Vol. 13 (September 1986), pp. 174–195; Gary L. Sullivan and Kenneth J. Burger, "An Investigation of the Determinants of Cue Utilization," *Psychology & Marketing*, Vol. 4 (Spring 1987), pp. 63–74; R. L. Celsi and J. C. Olson, "The Role of Involvement in Attention and Comprehension Processes," *Journal of Consumer Research*, Vol. 15 (September 1988), pp. 210–224; and Cathy Cobb-Walgren, "Tuning In and Turning Off: Trends in Television Viewing Behavior," in C. Haugtvedt and D. Rosen (eds.), *Proceedings of the Society for Consumer Psychology* (Knoxville: D. W. Schumann, 1991), pp. 73–75.

14. Jack Hairston, "Don't Look Up, Please," *Gainesville* (Florida) *Sun*, June 26, 1984, p. B1.

15. Ronald Alsop, "Advertisers See Big Gains in Odd Layouts," *The Wall Street Journal*, June 29, 1988, p. 25. See also Robert M. Schindler, Michael Berbaum, and Donna R. Weinzimer, "How an Attention Getting Device Can Affect Choice among Similar Alternatives," *Advances in Consumer Research*, Vol. 14 (1987), pp. 505–509; Ronald Hoverstad, "Vividness as a Means of Attracting Attention: A Revised Concept of Vividness," *AMA Winter Educators' Proceedings* (1987), pp. 245–248; and Jacqueline Hitchon, "'Headlines Make Ads Work': Highlights of the Special Topic Session," *Advances in Consumer Research*, Vol. 18 (1991), pp. 752–754.

16. "Packaging Research Probes Stopping Power, Label Reading, and Consumer Attitudes among the Targeted Audience," *Marketing News*, July 22, 1983, p. 8.

17. Dean Rotbart, "Store Designer Raises Profits for Retailers," *The Wall Street Journal*, December 5, 1980, p. 29.

18. For discussions of how consumer knowledge affects perceptual automaticity, see, for example, J. W. Alba and J. W. Hutchinson, "Dimensions of Consumer Expertise," *Journal of Consumer Research*, Vol. 13, No. 4 (1987), pp. 411–454; S. Ratneswar, David Mick, and Gail Reitinger, "Selective Attention in Consumer Infor-

mation Processing: The Role of Chronically Accessible Attributes," in *Advances in Consumer Research*, Vol. 17 (1990); and a series of studies by John A. Bargh and colleagues, for example, J. A. Bargh, Wendy Lombardi, and E. Troy Higgins, "Automaticitiy of Chronically Accessible Constructs...," *Journal of Personality and Social Psychology*, Vol. 55, No. 4 (1988), pp. 599–605.

19, See, for example, Norman Cousins, "Smudging the Subconscious," *Saturday Review*, October 5, 1957; also H. Brean, "What the Hidden Sell Is All About," *Life*, March 31, 1958, pp. 104–114. For a summary of this work, see Timothy E. Moore, "Subliminal Advertising: What You See Is What You Get," *Journal of Marketing*, Vol. 46 (Spring 1982), pp. 38–47; for further details and findings, see D. Hawkins, "The Effects of Subliminal Stimulations on Drive Level and Brand Preference," *Journal of Marketing Research*, Vol. 8 (August 1970), pp. 322–326; Norman F. Dixon, *Subliminal Perception: The Nature of a Controversy* (London: McGraw-Hill, 1971); Daniel Holender, "Semantic Activation without Conscious Activation in Dichotic Listening, Parafovial Vision and Pattern Masking: A Survey and Appraisal," *The Behavioral and Brain Sciences*, Vol. 9 (1986), pp. 1–66; John F. Kihlstrom, "The Cognitive Unconscious," *Science*, Vol. 237 (1987), pp. 1445–1452; Philip M. Merikle and Jim Chesman, "Current Status of Research on Subliminal Perception," *Advances in Consumer Research*, Vol. 14 (1987), pp. 298–302; Joel Saegert, "Why Marketing Should Quit Giving Subliminal Advertising the Benefit of the Doubt," *Psychology & Marketing*, Vol. 4 (Summer 1987), pp. 107–120. For an in-depth marketing look at this topic, see the Winter 1988 special issue of *Psychology & Marketing*, Vol. 5. For recent findings and discussion, see, for example, Anthony R. Pratkanis, "Subliminal Sorcery Then and Now, Who Is Seducing Whom?" in C. Haugtvedt and D. Rosen (eds.), *Proceedings of the Society for Consumer Psychology* (Knoxville: D. W. Schumann, 1991), pp. 84–86; and Jon A. Krosmick, Andrew Betz, Lee Jussim, and Ann Lynn, "Subliminal Conditioning of Attitudes," *Personality and Social Psychology Bulletin*, Vol. 18, No. 2 (April 1992), pp. 152–162; plus the references in Note 22.

20. For an accusation that the movie theater study reported results were fabricated, see Walter Weir, "Another Look at Subliminal Facts," *Advertising Age*, October 15, 1984.

21. M. L. DeFleur and R. M. Petranoff, "A Television Test of Subliminal Persuasion," *Public Opinion Quarterly*, Summer 1959, pp. 170–180.

22. The subliminal audiotape study is reported in Eric R. Spangenberg, Carl Obermiller, and Anthony Greenwald, "A Field Test of Subliminal Self-help Audiotapes: The Power of Expectancies," *Journal of Public Policy & Marketing*, Vol. 11, No. 1 (Fall 1992), pp. 26–36; and Anthony Greenwald, Eric R. Spangenberg, Anthony Pratkanis, and Jay Eskenazi, "Double-blind Tests of Subliminal Self-help Audiotapes," *Psychological Science*, Vol. 2, No. 2 (1991), pp. 119–122.

23. Albert S. King, "Pupil Size, Eye Direction, and Message Appeal: Some Preliminary Findings," *Journal of Marketing*, Vol. 36, No. 3 (July 1972), pp. 55–58. For recent research on preconscious processing, see Chris Janiszewski, "Preconscious Processing Effects: The Independence of Attitude Formation and Conscious Thought," *Journal of Consumer Research*, Vol. 15 (September 1988), pp. 199–209; Chris Janiszewski, "The Influence of Nonattended Material on the

Processing of Advertising Claims," *Journal of Marketing Research*, Vol. 27 (August 1990), pp. 263–278; and Stewart Shapiro and Deborah J. MacInnis, "Mapping the Relationship between Preattentive Processing and Attitudes," *Advances in Consumer Research*, Vol. 19 (1991), pp. 505–513.

24. Key's charges can be found in W. B. Key, *Subliminal Seduction* (Englewood Cliffs, N.J.: Signet, 1973), W. B. Key, *Media Sexploitation* (Englewood Cliffs, N.J.: Prentice Hall, 1976); and W. B. Key, *The Clamplate Orgy* (Englewood Cliffs, N.J.: Prentice Hall, 1980); for reports on the national survey and recent advertiser reaction, see Michael Lev, "No Hidden Meaning Here: Survey Sees Subliminal Ads," *New York Times*, May 3, 1991, p. C6.

25. G. S. Bagley and B. J. Dunlap, "Subliminally Embedded Ads: A 'Turn On'?" in J. H. Summey and R. D. Taylor (eds.), *Evolving Marketing Thought for 1980* (Carbondale, Ill.: Southern Marketing Association, 1980), pp. 296–298.

26. J. S. Kelly, "Subliminal Embeds in Print Advertising: A Challenge to Advertising Ethics," *Journal of Advertising*, Vol. 8, No. 3 (1979), pp. 20–24; J. G. Caccavale, T. C. Wanty, and J. A. Edell, "Subliminal Implants in Advertisements: An Experiment," *Advances in Consumer Research*, Vol. 9 (1982), pp. 418–423; and Rajeev Kohli and Deborah MacInnis, "Subliminal Advertising: An Empirical Investigation of its Effects in Print Media," Working Paper, University of Arizona, Tucson, 1989. For basic discussion of how persuasion might occur in this area, see R. B. Zajonc, "Feeling and Thinking: Preferences Need No Inferences," *American Psychologist*, Vol. 35 (February 1980), pp. 151–175; Stephan C. George and Luther B. Jennings, "Effect of Subliminal Stimuli on Consumer Behavior: Negative Evidence," *Perceptual and Motor Skills*, Vol. 41 (1975), pp. 847–854; and Ronnie Cuperfain and T. K. Clarke, "A New Perspective on Subliminal Perception," *Journal of Advertising*, Vol. 14, No. 1 (1985), pp. 36–41. See also William E. Kilbourne, Scott Painton, and Danny Ridley, "The Effect of Sexual Embedding on Responses to Magazine Advertisements," *Journal of Advertising*, Vol. 14, No. 2 (1985), pp. 48–56.

27. Raymond Serfin and Gary Levin, "Ad Industry Suffers Crushing Blow," *Advertising Age*, November 12, 1990, p. 1; Jennifer Lawrence, "How Volvo's Ad Collided with the Truth," *Advertising Age*, November 12, 1990, p. 76; and Joann Lublin, "WPP's Scali Gives Up the Volvo Account," *The Wall Street Journal*, November 14, 1990, p. B6. See also Krystal Miller and Jacqueline Mitchell, "Car Marketers Test Grey Area of Truth in Advertising," *The Wall Street Journal*, November 19, 1990, p. B1; and Raymond Serfin and Jennifer Lawrence, "Four More Volvo Ads Scrutinized," *Advertising Age*, November 26, 1990, p. 4.

28. Dena Kleiman, "The Artists Who Create Food Fantasies," *New York Times*, November 7, 1990, p. B1.

29. David E. Kalish, "Consumers Rap Shrinking Food Packages," *Associated Press Wire*, January 6, 1991.

30. David Kiley, "Shrinking the Brand to Fit the Hard Times," *Marketing Week*, November 26, 1990, p. 6. To learn about further criticisms of downsizing, see also Laurie Petersen, "A Misguided Defense," *Marketing Week*, February 25, 1991, p. 9; Judann Dagnoli, "State AGs Attack Downsized Brands," *Advertising Age*, February 18, 1991, p. 1.; Hall Farahi, "Sometimes Less Is Less," *Washington Post National Weekly Edition*, February 11, 1991, p. 23; and Anthony Adams, C. Anthony diBenedetto, and Rajan Chandran, "Can You

Reduce Your Package Size without Damaging Sales?" *Long Range Planning*, Vol. 24, No. 4 (August 1991), pp. 86–96.

31. A number of fascinating readings are available on these topics. See, for example, "Color Cues!" *Marketing Insights*, Spring 1990, pp. 42–46; Pamela J. Black, "No One Sniffing at Aroma Research Now," *Business Week*, December 23, 1991, pp. 82–83; Molly O'Neill, "Taming the Frontier of the Senses: Using Aroma to Manipulate Moods," *New York Times*, November 27, 1991, B1; and Gene Bylinsky, "A Sixth Sense That Affects How You Feel," *Fortune*, January 27, 1992, p. 99.

Chapter 9

Consumer Perception (II): Interpreting Marketing Cues

1. Gregory Witcher, "Department of Shattered Illusions: Coreenthian Leather Is Made in . . . ," *The Wall Street Journal*, April 11, 1988, p. 21.

2. This section is based on discussions in J. R. Hayes, *Cognitive Psychology: Thinking and Creating* (Homewood, Ill.: Dorsey, 1978, pp. 52–73); H. R. Schiffman, *Sensation and Perception: An Integrated Approach* (New York: John Wiley & Sons, 1976); D. A. Aaker and J. G. Myers, *Advertising Management*, 2d ed. (Englewood Cliffs, N.J.: Prentice Hall, 1982); and Carolyn Simmons, "Perceptual Issues in Consumer Behavior," Working Paper, University of Florida, Gainesville, 1981.

3. Wolfgang Kohler, *The Mentality of Apes* (London: Routledge and Kegan Paul, 1925); and Wolfgang Kohler, *Dynamics of Psychology* (New York: Liveright, 1940), as reported in Hayes, *Cognitive Psychology*.

4. Anthony Ramirez, "Soap Sellers' New Credo: Less Powder, More Power," *New York Times*, February 1, 1991, p. A1.

5. Charles G. Burck, "Plain Labels Challenge the Supermarket Establishment," *Fortune*, March 26, 1979, pp. 70–75.

6. "Gerber Goes Global with 'Superbrand' Concept," *Marketing News*, September 16, 1991, p. 21; and Gail Bronson, "Baby-Food It Is, but Gerber Wants Teen-Agers to Think of It as Dessert," *The Wall Street Journal*, July 17, 1981, p. 29.

7. "Safety First in Sampling," *Advertising Age*, July 26, 1981.

8. The concept of "schema" was developed over 50 years ago by F. C. Bartlett, *Remembering* (Cambridge, Mass.: Harvard University Press, 1932). For a comprehensive background on schema theories, see Joseph W. Alba and Lynn Hasher, "Is Memory Schematic?" *Psychological Bulletin*, Vol. 93 (1983), pp. 203–231; and W. F. Brewer and G. V. Nakamura, "The Nature and Functions of Schemas," in R. S. Wyer and T. K. Srull (eds.), *Handbook of Social Cognition* (Hillsdale, N.J.: Erlbaum, 1984). For applications to consumer behavior, see Mita Sujan and James R. Bettman, "The Effects of Brand Positioning Strategies on Consumers' Brand and Category Perceptions: Some Insights from Schema Research," *Journal of Marketing Research*, Vol. 26 (November 1989), pp. 454–467; Steven A. Taylor, J. Joseph Cronin, and Randall S. Hansen, "Schema and Script Theory in Channels," *AMA Winter Educators' Proceedings* (1991), pp. 15–24; Tom J. Brown, "Schemata in Consumer Research: A Connectionist Approach," *Advances in Consumer Research*, Vol. 19 (1992), pp. 787–794; and Douglas M. Stayman, Dana L. Alden, and Karen H. Smith,

"Some Effects of Schematic Processing on Consumer Expectations and Disconfirmation Judgments," *Journal of Consumer Research*, Vol. 19, No. 2 (September 1992), pp. 240–255.

The basis of script theory is well described in Robert P. Abelson, "Script Processing in Attitude Formation and Decision-making," in J. S. Carroll and J. W. Payne (eds.), *Cognition and Social Behavior* (Hillsdale, N.J.: Erlbaum, 1976). Applications within consumer behavior are provided in Ruth Ann Smith and Michael J. Houston, "A Psychometric Assessment of Measures of Scripts in Consumer Memory," *Journal of Consumer Research*, Vol. 12 (September 1985), pp. 214–224. See also Lauette Dube-Rioux, Dennis T. Regan, and Bernd H. Schmitt, "The Cognitive Representation of Services Varying in Concreteness and Specificity," *Advances in Consumer Research*, Vol. 17 (1990), pp. 861–865.

9. Jerome S. Bruner, "On Perceptual Readiness," *Psychological Review*, Vol. 64 (1957), pp. 123–152.

10. See Joel B. Bohen and Kunal Basu, "Alternative Models of Categorization: Toward a Contingent Processing Framework," *Journal of Consumer Research*, Vol. 13 (March 1987), pp. 455–472; and Joseph W. Alba and J. Wesley Hutchinson, "Dimensions of Consumer Expertise," *Journal of Consumer Research*, Vol. 13 (March 1987), pp. 411–454. For recent findings, see, for example, Barbara Loken and James Ward, "Alternative Approaches to Understanding the Determinants of Typicality," *Journal of Consumer Research*, Vol. 17, No. 2 (September 1990), pp. 111–126; Cynthia D. Huffman, Barbara Loken, and James Ward, "Knowledge and Context Effects on Typicality and Attitude Judgements," *Advances in Consumer Research*, Vol. 17 (1990), pp. 257–265; W. Steven Perkins and Valerie F. Reyna, "The Effects of Expertise on Preference and Typicality in Investment Decision Making," *Advances in Consumer Research*, Vol. 17 (1990), pp. 355–360; Joseph Cherian, "Some Processes in Brand Categorizing: Why One Person's Noise Is Another Person's Music," *Advances in Consumer Research*, Vol. 18 (1991), pp. 77–83; Don Saunders, Steve Tax, James Ward, Kym Court, and Barbara Loken, "The Family Resemblance Approach to Understanding Categorization of Products: Measurement Problems, Alternative Solutions, and Their Assessment," *Advances in Consumer Research*, Vol. 18 (1991), pp. 84–89; Deborah J. MacInnis, Kent Nakamoto, and Gayathri Mani, "Cognitive Associations and Product Category Comparisons: The Role of Knowledge Structure and Context," *Advances in Consumer Research*, Vol. 19 (1991), pp. 260–267; Richard Ettenson and Gary Gaeth, "Consumer Perceptions of Hybrid (Bi Natural) Products," *The Journal of Consumer Marketing*, Vol. 8, No. 4 (Fall 1991), pp. 13–18; Jean B. Romeo and Todd A. Mooradian, "Broadening the Cognitive Structure of a Brand Category: A Pilot Study," *AMA Winter Educators' Proceedings* (1992), Vol. 3, pp. 132–133; and Shantanu Dutta, Mark Bergen, Madhubalan Viswanathan, and Terry Childers, "Categorization: A Fuzzy Set Conceptualization," *AMA Winter Educators' Proceedings* (1993), pp. 78–82.

11. Pierre Martineau, *Motivation in Advertising* (New York: McGraw-Hill, 1957), p. 114.

12. Carl McDaniel and R. C. Baker, "Convenience Food Packaging and the Perception of Product Quality," *Journal of Marketing*, October 1977, pp. 57–58. For broader discussions, see Ernest Dichter, "What's in an Image," *Journal of Consumer Marketing*, Vol. 2 (Winter 1985), pp. 75–91; Roberto Friedmann, "Psychological Meaning of Products: Identification and Marketing Applications," *Psychology & Marketing*, Vol. 3 (Spring 1986), pp. 1–16; and Robert W. Veryzer,

Jr., "Aesthetic Response and the Influence of Design Principles on Product Preferences," *Advances in Consumer Research*, Vol. 20 (1993), pp. 224–228.

13. Donald A. Laird, "How the Consumer Estimates Quality by Subconscious Sensory Impressions—With Special Reference to the Role of Smell," *Journal of Applied Psychology*, Vol. 16 (June 1932), pp. 241–246.

14. William Safire, "On Language" *The New York Times News Service*, June 10, 1984.

15. John Bussey and Joseph White, "Nissan Cuts U.S. Exports as Marketing Effort Lags," *The Wall Street Journal*, April 13, 1988, p. 27; Sheryl Harris, "Infiniti Eyes Young, Affluent Crowd," *Advertising Age*, February 29, 1988, pp. 5–16; "Beer Bash," *Marketing Week*, December 14, 1987, p. 62; Alice Cuneo, "AIDS Prompts Ayds Move," *Advertising Age*, May 30, 1988, p. 66; Carl Obermiller, "A Brownie by Any Other Name Would Smell as Sweet: A Field Test of the Effect of Brand Name Meaningfulness," *AMA Winter Educators' Proceedings* (1992), Vol. 3, pp. 134–139; Kim Robertson, "Strategically Desirable Brand Name Characteristics," *The Journal of Product & Brand Management*, Vol. 1, No. 3 (Summer 1992), pp. 62–72; and Teresa Pavia and Janeen A. Costa, "The Winning Number: Consumer Perceptions of Alpha-Numeric Brand Names," *Journal of Marketing*, Vol. 57 (July 1993), pp. 85–98.

16. J. Neher, "Toro Cutting a Wider Swath in Outdoor Appliance Market," *Advertising Age*, February 25, 1978, p. 21.

17. "Goodbye to the F-word," *USA Today*, March 27, 1991, p. B2, "Burgers? What Burgers?" *Forbes*, April 30, 1990, p. 12.

18. Robert D. Hof, "A Washout for Clorox?" *Business Week*, July 9, 1990, p. 32; and Bill Abrams, "Exploiting Proven Brand Names Can Cut Risk of New Products," *The Wall Street Journal*, January 22, 1981. See also Kenneth N. Thompson, James E. Nelson, and Calvin P. Duncan, "A Moderator Variables Model of Brand Extension Behavior," *AMA Winter Educators' Proceedings* (1987), pp. 45–49; David A. Aaker and Kevin Lane Keller, "Consumer Evaluations of Brand Extensions," *Journal of Marketing*, Vol. 54, No. 1 (January 1990), pp. 27–41; Cathy L. Hartman, Linda L. Price, and Calvin P. Duncan, "Consumer Evaluation of Franchise Extension Products: A Categorization Processing Perspective," *Advances in Consumer Research*, Vol. 17 (1990), pp. 120–127; George Miaoulis, Valerie Free, and Henry Parsons, "TURF: A New Planning Approach for Product Line Extensions," *Marketing Research*, Vol. 2, No. 1 (March 1990), pp. 28–40; Peter H. Farquhar, Paul M. Herr, and Russell H. Fazio, "A Relational Model for Cateogry Extensions of Brands," *Advances in Consumer Research*, Vol. 17 (1990), pp. 856–860; Dipankar Chakravati, Deborah J. MacInnis, and Kent Nakamoto, "Product Category Perceptions, Elaborative Processing and Brand Name Extension Strategies," *Advances in Consumer Research*, Vol. 17 (1990), pp. 910–916; David M. Boush and Barbara Loken, "A Process-tracing Study of Brand Extension Evaluation," *Journal of Marketing Research*, Vol. 28 (February 1991), pp. 16–28; Laurette Dube, Bernd H. Schmitt, and Sheri Bridges, "Categorization Research and Brand Extensions," *Advances in Consumer Research*, Vol. 19 (1991), pp. 255–259; A. V. Muthukrishnan and Barton A. Weitz, "Role of Product Knowledge in Evaluation of Brand Extensions," *Advances in Consumer Research*, Vol. 18 (1991), pp. 407–413; Frank R. Kardes and Chris T. Allen, "Perceived Variability and Inferences about Brand Extensions," *Advances in Consumer Research*, Vol. 18 (1991), pp. 392–398; and Jean B. Romeo, "The Effect of Negative Information on the Evaluations of Brand Extensions and the Family Brand," *Advances in Consumer Research*, Vol. 18 (1991), pp. 399–406.

19. Philip Kotler, "Atmospherics as a Marketing Tool," *Journal of Retailing*, Vol. 49 (Winter 1973–74), pp. 48–64.

20. For discussions on perceptual inferences drawn from advertising, see, for example, Larry Percy, "The Often Subtle Linguistic Cues in Advertising," *Advances in Consumer Research*, Vol. 15 (1988), pp. 269–274; Danny L. Moore, Douglas Hausknecht, and Kanchana Thamodaran, "Time Compression, Response Opportunity, and Persuasion," *Journal of Consumer Research*, Vol. 13, No. 1 (1986), pp. 85–99; Roberto Friedmann and Mary R. Zimmer, "The Role of Psychological Meaning in Advertising," *Journal of Advertising*, Vol. 17 (November 1988), pp. 31–40; Amna Kirmani and Peter Wright, "Money Talks: Perceived Advertising Expense and Expected Product Quality," *Journal of Consumer Research*, Vol. 16, No. 3 (December 1989), pp. 344–353; Amna Kirmani, "The Effect of Perceived Advertising Costs on Brand Perceptions," *Journal of Consumer Research*, Vol. 17, No. 2 (September 1990), pp. 160–171; Cynthia Fraser Hite, Robert E. Hite, and Tamra Minor, "Quality Uncertainty, Brand Reliance, and Dissipative Advertising," *Journal of the Academy of Marketing Science*, Vol. 19, No. 2 (Spring 1991), pp. 115–122; Ruth Ann Smith, "What You See Is Not Necessarily What You Get: The Effects of Pictures and Words on Consumers' Inferences," *Advances in Consumer Research*, Vol. 19 (1991), pp. 296–298; Douglas M. Stayman and Frank R. Kardes, "Spontaneous Inference Processes in Advertising: Effects of Need for Cognition and Self-monitoring on Inference Generation and Utilization," *Journal of Consumer Psychology*, Vol. 1, No. 2 (1992), pp. 125–142; Priya Raghubir Das, "Semantic Cues and Buyer Evaluation of Promotional Communication," *AMA Summer Educators' Proceedings* (1992), pp. 12–17; and Richard Jackson Harris, Julia C. Pounds, Melissa J. Mairoelle, and Maria Mermis, "The Effect of Type of Claim, Gender, and Buying History on the Drawing of Pragmatic Inferences from Advertising Claims," *Journal of Consumer Psychology*, Vol. 2, No. 1 (1993), pp. 83–95.

21. Cyndee Miller, "The Green Giant: An Enduring Figure Lives Happily Ever After," *Marketing News*, April 15, 1991, p. 2; "The Birth of a Sprout," *Advertising Age*, October 25, 1982, p. M5.

22. Lenore Skenazy, "Political Touch-ups: Special Effects Benefit Bush," *Advertising Age*, April 18, 1988, p. 3.

23. An interesting related marketing question is whether *temporary* price promotions have any impacts on a brand's perceived quality. Research here is difficult and results are mixed: on balance, however, the evidence seems to show little negative impact on inferences about a brand's quality (see, for example, Scott Davis, Jeffrey Inman, and Leigh McAlister, "Promotion Has a Negative Effect on Brand Evaluations—Or Does It? Additional Disconfirming Evidence," *Journal of Marketing Research*, Vol. 23 (February 1992), pp. 143–148).

However, researchers in the field have studied the topic of price quality inferences in considerable detail, and evidence is not nearly so mixed. For a fine overview of this research, see Akshay R. Rao and Kent B. Monroe, "The Effect of Price, Brand Name, and Store Name on Buyers' Perceptions of Product Quality: An Integrative Review," *Journal of Marketing Research*, Vol. 26 (August 1989), pp. 351–357; and Valarie A. Zeithaml, "Consumer Perceptions of Price, Quality, and Value: A Means-End Model and Synthesis of Evidence," *Journal of Marketing*, Vol. 52 (July 1988), pp. 2–22. For

further recent findings, see, for example, William B. Dodds, "In Search of Value: How Price and Store Name Information Influence Buyer's Product Perceptions," *The Journal of Consumer Marketing*, Vol. 8, No. 2 (Spring 1991), pp. 15–24; Merrie Brucks and Valarie Zeithaml, "Price and Brand Name as Indicators of Quality Dimensions," *Marketing Science Institute*, Paper 91–130, December 1991; Richard Sjolander, "A Cross-cultural Study on the Effect of Price and Perceptions of Product Quality," *AMA Summer Educators' Proceedings* (1992), pp. 344–351; Glenn B. Voss, "Modeling Value Determination: The Role of Perceived Price and Quality," in Robert L. King (ed.), *Marketing: Perspectives for the 1990s* (Richmond, Va: Southern Marketing Association, 1992), pp. 94–97; and Katherine Fraccastoro, Scot Burton, and Abhijit Biswas, "Effective Use of Advertisements Promoting Sale Prices," *Journal of Consumer Marketing*, Vol. 10, No. 1 (1993), pp. 61–70.

Beyond perceptions, there is also the question of how well actual product quality correlates with price. Does it go up as price goes up? Results here are surprising and controversial. See R. T. Morris and C. S. Bronson, "The Chaos in Competition Indicated by Consumer Reports," *Journal of Marketing*, Vol. 33, No. 3 (July 1969), pp. 26–34; George B. Sproles, "New Evidence on Price and Product Quality," *Journal of Consumer Affairs*, Vol. 11 (Summer 1977), pp. 63–77; Ellen Day and Stephen B. Castleberry, "Defining and Evaluating Quality: The Consumer's View," *Advances in Consumer Research*, Vol. 13 (1986); David J. Curry and David J. Faulds, "Indexing Product Quantity: Issues, Theory, and Results," *Journal of Consumer Research*, Vol. 13 (June 1986), pp. 134–145; David J. Curry and Peter C. Riesz, "Prices and Price/Quality Relationships: A Longitudinal Analysis," *Journal of Marketing*, Vol. 52 (January 1988), pp. 35–51; Monroe Friedman, "Agreement between Product Ratings Generated by Different Consumer Testing Organizations: A Statistical Comparison of *Consumer Reports* and *Which?* from 1957 to 1986," *The Journal of Consumer Affairs*, Vol. 24, No. 1 (Summer 1990), pp. 44–68; Donald R. Lichtenstein and Scot Burton, "The Relationship between Perceived and Objective Price-Quality," *Journal of Marketing Research*, Vol. 26 (November 1989), pp. 429–443; Scot Burton and Donald R. Lichtenstein, "Assessing the Relationship between Perceived and Objective Price-Quality: A Replication," *Advances in Consumer Research*, Vol. 17 (1990), pp. 715–722; Brian T. Ratchford and Pola Gupta, "On the Interpretation of Price-Quality Relations," in R. N. Mayer (ed.), *Enhancing Consumer Choice* (Columbia, Mo.: American Council on Consumer Interests, 1991), pp. 515–524; Akshay R. Rao and Mark E. Bergen, "Price Premium Variations as a Consequence of Buyers' Lack of Information," *Journal of Consumer Research*, Vol. 19, No. 3 (December 1992), pp. 412–423.

24. This area has also received considerable research attention. For useful insights and findings, see Robert M. Schindler and Diana M. Bauer, "The Uses of Price Information: Implications for Marketers," *AMA Summer Educators' Proceedings* (1988), pp. 68–73; Susan M. Petroshius and Kent B. Monroe, "Effect of Product-Line Pricing Characteristics on Product Evaluations," *Journal of Consumer Research*, Vol. 13 (March 1987), pp. 511–519; Judith Lynne Zaichkowsky, "Involvement and the Price Cue," *Advances in Consumer Research*, Vol. 15 (1988), pp. 323–327; Donald R. Lichenstein, Peter H. Bloch, and William C. Black, "Correlates of Price Acceptability," *Journal of Consumer Research*, Vol. 15 (September 1988), pp. 243–252; Rustan Kosenko and Don Rahtz, "Buyer Market Price Knowledge Influence on Acceptable Price Range and Price Limits," *Advances in Consumer Research*, Vol. 15 (1988), pp. 328–333;

Patricia Sorce and Stanley M. Widrick, "Individual Differences in Latitude of Acceptable Prices," *Advances in Consumer Research*, Vol. 18 (1991), pp. 802–805; and Tridib Mazumdar and Cheoul Ryon Kim, "Effects of Prior Belief on Feature-based Price Estimates," *Advances in Consumer Research*, Vol. 20 (1993), pp. 586–590.

For specific findings in the area of reference pricing, see, for example, James M. Lattin and Randolph E. Bucklin, "Reference Effects of Price and Promotion on Brand Choice Behavior," *Journal of Marketing Research*, Vol. 26 (August 1989), pp. 299–310; Robert Jacobson and Carl Obermiller, "The Formation of Reference Price," *Advances in Consumer Research*, Vol. 16 (1989), pp. 234–240; William D. Diamond and Leland Campbell, "The Framing of Sales Promotions: Effects on Reference Price Change," *Advances in Consumer Research*, Vol. 16 (1989), pp. 241–247; Joel E. Urbany, William O. Bearden, and Dan C. Weilbaker, "The Effect of Plausible and Exaggerated Reference Prices on Consumer Perceptions and Price Search," *Journal of Consumer Research*, Vol. 15 (June 1988), pp. 95–110; Donald R. Lichtenstein and William O. Bearden, "Contextual Influences on Perceptions of Merchant-supplied Reference Prices," *Journal of Consumer Research*, Vol. 15 (March 1989), pp. 55–66; Abhijit Biswas and Edward A. Blair, "Contextual Effects of Reference Prices in Retail Advertisements," *Journal of Marketing*, Vol. 55, No. 3 (July 1991), pp. 1–12; William O. Bearden, Ajit Kaicker, Melinda Smith de Borrero, and Joel E. Urbany, "Examining Alternative Operational Measures of Internal Reference Prices," *Advances in Consumer Research*, Vol. 19 (1991), pp. 629–635; Donald R. Lichtenstein, Scot Burton, and Eric J. Karson, "The Effect of Semantic Cues on Consumer Perceptions of Reference Price Ads," *Journal of Consumer Research*, Vol. 18, No. 3 (December 1991), pp. 380–391; Glenn E. Mayhew and Russell S. Winer, "An Empirical Analysis of Internal and External Reference Prices Using Scanner Data," *Journal of Consumer Research*, Vol. 19, No. 1 (June 1992), pp. 62–70; James I. Gray, "The Effect of Order of Presentation on the Formation of Internal Reference Prices," in T. J. Page, Jr., and S. E. Middlestadt (eds), *Proceedings of the Society for Consumer Psychology* (Clemson, S.C.: CtC Press, 1992), pp. 57–58; Daniel C. Lockhart and Roger Tourangeau, "The Effect of Suggested Price Points on Open-ended Price Estimates," ibid. pp. 59–64; and Abhay Shah, "Reference Price and Just Noticeable Difference: A Study with Some Implications for Retail Pricing," in Robert L. King (ed.), *Marketing: Perspectives for the 1990s* (Richmond, Va.: Southern Marketing Association, 1992), pp. 463–466.

25. Bernard F. Whalen, "Strategic Mix of Odd, Even Prices Can Lead to Retail Profits," *Marketing News*, March 7, 1980, p. 24; see also Robert M. Schindler, "Symbolic Meanings of a Price Ending," *Advances in Consumer Research*, Vol. 18 (1991), pp. 794–801; and Robert M. Schindler and Thomas Kobarian, "Testing for Perceptual Underestimation of 9-Ending Prices," *Advancing in Consumer Research*, Vol. 20 (1993), pp. 580–585.

26. Thanks to Deborah MacInnis for this illustration. For interesting reading on this topic, see C. Whan Park, Bernard J. Jaworski, and Deborah J. MacInnis, "Strategic Brand Concept—Image Management," *Journal of Marketing*, Vol. 50 (October 1986), pp. 135–145.

27. Inference making is a broad topic that has received much attention in recent consumer research. For theoretical and empirical background, see E.T. Higgins and J. A. Bargh, "Social Cognition and Social Perception," *Annual Review of Psychology*, Vol. 38 (1987), pp. 369–425; and Joseph W. Alba and J. Wesley Hutchinson, "Dimensions of Consumer Expertise," *Journal of Consumer Research*, Vol. 13 (March 1987), pp. 411–454. For interesting applications and findings, see, for example, Raymond R. Burke, Wayne S. DeSarbo, Richard L. Oliver, and Thomas S. Robertson, "Deception by Implication: An Experimental Investigation," *Journal of Consumer Research*, Vol. 14 (March 1988), p. 483–494; Frank R. Kardes, "Spontaneous Inference Processes in Advertising: The Effects of Conclusion Omission and Involvement on Persuasion," *Journal of Consumer Research*, Vol. 15 (September 1988), pp. 225–233; Jeen-Su Lim, Richard W. Olshavsky, and John Kim, "The Impact of Inferences on Product Evaluations: Replication and Extension," *Journal of Marketing Research*, Vol. 25 (August 1988), pp. 308–316; Amitava Chattopadhyay and Joseph W. Alba, "The Situational Importance of Recall and Inference in Consumer Decision Making," *Journal of Consumer Research*, Vol. 15 (June 1988), pp, 1–12; Paula Fitzgerald Bone, Terence A. Shimp, and Subhash Sharma, "Assimilation and Contrast Effects in Product Performance Perceptions: Implications for Public Policy," *Journal of Public Policy & Marketing*, Vol. 9 (1990), pp. 100–110; Keith B. Murray and John L. Schlacter, "The Impact of Services versus Goods on Consumers' Assessment of Perceived Risk and Variability," *Journal of the Academy of Marketing Science*, Vol. 18, No. 1 (Winter 1990), pp. 51–66; Carolyn J. Simmons and John G. Lynch, Jr., "Inference Effects without Inference Making? Effects of Missing Information on Discounting and Use of Presented Information," *Journal of Consumer Research*, Vol. 17, No. 4 (March 1991), pp. 477–491; Robert W. Bozer, David C. Wyld, and James Grant, "Using Metaphor to Create More Effective Sales Messages," *The Journal of Consumer Marketing*, Vol. 8, No. 2 (Spring 1991), pp. 59–68; Michael Lynn, "Theoretical Explanations for Scarcity's Enhancement of Perceived Value," *AMA Winter Educators' Proceedings* (1991), pp. 25–26; Deepak Sirdeshmukh and H. Rao Unnava, "The Effects of Missing Information on Consumer Product Evaluations," *Advances in Consumer Research*, Vol. 19 (1991), pp. 284–289; John Kim and Frank R. Kardes, "Consumer Inference," *Advances in Consumer Research*, Vol. 19 (1991), pp. 407–410; Robert E. Kleine III and Jerome B. Kernan, "Contextual Influences on the Meanings Ascribed to Ordinary Consumption Objects," *Journal of Consumer Research*, Vol. 18, No. 3 (December 1991), pp. 331–324; J. Wesley Hutchinson and Joseph W. Alba, "Ignoring Irrelevant Information: Situational Determinants of Consumer Learning," *Journal of Consumer Research*, Vol. 18, No 3 (December 1991), pp. 325–345; Cornelia Pechmann and S. Ratneshwar, "Consumer Covariation Judgments: Theory or Data Driven?" *Journal of Consumer Research*, Vol. 19, No. 3 (December 1992), pp. 373–386; and William Boulding and Amna Kirmani, "A Consumer-Side Experimental Examination of Signaling Theory: Do Consumers Perceive Warranties as Signals of Quality?" *Journal of Consumer Research*, Vol. 20, No. 1 (June 1993), pp. 111–123.

28. If you decided in favor of the new competitor in the first four cases, you agreed with the court, which felt that consumer confusion was not likely in any of these instances. For further discussion, see Sidney A. Diamond, "Marked for Dispute," *Advertising Age*, July 5, 1982, p. M26.

The two McDonald's cases were decided in favor of McDonald's. Even though the owner of McBagel's name was Ken McShea, the judge ruled that products such as McNuggets, McMuffin, and McD.L.T. had created a "family" of trademarks for food products. In the McSleep Inn case, the head of the chain had been quoted in early news stories as saying, "Obviously, the name is a takeoff on McDonald's and quality at a consistent price." (For further details, see "Judge's McPinion...," *Marketing News*, October 10, 1988, p. 5; and David Kiley, "McDonald's Bares Teeth over Prefix," *Marketing Week*, October 26, 1987, p. 2.)

The Jordache case was decided in favor in Lardashe Jeans, on the grounds that although it was a parody of the Jordache name, it would not confuse consumers and tarnish the Jordache trademark. The producers of Lardashe, Oink, Inc., indicated they would resume production of the "resigner" jeans after the verdict. (See "Lardashe Jeans Wins Big Court Fight...," *Marketing News*, September 25, 1987, p. 24.)

29. "P & G will Fight Court Order on Tide Copycats," *Advertising Age*, July 9, 1984, p. 40. For related readings, see Barbara Loken, Ivan Ross, and Ronald L. Hinkle, "Consumer 'Confusion' of Origin and Brand Similarity Perceptions," *Journal of Public Policy & Marketing*, Vol. 5 (1986), pp. 195–211; James Cross, James Stephens, and Robert E. Benjamin, "Gray Markets: A Legal Review and Public Policy Perspective," *Journal of Public Policy & Marketing*, Vol. 9, 1990, pp. 183–194; Ellen R. Foxman, Darrel D. Muehling, and Phil W. Berger, "An Investigation of Factors Contributing to Consumer Brand Confusion," *The Journal of Consumer Affairs*, Vol. 24, No. 1 (Summer 1990), pp. 170–189; and Dorothy Cohen, "Trademark Strategy Revisited," *Journal of Marketing*, Vol. 55, No. 3 (July 1991), pp. 46–59.

Chapter 10

Consumer Learning

1. An excellent overview of the major learning theories and their points of agreement and dispute can be found in Ernest R. Hilgard and Gordon H. Bower, *Theories of Learning* (New York: Appleton-Century-Crofts, 1966). See also Winfred F. Hill, *Learning: A Survey of Psychological Interpretations*, 3d ed. (New York: Thomas Crowell, 1977).

2. Jean Piaget, *The Child's Conception of the World* (New York: Harcourt Brace, 1928); and Jean Piaget, *The Construction of Reality in the Child* (New York: Basic Books, 1954).

3. Much of the work on children with marketing and consumer behavior has been inspired by Scott Ward. See, for example, Scott Ward, "Consumer Socialization," *Journal of Consumer Research*, Vol. 1 (September 1974), pp. 1–14; and Scott Ward, Daniel B. Wackman, and Ellen Wartella, *How Children Learn to Buy* (Beverly Hills: Sage, 1977).

4. For a comprehensive recent review, see P. S. Raju and Subhash C. Lonial, "Advertising to Children: Findings and Implications," *Current Issues & Research in Advertising*, Vol. 12, Ann Arbor: University of Michigan 1990, pp. 231–274. Research since Piaget has identified three levels of CIP skills in children: strategic, cued, and limited. **Strategic processors** (children ages 10 to 11 and older) *are able* to store and retrieve information from LTM to process ads well. **Cued processors** (age 6 to 9) are *sometimes able* to use appropriate storage and retrieval strategies, but only when reminded to do so. **Limited processors** (children below 6 years old) are *unable* to use these strategies effectively. See Deborah L. Roedder, "Age Differences in Children's Responses to Television Advertising: An Information-processing Approach," *Journal of Consumer Research*, Vol. 8 (September 1981), pp. 144–153. In addition, con-

sumer researchers have addressed a number of further topics in this area. For recent findings, see, for example, Deborah Roedder John and Mita Sujan, "Age Differences in Product Categorization," *Journal of Consumer Research*, Vol. 16, No. 4 (March 1990), pp. 452–460; Catherine A. Cole and Gary J. Gaeth, "Cognitive and Age-related Differences in the Ability to Use Nutritional Information in a Complex Environment," *Journal of Marketing Research*, Vol. 27 (May 1990), pp. 175–184. See also the special issue of *Psychology & Marketing*, Vol. 7 (Winter 1990), which includes P. Greenfield, E. Yut, M. Chung, D. Land, M. Kreider, M. Pantoja, and K. Horsley, "The Program-Length Commercial: A Study of the Effects of Television/Toy Tie-ins on Imaginative Play," pp. 237–255; Laura A. Peracchio, "Designing Research to Reveal the Young Child's Emerging Competence," pp. 257–276; Deborah R. John and Mita Sujan, "Children's Use of Perceptual Cues in Product Categorization," pp. 277–294; M. Carole Macklin, "The Influence of Model Age on Children's Reactions to Advertising Stimuli," pp. 295–310; and Karen F. A. Fox and Trudy Kehret-Ward, "Naive Theories of Price: A Developmental Model," pp. 311–329; and see Kenneth D. Bahn and M. Joseph Sirgy, "Attribute Similarity between Brand Discrimination and Brand Preferences Tasks in Children: An Extension," *AMA Summer Educators' Proceedings* (1991), pp. 432–437; Judy A. Harrigan, "Children's Research: Where It's Been, Where It Is Going," *Advances in Consumer Research*, Vol. 18 (1991), pp. 11–17; Langbourne Rust and Carole Hyatt, "Qualitative and Quantitative Approaches to Child Research," *Advances in Consumer Research*, Vol. 18 (1991), pp. 18–22; M. Carole Macklin, Emily Crawford, and Carol R. Carlson, "Multitheoretical Perspectives Applicable to Children's Consumer Research: Another Viable Alternative," in C. Haugtvedt and D. Rosen (eds.), *Proceedings of the Society for Consumer Psychology* (Knoxville: D. W. Schumann, 1991), pp. 109–115; M. Elizabeth Blair and Mark N. Hatala, "The Use of Rap Music in Children's Advertising," *Advances in Consumer Research*, Vol. 19 (1992), pp. 719–724; Laura A. Peracchio, "How Do Young Children Learn to Be Consumers? A Script-processing Approach," *Journal of Consumer Research*, Vol. 18, No. 4 (March 1992), pp. 425–440; Joanne Burke, "Children's Research and Methods: What Media Researchers Are Doing," *Journal of Advertising Research*, Vol. 32, No. 1 (January/February 1992), pp. RC2–RC3; Deborah Roedder John and Ramnath Lakshmi-Ratan, "Age Differences in Children's Choice Behavior: The Impact of Available Alternatives," *Jounal of Marketing Research*, Vol. 29, No. 2 (May 1992), pp. 216–226; and Srivatsa Seshadri and C. P. Rao, "Considerations in Advertising Directed to Children," *AMA Summer Educators' Proceedings* (1992), pp. 242–248.

5. Scott Ward, "Researchers Look at the 'KidVid' Rule: Overview of Session," *Advances in Consumer Research*, Vol. 6 (1979), pp. 7–8. For more recent policy discussions, see also Bonnie B. Reece, "Children and Shopping: Some Public Policy Questions," *Journal of Public Policy & Marketing*, Vol. 5 (1986), pp. 185–194; Gary M. Armstrong and Merrie Brucks, "Dealing with Children's Advertising: Public Policy Issues and Alternatives," *Journal of Public Policy & Marketing*, Vol. 7 (1988), pp. 98–113; and Marvin Goldberg, "The Elimination of Advertising Directed to Children in Quebec: A Quasi-Experiment," *Advances in Consumer Research*, Vol. 16 (1989), p. 790.

6. Steven Colford, "Top Kid TV Offender: Premiums," *Advertising Age*, April 29, 1991, p. 52.

7. See, for example, Edmund L. Andrews, "F.C.C. Adopts Limits on TV Ads Aimed at Children," *New York Times*, April 10,

1991, p. C6; and Carrie Goerne, "Season Finale for TV Watchdog Group...," *Marketing News*, March 16, 1992, p. 5.

8. For recent discussions, see, for example, Rajesh Kanwar, Lorna Grund, and Jerry C. Olson, "When Do the Measures of Knowledge Measure What We Think They Are Measuring?" *Advances in Consumer Research*, Vol. 17 (1990), pp. 603–608; Mariea Grubbs Hoy, "The Emergence of Script-related Knowledge," *AMA Winter Educators' Proceedings* (1991), pp. 387–394; Lawrence Feick, C. Whan Park, and David L. Mothersbaugh, "Knowledge and Knowledge of Knowledge: What We Know, What We Think We Know, and Why the Difference Makes a Difference," *Advances in Consumer Research*, Vol. 19 (1992), pp. 190–192; and C. Whan Park, Lawrence Feick, and David L. Mothersbaugh, "Consumer Knowledge Assessment: How Product Experience and Knowledge of Brands, Attributes, and Features Affects What We Think We Know," *Advances in Consumer Research*, Vol. 19 (1992), pp. 193–198.

9. Given our topic, learning, we should note that cognitive response research reflects what consumers are "thinking" rather than exactly what they may be "learning" from an ad. However, this research is quite useful for studying advertising effects. A thorough review of work on "direct monitoring" is provided in Peter Wright, "Message-evoked Thoughts: Persuasion Research Using Thought Verbalizations," *Journal of Consumer Research*, Vol. 7 (September 1980), pp. 151–175; Manoj Hastak and Jerry C. Olson, "Assessing the Role of Brand-related Cognitive Responses as Mediators of Communication Effects on Cognitive Structure," *Journal of Consumer Research*, Vol. 15 (March 1989), pp. 444–456; Paul L. Sauer, Peter R. Dickson, and Kenneth Lord, "A Multiphase Thought Elicitation Coding Scheme for Cognitive Response Analysis," *Advances in Consumer Research*, Vol. 19 (1991), pp. 826–834; Debra L. Stephens and J. Edward Russo, "Predicting Post-Advertisement Attitudes," Working Paper 92-109, Marketing Science Institute, 1992; and J. Craig Andrews, Richard G. Netemeyer, and Srinivas Durvasula, "The Role of Cognitive Responses as Mediators of Alcohol Warning Label Effects," *Jounal of Public Policy & Marketing*, Vol. 12, No. 1 (Spring 1993), pp. 57–68.

10. An excellent analysis of the FTC's policy statement on deception is available in Gary T. Ford and John E. Calfee, "Recent Developments in FTC Policy on Deception," *Journal of Marketing*, Vol. 50 (July 1986), pp. 82–103. See also Debra K. Owen and Joyce E. Plyler, "The Role of Empirical Evidence in the Federal Regulation of Advertising," *Journal of Public Policy & Marketing*, Vol. 10, No. 1 (Spring 1991), pp. 1–14; and Thomas J. Maronick, "Copy Tests in FTC Deception Cases: Guidelines for Researchers," *Journal of Advertising Research*, Vol. 31, No. 6 (December 1991), pp. 9–17.

11. See David M. Gardner, "Deception in Advertising: A Conceptual Approach," *Journal of Marketing*, Vol. 39 (January 1975), pp. 40–46; and Fredric L. Barbour and David M. Gardner, "Deceptive Advertising: A Practical Approach to Measurement," *Journal of Advertising*, Vol. 11, No. 1 (1982), pp. 21–30.

12. See the references in Notes 10 and 11, plus Jacob Jacoby and Constance Small, "The FDA Approach to Defining Misleading Advertising," *Journal of Marketing*, Vol. 39 (October 1975), pp. 65–68; Michael T. Brandt and Ivan L. Preston, "The Federal Trade Commission's Use of Evidence to Determine Deception," *Journal of Marketing*, Vol. 41 (January 1977), pp. 54–62; Terence A. Shimp, "Social Psychological (Mis)-representations in Advertising," *Journal of Consumer Research*, Vol. 13 (1979), pp. 28–40; Edward J. Russo,

Barbara L. Metcalf, and Debra Stephens, "Identifying Misleading Advertising," *Journal of Consumer Research*, Vol. 8 (September 1981), pp. 119–131; Gary J. Gaeth and Timothy B. Heath, "The Cognitive Processing of Misleading Advertising in Young and Old Adults," *Journal of Consumer Research*, Vol. 14 (June 1987), pp. 43–54; Raymond R. Burke, Wayne S. DeSarbo, Richard L. Oliver, and Thomas S. Robertson, "Deception by Implication: An Experimental Investigation," *Journal of Consumer Research*, Vol. 14 (March 1988), pp. 483–494; David M. Gardner and Nancy H. Leonard, "Research in Deceptive and Corrective Advertising: Progress to Date and Impact on Public Policy," in J. Leigh and C. Martin (eds.), *Current Issues & Research in Advertising*, Vol. 12 (Ann Arbor: University of Michigan, 1990), pp. 275–309; Jef I. Richards, "A 'New and Improved' View of Puffery," *Journal of Public Policy & Marketing*, Vol. 9 (1990), pp. 73–84; Russell N. Laczniak and Sanford Grossbart, "An Assessment of Assumptions Underlying the Reasonable Consumer Element in Deceptive Advertising Policy," *Journal of Public Policy & Marketing*, Vol. 9 (1990), pp. 85–99; Gary T. Ford, Darlene B. Smith, and John L. Swasy, "Consumer Skepticism of Advertising Claims: Testing Hypotheses from Economics of Information," *Journal of Consumer Research*, Vol. 16, No. 4 (March 1990), pp. 433–441; Bruce Buchanan and Ronald H. Smithies, "Taste Claims and Their Substantiation," *Journal of Advertising Research*, Vol. 31, No. 3 (June/July 1991), pp. 19–35; Judith Lynne Zaichkowsky and Deborah Patricia Sadlowsky, "Misperceptions of Grocery Advertising," *The Journal of Consumer Affairs*, Vol. 25, No. 1 (Summer 1991), pp. 98–109; John Richardson and Judy Cohen, "A Grecian Pragmatic Approach to Advertising Comprehension and Deception in Advertising," *AMA Summer Educators' Proceedings* (1992), pp. 235–241; and Mary Anne Milward, "The Dynamics of Deception in Political Advertising," *AMA Winter Educators' Proceedings* (1993), pp. 187–192.

13. Kevin Kerr, "Just Exactly How Weighty Are the Slogans of Our Times?" *Marketing Week*, March 26, 1990, pp. 6–7.

14. Jacob Jacoby and Wayne D. Hoyer, "Viewer Miscomprehension of Televised Communication: Selected Findings," *Journal of Marketing*, Vol. 46, No. 4 (Fall 1982), pp. 12–26. For results of a similar study on print media, see Jacob Jacoby and Wayne D. Hoyer, "The Comprehension/Miscomprehension of Print Communicaiton: Selected Findings," *Journal of Consumer Research*, Vol. 15 (March 1989), pp. 434–443. See also Jacob Jacoby and Wayne D. Hoyer, "The Miscomprehension of Mass-media Advertising Claims: A Re-Analysis of Benchmark Data," *Journal of Advertising Research*, Vol. 30, No. 3 (June/July 1990), pp. 9–16.

15. For an interesting set of readings in this area, you might begin with the original Jacoby and Hoyer article listed in Note 14 and then proceed to critical comments and replies from the study's authors. Critical comments were offered by Richard W. Mizerski, "Major Problems in 4As Pioneering Study of TV Miscomprehension," *Marketing News*, Vol. 14 (June 12, 1981), pp. 7–8; Gary T. Ford and Richard Yalch, "Viewer Miscomprehension of Televised Communication—A Comment," *Journal of Marketing*, Vol. 46, No. 4 (Fall 1982), pp. 27–31; and Richard Mizerski, "Viewer Miscomprehension Findings Are Measurement Bound," *Journal of Marketing*, Vol. 46, No. 4 (Fall 1982), pp. 32–34. Responses to these criticisms are available in Jacob Jacoby and W. D. Hoyer, "Reply to Mizerski's Criticisms: Some Mislead, Others Misrepresent Facts," *Marketing News*, Vol. 15 (July 24, 1981), pp. 35–36; and Jacob Jacoby and Wayne D. Hoyer, "On Miscomprehending Televised Communication: A Rejoinder," *Journal of Marketing*, Vol. 46, No. 4 (Fall 1982), pp. 35–43.

See also David C. Schmittlein and Donald G. Morrison, "Measuring Miscomprehension for Televised Communications Using True-False Questions," *Journal of Consumer Research*, Vol. 10 (September 1983), pp. 147–156; Mark I. Alpert, Linda L. Golden, and Wayne D. Hoyer, "The Impact of Repetition on Advertising Miscomprehension and Effectiveness," *Advances in Consumer Research*, Vol. 10 (1983), pp. 130–135; and two articles in *Advances in Consumer Research*, Vol. 13 (1986): Fliece R. Gates and Wayne D. Hoyer, "Measuring Miscomprehension: A Comparison of Alternative Formats," pp. 143–146; and Ivan L. Preston and Jeff I. Richards, "The Relationship of Miscomprehension to Deceptiveness in FTC Cases," pp. 138–142.

16. John B. Watson, "The Place of the Conditioned Reflex in Psychology," *Psychological Review*, Vol. 23 (1916), pp. 89–116. For an interesting perspective, see Peggy J. Kreshel, "John B. Watson at J. Walter Thompson: The Legitimation of 'Science' in Advertising," *Journal of Advertising*, Vol. 19, No. 2 (1990), pp. 49–59.

17. The description provided in the chapter is a traditional one, which stresses particular aspects of the approach. In fact, it appears that Pavlovian conditioning can also be represented within a modern framework of thinking, in which it would not appear so distinct. See Robert A. Rescorla, "Pavlovian Conditioning: It's Not What You Think It Is," *American Psychologist*, March 1988, pp. 151–160.

18. "Coca-Cola Turns to Pavlov . . . ," *The Wall Street Journal*, January 19, 1984.

19. Gerald J. Gorn, "The Effects of Music in Advertising on Choice Behavior: A Classical Conditioning Approach," *Journal of Marketing*, Vol. 46, No. 1 (Winter 1982), pp. 94–101; see also the discussion in Note 20.

20. The study using attractive water scenes is Elnora W. Stuart, Terence A. Shimp, and Randall W. Engle, "Classical Conditioning of Consumer Attitudes: Four Experiments in an Advertising Context," *Journal of Consumer Research*, Vol. 14 (December 1987), pp. 334–349. For an excellent advanced discussion of recent research developments on classical conditioning, see Terence A. Shimp, "Neo-Pavlovian Conditioning and Its Implications for Consumer Theory and Research," in T. Robertson and H. Kassarjian, *Handbook of Consumer Behavior* (Englewood Cliffs, N.J.: Prentice Hall, pp. 162–187; for a related discussion of classical conditioning's impact on affect acquisition, see Joel B. Cohen and Charles S. Areni, "Affect and Consumer Behavior," ibid, pp. 188–240. In addition to further studies, Gorn's results sparked a number of new issues and criticisms as to the exact nature of the effect. See, for example, Chris T. Allen and Thomas J. Madden, "A Closer Look at Classical Conditioning," *Journal of Consumer Research*, Vol. 12 (December 1985), pp. 301–315; two articles in *Advances in Consumer Research*, Vol. 14 (1987): L. R. Kahle, Sharon E. Beatty, and Pat Kennedy, "Comment on Classically Conditioning Human Consumers," pp. 411–414, and Gerald J. Gorn, W. J. Jacobs, and Michael J. Mana, "Observations on Awareness and Conditioning," pp. 415–416; Judy I. Alpert and Mark I. Alpert, "Background Music as an Influence in Consumer Mood and Advertising Responses," *Advances in Consumer Research*, Vol. 16 (1989), pp. 485–491; James J. Kellaris and Anthony D. Cox, "The Effects of Background Music in Advertising: A Reassessment," *Journal of Consumer Research*, Vol. 15 (March 1989), pp. 113–118; Chris T. Allen and Chris A. Janiszewski, "Assessing the Role of Contingency Awareness in Attitudinal Conditioning

with Implications for Advertising Research," *Journal of Marketing Research*, Vol. 26 (February 1989), pp. 30–43; Deborah J. MacInnis and C. Whan Park, "The Differential Role of Music on Consumers' Processing of and Reactions to Ads," Working Paper, University of Arizona, Tucson, 1989; Susan E. Middlestadt, "The Effect of Background and Ambient Color on Product Attitudes and Beliefs," *Advances in Consumer Research*, Vol. 17 (1990), pp. 244–249; Kunal Basu, Marvin Goldberg, and Gerald J. Gorn, "The Effects of Music in Conditioning Brand Preference: Replication and Extension," *Advances in Consumer Research*, Vol. 17 (1990), p. 535; Terence A. Shimp, Elnora W. Stuart, and Randall W. Engle, "A Program of Classical Conditioning Experiments Testing Variations in the Conditioned Stimulus and Contents," *Journal of Consumer Research*, Vol. 18, No. 1 (June 1991), pp. 1–12; and Basil G. Englis, "Classically Conditioned Responses to Television Advertising," in C. Haugtvedt and D. Rosen (eds.), *Proceedings of the Society for Consumer Psychology* (Knoxville: D. W. Schumann, 1991), pp. 80–83.

For earlier discussions, speculations on how marketers might use CC, and debates about it, see Frances K. McSweeney and Calvin Bierley, "Recent Developments in Classical Conditioning," *Journal of Consumer Research*, Vol. 11 (September 1984), pp. 619–631; Walter R. Nord and J. Paul Peter, "A Behavior Modification Perspective on Marketing," *Journal of Marketing*, Vol. 44, No. 2 (Spring 1980), pp. 36–47; and Werner Kroeber-Riel, "Emotional Product Differentiation by Classical Conditioning," *Advances in Consumer Research*, Vol. 11 (1984), pp. 538–543; Feinberg, R., "Credit Cards as Spending Facilitating Stimuli," *Journal of Consumer Research*, Vol. 13 (1986), pp. 348–356; J. Hunt, R. Florsheim, A. Chatterjee, and J. Kernan, "Credit Cards as Spending-Facilitating Stimuli: A Test and Extension of Feinberg's Classical Conditioning Hypothesis," *Psychological Reports*, Vol. 67 (1990), pp. 323–330; and Richard A. Feinberg, "The Social Nature of the Classical Conditioning Phenomena in People: A Comment on Hunt, Florsheim, Chatterjee, and Kernan," *Psychological Reports*, Vol. 67 (1990), pp. 331–334.

21. Skinner wrote a number of articles and books. Some of these are written in nontechnical language and are interesting to read. See, for example, B. F. Skinner, *Walden Two* (New York: Macmillan, 1948); B. F. Skinner; "How to Teach Animals," *Scientific American*, Vol. 185 (December 1951); pp. 26–29; B. F. Skinner, "Teaching Machines," *Science*, Vol. 128 (1958), pp. 969–977; and Carl R. Rogers and B. F. Skinner, "Some Issues Concerning the Control of Human Behavior," *Science*, Vol. 124 (1956), pp. 1057–1066. See also two of his famous books: B. F. Skinner, *Science and Human Behavior* (New York: The Free Press, 1953); and B. F. Skinner, *Beyond Freedom and Dignity* (New York: Alfred A. Knopf, 1972).

22. This section is based upon the discussion by Walter R. Nord and J. Paul Peter, "A Behavior Modification Perspective." For further suggestions and clarification of issues, see Michael L. Rothschild and William C. Gaidis, "Behavioral Learning Theory: Its Relevance to Marketing and Promotions," *Journal of Marketing*, Spring 1981, pp. 70–78; and J. Paul Peter and Walter R. Nord, "A Clarification and Extension of Operant Conditioning Principles in Marketing," *Journal of Marketing*, Vol. 46, No. 3 (Summer 1982), pp. 102–107. For a recent overview, see Gordon R. Foxall, "The Behavioral Perspective Model of Purchase and Consumption: From Consumer Theory to Marketing Practice," *Journal of the Academy of Marketing Science*, Vol. 20, No. 2 (Spring 1992), pp. 189–198.

23. J. R. Carey, S. H. Clicque, B. A. Leighton, and F. Milton, "A Test of Positive Reinforcement of Customers," *Journal of Marketing*, Vol. 40, No. 4 (October 1976), pp. 98–100.

24. This section is based upon the discussion in Nord and Peter, "A Behavior Modification Perspective." See also Albert Bandura, *Principles of Behavior Modification* (New York: Holt, Rinehart and Winston, 1969).

25. Nord and Peter, "A Behavior Modification Perspective." See also Mary Jo Bitner, "Servicescapes: The Impact of Physical Surroundings on Customers and Employees," *Journal of Marketing*, Vol. 56, No. 2 (April 1992), pp. 57–71; Dhruv Grewal and Julie Baker, "Do Retail Store Environment Cues Affect Consumer Price Perceptions?: An Empirical Examination," *International Journal of Research & Marketing*, 1993; and Syed H. Akhter, J. Craig Andrews, and Srinivas Durvasula, "Examining the Influence of Retail Store Environment on Brand Beliefs, Attitude, Evaluation, and Intentions," *AMA Winter Educators' Proceedings* (1993), pp. 98–99.

26. "Mindbenders," *Money Magazine*, September 1978, p. 24.

27. Ronald E. Milliman, "Using Background Music to Affect the Behavior of Supermarket Shoppers," *Journal of Marketing*, Vol. 46, No. 3 (Summer 1982), p. 86–91. For more recent results and extensions, see Richard Yalch and Eric Spangenberg, "Effects of Store Music on Shopping Behavior," *The Journal of Consumer Marketing*, Vol. 7, No. 2 (Spring 1990), pp. 55–60; Gail Tom, "Marketing with Music," *The Journal of Consumer Marketing*, Vol. 7, No. 2 (Spring 1990), pp. 49–54; Gordon C. Bruner II, "Music, Mood, and Marketing," *Journal of Marketing*, Vol. 54, No. 4 (October 1990) pp. 94–104; James J. Kellaris and Robert J. Kent, "The Influence of Music on Consumers' Temporal Perceptions: Does Time Fly When You're Having Fun?" *Journal of Consumer Psychology*, Vol. 1, No. 4 (1992), pp. 365–376; and Charles S. Areni and David Kim, "The Influence of Background Music on Shopping Behavior: Classical versus Top-Forty Music in a Wine Store," *Advances in Consumer Research*, Vol. 20 (1993), pp. 336–340.

28. Francine Schwadel, "Kmart Testing 'Radar' to Track Shopper Traffic," *The Wall Street Journal*, September 24, 1991, p. B1; Joanne Lipman, "Scents That Encourage Buying Couldn't Smell Sweeter to Stores," *The Wall Street Journal*, January 9, 1990, p. B5; DeeAnn Glamser, "Mozart Plays to Empty Lot," *USA Today*, August 24, 1990, p. 3A.

29. Nord and Peter, "A Behavior Modification Perspective," p. 45.

30. There is little literature pointed to the specific issues raised in this section. However, a useful overview of thinking in the area of marketing ethics is provided in Gene R. Laczniak and Patrick E. Murphy, *Ethical Marketing Decisions: The Higher Road* (Needham Heights, Mass.: Allyn & Bacon, 1993). In addition, a thoughtful discussion of IC in marketing is provided by Rom J. Markin and Chem L. Narayana, "Behavior Control: Are Consumers beyond Freedom and Dignity?" *Advances in Consumer Research*, Vol. 3 (1976), pp. 222–228. See also Douglas Hoffman and Vince Howe, "Ethical Issues in Services Marketing," in Robert L. King (ed.), *Marketing Perspectives for the 1990s* (Richmond, Va.: Southern Marketing Association, 1992), pp. 406–410.

31. Joe A. Dodson, Alice M. Tybout, and Brian Sternthal, "Impact on Deals and Deal Retraction on Brand Switching," *Journal of Marketing Research*, Vol. 15, No. 1 (February 1978), pp. 72–81. For a comprehensive look at this area of research, see Robert J. Meyer

and Barbara E. Kahn, "Probabilistic Models of Consumer Choice Behavior," in T. Robertson and H. Kassarjian (eds.) *Handbook of Consumer Behavior*, (Englewood Cliffs, N.J.: Prentice Hall, 1991), pp. 85–123.

32. Readers interested in pursuing this area are encouraged to begin with Jacob Jacoby and Robert Chestnut, *Brand Loyalty Measurement and Management* (New York: Ronald/John Wiley, 1978). This volume contains numerous citations of further work on brand loyalty. See also Richard E. DuWors, Jr., and George H. Haines, Jr., "Event History Analysis Measures of Brand Loyalty," *Journal of Marketing Research*, Vol. 27 (November 1990), pp. 485–493; Barry L. Bayus, "Brand Loyalty and Marketing Strategy: An Application to Home Appliances," *Marketing Science*, Vol. 11, No. 1 (Winter 1992), pp. 21–38; and Barbara Olsen, "Brand Loyalty and Lineage: Exploring New Dimensions for Research," *Advances in Consumer Research*, Vol. 20 (1993), pp. 575–579.

33. See, for example, Scott Hume, "Brand Loyalty Steady," *Advertising Age*, March 2, 1992, p. 19; Julie Liesse, "Brands in Trouble," *Advertising Age*, December 2, 1991, p. 16.

34. The newsletter is entitled *Colloquy* and is published by Frequency Marketing, Inc., PO Box 3920, Milford, Ohio, 45150; telephone number (513) 248-9184.

35. Laurie Pertersen, "Marketing Dig Deep for Loyalty," *Marketing Week*, June 29, 1987, pp. 1ff; Nancy Youman, "Trying Frequent-Drinker Programs," *Adweek*, September 12, 1988, p. 60; and Terrence J. Kearney, "Frequent Flyer Programs: A Failure in Competitive Strategy, with Lessons for Management," *The Journal of Consumer Marketing*, Vol. 7, No. 1 (Winter 1990), pp. 31–40.

Chapter 11

Consumer Attitudes

1. B. G. Yovovich, "What Is Your Brand Really Worth?" *Marketing Week*, August 8, 1988, pp. 18–24. For some recent developments, see "Brands on the Run," *Business Week*, April 19, 1993, pp. 26ff.

2. Gordon W. Allport, "Attitudes," in C. A. Murchinson (ed.), *A Handbook of Social Psychology* (Worcester, Mass.: Clark University Press, 1935), pp. 798–844.

3. Scholars, especially those in the field of social psychology, have for many years been concerned about the nature of attitudes and the relationships among the components. For excellent recent overviews of thinking in this area, see Alice H. Eagly and Shelly Chaiken, *The Psychology of Attitudes* (Chicago: Harcourt Brace Jovanovich, 1993); and Joel B. Cohen and Charles S. Areni, "Affect and Consumer Behavior," in T. Robertson and H. Kassarjian (eds.), *Handbook of Consumer Behavior* (Englewood Cliffs, N.J.: Prentice Hall, 1991), pp. 188–240. In the same volume two other articles are also significant: for implications regarding marketers' changing attitudes through persuasion, see Richard E. Petty, Rao H. Unnava, and Alan J. Strathman, "Theories of Attitude Change," pp. 241–280; and for analysis of how consumers' expectations affect behavior, see W. Fred van Raaij, "The Formation and Use of Expectations in Consumer Decision Making," pp. 401–418. See also the ideas in Youjae Yi and Ken Gray, "New Perspectives in Attitude Research," *Advances in Consumer Research*, Vol. 19 (1991), pp. 319–322.

4. For further discussions of the functional approach, see Richard J. Lutz, "The Role of Attitude Theory in Marketing," in H. Kassarjian and T. Robertson (eds.), *Perspectives in Consumer Behavior*, 4th ed. (Englewood Cliffs, N.J.: Prentice Hall, 1991), pp. 317–339; Mark P. Zanna, "Attitude Function: Is It Related to Attitude Structure?" *Advances in Consumer Research*, Vol. 17 (1990), pp. 98–100; and Richard Ennis and Mark Zanna, "Attitudes, Advertising, and Automobiles: A Functional Approach," *Advances in Consumer Research*, Vol. 20 (1993), pp. 662–666.

5. "Revive Sluggish Brand with Seven-Step Plan," *Marketing News*, October 9, 1987, p. 28. The figure is adapted from discussion in this article.

6. Martha T. Moore, "What's in a Name? Billions!" *USA Today*, August 12, 1992, p. B1.

7. Discussion of the brand equity concept and other examples are drawn from B. G. Yovovich, "What Is Your Brand Really Worth?" *Marketing Week*, August 8, 1988, pp. 18–24; and Lance Leuthesser, "Defining, Measuring, and Managing Brand Equity," Report 88-104, Marketing Science Institute, May 1988.

8. The Marriott example is provided in Peter H. Farquhar, "Managing Brand Equity," *Marketing Research*, Vol. 1, No. 3 (September 1989), pp. 24–33; B. G. Yovovich, "What Is Your Brand Really Worth?"

9. Exhibit 11-1 answers are as follows. Top ten, in order: Coca-Cola, Campbell's, Disney, Pepsi-Cola, Kodak, NBC, Black & Decker, Kellogg's, McDonald's, Hershey's; bottom ten, in order: Canadian cigarettes, loudspeakers, diversified financial services, Danish consumer electronics, Japanese beer, pet food, Korean electronics, German cooking equipment, Swiss cough drops, batteries. Competitive rankings: Duracell (no. 23) shocked Energizer (no. 69), Burger King (43) drove by Wendy's (134), Nike (73) trampled Reebok (122), UPS (40) outdelivered Federal Express (139), and Maxwell House (101) ground by Folgers (143). The consumer surveys were conducted by Landor Associates, a San Francisco research firm. The top ten and competitive brand rankings are based on the report by Laura Bird, "The New Secret Weapon: Consumer Esteem," *Marketing Week: Superbrands*, 1990, pp. 70–71. The bottom ten brands are based on the report by Edward C. Baig, "Name That Brand," *Fortune*, July 4, 1988, pp. 9ff.

10. B. G. Yovovich, "What Is Your Brand Really Worth?"

11. There are many good articles available on various aspects of brand equity. For some recent writings, see, for example, Peter Doyle, "Building Successful Brands: The Strategic Options," *The Journal of Consumer Marketing*, Vol. 7, No. 2 (Spring 1990), pp. 5–20; Allan L. Baldinger, "Defining and Applying the Brand Equity Concept: Why the Researcher Should Care," *Journal of Advertising Research*, Vol. 30, No. 3 (June/July 1990), pp. RC-2–RC-5; Max Blackston, "Price Trade-offs as a Measure of Brand Value," *Journal of Advertising Research*, Vol. 30, No. 4 (August/September 1990), pp. RC-3–RC-6; Peter H. Farquhar, "Managing Brand Equity," *Journal of Advertising Research*, Vol. 30, No. 4 (August/September 1990), pp. RC-7–RC-12; Peter Kim, "A Perspective on Brands," *The Journal of Consumer Marketing*, Vol. 7, No. 4 (Fall 1990), pp. 63–67; Chris A. Abernathy, "Building Networks of Small Brands," *The Journal of Consumer Marketing*, Vol. 8, No. 2 (Spring 1991), pp. 25–30; Eliot Maltz, "Managing Brand Equity," Marketing Science Institute Conference, November 28–30, 1990, Austin. Report No. 91-110 (April 1991); James R. Tindall, "Marketing Established Brands," *The Journal of Consumer Marketing*, Vol. 8, No. 4 (Fall 1991), pp. 5–12; Steven

King, "Brand-Building in the 1990s," *The Journal of Consumer Marketing*, Vol. 8, No. 4 (Fall 1991), pp. 43–52; C. Whan Park, Sandra Milberg, and Robert Lawson, "Evaluation of Brand Extensions: The Role of Product Feature Similarity and Brand Concept Consistency," *Journal of Consumer Research*, Vol. 18, No. 2 (September 1991), pp. 185–193; Kevin Lane Keller and David A. Aaker, "The Effects of Sequential Introduction of Brand Extensions," *Journal of Marketing Research*, Vol. 29, No. 1 (February 1992), pp. 35–50; Norman C. Berry, "Revitalizing Brands," *The Journal of Product & Brand Management*, Vol. 1, No. 2 (Spring 1992), pp. 19–24; James C. Crimmins, "Better Measurement and Management of Brand Value," *Journal of Advertising Research*, Vol. 32, No. 4 (July/August 1992), pp. 11–19; Daniel C. Smith and C. Whan Park, "The Effects of Brand Extensions on Market Share and Advertising Efficiency," *Journal of Marketing Research*, Vol. 29, No. 3 (August 1992), pp. 296–313; Peter H. Farquhar, Julia Y. Han, Paul M. Herr, and Yuji Ijiri, "Strategies for Leveraging Master Brands," *Marketing Research*, Vol. 4, No. 3 (September 1992), pp. 32–43; Carol J. Simon and Mary W. Sullivan, "The Measurement and Determinants of Brand Equity: A Financial Approach," *Marketing Science*, Vol. 12, No. 1 (Winter 1993), pp. 28–52; Peter A. Dacin and Daniel C. Smith, "The Effects of Adding Products to a Brand on Consumers' Evaluations of New Brand Extensions," *Advances in Consumer Research*, Vol. 20 (1993), pp. 594–598; Kalpesh Kaushik Desai and Wayne D. Hoyer, "Line Extensions: A Categorization and an Information Processing Perspective," *Advances in Consumer Research*, Vol. 20 (1993), pp. 599–606; Sandy D. Jap, "An Examination of the Effects of Multiple Brand Extensions on the Brand Concept," *Advances in Consumer Research*, Vol. 20 (1993), pp. 607–611; Gabriella Stern, "Brand Names Are Getting Steamed Up to Peel Off Their Private-Label Rivals," *The Wall Street Journal*, April 21, 1993, p. B1; and Barbara Loken and Deborah Roedder John, "Diluting Brand Beliefs: When Do Brand Extensions Have a Negative Impact?" *Journal of Marketing*, Vol. 57, No. 3 (July 1993), pp. 71–84.

12. For detailed reviews of these issues and results on them, see William L. Wilkie and Edgar A. Pessemier, "Issues in Marketing's Use of Multi-attribute Attitude Models," *Journal of Marketing Research*, Vol. 10 No. 4 (November 1973), pp. 428–441; and Richard J. Lutz and James R. Bettman, "Multi-attribute Models in Marketing: A Bicentennial Review," in A. Woodside, J. Sheth, and B. Bennett (eds.), *Consumer and Industrial Buying Behavior* (New York: North Holland, 1977), pp. 137–150. For theoretical background and applications of related models in psychology, see Martin Fishbein and Icek Ajzen, *Attitude, Intention and Behavior: An Introduction to Theory and Research* (Reading, Mass.: Addison-Wesley, 1975); Icek Ajzen and Martin Fishbein, *Understanding Attitudes and Predicting Social Behavior* (Englewood Cliffs, N.J.: Prentice Hall, 1980); and Milton J. Rosenberg, "Cognitive Structure and Attitudinal Affect," *Journal of Abnormal and Social Psychology*, November 1956, pp. 367–372. Other significant alterations in the Fishbein model have also been proposed. See, for example, Olli T. Ahtola, "The Vector Model of Preferences: An Alternative to the Fishbein Model," *Journal of Marketing Research*, Vol. 12, No. 1 (February 1975), pp. 52–59, and the more recent proposals of Kari Edwards, "The Interplay of Affect and Cognition in Attitude Formation and Change," *Journal of Personality and Social Psychology*, Vol. 59, No. 2 (1990), pp. 202–216.

For more detailed discussions of specific issues, see also Daniel R. Denison and Claes Fornell, "Modeling Distance Structures in

Consumer Research: Scale versus Order in Validity Assessment," *Journal of Consumer Research,* Vol. 16, No. 4 (March 1990), pp. 479–489; Youjae Yi, "The Indirect Effects of Advertisements Designed to Change Product Attribute Beliefs," *Psychology & Marketing,* Vol. 7, No. 1 (Spring 1990), pp. 47–64; William L. Moore, "Factorial Preference Structures," *Journal of Consumer Research,* Vol. 17, No. 1 (June 1990), pp. 94–104; Stephen B. Castleberry and Andrew S. C. Ehrenberg, "Brand Usage: A Factor in Consumer Beliefs," *Marketing Research,* Vol. 2, No. 2 (June 1990), pp. 14–20; Neil R. Barnard and Andrew S. C. Ehrenberg, "Robust Measures of Consumer Brand Beliefs," *Journal of Marketing Research,* Vol. 27 (November 1990), pp. 477–484; Sharon Shavitt and Russell H. Fazio, "Effects of Attribute Salience on the Consistency of Product Evaluations and Purchase Predictions," *Advances in Consumer Research,* Vol. 17 (1990), pp. 91–97; Randall L. Rose, Paul W. Miniard, and Sunil Bhatla, "Brand Cognitions as Determinants of Brand Attitudes: The Influence of Measurement and Processing Involvement," *Advances in Consumer Research,* Vol. 17 (1990), pp. 128–134; Roxanne Lefkoff-Hagius and Charlotte H. Mason, "The Role of Tangible and Intangible Attributes in Similarity and Preference Judgements," *Advances in Consumer Research,* Vol. 17 (1990), pp. 135–143; Calvin P. Duncan, "Consumer Market Beliefs: A Review of the Literature and an Agenda for Future Research," *Advances in Consumer Research,* Vol. 17 (1990), pp. 729–736; Itamar Simonson, "The Effect of Buying Decisions on Consumers' Assessment of Their Tastes," *Marketing Letters,* Vol. 2, No. 1 (January 1991), pp. 5–14; Gary J. Gaeth, Irwin P. Levin, Goutam Chadraborty, and Aron M. Levin, "Consumer Evaluation of Multi-product Bundles: An Information Integration Analysis," *Marketing Letters,* Vol. 2, No. 1 (January 1991), pp. 47–59; Richard P. Bagozzi and Youjae Yi, "Multitrait-Multimethod Matrices in Consumer Research,"*Journal of Consumer Research,* Vol. 17, No. 4 (March 1991), pp. 426–439; Paul M. Herr, Frank R. Kardes, and John Kim, "Effects of Word-of-Mouth and Product-Attribute Information on Persuasion: AN Accessibility-Diagnosticity Perspective," *Journal of Consumer Research,* Vol. 17, No. 4 (March 1991), pp. 454–462; Kevin M. Elliott, "Are Consumers Evaluating Your Products the Way You Think and Hope They Are?" *The Journal of Consumer Marketing,* Vol. 8, No. 2 (Spring 1991), pp. 5–14; Laura Yale and Kenneth C. Gehrt, "The Multidimensionality of the Construct of Convenience: An Exploratory Investigation," *AMA Summer Educators' Proceedings* (1991), pp. 369–370; Kwangsu Kim and Girish N. Punj, "Discriminant Validity of Determinants of Brand Attitude in New Brand Commercials," *AMA Summer Educators' Proceedings* (1991), pp. 380–389; David J. Curry, Michael B. Menasco, and James W. Van Ark, "Multiattribute Dyadic Choice: Models and Tests," *Journal of Marketing Research,* Vol. 28 (August 1991), pp. 259–267; William B. Dodds, Kent B. Monroe, and Dhruv Grewal, "Effects of Price, Brand, and Store Information on Buyers' Product Evaluations," *Journal of Marketing Research,* Vol. 28 (August 1991), pp. 307–319; Niraj Dawar, S. Ratneshwar, and Alan G. Sawyer, "The Use of Multiple Methods to Explore Three-way Person, Brand and Usage Context Interactions," *Advances in Consumer Research,* Vol. 19 (1992), pp. 116–122; Linda Golden and Mayur Sirdesai, "'Chernoff Faces': A Useful Technique for Comparative Image Analysis and Representation," *Advances in Consumer Research,* Vol. 19 (1992), pp. 123–128; Norbert Schwarz and Herbert Bless, "Assimilation and Contrast Effects in Attitude Measurement: An Inclusion/Exclusion Model," *Advances in Consumer Research,* Vol. 19 (1992), pp. 72–77; Richard F. Yalch, "Comment on Factors Affecting Evaluations,"*Advances in Consumer Research,* Vol. 19 (1992), pp. 276–278; Paul E. Green and Catherine M. Schaffer, "Importance Weight Effects on Self-explicated Preference Models: Some Empirical Findings," *Advances in Consumer Research,* Vol. 18 (1991), pp. 476–482; Eric A. Greenleaf, "Improving Rating Scale Measures by Detecting and Correcting Bias Components in Some Response Styles," *Journal of Marketing Research,* Vol. 29, No. 2 (May 1992), pp. 176–188; G. Ray Funkhouser, "Using Consumer Expectations as an Input to Pricing Decisions," *The Journal of Product & Brand Management,* Vol. 1, No. 2 (Spring 1992), pp. 47–53; David J. Ortinau and Ronald P. Bresinger, "An Empirical Investigation of Perceived Quality's Intangible Dimensionality through Direct Cognitive Structural (DCS) Analysis," in Robert L. King (ed.), *Marketing Perspectives for the 1990s* (Richmond, Va.: Southern Marketing Association, 1992), pp. 214–219; Amy J. Morgan, "Exploring Customer Satisfaction with Television Home Shopping: An Importance-Performance Approach," ibid., pp. 220–223; Joel Huber, Dick R. Wittink, John A. Fiedler, and Richard Miller, "The Effectiveness of Alternative Preference Elicitation Procedures in Predicting Choice," *Journal of Marketing Research,* Vol. 30, No. 1 (February 1993), pp. 105–114; Robert Underwood, "Packaging as an Extrinsic Product Attribute: An Examination of Package Utility and Its Effect on Total Product Utility in a Consumer Purchase Situation," *AMA Winter Educators' Conference* (1993), pp. 212–217; Hans Baumgartner, "An Exploratory Investigation of Holistic and Analytic Modes of Product Perception," *Advances in Consumer Research,* Vol. 20 (1993), pp. 673–677; and Roxanne Lefkoff-Hagius and Charlotte H. Mason, "Characteristic, Beneficial, and Image Attributes in Consumer Judgements of Similarity and Preference," *Journal of Consumer Research,* Vol. 20, No. 1 (June 1993), pp. 100–110.

13. For further discussion of these strategy approaches, see Harper W. Boyd, Michael L. Ray, and Edward C. Strong, "An Attitudinal Framework for Advertising Strategy," *Journal of Marketing,* Vol. 36, No. 2, April 1972, pp. 27–33. See also C. Whan Park, Bernard J. Jaworski, and Deborah J. MacInnis, "Strategic Brand Concept—Image Management," *Journal of Marketing,* Vol. 50 (October 1986), pp. 135–145; and Robert Jacobson and David Aaker, "The Strategic Role of Product Quality," *Journal of Marketing,* Vol. 51 (October 1987), pp. 31–44.

14. Paul L. Edwards, "Mailing by Six Flags Seeks to Reinforce Park's Safety," *Advertising Age,* August 23, 1984, p. 8.

15. "P&G Rides Crest with Leverage," *Marketing Week,* October 5, 1987, p. 58; Thomas Jaffe, "Lighting Up the Skies," *Forbes,* February 15, 1993, p. 20.

16. Peter Nulty, "No Product Too Dull to Shine," *Fortune,* July 27, 1992, pp. 95–96; Laura Bird, "Arm & Hammer Stakes Its Name on the Environment," *Marketing Week,* November 19, 1990, p. 4; Jack J. Honomichl, "The Ongoing Saga of 'Mother Baking Soda,'" *Advertising Age,* September 20, 1982, pp. M2ff.

17. "The War in Military Ads? What War?" *New York Times,* March 8, 1991, p. C1.

18. William L. Wilkie and Paul W. Farris, *Consumer Information Processing: Perspectives and Implications for Advertising* (Cambridge, Mass.: Marketing Science Institute, 1976).

19. Ibid.

20. Jack Trout and Al Ries, "Positioning Cuts through Chaos in Marketplace," *Advertising Age,* May 1, 1972; and Al Ries and Jack

Trout, *Positioning: The Battle for Your Mind* (New York: McGraw-Hill, 1981). See also Dawn Dobni and George M. Zinkhan, "In Search of Brand Image: A Foundations Analysis," *Advances in Consumer Research*, Vol. 17 (1990), pp. 110–119; Melvin Prince, "How Consistent Is the Information in Positioning Studies?" *Journal of Advertising Research*, Vol. 30, No. 3 (June/July 1990), pp. 25–30; Gail Tom, Michelle Dragics, and Christi Holderegger, "Using Visual Presentation to Assess Store Positioning: A Case Study of J.C. Penney," *Marketing Research*, Vol. 3, No. 3 (September 1991), pp. 48–52; Richard F. Chay, "How Marketing Researchers Can Harness the Power of Brand Equity," *Marketing Research*, Vol. 3, No. 2 June 1991, pp. 30–37; Eugene W. Anderson and Steven M. Shugan, "Repositioning for Changing Preferences: The Case of Beef versus Poultry," *Journal of Consumer Research*, Vol. 18, No. 2 (September 1991), pp. 219–232; Jeffrey F. Durgee, "Contrarian Marketing," *The Journal of Consumer Marketing*, Vol. 9, No. 1 (Winter 1992), pp. 51–60; Susan M. Keaveney and Kenneth A. Hunt, "Conceptualization and Operationalization of Retail Store Image: A Case of Rival Middle-Level Theories," *Journal of the Academy of Marketing Science*, Vol. 20, No. 2 (Spring 1992), pp. 165–176; Dan Horsky and Paul Nelson, "New Brand Positioning and Pricing in an Oligopolistic Market," *Marketing Science*, Vol. 11, No. 2 (Spring 1992), pp. 133–153; Mark B. Traylor, "Cannibalism in Multibrand Firms," *The Journal of Product & Brand Mangement*, Vol. 1, No. 3 (Summer 1992), pp. 17–23; Sallie H. Bogs, "The Construct of Retail Crowding in Store Image Literature: Development and Directions," in Robert L. King (ed.), *Marketing Perspectives for the 1990s* (Richmond, Va.: Southern Marketing Association, 1992), pp. 57–60; Sandra McCurley Hortman, "Repositioning the Regional Symphony Orchestra: How Joint Ventures of Marketing Professionals are Fine Arts Administrators Can Benefit Both Town and Gown," ibid., pp. 358–361; and Peter N. Golder and Gerald J. Tellis, "Pioneer Advantage: Marketing Logic or Marketing Legend?" *Journal of Marketing Research*, Vol. 30 (May 1993), pp. 158–170.

21. David A. Aaker and J. Gary Shansby, "Positioning Your Product," *Business Horizons*, May-June 1982, pp. 56–62.

22. Allan D. Shocker and V. Srinivasan, "Multiattribute Approaches for Product Concept Evaluation and Generation: A Critical Review," *Journal of Marketing Research*, Vol. 16, No. 2 (May 1979), pp. 159–180. For excellent recent discussions and applications, see, for example, Paul E. Green and Jonathan S. Kim, "Beyond the Quadrant Chart: Designing Effective Benefit Bundle Strategies," *Journal of Advertising Research*, Vol. 31, No. 6 (December 1991), pp. 56–63; Paul E. Green and Abba M. Krieger, "An Application of a Product Positioning Model to Pharmaceutical Products," *Marketing Science*, Vol. 11, No. 2 (Spring 1992), pp. 117–132; and Abbie Griffin and John R. Hauser, "The Voice of the Customer," *Marketing Science*, Vol. 12, No. 1 (Winter 1993), pp. 1–27.

23. For discussions of determinant attributes, see Mark I. Alpert, "Definition of Determinant Attributes: A Comparison of Methods," *Journal of Marketing Research*, Vol. 8, No. 2 (May 1971), pp. 184–191; James H. Meyers, "Benefit Structure Analysis: A New Tool for Product Planning," *Journal of Marketing*, October 1976, pp. 23–32; and Mark I. Alpert, "Unresolved Issues in Identification of Determinant Attributes," *Advances in Consumer Research*, Vol. 7 (1980), pp. 83–88.

24. This is an important sector of work. It stresses how consumers' subjective ratings can be transformed into objective dimensions that marketing managers can control in their marketing mixes, and it

has therefore attracted the interest of quantitatively oriented marketers. For recent overviews, see Paul E. Green and V. Srinivasan, "Conjoint Analysis in Marketing Research: New Developments and Directions," *Journal of Marketing*, Vol. 54, No. 4 (October 1990), pp. 3–19; and Mitch Griffin, Jill S. Attaway, and Barry J. Babin, "Conjoint Analysis in Academic Research: A Survey of Marketing Literature," *AMA Summer Educators' Proceedings* (1991), pp. 683–692. For some early readings presenting various viewpoints and alternative methodologies, see Paul E. Green and Yoram Wind, *Multi-attribute Decisions in Marketing* (Hinsdale, Ill.: Dryden Press, 1973); Paul E. Green and V. Srinivasan, "Conjoint Analysis in Consumer Research: Issues and Outlook," *Journal of Consumer Research*, Vol. 5 (September 1978), pp. 103–123; and Rajendra K. Srivastava, Mark I. Alpert, and Allan D. Shocker, "A Customer Oriented Approach for Determining Market Structures," *Journal of Marketing*, Vol. 48, No. 2 (Spring 1984), pp. 32–45.

For recent developments, see, for example, R. Kenneth Teas and Andrea L. Perr, "A Test of a Decompositional Method of Multiattribute Perceptions Measurement," *Journal of Consumer Research*, Vol. 16, No. 3 (December 1989), pp. 384–391; Amiya K. Basu and Manoj Hastak, "Multiattribute Judgements under Uncertainty: A Conjoint Measurement Approach," *Advances in Consumer Research*, Vol. 17 (1990), pp. 554–562; Michael Tharp and Lawrence Marks, "An Examination of the Effects of Attribute Order and Product Order Biases in Conjoint Analysis," *Advances in Consumer Research*, Vol. 17 (1990), pp. 563–570; Joel N. Axelrod and Norman Frendberg, "Conjoint Analysis: Peering behind the Jargon," *Marketing Research*, Vol. 2, No. 2 (June 1990), pp. 28–35; Rajeev Kohli and Vijay Mahajan, "A Reservation-Price Model for Optimal Pricing of Multiattribute Products in Conjoint Analysis," *Journal of Marketing Research*, Vol. 28 (August 1991), pp. 347–354; Mitch Griffin, Jill S. Attaway, and Barry J. Babin, "Conjoint Analysis in Academic Research: A Survey of Marketing Literature," *AMA Summer Educators' Proceedings* (1991), pp. 683–692; Rajan Natarajan and Paul R. Warshaw, "Are the Models Compatible for Empirical Comparison? An Illustration with an Intensions Model, an Expectations Model, and Traditional Conjoint Analysis," *Advances in Consumer Research*, Vol. 19 (1992), pp. 472–481; Alan Strathman, David S. Boninger, and Sara M. Baker, "The Influence of Level of Involvement on the Feature Matching Process in Consumer Preference Judgments," *Advances in Consumer Research*, Vol. 19 (1992), pp. 777–781; Ishmael P. Akaah, "Predictive Performance of Self-explicated, Traditional Conjoint, and Hybrid Conjoint Models under Alternative Data Collection Models," *Journal of the Academy of Marketing Science*, Vol. 19, No. 4 (Fall 1991), pp. 309–314; Rene Y. Darmon and Dominique Rouzies, "Internal Validity Assessment of Conjoint Estimated Attribute Importance Weights," *Journal of the Academy of Marketing Science*, Vol. 19, No. 4 (Fall 1991), pp. 315–322; Michael J. Dorsch and R. Kenneth Teas, "A Test of the Convergent Validity of Self-explicated and Decompositional Conjoint Measurement," *Journal of the Academy of Marketing Science*, Vol. 20, No. 1 (Winter 1992), pp. 27–36; Terry Elrod, Jordan J. Louviere, and Krishnakumar S. Davey, "An Empirical Comparison of Ratings-based and Choice-based Conjoint Models," *Journal of Marketing Research*, Vol. 29, No. 3 (August 1992), pp. 368–377; Raj Mehta, William L. Moore, and Teresa M. Pavia, "An Examination of the Use of Unacceptable Levels in Conjoint Analysis," *Journal of Consumer Research*, Vol. 19, No. 3 (December 1992), pp. 470–476; Paul E. Green, Abba M. Krieger, and Catherine M. Schaffer, "A Hybrid Conjoint Model with Individual-Level Interaction

Estimation," *Advances in Consumer Research*, Vol. 20 (1993), pp. 149–154; Paul L. Sauer and Alan Dick, "Using Moderator Variables in Structural Equations Models," *Advances in Consumer Research*, Vol. 20 (1993), pp. 637–640; Banwari Mittal, "Testing Consumer Behavior Theories: LISREL Is Not a Panacea," *Advances in Consumer Research*, Vol. 20 (1993), pp. 647–653; and Ishmael P. Akaah and Attila Yaprak, "Assessing the Influence of Country of Origin on Product Evaluations: An Application of Conjoint Methodology," *Journal of International Consumer Marketing*, Vol. 5, No. 2 (1993), pp. 39–54.

25. For an excellent recent overview, see Glen L. Urban and John Hauser, *Design and Marketing of New Products*, 2d ed. (Englewood Cliffs, N.J.: Prentice Hall, 1994). For a useful (but advanced) discussion tying academic research on modeling with consumer behavior, see K. Sridhar Moorthy, "Theoretical Modeling in Marketing," *Journal of Marketing*, Vol. 57, No. 2 (April 1993), pp. 92–106.

26. Richard Johnson, "Market Segmentation: A Strategic Management Tool," *Journal of Marketing Research*, February 1971, pp. 13–19. For recent discussions of related issues and possibilities, see Donna L. Hoffman and George R. Franke, "Correspondence Analysis Graphical Representation of Categorical Data in Marketing Research," *Journal of Marketing Research*, Vol. 23 (August 1986), pp. 213–227; Steven M. Shugan, "Estimating Brand Positioning Maps Using Supermarket Scanning Data," *Journal of Marketing Research*, Vol. 24 (February 1987), pp. 1–18; Naresh K. Malhotra, "Validity and Structural Reliability of Multidimensional Scaling," *Journal of Marketing Research*, Vol. 24 (May 1987), pp. 164–173; Wayne S. DeSarbo and Richard R. Batsell, "A New Multidimensional Scaling Methodology for the Representation of Inter-Product Substitutability," *Advances in Consumer Research*, Vol. 15 (1988), pp. 518–527; Haim Mano and Scott M. Davis, "The Effects of Familiarity on Cognitive Maps," *Advances in Consumer Research*, Vol. 17 (1990), pp. 275–282; Pierre Valette-Florence and Bernard Rapacchi, "Improvements in Means-End Chain Analysis Using Graph Theory and Correspondence Analysis," *Journal of Advertising Research*, Vol. 31, No. 1 (February/March 1991), pp. 30–45; Randolph E. Bucklin and V. Srinivasan, "Determining Interbrand Substitutability through Survey Measurement of Consumer Preference Structures," *Journal of Marketing Research*, Vol. 28 (February 1991), pp. 58–71; S. Ratneshwar and Allan D. Shocker, "Substitution in Use and the Role of Usage Context in Product Category Structures," *Journal of Marketing Research*, Vol. 28 (August 1991), pp. 281–295; and R. Kenneth Teas and John K. Wong, "Item Context and the Stability of Entity-based and Attribute-based Multiattribute Scaling Methods," *Journal of Consumer Research*, Vol. 18, No. 4 (March 1992), pp. 536–545.

27. Allan D. Shocker and V. Srinivasan, "Multiattribute Approaches for Product Concept Evaluation and Generation: A Critical Review," *Journal of Marketing Research*, Vol. 16, No. 2 (May 1979), pp. 159–180; see also "A-B Miller Brews Continue to Barrel Ahead," *Advertising Age*, August 4, 1980, p. 4; and "These Days It's Miller Time Less Often, Worrying Brewer," *The Wall Street Journal*, February 10, 1983, p. 33.

28. See, for example, Patrick E. Murphy and William L. Wilkie (eds.), *Marketing and Advertising Regulation: The Federal Trade Commission in the 1990s* (Notre Dame, Ind.: University of Notre Dame Press, 1990); William L. Wilkie, Dennis L. McNeill, and Michael B. Mazis, "Marketing's 'Scarlet Letter': The Theory and Practice of Corrective Advertising," *Journal of Marketing*, Vol. 48, No. 2 (Spring

1984), pp. 11–31; and Fred W. Morgan, "Judicial Standards for Survey Research: An Update and Guidelines," *Journal of Marketing*, Vol. 54, No. 1 (January 1990), pp. 59–70.

29. Alvin Achenbaum, "Knowledge Is a Thing Called Measurement," in L. Adler and I. Crespi (eds.), *Attitude Research at Sea* (Chicago: American Marketing Association, 1966), pp. 111–126; and Alvin Achenbaum, "Advertising Doesn't Manipulate Consumers," *Journal of Advertising Research*, Vol. 12, No. 2 April/May 1972, pp. 3–13. See also William D. Wells, "Attitude and Behavior: Lessons from the Needham Life Style Study," *Journal of Advertising Research*, Vol. 25, No. 1 (February–March 1985), pp. 40–44; Murray G. Millal and Abraham Tesser, "Attitudes and Behavior: The Cognitive-Affective Mismatch Hypothesis," *Advances in Consumer Research*, Vol. 17 (1990), pp. 86–90; and Mahmood M. Hajjat, "The Conceptual Organization of Behavior and Attitude-Behavior Consistency," *Advances in Consumer Research*, Vol. 17 (1990), pp. 777–784.

30. R. H. Fazio and M. P. Zanna, "Attitudinal Qualities Relating to the Strength of the Attitude-Behavior Relationship," *Journal of Experimental Social Psychology*, Vol. 14 (1978), pp. 398–408. See also R. H. Fazio and M. P. Zanna, "Direct Experience and Attitude-Behavior Consistency," in L. Berkowitz (ed.), *Advances in Experimental Social Psychology*, Vol. 14 (New York: Academic Press, 1981), pp. 162–202. For results in marketing, see Robert E. Smith and William R. Swinyard, "Attitude-Behavior Consistencies: The Impact of Product Trial versus Advertising," *Journal of Marketing Research*, Vol. 20, No. 3 (August 1983), pp. 257–267; Michael A. Kamins and Larry J. Marks, "The Effects of Framing and Advertising Sequencing on Attitude Consistency and Behavioral Intentions," *Advances in Consumer Research*, Vol. 14 (1987), pp. 168–172; Mark P. Zanna, "Attitude-Behavior Consistency: Fulfilling the Need for Cognitive Structure," *Advances in Consumer Research*, Vol. 16, (1989), pp. 318–320; and Chris T. Allen, Karen A. Machleit, and Susan Schultz Kleine, "A Comparison of Attitudes and Emotions as Predictors of Behavior at Diverse Levels of Behavioral Experience," *Journal of Consumer Research*, Vol. 18, No. 4 (March 1992), pp. 493–504.

31. See, for example, work by Richard E. Petty and John T. Cacioppo and their colleagues. A useful review and perspective appears in their chapter in T. Robertson and H. Kassarjian (eds.), *Handbook of Consumer Behavior* (Englewood Cliffs, N.J.: Prentice Hall, 1991), pp. 241–280. See also Jack M. Feldman and John G. Lynch, "Self-generated Validity and Other Effects of Measurement on Belief, Attitude Intention, and Behavior," *Journal of Applied Psychology*, Vol. 73, No. 3 (1988), pp. 421–435; Sandrudin A. Ahmed, "Attitude Behavior Consistency: The Moderating Effect of Cognitive Style," *AMA Summer Educators' Proceedings* (1985), pp. 7–10; Brian Wansink and Michael L. Ray, "Goal-Related Consumption and Extension Advertising: The Impact on Memory and Consumption," *Advances in Consumer Research*, Vol. 19 (1991), pp. 806–812; Richard J. Harnish, "Role of Affect in Consumer Behavior: The Effect of Self-monitoring," in T.J Page, Jr., and S.E. Middlestadt (eds.), *Proceedings of the Society for Consumer Psychology*, (Clemson, S.C.: CtC Press, 1992), pp. 7–11; Curtis P. Haugtvedt and Richard E. Petty, "Personality and Persuasion: Need for Cognition Moderates the Persistence and Resistence of Attitude Changes," *Journal of Personality and Social Psychology*, Vol. 63, No. 2 (1992), pp. 308–319; and Sharon Shavitt, Tina M. Lowrey, and Sang-Pil Han, "Attitude Functions in Advertising: The Interactive Role of Products and Self-monitoring," *Journal of Consumer Psychology*, Vol. 1, No. 4 (1992), pp. 337–364.

32. This point, together with related insights, has drawn considerable attention from researchers in marketing; see, for example, Icek Ajzen and Martin Fishbein, *Understanding Attitudes and Predicting Social Behavior* (Englewood Cliffs, N.J.: Prentice Hall, 1980). Within marketing an especially useful basic discussion is provided in Michael J. Ryan and E. H. Bonfield, "The Fishbein Extended Model and Consumer Behavior," *Journal of Consumer Research*, Vol. 2 (August 1975), pp. 118–136.

This area has seen a number of heated debates and controversies, because the issues of how social influences operate and how attitudes relate to behavior are complex. These issues are important to theorists and to those concerned with obtaining precise and valid measures with which to diagnose specific causes of consumer intentions and behaviors. If your would like to pursue these more abstract issues to understand better the nuances of this model, see the following articles in *Advances in Consumer Research*, Vol. 4, (1976): Olli T. Ahtola, "Toward a Vector Model of Intentions," pp. 481–484, Richard J. Lutz, "Conceptual and Operational Issues in the Extended Fishbein Model," pp. 469–476, and Martin Fishbein, "Extending the Extended Model: Some Comments," pp. 491–497.

Also, for a heated debate featuring strong disagreements about the model, see Paul W. Miniard and Joel B. Cohen, "An Examination of the Fishbein-Ajzen Behavioral Intentions Model's Concepts and Measures," *Journal of Experimental Social Psychology*, Vol. 17 (July 1981), pp. 309–339; Martin Fishbein and Icek Ajzen, "On Construct Validity: A Critique of Miniard and Cohen's Paper," *Journal of Experimental Social Psychology*, Vol.17 (July 1981), pp. 340–350; and Paul W. Miniard and Joel B. Cohen, "Modeling Personal and Normative Influences on Behavior," *Journal of Consumer Research*, Vol. 10 (September 1983), pp. 169–180.

For recent empirical findings and extensions in consumer behavior, see Blair H. Sheppard, John Hartwick, and Paul R. Warshaw, "The Theory of Reasoned Action: A Meta-analysis of Past Research with Recommendations for Modifications and Future Research," *Journal of Consumer Research*, Vol. 15 (December 1988), pp. 325–343; Chol Lee, "Modifying an American Consumer Behavior Model for Consumers in Confucian Culture: The Case of the Fishbein Behavioral Intention Model," *Journal of International Consumer Marketing*, Vol. 3, No. 1 (1990), pp. 27–50; Richard P. Bagozzi, Hans Baumgartner, and Youjae Yi, "State versus Action Orientation and the Theory of Reasoned Action: An Application to Coupon Usage," *Journal of Consumer Research*, Vol. 18, No. 4 (March 1992), pp. 505–518; Richard G. Netemeyer and William O. Bearden, "A Comparative Analysis of Two Models of Behavioral Intention," *Journal of the Academy of Marketing Science*, Vol. 20, No. 1 (Winter 1992), pp. 49–60; Mark R. Young and Rosemary R. Lagace, "The Theory of Reasoned Action Revisited: A Case of Highly Involved, Long-Term Voluntary Behavior," *AMA Summer Educators' Proceedings* (1992), pp. 547–554; Icek Ajzen and B. L. Driver, "Contingent Value Measurement: On the Nature and Meaning of Willingness to Pay," *Journal of Consumer Psychology*, Vol. 1, No. 4 (1992), pp. 297–316; Richard G. Netemeyer, J. Craig Andrews, and Srinivas Durvasula, "A Comparison of Three Behavioral Intention Models: The Case of Valentine's Day Gift-giving," *Advances in Consumer Research*, Vol. 20 (1993), pp. 135–141; and Vicki G. Morwitz, Eric Johnson, and

David Schmittlein, "Does Measuring Intent Change Behavior?" *Journal of Consumer Behavior*, Vol. 20, No. 1 (June 1993), pp. 46–61.

33. Russell H. Fazio, Martha C. Powell, and Carol J. Williams, "The Role of Attitude Accessibility in the Attitude-to-Behavior Process," *Journal of Consumer Research*, Vol. 16, No. 3 (December 1989), pp. 280–288. For a broader review of this approach, see R. H. Fazio, "On the Power and Functionality of Attitudes: The Role of Attitude Accessibility," in A. Pratkanis, S. Breckler, and A. Greenwald (eds.), *Attitude Structure and Function* (Hillsdale, N.J.: Erlbaum, 1989), pp. 153–179. See also Ida E. Berger and Andrew A. Mitchell, "The Effect of Advertising on Attitude Accessibility, Attitude Confidence, and the Attitude-Behavior Relationship," *Journal of Consumer Research*, Vol. 16, No. 3 (December 1989), pp. 269–279; Timothy D. Wilson, Douglas J. Lisle, and Dolores Kraft, "Effects of Self-Reflection on Attitudes and Consumer Decisions," *Advances in Consumer Research*, Vol. 17 (1990), pp. 79–85; and Ida E. Berger, "The Nature of Attitude Accessibility and Attitude Confidence: A Triangulated Experiment," *Journal of Consumer Psychology*, Vol. 1, No. 2 (1992), pp. 103–124.

34. Academic researchers have been very interested in developing a deeper understanding of the attitude-behavior relationship. In addition to the references in Notes 29–33, for recent advanced, excellent discussions of these topics, see Paul M. Herr and Russell H. Fazio, "The Attitude-to-Behavior Process: Implications for Consumer Behavior," in Andrew Mitchell (ed.), *Advances in Consumer Behavior: Ad Exposure, Memory and Choice* (Hillsdale, N.J.: Erlbaum, 1992), pp. 119–140; Richard P. Bagozzi, "The Self-regulation of Attitudes, Intentions, and Behavior," *Social Psychology Quarterly*, Vol. 55, No. 2 (1992), pp. 178–204; Icek Ajzen, "From Intentions to Actions: A Theory of Planned Behavior," in J. Kuhl and J. Beckmann (eds.), *Action Control: From Cognition to Behavior* (New York: Springer-Verlag, 1985); Icek Ajzen, "The Theory of Planned Behavior: Some Unresolved Issues," *Organizational Behavior and Human Decision Processes*, Vol. 50 (1991), pp. 179–211; Richard P. Bagozzi and Paul R. Warshaw, "Trying to Consume," *Journal of Consumer Research*, Vol. 17 (1990), pp. 127–140; and Richard G. Netemeyer, Scott Burton, and Mark Johnston, "A Comparison of Two Models for the Prediction of Volitional and Goal-directed Behaviors: A Confirmatory Analysis Approach," *Social Psychology Quarterly*, Vol. 54 (1991), pp. 87–100.

Chapter 12

Cultural Influences

1. Ernest L. Schusky and T. Patrick Culbert, *Introducing Culture*, 3d ed. (Englewood Cliffs, N.J.: Prentice Hall, 1978).

2. A. L. Kroeber and Clyde Kluckhohn, *Culture: A Critical Review of Concepts and Definitions* (New York: Random House, 1963).

3. Mavis H. Biesanz and John Biesanz, *Introduction to Sociology*, 3d ed. (Englewood Cliffs, N.J.: Prentice Hall, 1978), pp. 34–53. See also Thomas C. O'Guinn, Ronald J. Faber, Nadine J. J. Curias, and Kay Schmitt, "The Cultivation of Consumer Norms," *Advances in Consumer Research*, Vol. 16 (1989), pp. 779–785; Michael K. Hui, Annamma Joy, Chankon Kim, and Michael Laroche, "Acculturation as a Determinant of Consumer Behavior: Conceptual and Methodological Issues," *AMA Winter Educators' Proceedings* (1992), Vol. 3, pp. 466–473; and Sunkyu Jun, A. Dwayne Ball, and James W. Gentry, "Modes of Consumer Acculturation," *Advances in Consumer Research,* Vol. 20 (1993), pp. 76–82.

4. The following discussion is based upon George P. Murdoch, "The Common Denominator of Cultures," in Ralph Linton (ed.), *The Science of Man in the World Crisis* (New York: Columbia University Press, 1945), pp. 123–142.

5. Ibid., p. 125.

6. For an excellent discussion of further aspects of culture as they apply to marketing, see Frederick D. Sturdivant, "Subculture Theory: Poverty, Minorities, and Marketing," in Scott Ward and Thomas Robertson (eds.), *Consumer Behavior: Theoretical Sources* (Englewood Cliffs, N.J.: Prentice Hall, 1973), pp. 470–520. For recent discussions, see Grant McCracken, "Culture and Consumption: A Theoretical Account of the Structure and Movement of the Cultural Meaning of Consumer Goods," *Journal of Consumer Research,* Vol. 13 (June 1986), pp. 71–84; Alan R. Andreasen, "Cultural Interpenetration: A Critical Consumer Research Issue for the 1990s," *Advances in Consumer Research,* Vol. 17 (1990), pp. 847–849; and Lance Strate, "The Cultural Meaning of Beer Commercials," *Advances in Consumer Research,* Vol. 18 (1991), pp. 115–119.

7. Robin M. Williams, *American Society: A Sociological Interpretation,* 3d ed. (New York: Alfred A. Knopf, 1970), pp. 438–639.

8. Josh Levine, "Hard Sell Falls Flat for S.E. Asians," *Advertising Age,* June 21, 1981, p. 35.

9. The examples in this section are derived from several sources, most prominently an interesting book by David A. Ricks, *Big Business Blunders: Mistakes in Multinational Marketing* (Homewood, Ill.: Dow Jones-Irwin, 1983).

10. Doreen Lee, "Are Tokyo Tastes Ready for Tacos and Tostadas?" *Marketing Week,* September 14, 1987, p. 32.

11. The noted anthropologist Edward T. Hall has made numerous contributions to the study of issues related to "hidden languages." His books have been widely read by marketers. You might enjoy reading E. T. Hall, *Beyond Culture* (Garden City, N.Y.: Anchor/Doubleday, 1976); E. T. Hall, *The Silent Language* (Garden City, N.Y.: Doubleday, 1973); E. T. Hall, *The Hidden Dimension* (Garden City, N.Y.: Doubleday, 1969); and Edward T. Hall and Mildred R. Hall, *Hidden Differences: Doing Business with the Japanese* (Garden City, N.Y.: Anchor Press/Doubleday, 1987). For related discussions, see also John Tsalikis, Eric R. Reidenbach, and Donald P. Robin, "Foreign Business 'Payments': A Cross-cultural Comparison of Greek and American Ethical Evaluations," *Journal of International Consumer Marketing,* Vol. 4, Nos. 1/2 (1991), pp. 91–120; Carol J. Kaufman and Paul M. Lane, "The Language of Time in the Global Marketplace," *AMA Summer Educators' Proceedings* (1991), pp. 229–237; and Dana-Nicolet Lascu, "Assessing Consumer Ethics: Scale Development Considerations for International Marketing," *AMA Winter Educators' Proceedings* (1993), pp. 57–61.

12. Wasief Djajanto, "Indonesia Government Expands Ad Ban," *Advertising Age,* March 16, 1981, p. 22.

13. John Karevoll, "Singapore Girl Nixed in Norway," *Advertising Age,* March 23, 1981, p. 48.

14. This issue has recently arisen also in Saudi Arabia: see Tony Horwitz, "With Gulf War Over, Saudi Fundamentalists Reassert Themselves," *The Wall Street Journal,* May 2, 1991, p. A1; and David Kline, "How Islam Collides with Advertising," *Advertising Age,* Au-

gust 2, 1982, pp. M2–M3. For related discussions, see also Robert J. Thomas, "Patent Infringement of Innovations by Foreign Competitors: The Role of the U.S. International Trade Commission," *Journal of Marketing,* Vol. 53, No. 4 (October 1989), pp. 63–75; Charles F. Keown, Laurence W. Jacobs, Roger A. Layton, and Junge-Bae Kim, "A Cross-National Survey of Attitudes toward Marketing's Role in Society," *Journal of International Consumer Marketing,* Vol. 2, No. 4 (1990), pp. 37–56; Michael Kublin, "Obstacles to Soviet-American Joint Ventures," *The Journal of Consumer Marketing,* Vol. 8, No. 3 (Summer 1991), pp. 47–56; M. Sahlins, "Rationality of the Culture of Goods," *Advances in Consumer Research,* Vol. 19 (1992), pp. 78–80; Bruce Keillor and Jamal Al-Khatib, "Japanese National Character and the Role of Shinto: Implications for Marketers," in Robert L. King (ed.), *Marketing: Perspectives for the 1990s* (Richmond, Va.: Southern Marketing Association, 1992), pp. 141–144; Kenneth A. LeClaire, "Ethnic Attitudes and Hong Kong Chinese Consumption Values," *Journal of International Consumer Marketing,* Vol. 4, No. 4 (1992), pp. 73–88; Srinivas Durvasula, J. Craig Andrews, Steven Lysonski, and Richard G. Netemeyer, "Assessing the Cross-National Applicability of Consumer Behavior Models: A Model of Attitude toward Advertising in General," *Journal of Consumer Research,* Vol. 19, No. 4 (March 1993), pp. 626–636; Avraham Shama, Jana Matesova, Tamas Mellar, Bogdan Radomski, and Sergey Sementsov, "The Transformation of Management in Eastern Europe: Status Report," *AMA Winter Educators' Proceedings* (1993), pp. 433–434; Nittaya Wongtada, "Forces Controlling the Compliance of the Gentlemen's Agreement among Overseas Chinese Businessmen," *Journal of International Consumer Marketing,* Vol. 5, No. 2 (1993), pp. 69–83; William K. Darley and Denise M. Johnson, "Cross-National Comparison of Consumer Attitudes toward Consumerism in Four Developing Countries," *The Journal of Consumer Affairs,* Vol. 27, No. 1 (Summer 1993), pp. 37–54; and M. Sami Kassem, Dean Ludwig, and Don R. Beeman, "Segmenting the Arab World: The Gulf Cooperation Council as a Target Market," *Journal of International Consumer Marketing,* Vol. 5, No. 3 (1993), pp. 105–125.

15. J. J. Boddewyn, *Premiums, Gifts, Competitions, and Other Sales Promotions: Regulation and Self-Regulation in 42 Countries* (New York: International Advertising Association, 1988).

16. Bryant Robey, "The Year 2020: Populations Double Abroad," *Marketing Week,* June 19, 1989, p. 57.

17. Madlyn Resener, "Europe's New Mass-Market Appeal," *Adweek,* June 1, 1987, pp. 6ff; see also Martin van Mesdag, "Winging It in Foreign Markets," *Harvard Business Review* (January–February 1987), pp. 71–74. Considerable attention has been given to those issues in recent years. See, for example, Arvind Rangaswamy, Jehoshua Eliashberg, Raymond R. Burke, and Jerry Wind, "Developing Marketing Expert Systems: An Application to International Negotiations," *Journal of Marketing,* Vol. 53, No. 4 (October 1989), pp. 24–39; John H. Holmes, "Toward More Effective International Advertising," *Journal of International Consumer Marketing,* Vol. 3, No. 1 (1990), pp. 51–66; Gary Ko and James W. Gentry, "The Development of Time Orientation Measures for Use in Cross-cultural Research," *Advances in Consumer Research,* Vol. 18 (1991), pp. 135–142; Tiger Li and S. Tamer Cavusgil, "International Marketing: A Classification of Research Streams and Assessment of Their Development since 1982," *AMA Summer Educators' Proceedings* (1991), pp. 592–607; Richard G. Netemeyer, Srinivas Durvasula, and Donald R. Lichtenstein, "A Cross-National Assessment of the Reliability and Validity of the CETSCALE," *Journal of Marketing Research,* Vol. 28 (August 1991), pp. 320–327; Michael Minor, "Replication and the Extension of Cross-national Research: An Example from Advertising," *AMA Winter Educators' Proceedings* (1992), Vol. 3, pp. 27–31; Melissa Martin Young, "Synthesis of Cross-cultural Consumer Behavior Sessions," *AMA Winter Educators' Proceedings* (1992), Vol. 3, pp. 392–396; David K. Tse and John K. Wong, "Instrumental Values and Consumption Behavior among Asia Pacific Consumers; There Are Differences and Commonalities," *AMA Winter Educators' Proceedings* (1992), Vol. 3, pp. 397–398; Paul H. Schurr and Angelica C. Cortes, "Developing Knowledge about Cross-cultural Interpersonal Interactions in Marketing," *AMA Winter Educators' Proceedings* (1992), Vol. 3, pp. 450–456; C. Anthony diBenedetto, Mariko Tamate, and Rajan Chandran, "Developing Creative Advertising Strategy for the Japanese Marketplace," *Journal of Advertising Research,* January/February 1992, pp. 39–48; and Yoo S. Yang, Robert P. Leone, and Dana L. Alden, "A Market Expansion Ability Approach to Identify Potential Exporters," *Journal of Marketing,* Vol. 56, No. 1 (January 1992), pp. 84–96.

In addition, the *Journal of Advertising Research* presented a special issue on international advertising in Vol. 32 (January/February 1992), including Ali Kanso, "International Advertising Strategies: Global Commitment to Local Vision," pp. 10–14; Barbara Mueller, "Standardization vs. Specialization: An Examination of Westernization in Japanese Advertising," pp. 15–24; Fred Zandpour, Cypress Chang, and Joelle Catalano, "Stories, Symbols, and Straight Talk: A Comparative Analysis of French, Taiwanese, and U.S. TV Commercials," pp. 25–38; C. Anthony diBenedetto, Mariko Tamate, and Rajan Chandran, "Developing Creative Advertising Strategy for the Japanese Marketplace," pp. 39–48; Alan T. Shao and John S. Hill, "Executing Transnational Advertising Campaigns: Do U.S. Agencies Have the Overseas Talent?" pp. 49–58; Jyotika Ramaprasad and Kazumi Hasegawa, "Creative Strategies in American and Japanese TV Commercials: A Comparison," pp. 59–70; and Bob D. Cutler and Rajshekhar G. Javalgi, "A Cross-cultural Analysis of the Visual Components of Print Advertising: The United States and the European Community," pp. 71ff. See also the following articles in Robert L. King (ed.), *Marketing: Perspectives for the 1990s* (Richmond, Va: Southern Marketing Association, 1992): James B. Hunt and Judy A. Siguaw, "The Effect of Patriotism on Product Evaluation and Choice," pp. 98–101; Robert D. Mackoy, "Empirical Studies of International Consumers: 1970–1991," pp. 124–128; Erdener Kaynak and Orsay Kucukemiroglu, "Holiday Destination Choice Behavior of Hong Kong Residents: First and Multiple Time Visitors Contrasted," pp. 135–140; and Massoud M. Saghafi, "Maquiladora Industry: History and Life after NAFTA," pp. 153–156. See also Saeed Samiee and Kendall Roth, "The Influence of Global Marketing Standardization on Performance," *Journal of Marketing,* Vol. 56, No. 2 (April 1992), pp. 1–17; Gianluigi Guido, "What U.S. Marketers Should Consider in Planning a Pan-European Approach," *The Journal of Consumer Marketing,* Vol. 9, No. 2 (Spring 1992), pp. 29–34; Alan T. Shao, Lawrence P. Shao, and Dale H. Shao, "Are Global Markets with Standardized Advertising Campaigns Feasible?" *Journal of International Consumer Marketing,* Vol. 4, No. 3 (1992), pp. 5–16. In *AMA Summer Educators' Proceedings* (1992) see Yangjin Yoo, "Country of Origin Effect: The New Conceptualization and Alternative Models," pp. 28–34; Brian D. Ottum and Richard J. Semenik, "International Market Assessment: The 'Demand-Side' Effects of Infrastructure," pp. 265–273; Wai-kwan

Li and Kent B. Monroe, "The Role of Country of Origin Information on Buyers' Product Evaluation: An In-depth Interview Approach," pp. 274–280; and Tom Duncan, "Standardized Global Marketing Communication Campaigns Are Possible, They're Just Hard to Do," pp. 352–358. In the *Journal of International Consumer Marketing,* Vol. 4, No. 4 (1992), see Nejdet Delener, "Consumer-Related Marital Role Orientations among Hispanic, Irish and Italian-American Wives: A Subcultural Comparison," pp. 7–32; T. S. Chan and Gong-shi Lin, "An Empirical Analysis of Consumer Decision Processes in the People's Republic of China," pp. 33–48; Sung-Tai Hong and Youjae Yi, "A Cross-national Comparison of Country-of-Origin Effects on Product Evaluations," pp. 49–72; and Gordon E. Miracle, Charles R. Taylor, and Kyu Yeol Chang, "Culture and Advertising Executions: A Comparison of Selected Characteristics of Japanese and U.S. Television Commercials," pp. 89–114.

In the *Journal of International Consumer Marketing,* Vol. 5, No. 1 (1993), see C. M. Kochunny, Emin Babakus, Robert Berl, and William Marks, "Schematic Representation of Country Image: Its Effects on Product Evaluations," pp. 5–26; Alma T. Mintu, Roger J. Calantone, and Jule B. Gassenheimer, "International Mail Surveys: Some Guidelines for Marketing Researchers," pp. 69–84; Noel M. Murray and Lalita A. Manrai, "Exploratory Consumption Behavior: A Cross Cultural Perspective," pp. 101–120; and Victor V. Cordell, "Interaction Effects of Country of Origin with Branding, Price, and Perceived Performance Risk," pp. 5–20. In *Advances in Consumer Research,* Vol. 20 (1993), see Siew Meng Leong and Swee Hoon Ang, "The Visible Hand in Marriage: An Exploratory Assessment of the Marriage Promotion Campaign in Singapore," pp. 559–564; Irwin P. Levin, J. D. Jasper, John D. Mittelstaedt, and Gary J. Gaeth, "Attitudes toward 'Buy America First' and Perferences for American and Japanese Cars: A Different Role for Country-of-Origin Information," pp. 625–629; Dana L. Alden, Wayne D. Hoyer, and Ayn E. Crowley, "Country-of-Origin, Perceived Risk and Evaluation Strategy," pp. 678–683; and Wai-kwan Li, Kwok Leung, and Robert S. Wyer, Jr., "The Roles of Country of Origin on Buyers' Product Evaluations: Signal or Attribute?" pp. 684–689. See also Lyn S. Amine, "Linking Consumer Behavior Constructs to International Marketing Strategy: A Comment on Wills, Samli, and Jacobs and an Extension," *Journal of Academy of Marketing Science,* Vol. 21, No. 1 (Winter 1993), pp. 71–78; A. Coskun Samli, James R. Wills, Jr., and Laurence Jacobs, "Developing Global Products and Marketing Strategies: A Rejoinder," *Journal of the Academy of Marketing Science,* Vol. 21, No. 1 (Winter 1993), pp. 79–84; Dana L. Alden, Wayne D. Hoyer, and Chol Lee, "Identifying Global and Culture-Specific Dimensions of Humor in Advertising: A Multinational Analysis," *Journal of Marketing,* Vol. 57, No. 2 (April 1993), pp. 64–75; and Srinivas Durvasula, Steven Lysonski, and J. Craig Andrews, "Cross-Cultural Generalizability of a Scale for Profiling Consumers' Decision-making Styles," *The Journal of Consumer Affairs,* Vol. 27, No. 1 (Summer 1993), pp. 55–65. Finally, *Journal of International Consumer Marketing,* Vol. 5, No. 3 (1993), is a special issue on consumer behavior in Canada and includes Richard M. Sparkman and Nan Zhou, "Consumer Behavior in Canada's Cultural Mosaic: An Introduction to the Special Issue," pp. 9–14; Michael Hui, Annamma Joy, Chankon Kim, and Michel Laroche, "Equivalence of Lifestyle Dimensions across Four Major Subcultures in Canada," pp. 15–36; Emmanuel J. Cheron and Thomas E. Muller, "Relative Importance of Values as Determinants of Ownership Patterns: Comparisons between the Canadian Provinces of

Ontario and Quebec," pp. 37–54; Nan Zhou, Richard M. Sparkman, Jr., and Scott B. Follows, "What Types of Product Information Do Nova Scotians Want from Advertising?" pp. 55–68; and Gordon H. G. McDougall, "The Green Movement in Canada: Implications for Marketing Strategy," pp. 69–88. In this same issue, see also Arch G. Woodside and Ilkka A. Ronkainen, "Consumer Memory and Mental Categorization in International Travel Destination Decision Making," pp. 89–104.

18. The retailing setting is continuing to change dramatically during the 1990s. See, for example, "Retailing Will Never Be the Same," *Business Week,* July 26, 1993, pp. 54–60; Michael J. McDurmott, "Killers Stalk a Shifting Landscape," *Marketing Week,* October 28, 1991, p. 24; "Shopping Centers Will Be America's Towns of Tomorrow," *Marketing News,* November 28, 1980, pp. 1ff.

19. See, for example, "Hair Spray, Yes: Hair Coloring, No," *Marketing Week,* November 5, 1990, p. 43. See also Terry Anderson, "Men's Cosmetic Industry Is Groomed for Success," *USA Today,* March 30, 1989, p. 6D; and Mary McCabe English, "The Face of the '80's: What's Ahead?" *Advertising Age,* March 1, 1982, pp. M9–M11.

20. Stratford P. Sherman, "America Won't Win Till It Reads More," *Fortune,* November 18, 1991, pp. 201–204; "Sights and Sounds," *The Wall Street Journal,* July 6, 1987, p. 13; *The Statistical Abstract of the United States,* 1981 (Washington D.C.: U.S. Government Printing Office, 1982), p. 559; and William F. Gloede, "Industry Delivers Solution to Bad News," *Advertising Age,* July 25, 1985, pp. 15–16. See also Basil G. Englis, "Music Television and Its Influences on Consumers, Consumer Culture, and the Transmission of Consumption Messages," *Advances in Consumer Research,* Vol. 18 (1991), pp. 111–114.

21. Robert Lewis, "U.S. Index Shows Bargains of 1990s," Newhouse News Service, August 6, 1990; Ralph Blumenthal, "Despite Soaring Inflation, Some Things Are Cheaper," *The New York Times* News Service, March 8, 1981.

22. Eric Hollreiser, "Mellow Booze," *Marketing Week,* December 16, 1991, p. 24; "Cutty's Image Riding on New Club," *Marketing Week,* March 14, 1988, p. 5; George Lazarus, "Cigar Biz Gasps in New Climate," *Marketing Week,* November 16, 1987, p. 34; George Allen, "Investing in Fitness," *Advertising Age,* February 8, 1982, p. M12; and Ed Fitch, "Distillers Try Tactics to Brake Sales Slide," *Advertising Age,* July 18, 1985, pp. 13–14.

23. Ed Zotti, "Consumers Toast to a Vintage Future," *Advertising Age,* March 29, 1982, pp. M13–M14, and John Maxwell, "U.S. Wine Industry Uncorks Sales Hike," *Advertising Age,* June 4, 1984, p. 50.

24. Harold H. Kassarjian, "Content Analysis in Consumer Research," *Journal of Consumer Research,* June 1977, pp. 8–18.

25. B. G. Yovovich, "His Crystal Ball: The Daily Newspaper," *Advertising Age,* October 11, 1982, pp. M4ff; Randall Poe, "Who Will Make the 'Fortunate' 500?" *Consumers' Digest,* March–April 1985, pp. 55, 73; Emily Yoffe, "Naisbitt's Clip Joint: The Selling of Content Analysis and Megatrends," *Marketing News,* March 16, 1984, pp. 2–1ff; and John Naisbitt, *Megatrends* (New York: Warner Books, 1982). For related readings, see Ronald D. Michman, "Why Forecast for the Long Term?" *Journal of Business Strategy,* September/October 1989, pp. 36–40; Martin G. Letscher, "Fad or Trend? How to Distinguish Them and Capitalize on Them," *The Journal of Consumer Marketing,* Vol. 7, No. 2 (Spring 1990), pp. 21–26; Kenneth

Traynor and Susan C. Traynor, "Long-Range Scenario Research as A Factor in Long-Range Consumer Marketing Planning," *The Journal of Consumer Marketing,* Vol. 7, No. 1 (Winter 1990), pp. 5–14; Allen M. Clark, "'Trends' That Will Impact New Products," *The Journal of Consumer Marketing,* Vol. 8, No. 1 (Winter 1991), pp. 35–40; and Herb Brody, "Great Expectations: Why Predictions Go Awry," *Journal of Consumer Marketing,* Vol. 10, No. 1 (1993), pp. 23–27.

26. This listing is based upon discussions in *The Public Pulse* (New York: Roper Organization, 1991); Rance Crain, "Swords Back into Plowshares," *Advertising Age,* November 18, 1991, p. 24; Gary M. Stern, "Future Forecasts," *USAir Magazine,* March 1991, pp. 28–33; "31 Major Trends Shaping Future of American Business," *Roper's Public Pulse,* 1988; "Popcorn: Trends Last, but Fads Fade Fast," *Marketing News,* March 14, 1988, p. 29; "Scan Social Trends to Develop Effective Marketing Communications," *Marketing News,* November 13, 1981, p. 12; "Smith Outlines Eight Trends to Watch," *Advertising Age,* August 24, 1981, pp. 22ff; and "Rules a Glimpse into the New World," *Advertising Age,* July 20, 1981, p. 44.

27. "Food Marketer: Slow the Frenetic Pace of New Product Introductions," *Marketing News,* March 28, 1988, p. 17; and George Lazarus, "Microwaves Heat Up Lunch Biz," *Marketing Week,* November 2, 1987, p. 30. For broader discussions, see Steven C. Wheelwright and W. Earl Sasser, Jr., "The New Product Development Map," *Harvard Business Review,* No. 3 (May–June 1989), pp. 112–127; Ashok K. Gupta and Everett M. Rogers, "Internal Marketing: Integrating R&D and Marketing within the Organization," *The Journal of Consumer Marketing,* Vol. 8, No. 3 (Summer 1991), pp. 5–18; Stanley F. Stasch, Ronald T. Lonsdale, and Noel M. LaVenka, "Developing a Framework for Sources of New Product Ideas," *The Journal of Consumer Marketing,* Vol. 9, No. 2 (Spring 1992), pp. 5–16; Andrew Parsons, "Building Innovativeness in Large U.S. Corporations," *The Journal of Consumer Marketing,* Vol. 9, No. 2 (Spring 1992), pp. 35–50; Larry A. Constantineau, "The Twenty Toughest Questions for New Product Proposals," *The Journal of Consumer Marketing,* Vol. 9, No. 2 (Spring 1992), pp. 51–54; Gloria J. Barczak, Daniel C. Bello, and Everett S. Wallace, "The Role of Consumer Shows in New Product Adoption," *The Journal of Consumer Marketing,* Vol. 9, No. 2 (Spring 1992), pp. 55–68; John H. Summey and Brian T. Engelland, "Barriers to Innovative Thinking: The Influence of Cognitive Communities on New Product Innovation," in Robert L. King (ed.), *Marketing: Perspectives for the 1990s* (Richmond, Va: Southern Marketing Association, 1992), pp. 437–442; Patrick Hetzel, "Fashion, Creation and Firms' Competition," *AMA Winter Educators' Proceedings* (1993), pp. 125–132; and Tridib Mazumdar, "A Value-based Orientation to New Product Planning," *Journal of Consumer Marketing,* Vol. 10, No. 1 (1993), pp. 28–41.

28. For a comprehensive overview of research in this area, see Hubert Gatignon and Thomas S. Robertson, "Innovative Decision Processes," in T. Robertson and H. Kassarjian (eds), *Handbook of Consumer Behavior* (Englewood Cliffs, N.J.: Prentice Hall, 1991), pp. 316–348. The framework here was introduced by Thomas S. Robertson, "The Process of Innovation and the Diffusion of Innovation," *Journal of Marketing,* Vol. 31 (January 1967), pp. 14–19. See also Pam Scholder Ellen, William O. Bearden, and Subhash Sharma, "Resistance to Technological Innovations: An Examination of the Role of Self-Efficacy and Performance Satisfaction," *Journal of the Academy of Marketing Science,* Vol. 19, No. 4 (Fall 1991), pp. 297–308; Roger J. Calantone, C. Anthony diBenedetto, and

Sriraman Bhoovaragavan, "Examining the Relationship between Degree of Innovation and New Product Success," in Robert L. King (ed.), *Marketing: Perspectives for the 1990s* (Richmond, Va.: Southern Marketing Association, 1992), pp. 443–448; and David F. Midgley and Grahame R. Dowling, "A Longitudinal Study of Product Form Innovation: The Interaction between Predispositions and Social Messages," *Journal of Consumer Research*, Vol. 19, No. 4 (March 1993), pp. 611–625.

29. There is a large, but technical, literature on new product models and market forecasting. You may wish to begin by consulting Vijay Mahajan, Eitan Muller, and Frank M. Bass, "New Product Diffusion Models in Marketing: A Review and Directions for Research," *Journal of Marketing*, Vol. 54, No. 1 (January 1990), pp. 1–26; and Fareena Sultan, John U. Farley, and Donald Lehmann, "A Meta-Analysis of Applications of Diffusion Models," *Journal of Marketing Research*, Vol. 27 (February 1990), pp. 70–77. For related discussions, see also J. Scott Armstrong, "Prediction of Consumer Behavior by Experts and Novices," *Journal of Consumer Research*, Vol. 18, No. 2 (September 1991), pp. 251ff; Rick Brown, "Managing the 'S' Curves of Innovation," *The Journal of Consumer Marketing*, Vol. 9, No. 1 (Winter 1992), pp. 61–72; Madhavan Parthasarathy and Ronald Hampton, "The Role of Piracy in the Diffusion of a Software Product: A Propositional Framework," *AMA Winter Educators' Proceedings* (1993), p. 91; Christopher M. Miller, Shelby M. McIntyre, and Murali K. Mantrala, "Toward Formalizing Fashion Theory," *Journal of Marketing Research*, Vol. 30, May 1993, pp. 142–157; and Glen L. Urban, John S. Hulland, and Bruce D. Weinberg, "Premarket Forecasting for New Consumer Durable Goods: Modeling Categorization, Elimination, and Consideration Phenomena," *Journal of Marketing*, Vol. 57, No. 2 (April 1993), pp. 47–63.

30. Rogers and Shoemaker, *Communication of Innovations* (New York: Free Press, 1971). For further findings, see *Advances in Consumer Research*, Vol. 14 (1987): David Midgley, "A Meta-Analysis of the Diffusion of Innovations Literature," pp. 204–207, S. Ram, "A Model of Innovation Resistance," pp. 208–212; and S. Ram and Jagdish N. Sheth, "Consumer Resistance to Innovations: The Marketing Problem and Its Solutions," *The Journal of Consumer Marketing*, Vol. 6 (Spring 1989), pp. 5–14; Susan L. Holak and Y. Edwin Tang, "Advertising's Effect on the Product Evolutionary Cycle," *Journal of Marketing*, Vol. 54, No. 3 (July 1990), pp. 16–29; Hirokazu Takada and Dipak Jain, "Cross-national Analysis of Diffusion of Consumer Durable Goods in Pacific Rim Countries," *Journal of Marketing*, Vol. 55, No. 2 (April 1991), pp. 48–54; Tina M. Lowrey, "The Use of Diffusion Theory in Marketing: A Qualitative Approach to Innovative Consumer Behavior," *Advances in Consumer Research*, Vol. 18 (1991), pp. 644–650; and Michael S. LaTour and Scott D. Roberts, "Cultural Anchoring and Product Diffusion," *The Journal of Consumer Marketing*, Vol. 9, No. 4 (Fall 1992), pp. 29–34.

31. Rogers and Shoemaker, *Communication of Innovations*; and John A. Howard and Lyman E. Ostland, *Buyer Behavior: Theoretical and Empirical Foundations* (New York: Alfred A. Knopf, 1973).

32. Everett M. Rogers and Floyd Shoemaker, *Communication of Innovations* (New York: Free Press, 1971). See also Vijay Mahajan, Eitan Muller, and Rajendra K. Srivastava, "Determination of Adopter Categories by Using Innovation Diffusion Models," *Journal of Marketing Research*, Vol. 27 (February 1990), pp. 37–50.

33. There is an interesting literature on issues involving the characteristics and actions of the various adopter types. Our discussion in the remainder of this chapter draws upon these sources. See, for example, J. Arndt, "Profiling Consumer Innovations," in J. Arndt (ed.), *Insights into Consumer Behavior* (Boston: Allyn & Bacon, 1968), pp. 71–83; and T. S. Robertson, *Innovative Behavior and Communication* (New York: Holt, Rinehart & Winston, 1971), pp. 75–77. For recent findings and discussions, see Kenny K. Chan and Shekhar Misra, "Characteristics of the Opinion Leader: A New Dimension," *Journal of Advertising*, Vol. 19, No. 3 (1990), pp. 53–60; and three articles in *Advances in Consumer Research*, Vol. 17 (1990): Mark E. Slama and Terrell G. Williams, "Generalization of the Market Maven's Information Provision Tendency across Product Categories," pp. 48–52; Donald R. Lichtenstein and Scot Burton, "An Assessment of the Moderating Effects of Market Mavenism and Value Consciousness on Price-Quality Perception Accuracy," pp. 53–59; and Meera P. Venkatraman, "Opinion Leadership, Enduring Involvement and Characteristics of Opinion Leaders: A Moderating or Mediating Relationship?" pp. 60–67. See also David M. Andrus, Jay L. Laughlin, and Vashti Balkisson-Jutla, "Market Penetration and Customer Retention Strategies in the U.S. Cable Television Industry," in Robert L. King (ed.), *Marketing: Perspectives for the 1990s* (Richmond, Va.: Southern Marketing Association, 1992), pp. 281–284; Dale A. Lunsford and Melissa S. Burnett, "Marketing Product Innovations to the Elderly: Understanding the Barriers to Adoption," *The Journal of Consumer Marketing*, Vol. 9, No. 4 (Fall 1992), pp. 53–63; Robert J. Fisher and Linda L. Price, "An Investigation into the Social Context of Early Adoption Behavior," *Journal of Consumer Research*, Vol. 19, No. 3 (December 1992), pp. 477–486; Susan Schultz Kleine and Amy R. Hubbert, "How Do Consumers Acquire a New Food Consumption System: When It Is Vegetarian," *Advances in Consumer Research*, Vol. 20 (1993), pp. 196–201; and Michael T. Elliott and Anne E. Warfield, "Do Market Mavens Categorize Brands Differently?" *Advances in Consumer Research*, Vol. 20 (1993), pp. 202–208.

34. Elizabeth C. Hirschman, "Innovativeness, Novelty Seeking, and Consumer Creativity," *Journal of Consumer Research*, December 1980, pp. 283–295; and Les Carlson and Sanford Grossbart, "Toward a Better Understanding of Inherent Innovativeness," *AMA Educators' Proceedings* (1984), pp. 88–91.

35. David F. Midgley and Grahame R. Dowling, "Innovativeness: The Concept and Its Measurement," *Journal of Consumer Research*, Vol. 4 (March 1978), pp. 229–242. See also Ronald E. Goldsmith and Charles F. Hofacker, "Measuring Consumer Innovativeness," *Journal of the Academy of Marketing Science*, Vol. 19, No. 3 (Summer 1991), pp. 209–222; Suresh Subramanian and Robert A. Mittelstaedt, "Conceptualizing Innovativeness as a Consumer Trait: Consequences and Alternatives," *AMA Summer Educators' Proceedings* (1991), pp. 352–360; and Suresh Subramanian and Robert A. Mittelstaedt, "Reconceptualizing and Measuring Consumer Innovativeness," *AMA Summer Educators' Proceedings* (1992), pp. 300–307.

36. Kenneth Uhl, Roman Andrus, and Lance Poulson, "How Are Laggards Different? An Empirical Inquiry," *Journal of Marketing Research*, February 1970, pp. 51–54.

37. Richard K. Manoff, "When the 'Client' Is Human Life Itself," *Advertising Age*, August 22, 1983, pp. M4–M5. For related topics, see P. Rajan Varadarajan and Anil Menon, "Cause-Related Marketing: A Coalignment of Marketing Strategy and Corporate Philanthropy," *Journal of Marketing*, Vol. 52 (July 1988), pp. 58–74; and

Bonnie S. Guy and Wesley E. Patton, "The Marketing of Altruistic Causes: Understanding Why People Help," *The Journal of Consumer Marketing*, Vol. 6 (Winter 1989), pp. 19–30; Elizabeth Cooper-Martin and Debra Lynn Stephens, "AIDS Preventions through Consumer Communication: Ideas from Past and Current Research," *Advances in Consumer Research*, Vol. 17 (1990), pp. 288–293; Ronald Paul Hill, "AIDS and the Arts," *Advances in Consumer Research*, Vol. 17 (1990), pp. 294–297; Lalita A. Manrai and Meryl P. Gardner, "Consumer Processing of Social Ideas Advertising: A Conceptual Model," *Advances in Consumer Research*, Vol. 19 (1992), pp. 15–22; and John K. Ross III, Larry T. Patterson, and Mary Ann Stutts, "Consumer Perceptions of Organizations That Use Cause-related Marketing," *Journal of the Academy of Marketing Science*, Vol. 20, No. 1 (Winter 1992), pp. 93–98.

38. For an excellent recent overview of social dimensions related to this area, see Alan R. Andreasen, "Consumer Behavior Research and Social Policy," in T. Robertson and H. Kassarjian (eds.), *Handbook of Consumer Behavior* (Englewood Cliffs, N.J.: Prentice Hall, 1991), pp. 459–506; and Everett M. Rogers, "New Product Adoption and Diffusion," *Journal of Consumer Research*, March 1976, pp. 290–301.

39. Lloyd Shearer, "Censorship in Finland," *Parade,* July 1, 1990, p. 11.

40. Max Weber, "Class, Status, Party," in H. Gerth and C. W. Mills (eds.), *From Max Weber: Essays in Sociology* (New York: Oxford University Press, 1946), Chap. 7. See also Max Weber, *General Economic History*, trans. by F. H. Knight (New York: Greenberg, 1927).

41. Survey conducted by the Carnegie Commission on the Future of Higher Education. These results were reported in John Helmer, *The Daily Simple Mechanics of Society* (New York: Seabury Press, 1974), pp. 66.

42. This distinction was originally made by Ralph Linton, *The Study of Man* (New York: Appleton-Century-Crofts, 1936), Chap. 8. His terms for the two status types were *ascribed status* and *achieved status.*

43. See, for example, J. H. Hutton, *Caste in India: Its Nature, Function, and Origins*, 4th ed. (London: Oxford University Press, 1962); James Silverberg (ed.), *Social Mobility in the Caste System in India* (The Hague: Mouton Press, 1968); and Gerald D. Berreman, *Caste in the Modern World* (Morristown, N.J.: General Learning Press, 1973). The author also wishes to acknowledge the suggestions of his Indian colleagues.

44. This section is based upon Norman Goodman and Gary Marx, *Society Today*, 3d ed. (New York: CRM/Random House, 1978), pp. 246–251. See also Gerhard Lenski, *Power and Privilege: The Theory of Social Stratification* (New York: McGraw-Hill, 1966); Reinhard Bendix and Seymour M. Lipset (eds.), *Class, Status, and Power* (New York: Free Press, 1966); Thomas B. Bottomore, *Classes in Modern Society* (New York: Vantage, 1966); Robin M. Williams, Jr., *American Society: A Sociological Interpretation*, 3d ed.; Samuel N. Eisenstadt, *Social Differentiation and Stratification* (Glenview, Ill.: Scott, Foresman, 1971); Lewis A. Coser, *Masters of Sociological Thought*, 2nd ed. (New York: Harcourt Brace Jovanovich, 1977); and Metta Spencer, *Foundations of Modern Sociology* (Englewood Cliffs, N.J.: Prentice Hall, 1976).

45. Karl Marx and Fredrich Engels, *The Communist Manifesto* (1848)(Chicago: Regenery, 1960). See also John Mager and John F. Hulpke, "Social Class in a Classless Society: Marketing Implications for China," *Journal of International Consumer Marketing*, Vol. 2, No. 4 (1990), pp. 57–88; and Sherri M. Stevens, "Communism Meets Capitalism: Soviet Immigrants in the United States," *AMA Winter Educators' Proceedings* (1992), Vol. 3, p. 365.

46. See Kingsley Davis and Wilbert E. Moore, "Some Principles of Stratification," *American Sociological Review*, Vol. 10 (April 1945), pp. 242–249.

47. Richard P. Coleman, "The Continuing Significance of Social Class to Marketing," *Journal of Consumer Research*, Vol. 10 (December 1983), pp. 265–280. See also James E. Fisher, "Social Class and Consumer Behavior: The Relevance of Class and Status," *Advances in Consumer Research*, Vol. 14 (1987), pp. 492–496; Kjell Gronhaug and Paul S. Trapp, "Perceived Social Class Appeals of Branded Goods and Services," *The Journal of Consumer Marketing*, Vol. 6 (Winter 1989), pp. 13–18; and Scott Dawson, Bruce Stern, and Tom Gillpatrick, "An Empirical Update and Extension of Patronage Behaviors across the Social Class Hierarchy," *Advances in Consumer Research*, Vol. 17 (1990), pp. 833–838.

48. Richard P. Coleman, "The Significance of Social Stratification in Selling," in M. L. Bell (ed.), *Marketing: A Maturing Discipline* (Chicago: American Marketing Association, 1960), pp. 171–184, and Richard P. Coleman, "The Continuing Significance of Social Class to Marketing," p. 274. For further applications, see W. H. Peters, "Relative Occupational Class Income: A Significant Variable in the Marketing of Automobiles," *Journal of Marketing* (April 1970), pp. 74–82; and R. E. Klippel and J. F. Monoky, "A Potential Segmentation Variable for Marketers: Relative Occupational Class Income," *Journal of the Academy of Marketing Science* (Spring 1974), pp. 351–356.

49. For discussions of the forecasting potentials of income versus social class measures, see, for example, James H. Myers, Roger R. Stanton, and Arne F. Haug, "Correlates of Buying Behavior: Social Class vs. Income," *Journal of Marketing*, Vol. 35 (October 1971); Frederick E. May, "The Effect of Social Class on Brand Loyalty," *California Management Review*, Vol. 14 (Fall 1971), pp. 81–87; John W. Slocum and H. Lee Matthews, "Social Class and Income as Indicator of Consumer Credit Behavior," *Journal of Marketing*, Vol. 34 (April 1970), pp. 69–73; William W. Curtis, "Social Class or Income?" *Journal of Marketing*, Vol. 36 (January 1972), pp. 67–68; H. Lee Matthews and John W. Slocum, Jr., "A Rejoinder to 'Social Class or Income?'" *Journal of Marketing*, Vol. 36 (January 1972), pp. 69–70; James H. Myers and John F. Mount, "More on Social Class vs. Income as Correlates of Buying Behavior," *Journal of Marketing*, Vol. 37 (April 1973), pp. 71–73; and Robert D. Hisrich and Michael P. Peters, "Selecting the Superior Segmentation Correlate," *Journal of Marketing*, Vol. 38 (July 1974), pp. 60–63.

50. The description of the social classes is based on a number of sources. See Richard Coleman, "The Continuing Significance of Social Class to Marketing"; and Burleigh Gardner, "Social Status and Consumer Behavior," in Lincoln H. Clark (ed.), *The Life Cycle and Consumer Behavior* (New York: New York University Press, 1955); Pierre Martineau, "Social Class and Spending Behavior," *Journal of Marketing*, Vol. 23 (October 1958), pp. 121–130; Joseph N. Fry and Frederick H. Siller, "A Comparision of Housewife Decision Making in Two Social Classes," *Journal of Marketing Research*, Vol. 7

(August 1970), pp. 333–337; Sidney J. Levy, "Social Class and Consumer Behavior," in John A. Howard and Lyman E. Ostland (eds.), *Buyer Behavior* (New York: Alfred J. Knopf, 1973); Walter A. Henry, "Cultural Values Do Correlate with Consumer Behavior," *Journal of Marketing Research*, Vol. 13 (May 1976), pp. 121–127; J. Michael Munson and W. Austin Spivey, "Product and Brand-User Stereotypes among Social Classes: Implications for Advertising Strategy," *Journal of Advertising Research*, Vol. 21, No. 4 (August 1981), pp. 37–45; Terrence A. Shimp and J. Thomas Yokum, "Extensions of the Basic Social Class Model Employed in Consumer Behavior," *Advances in Consumer Research*, Vol. 8, pp. 702–707; Luis V. Dominguez and Albert L. Page, "Stratification in Consumer Behavior Research: A Re-Examination," *Journal of the Academy of Marketing Science*, Vol. 9 (Summer 1981), pp. 250–273; Matthew C. Sonfield, "Marketing to the Carriage Trade," *Harvard Business Review*, No. 3 (May–June 1990), pp. 112–117; Elizabeth C. Hirschman, "Consumption Styles of the Rich and Famous: The Semiology of Saul Steinberg and Malcolm Forbes," *Advances in Consumer Research*, Vol. 17 (1990), pp. 850–855; Rajesh Kanwar and Notis Pagiavlas, "When Are Higher Social Class Consumers More and Less Brand Loyal than Lower Social Class Consumers?: The Role of Mediating Variables," *Advances in Consumer Research*, Vol. 19 (1992), pp. 589–595; and Louis S. Richman, "The Truth about the Rich and the Poor," *Fortune*, September 21, 1992, pp. 134ff.

51.   These examples are given in Michael Korda, *Power! How to Get It, How to Use It* (New York: Random House, 1975), Chap. 7.

52.   Kim B. Rotzoll, "The Effect of Social Stratification on Market Behavior," *Journal of Advertising Research*, Vol. 7 (March 1967), pp. 22–27.

53.   See the Andreasen review article in Note 38. See also, for example, Ronald Paul Hill and Mark Stamey, "The Homeless in America: An Examination of Possessions and Consumption Behaviors," *Journal of Consumer Research*, Vol. 17, No. 3 (December 1990), pp. 303–321; Jane Schuchardt, Julia Marlowe, Louise Parker, and Claudette Smith, "Low Income Families: Keys to Successful Outreach," *Advancing the Consumer Interest*, Vol. 3, No. 2 (1991), pp. 27–31; and Lisa M. Cotteleer and Ronald Paul Hill, "Access Denied: Consumer Behavior and the Poor," *AMA Winter Educators' Proceedings* (1993), pp. 151–156.

Chapter 13

Social and Situational Influences

1.   Alix M. Freedman, "Rumor Turns Fantasy into Bad Dream," *The Wall Street Journal*, May 10, 1991, p. B1.

2.   For more specific definitions, see Orville G. Brim, "Adult Socialization," in J. Clausen (ed.), *Socialization and Society* (Boston: Little, Brown, 1968), or Edward Zigler and Irwin L. Child, "Socialization," in Gardner Lindzey and Elliott Aronson (eds.), *The Handbook of Social Psychology, Vol. 3: The Individual in a Social Context* (Reading, Mass: Addison–Wesley, 1969), pp. 450–589. For basic insights, see also George Herbert Mead, *Mind, Self, and Society* (Chicago: University of Chicago Press, 1934). For recent results, see Scott Ward, Donna Klees, and Daniel B. Wackman, "Consumer Socialization Research: Content Analysis of Post-1980 Studies, and Some Implications for Future Work," *Advances in Consumer Research*, Vol. 17 (1990), pp. 798–803.

3.   Talcott Parsons, *The Social System* (Glencoe, Ill.: Free Press, 1951). See also David A. Goslin, *The School in Contemporary Societies* (Glenview, Ill: Scott, Foresman, 1965).

4.   Ruth Benedict, "Continuities and Discontinuities in Cultural Conditioning," *Psychiatry*, Vol. 1 (1938), pp. 161–167.

5.   You may enjoy reading, for example, Gail Sheehy, *Passages: Predictable Crises of Adult Life* (New York: E. P. Dutton, 1976). See also Lawrence R. Lepisto, "A Life Span Perspective of Consumer Behavior," *Advances in Consumer Research*, Vol. 12 (1985), pp. 47–52; and John W. Schouten, "Selves in Transition: Symbolic Consumption in Personal Rites of Passage and Identity Reconstruction," *Journal of Consumer Research*, Vol. 17, No. 4 (March 1991), pp. 412–425.

6.   William H. Whyte, Jr., "The Web of Word of Mouth," *Fortune*, November 1954, pp. 140–143. For further concepts and findings of this general topic, see, for example, Cathy L. Hartman and Pamela L. Kiecker, "Marketplace Influencers at the Point of Purchase: The Role of Purchase Pals in Consumer Decision Making," *AMA Summer Educators' Proceedings* (1991), pp. 461–469; Gloria Penn Thomas, "The Influence of Processing Conversational Information on Inference, Argument Elaboration, and Memory," *Journal of Consumer Research*, Vol. 19, No. 1 (June 1992), pp. 83–92; and Stephen S. Tax and Tim Christiansen, "Measuring Word-of-Mouth in Consumer Research: The Questions of Who and When?" *AMA Winter Educators' Proceedings* (1993), p. 370.

7.   Peter H. Reingen and Jerome B. Kernan, "Analysis of Referral Networks in Marketing: Methods and Illustration," *Journal of Marketing Research*, Vol. 23 (November 1986), pp. 370–378. For further insights, see Jacqueline Johnson Brown and Peter H. Reingen, "Social Ties and World-of-Mouth Referral Behavior," *Journal of Consumer Research*, Vol. 14 (December 1987), pp. 350–362; Dennis L. Rosen and Richard W. Olshavsky, "A Protocol Analysis of Brand Choice Strategies Involving Recommendations," *Journal of Consumer Research*, Vol. 14 (December 1987), pp. 440–444; Carl S. Bozman, Kathy L. Petit, and James Miner, "The Referral Method: An Inexpensive Means of Increasing Fund-Raising Efficiency by a Non-Profit Organization," *AMA Summer Educators' Proceedings* (1989), p. 50; William R. Wilson and Robert A. Peterson, "Some Limits on the Potency of World-of-Mouth Information," *Advances in Consumer Research*, Vol. 16 (1989), pp. 23–29; and James C. Ward and Peter H. Reingen, "Sociocognitive Analysis of Group Decision Making among Consumers," *Journal of Consumer Research*, Vol. 17, No. 3 (December 1990), pp. 245–262.

8.   Fred D. Reynolds and William R. Darden, "Mutually Adaptive Effects of Interpersonal Communication," *Journal of Marketing Research*, Vol. 8 (November 1971), pp. 449–454. See also Lawrence F. Feick, Linda L. Price, and Robin A. Higie, "People Who Use People: The Other Side of Opinion Leadership," *Advances in Consumer Research*, Vol. 13 (1986); and Pamela Kiecker and Cathy L. Hartman, "Purchase Pal Use: Why Buyers Choose to Stop with Others," *AMA Winter Educators' Proceedings* (1993), pp. 378–384.

9.   Marsha L. Richins and Teri Root-Shaffer, "The Role of Involvement and Opinion Leadership in Consumer Word-of-Mouth," in M. Houston (ed.), *Advances in Consumer Research*, Vol. 15 (Provo, Utah: Association for Consumer Research, 1988), pp. 32–36.

10.   This discussion is based upon the work John Sherry, "Some Implications of Consumer Oral Tradition for Reactive Marketing," Working Paper, Center for Consumer Research, University of Florida, Gainesville, 1983.

11. The first five quotes appeared in Sherry, "Some Implications of Consumer Oral Tradition for Reactive Marketing"; the sixth quote is adapted from a report in a "Dear Abby" column, April 2, 1989. The marketing examples are drawn from Alix M. Freedman, "Corona Beer Sales Are Down Sharply," *The Wall Street Journal,* August 17, 1988, p. 23; "Eatery Ad Hits Gossip," *Advertising Age,* August 3, 1987, p. 6; and Sid Astbury, "Pork Rumors Vex Indonesia," *Advertising Age,* February 6, 1989, p. 36.

12. For recent examples, see Amy E. Gross, "How Popeyes and Reebok Confronted Product Rumor," *Adweek's Marketing Week,* October 22, 1990, pp. 27–30. For alternative strategies that McDonald's might have used, see Alice Tybout, Bobby Calder, and Brian Sternthal, "Using Information Processing Theory to Design Effective Marketing Strategies," *Journal of Marketing Research* (February 1981), pp. 73–79. For related discussions, see Richard F. Yalch, John E. Butler, Jeremiah J. Sullivan, and Phillip H. Phan, "Responding to a Product Crisis: A Comparison of Memory Retrieval vs. Refutational Strategies," *AMA Summer Educators' Proceedings* (1992), pp. 56–63; Elisabeth Gilster, "Telling Stories: A Sociolinguistic Analysis of Language Use in a Marketplace," *Advances in Consumer Research,* Vol. 20 (1993), pp. 83–88; and Brian K. Jorgensen, "Company and Brand Image Following Company-Related Predicaments: Implications of Attribution and Impression Management Theories," *AMA Winter Educators' Proceedings* (1993), p. 85.

13. Joseph R. Mancuso, "Why Not Create Opinion Leaders for New Product Introductions?" *Journal of Marketing,* Vol. 33, No. 3 (July 1969), pp. 20–25. See also Hunter Hastings, "Introducing New Products without Advertising," *The Journal of Consumer Marketing,* Vol. 7, No. 3 (Summer 1990), pp. 19–26.

14. Laurie Freeman and Julie Erickson, "Doctored Strategy: Food Marketers Push Products through Physicians," *Advertising Age,* March 28, 1988, p. 12.

15. James Watson, "Brown Bag's Giveaway Works," *Advertising Age,* July 11, 1988, p. 39.

16. John P. Cortez, "Put People behind Wheel," *Advertising Age,* March 22, 1993, p. S28.

17. If you are interested in reading more about focus group research, see, for example, Edward F. Fern, "Focus Groups: A Review of Some Contradictory Evidence, Implications, and Suggestions for Future Research," *Advances in Consumer Research,* Vol. 10 (1983), pp. 121–126. See also D. N. Bellenger, K. L. Bernhardt, and Jac I. Goldstucker, *Qualitative Research in Marketing* (Chicago: American Marketing Association, 1976); B. J. Calder, "Focus Groups and the Nature of Qualitative Marketing Research," *Journal of Marketing Research* (August 1977), pp. 360ff; Edward F. McQuarrie and Shelby H. McIntyre, "Conceptual Underpinnings for the Use of Group Interviews in Consumer Research," *Advances in Consumer Research,* Vol. 15 (1988), pp. 580–586; David Checkman, "Focus Group Research as Theater: How it Affects the Players and Their Audience," *Marketing Research,* Vol. 1, No. 4 (December 1989), pp. 33–40; William j. McDonald, "The Influence of Moderator Philosophy on the Content of Focus Group Sessions: A Multivariate Analysis of Group Session Content," *AMA Summer Educators' Proceedings* (1992), pp. 540–545; Robert M. Schindler, "The Real Lesson of New Coke: The

Value of Focus Groups for Predicting the Effects of Social Influence," *Marketing Research,* Vol. 4, No. 4 (December 1992), pp. 22–27; and William J. McDonald, "Focus Group Research Dynamics and Reporting: An Examination of Research Objectives and Moderator Influences," *Journal of the Academy of Marketing Science,* Vol. 21, No. 2 (Spring 1993), pp. 161–168.

18. M. Deutsch and H. Gerard, "A Study of Normative and Informational Social Influences upon Individual Judgment," *Journal of Abnormal and Social Psychology,* Vol. 51 (1955), pp. 624–636. For applications in consumer behavior, see also Joel B. Cohen and Ellen Golden, "Informational Social Influence and Product Evaluation," *Journal of Marketing Research,* Vol. 8 (February 1972), pp. 54–59; Robert E. Burnkrant and Alain Cousineau, "Informational and Normative Social Influence in Buyer Behavior," *Journal of Consumer Research,* Vol. 2 (December 1975), pp. 206–215; Dennis L. Rosen and Richard W. Olshavsky, "The Dual Role of Informational Social Influence: Implications for Marketing Management," *Journal of Business Research,* Vol. 15 (1987), pp. 123–144; and Michael Tharp and Lawrence J. Marks, "The Relationship of Consumer Susceptibility to Normative Interpersonal Influence and Perceptions of Normative Beliefs to Consumer Ethnocentrism," *AMA Summer Educators' Proceedings* (1991), pp. 470–478.

19. This report uses our terms and group names and is based upon Stephen A. LaTour and Ajay K. Manrai, "Applying Attitude Theory to Donor Marketing Strategies: Interactive Effects of Informational and Normative Influence," Working Paper, Kellogg Graduate School, Northwestern University, Evanston, Ill., 1985. For further discussions, see Stephen A. LaTour and Ajay K. Manrai, "Interactive Impact of Informational and Normative Influence on Donations," *Journal of Marketing Research,* Vol. 26 (August 1989), pp. 327–335; William O. Bearden and Randall L. Rose, "Attention to Social Comparison Information: An Individual Difference Factor Affecting Consumer Conformity," *Journal of Consumer Research,* Vol. 16, No. 4 (March 1990), pp. 461–471; William O. Bearden, Richard G. Netemeyer, and Jesse E. Teel, "Further Validation of the Consumer Susceptibility to Interpersonal Influence Scale," *Advances in Consumer Research,* Vol. 17 (1990), pp. 770–776; Manoj K. Agarwal and Francis J. Yammarino, "Alumni Giving: A Conceptual Framework and Partial Test," *AMA Summer Educators' Proceedings* (1991), pp. 282–291; Denise D. Schoenbachler, "Toward More Effective Televised Anti-Drug PSAs," *AMA Winter Educators' Proceedings* (1991), pp. 158–164; Scott M. Smith and David S. Alcorn, "Cause Marketing: A New Direction in the Marketing of Corporate Responsibility," *Journal of Consumer Marketing,* Vol. 8, No. 3 (Summer 1991), pp. 19–36; Randall L. Rose, William O. Bearden, and Jesse E. Teel, "An Attributional Analysis of Resistance to Group Pressure Regarding Illicit Drug and Alcohol Consumption," *Journal of Consumer Research,* Vol. 19, No. 1 (June 1992), pp. 1–13; Kathleen Kelly and Ruth Edwards, "Observations: Does Discussion of Advertising Transform its Effects? Yes…Sometimes—A Case among College Students and Their Response to Anti-Drug Advertising," *Journal of Advertising Research,* Vol. 32, No. 4 (July/August 1992), pp. 79–83; and Daniel D. Butler and Jeff Allen, "Examining the Effects of Donation Frequency and Donors' Knowledge on the Perceived Risk of Giving Blood," in Robert L. King (ed.), *Marketing: Perspectives for the 1990s.* (Richmond, Va. Southern Marketing Association, 1992), pp. 351–357.

20. See, for example, George Homans, *Social Behavior: Its Elementary Forms* (New York: Harcourt Brace and World, 1961); P. Blau, *Exchange and Power in Social Life* (New York: John Wiley, 1964); and R. Nisbet, C. Caputo, C. Legany, and J. Maracek, "Behavior as Seen by the Actor and as Seen by the Observer," *Journal of Personality and Social Psychology*, Vol. 27 (1973), pp. 154–164.

21. Theodore R. Sarbin and Vernon L. Allen, "Role Theory," in G. Lindzey and E. Aronson (eds.), *The Handbook of Social Psychology* (Reading, Mass.: Addison-Wesley, 1968). For applications to consumer behavior and marketing, see David T. Wilson and Lorne Bozinoff, "Role Theory and Buying-Selling Negotiations: A Critical Overview," *Marketing in the 80's* (Chicago: American Marketing Association, 1980), pp. 118–121; Michael R. Solomon, Carol Suprenant, John A. Czepiel, and Evelyn A. Antman, "A Role Theory Perspective on Dyadic Interactions: The Service Encounter," *Journal of Marketing*, Vol. 49 (Winter 1985), pp. 99–111; Elaine Sherman and Ruth B. Smith, "Promising Interactions and Possible Behaviorial Effects," *Advances in Consumer Research*, Vol. 14 (1987), pp. 251–254; and Robert Prus, "Generic Social Processes: Implications of a Processual Theory of Action for Research on Marketplace Exchange," *Advances in Consumer Research*, Vol. 14 (1987), pp. 66–70.

22. See, for example, Russell W. Belk, Kenneth D. Bahn, and Robert N. Mayer, "Developmental Recognition of Consumption Symbols," *Journal of Consumer Research*, Vol. 9, No.1 (June 1982), pp. 4–17. Interested readers may wish to puruse the numerous references there for specific findings in specific product categories. For a discussion and debate over the role of possessions, see Russell W. Belk, "Possessions and the Extended Self," *Journal of Consumer Research*, Vol. 15 (September 1988), pp. 139–168; Joel B. Cohen, "An Over-Extended Self?" *Journal of Consumer Research*, Vol. 15 (March 1989), pp. 125–128; and Russell W. Belk, "Extended Self and Extending Paradigmatic Perspective," *Journal of Consumer Research*, Vol. 15 (March 1989), pp. 129–132.

23. Michael R. Solomon, "The Role of Products as Social Stimuli: A Symbolic Interactionism Perspective," *Journal of Consumer Research*, Vol. 10 (December 1983), pp. 319–329. For related discussions within consumer behavior, see Francesco M. Nicosia and Robert N. Mayer, "Toward a Sociology of Consumption," *Journal of Consumer Research*, Vol. 3 (September 1976), pp. 65–75; James H. Leigh and Terrance G. Gabel, "Symbolic Interactionism: Its Effects on Consumer Behavior and Implications for Marketing Strategy," *The Journal of Consumer Marketing*, Vol. 9, No. 1 (Winter 1992), pp. 27–38; Dong H. Lee, "Symbolic Interactionism: Some Implications for Consumer Self-Concept and Product Symbolism Research," *Advances in Consumer Research*, Vol. 17 (1990), pp. 386–393; Marsha L. Richins, "Social Comparison and the Idealized Images of Advertising," *Journal of Consumer Research*, Vol. 18, No. 1 (June 1991), pp. 71–83; Irfan Ahmed, "The Role of Status in Service Interactions," *AMA Winter Educators' Proceedings* (1992), Vol. 3, pp. 142–143; Elizabeth C. Hirschman, "Cocaine as Innovation: A Social-Symbolic Account," *Advances in Consumer Research*, Vol. 19 (1992), pp. 129–139; and Eva M. Hyatt, "Consumer Stereotyping: The Cognitive Bases of the Social Symbolism of Products," *Advances in Consumer Research*, Vol. 19 (1992), pp. 299–303.

24. Mason Haire, "Projective Techniques in Marketing Research," *Journal of Marketing*, Vol. 14, No. 2 (April 1950), pp. 649–652, and Frederick E. Webster and Frederick von Pechmann, "A Replication of the 'ShoppingList' Study," *Journal of Marketing*, Vol. 34 (April 1970), pp. 61–63. For an in-depth discussion of theories and research related to this topic, see Valerie S. Folkes and Tina Kiesler, "Social Cognition: Consumers' Inferences about the Self and Others," in T. Robertson and H. Kassarjian (eds.), *Handbook of Consumer Behavior* (Englewood Cliffs, N.J.: Prentice Hall, 1991), pp. 281–315.

25. Erving Goffman, *The Presentation of Self in Everyday Life* (Garden City, N.Y.: Doubleday/Anchor Books, 1959); Therese A. Louie, "Person Perception Carry-Over Effects; An Exploratory Look at How Our Partners' Traits Influence the Evaluation of Ourselves," *Advances in Consumer Research*, Vol. 19 (1992), pp. 81–84; Barbara B. Stern and Michael R. Solomon, "'Have You Kissed Your Professor Today?': Bumper Stickers and Consumer Self-Statements," *Advances in Consumer Research*, Vol. 19 (1992), pp. 169–173; Barbara B. Stern, "'All the World's a Stage': Drama and Consumer Research," *Advances in Consumer Research*, Vol. 19 (1992), pp. 450–451; Stephen J. Grove and Raymond P. Fisk, "The Service Experience as Theater," *Advances in Consumer Research*, Vol. 19 (1992), pp. 455–461; and John Deighton, "Sincerity, Sham and Satisfaction in Marketplace Performance," *Advances in Consumer Research*, Vol. 19 (1992), pp. 462–463.

26. See Thorstein Veblen, *The Theory of the Leisure Class* (New York: New American Library, Mentor Books, 1980), originally published in 1899.

27. John Brooks, *Showing Off in America* (Boston: Little, Brown, 1981).

28. The interested reader might wish to consult Brooks for a recent critique and Vance Packard, *The Status Seekers* (New York: David McKay, 1959), for an interesting, popularized account of the midcentury situation. See also Ottmar L. Braun and Robert A. Wicklund, "Psychological Antendents of Conspicuous Consumption," *Journal of Economic Psychology*, Vol. 10, No. 2 (1989), pp. 161–187; and Jacqueline C. Kilsheimer, Ronald E. Goldsmith, and Leisa Reinecke Flynn, "Status Consumption: The Concept and Its Measure," *AMA Summer Educators' Proceedings* (1992), pp. 341–342.

29. "How Grey Poupon Ignited Sales Surge with Spot Television," *Advertising Age*, September 23, 1992, p. T14. See also Michael Lynn, "Choose Your Own Price: An Exploratory Study Requiring an Expanded View of Price's Functions," *Advances in Consumer Research*, Vol. 17 (1990), pp. 710–714; and John C. Groth and Stephen W. McDaniel, "The Exclusive Value Principle: The Basis for Prestige Pricing," *Journal of Consumer Marketing*, Vol. 10, No. 1 (1993), pp. 10–16.

30. Dorwin Cartwright and Alvin Zander, *Group Dynamics* (New York: Harper & Row, 1968). For related discussions, see Melanie Wallendorf and Eric J. Arnould, "'We Gather Together': Consumption Rituals of Thanksgiving Day," *Journal of Consumer Research*, Vol. 18, No. 1 (June 1991), pp. 13–31; Douglas B. Holt, "Examining the Descriptive Value of 'Ritual' in Consumer Behavior: A View from the Field," *Advances in Consumer Research*, Vol. 19 (1992), pp. 213–218; and Stacey Levinson, Stacey Mack, Daniel Reinhardt, Helen Suarez, and Grace Yeh, "Halloween as Consumption Experience," *Advances in Consumer Research*, Vol. 19 (1992), pp. 219–228.

31. John French and Bertram Raven, "The Bases of Social Power," in D. Cartwright (ed.), *Studies in Social Power* (Ann Arbor, Mich.: Institute for Social Research, 1959), pp. 150–167. Within consumer behavior, see, for example, Gary L. Sullivan and P. J. O'Connor,

"Social Power-based Print Advertising: Theoretical and Practical Considerations," *Psychology & Marketing*, Vol. 2 (Fall 1985), pp. 217ff; Jonathan E. Brill, "Scales to Measure Social Power in a Consumer Context," *Advances in Consumer Research*, Vol. 19 (1992), pp. 835–842.

32. Herbert C. Kelman, "Compliance, Identification, and Internalization: Three Processes of Attitude Change," *Journal of Conflict Resolution*, Vol. 2 (1958), pp. 51–60. See also Cathy Goodwin, "A Social Influence Theory of Consumer Cooperation," *Advances in Consumer Research*, Vol. 14 (1987), pp. 378–381.

33. Ellen Graham, "Tupperware Parties Create a New Breed of Super Saleswoman," *The Wall Street Journal*, May 21, 1971, p. 1; and John Birmingham, "The New American Office Party . . . ," *Marketing Week*, June 13, 1988, pp. 28–30. See also Brenda Gainer and Eileen Fischer, "To Buy or Not to Buy? That Is Not the Question: Female Ritual in Home Shopping Parties," *Advances in Consumer Research*, Vol. 18 (1991), pp. 597–602.

34. Jack W. Brehm, "Psychological Reactance: Theory and Applications," *Advances in Consumer Research*, Vol. 16 (1989), pp. 72–75; Greg Lessne and M. Venkatesan, "Reactance Theory in Consumer Research: The Past, Present, and Future," *Advances in Consumer Research*, Vol. 16 (1989), pp. 76–78; and Greg Lessne and Elaine M. Notarantonio, "The Effect of Limits in Retail Advertisements: A Reactance Theory Perspective," *Psychology & Marketing*, Vol. 5 (Spring 1988), pp. 33–44. See also Michael B. Mazis, Robert B. Settle, and Dennis C. Leslie, "Elimination of Phosphate Detergents and Psychological Reactance," *Journal of Marketing Research*, Vol. 10, No. 4 (November 1973), pp. 390–395; and Mona A. Clee and Robert A. Wicklund, "Consumer Behavior and Psychological Reactance," *Journal of Consumer Research*, Vol. 6, No. 4 (March 1980), pp. 389–405.

35. See, for example, Michael L. Ray and William L. Wilkie, "Fear: The Potential of an Appeal Neglected by Marketing," *Journal of Marketing*, Vol. 34, No. 1 (January 1970), pp. 54–62; Brian Sternthal and C. Samuel Craig, "Fear Appeals: Revisited and Revised," *Journal of Consumer Research*, Vol. 1 (December 1974), pp. 23–34; John F. Tanner, Jr., James B. Hunt, and David R. Eppright, "The Protection Motivation Model: A Normative Model of Fear Appeals," *Journal of Marketing*, Vol. 55, No. 3 (July 1991), pp. 36–45; and Charles R. Duke, Gregory M. Pickett, Les Carlson, and Stephen J. Grove, "A Method for Evaluating the Ethics of Fear Appeals," *Journal of Public Policy & Marketing*, Vol. 12, No. 1 (Spring 1993), pp. 120–129.

36. Bill Abrams, "Ring Around the Collar Ads Irritate Many, Yet Get Results," *The Wall Street Journal*, November 4, 1982, p. 33; "Lever Assigns Wisk to JWT," *Marketing Week*, August 14, 1989, p. 5; Gary Levin, "On Wisk Account, It's Like Father, Like Son," *Advertising Age*, October 2, 1989, p. 48.

37. The term reference group was coined in 1942 by a psychologist, Herbert Hyman, who was studying social status. According to Hyman, a reference group was the group against which a person would compare himself or herself (that is, "refer to") to determine his or her own social standing in the community. Since that time, however, the concept has broadened considerably in the field of consumer behavior. Today, the term has come to mean a group to whom we look ("refer to") for guidance for our own behavior. See Herbert Hyman, "The Psychology of Status," *Archives of Psychology*, Vol. 38, No. 269 (1942). See also Scott Dawson and Jill Cavell,

"Status Recognition in the 1980's: Invidious Distinction Revisited," *Advances in Consumer Research*, Vol. 14 (1987), pp. 487–491.

38. See William O. Bearden and Michael J. Etzel, "Reference Group Influence on Product and Brand Purchase Decisions," *Journal of Consumer Research*, Vol. 9 (September 1982), pp. 183–194. This paper builds upon the early classification by Francis S. Bourne, "Group Influences in Marketing and Public Relations," in R. Likert and S. P. Hayes (eds.), *Some Applications of Behavioral Research* (Basel, Switzerland: UNESCO, 1957). For a recent extension and empirical results, see also Terry L. Childers and Akshay R. Rao, "The Influence of Familial and Peer-based Reference Groups on Consumer Decisions," *Journal of Consumer Research*, Vol. 19, No. 2 (September 1992), pp. 198–211; and Gwen Rae Bachman, Deborah Roedder John, and Akshay R. Roe, "Children's Susceptibility to Peer Group Purchase Influence: An Exploratory Investigation," *Advances in Consumer Research*, Vol. 20 (1993), pp. 463–468.

39. Judann Dagnoli, "Weight Watchers Gaining . . . ," *Advertising Age*, July 13, 1987, p. 4. See also Grant McCracken, "Who Is the Celebrity Endorser? Cultural Foundations of the Endorsement Process," *Journal of Consumer Research*, Vol. 16, No. 3 (December 1989), pp. 310–321; Michael A. Kamins, "An Investigation into the 'Match-Up' Hypothesis in Celebrity Advertising: When Beauty May Be Only Skin Deep," *Journal of Advertising*, Vol. 19, No. 1 (1990), pp. 4–13; Roobina Ohanian, "Construction and Validation of a Scale to Measure Celebrity Endorsers' Perceived Expertise, Trustworthiness, and Attractiveness," *Journal of Advertising*, Vol. 19, No. 3 (1990), pp. 39–52; Lynn Langmeyer and Mary Walker, "A First Step to Identify the Meaning in Celebrity Endorsers," *Advances in Consumer Research*, Vol. 18 (1991), pp. 364–371; Linda M. Scott, "The Troupe: Celebrities as *Dramatis Personae* in Advertisements," *Advances in Consumer Research*, Vol. 18 (1991), pp. 355–363; Laura J. Yale, "The Role of Expertise and Coorientation in Personal Source Selection," *AMA Winter Educators' Proceedings* (1991), pp. 395–403; Roobina Ohanian, "The Impact of Celebrity Spokespersons' Perceived Image on Consumers' Intention to Purchase," *Journal of Advertising Research*, Vol. 31, No. 1 (February/March 1991), pp. 46–54; Mary Walker, Lynn Langmeyer, and Daniel Langmeyer, "Celebrity Endorsers: Do You Get What You Pay For?" *The Journal of Consumer Marketing*, Vol. 9, No. 2 (Spring 1992), pp. 69–76; and Gail Tom, Rebecca Clark, Laura Elmer, Edward Grech, Joseph Massetti, Jr., and Harmona Sandhhar, "The Use of Created versus Celebrity Spokespersons in Advertisements," *The Journal of Consumer Marketing*, Vol. 9, No. 4 (Fall 1992), pp. 45–51.

40. "Update," *USA Today*, April 14, 1993, p. 13C.

41. Tatiana Pouschine, "Cruising on Ray-Ban," *Forbes*, August 3, 1992, pp. 53–54; John Birmingham, "How Bausch & Lomb Keeps Ray-Ban in the Limelight," *Marketing Week*, July 4, 1988, pp. 27–28.

42. It is generally agreed that a situation comprises a point in time and space and is a more narrow concept than either a "behavior setting" or an "environment." Roger G. Barker, *Ecological Psychology: Concepts and Methods for Studying the Environment of Human Behavior* (Stanford, Calif.: Stanford University Press, 1968). There is, however, some disagreement about whether to define a situation in objective terms (e.g., physical or social surroundings that affect consumer behavior) or in subjective terms (i.e., focusing on a consumer's internal interpretations and responses). For our purposes we need not resolve this question, though it does remain an issue in this field. For a presentation of the "objective" position, see Russell W. Belk, "Situational Variables and Consumer Behavior," *Journal of Consumer Research,* Vol. 2 (December 1975), pp. 157–164; and comments by Roger Barker and Allan Wicker on pp. 165–167 of the same *Journal of Consumer Research* issue, and by James A. Russell and Albert Mehrabian, "Environmental Variables in Consumer Research," *Journal of Consumer Research,* Vol. 3 (June 1976), pp. 62–63, with replay by Belk, "Situational Mediation and Consumer Behavior: A Reply to Russell and Mehrabian," *Journal of Consumer Research,* Vol. 3 (December 1976), pp. 175–177. For a presentation of the "subjective" position, see Richard J. Lutz and Pradeep Kakkar, "The Psychological Situation as a Determinant of Consumer Behavior," *Advances in Consumer Research,* Vol. 2 (1975), pp. 439–454.

43. George Katona, "Psychology and Consumer Economics," *Journal of Consumer Research,* Vol. 1 (June 1974), pp. 1–8; "Appliance Shipments Set Records," *USA Today,* March 14, 1984, p. 1; see also Richard T. Curtin and Christopher J. Gordon, "Coping with Economic Adversity," *Advances in Consumer Research,* Vol. 10 (1983), pp. 175–181; Andrew S. C. Ehrenberg, "A Case of Seasonal Segmentation," *Marketing Research,* Vol. 2, No. 2 (June 1990), pp. 11–13; Scott D. Roberts, "Consumption Responses to Involuntary Job Loss," *Advances in Consumer Research,* Vol. 18 (1991), pp. 40–42; Joyce A. Young, Faye W. Gilbert, and Scott J. Vitell, "A Theoretical Framework of Consumer Coping under Conditions of Constrained Purchasing Behavior," in Robert L. King (ed.), *Marketing: Perspectives for the 1990s* (Richmond, Va.: Southern Marketing Association, 1992), pp. 70–73; T. Bettina Cornwell and O. C. Ferrell, "Coping With the Threat of an Earthquake: An Examination of Consumption Pattern Changes," in King (ed.), *Marketing: Perspectives for the 1990s,* pp. 74–78; and James W. Gentry, Patriya S. Tansuhaj, and Gary Ko, "Searching for Etic and Emic Notions in Measures of Personal Time Orientation," *AMA Winter Educators' Proceedings* (1993), pp. 309–310.

44. National Income and Product Accounts of the United States, Government Printing Office, Washington, D.C., July 1983.

45. William L. Wilkie and Peter R. Dickson, "Patterns of Consumer Information Search and Shopping Behavior for Household Durables," Working Paper Series, Marketing Research Institute, Cambridge, Mass., 1985.

46. There are a number of interesting points and findings on usage situation's impact on consumer behavior. For further reading of an overview of the issues, you may wish to pursue Pradeep Kakkar and Richard J. Lutz, "Situational Influence on Consumer Behavior: A Review." in H. H. Kassarjian and T. S. Robertson (eds.), *Perspectives in Consumer Behavior,* 3d ed. (Glenview, Ill.: Scott Foresman, 1981), pp. 204–214; and P. Greg Bonner, "Considerations for Situational Research," *Advances in Consumer Research,* Vol. 12 (1985), pp. 368–373. For further concepts and recent findings, see Simeon Chow, Richard L. Celsi, and Robin Abel, "The Effects of Situational and Intrinsic Sources of Personal Relevance on Brand Choice Decisions," *Advances in Consumer Research,* Vol. 17 (1990), pp. 755–760; Jeffrey J. Stoltman, Linda K. Anglin, and Fred W. Morgan, "An Expanded Consideration of Situational Influence: An Investigation of Retail Shopping Situations," *AMA Winter Educators' Proceedings* (1991), pp. 294–295; Aaron Bernard, Mara B. Adelman, and Jonathan E. Schroeder, "Two Views of Consumption in Mating and Dating," *Advances in Consumer Research,* Vol. 18 (1991), pp. 532–537; Nancy M. Ridgway and Linda L. Price, "Creativity under Pressure: The Importance of Consumption Situations on Consumer

Product Use," *AMA Summer Educators' Proceedings* (1991), pp. 361–368; and Deborah A. Cours and Harold H. Kassarjian, "Situational Influences and the Academy Awards: Approach or Avoidance?" *AMA Winter Educators' Proceedings* (1993), p. 83.

47. John Birmingham, "Dial's Hearty Office Meal," *Marketing Week,* June 27, 1988, pp. 20–23.

48. Peter R. Dickson, "Person-Situation: Segmentation's Missing Link," *Journal of Marketing,* Vol. 46 (Fall 1982), pp. 56–64. See also Roger J. Calantone and Alan G. Sawyer, "The Stability of Benefit Segments," *Journal of Marketing Research,* Vol. 15 (August 1978), pp. 395–404.

49. Sharon K. Banks, "Gift-Giving: A Review and an Interactive Paradigm," *Advances in Consumer Research,* Vol. 6 (1979), pp. 319–324, and Jeffrey H. Birnbaum, "Christmas Sales Get Off to a Slow Start, but Stores Hope for the Usual Late Surge," *The Wall Street Journal,* November 20, 1981, p. 56.

50. Russell Belk, "Gift-Giving Behavior," in J. Sheth (ed.), *Research in Marketing,* Vol. 2 (Greenwich, Conn.: JAI Press, 1979), pp. 95–126.

51. An interesting overview of this area is presented in John F. Sherry "Gift Giving in Anthropological Perspective," *Journal of Consumer Research* (September 1983), pp. 157–168. For recent discussions, see Alice James and William L. James, "Gift Giving in Rural Ireland: An Analysis," *AMA Educators' Proceedings* (1985), pp. 26–29; David M. Andrus, Edward Silver, and Dallas E. Johnson, "Status Brand Mangement and Gift Purchase: A Discriminant Analysis," *The Journal of Consumer Marketing,* Vol. 3 (Winter 1986), pp. 5–14; Christian Dussart, "Pre-Christmas Toy Guides: A Cross-Sectional Research Study," *Advances in Consumer Research,* Vol. 16 (1989), pp. 374–383; Janet Wagner, Richard Ettenson, and Sherri Verrier, "The Effect of Donor-Recipient Involvement on Consumer Gift Decisions," *Advances in Consumer Research,* Vol. 17 (1990), pp. 683–689; Cathy Goodwin, Kelly L. Smith, and Susan Spiggle, "Gift Giving: Consumer Motivation and the Gift Purchase Process," *Advances in Consumer Research,* Vol. 17 (1990), pp. 690–698; Mary Finley Wolfinbarger, "Motivations and Symbolism in Gift-Giving Behavior," *Advances in Consumer Research,* Vol. 17 (1990), pp. 699–706; Scott D. Roberts, "Symbolism, Obligation, and Fiber Choice: The Macro to Micro Continuum of Understanding Gift Giving," *Advances in Consumer Research,* Vol. 17 (1990), pp. 707–709; John A. McCarty, L. J. Shrum, Tracey E. Conrad-Katz, and Zacho Kanne, "Tipping as a Consumer Behavior: A Qualitative Investigation," *Advances in Consumer Research,* Vol. 17 (1990), pp. 723–728; David Glen Mick and Michelle DeMoss, "Self-Gifts: Phenomenological Insights from Four Contexts," *Journal of Consumer Research,* Vol. 17, No. 3 (December 1990), pp. 322–332; Eileen Fischer and Stephen J. Arnold, "More than a Labor of Love: Gender Roles and Christmas Gift Shopping," *Journal of Consumer Research,* Vol. 17, No. 3 (December 1990), pp. 333–345; Terrence H. Witkowski and Yoshito Yamamoto, "Omiyage Gift Purchasing by Japanese Travelers in the U.S.," *Advances in Consumer Research,* Vol. 18 (1991), pp. 123–128; Russell W. Belk and Gregory S. Coon, "Can't Buy Me Love: Dating, Money, and Gifts," *Advances in Consumer Research,* Vol. 18 (1991), pp. 521–527; Margaret Rucker, L. Leckliter, S. Kivel, M. Dinkel, T. Freitas, M. Wynes, and H. Prato, "When the Thought Counts: Friendship, Love, Gift Exchanges and Gift Returns," *Advances in Consumer Research,* Vol. 18 (1991), pp. 528–531; David Mick and Michelle DeMoss, "Further Findings on Self-Gifts: Products, Qualities, and

Socioeconomic Correlates," *Advances in Consumer Research*, Vol. 19 (1992), pp. 140–146; Anil M. Pandya and A. Venkatesh, "Symbolic Communication among Consumers in Self-Consumption and Gift Giving: A Semiotic Approach," *Advances in Consumer Research*, Vol. 19 (1992), pp. 147–154; Anil Mathur, Kelly L. Smith, and George P. Moschis, "The Elderly's Motivations for Charity Gift-Giving: An Exchange Theory Perspective," *AMA Winter Educators' Proceedings* (1992), Vol. 3, pp. 430–431; Bodo B. Schlegelmilch, Adamantios Diamantopoulos, and Alix Love, "Determinants of Charity Giving: An Interdisciplinary Review of the Literature and Suggestions for Future Research," *AMA Winter Educators' Proceedings* (1992), Vol. 3, pp. 507–516; Cele Otnes, Young Chan Kim, and Tina M. Lowrey, "Ho, Ho, Woe: Christmas Shopping for 'Difficult' People," *Advances in Consumer Research*, Vol. 19 (1992), pp. 482–487; Thesia I. Garner and Janet Wagner, "Economic Dimensions of Household Gift Giving," *Journal of Consumer Research*, Vol. 18, No. 3 (December 1991), pp. 368–379; Audrey Guskey Federouch, "The Santa Phenomenon—Helping Others by Giving Gifts: Conceptualization of Self-Initiated Gift-Giving," in T. J. Page, Jr. and S. E. Middlestadt (eds.), (Clemson, S.C.: CtC Press, 1992) *Proceedings of the Society for Consumer Psychology*, pp. 31–33; Lise Heroux and Nancy J. Church, "Wedding Anniversary Celebration and Gift-Giving Rituals: The Dialectic of Intimacy," in Robert L. King (ed.), *Marketing: Perspectives for the 1990s* (Richmond, Va.: Southern Marketing Association, 1992), pp. 43–47; Anthony D. Miyazaki, "How Many Shopping Days until Christmas?: A Preliminary Investigation of Time Pressures, Deadlines, and Planning Levels on Holiday Gift Purchases," *Advances in Consumer Research*, Vol. 20 (1993), pp. 331–335; Kim K. R. McKeage, Marsha L. Richins, and Kathleen Debevec, "Self-Gifts and the Manifestation of Material Values," *Advances in Consumer Research*, Vol. 20 (1993), pp. 359–364; Mitch Griffin, Barry J. Babin, Jill S. Attaway, and William R. Darden, "Hey You, Can Ya Spare Some Change? The Case of Empathy and Personal Distress as Reactions to Charitable Appeals," *Advances in Consumer Research*, Vol. 20 (1993), pp. 508–514; Janet Wagner and Thesia I. Garner, "Extrahousehold Giving in Popular Gift Categories: A Socioeconomic and Demographic Analysis," *Advances in Consumer Research*, Vol. 20 (1993), pp. 515–519; Mary Finley Wolfinbarger and Laura J. Yale, "Three Motivations for Interpersonal Gift Giving: Experiential, Obligated, and Practical Motivations," *Advances in Consumer Research*, Vol. 20 (1993), pp. 520–526; Cele Otnes, Julie Ruth, and Connie Milbourne, "The Influence of Gender and Self-Acceptance on Valentine's Day Gift Exchange," *AMA Winter Educators' Proceedings* (1993), p. 54; Margaret Rucker and Jamie Dolstra, "Gifts as Tokens of Appreciation: New Tests for Old Models," *AMA Winter Educators' Proceedings* (1993), pp. 55–56; and Adamantios Diamantopoulos, Bodo B. Schlegelmilch, and Alix Love, "Giving to Charity: Determinants of Cash Donations through Prompted Giving," *AMA Winter Educators' Proceedings* (1993), p. 133.

Chapter 14

Household Influences

1. *Statistical Abstract of the United States* (Washington, DC: U.S. Government Printing Office, 1992).

2. "Demographics," *U.S. News & World Report*, July 27, 1992, p. 12; see also Kathryn A. London and Barbara F. Wilson, "Divorce," *American Demographics*, October 1988, pp. 23–26, and "Marital Status and Living Arrangements: March 1987," report, U.S. Census Bureau, 1988.

3. Richard Morin, "Family Life Makes a Comeback," *Washington Post National Weekly*, November 25, 1991, p. 37; "Unflattering Portrait," *Parade Magazine*, July 14, 1991, p. 17; Urie Bronfenbrenner, "What Do Families Do?" *Family Affairs*, Vol. 4 (Winter/Spring 1991), pp. 1–6; Glenn Collins, "Family Attitudes Show Marked Changes," *The New York Times New Service*, June 17, 1987; Nanci Hellmich, "Marriage Outranks a Career," *USA Today*, October 5, 1988, p. D-1; "Birth Expectations," report, U.S. Census Bureau, January 1988.

4. Scott Ward, "Consumer Socialization," *Journal of Consumer Research*, Vol. 1 (September 1974), p. 2.

5. Scott Ward, Daniel Wackman, and Ellen Wartella, *How Children Learn to Buy* (Beverly Hills, Calif.: Sage, 1977), pp. 175–197. See also Les Carlson, Sanford Grossbart, and Ann Walsh, "Mothers' Communication Orientations and Consumer-Socialization Tendencies," *Journal of Advertising*, Vol. 19, No. 3 (1990), pp. 27–38; Les Carlson, Sanford Grossbart, and Carolyn Tripp, "An Investigation of Mothers' Communication Orientations and Patterns," *Advances in Consumer Research*, Vol. 17 (1990), pp. 804–812; and Sanford Grossbart, Les Carlson, and Ann Walsh, "Consumer Socialization and Frequency of Shopping with Children," *Journal of the Academy of Marketing Science*, Vol. 19, No. 3 (Summer 1991), pp. 155–164.

6. Scott Ward, "Consumer Socialization," *Journal of Consumer Research*, Vol. 1 (September 1974), p. 2; see also Kenneth D. Bahn, "How and When Do Brand Perceptions and Preferences First Form? A Cognitive Developmental Investigation," *Journal of Consumer Research*, Vol. 13 (December 1986), pp. 382–393; Karin M. Ekstrom, Patriya S. Tansuhaj, and Ellen R. Foxman, "Children's Influence in Family Decisions and Consumer Socialization: A Reciprocal View," *Advances in Consumer Research*, Vol. 14 (1987), pp. 283–287; Les Carlson and Sanford Grossbart, "Parental Style and Consumer Socialization of Children," *Journal of Consumer Research*, Vol. 15 (June 1988), pp. 77–94; Newell D. Wright and Jon Shapiro, "Consumption and the Crisis of Teen Pregnancy: A Critical Theory Approach," *Advances in Consumer Research*, Vol. 19 (1992), pp. 404–406; Jane P. Wayland and Cathy Owens Swift, "Children of Divorce and Consumer Socialization," in Robert L. King (ed.), *Marketing: Perspectives for the 1990s* (Richmond, Va.: Southern Marketing Association, 1992), pp. 52–56; and Oswald A. J. Mascarenhas and Mary A. Higby, "Peer, Parent, and Media Influences in Teen Apparel Shopping," *Journal of Academy of Marketing Science*, Vol. 21, No. 1 (Winter 1993), pp. 53–58.

7. Reuben Hill, *Family Development in Three Generations* (Cambridge, Mass.: Schenkman, 1970).

8. The 40 percent figure is based on those who answered the question: 18 percent of the sample did not know which policy their parents held. See Larry G. Woodson, Terry L. Childers, and Paul R. Winn, "Intergenerational Influences in the Purchase of Auto Insurance," in W. Locander (ed.), *Marketing Looks Outward: 1976 Business Proceedings* (Chicago: American Marketing Association, 1976), pp. 43–49.

9. Carlee Scott and Carrie Dolan, "Funeral Homes Hope to Attract Business by Offering Services after the Service," *The Wall Street Journal*, April 11, 1991, p. B1; "Brand Formations of the Average Product," study conducted for *Seventeen* magazine by Yankelovich, Skelly, and White, March 1980.

10. Doron P. Levin, "Detroit Strives to Reclaim Lost Generation of Buyers," *New York Times,* April 9, 1991, p. A1.

11. See, for example, Terry L. Childers and Akshay R. Rao, "The Influence of Familial and Peer-based Reference Groups on Consumer Decision," *Journal of Consumer Research,* Vol. 19 (September 1992), pp. 198–211; Susan E. Heckler, Terry L. Childers, and Ramesh Arunachalam, "Intergenerational Influence in Adult Buying Behaviors: An Examination of Moderating Factors," *Advances in Consumer Research,* Vol. 16 (1989), pp. 276–284; two articles in *Advances in Consumer Research,* Vol. 15 (1988): Elizabeth S. Moore-Shay and Richard J. Lutz, "Intergenerational Influences in the Formation of Consumer Attitudes and Beliefs about the Marketplace: Mothers and Daughters," pp. 461–467; and George P. Mochis, "Methodological Issues in Studying Intergenerational Influences on Consumer Behavior," pp. 569–573; Patricia Sorce, Philip R. Tyler, and Lynette Loomis, "Intergenerational Influence on Consumer Decision Making," *Advances in Consumer Research,* Vol. 16 (1989), pp. 271–275; Mary M. Walker and M. Carole Macklin, "The Use of Role Modeling in Targeting Advertising to Grandparents," *Journal of Advertising Research,* Vol. 32, No. 4 (July/August 1992), pp. 37–44; and Patriya S. Tansuhaj, Ellen R. Foxman, and Jong Hee Park, "Intergenerational Differences in Product Importance Perceptions: The Role of Societal Change," *Journal of International Consumer Marketing,* Vol. 5, No. 2 (1993), pp. 21–38.

12. Howard Schlossberg, "Kids Teach Parents How to Change Their Buying Habits," *Marketing News,* March 2, 1992, p. 8. See also Tamara F. Mangleburg, "Children's Influence in Purchase Decisions: A Review and Critique," *Advances in Consumer Research,* Vol. 17 (1990), pp. 813–825; and Chankon Kim, Hanjoon Lee, and Katherine Hall, "A Study of Adolescents' Power, Influence Strategy, and Influence on Family Purchase Decisions," *AMA Winter Educators' Proceedings* (1991), pp. 37–45.

13. See *Rolling Stone* April 7 and May 5, 1988, issues for description of results from this survey entitled "Portrait of a Generation." See also William Strauss and Neil Howe, "Generations," *American Demographics,* April 1991, pp. 25–33.

14. Much of the framework for this section is based upon the seminal article by Harry L. Davis, "Decision Making within the Household," in R. Ferber (ed.), *Selected Aspects of Consumer Behavior* (Washington, D.C.: U.S. Government Printing Office, National Science Foundation, 1977), pp. 73–97. For related recent findings and perspectives, see Alvin C. Burns and James W. Gentry, "Toward Improving Household Consumption Behavior Research: Avoidance of Pitfalls in Using Alternative Household Data Collection Procedures," *Advances in Consumer Research,* Vol. 17 (1990), pp. 518–530; Jong-Hee Park, Patriya S. Tansuhaj, and Richard H. Kolbe, "The Role of Love, Affection, and Intimacy in Family Decision Research," Advances in Consumer Research, Vol. 18 (1991), pp. 651–656; Amardeep Assar and George S. Bobinski, Jr., "Financial Decision Making of Babyboomer Couples," *Advances in Consumer Research,* Vol. 18 (1991), pp. 657–665; Jeffrey J. Stoltman and James W. Gentry, "Using Focus Groups to Study Household Decision Processes and Choices," *AMA Summer Educators' Proceedings* (1992), pp. 257–263; and Chankon Kim, Michel Laroche, and Lianxi Zhou, "An Investigation of Ethnicity and Sex-Role Attitude as Factors Influencing Household Financial Task Sharing Behavior," *Advances in Consumer Research,* Vol. 20 (1993), pp. 52–58.

15. Bernard Berelson and Gary Steiner, *Human Behavior: An Inventory of Scientific Findings* (New York: Harcourt, Brace & World, 1964).

16. "He Wears the Pants," *The Wall Street Journal,* May 17, 1990, p. A1; P. Sloan, "Matchabelli Name Readied for Men's Fragrance Line," *Advertising Age,* April 21, 1980, p. 69.

17. Fred D. Reynolds and William D. Wells, *Consumer Behavior* (New York: McGraw-Hill, 1977), pp. 282–283.

18. Susan Hayward, "Men (Finally) Beginning to Redefine Roles," *Advertising Age,* November 18, 1991, p. 20; and "Marketing to the Family," *Advertising Age,* July 30, 1990, pp. 26ff. See also Mary Lou Roberts and Lawrence H. Wortzel, "Role Transferral in the Household: A Conceptual Model and Partial Test," *Advances in Consumer Research,* Vol. 9 (1982), pp. 261–266. For recent findings, see John J. Burnett and Julie Baker, "The Roberts–Wortzel Hierarchical Model: An Extension through Methodological and Variable Delineation Considerations," *AMA Summer Educators' Proceedings* (1989), p. 265; and three papers in *Advances in Consumer Research,* Vol. 16, (1989): W. Thomas Anderson, Jr., Linda L. Golden, William A. Weeks, and U. M. Umesh, "The Five Faces of Eve: Women's Timestyle Typologies," pp. 346–353; Irene Raj Foster and Richard W. Olshavsky, "An Exploratory Study of Family Decision Making Using a New Taxonomy of Family Role Structure," pp. 665–670; and Chankon Kim and Hanjoon Lee, "Sex Role Attitudes of Spouses and Task Sharing Behavior," pp. 671–679. See also Ved Prakash, "Sex Roles and Advertising Preferences," *Journal of Advertising Research,* Vol. 32, No. 3 (May/June 1992), pp. 43–52; Carol J. Kaufman, "Usage versus Ownership: Suggestions for Refining Studies of Time Savings and Wives' Employment," *The Journal of Consumer Marketing,* Vol. 7, No. 1 (Winter 1990), pp. 23–30; Sharon M. Danes and Mary Winter, "The Impact of the Employment of the Wife on the Achievement of Home Ownership," *The Journal of Consumer Affairs,* Vol. 24, No. 1 (Summer 1990), pp. 148–169; Craig J. Thompson, William B. Locander, and Howard R. Pollio, "The Lived Meaning of Free Choice: An Existential-Phenomenological Description of Everyday Consumer Experiences of Contemporary Married Women," *Journal of Consumer Research,* Vol. 17, No. 3 (December 1990), pp. 346–361; Gail DeWeese and Marjorie J. T. Norton, "Impact of Married Women's Employment on Individual Household Member Expenditures for Clothing," *The Journal of Consumer Affairs,* Vol. 25, No. 2 (Winter 1991), pp. 235–257; Joseph A. Bellizzi and Laura Milner, "Gender Positioning of a Traditionally Male-Dominant Product," *Journal of Advertising Research,* Vol. 31, No. 3 (June/July 1991), pp. 72–79; Melissa Martin Young, "Disposition of Possessions during Role Transitions," *Advances in Consumer Research,* Vol. 18 (1991), pp. 33–39; James H. McAlexander, "Divorce, the Disposition of the Relationship, and Everything," *Advances in Consumer Research,* Vol. 18 (1991), pp. 43–48; Shreekant G. Joag, James W. Gentry, and Karin Ekstrom, "An Investigation of a Role/Goal Model of Wives' Role Overload Reduction Strategies," *Advances in Consumer Research,* Vol. 18 (1991), pp. 666–672; Carol Felker Kaufman, Paul M. Lane, and Jay D. Lindquist, "Exploring More than 24 Hours a Day: A Preliminary Investigation of Polychronic Time Use," *Journal of Consumer Research,* Vol. 18, No. 3 (December 1991), pp. 392–401; KerenAmi Johnson and Scott D. Roberts, "Incompletely-Launched and Returning Young Adults: Social Change, Consumption, and Family Environment," *AMA Summer Educators' Proceedings* (1992), pp. 249–254; Ritha Fellerman and Kathleen Debevec, "Till Death Do

We Part: Family Dissolution, Transition, and Consumer Behavior," *Advances in Consumer Research*, Vol. 19 (1992), pp. 514–521; James H. McAlexander, John W. Schouten, and Scott D. Roberts, "Consumer Behavior in Coping Strategies for Divorce," *Advances in Consumer Research*, Vol. 19 (1992), pp. 555–556; Nejdet Delener, "Cultural Determinants of Power for Women Within the Family: A Neglected Aspect of Family Decision Making Research," *AMA Winter Educators' Proceedings* (1992), pp. 464–465; R. S. Oropesa, "Female Labor Force Participation and Time-saving Household Technology: A Case Study of the Microwave from 1978 to 1989," *Journal of Consumer Research*, Vol. 19, No. 4 (March 1993), pp. 567–579; Ritha Fellerman and Kathleen Debevec, "Kinship Exchange Networks and Family Consumption," *Advances in Consumer Research*, Vol. 20 (1993), pp. 458–462; Roshan D. Ahuja and Kandi M. Stinson, "Female-Headed Single Parent Families: An Exploratory Study of Children's Influence in Family Decision Making," *Advances in Consumer Research*, Vol. 20 (1993), pp. 469–474; and Judith J. Marshall and Frances Woolley, "What's Mine Is Mine and What's Yours Is Ours: Challenging the Income Pooling Assumption," *Advances in Consumer Research*, Vol. 20 (1993), pp. 541–545.

19. Harry L. Davis and Benny P. Rigaux, "Perception of Marital Roles in Decision Processes," *Journal of Consumer Research*, Vol 1 (June 1974), pp. 51–62. See also E. H. Bonfield, "Perception of Marital Roles in Decision Processes: Replication and Extension," *Advances in Consumer Research*, Vol. 5 (1978), pp. 300–307; Charles B. Weinberg and Russell S. Winer, "Working Wives and Major Family Expenditures: Replication and Extension," *Journal of Consumer Research*, Vol. 10 (September 1983), pp. 259–263; W. Keith Bryant, "Durables and Wives' Employment Yet Again," *Journal of Consumer Research*, Vol. 15 (June 1988), pp. 37–47; Michael S. LaTour, Tony L. Henthorne, and John B. Ford, "Marital Role Influence in the Purchase Decision Process: The Chinese Perspective," *AMA Winter Educators' Proceedings* (1991), pp. 80–81; and Cynthia Webster, "Observation of Marital Roles in Decision Making: A Third World Perspective," *AMA Summer Educators' Proceedings* (1992), pp. 513–519.

20. Arch Woodside and William Motes, "Husband and Wife Perceptions of Marital Roles in Consumer Decision Processes for Six Products," *AMA Educators' Proceedings* (1979).

21. This discussion is based upon the Davis framework (see Note 14): Table 14–1 is adapted from that source, p. 89. For other useful frameworks and findings, see David Brinberg and Nancy Schwenk, "Husband-Wife Decision Making: An Exploratory Study of the Interaction Process," *Advances in Consumer Research*, Vol. 12 (1985), pp. 487–491; Alvin C. Burns and Jo Anne Hopper, "An Analysis of the Presence, Stability, and Antecedents of Husband and Wife Purchase Decision Making Influence Assessment: Agreement and Disagreement," *Advances in Consumer Research*, Vol. 13 (1986); Elizabeth S. Moore-Shay and William L. Wilkie, "Recent Developments in Research on Family Decisions," *Advances in Consumer Research*, Vol. 15 (1988), pp. 454–460; Michael B. Menasco and David J. Curry, "Utility and Choice: An Empirical Study of Wife/Husband Decision Making," *Journal of Consumer Research*, Vol. 15 (March 1989), pp. 87–97; Ellen R. Foxman, Patriya S. Tansuhaj, and Karin M. Ekstrom, "Family Members' Perceptions of Adolescents' Influence in Family Decision Making," *Journal of Consumer Research*, Vol. 15 (March 1989), pp. 482–491; Rama Yelkur and Louis M. Capella, "Joint Adoptions Decisions by the Family: An Overview of Influencing

Factors," in Robert L. King (ed.), *Marketing: Perspectives for the 1990s* (Richmond, Va.: Southern Marketing Association, 1992), pp. 48–51; and Jacob Hornik, "Measuring Cohort Role on Husband-Wife Differences in Temporal Behavior," *Advances in Consumer Research*, Vol. 20 (1993), pp. 527–533.

22. Rosann L. Spiro, "Persuasion in Family Decisionmaking," *Journal of Consumer Research*, Vol. 10 (March 1983), pp. 393–402. See also Daniel Seymour and Greg Lessne, "Spousal Conflict Arousal: Scale Development," *Journal of Consumer Research*, Vol. 11 (December 1984), pp. 810–821; Daniel T. Seymour, "Forced Compliance in Family Decision-Making," *Psychology & Marketing*, Vol. 3 (Fall 1986), pp. 223ff.; and William J. Qualls and Francoise Jaffe, "Measuring Conflict in Household Decision Behavior: Read My Lips and Read My Mind," *Advances in Consumer Research*, Vol. 19 (1992), pp. 522–531.

23. Margaret C. Nelson, "The Resolution of Conflict in Joint Purchase Decisions by Husbands and Wives: A Review and Empirical Test," *Advances in Consumer Research*, Vol. 15 (1988), pp. 436–441.

24. C. Whan Park, "Joint Decisions in Home Purchasing: A Muddling-Through Process," *Journal of Consumer Research*, Vol. 9 (September 1982), pp. 151–62. See also C. Whan Park, "A Conflict Resolution Choice Model," *Journal of Consumer Research*, Vol. 5 (September 1978), pp. 124–135.

25. Harry L. Davis, Stephen J. Hoch, and E. K. Easton Ragsdale, "An Anchoring and Adjustment Model of Spousal Predictions," *Journal of Consumer Research*, Vol. 13 (June 1986), pp. 25–37, and Kim P. Corfman, "Measures of Relative Influence in Couples: A Typology and Predictions for Accuracy," *Advances in Consumer Research*, Vol. 16 (1989), pp. 659–664.

26. Recent research from family studies supports the difficulty of this issue: one recent study comparing spouse interviews with both partners present with interviews of one partner at a time showed differences in response on such issues as happiness, premarital cohabitation, frequency of sex, frequency of fighting, and earnings (men reported lower earnings with wife present, while wives reported higher earnings with husbands present). See Alan L. Otten, "Spousal Audience Colors Scenes from a Marriage," *The Wall Street Journal*, February 28, 1992, p. B1.

27. Lincoln H. Clark (ed.), *The Life Cycle and Consumer Behavior* (New York: New York University Press, 1955).

28. The following discussion is based upon the FLC framework presented in William D. Wells and George Gubar, "Life Cycle Concept in Marketing Research," *Journal of Marketing Research*, Vol. 3 (November 1966), pp. 355–363. See also Ronald W. Stampfl, "The Consumer Life Cycle," *The Journal of Consumer Affairs*, Vol. 12 (Winter 1978), pp. 209–219.

29. Sarah Stiansen, "A Marriage Made in Heaven," *Advertising Age*, October 25, 1982, p. M56.

30. "Just Think of It All as Another Mortgage," *The Wall Street Journal*, June 2, 1993, p. B1.

31. Patrick E. Murphy and William A. Staples, "A Modernized Family Life Cycle," *Journal of Consumer Research*, Vol. 6 (June 1979), pp. 12–22.

32. Mary C. Gilly and Ben J. Enis, "Recycling the Family Life Cycle: A Proposal for Redefinition," *Advances in Consumer Research*,

Vol. 9 (1982), pp. 271–276. See also Frederick W. Derrick and Alane K. Lehfeld, "The Family Life Cycle: An Alternative Approach," *Journal of Consumer Research*, Vol. 7 (September 1980), pp. 214–217; Karen S. Reilly, Sevgin A. Eroglu, Karen A. Machleit, and Glenn S. Omura, "Consumer Decision Making across Family Life Cycle Stages," *Advances in Consumer Research*, Vol. 11 (1984), pp. 400–404; Alan R. Andreasen "Life Status Changes and Changes in Consumer Preferences and Satisfaction," *Journal of Consumer Research*, Vol. 11 (December 1984), pp. 784–794; Lawrence R. Lepisto, "A Life-Span Perspective of Consumer Behavior," *Advances in Consumer Research*, Vol. 12 (1985), pp. 47–52; and Caroline Chua, Joseph A. Cote, and Siew Meng Leong, "The Antecedents of Cognitive Age," *Advances in Consumer Research*, Vol. 17 (1990), pp. 880–885.

33. The direct framework comparisons are reported in Janet Wagner and Sherman Hanna, "The Effectiveness of Family Life Cycle Variables in Consumer Expenditure Research," *Journal of Consumer Research*, Vol. 10 (December 1983), pp. 281–291; and Charles M. Schaninger and William D. Danko, "A Conceptual and Empirical Comparison of Alternative Household Life Cycle Models," *Journal of Consumer Research*, Vol. 19, No. 4 (March 1993), pp. 580–594. See also Robin A. Douthitt and Joanne M. Fedyk, "Family Composition, Parental Time, and Market Goods: Life Cycle Trade-offs," *The Journal of Consumer Affairs*, Vol. 24, No. 1 (Summer 1990), pp. 110–133.

34. This example is based upon definitions and figures provided in *Targeting Consumers at the Crossroads of Their Lives: Lifestage Marketing* (New York: Media Mark Research, Inc., 1990).

35. See, for example, Donald H. Granbois, "The Role of Communication in the Family Decision-Making Process" in S. Greyser (ed.), *AMA Educators' Proceedings* (Chicago: American Marketing Association, 1963), pp. 44–57; and Harry L. Davis, "Decision Making within the Household," *Journal of Consumer Research*, March 1976, pp. 241–260.

36. Scott Ward and Daniel Wackman, "Children's Purchase Influence Attempts and Parental Yielding," *Journal of Marketing Research*, Vol. 9 (August 1972), pp. 316–319. For related results, see also William K. Darley and Jeen Su Lim, "Family Decision Making in Leisure-Time Activities: An Exploratory Investigation of the Impact of Locus of Control and Parental Type on Perceived Child Influence," *Advances in Consumer Research*, Vol. 13 (1986); Kenneth Bahn, "Do Mothers and Children Share Cereal and Beverage Preference and Evaluative Criteria?" *Advances in Consumer Research*, Vol. 14 (1987), pp. 279–282; and Joseph R. Murphy, "Parent–Adult–Child Segments in Marketing," *Journal of Advertising Research*, Vol. 27 (April/May 1987), pp. 38–42.

Chapter 15

Salespersons' Influences

1. William L. Wilkie and Peter R. Dickson, "Consumer Information Search and Shopping Behavior," Marketing Science Institute paper series, Cambridge, Mass., 1985.

2. Jon G. Udell, *Successful Marketing Strategies in American Industry* (Madison: Mimir, 1972).

3. Franklin B. Evans, "Selling as a Dyadic Relationship," *American Behavioral Scientist*, May 1963, pp. 76–79.

4. Robert F. Bales, "A Set of Categories for the Analysis of Small Group Interaction," *American Sociological Review*, April 1950.

5. Ronald P. Willett and Allan L. Pennington, "Customer and Salesman: The Anatomy of Choice and Influence in a Retail Setting," in Raymond M. Haas (ed.), *Science, Technology, and Marketing*. (Chicago: American Marketing Association, 1966), pp. 598–616.

6. Richard W. Olshavsky, "Customer-Salesman Interaction in Appliance Retailing," *Journal of Marketing Research*, Vol. 10 (May 1973), pp. 208–212.

7. Adam Bryant, "In Search of Greener Showrooms," *New York Times*, October 1, 1991, p. C1; and David Kiley, "Chrysler Is Set to Grade the Sales Staff," *Marketing Week*, October 8, 1990, p. 35.

8. James L. Taylor and Arch G. Woodside, "An Examination of the Structure of Buying-Selling Interactions among Insurance Agents and Prospective Customers," *Advances in Consumer Research*, Vol. 7 (1980), pp. 387–392. See also Arch G. Woodside and James L. Taylor, "Identity Negotiations in Buyer-Seller Interactions," *Advances in Consumer Research*, Vol. 12 (1985), pp. 443–449.

9. Kenneth A. Anglin, Jeffrey J. Stoltman, and James W. Gentry, "Salesperson Communication Strategy and Adaptive Selling," *AMA Winter Educators' Proceedings* (1991), pp. 303–309; Thomas W. Leigh and Patrick F. McGraw, "Mapping the Procedural Knowledge of Industrial Sales Personnel: A Script-Theoretic Investigation," *Journal of Marketing*, Vol. 53 (January 1989), pp. 16–34; Siew Meng Leong, Paul S. Busch, and Deborah Roedder John, "Knowledge Bases and Salesperson Effectiveness: A Script-Theoretic Analysis," *Journal of Marketing Research*, Vol. 26 (May 1989), pp. 164–178; David M. Szymanski, "Determinants of Selling Effectiveness: The Importance of Declarative Knowledge to the Personal Selling Concept," *Journal of Marketing*, Vol. 52 (January 1988), pp. 64–77; David M. Szymanski and Gilbert A. Churchill, Jr., "Client Evaluation Cues: A Comparison of Successful and Unsuccessful Salespeople," *Journal of Marketing*, Vol. 27 (May 1990), pp. 163–174; and Harish Sujan, Mita Sujan, and James R. Bettman, "Knowledge Structure Differences between More Effective and Less Effective Salespeople," *Journal of Marketing Research*, Vol. 25 (February 1988), pp. 81–86.

10. This discussion and Figure 15–1 are adapted from Barton A. Weitz, "The Relationship between Salesperson Performance and Understanding of Customer Decision Making," *Journal of Marketing Research*, Vol. 15 (November 1978), pp. 501–516. See also Barton A. Weitz, "Effectiveness in Sales Interactions: A Contingency Framework," *Journal of Marketing*, Vol. 45, No.1, (Winter 1981), pp. 85–103; Robert Saxe and Barton Weitz, "The SOCO Scale: A Measure of the Customer Orientation of Salespeople," *Journal of Marketing Research*, Vol. 19 (August 1982), pp. 343–351; Rosann L. Spiro and Barton A. Weitz, "Adaptive Selling: Conceptualization, Measurement, and Nomological Validity," *Journal of Marketing Research*, Vol. 27 (February 1990), pp. 61–69; Fred Morgan and Jeffrey Stoltman, "Adaptive Selling–Insights from Social Cognition," *Journal of Personal Selling and Sales Management*, Vol. 10 (1990), pp. 43–54; Alain D'Astous and Helene Kettler, "Perceptions of an Ongoing Sales Interaction by Expert and Novice Salespersons," *Proceedings of the Annual Conference of the Administrative Sciences Association of Canada* (Halifax, N.S.: St. Mary's University, 1988); David J. Urban, "Neuro-Linguistic Programming Revisited: A Critical Literature Review and Its Implications for Sales," *AMA Winter Educators' Proceedings* (1991), pp. 212–219; Dan C. Weilbaker, "An Empirical Test of the Relationship between Adaptive Selling Behavior and Sales-People's Knowledge Structures," *AMA Winter Educators' Proceedings* (1991), pp. 310–316; Gene Brown, Robert E. Widing II, and Ronald L. Coulter, "Customer Evaluation of Retail Salespeople Utilizing the SOCO Scale: A Replication, Extension, and Application," *Journal of the Academy of Marketing Science*, Vol. 19, No. 4 (Fall 1991), pp. 347–352; Leslie M. Fine, "Refining the Concept of Salesperson Adaptability," *AMA Winter Educators' Proceedings* (1992), pp. 42–49; Dong Hwan Lee and Richard W. Olshavsky, "Adapting to What?: A Contingency Approach to Sales Interactions Based on a Comprehensive Model of Consumer Choice," *AMA Summer Educators' Proceedings* (1992), pp. 224–232; James A. Henley, Jr., and Danny R. Arnold, "Influence Strategies in Personal Selling: A Contingency Approach Based on the Communication/Social Style of the Potential Customer," in Robert L. King (ed.), *Marketing: Perspectives for the 1990s* (Richmond, Va.: Southern Marketing Association, 1992), pp. 265–270; and Harry A. Harmon and Gene Brown, "Antecedents and Consequences of Multiple Ambiguities of Salespeople: A Proposed Model," in King, *Marketing: Perspectives for the 1990s*, pp. 271–275. For an interesting recent book on the nature of selling as seen by an anthropologist, see Robert C. Prus, *Making Sales* (Newbury Park, Calif.: Sage, 1989).

11. Table 15–1 is adapted from Joseph W. Thompson, "A Strategy of Selling," in Steven J. Shaw and Joseph W. Thompson (eds.), *Salesmanship* (New York: Holt, Rinehart & Winston, 1966), pp. 13–25. For a detailed study of search tips of auto buyers, see David H. Furse, Girish N. Punj, and David W. Stewart, "A Typology of Individual Search Strategies among Purchasers of New Automobiles," *Journal of Consumer Research*, Vol. 10 (March 1984), pp. 417–431. See also Saul W. Gellerman, "The Tests of a Good Salesperson," *Harvard Business Review*, No. 3 (May–June 1990), pp. 64–69.

12. Arch G. Woodside and William J. Davenport, "The Effect of Salesman Similarity and Expertise on Consumer Purchasing Behavior," *Journal of Marketing Research*, Vol. 11 (May 1974), pp. 198–202. For recent findings, see also Lawrence A. Crosby, Kenneth R. Evans, and Deborah Cowles, "Relationship Quality in Services Selling: An Interpersonal Influence Perspective," *Journal of Marketing*, Vol. 54, No. 3 (July 1990), pp. 68–81; Cynthia R. Jasper and Michael L. Klassen, "Perceptions of Salespersons' Appearance and Evaluation of Job Performance," *Perceptual and Motor Skills*, Vol. 71 (1990), pp. 563–566; Pratibha A. Dabholkar, "Role of Affect and Need for Interaction in On-Site Service Encounters," *Advances in Consumer Research*, Vol. 19 (1992), pp. 563–569; Michael Guiry, "Consumer and Employee Roles in Service Encounters," *Advances in Consumer Research*, Vol. 19 (1992), pp. 666–672; Avraham Shama, "Service Selling and Buying: The Impact of Selected Seller and Buyer Characteristics," *AMA Summer Educators' Proceedings* (1992), pp. 563–567; Leslie M. Fine and David W. Schumann, "The Nature and Role of Salesperson Perceptions: The Interactive Effects of Salesperson/Customer Personalities," *Journal of Consumer Psychology*, Vol. 1, No. 3 (1992), pp. 285–296; Laura M. Milner, Dale D. Fodness, and Mark Speece, "Women in the Global Sales Force: A Call for Research," *AMA Summer Educators' Proceedings* (1992) pp. 359–365; James E. Ricks and Paul Hensel, "Exploratory Propositions Concerning the Role of Salesperson Empathy," in Robert L. King (ed.), *Marketing: Perspectives for the 1990s* (Richmond, Va.: Southern Marketing Association, 1992), pp. 333–336; Harper Roehm, Leslie M. Fine, and Peter R. Dickson, "'You're Great, I'm Great': Salesperson Self-Presentation Tactics," *AMA Winter Educators' Proceedings* (1993) pp. 245–251; and Peter H. Reingen and Jerome B. Kernan, "Social Perception and Interpersonal Influence: Some Consequences of the Physical Attractiveness Stereotype in a Personal Selling Setting," *Journal of Consumer Psychology*, Vol. 2, No. 1 (1993), pp. 25–38.

13. For an overview of findings, see Gilbert A. Churchill, Jr., Neil M. Ford, Steven W. Hartley, and Orville C. Walker, "The Determinants of Salesperson Performance: A Meta–Analysis," *Journal of Marketing Research*, Vol. 22 (May 1985), pp. 103–118. For recent findings and discussions, see William T. Ross, Jr. "Performance against Quota and the Call Selection Decision," *Journal of Marketing Research*, Vol. 28 (August 1991), pp. 296–306; Deborah Y. Cohn and Delia A. Sumrall, "Salesperson Initiation: Rookie to Producer," in Robert L. King (ed.), *Marketing: Perspectives for the 1990s* (Richmond, Va.: Southern Marketing Association, 1992), pp. 276–280; James T. Strong, Michael F. d'Amico, and Khalid M. Dubas, "A Comparison of Closing Techniques: Persuasion Theory Explanations and Preliminary Data," in King, *Marketing: Perspectives for the 1990s*, pp. 314–318; and Jhinuk Chowdhury, "The Motivational Impact of Sales Quotas on Effort," *Journal of Marketing Research*, Vol. 5, No. 1. February 1993, pp. 28–41.

14. Sylvia Porter, "Skills in Negotiation Can't Be Overlooked," *South Bend Tribune*, September 18, 1990, p. C6.

15. E. Scott Maynes, *Decision-Making for Consumers* (New York: Macmillan, 1976).

16. Walter J. Primeaux, "The Effect of Consumer Knowledge and Bargaining Strength on Final Selling Price," *Journal of Business*, October 1970. See also W. Wossen Kassaye, "The Role of Haggling in Marketing: An Examination of Buyer Behavior," *The Journal of Consumer Marketing*, Vol. 7, No. 4 (Fall 1990), pp. 53–62; and Hugh E. Kramer and Paul A. Herbig, "The Suq Model of Haggling: Who, What, When and Why?" *Journal of International Consumer Marketing*, Vol. 5, No. 2 (1993), pp. 55–68.

17. G. David Hughes, Joseph B. Juhasz, and Bruno Contini, "The Influence of Personality on the Bargaining Process," *Journal of Business*, October 1973, pp. 593–603. See also Marsha L. Richins, "An Analysis of Consumer Interaction Styles in the Marketplace," *Journal of Consumer Research*, Vol. 10 (June 1983), pp. 73–82; George Coan, Jr., "Rapport: Definition and Dimensions," *Advances in Consumer Research*, Vol. 11 (1984), pp. 333–336; Mark A. Pavelchak, "When Salespersons Are Typical: Does Stereotype Consistency Increase or Decrease Customers' Attention to Sales Presentations?" *AMA Summer Educators' Proceedings* (1991), pp. 549–557; Robert Baer and Rustan Kosenko, "Consumers' Belief in Their Ability to Judge the Truthfulness of Sales Claims," *Advances in Consumer Research*, Vol. 18 (1991), pp. 310–316; and Rosemary R. Lagace and Jule B. Gassenheimer, "An Exploratory Study of Trust and Suspicion toward Salespeople: Scale Validation and Replication," *AMA Winter Educators' Proceedings* (1991), pp. 121–127.

18. Kathleen Kerwin, "More and More No-Dicker Sticker," *Business Week*, September 28, 1992, p. 35; and Joseph B. White, "Dealer Plays Tag to Run after Sales," *The Wall Street Journal*, January 31, 1991, p. B1.

19. John R. Dorfman, "Special Sales Pitches Put Extra Cash in Brokers' Pockets," *The Wall Street Journal*, April 30, 1991, p. C1; and Alexandra Peers, "Commissions on Financial Products Are Often High–And Confusing," *The Wall Street Journal*, January 21, 1988,

p. 33. For the same issues in a related industry, see Mike Clary, "A Cash Bonus for Travel Agents," *Marketing Week*, July 17, 1989, p. 21. For broader discussions, see Robert Baer, "Overestimating Salesperson Truthfulness: The Fundamental Attribution Error," *Advances in Consumer Research*, Vol. 17 (1990), pp. 501–507; and Vince Howe, K. Douglas Hoffman, and Donald W. Hardigree, "The Relationship between Ethical and Customer-Oriented Behavior and Their Effects on the Selling of Complex Service," *AMA Winter Educators' Proceedings* Vol. 4 (1993) pp. 401–402.

20.   Warren G. Magnuson and Jean Carper, "Caveat Emptor," in D. A. Aaker and G. S. Day, (eds.), *Consumerism: Search for the Consumer Interest*, 4th ed. (New York: Free Press, 1982), pp. 267–278. See also Alan J. Resnik and Marjorie J. Caballero, "Exploring the Unthinkable: Do Marketers Manipulate?" *AMA Educators' Proceedings* (1984), pp. 332–336; Alan J. Dubinsky and Michael Levy, "Ethics in Retailing: Perceptions of Retail Salespeople," *Journal of the Academy of Marketing Science*, Vol. 13 (Winter 1985), pp. 1–16; Joseph A. Bellizzi and Robert E. Hite, "Supervising Unethical Salesforce Behavior," *Journal of Marketing*, Vol. 53 (April 1989), pp. 36–47; Nancy M. Ridgway and Scott A. Dawson, "Misinformation Provided by Retail Salespeople: An Overlooked Aspect of the Information Environment," *AMA Summer Educators' Proceedings* (1992), pp. 168–175; Brooke Hamilton and David Strutton, "A Philosophical Essay on Truth-Telling in the Personal Selling Role," in Robert L. King (ed.), *Marketing: Perspectives for the 1990s* (Richmond, Va.: Southern Marketing Association, 1992), pp. 305–309; and Douglas Hoffman and Vince Howe, "Ethical Issues in Services Marketing," in King, *Marketing: Perspectives for the 1990s*, pp. 406–410.

21.   Magnuson and Carper, "Caveat Emptor."

22.   *In the matter of Encyclopedia Britannica*, Inc., et al. (Docket 8908, 87 F.T.C. 453).

23.   Diane Henry, "FTC Tells Sears to Change Practice in Appliance Sales," *The New York Times*, October 22, 1976, p. A12.

24.   See, for example, *In the matter of William D. Campbell et al. t/a Rhode Island Carpets* (84 F.T.C. 567). For an interesting discussion of the related technique of "low balling," see William Motes, Reginald Brown, Hazel Ezell, and Gail Hudson, "The Influence of Low-Balling on Buyers' Compliance: Revisited," *Psychology & Marketing*, Vol. 3, No. 3 (Summer 1986), pp. 79–86. For a surprising discussion on bait and switch, see Eitan Gerstner and James D. Hess, "Can Bait and Switch Benefit Customers?" *Marketing Science*, Vol. 9, No. 2 (Spring 1990), pp. 114–124. For a broader look at this area, see Karl A. Boedecker, Fred W. Morgan, and Jeffrey J. Stoltman, "Legal Dimensions of Salespersons' Statements: A Review and Managerial Suggestions," *Journal of Marketing*, Vol. 55, No. 1 (January 1991), pp. 70–80.

25.   An excellent article in this regard is Cynthia J. Frey and Thomas C. Kinnear, "Legal Constraints and Marketing Research: Review and Call to Action," *Journal of Marketing Research*, Vol. 16 (August 1979), pp. 295–302. For broader issues on the responsibilities of researchers, see Alice M. Tybout and Gerald Zaltman, "Ethics in Marketing Research: Their Practical Relevance," *Journal of Marketing Research*, Vol. 11 (November 1974), pp. 357–368; Robert L. Day, "A Comment on Ethics in Marketing Research," *Journal of Marketing Research*, Vol. 12 (May 1975), pp. 232–233; and Alice M. Tybout and Gerald Zaltman, "A Reply to Comments on Ethics in Marketing Research," *Journal of Marketing Research*, Vol. 12 (May 1975), pp. 234–237.

Chapter 16

Advertising's Influences on Consumer Behavior

1.   Fred Danzig, "The Big Idea," *Advertising Age*, November 9, 1988, p. 16.

2.   "Oops! Marketers Blunder Their Way through the 'Herb Decade,'" *Advertising Age*, February 13, 1989, p. 3; and James Cox, "New Ads Aim to Whop McDonald's," *USA Today*, February 17, 1988, p. B1.

3.   Michael J. McCarthy, "Mind Probe: What Makes an Ad Memorable," *The Wall Street Journal*, March 22, 1991, p. B3.

4.   This framework is an extension of that provided in Russell H. Colley, *Defining Advertising Goals for Measured Advertising Results* (New York: Association of National Advertisers, 1961), pp. 61–68. For related discussions, see also Robert R. Johnson and Donald J. Messmer, "The Effect of Advertising on Hierarchical Stages in Vacation Destination Choice," *Journal of Advertising Research*, Vol. 31, No. 6 (December 1991), pp. 18–25; and Peter Kim, "Does Advertising Work: A Review of the Evidence," *The Journal of Consumer Marketing*, Vol. 9, No. 4 (Fall 1992), pp. 5–21.

5.   Ronald Alsop, "In TV Viewers' Favorite Ads, Offbeat Characters Were the Stars," *The Wall Street Journal*, March 3, 1988, p. 17.

6.   Jagdish Sheth, "The Measurement of Advertising Effectiveness: Some Theoretical Considerations," *Journal of Advertising*, Vol. 3 (1974), pp. 6–11. See also Josh McQueen, "The Different Ways Ads Work," *Journal of Advertising Research*, Vol. 30, No. 4 (August/September 1990), pp. RC13–RC16; and Arjun Chaudhuri, "A Theoretical Framework for Advertising," *AMA Summer Educators' Proceedings* (1992), pp. 442–446.

7.   Scott Hume, "Burger King Tinkers with 'Break the Rules,'" *Advertising Age*, September 10, 1990, p. 3.

8.   Ibid.

9.   Avery Abernethy and Herbert Rotfeld, "Zipping through TV Ads Is Old Tradition—But Viewers Are Getting Better at It," *Marketing News*, January 7, 1991, p. 6; Howard Schlossberg, "Case of the Missing TV Viewers: Everyone Knows They're Gone, but No One Knows Why," *Marketing News*, September 17, 1990, p. 1; Cathy J. Cobb-Walgren, "Tuning In and Turning Off: Trends in Television Viewing Behavior," in C. Haugtvedt and D. Rosen (eds.), *Proceedings of the Society for Consumer Psychology*, (Knoxville: D.W. Schumann, 1991), pp. 73–75; Dennis Kneale, "Zapping of TV Ads Appears Pervasive," *The Wall Street Journal*, April 25, 1988, p. 21; and Patricia A. Stout and Benedicta L. Burda, "Zipped Commericals: Are They Effective?" *Journal of Advertising*, Vol. 18, No. 4 (1989), pp. 23–32.

10.   William J. McGuire, "An Information Processing Model of Advertising Effectiveness," in H. Davis and A. Silk (eds.), *Behavioral and Management Sciences in Marketing* (New York: Ronald Press/John Wiley, 1978), p. 161. See also Brian Wansink and Michael L. Ray, "Estimating an Advertisement's Impact on One's Consumption of a Brand," *Journal of Advertising Research*, Vol. 32, No. 3 (May/June 1992), pp. 9–16.

11.   The Starch study was reported in sworn testimony in a Federal Trade Commission advertising case against the Firestone Tire and Rubber Company (81 F.T.C. 398). The study found that, of

persons who had been watching during the time that a commercial had been broadcast two hours before the interview, only 32 percent remembered having seen the average ad. When asked to identify the brand, only half of this group—or only 16 percent of the entire consumer sample—was able to identify the sponsoring brand correctly. One-fourth of this group believed that they knew the sponsor, then gave the wrong brand name! The other one-fourth remembered the contents, but didn't venture a guess as to which brand sponsored it. Commentators pointed out that this meant that the average advertiser was spending only one-sixth of his or her budget to communicate effectively even the most basic information about the brand, and was spending half of this amount to advance the cause of competing brands! More recent research using a slightly different "day after recall" identification method by Sami/Burke Research shows similar results (the numbers are not directly comparable due to different methods than Starch used: Burke scores show the average recall to be 21 percent). See Jeffrey A. Trachtenberg, "Viewer Fatigue?" *Forbes*, December 26, 1988, pp. 120–122. For further reading about advertising research and these types of issues, an extensive literature is available. See, for example, Kevin Celuch, "A Conceptual Model for Examining the Effects of Advertising Communications," *AMA Summer Educators' Proceedings* (1986), pp. 81–85; Surendra N. Singh and Catherine A. Cole, "Advertising Copy Testing in Print Media," in J. Leigh and C. Martin (eds.), *Journal of Current Issues and Research in Advertising*, Vol. 11 (Ann Arbor: University of Michigan, 1988), pp. 215–284; Susan E. Heckler, "Bridging the Gap: The Challenge of Integrating Consumer Behavior Research with the Practice of Advertising," *Advances in Consumer Research*, Vol. 15 (1988), pp. 265–268; David W. Stewart, "Measures, Methods, and Models in Advertising Research," *Journal of Advertising Research*, Vol. 29 (June–July 1989), pp. 54–60; Lauranne Buchanan and Amiya Basu, "The Impact of Advertising Copy Testing: Is the Advertiser Getting More Than He Bargained For?" *Advances in Consumer Research*, Vol. 16 (1989), pp. 479–484; Robert J. Lavidge, "Seven Tested Ways to Abuse and Misuse Strategic Advertising Research," *Marketing Research*, Vol. 2, No. 1 (March 1990), pp. 41–48; Robin A. Higie and Murphy A. Sewall, "Using Recall and Brand Preference to Evaluate Advertising Effectiveness," *Journal of Advertising Research*, Vol. 31, No. 2 (April/May 1991), pp. 56–63; David A. Aaker and Douglas M. Stayman, "Measuring Audience Perceptions of Commercials and Relating Them to Ad Impact," *Journal of Advertising Research*, Vol. 30, No. 4 (August/September 1990), pp. 7–18; Sharon Shavitt and Timothy C. Brock, "Delayed Recall of Copytest Responses: The Temporal Stability of Listed Thoughts," *Journal of Advertising*, Vol. 19, No. 4 (1990), pp. 6–17; Ian Fenwick and Marshall D. Rice, "Reliability of Continuous Measurement Copy-testing Methods," *Journal of Advertising Research*, Vol. 31, No. 1 (February/March 1991), pp. 23–29; Thomas J. Reynolds and Charles Gengler, "A Strategic Framework for Assessing Advertising: The Animatic vs. Finished Issue," *Journal of Advertising Research*, Vol. 31, No. 5 (October/November 1991), pp. 61–72; Gabriele S. Haberland and Peter A. Dacin, "The Development of a Measure to Assess Viewers' Judgments of the Creativity of an Advertisement: A Preliminary Study," *Advances in Consumer Research*, Vol. 19 (1992), pp. 817–825; Adam Finn, "Print Ad Readership Scores: Extending the Information Processing Perspective to Recall Scores," *AMA Winter Educators' Proceedings* (1992), Vol. 3, pp. 32–41; Ved Prakash, "Some Measurement Issues in Consumer Research," *Advances in Consumer Research*, Vol. 19 (1992), pp. 813–816; James A. Muncy and Roger Gomes, "The

Development of Advertising-centered versus Individual-centered Scales," *Journal of Current Issues and Research in Advertising*, Vol. 14, No. 1 (Spring 1992), pp. 59–66; Simeon Chow, Randall L. Rose, and Darral G. Clarke, "SEQUENCE: Structural Equations Estimation of New Copy Effectiveness," *Journal of Advertising Research*, Vol. 32, No. 4 (July/August 1992), pp. 60–72; Arjun Chaudhuri and Ross Buck, "Advertising Variables That Predict Consumer Responses," *AMA Summer Educators' Proceedings* (1992), pp. 19–25; and G. David Hughes, "Realtime Response Measures of Television Commercials: Reliability, Construct Validity, New Approaches to Wearout, and Potential Applications for Pretesting," Marketing Science Institute Working Paper 92–100, May 1992.

12. Testimony delivered in the Firestone Tire and Rubber Company case (81 F.T.C. 398).

13. Michael L. Ray, *Advertising and Communication Management* (Englewood Cliffs, N.J.; Prentice Hall, 1982), pp. 182–188. The original conceptualization of advertising's impact in low-involvement situations was developed by Herbert E. Krugman, "The Impact of Television Advertising: Learning without Involvement," *Public Opinion Quarterly*, Vol. 29 (1965), pp. 349–356; and Herbert E. Krugman, "Points of View: Limits of Attention to Advertising," *Journal of Advertising Research*, Vol. 28 (October/November 1988), pp. 47–49. For more recent discussions, see also David W. Lloyd and Kevin J. Clancy, "Television Program Involvement and Advertising Response," *The Journal of Consumer Marketing*, Vol. 8, No. 4 (Fall 1991), pp. 61–68; and Debra L. Stephens and J. Edward Russo, "Predicting Post-Advertisement Attitudes," Marketing Science Institute Working Paper 92–109, May 1992.

14. Adapted from Stephen S. Bell, "Evaluating the Effects of Consumer Advertising on Market Position over Time…," Marketing Science Institute Report 88–107, July 1988, pp. 18–19.

15. Adapted from ibid., pp. 12–13. For further reading on this interesting topic, see Robert E. Smith and William R. Swinyard, "Cognitive Response to Advertising and Trial: Belief Strength, Belief Confidence and Product Curiosity," *Journal of Advertising*, Vol. 17 (November 1988), pp. 3–14; Stephen J. Hoch and John Deighton, "Managing What Consumers Learn from Experience," *Journal of Marketing*, Vol. 53 (April 1989), pp. 1–20; John Deighton, Daniel Romer, and Josh McQueen, "Using Drama to Persuade," *Journal of Consumer Research*, Vol. 16, No. 3 (December 1989), pp. 335–343; Young-Won Ha and Stephen J. Hoch, "Ambiguity, Processing Strategy, and Advertising-Evidence Interactions," *Journal of Consumer Research*, Vol. 16, No. 3 (December 1989), pp. 354–360; Gregory W. Boller, "The Vicissitudes of Product Experience: 'Songs of Our Consuming Selves' in Drama Ads," *Advances in Consumer Research*, Vol. 17 (1990), pp. 621–626; and David G. Mick and Claus Buhl, "A Meaning-based Model of Advertising Experiences," *Journal of Consumer Research*, Vol. 19, No. 3 (December 1992), pp. 317–338.

16. For a recent, advanced overview of the ELM and its treatment of a large number of research issues, see Richard E. Petty, Rao Unnava, and Alan J. Strathman, "Theories of Attitude Change," in T. Robertson and H. Kassarjian (eds.), *Handbook of Consumer Behavior* (Englewood Cliffs, N.J.: Prentice Hall, 1991), pp. 241–280. For an interesting related topic in marketing, see Deborah J. Macinnis, Christine Moorman, and Bernard J. Jaworski, "Enhancing and Measuring Consumers' Motivation, Opportunity, and Ability to Process Brand Information from Ads," *Journal of Marketing*, October 1991, pp. 42–53. See also Jerry B. Gotlieb and John E. Swan, "An Application of the Elaboration Likelihood Model," *Journal of the Academy of Marketing Science*, Vol. 18, No. 3 (Summer 1990), pp. 221–228; David W. Schumann, Richard E. Petty, and D. Scott Clemons, "Predicting the Effectiveness of Different Strategies of Advertising Variation: A Test of the Repetition-Variation Hypotheses," *Journal of Consumer Research*, Vol. 17, No. 2 (September 1990), pp. 192–202; J. Craig Andrews and Terence A. Shimp, "Effects of Involvement, Argument Strength, and Source Characteristics on Central and Peripheral Processing of Advertising," *Psychology & Marketing*, Vol. 7, No. 3 (Fall 1990), pp. 195–214; four articles in *Advances in Consumer Research*, Vol. 17 (1990): Karen A. Machleit, Thomas J. Madden, and Chris T. Allen, "Measuring and Modeling Brand Interest as an Alternative Ad Effect with Familiar Brands," pp. 223–230; Catherine Cole, Richard Ettenson, Suzanne Reinke, and Tracy Schrader, "The Elaboration Likelihood Model (ELM): Replications, Extensions and Some Conflicting Findings," pp. 231–236; Judith E. Hennessey and Shirley C. Anderson, "The Interaction of Peripheral Cues and Message Arguments on Cognitive Responses to an Advertisement," pp. 237–243; and Amitava Chattopadhyay and Prakash Nedungadi, "Ad Affect, Brand Attitude and Choice: The Moderating Roles of Delay and Involvement," pp. 619–620; Joan Meyers-Levy, "Elaborating on Elaboration: The Distinction between Relational and Item-specific Elaboration," *Journal of Consumer Research*, Vol. 18, No. 3, (December 1991), pp. 358–367; David W. Schumann, Linda Wright, and Esther Thorson, "Initial Tests of the Selection-processing Model of Television Program Context Effects: Identifying and Measuring Scene Response Variables," in *Proceedings of the Society for Consumer Psychology*, (Clemson, S. C.: CtC Press, 1992), pp. 76–77; Scott A. Hawkins and Stephen J. Hoch, "Low-Involvement Learning: Memory without Evaluation," *Journal of Consumer Research*, Vol. 19, No. 2 (September 1992), pp. 212–225; Paul W. Miniard, Deepak Sirdeshmukh, and Daniel E. Innis, "Peripheral Persuasion and Brand Choice," *Journal of Consumer Research*, Vol. 19, No. 2 (September 1992), pp. 226–239; and Sunil Bhatla, "Understanding the Antecedents of Felt Involvement during Ad Processing," *AMA Winter Educators' Proceedings* (1993), pp. 340–346.

17.   For early discussions of the "Attitude toward the Ad" concept, see Terence A. Shimp, "Attitude toward the Ad as a Mediator of Consumer Brand Choice," *Journal of Advertising*, Vol. 10, No. 2 (1981), pp. 9–15 ff; and Andrew A. Mitchell and Jerry C. Olson, "Are Product Attribute Beliefs the Only Mediator of Advertising Effects on Brand Attitude?" *Journal of Marketing Research*, August 1981, pp. 318–332. For a recent critical discussion of the concept, see Larry Percy and John R. Rossiter, "Advertising Stimulus Effects: A Review," *Journal of Current Issues and Research in Advertising*, Vol. 14, No. 1 (Spring 1992), pp. 75–90. For recent findings, discussions, and extensions, see Pamela M. Homer, "The Mediating Role of Attitude toward the Ad: Some Additional Evidence," *Journal of Marketing Research*, Vol. 27 (February 1990), pp. 78–86; Paul W. Miniard, Sunil Bhatla, and Randall L. Rose, "On the Formation and Relationship of Ad and Brand Attitudes: An Experimental and Casual Analysis," *Journal of Marketing Research*, Vol. 27 (August 1990), pp. 290–303; Banwari Mittal, "The Relative Roles of Brand Beliefs and Attitude toward the Ad as Mediators of Brand Attitude," *Journal of Marketing Research*, Vol. 27 (May 1990), pp. 209–219; Thomas J. Olney, Morris B. Holbrook, and Rajeev Batra, "Consumer Responses to Advertising: The Effects of Ad Content,

Emotions, and Attitude toward the Ad on Viewing Time," *Journal of Consumer Research*, Vol. 17, No. 4 (March 1991), pp. 440–453; Mark A. Pavelchak, Meryl P. Gardner, and V. Carter Broach, "Effect of Ad Pacing and Optimal Level of Arousal on Attitude toward the Ad," *Advances in Consumer Research*, Vol. 18 (1991), pp. 94–99; Joseph Phelps and Esther Thorson, "Brand Familiarity and Product Involvement Effects on the Attitude toward an Ad–Brand Attitude Relationship," *Advances in Consumer Research*, Vol. 18 (1991), pp. 202–209; Larry Percy and John Rossiter, "The Role of Emotion in Processing Advertising," in C. Haugtvedt and D. Rosen (eds.), *Proceedings of the Society for Consumer Psychology* (Knoxville: D.W. Schumann, 1991), pp. 54–58; Karen A. Machleit and Arti Sahni, "The Impact of Measurement Context on the Relationship between Attitude toward the Ad and Brand Attitude for Familiar Brands," *Advances in Consumer Research*, Vol. 19 (1992), pp. 279–283; John P. Murry, Jr., John L. Lastovicka, and Surendra N. Singh, "Feeling and Liking Responses to Television Programs: An Examination of Two Explanations for Media-Context Effects," *Journal of Consumer Research*, Vol. 18, No. 4 (March 1992), pp. 441–451; Scott B. MacKenzie and Richard A. Spreng, "How Does Motivation Moderate the Impact of Central and Peripheral Processing on Brand Attitudes and Intentions?" *Journal of Consumer Research*, Vol. 18, No. 4 (March 1992), pp. 519–529; Amitava Chattopadhyay and Prakash Nedungadi, "Does Attitude toward the Ad Endure? The Moderating Effects of Attention and Delay," *Journal of Consumer Research*, Vol 19, No. 1 (June 1992), pp. 26–33; Darrel D. Muehling and Russell N. Laczniak, "An Examination of Factors Mediating and Moderating Advertising's Effect on Brand Attitude Formation," *Journal of Current Issues and Research in Advertising*, Vol. 14, No. 1 (Spring 1992), pp. 23–34; and Steven P. Brown and Douglas M. Stayman, "Antecedents and Consequences of Attitude toward the Ad: A Meta-analysis," *Journal of Consumer Research*, Vol. 19, No. 1 (June 1992), pp. 34–51.

18.   This study was conducted by the Advertising Research Foundation; see Russell I. Haley and Allan L. Baldinger, "The ARF Copy Research Validation Project," *Journal of Advertising Research*, Vol. 31, No. 2 (1991), pp. 11–32. This study has generated considerable interest in the advertising field; see, for example, the following three articles in *Journal of Advertising Research*, (March/April 1992): William A. Cook, "Editorial: Love, Hate, and Likability," pp. 7–9; Valentine Appel, "More on the Liking of Television Commercials," pp. 49–50; and William F. Greene, "Observations: What Drives Commercial Liking?" pp. 65–68.

19.   "Raisin Expectations," *Promote*, April 11, 1988, p. 7.

20.   Jennifer Lawrence, "P&G's Artzt on Ads: Crucial Investment," *Advertising Age*, October 28, 1991, p. 1.

21.   For brief descriptions of industry views concerning integrated marketing, see, for example, Timm Crull, "Nestle to Agencies: Shake Mindset," *Advertising Age*, May 3, 1993, p. 26; Scott Hume, "Burnett's Big Event: Integration Expands," *Advertising Age*, March 4, 1991, p. 27; Faye Rice, "A Cure for What Ails Advertising?" *Fortune*, December 16, 1991, pp. 119–122; Scott Hume, "Redefining Promotion's Role," *Advertising Age*, August 13, 1990, p. 54.

22.   The analysis of sales results from advertising and promotion can quickly become complex: it is the province of some of the best work in marketing science. For good articles aimed at a general audience, see Magid M. Abraham and Leonard M. Lodish,

"Getting the Most out of Advertising and Promotion," *Harvard Business Review*, Vol. 68, No. 3 (May–June 1990), pp. 50–60; John P. Jones, "The Double Jeopardy of Sales Promotions," *Harvard Business Review*, Vol. 68, No. 5 (September–October 1990), pp. 145–152; and George S. Low and Jakki J. Mohr, "The Advertising Sales Promotion Trade-off: Theory and Practice," Marketing Science Institute Report 92–127, October 1992. Other interesting discussions are presented in, for example, Robert Blattberg and Stephen Hoch, "Database Models and Managerial Intuition: 50% Model + 50% Manager," *Management Science*, Vol. 36 (August 1990), pp. 887–899; Scott Davis, J. Jeffrey Inman, and Leigh McAlister, "Promotion Has a Negative Effect on Brand Evaluations—Or Does It?" *Journal of Marketing Research*, Vol. 29 (February 1992), pp. 143–148; Peter Fader and Leonard Lodish, "A Cross-Category Analysis of Category Structure and Promotional Activity for Grocery Products," *Journal of Marketing*, Vol. 54 (October 1990), pp. 52–65; Aradhna Krishna, Imran Currim, and Robert Shoemaker, "Consumer Perceptions of Promotional Activity," *Journal of Marketing*, Vol. 55 (April 1991), pp. 4–16; and William Boulding, Eunkyu Lee, and Richard Staelin, "The Long-Term Differentiation Value of Marketing Communication Actions," Marketing Science Institute Report, 92–133, December 1992.

23. Skip Wollenberg, "ABC Seeks to Relax Advertising Guidelines," *Marketing News*, October 14, 1991, p. 5; Joanne Lipman, "ABC to Relax Longstanding Guidelines for Ad Content," *The Wall Street Journal*, September 5, 1991, p. B1; and William M. Weilbacher, *Advertising* (New York: Macmillan, 1979), pp. 264–265, 610–611. See also Patrick R. Parsons and Herbert J. Rotfeld, "Infomercials and Television Station Clearance Practices," *Journal of Public Policy & Marketing*, Vol. 9, 1990, pp. 62–72.

24. National Advertising Division, "Case Report" (New York: Council of Better Business Bureaus, July 15, 1983), pp. 20–23. See also Gordon E. Miracle and Terence R. Nevett, "Improving NAD/NARB Self-regulation of Advertising," *Journal of Public Policy & Marketing*, Vol. 7 (1988), pp. 114–126; Jean J. Boddewyn, "Advertising Self-Regulation: True Purpose and Limits," *Journal of Advertising*, Vol. 18 (November 1989), pp. 19–27; Herbert J. Rotfeld, Avery M. Abernethy, and Patrick R. Parsons, "Self-regulation and Television Advertising," *Journal of Advertising*, Vol. 19, No. 4 (1990), pp. 18–26; and Alison Masson, "Direct-to-Consumer Advertising: A Continuing Controversy," in R. N. Mayer (ed.), *Enhancing Consumer Choice* (Columbia, Mo.: American Council on Consumer Interests, 1991), pp. 159–168.

25. The debates on each of these issues often involve advanced quantitative analyses that are beyond the scope of this text. If you are interested in learning more about how each issue is treated, excellent discussions are provided in Mark S. Albion and Paul W. Farris, *The Advertising Controversy: Evidence on the Economic Effects of Advertising* (Boston: Auburn House, 1981). See also Gert Assmus, John U. Farley, and Donald R. Lehmann, "How Advertising Affects Sales: Meta-Analysis of Econometric Results," *Journal of Marketing Research*, Vol. 20 (February 1984), pp. 65–74; Robert L. Steiner, "Point of View: The Paradox of Increasing Returns of Advertising," *Journal of Advertising Research*, Vol. 27 (February/March 1987), pp. 45–53; and Siva K. Balasubramanian and V. Kumar, "Analyzing Variations in Advertising and Promotional Expenditures: Key Correlates in Consumer, Industrial, and Services Marketing," *Journal of Marketing*, Vol. 54, No. 2 (April 1990), pp. 57–68.

26. Raymond A. Bauer and Stephen A. Greyser, *Advertising in America: The Consumer View* (Boston: Research Division, Harvard Business School, 1968). For a recent national poll indicating similar results, see "Roper's America: On Advertising, More Good Than Bad," *Marketing Week*, August 7, 1989, p. 11. For recent findings on related issues, see also Robert E. Hite and Cynthia Fraser, "Meta-analyses of Attitudes toward Advertising by Professionals," *Journal of Marketing*, Vol. 52 (July 1988), pp. 95–105; John E. Calfee and Debra Jones Ringold, "Consumer Skepticism and Advertising Regulation: What Do the Polls Show?" *Advances in Consumer Research*, Vol. 15 (1988), pp. 244–248; J. Craig Andrews, "The Dimensionality of Beliefs toward Advertising in General," *Journal of Advertising*, Vol. 18 (November 1989), pp. 26–35; and Richard W. Pollay and Banwari Mittal, "Here's the Beef: Factors, Determinants, and Segments in Consumer Criticism of Advertising," *Journal of Marketing*, Vol. 57, No. 3 (July 1993), pp. 99–114.

27. Several of these categories were developed from the discussion in *Appraising the Economic and Social Effects of Advertising: Staff Report of the Marketing Science Institute* (Cambridge, Mass.: Marketing Science Institute, 1971). For further reading on this topic, see Richard W. Pollay, "The Distorted Mirror: Reflections on the Unintended Consequences of Advertising," *Journal of Marketing*, Vol. 50 (April 1986), pp. 18–36; Morris B. Holbrook, "Mirror, Mirror, on the Wall, What's Unfair in the Reflections on Advertising?" *Journal of Marketing*, Vol. 51, No. 3 (July 1987), pp. 95–103; Richard W. Pollay, "On the Value of Reflections on the Values in 'The Distorted Mirror'" *Journal of Marketing*, Vol. 51, No. 3 (July 1987), pp. 104–110; Geoffrey P. Lantos, "Advertising: Looking Glass or Molder of the Masses?" *Journal of Public Policy & Marketing*, Vol. 6 (1987), pp. 104–128; Donald P. Robin and R. Eric Reidenbach, "Social Responsibility, Ethics and Marketing Strategy: Closing the Gap between Concept and Application," *Journal of Marketing*, Vol. 51 (January 1987), pp. 44–58; James H. Barnes, Jr., and Michael J. Dotson, "An Exploratory Investigation into the Nature of Offensive Television Advertising," *Journal of Advertising*, Vol. 19, No. 3 (1990), pp. 61–69; E. Lincoln James and Bruce G. Vanden Bergh, "An Informational Content Comparison of Magazine Ads across a Response Continuum from Direct Response to Institutional Advertising," *Journal of Advertising*, Vol. 19, No. 2 (1990), pp. 23–29; Bruce L. Stern and Alan J. Resnik, "Information Content in Television Advertising: A Replication and Extension," *Journal of Advertising Research*, Vol. 31, No. 3 (June/July 1991), pp. 36–48; Marsha L. Richins, "Social Comparison and the Idealized Images of Advertising," *Journal of Consumer Research*, Vol. 18, No. 1 (June 1991), pp. 71–83; L. J. Shrum, Thomas C. O'Guinn, Richard J. Semenik, and Ronald J. Faber, "Processes and Effects in the Construction of Normative Consumer Beliefs: The Role of Television," *Advances in Consumer Research*, Vol. 18 (1991), pp. 755–763; Charles R. Taylor and Stephen W. Kopp, "Games, Contests, and Sweepstakes Run Afoul: A State Legal Disorder," *Journal of Public Policy & Marketing*, Vol. 10, No. 1 (Spring 1991), pp. 199–213; Denise Schoenbachler and Margaret U. Dsilva, "Persuasion and the News Media: Agenda Setting Effects on Consumer Behavior," in Robert L. King (ed.), *Marketing: Perspectives for the 1990s* (Richmond, Va.: Southern Marketing Association, 1992), pp. 83–88; Retha A. Price and Danny R. Arnold, "An Indexing System for the Analysis of Advertising Information Content," in King, *Marketing: Perspectives for the 1990s*, pp. 319–323; Barry Vacker, "Beauty and the Beast (of Advertising)," *Advances in Consumer Research*, Vol. 20 (1993), pp. 345–351; Marsha L. Richins,

"Materialism and the Idealized Images of Advertising," *AMA Winter Educators' Proceedings* (1993), pp. 53; and Diana L. Haytko and Erika Matulich, "The Conceptualization and Measurement of Consumer Attitudes toward Advertising in General," *AMA Winter Educators' Proceedings* (1993), pp. 411–419. For a discussion of a different set of "Seven Sins," see Clarke L. Caywood and Frederick W. Langrehr, "Definitional Issues Related to Using the Seven Sins and Seven Virtues as a Model for Advertising Analysis," in James H. Leigh and Claude R. Martin (eds.), *Journal of Current Issues and Research in Advertising*, Vol. 12 (Ann Arbor: University of Michigan, 1990), pp. 43–73.

For analyses of racial issues in advertising, see, for example, Robert E. Wilkes and Humberto Valencia, "Hispanics and Blacks in Television Commercials," *Journal of Advertising*, Vol. 18 (November 1989), pp. 19–25; William J. Qualls and David J. Moore, "Stereotyping Effects on Consumers' Evaluation of Advertising: Impact of Racial Differences between Actors and Viewers," *Psychology & Marketing*, Vol. 7, No. 2 (Summer 1990), pp. 135–151; Rita Snyder, James Freeman, and Susan Condray, "Magazine Ad Portrayal of Blacks: Gender and Readership Effects," in C. Haugtvedt and D. Rosen (eds.), *Proceedings of the Society for Consumer Psychology* (Knoxville, D. W. Schumann 1991), pp. 81–87; Tommy E. Whittler and Joan DiMeo, "Viewers' Reactions to Racial Cues in Advertising Stimuli," *Journal of Advertising Research*, Vol. 31, No. 6 (December 1991), pp. 37–46; Thaddeus H. Spratlen, "Targeting Blacks in Cigarette Advertising: Knowledge of Externalities Using Secondary Research," *AMA Winter Educators' Proceedings* (1992), Vol. 3, pp. 517–524; and Thomas H. Stevenson, "A Content Analysis of the Portrayal of Blacks in Trade Publication Advertising," *Journal of Current Issues and Research in Advertising*, Vol. 14, No. 1 (Spring 1992), pp. 67–74.

For recent discussions of gender issues in advertising, see, for example, Jill Hicks Ferguson, Peggy J. Kreshel, and Spencer F. Tinkham, "In the Pages of *Ms.*: Sex Role Portrayals of Women in Advertising," *Journal of Advertising*, Vol. 19, No. 1 (1990), pp. 40–51; John Mager and Linda Summers-Hoskins, "The Portrayal of Women in Advertising: A Review and Critique," *AMA Winter Educators' Proceedings* (1991), pp. 150–157; John B. Ford, Michael S. LaTour, and William J. Lundstrom, "Contemporary Women's Evaluation of Female Role Portrayals in Advertising," *The Journal of Consumer Marketing*, Vol. 8, No. 1 (Winter 1991), pp. 15–28; Nancy Artz and Alladi Venkatesh, "Gender Representation in Advertising," *Advances in Consumer Research*, Vol. 18 (1991), pp. 618–623; Julia M. Bristor and Eileen Fischer, "Feminist Thought: Implications for Consumer Research," *Journal of Consumer Research*, Vol. 19, No. 4 (March 1993), pp. 518–536; Elizabeth C. Hirschman, "Ideology in Consumer Research, 1980 and 1990: A Marxist and Feminist Critique," *Journal of Consumer Research*, Vol. 19, No. 4 (March 1993), pp. 537–555; and Barbara B. Stern, "Feminist Literary Criticism and the Deconstruction of Ads: A Postmodern View of Advertising and Consumer Responses," *Journal of Consumer Research*, Vol. 19, No. 4 (March 1993), pp. 556–566.

For discussions of sex in advertising, see, for example, Jessica Severn, George E. Belch, and Michael A. Belch, "The Effects of Sexual and Non-sexual Advertising Appeals and Information Level on Cognitive Processing and Communication Effectiveness," *Journal of Advertising*, Vol. 19, No. 1 (1990), pp. 14–22; Michael S. LaTour, "Female Nudity in Print Advertising: An Analysis of Gender Differences in Arousal and Ad Response," *Psychology & Marketing*, Vol. 7, No. 1 (Spring 1990), pp. 65–81; Michael S. LaTour, Robert E.

Pitts, and David C. Snook-Luther, "Female Nudity, Arousal, and Ad Response: An Experimental Investigation," *Journal of Advertising*, Vol. 19, No. 4 (1990), pp. 51–62; and Barbara B. Stern, "Two Pornographies: A Feminist View of Sex in Advertising," *Advances in Consumer Research*, Vol. 18 (1991), pp. 384–391.

For heated debates about cigarette advertising and related issues, see the following three articles in the *Journal of Public Policy & Marketing*, Vol. 8 (1989): Debra Jones Ringold and John E. Calfee, "The Information Content of Cigarette Advertising: 1926–1986," pp. 1–23; Joel B. Cohen, "Counting Advertising Assertions to Assess Regulatory Policy: When It Doesn't Add Up," pp. 24–29; and Richard W. Pollay, "Filters, Flavors…Flim-Flam, Too! On 'Health Information' and Policy Implications in Cigarette Advertising," pp. 30–39; and the response by the original authors, Debra Jones Ringold and John E. Calfee, " What Can We Learn from the Informational Content of Cigarette Advertising? A Reply and Further Analysis," *Journal of Public Policy & Marketing*, Vol. 9, (1990), pp. 30–41; See also the following three papers in *Advances in Consumer Research*, Vol. 17 (1990): John E. Calfee and Debra Jones Ringold, "What Would Happen If Cigarette Advertising and Promotion Were Banned?" pp. 474–479; Paul N. Bloom, "Banning Cigarette Advertising: A Cure That Will Aggravate the Disease," pp. 480–481; and Edward T. Popper, "The Regulation of Cigarette Advertising in the United States: Some Alternatives," pp. 482–487; Gary B. Wilcox, "Cigarette Brand Advertising and Consumption in the United States: 1949–1985," *Journal of Advertising Research*, Vol. 31, No. 4 (August/September 1991), pp. 61–67; Rick Andrews and George R. Franke, "The Determinants of Cigarette Consumption: A Meta-analysis," *Journal of Public Policy & Marketing*, Vol. 10, No. 1 (Spring 1991), pp. 81–100; Karen Whitehall King, Leonard N. Reid, Young Sook Moon, and Debra Jones Ringold, "Changes in the Visual Imagery of Print Cigarette Ads, 1954–1986," *Journal of Public Policy and Marketing*, Vol. 10, No. 1 (Spring 1991), pp. 63–80; Leopoldo G. Arias-Bolzmann and John C. Mowen, "Absurd Images in Cigarette Advertisements: An Empirical Investigation," in Robert L. King (ed.), *Marketing: Perspectives for the 1990s* (Richmond, Va.: Southern Marketing Association, 1992), pp. 295–299; and Michael B. Mazis, Debra Jones Ringold, Elgin S. Perry, and Daniel W. Denman, "Perceived Age and Attractiveness of Models in Cigarette Advertisements," *Journal of Marketing*, Vol. 56, No. 1 (January 1992), pp. 22–37.

For historical analyses and related discussions, see Barbara L. Bross and Jagdish N. Sheth, "Time-oriented Advertising: A Content Analysis of United States Magazine Advertising, 1890–1988," *Journal of Marketing*, Vol. 53, No. 4 (October 1989), pp. 76–83; three articles in *AMA Summer Educators' Proceedings* (1991): Erik L. Olson, "The Unintended Negative Consequences of Advertising during the Early Years of the Modern Advertising Era: An Editorial Content Analysis of Popular Magazines: 1900–1940," pp. 726–727; T. N. Somasundaram and C. David Light, "A Cross-cultural and Media Specific Analysis of Student Attitudes toward Advertising," pp. 669–677; and Jagdip Singh, "Consumer Alienation and Discontent: A Review and Prospectus," pp. 678–682; and A. N. M. Waheeduzzaman, "Changing Pattern of Car Advertisements in Magazines: The Past 30 Years," *AMA Summer Educators' Proceedings* (1992), pp. 121–129.

28. The classic paper on this topic is Carl Hovland and Walter Weiss, "The Influence of Source Credibility on Communication Effectiveness," *Public Opinion Quarterly*, Vol. 15 (1951), pp. 635–650.

For insights and debate on experimental methods and results, see R. Dholakia and B. Sternthal, "Highly Credible Sources: Persuasive Facilitators or Persuasive Liabilities?" *Journal of Consumer Research*, Vol. 3 (1977), pp. 223–232; Thomas J. Stanley, "Are Highly Credible Sources Persuasive?" *Journal of Consumer Research*, Vol. 5 (1978), pp. 66–67; and B. Sternthal and R. Dholakia, "Rejoinder," *Journal of Consumer Research*, Vol. 5 (1978); pp. 67–69. For recent developments, see Pamela M. Homer and Lynn R. Kahle, "Source Expertise, Time of Source Identification, and Involvement in Persuasion: An Elaborative Processing Perspective," *Journal of Advertising*, Vol. 19, No. 1 (1990), pp. 30–39; Marvin E. Goldberg and Jon Hartwick, "The Effects of Advertiser Reputation and Extremity of Advertising Claim on Advertising Effectiveness," *Journal of Consumer Research*, Vol. 17, No. 2 (September 1990), pp. 172–179; S. Ratneshwar and Shelly Chaiken, "Comprehension's Role in Persuasion: The Case of Its Moderating Effect on the Persuasive Impact of Source Cues," *Journal of Consumer Research*, Vol. 18, No. 1 (June 1991), pp. 52–62; three articles in *Advances in Consumer Research*, Vol. 19 (1992): Michel Tuan Pham, "Effects of Involvement, Arousal, and Pleasure on the Recognition of Sponsorship Stimuli," pp. 85–93; Jean-Charles Chebat, Michel Laroche, Pierre Filiatrault, and Daisy Baddoura, "Effects of Source Likability on Attitude Change through Message Repetition," pp. 353–358; and Barry Vacker, "The Marlboro Man as a 20th Century David: A Philosophical Inquiry into the Aristotelian Aesthetic of Advertising," pp. 746–755; Robert A. Peterson, William A. Wilson, and Steven P. Brown, "Effects of Advertised Customer Satisfaction Claims on Consumer Attitudes and Purchase Intention," *Journal of Advertising Research*, (March/April 1992), pp. 34–40; Timothy B. Heath, David L. Mothersbaugh, and Michael S. McCarthy, "Spokesperson Effects in High Involvement Markets," *Advances of Consumer Research*, Vol. 20 (1993), pp. 704–708; and Elizabeth J. Wilson and Daniel L. Sherrel, "Source Effects in Communication and Persuasion Research: A Meta-analysis of Effect Size," *Journal of the Academy of Marketing Science*, Vol. 21, No. 2 (Spring 1993), pp. 101–112.

29. See, for example, W. Benoy Joseph, "The Credibility of Physically Attractive Communicators: A Review," *Journal of Advertising*, Vol. 11, No. 3 (1982), pp. 15–23; Michael B. Mazis, Debra Jones Ringold, Elgin S. Perry, and Daniel W. Denman, "Perceived Age and Attractiveness of Models in Cigarette Advertisements," *Journal of Marketing*, Vol. 56, No. 1 (January 1992), pp. 22–37; Judy Cohen, "White Consumer Response to Asian Models in Advertising," *The Journal of Consumer Marketing*, Vol. 9, No. 2 (Spring 1992), pp. 17–28; and Anne M. Brumbaugh, "Physical Attractiveness and Personality in Advertising: More Than Just a Pretty Face?," *Advances in Consumer Research*, Vol. 20 (1993), pp. 155–158.

30. The classic overviews of research in this area are C. I. Hovland, I. L. Janis, and H. H. Kelley, *Communication and Persuasion* (New Haven, Conn.: Yale University Press, 1953), and Dorwin Cartwright, "Some Principles of Mass Persuasion: Selected Findings of Research on the Sale of United States War Bonds," *Human Relations*, Vol. 1 (1949), pp. 253–267.

For more recent comprehensive overviews of findings and approaches, see Kjell Gronhaug, Olav Kvitastein, and Sigmund Gronmo, "Factors Moderating Advertising Effectiveness As Reflected in 333 Tested Advertisements," *Journal of Advertising Research*, Vol. 31, No. 5 (October/November 1991), pp. 42–50; and Larry Percy and John R. Rossiter, "Advertising Stimulus Effects: A

Review," *Journal of Current Issues and Research in Advertising*, Vol. 14, No. 1 (Spring 1992), pp. 75–90.

For recent developments in specific topics, see also Punam Anand and Brian Sternthal, "Ease of Message Processing as a Moderator of Repetition Effects in Advertising," *Journal of Marketing Research*, Vol. 27 (August 1990), pp. 345–353; Meera P. Venkatraman, Deborah Marlino, Frank R. Kardes, and Kimberly B. Sklar, "The Interactive Effects of Message Appeal and Individual Differences on Information Processing and Persuasion," *Psychology & Marketing*, Vol. 7, No. 2 (Summer 1990), pp. 85–96; six papers in *Advances in Consumer Research*, Vol. 17 (1990): Barbara B. Stern, "Beauty and Joy in Metaphorical Advertising: The Poetic Dimension," pp. 71–77; Manoj Hastak and John-Won Park, "Mediators of Message Sidedness Effects on Cognitive Structure for Involved and Uninvolved Audiences," pp. 329–336; Karen A. Berger and Robert F. Gilmore, "An Introduction to Semantic Variables in Advertising Messages," pp. 643–650; Siva K. Balasubramanian, "Temporal Variations in the Evaluation of Television Advertisements: The Role of Key Nonverbal Cues," pp. 651–657; Edward F. McQuarrie, "How Does an Advertisement Mean—Cue, Claim, Metaphor, Resonance?" pp. 658–661; and James Ward and William Gaidis, "Metaphor in Promotional Communication: A Review of Research on Metaphor Comprehension and Quality," pp. 636–642; Melvin R. Crask and Henry A. Laskey, "A Positioning-based Decision Model for Selecting Advertising Messages," *Journal of Advertising Research*, Vol. 30, No. 4 (August/September 1990), pp. 32–38; Carolyn L. Costley and Duane DeWald, "Cue Modality: Video and Audio Effects on Recall," *Advances in Consumer Research*, Vol. 18 (1991), pp. 819–825; three articles in *AMA Summer Educators' Proceedings* (1991): John E. Weiss and Jakki Mohr, "Communication Style: Looking beyond Content in Designing Influence Strategies," pp. 33–45; Arch G. Woodside and Richard Brookes, "Advertising Effects on Consumer Awareness and Purchase Decisions at Different Stages of the Product Life Cycle," pp. 438–447; and Knog Fah Cheng, "The Effects of Product-Celebrity Congruency and Endorsement Strength on Cognitive Responses," pp. 667–668; Paul M. Herr and Russell H. Fazio, "On the Effectiveness of Repeated Positive Expressions as an Advertising Strategy," *Advances in Consumer Research*, Vol. 18 (1991), pp. 30–32; Gordon L. Patzer, "Multiple Dimensions of Performance for 30-Second and 15-Second Commercials," *Journal of Advertising Research*, Vol. 31, No. 4 (August/September) 1991, pp. 18–25; James W. Peltier and John A. Schibrowsky, "The Relationship between Distractor Similarity and the Recognition of Print Advertisements," *Advances in Consumer Research*, Vol. 19 (1992), pp. 94–100; Lydia J. Price, "The Effects of Message Valence on Inferential Processes," *Advances in Consumer Research*, Vol. 19 (1992), pp. 359–365; V. Carter Broach, Jr., Thomas J. Page, Jr., and R. Dale Wilson, "TV Program Effects on Commercial Position: The Role of Program Pleasure," *AMA Winter Educators' Proceedings* (1992), Vol. 3, pp. 23–26; Larry Percy, "Thoughts on the Importance of Psycholinguistics to the Understanding of Effective Advertising Communication," *Advances in Consumer Research*, Vol. 19 (1992), pp. 268–269; Tina M. Lowrey, "The Relation between Syntactic Complexity and Advertising Persuasiveness," *Advances in Consumer Research*, Vol. 19 (1992), pp. 270–274; Slimen Saliba, "Using Syntax to Direct Processing Resources," *Advances in Consumer Research*, Vol. 19 (1992), p. 275; Lynn J. Jaffe, Linda F. Jamieson, and Paul D. Berger, "Impact of Comprehension, Positioning, and Segmentation on Advertising Response," *Journal of Advertising Research*, Vol. 32 No. 3 (May/June 1992), pp. 24–33;

J. Craig Andrews, Syed H. Akhter, Srinivas Durvasula, and Darrel D. Muehling, "The Effects of Advertising Distinctiveness and Message Content Involvement on Cognitive and Affective Responses to Advertising," *Journal of Current Issues and Research in Advertising,* Vol. 14, No. 1 (Spring 1992), pp. 45–58; Edward F. McQuarrie and David G. Mick, "On Resonance: A Critical Pluralistic Inquiry into Advertising Rhetoric," *Journal of Consumer Research,* Vol. 19, No. 2 (September 1992), pp. 180–197; Lalita A. Manrai, V. Carter Broach, and Ajay K. Manrai, "Program Induced Contextual Effects in Processing of Embedded Commericals: An Integrated Approach," in T. J. Page, Jr. and S. E. Middlestadt (eds.), *Proceedings of the Society for Consumer Psychology,* (Clemson, S.C.: CtC Press, 1992), pp. 69–75; Surendra N. Singh and Catherine A. Cole, "The Effects of Length, Content, and Repetition on Television Commercial Effectiveness," *Journal of Marketing Research,* February 1993, pp. 91–104; and Arjun Chaudhuri and Ross Buck, "The Relationship of Advertising Variables to Analytic and Syncretic Cognitions," *AMA Winter Educators' Proceedings* (1993), pp. 193–198.

31. Raymond R. Burke, Arvind Rangaswamy, Jerry Wind, and Jehoshua Eliashberg, "A Knowledge-based System for Advertising Design," *Marketing Science,* Vol. 9, No. 3 (Summer 1990), pp. 212–229.

32. Fear appeals are discussed and reviewed in Michael L. Ray and William Wilkie, "Fear: The Potential of an Appeal Neglected by Marketing," *Journal of Marketing,* Vol. 34 (January 1970), pp. 54–62; and Brian Sternthal and C. Samuel Craig, "Fear Appeals: Revisited and Revised," *Journal of Consumer Research,* Vol. 1 (December 1974), pp. 22–34. For further insights and recent results, see also John F. Tanner, Jr., James B. Hunt, and David R. Eppright, "The Protection Motivation Model: A Normative Model of Fear Appeals," *Journal of Marketing,* Vol. 55, No. 3 (July 1991), pp. 36–45; and Ken Chapman, "Fear Appeal Research: Perspective and Application," *AMA Summer Educators' Proceedings* (1992), pp. 1–9.

The use of humorous appeals is discussed and reviewed in Brian Sternthal and C. Samuel Craig, "Humor in Advertising," *Journal of Marketing,* Vol. 37 (October 1973), pp. 12–18; and P. Kelly and P. J. Solomon, "Humor in Television Advertising," *Journal of Advertising,* Vol. 4 (1975), pp. 33–35. For recent discussions and results, see, for example, Cliff Scott, David M. Klein, and Jennings Bryant, "Consumer Response to Humor in Advertising: A Series of Field Studies Using Behavioral Observation," *Journal of Consumer Research,* Vol. 16, No. 4 (March 1990), pp. 498–501; Amitava Chattopadhyay and Kunal Basu, "Humor in Advertising: The Moderating Role of Prior Brand Evaluation," *Journal of Marketing Research,* Vol. 27 (November 1990), pp. 466–476; George M. Zinkhan and Betsy D. Gelb, "Repetition, Social Settings, Perceived Humor, and Wearout," *Advances in Consumer Research,* Vol. 17 (1990), pp. 438–441; Marc G. Weinberger and Leland Campbell, "The Use and Impact of Humor in Radio Advertising," *Journal of Advertising Research,* Vol. 30, No. 6 (December 1990/January 1991), pp. 44–52; Yong Zhang and George M. Zinkhan, "Humor in Television Advertising: The Effects of Repetition and Social Setting," *Advances in Consumer Research,* Vol. 18 (1991), pp. 813–818; Stephen M. Smith, "Does Humor in Advertising Enhance Systematic Processing?" *Advances in Consumer Research,* Vol. 20 (1993), pp. 155–158; and Paul Surgi Speck and Mary Jane Burns, "Gender Effects on Humor Appreciation: Implications for Advertising," *AMA Summer Educators' Proceedings* (1991), pp. 219–228.

Much research has focused on receiver factors as well. See, for example, Durairaj Maheswaran and Brian Sternthal, "The Effects of Knowledge, Motivation, and Type of Message on Ad Processing and Product Judgments," *Journal of Consumer Research,* Vol. 17, No. 1 (June 1990), pp. 66–73; Rajeev Batra and Douglas M. Stayman, "The Role of Mood in Advertising Effectiveness," *Journal of Consumer Research,* Vol. 17, No. 2 (September 1990), pp. 203–214; Kevin Lane Keller, "Memory and Evaluation Effects in Competitive Advertising Environments," *Journal of Consumer Research,* Vol. 17, No. 4 (March 1991), pp. 463–476; Punam Anand and Brian Sternthal, "The Effects of Program Involvement and Ease of Message Counterarguing on Advertising Persuasiveness," *Journal of Consumer Psychology,* Vol. 1, No. 3 (1992), pp. 225–238; Mark A. Pavelchak, John H. Antil, and James M. Munch, "Why Do People Recall TV Ads? A Comparison of Viewer Beliefs and Objective Contextual Determinants of Recall," *AMA Winter Educators' Proceedings* (1993), pp. 179–186; Alice A. Wright and Richard J. Lutz, "Effects of Advertising and Experience on Brand Judgments: A Rose by Any Other Frame...," *Advances in Consumer Research,* Vol. 20 (1993), pp. 165–169; and David B. Wooten and Tiffany Galvin, "A Preliminary Examination of the Effects of Context-induced Felt Ethnicity on Advertising Effectiveness," *Advances in Consumer Research,* Vol. 20 (1993), pp. 253–256. For additional related perspectives, see also Donna L. Hoffman and Rajeev Batra, "Viewer Response to Programs: Dimensionality and Concurrent Behavior," *Journal of Advertising Research,* Vol. 31, No. 4 (August/September) 1991, pp. 46–60; Deborah E. Rosen, David W. Schumann, and Jennifer Grayson, "Attention to Television Programs and Commercials: A Viewer Response Approach," in C. Haugtvedt and D. Rosen (eds.), *Proceedings of the Society for Consumer Psychology* (Knoxville: D.W. Schumann, 1991), pp. 98–104; David Glen Mick, "Levels of Subjective Comprehension in Advertising Processing and Their Relations to Ad Perceptions, Attitudes, and Memory," *Journal of Consumer Research,* Vol. 18, No. 4 (March 1992), pp. 411–424; and Michael R. Solomon and Basil G. Englis, "Consumption Constellations: Implications for Advertising Strategy," in T. J. Page, Jr., and S. E. Middlestadt (eds.), *Proceedings of the Society for Consumer Psychology,* (Clemson, S.C.: CtC Press, 1992), pp. 23–30.

33. The topic of comparison (comparative) advertising is interesting in a number of respects. To trace the development of work in this area, see, for example, William L. Wilkie and Paul W. Farris, "Comparison Advertising: Problems and Potential," *Journal of Marketing,* Vol. 39 (November 1975), pp. 7–15; Stephen B. Ash and Chou-Hou Wee, "Comparative Advertising: A Review with Implications for Further Research," *Advances in Consumer Research,* Vol. 10 (1983), pp. 370–376; Bruce Buchanan and Doron Goldman, "Us vs. Them: The Minefield of Comparative Ads," *Harvard Business Review,* Vol. 67, No. 3 (May–June 1989), pp. 38–53; John C. Rogers and Terrell G. Williams, "Comparative Advertising Effectiveness: Practitioners' Perceptions versus Academic Research Findings," *Journal of Advertising Research,* Vol. 29, No. 5 (October/November 1989), pp. 22–37; and Darrel D. Muehling, Donald E. Stem, Jr., and Peter Raven, "Comparative Advertising: Views from Advertisers, Agencies, Media, and Policy Makers," *Journal of Advertising Research,* Vol. 29, No. 5 (October/November 1989), pp. 38–48. For recent findings and discussions, see Caryn L. Beck-Dudley and Terrell G. Williams, "Legal and Public Policy Implications for the Future of

Comparative Advertising: A Look at U-Haul vs. Jartran," *Journal of Public Policy & Marketing*, Vol. 8 (1989), pp. 124–142; Michael B. Bixby and Douglas J. Lincoln, "Legal Issues Surrounding the Use of Comparative Advertising: What the Non-Prescriptive Drug Industry Has Taught Us," *Journal of Public Policy & Marketing*, Vol. 8 (1989), pp. 143–160; Darrel D. Muehling, Jeffrey J. Stoltman, and Sanford Grossbart, "The Impact of Comparative Advertising on Levels of Message Involvement," *Journal of Advertising*, Vol. 19, No. 4 (1990), pp. 41–50; Cornelia Pechmann and David W. Stewart, "The Effects of Comparative Advertising on Attention, Memory, and Purchase Intentions," *Journal of Consumer Research*, Vol. 17, No. 2 (September 1990), pp. 180–191; Beth A. Walker and Helen H. Anderson, "Reconceptualizing Comparative Advertising: A Framework and Theory of Effects," *Advances in Consumer Research*, Vol. 18 (1991), pp 342–347; Cornelia Pechmann and S. Ratneshwar, "The Use of Compartative Advertising for Brand Positioning: Association versus Differentiation," *Journal of Consumer Research*, Vol. 18, No. 2 (September 1991), pp. 145–160; Cornelia Pechmann and David W. Stewart, "How Direct Comparative Ads and Market Share Affect Brand Choice," *Journal of Advertising Research*, Vol. 31, No. 6 (December 1991), pp. 47–55; Kathy L. Pettit-O'Malley and Mark S. Johnson, "Differentiative Comparative Advertising: Some Positive Results Revealed by Measurement of Simutaneous Effects on the Ad-Sponsoring and Comparison Brands," *Journal of Current Issues and Research in Advertising*, Vol. 14, No. 1 (Spring 1992), pp. 35–44; and Tahi J. Gnepa, "An Empirical Investigation of Explicit Verbal and Visual References to Competition in Magazine Advertisements," in Robert L. King (ed.), *Marketing: Perspectives for the 1990s* (Richmond, Va.: Southern Marketing Association, 1992), pp. 300–304.

Chapter 17

Consumer Decisions (I): Prepurchase Processes

1. These quotes were provided by courtesy of Professor Patrick E. Murphy, University of Notre Dame.

2. Jennifer Alter, "Sales of Tampons Dip 20%," *Advertising Age*, December 22, 1980, pp. 2ff. See also Raymond R. Burke, Jaewun Cho, Wayne S. DeSarbo, and Vijay Mahajan, "The Impact of Product-related Announcements on Consumer Purchase Intentions," *Advances in Consumer Research*, Vol. 17 (1990), pp. 342–350; David P. Fan and Carol L. Shaffer, "Effects of the Mass Media News on Trends in the Consumption of Caffeine-Free Colas," *Advances in Consumer Research*, Vol. 17 (1990), pp. 406–414; and Mitch Griffin, Barry J. Babin, and Jill S. Attaway, "An Empirical Investigation of the Impact of Negative Public Publicity on Consumer Attitudes and Intentions," *Advances in Consumer Research*, Vol. 18 (1991), pp. 334–341.

3. Laurie Freeman, "Sales of Aspirin Soar after Study," *Advertising Age*, March 28, 1988, p. 3. See also Ronald J. Adams and Kenneth M. Jennings, "Media Advocacy: Case Study of Philip Sokolof's Cholesterol Awareness Campaigns," *The Journal of Consumer Affairs*, Vol. 27, No. 1 (Summer 1993), pp. 145–165.

4. John A. Howard, *Consumer Behavior: Application of Theory* (New York: McGraw-Hill, 1977); and John A. Howard and Jagdish N. Sheth, *The Theory of Buyer Behavior* (New York: John Wiley & Sons, 1969).

5. As noted in earlier chapters, the decision process perspective has had an enormous impact on consumer behavior thought and research. Among the most influential proponents of this approach were James Engel, David Kollatt, and Roger Blackwell. Other influential early models incorporating a decision process perspective included those by Franco Nicosia, by John Howard and Jagdish Sheth, and by Flemming Hansen. See, for example, James F. Engel, David T. Kollat, and Roger D. Blackwell, *Consumer Behavior*, 2d ed. (New York: Holt, Rinehart & Winston, 1973); Francesco M. Nicosia, *Consumer Decision Processes: Marketing and Advertising Implications* (Englewood Cliffs, N.J.: Prentice Hall, 1966); Howard and Sheth, *The Theory of Buyer Behavior*; and Flemming Hansen, *Consumer Choice Behavior: A Cognitive Theory* (New York: Free Press, 1972).

See, however, Richard W. Olshavsky and Donald H. Granbois, "Consumer Decision Making—Fact or Fiction?" *Journal of Consumer Research*, Vol. 6 (September 1979), pp. 93–100; a comment on this article by Michael Ursic, "Consumer Decision Making—Fact or Fiction?" *Journal of Consumer Research*, Vol. 7 (December 1980), pp. 331–333; and the rejoinder by the authors on page 33 of the same volume; and Richard W. Olshavsky, "Toward a More Comprehensive Theory of Choice," *Advances in Consumer Research*, Vol. 12, (1985), pp. 465–470.

6. "Marketing Briefs," *Marketing News*, August 31, 1984, p. 27. For related readings, see Girish Punj and Narasimhan Srinivasan, "Influence of Problem Recognition on Search and Other Decision Process Variables: A Framework for Analysis," *Advances in Consumer Research*, Vol. 19 (1992), pp. 491–497; and Gordon C. Bruner II and Richard J. Pomazal, "Problem Recognition: The Crucial First Stage of the Consumer Decision Process," *The Journal of Product & Brand Management*, Vol. 1, No. 2 (Spring 1992), pp. 70–80.

7. Lee W. Dyer, "Display Contest Adds Big Slice to Cheese Sales," *Progressive Grocer*, Vol. 60, No. 6 (June 1981), pp. 89–94.

8. Lee W. Dyer, "How to Win Display Contests . . . and Win Extra Sales Too!" *Progressive Grocer*, Vol. 60, No. 9 (September 1981), pp. 130–132.

9. See Lauranne Buchanan and Wanru Su, "Coping with the Uncertainty of Consumer Markets," *Advances in Consumer Research*, Vol. 15 (1988), pp. 396–402; Dipak C. Jain and Naufel J. Vilcassim, "Investigating Household Purchase Timing Decisions: A Conditional Hazard Function Approach," *Marketing Science*, Vol. 10, No. 1 (Winter 1991), pp. 1–23; Eric Greenleaf and Donald Lehmann, "Causes of Delay in Consumer Decision Making: An Exploratory Study," *Advances in Consumer Research*, Vol. 18 (1991), pp. 470–475; and Ziv Carmon, "Recent Studies of Time in Consumer Behavior," *Advances in Consumer Research*, Vol. 18 (1991), pp. 703–705.

10. Adrienne Ward, "Americans Step into a New Fitness Market," *Advertising Age*, December 3, 1990, p. 33; Jon Berry, "Owens Dusts Off 'Energy Crunch' Ads As Oil Price Climbs," *Marketing Week*, November 5, 1990, p. 10; and Gene Koretz, "This Generation Gap Could Jump-Start Detroit," *Business Week*, March 4, 1991, p. 12.

11. Martin Sloane, "Hoosier Wins Longest Tape Contest," United Features, April 13, 1987; "Coupon Fanatic Spends $125 for over $1800 in Groceries," Associated Press, New York, December 28, 1982; Caroline M. Henderson, "Modeling the Coupon Redemption Decision," *Advances in Consumer Research*, Vol. 12 (1985), pp. 138–143; and Linda L. Price, Lawrence F. Feick, and Audrey Guskey-Federouch, "Couponing Behaviors of the Market Maven: Profile of

a Super Couponer," *Advances in Consumer Research,* Vol. 15 (1988), pp. 354–359.

12. William L. Wilkie, *How Consumers Use Product Information: A Report Prepared for the National Science Foundation* (Washington, D.C.: U.S. Government Printing Office, 1975); see also Joel E. Urbany, Peter R. Dickson, and William L. Wilkie, "Buyer Uncertainty and Information Search," *Journal of Consumer Research,* Vol. 16 (September 1989), pp. 208–215.

13. See, for example, Jeffrey J. Stoltman, James W. Gentry, and Kenneth A. Anglin, "Shopping Choices: The Case of Mall Choice," *Advances in Consumer Research,* Vol. 18 (1991), pp. 434–440; Jennifer Meoli, Richard A. Feinberg, and Lori Westgate, "A Reinforcement-Affect Model of Mall Patronage," *Advances in Consumer Research,* Vol. 18 (1991), pp. 441–444; Peter H. Bloch, Nancy M. Ridgway, and James E. Nelson, "Leisure and the Shopping Mall," *Advances in Consumer Research,* Vol. 18 (1991), pp. 445–452; Peter A. Doherty and Judith E. P. Kulikowski, "Consumer Research and Its Role in Shopping Center Development," *Advances in Consumer Research,* Vol. 18 (1991), pp. 453–461; Elizabeth J. Wilson and Arch G. Woodside, "A Comment on Patterns of Store Choice and Customer Gain/Loss Analysis," *Journal of the Academy of Marketing Science,* Vol. 19, No. 4 (Fall 1991), pp. 377–382; and two papers in Robert L. King (ed.), *Marketing: Perspectives for the 1990s* (Richmond, Va.: Southern Marketing Association, 1992): David Strutton, Sheb True, and R. Keith Tudor, "An Investigation of the Relationship between Retailer Attributes and the Outshopping Behavior of Consumers in the Rural South," pp. 254–258; and Jill S. Attaway, Mitch Griffin, and Roger B. Singley, "How Do Consumers Decide Which Retailer to Visit? An Examination of Consumers' Choice Set Formation Processes," pp. 259–264.

14. See Francis Piron, "Defining Impulse Purchasing," *Advances in Consumer Research,* Vol. 18 (1991), pp. 509–514.

15. The entries in this table were developed from a number of sources, including especially Donald H. Granbois, "Shopping Behavior and Preferences," in R. Ferber (ed.), *Selected Aspects of Consumer Behavior* (Washington, D.C.: U.S. Government Printing Office, 1977), pp. 259–298; Joseph W. Newman, "Consumer External Search: Amount and Determinants" in A. Woodside, J. Sheth, and P. Bennett (eds.), *Consumer and Industrial Buying Behavior* (New York: North-Holland, 1977), pp. 79–94; and William L. Wilkie, *How Consumers Use Product Information: A Report Prepared for the National Science Foundation* (Washington, D.C.: U.S. Government Printing Office, 1975). See also Banwari Mittal, "Must Consumer Involvement Always Imply More Information Search?" *Advances in Consumer Research,* Vol. 16 (1989), pp. 167–172.

16. See, for example, E. Scott Maynes, "Towards Market Transparency," Working Paper, Cornell University, Ithaca, N.Y., 1985; Gary T. Ford, Darlene B. Smith, and John L. Swasy, "An Empirical Test of the Search, Experience and Credence Attributes Framework," *Advances in Consumer Research,* Vol. 15 (1988), pp. 239–243; and Joel E. Urbany, Peter R. Dickson, and William L. Wilkie, "Buyer Uncertainty and Information Search," *Journal of Consumer Research,* Vol. 16 (September 1989), pp. 208–215; Darlene Branigan Smith, "The Economics of Information: An Empirical Approach to Nelson's Search-Experience Framework," *Journal of Public Policy & Marketing,* Vol. 9 (1990), pp. 111–128; Arni Arnthorsson, Wendall E. Berry, and Joel E. Urbany, "Difficulty of Pre-Purchase Quality Inspection: Conceptualization and Measurement," *Advances in*

Consumer Research, Vol. 18 (1991), pp. 217–224; Cynthia Fraser Hite, Robert E. Hite, and Tamra Minor, "Quality Uncertainty, Brand Reliance, and Dissipative Advertising," *Journal of the Academy of Marketing Science,* Vol. 19, No. 2 (Spring 1991), pp. 115–122; three articles in *AMA Summer Educators' Proceedings* (1991): James Lynch and Drue Schuler, "Operationalizing Economics of Information Theory: Consumer Quality Judgments and Advertising Credibility," pp. 412–421; Frank H. Wadsworth and Peter A. Dacin, "Perceived Food Product Value Judgments: A Measurement Approach," pp. 422–431; and Brent G. Goff and Rajan Nataraajan, "Toward a Generalizable Customer Typology for Experiential and Credence Financial Services," pp. 760–770; and three articles in *Journal of Public Policy & Marketing,* Vol. 10, No. 1 (Spring 1991): Pauline M. Ippolito and Alan D. Mathios, "Health Claims in Food Marketing: Evidence on Knowledge and Behavior in the Cereal Market," pp. 15–32; John E. Calfee and Janis K. Pappalardo, "Public Policy Issues in Health Claims for Foods," pp. 33–53; and Bruce A. Silverglade, "A Comment on Public Policy Issues in Health Claims for Foods," pp. 54–62.

17. See Jon B. Freiden and Ronald E. Goldsmith, "Prepurchase Information Seeking for Professional Services," *Journal of Services Marketing,* Vol. 3 (Winter 1989), pp. 45–55; Drew Hyman, "The Hierarchy of Consumer Participation: Knowledge and Proficiency in Telecommunications Decision Making," *The Journal of Consumer Affairs,* Vol. 24, No. 1 (Summer 1990), pp. 1–23; Keith B. Murray, "A Test of Services Marketing Theory: Consumer Information Acquisition Activities," *Journal of Marketing,* Vol. 55, No. 1 (January 1991), pp. 10–25; Elizabeth Cooper-Martin, "Consumers and Movies: Information Sources for Experiential Products," *Advances in Consumer Research,* Vol. 19 (1992), pp. 756–761; Alain d'Astous and Diane Miquelon, "Helping Consumers Choose a Credit Card," *The Journal of Consumer Affairs,* Vol. 25, No. 2 (Winter 1991), pp. 278–294; H. David Strutton and James R. Lumpkin, "Information Sources Used by Elderly Health Care Product Adopters," *Journal of Advertising Research,* Vol. 32, No. 4 (July/August 1992), pp. 20–29; Ronald Paul Hill, Maria Cacia, and John Shamsey, "Managed Care and the Physician: An Exploratory Study," *AMA Summer Educators' Proceedings* (1992), pp. 557–562; Alice Ford and Warren French, "The Influence of Familiarity and Involvement on Service Quality Expectations," in Robert L. King (ed.), *Marketing: Perspectives for the 1990s* (Richmond, Va.: Southern Marketing Association, 1992), pp. 372–376; and Michael Dotson and W. E. Patton III, "Segment Differences in the Structure of the Service Component of Department Store Image: An Exploratory Study," in King, *Marketing: Perspectives for the 1990s,* pp. 386–389.

18. William L. Wilkie and Peter R. Dickson, "Consumer Information Search and Shopping Behavior," in H. Kassarjian and T. Robertson (eds.), *Perspectives in Consumer Behavior,* 4th ed. (Englewood Cliffs, N.J.: Prentice Hall, 1991), pp. 1–26.

19. Since these results are based upon consumers' recollections of their past behavior, they may be prone to understate somewhat the actual amount of information search (since some elements may have been forgotten). One study provided evidence on this possibility by first *observing* consumers while they were purchasing shoes and then later *asking* them about their search and decision processes. See Joseph W. Newman and Bradley D. Lockeman, "Measuring Prepurchase Information Seeking," *Journal of Consumer Research,* Vol. 2 (December 1975), pp. 216–222. Results showed that the survey method led to less reported search than the researchers had actually observed. For recent discussions and findings, see Jeffrey J. Stoltman, Shelley R. Tapp, and Richard S. Lapidus, "An Examination of Shopping Scripts," *Advances in Consumer Research*, Vol. 16 (1989), pp. 384–391; Barry L. Bayus, "The Consumer Durable Replacement Buyer," *Journal of Marketing*, Vol. 55, No. 1 (January 1991), pp. 42–51; Jeff Blodgett and Donna Hill, "An Exploratory Study Comparing Amount-of-Search Measures to Consumers' Reliance on Each Source of Information," *Advances in Consumer Research*, Vol. 18 (1991), pp. 773–779; Paul H. Schurr and Merrie Brucks, "Deal Search: An Approach for Computer-Controlled Information Processing Experiments Involving Bargainable Attributes," *Advances in Consumer Research*, Vol. 18 (1991), pp. 591–596; Patrick G. Buckley, "An S-O-R Model of the Purchase of an Item in a Store," *Advances in Consumer Research*, Vol. 18 (1991), pp. 491–500; James Bailey and Michael Strube, "Effects of Need for Cognition on Patterns of Information Acquisition," in C. Haugtvedt and D. Rosen (eds.), *Proceedings of the Society for Consumer Psychology* (Knoxville: D.W. Schumann, 1991), pp. 41–45; Narasimhan Srinivasan and Brian T. Ratchford, "An Empirical Test of a Model of External Search for Automobiles," *Journal of Consumer Research*, Vol. 18, No. 2 (September 1991), pp. 233–242; Jhinuk Chowdhruy and Varinder M. Sharma, "Consumer Choices of Information Sources: A Contingency Approach," *AMA Summer Educators' Proceedings* (1991), pp. 479–486; Narasimhan Srinivasan and Surinder Tikoo, "Effect of Locus of Control on Information Search Behavior," *Advances in Consumer Research*, Vol. 19 (1992), pp. 498–504; Julie L. Ozanne, Merrie Brucks, and Dhruv Grewal, "A Study of Information Search Behavior during the Categorization of New Products," *Journal of Consumer Research*, Vol. 18, No. 4 (March 1992), pp. 452–463; Carolyn L. Costley and Merrie Brucks, "Selective Recall and Information Use in Consumer Preferences" *Journal of Consumer Research*, Vol. 18, No. 4 (March 1992), pp. 464–474; Devavrat Purohit, "Exploring the Relationship between the Markets for New and Used Durable Goods: The Case of Automobiles," *Marketing Science*, Vol. 11, No. 2 (Spring 1992), pp. 154–167; Raymond R. Burke, Bari A. Harlam, Barbara E. Kahn, and Leonard M. Lodish, "Comparing Dynamic Consumer Choice in Real and Computer-simulated Environments," *Journal of Consumer Research*, Vol. 19, No. 1 (June 1992), pp. 71–83; Daniel D. Butler, "Perceived Risk and Subjective Knowledge Effects on External Search Behavior," *AMA Winter Educators' Proceedings* (1993), p. 253; Rajan Sambandam, "Using Information Search to Study the Consequences of the Satisfaction Judgement," *AMA Winter Educators' Proceedings* (1993), pp. 254–259; Brian T. Ratchford and Narasimhan Srinivasan, "An Empirical Investigation of Returns to Search," *Marketing Science*, Vol. 12, No. 1 (Winter 1993), pp. 73–87; Robert E. Smith, "Integrating Information from Advertising and Trial: Processes and Effects on Consumer Response to Product Information," *Journal of Marketing Research*, Vol. 30 (May 1993), pp. 204–219; and Donald R. Lichtenstein, Nancy M. Ridgway, and Richard G. Netemeyer, "Price Perceptions and Consumer Shopping Behavior," *Journal of Marketing Research*, Vol. 30 (May 1993), pp. 234–245.

20.   See, for example, John D. Claxton, Joseph N. Fry, and Bernard Portis, "A Taxonomy of Prepurchase Information Gathering Patterns," *Journal of Consumer Research*, Vol. 1 (December 1974), pp. 35–42; and David H. Furse, Girish N. Punj, and David W. Stewart, "A Typology of Individual Search Strategies among Purchasers of New Automobiles," *Journal of Consumer Research* (March 1984),

pp. 417–431. See also David F. Midgley, Grahame R. Dowling, and Pamela D. Morrison, "Consumer Types, Social Influence, Information Search and Choice," *Advances in Consumer Research*, Vol. 16 (1989), pp. 137–143.

21.   Robert A. Westbrook and Claes Fornell, "Patterns of Information Source Usage among Durable Goods Buyers," *Journal of Marketing Research*, Vol. 16 (August 1970), pp. 303–312.

22.   See, for example, Hans G. Thorelli and Jack L. Engledow, "Information Seekers and Information Systems: A Policy Perspective," *Journal of Marketing*, Vol. 44 (Spring 1980), pp. 9–27; and Ronald D. Anderson and Jack Engledow, "A Factor Analytic Comparison of U.S. and German Information Seekers," *Journal of Consumer Research*, Vol. 3 (March 1977), pp. 185–196.

23.   See Calvin P. Duncan, "Consumer Market Beliefs: A Review of the Literature and an Agenda for Future Research," *Advances in Consumer Research*, Vol. 17 (1990), pp. 729–736; Calvin P. Duncan and Richard W. Olshavsky, "External Search: The Role of Consumer Beliefs," *Journal of Marketing Research*, Vol. 19 (February 1982), pp. 32–43; and James A. Muncy, "Beliefs and External Information Search: A Replication," *AMA Summer Educators' Proceedings* (1986), pp. 62–67.

24.   Randall Bloomquist, "Consumer Libraries: New Way to Advertise Real Estate," *Marketing Week*, October 5, 1987, p. 25. See also Mary Gardiner Jones and Helen Ewing Nelson, "New Information Technologies and Consumer Choice," *Advancing the Consumer Interest*, Vol. 3, No. 2 (1991), pp. 20–26; and Robert E. Widing II and W. Wayne Talarzyk, "Electronic Information Systems for Consumers: An Evaluation of Computer-assisted Formats in Multiple Decision Environments," *Journal of Marketing Research*, Vol. 30 (May 1993), pp. 125–141.

25.   See, for example, Monroe P. Friedman, "Consumer Confusion in the Selection of Supermarket Products," *Journal of Applied Psychology*, Vol. 50 (December 1966), pp. 529–534; and Michael J. Houston, "The Effect of Unit Pricing on Choices of Brand and Size in Economic Shopping," *Journal of Marketing*, Vol. 36 (July 1972), pp. 51–54. For related discussions, see especially Joseph W. Alba and J. Wesley Hutchinson, "Dimensions of Consumer Expertise," *Journal of Consumer Research*, Vol. 13 (March 1987), pp. 411–454, and Joseph W. Alba and Howard Marmorstein, "The Effects of Frequency Knowledge on Consumer Decision Making," *Journal of Consumer Research*, Vol. 14 (June 1987), pp. 14–25.

26.   J. Edward Russo, Gene Krieser, and Sally Miyashita, "An Effective Display of Unit Price Information," *Journal of Marketing*, Vol. 39 (April 1975), pp. 11–19. For a review of the experience with unit pricing programs, see David A. Aaker and Gary T. Ford, "Unit Pricing Ten Years Later: A Replication," *Journal of Marketing*, Vol. 47 (Winter 1983), pp. 118–122. For related discussions, see Gerard J. Tellis and Gary J. Gaeth, "Best Value, Price-seeking, and Price Aversion: The Impact of Information and Learning on Consumer Choices," *Journal of Marketing*, Vol. 54, No. 2 (April 1990) pp. 34–45; Jane Kolodinsky, "Time as a Direct Source of Utility: The Case of Price Information Search for Groceries," *The Journal of Consumer Affairs*, Vol. 24, No. 1 (Summer 1990), pp. 89–109; Christine Moorman, "The Effects of Stimulus and Consumer Characteristics on the Utilization of Nutrition Information," *Journal of Consumer Research*, Vol. 17, No. 3 (December 1990), pp. 362–374; William B. Dodds, Kent B. Monroe, and Dhruv Grewal, "Effects of Price, Brand, and Store Information on Buyers' Product Evaluations," *Journal of Marketing Research,* Vol. 28 (August 1991), pp. 307–319; Siva K. Balasubramanian, Catherine Cole, and Nadine M. Castellano, "Consumer Behavior Research and Its Implications for Product/Nutritional Information Programs," *Advances in Consumer Research,* Vol. 19 (1992), pp. 489–490; Howard Marmorstein, Dhruv Grewal, and Raymond P. H. Fishe, "The Value of Time Spent in Price-Comparison Shopping: Survey and Experimental Evidence," *Journal of Consumer Research,* Vol. 19, No. 1 (June 1992), pp. 52–61; Akshay R. Rao and Wanda A. Sieben, "The Effect of Prior Knowledge on Price Acceptability and the Type of Information Examined," *Journal of Consumer Research,* Vol. 19, No. 2 (September 1992), pp. 256–270; and David L. Mothersbaugh, Robert O. Herrmann, and Rex H. Warland, "Perceived Time Pressure and Recommended Dietary Practices: The Moderating Effect of Knowledge of Nutrition," *The Journal of Consumer Affairs,* Vol. 27, No. 1 (Summer 1993), pp. 106–126.

27.   For a comprehensive coverage of this topic, see Jacob Jacoby, Donald E. Speller, and Carol A. Kohn, "Brand Choice Behavior as a Function of Information Load," *Journal of Marketing Research,* Vol. 11 (February 1974), pp. 63–69; William L. Wilkie, "Analysis of Effects of Information Load," *Journal of Marketing Research,* Vol. 11 (November 1974), pp. 462–466; John O. Summers, "Less Information Is Better!" *Journal of Marketing Research,* Vol. 11 (November 1974), pp. 467–468; Jacob Jacoby, Donald E. Speller, and Carol A. Kohn, "Brand Choice Behavior as a Function of Information Load: Replication and Extension," *Journal of Consumer Research,* Vol. 3 (March 1974), pp. 33–42; J. Edward Russo, "More Information Is Better: A Reevaluation of Jacoby, Speller, and Kohn," *Journal of Consumer Research,* Vol. 1 (December 1974) pp. 68–72; Jacob Jacoby, "Information Load and Decision Quality: Some Contested Issues," *Journal of Marketing Research,* Vol. 14 (November 1977), pp. 569–577; Richard Staelin and John W. Payne, "Studies of the Information-seeking Behavior of Consumers," in John S. Carroll and John W. Payne (eds.), *Cognition and Social Behavior* (Hillsdale, N.J.: Erlbaum, 1976), pp. 185–201; Debra L. Scammon, "'Information Load' and Consumers," *Journal of Consumer Research,* Vol. 4 (December 1977), pp. 148–155; Naresh K. Malhotra, "Information Load and Consumer Decision Making," *Journal of Consumer Research,* Vol. 9 (March 1982), pp. 419–430; Naresh K. Malhotra, Arun K. Jain, and Stephen Lagakos, "The Information Overload Controversy: An Alternative Viewpoint," *Journal of Marketing,* Vol. 46 (Spring 1982), pp. 27–37; Jacob Jacoby, "Perspectives on Information Overload," *Journal of Consumer Research,* Vol. 10 (March 1984), pp. 432–435; Naresh K. Malhotra, "Reflections on the Information Overload Paradigm in Consumer Decision Making," *Journal of Consumer Research,* Vol. 10 (March 1984), pp. 436–440; Roger J. Best and Michael Ursic, "The Impact of Information Load and Variability on Choice Accuracy," *Advances in Consumer Research,* Vol. 14 (1987), pp. 106–108; Kevin Lane Keller and Richard Staelin, "Effects of Quality and Quantity of Information on Decision Effectiveness," *Journal of Consumer Research,* Vol. 14 (September 1987), pp. 200–213; Robert J. Meyer and Eric J. Johnson, "Information Overload and the Nonrobustness of Linear Models: A Comment on Keller and Staelin," *Journal of Consumer Research,* Vol. 15 (March 1989), pp. 498–503; and Kevin Lane Keller and Richard Staelin, "Assessing Biases in Measuring Decision Effectiveness and Information Overload," *Journal of Consumer Research,* Vol. 15 (March 1989), pp. 504–508; Robert S. Owen, "Clarifying the Simple Assumption of the Information Load

Paradigm," *Advances in Consumer Research,* Vol. 19 (1992), pp. 770–776; and James G. Helgeson and Michael L. Ursic, "Information Load, Cost/Benefit Assessment and Decision Strategy Variability," *Journal of the Academy of Marketing Science,* Vol. 21, No. 1 (Winter 1993), pp. 13–20.

28.   Dennis L. McNeill and William L. Wilkie, "Public Policy and Consumer Information: Impacts of the New Energy Labels," *Journal of Consumer Research,* Vol. 6 (June 1979), pp. 1–11. For related discussions, see also R. Bruce Hutton, Gary A. Mauser, Pierre Filiatrault, and Olli T. Ahtola, "Effects of Cost-related Feedback on Consumer Knowledge and Consumption Behavior: A Field Experimental Approach," *Journal of Consumer Research,* Vol. 13 (December 1986), pp. 327–336; Robert F. Dyer and Thomas J. Maronick, "An Evaluation of Consumer Awareness and Use of Energy Labels in the Purchase of Major Appliances—A Longitudinal Analysis," *Journal of Public Policy & Marketing,* Vol. 7 (1988), pp. 83–97; and Jeannet H. van Houwelingen and W. Fred van Raaij, "The Effects of Goal-Setting and Daily Electronic Feedback on In-Home Energy Use," *Journal of Consumer Research,* Vol. 15 (March 1989), pp. 98–105.

For findings in related areas, see also Craig A. Kelley, William C. Gaidis, and Peter H. Reingen, "The Use of Vivid Stimuli to Enhance Comprehension of the Content of Product Warning Messages," *The Journal of Consumer Affairs,* Vol. 23, No. 2 (Winter 1989), pp. 243–266; Louis A. Morris, Michael B. Mazis, and David Brinberg, "Risk Disclosures in Televised Prescription Drug Advertising to Consumers," *Journal of Public Policy & Marketing,* Vol. 8 (1989), pp. 64–80; Edward T. Popper and Keith B. Murray, "Communication Effectiveness and Format Effects on In-Ad Disclosure of Health Warnings," *Journal of Public Policy & Marketing,* Vol. 8 (1989), pp. 109–123; Paul N. Bloom, "A Decision Model for Prioritizing and Addressing Consumer Information Problems," *Journal of Public Policy & Marketing,* Vol. 8 (1989), pp. 161–180; five papers in R. N. Mayer (ed.), *Enhancing Consumer Choice* (Columbia, Mo.: American Council on Consumer Interests, 1991): Robert N. Mayer, Ken R. Smith, and Debra L. Scammon, "Read Any Good Labels Lately? Evaluating the Impact of Alcohol Warning Labels," pp. 149–158; Janet E. Fast, "The Effect of Plain Language Billing Procedures on Residential Energy Consumption," pp. 169–188; Loren V. Geistfeld, "Enhancing Consumer Choice through Decision-making Aids," pp. 477–484; Sherman Hanna, "Academic Participation in Development of Expert Systems for Consumers," pp. 485–490; and E. Scott Maynes, "An Information Desiderata Evaluation of Sources of Consumer Information," pp. 491–514; three articles in the *Journal of Public Policy & Marketing,* Vol. 10, No. 1 (Spring 1991): R. Bruce Hutton and Olli T. Ahtola, "Consumer Response to a Five-Year Campaign to Combat Air Pollution," pp. 242–256; Debra L. Scammon, Robert N. Mayer, and Ken R. Smith, "Alcohol Warnings: How Do You Know When You Have Had One Too Many?" pp. 214–228; and Michael B. Mazis, Louis A. Morris and John L. Swasy, "An Evaluation of the Alcohol Warning Label: Initial Survey Results," pp. 229–241; J. Craig Andrews, Richard G. Netemeyer, and Srinivas Durvasula, "Effects of Consumption Frequency on Believability and Attitudes toward Alcohol Warning Labels," *The Journal of Consumer Affairs,* Vol. 25, No. 2 (Winter 1991), pp. 323–338; Robert E. Widing II, Erik Olson, and W. Wayne Talarzyk, "The ADE Scales: Measures of Accuracy, Difficulty, and Effort for Evaluating Decisions Aids and Information Formats," *AMA Summer Educators' Proceedings* (1992), pp. 205–206; Michael E. Hilton, "An Overview of Recent Findings on Alcoholic Beverage Warning Labels," *Journal of Public Policy & Marketing*, Vol. 12, No. 1 (Spring 1993), pp. 1–9; Scot Burton and Abhijit Biswas, "Preliminary Assessment of Changes in Labels Required by the Nutrition Labeling and Education Act of 1990," *The Journal of Consumer Affairs*, Vol. 27, No. 1 (Summer 1993), pp. 127–144; and Robert N. Mayer, Debra L. Scammon, and Jason Gray-Lee, "Will the FTC Guides on Environmental Marketing Affect the Hue of Green Marketing? An Audit of Claims on Product Labels," in M. J. Sheffet (ed.) *Proceedings of the 1993 Public Policy and Marketing Conference* (East Lansing: Michigan State University, Eli Broad Graduate School of Management, 1993), pp. 19–30.

29. R. Bruce Hutton and William L. Wilkie, "Life Cycle Cost: A New Form of Consumer Information," *Journal of Consumer Research*, Vol. 6 (March 1980), pp. 349–360.

Chapter 18
Consumer Decisions (II): Purchase Processes

1. These quotes are provided by courtesy of Professor Patrick E. Murphy, University of Notre Dame.

2. Dan Koeppel, "Even Häagen Dazs Gets Lost in the Crowd," *Marketing Week*, October 22, 1990, p. 9.

3. Gretchen Morgenson, "The Buyout That Saved Safeway," *Forbes*, November 12, 1990, pp. 88–92.

4. See, for example, John G. Lynch, "Adventures in Paramorphic Modeling: Models of Consumers' Processing of Negative Information," Working Paper, Center for Consumer Research, University of Florida, Gainesville, 1984; For general considerations, see Alan G. Sawyer, "Demand Artifacts in Laboratory Experiments in Consumer Research," *Journal of Consumer Research*, Vol. 1 (March 1975), pp. 20–30; and Frank R. Kardes, Chris T. Allen, and Manuel J. Pontes, "Effects of Multiple Measurement Operations on Consumer Judgment: Measurement Reliability or Reactivity?" *Advances in Consumer Research*, Vol. 20 (1993), pp. 280–283.

5. See James R. Bettman, *An Information Processing Theory of Consumer Choice* (Reading, Mass.: Addison-Wesley, 1979); James R. Bettman and C. Whan Park, "Effects of Prior Knowledge and Experience and Phase of the Choice Process on Consumer Decision Processes: A Protocol Analysis," *Journal of Consumer Research*, Vol. 7 (1980), pp. 234–248; Gabriel Biehal and Dipankar Chakravarti, "Experiences with the Bettman-Park Verbal Protocol Coding Scheme," *Journal of Consumer Research*, Vol. 8 (1982), pp. 442–448; Gabriel Biehal and Dipankar Chakravarti, "The Effects of Concurrent Verbalization on Choice Processing," *Journal of Marketing Research*, Vol. 26 (February 1989), pp. 84–96; Richard W. Olshavsky and Anand Kumar, "Toward A More Comprehensive Coding Scheme for the Analysis of Protocol Data in Studies of Brand Choice," *AMA Winter Educators' Proceedings* (1992), pp. 122–131; and James H. Barnes, "Ethono: A Methodology for Studying Process Information," *Advances in Consumer Research*, Vol. 20 (1993), pp. 63–69.

6. Jacob Jacoby, "Perspectives on a Consumer Information Processing Research Program," *Communication Research*, Vol. 2 (July 1975), pp. 203–215.

7. James R. Bettman and Jacob Jacoby, "Patterns of Processing in Consumer Information Acquisition," *Advances in Consumer Research*, Vol. 3 (1976), pp. 315–320; James R. Bettman and Pradeep Kakkar, "Effects of Information Presentation Format on Consumer Information Acquisition Strategies," *Journal of Consumer Research*, Vol. 3 (March 1977), pp. 233–240; Russell G. Wahlers, "Number of Choice Alternatives and Number of Product Characteristics as Determinants of the Consumer's Choice of an Evaluation Process Strategy," *Advances in Consumer Research*, Vol. 9 (1982), pp. 544–549; and Ann McGill and Punam Anand, "Processing by Attribute versus Brand: The Mediating Role of Imagery," *Advances in Consumer Research*, Vol. 15 (1988), pp. 184 ff.

8. J. E. Russo, "Eye Fixations Can Save the World: A Critical Evaluation and a Comparison between Eye Fixations and Other Information," *Advances in Consumer Research*, Vol. 5 (1978), pp. 561–570; Raymond J. Smead, James B. Wilcox, and Robert E. Wilkes, "An Illustration and Evaluation of a Joint Process Tracing Methodology: Eye Movement and Protocols," *Advances in Consumer Research*, Vol. 7 (1980), pp. 507–512.

9. Gabriel Biehal and Dipankar Chakravarti, "Consumers' Use of Memory and External Information in Choice: Macro and Micro Perspectives," *Journal of Consumer Research*, Vol. 13 (March 1986), pp. 382–405. See also John G. Lynch, Jr., and Thomas K. Srull, "Memory and Attentional Factors in Consumer Choice: Concepts and Research Methods," *Journal of Consumer Research*, Vol. 9 (June 1982), pp. 18–37; Alan Dick, Dipankar Chakravarti, and Gabriel Biehal, "Memory-based Inferences during Consumer Choice," *Journal of Consumer Research*, Vol. 17, No. 1 (June 1990), pp. 82–93; Sandra J. Burke, "The Effects of Missing Information on Decision Strategy Selection," *Advances in Consumer Research*, Vol. 17 (1990), pp. 250–256; Carolyn J. Simmons and Nancy H. Leonard, "Inferences about Missing Attributes: Contingencies Affecting the Use of Alternative Information Sources," *Advances in Consumer Research*, Vol. 17 (1990), pp. 266–274; Sarah Fisher Gardial and David W. Schumann, "In Search of the Elusive Consumer Inference," *Advances in Consumer Research*, Vol. 17 (1990), pp. 283–287; Carolyn J. Simmons and John G. Lynch, Jr., "Inference Effects without Inference Making? Effects of Missing Information on Discounting and Use of Presented Information," *Journal of Consumer Research*, Vol. 17, No. 4 (March 1991), pp. 477–491; and William T. Ross, Jr., and Elizabeth H. Creyer, "Making Inferences about Missing Information: The Effects of Existing Information," *Journal of Consumer Research*, Vol. 19, No. 1 (June 1992), pp. 14–25.

10. We should note that consumers may well employ different rules when evaluating products and brands (that is, making judgments about them) than when deciding which particular brands to buy. For example, it is easy to like several brands, but it is difficult to buy all the brands we like at one time. The rules we use to judge liking can thus easily be different from the rules we might use when faced with an actual decision. For further discussion of these rules and their settings, see Peter L. Wright, "Consumer Judgment Strategies: Beyond the Compensatory Assumption," in M. Venkatesan (ed.), *Proceedings of the Third Annual Conference* (Chicago: Association for Consumer Research, 1972), pp. 316–324; and Hillel J. Einhorn, "Use of Nonlinear, Noncompensatory Models in Decision Making," *Psychological Bulletin*, Vol. 73 (1970), pp. 221–230. For related discussions, see also Chezy Ofir and John G. Lynch, Jr., "Context Effects on Judgment under Uncertainty," *Journal of Consumer Research*, Vol. 11 (September 1984), pp. 668–679; Eric J. Johnson and Robert J. Meyer, "Compensatory Choice Models of Noncompensatory Processes: The Effect of Varying Context," *Journal of Consumer Research*, Vol. 11 (June 1984), pp. 528–541; Wayne D. Hoyer and Cathy J. Cobb-Walgren, "Consumer Decision Making across Product Categories: The Influence of Task Environment," *Psychology & Marketing*, Vol. 5 (Spring 1988), pp. 45–70; Elizabeth Cooper-Martin, "The Effect of Three Contingency Factors on Consumer Choice Strategies: A Test of Awareness of Cost and Benefit," *Advances in Consumer Research*, Vol. 16 (1989), pp. 130–136; Yaacov Schul and David Mazursky, "Conditions Facilitating Successful Discounting in Consumer Decision Making," *Journal of Consumer Research*, Vol. 16, No. 4 (March 1990), pp. 442–451; Michael D. Johnson, "The Differential Processing of Product Category and Noncomparable Choice Alternatives," *Journal of Consumer Research*, Vol. 16, No. 3 (December 1989), pp. 300–309; Barbara E. Kahn and Robert J. Meyer, "Consumer Multiattribute Judgments under Attribute-Weight Uncertainty," *Journal of Consumer Research*, Vol. 17, No. 4 (March 1991), pp. 508–522; Kim P. Corfman, "Comparability and Comparison Levels Used in Choices among Consumer Products," *Journal of Marketing Research*, Vol. 28 (August 1991), pp. 368–374; five papers in *Advances in Consumer Research*, Vol. 19 (1992): Barbara Bickart, Geeta Menon, Seymour Sudman, and Johnny Blair, "Context Effects in Proxy Judgments," pp. 64–71; David E. Hansen, "Issues in Consumer Choice with Uncertain Product Outcomes," pp. 175–176; James Shanteau, "Decision Making under Risk: Applications to Insurance Purchasing," pp. 177–181; John C. Mowen, "The Time and Outcome Valuation Model: Implications for Understanding Reactance and Risky Choices in Consumer Decision Making," pp. 182–189; and Ravi Dhar, "To Choose or Not to Choose: This Is the Question," pp. 735–738; Joel Huber and Noreen M. Klein, "Adapting Cutoffs to the Choice Environment: The Effects of Attribute Correlation and Reliability," *Journal of Consumer Research*, Vol. 18, No. 3 (December 1991), pp. 346–357; John C. Mowen and Gary J. Gaeth, "The Evaluation Stage in Marketing Decision-making," *Journal of the Academy of Marketing Science*, Vol. 20, No. 2 (Spring 1992), pp. 177–188; Itamar Simonson, "The Influence of Anticipating Regret and Responsibility on Purchase Decisions," *Journal of Consumer Research*, Vol. 19, No. 1 (June 1992), pp. 105–118; Itamar Simonson and Amos Tversky, "Choice in Context: Tradeoff Contrast and Extremeness Aversion," *Journal of Marketing Research*, Vol. 29, No. 3 (August 1992), pp. 281–296; Scott A. Spira, "Context Effects, Halo Effects," in T. J. Page, Jr., and S. E. Middlestadt (eds.), *Proceedings of the Society for Consumer Psychology* (Clemson, S.C.: CtC Press, 1992), p. 68; Durairaj Maheswaran, Diane M. Mackie, and Shelly Chaiken, "Brand Name as a Heuristic Cue: The Effects of Task Importance and Expectancy Confirmation on Consumer Judgments," *Journal of Consumer Psychology*, Vol. 1, No. 4 (1992), pp. 317–336; Frank R. Kardes and David M. Sanbonmatsu, "Direction of Comparison, Expected Feature Correlation, and the Set-Size Effect in Preference Judgment," *Journal of Consumer Psychology*, Vol. 2, No. 1 (1993), pp. 39–54; and Gita V. Johar and Elizabeth H. Creyer, "The Impact of Direction-of-Comparison on the Formation of Preference," *Advances in Consumer Research*, Vol. 20 (1993), pp. 284–287.

11. If Sandy turns to her dictionary she'll easily see the answer, since the term *lexicography* refers to the principles used in making a dictionary. If we consider these principles briefly, we can recognize the basic rule used to "order" the alternative words in the dictionary: the first letter is most important, followed by the second, the third, and so forth. Thus, in making a dictionary, Sandy would first consider all possible words on the "most important attribute" (that is, that the starting letter is an *A*). All words with other starting letters are dropped from consideration at this point. All those

that have a starting *A* remain in the set. Sandy will then turn to her second most important attribute and continue with her choice process to pick the word that will have the honor of starting out her dictionary of the English language! After choosing this word, she'll then begin a new choice process to discover the second word in her listing, and will again employ the lexicographic choice rule. By the way, what's your guess on the first and second words she'll discover? (As an aside, Sandy bought a Comfort Case.)

12. John G. Lynch, Jr., "Adventures in Paramorphic Modeling: Models of Consumers' Processing of Negative Information," Working Paper, Center for Consumer Research, University of Florida, Gainesville, 1984. (The other consumers' purchases: Paul bought a Beauty Brief, and Ed bought an Air Attache.)

13. These are also termed *phased strategies*. See Amos Tversky, "Elimination by Aspects: A Theory of Choice," *Psychological Review*, Vol. 79 (1972), pp. 281–299; Peter Wright and Fredric Barbour, "The Relevance of Decision Process Models in Structuring Persuasive Messages," *Communication Research*, Vol. 2 (July 1975), pp. 246–259; Denis A. Lussier and Richard W. Olshavsky, "Task Complexity and Contingent Processing in Brand Choice," *Journal of Consumer Research*, Vol. 6 (1979), pp. 154–165; and Frank R. Kardes and Paul M. Herr, "Order Effects in Consumer Judgment, Choice, and Memory: The Role of Initial Processing Goals," *Advances in Consumer Research*, Vol. 17 (1990), pp. 541–546.

14. Alain d'Astous and Dominique Rouzies, "Selection and Implementation of Processing Strategies . . . ," *International Journal of Marketing*, Vol. 4 (1987), pp. 99–110; Gabriel Biehal and Dipankar Chakravarti, "Consumers' Use of Memory and External Information in Choice: Macro and Micro Perspectives," *Journal of Consumer Research*, Vol. 13 (March 1986), pp. 382–405; James R. Bettman and Michael A. Zins, "Constructive Processes in Consumer Choice," *Journal of Consumer Research*, Vol. 4, No. 2 (September 1977), pp. 75–85; Noreen M. Klein and Manjit S. Yadiv, "Context Effects on Effort and Accuracy in Choice: An Inquiry into Adaptive Decision Making," *Journal of Consumer Research*, Vol. 15 (March 1989), pp. 411–421; Robert A. Bjork and Marc Vanhuele, "Retrieval Inhibition and Related Adaptive Peculiarities of Human Memory," *Advances in Consumer Research*, Vol. 19 (1992), pp. 155–160; and Mary Frances Luce, "Consideration of Inhibition as a Mechanism in Decision Processes," *Advances in Consumer Research*, Vol. 19 (1992), pp. 161–165.

15. Peter L. Wright, "Consumer Choice Strategies: Simplifying versus Optimizing," *Journal of Marketing Research*, Vol. 11 (1975), pp. 60–67. See also John G. Lynch, Jr., Howard Marmorstein, and Michael F. Weigold, "Choices from Sets Including Remembered Brands: Use of Recalled Attributes and Prior Overall Evaluations," *Journal of Consumer Research*, Vol. 15 (September 1988), pp. 169–184.

16. Merrie Brucks, "The Effects of Product Class Knowledge on Information Search Behavior," *Journal of Consumer Research*, Vol. 12 (June 1985), pp. 1–16. For related issues, see also Amardeep Assar and Dipankar Chakravarti, "Attribute Range Knowledge: Effects on Consumers' Evaluation of Brand-Attribute Information and Search Patterns in Choice," *AMA Summer Educators' Proceedings* (1984), pp. 62–67; Mita Sujan, "Consumer Knowledge: Effects on Evaluation Strategies Mediating Consumer Judgments," *Journal of Consumer Research*, Vol. 12 (June 1985), pp. 31–46. For related discussions, see also Lawrence J. Marks, Michael A. Kamins, and Donna

Murphy, "The Effects of Level of Expertise on the Processing of Framed and Unframed Pictorial Print Advertisements," *AMA Summer Educators' Proceedings* (1986), pp. 57–61; James R. Bettman and Mita Sujan, "Effects of Framing on Evaluation of Comparable and Noncomparable Alternatives by Expert and Novice Consumers," *Journal of Consumer Research*, Vol. 14 (September 1987), pp. 141–154; Itamar Simonson, Joel Huber, and John Payne, "The Relationship between Prior Brand Knowledge and Information Acquisition Order," *Journal of Consumer Research*, Vol. 14 (March 1988), pp. 566–578; Merrie Brucks, "Search Monitor: An Approach for Computer-controlled Experiments Involving Consumer Information Search," *Journal of Consumer Research*, Vol. 15 (June 1988), pp. 117–121; Merrie Brucks and Paul H. Schurr, "The Effects of Bargainable Attributes and Attribute Range Knowledge on Consumer Choice Processes," *Journal of Consumer Research*, Vol. 16, No. 4 (March 1990), pp. 409–419; Frank R. Kardes, David M. Sanbonmatsu, and Paul M. Herr, "Consumer Expertise and the Feature-Positive Effect: Implications for Judgment and Inference," *Advances in Consumer Research*, Vol. 17 (1990), pp. 351–354; Akshay R. Rao and Eric M. Olson, "Information Examination as a Function of Information Type and Dimension of Consumer Expertise: Some Exploratory Findings," *Advances in Consumer Research*, Vol. 17 (1990), pp. 361–366; Merrie Brucks, "Computer-controlled Experimentation in Consumer Decision Making and Judgment," *Advances in Consumer Research*, Vol. 17 (1990), pp. 905–909; John Kim, Frank R. Kardes and Paul M. Herr, "Consumer Expertise and the Vividness Effect: Implications for Judgment and Inference," *Advances in Consumer Research*, Vol. 18 (1991), pp. 90–93; and Judy A. Wagner and Noreen M. Klein, "The Effect of Familiarity on Consumers' Choice Agendas," *Advances in Consumer Research*, Vol. 20 (1993), pp. 209–214.

17. For three excellent (but advanced) overviews of research on consumer decision making, see Joseph W. Alba, J. Wesley Hutchinson, and John G. Lynch, "Memory and Decision Making," James R. Bettman, Erie J. Johnson, and John W. Payne, "Consumer Decision Making," and Robert J. Meyer and Barbara Kahn, "Probabilistic Models of Consumer Choice Behavior," all in T. Robertson and H. Kassarjian (eds.), *Handbook of Consumer Behavior* (Englewood Cliffs, N.J.: Prentice Hall, 1991), pp. 1–49, 50–84, and 85–123, respectively. See also David W. Stewart, "A Commentary on New Theoretical Perspectives on Consumer Behavior," *Advances in Consumer Research*, Vol. 17 (1990), pp. 750–754.

18. Philip M. Boffey, "Subtle Factors Influence Simplest Choices of Our Lives," The New York Times News Service, December 20, 1983; and Amos Tversky and Daniel Kahneman, "The Framing of Decisions and the Psychology of Choice," *Science* (1981), pp. 453–458. For further in-depth discussions, see Daniel Kahneman and Amos Tversky, "Prospect Theory: An Analysis of Decision under Risk," *Econometrica*, Vol. 47 (March 1979), pp. 263–291; and Daniel Kahneman and Amos Tversky, "Choices, Values, and Frames," *American Psychologist*, Vol. 39 (April 1984), pp. 341–350.

19. Readings might best begin with the *Science* article in Note 18. For extensions, see Richard Thaler, "Mental Accounting and Consumer Choice," *Marketing Science*, Vol. 4 (Summer 1985), pp. 199–214; Irwin P. Levin, Richard D. Johnson, Craig P. Russo, and Patricia J. Deldin, "Framing Effects in Judgment Tasks with Varying Amount of Information," *Organizational Behavior and Human Decision Processes*, Vol. 36 (December 1985), pp. 366–377; Christopher P. Puto, "The Framing of Buying Decisions," *Journal of Consumer Research*, Vol. 14 (December 1987), pp. 301–315; William D. Diamond, "The Effect of Probability and Consequence Levels on the Focus of Consumer Judgments in Risky Situations," *Journal of Consumer Research*, Vol. 15 (September 1988), pp. 280–283; Irwin P. Levin and Gary J. Gaeth, "How Consumers Are Affected by the Framing of Attribute Information before and after Consuming the Product," *Journal of Consumer Research*, Vol. 15 (December 1988), pp. 374–378; Scot Burton and Laure A. Babin, "Decision-framing Helps Make the Sale," *The Journal of Consumer Marketing*, Vol. 6 (Spring 1989), pp. 15–24; Stephen J. Hoch and John Deighton, "Managing What Consumers Learn from Experience," *Journal of Marketing*, Vol. 53 (April 1989), pp. 1–20; Itamar Simonson, "Choice Based on Reasons: The Case of Attraction and Compromise Effects," *Journal of Consumer Research*, Vol. 16 (September 1989), pp. 158–174; Durairaj Maheswaran and Joan Meyers-Levy, "The Influence of Message Framing and Issue Involvement," *Journal of Marketing Research*, Vol. 27 (August 1990), pp. 361–367; Thomas S. Gruca, "How Regular Is Regularity? An Empirical Test of the Regularity Assumption," *Advances in Consumer Research*, Vol. 17 (1990), pp. 398–405; Jennifer Aaker, "The Negative Attraction Effect? A Study of the Attraction Effect under Judgment and Choice," *Advances in Consumer Research*, Vol. 18 (1991), pp. 462–469; Ajit Kaicker and Brian D. Till, "The Framing Effect: Attribute Information and Product Experience," *AMA Winter Educators' Proceedings* (1991), pp. 404–410; Kevin Lane Keller, "Cue Compatibility and Framing in Advertising," *Journal of Marketing Research*, Vol. 28 (February 1991), pp. 42–57; Timothy B. Heath and Subimal Chatterjee, "How Entrants Affect Multiple Brands: A Dual Attraction Mechanism," *Advances in Consumer Research*, Vol. 18 (1991), pp. 768–772; Brian Wansink, "Consumption Framing and Extension Advertising: The Impact on Memory and Consumption," in C. Haugtuedt and D. Rosen (eds.), *Proceedings of the Society for Consumer Psychology* (Knoxville: D. W. Schumann, 1991), pp. 76–80; John G. Lynch, Jr., Dipankar Chakravarti, and Anusree Mitra, "Contrast Effects in Consumer Judgments: Changes in Mental Representations or in the Anchoring of Rating Scales?" *Journal of Consumer Research*, Vol. 18, No. 3 (December 1991), pp. 284–297; Priya Raghubir Das, "Semantic Cues and Buyer Evaluation of Promotional Communication," *AMA Summer Educators' Proceedings* (1992), pp. 12–17; Kathleen Seiders, "Managing the Evidence for the Inexperienced Service Customer," *AMA Summer Educators' Proceedings* (1992), pp. 176–182; Gerald E. Smith, "The Effect of Framing on Perceptions of Value and Likelihood of Purchase," in T. J. Page, Jr., and S. E. Middlestadt, *Proceedings of the Society for Consumer Psychology*, 1992, pp. 65–67; Alice A. Wright and Richard J. Lutz, "The Framing of Brand Judgments after Direct Product Experience and Advertising: An Empirical Investigation," *AMA Winter Educators' Proceedings* (1993), pp. 172–178; Karen H. Smith, "The Moderating Influence of Depth of Processing on Order of Entry Framing Effects," *Advances in Consumer Research*, Vol. 20 (1993), pp. 219–223; and Donald J. Hempel and Harold Daniel, "Framing Dynamics: Measurement Issues and Perspectives," *Advances in Consumer Research*, Vol. 20 (1993), pp. 273–279. For a discussion of ethical considerations, see also Alan E. Singer, Steven Lysonski, Ming Singer, and David Hayes, "Ethical Myopia: The Case of 'Framing' by Framing," *Journal of Business Ethics*, Vol. 10 (1991), pp. 29–36.

20. Prakash Nedungadi, "Recall and Consumer Consideration Sets: Influencing Choice without Altering Brand Evaluations," *Journal of Consumer Research*, Vol. 17, No. 3 (December 1990),

pp. 263–276; C. Whan Park and Daniel C. Smith, "Product-Level Choice: A Top-Down or Bottom-Up Process?," *Journal of Consumer Research*, Vol. 16, No. 3 (December 1989), pp. 289–299; John R. Hauser and Birger Wernerfelt, "The Competitive Implications of Relevant-Set/Response Analysis," *Journal of Marketing Research*, Vol. 26 (November 1989), pp. 391–405; Prakash Nedungadi and Vinay Kanetkar, "Incorporating Consideration Sets into Models of Brand Choice," *Advances in Consumer Research*, Vol. 19 (1992), pp. 251–252; and John S. Hulland, "An Empirical Investigation of Consideration Set Formation," *Advances in Consumer Research*, Vol. 19 (1992), pp. 253–254.

21.   William L. Wilkie and Peter R. Dickson, "Consumer Information Search and Shopping Behavior," in H. Kassarjian and T. Robertson (eds.), *Perspectives in Consumer Behavior*, 4th ed. (Englewood Cliffs, N.J.: Prentice Hall, 1991), pp. 1–26.

22.   The discussion on "The Information Accelerator" is primarily based upon Raymond Serafin, "The Information Accelerator and Me," *Advertising Age*, March 22, 1993, p. 47. The discussion on "The Visionary Shopper" is primarily based upon Howard Schlossberg, "Shoppers Virtually Stroll through Store Aisles to Examine Packages," *Marketing News*, June 7, 1993, p. 2. For detailed considerations of how such simulations might depart from realistic consumer responses, see especially Raymond R. Burke, Bari A. Harlam, Barbara E. Kahn, and Leonard M. Lodish, "Comparing Dynamic Consumer Choice in Real and Computer-simulated Environments," *Journal of Consumer Research*, Vol. 19, June 1992, pp. 71–82. See also John E. G. Bateson and Michael K. Hui, "The Ecological Validity of Photographic Slides and Videotapes in Simulating the Service Setting," *Journal of Consumer Research*, Vol. 19, No. 2 (September 1992), pp. 271–281.

23.   K. W. Kendall and Ian Fenwick, "What Do You Learn Standing in a Supermarket Aisle?" *Advances in Consumer Research*, Vol. 6 (1979), pp. 153–160. See also Wayne D. Hoyer, "An Examination of Consumer Decision Making for a Common Repeat Purchase Product," *Journal of Consumer Research*, Vol. 11 (December 1984), pp. 822–829; Cathy J. Cobb and Wayne D. Hoyer, "Direct Observation of Search Behavior," *Psychology & Marketing*, Vol. 2 (Fall 1985), pp. 161–179; Patricia M. Anderson, "Personality, Perception, and Emotional-State Factors in Approach-Avoidance Behavior in the Store Environment," *AMA Summer Educators' Proceedings* (1986), pp. 35–39; Adam Finn, "A Consumer Acceptance of Unobstrusive Observation in a Shopping Center," *AMA Summer Educators' Proceedings* (1989), pp. 176–181; Laurette Dube-Rioux, Bernd H. Schmitt, and France Leclerc, "Consumers' Reactions to Waiting: When Delays Affect the Perception of Service Quality," *Advances in Consumer Research*, Vol. 16 (1989), pp. 59–63; Alain D'Astous, Idriss Bensouda, and Jean Guindon, "A Re-Examination of Consumer Decision Making for a Repeat Purchase Product: Variations in Product Importance and Purchase Frequency," *Advances in Consumer Research*, Vol. 16 (1989), pp. 433–438; Cathy Goodwin and Charles D. Frame, "Social Distance within the Service Encounter: Does the Consumer Want to Be Your Friend?" *Advances in Consumer Research*, Vol. 16 (1989), pp. 64–71; and C. Whan Park, Easwar S. Iyer, and Daniel C. Smith, "The Effects of Situational Factors on In-Store Grocery Shopping Behavior: The Role of Store Environment and Time Available for Shopping," *Journal of Consumer Research*, Vol. 15 (March 1989), pp. 422–433.

24.   C. Whan Park, Easwar S. Iyer, and Daniel C. Smith, "The Effects of Situational Factors on In-Store Grocery Shopping Behavior: The Role of Store Environment and Time Available for Shopping," *Journal of Consumer Research*, Vol. 15 (March 1989), pp. 422–433.

25.   Laurie Petersen, "Study Confirms Impulse Buying on Rise," *Promote*, October 12, 1987, pp. 6–10.

26.   Kathleen Deveny, "Displays Pay Off for Grocery Marketers," *The Wall Street Journal,* October 15, 1992, p. B1. See also Michel Chevalier, "Increase in Sales due to In-Store Display," *Journal of Marketing Research*, Vol. 12 (November 1975), pp. 426–431.

27.   "Is Type Size Key Factor in Ads?" *Chain Store Age Executive,* February 1977, p. 12. For further review of this area, together with more sophisticated analyses, see J. B. Wilkinson, J. Barry Mason, and Christie H. Paksoy, "Assessing the Impact of Short-Term Supermarket Strategy Variables," *Journal of Marketing Research*, Vol. 9 (February 1982), pp. 72–86; P. S. Raju and Manoj Hastak, "Consumer Response to Deals: A Discussion of Theoretical Perspectives," *Advances in Consumer Research*, Vol. 7 (1980), pp. 296–301; Meryl P. Gardner and Roger A. Strang, "Consumer Response to Promotions: Some New Perspectives," *Advances in Consumer Research*, Vol. 11 (1984), pp. 420–425; Bruce E. Mattson and Alan J. Dubinsky, "Shopping Patterns: An Exploration of Some Situational Determinants," *Psychology & Marketing,* Vol. 4 (Spring 1987), pp. 47–62; Catherine Cole and Goutam Chakraborty, "Laboratory Studies of Coupon Redemption Rates and Repeat Purchase Rates," *AMA Summer Educators' Proceedings* (1987), pp. 51–54; Sunil Gupta, "Impact of Sales Promotions on When, What, and How Much to Buy," *Journal of Marketing Research*, Vol. 25 (November 1988), pp. 342–355; Jerry N. Conover, "The Influence of Cents-Off Coupons on Brand Choice Decisions at the Point of Purchase," *Advances in Consumer Research*, Vol. 16 (1989), pp. 443–446; and Kapil Bawa and Robert W. Shoemaker, "Analyzing Incremental Sales from a Direct Mail Coupon Promotion," *Journal of Marketing*, Vol. 53 (July 1989), pp. 66–78; Peter S. Fader and Leonard M. Lodish, "A Cross-Category Analysis of Category Structure and Promotional Activity for Grocery Products," *Journal of Marketing*, Vol. 54, No. 4 (October 1990), pp. 52–65; Leland Campbell and William D. Diamond, "Framing and Sales Promotions: The Characteristics of a 'Good Deal,'" *The Journal of Consumer Marketing*, Vol. 7, No. 4 (Fall 1990), pp. 25–31; Rajiv Lal, "Manufacturer Trade Deals and Retail Price Promotions," *Journal of Marketing Research*, Vol. 27 (November 1990), pp. 428–444; Barbara E. Kahn and Therese A. Louie, "Effects of Retraction of Price Promotions on Brand Choice Behavior for Variety-seeking and Last-Purchase-Loyal Consumers," *Journal of Marketing Research*, Vol. 27 (August 1990), pp. 279–289; Peter S. Fader and Leigh McAlister, "An Elimination by Aspects Model of Consumer Response to Promotion Calibrated on UPC Scanner Data," *Journal of Marketing Research*, Vol. 27 (August 1990), pp. 322–332; William D. Diamond and Abhijit Sanyal, "The Effect of Framing on the Choice of Supermarket Coupons," *Advances in Consumer Research*, Vol. 17 (1990), pp. 488–493; William D. Diamond and Robert R. Johnson, "The Framing of Sales Promotions: An Approach to Classification," *Advances in Consumer Research*, Vol. 17 (1990), pp. 494–500; Rockney G. Walters, "Assessing the Impact of Retail Price Promotions on Product Substitution, Complementary Purchase, and Interstore Sales Displacement," *Journal of Marketing*, Vol. 55, No. 2 (April 1991), pp. 17–28; H. Bruce Lammers, "The Effect of Free Samples on Immediate Consumer Purchase," *The*

Journal of Consumer Marketing, Vol. 8, No. 2 (Spring 1991), pp. 31–38; William D. Diamond, "The Effects of Different Types of Supermarket Coupons on Purchase Intention," *AMA Summer Educators' Proceedings* (1991), pp. 54–58; Ajay K. Manrai and Lalita A. Manrai, "A Model of Preference of Department Stores," *AMA Summer Educators' Proceedings* (1991), pp. 145–153; Lakshman Krishnamurthi, Tridib Mazumdar, and S.P. Raj, "Asymmetric Response to Price in Consumer Brand Choice and Purchase Quantity Decisions," *Journal of Consumer Research,* Vol. 19, No. 3 (December 1992), pp. 387–400; Sunil Gupta and Lee G. Cooper, "The Discounting of Discounts and Promotion Thresholds," *Journal of Consumer Research,* Vol. 19, No. 3 (December 1992), pp. 401–411; and Donald R. Lichtenstein, Richard G. Netemeyer, and Scot Burton, "Using a Theoretical Perspective to Examine the Psychological Construct of Coupon Proneness," *Advances in Consumer Research,* Vol. 18 (1991), pp. 501–508.

28. Examples and discussion in this Exhibit are based on Kerry J. Smith, "In-Store Marketing," *PROMO Magazine,* January 1993, pp. 6ff; Glenn Heitsmith, "Making Instant In-Store Impact," *PROMO Magazine,* October 1992, pp. 24ff; Larry Armstrong, "What's That Noise in Aisle 5?" *Business Week,* June 8, 1992; Laurie Petersen, "Buying French Fries with Plastic," *Marketing Week,* October 28, 1991; Judann Dagnoli, "Impulse Governs Shoppers," *Advertising Age,* October 5, 1987, p. 93; "Ideas From POPAI's Marketplace '87," *Promote,* December 14, 1987, p. 12; Laurie Freeman and Judann Dagnoli, "Point-of-Purchase Rush Is On," *Advertising Age,* February 8, 1988, p. 47; Jim Connolly, "POP Radio: It's Music to the Ears . . . ," *Marketing Week,* May 2, 1988, p. 17; Lori Kesler, "Catalina Cuts Couponing Clutter," *Advertising Age,* May 9, 1988, p. S30, and David Kiley, "Sales Promotion in a Flash," *Marketing Week,* December 21, 1987, p. 1; "VideOCart Shopping Cart with Computer Screen Creates New Ad Medium . . . ," *Marketing News,* May 9, 1988, p. 1; and Michael Burgi, "Coupon Machine Off at a Fast Clip," *Advertising Age,* May 6, 1991, p. 31. See also David W. Schumann, Jennifer Grayson, Johanna Ault, Kerri Hargrove, Lois Hollingsworth, Russell Ruelle, and Sharon Seguin, "The Effectiveness of Shopping Cart Signage: Perceptual Measures Tell a Different Story," *Journal of Advertising Research,* Vol. 31, No. 1 (February/March 1991), pp. 17–22; and Ron Garland, "Price Accuracy in New Zealand's Scanning Supermarkets," *Journal of International Consumer Marketing,* Vol. 5, No. 1 (1993), pp. 85–100.

29. See Dudley M. Ruch, "Effective Sales Promotion Lessons for Today," *Marketing Science* Institute Report 87-108, 1987; Kenneth G. Hardy, "Key Success Factors for Manufacturers' Sales Promotions in Package Goods," *Journal of Marketing,* Vol. 50, No. 3 (July 1986), pp. 13–23; J. Jeffrey Inman, Leigh McAlister, and Wayne D. Hoyer, "Promotion Signal: Proxy for a Price Cut?" *Journal of Consumer Research,* Vol. 17 (June 1990), pp. 74–81; Harry Levinson and Nan Stone, "The Case of the Perplexing Promotion," *Harvard Business Review,* No. 1 (January–February 1990), pp. 11–21; Robert D. Buzzell, John A. Quelch, and Walter J. Salmon, "The Costly Bargain of Trade Promotion," *Harvard Business Review,* No. 2 (March–April 1990), pp. 141–149; and John Philip Jones, "The Double Jeopardy of Sales Promotions," *Harvard Business Review,* (September–October 1990), pp. 145–152.

30. Peter R. Dickson and Alan G. Sawyer, "The Price Knowledge and Search of Supermarket Shoppers," *Journal of Marketing,* Vol. 54, No. 3 (July 1990), pp. 42–53. See also Valarie A. Zeithaml, "Consumer Response to In-Store Price Information Environments," *Journal of Consumer Research,* Vol. 8 (March 1982), pp. 357–369; Rosemary Walker and Brenda Cude, "In-Store Shopping Strategies: Time and Money Costs in the Supermarket," *The Journal of Consumer Affairs,* Vol. 17 (Winter 1983), pp. 356–369; Olli T. Ahtola, "Price as a 'Give' Component in an Exchange Theoretic Multicomponent Model," *Advances in Consumer Research,* Vol. 11 (1984), pp. 623–626; Easwar S. Iyer and Sucheta S. Ahlawat, "Deviations from a Shopping Plan: When and Why Do Consumers Not Buy Items As Planned," *Advances in Consumer Research,* Vol. 14 (1987), pp. 246–250; Jerry N. Conover, "Shoppers Recall of Grocery Product Prices," *AMA Summer Educators' Proceedings* (1988), pp. 62–67; Donald R. Lichtenstein, Richard G. Netemeyer, and Scot Burton, "Distinguishing Coupon Proneness from Value Consciousness: An Acquisition-Transaction Utility Theory Perspective," *Journal of Marketing,* Vol. 54, No. 3 (July 1990), pp. 54–67; Wayne D. Hoyer and Steven P. Brown, "Effects of Brand Awareness on Choice for a Common, Repeat-Purchase Product," *Journal of Consumer Research,* Vol. 17, No. 2 (September 1990), pp. 141–148; Jonathan K. Frenzen and Harry L. Davis, "Purchasing Behavior in Embedded Markets," *Journal of Consumer Research,* Vol. 17, No. 1 (June 1990), pp. 1–12; Robert Jacobson and Carl Obermiller, "The Formation of Expected Future Price: A Reference Price for Forward-Looking Consumers," *Journal of Consumer Research,* Vol. 16, No. 4 (March 1990), pp. 420–432; Joel E. Urbany and Peter R. Dickson, "Consumer Normal Price Estimation: Market versus Personal Standards," *Journal of Consumer Research,* Vol. 18, No. 1 (June 1991), pp. 45–51; Joel E. Urbany, Peter R. Dickson, and Rosemary Key, "Actual and Perceived Consumer Vigilance in the Retail Grocery Industry," *Marketing Letters,* Vol. 2, No. 1 (January 1991), pp. 15–26; Rosemary Kalapurakal, Peter R. Dickson, and Joel E. Urbany, "Perceived Price Fairness and Dual Entitlement," *Advances in Consumer Research,* Vol. 18 (1991), pp. 788–793; Michael K. Hui and John E. G. Bateson, "Perceived Control and the Effects of Crowding and Consumer Choice on the Service Experience," *Journal of Consumer Research,* Vol. 18, No. 2 (September 1991), pp. 174–184; and Richard Parker, G. Ray Funkhouser, and Anindya Chatterjee, "Consumer Cost Orientations: An Exploratory Empirical Investigation," *AMA Winter Educators' Proceedings* (1993), pp. 385–391.

Chapter 19

Consumer Decision (III) Postpurchase Processes

1. Quotes are courtesy of Professor Patrick E. Murphy, University of Notre Dame.

2. This section is adapted from material presented in Philip E. Hendrix, "Product/Service Consumption: Key Dimensions and Implications for Marketing," Working Paper, Emory University, Atlanta, August 1984.

3. See Melissa Martin Young, "Emotional Reactions to Possession Disposition: Protest, Retrospective, and Relief Factors," *AMA Winter Educators' Proceedings* (1991), pp. 176–185; and Jacob Jacoby, Carol Berning, and Thomas Dietvorst, "What about Disposition?" *Journal of Marketing,* Vol. 41 (April 1977), pp. 22–28. For other readings in this area, see also James W. Hanson, "A Proposed Paradigm for Consumer Product Disposition Processes," *The Journal of Consumer Affairs* Vol. 14, No. 1 (Summer 1980), pp. 49–67.

4. The "Eco-logic" framework was developed by the author of this text. The points made are based upon Jacquelyn Ottman, "Use Less, Make It More Durable, and Then Take It Back," *Marketing News*, April 30, 1992, p. 14. Ms. Ottman is president of J. Ottman Consulting, Inc., an environmental marketing consulting firm in New York City. Developments in this area are rapidly changing. For excellent discussions of the FTC's *Guides for Environmental Marketing*, see Jason W. Gray-Lee, Debra L. Scammon, and Robert N. Mayer, "A Guilding Light: Illuminating the Green Marketing Guides," and Robert N. Mayer, Debra L. Scammon, and Jason W. Gray-Lee, "Will the FTC Guidelines on Environmental Marketing Affect the Hue of Green Marketing? An Audit of Claims on Product Labels," both in M. J. Sheffet (ed.), *Proceedings of the 1993 Marketing and Public Policy Conference* (East Lansing: Michigan State University, Eli Broad Graduate School, 1993), pp. 75–91 and 19–30, respectively. See also Norman Kangun, Stephen Grove, and Williams Kilbourne, "The Green Alternative: A Prognosis for Further Development and Its Marketplace Impact," *AMA Winter Educators' Proceedings* (1991), pp. 233–236; Jaclyn Fierman, "The Big Muddle in Green Marketing," *Fortune*, June 3, 1991, p. 91ff; Jennifer Lawrence and Pat Sloan, "Toiletries to Strip Excess Packaging," *Advertising Age*, May 13, 1991, pp. 3ff; and Bentham Paulos and Andrew Stoeckle, "FTC Green Marketing Guides Are Not Optional," *Marketing News*, Vol. 27, No. 13 (June 21, 1993), pp. 4–5.

For related academic perspectives, see also Patrick L. Brockett, Linda L. Golden, and Paul R. Aird, "How Public Policy Can Define the Marketplace: The Case of Pollution Liability Insurance in the 1980's," *Journal of Public Policy & Marketing*, Vol. 9 (1990), pp. 211–226; Michael Naughton, Fredrick Sebold, and Thomas Mayer, "Impacts of the California Beverage Container Recycling and Litter Reduction Act on Consumers," *The Journal of Consumer Affairs*, Vol. 24, No. 1 (Summer 1990), pp. 190–220; George C. Lodge and Jeffrey F. Rayport, "Knee-deep and Rising: America's Recycling Crisis," *Harvard Business Review*, September–October 1991, pp. 128–139; T. J. Olney and Wendy Bryce, "Consumer Responses to Environmentally Based Product Claims," *Advances in Consumer Research*, Vol. 18 (1991), pp. 693–696; R. Bruce Hutton and Frank Markley, "The Effects of Incentives on Environment-Friendly Behaviors: A Case Study," *Advances in Consumer Research*, Vol. 18 (1991), pp. 697–702; three papers in *AMA Summer Educators' Proceedings* (1991): Kent L. Granzin and Janeen E. Olsen, "An Investigation of the Characteristics of Participants in Conservation and Environmental Protection: An Emphasis on Helping Behavior," pp. 177–186; Hazel T. Suchard and Michael Jay Polonsky, "A Theory of Environmental Buyer Behavior and Its Validity: The Environmental Action-Behavior Model," pp. 187–201; and Michael H. Morris and Pamela S. Lewis, "The Determinants of Societal Entrepreneurship: An Environmental Perspective," pp. 583–591; Ken Geiser, "The Greening of Industry," *Technology Review*, August/September 1991, pp. 64ff; "Diapers: Disposable and Cloth," *Consumer Reports*, Vol. 56, No. 8 (August 1991), pp. 551–557; Ed Petkus, Jr., "Implications of the Symbolic Interactionism Perspective for the Study of Environmentally-Responsible Consumption," *Advances in Consumer Research*, Vol. 19 (1992), pp. 861–869; four articles in *AMA Winter Educators' Proceedings* (1992): Gregory M. Pickett, Stephen J. Grove, and Norman Kangun, "An Analysis of the Conserving Consumer: A Public Policy Perspective," pp. 151–153; Amardeep Assar and George S. Bobinski, Jr., "Issues in Voluntary Simplicity: Concepts, Measurement, and Determinants," pp. 237–243; Annamma Joy and Barbara Motzney, "Ecotourism and Ecotourists: Preliminary Thoughts on the New Leisure Traveller," pp. 457–463; and Ida E. Berger, "A Framework for Understanding the Relationship between Environmental Attitudes and Consumer Behaviors," pp. 157–164; Kim A. Nelson, "The Role of Cognitive Moral Development in Socially Responsible Consumer Choice," *AMA Winter Educators' Proceedings* (1993), pp. 165–171; Donald A. Fuller, "Developing Ecologically Responsible Products: The Marketing-Industrial Design Interface," *AMA Winter Educators' Proceedings* (1993), pp. 204–205; Easwar Iyer and Bobby Banerjee, "Anatomy of Green Advertising," *Advances in Consumer Research*, Vol. 20 (1993), pp. 494–501; Harvey Alter, "Cost of Recycling Municipal Solid Waste with and without a Concurrent Beverage Container Deposit Law," *The Journal of Consumer Affairs*, Vol. 27, No. 1 (Summer 1993), pp. 166–186; Kenneth P. Dupré and Louis M. Capella, "The New Environmental Market: Pricing Implications for Ecopreneurial Firms," in Robert L. King (ed.), *Marketing: Perspectives for the 1990s*, (Richmond, Va.: Southern Marketing Association, 1992), pp. 467–470; and two articles in M. J. Sheffet (ed.), *Proceedings of the 1993 Public Policy and Marketing Conference* (East Lansing: Michigan State University, Eli Broad Graduate School of Management, 1993): Donald A. Fuller, "The Role of Ecological-Legal Sanctions in Fostering Post-Consumer Recycling: A Marketing Commentary," pp. 7–16; and Karl Moore, "An Emergent Model of Consumer Response to Green Marketing," pp. 109–122.

5. Alan Farnham, "State Your Values, Hold the Hot Air," *Fortune*, April 19, 1993, pp. 117ff. See also Robert N. Mayer, Debra L. Scammon, and Cathleen D. Zick, "Poisoning the Well: Do Environmental Claims Strain Consumer Credulity?" *Advances in Consumer Research*, Vol. 20 (1993), pp. 698–703.

6. This discussion is based upon "For Growing Band of Shoppers, Clean Means Green," *The Wall Street Journal*, April 6, 1993, p. B1; "Our Garbage I.Q. is Low," *USA Today*, November 1, 1991, p. 12A; David Stipp, "Consumers' Improper Sorting of Trash is a Messy Problem for Recycling Industry," *The Wall Street Journal*, May 9, 1991, B1; and Rebecca Piirto, *Beyond Mind Games: The Marketing Power of Psychographics* (Ithaca, N.Y.: American Demographics Books, 1991), pp. 190–195. See also Duane L. Davis and Jeff Allen, "The Effects of Economic Incentives on the Reverse Distribution of Aluminum: A Field Experiment," *AMA Winter Educators' Proceedings* (1991), pp. 72–79; Royce Anderson, "Consumer Response to Mandatory Recycling," *AMA Winter Educators' Proceedings* (1993), pp. 206–211; and three papers in *Advances in Consumer Research*, Vol. 20 (1993): Anita L. Jackson, Janeen E. Olsen, Kent L. Granzin, and Alvin C. Burns, "An Investigation of Determinants of Recycling Consumer Behavior," pp. 481–487; Prem Shamdasani, Gloria Ong Chon-Lin, and Daleen Richmond, "Exploring Green Consumers in an Oriental Culture: Role of Personal and Marketing Mix Factors," pp. 488–493; and John A. McCarty and L. J. Shrum, "A Structural Equation Analysis of the Relationships of Personal Values, Attitudes and Beliefs about Recycling, and the Recycling of Solid Waste Products," pp. 641–646.

7. Leon Festinger, *A Theory of Cognitive Dissonance* (Stanford, Calif.: Stanford University Press, 1957). See also A. G. Greenwald and D. L. Ronis, "Twenty Years of Cognitive Dissonance: Case Study of the Evolution of a Theory," *Psychological Review*, Vol. 85 (1978), pp. 53–57, and J. Beauvois and R. Joule, "Dissonance versus Self-perception Theories: A Radical Conception of Festinger's Theory," *Journal of Social Psychology*, Vol. 117 (1982), pp. 99–113.

8. Readers interested in the controversies should be aware of three key points: (1) In technical terms, dissonance theory is not highly specific. (2) It is difficult to create research conditions to allow clear tests of whether or not dissonance is the only factor that is operating in a study. (3) Finally, everyone recognizes that many factors beyond dissonance will affect a consumer's behavior in the real world. For example, if Kevin Baker's new Camaro won't start easily, the fact that he's motivated to like the car probably won't stand up against his knowledge that he's being stranded on a regular basis. In addition to the readings in Note 7, there is an interesting literature in marketing. See Joel B. Cohen and Danny L. Moore, "Postdecision Consistency Enhancing Processes," Paper, University of Florida, Gainesville, Center for Consumer Research, 1988, for an overview. See also William H. Cummings and M. Venkatesan, "Cognitive Dissonance and Consumer Behavior: A Review of the Evidence," *Journal of Marketing Research*, Vol. 13 (August 1976), pp. 303–308; and Valerie S. Folkes and Barbara Kotsos, "Buyers' and Sellers' Explanation for Product Failure: Who Done It?" *Journal of Marketing*, Vol. 50 (April 1986), pp. 74–80.

9. A useful overview of this field is available in E. Scott Maynes et al. (eds.), *Research in the Consumer Interest: The Frontier* (Columbia, Mo.: American Council on Consumer Interests, 1988). In this volume see especially H. Keith Hunt, "Consumer Satisfaction/Dissatisfaction and the Consumer Interest," pp. 731–748; Robert A. Westbrook, "Consumer Satisfaction: An Affirmation of Possibilities," pp. 760–770; and Folke Olander, "Consumer Satisfaction/Dissatisfaction and the Consumer Interest," pp. 753–759.

Long before the business world at large discovered Total Quality Management, (TQM), consumer researchers were stressing consumer satisfaction. Very many papers are available on this topic. The *Journal of Consumer Satisfaction, Dissatisfaction and Complaining Behavior* is an annual publication presenting relevant work in this area. For information on how you or your library can obtain this publication, contact Professor H. Keith Hunt, Marriott School of Management, Brigham Young University, Provo, UT 84602 (phone: 801-378-2080). Some articles of interest in Volume 5 (1992) include Diane Halstead and Thomas J. Page, Jr., "The Effects of Satisfaction and Complaining Behavior on Consumer Repurchase Intentions," pp. 1–11; Hudson P. Rogers, Reginald M. Peyton and Robert L. Berl, "Measurement and Evaluation of Satisfaction Processes in a Dyadic Setting," pp. 12–23; Denyse Laberge Dagenais and Carole P. Duhaime, "Estimating Models of Determination of Consumer Satisfaction: An Alternative Approach," pp. 24–35; Jane Kolodinsky, "A System for Estimating Complaints, Complaint Resolution, and Subsequent Purchases of Professional and Personal Services," pp. 36–44; Richard A. Spreng and Richard W. Olshavsky, "A Desires-as-Standard Model of Consumer Satisfaction: Implications for Measuring Satisfaction," pp. 45–54; Stephen S. Tax and Murali Chandrashekaran, "Consumer Decision Making following a Failed Service Encounter: A Pilot Study," pp. 55–68; John Swan, "Satisfaction Work: The Joint Production of Patient Satisfaction by Health Care Providers and Patients," pp. 69–80; John C. Rogers, Steven C. Ross, and Terrell G. Williams, "Personal Values and Purchase Dissatisfaction Response," pp. 81–92; Jeffrey G. Blodgett and Donald H. Granbois, "Toward an Integrated Conceptual Model of Consumer Complaining Behavior," pp. 93–103; Sunil Erevelles and Clark Leavitt, "A Comparison of Current Models of Consumer Satisfaction/Dissatisfaction," pp. 104–114; Brent G.

Goff and Manton C. Gibbs, "The Effects of Denominational Dissatisfaction and Anomie on Involvement and Complaint Intentions: An Exploratory Model for Religious Services," pp. 115–126; Eivind Sto and Sidsel Glefjell, "Consumer Satisfaction, Dissatisfaction and Advertising Complaints," pp. 127–138; Norleen M. Ackerman and Leona K. Hawks, "Product Satisfaction Explained by Satisfaction and Complaints Regarding Product Characteristics," pp. 139–147; A.K. Srivastava, "Effect of Disconfirmed Expectancy on Consumer Attributions: A Study of Durable Products," pp. 148–161; Sally K. Francis, "Effect of Clothing Interest on Clothing Deprivation/Dissatisfaction," pp. 162–167; Ann Marie Fiore and Mary Lynn Damhorst, "Intrinsic Cues as Predictors of Perceived Quality of Apparel," pp. 168–178; William M. Strahle, Sigfredo A. Hernandez, Hector L. Garcia and Robert C. Sorensen, "A Study of Consumer Complaining Behavior: VCR Owners in Puerto Rico," pp. 179–191; Soyeon Shim and Marianne Y. Mahoney, "Differentiation of Satisfied Users and Dissatisfied Users of In-Home Electronic Shopping Mode: An Exploratory Study," pp. 192–200; Katherine V. Diaz-Knauf, Howard G. Schutz and Roberta Y. Almeida, "Hispanic Consumer Attitudes toward Occupational Service Providers: Satisfaction, Quality, and Selection Criteria," pp. 201–212; James Kent Pinney and Larry Strate, "A&B Telemarketing: A Case Study in Consumer Dissatisfaction and Complaining Behavior," pp. 213–222; Ralph L. Day and Debra S. Perkins, "Roots: A Folk History of the Consumer Satisfaction Literature," pp. 223–227; and Jonathan C. Huefner and H. Keith Hunt, "Brand and Store Avoidance: The Behavioral Expression of Dissatisfaction," pp. 228–232.

Some relevant articles in Volume 4 (1991) include Jagdip Singh and Robert E. Wilkes, "A Theoretical Framework for Modeling Consumers' Response to Marketplace Dissatisfaction," pp. 1–12; Thomas E. Muller, David K. Tse, and Ramesh Venkatasubramaniam, "Post-Consumption Emotions: Exploring Their Emergence and Determinants," pp. 13–20; James H. Drew and Ruth N. Bolton, "The Structure of Customer Satisfaction: Effects of Survey Measurement," pp. 21–31; William R. Forrester, Jr., and Manfred F. Maute, "Effects of Response Delay on the Quality of Satisfaction Data in Mail Surveys," pp. 32–38; Andy R. McGill, "Treating Consumer Depression to Create Infiniti Potential," pp. 39–49; Alex Simonson, "Examining Consumer Losses and Dissatisfaction due to Broken Sales and Service Agreements," pp. 50–61; Dennis E. Garrett, Renee A. Meyers, and John Camey, "Interactive Complaint Communication: A Theoretical Framework and Research Agenda," pp. 62–79; Dirk Standop, "Manufacturers' Concern for Product Risks after the Sale: Do Product Recalls Really Cause Consumers' Dissatisfaction?," pp. 80–83; Deepak Sirdeshmukh, Dev S. Pathak, Susan Kucukarslan, Richard Segal, Karen L. Kier, and Sheri L. Aversa, "Patient Satisfaction/Dissatisfaction and Post-Exchange Actions in the High–Blood Pressure Prescription Drug Market: A Preliminary Report," pp. 84–92; Yves Evrard, "A Two-Step Model of Satisfaction with Public Transportation," pp. 93–102; Robert B. Woodruff, D. Scott Clemons, David W. Schumann, Sarah F. Gardial and Mary Jane Burns, "The Standards Issue in CS/D Research: A Historical Perspective," pp. 103–109; Ved Prakash, "Intensity of Dissatisfaction and Consumer Complaint Behaviors," pp. 110–122; Robert East, Wendy Lomax, and Will Willson, "Factors Associated with Service Delay in Supermarkets and Post Offices," pp. 123–128; Cathy Goodwin, Kelly L. Smith, and Bronislaw J. Verhage, "An Equity Model of Consumer Response to Waiting Time," pp. 129–138; Sally K. Francis and Beverly Browne, "Effect of User

Orientation on Disconfirmation Processing," pp. 139–143; Teresa N. Malafi, "The Impact of Social Influence on Consumer Complaint Behavior," pp. 144–150; James Kent Pinney, "The Decision Making Process of Cancer Patients: Through a Model Still More Clearly," pp. 151–160; Douglas Hausknecht and James R. Webb, "Homeowner Satisfaction," pp. 161–166; Mark E. Slama and Terrell G. Williams, "Consumer Interaction Styles and Purchase Complaint Interactions," pp. 167–174; Gail Tom, Stoakley Swanson, Bruce McElroy, and Jenney Lim, "The Role of Situational Variables in Consumer Choice Satisfaction," pp. 175–179; Dianne S. P. Cermak, Karen Maru File, and Russ Alan Prince, "Complaining and Praising in Non-profit Exchanges: When Satisfaction Matters Less," pp. 180–187; J. Patrick Kelly, Jonathan C. Huefner, and H. Keith Hunt, "Frequency of Use and Level of Satisfaction with Rainchecks," pp. 188–193; and "A Consumer Satisfaction, Dissatisfaction and Complaining Behavior Bibliography: 1982–1990," pp. 194–228.

10.   This section is based on discussions in Richard L. Oliver, "A Cognitive Model of the Antecedents and Consequences of Satisfaction Decisions," *Journal of Marketing Research*, Vol. 17 (November 1980), pp. 460–469; H. Keith Hunt, "CS/D: Overview and Future Research Directions," in H. K. Hunt (ed.), *Conceptualization and Measurement of Consumer Satisfaction and Dissatisfaction* (Cambridge, Mass.: Marketing Science Institute, 1977); and the following articles in Ralph L. Day and H. Keith Hunt (eds.), *International Fair in Consumer Satisfaction and Complaining Behavior* (Bloomington: Indiana University Division of Research, 1983): Robert A. Westbrook, "Consumer Satisfaction and the Phenomenology of Emotions during Automobile Ownership Experiences," pp. 2–9; Ralph L. Day, "The Next Step: Commonly Accepted Constructions for Satisfaction Research," pp. 113–117; Robert B. Woodruff, Ernest R. Cadotte, and Roger L. Jenkins, "Charting a Path for CS/D Research," pp. 118–123; John E. Swan, "Consumer Satisfaction Research and Theory: Current Status and Future Directions," pp. 124–129, and H. Keith Hunt, "A '10' Based on Expectations, but Normatively a '3.6371,'" pp. 130–131.

For additional recent perspectives on the nature of CS/D, see, for example, Daniel J. Howard and Thomas E. Barry, "The Evaluative Consequences of Experiencing Unexpected Favorable Events," *Journal of Marketing Research*, Vol. 27 (February 1990), pp. 51–60; David K. Tse, Franco M. Nicosia, and Peter C. Wilton, "Consumer Satisfaction as a Process," *Psychology & Marketing*, Vol. 7, No. 3 (Fall 1990), pp. 177–194; Robert A. Westbrook and Richard L. Oliver, "The Dimensionality of Consumption Emotion Patterns and Consumer Satisfaction," *Journal of Consumer Research*, Vol. 18, No. 1 (June 1991), pp. 84–91; Ann L. McGill, "Predicting Consumers' Reactions to Product Failure: Do Responsibility Judgments Follow from Consumers' Causal Explanations?" *Marketing Letters*, Vol. 2, No. 1 (January 1991), pp. 59–70; Jagdip Singh, "Understanding the Structure of Consumers' Satisfaction Evaluations of Service Delivery," *Journal of the Academy of Marketing Science*, Vol. 19, No. 3 (Summer 1991), pp. 223–244; Laurette Dube and Bernd H. Schmitt, "The Processing of Emotional and Cognitive Aspects of Product Usage in Satisfaction Judgments," *Advances in Consumer Research*, Vol. 18 (1991), pp. 52–56; Lalita A. Manrai and Meryl P. Gardner, "The Influence of Affect on Attributions for Product Failure," *Advances in Consumer Research*, Vol. 18 (1991), pp. 249–254; Michael A. McCollough and Sundar G. Bharadwaj, "The Recovery Paradox: An Examination of Consumer Satisfaction in Relation to Disconfirmation, Service

Quality, and Attribution Based Theories," *AMA Winter Educators' Proceedings* (1992), p. 119; David J. Burns, " 'It Wasn't My Fault,' or the Role of Excuses in Post-Purchase Behavior," *AMA Winter Educators' Proceedings* (1992), p. 236; D. Scott Clemons and Robert B. Woodruff, "Broadening the View of Consumer (Dis)Satisfaction: A Proposed Means-End Disconfirmation Model of CS/D," *AMA Winter Educators' Proceedings* (1992), pp. 413–421; Robert A. Peterson and William R. Wilson, "Measuring Customer Satisfaction: Fact and Artifact," *Journal of the Academy of Marketing Science*, Vol. 20, No. 1 (Winter, 1992), pp. 61–72; Richard A. Spreng and Andrea L. Dixon, "Alternative Comparison Standards in the Formation of Consumer Satisfaction/Dissatisfaction," *AMA Summer Educators' Proceedings* (1992), pp. 85–91; Randall G. Chapman, "Assessing Nonresponse Bias the Right Way: A Customer Satisfaction Case Study," *AMA Summer Educators' Proceedings* (1992), pp. 322–326; Kevin M. Elliott and Carolyn Tripp, "Customer Satisfaction within the Airline Industry: How Do Airlines Rate with Regard to Meeting Consumer Expectations?" in R. King (ed.), *Marketing: Perspectives for the 1990s* (Richmond, Va.: Southern Marketing Association, 1992), pp. 382–385; Mary L. Carsky and Margery S. Steinberg, "Customer Satisfaction—Where Are We Going? Where Have We Been?," *AMA Winter Educators' Proceedings* (1993), pp. 362–369; and Diane Halstead, "The Expectations-Satisfaction Relationship Revisited: An Empirical Test and Directions for Future Research," *AMA Winter Educators' Proceedings* (1993), pp. 371–373.

11.   For the Sears results, see Donald A. Hughes, "Considerations in the Measurement and Use of Consumer Satisfaction Ratings," in William Locander (ed.), *Marketing Looks Outward* (Chicago: American Marketing Association, 1977).

12.   For interesting discussions and debates about the Power method, see Alex Taylor, "More Power to J.D. Power," *Fortune*, May 18, 1992, pp. 103–106; Larry Armstrong, "Who's the Most Pampered Motorist of All?" *Business Week*, June 10, 1991, pp. 90–92; Raymond Serafin and Cleveland Horton, "Is There Too Much Power in Auto Ads?" *Advertising Age*, July 23, 1990, pp. 3ff; and Joel Newman, "J.D. Power Play: It's the Auto-Marketing Authority," *Marketing Week*, February 8, 1988, p. 21.

13.   Marc A. Grainer, Kathleen A. McEvoy, and Donald King, "Consumer Problems and Complaints: A National View," *Advances in Consumer Research*, Vol. 6 (1979), p. 496. See also Jagdip Singh, "Industry Characteristics and Consumer Dissatisfaction," *The Journal of Consumer Affairs*, Vol. 25, No. 1 (Summer 1991), pp. 19–56; and Claes Fornell, "A National Customer Satisfaction Barometer: The Swedish Experience," *Journal of Marketing*, Vol. 56, No. 1 (January 1992), pp. 6–21.

14.   Alan R. Andreasen and Arthur Best, "Consumers Complain—Does Business Respond?" *Harvard Business Review* (July–August 1977), pp. 94–104. See also Dan Finkelman and Tony Goland, "The Case of the Complaining Customer," *Harvard Business Review*, No. 3 (May–June 1990), pp. 9–25.

15.   E. Laird Landon, "A Model for Consumer Complaint Behavior," in R. Day (ed.), *Consumer Satisfaction, Dissatisfaction, and Complaining Behavior* (Bloomington: School of Business, Indiana University, 1977). For an excellent discussion on consumer complaining, see Alan R. Andreasen, "Consumer Complaints and Redress: What We Know and What We Don't Know," in E. Scott Maynes (ed.), *The Frontier of Research in the Consumer Interest* (Columbia, Mo.:

American Council on Consumer Interests, 1988), pp. 675–722. In this same volume see also W. Keith Bryant, "Consumer Complaints and Redress: Some Directions for Future Research," pp. 723–726, and Robert O. Herrmann, "Consumer Complaints and Redress— What We Know and What We Don't Know," pp. 727–730. See also Ingrid Martin, "Expert-Novice Differences in Complaint Scripts," *Advances in Consumer Research*, Vol. 18 (1991), pp. 225–231; Jagdip Singh, "Determinants of Consumers' Decisions to Seek Third Party Redress: An Empirical Study of Dissatisfied Patients," *The Journal of Consumer Affairs*, Vol. 23, No. 2 (Winter 1989), pp. 329–363; T. Bettina Cornwell, Alan David Bligh, and Emin Babakus, "Complaint Behavior of Mexican-American Consumers to a Third-Party Agency," *The Journal of Consumer Affairs*, Vol. 25, No. 1 (Summer 1991), pp. 1–18; Diane Halstead and Cornelia Droge, "Consumer Attitudes toward Complaining and the Prediction of Multiple Complaint Responses," *Advances in Consumer Research*, Vol. 18 (1991), pp. 210–216; Nancy Ryan McClure and Pamela Kiecker, "Explaining Differences in Individuals' Prospensity to Complain," *AMA Summer Educators' Proceedings* (1992), pp. 79–84; Ved Prakash, "Mood States and Consumer Complaint Behaviors," *AMA Summer Educators' Proceedings* (1992), pp. 148–150; and T. N. Somasundaram, "Consumers Reaction to Product Failure: Impact of Product Involvement and Knowledge," *Advances in Consumer Research*, Vol. 20 (1993), pp. 215–218.

16.   John A. Czepiel, "Managing Customer Satisfaction in Consumer Service Businesses," Working Paper, Marketing Science Institute, September 1980; Frank E. Camacho and D. Matthew Knain, "Listening to Customers: The Market Research Function at Marriott Corporation," *Marketing Research* (March 1989), pp. 5–14; and Craig Cina, "Creating an Effective Customer Satisfaction Program," *The Journal of Consumer Marketing*, Vol. 6, No. 4 (Fall 1989), pp. 31–40.

17.   J. A. Presbo, "At Procter & Gamble, Success Is Largely due to Heeding the Consumer," *The Wall Street Journal*, April 29, 1980, p. 23; and P. A. Engelmayer, "Before You Discard That Soda Can, You Might Look for This Machine," *The Wall Street Journal*, September 7, 1983, p. 33.

18.   "Detroit's Tonic for Lemon Buyers," *Business Week*, April 4, 1983, pp. 54–55.

19.   "Coke Drinkers Talk a Lot . . . ," *The Wall Street Journal*, October 22, 1981, p. 29. See also Steven P. Brown and Richard F. Beltramini, "Consumer Complaining and Word of Mouth Activities: Field Evidence," *Advances in Consumer Research*, Vol. 16 (1989), pp. 9–16; Jagdip Singh, "Voice, Exit, and Negative Word-of-Mouth Behaviors: An Investigation across Three Service Categories," *Journal of the Academy of Marketing Science*, Vol. 18, No. 1 (Winter 1990), pp. 1–16; Teresa N. Malafi, "Exit, Voice, Loyalty, & Neglect: A New Approach to Consumer Dissatisfaction," in C. Haugtvedt and D. Rosen (eds.), *Proceedings of the Society for Consumer Psychology* (Knoxville: D.W. Schumann, 1991), pp. 87–94; and Paula Fitzgerald Bone, "Determinants of Word-of-Mouth Communications during Product Consumption," *Advances in Consumer Research*, Vol. 19 (1992), pp. 579–583.

20.   Daniel Pearl, "More Firms Pledge Guaranteed Service," *The Wall Street Journal*, July 17, 1991, p. B1; Amanda Bennett, "Give Them Anything, but Promise Satisfaction," *The Wall Street Journal*, February 13, 1991, p. B1.

21.   These reports are based on Amanda Bennett, "Give Them Anything, but Promise Satisfaction," *The Wall Street Journal*, February 13, 1991, p. B1; Joshua Levine, "How'm I Doing?" *Forbes*, December 24, 1990, pp. 106–109; and "Domino's Great Delivery Deal . . ." *Adweek*, August 3, 1987, p. 35.

22.   Discussion in this section was based on Jerry Plymire, "Complaints as Opportunities," *Journal of Product and Brand Management*, Vol. 1, No. 3 (Summer 1992), pp. 73–77; Dan Wascoe, "Toll-Free Numbers Prove to Be Good Marketing Tool," *South Bend Tribune*, April 14, 1992; Lewis C. Winter, "Satisfaction Research," *Marketing Research*, September 1991, pp. 70–74; Micheline Maynard, "Infiniti Drives into a Second Year with New Sedan," *USA Today*, November 8, 1990, p. 6B. Interview with Tom Peters on "Business Times Management Report," November 1984; J. A. Prestbo, "At Procter & Gamble, Success is Largely due to Heeding the Consumer," *The Wall Street Journal*, April 29, 1980, p. 23; Patricia Sellers, "How to Handle Customers' Gripes," *Fortune*, October 24, 1988, pp. 89ff.; and Eileen Norris, "Applying Know-how to Appliances," *Advertising Age*, August 30, 1984, p. 19.

23.   This section is based on Frank Rose, "Now Quality Means Service Too," *Fortune*, April 22, 1991, pp. 99ff; Patricia Sellers, "What Consumers Really Want," *Fortune*, June 4, 1990; pp. 58ff; Frederick Reichheld, "Making Sure Customers Come Back for More," *The Wall Street Journal*, March 12, 1990, p. A8; John A. Czepiel, "Managing Customer Satisfaction in Consumer Service Businesses," Working Paper, Marketing Science Institute, September 1980; and Alan J. Resnik and Robert R. Harmon, "Consumer Complaints and Managerial Response: A Holistic Approach," *Journal of Marketing*, Vol. 47 (Winter 1983), pp. 86–97. For further discussion of useful actions in this area, see also Nessim Hanna and John S. Wagle, "Who Is Your Satisfied Customer?" *The Journal of Consumer Marketing*, Vol. 6 (Winter 1989), pp. 53–62; Stephen W. Brown and Teresa A. Swartz, "A Gap Analysis of Professional Service Quality," *Journal of Marketing*, Vol. 53 (April 1989), pp. 92–98; Mary Jo Bitner, "Evaluating Service Encounters: The Effects of Physical Surroundings and Employee Responses," *Journal of Marketing*, Vol. 54 (April 1990) pp. 69–82; Mary Jo Bitner, Bernard M. Booms, and Mary Stanfield Tetreault, "The Service Encounter: Diagnosing Favorable and Unfavorable Incidents," *Journal of Marketing*, Vol. 54 (January 1990), pp. 71–84; Lawrence A. Crosby, Kenneth R. Evans, and Deborah Cowles, "Relationship Quality in Services Selling: An Interpersonal Influence Perspective," *Journal of Marketing*, Vol. 54 (July 1990), pp. 68–81; Cathy Goodwin and Ivan Ross, "Consumer Evaluations of Responses to Complaints: What's Fair and Why," *The Journal of Consumer Marketing*, Vol. 7, No. 2 (Spring 1990), pp. 29–48; Diane Halstead, Cornelia Droge, and M. Bixby Cooper, "Warranties, Postpurchase Service, and Consumer Satisfaction with Complaint Resolution: The Role of Expectations and Disconfirmation Beliefs," *AMA Winter Educators' Proceedings* (1991), pp. 27–36; Craig A. Kelley and Jeffrey S. Conant, "Extended Warranties: Consumer and Manufacturer Perceptions," *The Journal of Consumer Affairs*, Vol. 25, No. 1 (Summer 1991), pp. 68–83; four papers in *Advances in Consumer Research*, Vol. 18 (1991): David W. Finn and Charles W. Lamb, Jr., "An Evaluation of the SERVQUAL Scales in a Retailing Setting," pp. 483–490; Lois A. Mohr and Mary Jo Bitner, "Mutual Understanding between Customers and Employees in Service Encounters," pp. 611–617; Daniel E. Innis and H. Rao Unnava, "The Usefulness of Product Warranties for Reputable and New Brands," pp. 317–322; and Rama Jayanti and Anita Jackson, "Service Satisfaction: An Exploratory Investigation of Three Models," pp. 603–610; and three papers in *Advances in Consumer Research*, Vol. 19 (1992): Ann L. McGill and Dawn Iacobucci, "The Role of Post-Experience Comparison Standards in the Evaluation of Unfamiliar Services," pp. 570–578; Glenn B. Voss and Irfan Ahmed, "Extended Warranties: A Behavioral Perspective," pp. 879–886; and Donna J. Hill, Robert Baer, and Rustan Kosenko, "Organizational Characteristics and Employee Excuse Making: Passing the Buck for Failed Service Encounters," pp. 673–678.

For related managerial perspectives and findings, see also Dwayne Gremler and Mary Jo Bitner, "Classifying Service Encounter Satisfaction across Industries," *AMA Winter Educators' Proceedings* (1992), Vol. 3, pp. 111–118; John Ozment and Edward A. Morash, "Managing Service Quality," *AMA Winter Educators' Proceedings* (1992), pp. 120–121; Scott W. Kelley, "Developing Customer Orientation among Service Employees," *Journal of the Academy of Marketing Science*, Vol. 20, No. 1 (Winter 1992), pp. 27–36; Mary C. Gilly, William B. Stevenson, and Laura J. Yale, "Dynamics of Complaint Management in the Service Organization," *The Journal of Consumer Affairs*, Vol. 25, No. 2 (Winter 1991), pp. 295–322; J. Joseph Cronin, Jr., and Steven A. Taylor, "Measuring Service Quality: A Reexamination and Extension," *Journal of Marketing*, Vol. 56, No. 3 (July 1992), pp. 55–68; Terence A. Oliva, Richard L. Oliver, and Ian C. MacMillan, "A Catastrophe Model for Developing Service Satisfaction Strategies," *Journal of Marketing*, Vol. 56, No. 3 (July 1992), pp. 83–95; Jeff Allen, Duane Davis, Garland Keesling, and William Grazer, "Segmenting the Mature Market by Characteristics of Organizational Response to Complaint Behavior," *AMA Summer Educators' Proceedings* (1992), pp. 72–78; Claire Bolfing and Andrew M. Forman, "Assessing the Role of Guilt in Service Marketing Evaluations," *AMA Summer Educators' Proceedings* (1992), pp. 140–147; Mary C. Gilly and Richard W. Hansen, "Consumer Complaint Handling as a Strategic Marketing Tool," *The Journal of Product & Brand Management*, Vol. 1, No. 3 (Summer 1992), pp. 5–16; three papers in Robert L. King (ed.), *Marketing: Perspectives for the 1990s* (Richmond, Va.: Southern Marketing Association, 1992): Elise Truly and Steve Walker, "Service Quality, Satisfaction, and Value: A Research Summary," pp. 377–381; Barry E. Langford and Susan Lee Taylor, "Toward Service Firm Satisfaction: A Conceptual, Integrated Model," pp. 390–395; and Steven A. Taylor, Randall Hansen, and Richard Heiens, "Service Quality: An Examination Using Multidimensional Scaling," pp. 401–405; William Boulding, Ajay Kalra, Richard Staelin, and Valarie A. Zeithaml, "A Dynamic Process Model of Service Quality: From Expectations to Behavioral Intentions," *Journal of Marketing Research*, Vol. 30, No. 1 (February 1993), pp. 7–27; and Ellen M. Moore and F. Kelly Shuptrine, "Warranties: Continued Readability Problems after the 1975 Magnuson-Moss Warranty Act," *The Journal of Consumer Affairs*, Vol. 27, No. 1 (Summer 1993), pp. 23–36.

24. Lawrence Kanter et al., *Briefing Book for Policy Review Session* (Washington, D.C.: Federal Trade Commission, April 1980). Examples that extend beyond the Federal Trade Commission were not drawn from this source; see Walter Guzzardi, "The Mindless Pursuit of Safety," *Fortune*, April 9, 1979, pp. 54–64.

25. The first two cases were decided in favor of the injured consumers. (1) In the candle case Fabergé argued that it should not be expected to foresee that someone might attempt to pour perfume into a flame and thus should not be liable. On the other hand, the court ruled that the flammability was a significant concern for this type of product and that consumers should be warned about this potential hazard. The injured student was awarded $27,000. (2) In the football case the jury agreed with the player and awarded a $5 million judgment against the helmet maker. (3) In the killing case, the jury ordered the magazine to pay Mrs. Black's family $9.4 million because it neglected to check on the meaning of the ad! See "An Impossible Liability Standard," *Advertising Age*, March 14, 1988; and "The Devils in the Product Liability Laws," *Business Week*, February 12, 1979, pp. 72–79. For a useful broader perspective, see Jeffrey J. Stoltman, Fred W. Morgan, and Karl A. Boedecker, "Expanding the Perspective on Product Safety Problems," in M.J. Sheffet (ed.), *Proceedings of the 1993 Public Policy and Marketing Conference* (East Lansing: Michigan State University, Eli Broad Graduate School of Management, 1993), pp. 72–74.

26. This typology and the ensuing discussion on strict liability follows that given by Louis W. Stern and Thomas L. Eovaldi, *Legal Aspects of Marketing Strategy* (Englewood Cliffs, N.J.: Prentice Hall, 1984), pp. 89–99. See also Leslie Spencer, "The Tort Tax," *Forbes*, February 17, 1992, pp. 40–41.

27. The legal issues in product liability are continuing to evolve. For interesting recent news articles, see Catherine Yang, "Will the High Court Make Damages Less Punitive?" *Business Week*, March 15, 1993, pp. 83–84; Ted Gest, "Product Liability: Making the Case for New Legislation," *USA Today*, November 7, 1991, pp. 11A; Amy Marcus, "Limits on Personal Injury Suits Urged," *The Wall Street Journal*, April 23, 1991, p. B1; and Amy Marcus, "Grandchild May Widen Liability with DES Suit," *The Wall Street Journal*, January 7, 1991, p. B1.

For academic articles providing overviews of this topic, see Phillip E. Downs and Douglas N. Behrman, "The Products Liability Coordinator: A Partial Solution," *Journal of the Academy of Marketing Science*, Vol. 14 (Fall 1986), pp. 58ff.; Fred W. Morgan, "Strict Liability and the Marketing of Services vs. Goods: A Judicial Review," in *Journal of Public Policy & Marketing*, Vol. 6 (1987), pp. 43–57; Candace Croucher Dugan, "Advertising, the Consumer Researcher and Products Liability," *Journal of Public Policy & Marketing*, Vol. 8 (1989), pp. 227–241; and Fred W. Morgan, "The Evolution of Punitive Damages in Product Liability Litigation for Unprincipled Marketing Behavior," *Journal of Public Policy & Marketing*, Vol. 8 (1989), pp. 279ff. For related discussions, see also Mitch Griffin, Barry J. Babin, and William R. Darden, "Consumer Assessments of Responsibility for Product-related Injuries: The Impact of Regulations, Warnings, and Promotional Policies," *Advances in Consumer Research*, Vol. 19 (1992), pp. 870–878; and Patricia A. Bonner and Edward J. Metzen, "Probabilities of Small Claims Judgment Satisfaction and Factors Influencing Success," *The Journal of Consumer Affairs*, Vol. 27, No. 1 (Summer 1993), pp. 66–86.

Chapter 20

Public Policy and Consumer Behavior

1. Vermont Royster, "Regulation Isn't a Dirty Word," *The Wall Street Journal*, September 9, 1987, p. 30. For an excellent overview of many of the topics in this chapter, see Alan R. Andreasen, "Consumer Behavior Research and Social Policy," in T. Robertson and H. Kassarjian (eds.), *Handbook of Consumer Behavior* (Englewood Cliffs, N.J.: Prentice Hall, 1991), pp. 459–506.

2. This section's discussion of consumer rights is based upon David A. Aaker and George S. Day, "A Guide to Consumerism," in D. Aaker and G. Day (eds.), *Consumerism: Search for the Public Interest*, 4th ed. (New York: Free Press, 1982), pp. 2–20. For related readings, see Robert W. Nason, "The Social Consequences of Marketing: Macromarketing and Public Policy," *Journal of Public Policy & Marketing*, Vol. 8 (1989), pp. 242–251; three papers in R. N. Mayer (ed.), *Enhancing Consumer Choice* (Columbia, Mo.: American Council on Consumer Interests, 1991): Gregory T. Gundlach and William L. Wilkie, "The Marketing Literature in Consumer Policy: 1970–1989," pp. 551–560; E. Scott Maynes, "The Becker 'Revolution': Challenges for Tomorrow's Researchers and Educators in the Consumer Interest," pp. 569–572; and Edward J. Metzen, "The Future of the Consumer Policy Research," pp. 573–575; and Richard L. Priem, "Industrial Organization Economics and Alderson's General Theory of Marketing," *Journal of the Academy of Marketing Science*, Vol. 20, No. 2 (Spring 1992), pp. 135–142.

3. Hans B. Thorelli, "Consumer Information as Consumer Protection," in J. Cady (ed.), *Marketing and the Public Interest* (Cambridge, Mass.: Marketing Science Institute, 1978), pp. 269–290. See also Francis J. Mulhern, "Consumer Wants and Consumer Welfare," *AMA Winter Educators' Proceedings* (1992), pp. 407–412; and Peter S. Carusone, Paula M. Saunders, and Herbert E. Brown, "Value-driven Marketing: Beyond Social Responsibility," *AMA Summer Educators' Proceedings* (1992), pp. 183–188.

4. Warren G. Magnuson and Jean Carper, "Caveat Emptor," in D. Aaker and G. Day (eds.), *Consumerism: Search for the Consumer Interest*, 4th ed. (New York: Free Press, 1982), pp. 267–278.

5. Doris Chandler, "Fraud by Mail Still Is Bilking Consumers," *Gainesville* (Florida) *Sun*, July 8, 1985, p. 1C. See also Linda F. Golodner, "Telemarketing: Enhancing Consumer Choice of the Market Place: Enhancing Opportunities for Fraud," in R. N. Mayer (ed.), *Enhancing Consumer Choice* (Columbia, Mo.: American Council on Consumer Interests, 1991), pp. 315–324.

6. David Horowitz, "Dream-Away Diet Pills Banned," *Gainesville* (Florida) *Sun*, May 23, 1985, p. 10C.

7. Milt Freudenheim, "Bolar Plans Guilty Plea on Generics," *New York Times*, February 28, 1991, p. C2.

8. Scott Hume, "Redeeming Feature," *Advertising Age*, February 4, 1991, p. 35; Judith Farrel, "Cracking Down on Coupon Fraud," *Marketing Week*, June 12, 1989, p. P28; Nancy Giges, "Coupon Loss Put at $500,000,000," *Advertising Age*, February 13, 1984, p. 75. For additional discussions of consumer slippage topics, see Noel B. Zabriskie, "Fraud by Consumers," *Journal of Retailing*, Vol. 48 (Winter 1972), pp. 22–27; Marvin A. Jolson, "Consumers as Offenders," *Journal of Business Research*, Vol. 2 (January 1974), pp. 89–98; Robert E. Wilkes, "Fraudulent Consumer Behavior," *Journal of Marketing*, Vol. 42 (October 1978), pp. 67–75; Lawrence J. Marks and Michael A. Mayo, "An Empirical Test of a Model of Consumer Ethical Dilemmas," *Advances in Consumer Research*, Vol. 18 (1991), pp. 720–728; and Dena Cox, Anthony D. Cox, and George P. Moschis, "When Consumer Behavior Goes Bad: An Investigation

of Adolescent Shoplifting," *Journal of Consumer Research*, Vol. 17, No. 2 (September 1990), pp. 149–159.

9. Josh Barbanel, "Shake-up Follows News of Unread Cancer Test," *New York Times News Service*, July 24, 1990.

10. Consumer Product Safety Commission, Annual Report (Washington, D.C.: U.S. Government Printing Office, 1981), pp. 223–226.

11. See Helen B. Taussig, "The Thalidomide Syndrome," *Scientific American*, August 1962, pp. 29–35; "The Thalidomide Disaster," *Time*, August 10, 1962, p. 32; "Thalidomide Homocide," *Time*, November 16, 1962, p. 67; and Steven M. Spencer, "The Untold Story of the Thalidomide Babies," *Saturday Evening Post*, October 20, 1962, pp. 19–27.

12. Because health and safety issues are so significant, the FDA is an interesting government agency to follow. For some interesting readings, see, for example, (bribery of government officials) Zina Sawyer, "Getting Even," *Forbes*, April 29, 1991, pp. 92–95; "How Far Has the Cancer Spread at the FDA?" *Business Week*, September 18, 1989, pp. 30–31; (conflict over speed of approval versus safe testing) Marilyn Chase, "Cooper Resigns Post as Top Regulator for AIDS Drugs, Citing Stress, Fatigue," *The Wall Street Journal*, December 24, 1990, p. 10; (on legal liability and health warnings) Jeff Bailey, "FDA Says Pfizer Inadequately Warned Heart-Valve Recipients of Risk of Death," *The Wall Street Journal*, December 10, 1990, p. B4; (increased activism) Malcolm Gladwell, "The FDA's Eliot Ness: David Kessler Is a Man on a Mission," *Washington Post National Weekly Edition*, November 18–24, 1991, p. 12; (product names having to meet standards) Steven W. Colford, "FDA Getting Tougher: Seizure of Citrus Hill Is Signal to Marketers," *Advertising Age*, April 29, 1991, p. 1ff; (moving pharmaceuticals closer to consumers) Bruce Ingersoll, "FDA Decision on Hydrocortisone Buoys Drug Industry," *The Wall Street Journal*, September 9, 1991, p. B1; and "More Prescription Drugs Going over the Counter," *USA Today*, October 8, 1991, p. 9A.

For related readings across a range of topic areas that underpin regulation and ethics, see R. Eric Reidenbach, Donald P. Robin, and Lyndon Dawson, "An Application and Extension of a Multidimensional Ethics Scale to Selected Marketing Practices and Marketing Groups," *Journal of the Academy of Marketing Science*, Vol. 19, No. 2 (Spring 1991), pp. 83–92; Elizabeth C. Hirschman, "Babies for Sale: Market Ethics and the New Reproductive Technologies," *The Journal of Consumer Affairs*, Vol. 25, No. 2 (Winter 1991), pp. 358–390; Joseph P. Cannon and Paul N. Bloom, "Are Slotting Allowances Legal under Antitrust Laws?" *Journal of Public Policy & Marketing*, Vol. 10, No. 1 (Spring 1991), pp. 167–186; Kenneth Kelly, "Antitrust Analysis of Grocery Slotting Allowances: The Procompetitive Case," *Journal of Public Policy & Marketing*, Vol. 10, No. 1 (Spring 1991), pp. 187–198; Ed Petkus, Jr. and Robert B. Woodruff, "A Model of the Socially Responsible Decision-making Process in Marketing: Linking Decision Makers and Stakeholders," *AMA Winter Educators' Proceedings* (1992), pp. 154–161; Patrick E. Murphy and Mark G. Dunn, "Marketing Research Ethics: An Update," *AMA Winter Educators' Proceedings* (1992), pp. 326–327; Ronald Paul Hill, "Helping the Homeless: A Radical Consumer Behavior–Oriented Solution," *Advances in Consumer Research*, Vol. 19 (1992), pp. 550–553; Jerry R. Goolsby and Shelby D. Hunt, "Cognitive Moral Development and Marketing," *Journal of Marketing*,

Vol. 56, No. 1 (January 1992), pp. 55–68; Patrick E. Murphy and Gene R. Laczniak, "Emerging Ethical Issues Facing Marketing Researchers," *Marketing Research*, Vol. 4, No. 2 (June 1992), pp. 6–11; Ralph W. Jackson and Steve Cashon, "The Inherent Ethical Conflicts in the Corporate Setting," *AMA Winter Educators' Proceedings* (1993), pp. 394–400; Gene R. Laczniak, "Marketing Ethics: Onward toward Greater Expectations," *Journal of Public Policy & Marketing*, Vol. 12, No. 1 (Spring 1993), pp. 91–96; Donald P. Robin and R. Eric Reidenbach, "Searching for a Place to Stand: Toward a Workable Ethical Philosophy for Marketing," *Journal of Public Policy & Marketing*, Vol. 12, No. 1 (Spring 1993), pp. 97–105; and Jerome D. Williams, "Alcohol Promotion and Ethnic Minority Target Marketing: A Review of Policy and Research Issues," in M. J. Sheffet (ed.), *Proceedings of the 1993 Public Policy and Marketing Conference* (East Lansing: Michigan State University, Eli Broad Graduate School of Management, 1993), pp. 69–70.

13. Pete Engardio, "Companies Are Knocking Off the Knockoff Outfits," *Business Week*, September 26, 1988, pp. 86–88. See also Victor V. Cordell and Nittaya Wongtada, "Consumer Responses to Counterfeit Products," *AMA Winter Educators' Proceedings* (1991), p. 247.

14. Edwin McDowell, "Oh, for the Good Old Days of Brand X," in Roy Adler, Larry Robinson, and Jan Carlson (eds.), *Marketing and Society: Cases and Commentaries* (Englewood Cliffs, N.J.: Prentice Hall, 1981), pp. 200–204.

15. William L. Wilkie and David M. Gardner, "The Role of Marketing Research in Public Policy Decision Making," *Journal of Marketing*, Vol. 38 (January 1974), pp. 38–47. See also Jutta M. Joesch and Cathleen D. Zick, "Regulate? Deregulate? Reregulate? The Impact of Regulatory Reform on Consumer Welfare in the Airline Market," in R. N. Mayer (ed.), *Enhancing Consumer Choice* (Columbia, Mo.: American Council on Consumer Interests, 1991), pp. 335–348; and Denise T. Smart, Jeffrey S. Conant, and Miguel G. Pflucker, "Deregulation and the Information Content of Advertising: Illustrations from the Airline and Banking Industries," in Robert L. King (ed.), *Marketing: Perspectives for the 1990s* (Richmond, Va.: Southern Marketing Association, 1992), pp. 285–289.

16. To read the entire 1989 ABA report on the FTC, together with many interesting discussions of it, see Patrick E. Murphy and William L. Wilkie (eds.), *The FTC in the 1990's* (Notre Dame, Ind.: University of Notre Dame Press, 1990).

17. For the sources of quotes in this report, see Christi Harlan, "Texas Law Official Stirs Up Marketers," *The Wall Street Journal*, June 6, 1991, p. B1; Margaret E. Kriz, "Leashed Watchdog," *National Journal*, October 24, 1987, pp. 2663–2665; "FTC Member Hints of Attack on Food Ads," *Advertising Age*, November 21, 1988, p. 60; and Paul M. Barrett, "Attorneys General Flex Their Muscles," *The Wall Street Journal*, July 13, 1988, p. 22. For related discussions, see also J. Howard Beales III, "What State Regulators Should Learn from FTC Experience in Regulating Advertising," *Journal of Public Policy & Marketing*, Vol. 10, No. 1 (Spring 1991), pp. 101–117; and Jef I. Richards, "FTC or NAAG, Consumers or Advertisers: Who Will Win the Territorial Battle?" *Journal of Public Policy & Marketing*, Vol. 10, No. 1 (Spring 1991), pp. 118–132.

18. Adapted from "Need for Government Oversight," *Adweek*, October 12, 1987, p. 78. For an excellent source of current research on public policy matters in marketing, see the *Journal of Public Policy & Marketing*, published by the American Marketing Association (Chicago) and edited by Michael Mazis, American University. For further discussion of these issues, see John F. Gaski and Michael J. Etzel, "The Index of Consumer Sentiment toward Marketing," *Journal of Marketing*, Vol. 50 (July 1986), pp. 71–80; Ronald Paul Hill, "A Primer for Ethnographic Research with a Focus on Social Policy Issues Involving Consumer Behavior," *Advances in Consumer Research*, Vol. 20 (1993), pp. 59–62; and John R. Burton, Cathleen D. Zick, and Robert N. Mayer, "Consumer Views of the Need for Government Intervention in the Airline Market," *The Journal of Consumer Affairs*, Vol. 27, No. 1 (Summer 1993), pp. 1–22.

19. Figure 20-2 and the discussion are based upon Michael B. Mazis, Richard Staelin, Howard Beales, and Steven Salop, "A Framework for Evaluating Consumer Information Regulation," *Journal of Marketing*, Vol. 44 (Winter 1981), pp. 11–21. This framework has a wide range of applications. For related discussions, see, for example, Gary T. Ford, Darlene B. Smith, and John L. Swasy, "Consumer Skepticism of Advertising Claims: Testing Hypotheses from Economics of Information," *Journal of Consumer Research*, Vol. 16, No. 4 (March 1990), pp. 433–441; Fred W. Morgan, "Judicial Standards for Survey Research: An Update and Guidelines," *Journal of Marketing*, Vol. 54, No. 1 (January 1990), pp. 59–70; two papers in R. N. Mayer (ed.), *Enhancing Consumer Choice* (Columbia, Mo.: American Council on Consumer Interests, 1991): Robin A. Douthitt, "Biotechnology and Consumer Choice in the Market Place: Should There Be Mandatory Product Labeling?" pp. 97–104; and Joel Rudd and Karen Glanz, "Providing Consumers with Quality of Health-Care Information: A Critical Review and Media Content Analysis," pp. 229–238; John P. Murry, Jr., "Youthful Drinking and Driving: Policy Implications from Mass Media Research," *Advances in Consumer Research*, Vol. 18 (1991), pp. 120–122; Ronald Paul Hill, "Political Advertising in the 1990s: Expected Strategies, Voter Responses, and Public Policy Implications," *Advances in Consumer Research*, Vol. 18 (1991), pp. 715–719; Jeffrey Stoltman and Fred Morgan, "Psychological Dimensions of (Un)Safe Product Usage," *AMA Winter Educators' Proceedings* (1993), pp. 143–150; and Martha Rogers and Jackie Jackson, "Advertising and the First Amendment: A Practical Test for Distinguishing Commercial Speech from Full-Protected Speech," in M. J. Sheffet (ed.), *Proceedings of the 1993 Public Policy and Marketing Conference* (East Lansing: Michigan State University, Eli Broad Graduate School of Management, 1993), pp. 36–61.

20. See, for example, Lee Benham and Alexandra Benham, "Regulating through the Professions: A Perspective on Information Control," *Journal of Law and Economics*, Vol. 18 (October 1975), pp. 421–447, and Alex R. Maurizi, Ruth L. Moore, and Lawrence Shepard, "The Impact of Price Advertising: The California Eyewear Market after One Year," *The Journal of Consumer Affairs*, Vol. 15 (Winter 1981), pp. 290–300; and Sandra E. Gleason and Ronald Stiff, "The Federal Trade Commission's Contact Lens Study: Implications for Public Policy," *Journal of Public Policy & Marketing*, Vol. 5 (1986), pp. 163–170. See also Mary Jane Sheffet and Steven W. Kopp, "Advertising Prescription Drugs to the Public: Headache or Relief?" *Journal of Public Policy & Marketing*, Vol. 9, 1990, pp. 42–61.

21. William L. Wilkie, "Affirmative Disclosure: Perspectives on FTC Orders," *Journal of Public Policy & Marketing*, Vol. 1 (Winter 1982), pp. 95–110. For further discussions related to this area, see, for example, Gaurav Bhalla and John L. Lastovicka, "The Impact of Changing Cigarette Warning Message Content and Format," *Advances in Consumer Research*, Vol. 11 (1984), pp. 305–310; G. Ray Funkhouser, "An Empirical Study of Consumers' Sensitivity to the Wording of Affirmative Disclosure Messages," *Journal of Public Policy & Marketing*, Vol. 3, No. 1 (1984), pp. 26–37; James R. Bettman, John W. Payne, and Richard Staelin, "Cognitive Considerations in Designing Effective Labels for Presenting Risk Information," *Journal of Public Policy & Marketing*, Vol. 5 (1986), pp. 1–28; William L. Wilkie, "Affirmative Disclosure at the FTC: Strategic Dimensions," *Journal of Public Policy & Marketing*, Vol. 5 (1986), pp. 123–145; William L. Wilkie, "Affirmative Disclosure at the FTC: Communication Decisions," in *Journal of Public Policy & Marketing*, Vol. 6 (1987) pp. 33–42; Richard F. Beltramini, "Perceived Believability of Warning Label Information Presented in Cigarette Advertising," *Journal of Advertising*, Vol. 17 (November 1988), pp. 26–32; Edward T. Popper and Keith B. Murray, "Format Effects on an In-Ad Disclosure," *Advances in Consumer Research*, Vol. 16 (1989), pp. 221–230; James H. McAlexander and Debra L. Scammon, "Are Disclosures Sufficient? A Micro Analysis of Impact in Financial Services Market," *Journal of Public Policy & Marketing*, Vol. 7 (1988), p. 185–202; Ellen R. Foxman, Darrel D. Muehling, and Patrick A. Moore, "Disclaimer Footnotes in Ads: Discrepancies between Purpose and Performance," *Journal of Public Policy & Marketing*, Vol. 7 (1988), pp. 127–137; J. Craig Andrews, Richard G. Netemeyer, and Srinivas Durvasula, "Believability and Attitudes toward Warning Label Information: The Role of Persuasive Communications Theory," *Journal of Public Policy & Marketing*, Vol. 9, 1990, pp. 1–15; Vernon Brown, Craig A. Kelley, and Ming-Tung Lee, "The State-of-the-Art in Labeling Research Revisited: Development in Labeling Research 1978–1990," *AMA Summer Educators' Proceedings* (1991), pp. 717–726; Thomas A. Durkin and Gregory E. Elliehausen, "The Issue of Market Transparency: Truth-in-Lending Disclosure Requirements as Consumer Protections in the United States," in R. N. Mayer (ed.), *Enhancing Consumer Choice* (Columbia, Mo.: American Council on Consumer Interests, 1991), pp. 255–266; Michael E. Hilton, "An Overview of Recent Findings on Alcoholic Beverage Warning Labels," *Journal of Public Policy & Marketing*, Vol. 12, No. 1 (Spring 1993), pp. 1–9; and Kenneth R. Laughery, N. Kimberly Bohannon, and Stephen L. Young, "Age Factors in the Effects of Alcohol Warnings in Advertisements," in M. J. Sheffet (ed.), *Proceedings of the 1993 Public Policy and Marketing Conference* (East Lansing: Michigan State University, Eli Broad Graduate School of Management, 1993), pp. 124–130.

22. William L. Wilkie, "Applying Attitude Research in Public Policy," in W. Wells (ed.), *Attitude Research at Bay* (Chicago: American Marketing Association, 1976). See also Stanley I. Ornstein and Dominique M. Hanssens, "Alcohol Control Laws and the Consumption of Distilled Spirits and Beer," *Journal of Consumer Research*, Vol. 12 (September 1985), pp. 200–213; Susan L. Holak and Srinivas K. Reddy, "Effects of a Television and Radio Advertising Ban: A Study of the Cigarette Industry," *Journal of Marketing*, Vol. 50 (October 1986), pp. 219–227; George P. Moschis, "Point of View: Cigarette Advertising and Young Smokers," *Journal of Advertising Research*, Vol. 29 (April–May 1989), pp. 51–60; and the extensive citations in Note 27 of Chapter 16.

23. Gene Koretz, "Canada Makes Smoking Hazardous to the Wallet," *Business Week*, May 20, 1991, p. 24; Joann Lipman, "Decline of Tobacco Sales in Canada Fuels Ad Debate," *The Wall Street Journal*, June 12, 1990, p. B1; Barry Brown, "We Will Advertise," *Advertising Age*, August 6, 1991, p. 9; Sonia Nazario, "California Anti-Cigarette Ads Seem to Reduce Smoking," *The Wall Street Journal*, October 31, 1990, p. B1; and Marvin Goldberg, "The Elimination of Advertising Directed at Children in Quebec: A Quasi-Experiment," *Advances in Consumer Research*, Vol. 16 (1989), p. 790. See also Rick Andrews and George R. Franke, "The Determinants of Cigarette Consumption: A Meta-analysis," *Journal of Public Policy & Marketing*, Vol. 10, No. 1 (Spring 1991), pp. 81–100; and William Krumske, Jr., "When Medical Doctors Conduct Marketing Research: JAMA and Old Joe, the Camel," *AMA Winter Educators' Proceedings* (1993), pp. 405–410.

24. Evan I. Schwartz, "The Rush to Keep Mum," *Business Week*, June 8, 1992, p. 36; Richard Edel, "The Privacy Debate," *Advertising Age*, October 17, 1988, p. S12. See also Ellen R. Foxman and Paula Kilcoyne, "Information Technology, Marketing Practice, and Consumer Privacy: Ethical Issues," *Journal of Public Policy & Marketing*, Vol. 12, No. 1 (Spring 1993), pp. 106–119.

25. The savings and loan crisis of the 1980s raises serious issues about regulation of marketing. *Fortune* magazine and the *The Wall Street Journal* have both produced extensive, interesting reviews (further coverage can easily be found through your reference librarian). See Charles McCoy, Richard Schmitt, and Jeff Bailey, "Hall of Shame . . . ," *The Wall Street Journal*, November 2, 1990, pp. 1ff; and Alan Farnham, "The S & L Felons," *Fortune*, November 5, 1990, pp. 90–108.

26. See Alan R. Andreasen, "Consumer Behavior Research and Social Policy," in T. Robertson and H. Kassarjian (eds.), *Handbook of Consumer Behavior* (Englewood Cliffs, N.J.: Prentice Hall, 1991), pp. 459–506; and K. Douglas Hoffman, Donald W. Hardigree, and Robert J. Aalberts, "The Americans with Disabilities Act: Overview and Marketing Implications," *AMA Winter Educators' Proceedings* (1993), pp. 202–203.

27. This section is based upon William L. Wilkie, Dennis L. McNeill, and Michael B. Mazis, "Marketing's 'Scarlet Letter': The Theory and Practice of Corrective Advertising," *Journal of Marketing*, Vol. 48 (Spring 1984), pp. 11–31. For an excellent review see also Debra L. Scammon and Richard J. Semenik, "Corrective Advertising: Evolution of the Legal Theory and Application of the Remedy," *Journal of Advertising*, Vol. 11, No. 1 (1982), pp. 10–20. For additional findings in this most interesting area, see H. Keith Hunt, "Effects of Corrective Advertising," *Journal of Advertising Research*, October 1973, pp. 15–24; Robert F. Dyer and Philip G. Kuehl, "The Corrective Advertising Remedy of the FTC: An Experimental Evaluation," *Journal of Marketing*, Vol. 38 (January 1974), pp. 48–54; Harold H. Kassarjian, Cynthia Carlson, and Paula Rosin, "A Corrective Advertising Study," *Advances in Consumer Research*, Vol. 2 (1974), pp. 631–642; Gary M. Armstrong, Metin N. Gurol, and Frederick A. Russ, "Detecting and Correcting Deceptive Advertising," *Journal of Consumer Research*, Vol. 6 (December 1979), pp. 237–246; Neil K. Allison and Richard W. Mizerski, "The Effects of Recall on Belief Change: The Corrective Advertising Case," *Advances in Consumer Research*, Vol. 8 (1981), pp. 419–422; Tyzoon T. Tyebjee, "The Role of Publicity in FTC Corrective Advertising Remedies," *Journal of Public Policy & Marketing*, Vol. 1, No. 1 (1982), pp. 111–122; George F. Belch, Michael A. Belch, Robert B. Settle, and Lisa M.

De Lucchi, "An Examination of Consumers' Perceptions of Purpose and Content of Corrective Advertising," *Advances in Consumer Research,* Vol. 9 (1982), pp. 327–332; Kenneth L. Bernhardt, Thomas C. Kinnear, Michael B. Mazis, and Bonnie B. Reece, "Impact of Publicity on Corrective Advertising Effects," *Advances in Consumer Research,* Vol. 8 (1981), pp. 414–415; Jacob Jacoby, Margaret C. Nelson, and Wayne D. Hoyer, "Correcting Corrective Advertising," *Advances in Consumer Research,* Vol. 8 (1981), pp. 416–418; three articles in *Journal of Public Policy & Marketing,* Vol. 2, No. 1 (1983), Gary M. Armstrong, Metin N. Gurol, and Frederick A. Russ, "A Longitudinal Evaluation of the Listerine Corrective Advertising Campaign," pp. 16–28; Michael B. Mazis, Dennis L. McNeill, and Kenneth L. Bernhardt, "Day-After Recall of Listerine Corrective Commercials," pp. 29–37; Thomas C. Kinnear, James R. Taylor, and Oded Gur-Arie, "Affirmative Disclosure: Long-Term Marketing Monitoring of Residual Effects," pp. 38–45; and Kenneth L. Bernhardt, Thomas C. Kinnear, and Michael B. Mazis, "A Field Study of Corrective Advertising Effectiveness," *Journal of Public Policy & Marketing,* Vol. 5 (1986), pp. 146–162.

Chapter 21

Organizational Buying Behavior

1. "Philip Kotler Explores the New Marketing Paradigm," *Marketing Science Institute Review,* Vol. 1 (Spring 1991), p. 1.

2. Table 21-1 is adapted from the discussion in Geoffrey W. Thompson, "Benefit Marketing Makes Technical Products Appealing," *Marketing News,* March 4, 1991, p. 22.

3. Vicky Crittendon, Carol A. Scott, and Rowland T. Moriarity, "The Role of Prior Product Experience in Organizational Buying Behavior," *Advances in Consumer Research,* Vol. 14 (1986), pp. 387–391. See also Edward Fern and James Brown, "The Industrial/Consumer Marketing Dichotomy: A Case of Insufficient Justification," *Journal of Marketing,* Vol. 48 (Spring 1984), pp. 68–77; Fahri Karakaya and Michael J. Stahl, "Barriers to Entry and Market Entry Decisions in Consumer and Industrial Goods Markets," *Journal of Marketing,* Vol. 53 (April 1989), pp. 80–91.

4. Larry Riggs, "A Must for Today's Marketers," *Sales and Marketing Management,* April 22, 1985, p. 36. See also Jakki Mohr and J. Paul Peter, "Organizational Buyer-Seller Communications: A Review of Recent Literature," *AMA Summer Educators' Proceedings* (1988), pp. 84–89; Kaylene Williams and Rosann Spiro, "Communication Style in the Salesperson-Customer Dyad," *Journal of Marketing Research,* Vol. 22 (November 1985), pp. 434–442; and R. Dale Wilson, "Segmentation and Communication in the Industrial Marketplace," *Journal of Business Research,* Vol. 14 (December 1986), pp. 487–500.

5. Kerry J. Smith, "Promotion Plays Major Role in '92 ECHO Award," *PROMO Magazine,* November 1992, pp. 43–44.

6. Patrick J. Robinson, Charles Faris, and Yoram Wind, *Industrial Buying and Creative Marketing* (Boston: Allyn & Bacon, 1967). See also Marian B. Wood and Evelyn Ehrlich, "Segmentation: Five Steps to More Effective Business-to-Business Marketing," *Sales & Marketing Management,* April 1991, pp. 59–63; George S. Day, "Learning about Markets," Marketing Science Institute Report 91–117, June 1991; "The Changing World of Marketing: A Conference Summary," Marketing Science Institute Report 92-112, May 1992; Paul A. Herbig and John C. Milewicz, "Signaling in Business-to- Business Markets," in R. King (ed.), *Marketing: Perspectives for the 1990s* (Richmond, Va. Southern Marketing Association, 1992), pp. 16–19; V. Kasturi Rangan, Rowland T. Moriarty, and Gordon S. Swartz, "Segmenting Consumers in Mature Industrial Markets," *Journal of Marketing,* Vol. 56, No. 4 (October 1992), pp. 72–82; and Michele D. Bunn and Ben Shaw-Ching Liu, "Defining Purchase Types through Situational Assessment," *AMA Winter Educators' Proceedings* (1993), pp. 392–393.

7. Frederick E. Webster and Yoram Wind, "A General Model for Understanding Organizational Buying Behavior," *Journal of Marketing,* Vol. 36, No. 2 (1973), pp. 12–19. For recent research results, see, for example, Donald L. McCabe, "Buying Group Structure: Constriction at the Top," *Journal of Marketing,* Vol. 51, No. 4 (October 1987), pp. 89–98; Harvey B. Mackay, "The CEO Hits the Road (and Other Sales Tales)," *Harvard Business Review,* No. 2 (March-April 1990), pp. 32–44; Patricia A. Knowles and Gwen Hanks, "A Living Systems Approach within Marketing: Understanding the Buying Center," *AMA Winter Educators' Proceedings* (1992), pp. 495–497; and Barbara Samuel Loftus and Patricia W. Meyers, "Launching Emerging Technologies to Create New Markets: Identifying Industrial Buyers During the Early Development of Marketing Relationships," *AMA Winter Educators' Proceedings* (1993), pp. 312–313.

8. Susan Caminiti, "Finding New Ways to Sell More," *Fortune,* July 27, 1992, pp. 100–103.

9. "The 'Short Reach' of Salespeople," *Sales & Marketing Management,* July 2, 1984, p. 24. See also David F. Midgley, Pamela D. Morrison and John H. Roberts, "The Nature of Communication Networks between Organizations Involved in the Diffusion of Technological Innovations," *Advances in Consumer Research,* Vol. 18 (1991), pp. 635–643; Geoffrey L. Gordon, Roger J. Calantone, and C. Anthony diBenedetto, "A Conceptual Integration of Innovation and Diffusion Drivers of Industrial New Product Success," *AMA Winter Educators' Proceedings* (1991), pp. 102–110; and Allen M. Weiss and Jan B. Heide, "The Nature of Organizational Search in High Technology Markets," *Journal of Marketing Research,* Vol. 30 (May 1993), pp. 220–233.

10. "Positioning Reigns for Consumer or Industrial Products," *Marketing News,* May 9, 1986, p. 14. See also Gary L. Frazier, Robert E. Spekman, and Charles R. O'Neal, "Just-in-Time Exchange Relationships in Industrial Markets," *Journal of Marketing,* Vol. 52 (October 1988), pp. 52–67; James C. Anderson and James A. Narus, "Model of Distributor Firm and Manufacturer Firm Working Partnerships," *Journal of Marketing,* Vol. 54 (January 1990), pp. 42–58; Jan B. Heide and George John, "Alliances in Industrial Purchasing: The Determinants of Joint Action in Buyer-Supplier Relationships," *Journal of Marketing Research,* Vol. 27 (February 1990), pp. 24–36; Thomas G. Noordewier, George John, and John R. Nevin, "Performance Outcomes of Purchasing Arrangements in Industrial Buyer-Vendor Relationships," *Journal of Marketing,* Vol. 54 (October 1990), pp. 80–93; Pushkala Raman, "A Relationship Marketing: The Chicken or the Egg? A Theoretical Framework of Relational Exchanges in Marketing," in Robert L. King (ed.), *Marketing: Perspectives for the 1990s* (Richmond, Va.: Southern Marketing Association,

1992), pp. 38–42; Sandy D. Jap (ed.), "Evolving Relationships of Retailers and Manufacturers: A Conference Summary," Marketing Science Institute Report 92–113, May 1992; Peter Jancourtz and Gil Press, "Digital Hears the Voice of the Market," *Marketing Research*, Vol. 4, No. 4 (December 1992), pp. 28–33; Gerald A. Athaide and Patricia W. Meyers, "The Role of Relationship Marketing in the Commercialization of Technological Process Innovations," *AMA Winter Educators' Proceedings* (1993), p. 311; and James F. Wolter, Steven A. Melnyk, Robert W. Nason, and Cyrus P. Olsen, "Managing Fusion Selling: Innovative and Entrepreneurial Buyer/Seller Relationships," *AMA Winter Educators' Proceedings* (1993), p. 314.

11. Patrick J. Robinson, Charles Faris, and Yoram Wind, *Industrial Buying and Creative Marketing* (Boston: Allyn & Bacon, 1967).

12. For an informative overview of this topic, see Scott Ward and Frederick E. Webster, "Organizational Buying Behavior," in T. Robertson and H. Kassarjian (eds.), *Handbook of Consumer Behavior* (Englewood Cliffs, N.J.: Prentice Hall, 1991), pp. 419–458. See also Joe F. Alexander, Patrick L. Schul, and Emin Babakus, "Analyzing Interpersonal Communications in Industrial Marketing Negotiations," *Journal of the Academy of Marketing Science*, Vol. 19, No. 2 (Spring 1991), pp. 129–140; Bruce Buchanan and Paul C. Michell, "Using Structural Factors to Assess the Risk of Failure in Agency-Client Relations," *Journal of Advertising Research*, Vol. 31, No. 4 (August/September 1991), pp. 68ff; Rajiv P. Dant and Patrick L. Schul, "Conflict Resolution Processes in Contractual Channels of Distribution," *Journal of Marketing*, Vol. 56 (January 1992), pp. 38–54; Edward F. McQuarrie, "The Customer Visit: Qualitative Research for Business-to-Business Marketers," *Marketing Science Institute*, Report 92-114, May 1992; Michael Minor and Marion E. Deaton, "An Expected Utility Approach to Modeling Organizational Buying Decisions," *AMA Winter Educators' Proceedings* (1992), pp. 78–84; J. Joseph Cronin, Jr., Allen W. Imershein, and Steven A. Taylor, "Organizational Theory and Paradigms of Organizational Behavior," *AMA Winter Educators' Proceedings* (1992), Vol. 3, pp. 162–176; Frank H. Alpert, Michael A. Kamins, and John L. Graham, "An Examination of Reseller Buyer Attitudes toward Order of Brand Entry," *Journal of Marketing*, Vol. 56 (July 1992), pp. 25–37; V. Kasturi Rangan, Melvyn A. J. Menezes, and E.P. Maier, "Channel Selection for New Industrial Products: A Framework, Method, and Application," *Journal of Marketing*, Vol. 56 (July 1992), pp. 69–82; Paul Herbig and Hugh E. Kramer, "The Importance of Cross-cultural Negotiations for Successful International Marketing Activities," in Robert L. King (ed.), *Marketing: Perspectives for the 1990s* (Richmond, Va.: Southern Marketing Association, 1992), pp. 110–113; and Alan T. Shao, "Client Desires and Cooperation with U.S. Advertising Agencies in Foreign Markets," in King, *Marketing: Perspectives for the 1990s*, pp. 114–117.

13. Jagdish N. Sheth, "A Model of Industrial Buyer Behavior," *Journal of Marketing*, Vol. 37, No. 4 (1973), p. 52. For related discussions, see Jakki Mohr (ed.), "Communicating with Industrial Customers: A Conference Summary," *Marketing Science Institute Report* 89–112, August 1989; Susan H. Godar, "Same Time Next Year? Why Industrial Buyers Go to Trade Shows," in *Marketing: Perspectives for the 1990s*, Robert L. King (ed.), (Richmond, Va.: Southern Marketing Association, 1992), pp. 33–37; Cathy Owens Swift and Barbara J. Coe, "Negotiation Style among Purchasing

Managers: Are Some Purchasing Managers More Collaborative Than Others?" in King, *Marketing: Perspectives for the 1990s*, pp. 29–32; John F. Tanner, Jr., and Lawrence B. Chonko, "Territorial Behaviors in Organizational Buyers: Vigilance, Encroachment and Defense," *AMA Winter Educators' Proceedings* (1992), pp. 71–77; Jose Antonio Rosa and William J. Qualls, "The Effects of Dispositional and Situational Variables on the Motivation of Industrial Buyers," Faculty Working Paper 93-0101, University of Illinois; and Jill Joyce, "The Industrial Buyer's Use of Information Sources: An Empirical Investigation of Source Type and Topic Interrelationships," *AMA Winter Educators' Proceedings* (1993), pp. 260–265.

14. Figure 21-4 is adapted from Thomas Bonoma, Gerald Zaltman, and Wesley Johnston, *Industrial Buying Behavior* (Cambridge, Mass.: Marketing Science Institute, 1977), p. 27. See also Randall L. Rose and Murray Young, "Competitive versus Cooperative Motives in Buyer-Seller Negotiations," *AMA Summer Educators' Proceedings* (1991), pp. 618–625; Lloyd M. Rinehart and Thomas J. Page, Jr., "The Development and Test of a Model of Transaction Negotiation," *Journal of Marketing*, Vol. 56, No. 4 (October 1992), pp. 18–32; P. V. (Sundar) Balakrishnan, Charles Patton, and Phillip A. Lewis, "Toward a Theory of Agenda Setting in Negotiations," *Journal of Consumer Research*, Vol. 19, No. 4 (March 1993), pp. 637–654; and Shankar Ganesan, "Negotiation Strategies and the Nature of Channel Relationships," *Journal of Marketing Research*, Vol. 30 (May 1993), pp. 183–203.

15. This table reports partial results from the study in James R. Moore, Donald Eckrich, and Lorry T. Carlson, "A Hierarchy of Industrial Selling Competencies," *Journal of Marketing Education* (Spring 1986), pp. 79–88. For related findings, see Thomas W. Leigh and Patrick F. McGraw, "Mapping the Procedural Knowledge of Industrial Sales Personnel: A Script-Theoretic Investigation," *Journal of Marketing*, Vol. 53 (January 1989), pp. 16–34; Siew Meng Leong, Paul S. Busch, and Deborah Roedder John, "Knowledge Bases and Salesperson Effectiveness: A Script-Theoretic Analysis," *Journal of Marketing Research*, Vol. 26 (May 1989), pp. 164–178; Robert W. Cook and Robert J. Corey, "A Confirmatory Investigation of Industrial Buyer Image of the Saleswoman," *Journal of the Academy of Marketing Science*, Vol. 19, No. 3 (Summer 1991), pp. 199–208; Jagdip Singh and Gary K. Rhoads, "Boundary Role Ambiguity in Marketing-oriented Positions: A Multidimensional, Multifaceted Operationalization," *Journal of Marketing Research*, Vol. 28 (August 1991), pp. 328–338; and Patrick L. Schul and Brent M. Wren, "The Emerging Role of Women in Industrial Selling: A Decade of Change," *Journal of Marketing*, Vol. 56 (July 1992), pp. 38–54.

16. "King Customer," *Business Week*, March 12, 1990, pp. 88–94.

17. John Swan and Fredrick Trawick, Jr., "Building Industrial Trust in the Industrial Salesperson," in Arch Woodside (ed.), *Advances in Business Marketing* (Greenwich, Conn.: JAI Press, 1987). See also Syed Saad Andaleeb, "Trust and Dependence in Channel Relationships: Implications for Satisfaction and Perceived Stability," *AMA Summer Educators' Proceedings* (1991), pp. 249–250; and Greg S. Martin, "The Concept of Trust in Marketing Channel Relationship: A Review and Synthesis," *AMA Summer Educators' Proceedings* (1991), pp. 251–259.

18. Darrel Miller, "Long-Term Trusting Relationships in Channels of Distribution: A Proposed Model," unpublished manuscript, University of Florida, Gainesville, 1988.

19.   John Browning and Noel Zabriskie, "How Ethical Are Industrial Buyers?" *Industrial Marketing Management*, Vol. 12 (1983), pp. 219–224. See also Richard F. Beltramini, "Exploring the Effectiveness of Business Gifts: A Controlled Field Experiment," *Journal of the Academy of Marketing Science*, Vol. 20, No. 1 (Winter 1992), pp. 87–92.

20.   For an introduction and overview of many of the ethical issues confronted by marketing managers, see the various topic chapters in Gene R. Laczniak and Patrick E. Murphy, *Ethical Marketing Decisions: The Higher Road* (Needham Heights, Mass: Allyn & Bacon, 1993). For further discussions, see Lawrence Chonko, James R. Lumpkin, and Marjorie J. Caballero, "Perceptions of Ethical Situations by Purchasing Managers: A Preliminary Explanation of Differences," *AMA Summer Educators' Proceedings* (1986), pp. 93–98; Joseph A. Bellizzi and Robert E. Hite, "Supervising Unethical Salesforce Behavior," *Journal of Marketing*, Vol. 53 (April 1989), pp. 36–47; Shelby D. Hunt, Van R. Wood, and Lawrence B. Chonko, "Corporate Ethical Values and Organizational Commitment in Marketing," *Journal of Marketing*, Vol. 53 (July 1989), pp. 79–90; Ismael P. Akaah and Edward A. Riordan, "Judgments of Marketing Professionals about Ethical Issues in Marketing Research: A Replication and Extension," *Journal of Marketing Research*, Vol. 26 (February 1989), pp. 112–120; and Ishmael P. Akaah, "Organizational Culture and Ethical Research Behavior," *Journal of the Academy of Marketing Science*, Vol. 21, No. 1 (Winter 1993), pp. 59–64.

GLOSSARY

A

A-C-V model The representation of the simple means-end chain used in the laddering research approach: product attributes are linked to consequences, which are linked to values. (p. 161)

absolute sensory threshold The minimum amount of energy that can be detected by a particular sensory receptor (cf. *differential sensory threshold*). (p. 209)

accommodative decision A family decision in which different members have different goals: conflict resolution has to occur because the goal differences have to be resolved in some manner (cf. *consensual decision*). (p. 402)

acculturation The learning of a different culture, as when a person emigrates or is transferred to work in a different land (cf. *enculturation*). (p. 313)

action-oriented consumers Within the VALS-2 system, consumers who are guided by a desire for social or physical activity, variety, and risk taking. (p. 115)

activation In consumer information processing theory, energy flow into particular nodes to bring them into short-term memory. (p. 187)

adaptation theory A theory of perception that states that consumers become accustomed to constant levels of stimuli and thus pay less attention to them over time. (p. 220)

adaptive Able to adjust to the requirements of different circumstances; adaptivity is an important quality of the human consumer information processing system. (p. 182)

adjustment In adaptive selling, this stage suggests that the salesperson should continually "customize" his or her presentation to reflect the customer's reactions during the sales interaction. (p. 423)

adjustment function One of four useful roles that attitudes may serve: to help consumers to adjust their likes and dislikes to the realities of their external environment (cf. *ego-defense function, object-appraisal function,* and *value-expressive function*). (p. 283)

adoption-process model A modified hierarchy of effects model to reflect the stages consumers pass through to adopt an innovation: adds trial and use evaluation stages (cf. *hierarchy of effects*). (p. 333)

advertising approval processes Internal steps at companies and ad agencies to review, modify, and approve advertising themes and copy prior to release of a campaign. (p. 461)

advertising industry codes Guidelines developed by advertising industry groups to provide suggestions and standards for advertising practices: provide a basis for self-regulation. (p. 460)

advertising self-regulatory system See *NAD/NARB system*. (p. 462)

affect referral A special form of decision heuristic in which a consumer chooses a very familiar brand by simply recalling his or her favorable attitude toward the brand. (p. 513)

affective component A dimension of attitude: refers to emotional or feeling states (cf. *cognitive component* and *conative component*). (pp. 177, 282)

affective involvement The degree of arousal of feelings and emotions during an episode. (p. 167)

affirmative disclosures A public policy program that requires marketers to disclose certain information to consumers, as in product warning levels or ingredient listings. (p. 586)

aggregate perspective One significant approach to consumer behavior: stresses descriptive consumer research on markets and trends. (p. 56)

aggregate versus individual-level views One of the distinctions between the marketer's perspective and the consumer's perspective: stems from the fact that consumers view themselves as individuals, whereas marketers tend to view consumers as part of a market. (p. 43)

aggressive In Cohen's CAD personality scale, this category is for those who move against people (i.e., compete against others). (p. 152)

AIO (activities, interests, and opinions) A name given to measurement scales used by marketers to study consumer life-styles. (p. 97)

American mainstream In social stratification, a term applied to the three social classes that comprise 83 percent of the population: the upper-middle, middle, and working classes. (p. 348)

antitrust regulation An area of public policy that promotes competition by policing the dealings one firm has with other firms. (p. 579)

appearance-only endorsements Advertisements in which a celebrity acts as a spokesperson for the brand, but does not pretend to offer any special expertise with the product (cf. *testimonial*). (p. 378)

applications only, please One of the "4 Pitfalls" in the study of consumer behavior: the natural tendency to look for helpful marketing hints becomes a pitfall if it drives out an appreciation for learning the basic concepts and research methods of consumer behavior, since these are what persist across time and marketing situations. (p. 24)

approach-approach A class of motivational conflicts that can occur when a consumer is attempting to decide between two alternatives and is concentrating only on their attractive features. (p. 133)

approach-avoidance A class of motivational conflicts in which a consumer wishes to move both toward and away from an object. In consumer behavior such conflict often occurs when a consumer is considering both positive and negative features of a single alternative. (p. 133)

arrival problems gap The third stage of the STAIR system of potential advertising problems: reflects any difficulties that may occur in the physical transmission or delivery of an ad to the consumer. (p. 448)

atmospherics The creation of a planned environment in which cues are used by a marketer to stimulate particular perceptions and behaviors on the part of consumers. (p. 249)

attention The momentary focusing of our information processing capacity on a particular stimulus (cf. *planned attention, spontaneous attention,* and *involuntary attention*). (p. 217)

attitude A learned predisposition to respond to an object or class of objects in a consistently favorable or unfavorable way. (p. 281)

attitude accessibility The extent to which an attitude is likely to "come to mind" (i.e., be accessed, and move from LTM to STM) when a purchase is being made. (p. 304)

attitude toward the ad (A/ad) In contrast to attitude toward the brand, this reflects a consumer's evaluations of an advertisement. (p. 457)

attitudinal segmentation A special form of behavioral segmentation that groups together consumers who hold similar beliefs, attitudes, or preferences within a particular product category. (p. 107)

attractiveness A general term in the advertising source literature to reflect a consumer's perceptions of how prestigious the source is, how empathic (similar to the consumer) the source is, or how physically attractive the source may be. (p. 470)

attribution theory A theory based on the premise that people desire order in their lives and therefore attempt to estimate the reasons or causes for events they encounter. (p. 140)

automaticity In perception, refers to attentional processes that have been learned so strongly over time that they are performed without conscious control and with minimal effort (cf. *preconscious attention*). (p. 221)

average amount consumed A measure of the typical quantity of a product or service used per usage occasion. This can be the target of marketing strategies to increase sales, as in special prices for larger quantities. (p. 532)

avoidance-avoidance A class of motivational conflicts that can occur when a consumer is involved in a choice between two behaviors with negative valences. (p. 133)

B

baby boom generation The people born in the explosion in births between the years 1946 and 1964: constitutes some 76 million people in the United States. (p. 62)

baby bust generation Those people born between 1965 and 1976, when the birth rate was low: consists of 43 million people in the United States. (p. 62)

bait and switch An illegal combination of advertising and personal selling. The advertising sets the bait in the form of an extremely low price. When the consumer takes the bait and comes to the store, the salesperson switches the consumer to a more expensive model. This method is illegal when the advertised product is not available for purchase. (p. 436)

bargaining strategy A broad set of family decision approaches used when different members have different goals: these involve give and take, and creating conditions under which the member will want to make the decision. (p. 403)

barrier to entry In economic theory, something that hinders a potential competitor from entering a product class, such as high costs for advertising. (p. 466)

behavior The third level of our segmentation behavioral system: classifies each consumer on the basis of his or her actual behavior in the marketplace. (p. 91)

behaviorism See *learning as behavior (LAB).* (p. 258)

benefit segmentation A popular approach to segmentation that identifies segments in terms of what consumers need, or are seeking to obtain, from a product or service. (p. 103)

benefits sought The second level of our segmentation behavioral system: refers to measures of what consumers are seeking in a product or service. (p. 90)

black box model A frequently used approach to studying consumer behavior: concentrates on external inputs and the outputs that seem to ensue from them (e.g., sales increase due to coupons). (p. 178)

brand and style decisions One of four basic types of consumer decisions: the details of exactly which items are purchased. (p. 479)

brand attitudes The feelings and evaluations consumers hold about a brand. (p. 284)

brand-choice involvement The specific arousal during a purchase process involving the choice of a single alternative. (p. 166)

brand equity The value of a brand name for the company that owns it. (p. 284)

brand extension A new product offering that uses an existing brand's name to capitalize on that brand name's high brand equity (can range from a minor change, such as a new flavor, to an entirely new product line). (p. 286)

brand loyalty A term used to reflect a consistent pattern of brand purchases: reflects consumers' having learned specific purchase behaviors and having found these to be rewarding. (p. 276)

brand-specific versus best alternative One of the distinctions between the marketer's perspective and the consumer's perspective: stems from the fact that marketers act as if the best purchase for a particular consumer should be the brand that they are offering, whereas the consumer is interested in obtaining the alternative that is best for himself or herself. (p. 44)

budget allocation One of four basic types of consumer decisions: involves choices of how to spend (or save) available funds, how to time spending, and whether to borrow in order to buy. (p. 478)

bundle of attributes The set of important characteristics offered by a product to consumers. (p. 296)

bundle of benefits A phrase indicating that consumer purchases are made to achieve a set of goals or benefits that are being sought. Products and services can thus be seen as providing a set of attributes (or characteristics) to satisfy consumers' wants and needs. (p. 15)

buying center In organizational buying, another term for the decision-making unit (DMU). (p. 603)

buyer/seller dyad The pairing of salesperson and purchaser, whose interrelationships are studied with respect to the exchanges taking place. (p. 609)

C

Capacity limitations Within the CIP system, refers to constraints on how much information we can take in or think about in a given period of time, primarily because of the STM (cf. *time constraints* and *size constraints*). (p. 184)

caste system An extreme type of social stratification, in which classes are very rigid structures, social inequality is a core value in the society, and very little social mobility is possible (cf. *class system* and *estate system*). (p. 345)

categorization The second of three stages in interpreting external stimuli: the process of translating sensory inputs into an identification of a stimulus (cf. *perceptual organization* and *inference*). (p. 239)

central route to persuasion In the ELM model, the high-involvement process reflecting a consumer who pays attention to the major points in an ad, thinks about (elaborates) them, and strengthens or changes his or her attitude toward the brand. (p. 456)

channels One of the 5 C's, or uncontrollable factors to which a marketer must adapt: recognizes that the distribution system consists of independent wholesalers and retailers, who will not necessarily do what a manufacturer desires for his or her product. (p. 39)

Checkout Coupon computer system A computerized system hooked to a supermarket's scanner display that analyzes a customer's purchases as they are being made and spits out coupons tailored to that buyer. (p. 524)

chunking In CIP, the mental process of grouping together several pieces of information and treating them as a set. (p. 185)

CIP approach Extends the black box model to concentrate on the thoughts consumers have: not as strong at analyzing inputs and outputs. (p. 179)

CIP system A common acronym for consumer information processing system; it consists of three sectors: the sensory register, short-term memory (STM), and long-term memory (LTM). (p. 181)

claim-belief interaction A category of deceptive advertising: occurs when all the information in an ad is literally correct but might be expected to be interpreted in a misleading way by consumers because of their existing knowledge and beliefs (cf. *unconscionable lie* and *claim-fact discrepancy*). (p. 264)

claim-fact discrepancy A category of deceptive advertising: reflects a situation in which an ad's description needs some further information to be added so as to avoid misleading implications (cf. *unconscionable lie* and *claim-belief interaction*). (p. 264)

class system A type of social stratification that conforms in most respects to an open system: relies on a mixture of inherited and earned status, offers moderate opportunities for social mobility, and is found in industrialized societies (cf. *caste system* and *estate system*). (p. 347)

classical conditioning (CC) A type of learning in which new response behaviors are created by repetitively pairing a neutral stimulus with another stimulus that is known to evoke the desired response (cf. *instrumental conditioning*). (p. 267)

closed systems Societies in which inherited status dominates, offering little opportunity for social mobility (cf. *open systems*). (p. 345)

coercive power A type of social power or influence: rests on the threat, real or imagined, that the group can punish the member if he or she does not comply with the recommended behavior. (p. 374)

cognitive component A dimension of attitude: refers to the knowledge or beliefs a consumer has about the attitude object (cf. *affective component* and *conative component*). (pp. 177, 282)

cognitive consistency The concept that consumers strive for harmonious (or consistent) relationships among their thoughts and feelings. (p. 282)

cognitive dissonance theory An influential theory that posits that (1) dissonant cognitions cause psychological discomfort, (2) dissonance is likely to occur after a choice has been made, and (3) consumers are motivated to reduce their unpleasant feelings by changing their perceptions and attitudes. (p. 539)

cognitive involvement The degree of thinking aroused during an episode. (p. 167)

cognitive responses Thoughts that consumers have in response to an ad or other message: commonly studied as counterarguments, support arguments, and source derogations. (p. 263)

communicability In the study of diffusion, this represents the ease with which the essence of an innovation can be conveyed to potential adopters; the greater the communicability, the faster diffusion tends to be. (p. 332)

company One of the 5 C's, or uncontrollable factors to which a marketer must adapt: recognizes that companies and their cultures are different, and that what is best for one company may not be possible for another. (p. 37)

comparative fault doctrine An emerging rule in liability law that is in some respects a compromise between the negligence and strict liability doctrines: here damages depend on the extent to which the injured party has contributed to the problem. (p. 557)

comparison advertising A type of advertising that (1) compares two or more specifically named (or recognizably presented) brands of the same product class and

(2) makes such a comparison in terms of one or more specific product attributes. (p. 471)

compatibility In the study of diffusion, this represents how well an innovation fits the existing beliefs and practices of potential adopters; the higher the compatibility, the faster the diffusion. (p. 332)

compensatory rule A decision rule aimed at selecting the best overall brand: all brand ratings are considered on all attributes, with an overall score calculated as in a multiattribute model. (p. 510)

competitors One of the 5 C's, or uncontrollable factors to which a marketer must adapt: refers to other marketers who are also appealing to consumers to purchase rival offerings in the marketplace. Marketers frequently need to alter a marketing mix to match or surpass a competitor's tactic. (p. 36)

complexity In diffusion of innovations, a characteristic that slows the rate of diffusion: the inherent difficulty associated with the new idea or product. (p. 332)

compliance A type of group influence process: here a person goes along with the group because of the group's power to reward or punish (either physically or socially). (p. 374)

compliant In Cohen's CAD personality scale, this category is for those who move toward people (i.e., those who desire to be loved, wanted, and appreciated by others). (p. 152)

conative component A dimension of attitude: involves the tendency to action or behavior (cf. *affective component* and *cognitive component*). (pp. 177, 282)

conceptual system The human system for dealing with mental concepts: it is the means by which we think (cf. *sensory system*). (p. 179)

conditions One of the 5 C's, or uncontrollable factors to which a marketer must adapt: refers to a host of broader economic and social forces that can affect the success or failure of marketing programs. (p. 40)

confirmation/disconfirmation In consumer satisfaction research, the results of mental comparison between the consumer's prior expectations and the actual level of performance: a confirmation results when the levels are equal, while a disconfirmation results when the levels are unequal (cf. *discrepancy*). (p. 541)

conforming behavior An action that follows and is similar to the behavior of others: it is sometimes controversial, and it has numerous causes. (p. 380)

conjunctive rule A form of decision rule in which the consumer sets a minimum standard for product performance on each attribute and then evaluates brands as to whether they pass each standard. If a brand fails on any standard, it is dropped from consideration. (p. 511)

consciousness levels A three-part framework for motivation. Consumers are aware of motives at the conscious level, whereas motives at the preconscious level are not currently known but can be brought to consciousness if they can be located; motives at the unconscious level are deeply buried and cannot be expected to emerge in consumer research. (p. 126)

consensual decision A class of family decisions in which different members share the same goal, but the details need to be settled (cf. *accommodative decision*). (p. 402)

consonant cognitions Beliefs or opinions that are related and are logically consistent with each other (cf. *dissonant cognitions*). (p. 539)

consumer behavior The mental, emotional, and physical activities that people engage in when selecting, purchasing, using, and disposing of products and services so as to satisfy needs and desires. (p. 14)

consumer Bill of Rights Four basic consumer rights recognized by President Kennedy: the right to be informed, to choose freely, to be safe, and to be heard. (p. 568)

consumer database A computerized record of individual consumers or households, their addresses, and information concerning their interests or buying histories. As computers have developed, this approach to monitoring the marketplace has grown rapidly, as it allows direct targeting of high-potential customers. (p. 109)

consumer dissatisfaction A negative emotional response to an evaluation of a product or service consumption experience. (p. 541)

consumer dissaving A technical term for spending more than one earns. On average, younger households (especially those whose heads are under 25) and older households (over 65) engage in this. (p. 77)

consumer folklore The total set of consumer beliefs, opinions, and stories across a society or subculture. (p. 358)

consumer inertia The tendency for consumers to continue in the same behavioral mode over time. This tendency makes it difficult for marketers to induce changes in behavior. (p. 124)

consumer information In public policy, a category of programs aimed at assisting consumers by having pertinent facts available during their purchase decisions: a popular option because of its nonrestrictive nature. (p. 582)

consumer information overload A potential danger from providing too much information to consumers, such that their CIP systems are stretched beyond capacity: can lead either to confusion or to avoiding available information. (p. 497)

consumer information processing The sequences of mental activities that people use within consumption contexts. (p. 179)

consumer information search A deliberate attempt to gain knowledge about a product, store, or purchase. (p. 488)

consumer involvement A concept relating to personal relevance: a state of energy (arousal) that a person experiences in regard to a consumption-related activity. (pp. 164, 302)

consumer life cycle (CLC) A framework of stages that a consumer passes through as he or she moves through life: concentrates on the systematic effects that age, marital status, and the presence of children have on a household's consumer behaviors. (p. 406)

consumer panel data Information gathered from samples of consumers who provide records of all their purchases over an extended period of time. (p. 275)

consumer protection An area of public policy concerned with protecting consumers' rights through regulating marketers' actions toward consumers. (p. 579)

consumer purchase patterns Regularities in a consumer's (or household's) brand purchases over a certain time period. (p. 275)

consumer role A part to be played within a consumer decision process. One simple role set allows a person to be an influencer, purchaser, and/or user. More complex role structures are also frequently used. (p. 18)

consumer satisfaction A positive emotional response to an evaluation of a product or service consumption experience. (p. 541)

consumer social integration A framework for understanding consumer word-of-mouth behavior in a product class: consists of four categories based upon whether a consumer is high or low on both opinion-giving and opinion-seeking. (p. 357)

consumer socialization The process by which young people acquire skills, knowledge, and attitudes relevant to their functioning as consumers in the marketplace. (p. 393)

consumerist economies A phrase used by social critics to describe societies in which the pursuit of material goods can become so strong that people may give up some personal and social virtues (family time, volunteering) in a drive for more income to make more purchases. (p. 47)

consumer's perspective The standpoint of the consumer in viewing consumer behavior. It is helpful for marketers (and students of consumer behavior) to be able to adopt this perspective so as better to understand marketplace behavior and reactions (cf. *marketing perspective* and *public policy perspective*). (p. 43)

consummation phase The third and last stage of a sales interaction: here the consumer decides either to buy or not. If a positive decision is reached, payment, credit, and delivery are determined. (p. 417)

consumption frequency A measure of how often a product is purchased or used. This can be the target of marketing strategies to increase sales, such as by increasing the number of perceived use occasions. (p. 532)

consumption purposes The precise uses that consumers see as appropriate for a product: Arm & Hammer increased its sales dramatically by expanding these, for example. (p. 534)

content analysis A systematic method of objectively studying what is contained in a given set of communications: often used to infer social trends and values. (p. 327)

continuous innovation A weak category of innovation: here a product is modified or improved, but consumers can continue their present behaviors with only minor changes in product benefits. (p. 330)

contrast In perception, represents a change to our sensory systems, which activates our sensory receptors and stimulates attentional processes. (p. 220)

controllable factors Decisions that a marketing manager makes. They fall into four basic categories, popularly known as the 4 P's: product, place, price, and promotion (cf. *uncontrollable factors*). (p. 31)

convenience goods Products that consumers tend to purchase where available, such as foods and household supplies: they will not go to another store to obtain a different brand. (p. 489)

cooling-off laws A moderately restrictive public policy program: allow three days for consumers to cancel sales agreements that they may have made under high-pressure selling conditions. (pp. 437, 585)

copy testing Advertising research that helps advertisers to choose which ad ideas to run and how they might be modified. Day-after recall tests and ad recognition tests are two types. (p. 263)

cost-benefit analysis A potentially complex approach to decision making in which all the costs (direct and indirect) of an alternative strategy are compared against all the benefits (direct and indirect) of that alternative. (p. 573)

counterarguments A category of cognitive responses in which a consumer disagrees with and resists claims being made in an ad. (p. 263)

credence characteristics A category of product attributes or claims: those that typical consumers will never be able to evaluate precisely, even after purchase and use, such as the quality of internal stitches during an operation. (p. 490)

culture The complex whole that includes knowledge, belief, art, morals, customs, and any other capabilities and habits acquired by a person as a member of society (cf. *external, material culture* and *internal mental culture*). (p. 311)

cultural conventions The normal (conventional) ways in which consumers of a given culture have learned to think and act. (p. 317)

cultural universals Elements common to all known cultures: represent the nature of human life. (p. 313)

current state In the problem recognition process, a term representing the consumer's actual situation with respect to a product or service. (p. 482)

customer One of the 5 C's, or uncontrollable factors to which a marketer must adapt: can refer to the needs and preferences of either personal consumers (who buy goods and services for their own use) or organizational consumers (who buy products, equipment, and services in order to run their organizations). (p. 40)

customer trust A key determinant of long-term success for a salesperson, it develops from five attributes of a salesperson: dependability, honesty, competence, customer orientation, and likability. (p. 610)

D

data-driven view This perception research approach stresses the influence of external stimuli on the process: is sometimes termed the "bottom-up" view (cf. *theory-driven view*). (p. 207)

decision heuristics The rules of thumb that consumers use to help them make up their minds about purchases. (p. 510)

decision-making unit (DMU) The center for organizational purchasing: can consist of a single individual or any number of individuals in a variety of subunits in the organization. (p. 597)

decision process approach A framework that studies consumer behavior as a sequence of activities: stresses that the prepurchase, purchase, and postpurchase stages are all important. (p. 17)

decision rules Strategies that consumers use to provide guidance while making decisions. (p. 510)

decision simplifiers Heuristics, or rules of thumb, that consumers use to help make decisions more easily. Some common ones include aiming for a merely satisfactory decision rather than the best one possible, reliance on other people's recommendations, and becoming brand loyal. (p. 18)

decoding In communication theory, the process of a message receiver's interpreting the message's symbols so as to take away meaning. (p. 368)

deliberate consumer behaviors Activities we undertake for a specific purpose involving purchase or consumption (cf. *incidental consumer behaviors*). (p. 17)

demographic profile A listing of the characteristics of the audience for a particular television show, magazine, or other medium: used by marketers to decide on advertising placement. (p. 80)

demographic segmentation The creation of segments based on demographic categories, such as gender, ethnic group, age, income, and occupation. (p. 92)

demographics The statistical study of human populations in terms of age, gender, location, and so on. (p. 56)

depletion The using up of the stock of a product during consumption: serves to stimulate considerable consumer replacement purchasing in the economy. (p. 384)

deregulation The deliberate reduction of government control of business activities, based on the belief that the marketplace works best when individuals are most free to operate in their own self-interest: in vogue during the 1980s in the United States. (p. 580)

descriptive consumer research Research that describes the actual state of the consumer marketplace (cf. *inferential consumer research*). (p. 8)

desired state In the problem recognition process, a term representing a state the consumer wishes to achieve with respect to a product or service. When sufficiently different from the current state, a problem is recognized. (p. 482)

detached In Cohen's CAD personality scale, this category is for those who move away from people (i.e., *desire independence*). (p. 152)

determinant attributes Those product characteristics that are most crucial in determining which exact brand a consumer will choose. (p. 297)

differential sensory threshold The minimum amount of change necessary for our sensory systems to detect differences in stimuli: also known as the just noticeable difference (cf. *absolute sensory threshold*). (p. 211)

diffusion of innovation The process by which new ideas, products, or practices spread through a culture. (p. 328)

direct-response segmentation An approach that targets promotions to specific consumers who are expected to react favorably, with an opportunity for them to respond directly (e.g., by mail or telephone) with a purchase. (p. 109)

directed search The conscious search for information to help make a particular consumer decision. (p. 488)

discontinuous innovation The strongest category of innovation: a new product or service that represents a major change in benefits offered to consumers or in the behaviors

necessary to use the product (i.e., consumers must discontinue their past patterns to fit the new product into their lives). (p. 329)

discrepancy In postpurchase evaluation, the extent to which the actual product performance differs from expectations: the larger a positive discrepancy, the greater the satisfaction, the larger a negative discrepancy, the greater the dissatisfaction. (p. 541)

discretionary funds The remainder of funds available to a consumer after spending for necessities. (p. 478)

discriminative stimuli Those stimuli that, when present, increase the probability of purchase behavior (e.g., the "golden arches" or a "clearance sale" sign). (p. 271)

dissonant cognitions Beliefs or opinions that are related but are logically inconsistent with each other (cf. *consonant cognitions*). (p. 539)

DITF technique In the door-in-the-face technique, based on self-perception theory, the consumer is asked to comply with a very large request; after being turned down, it makes it more likely that a smaller, more reasonable request (the one actually desired by the seller) will be accepted. (p. 141)

divisibility Sometimes termed "trialability" in the study of diffusion, this refers to an innovation's capability of being tried out in smaller doses by potential adopters: the higher the divisibility, the faster the diffusion. (p. 332)

downsizing A marketing practice that involves decreasing contents or ingredients, often while maintaining prices at a constant level. (p. 212)

durable goods Products that provide benefits over long time periods, such as houses, autos, and appliances. (p. 491)

dynamically continuous innovation A moderately strong category of innovation: here consumers have to alter their behaviors somewhat for the new product, but not greatly. (p. 330)

E

early adopters Those persons who adopt an innovation just after the innovators, but before the rest of the population: comprise 13.5 percent of all adopters, and most opinion leaders. (p. 336)

early majority Those persons who adopt an innovation after the innovators and early adopters, but before the rest of the population: a sizable group comprising just over one-third of all adopters. (p. 336)

earned status A position in the social hierarchy, usually accorded in adulthood, that is based on a person's actions and performance (cf. *inherited status*). (p. 345)

ecological design The deliberate design of environments and stimuli to modify human behavior (sometimes also termed atmospherics). (p. 273)

economic infrastructures The physical resource systems (e.g., roads and electric systems) and financial resource systems available to support economic activities. (p. 314)

efficiency potential One of our three criteria for a true market segment: asks the practical question whether or not a marketing mix can be developed to reach efficiently and appeal differentially to the possible segment grouping. (p. 89)

ego In Freud's theory, this is the system that is in contact with the external world and that develops to take charge of the person's behavior according to the reality principle. (p. 127)

ego-defense function One of four useful roles that attitudes may serve: to help in protecting consumers' egos from threats to their self-identities (cf. *adjustment function*, *object-appraisal function*, and *value-expressive function*). (p. 283)

elaboration Thinking about the information provided, as in an advertising message. (p. 456)

elaboration likelihood model (ELM) An advertising effects framework based on the premise that persuasion can occur in two fundamentally different ways: the central path (thinking about or elaborating on the points made in the ad) or the peripheral path (responding to the pleasant features of the ad itself). (p. 456)

embeds Symbols or photos deliberately placed in advertising to influence evaluations subtly with low or no levels of conscious awareness: sometimes termed implants. (p. 225)

emotion The state of feeling that we experience in reaction to some cause. (p. 167)

empathy A term that reflects how closely another person is able to relate (in terms of value judgements or understanding) to another person's views or situations: one of the bases for informational social influence. (p. 365)

encoding (*a*) In consumer information processing theory, the process of categorizing a stimulus and then choosing a storage location for it in long-term memory. (p. 189); (*b*) In communication theory, the choice and arrangement of symbols to represent the intended meaning of a communicator. (p. 368)

enculturation The learning of a person's own culture (cf. *acculturation*). (p. 312)

enforcement remedies A category of public policies that ensures that the rights of consumers are protected if they encounter postpurchase problems. (p. 554)

environmental factors In organizational purchasing, these are factors external to the organization that yet impact the purchase decision process, such as labor unions, governmental regulations, or business competitors. (p. 606)

episodic memory A type of long-term memory that reflects the picture form in which we remember events or episodes out of our personal life experiences (cf. *semantic memory*). (p. 186)

errors of commission In public policy, unwise or bad actions committed by policymakers. (p. 573)

errors of omission In public policy, a lack of activity when activity is warranted. (p. 572)

estate system An historical category in social stratification in which a few nobles (kings, dukes, and barons) held high status and almost everyone else (peasants, serfs, etc.) held low status (cf. *caste system* and *class system*). (p. 347)

ethical behavior Actions that are carried out in accordance with a personal code of justice and morality that does not violate acceptable standards of society as a whole. (p. 611)

evaluation phase The second stage of a sales interaction: here the alternative products are examined. (p. 417)

evocative symbol A symbol that leads a person to bring forth further interpretations or emotions. (p. 198)

evoked set Those few brands that come to mind (enter STM) when a consumer considers a purchase decision: sometimes called a "consideration set." (pp. 191, 515)

exchange function A benefit often offered by salespersons, who allow the transaction to occur in which the marketer obtains funds in return for a product or service whose benefit is valued by consumers. (p. 416)

exemplar strategy A marketing strategy that helps consumers to categorize a new product by associating it with an already well-known, well-liked product, as in "If you like Honey-Nut Cheerios, you'll love . . . ." (cf. *feature-based strategy*). (p. 243)

expectancy × value theory Based on the premise that goals lead to specific behaviors, its major proposition is that the tendency to act is based upon the "expectation" that the act will lead to specific consequences and the "value" of those consequences to the individual. (p. 135)

expectations Consumers' beliefs about what they will receive from a product: these provide the baselines for judgments of consumer satisfaction or dissatisfaction. (p. 541)

experience characteristics A category of product attributes or claims: those for which the consumer must purchase the good and try it out before being able to evaluate its quality, such as the taste of a food product. (p. 490)

expert power A source of interpersonal or selling influence that arises when the consumer believes that another person has superior knowledge or skills regarding the product or service. (pp. 373, 424)

expertise Regarding both source credibility and informational social influence, a high level of qualifications enabling knowledgeable recommendations about a product or service. (pp. 365, 470)

expressive behaviors Actions that stress family affection and pleasure. (p. 399)

extended family A family structure in which grandparents or perhaps other relatives are present in the household. (p. 395)

extensive problem solving The most involved of three categories of purchase processes: this mode of decision making requires much effort, can take a long time, and is complex. (p. 480)

external conditions Influences on consumer behavior that are large-scale social and economic factors, such as inflation, unemployment, credit availability, and so forth. (p. 21)

external influences Outside factors that can help to determine or affect consumer behavior: can include culture, subculture, social class, friends and family, salespersons, advertising and promotion, and situational characteristics. (p. 26)

external, material culture The tangible objects of our world—the things that we can see, touch, and use in our day-to-day living (cf. *internal, mental culture*). (p. 311)

external retrieval cues Stimuli, whose nodes are known to be stored in consumers' memories, that are used to evoke those nodes from LTM (e.g., jingles that evoke a brand name, photos or characters on boxes on a store shelf). (p. 189)

external versus internal views One of the distinctions between the marketer's perspective and the consumer's perspective: consumers are internally focused and driven, whereas marketers exist and act in the external world of the consumer. Consumer research is often used in order to gain a better internal view of consumer behavior. (p. 43)

F

fads and fashions A category of social norms that persist for only a short period (fashions) or a very short period (fads). During that time, however, enthusiastic forces for conforming can exist. (p. 312)

family branding The marketing strategy of placing a strong brand name on a number of products so as to stimulate positive inferences by consumers (e.g., Campbell's and General Electric). (p. 249)

family household A living unit having at least two people related by blood or marriage living together: such households make up 70 percent of all households. (p. 391)

feature-based strategy A popular marketing strategy that helps consumers to categorize a new product by stressing its special appeals or features (cf. *exemplar strategy*). (p. 244)

fertility The technical term for birthrate. It is measured in several ways: e.g., the fertility rate is the number of live births per 1,000 women of child-bearing age, and the total fertility rate is the total number of children an average woman would bear in her lifetime. (p. 57)

field theory Lewin's system based on the premise that behavior is a function of both the person and his or her environment. (p. 132)

First Amendment protection A principle in public policy: reminds regulators to strive to maintain freedom of speech for marketers to the extent that this is possible. (p. 584)

FITD technique In the foot-in-the-door approach, based upon self-perception theory, the consumers are asked to agree to a small request: once they've done this, their chances of agreeing to a larger request (the one actually desired by the seller) are higher than if the large request alone had been made. (p. 141)

5 C's A framework for analyzing the uncontrollable factors facing a marketer: refers to competitors, conditions, company, customers, and channels. (p. 36)

focus group A popular research technique in marketing: a trained moderator brings together 8 to 12 consumers from the target market, seats them in a conversational setting, and asks them to talk freely about the subject. (pp. 128, 364)

folkways A category of mild social norms for most routine activities in our everyday life (e.g., greeting someone on the street); these define what is socially correct and are subject to only informal sanctions. (p. 312)

frame of reference The mental perspective from which a consumer subjectively evaluates a decision problem: can lead to different choices even though the objective values are equal (e.g., expressing ground beef as "percent fat" rather than "percent lean"). (p. 514)

free speech A right guaranteed for both consumers and marketers by the First Amendment: public policy must carefully consider any programs that restrict this, such as advertising bans. (p. 586)

frequency marketing Activities aimed at identifying, maintaining, and increasing sales to and profits from a firm's best customers through encouraging long-term, interactive value-added relationships. (p. 277)

functional illiteracy A condition in which an adult lacks the reading and writing skills needed to handle the minimal demands of daily living in an effective manner: estimated to include as many as one in five adults in the United States. (p. 69)

functional motives Reasons for a purchase that relate to the product's performance in order to reach a goal: for example, tools are purchased to build or repair items (cf. *self-expressive motives*). (p. 15)

functionalist theory In social stratification, a theory that prestige and property must be unequal in order to provide incentives for society's members to work hard and perform well: supports the marketplace system of capitalism. (p. 347)

G

gatekeeper A role within an organization in which a person controls the flow of information about products or purchases, thus strongly influencing what options are considered. (p. 400)

geodemographic clustering A segmentation approach that combines geography (zip codes) and demographics (age, income, occupation, etc.) to identify neighborhoods that are similar to one another across a nation; see the PRIZM examples in Exhibit 4-1. (p. 100)

geographic segmentation The creation of market segments based upon residential location. (p. 100)

Gestalt school A school of perceptual psychology, which began about 75 years ago in Germany. The primary principle is that people wish to perceive entire objects rather than the separate parts of them: to have perceptions that are simple, complete, and meaningful. (p. 232)

Greenback Greens In the environmental area, these are the consumers who are willing to pay more for environmentally safe products but who are not willing to change their own disposition behaviors much: constitute about 10 percent of consumers (cf. *True Blue Greens*). (p. 537)

group Two or more individuals who (*a*) share a set of norms, values, or beliefs; (*b*) have certain role relationships; and (*c*) behave interdependently. (p. 373)

group identity One of our three criteria for a true market segment: to ensure good groupings, members of a segment have to be similar to other consumers in that same segment and to be different from consumers who are in other segments. (p. 89)

H

heavy-users segment Those consumers who consume a product or service at a much higher than usual rate: in marketing these consumers often account for a very large percentage of all sales (e.g., 20 percent of all households buy 80 percent of the product) and are avidly sought after by marketers. (p. 107)

hedonic consumption The sensory, fantasy, and emotive aspects of a person's experiences with products. (p. 168)

hidden languages A term that refers to the fact that people in a culture learn to communicate with each other through means beyond spoken language (e.g., eye contact, body movement, and clothing). (p. 321)

hierarchy of effects A marketing framework outlining a logical process of how a consumer moves from an advertising exposure to a brand purchase. Stages include unaware, aware, knowledge, liking, preference, conviction, and purchase. (p. 176)

high involvement Requires that high levels of energy are aroused within the consumer and that this energy is directed toward a particular consumer activity, such as thinking more about a purchase or feeling more strongly. (p. 164)

household A technical term referring to an occupied housing unit. (pp. 73, 391)

hypodermic needle approach A term sometimes used to describe a one-way flow of communication, bringing to mind a picture of a needle through which the source injects the audience with his or her message. (p. 444)

I

id In Freud's theory of motivation, this is the source of the psychic energy behind all behavior. It relies upon the pleasure principle, desires immediate gratification, is entirely unconscious, and is very powerful. (p. 127)

ideal point A consumer's most preferred combination of available attributes. (p. 298)

identification A group influence process that represents a social response: here the individual goes along with the group because he or she desires to create a close relationship with the group, but has little interest in the group's norms themselves. (p. 374)

image management A strategy of marketers that coordinates each of the elements of the marketing mix to work together to influence consumer inferences. (p. 253)

impression management Sometimes termed self-presentation, the theory that people manage the signals they send out in order to create symbolic messages about themselves. (p. 370)

impulse decisions Decisions stimulated by an external stimulus display but having very little external search and receiving very little impact from LTM: tend to be made quickly. (p. 489)

incentive compatibility A principle in public policy: to create regulations that marketers would like to comply with rather than regulations they will fight against. (p. 583)

incidental consumer behaviors Learning or purchases that occur as by-products of other, nonconsumer, activities (cf. *deliberate consumer behaviors*). (p. 17)

incidental learning Gaining information when we're not actually making a consumer decision, as in browsing through a mall. (p. 488)

individual differences A formal term to indicate the analysis of why each consumer undertakes somewhat different activities, makes somewhat different purchases, and has somewhat different preferences. (p. 22)

industry self-regulation Rather than submitting disputes and complaints to government agencies or courts, marketers develop a voluntary system of resolution (cf. *NAD/NARB system*). (p. 575)

inference A belief we develop based on other information. In perception, it is the third stage of interpreting external stimuli, in which a consumer reaches tentative conclusions about stimulus objects. (p. 244)

inferential consumer research Research that helps the marketer to discover why consumers behave the way they do or how they will likely react to new products or services (cf. *descriptive consumer research*). (p. 8)

influence The voluntary alteration of a person's attitudes, preferences, or behaviors by an outside force. Because consumer behavior is adaptive, influences can be powerful and can come from many sources. (p. 20)

influencing behavior versus handling behavioral influence One of the distinctions between the marketer's perspective and the consumer's perspective: stems from the fact that every marketing manager's role is to influence consumers, while consumers must find ways to adapt to the enormous number of marketing stimuli, each of which is attempting to influence them in a different direction. (p. 45)

influentials' stimulation A marketing strategy to create favorable consumer word-of-mouth for a new product through a two-step flow of communication: locates opinion leaders for a particular product category, promotes the new product to them, then relies on them promote it in their social networks. (p. 360)

information acquisition One of three basic types of CIP research in marketing: focuses on consumers' active search for information in the marketplace. (p. 192)

information decoding gap The fourth stage of the STAIR system of advertising problems: refers to any problem that may occur during consumers' perceptions of each ad as it is delivered to them, including attention, comprehension, and interpretation. (p. 450)

information integration One of three basic types of CIP research in marketing: focuses on what happens to information once it has entered working memory, including how new information is handled, how information is combined, and how attitudes are formed or changed. (p. 193)

information school An economic view of advertising that stresses its informative aspects and argues that it contributes to heightened competition and lower prices (cf. *market power school*). (p. 466)

information search and alternative evaluation The second stage of the consumer decision process. Here the necessary information is gathered and used to evaluate mentally the options that are open to us. (p. 481)

informational motivations In the Rossiter-Percy advertising framework, refers to the consumer's desires to relieve negative states (cf. *transformational motivations*). (p. 168)

informational remedies A category of public policy that aims at having consumers know about products and how to use them. (p. 554)

informational social influence A form of social influence: the consumer is influenced by the contents of knowledge gained from other people, rather than by social pressures (cf. *normative social influence*). (p. 365)

inherent responsibilities The other side of rights and freedoms: the responsibilities marketers have to conduct business in accord with the spirit and laws of our system. (p. 569)

inherited status A position in the social hierarchy that is automatically assigned to individuals at birth, without any control on their part or any possibility of their influencing the process: usually based on gender, race, religion, and parents' social position (cf. *earned status*). (p. 345)

initial information processing One of three basic types of CIP research in marketing: is focused especially on how consumers receive and process advertising. (p. 193)

innovation An idea, invention, or process that is new and different. (p. 328)

innovators Those persons who adopt an innovation at a very early time: the first 2.5 percent of adopters. (p. 336)

input-output approach In research on consumer decisions, involves providing a stimulus input to consumers and observing their behavioral responses as outputs: often done as an experiment. (p. 506)

instrumental behaviors Actions intended to complete the basic tasks of a group successfully. (p. 399)

instrumental conditioning (IC) A type of learning that is goal directed: a new response behavior is learned as a result of positive experience (reinforcement) resulting from the consumer engaging in this behavior over time. (p. 270)

instrumental (or means) values Beliefs about desirable ways of behaving to help us attain terminal values (e.g., behaving honestly or accepting responsibility). (p. 159)

integrated marketing The creation of promotional programs that unify the themes and planning of traditional advertising, packaging, in-store promotions, direct mail, direct response, database marketing, and so forth. (p. 460)

interaction dyad A pair of individuals engaged in a common activity, such as a selling interaction between a salesperson and consumer. (p. 416)

interference The CIP process in which the presence of certain nodes in LTM seems to block or hinder the retrieval of other nodes (e.g., advertising by a competitor can make it more difficult for your ad to be recalled). (p. 189)

intergenerational influences Consumer socialization as passed along within the generations of a family: from grandparents to parents to children, though time. (p. 394)

internal, mental culture The ideas and points of view that are shared by most members of a society (cf. *external, material culture*). (p. 311)

internal processes Consumers' mental and emotional processes that determine their behaviors: include motivations, emotions, information processing, perceptions, learning, attitude formation and change, and decision making. (p. 26)

internalization A type of group influence process: here an individual goes along with a group because he or she personally agrees with the group's values. (p. 374)

interpersonal determinants In organizational purchasing, these reflect social influences within the buying center. (p. 606)

intervals between consumption occasions The time between consumer use episodes: shortening this can be the target of marketing strategies. (p. 533)

intrusive medium An advertising carrier that forces itself into consumers' awareness, such as loud television or a prominent billboard. (p. 193)

intrusive stimuli Particular types of marketing stimuli so called because they tend to force themselves into consumers' spheres of attention: television ads are more intrusive than newspaper ads, for example. (p. 45)

involuntary attention A type of attention: occurs when an external stimulus literally forces its way into a consumer's consciousness, as with a loud bang (cf. *planned attention* and *spontaneous attention*). (p. 218)

involvement The state of energy (arousal) that a person experiences. (p. 164)

ISTEA A five-stage model of adaptive selling: consists of impression formation, strategy formulation, transmission of selling messages, evaluation of consumer responses, and adjustment of the strategy to adapt to the responses. (p. 423)

J

just noticeable difference (JND) Another term for the differential sensory threshold. (p. 211)

L

laddering A marketing research technique that traces the linkages between a consumer's values and the particular product attributes managed by marketers. (p. 161)

laggards Those consumers who are the last to adopt an innovation: constitute one-sixth of all adopters. (p. 336)

late majority Those persons who adopt an innovation just following the median time for adoption; a sizable group comprising over one-third of all adopters. (p. 336)

laws A category of social norms: represent specific rules of behavior created and enforced by special power in the culture. (p. 312)

learning The relatively permanent changes in behavior, feelings, and thoughts as the effects of information and experience. (p. 257)

learning as behavior (LAB) One of the two major approaches to studying learning: concentrates on the stimuli (S) and the response behaviors (R) made over time (T). (p. 258)

learning is knowledge (LIK) One of the two major approaches to studying learning: stresses knowledge rather than behavior as the best measure of learning. Emphasizes the internal world of learning, stressing the role of memory and knowledge (K) and internal thinking processes (I). (p. 258)

legitimated power A type of social power or influence: stems from a person's acceptance that another person has the right to suggest (or even order) a particular behavior, perhaps because of his or her position in an organization. (p. 373)

lexicographic rule A form of decision rule that uses only some of the information available: here a consumer ranks the attributes according to their importance and then selects the brand that is superior on that attribute. If two or more brands are tied, attention shifts to the next most important attribute, and so on. (p. 511)

libido Freud's term for psychic energy. (p. 127)

life chances One consequence of social stratification: this concept stresses the inequality that is present in the futures of babies born into different social classes. (p. 344)

life-cycle cost (LCC) Rather than merely providing purchase price, this information form provides consumers with the expected cost of ownership over the time they are likely to own a product. (p. 500)

life space Sometimes termed psychological field, a central concept in Lewin's field theory: represents the totality of all forces acting on a person at a point in time. (p. 132)

life-style Patterns of activities, interests, and opinions that represent the ways different consumers prefer to live their daily lives: often used by marketers as a basis for segmentation. (pp. 97, 344)

life-style/psychographic segmentation The creation of market segments based on consumers' patterns of activities, interests, opinions, or psychological measures. (p. 97)

limited problem solving The intermediate of three categories of purchase processes: here the consumer already knows about the product category, but needs to find out about the exact brand, style, and price options that are currently available. (p. 480)

linkage In long-term memory, represents the degree of association between nodes: provides a basis for efficient thinking. (p. 186)

long-term memory (LTM) The storage center of the CIP system, it contains unlimited capacity for permanent records. (p. 183)

low involvement Occurs when consumers invest lower levels of energy into their thoughts or feelings concerning an object or purchase. (p. 165)

lower Americans In social stratification, a term applied to the very diverse one-sixth of the population whose major common characteristic is their very low incomes. (p. 350)

loyalty decisions A type of well-practiced internal search decision: occur when our LTM has strong experience and a single strong brand preference to guide it. (p. 488)

M

mandatory PPRs The strongest category of postpurchase remedy in public policy: here the government steps directly into the terms and conditions for contracts, as with product bans or required trial periods. (p. 555)

market patronage The selection decision of exactly which stores and service providers to use. (p. 72)

market power school An economic view of advertising that stresses its persuasive aspects and argues that it frequently contributes to lessened competition and higher prices (cf. *information school*). (p. 466)

market segmentation A managerial strategy that adapts a firm's marketing mix to best fit the various consumer demand curves existing in a market. It consists of a three-stage process: (1) identifying segments, (2) selecting segment targets, and (3) creating marketing mixes for each target. (p. 88)

market system The type of economic system generally found in Western nations: marketers are granted considerable freedoms to produce and sell, while consumers are given considerable freedoms to buy. (p. 568)

marketing concept The philosophy that a firm should focus on serving the wants and needs of its customers: summarized in the saying, "Rather than making what you've always made and then trying to sell it, find out what will sell and try to make it." (p. 8)

marketing-consumer environment The setting within which consumer transactions occur: the primary goal for public policy is that this be efficient but fair for marketers and consumers alike. (p. 567)

marketing environment The "setting" created by marketers to reach and influence consumer decisions: includes attractively designed packages, advertising, displays, salespersons, prices, and the design of the store itself, but it also includes the presence of competitors' efforts. (p. 21)

marketing mix The entire set of decisions a firm makes in developing its offerings to the market: blends product, place, promotion, and price. (p. 31)

marketing perspective The standpoint of the seller in viewing consumer behavior: usually reflects the marketing concept—that every firm needs to match its products and services to meet the needs of potential customers (cf. *consumer perspective* and *public policy perspective*). (p. 31)

marketplace theory A basis for capitalism in society, reflecting the belief that consumers' and producers' decisions, based on self-interest, will best allocate society's resources. (p. 347)

"me" mentality One of the "4 Pitfalls" in the study of consumer behavior: warns against a sole reliance on our own opinions and experience as being representative of the consumer marketplace (guarding against this pitfall is a major reason marketers use consumer research). (p. 24)

means-end chain The linkages used in the laddering research approach: product attributes are linked to consequences, which are linked to values. (p. 161)

means to an end The concept that consumer behavior is the way by which (the means) a person can achieve a particular goal (the end). (p. 15)

media clearance procedures Review and modification requests on the part of advertising media (TV, radio, newspapers, etc.) prior to acceptance of an advertisement. (p. 461)

media exposure segmentation The creation of market segments based on audience membership for a particular advertising medium. (p. 96)

median age That age at which half the population is younger and half is older: currently about 33 years in the United States. (p. 61)

metamotives The highest level of Maslow's system: these are the ultimate values that humans seek, including truth, beauty, "aliveness," goodness, justice, and unity. (p. 143)

miscomprehension A state of mislearning that results when the receiver of a message extracts an incorrect or confused meaning from it. (p. 265)

mislearning An instance in which what a consumer learns about his or her environment is incorrect. (p. 264)

mix of motivations A phrase indicating that most consumer behaviors have more than one goal, often including functional, social, and self-expressive motives. Toothpaste, for example, is purchased to clean teeth, as well as to brighten teeth, to give fresh breath, to prevent tooth decay, and so on. (p. 15)

mixed strategies The use of several consumer decision rules in a sequence: frequently, for example, the conjunctive rule is used first to eliminate numerous alternatives, then the consumer will shift to a form of the lexicographic or the compensatory rule to make a final decision. (p. 512)

mobility The technical term for change of residence. (p. 70)

modeling A form of learning achieved by having a person observe the actions of others (the models) and the consequences of the models' behaviors (cf. *vicarious reinforcement*). (p. 272)

modified rebuy One of three types of organizational purchases: a routine purchase, but one for which the organization has decided to change product specifications or suppliers. (p. 603)

mood A feeling state that is subjectively perceived by the individual and that lasts for a relatively short time period. Compared with emotions, moods are usually less intense and are less related to a particular stimulus. (p. 168)

mores A category of significant behavior norms that are subject to intense social sanctions if violated (e.g., concerning nudity on the street). (p. 312)

mortality The technical term referring to death. (p. 60)

motivation The processes that move a person to behave in certain ways. The study of motivation deals with how behavior gets started and is energized, sustained, directed, and stopped. (p. 123)

motive A concept used by researchers to explain the reasons for behavior. Consumers are expected to have multiple motives for a behavior, some of which are overt, or known, and some of which are hidden to the consumer. (p. 125)

muddling through A description of husband-wife decision making that indicates that the process is not highly rational and well planned: instead, the spouses are unsure of both their own and each other's preferences and work to avoid conflict. (p. 404)

multiattribute model A major research approach to measuring consumer attitudes that views an object (e.g, brand) as possessing many attributes (or characteristics): consumers' attitudes depend on how important each attribute is and on their beliefs about how well the brand provides that attribute. (p. 287)

multidimensional scaling (MDS) A special analysis program that produces a perceptual map: uses mathematical procedures to obtain a "best fit" of the ratings that the consumers have provided. (p. 298)

Murray's needs Henry Murray's list of basic motivating forces for people. (p. 144)

N

NAD/NARB system A very successful program of industry self-regulation for advertising, in which companies agree to have complaints about their advertising heard by two groups, first the National Advertising Division (NAD) and then, if appealed, the National Advertising Review Board (NARB). (p. 462)

need A force in the brain region that influences a person to perceive and act in ways to turn unsatisfying situations into more satisfying ones. (p. 144)

need hierarchy The basis for Maslow's framework: asserts that some needs will be evoked before others, based upon their level within the system. (p. 142)

negligence doctrine The former rule in liability law, under which an injured consumer had to prove that a marketer had acted negligently in order to recover for an injury (cf. *doctrine of strict liability*). (p. 556)

neo-Freudian views In personality theory, these approaches extend Freud's work: they stress that people's personalities continue to develop as adults and that the role of interpersonal (social) factors is extremely important. (p. 150)

net immigration The net increase or decrease in population accounted for by people moving into or out of a country. (p. 60)

network organization The format for storage in long-term memory. Consists of nodes connected by linkages based on association of concepts. (p. 186)

neutral view of actual choice A public policy concept: in a free market, the government does not discriminate on behalf of some consumer purchases rather than others. (p. 567)

new buy The most complex of the three types of organizational purchases: since the item has never been purchased before by the organization, specifications must be developed and vendors must be evaluated. (p. 603)

node In long-term memory, a center that represents a word, idea, or concept. Nodes are connected to selected other nodes through linkages: these depend on whether or not they are associated with one another (e.g., the node for "water" would likely not be linked to the "sugar" node, but the node for "sweet" would). (p. 186)

nondurables Products that are consumed quickly and are repurchased frequently. (p. 490)

normative social influence A form of social influence that reflects a heavy effect of social pressure on the decision that a consumer makes (cf. *informational social influence*). (p. 365)

norms Social guides or rules for behaving in certain situations or for adopting a particular role: range includes fads, folkways, mores, and laws. (p. 312)

nuclear family A household with parent(s) and children residing together. (p. 395)

O

object-appraisal function One of four useful roles that attitudes may serve: to help consumers to organize their perceptions of familiar stimuli in their external world; this is sometimes termed the knowledge function (cf. *adjustment function*, *ego-defense function*, and *value-expressive function*). (p. 283)

objective symbol A symbol that simply transmits information by describing or identifying an object: does not lead to elaboration. (p. 198)

observational monitoring methods A type of process monitoring research in which consumers are observed as they act: examples include eye cameras and in-store observation. (p. 509)

one-way communication flow Descriptive of most advertising, the flow of a message from a source to a receiver without a return message from the receiver (cf. *hypodermic needle approach*). (p. 443)

open systems Societies in which earned status is dominant and opportunity for social mobility is high (cf. *closed systems*). (p. 345)

opinion follower A consumer in a particular product category who is ranked low in influencing others, but high in being influenced by other consumers: sometimes termed social dependent. (p. 357)

opinion leader A consumer who offers advice and has influence on others in his or her social system. (pp. 338, 357)

organization A group interacting together on the basis of shared identity and goals. (p. 603)

organizational buying The purchasing processes and decisions within industrial firms, government agencies, retail businesses, service organizations, and so forth. (p. 595)

organizational determinants In organizational purchasing, these are the internal equivalents of environmental factors: they consist of relevant technology, structure, goals, and people. (p. 606)

orientation phase The first of three stages in a sales interaction: here the salesperson is learning about the consumer's interests, and the consumer is learning about the store's offerings. (p. 417)

overall evaluation In attitude theory, a single measure of how much a consumer likes or dislikes an attitude object. (p. 287)

P

parity products Products that are virtually equal: the actual differences between the brands are very slight. Parity products are found in certain food and drug categories. (p. 213)

passive processing The mode of information processing created by television: consumers tend to sit back and observe rather than sit up and participate. (p. 195)

perceived risk A consumer judgment of the negative social, economic, or physical consequences that are possible with a purchase: in the study of diffusion, the higher the perceived risk, the slower the diffusion of an innovation. (p. 333)

perceived quality inference A tentative conclusion about the quality of a product in the absence of direct information (e.g., the belief that a higher price on a product indicates that it is of higher quality). (p. 252)

perceived use occasions Those situations in which a consumer thinks of a certain product as being appropriate for use, as with orange juice for breakfast. (p. 532)

perception The process of sensing, selecting, and interpreting consumer stimuli in the external world. (p. 205)

perceptual constancy A concept that stresses how strongly our past experience influences our perceptions of the present: refers to the fact that we strive to perceive our world as a relatively unchanging environment, even though our sensory receptors are providing us with changing sensory impressions. (p. 237)

perceptual context The principle that various stimuli will affect our perceptions, even if we are not conscious of this happening. (p. 234)

perceptual map A graphical depiction of how competing brands are perceived by consumers, in terms of similarities and differences in the bundle of attributes they offer (cf. *preference map*). (p. 298)

perceptual organization The first of three stages in interpreting external stimuli: determines which of the huge numbers of molecules in our environment actually belong together (cf. *categorization* and *inference*). (p. 232)

perceptual set The readiness to perceive or act in particular ways in a situation. (p. 237)

peripheral route to persuasion In the ELM model, the low-involvement process that involves little or no thinking about the ad's points about the brand but instead results in a weaker form of persuasion because of attention to favorable cues in the ad itself, such as a positive spokesperson or attractive scenery. (p. 456)

person-situation segmentation A marketing strategy that reflects that certain types of people place themselves into certain types of usage situations that call for certain types of product benefits to be offered. (p. 385)

personal characteristics The first level of our segmentation behavioral system: represents measures that can be used to identify or describe particular individuals as people or as consumers (e.g., age, income, lifestyle, and media habits). (p. 90)

personality A class of theories that classify people into types that represent an individual's consistency in behaviors and reactions to events in various phases of their lives. (p. 150)

perspective A term derived from the Latin word *prospectus*, meaning a mental view of a scene: the standpoint from which we choose to analyze something. (p. 30)

persuasion goal One of four types of advertising goals: to develop new or improved attitudes and beliefs about a brand. (p. 445)

persuasion strategy A broad set of family decision approaches when different members have different goals: here a member is led to make a decision that he'd rather not make. (p. 403)

persuasion without awareness An instance in which a stimulus that could have been consciously perceived, but which was not, nonetheless affects consumers' feelings and evaluations. (p. 224)

physical monitoring methods Process monitoring research in which the progress of a consumer decision is measured through physical means, as in removing tabs in an information display board. (p. 508)

physiological differences An area of study that stresses the effects of bodily characteristics on behavior. (p. 155)

planned attention A type of attention: occurs when consumers consciously direct their attentional processes so as to help with their consumption activities (cf. *spontaneous attention* and *involuntary attention*). (p. 218)

pleasure principle Freud's description of the basis on which the id operates: geared to achieving immediate pleasure and avoiding pain. (p. 127)

positioning The deliberate design of a marketing mix that will lead consumers to perceive the brand as having a distinctive image in comparison to competitors. (p. 296)

postmodernism A growing approach in consumer research: stresses a broadened, rich view of consumption. (p. 197)

postpurchase evaluation The judgments that are made about a purchase after it has been made, often during consumption. Postpurchase evaluation often provides the basis for future actions with respect to the same or similar products. (p. 18)

postpurchase learning The discovery of new knowledge about a product or service following its purchase, often through use or storage experience: can have a strong impact on future behavior. (p. 538)

postpurchase processes The fourth and final stage of the consumer decision process: here our interest is in what happens after a purchase is made. (p. 481)

postpurchase remedies (PPRs) The set of legal and public policies aimed at minimizing or resolving problems between marketers and consumers after purchase of a product or service. (p. 553)

power differences In Weber's theory of social stratification, these represent degrees to which persons can generate obedience in others; power differences create parties or political interest groups in society. (p. 344)

preconscious attention In perception, attentional processes that occur without conscious control (cf. *automaticity*). (p. 221)

predisposition to respond The tendency to behave toward a particular object in a particular manner in the future: relates to consumer attitudes. (p. 282)

preference map A graphical depiction of the preferences that consumers have for various bundles of attributes (cf. *perceptual map*). (p. 298)

prepurchase activities Mental, physical, and emotional activities that occur before a purchase is made: can include shopping, attending to ads, discussions with friends, comparing alternatives, meeting with salespersons, and so forth. Can be deliberate or incidental, extensive or brief. (p. 17)

prestige differences In Weber's theory of social stratification, these reflect degrees of admiration held by others for a person and his or her role; they generate status levels in society. (p. 344)

price discrimination The theory or practice in which revenues are maximized by charging different customers different prices, reflecting the highest level that each is willing to pay; it is often accomplished through personal selling. (pp. 87, 431)

price lining The retail practice of pricing at the top of several price ranges that consumers see as reasonable for a product. (p. 252)

primary motives. The purposes behind consumers' decisions to purchase a product or service category (cf. *selective motives*). (p. 124)

principle-oriented consumers Within the VALS-2 system, consumers who are guided in their choices by their beliefs, rather than by feelings or desire for approval. (p. 115)

private luxuries Products that are exclusively owned, but not easily visible to others: reference groups should be influential on product ownership, but weak in influence on brand purchased. (p. 377)

private necessities Products that are required by almost everyone and are not easily visible to others: the least susceptible to reference group influence. (p. 377)

privilege level In social stratification, the concept that within each social class, those with higher income levels will exhibit systematically different life-styles and consumption patterns than those with lower income levels. (p. 348)

PRIZM system A commercial service for geodemographic segmentation: stands for *potential rating index by zip market.* See Exhibit 4-1. (p. 101)

probabilistic linkage In hierarchical models, the concept that only some persons will progress to a given stage, and then only some of those will move to the following stage: implies a multiplicative relationship of probabilities among stages. (p. 452)

probability models Also termed stochastic models, these mathematical systems are developed and tested to predict marketplace behavior, such as the probability a consumer will purchase a particular brand at a particular time. (p. 276)

problem recognition The first stage of a decision process. Here the consumer perceives a need and becomes motivated to solve "the problem" just recognized: stimulated by the "current state" being below the "desired state." (p. 481)

problem-solving strategy A set of family decision approaches when the goals are agreed upon but details remain to be settled: options can include reliance on expertise, family discussions, or multiple purchases. (p. 402)

process monitoring A general approach to research on consumer decisions: focuses on measuring the decision process itself, as it occurs. (p. 507)

processing by attributes (PBA) An information gathering strategy in which a consumer compares alternatives on one attribute (say, price), then on another (say, location), then on another, and so on. (p. 509)

processing by brands (PBB) An information gathering strategy in which a consumer learns much about one brand (by examining its ratings across several attributes) before moving to another brand. (p. 509)

product-class involvement The average interest a consumer has in a product category on a day-to-day basis. (p. 166)

product disposition The final stage in a product's life with a particular owner: an important issue because of environmental concerns. (p. 534)

product portfolio A term used to describe a firm's range of offerings, usually aimed at different consumer segments in the market. (p. 31)

product purchase or not One of four basic types of consumer decisions: reflects choices to buy or not buy each product or service category. (p. 478)

product-specific versus across-product orientation One of the distinctions between the marketer's perspective and the consumer's perspective: stems from the fact that a consumer purchases items from all important product and service categories, whereas a marketer specializes in only certain categories of products or services. (p. 44)

product standards Required measures, ingredients, and sizes that are used to identify products and quality levels: examples include the calorie, pound, and meat grade. (p. 585)

product use customs Systematic ways consumers have learned to use or prepare a particular product: can differ among cultures. (p. 318)

product use experience An episode or trial of a product: can be a significant factor in forming or changing consumers' attitudes toward a brand. (p. 302)

projective tests A set of research methods that present consumers with ambiguous or unfinished tasks in which right or wrong answers are not possible: the researcher hopes that the consumer will project his or her own pre-conscious motivations into the answers. (p. 129)

promotion The chief communication link between the firm and its customers: informs potential customers about the marketing mix and encourages them to purchase the firm's product. (p. 34)

property differences In Weber's theory of social stratification, these differences in money, land, and material possessions are the key basis for the creation of classes in a society. (p. 344)

prospect theory A theory built around the concept of frame of reference: stresses the process by which a consumer's subjective estimates of decision alternatives are formed. (p. 514)

psychographics A popular name for quantitative research intended to place consumers on psychological—as distinguished from demographic—dimensions. (p. 97)

psychological reactance A theory that consumers will sometimes resent receiving social pressures (because of a perceived loss of freedom), leading to a "boomerang effect" experienced by marketers as people resist an attempt to influence them. (p. 375)

psychophysics The science that studies how the actual physical environment is translated into our psychological environments. (p. 209)

psychophysiological approaches The use of physiological measures of the body (such as brain waves, eye dilation, eye direction, and skin response) to better understand the emotional and thinking processes that consumers are experiencing. (p. 168)

public luxuries Products that are both visible to others and are exclusively owned: reference group influences should be strong for both product ownership and brand or style choice. (p. 377)

public necessities Products that are required by almost everyone and are easily visible to others: reference group influences should be weak for product ownership, but strong for the brand or style. (p. 377)

public policy view The perspective taken by public policy on the consumer marketplace: external, aggregate, across-products, and neutral with respect to choice. (p. 567)

purchase precipitation advertising One of the four types of goals for advertising: aimed at encouraging consumers to buy now. (p. 445)

purchase precipitators Situations that stimulate or cause consumer purchases: two prime categories are depletion and product failure. (p. 384)

purchase processes The third stage of the consumer decision process: the activities that occur during the final decision making and the actual purchase of the product or service. (p. 481)

Q

qualitative research The use of nonstatistical, unstructured research methods in which consumers are enticed to reveal what they can about their thoughts and feelings. (p. 128)

quantitative era Still in existence today, refers to the use of large samples, many survey questions, and sophisticated statistical analyses in consumer research. (p. 151)

R

reality principle Freud's term for the operation of the ego, as it seeks to achieve the pleasurable demands of the id in as realistic a way as possible given the reality of the person's world. (p. 127)

reciprocity The principle that a person who receives something from another should in some manner repay that person in the future: often active in gift-giving behavior. (p. 386)

reference group A group to whom a consumer looks (refers) for guidance for his or her values and behavior. (p. 376)

reference price A benchmark expected, or normal, price, sometimes provided in a consumer's memory and sometimes by a marketer: can be used to encourage perceptual inferences of special savings. (p. 252)

referent other A term for an individual who performs the same functions as a reference group. (p. 376)

referent power (*a*) A type of social power or influence: reflects a person's desire to feel that he or she belongs with another individual or group and to act so as to express this identity. (p. 373) (*b*) In selling, a source of salesperson influence that arises from a consumer's feelings of identification with, or similarity to, the salesperson. (p. 424)

referral fee A practice, common in professional services, in which a person providing advice about where to seek service will receive a payment from the marketer (lawyer, contractor, etc.) who gains the new client. (p. 363)

referral network An analytical map of the set of consumer word-of-mouth discussions that lead to the selection of a new service provider or store. (p. 355)

reinforcement advertising One of four types of advertising goals: to assist continuing favorable consumer evaluation of a brand on the part of people who have purchased it. (p. 445)

reinforcement schedules The planned timing of positive experiences for consumers who behave in certain ways. (p. 271)

rejectors A term to describe those consumers who consider an innovation at the same very early time as innovators, but who decide not to adopt it. (p. 337)

relationship marketing An emerging force in organizational buying and selling, this is an arrangement in which suppliers and customers cooperate for long-term advantages for each. (p. 605)

relative advantage The degree of improvement that a new innovation represents over existing alternatives: increases speed of diffusion. (p. 332)

reminder advertising One of four goals of advertising: aimed at consumers already favorable to a brand, to keep it alive in their evoked sets so that they continue to purchase it in the future. (p. 445)

resources Within the VALS-2 system, refers to the full range of capacities (material, physical, psychological, etc.) consumers have to draw upon. (p. 115)

response problems gap The fifth and final stage of the STAIR system of advertising problems: refers to any difficulties the advertiser has with respect to consumers' retaining the message, being influenced by it, and behaving in the manner desired. (p. 451)

retrieval In CIP, the process of finding the proper nodes in long-term memory and bringing them into short-term memory. (p. 189)

reward power A type of social power or influence: a person will comply because he or she expects to receive material benefits, praise, or other positive recognition. (p. 374)

right to an environment that enhances the quality of life A further proposed consumer right beyond the basic four in the Consumer Bill of Rights: reflects increased recent concerns for ecology, pollution, and hazardous waste issues. (p. 569)

right to consumer education A further proposed consumer right beyond the basic four in the Consumer Bill of Rights: to assist consumers to buy wisely and well. (p. 569)

right to consumer recourse and redress A further proposed consumer right beyond the basic four in the Consumer Bill of Rights: the right to a fair settlement of problems that consumers encounter. (p. 569)

role A set of accepted rules for appropriate behaviors in a particular situation. (p. 367)

role repertoire The set of all roles that an individual possesses. (p. 368)

role specialization In family decision making, a state in which one spouse acts as the dominant factor in purchases of a particular product category. (p. 401)

role structure A relatively fixed organizational arrangement in which particular persons adopt specific roles and functions, as in a family or firm. (p. 399)

role structure strategy A family decision type in which one member assumes the role of a specialist and handles decisions in a particular category on a routine basis. (p. 402)

role transitions In socialization, the shifts that take place as a person changes roles, as in moving from childhood to adulthood. (p. 354)

routinized response behavior The least complex of the three categories of purchase processes: here the consumer has purchased the product frequently in the past, knows what it can do, and has clear likes and dislikes among the brands available. (p. 480)

rule strategy A family decision type in which a rule can be set up by members and simply followed in the future. (p. 402)

S

s-shaped diffusion curve The basis for mathematical models of new product diffusion, this empirical finding suggests that the cumulative adoption of an innovation will be slow at the start, then increase rapidly, and then be slow again as a ceiling is reached. (p. 331)

salesperson power A term that reflects the empirical finding that the salesperson exerts considerable control over the direction of sales interactions and on the choice of the exact item purchased. (p. 417)

sanctions Actions used to enforce norms for appropriate social behavior: can be either rewards or punishments. (p. 312)

satisficing A common goal for consumer purchases: to obtain a product that is good enough, even if it does not represent the absolutely best buy that might be available if a consumer would work hard enough to find it. (p. 480)

scanners Computerized devices used to register every brand and purchase price as it is sold at the checkout: this provides marketers with instantaneous information on sales and consumer behaviors. (p. 276)

schema A cognitive structure that represents a person's knowledge about a given object or behavior (cf. *script*). (p. 241)

script (*a*) A form of cognitive schema that is an organized sequence of behavioral events, such as a set of comic page panels. (p. 241) (*b*) In selling, organized memory structures that describe a sequence of sales activities: used by salespersons to plan and carry out effective sales presentations. (p. 421)

search characteristics A category of product attributes or claims: those that consumers can evaluate through search and shopping, such as the style of a dress. (p. 490)

selective attention The perceptual concept that consumers determine which stimuli they will attend to from all that are available. (p. 216)

selective exposure The perceptual concept that consumers decide which situations and stimuli they are exposed to. (p. 216)

selective interpretation The perceptual concept that consumers determine how a stimulus is to be categorized and encoded: the categorization and interpretation are based in part on the consumer's long-term memory and in part on which cues are taken from the stimulus. (p. 216)

selective motives The reasons behind consumers' decisions as to exactly which stores, brands, and model features are chosen. (cf. *primary motives*). (p. 124)

selective retention and retrieval The perceptual concept that consumers selectively determine what is remembered and recalled at later times. (p. 216)

selectivity operators An overall term to describe the perceptual operations of selective exposure, selective attention, selective interpretation, and selective retention and retrieval. (p. 216)

self-concept An area of research related to motivation and personality: based on the premise that a consumer prefers those products that help to express that consumer's image of himself or herself, either as an "actual self" or an "ideal self." (p. 156)

self-expressive motives Reasons for consumer behaviors that relate to people's desire to express something about themselves or their feelings, as sometimes with gifts, perfume, clothing, and so on. (cf. *functional motives*). (p. 15)

self-monitoring The process of noting how one's actions are being perceived by other people. (p. 158)

self-orientation Within the VALS-2 system, refers to each person's social self-image and the patterns of attitudes and activities that a person undertakes to help reinforce or act out that image. (p. 115)

self-perception A theory based on the premise that people examine their own behavior after they've undertaken it, and that this examination helps them to infer their own beliefs and attitudes. (p. 140)

semantic memory A type of long-term memory that reflects the facts and other information that we store through language (cf. *episodic memory*). (p. 186)

semiotics The study of signs and their meanings. (p. 197)

sensory receptors The human sensory organs (eyes, ears, mouth, nose, and skin), which receive input from the environment. (p. 207)

sensory register The CIP sector in which external stimuli are gathered by our senses. (p. 182)

sensory system The collection and operations of the five human senses, sight, touch, smell, hearing, and taste: provides the means by which humans contact all aspects of their external world (cf. *conceptual system*). (p. 179)

services Purchase offerings that are often intangible in nature, and are often customized for each consumer. (p. 490)

7 M's A framework of seven factors in advertising management: merchandise, markets, motives, messages, money, media, and measurement. (p. 443)

shaping The reinforcement of a series of successive approximations of behaviors that will gradually bring the consumer to the desired final behavior. (p. 271)

shopping goods Products, such as appliances and audio equipment, for which consumers are expected to engage in prepurchase search at several stores, to learn about products, options, and prices. (p. 490)

short-term memory (STM) The CIP sector that is the working center of the system where thinking occurs (also termed working memory). (p. 182)

single-minded explanation One of the "4 Pitfalls" in the study of consumer behavior: the temptation to assume that a single factor alone causes a consumer behavior. (p. 23)

situational effects Temporary forces that stem from particular settings in which consumers find themselves for short periods of time. (p. 21)

situational influences Immediate forces that stem from particular settings or conditions, not from within the person. (p. 381)

situational segmentation An approach related to benefit segmentation: refers to grouping consumers according to the similarities of the situations they encounter, since situations give rise to specific needs. (p. 105)

size constraints Within CIP, refers to limits on the number of information items that can be handled in STM at any given time: the "magic number 7, plus or minus two," more recently found to be three or four pieces of information (cf. *capacity limitations, time constraints*). (p. 185)

slice-of-life approach Used in advertising, this depicts two or more normal-appearing consumers conversing about a typical consumer problem and the value of the sponsoring brand. (p. 364)

Sniff-Teaser device Equipment used by a retailer or brand marketer to spread the scent of a product (e.g., coffee, baked goods) in the store aisle near its display. (p. 523)

social dependents Consumers who score low in a product category on influencing others, but high on being influenced by others (cf. *opinion follower*). (p. 357)

social exchange A basic element in many social interactions: occurs when one person provides benefits of some sort to the other, usually with the expectation of some reciprocal benefits that will be returned. (p. 366)

social fear advertising The use of the theme that embarrassing social consequences lie ahead if a certain product is not used: sometimes controversial. (p. 375)

social independents Consumers who score high in a product category on influencing others, but low on being influenced themselves. (p. 357)

social integrateds Consumers who score high in a product category for both giving opinions to others and seeking information from others. (p. 357)

social interactions The natural intermingling of people, often with consumer roles to enact. Can serve as a powerful source of information and influence on consumer behavior. (p. 19)

social isolates Consumers in a particular product category who score low on both giving and receiving influence: they are less involved in the web of word of mouth for that product. (p. 357)

social marketing The use of advanced techniques to market new ideas and social practices on behalf of not-for-profit organizations, such as government agencies and charities. (p. 339)

social mobility The shifting, up or down, of a person's status in the social hierarchy. (p. 345)

social power The potential influence that an individual or group can have over a person. (p. 373)

social stratification The key concept for analyzing the internal organization of a society: refers to groups (or strata) of people who are arranged in some sort of ranked order of social classes, based on differences in property, prestige, and power. (p. 344)

socialization The process by which each individual learns to live and behave effectively as a person among other people. (p. 353)

socializing institution Any type of organization that has a strong influence in socializing the members of a society: includes the family, schools, mass media, organized religions, work centers, and social groups. (p. 353)

source credibility The believability of a source of information, based on a consumer's perception of trustworthiness and expertise. (p. 470)

source derogations A category of cognitive responses in which a consumer disagrees with the ad, but does so by reacting negatively to its source rather than the message contents. (p. 263)

specialty goods Products for which consumers have a strong brand or type preference and for which they will seek out a particular outlet from which to buy, such as musical instruments and some clothing lines. (p. 489)

specifications The frequent basis for organizational buying by bids from competing suppliers: these detail the exact product to be purchased. (p. 598)

spiff A marketing technique to obtain more "push" for a brand at the point of sale: consists of an added bonus paid to a salesperson by a manufacturer if a particular brand or model is purchased by a consumer. Also termed "push money." (p. 427)

spontaneous attention A type of attention that arises at a point in time, in part determined by an external stimulus and in part by a consumer's interests (cf. *planned attention, involuntary attention*). (p. 218)

STAIR system A framework to highlight five potential gaps, or pitfalls, that can occur in advertising: strategy problems, tactical problems, arrival problems, information decoding problems, and response problems. (p. 447)

start point Related to the analysis of the pathway a consumer follows to a purchase, this concept stresses that the first step taken is an important determinant of which purchase will be made. (p. 515)

status-oriented consumers Within the VALS-2 system, consumers who are heavily influenced by the actions, approval, and opinions of others. (p. 115)

status symbols Products or possessions that serve to send others a message about the elevated social status of a person. (p. 371)

store patronage One of four basic types of consumer decisions: the choice of which sources to shop at to obtain a product or service. (p. 478)

store-specific marketing A new technology approach in which a major food marketer might use data from individual stores' checkout scanners to plan different specific promotions for the shoppers in those stores. (p. 101)

straight rebuy One of three types of organizational purchases: simply the reordering of an item that has been purchased before by the organization. (p. 603)

strategy problem pitfall The first gap in the STAIR system of potential problems with advertising: represents an instance in which the chosen advertising strategy is not capable of achieving the goals that have been set for the campaign. (p. 447)

strict liability doctrine An extremely controversial rule in liability law, currently in force, that allows consumers to recover for injuries with proof that a product was unreasonably dangerous or in a defective condition when sold (cf. *negligence doctrine*). (p. 557)

subcultures A group of people within a culture who share an identity and particular patterns of values and behaviors. (p. 20)

subliminal perception The perception of a stimulus that is presented below the threshold of conscious awareness. (p. 223)

superego In Freud's theory, the last of the three structures to develop. It has two functions: to reward good behavior and to punish unacceptable behavior by creating guilt. Thus the superego represents a person's "conscience" and works against the unacceptable impulses of the id (rather than seeking to manage them, as does the ego). (p. 128)

supermarket scanners The computerized checkout systems that read prices, total the bill, control the store's inventory, and provide detailed records of consumer purchases for marketing research purposes. (p. 506)

support arguments A category of cognitive responses in which a consumer agrees with the points being made in an ad. (p. 263)

support system A set of resources sometimes required in the postpurchase stage: can include storage, servicing, and energy use. (p. 531)

symbol An external object that stands for or represents something else to us. (p. 197)

symbolic interaction theory An area in consumer research that studies how individuals interact with the symbols in their environment and how products play symbolic roles. (p. 368)

systematic behaviors One of our three criteria for a true market segment: refers to the need for members of a segment to behave similarly and to respond similarly to a particular marketing mix. (p. 89)

T

tactical problems gap The second stage of the STAIR system of potential advertising problems: occurs when the actual advertising does not adequately reflect the intended strategy or when a mistake is made in the ad. (p. 448)

task factors Aspects of the setting or problem to which the consumer must react in order to resolve an issue successfully: examples include time pressure, number of alternatives, and amount of information available. (p. 512)

terminal (or end-state) values Beliefs we have about the goals or end states for which we strive (e.g., happiness, wisdom). (p. 159)

testimonial Advertisements in which a celebrity has personally used the product in his or her field of expertise and is attesting to its quality and usefulness (cf. *appearance-only endorsements*). (p. 378)

theory-driven view This perception research approach stresses the influence of a consumer's personal characteristics (such as expectations) in directing the process: is sometimes termed the top-down view (cf. *data-driven view*). (p. 207)

threshold The level at which an effect begins to occur. (p. 209)

time constraints Within the CIP system, refers to limitations on how long sensory representations and thoughts can remain in the sensory register or STM (cf. *capacity limitations* and *size constraints*). (p. 184)

tort liability A legal term referring to the compensation due an injured party for the wrongs committed by another party. (p. 555)

total fertility rate A technical measure of fertility: represents the total number of children the average woman would have in her lifetime. (p. 58)

trait A relatively enduring characteristic in which people differ from each other. (p. 150)

trait theories In personality research, these represent quantitative studies in which survey answers are statistically analyzed to best distinguish types of people: frequently used in marketing research on personality. (p. 150)

transaction strategy One of the three principles for being an effective consumer in a sales interaction requires that this be brought to the interaction: reflects an awareness of the salesperson's situation and goals as well as some form of negotiating approach. (p. 432)

transformational effect One possible result from advertising: leading consumers to look forward to certain effects from using a brand, thereby changing (transforming) the use experiences they have. (p. 455)

transformational motivations In the Rossiter-Percy advertising framework, refers to the consumer's desires to achieve positive states, such as excitement and elation. (cf. *informational motivations*). (p. 169)

transmission In communication theory, the actual movement (through light waves, sound waves, TV systems, etc.) of a message from the sender to the receiver. (p. 368)

trial A consumer effort to try out a new product or service without making a long-term commitment: a stage in the adoption process model. (p. 334)

True Blue Greens In the environmental area, these are the consumers who try to "buy green," recycle, and support new ecology initiatives: constitute about 10 percent of consumers (cf. *Greenback Greens*). (p. 537)

trustworthiness Relates to the presence or absence of a manipulative intent on the part of an influencer: one basis for informational social influence. (pp. 365, 470)

24-hour recall A common form of television advertising research in which consumers are interviewed the day after being exposed to a commercial to ascertain what, if anything, is recalled. (p. 454)

two-way flow of communication A characteristic of consumer word-of-mouth and salesperson-consumer interactions, but not media advertising: allows each party to a discussion to ask or answer questions, offer clarifications, modify earlier comments, and so on. (p. 356)

U

unconscionable lie A category of deceptive advertising: reflects an ad that contains statements that simply are not true (cf. *claim-belief interaction* and *claim-fact discrepancy*). (p. 264)

uncontrollable factors Those forces that a manager does not control but that help determine success or failure, and which must be accounted for: organized in this text as the 5 C's. (p. 36)

unspecified focus One of the "4 Pitfalls" in the study of consumer behavior: warns us that terms such as *the consumer* or *purchase* can exist at different levels of analysis, and we need to be specific when we use them. (p. 23)

usage situation The exact purposes, settings, and conditions under which a consumer expects to be consuming a product: helps to determine the type of purchase to be made. (p. 385)

V

valence In Lewin's field theory, a measure of the degree of attractiveness (positive or negative) that a particular object, such as a product, holds for a consumer. (p. 132)

VALS-2 The revised version of SRI International's national segmentation system, it stands for *values and life-styles* and consists of eight segments. See Appendix 4A for a detailed description. (p. 115)

value-expressive function One of four useful roles that attitudes may serve: to allow strongly held personal values to be expressed in consumer behavior (cf. *adjustment*, *ego-defense function*, and *object-appraisal function*). (p. 283)

values The mental representations of underlying needs after they have been transformed to take into account the realities of the world. (p. 159)

verbal monitoring methods A type of process monitoring research: methods that ask the consumer to verbalize his or her thinking about the decision as it occurs or just after. (p. 508)

vicarious reinforcement A type of learning achieved when a consumer observes the positive outcomes of behaviors undertaken by others (cf. *modeling*). (p. 273)

videOcarts Supermarket shopping carts equipped with small computer displays that can present individualized stimuli while a shopper moves through the store (e.g., identify sales promotions or show ads as the shopper nears a brand on the shelf). (p. 524)

W

web of word of mouth A distinct social network for the transmission of social influence among consumers. (p. 354)

word-of-mouth advice Communication between one consumer and another in which personal influence is exerted. (p. 72)

word-of-mouth communication Discussions among consumers regarding marketplace phenomena: a powerful influence on consumer behavior. (p. 355)

working memory Another term for short-term memory (STM) in the CIP system. (p. 182)

Z

zapping A modern problem for television advertisers: the consumer practice of flipping channels to check on other programs when a commercial break begins. (p. 449)

zipping A modern problem for television advertisers: the consumer practice of running the VCR on fast forward through commercials. (p. 449)

PHOTO CREDITS

of Panasonic. **Page 330:** Used with permission of TV Answer, Inc. **Page 335:** Courtesy of American Marketing Association.

Chapter 13　**Page 355:** George Hall/Woodfin Camp & Associates. **Page 361:** Courtesy of Reebok. **Page 362:** Courtesy of Chrysler Corporation. **Page 371:** Created by Markin/Williams Advertising, Inc. **Page 372:** Courtesy of Nabisco. **Page 373:** Brian Smith. **Page 378:** DDB Needham for Weight Watchers International, Inc. **Page 379:** Copyright Rich Pilling, The *Sporting News.*

Chapter 14　**Page 394 (left):** Jerry Howard/Stock, Boston. **Page 394 (center):** Dorothy Littell/Stock, Boston. **Page 394 (right):** Jeffry W. Myers/Stock, Boston. **Page 398:** Courtesy of *Seventeen* Magazine. **Page 402:** Joel Gordon. **Page 405:** Frederik D. Bodin/Stock, Boston. **Page 408:** David Strickler/The Image Works. **Page 411:** Courtesy of Mediamark Research Inc.

Chapter 15　**Page 417:** Andy Mercado/Jeroboam. **Page 421:** Michael Weisbrot & Family/Stock, Boston. **Page 421:** Bart Bartholemew/NYT Pictures.

Chapter 16　**Page 446:** Courtesy of Roto Rooter. **Page 450:** Reprinted with permission from *Marketing News,* published by the American Marketing Association. **Page 453:** Courtesy of Hal Riney & Partners Inc. and Saturn Corporation. **Page 458:** Courtesy of Hardee's Food Systems, Inc., and The California Raisins. **Page 459:** Courtesy of Catalina Marketing. **Page 461:** Courtesy of American Association of Advertising Agencies, Inc.

PART IV OPENER:　Toni Michaels/The Image Works.

Chapter 17　**Page 478:** Michael Dwyer/Stock, Boston. **Page 479:** Mark Antman/The Image Works. **Page 484:** Courtesy of Easy Spirit Shoes, U.S. Shoe Corp. **Page 487:** Courtesy of Embassy Suites, Inc. of Irving, Texas. **Page 490:** Bernard Pierre Wolff/Photo Researchers, Inc. **Page 496:** © 1993 Rocky Thies. **Page 499:** Courtesy of Del Monte Foods.

Chapter 18　**Page 505:** Comstock, Inc. **Page 517:** Glen L. Urban/John R. Hauser, *Design and Marketing of New Products,* 2e, © 1993, pp. 328, 329. Prentice Hall, Englewood Cliffs, New Jersey. **Page 519:** Courtesy of Marketware Corp. and Professor Burke. **Page 520:** Larry Fleming. **Page 521:** Courtesy of *Promo: The International Magazine for Promotion Marketing.* **Page 523:** Courtesy of Noxell Corp., Hunt Valley, Md. **Page 524:** Courtesy of ACTMEDIA. **Page 525:** Courtesy of VideOcart, Inc.

Chapter 19　**Page 532:** From *Business Week,* April 29, 1991, p. 59. Used with Permission.. **Page 533:** Courtesy of State of Florida, Dept. of Citrus. **Page 537:** Steve Woit. **Page 538:** Robbie McClaran. **Page 543:** Reprinted with permission of Dell Computer Corporation. Reproduction in any manner whatsoever without the written permission of Dell Computer Corporation is strictly forbidden. **Page 550:** Courtesy of Hampton Inn/Homewood Suites, Inc. **Page 552:** Courtesy of Bob Thomas & Associates for Nissan Motor Corporation.

PART V OPENER:　Bill Binzen/The Stock Market.

Chapter 20　**Page 572:** Reprinted courtesy of Nestle. **Page 578:** Elizabeth Crews/Stock, Boston. **Page 581:** Alan Dorow. **Page 585:** Courtesy of Precision LensCrafters. **Page 586:** Caheim Drake, 4th-grade winner in the NYC Smoke-Free Ad Contest. Coalition for a Smoke-Free City. **Page 587 (top):** Herman LeRoy Emmet/Photo Researchers. **Page 587 (bottom):** Focus on Sports Inc. **Page 595:** Courtesy of Maxon Marine. **Page 597:** Jeffrey Dunn Studio/The Picture Cube.

Chapter 21　**Page 598:** Courtesy of *Promo: The International Magazine for Promotion Marketing.* **Page 599 (top):** Richard Pasley/Stock, Boston. **Page 599 (bottom):** Barbara Rios/Photo Researchers. **Page 604:** Will Van Overbeek.

COLOR INSERT 1:　**Page 1:** Alan D. Levenson Photography. **Page 2:** Louis Psihoyos/Matrix. **Page 3 (top):** ©1993 Rocky Thies. **Page 3 (bottom):** Glenn Triest. **Page 4:** Francoise Sauze/Science Photo Library/Photo Researchers.

COLOR INSERT 2:　**Page 1:** Used by Permission of Parker Pen USA Limited. **Page 2:** Courtesy of State Farm Insurance. **Page 3:** Courtesy of Focus Suites. **Page 4:** Courtesy of Chiat Day.

COLOR INSERT 3:　**Page 1:** Courtesy of Magazine Publishers of America. **Page 2:** ©1993 Rich Sorgel/Bernard Groefsema. **Page 3:** Courtesy of American Honda Motor Co. **Page 4:** Ad created by Ogilvy & Mather for Seagram's Extra Dry Gin, America's #1 selling gin.

COLOR INSERT 4:　**Page 1:** Courtesy of Range Rover. **Page 2 (top):** Courtesy of Kaytee Products, Inc. and Murrie Leinhardt and Drummond. **Page 2 (bottom):** Courtesy of Rayovac Corporation. **Page 3 (top):** Courtesy of Sutter Home Winery. **Page 3 (bottom):** Courtesy of Andrew Jergens Co. **Page 4:** Courtesy of the Office of the Attorney General.

COLOR INSERT 5:　**Page 1:** Courtesy of Henkel Group. **Page 2:** Courtesy of Edwards Martin Thornton. **Page 3:** Courtesy of Hal Riney & Partners Inc. and Saturn Corp. **Page 4:** Courtesy of Mediamark Research, Inc.

COLOR INSERT 6:　**Page 1:** Courtesy of Roto Rooter. **Page 2 (top):** Courtesy of California Raisin Advisory Board. **Page 2 (bottom):** Courtesy of DuPont. **Page 3:** Courtesy of Campbell Soup Company. **Page 4:** Larry Fleming.

COLOR INSERT 7:　**Page 1:** Ogust/The Image Works. **Page 2:** Courtesy of ACTMEDIA. **Page 3:** Courtesy of Catalina Marketing. **Page 4:** Courtesy of Del Monte.

COLOR INSERT 8:　**Page 1:** Steve Woit. **Page 2:** Caheim Drake, 4th Grade Winner in the NYC Smoke-Free Ad Contest, Coalition for a Smoke-Free City. **Page 3:** Focus on Sports. **Page 4:** Courtesy of *Promo: The International Magazine for Promotion Marketing.*

NAME INDEX

SUBJECT INDEX